International Conferences e-Society 2023 and Mobile Learning 2023

Lisbon, Portugal
11-13 March 2023

Editors:

Piet Kommers
Inmaculada Arnedillo Sánchez
Pedro Isaías

ISBN: 978-1-7138-8464-4

Printed from e-media with permission by:

Curran Associates, Inc.
57 Morehouse Lane
Red Hook, NY 12571

Some format issues inherent in the e-media version may also appear in this print version.

Printed with permission by Curran Associates, Inc. (2024)

For permission requests, please contact International Association for Development of the Information Society (IADIS) at the address below.

International Association for Development of the Information Society (IADIS)
Rua Sao Sebastiao Da Pedreira
No. 100, 30, 1050-209
Lisbon, Portugal

Phone: 351 21 3151373
Fax: 351 21 3151244

secretariat@iadis.org

Additional copies of this publication are available from:

Curran Associates, Inc.
57 Morehouse Lane
Red Hook, NY 12571 USA
Phone: 845-758-0400
Fax: 845-758-2633
Email: curran@proceedings.com
Web: www.proceedings.com

TABLE OF CONTENTS

FULL PAPERS

SHORT PAPERS

REFLECTION

POSTERS

FULL

PAPERS

AR-BASED LEARNING RESOURCE: A DIFFERENT WAY TO LEARN DATA-STRUCTURES

Lázaro Vinicius de Oliveira Lima[1], Luis Gonzaga Magalhaes[2], Pedro Rangel Henriques[2] and Alexandre Cardoso[3]
[1]*Instituto Federal de Brasılia (IFB) Brasılia – DF – Brazil*
[2]*Algoritmi Research Centre/ LASI Universidade do Minho Braga - Portugal*
[3]*Universidade Federal de Uberlandia Engenharia Eletrica – Uberlandia, MG – Brazil*

ABSTRACT

Considering the difficulties in the teaching/learning process of computerprogramming, the development of skills related to Computational Thinking (CT) toprepare people to better solve problems stands out. Augmented Reality (AR) allows for the insertion and interaction with virtual information in the real world. AR is becoming ordinary to humanity, including the design of new teaching/learning strategies that enable the creation of metaphors with virtual information. In this way, it can be said that AR provides a framework for the creation of analogies of complex concepts facilitating their comprehension. This article describes an interactive way of understanding computer instructions (a program) to manipulate data structures (lists, stacks, and queues). The objective of this study is to useAugmented Reality to visualize high-level program statements through a mobile animation system. User instructions are animated in real-time creating virtual 3D representations to help understand operations that handle abstract data-structures used in classic programming. This approach contributes substantially to the construction of educational resources aimed at supporting novice programmers that face critical difficulties to learn adequately Computer Programming. The work described here shows that with effective AR-based Learning Resources, it is possibleto train skills such as analyzing, representing information, planning strategies, andsystematizing resolution schemes, that are crucial to solve problems.

KEYWORDS

Augmented Reality, Learning Resource, Learning Active, Mobile, Computational Thinking, Experiment

1. INTRODUCTION

In the Age where computational knowledge is a keyword, the community should be concerned with developing the skills related to programming. There is a concern to help peopledeveloping skills related to Computational Thinking. Therefore, there is also the concern of the hermeneutic dialogue of teaching-learning in the construction of adequate learning resources (LR). Technologies help us to build appropriate resources. One technology that has been showing great impact on students motivation is Augmented Reality (AR). AR is defined as the insertion of virtual information (created by computer) in a real environment inreal time (Azuma 1997). In line with the great popularity of Augmented Reality, we identified potential to create interactive environments that allow students to absorb programming concepts and how instructions manipulate data structures.

We present LVL (Learning Virtual Language), a language and an AR-based artifact to explore data structures (lists, stacks and queues), to help students in the introductory steps to learn computer programming. Our goal in this work is to show a different process of visualizing high-level program statements using handle-mobile AR to manipulate data structures, a new approach to support novice programmers. We want to demonstrate that a tool can help in visualizing the effects that a code and its operations have on a system.

This paper is organized as follows: Section 2 discusses the ideas and motivations that lead to the project; then Section 3 presents an overview of the system we built aiming at resorting to AR to develop a tool that can help novice programming students; Section4 presents the LVL language processor developed; Section 5 introduces the programming language LVL designed to be used in our tool and demonstrate how the proposal can be realized; Section 6 illustrates with examples the tool actually built; Section 7 discusses an experiment conducted in a classroom; Section 8 concludes the paper with a summary, main lessons learned and future work.

2. THINKING ABOUT DATA-STRUCTURES

First, we need to talk about Learning Resources and new educational strategies that support us. This work have intention to create new Learning Resources to help programmers. Work by (Neamtiu et al. 2005) presents a tool to compare source code from different versions of a C program using the partial abstract syntax tree matching approach. The author explores an interesting approach to show us how important it is to follow software evolution issues. In the evolution of technologies, in the paper (Teng et al. 2018), the authors present an AR learning system for visual representation and interaction in 3D programming... In that work it was demonstrated that AR-based resources, the students have better learning efficiency than with common tools. The authors of (Dass et al. 2018) evaluatedtwo interactive AR coding environments:(1) head-mounted AR with Microsoft HoloLens, (2) mobile AR with ARKit on an iPhone. The author reported that participants enjoyed using mobile AR the most, emphasizing the easy access and manipulation of the system. Another author (Agrahari and Chimalakonda 2020) proposes an Augmented Reality-based software application to teach data structures with the help of abstract syntax trees. Using Unity with Vuforia to show concepts of data structures, Narman and colleagues developed an AR application that visualizes some operations in Array list, Linked list, and Stack (Narman et al. 2020). The author creates a learning environment for students based on AR. The author (Card 1999) says: "Visualization holds great promise for computational science and engineering, provided we can meet the immediate and long-term needs of both toolmaker and tool users." But there are different types of visual representation of this information. This information is usually classified into 3 categories: one-dimensional, two- dimensional and three-dimensional (Freitas et al., 2001). In the work (Lima et al. 2021), the authors search for ways to visualize different types of data, their connections and relationships. Using family tree analogies and text structures to present information and its relationships, this work allowed to investigate information arrangements and organizations in a 3D environment.

Works like those discussed above have inspired the work presented in this paper. Inthe next section, we will present the proposed system and its architecture.

3. PROPOSED SYSTEM

A first attempt used the idea of presenting queue, list and stacks and their concepts related to data structure. Each data structure has its own set of methods to perform operations suchas Inserting or deleting elements to introduce the different Data Structure concepts. So, it was possible to choose the type of structure, and the values to be placed in each position. Asimilar work was done by (Narman et al. 2020), but we believe that it is necessary and feasible to go further. In the investigation, we look for greater freedom in textual writing and animmersion in the visual representation of interaction in structures. Bearing these important points in mind, LVL, a small language capable of supporting the declaration and operation with data structures was designed. That language allows the Programmer to declare structures such as lists, stacks and queues, as well as it provides special operators to handle thesestructures.

Figure 1 shows the architecture of the overall system that can recognizes a program given as input (the 'code.txt' block in the image) and creates an Augmented Reality interactive scenario to help people comprehending the semantics of that input program.

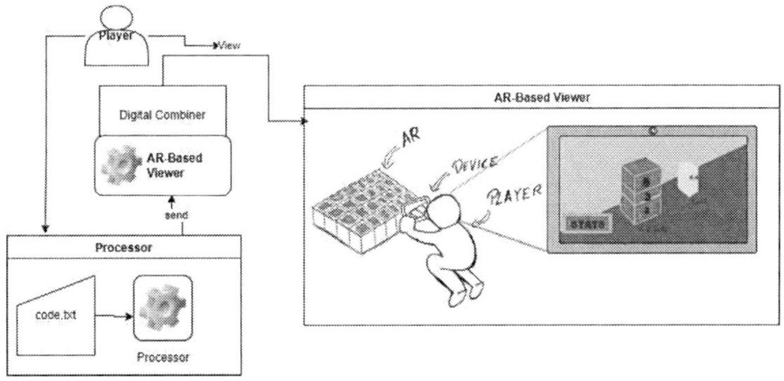

Figure 1. System Architecture

In the sequence of our previous work (see (Lima et al. 2022, Lima et al. 2021, Saraiva et al. 2021) for details) we have decided to use of mobile devices because of their great popularity and the effective power of their technological components. Moreover, that choice offers a low cost solution when compared to Head-mounted display devices. The developed solution can be used on cell phones and tablets that have a camera. The developed mobile APP can be compiled for different platforms simply by configuring the Unity compiler. The system is split into two parts: (1) the analyzer plus translator; and (2) the AR-viewer App.

To implement the ideas, we used Unity 3-D® v.2018.4, that builds Augmented Reality systems supported by the Vuforia® version 9.8 library. Vuforia is a robust library that enables rapid prototyping. The parser and translator were built with Lark, a parsing library forPython. The work aims to create an immersion in textual programming similar to immersionin the use of virtual systems. In the next sections, the implementation of the proposed systemis discussed.

4. LVL PROCESSOR

As said above, the overall system is divided into two parts: the input Language Processor (a Translator composed of a lexical-syntactic analyzer plus a code generator); and the AR-based Viewer to display the animation. This section and the next one deal with the language and its processor. LVL is a simple, imperative (or procedural) programming language, speciallydesigned for this project aimed at supporting the creation of sequential one-dimensional Data-structures.

A parser is capable of transforming the input text (the language sentences) into a syntax tree that synthesizes the meaning of the input program and is available for the APP to use this information. After the code is analyzed, the tree is traversed and the information of the input program relevant for the animation (variable declarations and variable manipulations) is extracted and converted to an internal representation in JSON (JavaScript Object Notation)format. After that, JSON description is then transformed into a QR-Code. In that way it can be said that the generated QR-code contains the input statements that the AR viewer can understand and recreate. Pointing the camera of the mobile device to the QR-Code image, the system is able to collect the information extracted by the processor.

A simple-to-use interface was created to work in a web-browser. The user writes the code and presses the button to process the code and generate the corresponding QR- code. With this QR-code, the user points his AR viewer to visualize the result of his program.

5. LVL LANGUAGE

At the present moment LVL system only supports three data structures—LIST, QUEUE and STACK—to represent in the program visualization. Of course, variables of atomic data types(integer, real, and string) can be declared and used, and so will be displayed as componentsof the system state. We use colored cubes to represent those structures. After declaring the program variables and their respective data types, it is possible to write statements to assignthem values. For List, we have the operations Insert(n) and Remove(). Stacks are based on the LIFO principle (Last In First Out), the element inserted at the last, is the first element to come out of the list. The language provides operators Push(n)and Pop().

The language also allows the use of Queues. The queues are based on the FIFO (First In First Out) principle, the first element inserted, is the first element to come out of the list. To work with Queues, the language provides the operators Enqueue(n)and Dequeue().

Listing 1 illustrates a program written in LVL language that declares a variable Stack, and operates with it. Figure 2 shows the visual environment produced by LVL system for the stack code listed.

```
VARS
    a, b, c: INT;
    pilha : STACK( int )
STATS
    a=2;b=4;c=6;
    pilha.push(2);
    pilha.push(4);
    pilha . pop() ;
    pilha . push(6)
END
```

Listing 1. Example of a program using a Stack structure

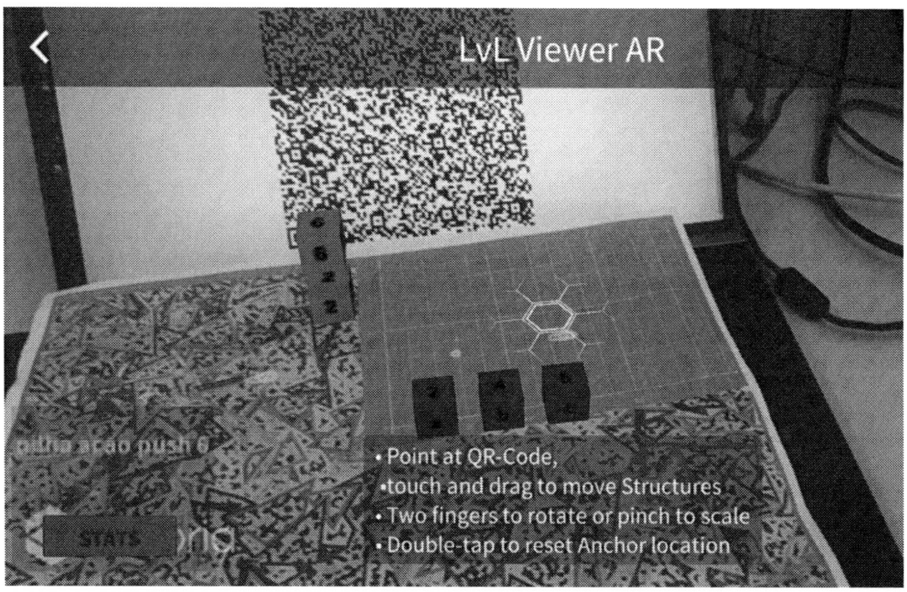

Figure 2. Screen capture of LVL animating the Stack program example

Next, more examples of LVL programs and a description of the AR-Viewer will be provided.

6. AR-BASED VIEWER

AR Viewer uses the QR-code to read the information processed by the Compiler/Processor. This section explains how the user views the information through the App. Figure 3, illustrates how to use the mobile.

The user detects with mobile the ground and then reads the QR-code. The App is very simple to use.

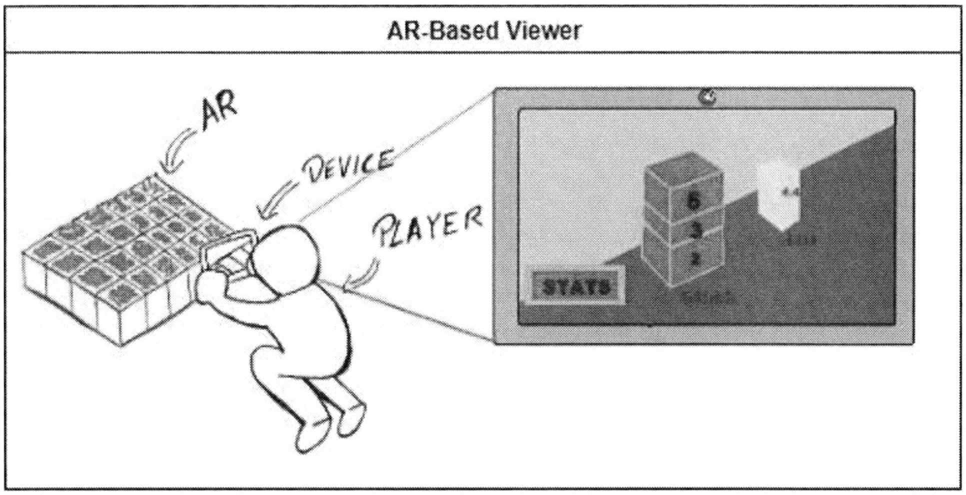

Figure 3. AR viewer app

First access the menu to turn on the camera, then point to the generated QR-code. The viewer reads the instructions and projects the structures without a marker. The system was built to be able to show the effects of each instruction manipulating the data.Examples of a short program and visual results are shown in Listings 2 and 3 and respectivelyin Figure 4 and Figure 5.

```
VARS
    a, b, c: INT;
    lista:list(int)
STATS
    a=2; b=4; c=6;
    lista.insert(2);
    lista.insert(4);
    lista.remove();
    lista.insert(6)
END
```

Listing 2. Example of a program using a List

```
VARS
    a, b, c: INT;
    fila: queue(str);
    pilha: stack(int)
STATS
    a=2;    b=4;
    c=6;
    pilha.push(5);
    pilha.push(a);
    pilha.push(6);
    fila.enqueue("a");
    pilha.pop()
END
```

Listing 3. Example of a program using a Queue

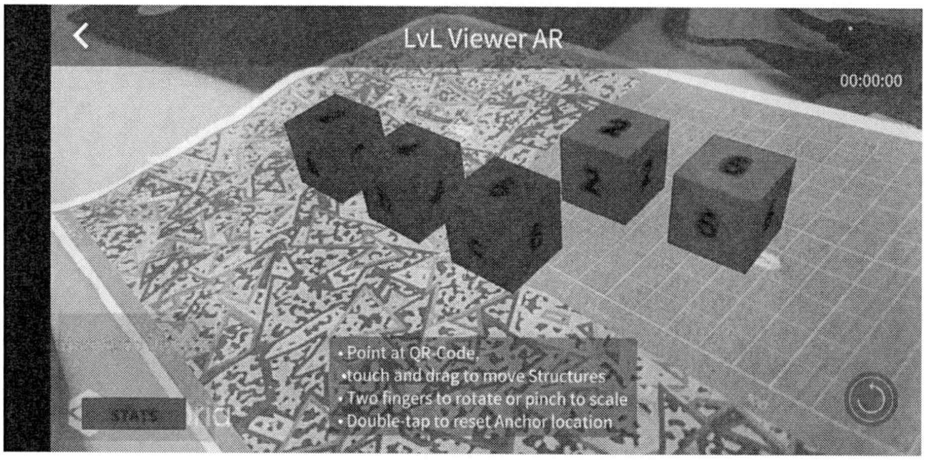

Figure 4. Screen capture of LVL animating the List program example

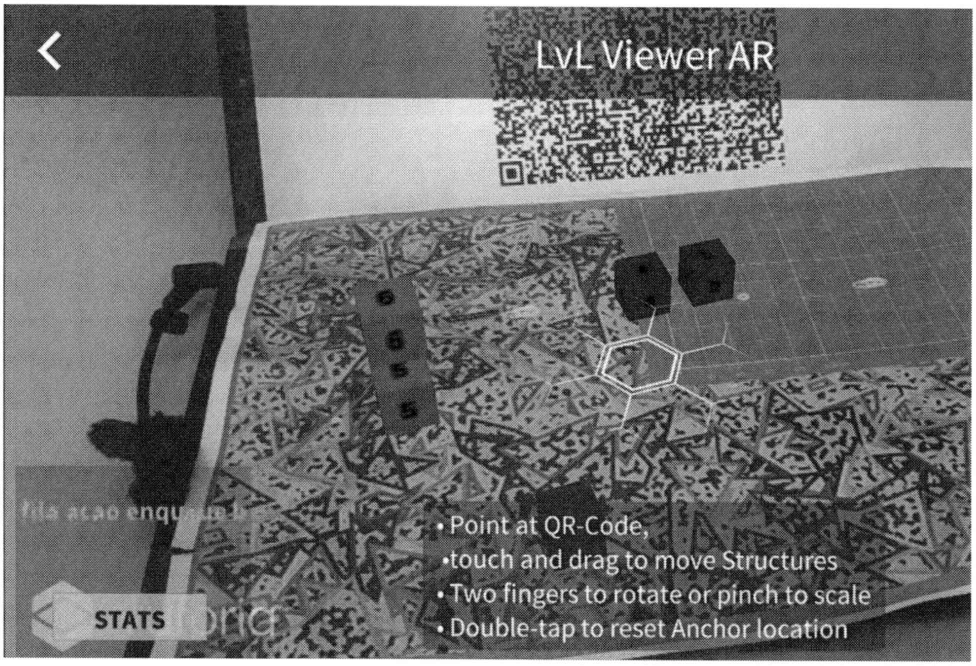

Figure 5. Screen capture of LVL animating the Queue program example

Using the screen of the mobile device, the user can touch and navigate through the program statements, observing how the content of the various data structures (the values stored in each one) evolve.

7. RESULTS AND DISCUSSIONS

To validate the AR-based Learning Resource created, an experiment in a real classroom was conducted. That experiment took place with a group of students graduating from the IT course at University in Brasilia. A total of 7 male students participated in the experiment, aged between 20 and 24 years. The presentation was carried out in the classroom. After introducing the Language LVL, a link was shared to download the activity and the app. The activity consisted of using the LVL language to write a small program manipulating the 3 different structures available in the system (List, Stack and Queue). To carry out the activity, the students spent an hour writing the script and compiling it with the LVLprocessor available online. At the end of that one hour task, the students answered a questionnaire prepared/designed according to Evaluation of a Mobile Augmented Reality Application (MAREEA) (Pombo et al. 2022) as an Outdoor Learning Tool. Four evaluation factors are defined in the MAREEA evaluation model: *Usability, engagement, motivation, and active learning*. All students were able to successfully complete the activities. As response format,the use of the Likert scale is defined. Student feedback indicates that all students agree withthe statements contained in the MAREEA questionnaire. In the open question, one student wrote that the system was "Good for Learning". Corroborating with the thesis that an Augmented Reality tool can help in understanding complex problems. The experiment had goodfeedback showing that all students were able to understand the language and manipulate thevisualization tool. Interface improvements were suggested to improve the visualization of subtitles in structures. It is necessary to expand the experiments with a more significant number of students.

8. CONCLUSION

This paper reports the design and development of an immersive tool to explore the manipulation of data structures through an imperative programming language. The proposed system is able to represent, in an interactive virtual environment, variables of different types—atomic,lists, stacks, or queues—defining the state of a program. We believe that this system, with the AR-Based viewer, can be used as a Learning Resource allowing the user to inspect his programs with a mobile device in order to better absorb concepts related to data structures. Vuforia library allows for surface recognition removing the need for markers. Taking advantage of the best practices of AR, one can align the objectives of teaching algorithms and data structures with 3D visualization so that the teacher can write a program with declarations and operations and thereafter the students can visualize their effects, this is the program behavior. Similar to some high-level debuggers, the AR-based Viewer showsall declared variables and allows to evolve step-by-step along the sequence of the program statements, providing a new and attractive environment to understand through the visual aidhow statements change the value of the declared structures.

One of the biggest challenges in the development of this project was the questionof how to transmit the information extracted from the input program by the LVL processor to the Viewer so that it can render and display that data. Initially, wireless transmission approaches were considered, but as the device camera is already used for the creation of the AR immersive scenario, we decided to resort to QR-code technology to overcome that issue. It was actually a nice solution but we are aware that may pose scalability problems. Another interesting challenge was related to the visual organization of all the objects in the 3D scenario. It was necessary to build specific scripts in Unity to perform the layout of one or many structures of the supported types aiming at the construction of a nice and clearscenario. With the arrangements made, objects are grouped keeping their relative position ina stable image. Moreover, a color mapping is used so that the user can easily identify each data structure type. The ideas and the proof-of-concept presented and discussed along the paper proved that the development of Learning Resources with new technologies such as ARis a promising approach. AR allows total control of the environment. This means that the user can move around the surface of the chosen projection, pause or repeat all simulations tobetter visualize the structures. Summing up, we can say that Augmented Reality allows us tocreate analogies of simple or complex concepts enhancing their comprehension. As future work, it is intended to extend LVL language with conditional and cyclic statements, not yet included. Also, improvements in the LVL Processor are planned to decrease the processing effort in the mobile device side. Actually, the JSON description generated can contain more information about the program behavior avoiding its inference by the mobile APP, reducingtime and power consumption. The user interface can also be improved using guided audio.

ACKNOWLEDGMENT

This work has been supported by FCT – Fundação para a Ciência e Tecnologia within the Project Scope: "UIDB/00319/2020".

REFERENCES

Agrahari, V. and Chimalakonda, S. (2020). Ast (ar)–towards using augmented reality and abstract syntax trees for teaching data structures to novice programmers. In *2020 IEEE 20th International Conference on Advanced Learning Technologies (ICALT)*, pages 311–315. IEEE.

Azuma, R. T. (1997). A survey of augmented reality. *Presence: teleoperators & virtual environments*, 6(4):355–385.

Card, M. (1999). *Readings in information visualization: using vision to think*. Morgan Kaufmann.

Dass, N., Kim, J., Ford, S., Agarwal, S., and Chau, D. H. (2018). Augmenting coding: Augmented reality for learning programming. In *Proceedings of the Sixth International Symposium of Chinese CHI*, pages 156–159.

Freitas, C. M. D. S. and et, a. (2001). Introducao a Visualização de Informação. *Revista de Informtica Teica e Aplicada*, 2:143–158.

Lima, L. V., Sousa, M., Magalhes, L. G., and Henriques, P. R. (2021). Understanding effects of the algorithm visualized with ar techniques (short paper). In *Second International Computer Programming Education Conference (ICPEC 2021)*. Schloss Dagstuhl-Leibniz-Zentrum fur Informatik.

Lima, L. V. O., Saraiva, F., Magalhães, L. G., Henriques, P. R., and Cardoso, A. (2022). AR- based Resources to train Computational Thinking Skills. In *International Conference in Information Technology Educations - (ICITED 22)*.(to be published).

Narman, H. S., Berry, C., Canfield, A., Carpenter, L., Giese, J., Loftus, N., and Schrader, I. (2020). Augmented reality for teaching data structures in computer science. In *2020 IEEE Global Humanitarian Technology Conference (GHTC)*, pages 1–7. IEEE.

Neamtiu, I., Foster, J. S., and Hicks, M. (2005). Understanding source code evolution usingabstract syntax tree matching. In *Proceedings of the 2005 international workshop on Mining software repositories*, pages 1–5.

Pombo, L., Marques, M., Afonso, L., Dias, P., and Madeira, J. (2022). *Evaluation of a Mobile Augmented Reality Game Application as an Outdoor Learning Tool*, pages 321–343.

Saraiva, F., Lima, L. V. O., Araújo, C., Magalhães, L. G., and Henriques, P. R. (2021). SHREWS: A Game with Augmented Reality for Training Computational Thinking. In Henriques, P. R., Portela, F., Queirós, R., and Simões, A., editors, *Second International Computer Programming Education Conference (ICPEC 2021)*, volume 91 of *Open Access Series in Informatics (OASIcs)*, pages 14:1–14:10, Dagstuhl, Germany. Schloss Dagstuhl – Leibniz-Zentrum für Informatik.

Teng, C.-H., Chen, J.-Y., and Chen, Z.-H. (2018). Impact of augmented reality on programming language learning: Efficiency and perception. *Journal of Educational Computing Research*, 56(2):254–271.

MULTIDIMENSIONAL DIH4CPS ONTOLOGY

Damien Nicolas, Christophe Feltus and Djamel Khadraoui
Luxembourg Institute of Science and Technology, 5, avenue des Hauts-Fourneaux, L-4362 Esch-sur-Alzette, Luxembourg

ABSTRACT

Digital Innovation Hub are of utmost importance when they sustain cooperation in innovative technological domains like the Cyber-Physical System. In this paper, we introduce, in a first part, a DIH ontology that we extend with CPS entities. For this, we remind the questions that the ontology must answer, deploy the methodology proposed by Noy and McGuinness, to identify the classes and the associations between classes, and integrate the new CPS ontological extensions. In the second part, we implement the full innovative DIH4CPS ontology within Protégé, and we instantiate it to a real company.

KEYWORDS

Digital Innovation Hub, CPS, Cyber-Physical System, Ontology, Protégé, Network, Capability, SME, Enterprise

1. INTRODUCTION

A Digital Innovation Hub (DIH) is defined by Crupi et al. (2020) as a one-stop shops that can help companies become more competitive with regard to their business/production processes, products or services by using digital technologie. DIH have for purpose to guarantee that all companies, whatever their sizes, can benefit from the advantages of new digital technologies1 and thereby, that they are able to find the appropriate competence regarding digital technologies and IT, which, for Rübmann (2015), is paramount for manufacturing industry. DIH are by essence strongly associated to network of partners, and it is essential for DIH to set up the more efficient tools as possible to support the market in discovering the digital information (technological, business or even scientific) in an accurate and prompt manner since both are essential for the existence of the company. Moreover, has already observed, DIH are especially of utmost importance when they are encouraging and sustaining cooperation (Sassanelli & Terzi, 2022) in cutting-edge technological domains like the cyber-physical system (CPS) (Gunes et al., 2014). In this context, an ontological representation of a DIH4CPS may be perceived as a contribution with high impact since it offers an "explicit specifications of conceptualizations" and, as a result contribute to sustain the networking environment in which DIH behaves. Unfortunately, as far of our knowledge, such ontology for specifying the DIH surrounding the promotion, the strengthening, the cooperation, and the co-development of CPS2 networks have never been developed so far.

Acknowledging this, the paper aims to describe and instantiate the ontology by formalizing the existing knowledge on DIHs competences, organization, experience, technologies, network, and the interoperability requirements of their networks and with their partners. Accordingly, this paper targets the development of the DIH4CPS ontology, including a dimension related to inner consortiums development and cooperation, as well as inner networking activities among the partner from a DIH. As a matter of fact, the target audience of this paper is far beyond traditional academic audience but also target directly project consortiums and the project partners responsible for the development of the DIH4CPS models. Those partners will use the ontological model described in the paper for achieving several development processes later. The paper also allows to understand how the ontology was built and its potential links with existing ontologies. Therefore, in the paper we remind an ontology for the CPS. This ontology has the particularity to be oriented to the surrounding network of the CPS organizational management that is addressed by the lens of Digital Innovation Hub.

---

[1] [1] Pan-European network of Digital Innovation Hubs (DIHs). Available: https://ec.europa.eu/digital-single-market/en/digital-innovation-hubs; 2016

[2] A Cyber-Physical System (CPS) is, according to Wikipedia, a computer system in which a mechanism is controlled or monitored by computer-based algorithms

This paper is structured as following: After having remind the related work in Section 2 and put in exergue the lack of existing DIH for CPS ontology, we present an innovative DIH ontology with a CPS extension in Section 3. In Section 4, the complete ontology is validated by means of inferences in the context of a real case study. And Section 5 concludes the paper and propose few future works.

2. RELATED WORKS

While CPS exist for few decades, scientific contributions directly addressing the inter-relation between physical and cybernetic knowledge entities dates from 20 years with an acceleration in the volume of publications since 2018. This includes but is not limited to CPS for a plethora of areas such as traffic light and mobility (Shih et al., 2016), facilities management tools (door opening, conditioning system) (Terreno et al., 2020), robotics and healthcare cyber-robots (Yang et al., 2020; Zhang et al., 2015), mobility and self-driving car (Kim et al., 2013), telecommunication (Kim et al., 2017), etc. Accordingly, and as it is usual to do in the academic field, a large number of authors have produced state of the arts in this field, among which some are very good and well documented, like Jamaludin & Rohani (2018) analyzed CPS through two criteria: CPS's characteristic and architectures, Kumar et al. (2020) that stresses out how attacks on CPS (CPS) continue to grow in frequency and that accordingly, identifies a set of relevant research opportunities or Sun et al. (2018) that specially focus on CPS security and describes future research directions to secure critical CPS. Although the impressive number of existing publications dealing with CPS, little research has been focused so far to the modeling of the CPS system, which is paramount to understand the underlying structure and communication mechanisms between the CPS sub-components. In that regards, Weyer et al. (2016) proposes a framework for modeling and simulation of CPS-based factories and applied it to the automotive industry that the authors consider as the most competitive, advanced and complex industrial sector, Jeon et al. (2012) developed a CPS dedicated Meta Modeler (CMM) allowing to design complex and large scale systems, and Yu et al. (2011) proposed (1) a method to model and analyze CPS using a hierarchical and compositional modeling approach contributing to solve the tight coupling between physical and cyber world and (2) basic transformation rules to translate the CPS model into the networks of timed automata. Apart from these few contributions Weyer et al. (2016), Jeon et al. (2012), Yu et al. (2011), and some other less significant, modeling CPS remains a rather marginal area of research.

Modelling is a power tool to take a picture of the CPS and its environment. The project DIH4CPS goes one step further and proposes the elaboration of an ontologically structured knowledge base allowing reasoning based on CPS entities. Although CPS ontologies have already been proposed in the literature as well (Garetti et al., 2015; Petnga & Austin, 2016; Hildebrandt et al., 2018), the ontology proposed in this paper proposes to enrol a CPS ontology in the context of Digital Innovation Hubs competences and networking environment. As for of our knowledge such integration and integration-based reasoning has never been achieved before.

3. GENERIC DIH ONTOLOGY EXTENSION TO CPS

The DIH ontology that we extend to the CPS has been proposed in deliverable 3.3b of the DIH4CPS project. The global UML model of this DIH4CPS and further details are available in D3.3a and b3. To define the CPS ontology extension, we first had to determine and select the most appropriate method for ontology development. The review of the literature proposes therefore various approaches among which: Uschold & Gruninger (1996), Uschold & King (1995), Grüninger & Fox (1995), but also Methontology (Fernández-López et al., 1997), The Cyc Method (Fernández-López & Gómez-Pérez, 2002), KACTUS (Schreiber et al., 1995), SENSUS (Swartout et al., 1996), On-To-Knowledge2, ISO15504-based (Feltus & Rifaut, 2007; Rifaut & Feltus, 2006) and NeOn methodology (Rübmann, 2015; Terreno et al., 2020). For the CPS ontology, we have decided to work with the methodology proposed by Noy & McGuinness (2001). According to them, the development of ontologies requires the following steps: 1. Determine the domain and scope of the ontology, 2. Consider reusing existing ontologies, 3. Enumerate important terms, 4. Define the classes & class hierarchy, 5. Define the properties of classes, 6. Define the facets of the slots, 7. Create instances.

[3] All DIH4CPS deliverables are available at https://dih4cps.eu/ and considered by Eslami et al. (2020)

3.1 Determine the Domain and Scope of the Network Ontology Extension

This section aims to determine what the ontology is going to cover, for which purpose, and especially who will maintain and use this ontology. According to Noy & McGuiness (2001), one method to determine this domain and scope is to enumerate a list of question that the ontology must be able to answer afterwards. This list of question has been iteratively determined through working groups meeting. Examples of questions are: Who can give me advice in CPS technology application? Who can give advice for a specific technology? Which university can offer IT support? Which technologies uses organization A for data storage? Who has experience on sensor sensitivity and calibration? Who has expertise in working with Augmented Reality?

3.2 Consider Reusing Existing Ontologies

To extend the ontology to CPS, we have reviewed the state of the art in CPS ontologies, we have extracted the most important concepts, and we have proposed our own integrated model. Nine additional entities have been added to the DIH4CPS ontology to express that a CPS is a type of product, itself being a type of artefact. This CPS extension claims that CPS are composed of a Cyber Process entity, which is a type of Process and of a Physical Resource entity, which is a type of Resource (Zhang et al., 2015). According to Bertoli et al. (2021), characteristics of CPS are Sensors, Actuators, and HMI for the Physical part, and the Computing, The Software Communication and the Data storing and analytics for the Cyber part, as represented in Figure 1.

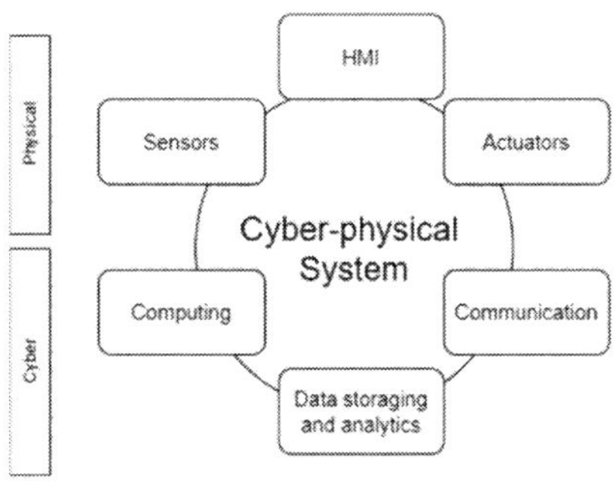

Figure 1. Key CPS characteristics extracted from Bertoli et al. (2021)

3.3 Enumerate Important Terms

Table 1. CPS terms

Concepts	Definition - Explanation
CPS	CPS are the key technology enabling Industry 4.0 and can be applied on different levels in the modern value chain (Bertoli et al., 2021). According to University of Yichita[4], CPS are engineered systems that are built from, and depend upon, the seamless integration of computational algorithms and physical components.
Cyber Process	According to Guo (2017), a cyber process system is a huge system with mass components and complex communication protocol.
Physical Resources	The Physical Resource system correspond to the integration of the physical components or mechanical parts of the CPS.
Computing	The realization of a set of algorithms having an impact on the stat and behavior of the physical system.
Software Communication	The exchange of messages between end-devices and a central network.
Data storing and analytics	The activity of analyzing, holding, deleting, backup organizing, and securing information to be compute to the purpose of the CPS.

[4] https://www.wichita.edu/research/netcpsreu/CPS.php

Sensors	A physical device that detects information form inputs from the physical environment and generate the expected responds.
Actuators	A physical device that achieves physical behavior in response to a cyber or physical order or command.
HMI	The hardware or software through which an operator interacts with a controller[5].

Based on these definitions and explanations, the hereabove concepts have been gather in an integrated ontology as represented on Figure 2.

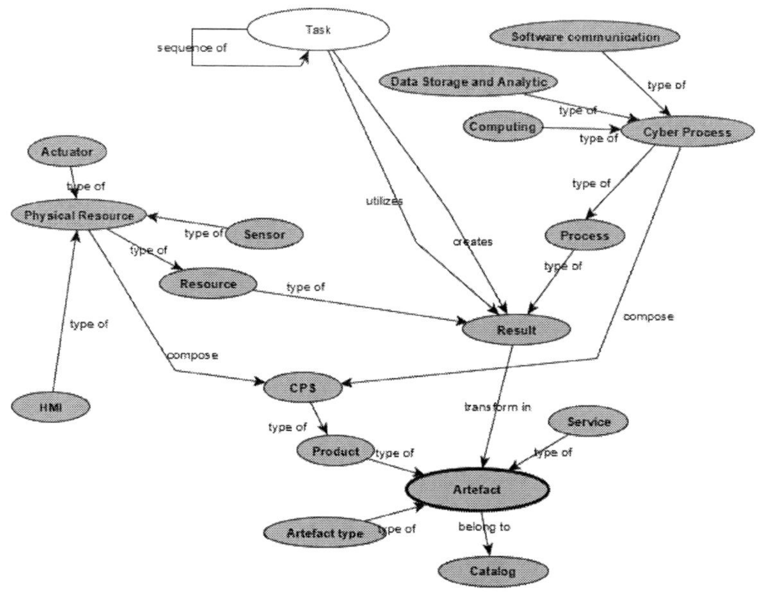

Figure 2. Integrated CPS ontology extension

3.4 Define the Classes & Class Hierarchy

Based on the important concepts enumerated in Table 1, the list of class and class hierarchy is the following: CPS are `type of` Product, Physical Resource and Cyber Process `compose` the CPS, Sensor, Actuator and HMI are `type of` Physical Resource, Data Storage and Analytic, Communication and Computing are `type of` Cyber Process, Physical Resource are `type of` Resource, Cyber Process are `type of` Process, and Sponsor `is an` Organization type.

3.5 Define the Properties of Classes

According to Noy & McGuiness (2001), the classes defined in section 3.3 do not contain enough information to fully and correctly answer all the questions listed in 3.1. Therefore, in this section, the methodology foresees to describe the internal structure of each concept. This step is important and has already partially been achieved in previous section. For instance, the structure of the Network concept has been explained based on the Network-type, the functioning rule and Status, and the relation with the Organization. It will not be further extended here.

[5] https://csrc.nist.gov/glossary/term/human_machine_interface

3.6 Define the Facets of the Slots

The cardinality defines, among others, the cardinalities and values a class may have. Accordingly, in this section, we will focus on defining the classes and associations cardinalities, as explained in Table 2.

Table 2. CPS cardinalities

Cardinality	Concepts	Association	Cardinality	Concepts
1	CPS	Type of	1	Product
1	Actuator, Sensor, HMI	Type of	1	Physical Resource
1	Data Storage and Analytic, Communication, Computing	Type of	1	Cyber Process
1	Physical Resource	Type of	1	Resource
1	Cyber Process	Type of	1	Process
1	Physical Resource	Compose	0 to n	CPS
1	Cyber Process	Compose	0 to n	CPS

3.7 Create Instances

This last step in the methodology is addressed in next section.

4. OPERATIONAL ONTOLOGY

The instantiation of the ontology for the one concrete company is realized with the tool Protégé, and the Luxembourg Institute for Science and Technology was chosen to test the instantiation of the DIH4CPS ontology because it covers a large set of services, competencies, domains, and skills.

4.1 Implementation in Protégé

According to Stanford University[6], Protégé is a "free, open-source ontology editor and framework for building intelligent systems", moreover, "Protégé is supported by a strong community of academic, government, and corporate users, who use Protégé to build knowledge-based solutions in areas as diverse as biomedicine, e-commerce, and organizational modelling". Using Protégé to support the exploitation of the DIH4CPS ontology, first, the 67 classes and 49 object properties have been encoded in Protégé.

In protégé, the relations between classes must be defined as object properties. For instance, as illustrated on Figure 3, the association name "is located" that associate the class "Region" and the class "Country" is the property named "isLocatedInCountry" and this property has for Domains Country and for Ranges Region. Given that all associations with a same name (e.g., "is located") have different Domains and Ranges, we must create as many associations as there exist cases. Therefore, for the "is located", we have three different properties: "isLocatedInCountry", "isLocatedIn- PostalAddress", and "isLocatedInRegion" (cf Figure 3).

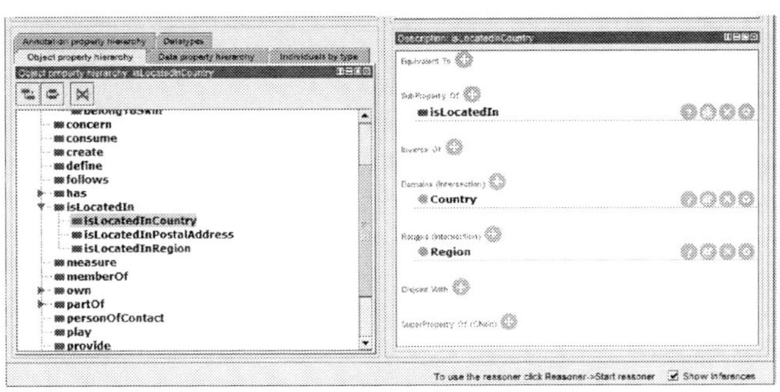

Figure 3. Example of property

[6] https://protege.stanford.edu/

4.2 Business Case Validation Using Inferences

To validate the ontology and to illustrate how it is possible to use it to infer new knowledge, we illustrate how an instance of the PME concept may also be an instance of an RTO using the inference mechanism. To do so, first we have created the individuals (instance of concepts) and data properties of these individuals in section 4.2.1, then, we have created rules in section 4.2.2, afterwards, we have launched the reasoning in section 4.2.3, and we have analyzed the new created knowledge base in Section 4.2.4.

4.2.1 Creation of Individuals

The creation of a new individual consists in defining a new direct instance of a class. For instance, we created an instance of the class PME by selecting the targeted class concept on the top left frame and pushing the mauve lozenge in the bottom left frame.

After the individual being created, it is possible to assign it with Data properties. Data properties need to be defined before being assigned. Therefore, in Protégé's Data property frame, we have defined 3 instances:

1. makesResearch, which is a property that may be assigned to a PME or an RTO, and which is of a type Boolean (True or False)
2. isPublic, which is a property that may also be assigned to a PME or an RTO, and which is of a type Boolean (True or False)
3. hasEmplosees, which is a property that may also be assigned to a PME or an RTO, and which is of a type integer.

Finally, these data properties may be asserted to created individuals. For example, we have asserted that LIST makes research, is public and has 750 employees.

4.2.2 Creation of Rules

The second step to create inference consists in generating inferring rules. There exist various options, therefore. In this paper, we have decided to express an "Equivale To" rule in the description of the RTO class. This rule, illustrated on Figure 4, shows that an RTO is equivalent to a class with the following characteristics: It is an individual of a class "PME" and it has, as data properties: to have more than 500 employees, to be public, and to make research. As illustrated on Figure 4, this is expressed by:

```
PME and (hasEmploees some xsd:integer[>=500] and (isPublic value true)
                    and (makesResearch value true)
```

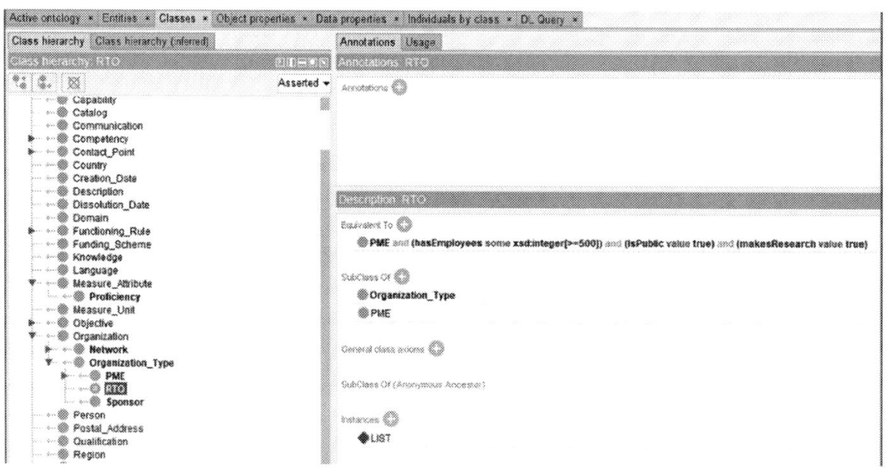

Figure 4. Example with inference

4.2.3 Reasoning

The last step in inferring new knowledge from the ontology consists in launching the reasoner. Before doing so, we observe that the RTO has not LIST individual as direct instance although LIST is an individual of PME.

To launch the reasoning, it is necessary to run a reasoner from the top menu of Protégé. In our case, we have worked with Pellet inference engine (reasoner) (Singh & Karwayun, 2010).

4.2.4 New Knowledge Base

After this reasoning, new inferences are automatically detected and ad to the existing knowledge base. For instance, in the case of LIST, Pellet has detected and a PME may also be considered has a subclass of RTO and that LIST fulfils the 3 conditions to be RTO, to know: to be public, to make research and to employ more than 500 employees. As illustrated on Figure 4, the newly inferred knowledge is highlighted in light yellow.

5. CONCLUSION AND FUTURE WORKS

This paper describes, as main result, the first part of the DIH4CPS ontology presented in D3.3, including its two dimensions, to know: competence and organization. In the second part (Section 3) we have developed the third area of the DIH4CPS ontology dedicated to networking. Therefore, we have reminded the questions the ontology is required to answer, we have developed the methodology proposed by Noy & McGuinness (2001), to identify the class and their associations, and we have integrated this networking area with the competence and organizational areas. Then, we have extended the Artefact Ontology with a CPS description using the same methodology than for defining the network one (Section 4). Finally, in the fourth part, we have encoded the full DIH4CPS ontology within Protégé, we have instantiated it to a real company case (to know: LIST), and we have validated its usability by means of inferences.

Based on the outcomes of this instantiation, updates on the DIH4CPS model could be foreseen if needed following by the instantiation of all the DIH4CPS network. This paper could also be used as a baseline for the development team of the DIH4CPS platform and for further use cases with other companies, and considering other technologies like the blockchain (Imeri et al., 2018).

ACKNOWLEDGEMENT

This work is supported by the project DIH4CPS: "Fostering DIHs for Embedding Interoperability in Cyber-Physical Systems of European SMEs" funded from the European Union's Horizon 2020 research and innovation program under the Grant Agreement no 872548.

REFERENCES

Bertoli, A., Cervo, A., Rosati, C. A., & Fantuzzi, C. (2021). Smart node networks orchestration: a new e2e approach for analysis and design for agile 4.0 implementation. *Sensors*, *21*(5), 1624.

Crupi, A., Del Sarto, N., Di Minin, A., Gregori, G. L., Lepore, D., Marinelli, L., & Spigarelli, F. (2020). The digital transformation of SMEs–a new knowledge broker called the digital innovation hub. *Journal of knowledge management*.

Eslami, Y., Lezoche, M., Semeraro, C., Panetto, H., Guédria, W., & Uhlenkamp, J. F. (2020). D3. 2: DIH4CPS deliverable-Elicitation and Modelling of Competences related to Embedded and Cyber Physical Systems (Doctoral dissertation, European Commission-Directorate-General for Communications Networks, Content and Technology).

Feltus, C., & Rifaut, A. (2007). An ontology for requirements analysis of managers' policies in Financial Institutions. In *Enterprise Interoperability II* (pp. 27-38). Springer, London.

Fernández-López, M., Gómez-Pérez, A. and Juristo, N., 1997. Methontology: from ontological art towards ontological engineering.

Garetti, M., Fumagalli, L., & Negri, E. (2015). Role of ontologies for CPS implementation in manufacturing. *Management and Production Engineering Review*.

Grüninger, M., & Fox, M. S. (1995). Methodology for the design and evaluation of ontologies.Noy, N. F., & McGuinness, D. L. (2001). Ontology development 101: A guide to creating your first ontology.

Gunes, V., Peter, S., Givargis, T., & Vahid, F. (2014). A survey on concepts, applications, and challenges in cyber-physical systems. *KSII Transactions on Internet and Information Systems (TIIS)*, *8*(12), 4242-4268.

Guo, X. (2017). Research on cyber-physical modeling for smart distribution grid. *Energy and Power Engineering*, *9*(04), 544.

Hildebrandt, C., Törsleff, S., Caesar, B., & Fay, A. (2018, August). Ontology building for cyber-physical systems: A domain expert-centric approach. In *2018 IEEE 14th international conference on automation science and engineering (CASE)* (pp. 1079-1086). IEEE.

Imeri, A., Feltus, C., Khadraoui, D., Agoulmine, N., & Nicolas, D. (2018, September). Solving the trust issues in the process of transportation of dangerous goods by using blockchain technology. In *Proceedings of the 11th International Conference on Security of Information and Networks* (pp. 1-2).

Jamaludin, J., & Rohani, J. M. (2018, November). Cyber-physical system (cps): State of the art. In *2018 International Conference on Computing, Electronic and Electrical Engineering (ICE Cube)* (pp. 1-5). IEEE.

Jeon, J., Chun, I., & Kim, W. (2012). Metamodel-based CPS modeling tool. In *Embedded and multimedia computing technology and service* (pp. 285-291). Springer, Dordrecht.

Kim, H., Kang, J., & Park, J. H. (2017). A light-weight secure information transmission and device control scheme in integration of CPS and cloud computing. *Microprocessors and Microsystems*, *52*, 416-426.

Kim, J., Kim, H., Lakshmanan, K., & Rajkumar, R. (2013, April). Parallel scheduling for cyber-physical systems: Analysis and case study on a self-driving car. In *Proceedings of the ACM/IEEE 4th international conference on cyber-physical systems* (pp. 31-40).

Kumar, C., Marston, S., & Sen, R. (2020). Cyber-physical Systems (CPS) Security: State of the Art and Research Opportunities for Information Systems Academics. *Communications of the Association for Information Systems*, *47*(1), 36.

Petnga, L., & Austin, M. (2016). An ontological framework for knowledge modeling and decision support in cyber-physical systems. *Advanced Engineering Informatics*, *30*(1), 77-94.

Rifaut, A., & Feltus, C. (2006). Improving Operational Risk Management Systems by Formalizing the Basel II Regulation with Goal Models and the ISO/IEC 15504 Approach. In *ReMo2V*

Rüßmann, M., Lorenz, M., Gerbert, P., Waldner, M., Engel, P., Harnisch, M., & Justus, J. (2015). Future of Productivity and Growth in Manufacturing. Boston Consulting.

Sassanelli, C., & Terzi, S. (2022). Building the Value Proposition of a Digital Innovation Hub Network to Support Ecosystem Sustainability. *Sustainability*, *14*(18), 11159.

Schreiber, G., Wielinga, B., & Jansweijer, W. (1995, August). The KACTUS view on the 'O'word. In *IJCAI workshop on basic ontological issues in knowledge sharing* (Vol. 20, p. 21).

Shih, C. S., Chou, J. J., Reijers, N., & Kuo, T. W. (2016). Designing CPS/IoT applications for smart buildings and cities. *IET Cyber-Physical Systems: Theory & Applications*, *1*(1), 3-12.

Singh, S., & Karwayun, R. (2010, April). A comparative study of inference engines. In *2010 seventh international conference on information technology: New generations* (pp. 53-57). IEEE Staab, S., & Studer, R. (Eds.). (2010). *Handbook on ontologies*. Springer Science & Business Media.

Sun, C. C., Hahn, A., & Liu, C. C. (2018). Cyber security of a power grid: State-of-the-art. *International Journal of Electrical Power & Energy Systems*, *99*, 45-56.

Swartout, B., Patil, R., Knight, K., & Russ, T. (1996, November). Toward distributed use of large-scale ontologies. In *Proc. of the Tenth Workshop on Knowledge Acquisition for Knowledge-Based Systems* (Vol. 138, No. 148, p. 25).

Terreno, S., Akanmu, A., Anumba, C. J., & Olayiwola, J. (2020). Cyber-physical social systems for facility management. In *Cyber-Physical Systems in the Built Environment* (pp. 297-308). Springer, Cham.

Uschold, M., & Gruninger, M. (1996). Ontologies: Principles, methods and applications. *The knowledge engineering review*, *11*(2), 93-136.

Uschold, M., & King, M. (1995). *Towards a methodology for building ontologies* (pp. 1-13). Edinburgh: Artificial Intelligence Applications Institute, University of Edinburgh.

Weyer, S., Meyer, T., Ohmer, M., Gorecky, D., & Zühlke, D. (2016). Future modeling and simulation of CPS-based factories: an example from the automotive industry. *Ifac-Papersonline*, *49*(31), 97-102.

Yang, G., Pang, Z., Deen, M. J., Dong, M., Zhang, Y. T., Lovell, N., & Rahmani, A. M. (2020). Homecare robotic systems for healthcare 4.0: visions and enabling technologies. *IEEE journal of biomedical and health informatics*, *24*(9), 2535-2549.

Yu, Z., Yunwei, D., Fan, Z., & Yunfeng, Z. (2011, September). Research on Modeling and Analysis of CPS. In *International Conference on Autonomic and Trusted Computing* (pp. 92-105). Springer, Berlin, Heidelberg.

Zhang, Y., Qiu, M., Tsai, C. W., Hassan, M. M., & Alamri, A. (2015). Health-CPS: Healthcare cyber-physical system assisted by cloud and big data. *IEEE Systems Journal*, *11*(1), 88-95.

MOTION SIMULATION AND VIRTUAL REALITY IN V-COMMERCE - HOW THE USE OF MOTION SIMULATION AFFECTS CUSTOMER VALUE, PURCHASE INTENTION, AND TRUST IN AUTONOMOUS VEHICLES

Roger Seiler, Riccardo Fiore and Stefan Koruna
Zurich University of Applied Sciences
St. Georgen- Platz 2, 8400 Winterthur, Switzerland

ABSTRACT

Autonomous vehicles (AVs) have captured the public imagination and may soon become an integral part of smart city concepts. Currently, preparations by city administrators, legislators, and politicians still lag behind technological developments. However, AVs may soon be capable of solving mobility issues and fundamentally extending micro-mobility concepts, including peer-to-peer taxi services such as Uber, in urban areas. As a result, mobility concepts could become more efficient, effective, and sustainable. Price acceptance, fuel efficiency, and mode of use (private or sharing) are relevant factors in determining the benefit of AVs for consumers. This paper focuses on the acceptance aspect. The Yaw 1 motion simulator was used to conduct a randomized control experiment (high vs. low motion simulation (MS)) to determine what driving style leads to higher acceptance and, thus, greater purchase intention. In addition, we examined how other aspects of virtual commerce (V-commerce) (customer value, purchase intention, trust, emotional involvement, and presence) might be affected by MS use. In particular driving style was found to be relevant and should be taken into account when designing mobility concepts that include AVs.

KEYWORDS

Purchase Intention, Smart City, Autonomous Vehicles, V-Commerce, Motion Simulation, Driving Style

1. INTRODUCTION

The technologies involved in creating smart cities, in particular those connected to autonomous vehicles (AVs), could help render mobility more sustainable. Smart mobility and the associated connectivity are ideally suited to meet the needs and expectations of the inhabitants of urban areas. Services such as Uber and micro-mobility (e.g., electro scooters such as Tier, Lime, and Bird) could help decongest busy city streets (Shahidehpour et al., 2018). In addition, AVs might also become a valuable aspect of smart cities as well as reducing the costs related to mobility services by dispensing with costly human drivers.

According to Perveen et al. (2017), societies all over the world are affected on an unprecedented scale by urban growth, and the effect on the environment is enormous. In fact, traffic in modern cities roughly accounts for one-third of emissions, which is why the potential of AVs in terms of their contribution to combatting climate change was found to be highly promising. In the literature, various scenarios have been developed that could help governments with this challenging task (Perveen et al., 2017).

2. LITERATURE REVIEW

In this part of the paper, the relevant constructs and the related literature are introduced from which a conceptual model and hypotheses were derived. While virtual reality (VR) has many useful applications, it can lead to cybersickness, which is especially true for MS due to vection. The paper further covers customer-related constructs such as customer value, purchase intention, trust, emotional involvement, and presence. Hence, these are all introduced in the following.

Vection is the concept of experiencing one's own motion (Ash et al., 2013). The body recognizes acceleration such as rotation, and this feeling of acceleration can lead to the illusion of movement (Colley et al., 2022). Empirical evidence suggests that a combination of rotation impulse and VR heightens the effect of vection (Colley et al., 2022; Rietzler et al., 2018; Wright, 2009), which can also increase motion sickness (Colley et al., 2022). Simulators with 13 degrees of freedom would eliminate the problem, but they come with a price tag of some 80 million dollars (Colley et al., 2022). Conveniently, simulators with lower degrees of freedom are sufficient for participants to experience the sensation of movement (Colley et al., 2022; Danieau et al., 2012; Gugenheimer et al., 2016).

SAE International recognizes six levels of automated driving: 0) No driving automation, 1) Driver assistance, 2) Partial driving automation, 3) Conditional driving automation, 4) High driving automation, and 5) Full driving automation (Kelechava, 2021). Autonomous driving is considered to be Level 5 (Faisal et al., 2019) because only at this level can drivers be considered real passengers in the true sense of the meaning without having to be "on standby to take over from the autopilot" as, for example, Tesla calls it.

As has already been stated above, the sensation of motion does not come without pitfalls. If the body's sensory perception is not completely in line with the movements seen in the head mounted display (HMD), motion sickness can occur (Caserman et al., 2021; Colley et al., 2022). Symptoms range from nausea and headaches to dizziness (Caserman et al., 2021). Similar problems can occur if technical details, such as the inter-pupillary distance, are not adjusted for correctly (Seiler et al., 2022). It is hardly surprising that these effects can have a negative impact on customer-related constructs such as customer value, net promoter score (NPS), consumers' trust in a vendor and purchase intentions (Seiler et al., 2022). Brand evaluation and purchase intention can negatively be affected by cybersickness (Breves and Dodel, 2021).

E-commerce has become an important feature of the Internet. As a result, VR is researched regarding its potential for commercial application. Martínez-Navarro et al. (2019) proposed a model which was generated by applying VR to the e-commerce setting. Other researchers, such as de Regt and Barnes (2019), have also conducted research on the topic, mainly focusing on the retail context. As depicted in Figure 1, emotions as well as affective appraisal play a vital role in presence and brand recall. This in turn can significantly affect purchase intention (Martínez-Navarro et al., 2019). Presence is the psychological sense of presence and people to behave like in the real world because the think they are actually there (Martínez-Navarro et al., 2019).

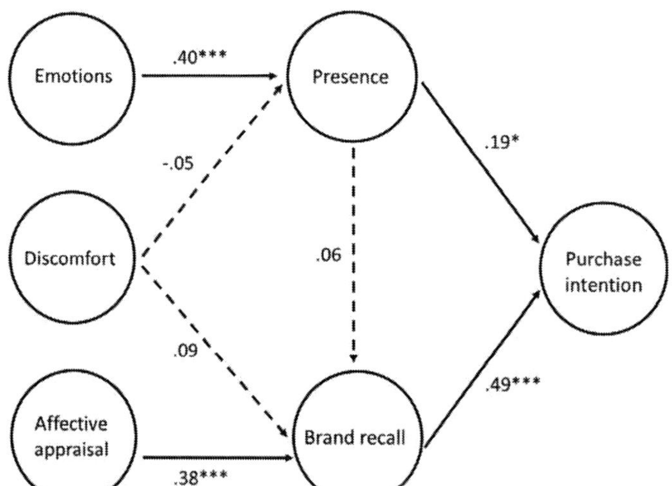

Figure 1. V-commerce model (Martinez et al., 2019)

The acceptance of autonomous driving vehicles depends on many factors according to Nastjuk et al. (2020). However, they considered neither VR nor MS. This study addresses this research gap by examining whether and how VR and MS affect customer value, purchase intention, trust, AV acceptance, emotional involvement, and presence.

We therefore asked the following research question (RQ): How can MS and VR be used in the context of virtual commerce (V-commerce) and AVs? In addition, we also formulated several sub-research questions: *How does the use of VR and MS in v-commerce affect customer value (SRQ1)?, How does the use of VR and*

MS in v-commerce affect purchase intention (SRQ2)?, How does the use of VR and MS in v-commerce affect trust (SRQ3)?, How does the use of VR and MS in v-commerce affect AV acceptance (SRQ4)?, How does the use of VR and MS in v-commerce affect emotional involvement (SRQ5)?, and how does the use of VR and MS in the context of AVs in v-commerce affect presence (SRQ6)?.

Hypotheses were derived from the literature, and an overview of the resulting conceptual model is given below (see Figure 2).

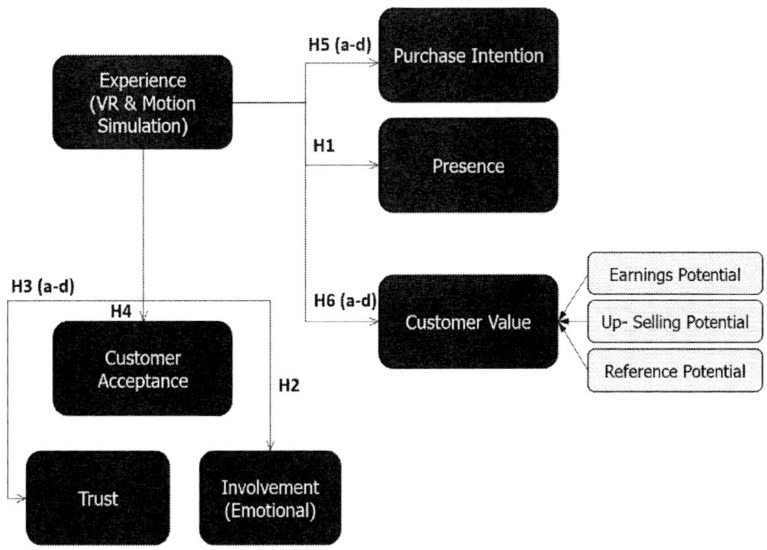

Figure 2. Conceptual model used in this paper

3. METHOD

We decided to conduct a randomized control experiment using the Yaw 1 motion simulator[1] (see Figure 3) and two speeds (driving styles) to take participants through a scenario. The parameterization of the intensity of the motion experienced in the one scenario is high (fast driving style with high levels of motion) and in the other one low. This is how the two speeds of driving styles are implemented. Previous research on the topic had been conducted by Yildirim et al. (2020), whose findings laid the foundations for our study as the source code was kindly provided. With the help of the authors of the source code (Cymmersion GmbH), the application was extended and adapted for our experiment. The application runs on Unity Engine (2019). The following adaptations were made: We reduced the time of the ride with the AV, integrated the Yaw 1 software development kit, and extended the ride to include a market scene.

The scenario starts at an open grocery market during a thunderstorm. Ginny, a digital companion, explains how the participant can get home by ordering an autonomous taxi. After this monologue, the participant uses a tablet to order an autonomous taxi (see Figure 5). After the taxi arrives (see Figure 5), the participant raises the HMD a little to sit in the motion simulator. The taxi then drives autonomously (without driver or passenger interaction) along the predefined route. The journey of the autonomous taxi is physically mapped by the motion simulator. After the car stops at the side of the road, the sequence ends.

[1] The Yaw 2 motion simulator (see Figure 4) is more advanced. Its design resembles that of a car seat, which makes it more comfortable than the half-sphere used for Yaw 1. However, at the time of conducting the experiment, Yaw 2 was not yet available.

Figure 3. Yaw 1 motion simulator

Figure 4. Yaw 2 motion simulator

To start the experiment, participants were asked to draw a random number (even numbers were assigned the parameterization of Script 1, odd ones of Script 2). Next, they were asked to fill out a pre-VR-experience questionnaire to serve as a base line. Then were they introduced to the VR gear (HTC Vive Pro Wireless) and strapped into the Yaw 1 for the actual experiment. After completing the driving sequence, participants filled out a post-VR-experience questionnaire.

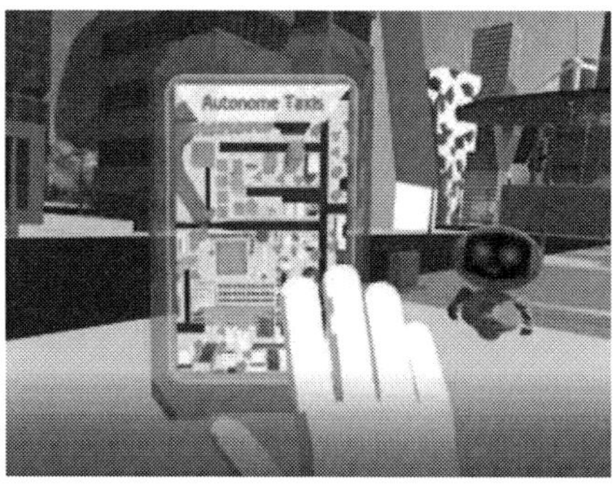

Figure 5. Autonomous taxi app in VR scenario

Figure 6. Picture of AV in VR scenario

The operationalization was based on existing literature (see Table 1). Three constructs are noteworthy as they are our own or were created based on constructs found in the existing literature. We used our own demographic variables and questions regarding mobility use. Customer value was adapted to the context of our study. The construct "customer value" was operationalized using three subdimensions: earnings, referral, and up-selling potential. Reichheld's (2003) NPS, recently extended for measuring emotions Müller et al. (2021) as net emotional value (NPV), measures referral potential and is often used in the context of customer satisfaction. Satisfaction is an antecedent to referral (Meilatinova, 2021). We decided to use NPS in this study because emotional value is already captured by a separate construct, and to enable comparisons to prior research.

Table 1. Overview of operationalization

Construct	Variable name (scale)	Author(s)
Demographic	ID (0-60) Age in years Gender	Own item
Mobility	Which means of transport do you use? (MC) [Car, electric car, public transport, car sharing, e-scooter, e-bike, bicycle, or other (open text)	Own item
Presence	6 items (Likert scale)	Usoh et al. (2000)
Emotional involvement	5 items (7-point Likert scale)	Martínez-Navarro et al. (2019)
Trust	6 items	Nastjuk et al. (2020)
Acceptance	Sum of trust and emotional involvement	
Purchase intention	3 items	Vieth (2008)
Customer value	Earnings potential Referral potential (NPS) Up-selling potential	Based on the existing literature

LimeSurvey was used as survey tool and R as well as R studio as tools for statistical analysis. openxlsx [Excel import], tidyverse [visualization], magrittr [linking of commands], psych [Cronbach's Alpha], broom [visualization], and reshape2 [restructuring and aggregation of data] were used as packages.

The highly parameterized setting (treatment group) had 25 participants (56.8 percent), the low parameterized scenario (control group) had 19 (43.2 percent). Highly parameterized means that the script controlling Yaw 1 hand X = 5, Y = 2, and Z= -3 and for the low parameterized version X =2, Y = 1 and Z = -1 as vector that is multiplied with a velocity vector.

4. RESULTS, DISCUSSION, FURTHER RESEARCH, AND LIMITATIONS

44 people participated in the experiment. Nobody had to abort due to cybersickness, and both questionnaires were completed in full by all participants. 36 percent were male and 64 percent female. The average age was 24. Regarding mobility, the following was reported: 77 percent (car), 0 percent (electric car), 95 percent (public transport), 7 percent (car sharing), 5 percent (e-scooter), 7 percent (e-bike), and 45 percent bicycle. One participant stated that they also walk.

Table 2. Comparison of pre- and post-VR-application questionnaire (mean values)

	Pre-VR (baseline)		**Post-VR**	
	Treatment	*Control*	*Treatment*	*Control*
Presence	*NA*	*NA*	2.88	2.88
Emotional involvement	*NA*	*NA*	3.81	3.75
Trust	4.12	3.96	4.19	3.93
Acceptance	*NA*	*NA*	4.05	3.87
Purchase intention	2.54	2.84	3.24	3.02
Earnings potential	3.58	3.12	3.26	3.24
Up-selling potential	3.42	3.64	3.32	3.44
Referral potential	*NA*	*NA*	3.55	3.60
Customer value	3.50	3.38	3.38	3.43

Cronbach's Alpha was used to check whether the constructs are reliable or not. Most constructs were above the cut-off value of .8 (Cronbach, 1951) and, except for "presence", all constructs were above the cut-off value of .7, proposed as sufficient by Nunally (1978). The Cronbach's Alpha values were as follows: .53 (presence) .71 (emotional involvement), .83 (trust), .7 (acceptance), .9 (purchase intention), and .76 (customer value).

A Shapiro Wilk test was also conducted. Presence, acceptance, and purchase intention were found to be normally distributed whereas emotional involvement, trust, and customer value were not. For further analysis of non-parametric or non-normally distributed constructs, a Wilcoxon test was used, as well as the t-test for normally distributed constructs (see Table 3).

The Hypotheses H1 to H7 (see Table 3 below) were tested accordingly, and the test statistics as well as the results were reported. Except for H5b and H5c regarding purchase intention, all other hypotheses were found not to be significant (H1 to H4 and H6 and H7).

It was found that neither high nor low parameterization in combination with VR affect presence or lead to emotional involvement, nor do they foster trust or customer value. Furthermore, a higher parameterized MS in combination with VR does not foster acceptance or purchase intention.

However, low parameterized MS positively affects purchase intention (H5b), and MS in combination with the VR experience presented in this study positively affects purchase intention (H5c). Earlier research pointed in the same direction, suggesting that VR positively affects purchase intention (Martínez-Navarro et al., 2019) or purchasing decisions (Harren et al., 2019).

Table 3. Overview of hypotheses, tests and results

#	**Path & test statistics**	**Result**
H1	High parameterized MS leads to higher presence values than MS with low parameterization (T[42] = 0.012, p = 0.495).	Rejected
H2	High parameterized MS leads to higher emotional involvement than MS with low parameterization (T[42] = -0.924, p = 0.361).	Rejected
H3a	High parameterized MS leads to higher trust than MS with low parameterization (T[24] = -0.511, p = 0.693).	Rejected
H3b	Low parameterized MS leads to higher trust than MS with high parameterization (T[18] = 0.794, p = 0.219).	Rejected
H3c	MS leads to higher trust in AV (T[43] = 0.081, p = 0.468).	Rejected
H4	High parameterized MS leads to higher acceptance than low parameterized MS (T[42] = -1.279, p = 0.896).	Rejected
H5a	High parameterized MS positively affects purchase intention (T[24] = 0.633, p = 0.266).	Rejected
H5b	Low parameterized MS positively affects purchase intention (T[18] = 2.466, p = 0.012).	Accepted
H5c	MS positively affects purchase intention (T[43] = 1.972, p = 0.028).	Accepted
H6a	High parameterized MS positively affects customer value (U = 140, p = 0.482).	Rejected
H6b	Low parameterized MS positively affects customer value (U = 96, p = 0.492).	Rejected
H6c	MS positively affects customer value (U = 454.5, p = 0.488).	Rejected
H7	High parameterized MS affects reference potential more than low parameterized MS (U = 253, p = 0.358).	Rejected

4.1 Further Research

Our study backs up earlier research and literature in suggesting that further research needs to be conducted to gain a deeper understanding of the constructs as well as their relationship to each other in the context of VR and MS. This is rather important as well as relevant because, in our study, VR and MS not only appear to have a positive effect on purchase intention but also on other business-relevant constructs such as customer value, trust, and emotional involvement. Positive effects have also been reported according to the empirical evidence. Hence, further research could focus on qualitative approaches to complement this study and identify the underlying reasons for its findings.

The low Cronbach's Alpha score of the construct "presence" may be addressed in further research by other forms of operationalization or qualitative research as to why this occurred in contradiction to prior research.

Further research may replicate this study using a representative sample as the sample in this study consists of rather young participants. Finally, replicating this study using more realistic hardware and haptics (e.g., the Yaw 2 rather than Yaw 1 simulator) may yield different results.

4.2 Limitations

The number of participants is rather low compared to other quantitative research and therefore, results may not be generalized unconditionally. Nevertheless, these results may be considered early stage and regarding method as well scenario a starting point and opportunity for further research. Also, the low Cronbach's Alpha score of "presence" must be mentioned because this construct is not reliable in the context of this study and one may speculate that this could be linked to the following point affecting the experience and thus the concept of presence.

Concerning the participants in the experiment, it could be possible that not everybody had the same experience because the motion simulator had to be adjusted for taller or larger participants (e.g., 1.90 m or 90 kg) to enable the motor to bring participants back into a centered position. Similarly, due to the physical dimensions of Yaw 1, not everybody (especially taller participants) could take the same seated position. Whereas smaller participants had no issues in sitting in an upright and seated position, taller participants were forced to lean back a bit (which may have been a further reason for the limitation regarding the position just mentioned, occurred, as the leverage increases and leads to a more imbalanced setting).

Finally, all participants were rather young, and results might have been different for a representative sample of the population.

5. CONCLUDING REMARKS

Our findings suggest that businesses looking to increase purchase intention among their customers might want to consider the use of VR and MS. However, a low parameterized MS is advisable because higher levels do not have the effect of increasing purchase intention. In addition, positive effects could not be reported for customer value, trust, and emotional involvement.

These preliminary results show that VR and MS can be relevant to businesses. In the light of the trend of consumers shopping in electronic settings, MS may be a further sales channel to complement classic retail showrooms or other forms of analogue sales approaches.

It must be pointed out that the results of our research apply to the context of AVs only. Results may vary if VR and MS are used in a consumer goods or B2B setting.

We hope our research may be of interest to the initiators of smart cities concepts considering autonomous vehicles as part of their mobility concept. In particular, cities planning to use AVs to fight climate change may find these results useful, especially considering that traffic accounts for a third of emissions in urban communities (Perveen et al., 2017).

REFERENCES

Ash, A., Palmisano, S., Apthorp, D., Allison, R.S., 2013. Vection in Depth during Treadmill Walking. Perception 42, 562–576. https://doi.org/10.1068/p7449

Breves, P., Dodel, N., 2021. The influence of cybersickness and the media devices' mobility on the persuasive effects of 360° commercials. Multimed Tools Appl 80, 27299–27322. https://doi.org/10.1007/s11042-021-11057-x

Caserman, P., Garcia-Agundez, A., Gámez Zerban, A., Göbel, S., 2021. Cybersickness in current-generation virtual reality head-mounted displays: systematic review and outlook. Virtual Reality 25, 1153–1170. https://doi.org/10.1007/s10055-021-00513-6

Colley, M., Jansen, P., Rukzio, E., Gugenheimer, J., 2022. SwiVR-Car-Seat: Exploring Vehicle Motion Effects on Interaction Quality in Virtual Reality Automated Driving Using a Motorized Swivel Seat. Proc. ACM Interact. Mob. Wearable Ubiquitous Technol. 5, 150:1-150:26. https://doi.org/10.1145/3494968

Cronbach, L., 1951. Coefficient alpha and the internal structure of tests. Psychometrika 16, 297–334. https://doi.org/10.1007/bf02310555

Danieau, F., Fleureau, J., Guillotel, P., Mollet, N., Lécuyer, A., Christie, M., 2012. HapSeat: producing motion sensation with multiple force-feedback devices embedded in a seat, in: Proceedings of the 18th ACM Symposium on Virtual Reality Software and Technology, VRST '12. Association for Computing Machinery, New York, NY, USA, pp. 69–76. https://doi.org/10.1145/2407336.2407350

de Regt, A., Barnes, S.J., 2019. V-Commerce in Retail: Nature and Potential Impact, in: tom Dieck, M.C., Jung, T. (Eds.), Augmented Reality and Virtual Reality: The Power of AR and VR for Business. Springer International Publishing, Cham, pp. 17–25. https://doi.org/10.1007/978-3-030-06246-0_2

Faisal, A., Yigitcanlar, T., Kamruzzaman, M., Currie, G., 2019. Understanding autonomous vehicles: A systematic literature review on capability, impact, planning and policy. Journal of Transport and Land Use 12. https://doi.org/10.5198/jtlu.2019.1405

Gugenheimer, J., Wolf, D., Haas, G., Krebs, S., Rukzio, E., 2016. SwiVRChair: A Motorized Swivel Chair to Nudge Users' Orientation for 360 Degree Storytelling in Virtual Reality, in: Proceedings of the 2016 CHI Conference on Human Factors in Computing Systems, CHI '16. Association for Computing Machinery, New York, NY, USA, pp. 1996–2000. https://doi.org/10.1145/2858036.2858040

Harren, B., Seiler, R., Müller, S., 2019. Augmented Reality und Virtual Reality im Premium- und Luxus-Retail, in: Uhl, A., Loretan, S. (Eds.), Digitalisierung in der Praxis. Springer Fachmedien Wiesbaden, Wiesbaden, pp. 183–195. https://doi.org/10.1007/978-3-658-26137-5_12

Kelechava, B., 2021. SAE Levels of Driving Automation. The ANSI Blog. URL https://blog.ansi.org/sae-levels-driving-automation-j-3016-2021/ (accessed 7.25.22).

Martínez-Navarro, J., Bigné, E., Guixeres, J., Alcañiz, M., Torrecilla, C., 2019. The influence of virtual reality in e-commerce. Journal of Business Research 100, 475–482. https://doi.org/10.1016/j.jbusres.2018.10.054

Meilatinova, N., 2021. Social commerce: Factors affecting customer repurchase and word-of-mouth intentions. International Journal of Information Management 57, 102300. https://doi.org/10.1016/j.ijinfomgt.2020.102300

Müller, S., Seiler, R., Völkle, M., 2021. Measuring emotions in customer relationships: Can NEV replace NPS? Presented at the EMAC Conference, Madrid, Spain.

Nastjuk, I., Herrenkind, B., Marrone, M., Brendel, A.B., Kolbe, L.M., 2020. What drives the acceptance of autonomous driving? An investigation of acceptance factors from an end-user's perspective. Technological Forecasting and Social Change 161, 120319. https://doi.org/10.1016/j.techfore.2020.120319

Nunally, J., 1978. Psychometric theory. McGraw-Hill, New York.

Perveen, S., Kamruzzaman, M., Yigitcanlar, T., 2017. Developing Policy Scenarios for Sustainable Urban Growth Management: A Delphi Approach. Sustainability 9, 1787. https://doi.org/10.3390/su9101787

Reichheld, F., 2003. The one Number You Need to Grow. Havard Business Review, 81 (12) 46–54.

Rietzler, M., Hirzle, T., Gugenheimer, J., Frommel, J., Dreja, T., Rukzio, E., 2018. VRSpinning: Exploring the Design Space of a 1D Rotation Platform to Increase the Perception of Self-Motion in VR, in: Proceedings of the 2018 Designing Interactive Systems Conference, DIS '18. Association for Computing Machinery, New York, NY, USA, pp. 99–108. https://doi.org/10.1145/3196709.3196755

Seiler, R., Brodmann, T., Keller, T., 2022. Trust and cybersickness in VR-marketing : investigating IPD and cybersickness, and their effects on trust, customer value, NPS, cross- and up-selling. Presented at the 20th International Conference e-Society 2022, Virtual, 12-14 March 2022, IADIS, pp. 99–106.

Shahidehpour, M., Li, Z., Ganji, M., 2018. Smart cities for a sustainable urbanization: Illuminating the need for establishing smart urban infrastructures. IEEE Electrification Magazine 6, 16–33. https://doi.org/10.1109/MELE.2018.2816840

Usoh, M., Catena, E., Arman, S., Slater, M., 2000. Using Presence Questionnaires in Reality. Presence: Teleoperators and Virtual Environments 9, 497–503. https://doi.org/10.1162/105474600566989

Vieth, M., 2008. Geld-zurück-Garantien: eine empirische Wirkungsanalyse aus Konsumentensicht, 1. Aufl. ed, Unternehmensführung und Marketing. Gabler, Wiesbaden.

Wright, W.G., 2009. Linear vection in virtual environments can be strengthened by discordant inertial input, in: 2009 Annual International Conference of the IEEE Engineering in Medicine and Biology Society. Presented at the 2009 Annual International Conference of the IEEE Engineering in Medicine and Biology Society, pp. 1157–1160. https://doi.org/10.1109/IEMBS.2009.5333425

Yildirim, O., Pidel, C., West, M., 2020. Future Mobility Solutions: A Use Case for Understanding How VR Influences User Perception, in: 2020 IEEE International Conference on Artificial Intelligence and Virtual Reality (AIVR). Presented at the 2020 IEEE International Conference on Artificial Intelligence and Virtual Reality (AIVR), pp. 184–187. https://doi.org/10.1109/AIVR50618.2020.00038

USER-ADAPTIVE NAVIGATION FOR ELDERLY PEDESTRIANS BASED ON PREFERENCE INFORMATION

Hiroshi Furukawa[1] and Ryotaro Mine[2]
[1]*Institute of Systems and Information Engineering, University of Tsukuba, 1-1-1 Tenoudai, Tsukuba, Ibaraki, 305-8577, Japan*
[2]*Department of Risk Engineering, University of Tsukuba, 1-1-1 Tenoudai, Tsukuba, Ibaraki, 305-8577, Japan*

ABSTRACT

The aim of our project is to develop a route planning method that can provide each user with an appropriate route, taking into consideration the walkability, safety, and pleasantness peculiar to the elderly. To achieve this goal, we constructed a quantitative model that expresses the relationship between the attributes of elderly users and their preference for route selection and proposed a method of individual adaptation of the model using post-walking preference evaluations of route factors. We used "acceptable detour time" to quantify user preferences. A paper survey and a walking experiment were conducted to examine the feasibility of the proposed method. It is confirmed that the targeted user attributes are useful in estimating the preferences of the elderly for the routes. In some situations, we were able to identify improvements in the participants' evaluation of the routes. The result indicates the feasibility of the user adaptation method. By adjusting the update parameters and using more data, it is expected to plan routes that are adapted to individuals with high accuracy.

KEYWORDS

Pedestrian Navigation, Elderly, User Adaptive Model, Preference Estimation, Intelligent Transport Systems

1. INTRODUCTION

Pedestrian navigation services have become standardized on mobile phone terminals with GPS functions. In addition, path-finding methods that incorporate demands other than the shortest distance have also been studied. On the other hand, researchers have reported numerous factors that hinder the outgoing activities of the elderly (Muronaga and Morozumi, 2003, Yoshikawa, 2011, Mizuno, 2011). To improve the quality of life (QOL) of the elderly, support methods that enhance outdoor activities are attracting attention. However, conventional pedestrian navigation systems that only provide the shortest routes are not sufficient to assist the elderly when they go out.

We are developing a route-finding method using a model that quantitatively considers physical difficulty, psychological vulnerability, sense of security, and preferences with respect to environmental factors on the route, i.e., an environmental factor cost model, in order to realize an effective route guidance method to improve the QOL of the elderly. In particular, we have attempted to identify factors that can consider the physical and mental conditions of elderly users and construct a quantitative cost function based on these factors. Here, we found that the difference in individual subjective evaluation is remarkable; therefore, using only the average value model is insufficient to obtain high user satisfaction (Furukawa, 2015).

As a countermeasure, we got the idea of personalized navigation considering the subjective evaluation of walkability, safety, and pleasantness (Furukawa and Wang, 2020). Although research on personal adaptation methods has been conducted worldwide, it has the potential to diverge from the actual situation of users due to limitations in model construction methods and lack of adaptability (Novack, et al., 2018, Torres, et al., 2018). The issue that we focused on for the practical application of this method is the "automatic response to individual differences of users." This target is particularly important in improving the quality of life of the elderly and in making emergency decisions during disaster evacuation.

The conditions set for the practical application of the proposed method are shown below.

- To eliminate the influence of individual differences, we create a "set of environmental factor cost models" for each user.

- In order to ensure the convenience of the navigation system, detailed interviews regarding user preferences will not be conducted.

- For the same reason, the hearing of evaluations of environmental factors to users at the time of use should be minimized.

Under these conditions, the research question is, "Is a model for estimating environmental factor costs that automatically adapts to each user using the user's attributes useful in finding a route that satisfies the requirements of each elderly person?" If this becomes possible, the cost model will be adjusted semi-automatically at the time of use, and the user will receive a personalized route guidance service with only a few responses to the evaluation mechanism.

2. RELATED WORKS

Research on personalized navigation has been conducted worldwide to improve pedestrian navigation services. The following is a summary of representative studies and their differences from this study.

Darko et al. proposed a route search method adapted to each user's physical condition for people with disabilities (Darko, 2022). A model based on the hierarchical analysis method is created for each user's preference for sidewalks, depending on the time of day, sidewalk conditions, weather, etc. It has some limitations, such as the fact that the target is limited to the evaluation of sidewalks, and the physical condition and the importance of each factor must be obtained from each user in advance. The advantage of our research is that it minimizes the amount of information acquired in advance and automatically adapts based on measurement data at the time of use.

Ertz et al. proposed a method to generate comfortable pedestrian routes in the presence of green spaces, social areas, and quiet roads (Ertz, 2021). Environmental factors and process methods are based on questionnaire surveys, and the necessity and sufficiency of route factors and the validity of quantification of each cost for factors have not been confirmed. Through multiple evaluation experiments, we have already obtained a wealth of reliable knowledge (Furukawa, 2015, 2020), which gives us an advantage. In this study, we focus on the user-adaptive method of quantitative cost.

Jonietz focused on the user's physical ability and preferences, similar to our study, and extracted environmental attribute data (aesthetic buildings, number of stairs, road surface conditions, green space, etc.) in the area visited by the user from walking history data, and proposed a route recommendation method using this (Jonietz, 2016). They do not use the "subjective evaluation by users," which is taken into account in our study. It also positions the visit as highly rated, which has the potential to deviate from the actual situation of the user. The cost used is also difficult to modify by the user.

3. A METHOD FOR QUANTIFYING PREFERENCES

Considering the diversity of users, it is difficult to quantify preferences (i.e., walkability, safety, and pleasantness) in a form that can be reflected in route guidance. In this study, we use the acceptable detour time proposed by Matsuda et al. (2004).

Two situations are assumed for the acceptable detour time (Matsuda, 2004). Figure 1 (a) shows the situation, where the detour time is the additional time accepted by the user to avoid a place with a high physical load (e.g., a steep slope) or high risk (e.g., a road without a sidewalk). In the situation shown in Figure 1 (b), the detour time is defined as the additional time that the user can accept to select the route with a preferred spot that is easier to walk, lower risk (e.g., an intersection with traffic signals), or more pleasure (e.g., a park).

Based on the concept of the acceptable detour time, the cost considering the user's preference is defined as Equations (1) and (2).

the revised cost of the detour path = α (the cost based on the physical distance of the detour path), (1)

α = (travel time for the shortest path) / (travel time for the shortest path + the acceptable detour time). (2)

When the value of the detour route for a user increases (that is, the acceptable detour time becomes longer), the revised cost decreases. The revised cost will be used instead of the original cost, when the path has one of the spots (described in Table 1 for this study). This cost function makes it possible to take pedestrian preferences into consideration in route planning.

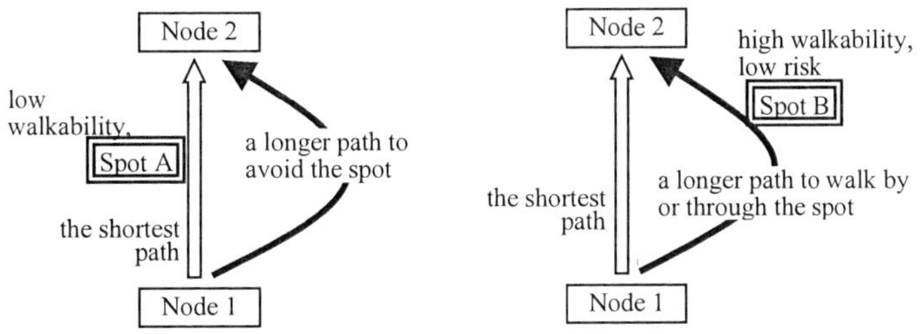

(a) a longer path to avoid a spot (b) a longer path to walk by or through a spot

Figure 1. The situations assumed for the definition of the acceptable detour time

4. PREFERENCE ESTIMATION MODEL USING THE ACCEPTABLE DETOUR TIME

4.1 Preference Estimation Model Based on User Attributes

As an approach for estimating personalized routes that meet the demands of the elderly, we propose a method for estimating preferences for route factors based on user attributes, i.e., a model for estimating the acceptable detour time for each route factor. As user attributes, it is conceivable to use the user's age, physical strength, and the like.

While age and gender are easy to use, physical fitness has many definitions and is difficult to quantify using a single standard. Considering the convenience of the system, it is not appropriate to measure the user's physical strength before use or to ask the user many questions. It is hard to say that it is a comfortable support if it takes a lot of time to prepare before use. Therefore, we aimed to develop a preference estimation model that uses the four attributes obtained from users in advance, such as age, gender, frequency of daily outings (at work, shopping, and recreation), and the interval at which they wish to take a break.

4.2 Building a Model Based on Reported Data on the Acceptable Detour Time

4.2.1 Paper Survey on Acceptable Detour Time

To reveal the relationship between user attributes and their preferences for route factors, we conducted a paper survey of the experiment participants to obtain the acceptable detour time for each route factor. In this study, we used the factors whose usefulness was confirmed in the related study (Furukawa and Wang, 2020). Further interviews were conducted and additional factors (e.g., routes with convenience stores) were added to the list of possible candidates. A total of 14 factors used are listed in Table 1, where each factor has relationships with walkability, safety, or pleasantness. A paper survey was conducted to answer the acceptable detour time for each factor. Fifty elderly people (over 60 years old) participated in the study and were paid an honorarium.

4.2.2 Building the Estimation Models from Acquired Data

For each of the 14 route factors, multiple regression analysis was conducted with user attributes (age, frequency of outings, desired break intervals, etc.), weather, and temperature as independent variables, and acceptable detour time as the dependent variable. The models were made separately for females and males. Based on the data obtained in advance, we evaluated the possibility of estimating the user's route preferences. Table 1 shows the adjusted R^2 values as results of the multiple regression analysis.

Table 1. Adjusted R2 values of the regression analysis models for the 14 route factors

Factors	adjusted R^2		Factors	adjusted R^2	
	male	female		male	female
1) steep slope/stairway	0.261	-0.09	8) school	0.223	0.186
2) crowded street	0.236	0.197	9) a park	0.230	0.331
3) a sidewalk	0.243	0.208	10) waterfront	0.199	0.345
4) an intersection with a traffic signal	0.277	0.158	11) a police box	0.266	0.327
5) road with guardrails	0.179	0.257	12) narrow road with poor visibility	0.230	0.408
6) a pedestrian overpass	0.258	0.178	13) convenience store	0.231	0.323
7) a bright path	0.207	0.244	14) a guide map	0.224	0.341

The results indicate that the factors that strongly influence male and female route selection are different and that separate models should be used for route finding for males and females.

The adjusted R^2 value for multiple regression analysis is quite low and the model is not highly reliable. The multiple regression model using the attributes targeted in this study does not have sufficient accuracy, and it is considered difficult to provide comfortable routes to users. There are two possible approaches to this improvement. One is to add other attributes to the model as independent variables that may have an impact. Another possible method is to adaptively improve the model for individual users by using the information after each walk. Considering the large individual differences in preferences, we use the constructed model as a basic model, and examine a method for sequentially improving the model by using each user's route evaluation and walking data.

5. AN ADAPTIVE IMPROVEMENT METHOD FOR THE ESTIMATION MODELS

To present routes that meet user preferences and are easy to walk, it would be effective to update the cost model by using information during walking and post-walking evaluations of the routes. On the other hand, considering the convenience of navigation, it is not appropriate to impose questions on the user that require time and attention to answer. It would be desirable to use simple questions that do not burden the user, or to use data that can be passively obtained from the user. Therefore, in this method, as a method for adapting the model to individual users, a method using the user's actual walking speed and the user's evaluation results for route factors was adopted. The former corresponds to data that can be acquired passively, and the latter corresponds to route evaluation by the user. In this research, we evaluate the basic effectiveness and feasibility of the idea by using a simple method.

5.1 Model Improvement by Modifying Actual Walking Speed

Since the acceptable detour time is used as a measure of preference, the user's walking speed is necessary for the calculation of the route cost. Walking speed is difficult to estimate accurately in advance, as it may vary with age, gender, exercise habits, and personality. In this study, the system measures the user's walking speed and uses it to generate the next route.

5.2 Model Improvement Based on Preference Evaluation Results

To improve the cost estimation model by adapting it to the individual, it is necessary to use subjective evaluation data on route factors that users prefer and reject. If users are asked to answer "acceptable detour time" for each factor while using a navigation service, they must make a generalized evaluation of each route factor independently of the situation in which they are traveling. This implementation is expected to require a certain amount of time and attention from the user, and may impair its convenience. In this method, instead of the "acceptable detour time," the evaluation value of the user's preference for the route factors that were present on the route traveled is used. The evaluation value is obtained on a 5-point scale (5: want to go through - 1: don't want to go through). The cost model is improved by using the results to adjust the acceptable detour time.

Specifically, the user's preference estimation model is updated by multiplying the "acceptable detour time" by the following cost update parameter. Different methods are used for positive factors and negative factors.

For favorable factors: [*cost update parameter*] = 1/4 * [*rating value of the factor*] + 1/4 (3)
For factors to be avoided: [*cost update parameter*] = -1/4 * [*rating value of the factor*] + 7/4 (4)

In these formulas, the correction is 1.5 times the current acceptable detour time when the preference evaluation value is maximum, i.e. 5, and 0.5 times the current acceptable detour time when the preference evaluation value is minimum, i.e. 1.

6. A VALIDATION EXPERIMENT ON THE MODEL IMPROVEMENT METHOD

The purpose of this experiment is to confirm the effectiveness of the proposed cost-improvement method in improving user walkability and comfort on the planned route. In this experiment, participants were asked to actually walk the routes planned by the model before the improvement and the routes planned after the improvement. Then, the comprehensive evaluation results for each route are compared. In addition, we tried to find out the user's burden and improvement points by interviewing the fatigue level after walking and the factors that bothered him/her while walking.

6.1 The Flow of the Experiment

(1) Using the estimation model based on the acceptable detour time created in Section 4, we planned routes for each participant.

(2) Using the navigation system, participants are asked to walk to three different destinations.

(3) For each route, we ask them to perform a comprehensive evaluation (0-100) of walkability, safety, and pleasantness.

(4) We ask participants to evaluate their preference (5 levels) for each of the route factors that existed on the route.

(5) Using the model improvement method, i.e., Equations (3) and (4), using the participant's preference values for the route factors, a set of the acceptable detour time for each participant is updated.

(6) Using each participant's updated acceptable detour time and the acquired walking speed data, a new route planning is performed for each participant.

(7) Using the navigation system, participants are asked to walk to the same three destinations as before.

(8) For each route, we ask them to perform a comprehensive evaluation (0-100) of walkability, safety, and pleasantness.

6.2 Experimental Conditions

The experiment participants were nine elderly people (female: 3 in their 60s, 2 in their 70s, male: 3 in their 70s, 1 in his 80s). The participants were chosen who were not familiar with the experimental areas, assuming that the user is a first-time visitor to the area. Before the experiment, the significance, purpose, methods, risks, and responses were explained to the experiment participants. Only those who consented actually participated in the experiment and paid a reward. This research plan was reviewed and approved by the Ethics Review Committee of the Institute of Systems and Information Engineering, University of Tsukuba (Review approval number 2019R349).

The proposed route planning method using the acceptable detour time requires accurate speed measurements because the travel time between nodes has a significant impact on the cost calculation. In this experiment, the participants were asked to wear a dedicated GPS device (i-gotU GT-600). Participants are asked to walk to their destinations while using a navigation application on a smartphone. The smartphone used is "SONY Xperia XZ3 SO-01L." The navigation application was originally created for this experiment using the map development kit "GeoTechnologies MapFan SDK."

6.3 Areas Covered by the Experiment

This experiment was conducted in the vicinity of Nagareyama Otakanomori Station in Nagareyama City, Chiba Prefecture, Japan (the corresponding area map is shown in Figure 2). This area has many target route factors such as school buildings, waterfront areas, and narrow and intricate roads.

Figure 2. Area covered by the walking experiment

Brief descriptions of the three areas walked by the participants follow.

6.3.1 Area 1: Wide and Well-Maintained Roads

This is the area surrounding the route from the starting point (1) to the destination (2). Many of the roads are quite well maintained. Since it is near a train station, there are many pedestrians and the sidewalks are quite wide. The road width is a little narrow in residential areas, but it is easy to walk without ups and downs. There are many factors related to the landscape, including riverfront roads and a relatively large number of parks.

6.3.2 Area 2: Narrow Busy Roads with Sidewalks

This is the area surrounding the route from the starting point (2) to the destination (3). Compared to Area 1, many roads are not well maintained. There are places where sidewalks are narrow and places where there are none. Some of the narrow roads have slopes.

6.3.3 Area 3: Busy Roads with No Sidewalks

This is the area surrounding the route from the starting point (3) to the destination (4). Many roads do not have sidewalks. There are a lot of pedestrians because it is near a hospital. Off the main streets, fairly narrow roads along the railroad tracks exist.

6.4 Analysis of Experimental Data and Results

A box-and-whisker diagram of the comprehensive evaluation (0-100) for each area is shown in Figure 3. As a result of the t-test, no significant difference was found in the mean of the comprehensive evaluation values for the routes of the initial model and the improved model (significance level 5%). Each participant's data in Area 1 showed little or no change between the two ratings or a decrease in value. For Area 3, the evaluation values of 8 out of 9 participants increased, indicating that the improvements in the cost model were successful. Since the initial routes were quite unsafe, model improvements based on participants' preference ratings would have greatly improved the safety of routes and increased their ratings.

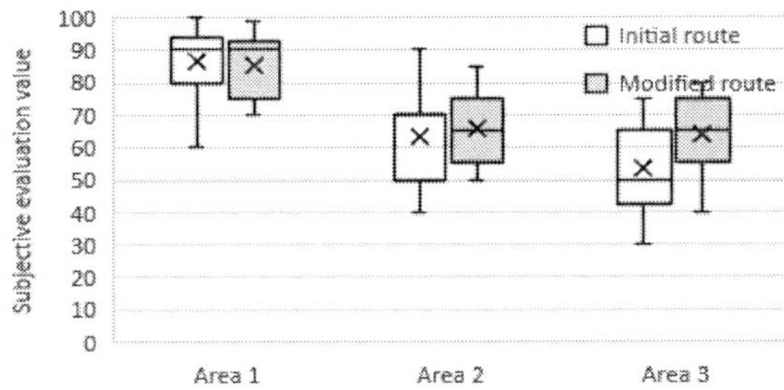

Figure 3. A box-and-whisker diagram of the comprehensive evaluation for each area

Next, statistical analysis of the data was conducted by classifying the participants' attributes as conditions. A t-test was conducted separately for males and females, and the results showed no significant differences in the means of the comprehensive evaluation values of the initial and improved models in each (5% level of significance). Box-and-whisker plots of the comprehensive ratings for each area for males and females are shown in Figures 4 and 5, respectively. For males, there is not much improvement in evaluation. Among females, there is a trend toward improved evaluations. Females' comprehensive evaluations of the initial routes are often low, suggesting that they may place more emphasis on the "safety" of routes. In analyses classified by other attributes (age and frequency of outings), no effect on comprehensive evaluations was found.

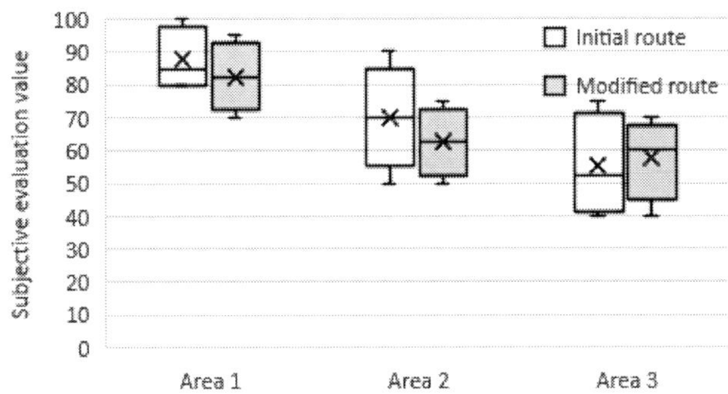

Figure 4. A box-and-whisker diagram of the comprehensive evaluation for males

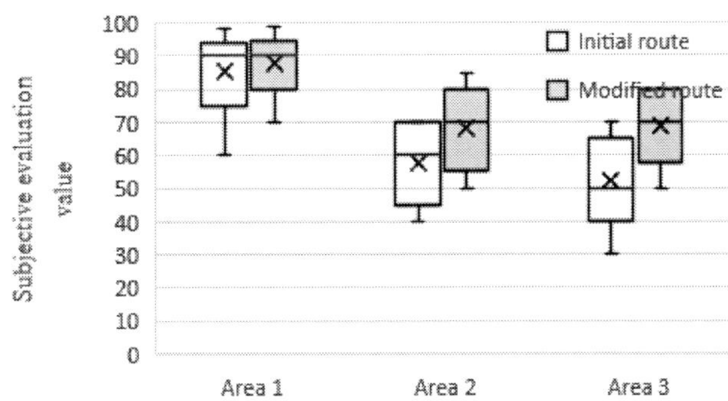

Figure 5. A box-and-whisker diagram of the comprehensive evaluation for females

6.5 Discussion

6.5.1 Effectiveness of the Cost Improvement Method

Although no statistically significant difference was observed in route evaluation, improvement in evaluation could be confirmed in some situations. In Areas 2 and 3, there were many roads that were dangerous or had cars on them in the initial route, and these were avoided in the updated route, which probably improved the evaluation from the viewpoint of safety. This trend is particularly noticeable in females' results.

In Area 1, many users rated the initial route highly, while the updated route received a lower rating. In the initial route, which was highly evaluated, there is a possibility that the accuracy of the model deteriorated due to the overcorrection of the model parameters based on the evaluation values of the participants. In this study, since we focused on confirming the "improvement of route evaluation by the proposed route modification method," we set the update parameter so that it can take a large value. To improve the versatility of the model, the variation range of the update parameters should be reduced, and the modification method should utilize a large number of evaluation data for the passage locations.

Since the comprehensive evaluation of walkability, safety, and pleasantness was used for the participant evaluation of the routes in this study, it may make the results vague and difficult to discuss the effects.

6.5.2 Appropriateness of Preference Evaluation Methods for Route Factors

In this study, a 5-point scale was used to obtain ratings of the route factors (cf. Section 5.2). Considering the burden on the user, the required time, and the improvement in model accuracy, this format can be said to be appropriate. In order to further reduce the user's burden, we are also considering a method of grouping route factors and reducing the number of evaluation items.

6.5.3 Appropriateness of Route Factors

In the route factors used, sidewalks, parks, and riverside areas were highly rated by many participants and had a significant impact on route selection and are therefore considered appropriate. On the other hand, many participants commented on the "amount of car traffic" and "narrowness of sidewalks," which were not included in the study, thus requiring the further study of different route factors.

7. CONCLUSION

7.1 Summary

In this project, we aim to develop a route planning method that can provide each user with an appropriate route, taking into consideration the preferences, i.e., walkability, safety, and pleasantness, peculiar to the elderly. To achieve this goal, we constructed a quantitative model that expresses the relationship between the attributes of elderly users and their preference for route selection, and examined the feasibility of a user adaptation method based on the user's preference evaluation for route factors.

In this study, we used "acceptable detour time" to quantify user preferences. The results of the paper survey of the elderly revealed that user attributes such as "age" and "the desired interval between breaks" influenced route selection, and that the impact of these attributes differed by gender. This suggests that the targeted user attributes are useful in estimating the preferences of the elderly for the routes. When planning user-friendly walking routes, separate models should be built for males and females.

Next, we proposed a method of individual adaptation of the model using post-walking evaluations of route factors, and verified its effectiveness through walking experiments. In some situations, we were able to identify improvements in the participants' evaluation of the routes. This indicates the feasibility of the user adaptation method based on the user's preference evaluation for route factors. On the other hand, there was also a route in which the evaluation by the participants declined. In this study, evaluation data after walking three routes were used to improve the cost model. By adjusting the update parameters and using more evaluation data, it is expected to plan routes that are adapted to individuals with high accuracy.

7.2 Future Works

The first work is to conduct a new validation experiment with a sufficient number of participants to confirm clear conclusions through statistical analysis. Also, in order to clarify the results, it is necessary to use dedicated evaluation indicators for walkability, safety, and pleasantness in the evaluation of planned routes. Second, it is necessary to obtain additional route factors. In order to deal with route factors not covered in this study, a comprehensive survey of factors affecting route selection is needed. The third is the improvement of the model adaptation method. To improve the versatility of the model, the update value from a single evaluation value by the user should be kept small, and updates from the accumulation of a large number of evaluation data should be employed.

The basic idea of the proposed method can be applied to evacuation route planning in the event of a disaster. As a tool to prevent panic among evacuees, the authors are developing a pedestrian navigation method with a model that quantitatively evaluates the fear that people feel during evacuation actions depending on the road conditions, with the goal of providing evacuees with a route that does not cause fear (Furukawa and Koshimizu, 2022). Although the results show that the mean value of the level of fear is lower for the revised method than for the shortest path, the significant individual differences in fear estimation should be addressed to improve the estimation accuracy. We believe that the method of individual adaptation of the model using post-walking evaluations of route factors has the potential to resolve the issue.

ACKNOWLEDGEMENT

This work was supported in part by Grants-Aid for Science Research 20K12074 of the Japanese Ministry of Education, Science, Sports, and Culture.

REFERENCES

Darko J. et al., 2022. Adaptive Personalized Routing for Vulnerable Road Users. *IET Intelligent Transport Systems*, Vol. 16, No. 8, pp. 1011-1025.

Ertz O. et al., 2021. Citizen Participation & Digital Tools to Improve Pedestrian Mobility in Cities. *Proc. of 6th International Conference on Smart Data and Smart Cities.* Stuttgart, Germany, pp. 29-34.

Furukawa H., 2015. Empirical Evaluation of the Pedestrian Navigation Method for Easy Wayfinding. *Proc. 6th International Conference and Workshop on Computing and Communication.* Vancouver, Canada, 7 pages.

Furukawa H. and Koshimizu R., 2022. Refinement of the Quantitative Models to Estimate User's Fear in Evacuation Route Planning: Introduction of User Attributes and Nonlinearization of the Model. *Proc. of 20th International Conference e-Society 2022.* Virtual event, pp. 45-52.

Furukawa H. and Wang Z., 2020. A Route Evaluation Method Considering the Subjective Evaluation on Walkability, Safety, and Pleasantness by Elderly Pedestrians. *Advances in Decision Sciences, Image Processing, Security and Computer Vision*. pp. 408-416.

Jonietz D., 2016. Learning Pedestrian Profiles from Movement Trajectories. *Proc. of the 13th International Conference on Location-Based Services.* Vienna, Austria, pp. 14-16.

Matsuda, M. et al., 2004. A Personalized Route Guidance System for Pedestrians. *IEICE Trans. on Fundamentals of Electronics, Communications and Computer Sciences*, Vol. 87, pp. 132-139. (in Japanese)

Mizuno E., 2011. Research on Anxiety and Intention of Elderly People to Go Out. *Research notes of The Dai-ichi Life Research Institute.* https://www.dlri.co.jp/pdf/ld/01-14/notes1107a.pdf (in Japanese)

Muronaga Y. and Morozumi M., 2003. A Case Study on the Elderly's Going-out Activities in Relation to Their Neighborhood Environment. *J. Archit. Plan. (Trans. AIJ)*, Vol. 68, pp. 63-70.

Novack T. et al, 2018. A System for Generating Customized Pleasant Pedestrian Routes Based on OpenStreetMap Data. *Sensors,* Vol. 18, No. 11, p. 3794 (19 pages).

Torres M. Et al., 2018. PRoA: An intelligent multi-criteria Personalized Route Assistant. *Engineering Applications of Artificial Intelligence*, Vol. 72, pp. 162-169.

Yoshikawa A., 2011. Senior citizens' adaptive strategies to get around in their communities: A case study of Yao City, Japan, A Doctoral Dissertation of the Graduate Studies of Texas A&M University.

CITIZEN SCIENCE AS A SERVICE? A REVIEW OF MULTI-PROJECT CITIZEN SCIENCE PLATFORMS

Carolin Stein, Alicia Wittmer, Jonas Fegert and Christof Weinhardt
FZI Research Center for Information Technology, KIT Karlsruhe Institute of Technology Haid-und-Neu-Straße 10-14, 76131 Karlsruhe, Germany

ABSTRACT

The upswing of projects, conducting citizen science (CS) by means of ICT has resulted in the development of numerous digital participation platforms. Recently platformization as a trend away from individual project platforms towards the domination of larger platforms enabling the support of generic citizen science initiatives could be observed. Through their design and functionality these multi-project platforms thus influence the way research initiatives can be conducted in a participatory manner. By performing a structured artifact review of multi-project citizen science platforms on the market, we provide clarity towards the question, which multi-project platforms exist and how they support research projects. The review identified 16 platforms, that assist the conduction of generic citizen science projects. Demonstrating significant differences in functionality and features of the investigated platforms, the review underlines that the choice of multi-project CS platform presents a key decision for project initiators.

KEYWORDS

Citizen Science, Platform Design, Artifact Review

1. INTRODUCTION

Citizen Science (CS), as the involvement of non-professionals in scientific research, is receiving more attention in academia as well as in media. It is considered to be a means to empower citizens to contribute meaningfully to research and thereby democratize scientific processes (De Albuquerque and Almeida, 2020). The academic discourse, recognizes its ability to generate unique insights and powering up research workforce (Shirk and Bonney, 2018), while presenting a source of learning opportunities to the public (Jennett et al., 2016; Sturm et al., 2018). Citizens have contributed to scientific achievements in a variety of disciplines, such as collecting and sharing geophysical data for earth observation research, or engaging in collective problem-solving and symptom or treatment surveillance in biomedicine (Shirk and Bonney, 2018). Especially in ecological research, it is only through the help of amateur scientists, that researchers have become access to large scale datasets, impossible to collect with traditional methods (Miller-Rushing and Bonney, 2012). This however shows, that the umbrella term, describes a broad range of different initiatives, ranging from crowdsourcing to collegial work with citizens (Shirk et al., 2012; Haklay, 2013). The variety makes it difficult for practitioners and policy makers to navigate the domain (Haklay et al., 2021) and complicates broad claims for learning and transformative effects (De Albuquerque and Almeida, 2020; Bela et al., 2016). The emerging of online or digital CS describing the involvement of citizens by means of ICT (Reed et al., 2012; Weinhardt et al., 2020), additional enriches the variety. While the call for digital support is high (Liu et al., 2021), the heterogeneity of CS initiatives complicates interoperability (Göbel et al., 2017; Liu et al., 2021). At the same time, CS initiatives have limited resources preventing them from developing important functionalities (Wald et al., 2016). As a result, a shift from individual to generic infrastructure can be observed (Baudry et al., 2022). A series of CS platforms with varying focus and functionalities emerged to serve different types of CS projects (Liu et al., 2021). While some platforms are only built for specific projects, others evolve into integrated platforms providing a rich set of functions for generic projects (Liu et al., 2021). These multi-project platforms influence the way digital CS projects are designed and conducted

(Baudry et al., 2022; Liu et al., 2021) what in turn determines project outcomes such as the democratic and transformative impact or learning (Sturm et al., 2018; Bela et al., 2016; De Albuquerque and Almeida, 2020). Navigating the large amount of digital platforms determining whether there is an appropriate solution for their project is a challenge to practitioners (Brenton et al., 2018). Likewise, for citizens the intransparent diversity of platforms can lead to confusion and create an image of competition (Brenton et al., 2018). While, some authors made efforts, to compare or categorize CS platforms (Liu et al., 2021; Wald et al., 2016; Luna et al., 2018; Skarlatidou et al., 2019; Yadav and Darlington, 2016), a structured review of their focus, functionalities and characteristics is yet missing. This however, is indispensable to help practitioners leverage the potential of the digital offer and for the research community to identify structural gaps. We thus turn towards the research question: *What multi-project CS platforms exist and how do they support the conduction of CS projects?*

To answer our research question, we conduct a structured artifact review, identifying 75 CS platforms, out of which 16 platforms qualify as multi-project platforms that allow to conduct generic CS projects. To provide guidance we review the 16 platforms, according to seven platform dimensions. As such, the review enables scientists, practitioners and citizens to understand and compare CS platforms based on key characteristics. Thereby, they can either find suitable platforms to support their needs or identify research gaps that are yet to fill.

2. THEORETICAL FOUNDATION

CS describes an umbrella term for civic engagement in research that is yet lacking a uniform definition (Haklay et al., 2021). The Socientize project characterizes CS as "the general public engagement in scientific research activities when citizens actively contribute to science either with their intellectual effort or surrounding knowledge or with their tools and resources" (Socientize, 2014). Originally, CS has been used especially in natural science, which is an important use case to date (Levy and Germonprez, 2017; Pettibone et al., 2017; Miller-Rushing et al., 2012). Nowadays however, it is a useful means to conduct research in various research domains (Pettibone et al., 2017). With the expansion of CS into a variety of fields of application, the heterogeneity of approaches has increased (Spasiano et al., 2021). Depending on the context, CS can be defined from a political, societal or scientific point of view (Haklay et al., 2021). At the heart of all classifications however, is the idea to define the extent and implementation of civic involvement in science (Haklay et al., 2021). The potential involvement can cover different parts of the research process from the creation of the research question and hypotheses, through data collection, to analysis and publication (Shirk et al., 2012). CS platforms, describe web-based infrastructures that are used to support CS initiatives (Liu et al., 2021). As for the term CS itself, CS platforms can comprise a variety of infrastructures that either present CS activities, display project information, provide support material and guidelines or best practices, offer tools, or a combination of the aforementioned (Liu et al., 2021). Different classifications for CS platforms differentiate for instance whether they are commercial or non-profit, domain specific or independent, national or international, or if their focus is on a single project (Brenton et al., 2018; Liu et al., 2021). Additionally, there are platforms for specific functions such as project finders, transcription or education tools (Brenton et al., 2018). Within the platform landscape, a platformization can be observed, describing a shift from individual projects to multi-project platforms (Baudry et al., 2022). These platforms enable the setup of new projects with their distinct goals, sharing a common infrastructure (Baudry et al., 2022). They thus standardize functions, as well as aspects such as community management (Baudry et al., 2022), which makes the choice of platform relevant to initiators. The suitability of the CS platform depends on the project's characteristics and should include several considerations. Brenton et al. (2018) for example highlights, data standards and the connection to open data portals, support features, options for customization and the organization and maintenance of the infrastructure as important platform features. Baudry et al. (2022) adds to this the dimensions of data representation and community management. To get guidance on the aspects that need to be considered when choosing a platform, one can also turn towards the rich literature on best practices for developing CS infrastructure. Several recurring motifs can be identified, that are summarized in Table 1.

Table 1. Key design dimensions identified in the digital CS literature

Dimension	Design Concept	Source
Platform aesthetics (PA)	Reduced information on the platform	(Jennett, 2014; Skarlatidou et al., 2019)
	Standardized naming and navigation	(Sturm et al., 2018; Skarlatidou et al., 2019)
Community organization (CO)	Enable communication between participants	(Sturm et al., 2018; Newman et al., 2010; Skarlatidou et al., 2019; Wald, Longo, and Dobell, 2016)
	Enable communication between participants and researchers	(Yadav and Darlington, 2016; Sturm et al., 2018; Newman et al., 2010; Skarlatidou et al., 2019).
	Validate the credibility of users	(Musto and Dahanayake, 2021; Newman et al., 2010)
Data standards (DS)	Enable secure handling of private data	(Yadav and Darlington, 2016; Sturm et al., 2018; Musto and Dahanayake, 2021)
	Validate user-generated data	(Skarlatidou et al., 2019; Musto and Dahanayake, 2021)
	Facilitate entering user-generated data	(Newman et al., 2010; Sturm et al., 2018; Skarlatidou et al., 2019)
	Enable data analysis and visualization	(Musto and Dahanayake, 2021; Newman et al., 2010; Skarlatidou et al., 2019; Wald, Longo, and Dobell, 2016)
Support information (SI)	Provide separate support pages	(Skarlatidou et al., 2019)
	Provide educational material	(Wald, Longo, and Dobell, 2016)
	Provide interactive tutorials and information	(Jennett, 2014; Skarlatidou et al., 2019)
Platforms usability (PS)	Provide simple and clear project main pages	(Skarlatidou, et al. 2019)
	Ease entry barriers	(Jennett, 2014; Sturm et al., 2018)
	Communicate project goals	(Jennett, 2014; Newman et al., 2010)
Platform utilization (PT)	Enable easy project creation	(Yadav and Darlington, 2016)
	Enable reusability of components	(Sturm et al., 2018; Yadav and Darlington, 2016)

3. A REVIEW OF CS PLATFORMS

3.1 Methodology

For the review of CS platforms, we follow the 7-step-methodology for reviewing software artifacts from practice by Gnewuch and Maedche (2022). The method aims at providing methodological guidance to the review of real-world artifacts in a systematic way, as it is a common practice for literature reviews (Gnewuch and Maedche, 2022). Starting with the problem formulation (1), the main objectives and conceptual boundaries for the review are defined. Based on these objectives potentially relevant artifacts are searched for (2) and based on predefined criteria screened for inclusion in the review (3). In a fourth step artifacts are assessed according to their practical quality (4) which can imply the development stage or user feedback. The first four steps of the methodology result in a list of artifacts, that are then used for data extraction (5) and documented and archived (6) for traceability. In a final step, collected data can be analyzed and synthesized (7) to present the findings of the artifact review. While step (1)-(6) has been conducted by one reviewer, for step (7) two independent reviewers have been engaged in coding the documentation. For data extraction and coding, we followed best-practices for structured-content analysis of web pages (Saraswat, 1999).

3.2 Implementation

We implement the review of CS platforms, to provide guidance in the CS platform landscape. Practitioners should be able to select an appropriate platform to conduct their CS initiative, based on necessary functionality and key characteristics. As such, the scope of our artifact review are multi-project CS platforms. This implies the platform must provide opportunities to create and host a new generic project (a) and provide active participation opportunities for project implementation (b). Based on these two inclusion criteria, our review does not focus on single-project platforms or project overview platforms (Brenton et al. 2018). For the software artifact search, we utilize three search directions, to provide a sufficiently extensive sample: First of all, we utilize provided overviews in the CS platform literature to identify 43 software artifacts (Liu et al., 2021; Brenton et al., 2018; Luna et al., 2018; Yadav and Darlington, 2016; Aristeidou and Herodotou, 2020; Skarlatidou et al., 2019). Additionally, we conduct a search using the commercial database provider Crunchbase, that is focused on technology companies. Through the filter option 'Citizen Science' 14 new platforms could be identified. As a third search direction, we utilized two webpages of national CS information platforms for Austria and the EU, resulting in 18 additional platforms. Thus, our initial sample includes 75 CS platforms, that we screened for inclusion based on (a) and (b). As indicated by the literature, the sample includes different types of CS platforms: 32 platforms were project overview platforms, while five platforms qualified as community exchange hubs for educational material and workshops. Additionally, 12 platforms were single project platforms and six platforms included several projects, however did not allow for the creation of new generic initiatives. After the screening this leaves 20 platforms that were further assessed in the quality assessment. When assessing quality in terms of practical usability for the review, four platforms had to be excluded because they were either not available in either English or German or could not be reviewed free of charge. This was the case for platforms, that were fee-based and did not offer a demo nor linked freely accessible project examples. Thus, the final review comprised 16 platforms, which were archived in *Archive.Today* [1] and can be seen in Table 2. For data extraction purposes, CS platforms were assessed and documented in a concept matrix, according to their offered participatory functionality based on Shirk et al. (2012) and key design dimensions identified in the literature (see Table 1). The matrix served as baseline for data analysis through two independent coders.

Table 2. List of multi-project platforms for the review

	Platform Name	Weblink
A	Biocollect-Atlas of Living Australia	https://www.ala.org.au/biocollect
B	CS Center Zürich	https://citizenscience.ch
C	CitSci	https://citsci.org
D	conserve.Io*	http://conserve.io
E	CyberTracker	https://cybertracker.org
F	DataCertus	https://datacertus.com
G	Epicollect5	https://five.epicollect.net
H	Inaturalist	https://www.inaturalist.org
I	Ispot	https://www.ispotnature.org
J	Just One Giant Lab (JOGL)	https://jogl.io
K	nQuire	https://nquire.org.uk
L	Pybossa	https://pb.citizenscience.ch
M	SciStarter	https://scistarter.org
N	Spotteron	https://www.spotteron.net
O	World Community Grid	https://www.worldcommunitygrid.org
P	Zooniverse	https://www.zooniverse.org

* The review of this platform is based on two freely viewable projects and thus limited.

3.3 Results

The structured artifact review allowed us to characterize 16 multi-project platforms according to key characteristics identified in the literature. This comprised the platforms aesthetics, usability and utilization, as well as functionality in terms of participatory functions, community organization, support information and data standards (see Table 1). In the following, results are reported by dimension:

1) Participatory functions: Platforms provide varying flexibility to support participatory research steps. As such, the lowest degree of participation was found for platform O, were citizens can only contribute to research projects by computational power. On the other hand, many platforms, focus on data collection and analysis: Four platforms (D, E, H, I) provide functionality to upload and classify observations, while one

[1] https://archive.ph

platform (F) allows to upload data sets and use tools for data analysis. Other platforms extend the possibilities for data collection e.g. to surveys (B, G, P), digital diaries (B), or different type of media (B, G, L). The opportunities for participatory data analysis range from functionalities for transcriptions (B, L, P), mapping or classification of images (B, L, P) to pattern recognition in sound or video material (L). In this context, four data collection and analysis platforms (A, C, M, N) stood out through their flexibility, which would potentially allow their usage for other participatory activities. This comprised one platform (M) offering a range of third-party tool integrations, another platform (C) with customizable data sheets and possible integrations, a further platform (A) providing multiple individual applications e.g. for evaluation or learning games, and a platform (N) with functionalities that can be customized on demand. Next to platforms for data collection and analysis, one platform (J) in the sample supports the participatory assignment of tasks, although tasks themselves are not conducted on the platform. This platform enables initiators to structure the project into several project phases. Another platform (K) enables users to define research questions, design a methodological approach and collect data, however except for data collection, activities are not undertaken participatory.

2) Platform aesthetics: To evaluate the platforms' aesthetics, we reviewed whether platforms had a concept for reducing text and for standardizing naming and navigation conventions. To reduce the information load, all platforms utilize pictures or icons, except for platform O, that is primarily text based. In particular, one platform (E) stood out, by replacing texts comprehensively through icons. Additionally, seven platforms (A, H, J, L, M, N, P) use expandable and collapsible text, to avoid information load on first sight. In terms of naming conventions, most platforms try to avoid technical terms and follow easy naming conventions such as 'Project or Community', 'Add' or 'Contribute'. An exception to this was found in the platform I, that uses individual names e.g. 'Spaces', 'Needs', 'Programs' or 'Claps' and technical terms for instance in search options. For the platform's navigation three platforms (B, C, F) allow to search for specific project names and one (E) for a specific web address. Besides that, three platforms enable users to search for names or categories (G, O, P) and three (D, K, L) platforms do not employ any search options. The majority of platforms (A, H, I, J, M, N) however allow for a broad search according to different characteristics such as age, activity or organization.

3) Community organization: Regarding community organization, concepts for the communication between participants, and between participants and researchers were reviewed. Five platforms (A, B, D, E, L) have no concept for a project-based debate of participants, while three platforms (D, E, L) additionally have no possibilities to contact researchers. Five platforms (H, J, M, N, P) enable exchange within the community and to researchers via direct chat options. Nine platforms (C, G, H, I, J, K, N, O, P) allow for communication via forums, either in project-based or general forums. Other concepts for community exchange comprised messages on newsfeeds (J, N), comment options (H, I, J, K, M, N, P) or project-based question and answer options (M). For the contact to researchers or project creators additionally many projects (A, B, C, F, G, K) offered an e-mail option. One platform in the sample (N) especially stood out due to a broad range of options for community exchange. Besides communication, platforms were reviewed for a concept of evaluating user credibility. For ten platforms, no concepts could be detected, while for platform D this could not be reviewed. Other platforms enable the appointment of expert users (N, P) or award collection based on completed learning units (M). Additionally, two platforms implement reputation models, either based on scores (I), or the collection of badges (I, O).

4) Data standards: In terms of data standards, platforms have been reviewed for their handling of private user data, and concepts for entering, validating, visualizing or analyzing data. For the handling of user data platforms differ in their concepts for registration and user profiles. For the registration platforms either require only a user name (E, N), a user name and an e-mail address (B, C, F, G, H, I, K, L, M, O, P), or more data (A, D, J), for instance the country of residence. The profile page of other users is either not visible (A, B, C, D, E, G), associates a user name with information about their contributions (K, L, P), or displays more information (F, H, I, J, M, N, O), for instance the level of education. Additionally, some platforms enable users to keep their user data private (C, M, N, O). For collecting project data, most platforms facilitate participation through specified entry masks that include for example drop-down menus, checkboxes or drag-and-drop (A, B, C, D, E, F, G, H, I, K, L, N, P). Additionally, some platforms provide extra help for the classification of data (E, H, I, N, P) in form of common mistakes, help information or automated proposals. Two platforms do not support data contributions (J, O) and one platform did not have standardized data entry options (M). In terms of data validation only four platforms present validation concepts: This comprised checking whether all necessary entries were filled (P), flagging of contributions through the community (N), a like and reputation system (I) or the differentiation between quality levels (H). For platform D data validation could not be reviewed. Regarding the analysis of project data, some platforms have integrated data analysis tools (A, B, C, E, F, K, L, N, O, P), while others focus only on data visualization (D, G, H, I). The tools are either available for project initiators and citizens, or only initiators. Two platforms additionally offer shared codebases for researchers (C, P), while two others (J, M) do not enable data analysis. Besides project data, five projects allow to analyze data about the projects' progress (B, H, N, O, P) and five projects analyze meta-data about the community (L, M, N, O, P).

5) Support information: Regarding support information, three design aspects were reviewed. The first one comprised a concept for a separate support page. Most platforms have help pages for several topics, such as guidelines on how to build a project (A, B, C, E, F, G, H, I, J, L, M, N, P), or general support pages for citizens (A, D, H, I, J, L, N, O). Additionally, most platforms employ an FAQ page for citizens (A, C, H, I, J, L, M, N, O, P). Five platforms (B, E, F, G, K) do not provide any separate help pages for participants. As a second aspect, platforms were reviewed for their provision of educational material. Implementations of this feature comprised workshops (A, M, P), training sections (A, C, D, H, I, M, P), blog or newsletter articles (C, E, H, I, O, P) and community spaces for learning (J). Six platforms did not integrate educational resources by design, however, project-based integrations are still possible. Third, concepts for interactive tutorials or help information were reviewed. Design features that were employed in this category, were pop-up tutorials leading through the platform (J, N, P), tutorials and videos on project pages (H, J, M, N, O, P), or additional information based on hovering over content (A, B, C, K, N, O). Six platforms do not include interactive help information.

6) Platform usability: Three design features, supporting platform usability were reviewed. First of all, as concepts for the design of the project main pages, most platforms follow the principle of deploying the same design for every project. Only two platforms (D, N) vary their design throughout different projects and one platform (E) has no project overview page by design. Five projects (B, H, N, O, P) give an overview over the projects' progress on the main page, while some platforms include information on contributing participants (B, C, E, H, J, M, N, P) or contributed data (A, C, D, E, G, H, I, K, L, N, P). Additionally, outstanding features that were noted are an overview of currently active participants in the project (I, N, P), or the proposition of similar projects (M). Second, for the ease of entry barriers, different concepts could be identified: Some platforms enable participation via the web browser (A, B, C, H, I, J, K, M, P), while the others require the installation of software. Above that, three platforms (D, J, N) include either pop-up explanations, upon registration or entering a project and ten platforms provide example pictures or explanations for project tasks (A, B, D, I, J, K, M, N, O, P). Additionally, four platforms (A, J, M, P) indicate the level of difficulty for tasks or indicate the required skills for participating. Third, in terms of communicating project goals, two different approaches could be identified. Three platforms (E, F, I) include general goals on the platforms main homepage, while other platforms include an explanation of project-specific goals on the individual project pages.

7) Platform utilization: In terms of platform utilization, platforms have been reviewed for their concepts of creating and maintaining projects, as well as their concept for reusability of components. Regarding the generation of new projects, we could identify two different types of platforms: Some platforms implement construction tools, that can be used to create new projects yourself (A, B, C, E, F, G, H, I, J, K, L, M, P). Another type of platform creates new projects only on request (D, N, O). Independent of this type, some platforms enable projects to utilize a mobile application (A, B, C, D, E, G, N). In terms of reusability three different level of openness could be detected. Some platforms are entirely based on open source software (A, B, G, H, J, L, O, P), while others were publicly usable and accessible, however not open source (C, E, F, I, K, M). A third platform type presents a chargeable service (D, N).

An overview of the results can be seen in Table 3.

Table 3. Summary of review results

Dimension	Platforms															
	A	B	C	D	E	F	G	H	I	J	K	L	M	N	O	P
Participatory Functions (PF): computational power (PF1) data collection (PF2), data analysis (PF3), task assignment (PF4) research questions and approach (PF5)																
PF	PF 2,3	PF 2,3	PF 2,3	PF 2	PF 2	PF 2,3	PF 2	PF 2	PF 2	PF 4	PF 5	PF 2,3	PF 2,3	PF 2,3	PF 1	PF 2,3
Platform Aesthetics (PA): reduced information (PA1) easy naming conventions (PA2) search options (PA3)																
PA	PA 1-3	PA 1-3	PA 1-3	PA 1,2	PA 1-3	PA 1-3	PA 1-3	PA 1-3	PA 1,3	PA 1-3	PA 1,2	PA 1,2	PA 1-3	PA 1-3	PA 2,3	PA 1-3
Community Organization (CO): communication between participants (CO1), communication between participants and researchers (CO2), user credibility evaluation (CO3)																
CO	CO 2	CO 2	CO 1,2	-	-	CO 1,2	CO 1,2	CO 1,2	CO 1-3	CO 1,2	CO 1,2	-	CO 1-3	CO 1-3	CO 1-3	CO 1-3
Data Standards (DS): limited private user data (DS1) eased data entering (DS2) data analysis and visualization (DS3) data validation (DS4)																
DS	DS 2,3	DS 1-3	DS 1-3	DS 2,3	DS 1-3	DS 1-3	DS 1-3	DS 1-4	DS 1-4	-	DS 1-3	DS 1-3	DS 1	DS 1-4	DS 1,3	DS 1-4
Support Information (SI): support page (SI1) educational material (SI2) interactive information and tutorials (SI3)																
SI	SI 1-3	SI 3	SI 1-3	SI 1,2	SI 2	-	-	SI 1-3	SI 1,2	SI 1-3	SI 3	SI 1	SI 1-3	SI 1,3	SI 1-3	SI 1-3
Platform Usability (PS): eased entry barriers (PS1) project goal communication on project page (PS2) similar project main pages (PS3)																
PS	PS 1-3	PS 1-3	PS 1-3	PS 1,2	-	PS 3	PS 2,3	PS 1-3	PS 1,3	PS 1-3	PS 1-3	PS 2,3	PS 1-3	PS 1,2	PS 1-3	PS 1-3
Platform Utilization (PT): project builder tools (PT1) mobile application (PT2) open source or free of charge software (PT3)																
PT	PT 1-3	PT 1-3	PT 1-3	PT 2	PT 1-3	PT 1,3	PT 1-3	PT 1,3	PT 1,3	PT 1,3	PT 1,3	PT 1,3	PT 1,3	PT 2	PT 3	PT 1,3

4. DISCUSSION

In this work we followed the 7-step framework for reviewing IT artifacts to provide a structured overview over the availability and functionality of multi-project CS platforms. As indicated by the literature we discovered a notable amount of project overview platforms, community platforms or single project platforms (Brenton et al., 2018), compared to which the share of multi-project platforms was rather small. Nevertheless, we identified and reviewed 16 platforms that enabled the generation and conduction of new CS projects, thus qualifying as multi-project platforms (Baudry et al., 2022). Assessing the platforms' functionalities, as well as their features for aesthetics, community organization, data standards, support information, usability and utilization, the review enabled us to draw a comprehensive understanding of the ways in which platforms support CS initiatives. Generally, a strong focus on functions and features for jointly collecting and analyzing scientific data was visible, which is however only a small part of the spectrum of possible research activities to include citizens (Shirk et al., 2012). Nevertheless, also within this narrow focus, the review showed that platforms present different opportunities and challenges and should be thus selected carefully based on the individual project's needs: First, variations in the platforms' aesthetic and usability allow practitioners to choose a platform according to their target audience characteristics, such as domain expertise or experience with digital platforms. Second, the varying options in the community organization and the provisioning of support enable the initiator to accurately design relationships to and the autonomy of participants. The design of these dimensions can have strong implications for learning or empowerment effects of citizens (De Albuquerque and Almeida 2020; Bela et al. 2016; National Academies of Sciences, Engineering, and Medicine, 2018). To this end, the results demonstrate that many innovative educational concepts from other educational settings such as extended reality (Garzón, Pavón, and Baldiris, 2019) or chatbots (Pérez, Daradoumis, and Puig, 2020; Okonkwo and Ade-Ibijola 2021) are yet missing on platforms. Third, different data standards could be suitable for collecting data of varying complexity, sensitivity or quality. While project initiators are free to choose a platform based on their preferences for the presented variations, their choice is further constrained by their financial budget and the requirement for transparency and flexibility of the platform.

Considering the multi-project platforms' diversity of feature and design choices, as a practical contribution, our work provides guidance to practitioners in need for a CS platform to conduct their projects. Based on their functional needs and project characteristics they can choose a platform that fits their initiative. Additionally, platform providers can benefit from the insights in different implementations and concepts to refine their digital offer. In terms of theoretical contributions, the structured artifact review is intended to enable scholars to explore the current artifact landscape in a specific domain, thereby demonstrating the need and novelty of new developments (Gnewuch and Maedche, 2022). As such, our work allows IS researchers to compare CS platforms and identify structural research gaps that are yet missing in the CS landscape. In addition, the overview of functionality and implementations for community management, support information, educational material and data standards can serve as a baseline to further research learning and empowerment opportunities for digital citizen scientists. When using the provided review on multi-project CS platforms, some limitations of our research should be named. Methodologically, the presented review is subject to natural limits in the search process as well as the data extraction. For the artifact search, a focus had been set to three search paths. As such, platforms outside this search base might not have been detected. Additionally, four platforms had to be excluded from the review due to their practical accessibility. For the description of CS platforms, data extraction is based on a single reviewer, which could imply that not every functionality or characteristic of a platform might be detected. For future work, it would thus be interesting to broaden this perspective with additional reviewers. The rapidly changing landscape makes it indispensable to constantly screen for additional needs of CS projects, as well as new platforms emerging. As such, our structured platform review provides a valuable baseline for assessing how multi-project platforms support the conduction of CS initiatives that other researchers can build upon. Future research could use the provided sample of platforms to further review aspects of interest or additionally add emerging platforms to the review. In addition, researchers could utilize the review to identify structural gaps and thus specifically develop new functionality for CS projects.

5. CONCLUSION

In this work we have presented a structured artifact review investigating what multi-project CS platforms are currently available in the digital landscape and how they support the conduction of CS projects. We have identified 16 platforms, that support the conduction of generic CS initiatives, presenting a considerable amount of support technology, CS project initiators can choose from. By reviewing the platforms according to seven dimensions, we present notable differences in their functionality and features for various design challenges, as well as structural gaps in the digital landscape. As a result, the choice of multi-project CS platform becomes a key decision for project initiators. Therefore, the artifact review presents a valuable baseline, both for researchers and practitioners to navigate, use and refine the digital CS landscape.

REFERENCES

Aristeidou, M. and Herodotou, C., (2020). Online Citizen Science: A Systematic Review of Effects on Learning and Scientific Literacy. *Citizen Science: Theory and Practice* 5 (1), pp.1–12.

Baudry, J. et al., (2022). Turning Crowds into Communities: The Collectives of Online Citizen Science. *Social Studies of Science,* Vol. 52, No. 3, pp. 399–424.

Bela, G. et al., (2016). Learning and the transformative potential of citizen science. *Conservation Biology,* Vol. 30, No. 5, pp. 990–99.

Brenton, P. et al., (2018). Technology Infrastructure for Citizen Science. In: *Citizen Science: Innovation in Open Science, Society and Policy,* pp. 63-80. UCL Press, London, England.

De Albuquerque, J., and Almeida, A., (2020). *Modes of Engagement: Reframing "Sensing" and Data Generation in Citizen Science for Empowering Relationships*. Manchester University Press.

Garzón, J. et al., (2019). Systematic Review and Meta-Analysis of Augmented Reality in Educational Settings. *Virtual Reality*, Vol. 23, No. 4, pp. 447–59.

Gnewuch, U., and Maedche, A. (2022). Toward a Method for Reviewing Software Artifacts from Practice. *International Conference on Design Science Research in Information Systems and Technology*. St. Petersburg, USA, pp. 337-350.

Göbel, C. et al., (2017). *Stakeholder Analysis: International Citizen Science Stakeholder Analysis on Data Interoperability. Final Report.* Woodrow Wilson International Center for Scholars. Washington, DC, USA.

Haklay, M. et al., (2021). What Is Citizen Science? The Challenges of Definition. In: *The Science of Citizen Science,* pp. 13-33. Springer International Publishing, Basel, Swiss.

Jennett, C., and Cox, A., (2016). Eight guidelines for designing virtual citizen science projects. *Second AAAI Conference on Human Computation and Crowdsourcing.* Pittsburgh, USA, pp. 16-17.

Jennett, C., et al., (2016). Motivations, Learning and Creativity in Online Citizen Science. *Journal of Science Communication* Vol. 15, No. 3.

Liu, H., et al., (2021). Citizen Science Platforms. In: The Science of Citizen Science, pp. 439-459 Springer, Cham, London, England.

Luna, S. et al, (2018). Developing Mobile Applications for Environmental and Biodiversity Citizen Science: Considerations and Recommendations. In: *Multimedia tools and applications for environmental & biodiversity informatics*. Springer, Cham. pp. 9-30

Miller-Rushing, A., Primack, R., & Bonney, R. (2012). The history of public participation in ecological research. *Frontiers in Ecology and the Environment*, Vol. 10 No. 6, pp. 285–290.

Musto, J., and Dahanayake, A. 2021. An Approach to Improve the Quality of User-Generated Content of Citizen Science Platforms. I*SPRS International Journal of Geo-Information* Vol. 10, No. 7, pp. 434.

National Academies of Sciences, Engineering, and Medicine. 2018. *Learning Through Citizen Science: Enhancing Opportunities by Design.* National Academies Press (US).

Newman, G., et al. (2010). User-Friendly Web Mapping: Lessons from a Citizen Science Website. *International Journal of Geographical Information Science,* Vol. 24, No. 12, pp. 1851–69.

Okonkwo, C. and Ade-Ibijola, A. (2021). Chatbots Applications in Education: A Systematic Review. *Computers and Education: Artificial Intelligence*, Vol 2.

Pérez, J., et al., (2020). Rediscovering the Use of Chatbots in Education: A Systematic Literature Review'. *Computer Applications in Engineering Education*, Vol. 28, No. 6, pp.1549–65.

Saraswat, Satya, (1999). Structured Content Analysis of Corporate Web-Sites: A Methodological Perspective. (1999). *AMCIS 1999 Proceedings*. Pittsburgh, USA, pp. 206-208.

Shirk, J. et al. (2012). Public Participation in Scientific Research: A Framework for Deliberate Design. *Ecology and Society* Vol. 17, pp. 29–48.

Shirk, J., and Bonney, R. (2018). Scientific Impacts and Innovations of Citizen Science. In *Citizen Science: Innovation in Open Science, Society and Policy*, pp. 41–51. UCL Press, London.

Skarlatidou, A. et al., (2019). What Do Volunteers Want from Citizen Science Technologies? A Systematic Literature Review and Best Practice Guidelines. *Journal of Science Communication,* Vol. 18, No. 1.

Sturm, U. et al., (2018). Mobile Learning in Environmental Citizen Science: An Initial Survey of Current Practice in Germany. *it-Information Technology,* Vol. 60, No. 1, pp. 3-9.

Sturm, U. et al., (2018). Defining Principles for Mobile Apps and Platforms Development in Citizen Science. *Research Ideas and Outcomes,* Vol. 4

Wald, D. et al., (2016). Design Principles for Engaging and Retaining Virtual Citizen Scientists. *Conservation Biology,* Vol. 30, No. 3, pp. 562–570.

Yadav, P. and Darlington, J., (2016). Design Guidelines for the User-Centred Collaborative Citizen Science Platforms'. *Human Computation*, Vol. 3, No. 1, pp. 205-211.

DETERMINATION OF COGNITIVE CRITERIA TO ENHANCE VISUALISATION DURING DESIGN REVIEW SESSION

Adlin Shaflina Azizo[1], Kherun Nita Ali[1], Noorminshah A. Iahad[2] and Chan Vei Siang[3]
[1]*Faculty of Built Environment and Surveying, Universiti Teknologi Malaysia, Johor Bahru, Malaysia*
[2]*Faculty of Management, Universiti Teknologi Malaysia, Johor Bahru, Malaysia*
[3]*Faculty of Computing, Universiti Teknologi Malaysia, Johor Bahru, Malaysia*

ABSTRACT

In the construction industry, it is a common practice to conduct a design review to uncover potential problems by comparing the designer's plan to the client's specifications before the construction begins. The design review involves cognitive process where conversation and debate help to cultivate effective decision-making. It also includes thinking and processing information to empower human communication. The designer's mental processes are crucial as they determine how designers address challenges and construct appropriate decisions. Hence, this study aims to investigate the cognitive criteria that can improve visualisation in the design review practice. This research conducted video interviews with a group of experts in the construction industry to elicit their feedback regarding the topic of virtual collaboration for quality assurance during the design review phase. The authors analysed the collected data using thematic analysis to develop cognitive criteria that improve decision-making during design review. The results uncover the possibilities of more future studies in this area. In conclusion, cognitive criteria with the aid of Virtual Reality (VR) have emerged as a potential solution for enhancing visualisation during the design review process.

KEYWORDS

Cognitive Process, Cognitive Criteria, Design Review, Visualisation, Virtual Reality

1. INTRODUCTION

Nowadays, the construction sector in Malaysia is embracing Industry Revolution 4.0 applications to reduce labour hours and achieve increased flexibility, efficiency, and quality production. Hence, design review during the design stage is critical to ensure that the design complies with all necessary operational, safety, environmental, and industry requirements. Design review is the process of reviewing the design according to the client's requirements to identify problems before the construction begins. In Malaysia, the construction firm still relies on traditional design review practices during the presentation stage of construction development. Thus, it is difficult to introduce a new intervention without exhibiting the advantages and limitations of its usability, especially for designers who follow conventional modus operandi (Czmoch & Pękala, 2014).

To achieve a better design review, the presentation of the design must be adequately assessed, and the design must be judged using reasoned and objective criteria rather than the designers' or developers' preferences. According to Balali *et al.* (2018), factors that will affect the project timeline during the regular design review session, such as changing orders, are due to a lack of understanding and communication between designers and stakeholders. As a result, the design review prizes high-quality visualisation and communication. Recently, the use of VR in design review is gaining momentum in integrating the workflow with 3D construction models and establishing a rapport between designers and clients. The VR environment allows the evaluation of unanticipated issues, typically caused by design mistakes, poor performance, and health and safety concerns in terms of time, costs, and resources (Goulding et al., 2012). It can also assist designers in reaching a mutually agreed settlement with stakeholders to expedite the flow of construction activity (Du et al., 2018). Hence, VR is capable of resolving difficulties regarding quality output during design review. However, it has inescapable obstacles and drawbacks that must be addressed (Fox & Felkey, 2017), including technical hardware issues, user-friendly interaction design, and incorporation of various data types for advanced VR analytics.

Therefore, this study aims to investigate the cognitive criteria in VR to improve the design review process which is one of the critical elements in the construction domain. It identified the cognitive criteria through interview sessions with experts and thematic analysis. The contribution of this study anticipates a means for effective discussion and empowering decision-making among the clients and designers or architects. The organisation of this article is as follows: Section 2 introduces the background of this study; Section 3 presents the research methodology; Sections 4 and 5 report the results and discussion, respectively; Section 6 concludes the article.

2. RELATED WORKS

2.1 Design Review

In the construction industry, the term 'design' encompasses drawings, design details, specifications, bills of quantities, and calculations created for the purpose of a design, which allows the project team to focus on safety and health issues and other vital aspects of the project ("Guidelines on Occupational Safety and Health in Construction Industry (Management)," 2017). Design review is a critical part of the planning process (Mathers et al., 2013) because it allows the designers and clients to share information and assess the project's design based on requirements to detect flaws before the construction begins. Most reviews are in the form of presentation sessions in which the design team and client present the plan to the evaluation panel and engage in conversation to obtain the comments from panels (Mathers et al., 2013). As part of the standard design process, the review process also allows the project team to focus on safety and health issues.

2.1.1 Virtual Reality and Its Adoption in the Design Review

Virtual reality (VR) is a virtual experience that is similar or completely distinct from reality, where users can communicate and interact in a simulated environment while analysing and collecting data from the 3D construction model. VR technology has been adopted to the construction industry for more than two decades (Thabet et al., 2002). The main reason for its high adoption rate in various businesses, including construction, is that VR enables designers to better comprehend the workflow, facilitates development, and increases operator safety (Park et al., 2018; Ray & Teizer, 2012).

One benefit of VR is that it enables powerful adaptive evaluation based on a multitude of design parameters and presents the outcome in a simulated environment. According to Lucko, Benjamin and Madden (2008), VR simulation of building operations is practicable, safe, less time-consuming, and cost-effective. In addition, it permits precise monitoring of the operation's driving factors and the parameters can be changed multiple times instantly to obtain the statistical mean and variance readings for choosing the optimal design.

Additionally, the realistic experience of VR technology is advantageous to the construction industry (Brioso et al., 2019). Whisker *et al.* (2020), discovered that a full-scale 3D virtual model of a construction project can aid designers and learners in comprehending, learning, and gaining experience by evaluating designs for their constructability and create suitable construction plan for complex buildings or infrastructure projects. Immersive VR also enables stakeholders to experience the full-scale representation of a virtual facility prototype in a realistic and accessible way through immersion and a sense of presence, hence facilitating the collection of input and feedback during usability-focused design review sessions (Ventura et al., 2020). Thus, incorporating virtual technology into the design review can provide effective yet interactive discussion.

2.2 Cognitive Process

Thinking, reasoning, learning, and remembering are all the end results of the human brain's cognitive process, which are defined by the way the brain receives and handles information. All designers' actions when analysing data or information are acts of cognition. Furthermore, understanding the scope of their own cognitive abilities is an essential part of the design process. The term "cognitive processes in design," as defined by Tschimmel (2004), encompasses the thinking and interacting abilities necessitated for design which include perceptual, creative, communication, learning, emotional, and collaborative processes. Therefore, it can overcome problems with reasoning, solution-seeking, conceptualization, and communication, as well as facilitate a more fruitful application of the creative design process by appreciating and accommodating individual differences in the cognitive process.

Nevertheless, most of the mental work involved in a design review can cause the developers' mental workload to increase, and thus, designers need to maintain open lines of communication to prevent cognitive burnout. Besides, it is inevitable that there are misunderstandings during the group discussion since every designer has a different degree of understanding. Another possibility is that the information supplied is only retained or comprehended at the time it is first encountered. Therefore, (Motte, Andersson and Bjärnemo (2004), argued the necessity to investigate the designer's cognitive process to better understand their abilities and explore the cognition weakness or limitation. Designers need to navigate the topics throughout the design review process, including coordinating with the developer to ensure clear and concise explanations.

In addition, the design skills and knowledges gained from studying fundamental processes, absorbing domain information, and examining previous satisfied examples can contribute to promising ideas before constructing the mock-ups for visualisation, comparison, and execution of the concepts (Gero, 1998). This cognitive process empowers humans to engage effectively with their environment and adapt to any circumstances. According to Gross and Medina-DeVilliers (2020), from a Bayesian perspective of cognitive process, individuals calculate the costs and benefits of a measure using their prior information and experience. Thus, consulting the experts can obtain a higher level of knowledge that can contribute to a more efficient identification of cognitive process compared to debate amongst peers.

2.3 Virtual Collaboration Quality (VCQ)

Advanced visuals can encourage people to interact and participate in discussion to reach a satisfactory decision. According to Hamrol (2015), the visual element is the centre of focus in most previous work. Hence, a VR system can promote advanced visual representation during client configuration, solving problems, and preventing communication crises. Besides, data visualisation is more effective in communication and understanding than writing or drawing (Cham et al., 2020). Meanwhile, dialogue can lead to decision-making or idea-exchanging (Gjerde, 2017). During the design review session, designers and clients discuss designs, ideas, and decisions through visualisation and dialogue. This research covers four aspects of Virtual Collaboration Quality (VCQ), including communication, decision, discussion, and visualisation, as depicted in Figure 1. These classifications determine the quality of cognitive process during the design review.

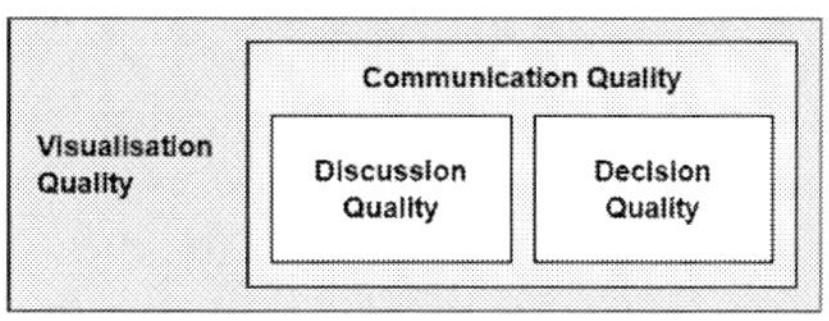

Figure 1 Virtual Collaboration Quality (VCQ) (Azizo & Ali, 2022; binti Azizo et al., 2022)

3. METHODOLOGY

To explore the cognitive criteria in VCQ during the conventional design review process, this study established a qualitative method by using an unstructured interview with an open-ended questionnaire for the experts in the construction industry to gather information and verify it (Berman, 2017; Creswell et al., 2011). Due to the Covid-19 pandemic, it is a necessity to use digital technologies (De et al., 2020) to collect the data via video meeting with industry experts. Since the goal of qualitative research is to construct knowledge from first-hand accounts of human experience and researchers need to follow a certain protocol to produce reliable and useful findings, this research chose qualitative research method for this investigation (Sandelowski, 2004). Five experts from the industry took part in the unstructured interview. Besides, the consultation and knowledge from the experts can improve the reliability of the interview results (Thakur, 2008; Wolfartsberger, 2019), because they had been involved in a wide range of experiences over the entirety of the construction process. Table 1 shows the information about experts invited for unstructured interviews.

Table 1. The details of experts of unstructured interviews

Experts	1 & 2	3	4	5	Total
Expertise	Architect	Architect (Government)	Civil Engineer	Quantity Surveyor	
Experience	> 10 years	> 10 years	> 10 years	> 10 years	
Total	**2**	**1**	**1**	**1**	5

4. RESULTS

This research conducted the thematic analysis by utilising NVivo software version 12.0 plus, a qualitative data analysis program that enables uncomplicated qualitative data analysis to aid researchers in acquiring a deeper understanding about specific research. All of the experts' feedbacks from the unstructured interview sessions was thematically analysed based on a six-step thematic analysis approach (Braun & Clarke, 2006), including (1) familiarisation with the data, (2) generating an initial code, (3) searching for preliminary themes, (4) reviewing themes, (5) defining and naming themes, and (6) summarising the thematic network in a mind map to easily identify the cognitive criteria in the design review (Mansor, 2021). According to Braun and Clarke (2006), thematic analysis is a suitable method for analysing the viewpoints of several respondents, uncovering similarities and contrasts, and delivering unexpected results. Figure 2 illustrates details of the thematic analysis.

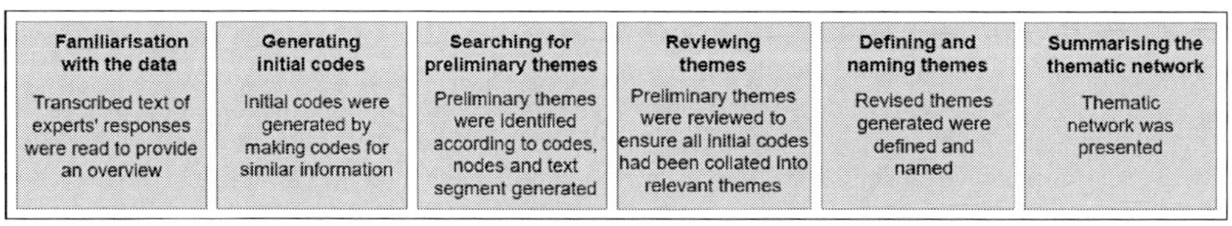

Figure 2. Phases of thematic analysis (Braun & Clarke, 2006; Mansor, 2021)

Azizo and Ali (2022) stated that incorporating an interview by involving three experts in the research can determine the cognitive processes. As a result, the interview outcomes showed the generation of initial codes that contain comparable information from all supplied data, including 'luxurious design', 'inviting design', 'grandeur design', and 'welcoming sense' that were combined under the code term 'quality of space.' Next, the initial theme for the 'quality of space' code was classified under 'vision and imagination'. Then, all preliminary themes were identified and described completely which encompasses 'design awareness', 'coordination', 'sharp discussion', 'firm', 'perceiving', 'understanding', 'teamwork processes', and 'evaluation'. In addition, under the 'visualisation quality' is the cognitive design that includes 'visual perception' theme (Sulaiman et al., 2020).

Lastly, this study created a thematic mind map to show the general theme-codes network link. The thematic network is a multi-actor organisation that combine existing knowledge on a focused issue for consultants, clients, and more. It is a method used for analysing text material thematically and illustrating the network's relationship graphically (Attride-Stirling, 2001). The use of colour encodings is as following: orange represents the initial codes, pink represents the codes, blue represents the preliminary themes, green represents revised themes, and white colour represents the VCQ's major parameter. Accordingly, the authors classified the ten codes into five revised themes from the five preliminary themes. Figure 3 provides a mind map summary of the additional data according to Braun and Clarke (2006) that utilise the thematic analysis.

5. DISCUSSION

The five revised themes are grouped under four VCQ's major parameters where 'visual perception' is under 'Visualisation Quality', 'synthesising' is under 'Communication Quality', 'knowledgeable' and 'leadership perspective' are under 'Discussion Quality', and 'decision making' is under 'Decision Quality'. During the design review, understanding the design specifications by all stakeholders is the first and most crucial step toward effective and quality communication. Hence, cognitive performance for all designers and stakeholders during the discussion is pivotal to reach an agreement from any problems. Furthermore, understanding the cognitive criteria can assist in the adoption of VR in design review to improve the design review process. According to Paes and Irizarry (2018), an immersive VR system improved decision-making during design review by improving the user's cognitive performance in expressing and comprehending the design ideas. Hence, the cognitive performance of designers and stakeholders throughout the dialogue is critical to obtain a consensus on any topics. In a nutshell, high-end technology can improve the efficacy of design reviews by assisting the stakeholders considerably in understanding their design and reducing cognitive strain (Frederiksen et al., 2020). Thus, the study of cognitive processes is necessary to enhance the use of VR in design review. The following sections explain the four VCQ's major parameters in detail.

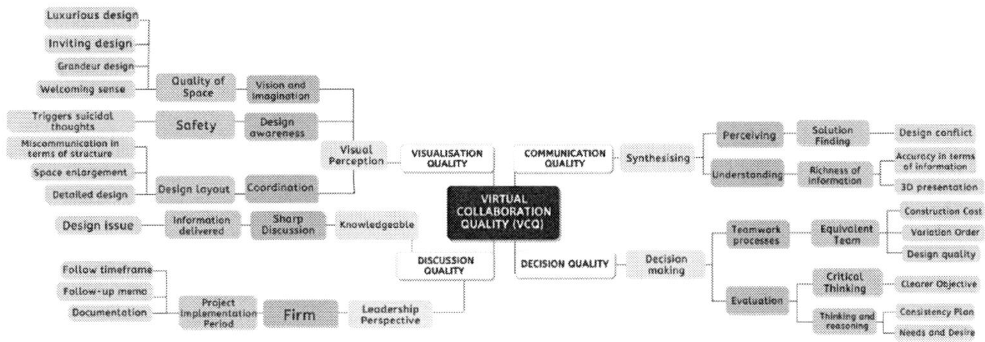

Figure 3. Summarisation of the thematic network mind map

5.1 Visualisation Quality

Visualisation is crucial in design review. As mentioned by Expert 1, the design review prizes the first visual impression of the building's entrance whether it has a welcoming and inviting presence that attracts the people to visit. Yee et al. (2012), indicated that visualisation improves decision-making where they are used internally to articulate findings and keep empathy for the client or context, as well as a communication tool with project stakeholders. By visualising the complete scale of architectural design (Liu et al., 2020), immersive VR can help with the decision-making process (Soust-verdaguer et al., 2021). Visual perception entails viewing, absorbing, and recognising an object or surrounding, and then, arranging the information mentally. Alhadad, (2018), argued that visual perception encodes the properties of the visualised information in the working memory. Through the design review process in VR, designers and stakeholders or clients are more aware of the building's structure or uncover existing problems in the design.

5.2 Communication Quality

Communication is the process of communicating information or knowledge between peoples through speaking, writing, viewing, or reading the media, nature, or other sources. Expert 2 stated that the accuracy of information is crucial to provide an efficient workflow because the contactor does not need to create a physical prototype if the visual is presented accurately. Hence, effective communication can facilitate productive discussion and decision-making. Communication can also produce hypotheses that can be tested which lead to experiment planning, changing hypotheses, and concluding a result. Synthesis is the process of making a new argument and a new point of view. It is one of the most important cognitive processes (Wang, 2015) for making good conclusions from communication. Besides, Paes and Irizarry (2018), asserted that a thorough understanding of design requirements by all designers and developers is the first and most crucial step toward effective communication in a design review scenario. Therefore, immersive VR was demonstrated to enhance communication between specialists and clients by bridging the construction site into the discussion room (Tibaldi et al., 2020).

5.3 Discussion Quality

Discussion is the method or procedure of discourse that leads to valuable results in conclusion. Typically, the discussion process leads to decision-making or the exchange of opinions concerning the discussed subjects (Gjerde, 2017). Thus, knowledge of cognition is essential because it comprises information about oneself as a learner, knowledge about learning approaches, and knowledge about when and why to employ a certain strategy. Bundeswehr and Padagogik (1982), stated that cognitive knowledge is related to a person's understanding of his or her own cognition. To guarantee that the debate is relevant to the issue at hand, it is necessary to possess the appropriate expertise. Moreover, Expert 1 said that the leadership perspective is a good quality and guiding concept that can achieve the goal and serve as a model for others to emulate. According to Eden and Leviatan (1975), which is referenced by Lord and Emrich (2000), most respondents feel that the leadership factor is essential to their everyday lives. Moreover, the impact of communication between designers and stakeholders or clients is significant to design negotiations, deliver an idea or thinking, and make decision. During the design review, designers use their understanding of the design to argue with other designers and discuss which facts and data are most beneficial.

5.4 Decision Quality

The designers and stakeholders meet during the design review meeting to examine the construction project's planning and the repercussions of project failure. Quality decision-making must occur during the meeting to reach a plausible conclusion. The reviewers must maintain a democratic balance of power to prevent unfavourable decisions that could affect the project's costs and time (Gjerde, 2017). Therefore, decision-making is one of the most basic cognitive processes in human behaviour, in which a preferred alternative or course of action is selected among a variety of alternatives based on predetermined criteria (Lee & Ostwald, 2020; Wang et al., 2004). Several factors that influence decision-making, such as past experiences, various cognitive impediments, the ability to engage and sunk performance, individual differences in age and socioeconomic status, and a sense of personal responsibility, can influence a decision-making process (Dietrich, 2010). The cognitive process of the designer's decision-making and problem-solving skills is also engaged in the growth of design concepts, according to Sun and Yao (2011), Individual behaviour is a significant aspect in the study of decision-making in psychology because an individual's reaction can influence their decision-making.

6. CONCLUSION

The findings of this study contribute to the expanding body of information regarding the cognitive criteria utilised by designers during traditional design reviews. It is crucial to organise the design review into revised themes based on cognitive criteria of the VCQ to enhance the design review experience. By developing a quality design review process, time and money can be saved because it can help produce effective decision-making amongst designers. A paucity of research on cognitive processes in VR-related architectural research, such as spatial or behavioural, visual perception, and other cognitive processes (Paes et al., 2017) may contribute to the knowledge gap in this area. The results from the unstructured interviews with construction experts can also be incorporated into new technologies, including VR, to compare the effectiveness with traditional methods in generating satisfied design review decisions. Hence, the authors anticipated that it could improve the productivity of designers in a construction project by analysing their cognition during design review, thereby maximising the use of VR for visualisation and, ultimately, contributing to the improvement of the construction industry, especially in Malaysia. For future work, the authors will create a questionnaire according to the revised VCQ thematic network and conduct an experiment on a group of construction experts to use the traditional method and VR technology in the design review. The outcome of this future study aims to identify the feasibility of VR technology in the design review process and how it affects the cognitive process of designers.

ACKNOWLEDGEMENT

This work was funded and supported by the Ministry of Higher Education (MoHE) Malaysia under the Fundamental Research Grant Scheme (Vote No. FRGS/1/2020/SS0/UTM/02/2) and Universiti Teknologi Malaysia (UTM). The authors would like to express their appreciation for the assistance of the sponsors.

REFERENCES

Alhadad, S. S. J. (2018). Visualizing Data to Support Judgement, Inference, and Decision Making in Learning Analytics: Insights from Cognitive Psychology and Visualization Science. *Journal of Learning Analytics*, *5*(2), 60–85.

Attride-Stirling, J. (2001). Thematic networks: An analytic tool for qualitative research. *Qualitative Research*, *1*(3), 385–405.

Azizo, A. S., & Ali, K. N. (2022). The Identification Of Cognitive Criteria In Design Review Decision Making. *9th International Graduate Conference on Engineering, Science and HUmanities*, 374–378.

Balali, V., Noghabaei, M., Heydarian, A., & Han, K. (2018). Improved Stakeholder Communication and Visualizations: Real-Time Interaction and Cost Estimation within Immersive Virtual Environments. *Construction Research Congress 2018*, 522–530.

Berman, E. (2017). An Exploratory Sequential Mixed Methods Approach to Understanding Researchers' Data Management Practices at UVM: Integrated Findings to Develop Research Data Services. *Journal of EScience Librarianship*, *6*(1), e1104.

binti Azizo, A. S., binti Ali, K. N., Iahad, N. B. A., Binti Mohd, N. I., Mat Dzahir, M. A. Bin, & Abdul Rahiman, N. B. (2022). A Methodology to Evaluate the Effectiveness of Designers' Cognitive Process when Using Multi-user Virtual Reality. *IOP Conference Series: Earth and Environmental Science*, *1067*(1), 012077.

Braun, V., & Clarke, V. (2006). Using thematic analysis in psychology,Qualitative Research in Psychology. *Journal of Chemical Information and Modeling*, *3*(2), 77–101.

Brioso, X., Calderon-hernandez, C., Irizarry, J., & Paes, D. (2019). *Using Immersive Virtual Reality to Improve Choosing by Advantages System for the Selection of Fall Protection Measures*. *June*.

Bundeswehr, H. der, & Padagogik, F. (1982). Cognitive Knowledge and Executive Control: Metacognition. *Animal Mind — Human Mind*, 201–224.

Cham, H., Malek, S., Milow, P., & Ramli, M. R. (2020). *Web-based system for visualisation of water quality index*.

Creswell, J., Klassen, A. C., Plano, V., & Smith, K. C. (2011). Best Practices for Mixed Methods Research in the Health Sciences. *Methods*, *29*, 1–39.

Czmoch, I., & Pękala, A. (2014). Traditional design versus BIM based design. *Procedia Engineering*, *91*(TFoCE), 210–215.

De, R., Pandey, N., & Pal, A. (2020). Impact of digital surge during Covid-19 pandemic: A viewpoint on research and practice. *International Journal of Information and Learning Technology*, *55*, 1–6.

Dietrich, C. (2010). Decision Making: Factors that Influence Decision Making, Heuristics Used, and Decision Outcomes. *Inquiries Journal*, *2*(2010), 2/3.

Du, J., Zou, Z., Shi, Y., & Zhao, D. (2018). Zero latency: Real-time synchronization of BIM data in virtual reality for collaborative decision-making. *Automation in Construction*, *85*(October 2017), 51–64.

Fox, B. I., & Felkey, B. G. (2017). Pharmacy automation and technology: Revisiting hospital readmissions. *Hospital Pharmacy*, *52*(2).

Frederiksen, J. G., Sørensen, S. M. D., Konge, L., Svendsen, M. B. S., Nobel-Jørgensen, M., Bjerrum, F., & Andersen, S. A. W. (2020). Cognitive load and performance in immersive virtual reality versus conventional virtual reality simulation training of laparoscopic surgery: a randomized trial. *Surgical Endoscopy*, *34*(3), 1244–1252.

Gero, J. (1998). Analysis of cognitive processes of a designer as the foundation for support tools. *Artificial Intelligence in Design '98, November*.

Gjerde, M. (2017). Informing design review: Discussion of the findings of a visual preference study in New Zealand. *Procedia Engineering*, *198*(September 2016), 562–569.

Goulding, J., Nadim, W., Petridis, P., & Alshawi, M. (2012). Construction industry offsite production: A virtual reality interactive training environment prototype. *Advanced Engineering Informatics*, *26*(1), 103–116.

Gross, E. B., & Medina-DeVilliers, S. E. (2020). Cognitive Processes Unfold in a Social Context: A Review and Extension of Social Baseline Theory. *Frontiers in Psychology*, *11*(March), 1–12.

Guidelines on Occupational Safety and Health in Construction Industry (Management). (2017). In *Department of Occupational Safety and Health Ministry of Human Resources*.

Hamrol, A. (2015). *Immersive City Bus Configuration System for Marketing and Sales Education Immersive City Bus Configuration System for Marketing and Sales Education. February 2016.*

Lee, J. H., & Ostwald, M. J. (2020). Creative decision-making processes in parametric design. *Buildings, 10*(12), 1–19.

Liu, Y., Ph, D., Castronovo, F., Ph, D., Asce, A. M., Messner, J., Ph, D., Asce, M., Leicht, R., Ph, D., & Asce, A. M. (2020). Evaluating the Impact of Virtual Reality on Design Review Meetings. *Journal of Computing in Civil Engineering, 34*(1).

Lord, R. G., & Emrich, C. G. (2000). Thinking outside the box by looking inside the box: Extending the cognitive revolution in leadership research. *Leadership Quarterly, 11*(4), 551–579.

Lucko, G., Benjamin, P. C., & Madden, M. G. (2008). Harnessing the Power of Simulation in the Project Management / Decision Support Aspects of the Construction Industry. *Proceedings - Winter Simulation Conference*, 2479–2487.

Mansor, R. (2021). *A Measurement Model Of Occupant Well-Being For Malaysian Office Building*.

Mathers, J., Illman, S., Brady, A., & Geraghty, D. P. (2013). Design Review Principles and Practice. *Design Council.*

Motte, D., Andersson, P., & Bjärnemo, R. (2004). Study of the designer ' s cognitive proc- esses during the later phases of the mechanical engineering design process. international design conference. *International Design Conference - Design 2004*, 1–8.

Paes, D., Arantes, E., & Irizarry, J. (2017). Immersive environment for improving the understanding of architectural 3D models: Comparing user spatial perception between immersive and traditional virtual reality systems. *Automation in Construction, 84*(September), 292–303.

Paes, D., & Irizarry, J. (2018). A Usability Study of an Immersive Virtual Reality Platform for Building Design Review: Considerations on Human Factors and User Interface. *Proceeding of Construction Research Congress 2018, 1996*(BuildingSMART 2007), 148–157.

Park, H., Panya, D. S., Goo, H., Kim, T., & Seo, J. (2018). BIM-based Virtual Reality and Human Behavior Simulation For Safety Design. *ECAADe, 2*, 823–832.

Ray, S. J., & Teizer, J. (2012). Real-time construction worker posture analysis for ergonomics training. *Advanced Engineering Informatics, 26*(2), 439–455.

Sandelowski, M. (2004). Using qualitative research. *Qualitative Health Research, 14*(10), 1366–1386.

Soust-verdaguer, B., Hollberg, A., Kiss, B., Martin, R., Wiberg, A. H., Lasvaux, S., Galimshina, A., & Habert, G. (2021). *Review of visualising LCA results in the design process of buildings. 190*(August 2020).

Sulaiman, H., Ibrahim, N., Latif, R. A., & Yusof, A. M. (2020). Students and Teachers' Perception on future use of Virtual Reality (VR) in learning Physics: A Preliminary Analysis. *2020 IEEE Conference on E-Learning, e-Management and e-Services, IC3e 2020*, 61–66.

Sun, G., & Yao, S. (2011). A New Framework of Studying the Cognitive Model of Creative Design. *Engineering, August.*

Thabet, W., Shiratuddin, M. F., & Bowman, D. A. (2002). *Virtual Reality in Construction* (Issue January).

Thakur, D. (2008). *Research Methodology In Social Science*. Deep & deep publications pvt. Ltd.

Tibaldi, A., Bonali, F. L., Vitello, F., Delage, E., Nomikou, P., Antoniou, V., Becciani, U., & Vries, B. V. W. De. (2020). *Real world – based immersive Virtual Reality for research , teaching and communication in volcanology*.

Tschimmel, K. (2004). A new discipline in design education: cognitive processes in design. *DS 33: Proceedings of E&PDE 2004, the 7th International Conference on Engineering and Product Design Education, Delft, the Netherlands, 02.-03.09. 2004, September 2004*.

Ventura, S. M., Castronovo, F., & Ciribini, A. L. C. (2020). A design review session protocol for the implementation of immersive virtual reality in usability-focused analysis. *Journal of Information Technology in Construction, 25*, 233–253.

Wang, Y. (2015). *On Cognitive Processes of Analysis and Synthesis in Cognitive Computing. 12*, 177–185.

Wang, Y., Liu, D., & Ruhe, G. (2004). Formal Description Of The Cognitive Process Of Decision Making. *Strategies.*

Whisker, V., Yerrapathruni, S., Messner, J., & Baratta, A. (2020). *Using Virtual Reality To Improve Construction Engineering Education*. 8.1266.1-8.1266.9.

Wolfartsberger, J. (2019). Automation in Construction Analyzing the potential of Virtual Reality for engineering design review. *Automation in Construction, 104*(March), 27–37.

THE USE OF MOBILE LEARNING IN THE PROFESSIONAL MASTER'S DEGREE IN CYBERSECURITY

Tayná Gabriela Araújo Albuquerque, Daniel Alves da Silva, Valéria Cristina Soares Alves, Danielle Alves de Oliveira Tabosa, Fábio Lúcio Lopes de Mendonça and Rafael Timóteo de Sousa Júnior
Universidade de Brasília, Brazil

ABSTRACT

Cybersecurity in Brazil and around the world has expanded due to the majority use of the world wide web through Information and Communications Technology (ICTs). In the educational field, the use of mobile devices during the COVID-19 pandemic was the common tool both students and teachers found to facilitate studies once the lockdown and the social distancing came into force, and remote teaching was adopted and implemented by universities. Notably, the Professional Graduate Program in Electrical Engineering (PPEE), at the University of Brasília (UnB), has a professional postgraduate program that aims to train its students in that cybersecurity—using mobile learning as one of its learning tools—which is relevant to public and private institutions.

KEYWORDS

Cyber Security, Remote Learning, Mobile Learning, Postgraduate Program, Master's Degree Program

1. INTRODUCTION

Currently, when we consider the high availability of access to global computer networks and the various information and communications technologies (ICTs), the digital world has exponentially grown—according to the International Telecommunication Union (ITU), in 2021, the number of global internet users reached 4,9 billion, which accounts for 63% of the world population (ITU, 2021)—encompassing, and developing the structure of several private and governmental entities. Conversely, the training of qualified professionals in the data protection and cybersecurity field has not followed this growth—in other words, the lack of qualified professionals creates breaches for cyber-attacks. According to the Security Report, Brazil was the 5th country with most of the cyber-attacks in the world, which brought financial losses to establishments as well as to their users.

Educational tools and strategies have also been redefined by ICTs, especially from 2020 onwards, when we had to adopt social distancing protocols due to the COVID-19 pandemic outbreak, and because of that, face-to-face activities were suspended to reduce the virus transmission. Educational activities were also suspended for a certain period of time, returning only remotely so that the damage was reduced as much as possible.

The dramatic increase of the use of easy-to-handle mobile devices—such as smartphones, tablets, laptops, and e-readers, for example—with the fifth generation of mobile network (5G) provides the student with a collaborative learning network, making it possible for them to experience new learning situations.

According to Al-Emran et al. (2018), mobile learning (M-learning) provides access to information, educational resources, and learning tools to students anytime and anywhere, and the learning process is not limited to a specific place (Corbeil & Valdes-Corbeil, 2007, as cited in Biswas et al). In addition, M-learning empowers and facilitates the shared knowledge in the teaching-learning process between learners and educators, bringing several opportunities for both without imposed restrictions (Al-Emran et al., 2020).

Encouraging the use of new technologies in the pedagogical scenario, by students and professors, within formal university learning had already been identified as a necessity (Bauer et al., 2020), nevertheless, it can be said that this use was propelled due to the pandemic with the implementation of remote teaching. And because of its greater scope and reach, reduced costs, and flexibility for the student to be able to balance study and private life; remote teaching has, therefore, contributed to the qualification of professionals (Maia & Meirelles, 2009).

Considering the challenges of cybersecurity and the need for courses on the subject at hand, our paper presents the experience of the Cybersecurity course—presently provided by the Professional Graduate Program in Electrical Engineering (PPEE) of the University of Brasília (UnB), in Brazil—during the years 2020-2021. The PPEE of UnB is developed by the Department of Electrical Engineering (ENE) of the Faculty of Technology (FT), and is ruled, where applicable, by the current legislation, as established by the provisions of the National Council of Education (CNE), by the Statute and General Regulations of the University of Brasília and by the Resolutions of the Teaching, Research and Extension Council (CEPE) nos. 0098/2020, 0080/2021, and 217/2016.

Our objective is to carry out a survey of the contributions that a Professional Training Program in Cybernetic Security can add to the training of qualified professionals and what is its impact on the labour market. And, also, we want to present to other graduate programs the methods and techniques supported by mobile technologies used by our PPEE, opening a communication network for dialogues about innovation between ours and graduate programs. Despite being a case study, the survey we herein conducted is instrumental in obtaining innovative alternatives and possibilities so that it is possible to increase the discussions on the capacity of the Brazilian professionals who are being trained.

The study is organised as follows: related works, course structure, extracurricular activities, professors, students, and intellectual production. Sections have been selected to cover all areas of the program and to provide insight into the surrounding categories.

2. RELATED WORKS

The works related to the case study herein presented are the ones that address the practice and introduction of M-learning applied in a context of higher education, at graduate level.

Bauer et al. (2020) state that a range of scenarios of different types of learning can be used in higher education, from individual M-learning units to virtual teaching. In their work, the authors used as example practical and pedagogical scenarios—videos, weblogs, e-portfolios, wikis, online research tools, and collaborative tools—developed and applied by participants of MINE Project in partner universities.

Farley et al. (2015), in *How Do Students Use Their Mobile Devices to Support Teaching? A Case Study from an Australian Regional University*, concluded in their case study at the University of Southern Queensland on the need for pedagogical approaches that are more focused on student's learning and the improvement of their critical thinking, collaboration, and communication. These approaches should encourage students to take responsibility for their own learning so they can apply theoretical concepts in real situations.

In Bangladesh, Biswas et al. (2020) shared a questionnaire by Google Docs, randomly distributed amongst several undergraduate and graduate students in universities in the region, about the perception of the use of M-learning during the beginning of the COVID-19 pandemic. The students were already familiar with M-learning, so the responses were quite positive. Amidst their findings, the authors concluded that mobile learning proved to be a useful tool during that first year of the pandemic, given that the place of study was limited to an environment outside the universities' grounds. In addition, the students also noticed an improvement in the relationship between them and the teachers.

3. COURSE STRUCTURE

The PPEE's mission is to promote personnel training and research on advanced professional practice that helps to evolve scientific and technological knowledge, allowing to train a professional capable of working in technical-scientific and innovative activities. With the inclination to work in any of the professional fields of electrical engineering, without coverage of its sister academic program, the Graduate Program in Electrical Engineering (PPGEE), the focus on cybersecurity makes it possible to meet the needs of the labour market.

In the Federal District of Brazil, it is possible to find a variety of institutions in which the training of professionals and applied research are of great interest. Therefore, the focus on cybersecurity is maintained as the only major area of concentration, despite being broken down into six strongly linked and complementary lines of research, namely: Information System and Networks Security; Science and Data Engineering; Security and Cyber Intelligence; Decision-making in security and cyber intelligence, processes, data engineering and artificial intelligence; Conceptions and developments of strategic and critical materials; and Security of information processing and Communications in electro-electronic-computer systems.

This structure has been attracting students from institutions or public agencies, generating technology transfer processes and knowledge.

As an assistance to the student's intellectual production, the Central Library of the UnB (BCE) has a collection of 563,069 volumes and 7,902 journal titles, of which 37,145 of the volumes and 2,143 of the journal titles address areas of exact sciences and engineering. On top of being connected to the world wide web, the BCE has a cataloguing and indexing system available for online consultations. The library offers an institutional repository, the Institutional Repository of the UnB (RIUnB), for the dissemination of scientific production carried out at the university. The library also has a Digital Library of Monographs, where an archive of theses, dissertations and monographs produced at the UnB can be found, including those that have been produced at the PPEE.

The update and access to the reference repositories, such as those in the BCE, are extremely important for the foundation of scientific knowledge, and the production of future academic works, as well as for consultations by companies.

It is noteworthy the number of laboratories of the Department of Electrical Engineering, along with classrooms, study rooms, professor's rooms, and administrative areas, with local wireless and affiliated computer networks included available. In three different points of presence of this network, there are routers with 1Gbps connection to the UnB Network (RedUnB), and from this network—via the Metropolitana GigaCandanga Network, with 10Gbps of connection—it is created the National Teaching and Research Network (RNO). Through this network, and using approximately one hundred computers and internet access booths, the student has access to scientific and technical information available through retrieval systems, both in the department itself and in the Dissertations and Theses Base of the Central Library of the UnB and on the Coordination of Superior Level Staff Improvement (CAPES) journal portal.

Although students are currently not using floor spaces of the university—since the use of the personal equipment allows, with the help of mobile networks, easy access from different locations—all classrooms are equipped with computers and multimedia equipment with internet access via wired and wireless network.

For this purpose, the environments of Microsoft Teams and Moodle (Aprender2) from UnB are used with the support of the Centre of Distance Learning (CEAD/UnB) along with Moodle from the Laboratory of Networks (LabRedes)—www.campusvirtual.unb.br. The laboratories remained fully functional during the pandemic of COVID-19 to provide support to professors and technical and administrative staff as well as to students—who are working from home.

The virtual laboratories for the students, important for the development of knowledge about communication networks, were carried out remotely during the pandemic. The students, under guidance, set up their own virtual laboratories, which provided them with greater computational processing capacity; conversely, the laboratories development relied on resources of commercial or personal devices, which, according to the students, led to numerous difficulties associated with hardware, software, capacity, compatibility, amongst others. The students themselves came up with a solution and suggested the assembly of the laboratories by the professors, making them available through VPN, speeding up the process.

The Decision-Making Technologies Laboratory (LATITUDE), where the physical structure of the PPEE is located, has resources from the Law of Information Technology ("Lei da Informática") of the Ministry of Science, Technology, and Innovation (MCTI) through the FUB-Dell contract—signed by the University of Brasília Foundation (FUB) and Dell Computadores do Brasil LDTA. The laboratory is an environment for cooperation between projects, such as: Audit System Project (SIGA), Budget Secretariat (SOF) Project, Integrated Planning and Budgeting System (SIAP) Project, Virtual School of SOF, National School of Public Administration (Enap) Project, Service Management System (SGS), amongst others. This interaction with government agencies, researchers and subjects is important and goes beyond the admission of students to the PPEE for they are able to interact and learn with senior members of various subjects.

The PPEE regulation has been adapted to meet the demands of academia and labour market, for example, currently, there are two mandatory disciplines, namely: Scientific Research Methodology, and Cybersecurity. These disciplines recycle, both in the production of academic works, and in the basic knowledge of the area of interest. The concern lies within the professionals who, numerous times, were estranged from their studies, and needed to become accustomed to the professional master's degree.

The other disciplines are adapted to the specificities and areas of knowledge of the professors, e.g., study of the Law of Guidelines and Bases ("Lei das Diretrizes e Bases"), Data Science, Cryptography, Application of Distributed Networks, and more.

4. EXTRACURRICULAR ACTIVITIES

The program has been helping in the training of professionals, specifically in the forensic sciences field, thus providing higher integration between academia and the productive sector. To that end, together with the Decision-Making Laboratory (LATITUDE), the PPEE connects institutions and government agencies through research projects in which students and professors exchange expertise in order to deliver a quality product.

It is possible to grant paid scholarships to the students participating in projects in partnerships with institutions such as the Brazilian Intelligence Agency (ABIN), the Ministry of Justice and Public Security (MJSP), the National School of Public Administration (Enap), and the Attorney General's Office (AGU). Those students tend to continue the course and have a better performance in other activities.

5. PROFESSORS

The faculty is composed mostly of PhD professors from the permanent personnel of UnB in effective exercise at the university. In general, these professors work in specific orientations and co-orientations, and also teach disciplines.

Intending to explore the synergy created between the university and the productive, and governmental sectors—the target of training and research products—the faculty addresses the professional demand and maintains the adequate adaptation to the program's proposal, allowing to achieve results with a high level of innovation and considerable applicability in the routine of the partner organisations. For this, new criteria of accreditation and tenure of professors were defined in accordance with the objective of obtaining a better evaluation by CAPES. As a result, the program has some of the professors as productivity fellows of the National Council for Scientific and Technological Development (CNPq), and several external participants and visitors who are highly qualified in the Cybersecurity field.

6. STUDENTS

The PPEE offers a professional master's degree, which is one of the few existing in the Midwest ("região Centro-Oeste"), cooperating with economic and social advancement of the region. In particular, the area of concentration of cybersecurity contributes greatly to the development of tools and innovations that boost Public Security and are also used to tackle new types of crime throughout the country as well as to support critical infrastructures of electricity, telecommunications, and internet.

These characteristics make the PPEE a highly sought-after program in its selection process and the candidates opening slots are always taken by the best ranked and approved candidates. Corroborating with this information, the PPEE has students working effectively in several relevant units in the field, with researchers with exclusive dedication in the production of academic content, clearly demonstrating the contribution of the program in these sectors.

Figure 1. Place of professional activity of the students. The figure exhibits a graph with the number of students with exclusive dedication placed in various units with due relevance to the program.

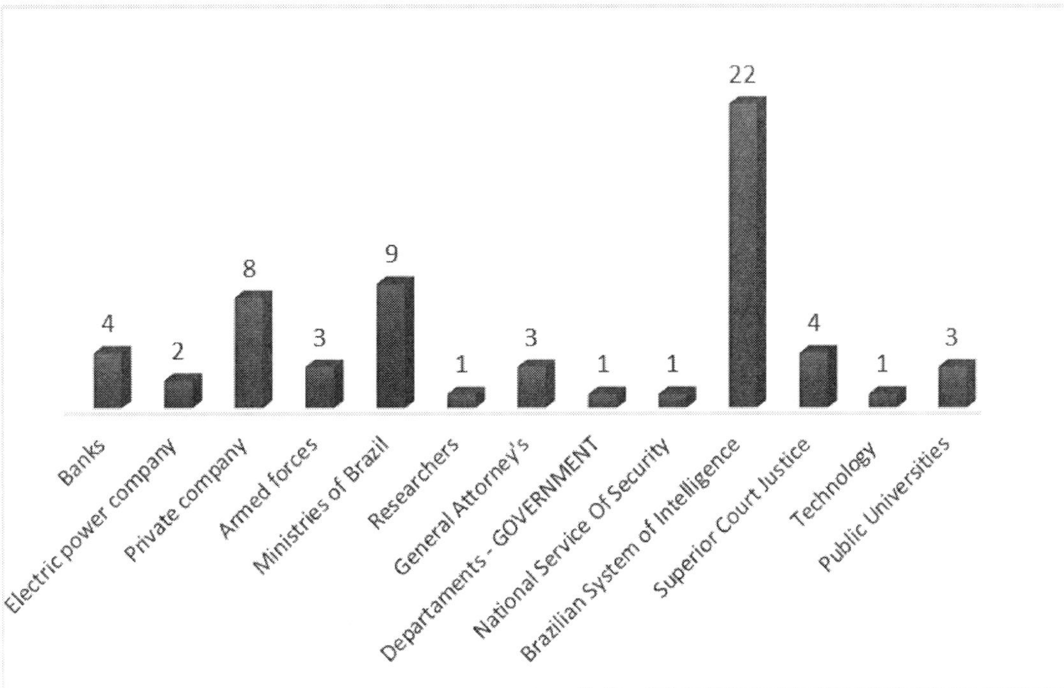

Figure 1. Place of professional activity of the students

7. RESULTS

We conducted a survey questionnaire amongst PPEE teachers and students about the teaching methods the PPEE had adopted during the COVID-19 pandemic, and we received 45 responses, 73.3% students and 26.7% professors. From the analysis of the answers, we gathered that 78.8% of the student respondents agreed that remote learning, synchronous and asynchronous, was appropriate enough to teach about cybersecurity, having the same percentage in terms of achieving the course objective. Amongst the open answers, we noted that students requested more synchronous activities, for longer periods, removing or increasing the deadline for activities outside of class hours.

Aiming to give visibility to the program, the PPEE developed and has been keeping its website updated (https://ppee.unb.br/) in order to disseminate the most significant information. The webpage also provides access to the previously produced master's essays in the program.

At present, the PPEE has almost 800 productions by professors that may have participation of students, as well as a total of 30 essays already defended. It is worth mentioning that due to the COVID-19 pandemic, the classes had a considerable loss in the completion of the course, therefore, with the gradual return of the activities, the students have been organising to defend their essays in the coming months.

Through the Sucupira Platform, from the Coordination for the Improvement of Higher Education Personnel, it is possible to issue an academic production report for the years 2018, 2019 and 2020. Thereby it is clear that most of the works produced are levels A1 and A3, considered the best pointers.

Figure 2. Academic productions. The figure presents a graphic demonstrating the number academic productions referring to the years 2018, 2019, and 2020 in relation to the level of the papers.

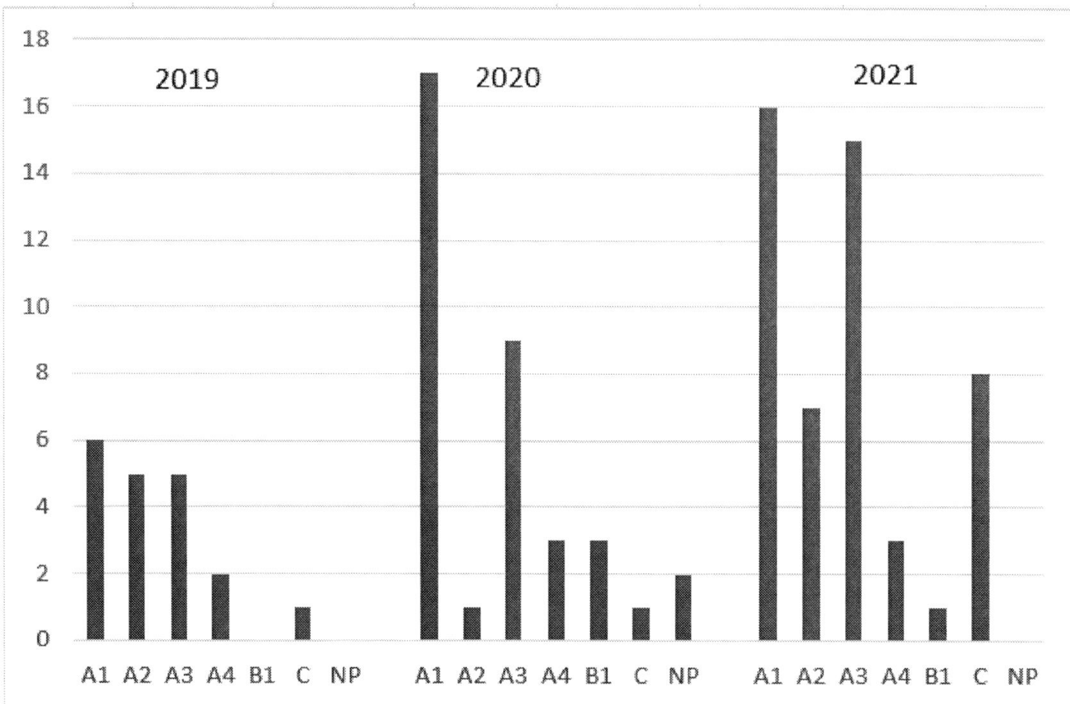

Figure 2. Academic productions

According to the Qualis Journals Report by the Coordination for the Improvement of Higher Education Personnel (2019), "Non-scientific journal" (NPC) means "vehicles that do not meet the definition of a scientific journal"; "C" refers to journals that do not meet the criteria of strata "A1" to "B4"; strata "A1", "A2", "A3", "A4", "B1", "B2", "B3", and "B4" are evaluated by strictly observing the percentage limits of journal distribution established by the Technical and Scientific Council of Higher Education (CTC – ES), with "A1" having the highest stratum (75%) and "B4" the lowest (40%).

The program supports, and has professors who participated in the organisation of technological and scientific events, such as the Simpósio Brasileiro de Segurança da Informação e de Sistemas Computacionais ("Brazilian Symposium on Information Security and Computer Systems") – SBSeg 2020 (Coordination of the Computational Forensics Workshop – WFC); SBrT 2020 (Financial Coordination); WCNPS 2020 – 5th Workshop on Communication Networks and Power Systems (General Chair, TP Chair, Local Organisation and Reviewers); Conferência Integrada ("Integrated Conference") ICCYBER and ICoFCS (partners and collaborators are organisers and committee members); CIARP 2021 (not held in 2020 due to COVID-19) and; o InterForensics 2021 (not held in 2020 due to COVID-19)—recognised as the largest integrated Forensic Sciences event in Latin America, amongst other forums in the region.

8. CONCLUSION

It is notable that information technology has grown in recent years, being linked to cybersecurity to solve current and future problems, and we can observe its impact in today's society with the use of technological resources.

As it is a relatively new program, we noted that the Graduate Program (PPG) achieved good stability in the structuring of its objectives, in the faculty and students, and, mainly, it has reached a high level of published academic productions.

Studies indicate that the PPEE has been helping in the training of qualified professionals in the cybersecurity field, and that the work developed, both by professors and students, are up-to-date and have contributions to the reality of the labour market.

We must pay attention to the research on related courses and contemporary demands post-pandemic. The current study shows the necessity to advance in the understanding of teaching techniques to professionals in the cybersecurity field.

Therefore, we intend in future studies to go deeper into education in cybersecurity, which is beneficial to our society as a whole.

ACKNOWLEDGMENT

This work counted on the support of the CNPq – National Research Council (Grants 312180/2019- 5 PQ-2 and 465741/2014-2 INCT in Cybersecurity), the Administrative Council for Economic Defense (Grant CADE 08700.000047/2019-14), the Attorney General's Office (Grant AGU 697.935/2019), of the National Department of Audit of the SUS (Grant DENASUS 23106.118410/2020-85), of the Attorney General's Office of the National Treasury (Grant PGFN 23106.148934/2019-67), of the Brazilian Intelligence Agency (Grant ABIN 08/2019), the University of Brasília (Grant FUB/COPEI 7129), and Projeto SISTER City – Sistemas Inteligentes Seguros e em Tempo Efetivo Real para Cidades Inteligentes (Secure near-real-time intelligent computing systems for Smart Cities) (Grant no. 625/2022).

REFERENCES

Al-Emran, M., Mezhuyev, V., & Kamaludin, A. (2018). Technology acceptance model in M-learning context: A systematic review. *Computers & Education, 125*, 389-412. https://doi.org/10.1016/j.compedu.2018.06.008

Al-Emran, M., Mezhuyev, V., & Kamaludin, A. (2020). Towards a conceptual model for examining the impact of knowledge management factors on mobile learning acceptance. *Technology in Society, 61*, 101247. https://doi.org/10.1016/j.techsoc.2020.101247

Bauer, P. B., Kolb, C., & Bastian, J. (2020). *16th International Conference Mobile Learning 2020*. IADIS Publications. https://www.iadisportal.org/components/com_booklibrary/ebooks/202004C012.pdf

Biswas, B., Roy, S. K., & Roy, F. (2020). Students Perception of Mobile Learning during COVID-19 in Bangladesh: University Student Perspective. *Aquademia, 4*(2), ep20023. https://doi.org/10.29333/aquademia/8443

Coordenação de Aperfeiçoamento de Pessoal de Nível Superior (Brasil). *Relatório do Qualis Periódicos: Área 26 Direito.* In: Relatório do Qualis Periódicos: Área 26 Direito. 26.dire@capes.gov.br: Diretoria de Avaliação, 2019. Disponível em: https://www.gov.br/capes/pt-br/centrais-de-conteudo/relatorio-qualis-direito-pdf. Acesso em: 12 dez. 2023.

Corbeil, J. R., & Valdes-Corbeil, M. E. (2007). Are you ready for mobile learning? *Educause Quarterly, 30*(2), 51-58. https://www.learntechlib.org/p/101389/

Farley, H., Murphy, A., Johnson, C., Carter, B., Lane, M., Midgley, W., ... Koronios, A. (2015). How Do Students Use Their Mobile Devices to Support Learning? A Case Study from an Australian Regional University. *Journal of Interactive Media in Education, 2015*(1), Art. 14. DOI: http://doi.org/10.5334/jime.ar

Maia, M. C., & Meirelles, F. (2009). *Tecnologia de Informação e Comunicação aplicada à Educação* [Information and Communication Technology applied to Education]. ACORN-Redecom (Américas Communication Research Network - Red Americana De Investigación e Información y Comunicación. https://www.academia.edu/28327579/Tecnologia_de_Informa%C3%A7%C3%A3o_e_Comunica%C3%A7%C3%A3o_aplicada_%C3%A0_Educa%C3%A7%C3%A3o

Measuring digital development: facts and figures 2021. (2021). International Telecommunication Union (ITU). https://www.itu.int/en/ITU-D/Statistics/Documents/facts/FactsFigures2021.pdf

Programa de Pós-Graduação Profissional em Engenharia Elétrica [Professional Graduate Program in Electrical Engineering]. (n.d). Universidade de Brasília (UnB). https://ppee.unb.br/?page_id=32

Redação. (2022, April 11). *Brasil foi o 5º país com mais ataques cibernéticos em 2021* [Brazil was the 5th country with the most cyberattacks in 2021]. Security Report. https://www.securityreport.com.br/overview/brasil-foi-o-5o-pais-com-mais-ataques-ciberneticos-em-2021/#.Y4u0ZHbMJPZ

Universidade de Brasília. (2020). *Resolução do Conselho de Ensino, Pesquisa e Extensão nº 0117/2020* [Resolution of the Teaching, Research and Extension Council no 0117/2020]. http://medicinatropical.unb.br/images/Normas/CEPE_117_2020_Planejamentodo_2-2020.pdf

Universidade de Brasília. (2020). *Resolução do Conselho de Ensino, Pesquisa e Extensão nº 0098/2020* [Resolution of the Teaching, Research and Extension Council no 0098/2020]. http://dpg.unb.br/images/Resoluo_CEPE_0098-2020_Regulamenta_os_Programas_de_Ps-Graduao_stricto_sensu.pdf

Universidade de Brasília. (2020). *Resolução do Conselho de Ensino, Pesquisa e Extensão nº 0080/2021* [Resolution of the Teaching, Research and Extension Council no 0080/2021]. https://drive.google.com/file/d/1sYD7oqxbDkYjAckpBVxTh4M89W7s3swr/view

Universidade de Brasília. (2020). *Resolução do Conselho de Ensino, Pesquisa e Extensão nº 0217/2016* [Resolution of the Teaching, Research and Extension Council no 0217/2016]. http://dpg.unb.br/images/Legislacao/RegulamentacaoUnB/Resoluo%20217-2016%20SEI_23106.076650_2016_19.pdf

Universidade de Brasília. (2021). *Regulamento do Programa de Pós-Graduação Profissional em Engenharia Elétrica* [Regulation on the Professional Graduate Program in Electrical Engineering]. https://ppee.unb.br/wp-content/uploads/2021/02/2021.02.22-2o-Regulamento-SEI_23106.006579_2021_74.pdf

A TECHNOLOGY ACCEPTANCE MODEL ANALYSIS OF METAVERSE TECHNOLOGY IN EDUCATION AND BEHAVIOURAL INTENTION TO USE IT AMONG UNIVERSITY STUDENTS. A COMPARATIVE ANALYSIS OF STUDENTS' BEHAVIOUR IN THE NETHERLANDS AND GREECE

Nikolaos Misirlis[1] and Yannis Nikolaidis[2]
[1]*HAN University of Applied Sciences, International School of Business, The Netherlands*
[2]*University of Macedonia, School of Applied Informatics, Greece*

ABSTRACT

The present study proposes a framework for university students' metaverse technologies in education acceptance and intention to use. The study is based on the Technology Acceptance Model (TAM). Data used are coming from two universities and are compared to each other. 311 university students from The Netherlands and 292 from Greece participated, gathering 513 valid answers to analyze (285 from The Netherlands and 228 from Greece).
The objectives of the study are to analyze the relationship between students' intention to use metaverse in education technologies (hereafter named **MetaEducation**) in correlation with selected constructs of TAM such as Attitude (ATT), Perceived Usefulness (PU), Perceived Ease of Use (PE), Self-efficacy (SE) of the metaverse technologies in education, and Subjective Norm (SN). Furthermore, we want to research any cultural differences between the two populations based on their answers. Therefore, we propose two different structural models from the SEM analysis, once for each country. For both proposed models, different and individual analysis is conducted. We decided not to combine the datasets, since the samples present several cultural differences.
The proposed models will be useful to universities' managers, policymakers, and professors to better incorporate the upcoming metaverse technology. The present study tests the correlations among the aforementioned constructs. Preliminary results show a hesitance to use MetaEducation technologies from university students from both countries. Self-efficacy and Subjective Norms affect Attitude and Perceived Usefulness positively, but on the other side, there is no strong correlation between Perceived Ease of Use and Attitude or Perceived Usefulness and Attitude. Authors believe that the weak ties among the study constructs have to do with the lack of knowledge of what really MetaEducation really is, and which are its advantages of use.

KEYWORDS

Metaverse, Technology Acceptance Model, University Students, E-Learning, MetaEducation, Greece, The Netherlands

1. INTRODUCTION

Metaverse is the last trend in technology representing a combination of virtual and augmented technology. With this technology, users will be able to immerse into a fully digital environment by obtaining a virtual identity through a digital avatar and acting as if this was the real world. They can meet other users, shop, buy real estate, visit bars and restaurants, and even flirt. Metaverse can be applied in several aspects of life such as (among others): Economy (with Metaverse entering into the cryptocurrency field), finance, social life, working environment, healthcare, real estate, and education. In the last two and a half years, during the COVID-19 pandemic, universities made immediate use of e-learning technologies, providing students with access to online learning content and platforms. Previous considerations on how to better integrate technology into university courses or how the institutions can be better prepared in terms of infrastructure vanished almost immediately due to the necessity of immediate actions towards the need for social distance and global health. Metaverse technology is constantly penetrating more and more fields of daily life. Starting 25 years ago, already, cinema industry was the first pioneer to introduce the term to a broader audience. Metaverse represents a combination of virtual and augmented reality, with augmented reality representing the biggest percentage (70%). The digital environment contains everything a 'real' world could have, including cities, real estate, schools, clubs, or restaurants. The fields that Metaverse can be applied is very broad as well. From economy to finance (Ko et al., 2021), to social life and work, eHealth (Misirlis et al., 2021) or even real estate (Terdiman, 2007), and lastly education (Collins, 2008) the possibilities keep on rising.

Regarding education, today more schools of all grades incorporate digital tools for their purposes. These facilities are not only a trend, but the post-covid-19 era made it necessary for the figurative function of schools (Park, 2009).

On the other hand, the process of integrating digital tools into education is not an easy process. Problems related to the technological knowledge and infrastructure of the institutions, the cost of new equipment, and the readiness of the personnel and students, may affect the usage of MetaEducation. Moreover, such technology is sometimes subject to acceptance from the involved entities. Faculty members and/ or students may not be aware of the benefits that this state-of-the-art technology may bring to their academic life.

On the other side, the acceptance of such technology is still under research, due to its innovative nature. Cultural differences between students from different countries, institutions' budgets, and different perspectives on the future of education can affect the levels of acceptance of MetaEducation.

2. RESEARCH OBJECTIVES

We present a comparison of the two populations regarding their demographics and their intended behavior towards new technologies and digital tools in daily activities related to wellbeing, leisure, education, and social life (Misirlis and Vlachopoulou, 2019, Misirlis et al., 2020). The results of this comparison may reveal differences in culture, perspective and acceptance of such new technologies and tools. The present study proposes a new framework based on the Technology Acceptance Model (TAM) on higher education students on whether the metaverse technology is accepted in the education field or not. Students from The Netherlands and Greece were chosen to answer a survey, in order to compare the results in two populations, that apparently, show cultural differences. Technology acceptance models were used before in the education field (Granić and Marangunić, 2019, Masrom, 2007, Scherer et al., 2019, Briz-Ponce and García-Peñalvo, 2015, Zaineldeen et al., 2020) but to the best of our knowledge, this is the first time that a study is focusing on MetaEducation, comparing two different populations with cultural differences.

The objective of this study is to calculate the correlation factors among students' intention to use MetaEducation and the rest of TAM components: *Attitude (ATT), Perceived Usefulness (PU), Perceived Ease of Use (PE), Self-efficacy (SE) of the metaverse technologies in education, and Subjective Norm (SN).* Furthermore, the students will answer general questions related to their relationship with the new technologies, not only for their education, but for their daily life, as well. That part of the survey, together with the TAM-related questions will provide an overall, more complete image on how students behave/ will behave toward MetaEducation.

Finally, the study presents two theoretical frameworks, one for each country to compare. The produced structural models provide insights to academic teachers, academic ethic committees, policymakers and managers, for further improving the infrastructures and formulating/ adapting the future of teaching.

3. LITERATURE REVIEW

The present research will use the well-known TAM, first introduced by Davis (1985) as an extension of Ajzen and Fishbein's Theory of reasoned action - TRA (Al-Suqri and Al-Kharusi, 2015). As aforementioned, TAM is using Subjective Norms, Perceived Usefulness, Perceived Ease of Use, Self-efficacy, and attitude as control variables, dependent and independent to predict the behavioural intention of users toward the use of technology and its acceptance. Several studies focusing on education have been already conducted (Scherer et al., 2019, Al-Emran et al., 2018, Weerasinghe and Hindagolla, 2017) , but to the best of our knowledge, this is the first one searching the acceptance behavior of technologies applied in education, related to the Metaverse. TAM is a model that explains individuals' intention to accept a certain technology.

The basic concept of TAM is the fact that every individual has the intention of particular behaviors. These behaviors are determined perceived ease of use (PE), perceived usefulness (PU), attitude (ATT), and Self-efficacy (SE). The outcome of the model presents the actual behavior of the individuals.

Metaverse represents a rather new field of research in science. Even if the term, and what this represents, is known for decades, the studies on that matter remain still limited. Despite this limitation, though, researchers understand already that the importance of use of metaverse technologies in education is crucial and important. The study of Collins (2008) examines the use of metaverse in education from a future and theoretical perspective. On the other side, the study of Hwang and Chien (2022) examines the subject from an artificial intelligence perspective. Tlili et al. (2022) start their research with an ethical dilemma, whether MetaEducation is a blessing or not. Together with those, several other studies examine the topic from a theoretical perspective, mostly (Singh et al., 2022, Contreras et al., 2022, Suh and Ahn, 2022). The results in the next paragraphs show several common behaviors but some differences, as well, mostly because of the different cultural backgrounds of our sample. The aforementioned review is based on the most current theories and definitions related to TAM, and in specific to the education field. Metaverse is a new technology to apply in education, therefore highly targeted articles are still difficult to find. Despite that, though, general articles related to education and technology acceptance were reviewed (Misirlis and Munawar, 2022).

4. RESEARCH HYPOTHESES

The study tests and supports the following hypotheses:

- University students' **Behavioural Intention** to use MetaEducation is affected by:

H1a: Attitude, H1b:Perceived Usefulness, H1c: Perceived Ease of Use, H1d: Self-efficacy, H1e: Subjective Norms.

- University students' **Attitude** toward the use of MetaEducation is affected by:

H2a: Perceived Usefulness, H2b: Perceived Ease of Use, H2c: Self-efficacy, H2d: Subjective Norms.

- University students' **Perceived Usefulness** to use MetaEducation is affected by:

H3a: Perceived Ease of Use, H3b: Self-efficacy, H3c: Subjective Norms.

- University students' **Perceived Ease of Use** towards the use of MetaEducation is affected by:

H4a: Self-efficacy, H4b: Subjective Norms.

5. METHODOLOGY

The proposed model with the hypotheses is tested with Structural Equation Modeling (SEM), using maximum likelihood estimation. SEM differs from other similar tools, and this is what makes SEM a more trustworthy model, since it includes an error on the measurements, assuming that the used variables cannot be measured with absolute precision. With SEM, a construction model is first used. This model represents the theoretical components to be observed, its components correlations with the estimated errors. In the first phase, the model is still theoretical. Once the structural equations are applied, a structural model is created, showing the weights among the components and whether these correlations can be accepted or rejected.

The proposed model with the hypotheses is tested with SEM, using maximum likelihood estimation. SEM differs from other similar tools, and this is what makes SEM a more trustworthy model, since it includes an error on the measurements, assuming that the used variables cannot be measured with absolute precision.

Based on previous research, a theoretical model was developed. Figure 1 presents the model to be tested and analyzed.

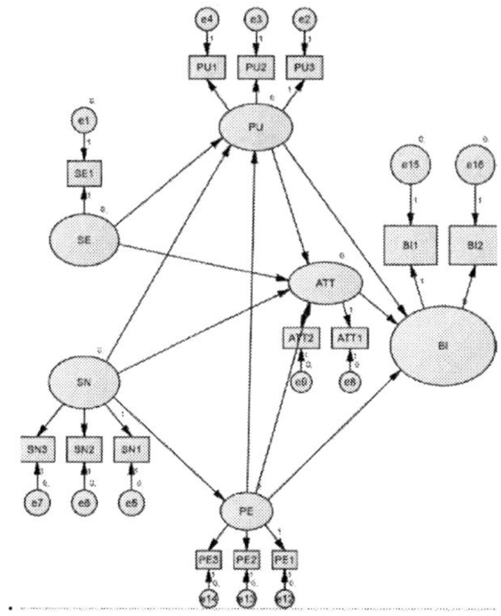

Figure 1. Theoretical model of our research

The directed arrows show the relationship between the latent variables and the observed ones. PE and PU can be considered cognitive constructs. Based on the above theoretical model, the dataset of our survey was applied to produce the measurement model (Figures 2 & 3).

5.1 Analysis of the Measurement Models

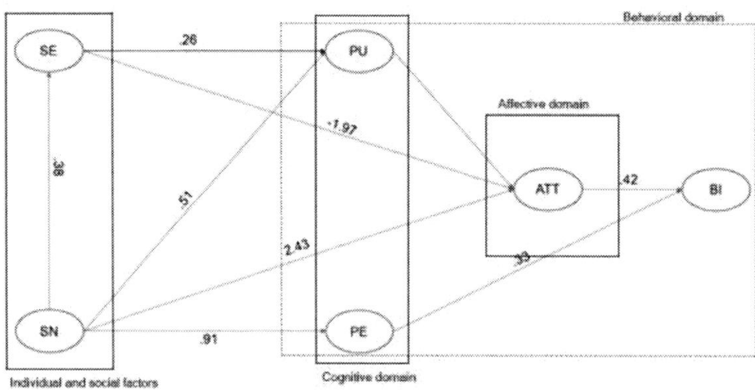

Figure 2. Structural model – Dutch dataset

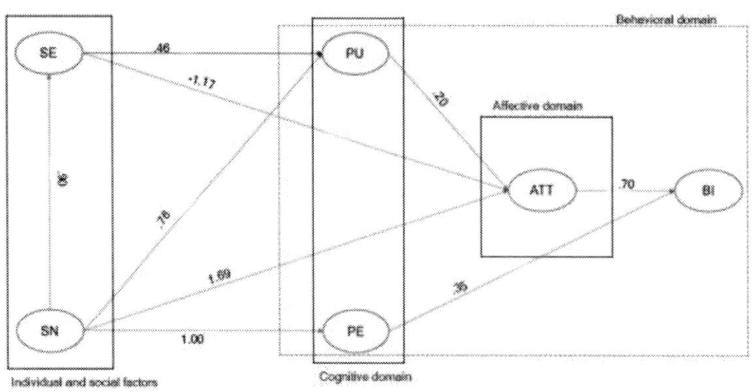

Figure. 3. Structural model – Greek dataset

5.2 Dutch Structural Model

Self-efficacy is negatively correlated to attitude, but on the contrary, subjective norms are positively correlated. There is no strong correlation between Perceived Ease of Use and Attitude or Perceived Usefulness and Attitude. The overall model is still weak, even if it is statistically acceptable. We notice that the final behavior of students is slightly affected by the Perceived ease of use but not by the perceived usefulness.

5.3 Greek Structural Model

Self-efficacy is negatively correlated to attitude, but on the contrary, subjective norms are positively correlated. There is no strong correlation between Perceived Ease of Use and Attitude or Perceived Usefulness and Attitude. The overall model is still weak, even if it is statistically acceptable.

In correlation with the Dutch sample, we notice a less strong correlation between SN and ATT for the Greeks, as well as between SE and ATT. The positive correlations between SN and PU, SE and PU, ATT and BI, and PE and BI, are stronger in the Greek sample.

6. DEMOGRAPHICS AND DATASETS

The present study obtained 513 valid answers from university students in The Netherlands (n:285) and Greece (n:228). Students were asked some preliminary questions in order to understand better their relationship to the digital world and how familiar they are with Metaverse and new/ upcoming technologies. Table 1 represents the gender balance of our sample in The Netherlands and in Greece.

Table 1. Gender percentages in both countries

	The Netherlands (n: 285)	**Greece (m: 228)**
Gender	Male: 63.4%	Male: 60.5%
	Female: 32.4%	Female: 38.2%
	Other/ prefer not to say: 3.2%	Other/ prefer not to say: 1.3%

Greeks are more positive, respect to the Dutch population, towards the future of how education will be conducted (92.1% vs. 72.4%). Greeks believe that their social life and their creativity depend more on technology, respect to the Dutch population (67.9% vs. 55.6% and 69.3% vs. 42.9%, respectively). Greeks turn to technology to unwind more than the Dutch do (85.6% vs, 66.1%). When it comes to partying, the Greeks prefer physical parties at 94.7%, respect to the Dutch who would not mind assisting a digital party a 30%. Analytically for the rest of the questions, we obtain:

7. STUDENTS AND DIGITAL WORLD - DISCUSSION

The two populations, with some slight differences present a common behavior toward the MetaEducation and the use of technology in their daily activities. We would expect some differences on the way people party or train physically, for example. Using the Hofstede's calculator for the two countries' cultural dimensions we obtain the following figure (the blue column represents Greece and the purple one the Dutch population).

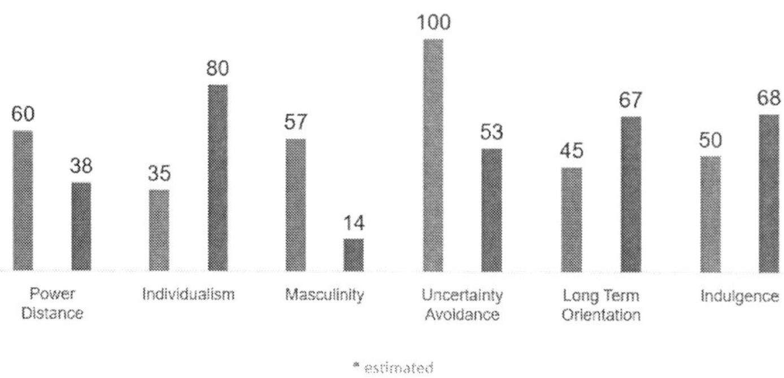

Figure 4. Cultural dimensions of Greece and The Netherlands (source: www.hofstede-insights.com)

Despite those differences, the majority of the findings as well as the correlations from the two structural models, is similar. An explanation for that, would be the lack of knowledge of what MetaEducation is and what can offer to the future of education, despite the fact that the vast majority of our respondents are Gen Zs, using technology for almost everything in their daily activities. The fact that the correlations of the structural models are weak, as well as the percentages to the generic questions, shows that students, trust the technology but probably ignore the usefulness, the easiness and the benefits of it. Metaverse represents the future. MetaEducation, inevitably, represents the future of education. Of course, it is still early to know how or when, as it is still early to know the cost and the infrastructure needed for that. On the other side, the education field which acted as a great pioneer during the Pandemic of COVID-19, being one of the first fields to incorporate the necessary technology and transform itself in hybrid or fully digital in a few days. We strongly believe that something similar will occur with the MetaEducation. When it will be the right, mature time, new technologies will be incorporated, adopted and accepted from Academia as it happened before.

REFERENCES

Al-Emran, M., Mezhuyev, V. & Kamaludin, A. (2018). Technology Acceptance Model in M-learning context: A systematic review. *Computers & Education,* 125, 389-412.

Al-Suqri, M. N. & Al-Kharusi, R. M. (2015). Ajzen and Fishbein's theory of reasoned action (TRA)(1980). *Information seeking behavior and technology adoption: Theories and trends.* IGI Global.

Briz-Ponce, L. & García-Peñalvo, F. J. (2015). An empirical assessment of a technology acceptance model for apps in medical education. *Journal of medical systems,* 39, 1-5.

Collins, C. (2008). Looking to the future: Higher education in the Metaverse. *Educause Review,* 43, 51-63.

Contreras, G. S., González, A. H., Fernández, M. I. S. & Martínez, C. B. 2022. The Importance of the Application of the Metaverse in Education. *Modern Applied Science,* 16, 1-34.

Davis, F. D. (1985). *A technology acceptance model for empirically testing new end-user information systems: Theory and results.* Massachusetts Institute of Technology.

Granić, A. & Marangunić, N. (2019). Technology acceptance model in educational context: A systematic literature review. *British Journal of Educational Technology,* 50, 2572-2593.

Hwang, G.-J. & Chien, S.-Y. (2022). Definition, roles, and potential research issues of the metaverse in education: An artificial intelligence perspective. *Computers and Education: Artificial Intelligence*, 100082.

Ko, S. Y., Chung, H. K., Kim, J.-I. & Shin, Y. (2021). A study on the typology and advancement of cultural leisure-based metaverse. *KIPS Transactions on Software and Data Engineering,* 10, 331-338.

Masrom, M. (2007). Technology acceptance model and e-learning. *Technology,* 21, 81.

Misirlis, N., Elshof, M. & Vlachopoulou, M. (2021). Modeling Facebook users' behavior towards the use of pages related to healthy diet and sport activities. *Journal of Tourism, Heritage & Services Marketing (JTHSM),* 7, 49-57.

Misirlis, N. & Munawar, H. B. An analysis of the technology acceptance model in understanding university students' behavioral intention to use metaverse technologies. 12th International Conference: The Future of Education, 2022. 159-163.

Misirlis, N. & Vlachopoulou, M. (2019). A unified framework for decision-making process on social media analytics. *Operational Research in the Digital Era–ICT Challenges.* Springer.

Misirlis, N., Zwaan, M., Sotiriou, A. & Weber, D. (2020). International students' loneliness, depression and stress levels in COVID-19 crisis. The role of social media and the host university. *Journal of Contemporary Education, Theory & Research,* 4, 20-25.

Park, S. Y. (2009). An analysis of the technology acceptance model in understanding university students' behavioral intention to use e-learning. *Journal of Educational Technology & Society,* 12, 150-162.

Scherer, R., Siddiq, F. & TONDEUR, J. (2019). The technology acceptance model (TAM): A meta-analytic structural equation modeling approach to explaining teachers' adoption of digital technology in education. *Computers & Education,* 128, 13-35.

Singh, J., Malhotra, M. & Sharma, N. (2022). Metaverse in Education: An Overview. *Applying Metalytics to Measure Customer Experience in the Metaverse*, 135-142.

Suh, W. & Ahn, S. (2022). Utilizing the Metaverse for Learner-Centered Constructivist Education in the Post-Pandemic Era: An Analysis of Elementary School Students. *Journal of Intelligence,* 10, 17.

Terdiman, D. (2007). *The entrepreneur's guide to Second Life: Making money in the metaverse*, John Wiley & Sons.

Tlili, A., Huang, R., Shehata, B., Liu, D., Zhao, J., Metwally, A. H. S., Wang, H., Denden, M., Bozkurt, A. & Lee, L.-H. (2022). Is Metaverse in education a blessing or a curse: a combined content and bibliometric analysis. *Smart Learning Environments,* 9, 1-31.

Weerasinghe, S. & Hindagolla, M. (2017). Technology acceptance model in the domains of LIS and education: A review of selected literature. *Library Philosophy and Practice*, 1-27.

Zaineldeen, S., Hongbo, L., Koffi, A. & Hassan, B. (2020). Technology acceptance model'concepts, contribution, limitation, and adoption in education. *Universal Journal of Educational Research,* 8, 5061-5071.

INVESTIGATING STAFF INFORMATION SECURITY POLICY COMPLIANCE IN ELECTRONIC IDENTITY SYSTEMS –THE GHANAIAN NATIONAL IDENTITY SYSTEM

Salim Awudu and Sotirios Terzis

Department of Computer and Information Sciences, University of Strathclyde, Glasgow, United Kingdom

ABSTRACT

Information Security Policy (ISP) compliance is key in securing organisational data. Although the factors that influence ISP compliance have been extensively studied, the emergence of Electronic Identity Systems (EIS) organisations like the Ghanaian National Identification Authority (NIA), have placed particular emphasis on the trustworthiness, privacy and security requirements. It is necessary to study these factors in this new context to ensure the security of the system. This paper presents the first study in this area. Prior research has shown the importance of staff attitude and motivation in ISP compliance, with motivation related to the perceived intrinsic benefits and extrinsic rewards for compliance. So, this study uses the NIA as a case study to explore the staff attitude towards ISP compliance and their perceived intrinsic and extrinsic rewards for compliance. A questionnaire-based study was conducted using adapted scales from literature. The results show that both experienced and inexperienced NIA staff recognise the necessity, benefits, importance, and usefulness of the ISP, and feel content, satisfied, accomplished, and fulfilled when complying with it. However, although experienced staff perceptions are clear that extrinsic rewards are not motivating compliance in the NIA, the inexperienced staff perceptions are unclear. These findings reinforce the need for clarity in EIS organisations regarding ISP compliance through formally approved policies and awareness training, they also point towards an opportunity to complement sanctions with rewards to motivate their staff.

KEYWORDS

Electronic Identity Systems, Information Security Policy, Information Security Policy Compliance

1. INTRODUCTION

Over the years, several countries have resorted to Electronic Identity Systems (EIS) to enhance the delivery of their services for citizens and residents. These systems collect and manage personal identification information. Despite the economic, social, and political benefits of such systems, their use has raised growing concerns about their security, privacy, and trustworthiness (Handforth and Matthew, 2019).

According to (Flowerday and Tuyikeze, 2016) "one important mechanism for protecting organizations' assets is the formulation and implementation of an effective Information Security Policy (ISP)". However, it is not enough for an organization to have an ISP, staff also need to comply with its provisions. According to (Alzahrani et al., 2018) "understanding the factors that influence employees' compliance with their organisational ISP is one of the fundamental challenges in (cyber) security management". Unsurprisingly, a lot of research has been devoted to this as a recent survey demonstrates (Ali et al., 2021). The research has explored a variety of factors that influence employee ISP compliance and has identified attitude towards compliance and motivation for compliance, with more focus on sanctions rather than rewards, as important factors.

In this paper we present the first study on attitude towards compliance and perceived intrinsic benefits and extrinsic rewards for ISP compliance in EIS organisations. We focus on benefits and rewards rather than sanction because of the limited attention they have received in the ISP compliance literature. The study explores these factors in the context of the Ghanaian National Identification Authority (NIA), a typical organisation that faces specific challenges that are not uncommon during the introduction of EIS. In addition to its focus on EIS organisations, the study is also novel in that, it explores how staff experience affects these factors, a question pertinent to the current circumstances of the NIA that has a lot of new and contracted staff joining the organisation recently. More specifically, a questionnaire-based study was conducted to answer the following research questions:

- What are the attitudes of NIA staff towards ISP compliance?
- What are their perceptions of the intrinsic and extrinsic rewards for ISP compliance?
- Does experience affect ISP compliance attitudes and reward perceptions of NIA staff?

The study built on the measures developed in (Bulgurcu et al, 2010) by focusing on intrinsic benefits and extrinsic rewards for ISP compliance. The results show that NIA staff recognise the necessity, benefits, importance, and usefulness of the ISP, and feel content, satisfied, accomplished and fulfilled when complying with it. This is the case for both experienced and inexperienced staff. However, although experienced staff perceptions are clear that extrinsic rewards are not used to motivate compliance, inexperienced staff are unclear about it. These findings further reinforce the need for clarity in EIS organisations in the form of formally approved policies and awareness training, both areas currently lacking in the NIA. Moreover, they highlight an opportunity in complimenting sanctions with rewards to further motivate staff.

This paper begins with literature review on EIS and ISP compliance in 2, followed by a description of our methodology in 3, presentation of our analysis and findings in 4, a discussion on the implications of our findings in 5, and closing with conclusion and directions for future work in 6.

2. LITERATURE REVIEW

EIS are "system[s] that involve the collection of information or attributes associated with a specific entity" (Wladawsky-Berger, 2016). Several countries, including Ghana, have fully operationalized EIS to collect such information for the purpose of providing services to people within their territory and beyond. Despite the potentially benefits of EIS, concerns have emerged about their potential negative effects, e.g. "once cards are mandatory, then they may be used to single out or even to harass visible minorities and those with alternative lifestyles" (Lyon and Bennett, 2013), or more importantly concerns about the Privacy, Trustworthiness, and Security of the data they collect, store and manage (Raggad, 2010).

To prevent security incidents organizations must have an ISP that reflects local information security philosophy and commitments (Johnson, 2006). More specifically, an ISP is a set of rules or requirements that are related to information security and enacted by an organization to be adhered to by all, to protect the confidentiality, integrity and availability of information and other valuable resources from security incidents (Tryfonas et al., 2001; Canavan, 2003).

It is not enough for organizations to have an ISP. Staff must also comply with it. The factors that affect ISP compliance have been studied extensively as a recent survey demonstrates (Ali et al., 2021). Although some of these studies focus on types of organisations, none on EIS, most are generic based on theories of human behaviour, like the Theory of Planned Behaviour (TPB), Protection Motivation Theory (PMT), Deterrence Theory (DT), etc. They typically take the form of questionnaire-based surveys. Most of them focus on participants' intention to comply with an organisation's ISP, a strong predictor of actual compliance. Comprehensive examples of such studies are (Bulgurcu, et al. 2010; Siponen and Vance 2010). Several studies have shown that attitude towards compliance, a key component of TPB, has a strong influence on people's intension to comply with the ISP (Ifinedo, 2012; Yun and Kim, 2013; Belager 2017). At the same time, several studies emphasise the importance of motivation in ISP compliance, most in the context of PMT and DT (Jai-Yeol, 2011; Ifinedo, 2012; Yoon and Kim, 2013; Sommestad et al., 2014). PMT puts emphasis on perceived risk with fear the main intrinsic/internal motivator, and fear appeals the extrinsic/external motivator. DT theory puts emphasis in the use of sanctions and punishment to deter non-compliance and extrinsically/externally motivate compliance. Both approaches have their limitations. First, studies have shown that intrinsic motivation has a stronger influence on ISP compliance intention rather than extrinsic motivation, but few studies have examined motivation more broadly covering both (Jai-Yeol, 2011; Padayachee, 2012). Second, research in organisations has shown that although sanctions and punishments are effective in motivating passive behaviours, rewards are more effective for active behaviours (Sharot, 2017).

In conclusion, staff attitudes and motivations for ISP compliance in EIS organisations have not been studied to date despite the importance of ISP compliance in securing the personal data they collect and manage. Both intrinsic and extrinsic motivations need to be studied. Of particular interest is the study of positive intrinsic motivations and rewards that have received little attention in the literature to date.

3. RESEARCH METHODOLOGY

To investigate staff attitudes and perceived motivations for ISP compliance in EIS organisations, we focus on the Ghanaian national identification authority (NIA) as a case study, and pose the following research questions:

- What are the attitudes of NIA staff towards ISP compliance?
- What are their perceptions of the intrinsic and extrinsic rewards for ISP compliance?
- Does experience affect ISP compliance attitudes and reward perceptions of NIA staff?

Despite the focus on the NIA, developing countries like Malaysia, Malawi, Nigeria, among others that have similar systems could potentially relate with the findings of this study.

3.1 The Ghanaian National Identification Authority (NIA)

The NIA was established in 2003 with a mandate to register and issue national identity cards to Ghanaian citizens and residents and manage the National Identification System (NIS). The NIA has been issuing citizens and residents with a smart card as a proof of identity that can be used to access basic services such as national health insurance, mobile phone accounts and banking services (Government of Ghana, 2006). The NIS collects and stores the personal data of card holders, including their biometric data.

The NIA management recognised the importance of securing the NIS from the outset. It developed a formally approved information security policy (ISP) and introduced formal ISP awareness training for all staff to boost ISP compliance. More recently, NIA management decided to update the ISP to better match international standards and a revised policy was drafted. However, the revised policy was never formally approved, while formal ISP awareness staff training was suspended until the formal approval.

In the meantime, the NIA has been growing with many staff being hired in recent years. Moreover, the NIA is currently conducting a nationwide identity registration exercise to ensure that all citizens and residents are issued with the national identity card, which has meant that additional staff have been contracted to register the population. Although new staff are made aware of ISP compliance expectations by their line managers, they have not had the clarity of a formal ISP and have not benefited from any awareness training.

The current situation with respect to new staff and the ISP raises some concerns about compliance in light of the personal data that NIS manages and makes the NIA an interesting case to study.

3.2 Study Structure and Procedures

To answer our research questions, similarly to past research, we have designed a questionnaire for NIA non-management staff to elicit their attitudes and their perceptions of motivation towards ISP compliance. Previous work shows that people's attitudes play an important role in determining their intention to comply and actual compliance to ISPs (Bulgurcu et al, 2010). Past research has also shown the significance of intrinsic in addition to extrinsic motivations in ISP compliance (Jai-Yeol, 2011), with focus mostly on negative motivation in terms of sanctions and punishments, and fear (S. Boss et al., 2015). However, positive motivation, intrinsic benefits and extrinsic rewards, has been shown to be more effective in motivating action which we consider essential for identity system organisation staff that must actively protect the personal data they manage (Posey, Roberts, and Lowry, 2015). So, we examine attitudes towards ISP compliance, and perceptions of intrinsic benefits and extrinsic rewards for ISP compliance.

Our questionnaire comprised three scales, one with 4 questions for attitude towards compliance, one with 4 questions for perceptions of intrinsic rewards for compliance, and one with 4 questions for perceptions of extrinsic awards for compliance. The questions were adapted from (Bulgurcu et al, 2010), preserving the actual questions, but using a uniform 7-point Likert scale from Strongly agree to Strongly disagree to conform to Stevens's measurement framework where Likert scale type items are summed or averaged and presented horizontally (Uebersax, 2006). We also solicited for participants' demographic data (Gender, Age range, Department or Unit, Years of work for the NIA, and Type of employment) to check the representativeness of the sample of employees that participated in the study according to the NIA Human Resources data.

Before distributing the questionnaire, we conducted a pilot study with 10 research students asking for their feedback on our study design. This exposed some minor issues with typographical errors that were corrected.

Due to the unstable nature of the Internet in Ghana, we decided to use paper-based questionnaires to ensure participant access. We printed and distributed 150 questionnaires to NIA staff who were not in managerial positions. To ensure fair participation of all NIA units and departments, we used a distribution formula based on the actual staff strength of each unit or department.

Finally, to conduct the research work, we sought prior ethics approval from our departmental Ethics Committee and obtained approval from the NIA to engage the staff. All participants were over the age of 18 and consented to participate in the study.

4. DATA ANALYSIS AND RESULTS

We obtained 115 questionnaires, 3 of which were excluded from the analysis because they were incomplete. We used the Statistical Package for Social Studies (SPSS) software to carry out our analysis by first, entering the data of the paper questionnaires to Qualtrics. Each participant was assigned a unique identifier. We then grouped each participant's data into Demographic and Non-Demographic Data. The former describes the profile of the participant, while the latter encompass the questions on attitude, perception of intrinsic benefits and perceptions of extrinsic rewards for ISP compliance.

4.1 Participants' Demographics

Table 1 provides an overview of the participants' demographic data (see column Participant Data) compared with NIA Human Resources data (see column Organization Reality). Despite some differences, we consider participants largely representative of the organization's employees.

Table 1. Overview of study demographic data

		Participant Data	Organization Reality
Gender	Male	55.3% (62)	74.0% (172)
	Female	44.6% (50)	26.0% (61)
Age Range	20-30	51.8% (58)	44.9% (96)
	31-40	38.4% (43)	45.8% (98)
	41-50	8.0% (9)	7.0% (15)
	51-60	1.8% (2)	2.3% (5)
Department or Unit	Human Resources	8.0% (9)	2.0% (9)
	Administration	6.3% (7)	52.0% (112)
	Technology and Biometrics	41. 1% (46)	22.0% (48)
	Operations	33.9% (38)	11.0% (35)
	Finance	4.5% (5)	6.0% (12)
	Internal Control	0.9% (1)	1.0% (3)
	Other	3.6% (4)	3.0% (6)
	Procurement	1.8% (2)	2.0 (5)
Years of NIA Work	Less than 1 year	55.4% (62)	32.0% (68)
	1-2 years	12.5% (14)	4.2% (9)
	3-6 years	1.8% (2)	1.4% (3)
	6-9 years	4.5% (3)	1.9% (4)
	More than 9 years	27.7% (31)	60.7% (130)
Employment Type	Permanent	30.4% (34)	64.0% (137)
	Contract	65.2% (73)	33.0% (73)
	Seconded	4.5% (5)	3.3% (7)

4.2 Information Security Policy Compliance Questions

The ISP compliance questions consisted of three scales, attitude towards ISP compliance (4 questions), ISP compliance perceived intrinsic benefits (4 questions), and ISP compliance perceived extrinsic rewards

(4 questions). We evaluated the reliability of these scales using Cronbach's Alpha. Table 2 shows the results that indicate acceptable reliability with Cronbach's Alpha above 0.6. We therefore included all three in our analysis.

Figure 1 shows the distribution of the participants' responses for their attitude towards ISP compliance with 79%, 79%, 85% and 87% of them agreeing that the ISP is necessary, beneficial, important, and useful, respectively, while 17%, 16% 10% and 13% disagreed, and 4%, 5%, 5% and 0% neither agree nor disagree.

Table 2. Summary of reliability analysis

	Cronbach's Alpha	Cronbach's Alpha Based on Standardized Items	No. of Items
Attitude towards ISP Compliance	0.654	0.654	4
Intrinsic Benefits of ISP Compliance	0.875	0.878	4
Extrinsic Rewards for ISP Compliance	0.893	0.893	4

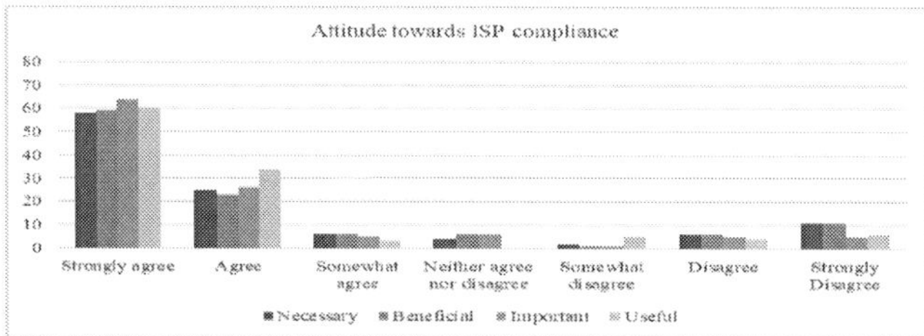

Figure 1. Distribution of participants' responses for attitude towards ISP compliance

Figure 2 shows the distribution for participants' responses for their perceived intrinsic benefits of ISP compliance with most staff agreeing that they feel content (68%), satisfied (73%), accomplished (70%), and fulfilled (69%), when complying with the ISP, while 19%, 13%, 20% and 16% respectively disagreed, and 13%,14%, 11%, and 15% neither agreed nor disagreed.

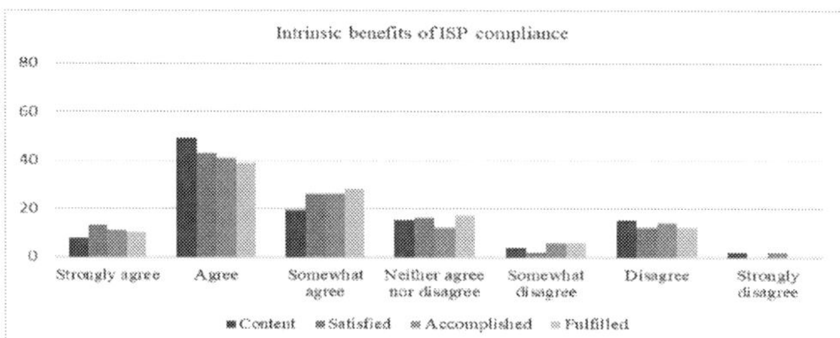

Figure 2. Distribution of participants' response for intrinsic benefits of ISP compliance

Figure 3 shows the distribution for participants' responses for their perceived extrinsic rewards for ISP compliance with the majority disagreeing that their ISP compliance will be rewarded in monetary/non-monetary (57%) or tangible/non-tangible awards (51%), with only 29% and 32% agreeing, and 17% and 14% neither agree nor disagree respectively. In addition to this, more participants disagree that their compliance will be rewarded with a pay rise/promotion (46%) than agree (35%), and the rest (19%) neither agree nor disagree. In contrast, more participants agree that their compliance will be rewarded with a personal mention/written assessment report (43%) than disagree (38%), and the rest (19%) neither agree nor disagree.

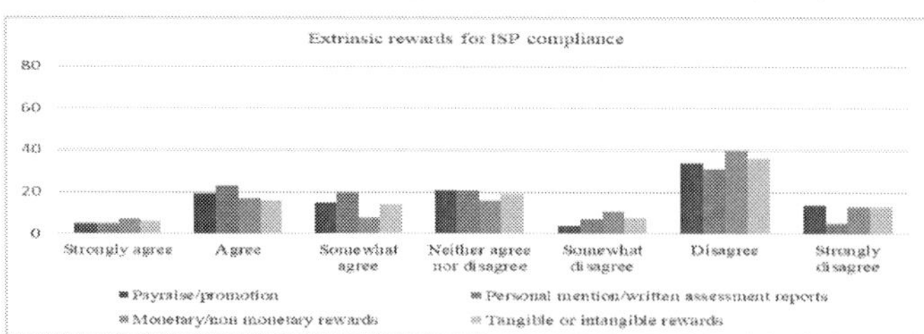

Figure 3. Distribution of participants' response for extrinsic rewards for ISP compliance

Comparing the first three figures we can say that, overall, although participants' attitudes and perceived intrinsic benefits of ISP compliance are positive, the former is much more positive than the latter. In contrast, their perceptions of extrinsic rewards for ISP compliance are negative. This is also supported by Table 3 which shows the Means and standard deviations for the corresponding questions with numbers below 4 indicating participant agreement levels with lower values indicating stronger agreement, while those above 4 indicate disagreement, with higher values indicating stronger disagreement.

Table 3. Means and standard deviations for the survey questions

		Mean	Std. dev.
Attitude towards ISP compliance	Necessary	2.37	2.022
	Beneficial	2.37	2.022
	Important	2.01	1.663
	Useful	1.99	1.636
Intrinsic benefit of ISP compliance	Content	3.10	1.582
	Satisfied	2.88	1.425
	Accomplished	3.10	1.582
	Fulfilled	3.05	1.432
Extrinsic rewards for ISP compliance	Pay rise/promotion	4.41	1.858
	Personal mention/written assessment report	4.03	1.732
	Monetary/non-monetary rewards	4.60	1.867
	Tangible/intangible rewards	4.49	1.836

Table 4. Means and standard deviations for the survey questions for experienced and inexperienced participants

		Experienced		Inexperienced	
		Mean	Std. dev.	Mean	Std. dev.
Attitude towards ISP compliance	Necessary	2.33	1.690	2.38	2.172
	Beneficial	2.36	1.743	2.37	2.153
	Important	2.25	1.746	1.89	1.621
	Useful	2.31	1.721	1.84	1.584
Intrinsic benefit of ISP compliance	Content	3.81	1.833	2.76	1.335
	Satisfied	3.22	1.726	2.72	1.239
	Accomplished	3.33	1.773	2.99	1.483
	Fulfilled	3.36	1.693	2.91	1.277
Extrinsic rewards for ISP compliance	Pay rise/promotion	5.44	1.594	3.92	1.780
	Personal mention/written assessment report	4.81	1.582	3.66	1.686
	Monetary/non-monetary rewards	5.42	1.538	4.21	1.838
	Tangible/intangible rewards	5.22	1.623	4.14	1.838

Table 5. T-test for inexperienced vs. experienced staff for extrinsic rewards for ISP compliance

	T	Df	Significance		Mean Difference	Std. Error Difference	95% Confidence Interval of the Difference	
			One-Sided p	Two-Sided p			Lower	Upper
Pay rise/promotion	-4.548	76.16	<.001	<.001	-1.523	0.335	-2.191	-0.856
Personal mention/written assessment report	-3.509	72.908	<.001	<.001	-1.148	0.327	-1.799	-0.496
Monetary/non-monetary rewards	-3.591	83.25	<.001	<.001	-1.206	0.336	-1.874	-0.538
Tangible/intangible rewards	-3.141	77.149	0.001	0.002	-1.077	0.343	-1.76	-0.395

We classified staff into two groups, experienced and inexperienced, based on the number of years they have been working for the NIA. Those working for 3 years, or more were classified as experienced and those with less than 3 years classified as inexperienced. Table 4 shows the means and standard deviations for the two groups across all the survey questions. There is a clear difference in the mean responses of experienced and inexperienced staff for their perceived extrinsic rewards for ISP compliance with inexperienced staff neither agreeing nor disagreeing while experienced staff disagreed. T-tests indicate that the difference is statistically significant with $p<0.05$, see Table 5. For perceived intrinsic benefits of ISP compliance, both experienced and inexperienced staff agree, with inexperienced staff in more agreement than experienced staff (i.e., lower means). However, t-tests show that the only difference is for feeling content which is statistically significant with $p<0.05$ ($t=-3.05$, $df=53.233$, one-sided $p=0.002$, two-sided $p=0.004$, mean difference=-1.042, std.

error=0.342. and 95% Confidence Interval of the Difference (-1.728, -0.357)). Finally, for both attitude towards ISP compliance both experienced and inexperienced staff agree with small means' differences that t-tests show aren't statistically significant.

5. DISCUSSION

The results are encouraging overall for the NIA. The attitude of NIA staff towards ISP compliance and their perceptions of the intrinsic benefits for it are positive, and literature shows that these are important factors for compliance (Bulgurcu, et al. 2010; Jai-Yeol, 2011). It is also reassuring that this is the case for both experienced staff who benefited from a formally approved ISP policy and ISP awareness training in the past, and inexperienced staff that lacked these benefits. In contrast, the NIA staff perceptions of the extrinsic benefits for ISP compliance are negative. This reflects the fact that the NIA is subjected to rigid government control procedures on financial budgetary allocations which include no officially accepted rewards for ISP compliance. Although in principle, it is possible for managers to offer financial incentives, these require the approval of both the board of Directors of the NIA, and the Parliament of Ghana or the government in power. Without such approval management is liable for misapplication or misappropriation of public funds. Although informal rewards like positive mentions either in personal or written assessment reports are possible, these are not as common, reflecting the fact that NIA management places more emphasis on deterrence. The statistically significant difference between experienced and inexperienced seems to result from lack of clarity on extrinsic awards for inexperienced staff, that could have been avoided if ISP awareness training was in place. Overall, extrinsic rewards is an area for improvement for the NIA, both in terms of providing more clarity to new staff and adopting a more balanced motivational approach between deterrence and rewards, going potentially as far as to introduce compliance as part of promotion decisions and financial reward packages.

Looking beyond the NIA for EIS organisations, our findings highlight the importance of clarity regarding the extrinsic motivation of staff for ISP compliance through formally approved ISP policy and ISP awareness training, especially for new staff. Although such training can also be beneficial in terms of attitude and intrinsic motivation, one should not forget that research shows that social factors can also promote a positive security culture in organisations (Warkentin and Johnston, 2010). More research is needed in establishing what the right balance between sanctions and rewards should be.

The main limitation of our work is that it focused on the NIA and the situation it currently faces with respect to the lack of formally approved ISP and ISP awareness training. Although we believe that the situation is not uncommon for EIS organisations as they grow, more research is needed to further validate our findings. The research will have been stronger if the questionnaire findings were combined with actual compliance monitoring to establish how attitudes and perceptions relate to tangible information security protection.

6. CONCLUSION AND FUTURE WORK

This paper presents the first study on attitude towards compliance and perceived motivations for ISP compliance in EIS through a case study of the NIA. The study explored perceived intrinsic benefits and perceived extrinsic rewards for ISP compliance. The study shows that despite the lack of formally approved ISP and ISP awareness training, there is a positive information security culture in the NIA with staff recognising the necessity, benefits, importance, and usefulness of the ISP and feeling content, satisfied, accomplished, and fulfilled when complying with it. However, things are less clear with extrinsic rewards. Although experienced staff perceptions are clear that, extrinsic rewards do not motivate compliance, inexperienced staff are unclear. This is where the lack of ISP awareness training is negatively impacting the NIA information security culture.

The study findings further reinforce the need for clarity in EIS organisations with a formally approved ISP and ISP awareness training. They also highlight an opportunity in complementing sanctions with rewards for extrinsic motivation of their staff and further cultivation of a positive information culture.

In terms of future work, similar research could be conducted in other EIS organisations to ascertain the generalizability of this research finding. Moreover, as this research focused on only non-management staff of the NIA, future research work could focus on the views of NIA management and external stakeholders.

REFERENCES

Ali, R.F. et al., (2021). *Information Security Behaviour and Information Security Policy Compliance: A Systematic Literature Review for Identifying the Transformation Process from Noncompliance to Compliance*, Applied Sciences, vol. 11, no. 3383, https://doi.org/10.3390/app11083383.

Alzahrani, A. et al., (2018). *Information security policy compliance: Investigating the role of intrinsic motivation towards policy compliance in the organisation*. In 4th International Conference on Information Management, pp. 125-132.

Belager, F. et al., (2017), *Determinants of early conformance with information security policies*. Information Management, vol. 54, pp. 887-901.

Boss, S. et al., (2015). *What do systems users have to fear? Using fear appeals to engender threats and fear that motivate protective security behaviors*, MIS Quarterly, vol. 39, pp. 837–864.

Bulgurcu, B. et al. (2010). *Information security policy compliance: an empirical study of rationality-based beliefs and information security awareness*, MIS Quarterly, pp. 523-548.

Canavan, S. (2003). *An information security policy development guide for large companies*, SANS Institute.

Flowerday, S. V. and Tuyikeze, T. (2016). *Information security policy development and implementation: The what, how and who*. Computers and Security, vol. no.61, pp. 169-183.

Government of Ghana, (2006). *National Identification Authority Act*, Act 707, Parliament of the Republic of Ghana, Accra, Ghana.

Handforth, C. and Matthew, W. (2019). *Digital Identity Country Report:* Malawi, available online at https://www.gsma.com/mobilefordevelopment/wp-content/uploads/2019/02/Digital-Identity-Country-Report.pdf, last accessed 25/08/2019.

Ifinedo, P. (2012). *Understanding information systems security policy compliance: An integration of the theory of planned behaviour and the protection motivation theory*, Computers and Security, vol. 31, pp. 83-95.

Jai-Yeol, S. (2011). *Out of fear or desire? Toward a better understanding of employees' motivation to follow IS security policies*, Information Management, vol. 48, pp. 296–302.

Johnson, E. C. (2006). *Security Awareness: Switch to a better programme*, Network security, vol.2, pp. 15-18.

Lyon, D. and Bennett, C. J. (2013).1 *Playing the ID Card: Understanding the significance of identity card systems*, in Playing the identity card: Surveillance, security and identification in global perspective, pp. 3-20.

Raggad, B. G. (2010). *Information security management: concepts and practice*, CRC Press.

Sharot, T. (2017). *What Motivates Employees More: Rewards or Punishments?* Harvard Business Review, available online at https://hbr.org/2017/09/what-motivates-employees-more-rewards-or-punishments, Last accessed 05/01/22023.

Siponen, M. and Vance, A. (2010). *Neutralization: New insights into the problem of employee information systems security policy violations*, MIS Quarterly, pp. 487-502.

Sommestad, T. et al., (2014). *Variables influencing information security policy compliance*. Information Management and Computer Security, vol. 22*, pp. 42–75.*

Padayachee, K. (2012). *Taxonomy of compliant information security behavior*, Computer Security*, vol.* 31*, pp. 673–680.*

Posey, C. Roberts, T.L. and Lowry, P.B. (2015). *The impact of organizational commitment on insiders' motivation to protect organizational information assets*. Journal of Management Information Systems, 32(4), 179-214.

Tryfonas, T. et al., (2001). *Embedding security practices in contemporary information systems development approaches*, Information Management and Computer Security, vol. 9, pp. 183-197, 2001.

Uebersax, J. S. (2006). *Likert scales: dispelling the confusion,* Statistical methods for rater agreement, vol. 31.

Warkentin, M. and Johnston, A.C. (2010). *Fear appeals and information security behaviors: An empirical study*. MIS Quarterly*,* vol. *34*, pp. 549–566.

Wladawsky-Berger, I. (2016). *Towards a Trusted Framework for Identity and Data Sharing*, https://blog.irvingwb.com/blog/2016/11/trusted-identity-and-data-ecosystems.html Accessed October 20, 2019.

Yoon, C. and Kim, H. (2013), *Understanding computer security behavioral intention in the workplace: An empirical study of Korean firms*, Information Technology and People, vol. *26*, pp. 401–419.

COMPARING BARRIERS TO DIGITAL TRANSFORMATION BETWEEN SMALL AND MEDIUM-SIZED AND LARGE ENTERPRISES

Philip Johannesson[1], John Sinha[1], Sven Packmohr[1] and Henning Brink[2]
[1]*Malmö University / Computer Science and Media Technology, Nordenskiöldsgatan 1, 211 19 Malmö, Sweden*
[2]*Osnabrück University / Organization and Information Systems, Katharinenstr. 1, 49069 Osnabrück, Germany*

ABSTRACT

With the rise of modern digital connectivity technologies, Digital Transformation (DT) is now an issue for most companies across almost all industries. DT is an evolution to digitalizing internal processes, offering digital services and products, and improving the customer experience. Prior studies have explored different barriers that hinder successful DT. Our study follows a quantitative design to explore further how these barriers are perceived by staff at small and medium-sized enterprises (SMEs) compared to larger enterprises (LEs). Our sample comprises participants from 189 SMEs and 221 LEs. In general, results indicate a somewhat similar perception of their DT processes. In detail, setting up new positions to manage DT poses a more intense barrier for SMEs.

KEYWORDS

Digital Transformation, Small and Medium-Sized Enterprises, Large Enterprises

1. INTRODUCTION

Implementing and adopting Digital Transformation (DT) within organizations is complex, but it could introduce countless benefits for the industries and sectors at hand. Leveraging DT can spark innovation and growth for the companies involved (Schmarzo, 2016). Literature defines DT as digitizing internal processes and offering digital services and products while enhancing the customer experience (Reis et al., 2018). Overall, DTs aim to improve capabilities, value, and innovation for businesses in the ever-evolving digital economy (Schmarzo, 2016).

Nevertheless, specific inabilities can obstruct the DT process and, if not recognized and sorted, may generate several obstacles, thereby hindering the business from succeeding and gaining substantial market power. Consulting companies report a failure rate to meet business objectives of 70% (Forth et al., 2020). DT obstacles may vary in intensity and significance depending on the sector or company size. These so-called hindrances have been identified as barriers to DT (Brink and Packmohr, 2022). Extensive studies and research have proposed instruments to measure the impact of these distinct complex barriers within organizational DT. Comparing different studies, recurring dimensions of barriers were recognized as: missing skills barriers, IT knowledge, information about, and decision on different technologies and process knowledge; the technical barriers with their dependency on other technologies, security when exchanging data, and the current infrastructure; individual barriers where the sample showed fear of data loss or data control, fear of transparency and acceptance along with a concern for job loss; the organizational barriers where holding on to traditional roles and principles, lack of any clear vision or strategy, and the resistance to cultural change, risk aversion, lack of financial resources and lack of time are some of the issues, and finally; the external barriers with its absence of standards and lack of laws are of significance (Jones et al., 2021).

Especially SMEs might face barriers in their DT, e.g., due to stronger financial constraints (Wonglimpiyarat, 2015). According to the European Union's standard, there are numerous variations and categories of companies depending on employee headcount, as well as either their turnover or their balance sheet total. These are classified as micro, small, and medium-sized enterprises, also known as SMEs

(Lu and Beamish, 2001). We follow these classifications and consider SMEs as enterprises employing less than 250 individuals. Subsequently, we consider companies above 250 employees as large enterprises (LEs).

This research aims to explore the additional component company size that might affect the DT barriers. Thus, our research question is: To what extent does company size affect the perception of the different barriers?

To answer our research question, we will first revise research on specific barriers regarding company size. After, we present the quantitative data collection and statistical methods used, which leads to the result section. In a discussion, we will revise the connection of our results to other scholars' studies before concluding and giving an outlook. SMEs are an essential economic factor (Roman et al., 2023). Thus, it is vital to understand their struggles. Compared to LEs, SMEs might need more help in DT from policymakers. Our research will contribute to a better understanding of the impact of company size-specific constraints. The literature shows that a considerable company size might be essential for extensive financial means but a limited agility (Caloghirou et al., 2004). We could argue that DT increases or levels out differences between SMEs and LEs. Thus, our research reveals new insights into this field of tension.

2. BACKGROUND

DT has become a buzzword that can have a multitude of different definitions. Scholars combined the various definitions: "Digital Transformation is the use of new digital technologies that enable major business improvements and influence all aspects of customer life" (Reis et al., 2018, p. 418). Vial assessed different DT definitions and specified the term as "a process that aims to improve an entity by triggering significant changes in its properties through combinations of information, computing, communication, and connectivity technologies" (Vial, 2019, p. 121). DT is a threat to existing organizations and should therefore be managed adequately (Pabst von Ohain, 2019).

According to the Oxford Dictionary (2021), barriers are obstacles that keep people or things apart or prevent communication or progress. The company's leaders are required to guide their organization through these barriers in the DT process. These leaders have the potential to either hinder or slow down the DT process, which makes them critical when it comes to managing the barriers. As DT is ubiquitous, managers should adopt a holistic approach to the barriers to DT. If the corporate managers can interweave these physical and digital layers, then the barriers can turn into facilitators, and failing to combine both assets instead leads to failure in long-term gains, which then leads to falling behind even more (Hadjimanolis, 2003; Hanelt et al., 2015). During the review of existing barrier research and literature, we came across studies on specific technologies (Radhakrishnan and Chattopadhyay, 2020), specific stakeholders or sectors (Liu et al., 2011), or unordered lists of different barriers (Bilgeri and Wortmann, 2017). Furthermore, a large proportion of the barrier studies follow a qualitative research design. Some quantitative studies exist. Again these publications often focus on specific sectors (Khanzode et al., 2021; Stentoft and Rajkumar, 2020) or specific company sizes (Bollweg et al., 2019; Koshal et al., 2019).

Therefore, we aim to extend the research by comparing different-sized companies from various sectors. Understanding which barriers slow down DT and the specific effect each barrier has on the DT, as well as analyzing how different-sized companies are affected by these barriers, are necessary when it comes to maturing the research field and providing an understanding of DT.

We hypothesize that LEs have it easier to implement DT into their work. LEs still face challenges that create barriers, but since LEs typically work with a higher budget and more resources than SMEs, they might perceive barriers as easier to work with.

2.1 Challenges for SMEs

DT is a strategic imperative for companies to remain competitive in a digitally disrupted and constantly changing business environment. Currently, SMEs are experiencing the effects of this DT (Skare et al., 2023), besides numerous other challenges such as in financing innovation and entrepreneurial activities (Wonglimpiyarat, 2015) or in finding suitable human resources poses challenges (Duan et al., 2002). Often, internationalization is an issue for SMEs (Lu and Beamish, 2001) as well as becoming more digital (Tarutė et al., 2018). DT for SMEs comes with changes in the competitive environment, novel technologies, digital skills development, and new requirements for leadership (Skare et al., 2023). DT is constantly changing SMEs' traditional business models and customers' value creation process (Matarazzo et al., 2021). The goal in every industry, regardless of company size – and not just tech giants - is to digitally transform. Besides experiencing the highest inflation rate in over a decade, SMEs face further challenges provoked by the increase in digital capabilities affecting leadership capabilities. Every step to DT opens new possibilities for extending the company's digital advantage most effectively. However, one dilemma regarding leadership capabilities within SMEs' is the lack of formal qualifications among SMEs' leaders compared to larger corporations. Instead, SME leaders are expected to learn on-site (Bolden and Rohini, 2020). Having technical and management skills that can adapt to and cope with an ever-changing environment is also fundamental, as well as the qualifications, abilities, and potential to train and develop staff. Given the many challenges of implementing DT while leading people, a lot of leaders of SMEs might fail because they might not possess the adequate skill set. Conducting a DT requires leaders to act strategically when recruiting employees. SMEs are already facing a lack of skilled labor, which is a critical constraint on their business activities. Thus, a crucial barrier to DT in SMEs is the shortage of human resources with the necessary knowledge and capabilities to meet the criteria of a DT process (Nguyen et al., 2015). A specific capability challenge is an ability to keep up to date with developments in digital marketing. Efforts could be wasted by focusing on procedures that used to work. Still, marketing activities are highly influenced by DT as DT opens new possibilities for understanding clients' and customers' behavior due to the placement of individually adapted advertisements, which is made possible due to algorithms and the automatically generated collection of data (Hausberg et al., 2019).

2.2 Challenges for LEs

Also, larger companies are facing challenges due to their size. One of the most common challenges these larger-sized companies face is the complexity of monitoring performances in all business areas. Choosing the right key performance indicators (KPIs) to provide the business with insights about success or failure is key. Most businesspeople are not experts in developing these KPIs but must understand their implications (Veleva, 2009). Also, enhanced digitalization can make KPIs more reliable, collect real-time data, and evolve into Business Activity Monitoring (BAM) (Wetzstein et al., 2008). Larger companies' complex structures can hinder innovation and change. Often, larger companies tend to have a more articulated list of desired outputs when compared to SMEs, making it more difficult to align with change or innovation and find a suitable balance between exploration and exploitation (Del Vecchio et al., 2018). Another challenge for larger companies is to work in different silos, meaning different departments work almost individually without adequate coordination. At best, these silos provoke specialization and make the work more effective. At worst, they can create a mentality where the departments are so separated that they don't share any knowledge or collaboration and only work towards their own department goals. Thus silos might prevent companies' achievements (de Waal et al., 2019).

3. METHOD

In a pre-study, we identified the main barrier dimensions regarding DT. The dimensions are missing skills, technical, individual, organizational, and external barriers (Brink and Packmohr, 2022). Based on the literature, we added the dimension DT process (Klötzer and Pflaum, 2017) as the dependent variable. The DT process is the aim companies strive for. It contains a value creation and a customer perspective. The DT process does not represent a barrier dimension but enables capturing a brief status quo of the DT in the respondents' companies. Based on our pre-study, we developed a questionnaire. We collected data between December 2019 and April 2021 (Brink and Packmohr, 2022) by applying a convenience sampling technique (Etikan, 2016) and putting out calls for participation on personal and professional network sites. All participants completed the same, anonymous, and voluntary questionnaire hosted by the online survey application LimeSurvey (2023).

After the collection, we cleaned and further organized the dataset. We removed 23 participants' data as some of the answers were missing or incomplete, especially regarding the size of the company. In total, 410 participants answered our questionnaire. Looking at the distribution, 189 came from SMEs and 221 from

LEs. Diversification allows one to gain the most insights from a sample (Yin, 2014). Therefore, we survey respondents with managerial responsibility, age, and sector affiliation differences. Our sample comprises data from sectors such as Automotive, Finance & Insurance, Food, Information and Communication Technology (ICT), and Mechanical & Plant Engineering. The broad sample allows for drawing generalized conclusions. Table 1 gives an overview of the sample.

The participants' responses from the questionnaire were collected and registered on a symmetric 5-point Likert Scale. The respondents specified their level of agreement or disagreement concerning the items of the barrier dimensions. The Likert Scale is the most widely used approach to scaling responses in quantitative survey research and measures perception. A 5-point scale is simple to understand and balances higher- and lower-point scales (Nemoto and Beglar, 2014). The scale used was ranging between "I disagree" (1) and "I agree" (5). In total, our quantitative questionnaire encompassed 36 items. To prevent contextual bias, we developed and separated 18 positive items along with 18 negatives. Therefore, we had to re-pole the reversed items for the later analyses. For the five barrier dimensions, we modified the positive ones by switching their Likert Scales symmetrically into negative connotations. This ensured the same scale orientation. A high value thus represents a high degree of the respective barrier. Since the dimension DT Process, in contrast to the barrier dimensions, represents something positive, we have reversed the polarity of the negatively formulated items to positive ones. Therefore, a high value in the DT process represents a high degree of DT in the company.

After the data preparation, we conducted a first exploratory data analysis by calculating means to answer our research question. We further performed a Mann-Whitney U test (MWU) to analyze whether the observed differences in the means between the SMEs and LEs data are statistically significant (sig.) or not (Pallant, 2005), as well as to compute the effect size (r). The effect size determines the magnitude of the difference. A high overlap of the two groups is expressed by a low r-value, and a low overlap of the sample is expressed by a high r-value (Fritz et al., 2012).

Table 1. Questionnaire sample

Sector distribution			**Position distribution**			**Age distribution**		
	SME	**LE**		**SME**	**LE**		**SME**	**LE**
Automotive	40%	21%	Executive Manager	11%	5%	61 or older	1%	1%
Logistics	2%	7%	Employee with personnel responsibility	25%	25%	51-60	8%	7%
Finance & Insurance	1%	25%				41-50	16%	18%
Food	1%	4%	Employee without personnel responsibility	47%	55%	31-40	22%	23%
ICT	10%	5%				21-30	49%	51%
Mechanical & plant eng.	16%	9%	Intern	7%	8%	20 or younger	4%	0%
Energy	6%	4%	Other	10%	7%			
Other	24%	25%						

4. RESULTS

Within our results, we compare the means on certain dimensions and characteristics between SMEs and LEs. We also check whether the differences in the mean values are significant and, if so, how extensive these differences are. At first glance, both groups score surprisingly similarly at every barrier dimension and the DT process, as shown in table 2. In detail, differences become visible.

In the DT process dimension, the most noticeable deviating results are regarding offers of significantly improved smart products/services to the customers (DT1) and the absence of roadmaps to use smart products/services internally (DT2). For DT2, the deviation is -0.66 (3.32 for SMEs compared to 3.98 for LEs) and 0.50 for DT3 (2.66 for SMEs compared to 2.16 for LEs). Both types of companies (DT5) move ahead regarding their DT but to different degrees. SMEs score 3.30 compared to 3.74 for LEs, leading to a difference of -0.44 between both groups. No significant differences could be observed in offering improved digital support for work. However, the mean values a relatively high in both groups.

Within the dimension of individual barriers, both groups' perceptions are relatively similar. A significant deviation is shown within the generation of data and the conclusion on work behavior (IND2). SMEs see this more as a problem than LEs (2.79 to 2.54), leading to a difference of 0.25 and a small effect size.

The Mann-Whitney U test doesn't show significant differences for the other items of this dimension, indicating a similar response behavior. Further, the mean values of the individual barrier items are relatively low, indicating a positive attitude of the participants towards DT.

Table 2. Questionnaire results

Dimension	(Code) Item	AVG.		MWU test	
		SME	LE	Sig.	r
DT Process	(DT1)* Company has no roadmap to offer smart products/services.	3.32	3.98	.000	.291
	(DT2) Company offers significantly improved smart products/services to customers.	2.66	2.16	.000	.211
	(DT3)* Company has no roadmap to use smart products/services internally.	2.37	2.10	.010	.128
	(DT4) Company offers improved digital support for my work.	3.30	3.17	.151	.071
	(DT5) Company is moving straight ahead in terms of a DT.	3.30	3.74	.000	.212
	(DT6)* Company still uses traditional methods for production/services.	2.53	2.28	.047	.098
Ind. Barriers	(IND1) DT is intimidating to me.	2.70	2.55	.211	.062
	(IND2)* I control the digital workspace and the data generated.	2.79	2.54	.005	.140
	(IND3) I am afraid that, during my work, data is generated in the background allowing conclusions about my work behavior.	1.83	1.73	.260	.056
	(IND4)* Traceability of my data does not influence my work behavior.	2.93	2.91	.837	.010
	(IND5) More jobs will be lost than gained through DT.	2.68	2.73	.754	.015
	(IND6) DT will have a negative effect on my job prospects.	1.92	1.91	.898	.006
	(IND7)* I am a strong advocate of DT as I expect process gains.	2.31	2.18	.156	.070
Orga. Barriers	(ORG1)* Senior management supports DT and is visibly engaged.	2.38	2.16	.031	.106
	(ORG2) We have no new roles in managing digitalization projects.	2.78	2.27	.000	.183
	(ORG3)* A clear strategy for DT is communicated.	2.90	2.47	.000	.192
	(ORG4)* Errors are used to improve work processes.	2.50	2.38	.220	.060
	(ORG5)* We strive to constantly learn and improve to master DT.	2.37	2.17	.146	.072
	(ORG6)* There is an openness to new ideas.	2.21	2.11	.280	.053
	(ORG7) We do not have enough resources to manage DT.	2.96	2.74	.041	.101
Tec. Barriers	(TEC1) My work suffers from a poor data connection.	3.26	3.41	.212	.139
	(TEC2) My work suffers from insufficient data interfaces.	3.19	3.50	.005	.178
	(TEC3) While exchanging information, my company fears data theft.	3.03	3.45	.000	.034
	(TEC4)* My confidential work data is sufficiently protected.	2.39	2.36	.485	.158
	(TEC5)* Company's infrastructure can handle DT.	2.57	2.23	.001	.091
	(TEC6)* Company's infrastructure is flexible for future developments.	2.61	2.37	.066	.139
Ext. Barriers	(EX1)* Through DT, data from different areas are more effectively integrated into my digital workspace.	2.36	2.35	.978	.001
	(EX2) There are enough standards to manage DT effectively.	3.16	3.45	.001	.157
	(EX3)* Legislation sufficiently protects companies in the digital world.	2.96	2.84	.361	.045
	(EX4) There are not enough laws to protect me in the digital workspace.	3.03	3.20	.130	.075
Missing Skills	(SKL1)* My IT knowledge is adequate to keep up with DT.	2.44	2.56	.192	.064
	(SKL2)* Company's IT knowledge is adequate to keep up with DT.	2.67	2.56	.338	.047
	(SKL3) There is a knowledge lack about the potential of DT.	2.96	2.89	.464	.036
	(SKL4) There is a knowledge lack to use digital technologies effectively.	3.61	3.73	.365	.045
	(SKL5) I would like to be more involved in the decision-making on the implementation of new technologies.	3.39	3.73	.001	.162
	(SKL6) Company should provide more training on technology skills.	3.88	4.05	.139	.073

*reversed item

In general, the dimension of Organizational barriers also shows relatively low means for both groups. At the more detailed level, we note significant deviations and small effect sizes in the missing roles to manage DT projects (ORG2) and an absence of clear strategies (ORG3). Both barriers are perceived as stronger within SMEs. Thus, ORG2 is 0.51 stronger and ORG3 0.43. We were also able to observe a significant difference in the perception of the existence of sufficient resources to manage the DT (ORG7) and the perception of supportive management (ORG1). Here, questionnaire participants from SMEs perceive a lack of resources and senior management support as slightly more severe barriers. For the other three items, we could not find any significant differences.

The technical barriers in general score a tad higher for LEs. While exchanging information, SMEs fear significantly less the theft of data than LEs (TEC3), with a difference of -0.42. Despite TEC3, both groups scored rather low and significantly differently on problems regarding infrastructure to handle DT (TEC5). SMEs perceive infrastructure as less problematic than LEs by a difference of 0.34. In LEs, participants significantly reported more insufficient data interfaces (TEC2). Again, the effect size is small. For TEC1 and TEC6, differences in response behavior are not observed.

External barriers are seemingly placed in the middle of the scores. However, the absence of standards (EX2) seems significantly more prevalent in LEs (-0.29). This is the only item of the external barriers for which we were able to demonstrate a significant difference with the help of the Mann-Whitney U test.

The highest mean values for both groups are observed in the dimension missing skills. Moreover, the dimension is of interest because we were only able to measure a significant difference between the groups for one item. The provision of more training on technologies (SKL6) scored remarkably high in both groups. Also, the question of involvement in decision-making on the implementation of new technologies (SKL5) is perceived as an important barrier. However, a significant deviation of -0.34 between SMEs (3.39) and LEs (3.73) can be observed. Surprisingly, employees in SMEs and LEs see their own IT knowledge as a minor barrier (SKL1). The response behavior for the other items in this dimension is also similar in both groups.

In sum, we identified differences and similarities in response behavior between SMEs and LEs. We found differences between both groups to be significant at 17 out of 36 items. However, the effect sizes show that although differences are significant, the overlap between the two groups is large, i.e., the differences are measurable but small.

5. DISCUSSION

The objective of our research is to gain an understanding of the perception of DT in SMEs contrasting LEs, and vice versa. Our proposition to start this research was that the company size might affect the perception of the different DT barriers. We used the same dimensions as identified in a pre-study, such as the DT process as target and individual, organizational, technical, external, and missing skills as barriers.

Within the DT process, an improvement regarding the offering of smart products and services to customers and implementing road maps for using smart product services internally seem of utmost importance. In our study, SMEs tend to have greater problems in offering smart products and services, which is surprising as we expect SMEs to be closer to the customer and better at exploring markets. SMEs might have to think more about engaging with the customer, as it will affect product and process innovation (Wahyuni and Sara, 2020). On the other hand, we see LEs more prepared to meet customer demands by forecasting (Del Vecchio et al., 2018). In contrast, SMEs are in lesser need of road maps. One reason for this may be that LEs have a more expanded and complex business structure which can hinder innovation and prevent any rapid changes within the business. The cause for this might be decelerations and delays of DT strategy announcements within LEs due to silos (de Waal et al., 2019). Silos might delimit departments from each other and make it harder to spread the word across silos' borders. Another lower-scoring item can emphasize this speculation for LEs to move less straight ahead in terms of DT than SMEs.

Within the individual dimension, employees in both groups are not very afraid of conclusions regarding their work behavior. Either employees trust their employers to be ethical, or the legal framework is substantially developed (Kidwell and Sprague, 2009). On the contrary, employees perceive a higher threat of being unable to control their digital workspace affecting more participants from SMEs. As IT adoption is normally slower in SMEs, this might lead to other insecurities also related to barriers we measure, such as fear of data theft.

Within the organizational barriers, we see the consequences of a lack of resources affecting SMEs to a higher degree when it comes to management roles for DT. Human resources especially pose a barrier for SMEs (Duan et al., 2002). Surprisingly are the results for the clear DT strategy. We expect a higher barrier perception for LEs, as silos hinder the communication of strategies (de Waal et al., 2019). A reason might be the keyword DT strategy. Without proper management roles for DT, a DT strategy might not evolve and, thus, cannot be communicated.

Since more staff and the different departments may be divided and segregated (de Waal et al., 2019), the data connections might also need to reach a wider area and include more people within LEs. This may create stability issues within the data connection and provoke a greater fear of theft while exchanging data. SMEs perceive higher barriers regarding their infrastructure, which we can relate to higher obstacles in acquiring resources (Wonglimpiyarat, 2015).

In the external barriers, the barrier of laws scores relatively high, which aligns with the rather high score of an absence of control in the digital workplace of the individual barriers. Thus, there is a need to implement digital workplace protection and a better legal framework (Forradellas and Garay Gallastegui, 2021). Especially technical standards, which pose a higher barrier for LEs, will contribute to many benefits for LEs. Anyways, without a proper cybersecurity strategy (Ani et al., 2017), it is bound to create a lot of vulnerable and assailable fronts for companies.

In Missing Skills, the perception of some sub-barriers is relatively high, especially within the knowledge of the use of technologies, involvement in decision-making, and training. Again, we can relate some barriers to the issue of resources. Interestingly, LEs tend to score higher on the aforementioned barriers. Regarding decision-making, employees in LEs tend to be less involved because of more hierarchy and bureaucracy (Bourdieu and Coleman, 2019). Regarding the training, we expect a higher value with SMEs because of a general lack of resources. This lack could lead to less formal training than on-the-job training. There is a need for more proper training planning (Hulla et al., 2021) to help employees to articulate their missing skills thoroughly. Otherwise, the pragmatic impacts of overcoming these DT barriers might be overlooked.

Since SMEs and LEs face different managerial implications, both can succeed by focusing on their unique strengths and opportunities. SMEs can leverage their agility, innovation, and entrepreneurial spirit, while LEs can leverage their resources, scale, and market position to achieve their business objectives (Analoui and Karami, 2003). SMEs are often more agile and flexible than LEs, enabling them to respond quickly to market or business environment changes. This can be advantageous in industries where speed and innovation are critical (Chan et al., 2019). Moreover, it would be wise for LEs to address the backlash of silos to remain competitive and agile in the rapidly changing business environment. By promoting collaboration, streamlining processes, leveraging technology, and providing effective leadership, LEs can break down silos and achieve greater innovation and efficiency (Tett, 2015).

6. CONCLUSION

Our study aimed to investigate the effects of company size on different DT barriers. SMEs perceivably are going through a smoother DT process than LEs. Interestingly, this is seemingly done despite the lack of different resources and capabilities within SMEs. Often, barriers such as building up leadership capabilities are handled on-site (Bolden and Rohini, 2020). Other than expected, SMEs are doing slightly better than the LEs with the DT implementation.

LEs might face struggles since these challenges exist due to the company's size. Larger companies' intense systems and networks can hinder innovation, change, and articulating strategies compared to SMEs.

Our study found some unexpected differences between SMEs and LEs regarding the perception of DT barriers. These unexpected differences might be because of bias in the data, although our sample is somewhat balanced between SMEs and LEs. We surveyed the companies' DT process but lacked deeper information on their maturity. In our discussion, we developed patterns for explanations. Further explorative research is needed to investigate these differences. Some additional, more substantial, and varied results between SMEs' and LEs' perception of the DT process and its implementation could transpire with a larger data sample. After collecting more data, narrowing this study down by emphasizing specific sectors, industries, age groups, and levels of responsibility might generate additional insights. Further research should also address ways of overcoming barriers to DT (Brink et al., 2022).

REFERENCES

Analoui, F., Karami, A., (2003). Strategic management in small and medium enterprises, 1st ed. ed. Thomson, London.

Ani, U.P.D., He, H. (Mary), Tiwari, A., (2017). Review of cybersecurity issues in industrial critical infrastructure: manufacturing in perspective. Journal of Cyber Security Technology 1, 32–74. https://doi.org/10.1080/23742917.2016.1252211

Bilgeri, D., Wortmann, F., (2017). Barriers to IoT Business Model Innovation. Proceedings of the 13th International Conference on Wirtschaftsinformatik 987–990.

Bolden, R., Rohini, T., (2020). Leadership Development in Small and Medium Sized Enterprises (No. 1). Centre for Leadership Studies, Exeter.

Bollweg, L., Lackes, R., Siepermann, M., Weber, P., (2019). Drivers and barriers of the digitalization of local owner operated retail outlets. Journal of Small Business & Entrepreneurship 0, 1–29. https://doi.org/10.1080/08276331.2019.1616256

Bourdieu, P., Coleman, J.S., (2019). Social theory for a changing society. Routledge, London.

Brink, H., Packmohr, S., (2022). Identifying Barriers to Digital Transformation and Measuring Their Impact - A Mixed-Method Study, in: PACIS 2022 Proceedings. Presented at the Pacific-Asian Conference on Information Systems, Taipei, pp. 1–17. https://aisel.aisnet.org/pacis2022/35

Brink, H., Packmohr, S., Paul, F.-H., (2022). Overcoming Barriers to Digital Transformation – Development of a Decision Matrix, in: Carroll, N., Nguyen-Duc, A., Wang, X., Stray, V. (Eds.), Software Business, Lecture Notes in Business Information Processing. Springer International Publishing, Cham, pp. 67–82. https://doi.org/10.1007/978-3-031-20706-8_5

Caloghirou, Y., Protogerou, A., Spanos, Y., Papagiannakis, L., (2004). Industry-Versus Firm-specific Effects on Performance: European Management Journal 22, 231–243. https://doi.org/10.1016/j.emj.2004.01.017

Chan, C.M.L., Teoh, S.Y., Yeow, A., Pan, G., (2019). Agility in responding to disruptive digital innovation: Case study of an SME. Info Systems J 29, 436–455. https://doi.org/10.1111/isj.12215

de Waal, Weaver, Day, van der Heijden, (2019). Silo-Busting: Overcoming the Greatest Threat to Organizational Performance. Sustainability 11, 6860. https://doi.org/10.3390/su11236860

Del Vecchio, P., Di Minin, A., Petruzzelli, A.M., Panniello, U., Pirri, S., (2018). Big data for open innovation in SMEs and large corporations: Trends, opportunities, and challenges. Creat Innov Manag 27, 6–22.

Duan, Y., Mullins, R., Hamblin, D., Stanek, S., Sroka, H., Machado, V., Araujo, J., (2002). Addressing ICTs skill challenges in SMEs: insights from three country investigations. Journal of European Industrial Training 26, 430–441. https://doi.org/10.1108/03090590210451524

Etikan, I., (2016). Comparison of Convenience Sampling and Purposive Sampling. AJTAS 5, 1. https://doi.org/10.11648/j.ajtas.20160501.11

Forradellas, R.F.R., Garay Gallastegui, L.M., (2021). Digital Transformation and Artificial Intelligence Applied to Business: Legal Regulations, Economic Impact and Perspective. Laws 10, 70. https://doi.org/10.3390/laws10030070

Forth, P., Reichert, T., de Laubier, R., Chakraborty, S., (2020). Flipping the Odds of Digital Transformation Success. BCG. https://www.bcg.com/publications/ (accessed 12.5.22).

Fritz, C.O., Morris, P.E., Richler, J.J., (2012). Effect size estimates: Current use, calculations, and interpretation. Journal of Experimental Psychology: General 141, 2–18. https://doi.org/10.1037/a0024338

Hadjimanolis, A., (2003). The Barriers Approach to Innovation, in: The International Handbook on Innovation. Elsevier, pp. 559–573. https://doi.org/10.1016/B978-008044198-6/50038-3

Hanelt, A., Piccinini, E., Gregory, R.W., Hildebrandt, B., Kolbe, L.M., (2015). Digital Transformation of Primarily Physical Industries-Exploring the Impact of Digital Trends on Business Models of Automobile Manufacturers., in: Wirtschaftsinformatik. pp. 1313–1327.

Hausberg, J.P., Liere-Netheler, K., Packmohr, S., Pakura, S., Vogelsang, K., (2019). Research streams on digital transformation from a holistic business perspective: a systematic literature review and citation network analysis. J Bus Econ 89, 931–963. https://doi.org/10.1007/s11573-019-00956-z

Hulla, M., Herstätter, P., Wolf, M., Ramsauer, C., (2021). Towards digitalization in production in SMEs – A qualitative study of challenges, competencies and requirements for trainings. Procedia CIRP 104, 887–892. https://doi.org/10.1016/j.procir.2021.11.149

Jones, M.D., Hutcheson, S., Camba, J.D., (2021). Past, present, and future barriers to digital transformation in manufacturing: A review. Journal of Manufacturing Systems 60, 936–948. https://doi.org/10.1016/j.jmsy.2021.03.006

Khanzode, A.G., Sarma, P.R.S., Mangla, S.K., Yuan, H., (2021). Modeling the Industry 4.0 adoption for sustainable production in Micro, Small & Medium Enterprises. Journal of Cleaner Production 279, 123489. https://doi.org/10.1016/j.jclepro.2020.123489

Kidwell, R.E., Sprague, R., (2009). Electronic surveillance in the global workplace: laws, ethics, research and practice. New Technology, Work and Employment 24, 194–208. https://doi.org/10.1111/j.1468-005X.2009.00228.x

Klötzer, C., Pflaum, A., (2017). Toward the development of a maturity model for digitalization within the manufacturing industry's supply chain, in: Proceedings of the 50th Hawaii International Conference on System Sciences. Presented at the HICSS, pp. 4210–4219. https://doi.org/10.24251/HICSS.2017.509

Koshal, A., Natarajarathinam, M., Johnson, M., (2019). Workforce Training and Industry 4.0 Adoption in Warehouses at SMEs, in: 2019 ASEE Annual Conference & Exposition Proceedings. Presented at the 2019 ASEE Annual Conference & Exposition, ASEE Conferences, Tampa, Florida, p. 33669. https://doi.org/10.18260/1-2--33669

LimeSurvey, (2023). Survey Maker. https://www.limesurvey.org/ (accessed 2.24.23).

Liu, D., Chen, S., Chou, T., (2011). Resource fit in digital transformation: Lessons learned from the CBC Bank global e-banking project. Management Decision 49, 1728–1742. https://doi.org/10.1108/00251741111183852

Lu, J.W., Beamish, P.W., (2001). The internationalization and performance of SMEs. Strat. Mgmt. J. 22, 565–586. https://doi.org/10.1002/smj.184

Matarazzo, M., Penco, L., Profumo, G., Quaglia, R., (2021). Digital transformation and customer value creation in Made in Italy SMEs: A dynamic capabilities perspective. Journal of Business Research 123, 642–656. https://doi.org/10.1016/j.jbusres.2020.10.033

Nemoto, T., Beglar, D., (2014). Developing Likert-scale questionnaires, in: JALT Conference Proceedings. Presented at the Japan Association for Language Teaching, Tokyo.

Nguyen, T.H., Newby, M., Macaulay, M.J., (2015). Information Technology Adoption in Small Business: Confirmation of a Proposed Framework. Journal of Small Business Management 53, 207–227.

Pabst von Ohain, B., (2019). Leader Attributes for Successful Digital Transformation. ICIS 2019 Proceedings.

Pallant, J., (2005). SPSS survival manual: a step by step guide to data analysis using SPSS for Windows (version 12), 2nd ed. ed. Open University Press, Maidenhead, Berkshire. U.K. ; New York, NY.

Radhakrishnan, J., Chattopadhyay, M., (2020). Determinants and Barriers of Artificial Intelligence Adoption – A Literature Review, in: Sharma, S.K., Dwivedi, Y.K., Metri, B., Rana, N.P. (Eds.), Re-Imagining Diffusion and Adoption of Information Technology and Systems: A Continuing Conversation, IFIP Advances in Information and Communication Technology. Springer International Publishing, Cham, pp. 89–99.

Reis, J., Amorim, M., Melão, N., Matos, P., (2018). Digital Transformation: A Literature Review and Guidelines for Future Research, in: Rocha, Á., Adeli, H., Reis, L.P., Costanzo, S. (Eds.), Trends and Advances in Information Systems and Technologies, Advances in Intelligent Systems and Computing. Springer International Publishing, Cham, pp. 411–421. https://doi.org/10.1007/978-3-319-77703-0_41

Roman, T., Marcu, N., Rusu, V.D., Doacă, E.M., Siriteanu, A.A., (2023). Tax Payment and the Performance of SMEs: A Longitudinal Analysis on EU Countries. Sustainability 15, 927. https://doi.org/10.3390/su15020927

Schmarzo, B., (2016). Big data MBA: driving business strategies with data science. Wiley, Indianapolis, Indiana.

Skare, M., de las Mercedes de Obesso, M., Ribeiro-Navarrete, S., (2023). Digital transformation and European small and medium enterprises (SMEs): A comparative study using digital economy and society index data. International Journal of Information Management 68, 102594. https://doi.org/10.1016/j.ijinfomgt.2022.102594

Stentoft, J., Rajkumar, C., (2020). The relevance of Industry 4.0 and its relationship with moving manufacturing out, back and staying at home. International Journal of Production Research 58, 2953–2973. https://doi.org/10.1080/00207543.2019.1660823

Tarutė, A., Duobienė, J., Klovienė, L., Vitkauskaitė, E., Varaniūtė, V., (2018). Identifying Factors Affecting Digital Transformation of SMEs, in: ICEB 2018 Proceedings. Guilin, China.

Tett, G., (2015). The silo effect: the peril of expertise and the promise of breaking down barriers, First Simon&Schuster hardcover edition. ed. Simon & Schuster, New York.

The Oxford Dictionary, (2021). Meaning of barrier in English. The Oxford Dictionary.

Veleva, V.R., (2009). Managing corporate citizenship: a new tool for companies. Corp. Soc. Responsib. Environ. Mgmt n/a-n/a. https://doi.org/10.1002/csr.206

Vial, G., (2019). Understanding digital transformation: A review and a research agenda. The Journal of Strategic Information Systems 28, 118–144. https://doi.org/10.1016/j.jsis.2019.01.003

Wahyuni, N.M., Sara, I.M., (2020). Market Orientation and Innovation Performance: Mediating Effects of Customer Engagement in SMEs. JEBAV 23. https://doi.org/10.14414/jebav.v23i1.2040

Wetzstein, B., Ma, Z., Leymann, F., (2008). Towards Measuring Key Performance Indicators of Semantic Business Processes, in: Abramowicz, W., Fensel, D. (Eds.), Business Information Systems, Lecture Notes in Business Information Processing. Springer Berlin Heidelberg, Berlin, Heidelberg, pp. 227–238.

Wonglimpiyarat, J., (2015). Challenges of SMEs innovation and entrepreneurial financing. World Journal of Entrepreneurship, Management and Sustainable Development 11, 295–311. https://doi.org/10.1108/WJEMSD-04-2015-0019

Yin, R.K., (2014). Case study research: design and methods, 5th ed. SAGE, Los Angeles.

ATTITUDES OF LIBRARIANS TOWARDS EMERGING TECHNOLOGIES – EFFECTS OF A MULTILINEAR SCENARIO

Elke Brucker-Kley, Samuel Keller and Thomas Keller
ZHAW School of Management and Law, Winterthur, Switzerland

ABSTRACT

A study examined the attitudes of 457 librarians in Germany and Switzerland towards emerging technologies that are likely to change the face of their profession. A multilinear narrative enabled participants to live through the future with these technologies. With their decisions, they could change the course and the end of the story. Before and after this intervention, participants were surveyed online about their attitudes. The results show a clear gap between imaginability and desirability of the technologies portrayed. The effect of the narrative is small but statistically relevant and shows a more differentiated attitude of the participants. The use of multilinear narrative scenarios to trigger a discourse about the consequences of digitalization on a profession can therefore be recommended.

KEYWORDS

Technology Assessment, Science Fiction Prototyping, Multilinear Storytelling, Field Study

1. INTRODUCTION

Libraries are not isolated institutions but have always been a social space and a mirror of how society deals with knowledge and information (Verma, 2015). The professional identity of librarians has been shaped over time by the purpose of libraries but also by the characteristics of the media they provide to their users. Thus, librarians have evolved from humanistic custodians of knowledge to socio-technical professionals who have long used technologies to acquire, maintain and supply information (Tîrziman, 2017). However, the massive digitization and virtualization of the global information landscape over the last thirty years has raised very fundamental questions about the role of librarians in the 21st century. The information seeking behavior of library users and the nature of library operations have been transformed by the digitization of content and technologies that have revolutionized the way information is organized and accessed (Lee, 2020). In response, librarians emphasize their relevance as navigators and gatekeepers in a user-centered information delivery model, advising their users rather than focusing primarily on their physical and digital collections (Dold, 2013). The mission to ensure equal access to information (American Library Association, 2014) has by no means lost its importance, but it requires new competencies and an open mind. The ability to deal with rapid technological change and to use innovations more proactively is demanded (Liu & Shen, 2018), (Noh, 2015), (Yeh & Walter, n.d.)(Kane, 2017), (Buhalis et al., 2019). Consequently, it is essential that librarians consciously engage with emerging technologies that will shape both their professional lives and the experiences of their users. Emerging technologies are defined as technologies that are characterized by novelty, fast growth, prominent impact, uncertainty and ambiguity (Rotolo et al., 2015). Scenarios can contribute to better envision the specific use of emerging technologies in everyday work and to think in terms of alternatives (Bradfield et al., 2005), (Bishop et al., 2007), (Boerjeson et al., 2005). Multilinear narratives represent a format to interact with a future scenario , to make decisions and to experience the consequences in a tangible way (Brunner et al., 2020a; Koenitz et al., 2015).

2. RESEARCH OBJECTIVES

The research presented in this paper aims at three objectives.

(1) The first objective is to survey the attitudes of librarians towards the potential use of relevant emerging technologies in their professional environment. Attitudes in the sense of subjective opinions or feelings towards a technologies comprise cognitive, affective and behavioral components (Eagly & Chaiken, 1993). The cognitive component shall be assessed through the dimension of imaginability, i.e. how tangible an emerging technology is or how concretely librarians can imagine it in their everyday future work life. The affective component shall be assessed through the dimension of desirability, i.e. to which extend librarians would like to see or not see an emerging technology as part of their future professional life. The behavioral component shall be extrapolated from the decisions that librarians actually make in relation to the use of technologies in the context of a multilinear narrative.

(2) The second objective is to investigate whether the multilinear story has an impact on the attitudes of the participating librarians towards the portrayed technologies (Brunner et al., 2020b), (Brucker-Kley & Keller, 2019). It is essential to the research design that the study is not based on a directional hypothesis. The question is not whether the narrative increases the desirability of a technology, but whether the narrative changes the attitude of the subjects regardless of the direction. The multilinear scenarios are not normative but deliberately show different variants of the future. The decision whether a future is desirable or not lies solely with the reader.

(3) A third subordinate objective is to determine whether there is a difference in attitudes and change in attitudes towards emerging technologies between academic and public librarians.

3. METHODOLOGY AND APPROACH

The design, creation and evaluation of the multilinear story followed the method of Science Fiction Prototyping, an approach fostering the critical reflection of consequences of technological innovations (Johnson, 2011), (Atherton & Johnson, 2016). Science Fiction Prototyping comprises three main phases (Merrie et al., 2018): (1) Identify and analyze the drivers shaping the future of the domain (in this case the librarian profession); (2) Develop the narrative to portray the impact of the technologies on people; (3) Expose the audience to the narrative and reflect on the impact and resulting learnings.

3.1 Select Relevant Technologies and "Build the Future World"

First, relevant emerging technologies which have the potential to change the librarian domain in the future were identified based on literature research. To design a plausible stage for the technologies in use also the political, economic and sociocultural drivers had to be determined via a PEST analysis (Sammut-Bonnici & Galea, 2015). The analysis led to the following five emerging technologies and technology-driven concepts which show great potential to change the future of the librarian profession. The majority of these are concepts driven by emerging technologies and not technologies per se. To reduce linguistic complexity, we will henceforth refer to them generally as "technologies":

- Smart glasses (Schweizer, 2014),
- Open Access (Homans & Wilen, 1997),
- Virtual Meetings (Laitinen & Valo, 2018),
- Artificial intelligence (AI) (Russell & Norvig, 2016), and
- Streaming services

Potential future manifestations of the key drivers and their impact were defined by applying the creative-narrative scenario technique according to Kosow and Gassner (Kosow & Gaßner, 2008). For each technology premises for light, moderate and extensive usage of the technology in libraries were formulated as well as the corresponding "stage design" in terms of assumed future political, economic and sociocultural conditions.

3.2 Develop the Narrative

Once the stage was set and the key technologies to be portrayed were selected, a multilinear story was developed in which librarians can make technology decisions and experience the consequences of those decisions. In this paper, only the structure of the story is outlined since the presentation of a multilinear story in a linear fashion does not correspond to the format. The English translation of the multilinear story is available online (*LibraryStory*, n.d.).

3.2.1 The Introduction:

The reader

- is placed in the role of a librarian,
- creates her/his own identity, by which she/he is addressed in the story, and
- is introduced to the future setting in which the story takes place.

3.2.2 The Main Part

The course of the narrative (following a working day) is outlined right at the beginning and basically portrays three possible narrative threads:

- Light usage of the technologies
- Moderate usage of the technologies
- Extensive usage of the technologies

The plot of the story follows various dialogues, which are personalized. The reader is addressed in the second person ("you") to create a certain intimacy and identification with the protagonist. The library plot is kept as general as possible, so that the everyday work situations can take place in a public library as well as in an academic library. The complexity of a daily work routine is simplified as much as possible but presented as tangible as possible so that librarians can familiarize with it. Decisions are built in the story whenever the librarian has a choice to use a technology more or less intensively. This leads to the splitting of individual narrative threads and increases the complexity of the possible storyline.

3.2.3 The End

Depending on the storyline driven by the decisions of the reader. The story leads to one of the following three open endings:

- "Obsolete": Rather dystopian with a negative impact, but with a professional reorientation as a silver lining on the horizon.
- "Irreplaceable": Rather conservative with few changes to the status quo.
- "Unburdened": Rather utopian with major technology-driven changes that open up new freedoms for self-fulfillment.

The multi-linear narrative was implemented as an interactive hypertext (Twine) accessible via any Internet browser. The quality of the artefact was validated via prototyping and think-aloud test-runs in four iterations along three dimensions: usability, immersion and transformational capability.

3.3 Analyse the Impact of the Narrative Intervention

The impact of the resulting narrative intervention was evaluated online. Subjects were recruited via digital channels from libraries and professional networks in the German-speaking part of Switzerland and Germany. Each participant went through a fully logged continuous online session that included a pre-survey, reading the hypertext story and a post-survey. Both survey rounds and the logging of the narrative intervention were conducted anonymously via a digital platform (Elke Brucker-Kley & Thomas Keller, n.d.).

For all the technologies mentioned above, one question each was asked about future imaginability ("Can you personally imagine that technology X will be dominant to perform tasks Y,Z in libraries?...") and desirability ("Do you personally want technology X to be part of your everyday work in the library?"). The responses to pre- and post-surveys were collected using a 5-point Likert scale Table 1. Applied five-point Likert scale (Table 1).

The post-survey was concluded by one additional open question, "What other thoughts and open questions does the story trigger in you? ". Number and content of answers to this optional question were used as a proxy to evaluate the effect of the narrative on the readers willingness to reflect and discuss. Both surveys were an integral part of the multilinear story and can be viewed online (*LibraryStory*, n.d.).

4. ANALYSIS AND FINDINGS

Statistical analysis was performed using SPSS. All data are available online (*Survey Data on OSF: Digital Futures - Library Story*, n.d.)

The verbal qualifiers of the 5-point Likert scale that were used for the pre and post survey were quantified as presented in Table 1.

Table 1. Applied five-point Likert scale

Imaginability	**Desirability**	**Value**
Very likely	Very desirable	5
Rather likely	Rather desirable	4
Possibly likely	Possibly desirable	3
Rather unlikely	Rather not desirable	2
Not likely at all	Not desirable at all	1

4.1 The Characteristics of the Participants

The total of 457 analyzable records can be grouped according to the following characteristics: Gender, age, and library type.

Table 2. Participants by gender

Gender	**No answer**	**Diverse**	**Male**	**Female**	**Total**
[#]	10	3	101	343	457
[%]	2.2	0.7	22.1	75	100

The gender distribution of the sample (Table 2) corresponds to the gender distribution of librarians in the surveyed geographies. Librarians are among the professions most influenced by gender. More than 80% of librarians in Switzerland and 75% of librarians in Germany are women (BfS, 2018; IAB - Institute for Labor Market and Profession Research, 2017).

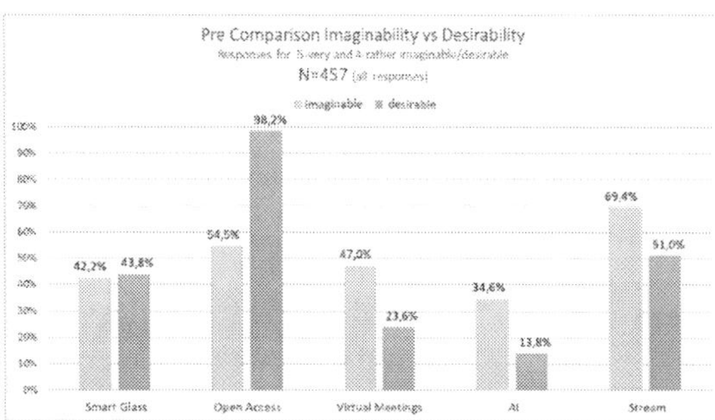

Figure 1. Imaginability and desirability of the portrayed technologies in the pre-survey

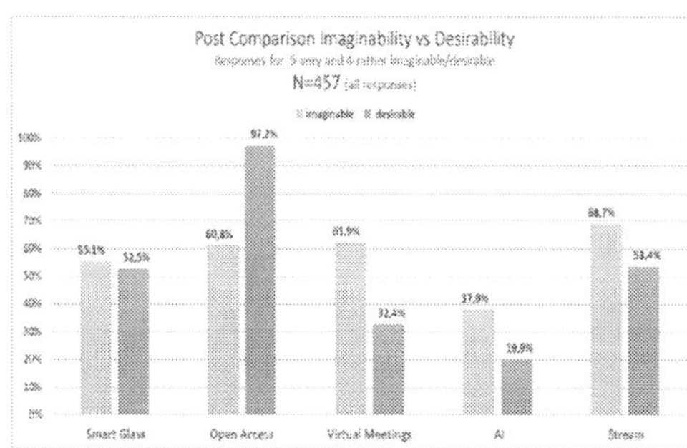

Figure 2. Imaginability and desirability of the portrayed technologies in the post-survey

The age distribution of the subjects does not reflect the age structure of librarians in the surveyed geographies. Librarians younger than 50 are more strongly represented in the survey than in reality. Age distribution data for information and documentation professions in Germany show that more than 47% of employees in that profession are 50 years and older, compared to 35% across all professions.

The sample shows that approximately ¼ of all participants work in a public library and almost ¾ in an academic library. The actual distribution of library staff according to Swiss library statistics (BfS, n.d.) is ⅔ in general public libraries and ⅓ in academic libraries. In Germany the jobs in public and scientific libraries are almost equally distributed (*02. German Library Statistics, Kerndaten, Engl. Ab 1999 - Bibliotheksstatistik - Hbz Service-Wiki*, n.d.). Thus, academic librarians are more strongly represented in the survey than in reality.

4.2 Imaginability Versus Desirability

The first objective was to identify the attitudes of the participating librarians towards the portrayed emerging technologies before reading the narrative scenario. Based on the results the cognitive aspect (imaginability) and the affective component (desirability) of the attitudes towards the technologies can be compared. For this purpose, the responses for "very likely" and "rather likely" as well as the responses for "very desirable" and "rather desirable" were cumulated. The responses for other options were not considered for this analysis.

The data show that smart glasses are equally imaginable and desirable for the participants before reading the scenario (Figure 1) . Practically all participants would like to see Open Access as the predominant paradigm to access scientific publications, but only 50% can imagine this for the future. For all other technologies, the gap between envisioning and embracing the technology in their everyday work life is the other way around. This is particular true for Virtual Meetings and AI. The participants consider it realistic that Virtual Meetings will dominate in libraries in the future but wish this to happen to a much lesser extent. The vision that AI could not only support but take over certain administrative and advisory processes in a library completely, is significantly less imaginable and clearly less desirable for the participants.

The second objective was to find out whether the multilinear narrative has an impact on the attitude towards the portrayed technologies. Figure 2 illustrates imaginability and desirability after the participants went through the multilinear narrative. Table 3 compares the data from the pre and post survey and shows the relative change for the positive responses presented in Figure 1 and Figure 2. Both imaginability and desirability have increased moderately for all of the technologies after reading the narrative except for the desirability of Open Access and the imaginability of Streaming. However, the clear gap between imaginability and desirability has remained. A more in-depth discussion of the impact of the multilinear narrative on the subjects' attitudes including the full spectrum of responses follows in the next section.

Table 3. Pre/Post survey comparison

	Pre survey		Post-survey	
	Very or rather desirable	Very or rather imaginable	Very or rather desirable	Very or rather imaginable
Smart Glass	43.76%	42.23%	52.52%	55.14%
Δ			20.00%	30.57%
Open Access	98.25%	54.49%	97.16%	60.83%
Δ			-1.11%	11.65%
Virtual Meetings	23.63%	47.05%	32.39%	61.93%
Δ			37.04%	31.63%
AI	13.79%	34.57%	19.91%	37.86%
Δ			44.44%	9.49%
Stream-ing	50.98%	69.37%	53.39%	68.71%
Δ			4.72%	-0.95%

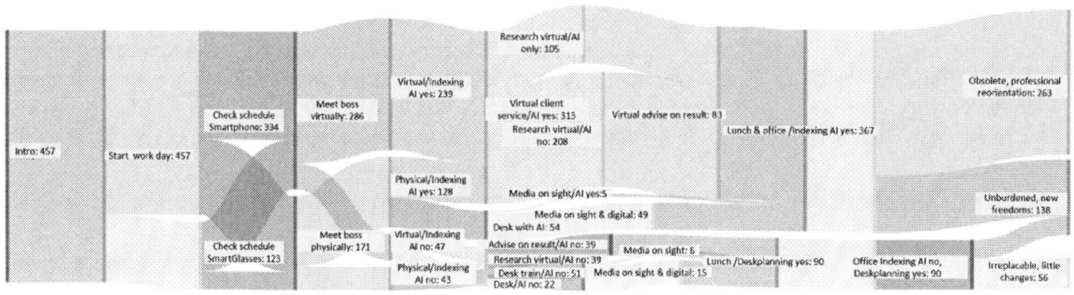

Figure 3. Sankey diagram illustrating the different paths the participants have taken in the story

4.3 The Impact of the Narrative

Based on the logged history of the individual paths of all participants (N=457) a Sankey diagram was generated (Figure 3). The thickness of the strands represents the quantity of the individuals who chose the different paths when interacting with the multilinear story. The Sankey diagram shows that many participants chose the strands with strong digitization. 313 participants opted for virtual customer service instead of supporting users on-sight at the customer service desk. Nevertheless only 105 participating librarians decided to leave the research for the user entirely up to AI in the virtual mode. 208 participants chose the virtual route but rejected the support of AI in conducting research. 263 participants closed the narrative experience with the rather dystopian ending (loss of job and professional reorientation). 138 experienced the rather utopian ending (freed up resources used for new ways of self-fulfillment). 56 participants left the experience with the rather conservative ending (light digital transformation resulting in little changes to the status-quo).

How did this predominantly dystopian narrative experience affect the attitude of the participants? The bubble charts visualize the change in attitude of the participants before and after the multilinear narrative for each portrayed technology, exemplarily for AI (Figure 4, Figure 6) and Smart Glasses (Figure 5, Figure 7) in this paper. The verbal qualifiers of the full Likert scale were recoded into numerical values (Table 1). Each datapoint is plotted in the coordinate system to express the response of the participant before (x-axis) and after (y-axis) the narrative experience. The bubble size represents the number of participants with the same response pattern. The bubbles along the diagonal of the diagram represent those participants whose attitudes remained the same before and after the narrative. The bubbles above the diagonal represent those participants who consider a technology more imaginable respectively more desirable after the narrative. The bubbles below the diagonal stand for negative changes in imaginability respectively desirability after the narrative.

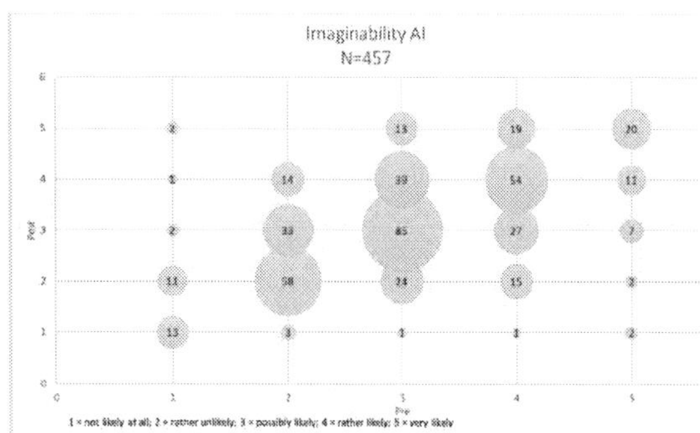

Figure 4. Imaginability of AI before and after reading the narrative

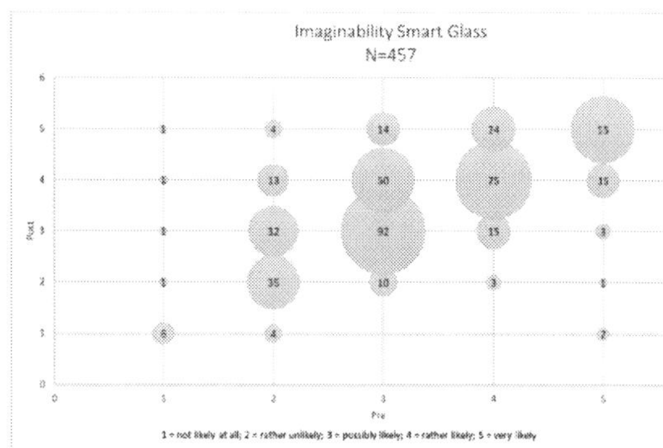

Figure 5. Imaginability of Smart Glasses before and after reading the narrative

The bubble diagrams clearly show the strikingly high proportion of users who have not changed their attitude according to pre- and post-survey. The bubbles along the diagonals in the case of smart glasses and AI represent more than half of the participants. The attitude towards Smart Glasses has not changed for 58% (imaginability) and 56% (desirability). Attitudes towards AI have not changed for 50% (imaginability) and 56% (desirability).

Overall, changes were small but nevertheless statistically significant. Significance was tested using the Wilcoxon signed ranked test, with a 0.05 significance level. For all technologies except for Streaming the measured differences between pre- and post-survey results were statistically significant for both imaginability and desirability. The null hypothesis that the narrative has no impact on the attitude of the participants can therefore be rejected for four of five technologies.

The bubble charts also show which technologies are more polarizing than others. In the case of the desirability of AI (Figure 6), for example, the bubble diagram reveals that almost one-third of the participants retained a negative attitude (rather not / not at all desirable). For Smart Glasses, the opinions are mainly in the indifferent and positive range and are more dynamic in terms of change from indifferent (3) to more desirable (4) (Figure 7).

To get an aggregated view on the strength of the changes in attitudes for each technology the sum of weighted positive and negative changes was calculated (v: variance in change, p: number of participants with the same variance in change)

$$\sum_{v+4}^{v-4} p_v \times v$$

The results are presented in Table 4. With the exception of the desirability of Open Access all technologies show an increase both of imaginability and desirability in the post-survey. Smart Glasses and Virtual Meetings became most tangible for the participants.

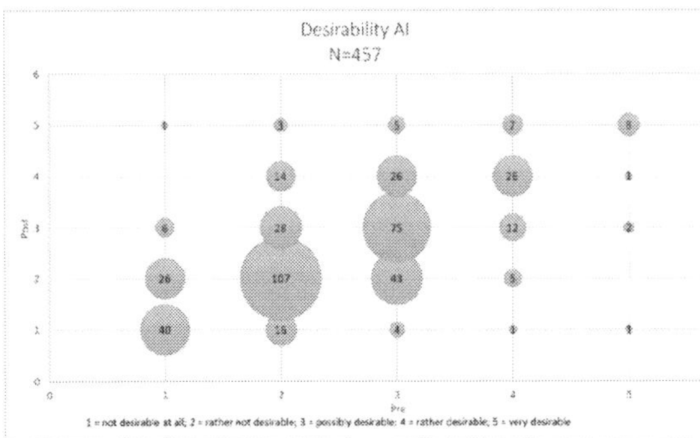

Figure 6. Desirability of AI before and after the narrative

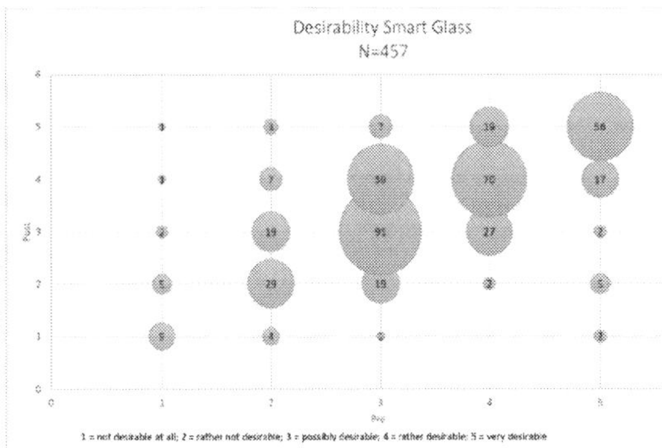

Figure 7. Desirability of Smart Glasses before and after the narrative

To compare and evaluate effect sizes in a standardized manner Pearson's r value was calculated based on the pre- and post-data (Table 5). Applying the classification for effect sizes in the social sciences according to Cohen (Cohen, 1988) (0.1=small, 03=medium, 0.5=large) to the results, it must be clearly declared that the effect size is small. For AI the effect is negligible, although statistically significant in the Wilcoxon test (0,04 for imaginability and 0,008 for desirability).

Table 4. Weighted changes of attitudes from pre to post survey

	Weighted change pre- to post survey	
	Imaginability	Desirability
Smart Glasses	+115	+50
Open Access	+60	-27
Virtual Meetings	+124	+76
AI	+43	+49
Streaming	+1	+18

Table 5. Effect sizes

	Effect size r	
	Imaginability	Desirability
Smart Glasses	0,20	0,10
Open Access	0,14	0,10
Virtual Meetings	0,21	0,15
AI	0,07	0,09
Streaming	0,00	0,04

4.4 Differences Based on Library Type

The Mann-Whitney U test with a significance level of 0,05 was applied to validate the statistical significance of differences between the attitudes and changes in attitudes of employees in public and academic libraries. Only for Virtual Meetings a statistically significant difference between public and scientific librarians could be identified. While 60% (52% post) of public librarians considered virtual meetings to be rather not or not at all desirable, only 37% (35% post) of scientific librarians shared the rather negative attitude. For all other technologies no statistically relevant difference could be observed The null hypothesis ("There is no difference in attitudes between employees of general public and academic libraries") thus can be confirmed.

5. DISCUSSION

One goal of this study was to determine librarians' attitudes towards emerging technologies that are likely to change the face of their profession. This revealed a clear gap between cognitive and affective attitudes both before and after reading the narrative scenario. The portrayed technologies, except for Smart Glasses, are overall more imaginable than desirable for the participating librarians. AI and Virtual Meetings are the technologies with the least desirability. The result for Virtual Meetings was probably also influenced by the pandemic. Libraries were either closed or reopened with heavy restrictions and a high share of librarians was working from home while the study was conducted. The desirability of Virtual Meetings nevertheless increased after reading the narrative. The futuristic version of meeting colleagues and clients virtually was seemingly more desirable than the current reality. With AI, attitudes were more entrenched. Here, there was not even a small effect on attitudes, neither on imaginability nor on desirability. With AI, nevertheless, the change in attitude among those who were in the middle of the Likert scale before the narrative (3 of 5) is noteworthy. 153 (33%) of participants considered AI "possibly desirable" before the narrative. Only 75 (16%) retained this indifferent opinion after the narrative, 31 changed their attitude to the more positive, 47 to the more negative. This example shows that despite statistically small effects, the narrative nevertheless enabled many participants to form an opinion. This is confirmed by the fact that 55% of the participants in this study used the optional free text field at the end of the survey to share thoughts and open questions triggered by the narrative.

For Smart Glasses, Open Access and Virtual Meetings the effects on imaginability were stronger than on desirability. The narrative was able to make these technologies and their impact on everyday professional life more tangible. The fact that the majority of participants opted for highly digitized paths of the multilinear narrative may have contributed to this effect.

However, it is questionable whether these decisions in the multilinear story are suitable as determinators for actual behavior. For example, the fact that 68% of participants chose virtual customer service might suggest that librarians do not mind the loss of customer contact. However, it can also simply mean that many librarians were curious to experience this version of customer service in the narrative. It is notable, however, that for 4 of 5 technologies desirability slightly increased, even though 58% of participants completed the story with the dystopian ending. This could indicate an insufficient level of immersion and believability of the story, which had been defined and testes as quality criteria for the narrative. However, it can also be taken as a positive indication that the story lives up to its claim of presenting different versions of the future as neutrally and descriptively as possible, rather than normatively convincing readers of good and bad versions of the future. The motivation behind this research was not to increase technology acceptance among librarians or to warn them about the consequences of digitization, but to promote a conscious engagement with emerging technologies.

6. CONCLUSIONS

Multilinear scenarios haven proven to be suited to make technologies imaginable. If we assume that imaginability is a prerequisite for engaging more consciously with technological change, multilinear narratives can contribute to a discourse on digitization and its consequences for the future of a profession.

We also consider the small changes in desirability to be relevant for this purpose, as they are an indicator that the readers of the narrative have developed a more differentiated attitude. Whether stronger effects are shown with more extreme scenarios is an interesting question for future inter- and transdisciplinary research. A multilinear narrative is a special form of intervention. It cannot be strictly controlled, even if it is created with the scientific methods outlined in this paper. The design of the narrative is ultimately also an artistic act and, despite testing, some bias in its creation cannot be prevented. The results of the study and feedback from readers suggests further design elements and design criteria worth exploring:

1. Avoid oversimplification. The attempt to make the experience fit for both public and scientific librarians did not work well. Public librarians found that the role of a library as a social space was underrepresented in the narrative.

2. Embed the possibility to experience the narrative from another perspective, e.g. of the library user. Roles and perspectives would allow to widen the scope of the audience and to pick or swop roles before and/or in the course of the story.

3. Reconsider the exclusive and irreversible choice of a path. Asking the readers at the end, whether they like this version of the future or whether they want to start the story again or return to a specific decision point, seems a promising new element both for the readers' experience and the research design.

4. Experiment with alternative formats for multilinear narratives. In the broader context of this study we experiment with immersive Virtual Reality (VR) to increase the emotional engagement of users. A "SciFi generator" allows to create VR experiences from textual Twines. Comparing the effects of textual twines versus immersive VR experiences is an interesting field of futures research.

REFERENCES

American Library Association (Ed.). (2014). *Library Bill of Rights*. https://crln.acrl.org/index.php/crlnews/article/view/17938

Atherton, E., & Johnson, B. D. (2016). Science Fiction Prototyping at Work. *Computer*, *49*(8), 109–111. https://doi.org/10.1109/MC.2016.229

BfS. (n.d.). *Swiss Library Statistics*. Swiss Federal Office of Statistics. Retrieved May 28, 2021, from https://www.bfs.admin.ch/bfs/de/home/statistiken/kultur-medien-informationsgesellschaft-port/erhebungen/chbs.html

BfS. (2018, January 31). *Employed persons aged 15 and over by occupation (nomenclature: SBN 2000), gender and nationality 1970-2016*. Swiss Federal Office of Statistics. /bfs/de/home/statistiken/kataloge-datenbanken/tabellen.assetdetail.4362784.html

Bishop, P., Hines, A., & Collins, T. (2007). The current state of scenario development: An overview of techniques. *Foresight*, *9*(1), 5–25. https://doi.org/10.1108/14636680710727516

Boerjeson, L., Hoejer, M., Dreborg, K.-H., Finnveden, G., & Ekvall, T. (2005). *Towards a user's guide to scenarios —A report on scenario types and scenario techniques*. https://www.osti.gov/etdeweb/biblio/20688312

Bradfield, R., Wright, G., Burt, G., Cairns, G., & Van Der Heijden, K. (2005). The origins and evolution of scenario techniques in long range business planning. *Futures*, *37*(8), 795–812. https://doi.org/10.1016/j.futures.2005.01.003

Brucker-Kley, E., & Keller, T. (2019). *Exploring the potential of immersive narrative scenarios to identify design criteria for our digital future(s)*. 499–504. https://doi.org/10.1109/IIAI-AAI.2019.00108

Brunner, M., Brucker-Kley, E., & Keller, T. (2020a). Eliciting personal attitude changes on predictive policing based on a multilinear narrative. *ECIAR Proceedings 2020*, 21–29. https://digitalcollection.zhaw.ch/handle/11475/21366

Brunner, M., Brucker-Kley, E., & Keller, T. (2020b). *Eliciting personal attitude changes on predictive policing based on a multilinear narrative*. 21–29. https://digitalcollection.zhaw.ch/handle/11475/21366

Buhalis, D., Harwood, T., Bogicevic, V., Viglia, G., Beldona, S., & Hofacker, C. (2019). Technological disruptions in services: Lessons from tourism and hospitality. *Journal of Service Management*, *30*(4), 484–506. https://doi.org/10.1108/JOSM-12-2018-0398

Cohen, J. (1988). *Statistical power analysis for the behavioral sciences*.

Dold, C. J. (2013). *The Role of Librarians in Academic Success*. 6.

Eagly, A. H., & Chaiken, S. (1993). *The psychology of attitudes* (pp. xxii, 794). Harcourt Brace Jovanovich College Publishers.

Elke Brucker-Kley & Thomas Keller. (n.d.). *A frame for responsible innovations*. Digital Futures. Retrieved May 19, 2021, from https://digitalfutures.ch/

German Library Statistics, Kerndaten, engl. Ab 1999—Bibliotheksstatistik—Hbz Service-Wiki. (n.d.). Retrieved May 31, 2021, from https://service-wiki.hbz-nrw.de

Homans, F. R., & Wilen, J. E. (1997). A Model of Regulated Open Access Resource Use. *Journal of Environmental Economics and Management*, *32*(1), 1–21. https://doi.org/10.1006/jeem.1996.0947

IAB - Institute for Labor Market and Profession Research. (2017). *Berufe im Spiegel der Statistik*. Berufe Im Spiegel Der Statistik. http://bisds.iab.de/Default.aspx?beruf=BG733&region=1&qualifikation=0

Johnson, B. D. (2011). Science Fiction Prototyping: Designing the Future with Science Fiction. *Synthesis Lectures on Computer Science*, *3*(1), 1–190. https://doi.org/10.2200/S00336ED1V01Y201102CSL003

Kane, G. C. (2017). The evolutionary implications of social media for organizational knowledge management. *Information and Organization*, *27*(1), 37–46. https://doi.org/10.1016/j.infoandorg.2017.01.001

Koenitz, H., Ferri, G., Haahr, M., Sezen, D., & Sezen, T. İ. (2015). *Interactive digital narrative: History, theory and practice*. Routledge.

Kosow, H., & Gaßner, R. (2008). *Methoden der Zukunfts-und Szenarioanalyse Überblick, Bewertung und Auswahlkriterien*.

Laitinen, K., & Valo, M. (2018). Meanings of communication technology in virtual team meetings: Framing technology-related interaction. *International Journal of Human-Computer Studies*, *111*, 12–22. https://doi.org/10.1016/j.ijhcs.2017.10.012

Lee, P.-C. (2020). Technological innovation in libraries. *Library Hi Tech*, *ahead-of-print*(ahead-of-print). https://doi.org/10.1108/LHT-07-2020-0163

LibraryStory. (n.d.). Survey and Twine - Future Scenario - Emerging Technologies in Libraries. Retrieved May 27, 2021, from https://library.digitalfutures.ch/wp-content/uploads/2021/05/LibraryStory_EN.html

Liu, S., & Shen, X.-L. (2018). Library management and innovation in the Big Data Era. *Library Hi Tech*, *36*(3), 374–377. https://doi.org/10.1108/LHT-09-2018-272

Merrie, A., Keys, P., Metian, M., & Österblom, H. (2018). Radical ocean futures-scenario development using science fiction prototyping. *Futures*, *95*, 22–32. https://doi.org/10.1016/j.futures.2017.09.005

Noh, Y. (2015). Imagining Library 4.0: Creating a Model for Future Libraries. *The Journal of Academic Librarianship*, *41*(6), 786–797. https://doi.org/10.1016/j.acalib.2015.08.020

Rotolo, D., Hicks, D., & Martin, B. (2015). *What Is an Emerging Technology?* (SSRN Scholarly Paper ID 2564094). Social Science Research Network. https://doi.org/10.2139/ssrn.2564094

Russell, S. J., & Norvig, P. (2016). *Artificial Intelligence: A Modern Approach*. Malaysia; Pearson Education Limited,. http://thuvienso.thanglong.edu.vn/handle/DHTL_123456789/4010

Sammut-Bonnici, T., & Galea, D. (2015). PEST analysis. In *Wiley Encyclopedia of Management* (pp. 1–1). Wiley. https://doi.org/10.1002/9781118785317.weom120113

Schweizer, H. (2014). Smart glasses: Technology and applications. *Ubiquitous Computing Seminar FS2014. Institute of Pervasive Computing*.

Tîrziman, E. (2017). The Librarian—A Redefined Profession for the 21st Century. *Revista Română de Biblioteconomie Şi Ştiinţa Informării*, *13*, 101–108. https://doi.org/10.26660/rrbsi.2017.13.4.101

Verma, M. K. (2015). Changing Role of Library Professional in Digital Environment: A Study. *International Journal of Library Science*, 9.

Yeh, S.-T., & Walter, Z. (n.d.). *Determinants of Service Innovation in Academic Libraries through the Lens of Disruptive Innovation | Yeh | College & Research Libraries*. https://doi.org/10.5860/crl.77.6.795

THE I-NERGY REFERENCE ARCHITECTURE FOR THE PROVISION OF NEXT GENERATION ENERGY SERVICES THROUGH ARTIFICIAL INTELLIGENCE

Evangelos Karakolis, Sotiris Pelekis, Spiros Mouzakitis, Georgios Kormpakis, Vasilis Michalakopoulos and John Psarras
Decision Support Systems Laboratory, National Technical University of Athens, Iroon Polytechneiou 9, 15772, Zografou, Greece

ABSTRACT

Recently the energy sector undergoes a rapid transformation that revolves around digitalization, decentralization and democratization. This is because global energy crisis contributes to rising poverty, raising prices and slowing economies. At the same time disrupting ICT technologies such as Artificial Intelligence (AI), Big Data Analytics, and Internet of Things (IoT) pose great potential towards improving several processes followed in the energy sector such as better forecasts for energy demand and consumption, that can contribute to significant energy savings. To this end, I-NERGY project aims at promoting and supporting AI in the energy sector through services and applications that support the entire energy value chain. In this publication, the I-NERGY big data reference architecture (RA) is presented, along with the most important technologies that have been used to cover the main requirements of I-NERGY platform. Moreover, I-NERGY is compared to other well-known big data RAs both general-purpose and energy sector specific, and the most important conclusions are presented in brief.

KEYWORDS

Artificial Intelligence, Big Data, Energy, AI on Demand, Data Governance, Energy Analytics

1. INTRODUCTION

People's well-being, industrial competitiveness and the overall functioning of society depend on safe, secure, sustainable and affordable energy. Hence, the energy sector and the underlying value chain are central in people's everyday life. Especially, in the last few years, with the advancements on technologies such as AI and Big Data Analytics, and due to the energy crisis, the energy sector undergoes a rapid transformation. In fact, AI and Big Data Analytics are expected to reshape drastically the entire energy value chain focusing mostly on digitalization, decentralization and democratization. Indicatively, General Electric estimates that the production of a wind farm can be increased by 20% through the use of AI (GeneralElectric, 2019). Moreover, McKinsey estimates that by 2030 Big Data, IoT and AI technologies can unlock 5.5 trillion to 12.6 trillion dollars in value globally (McKinsey, 2021). Also, there are already several examples that showcase the value that AI and Big Data technologies can unlock in the energy sector. For instance, Google Data Center operation achieved 40% energy savings through DeepMind AI (Yao, 2018).

Of course, there are several companies that already use such technologies and derive significant value from them, however in most cases they act as consolidated data siloes, unwilling to share neither their data nor the techniques, methodologies and technologies they are using. In this context, collaborative platforms and projects that combine data from different data sources and provide transparency about the techniques and technologies they are using are of utmost importance. In this direction, AI on Demand (AIoD) platform aims at bringing together the AI community and facilitate knowledge transfer from research to multiple business sectors (AI4EU, 2020). In addition GAIA-X project provides a federated and secure data infrastructure, in order to enable companies and citizens to share data, while they maintain control over them, while special attention is paid to data sovereignty (GAIA-X, 2022). The same objective of secure and sovereign data sharing poses also the International Data Space Association (IDSA) (IDSA, 2021).

All the above-mentioned projects focus on data and knowledge sharing for multiple business domains, however there is a variety of projects that focus on the value of AI and Big Data in the energy domain and their applications. For instance, the MATRYCS project focuses on big data analytics applications for smart buildings (MATRYCS, 2021). BD4NRG aims to exploit the full potential of Big Data to the entire energy value chain (BD4NRG, 2021). ENERSHARE aims at enabling secure and sovereign data sharing in the energy sector to facilitate the energy transition that was mentioned earlier (ENERSHARE, 2022).

The research presented in this publication, has been conducted under the context of the EU funded research project I-NERGY. The main objective of I-NERGY is the promotion and support of AI in the energy sector through novel AI services and applications that facilitate the entire energy value chain, as well as the reinforcement of AIoD platform with new knowledge and assets for energy (I-NERGY, 2021).

Specifically, in this paper, the I-NERGY high level architecture is presented along with its main components and building blocks based on which each component has been built, together with the main requirements that I-NERGY platform should cover. Moreover, a comparison with other similar big data architectures for the energy sector and other related works, is presented.

2. RELATED WORK

Recently Big Data Analytics, IoT and AI technologies are becoming popular in literature, leading to numerous publications and research work for relevant applications in the energy domain. Those include services about electrical load forecasting through AI (Pelekis et al., 2022), anomaly detection in smart buildings and smart grids (Karakolis, Alexakis, et al., 2022) predictive maintenance services, flexibility forecasting and demand response services (Ahmadiahangar et al., 2019) among others. Moreover, there are several publications on general purpose big data services, such as query engine applications (Alexakis et al., 2022) and visual analytics services (Kormpakis et al., 2022). However, most of them are focusing on specific problems rather than the entire architecture of a big data system.

On the other hand, there is a variety of publications and well-known big data architectures that have been proposed as general-purpose big data architectures that support a number of different and heterogeneous big data analytics and AI services. Such well-known architectures include BRIDGE (Lambert et al., 2021), IDS-Reference Architecture Model (IDS-RAM) (Otto et al., 2019) and GAIA-X (GAIA-X, 2022). Moreover, system architectures from similar projects in the energy domain are BD4NRG and MATRYCS architectures. All these architectures will be presented in a nutshell and compared to the one proposed in the following sections.

Specifically, BRIDGE initiative (BRIDGE, 2021) aims to address cross-cutting issues regarding smart grid, energy storage, islands and digitalization, by involving multiple stakeholders from a large number of related projects. The results of this initiative include BRIDGE Reference Architecture (RA), a multi-layered, cross-sectoral architecture model based on Smart Grid Architecture Model (SGAM). BRIDGE RA consists of five layers, namely the Component Layer, that includes all connected devices and data sources; the Communication layer that has to do with standardization of protocols and formats; the Information Layer that is responsible for forming the data according to the selected data models to facilitate interoperability; the Function Layer, which is responsible for decision making processes based on available data; and the Business Layer, which is responsible for business associations, roles and processes (Lambert et al., 2021).

BD4NRG architecture (Wehrmeister et al., 2022) has been designed on top of the BRIDGE architecture. Specifically, it consists of four layers illustrating the different layers of the data value chain and one vertical pillar that includes different dataspace enablers that are relevant with all the aforementioned layers. The layers include the Data Sources layer, which is similar to the component layer of BRIDGE RA, the Data Interoperability layer that accommodates the responsibilities of Communication and Information layers of BRIDGE RA, the Data Analytics Services layer, which is similar to the Function layer of BRIDGE RA, and the Business Actors layer that includes all the different stakeholders interacting with the platform. Regarding the vertical pillar (Data Space Enablers), it consists of all components and functions required for a distributed dataspace that is aligned with the design principles of IDSA and GAIA-X.

Furthermore, IDSA proposed their own architecture model, named IDS Reference Architecture Model (IDS-RAM) (Otto et al., 2019) that focuses on secure and trusted data exchange between organizations paying special attention to data sovereignty. The main building block for IDS-RAM is the IDS connector which acts as a gateway and enables peer to peer sovereign data exchange between users. The main participants of a data space are data owners, data providers, data consumers and data users. Similar to BRIDGE and BD4NRG RAs, IDS-RAM consists of several layers, namely the System Layer, the Information Layer, the Process Layer, the Functional Layer and the Business Layer. These layers provide similar functionalities to the layers of the previously presented architectures.

With respect to GAIA-X RA (GAIA-X, 2020), it focuses on decentralization and transparency and consists of a data ecosystem that provides data sharing services, as well as an infrastructure ecosystem that is responsible for portability, interoperability and interconnectivity. GAIA-X RA focuses more on cloud services and infrastructure compared to IDSA. Of course, these architectures can be integrated in a common approach (Otto, 2022), as IDS connectors can be used as secure gateways to GAIA-X RA nodes.

In addition, MATRYCS big data architecture is a high-level architecture focusing on big data management in the building domain, that facilitates data sharing, interoperability and seamless operation of big data-enabled services. It consists of four layers of functionalities, namely the Infrastructure Layer, the Data Governance Layer, the Processing Layer and the Analytics layer. All these layers are built, using well-known open-source technologies. MATRYCS high-level architecture, follows a similar approach to the one proposed in the publication at hand and the I-NERGY architecture. A brief comparison of all the presented reference architectures will be presented in section 5.

3. I-NERGY REQUIREMENTS

I-NERGY project provides AI-enabled analytical energy services to several pilot sites, covering the entire energy value chain, from TSOs, DSOs and ESCOs, to investors and policy makers, all of them posing different objectives and requirements. Specifically, the pilots include 9 pilot hubs and 15 different use cases, that have been described in detail in (Karakolis, Pelekis, et al., 2022). These use cases are distributed across three domains, namely, i) **AI for energy networks, aiming at the optimized operation of electricity and district heating networks**; ii) **AI for Renewable Energy Sources (RES) generation in buildings, districts and communities** and iii) **AI for enabling synergies and implications on other energy and non-energy domains**. Indicatively, the use cases under the first domain, include a use case for **AI enabled network assets predictive maintenance** and one for **AI enabled efficient operational planning through network load forecasting**. The use cases under the second domain include an **AI-based consumption and flexibility prediction for a local community** and an **AI for EV charging stations** use case. The third domain includes use cases such as **De-risking of energy efficiency investments through AI** and **AI-enabled prediction of climate change impact at a regional level.** Note here that the abovementioned use cases are indicative and the full list alongside their descriptions can be sought in (Karakolis, Pelekis, et al., 2022).

Given that there is a large number of different and heterogeneous pilots and use cases, that serve different stakeholder groups through the I-NERGY platform, a number of requirements should be satisfied in order for the platform to be able to serve all the aforementioned use cases. In particular, I-NERGY platform should be capable of:

Connecting with different and heterogeneous data sources. I-NERGY services are built on top of a variety of available data both static and streaming from multiple sources. Such data include weather data for different regions, sensor data from smart grids and smart buildings and data from network assets among others. To this end, the platform should be able to connect to different databases, use APIs and receive messages in real time through message broking technologies to facilitate near real-time services.

Preprocessing and harmonizing incoming data according to a common data model. As there are different data sources for different organizations and use cases, there is a requirement for storing information in a unified way, meaning that datasets that represent similar concepts and measurements should be represented in the same fashion, to establish interoperability and reusability, even though different organizations may use different models. Hence, a predefined commonly accepted data model should be established, in conjunction with a preprocessing and harmonization phase that brings the incoming data to a compliant form to the aforementioned common data model.

Providing efficient big data storage and querying capabilities. A variety of different data providers are envisaged to continuously send data to I-NERGY platform. These data should be stored efficiently and at a low latency to a database that is available for querying. Moreover, as several analytical and AI services are using these data, a mechanism for efficient querying is required, both in terms of low latency and high availability.

Accessing real-time data streams and facilitating access to the latter to related analytics services. Some of I-NERGY platform's services are near real-time services, such as real-time anomaly detection in smart buildings as well as fault detection in smart grid's network assets. To enable such services, incoming real-time data streams should be available to the services in near real-time.

Efficiently training, evaluating and serving AI models. Most of I-NERGY services heavily rely on AI, machine learning (ML) and deep learning (DL) models. As several of these models are very complex and require significant amounts of time and computational resources for training and inference, the platform should be able to provide efficient training, evaluation and serving capabilities (e.g. memory, GPUs etc.) to facilitate the development of these models.

Providing transfer learning capabilities. A common problem in energy related AI services is the insufficient amount or quality of available data, when it comes to training complex AI models. In such cases, the usage of transfer learning is often proposed by researchers (Sarmas et al., 2022), as it enables knowledge transfer from different domains to solve related problems.

Providing utilities for incremental (online) learning. It is commonly accepted that AI models that are trained offline tend to underperform, after a time period, due to the dynamic nature of the incoming data. To this end, I-NERGY platform should provide utilities for incremental learning, in order to dynamically adapt the developed models, once AI models stop performing as expected.

Serving multiple stakeholders, providing access to authorized users. I-NERGY assets (services, applications, data, etc.) should be available only to registered users, that have the appropriate permissions to access them.

Addressing cybersecurity. A complex big data platform with multiple stakeholders, and data from different organizations should be accompanied by high levels of security, including identification and prevention of malicious actions. Security measures should include service usage monitoring, vulnerability detection, access control and identity management and system monitoring among others.

Reinforcing the AIoD platform by sharing I-NERGY assets. One of the main objectives of I-NERGY project is to reinforce AIoD platform with a variety of energy analytics services. To this end, services, must be compliant with AIoD Experiments platform requirements, to be onboarded to the latter.

4. I-NERGY REFERENCE ARCHITECTURE

In Figure 1 the conceptual architecture of I-NERGY is illustrated alongside the interconnection with AIoD platform. It consists of several components responsible for different functionalities, namely the Data Management component, the AI models Training Component, the Energy Analytics component, and the Security and Access Control component. Moreover, the interconnection with the AIoD platform (formerly AI4EU) is presented, as I-NERGY project is tightly coupled with the AIoD platform. Hence, the main assets that are provided by I-NERGY platform (e.g., AI models, APIs, datasets, documentation) will also be available to AIoD platform, through the AI Catalog, and the AI Experiments platform.

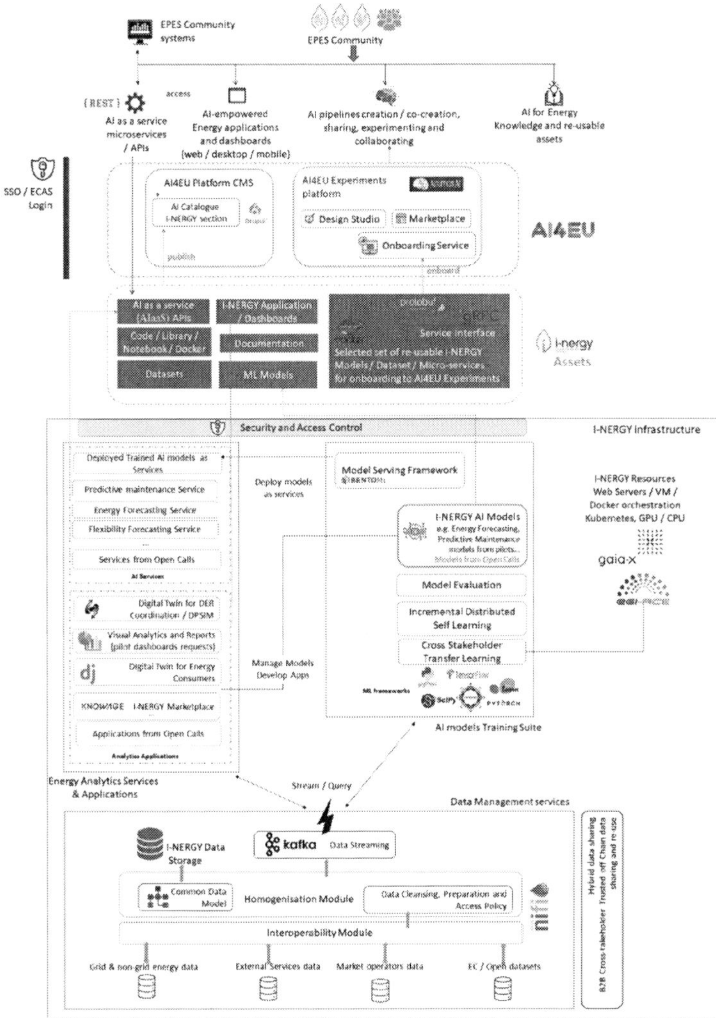

Figure 1. I-NERGY reference architecture

More specifically, the **Data Management component** is responsible for receiving incoming data from different data sources such as energy related data streams from smart grids and smart buildings and weather-related data and perform preprocessing, curation and harmonization procedures, in order to store these data in a commonly accepted form, according to a common data model. Additionally, this component is responsible for providing stored data, as well as real-time streaming data to the energy analytics services. The ingested data are also available to third parties and external stakeholders through a service based on blockchain and smart contracts that secures trusted data sharing and controlled access to data. The main technologies that are used in the Data Management component are Apache NiFi (Pandya et al., 2019), Apache Kafka (Kafka, n.d.) and MongoDB (MongoDB, 2018). Apache NiFi supports powerful directed graphs for data routing, transformation and system mediation logic, and within I-NERGY it facilitates the data ingestion and preprocessing phase. Apache Kafka is responsible for real-time data processing and, on the one hand, facilitates the reception of real-time data while, on the other hand, acts as a stream data provider for services that are based on streaming data. Finally, MongoDB, a highly scalable NoSQL database, is used for storing all the data, while analytics services are querying the latter.

The **AI models Training Suite** provides all the necessary tools for training evaluating and serving AI and ML models. Moreover, it provides capabilities for transfer learning and incremental learning, as well as storage of the aforementioned models. The main technology that is used for serving AI models is BentoML, while JupyterLab and MLFlow are used for model training and evaluation (Pelekis et al., 2022). Also, several technologies like TensorFlow, and Pytorch are used for transfer learning and incremental learning.

The **Energy Analytics services component** includes all analytics services that are available to the end-user. These services cover the entire energy value chain and include an electrical load forecasting service, an energy flexibility forecasting and demand response service, a service for real time anomaly detection in smart buildings, a predictive maintenance service, a service for evaluation and prioritization of energy efficiency investments in buildings, as well as a digital twin (DT) application for distributed energy resources (DER) coordination, and a DT application for electrical communities and energy consumers. On top of these services, a visual analytics service provides interactive data visualisations. All these services are available to external users through the I-NERGY Marketplace, which, on the one hand, enables the view of the project's available ML models and resources to promote their quick adaptation and reuse within different contexts, and on the other hand provides users with a graphical UI to develop in scale new services, algorithms, applications, and micro-services taking advantage of the available project assets such as datasets and ML models. For the development of AI models several python libraries are used such as TensorFlow, PyTorch, Darts, and Scikit-Learn. Moreover, for the DT for DER application DPSim simulator (Mirz et al., 2019) has been used, while DT for electrical communities as well as the Visual Analytics service were developed as web applications using the Django Python framework. Lastly, for the development of the marketplace the Knowage suite (Knowage, 2022) has been configured and deployed in accordance with user requirements.

The **Security and Access Control component** is responsible for ensuring that only authenticated users can access the platform services and data, on condition that they have the permission to access the requested resources. Moreover, this component is responsible for the overall security of I-NERGY platform, in order to protect platform data and services from cyber attacks. Identity and Access Control Management are achieved using Keycloak open-source identity and access management platform, while security is provided through Wazuh open-source security platform, which is installed on virtual machines of the project to provide endpoint security, threat and vulnerability detection, and continuous monitoring among others.

Of course, all these services require significant computational resources to operate smoothly. To this end, several cloud providers have been examined to be used for I-NERGY platform. Finally, EGI-ACE project's (EGI-ACE, 2021) cloud has been selected among the different cloud service providers. EGI-ACE is a project coordinated by EGI foundation (EGI, 2010) and is funded under EU Horizon 2020 research and innovation program. It provides free-at-point-of-use computing, storage resources, training and support for researchers and scientific projects. EGI is a federation of computation and storage resource providers that are united to provide computing and storage for analytics services and facilitate research and innovation across Europe.

The assets that I-NERGY provides are AI services available through APIs (AIaaS) and web interfaces, applications and dashboards, datasets, code and libraries, AI models and documentation. These assets can be utilised by different EPES stakeholders. All of them are planned to be published to AIoD catalogue, while several services amongst them will be onboarded as docker container-based pipelines to AIoD Experiments platform accompanied by the proper protobuf (Google, 2022) configuration as required by the platform for interoperability purposes. By publishing assets to AIoD catalogue and onboarding services to AIoD Experiments platform, more interested stakeholders can access them through the Single Sign On (SSO) mechanism of AIoD, which controls the identity of the users as well as their rights to the assets.

5. DISCUSSION

I-NERGY RA is the architecture of I-NERGY Big Data platform that provides energy analytics services and applications (static and near real-time) to the entire energy value chain, serving a variety of energy stakeholders. To this end, it gathers data from a number of different and heterogeneous data sources and then these data are preprocessed, harmonized according to a common data model, and stored to I-NERGY data storage. On top of that, different AI models and services are being developed utilizing an AI models' training suite, for training, evaluation, serving and storage of the models. Developed services, applications and other assets are available through both the I-NERGY and AIoD platforms. The usage of assets is protected by an Identity and Access Control Management component. All components of the presented architecture are deployed on EGI-ACE cloud, that offers storage and computational resources, such as CPUs and GPUs. The proposed architecture fulfills all the requirements presented in section 3, as illustrated also in section 4 that presents the architecture and provides a brief description of the most important components and services of I-NERGY platform.

Compared to other well-known big data architectures, both energy domain related and general-purpose ones, I-NERGY RA addresses the entire big data value chain, from data ingestion and governance to AI models and end-users' energy analytics services. It also proposes specific open-source technologies for each functionality instead of generic description of functionalities without related technologies and implementation details. On the other hand, IDS-RAM and GAIA-X RAs focus mostly on data exchange, sovereignty and transparency, neglecting other crucial functionalities of the big data value chain. Similarly, BRIDGE and BD4NRG RAs focus on smart grid applications of Big Data, without proposing specific technologies for addressing each layer of functionalities. Last but not least, contrary to the other RAs I-NERGY RA takes advantage of AIoD platform for knowledge transfer and sharing.

Regarding MATRYCS RA, it is the most similar RA to I-NERGY, as it provides components that cover the entire big data value chain, alongside the underlying technologies for each component. However, it does not cover all the requirements of I-NERGY project. For instance, MATRYCS, does not take into consideration AIoD platform, while neither transfer learning nor online learning issues are addressed.

6. CONCLUSION AND FUTURE OUTLOOK

In this paper, I-NERGY Big Data RA for the energy domain is presented, alongside the most important use cases and requirements that have been elicited and addressed by the architecture in question. Additionally, I-NERGY-RA is compared with other well-known big data RAs (both general purpose and energy specific) demonstrating the excellence of I-NERGY RA with respect to i) consideration of the entire energy value-chain compared to general purpose big data architectures that focus on data sharing, ii) proposition of specific open source technologies instead of generic high-level components and iii) consideration and addressing of novel AI concepts such as transfer learning and online learning.

Regarding, future extensions of the proposed RA, they include the validation of the entire platform by different energy stakeholders and the elicitation of new requirements for improvements. Finally, compliance with GAIA-X and IDSA will be further examined to facilitate efficient and effective data sharing among different organizations.

ACKNOWLEDGEMENT

This work has been funded by the European Union's Horizon 2020 research and innovation programme under the I-NERGY project, Grant Agreement No 101016508.

REFERENCES

Ahmadiahangar, R., Häring, T., Rosin, A., Korõtko, T., & Martins, J. (2019, June). Residential Load Forecasting for Flexibility Prediction Using Machine Learning-Based Regression Model. *Proceedings - 2019 IEEE International Conference on Environment and Electrical Engineering and 2019 IEEE Industrial and Commercial Power Systems Europe, EEEIC/I and CPS Europe 2019*. https://doi.org/10.1109/EEEIC.2019.8783634

AI4EU, P. (2020). *AI4EU - The European AI on Demand Platform.*

Alexakis, K., Kapsalis, P., Mylona, Z., Kormpakis, G., Karakolis, E., Ntanos, C., & Askounis, D. (2022). Intelligent Querying for Implementing Building Aggregation Pipelines. *13th International Conference on Information, Intelligence, Systems & Applications (IISA)*, 1–6.

BD4NRG, C. (2021). *BD4NRG - Big Data for Next Generation Energy.*

BRIDGE. (2021). *BRIDGE, Cooperation between Horizon 2020 projects in the fields of smart grid, energy storage, islands, and digitalisation.* https://op.europa.eu/en/publication-detail/-/publication/abf32809-143e-11ec-b4fe-01aa75ed71a1/language-en

EGI-ACE. (2021). *EGI-ACE.* https://www.egi.eu/project/egi-ace/

EGI. (2010). *EGI Foundation.* https://www.egi.eu/egi-foundation/

ENERSHARE. (2022). *ENERSHARE Project.* https://enershare.eu/

GAIA-X. (2022). *GAIA-X project.*

GAIA-X, P. (2020). *GAIA-X Technical Architecture.* https://www.data-infrastructure.eu/GAIAX/Redaktion/EN/Publications/gaia-x-technical-architecture.pdf?__blob=publicationFile&v=5

GeneralElectric. (2019). *General Electric GE Launches the Next Evolution of Wind Energy Making Renewables More Efficient, Economic.*

Google. (2022). *Protocol Buffers.* https://developers.google.com/protocol-buffers

I-NERGY. (2021). *I-NERGY project.* 2021.

IDSA. (2021). *International Data Spaces | The future of the data economy is here.*

Kafka. (n.d.). *Apache Kafka.*

Karakolis, E., Alexakis, K., Kapsalis, P., Mouzakitis, S., & Psarras, J. (2022). An end-to-end approach for scalable real time Anomaly detection in smart buildings. *13th International Conference on Information, Intelligence, Systems & Applications (IISA)*, 1–7.

Karakolis, E., Pelekis, S., Mouzakitis, S., Markaki, O., Papapostolou, K., Korbakis, G., & Psarras, J. (2022). Artificial Intelligence for Next Generation Energy Services across Europe – The I-NERGY Project. *20th International Conference E-Society 2022.*

Knowage. (2022). *Knowage Suite.* https://www.knowage-suite.com/site/

Kormpakis, G., Kapsalis, P., Alexakis, K., Pelekis, S., Karakolis, E., & Doukas, H. (2022). An Advanced Visualisation Engine with Role-Based Access Control for Building Energy Visual Analytics. *13th International Conference on Information, Intelligence, Systems & Applications (IISA)*, 1–8.

Lambert, E., Boultadakis, G., Kukk, K., Konstantinos, K., & Nikos, B. (2021). *European energy data exchange reference architecture.* https://energy.ec.europa.eu/bridge-reports_en

MATRYCS, C. (2021). *MATRYCS - Modular Big Data Applications for holistic energy services in buildingsNo Title.*

McKinsey. (2021). *IoT value set to accelerate through 2030: Where and how to capture it.*

Mirz, M., Vogel, S., Reinke, G., & Monti, A. (2019). DPsim—A dynamic phasor real-time simulator for power systems. *SoftwareX, 10.* https://doi.org/10.1016/j.softx.2019.100253

MongoDB. (2018). *MongoDB for GIANT Ideas | MongoDB.* MongoDB.

Otto, B. (2022). The Evolution of Data Spaces. *Designing Data Spaces.* https://library.oapen.org/bitstream/handle/20.500.12657/57901/1/978-3-030-93975-5.pdf#page=16

Otto, B., Steinbuß, S., Teuscher, A., & Lohmann, S. (2019). *IDSA Reference Architecture Model.* https://internationaldataspaces.org/wp-content/uploads/IDS-RAM-3.0-2019.pdf

Pandya, A., Kostakos, P., Mehmood, H., Cortes, M., Gilman, E., Oussalah, M., & Pirttikangas, S. (2019). Privacy preserving sentiment analysis on multiple edge data streams with Apache NiFi. *Proceedings of the 2019 European Intelligence and Security Informatics Conference, EISIC 2019.* https://doi.org/10.1109/EISIC49498.2019.9108851

Pelekis, S., Karakolis, E., Silva, F., Schoinas, V., Mouzakitis, S., Kormpakis, G., Amaro, N., & Psarras, J. (2022). In Search of Deep Learning Architectures for Load Forecasting: A Comparative Analysis and the Impact of the Covid-19 Pandemic on Model Performance. *13th International Conference on Information, Intelligence, Systems & Applications (IISA)*, 1–8.

Sarmas, E., Dimitropoulos, N., Marinakis, V., Mylona, Z., & Doukas, H. (2022). Transfer learning strategies for solar power forecasting under data scarcity. *Scientific Reports.*

Wehrmeister, K., Bothos, E., Marinakis, V., Magoutas, B., Pastor, A., Carreras, L., & Monti, A. (2022). The BD4NRG Reference Architecture for Big Data Driven Energy Applications. *13th International Conference on Information, Intelligence, Systems and Applications (IISA).*

Yao, W. (2018). *Analysis on the Application of the Artificial Intelligence Neural Network on the New Energy Micro Grid.* https://doi.org/10.2991/macmc-17.2018.144

SMART X: A DESCRIPTION FOR SMART ENVIRONMENTS

Richard Dabels
Department of Computer Science, University of Rostock, Rostock, Germany

ABSTRACT

In the Internet of Things, various terms are used to describe smart environments. These include Smart City, Smart Home, Smart Grid, Smart Industry and many more. However, they are often missing concrete definitions, which makes their use seem indiscriminate. The problem of horizontal integration describes that the different smart environments of the Internet of Things need to be brought together in order to gain a common advantage. But because we use a great abundance of terms describing smart environments, achieving horizontal integration between all of them seems almost impossible. Fortunately, the terms used for smart environments are often redundant, making the problem of horizontal integration more manageable. This theoretical study gives an overview of the current state of horizontal integration in smart environments. Its most well-known solutions and projects are presented and common problems of those solutions are discussed. After that, a new term is described based on the technological foundations prevalent in the smart environments in question. This term is *Smart X* and will be explained with some examples. Smart X as a concept is supposed to reduce the complexity of horizontal integration that arises from the inflationary vocabulary of smart environments that is currently used. Finally, further problems with existing projects and possible solution pathways are discussed.

KEYWORDS

Internet of Things, Horizontal Integration, Interoperability, Smart X, Smart Home, Smart City

1. INTRODUCTION

In recent years, the Internet of Things (IoT) has become a buzzword that extends into most areas of information technology. It consists of a wide variety of smart environments that are responsible for automating processes in their respective areas of application and are intended to make life and work easier for their users. New smart environments are constantly appearing in the literature, such as *Smart City*, *Smart Home*, *Smart Grid*, *Smart Infrastructure*, *Smart Health* and many, many more. A firm definition of these environments is often not given and *smart* mostly serves as a buzzword for modern communication systems. To better address the technological realities of our smart lives, we need a new way to talk about our connected world.

There is plenty of reason for this, as the economic impact of the IoT is immense, with the most significant areas in manufacturing and health care (Al-Fuqaha et al., 2015). Despite this, it is mostly impossible to share data efficiently between different smart environments, which poses a market risk, according to (Manyika et al., 2015). New technologies such as Thread are already trying to solve interoperability problems in their respective application areas, but are not able to cover them for the entire IoT domain.

This lack of interoperability is noticeable in various ways because end users are often confronted with multiple smart environments. For example, a lot of information is collected and processed in the Smart Home. Furthermore, municipal utilities are equipped with smart energy networks that enable more efficient use of resources. And last but not least, more and more Smart City initiatives exist, offering various functions for their residents. What is meant by "lack of interoperability" here is that there are no uniform interfaces between these environments and information is not aggregated.

This paper presents several options from the literature to address this lack of interoperability. It is also shown that the terms currently used to describe smart environments are inadequate to address the technological issues that arise with horizontal integration. A new term - *Smart X* - is elaborated to focus the discussion on the technological realities. Finally, some of the previously mentioned problems are identified and briefly discussed.

Smart X has one primary purpose: to reduce the complexity of horizontal integration. In the course of this theoretical study, a variety of smart environments will be highlighted. Connecting them for a common benefit is known as horizontal integration (Al-Fuqaha et al., 2015) and is a significant task due to the currently vast number of terms used in the literature. Smart X represents a subset of the terms used in the literature, which is limited to the main technological differences of each smart environment. The vocabulary currently used, which is partly redundant, mainly creates the impression that connecting all subsets of the IoT is an unattainable goal. Horizontal integration of the subsets of Smart X, on the other hand, seems more achievable.

2. RELATED WORKS

Interoperability of smart environments is a big problem of IoT and the process of connecting them is known as *horizontal integration* (Al-Fuqaha et al., 2015). This circumstance has developed because the requirements for the application areas of IoT differ significantly. For example, different promises are made regarding reliability, latency, jitter, and bandwidth (Qin et al., 2014), which is reflected in the respective protocols. Dave et al. describe in (Dave et al., 2020) that this interoperability is noticeable on different abstraction levels. It is shown that not only different protocols are problematic, but also the use of different network layers, platforms, and syntactic and semantic differences.

Technologically, this results in a variety of smart environments, which are mostly disconnected from each other. In the literature, these are often referred to as *vertices* or *vertical markets*, whose horizontal integration is a major problem (Filipponi et al., 2010; Prazeres and Serrano, 2016; Noura, Atiquzzaman and Gaedke, 2019). How these vertices are defined depends on the consideration of the respective authors. An overview can be seen in Table 1, although for some publications, the categorizations were adjusted. For example, a search for "smart" in (Stübinger and Schneider, 2020) yields 559 hits, but a generalization was also made within the publication itself, which is reflected in Table 1. Also, very similar categories were renamed. In other cases, single terms such as *Smart Garden* in (Noura, Atiquzzaman and Gaedke, 2019), which were used only once throughout the reviewed literature, have been omitted.

Table 1. Overview of different verticals mentioned in the literature

	(Al-Fuqaha et al., 2015)	(Noura, Atiquzzaman and Gaedke, 2019)	(Stübinger and Schneider, 2020)	(Hui, Sherratt and Sánchez, 2017)	(Marksteiner et al., 2015)	(Sidorov et al., 2019)
Home	X	X		X	X	X
City		X	X	X	X	X
Health	X	X	X	X		X
Grid/Energy	X	X		X	X	X
Vehicles	X					
Industry	X	X		X		
School	X					
Infrastructure	X		X			
Transportation	X	X			X	X
Sustainability			X			
Economy	X		X			
Agriculture	X					
Technology			X			
Office/ Buildings				X		X
Production					X	X
Factory				X		X

The sources used for Table 1 are mainly works that deal directly with horizontal integration (Al-Fuqaha et al., 2015; Noura, Atiquzzaman and Gaedke, 2019) or other literature that each provides overviews of the IoT and enabling technologies (Marksteiner et al., 2015; Stübinger and Schneider, 2020). Furthermore, in the case of (Sidorov et al., 2019), a paper was used that provides a broad overview of technologies of the IoT despite its focus on the project presented in it. Also, the available sources were selected because they each deal with a variety of smart environments. In this way, an overview that addresses a large number of terms used in the literature can be provided.

In addition to the categorization of Table 1, other possible classifications exist. For example, (Filipponi et al., 2010) uses a generalized representation of smart environments, where infrastructure and shopping are grouped as *smart city space*, home and office as *smart indoor space*. Marksteiner et al. also sees the above environments as parts of the Smart City (Marksteiner et al., 2017). Another category is *smart personal spaces*, which includes vehicles and presumably other technologies such as smartphones. Also, a variety of proposals exist to enable horizontal integration between the aforementioned vertices (Filipponi et al., 2010; Collina, Corazza and Vanelli-Coralli, 2012; Qin et al., 2014).

It is evident that there is to be a vast number of smart environments for which horizontal integration is desirable. The industry already combines Smart Grid functions with those of Smart Industry, so certain processes are only carried out when electricity prices are favorable. However, a stricter coupling to the power grid can also be useful for private individuals (Komninos, Philippou and Pitsillides, 2014). In corporate building automation, complicated and expensive solutions are met with acceptance if a financial incentive is present. This is particularly the case if installation and maintenance can be outsourced to external experts.

In the consumer market, however, solutions must be developed that are easy to implement and bring clear advantages. A complex configuration of gateways between each environment is only reasonable for very few end users. In addition, the number of environments to be linked seems so enormous that complete horizontal integration hardly seems possible. However, one thing the definition of Smart X in Section 3 is meant to show is that many existing smart environment definitions are essentially redundant and that the problem of horizontal integration might in fact be simpler than one thinks at first glance.

In the following, some approaches and projects are presented that deal with the topic of horizontal integration. Most of them use the MQTT protocol as the underlying technology, but there are also projects that propose more complex architectures. The present distinction is mainly based on the importance of MQTT in the proposed solutions.

2.1 MQTT Based Approaches

MQTT is a well-known publish-subscribe protocol for machine to machine (M2M) communication that is applied in many IoT architectures (Collina, Corazza and Vanelli-Coralli, 2012; Prazeres and Serrano, 2016; Gavrila et al., 2018; Dave et al., 2020). Information processing is organized around so-called *topics* to which clients subscribe and on which information can be published. It is particularly suitable for use in IoT systems and smart environments due to its low resource requirements and broad support. For these reasons, MQTT is the focus of many researchers studying horizontal integration.

In (Collina, Corazza and Vanelli-Coralli, 2012) two different concepts are combined: On the one hand, MQTT as a publish-subscribe protocol for energy-efficient M2M communication, and furthermore REST as a component of the Web of Things. The so-called QEST broker developed here thus makes it possible to provide REST resources as MQTT topics. This approach connects the concepts of the Web of Things with that of the Internet of Things and provides their resources in a unified way. The Ponte project (Dave et al., 2020) builds on QEST and extends it, among other things, with a CoAP interface.

2.2 Architecture Approaches

The area of the IoT is also characterized by the large number of technologies used, which can be seen just by looking at the Smart Home and the large number of wireless standards used there. For this reason, the more abstract approaches based on MQTT are always dependent on gateways taking over the translation into suitable formats and protocols. Complicated mesh network structures, as for example with ZigBee (Ondrej et al. 2006), are hidden from the higher layers of the MQTT service by these gateways.

The project SOFIA (Filipponi et al., 2010) proposes an architecture that loosely couples various producers and consumers of messages in so-called *smart spaces*. These producers and consumers are called *knowledge processors*, which in turn publish their information on, and consume information from, several interconnected publish-subscribe services - *semantic information brokers* - respectively. In this approach, applications each implement knowledge processors with which they can access the network of semantic information brokers.

A similar concept is that of the self-organized *Fog of Things* (FoT) (Prazeres and Serrano, 2016). Here, much of the information processing is shifted to the boundaries of the network to the FoT gateways, which receive it from sensors - the FoT devices. These gateways are also responsible for translating between different protocols and technologies or have advanced functionalities such as persistent storage of data (FoT servers). Again, MQTT-based Message Oriented Middleware is used for the connections of the devices.

Some approaches focus directly on the physical layer. One possibility here is the use of software-defined radios (SDR), as Gavrila et al. show in (Gavrila et al., 2018). Here, the authors developed an SDR gateway that supports various wireless protocols using a Universal Software Radio Peripheral. A similar project has also been developed by Lin et al. (Lin et al., 2013).

3. SMART X

In Table 1 different verticals are presented and ordered by the literature in which the corresponding terms are used. It should be emphasized here that depending on the literature used, authors come to very different conclusions regarding the respective categories. Although the research deals intensely with smart environments, it is apparently not possible to find a uniform vocabulary for it. The concrete problems that lead to this circumstance include the following:

- Depending on the nature of the underlying work, the interpretation of smart environments may vary. For example, a broad literature review by Stübinger and Schneider comes up with different keywords than one would have expected from a purely technological interpretation (Stübinger and Schneider, 2020). Technical surveys, on the other hand, usually map a variety of verticals (Al-Fuqaha et al., 2015; Noura, Atiquzzaman and Gaedke, 2019; Stübinger and Schneider, 2020).
- The choice of and focus on the level of abstraction is also relevant to the interpretation of the verticals. In (Collina, Corazza and Vanelli-Coralli, 2012) and (Dave et al., 2020), which present the MQTT solutions presented above, the terms of Table 1 are not mentioned at all. Instead of smart environments, they are using the term smart *objects* here. Similarly, this is also the case in the work of Gavrila et al., which in a sense deals with the other extreme of levels of abstraction: Here, too, the terms do not occur (Gavrila et al., 2018).

In order to deal with this circumstance, we propose to define a new term that does justice to the technical perspective. This term is *Smart X* and is based on the different technologies used in the respective smart environments or verticals. Smart X is thus a smart environment that is technologically distinct from other smart environments (Smart Xs). Horizontal integration between different Smart Xs is still a major problem (Noura, Atiquzzaman and Gaedke, 2019). However, a unified vocabulary here is intended to sharpen the problem definition and help overcome the boundaries of different Smart Xs. Some examples of this concept are discussed below.

3.1 Smart Home

First of all, the term *Smart Home* describes a network of sensors and actuators designed to assist its occupants in their daily lives (Bugeja, Jacobsso and Davidsson, 2016). They further target a user base that does not necessarily have sufficient technical skills to set up complicated home networks, which has implications on their design. For this reason, usability is a key factor when it comes to selecting a system for one's Smart Home. Other factors include security, privacy and, in particular, acquisition costs, since Smart Home devices are typically not critical services (Hui, Sherratt and Sánchez, 2017).

Due to their availability and user familiarity, protocols such as WiFi and Bluetooth are sometimes used for home automation. However, they involve considerable computational overhead, which makes them unsuitable for battery-powered devices. This problem is solved by technologies such as ZigBee, Z-Wave and

Homematic. Since the transmission power of especially the battery-powered devices is usually weaker and collision-avoidance methods would also mean a higher overhead, the respective networks are mostly organized as a mesh (Ondrej et al. 2006; Ondrej et al. 2006). Wired systems such as KNX on the other hand are very rarely used in homes due to their installation costs.

A requirement that arises of using specialized Smart Home protocols is that certain gateways must be used for interacting with the network. These are usually provided by the suppliers of the respective devices. However, community solutions such as *Home Assistant* (https://www.home-assistant.io/) or *OpenHAB* (https://www.openhab.org/) can also be used with adapters for the respective protocols. The use of Thread and Matter should make it easier to integrate Smart Home devices into IPv6 networks in the future (Unwala, Taqviand and Lu, 2018).

3.2 Smart Grid

The Smart Grid is closely related to the Smart Home because of the locality of data collection and communication. However, the interaction between these two Smart X often does not extend beyond the boundaries of the energy grid. Komninos, Philippou and Pitsillides show in (Komninos, Philippou and Pitsillides, 2014) several reasons why closer collaboration between Smart Home and Smart Grid is beneficial. Mainly discussed in the literature are the potential electricity savings (Hui, Sherratt and Sánchez, 2017). Among the technologies most often discussed are 5G, Narrowband IoT (Neagu and Hamouda, 2016) and WiMAX (Neagu and Hamouda, 2016; Marksteiner et al., 2017). However, the standardization of this Smart X is mainly through government specifications (U.S. Department of Commerce, 2020).

Since power grids are critical infrastructure, there is also interest from the government in securing and defining the Smart Grid. The National Institute of Standards (NIST) has launched an initiative to drive forward the standardization of Smart Grids. Among other things, it describes criteria by which industry standards will be considered for use in Smart Grids and a list of standards that meet those criteria. Some of the better-known protocols include MODBUS, BACnet, and DNP3. This detailed elaboration serves as the basis for the definition of this Smart X.

3.3 Smart City

In the literature, Smart City is often understood as a superset in which many other smart environments can be found (Marksteiner et al., 2017; Stübinger and Schneider, 2020). However, it is so differentiated from other smart environments by the requirements placed in and the technologies used by it that it is understood to be a Smart X in this paper. For example, Smart Cities often use wireless technologies that enable information exchange over many kilometers (Sidorov et al., 2019). Battery-powered devices are also used in some cases, which require low power consumption. One example is sensors that check soil moisture near urban greening to enable more efficient irrigation.

Relevant technologies that enable energy-efficient communication over many square kilometers include Narrowband IoT, LoRa and SigFox, which belong to LPWANs. Unlike Smart Home networks, here end devices connect to public base stations. In LoRaWAN, for example, high availability is ensured since messages can be received from several base stations.

While technologies such as ZigBee, Bluetooth and WiFi are also discussed as Smart City technologies in some publications (Jaloudi, 2015; Jawhar, Mohamed and Al-Jaroodi, 2018), they are not generally suitable for Smart City deployment due to high installation costs and short radio distance (Mekki et al., 2018; Sidorov et al., 2019). A concrete example of Smart City implementation is the Datenplatform Darmstadt (https://datenplattform.darmstadt.de), which can be used to query various information such as traffic status and particulate matter levels, and to track Corona infection events. In related publications such as (Poppe, 2021), 5G and LoRaWAN are mentioned as concrete technologies, but also WiFi as hotspots for citizens.

3.4 Further Smart X

This paper considers only the three mentioned Smart Xs in detail. However, a larger number of other Smart Xs is conceivable, which are defined by their technologies. Examples of these are partly given in Table 1. It should be noted, however, that these environments found in the literature do not have to be technologically delimited at all, and thus do not represent Smart X. It is likely that similar technologies will be used for Smart Industry, Building, Office, and School. In this sense, *Smart X* is intended to serve much more as a basis for discussion than as a fixed definition of already mentioned smart environments.

A specific example of the redundant categorization as a smart environment is the Smart Garden mentioned in (Noura, Atiquzzaman and Gaedke, 2019). Among others, ZigBee (Al-Ali et al., 2015) and WiFi (Hadi et al., 2020) can be used here, which are technologies that focus on the Smart Home domain. In addition to the work mentioned above, sensors for monitoring soil moisture and actuators for automated irrigation based on Smart Home technologies are now also available for end users. So from this perspective, Smart Garden is no additional Smart X, as it is not technologically different from the Smart X of Smart Home. Based on this information, Smart Garden is essentially the same as Smart Home.

This paper aims to introduce the term Smart X and to show examples of its usage. However, classifying the various terms shown in Table 1 into different Smart X will require further quantitative literature research.

4. FURTHER PROBLEMS AND PROPOSED SOLUTIONS

In Section 2, some projects have already been presented that offer solutions to the problem of horizontal integration. However, how existing technologies can be integrated into these solutions is often not considered. Underlying architectures, protocols, and management entities often do not allow for easy information exchange. Specifically, to the best of the author's knowledge, there is no architecture for gateways that can interconnect a large number of different Smart Xs.

Designing a gateway for a multitude of different Smart X is difficult because the respective technologies make certain tradeoffs due to their requirements (Qin et al., 2014) and representing this in a uniform system is presumably very complex. In environments with many battery-operated devices, it may not be possible to guarantee that telegrams reach their destination since acknowledgments are not defined in the respective protocol. Also, various network properties such as jitter, latency and reliability must be taken into account by a unified system. If information such as temperatures is made retrievable beyond the original publishing as in (Collina, Corazza and Vanelli-Coralli, 2012), expiration dates must also be considered. A careful examination of these properties and more must be the content of further work addressing the problem of horizontal integration.

In addition to the uniform representation of semantic information such as the coding of temperature or wind speed, it must also be known which devices can in principle be represented in IoT systems. Similar concepts are already used in ZigBee (Ondrej et al. 2006) and Bluetooth, where devices have a type that determines their role in the network. Again, a detailed definition of all possible devices in IoT applications is a tremendous task, but relevant to enable horizontal integration across Smart Xs. This can also be seen as a concretization of various concepts such as *semantic information brokers* (Filipponi et al., 2010) or *FoT devices* (Prazeres and Serrano, 2016), as these do not yet define tasks or device classes themselves.

However, the possible solution to the problem of horizontal integration must also adhere to certain quality parameters. For example, such systems are expected to be responsive enough for their tasks. Therefore, it is most likely necessary to have a decentralized architecture so that certain tasks can also be processed locally and at short notice. However, similar to blockchain concepts, it should be ensured in the long term that the overall system approaches a consistent state.

Last but not least, user privacy rights must also be taken into account in a unified system. According to (Hui, Sherratt and Sánchez, 2017), the Smart Home is the best opportunity for the Smart City to obtain personal information about its users. On the one hand, this personal information is of great value to other smart environments, but for the same reason, it does not necessarily want to be shared by the user. An attacker who can derive from Smart Home information, whether a user is at home or not, can generate great value for criminal their activity. However, for example, while an attacker might be able to derive certain information from a users Smart Home, it might still be advantageous to offer some of that information to the smart city's public transport system in case the user arrives late at the bus stop. A rights and privacy system must therefore be created that only allows certain parties access to sensitive information. Side channel attacks should also be considered in this context. An example of this could be that a Smart Home that does not transmit any information indicates that the user is not currently present.

Another special case is when information obtained in a smart environment does not belong to the actual user of the environment. This is the case, for example, when the landlord or municipal utilities read a tenant's consumption values to determine the electricity and heating costs. Here, too, a rights system must determine whether a user should still have access to consumption information.

5. CONCLUSION

This paper introduced Smart X: A description for different smart environments that are technologically distinct from each other. Previously used terms for smart environments were mostly historical and defining them precisely is difficult or even impossible. Therefore, the proposal was made to use a concept instead, which is aligned with the technological realities of smart environments. This refers to Smart X, which has been explained in this paper using three examples: Smart Home, Smart Grid and Smart City.

Also, various architectures were presented from the literature to solve problems in IoT systems, particularly horizontal integration. These are mostly based on MQTT and function as middleware for exchanging information from sensors and sending instructions to actuators. Although the presented proposals are quite relevant for unifying the IoT, they do not address the technological specificities of the underlying systems enough. Furthermore, issues such as privacy, information ownership, and semantics of information are often not addressed.

Smart X offers the possibility of reducing the complexity of the horizontal integration of a wide variety of smart environments. This is made possible by the fact that many smart environments can be grouped together by taking a technological view, since similar technologies characterize them. Horizontal integration of the remaining Smart X is thus a more manageable task than that of the more arbitrary smart environments mentioned in the literature. We hope that, on the basis of Smart X, the discussion will be further aligned with the technological foundations of such systems in the future.

REFERENCES

A. R. Al-Ali et al., (2015), ZigBee-based irrigation system for home gardens. *2015 International Conference on Communications, Signal Processing and their Applications (ICCSPA)*. Sharjah, United Arab Emirates, pp. 1-5

Ala Al-Fuqaha et al., (2015), Internet of Things: A Survey on Enabling Technologies, Protocols, and Applications. *In IEEE Communications Surveys & Tutorials.* Vol. 17, No. 4, pp. 2347–2376

Cassio Prazeres and Martin Serrano, (2016), SOFT-IoT: Self-Organizing FOG of Things. *In 2016 30th International Conference on Advanced Information Networking and Applications Workshops (WAINA)*. Crans-Montana, Switzerland, pp. 803-808

Cristinel Gavrila et al., (2018), Reconfigurable IoT Gateway Based on a SDR Platform. *2018 International Conference on Communications (COMM)*. Bucharest, Romania, pp. 345-348.

Imad Jawhar, Nader Mohamed, and Jameela Al-Jaroodi , (2018), Networking architectures and protocols for smart city systems. *In Journal of Internet Services and Applications*. Vol. 9, No. 1, p. 26.

Ishaq Unwala, Zafar Taqvi, and Jiang Lu, (2018), Thread: An IoT Protocol. *2018 IEEE Green Technologies Conference (GreenTech)*. Austin, TX, pp. 161-167.

J. Manyika et al., (2015), The internet of things: mapping the value beyond the hype. McKinsey Global Institute, New York, USA

Johannes Stübinger and Lucas Schneider, (2020), Understanding Smart City - A Data-Driven Literature Review. *In Sustainability*, Vol. 12, No. 20, p. 8460.

Joseph Bugeja, Andreas Jacobsson, and Paul Davidsson, (2016), On Privacy and Security Challenges in Smart Connected Homes. *2016 European Intelligence and Security Informatics Conference (EISIC)*. Uppsala, Sweden, pp. 172-175.

Kais Mekki et al., (2018), Overview of Cellular LPWAN Technologies for IoT Deployment: Sigfox, LoRaWAN, and NB-IoT. *2018 IEEE International Conference on Pervasive Computing and Communications Workshops (PerCom Workshops)*. Athens, Greece, pp. 197-202.

Luca Filipponi et al., (2010), Smart City: An Event Driven Architecture for Monitoring Public Spaces with Heterogeneous Sensors. *2010 Fourth International Conference on Sensor Technologies and Applications*. Venice, Italy, pp. 281-286.

Madhavi Dave et al., (2020), Ponte Message Broker Bridge Configuration Using MQTT and CoAP Protocol for Interoperability of IoT. *In Computing Science, Communication and Security*. Vol. 1235, pp.184-195.

Mahda Noura, Mohammed Atiquzzaman, and Martin Gaedke, (2019), Interoperability in Internet of Things: Taxonomies and Open Challenges. *In Mobile Networks and Applications*. Vol. 24, No. 3, pp. 769-809.

Matteo Collina, Giovanni Emanuele Corazza, and Alessandro Vanelli-Coralli, (2012), Introducing the QEST broker: Scaling the IoT by bridging MQTT and REST. *2012 IEEE 23rd International Symposium on Personal, Indoor and Mobile Radio Communications (PIMRC)*. Sydney, Australia, pp. 36-41

Michail Sidorov et al., (2019), LoRa-Based Precision Wireless Structural Health Monitoring System for Bolted Joints in a Smart City Environment, *In IEEE Access*. Vol. 7, pp. 179235-179251

Mokh. Sholihul Hadi et al., (2020), IoT Based Smart Garden Irrigation System. *2020 4th International Conference on Vocational Education and Training (ICOVET)*. Malang, Indonesia, pp. 361-365

Muneer Bani Yassein, Wail Mardini, and Ashwaq Khalil, (2016), Smart homes automation using Z-wave protocol. *2016 International Conference on Engineering & MIS (ICEMIS)*. Agadir, Morocco, pp. 1-6.

Nikos Komninos, Eleni Philippou, and Andreas Pitsillides, (2014), Survey in Smart Grid and Smart Home Security: Issues, Challenges and Countermeasures. *In IEEE Communications Surveys & Tutorials*, Vol. 16, No. 4, pp. 1933-1954.

Oana Neagu and Walaa Hamouda, (2016), Performance of WiMAX for smart grid applications. *2016 International Conference on Selected Topics in Mobile & Wireless Networking (MoWNeT)*. Cairo, Egypt, pp. 1-5.

S. Ondrej et al., (2006), ZigBee Technology and Device Design, *International Conference on Networking, International Conference on Systems and International Conference on Mobile Communications and Learning Technologies (ICNICONSMCL'06)*. Morne, Mauritius, pp 129-129.

S. Jaloudi, (2015), Open source software of smart city protocols current status and challenges. *2015 International Conference on Open Source Software Computing (OSSCOM)*. Amman, Jordan, pp. 1-6

Stefan Marksteiner et al., (2017), An overview of wireless IoT protocol security in the smart home domain. *2017 Internet of Things Business Models, Users, and Networks*. Copenhagen, Denmark, pp. 1-8.

Terence K.L. Hui, R. Simon Sherratt, and Daniel Díaz Sánchez, 2017, Major requirements for building Smart Homes in Smart Cities based on Internet of Things technologies. *In Future Generation Computer System,* Vol. 76, pp. 358-369.

Timo Poppe, (2021), Teamwork für smarte Regionen: Stadtwerke gestalten den digitalen Wandel für mehr Lebensqualität. *In Smart Region*. Wiesbaden, Germany, pp. 29-39.

U.S. Department of Commerce, 2020, *NIST Framework and Roadmap for Smart Grid Interoperability Standards, Release 4.0*

Yong Hua Lin et al., (2013), Wireless IoT Platform Based on SDR Technology, *2013 IEEE International Conference on Green Computing and Communications and IEEE Internet of Things and IEEE Cyber, Physical and Social Computing*. Beijing, China, pp. 2245-2246.

Zhijing Qin et al., (2014), A Software Defined Networking architecture for the Internet-of-Things. *IEEE Network Operations and Management Symposium (NOMS)*. Krakow, Poland, pp. 1-9

BD4NRG QUERY ENGINE – INTUITIVE, EFFICIENT AND FEDERATED QUERYING ON BIG DATA

Konstantinos Touloumis, Evangelos Karakolis, Panagiotis Kapsalis, Vangelis Marinakis and John Psarras
Decision Support Systems Laboratory, School of Electrical and Computer Engineering, National Technical University of Athens, 9 Iroon Polytechniou Str., 15773 Athens, Greece

ABSTRACT

Due to the rapid development of Internet of Things (IoT) technology during the last decade, there has been recorded a significant growth in the size of data collected by data warehouses, especially on the ones connected to sensors and meters on the energy sector. Querying such data, gathered by heterogeneous data sources is a complicated task in terms of space allocation, scalability, and integration. Big data analytics methods try to address the problem of querying big data by bringing together different data sources of different formats with a high level of abstraction. This paper presents a query engine that, on the one hand addresses the problem of querying big data stored on different and heterogeneous databases and on the other hand, simplifies the steps needed by the user for defining and executing queries on the aforementioned databases through an intuitive and easy to use interface, so as to facilitate high level analytical services. Particular attention is given to securing the tool by employing access resource management thus preventing unauthorized users from accessing the requested resources.

KEYWORDS

Big Data Querying, Big Data Analytics, Energy Sector, Federated Querying

1. INTRODUCTION

With the exponential growth of networking capabilities, there has been noticed a rapid growth in the volume of data collected in databases, gathering data from various sources on the energy sector such as energy consumption data (Mohammed et al., 2019). Traditional databases fail to scale up to the huge volumes of data collected, thus, making querying a complex and inefficient task (Nadikattu, 2020). Data warehouses try to bridge the gap by using multidimensional models to effectively represent the data they store. Still, with the evolution of IoT they fail to respond to the massive volumes of collected data on the energy sector, thus introducing difficulties in efficient storing, preprocessing, and querying (Marinakis & Doukas, 2018). Data lakes have been proposed as they maintain heterogenous data sets in their original format. They aim at providing scalable and flexible knowledge discovery and querying. Moreover, they reduce the cost of storing and integrating data. However, serious complexity is introduced during query execution (Endris et al., 2019).

In this context, big data analytics methods allow efficient querying of heterogeneous data sources. According to (Zhang et al., 2017) big data is characterized by its variety, velocity, volume, value and veracity (5V's of big data). Variety indicates that data comes from different sources and can be structured, semi-structured and unstructured. Volume indicates that the size of data is growing rapidly and is not easily manageable. Velocity indicates that big data can be used as streams to maximize its value. Veracity indicates that not all data on such high volume is going to be clean, hence the accuracy of data analysis is going to be affected. Value indicates that acquired data should be useful for knowledge mining and providing user related services, as investing in big data technologies comes at a high cost for interested companies.

One sector that can be highly benefited from big data analytics technologies is the energy sector. This is because recent developments in the energy domain such as smart grids and buildings result to the generation of vast amounts of data, that cannot be easily analyzed without big data analytics technologies and techniques. Of course, several energy companies are already benefitted from big data analytics, however there is still significant potential for novel services based on big data analytics and artificial intelligence (AI) and for improving already developed use cases (Chui et al., n.d.). To this end, there is a variety of projects that aim to unlock the full potential of big data analytics for the energy domain. This is done by private businesses internally, as well as globally by facilitating data sharing combining different data sources, instead of siloed approaches that are followed within a single organization. For instance, the I-NERGY project (Karakolis, et al., 2022) aims to unlock the full potential of AI on the energy sector through innovative services such as anomaly detection in smart buildings (Karakolis, et al., 2022), as well as electrical load forecasting (Pelekis et al., 2022), that cover the full energy value chain. Moreover, the MATRYCS project (MATRYCS, 2022) provides holistic energy services in smart buildings using big data. Also, BD4NRG project (BD4NRG, 2022) aims to establish new market opportunities in the energy sector using big data.

Such projects are huge and complicated, providing different and independent services on top of different and heterogeneous datasets gathered from different data sources and technologies. To derive value from these datasets, efficient querying technologies are required one the one hand, and on the other hand, combination of different and heterogeneous datasets should be made feasible. Moreover, querying is mostly related to programmers and data scientists, however energy domain experts can pose more relevant energy related queries as they are more familiar with this domain. In this context, an intuitive interface for creating and executing queries against the provided databases, without writing any SQL code is highly appreciated by domain experts. To deal with the huge volumes of data stored in data warehouses and assist data analysts and customers to extract useful and meaningful data, several query engine services and applications have been developed. However, they pose several limitations including ones related to compatibility with different technologies, security and access control management, efficiency and performance.

In this context, the research at hand presents the BD4NRG Query Engine application. This component is responsible for allowing its users explore, combine and express complex queries without any prior knowledge of any programming language, as well as executing these queries in an efficient manner, facilitating the execution of complex queries that combine different datasets from different and heterogeneous data sources and technologies including data streams alongside acceptable response time. This component can also be used by other applications through APIs as well as through direct connections to the main querying technology, to facilitate several data analytics applications with the requested data. It is worth mentioning that on top of these functionalities a security and access control management component has been employed to make sure that users have access only to data that are authorised to.

2. BACKGROUND AND RELATED WORK

According to (Mohammed et al., 2019) the challenges on big data querying are the following: Streaming of large-scale data from IoT, as the huge volumes of data during data acquisition phase makes it difficult to decide which data must be discarded and which to maintain. The data heterogeneity, as most data sources do not follow a structured format, thus, transforming a data source of unstructured format to structured is a major challenge. Pre-processing, cleaning and analyzing data is a complex task both due to scalability and complexity of data to be analyzed. Also, data storage and space allocation should be optimized. Security and privacy concerns are becoming extremely important for large scale integration and deployment of the IoT. Finally, visualizing querying results is very challenging as domain experts should be able to easily extract useful knowledge in a straightforward manner (Agrawal et al., 2015). This paper focuses mostly on big data querying.

Of course, a big data querying component should comply to certain functional and non-functional requirements as recognized in literature (Bohlouli et al., 2013). Some of the functional requirements include:

Integration: the query engine must be capable of being connected and fetching data from different data sources. This is because complex big data systems process data from different data sources that are not always stored in the same storage or database. There is a wide variety of SQL and NoSQL database technologies and each one focuses on different aspects, including general purpose big data databases focusing on performance (e.g. MongoDB (MongoDB, 2022)), timeseries databases (e.g. InfluxDB (influxdata, 2022)) for efficient timeseries operations, and conventional SQL ones for typical Online Transaction Processing (OLTP), as well as data lakes.

Statistical analysis: the query engine must be capable of performing simple and complex analysis like calculating statistics on aggregated data and providing Online Analytical Processing (OLAP) capabilities.

Exploration: the query engine should provide visual analytics for interacting with data to extract useful knowledge.

Decision support: the query engine should provide mechanisms for assisting decision making of stakeholders on both domain and non-domain decision problems.

Non-functional requirements include:

Scalability: the query engine should be able to handle large amounts of data.

Near real time monitoring: near real time monitoring is necessary especially for streaming data.

Resource efficiency: system resources should be utilized in an efficient way.

In this context, there are several big data querying technologies that address some of the presented functional and non-functional requirements. For instance, Trino (Trino, 2022) is a powerful distributed SQL query engine that facilitates big data analytics applications, offering low latency analytics, great scaling capabilities, query federation, simplicity (ANSI SQL compliant), as well as compatibility with the most well-known databases. Presto (Presto, 2022) offers similar functionalities, as it is fast, reliable, scalable and compatible the most well-known databases. Although Presto is a well-established solution in the market and Trino was built on top of it, the latter poses a few advantages over Presto. Specifically, it provides higher level of versatility when querying traditional data sources, non-relational databases and columnar databases. Moreover, it provides options to save resources. On the other hand, Presto provides better performance for processing specific file formats like ORC. It also, provides a library within Spark (Apache Spark, n.d.) executor (pandio, 2021). Since there are clear advantages in each technology, the selection of one option should be done according to the requirements of the specific use case. In this work, Trino was selected, as a large number of different database technologies is used, while the advantages of Presto are not relevant to the specific work.

In this context, several relevant query engine applications available in literature will be presented. Specifically, in (Linder et al., 2017) a big data system for collecting building data is presented. It depends on the notion of virtual objects. A virtual object is mapped to a real sensor through an ID by a specialized collector. A MySQL (Krogh, 2020) database is used to augment metadata with a virtual object and transmit it through Kafka (THEIN, 2014) messaging. Tokens are also used for securing data privacy. However, the research mentions that NoSQL (Atzeni et al., 2020) databases compromising between consistency, availability and partition tolerance and are not appropriate for acting at the storage level.

Similarly, in (Pau et al., 2022) and (Alexakis et al., 2022) another big data system for querying analytics on buildings sector is analyzed. The first step is data preprocessing to remove incomplete or inaccurate data. The transmission layer uses a Kafka broker for transmitting data. Kafka messaging offers high throughput and latency, but it is inefficient for time-based aggregation on data streams. Data is then harmonized and projected onto a common data model. A MongoDB service acts as the enriched data warehouse that stores the processed data. On top of this warehouse the Presto query engine is used for querying different data sources.

Besides SQL based query engines, several reasoning engines are presented in literature. They are based on semantic technologies to infer logical relations. Reasoning engine applications include the work of (Kapsalis et al., 2022) which presents a reasoning engine for smart building metadata management. The main technology that has been used is Neo4J graph database on top of RDF ontology data. Also (Anagnostopoulos et al., 2013) presented a reasoning engine for extracting qualitative temporal information using OWL language.

It is worth mentioning that a common problem that Big Data Analytics query engines (and projects) face is the identity and access control management on different data sources. Specifically, when there are many data providers, involved, alongside multiple other users from different organisations and levels of expertise, access to the available datasets should be restricted based on the provider's preferences. Hence, a user should have access only to resources he is authorised to. To this end, there are several technologies for identity and access control management such as FIWARE Keyrock (FIWARE, n.d.) and Keycloak (Keycloak, 2022), and several scientific publications addressing this aspect. For instance, (Kormpakis et al., 2022) present a framework for securing a visual analytics application for the energy sector, which enables only authorised access to energy related data, through Keycloak and role-based access control.

3. THE PROPOSED SOLUTION

In Figure 1 a high-level overview of the proposed big data architecture is presented focusing on the querying capabilities that BD4NRG Query Engine offers. It consists of several layers of functionalities, namely the data sources, the Data Storage, the Querying Component, the Querying and Analytics interfaces, alongside an Identity and Access Control Management layer and the main platform users.

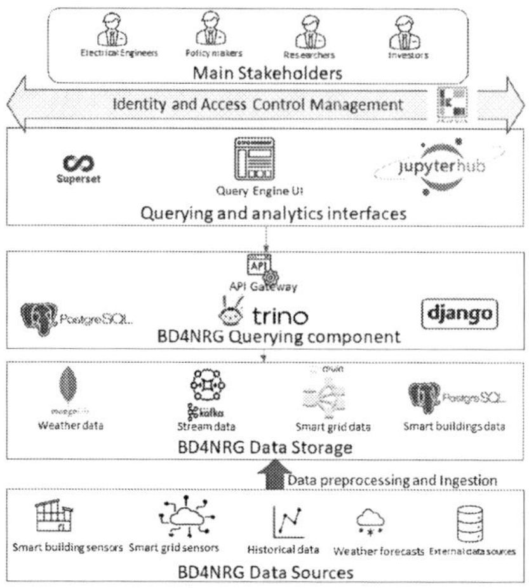

Figure 1. BD4NRG query engine high-level architecture

Specifically, the **BD4NRG data sources** include data from sensors and smart meters from both buildings and smart grids, weather related data including weather forecasts and actual weather measurements (e.g. temperature, humidity, wind speed), historical data of different kinds (e.g. fault incidents in smart grids) among others. All these data are pre-processed, curated, and harmonized to be stored to BD4NRG platform.

These data are stored to one of the databases of the **BD4NRG Data Storage layer**. Specifically, continuous flows of streaming data are ingested to BD4NRG platform through Kafka message broker, using protocols like MQTT and AMQP. Moreover, other types of data are stored to the databases into batches. Afterwards, all these data are stored to the database technologies employed for this component. In particular, weather data is stored to a MongoDB database, data from smart buildings are stored to a PostgreSQL database, while data from smart grids are stored to Apache Druid.

The **BD4NRG Querying component** is responsible for the execution of queries against the databases of the previous layer, and the combination of the available datasets. The main technology used in this component is Trino, a Big Data distributed Query Engine technology, which is an open-source, very efficient querying technology that can query exabytes of data and is used by some of the largest organizations in the world. Trino is able of connecting to all BD4NRG data sources, like the ones presented in the storage layer. Moreover, it allows query federation within a single query, and is compatible with the most well-known databases. Also, Trino enables queries to Kafka data streams, which is an important functionality for near real time analytics services. Also, it is ANSI SQL compliant and works with several well-known BI tools. It is worth mentioning that the BD4NRG Querying Component provides several APIs to execute queries on it. To this end, a Django web application has been developed to provide these APIs. Moreover, a PostgreSQL database has been employed to store dataset metadata. Several APIs of the Querying component are presented in Table 1.

Table 1. Querying component REST APIs

Description		HTTP Method	Endpoint URL	Params	Body
1.	Retrieve a list of the available datasets of the platform. For each dataset, some metadata are provided (e.g. title, a small description)	GET	/apis/get/datasources/	-	-
2.	Retrieve a list of all the available variables from all datasets of the platform.	GET	/apis/get/variables/	-	-
3.	Retrieve a list with all the variables that are included in a selected dataset. For each variable, some metadata are provided, such as its name, its dataset and its description.	GET	/apis/get/datasource/variables/	-	{ "catalog": "druid", "schema": "druid", "dataset": "lsp01" }
4.	Add a new dataset to the list of available datasets.	POST	/api/get/{datasource_id}/ datasource/	-	{ "dataset": "lsp01" }

The **Querying and Analytics interfaces layer's** main goal is to assist users in exploring the available datasets, building, executing custom queries and performing exploratory analysis. This is done through several ways. First, an intuitive, user-friendly web interface has been developed to facilitate easy query creation and execution by non-IT-related users. To this end, the Query Engine UI communicates with the Querying component through APIs and directs users in defining the query step by step, selecting datasets, aggregations on the data tables, and the logical expressions that will be used for filtering the selected data. Furthermore, Apache Superset is employed to allow high level visualizations for all data sources connected to Trino. By using Superset, users are able of making visualizations for inferring statistics and further discovering relations between data. Last, JupyterHub has been employed to serve Jupyter notebooks to multiple users for facilitating the creation of custom services on the project assets. It is worth mentioning that many BD4NRG analytical services communicate with the BD4NRG Querying component through APIs to execute efficient and low latency federated queries.

The **identity and access control management component** aims to manage resource access within the platform. Keyrock IdM is used for monitoring user access, roles and permissions on trusted applications. Keyrock Idm is an open-source identity management tool developed by FIWARE, that can register store and query identity data, with the purpose of providing and validating access tokens to users to authenticate them to trusted applications. Wilma PEP Proxy is a policy enforcement proxy server that validates the received access tokens with Keyrock IdM. The latter uses the OAuth 2.0 protocol for authorizing access of client users to the resources owned by a host user without knowing the host's credential. By using this protocol an application can obtain limited access to a resource, on behalf of the resource owner by orchestrating an approval interaction. These components are used for securing the custom BD4NRG user interface, Apache Superset and JupyterHub.

The most important **users/stakeholders** of the platform include among others several EPES stakeholders (electrical engineers, data scientists TSOs, DSOs etc.), investors, researchers and policy makers.

4. INDICATIVE USE CASE

A Greek island has hybrid power station of RES storage and a network of smart meters installed on the grid (e.g. in smart buildings). All sensors and smart meters are connected to BD4NRG platform through IoT technologies. A PostgreSQL database named "sensor_values" is used to store data from different kind of smart meters. Each row is identified by the sensor's name and contains the average value of the sensor, the unit of measurement and the date of the measurement. A MongoDB named "sensor_weather" is used to store weather data including forecasts for wind speed, temperature, humidity and pressure along with the timestamp of the measurement. A building manager can use the web interface of BD4NRG Query Engine to query data to assess the average consumption of a building on different weather conditions. The course of action is the following:

The user defines datasets and variables he intends to query: he first selects the datasets to be queried and afterwards the variables he is interested to view. He can also define aggregation for each field (e.g. MAX, AVERAGE, COUNT). In this use case, he selects a smart building dataset located on a Greek island, and afterwards selects to view all sensor values and measurements over time. So, he selects the mean column, which shows the measurement value, the statistic_id column, which indicates what is the measurement of a specific record (e.g. the total energy consumption of a building), the unit of measurement and the date of measurement (upper left section of Figure 2).

The user combines the smart building data with weather data: he selects the weather dataset, along with the variables temperature, wind speed, air pressure and the time of the measurements which will be the field to join with the previous dataset and is common for both data sources (upper right section of Figure 2).

The user intends to view only weather data for the place in which the buildings are located: so, he should define the filters that will be applied on the selected fields. Many kinds of operators are supported, i.e he can select the temperature and define that it should be within a range. The user is also able to combine expressions using logical operators. Finally, he selects to filter by the place (bottom left section of Figure 2).

The user inspects the created query, executes it, views and downloads the results. Once he has finished with the query, he can view the generated SQL, and execute the query. After a couple of seconds, he views the results which are downloadable to a csv file (bottom right section of Figure 2).

Of course, the Query Engine user interface enables many more functionalities such as data aggregations, group by and having statements, multiple joins and filters, limit, ordering and more. However, they will not be presented in the context of this publication. Superset and JupyterHub will not be presented either.

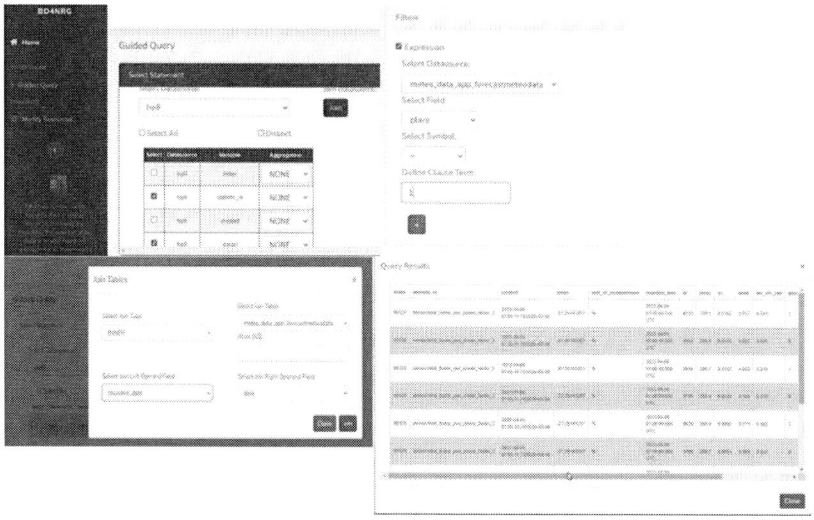

Figure 2. BD4NRG query engine web interface

5. DISCUSSION

BD4NRG Query Engine is a state-of-the-art big data query engine that fulfills all the functional and non-functional requirements of a big data analytics querying component, as presented in section 2. Specifically, in terms of functional requirements, it fulfills the requirement for **integration**, as it is capable of connecting and retrieving data from different and heterogeneous data sources. Moreover, it enables **statistical analysis** (second functional requirement) since it facilitates the creation and efficient execution of aggregation queries and can be used for OLAP. Furthermore, it provides functionalities for **exploration** (3rd functional requirement) through its intuitive user interface, as well as through APIs and a visual analytics service such as Apache Superset, which facilitates further the data exploration though data visualisations and dashboards. Last but not least, the proposed technical solution assists **decision support** (4th functional requirement) through its intuitive user interface, as it helps users build and save their own queries and results, as well as through Apache Superset and its data visualisation, dashboard and reporting capabilities, and also through JupyterHub, which enables users create their own custom services, using the BD4NRG Query Engine.

In terms of non-functional requirements, the proposed solution is **highly scalable** (1st non-functional requirement), as the main technology, that has been selected, is used by some of the largest organisations globally, and can query exabyte scale data lakes. Regarding the requirement for **near real-time monitoring**, the BD4NRG query engine enables not only near real-time monitoring but also near real-time querying, through queries to Kafka streams of data. Last, the proposed query engine is **efficient in terms of resources** (3rd requirement) as Trino is a highly parallel and distributed querying technology that facilitates efficient, low latency analytics queries.

Of course, the proposed query engine goes beyond the aforementioned requirements, as it facilitates also queries to Kafka streams in near real-time data and query federation between different and heterogeneous data sources and technologies. Moreover, it facilitates easy query creation and execution by stakeholders that are not experienced with programming and SQL. Beyond the user interface, the proposed solution provides several capabilities for data visualisations and custom services creation by users. Last but not least, usage of BD4NRG Query Engine is protected through an Access Control and Identity Management service, that secures that a user can view only the resources for which he has permission to view.

Compared to other query engine applications, the proposed one not only focuses on efficient querying of the available resources, but also on the accompanying services for maximizing user profit by providing also an intuitive, user-friendly interface, visual analytics, and custom service creation capabilities. Moreover, it provides security and access control, as these attributes are extremely important on any big data platform. Last but not least, it enables near real-time queries to data streams.

6. CONCLUSSION AND FUTURE OUTLOOK

In the publication at hand, BD4NRG Query Engine application for big data analytics querying to energy related big data was presented. It is a big data querying service that fulfills the requirements of a state-of-the-art big data query engine as presented in literature and constitutes an end-to-end solution on big data querying, providing also visual analytics and custom service creation capabilities as well as an intuitive web interface.

Regarding future extensions of this publication, they include the validation of the presented application on a production environment in terms of user experience, security and stress tests. To this end, also multi-node installations of the querying technologies will be examined. Future work will also employ metrics for benchmarking the time complexity for executing queries, along with the space utilization, to compare the proposed framework against similar approaches using alternative query engines. Moreover, the proposed solution is envisaged to be extended to support also queries against data sources that do not support SQL queries, such as graph databases and ontologies. Moreover, compatibility with IDSA data spaces will be examined to enable efficient and sovereign data sharing among different organisations (Á. Alonso et al., 2018).

ACKNOWLEDGEMENT

This research has been co-funded by European Union's Horizon 2020 research and innovation programme under grant agreement no. 872613.

REFERENCES

Agrawal, R., Kadadi, A., Dai, X., & Andres, F. (2015). Challenges and opportunities with big data visualization. *7th International ACM Conference on Management of Computational and CollEctive Intelligence in Digital EcoSystems, MEDES 2015*. https://doi.org/10.1145/2857218.2857256

Alexakis, K., Kapsalis, P., Mylona, Z., Kormpakis, G., Karakolis, E., Ntanos, C., & Askounis, D. (2022). Intelligent Querying for Implementing Building Aggregation Pipelines. *2022 13th International Conference on Information, Intelligence, Systems & Applications (IISA)*, 1–6. https://doi.org/10.1109/IISA56318.2022.9904384

Alonso, Á., Pozo, A., Cantera, J., de la Vega, F., & Hierro, J. (2018). Industrial Data Space Architecture Implementation Using FIWARE. *Sensors*, *18*(7), 2226. https://doi.org/10.3390/s18072226

Anagnostopoulos, E., Batsakis, S., & Petrakis, E. G. M. (2013). CHRONOS: A Reasoning Engine for Qualitative Temporal Information in OWL. *Procedia Computer Science*, *22*, 70–77. https://doi.org/10.1016/j.procs.2013.09.082

Apache Spark. (n.d.). Unified engine for large-scale data analytics. *Https://Spark.Apache.Org/*.

Atzeni, P., Bugiotti, F., Cabibbo, L., & Torlone, R. (2020). Data modeling in the NoSQL world. *Computer Standards and Interfaces*, *67*. https://doi.org/10.1016/j.csi.2016.10.003

BD4NRG. (2022). *https://www.bd4nrg.eu/*. Https://Www.Bd4nrg.Eu/.

Bohlouli, M., Schulz, F., Angelis, L., Pahor, D., Brandic, I., Atlan, D., & Tate, R. (2013). Towards an integrated platform for big data analysis. In *Integration of Practice-Oriented Knowledge Technology: Trends and Prospectives* (Vol. 9783642344718). https://doi.org/10.1007/978-3-642-34471-8_4

Chui, M., Collins, M., & Patel, M. (n.d.). *IoT value set to accelerate through 2030: Where and how to capture it*. Https://Www.Mckinsey.Com/Capabilities/Mckinsey-Digital/Our-Insights/Iot-Value-Set-to-Accelerate-through-2030-Where-and-How-to-Capture-It.

Endris, K. M., Rohde, P. D., Vidal, M. E., & Auer, S. (2019). Ontario: Federated Query Processing Against a Semantic Data Lake. *Lecture Notes in Computer Science (Including Subseries Lecture Notes in Artificial Intelligence and Lecture Notes in Bioinformatics)*, *11706 LNCS*. https://doi.org/10.1007/978-3-030-27615-7_29

FIWARE. (n.d.). *Identity Manager - Keyrock*. Https://Fiware-Idm.Readthedocs.Io/En/Latest/.

influxdata. (2022). *InfluxDB Time Series Data Platform*. Https://Www.Influxdata.Com/.

Kapsalis, P., Kormpakis, G., Alexakis, K., & Askounis, D. (2022). Leveraging Graph Analytics for Energy Efficiency Certificates. *Energies*, *15*(4), 1500. https://doi.org/10.3390/en15041500

Kapsalis, P., Kormpakis, G., Alexakis, K., Karakolis, E., Mouzakitis, S., & Askounis, D. (2022). A Reasoning Engine Architecture for Building Energy Metadata Management. *2022 13th International Conference on Information, Intelligence, Systems & Applications (IISA)*, 1–7. https://doi.org/10.1109/IISA56318.2022.9904419

Karakolis, E., Alexakis, K., Kapsalis, P., Mouzakitis, S., & Psarras, J. (2022). An end-to-end approach for scalable real time Anomaly detection in smart buildings. *2022 13th International Conference on Information, Intelligence, Systems & Applications (IISA)*, 1–7. https://doi.org/10.1109/IISA56318.2022.9904410

Karakolis, E., Pelekis, S., Mouzakitis, S., Markaki, O., Papapostolou, A., Korbakis, G., & Psarras, J. (2022). Artificial Intelligence for Next Generation Energy Services Across Europe - The I-NERGY Project. *IADIS International Conference E-Society 2022 (e-Society 2022).*

Keycloak. (2022). *Keycloak*. Https://Www.Keycloak.Org/.

Kormpakis, G., Kapsalis, P., Alexakis, K., Pelekis, S., Karakolis, E., & Doukas, H. (2022). An Advanced Visualisation Engine with Role-Based Access Control for Building Energy Visual Analytics. *2022 13th International Conference on Information, Intelligence, Systems & Applications (IISA)*, 1–8. https://doi.org/10.1109/IISA56318.2022.9904353.

Krogh, J. W. (2020). MySQL Workbench. In *MySQL 8 Query Performance Tuning*. https://doi.org/10.1007/978-1-4842-5584-1_11

Linder, L., Vionnet, D., Bacher, J. P., & Hennebert, J. (2017). Big Building Data-a Big Data Platform for Smart Buildings. *Energy Procedia*, *122*. https://doi.org/10.1016/j.egypro.2017.07.354

Marinakis, V. (2020). Big data for energy management and energy-efficient buildings. *Energies*, *13*(7). https://doi.org/10.3390/en13071555

Marinakis, V., & Doukas, H. (2018). An advanced IoT-based system for intelligent energy management in buildings. *Sensors (Switzerland)*, *18*(2). https://doi.org/10.3390/s18020610

MATRYCS. (2022). *The MATRYCS Project*. Https://Matrycs.Eu/.

Mohammed, T. A., Ghareeb, A., Al-Bayaty, H., & Aljawarneh, S. (2019). Big data challenges and achievements: Applications on smart cities and energy sector. *ACM International Conference Proceeding Series*. https://doi.org/10.1145/3368691.3368717

MongoDB. (2022). *MongoDB*. Https://Www.Mongodb.Com/Home.

Motlagh, N. H., Mohammadrezaei, M., Hunt, J., & Zakeri, B. (2020). Internet of things (IoT) and the energy sector. In *Energies* (Vol. 13, Issue 2). https://doi.org/10.3390/en13020494

Nadikattu, R. R. (2020). Data Warehouse Architecture – Leading the next generation Data Science. *International Journal of Computer Trends and Technology*, *67*(9). https://doi.org/10.14445/22312803/ijctt-v67i9p113

pandio. (2021). What's the Difference Between Trino and PrestoDB? *Https://Pandio.Com/Difference-between-Trino-and-Prestodb/.*

Pau, M., Kapsalis, P., Pan, Z., Korbakis, G., Pellegrino, D., & Monti, A. (2022). MATRYCS—A Big Data Architecture for Advanced Services in the Building Domain. *Energies*, *15*(7), 2568. https://doi.org/10.3390/en15072568

Pelekis, S., Karakolis, E., Silva, F., Schoinas, V., Mouzakitis, S., Kormpakis, G., Amaro, N., & Psarras, J. (2022). In Search of Deep Learning Architectures for Load Forecasting: A Comparative Analysis and the Impact of the Covid-19 Pandemic on Model Performance. *2022 13th International Conference on Information, Intelligence, Systems & Applications (IISA)*, 1–8. https://doi.org/10.1109/IISA56318.2022.9904363

PostgreSQL. (2022). *PostgreSQL*. Https://Www.Postgresql.Org/.

Presto. (2022). *Presto: Free, Open-Source SQL Query Engine for any Data*. Https://Prestodb.Io/.

Thein, K. M. M. (2014). Apache Kafka: Next Generation Distributed Messaging System KHIN ME ME THEIN. *International Journal of Scientific Engineering and Technology Rescearch*, *3*(47).

Trino. (2022). *Trino | Distributed SQL query engine for big data*. Https://Trino.Io/.

Zhang, Y., Ren, J., Liu, J., Xu, C., Guo, H., & Liu, Y. (2017a). A Survey on Emerging Computing Paradigms for Big Data. *Chinese Journal of Electronics*, *26*(1), 1–12. https://doi.org/10.1049/cje.2016.11.016

TWINP2G: A DIGITAL TWIN ARCHITECTURE FOR OPTIMAL POWER-TO-GAS PLANNING

Sotiris Pelekis, Elissaios Sarmas, Anna Georgiadou, Evangelos Karakolis, Christos Ntanos, Nikos Dimitropoulos, Georgios Kormpakis and Haris Doukas
Decision Support Systems Laboratory, National Technical University of Athens, Iroon Polytechneiou 9, 15772, Zografou, Greece

ABSTRACT

Power-to-Gas (P2G) is an emerging technology aiming to contribute towards addressing the climate change and environmental degradation. Yet, numerous factors need to be taken into consideration to for practical P2G applications. Digital Twins (DT) are used for simulation and optimization purposes, allowing investigation and prediction of their short-, medium- and long-term results. This paper presents a DT architecture, namely TwinP2G, that aims to couple the electrical power and natural gas sector by enabling multi-resolution simulations and optimization relating to the integration of P2G plants and regenerative hydrogen fuel cells (RHFC) in the power grid. The suggested solution is meant to be applied initially in the Greek energy system enabling data- and simulation-driven P2G and fuel cells optimal planning and techno-economic analyses. This piece of work concludes with future application plans and application development perspectives.

KEYWORDS

P2G, Digital Twin, Hydrogen, Sector Coupling, Natural Gas, Simulation, Optimization

1. INTRODUCTION

Climate change along with the growing population, the increase in electrical energy consumption and the depletion of resources have led to a large-scale deployment of Renewable Energy Sources (RES), increasing their energy share worldwide (Lewandowska-Bernat & Desideri, 2018). Numerous RES technologies have significantly progressed in technical and economic maturity over the past few decades. Yet, their fluctuating and intermittent nature raised concerns related to the balancing and capacity adequacy of an energy supply configuration relying mostly on RES (Varone & Ferrari, 2015). The necessity of increasing the flexibility of the existing bulk system has led researchers to investigate new methodologies to fully exploit the production of RES in the context of water pumping stations (Sarmas, Spiliotis, et al., 2022), supply to the energy system (Karakolis et al., 2022; Mazza et al., 2018) and so on.

Towards that end, the P2G technology has arisen unveiling various possibilities. P2G uses renewable or excess electricity to produce hydrogen via water electrolysis (Robles et al., 2018). This hydrogen can be used directly as a final energy carrier for electricity, mobility (fuel cells powering electric vehicles) and heat, converted to methane, liquid fuels, or chemicals (Gahleitner, 2013) or even stored in fuel cells to be later reconverted into electricity. Thus, they would satisfy the need for long-term energy storage by converting it to other easily storable energy carriers, and at the same time reduce the load of the electricity grid by their controlled operation.

Hydrogen offers a great variety of alternatives in its production, transportation, and distribution. Its multi-dimensional benefits triggered the development of multi-energy systems' modelling approaches to assess the technical, economic, and system-level challenges of integrating hydrogen into the overall energy system (Fu et al., 2020). Terms such as HIGG (Hydrogen Injection into the Gas Grid) soon arose along with a variety of research, modelling and real-life demonstrator projects exploring the possibilities of Green Hydrogen (hydrogen produced by renewable excess) in conjunction with other energy systems (ENTSO-G & ENTSO-E, 2018; Gondal, 2019; Quarton & Samsatli, 2018).

Over the past decades, several P2G plants have been developed (Quarton & Samsatli, 2018), numerous hydrogen demonstration projects have been funded (Diaz-Londono et al., 2020; *Everywh2ere*, 2022; *H2Haul*, 2022), and several studies and research efforts have been documented, exploring green hydrogen's potential and variations. P2G optimization and simulation techniques and models have been used in many scenarios over Europe. This paper aims to present the methodological approach towards developing a P2G digital twin (DT) in Greece with short-, medium- and long-term optimization goals and perspectives.

This paper presents a conceptual DT architecture, namely called TwinP2G, aiming to promote hydrogen and accelerate the energy transition via P2G technologies. Section 2 presents a literature review aiming to shed light on the current state-of-the-art P2G approaches and methodologies, DTs, and relevant software. In Section 3, the case study details, and application architecture are presented. Finally, Section 4 concludes with a discussion relating to the challenges of P2G and future steps related to the research objectives of this.

2. LITERATURE REVIEW

During the last few years many studies have focused on developing several optimization models for P2G applications (Quarton & Samsatli, 2018). Most of them develop complex optimization models, while others focus on simulation. With respect to optimization, the most widely used methods are Linear Programming (LP) (Dodds & Demoullin, 2013), Mixed Integer Linear Programming (MILP) (Almansoori & Shah, 2012) and Non-Linear Programming (NLP) (Clegg & Mancarella, 2016). Simulation, on the other hand, is the process of modeling a scenario and finding the outputs of a system based on a given set of inputs. Such models may run several different scenarios, as in the case of (Abeysekera et al., 2016) which provided a simulation method for gas networks with injection of upgraded biogas and hydrogen. Usually, simulation models are tightly linked with DTs. The selection of the objectives for P2G optimization problems is another interesting aspect. Although most of the developed models target towards minimizing the total operation costs, there are a few focusing on minimizing CO2 emissions (Mesfun et al., 2017) or even fuel consumption (Tabkhi et al., 2008). Moreover, the decisions supported by most of these models focus on long-term policy, proposing the degree of penetration of each technology per year or decade. A thorough techno-economic analysis of P2G scenarios is conducted in (Fambri et al., 2022). It seems that the existing state of the literature shows the urgent need for designing modern, data- or simulation- driven applications and models for assisting the successful penetration of P2G technologies. In this direction, the PLANET project (Schröder et al., 2018) aimed to leverage energy conversion technologies for optimal grid planning towards full energy system decarbonization. Specifically, Diaz-Londono et. al develop a real-time platform for P2G integration in electrical distribution grids, enabling a quasi-automatic creation of case studies and using digital simulation technologies and proprietary software, such as eMEGASIM, RT-LAB, and Matlab / Simulink (Diaz-Londono et al., 2020). Although most studies have focused on the process of converting surplus renewable energy into hydrogen gas, the case of fuel cells should be considered as well. Fuel cells operate like a conventional storage system, differing in that they do not need recharging (Smith, 2000). Fuel cells can produce electricity if enough fuel is supplied, thus being one of the most promising storage solutions for the near future. The optimization models used in the case of fuel cells do not significantly differ from the aforementioned ones. Typical examples of exploited optimization models are multi-objective genetic algorithms (Ehyaei & Rosen, 2019) and multi-objective probabilistic analysis algorithms (Zhou et al., 2022), among others.

With respect to DTs, they comprise digital representations of physical objects (processes, or services) which facilitate the planning, management, and optimization of complex and new activities (Batty, 2018). DTs are recently gaining significant popularity in the energy sector for purposes such as smart grid development, RES management, and distributed generation control (Borowski, 2021). It should be noted that a DT does not make any decisions by itself, but rather generates insights through post-processing that support decision making. As more and more data are becoming available through advancements in IoT devices and smart sensors, the combination of a physical object and its digital mapping in virtual space can be combined with big volumes of data to facilitate informed decision-making in the energy domain. A series of recent studies on DTs for energy-related topics is presented by (Onile et al., 2021). Some of the most recent studies include the development of a DT for hybrid renewable energy systems (Andryushkevich et al., 2019), a regression-based DT for university campus' power supply (Francisco et al., 2020) and DT-based energy management systems (Brosinsky et al., 2018), (Zhou, Yan and Feng, 2019). Gerrard et al. (Gerard et al., 2022) focused on a data-driven DT, for mitigating the uncertainties and risks associated with green hydrogen facilities design as an investment, which also calculates financial indicators (e.g., internal rate of return) through stochastic simulations using the Monte Carlo method.

From a technical perspective, in the domain of P2G oriented optimal grid planning (simulation and optimization), several open-source tools are currently available and used within a multitude of related research studies. A rather extensive review of those tools can be found in the PyPSA whitepaper (Brown et al., 2017). Indicatively, open-source grid simulation tools include PyPSA, Pandapower (Thurner et al., 2018), MATPOWER (Zimmerman et al., 2011) and DPSIM (Mirz et al., 2019), while Pandapipes (Lohmeier et al., 2020) can serve in creating coupled power and natural gas systems (Lu et al., 2021; Qadrdan, 2012). Several of them, such as PyPSA also include cost-based optimization capabilities usually leveraging optimization techniques and specifically tools such as Pyomo (Bynum et al., 2021). Some well-known solvers for linear programming are GLPK, CPLEX, and Gurobi (Meindl & Templ, 2014) and they can be used in these scenarios. Regarding macroscopical and long-term modelling and optimization, a variety of energy system modelling tools that are usually disconnected from optimal power flow analysis and are most linked with national energy planning strategies, are available. Linear programming remains the dominant optimization method within this scope of these applications, such as OseMosys (Howells et al., 2011) (written in GNU MathProg), Nemo (SEI, 2020) (written in Julia), and EnergyPLAN EU (Lund et al., 2021) (written in Delphi Pascal).

3. CASE STUDY AND APPLICATION ARCHITECTURE

The proposed case study takes place in Greece in the context of the ENERSHARE (*Enershare | The Energy Data Space for Europe*, 2022) project funded by the EC and involves both the natural gas and electrical power national transmission and distribution networks managed by DESFA (Desfa, 2022 and IPTO (IPTO, 2022) respectively. The objective of the case study is to form a digital simulation and optimization platform, named TwinP2G, coupling the electricity transmission system with natural gas demands, leveraging a DT architecture that will enable multi-resolution simulations involving P2G technologies and regenerative hydrogen fuel cells (RHFC) (Pellow et al., 2015). TwinP2G will enable data- and simulation-driven P2G and RHFC optimal planning for using the RES surplus for green hydrogen production via electrolysis.

3.1 High-Level Architecture

The TwinP2G architecture is shown in Figure 1. A Platform-as-a-Service (PaaS) design is proposed. The architecture serves multiple user roles while it is composed of various subcomponents using a many state-of-the-art technologies that is further analyzed in the following sections.

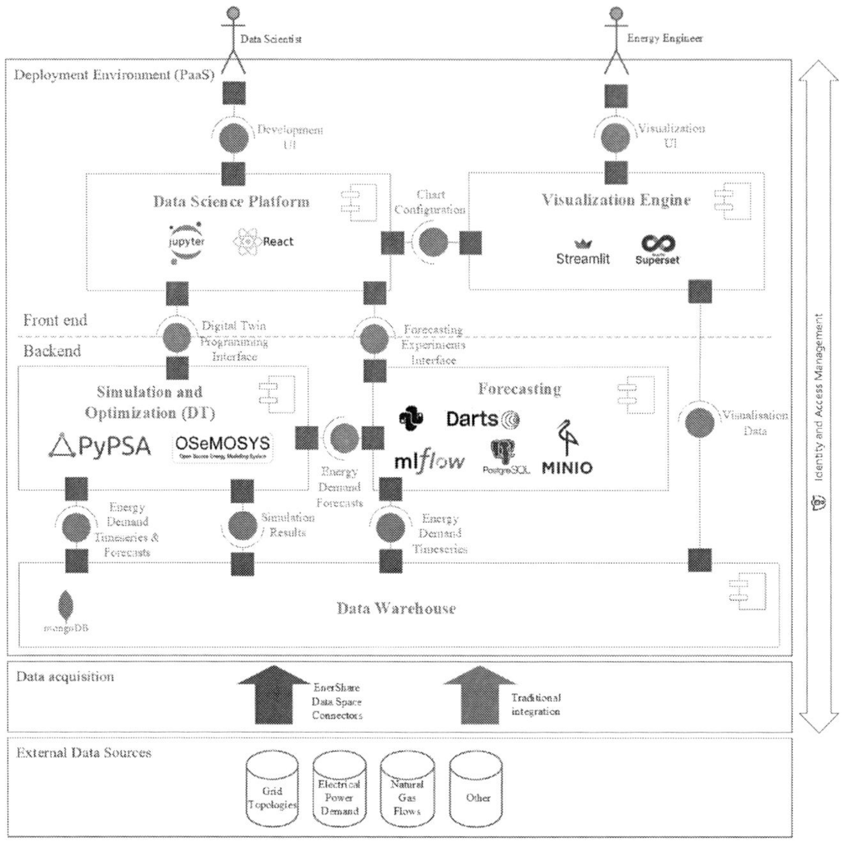

Figure 1. The high-level architecture of TwinP2G

3.1.1 Data Sources and Integration Process

For developing a DT application, data integration is a core process. It enriches the local data warehouse with new datasets that in turn improve the results of its main functionalities, therefore leading to up-to-date forecasts and simulation scenarios. TwinP2G mainly employs integration mechanisms based on Data Connectors (*IDSA Data Connector Report*, 2022; Qarawlus et al., 2021), as established by International Data Spaces (IDSA) (Otto et al., 2019) that will be further developed within the ENERSHARE project. In the conceptual architecture of Figure 1, TwinP2G receives data from IPTO (electrical power demand, RES generation, long-term grid planning, electrical grid topologies), DESFA (hourly / daily gas flows at entry and exit points, natural gas grid topologies) and other organizations (e.g. Eurostat, local and national grid topologies etc.) through Dataspace Connectors. Specifically, it acts as a data consumer, while the other organizations act as data providers. All the organizations involved need have a dataspace connector deployed in their infrastructure. Of course, traditional data ingestion methods are followed whenever the development of bidirectional Data Connectors is not feasible.

3.1.2 Multi-Horizon Simulation and Optimization

The Simulation core of the DT application involves physics- and data- driven simulation and optimization capabilities, allowing for extensive techno-economic analyses. In this context, the PyPSA open-source power system modelling tool is used as the short-term / mid-term simulation and optimization core of the DT. PyPSA can serve optimal power flow simulation based on network equations, security constraints and even least-cost (investment) optimization. Amongst the available models P2G and storage units with efficiency losses (suitable for RHFC) are of specific interest for the use case in question. Regarding multi-horizon dynamic investment optimization over several years (long-term projection), as PyPSA seems to have fallen behind, the OSeMOSYS open-source modelling system is selected, as it enables long-run integrated assessment and energy planning, also suitable for crisis modelling (Karamaneas A. et al., 2022). From a mathematical perspective, OSeMOSYS is a deterministic, long-term modeling framework based on linear optimization (linear programming and mixed-integer linear programming). The "Simulation and Optimization" component processes historical time series of renewable generation and production alongside power and gas demands originating from the data warehouse. It also uses forecasts produced by the "Forecasting" component creating projections within an optimization horizon. Local grid topologies in Greece with envisaged investments for P2G components is the main field of study within the "Simulator and Optimization" component. Pandapipes will also be considered if gas pipeline simulation is deemed necessary through the progress of the use case. With respect to optimization objectives, the following will be investigated in terms of optimal capacity and location: electrolysers (ENTSO-E, 2022), fuel cells, methanation reactors and hydrogen buffers (storage).

3.1.3 Forecasting

The forecasting component of TwinP2G is an MLOps (Sridhar et al., 2021) framework that has been developed within the I-NERGY H2020 project (Karakolis et al., 2022). The toolkit is based on a machine learning pipeline written in Python programming language that enables experimentation and evaluation of various machine learning and deep learning algorithms, such as XGBoost, Random Forest, NBEATS, Temporal Convolutional Networks (TCN) and Long Short-Term Memory (LSTM) networks as demonstrated in a recent work that dealt with a short-term load forecasting use case (Pelekis et al., 2022). The main technologies leveraged are MLflow (Alla & Adari, 2021) as the MLops platform, Darts (Herzen et al., 2021) as the time series forecasting framework, MinIO (MinIO, 2022) and PostgreSQL (PostgreSQL, 2022) as artifact storage and logging database respectively, FastAPI (*FastAPI*, 2022) as the API development framework, Javascript React (*React*, 2022) for developing the front-end. The forecasting platform in question can handle all type of time series and integrate new datasets with little to no extra development, hence allowing to easily handle the timeseries data ingested in TwinP2G (see Section 3.2.1) and providing forecasts of various (short-, mid-, long-term) horizons. Moreover, supplementing the existing forecasting models, novel practices in the field of machine learning can be used, including incremental analytics for periodically re-training existing models (Sarmas, Strompolas, et al., 2022), as well as transfer learning to handle cases with insufficient data (Sarmas, Dimitropoulos, et al., 2022).

3.1.4 Application Front-end and Security Framework

TwinP2G serves two main user roles/personas. The first persona is the "Data Scientist", who is assumed to be an experienced user with scientific and coding background alongside modelling capabilities of P2G use cases. This user can enter the "Data Science Platform" provided by TwinP2G to interface with the "Simulation and Optimization" component to develop P2G experiments and visualize their results (simulation and optimization results, forecasting accuracies, etc.). Additionally, the "Data Scientist" can configure the desired types of interactive analytics visualizations to be displayed to the Energy Engineer persona. Specifically, Streamlit (*Streamlit*, 2022) is a candidate high-level technology for serving this purpose. However, more advanced technologies, such as Apache Superset (*Superset*, 2022) and MATRYCS (Pau et al., 2022) Visualization Engine (Kormpakis et al., 2022) are also under investigation. The second persona is the "Energy Engineer" who is considered an end-user with knowledge and understanding of energy systems but limited coding and modelling skills. This persona uses the "Visualization Engine" component to monitor simulation and forecast results and metrics leveraging them for decision support regarding future P2G investments.

Ultimately, an identity/access management mechanism is the basis of TwinP2G's security. This has end-to-end processes, approaches, and technologies for user identification, authentication, and authorization. They ensure that the personas are allowed to access the appropriate resources. For this, the Keycloak (*Keycloak*, 2022) technology has been considered.

4. DISCUSSION

This work proposes a conceptual, innovative DT architecture, named TwinP2G to promote hydrogen and to accelerate the energy transition through P2G technologies. TwinP2G allows modelling multiple scenarios for green hydrogen production and storage as a flexibility provider and as an enabler for higher RES integration (directly through hydrogen fuel cells indirectly through the gas pipeline). The architecture has four main components, namely: i) a data warehouse that integrates open data mainly through IDSA technologies; ii) a simulation platform with state-of-the-art power and energy simulation and optimization technologies; iii) an MLOps-powered forecasting toolkit, for profiling, analyses and forecasts of electricity and gas quantities; iv) a front-end application that serves two user roles; a) a data scientist that can perform simulations and experiments by coding and b) an energy expert with limited coding skills that can inspect and visualize the high-level experiment results.

In conclusion, TwinP2G envisages addressing and overcoming some significant challenges posed in (ENTSO-G & ENTSO-E, 2018). Specifically, TwinP2G is expected to accelerate the learning curve effect within the P2G sector, allowing for experimentation with higher installed capacities at lower production rates of synthetic gas, hence contributing to the vision of much higher installed capacity by 2030. Finally, given that the current framework of regulations, market incentives and tariffs in Greece have not taken into account at all the opportunity of P2G, seasonal storage and other technologies. TwinP2G is expected to also promote the relevant national energy policies by establishing an innovative simulation platform that enables the experimentation with use cases that had been unfeasible until now.

ACKNOWLEDGEMENT

This work has been funded by the European Union's Horizon Europe research and innovation programme under the ENERSHARE project, Grant Agreement No 101069831.

REFERENCES

Abeysekera, M., Wu, J., Jenkins, N., & Rees, M. (2016). Steady state analysis of gas networks with distributed injection of alternative gas. Applied Energy, 164, 991–1002.

Alla, S., & Adari, S. K. (2021). Beginning MLOps with MLFlow. Apress.

Almansoori, A., & Shah, N. (2012). Design and operation of a stochastic hydrogen supply chain network under demand uncertainty. International Journal of Hydrogen Energy, 37(5), 3965–3977.

Andryushkevich, S. K., Kovalyov, S. P., & Nefedov, E. (2019). Composition and application of power system digital twins based on ontological modeling. IEEE International Conference on Industrial Informatics (INDIN), 2019-July, 1536–1542.

Batty, M. (2018). Digital twins. Environment and Planning B: Urban Analytics and City Science, 45(5), 817–820.

Borowski, P. F. (2021). Digitization, Digital Twins, Blockchain, and Industry 4.0 as Elements of Management Process in Enterprises in the Energy Sector. Energies 2021, Vol. 14, Page 1885, 14(7), 1885.

Brosinsky, C., Westermann, D., & Krebs, R. (2018). Recent and prospective developments in power system control centers: Adapting the digital twin technology for application in power system control centers. 2018 IEEE International Energy Conference, ENERGYCON 2018, 1–6.

Brown, T., Hörsch, J., & Schlachtberger, D. (2017). PyPSA: Python for Power System Analysis. Journal of Open Research Software, 6(1).

Bynum, M. L., Hackebeil, G. A., Hart, W. E., Laird, C. D., Nicholson, B. L., Siirola, J. D., Watson, J.-P., & Woodruff, D. L. (2021). Pyomo — Optimization Modeling in Python (Vol. 67). Springer International Publishing.

Clegg, S., & Mancarella, P. (2016). Storing renewables in the gas network: modelling of power-to-gas seasonal storage flexibility in low-carbon power systems. IET Generation, Transmission & Distribution, 10(3), 566–575.

Desfa. (2022). DESFA S.A. - desfa.gr. https://www.desfa.gr/en/

Diaz-Londono, C., Fambri, G., Mazza, A., Badami, M., & Bompard, E. (2020). A Real-Time Based Platform for Integrating Power-to-Gas in Electrical Distribution Grids. UPEC 2020 - 2020 55th International Universities Power Engineering Conference, Proceedings.

Digital twin and its application to power grid online analysis. (2019). CSEE Journal of Power and Energy Systems.

Dodds, P. E., & Demoullin, S. (2013). Conversion of the UK gas system to transport hydrogen. International Journal of Hydrogen Energy, 38(18), 7189–7200.

Ehyaei, M. A., & Rosen, M. A. (2019). Optimization of a triple cycle based on a solid oxide fuel cell and gas and steam cycles with a multiobjective genetic algorithm and energy, exergy and economic analyses. Energy Conversion and Management, 180, 689–708.

Enershare | The Energy Data Space for Europe. (2022). https://enershare.eu/

ENTSO-E. (2022). New ENTSO-E paper on the Role of Hydrogen - Facts about System Integration. https://www.entsoe.eu/2021/11/29/entso-e-publishes-new-paper-the-role-of-hydrogen-facts-about-system-integration/

ENTSO-G, & ENTSO-E. (2018). Power to gas | ENTSOG. https://www.entsog.eu/power-gas

Everywh2ere. (2022). https://www.everywh2ere.eu/

Fambri, G., Diaz-Londono, C., Mazza, A., Badami, M., Sihvonen, T., & Weiss, R. (2022). Techno-economic analysis of Power-to-Gas plants in a gas and electricity distribution network system with high renewable energy penetration. Applied Energy, 312, 118743.

FastAPI. (2022). https://fastapi.tiangolo.com/

Francisco, A., Asce, S. M., Mohammadi, N., Asce, A. M., Taylor, J. E., & Asce, M. (2020). Smart City Digital Twin–Enabled Energy Management: Toward Real-Time Urban Building Energy Benchmarking. Journal of Management in Engineering, 36(2).

Fu, P., Pudjianto, D., Zhang, X., & Strbac, G. (2020). Integration of Hydrogen into Multi-Energy Systems Optimisation. Energies 2020, Vol. 13, Page 1606, 13(7), 1606.

Gahleitner, G. (2013). Hydrogen from renewable electricity: An international review of power-to-gas pilot plants for stationary applications. International Journal of Hydrogen Energy, 38(5), 2039–2061.

Gerard, B., Carrera, E., Bernard, O., & Lun, D. (2022). Smart Design of Green Hydrogen Facilities: A Digital Twin-driven approach. E3S Web of Conferences, 334, 02001.

Gondal, I. A. (2019). Hydrogen integration in power-to-gas networks. International Journal of Hydrogen Energy, *44*(3), 1803–1815.

H2Haul. (2022). https://www.h2haul.eu/

Herzen, J., Lässig, F., Piazzetta, S. G., Neuer, T., Tafti, L., Raille, G., van Pottelbergh, T., Pasieka, M., Skrodzki, A., Huguenin, N., Dumonal, M., Kościsz, J., Bader, D., Gusset, F., Benheddi, M., Williamson, C., Kosinski, M., Petrik, M., & Grosch, G. (2021). Darts: User-Friendly Modern Machine Learning for Time Series.

Howells, M., Rogner, H., Strachan, N., Heaps, C., Huntington, H., Kypreos, S., Hughes, A., Silveira, S., DeCarolis, J., Bazillian, M., & Roehrl, A. (2011). OSeMOSYS: The Open Source Energy Modeling System. An introduction to its ethos, structure and development. Energy Policy, 39(10), 5850–5870.

IDSA Data Connector Report. (2022). https://internationaldataspaces.org/idsa-data-connector-report-published/

IPTO. (2022). Independent Power Transmission Operator | IPTO. https://www.admie.gr/en

Karakolis, E., Pelekis, S., Mouzakitis, S., Markaki, O., Papapostolou, K., Korbakis, G., & Psarras, J. (2022). Artificial Intelligence for Next Generation Energy Services Across Europe - THE I-NERGY PROJECT. ES 2021 : 19th International Conference e-Society 2021, 61–68.

Karamaneas A., Koasidis K., Frilingou N., Xexakis G., Nikas A., & Doukas H. (2022). A stakeholder-informed modelling study of Greece's energy transition amidst an energy crisis: the role of natural gas and climate ambition [Under Review]. Renewable & Sustainable Energy Transition.

Keycloak. (2022). https://www.keycloak.org/

Kormpakis, G., Kapsalis, P., Alexakis, K., Pelekis, S., Karakolis, E., & Doukas, H. (2022). An Advanced Visualisation Engine with Role-Based Access Control for Building Energy Visual Analytics. 13th International Conference on Information, Intelligence, Systems and Applications, IISA 2022.

Lewandowska-Bernat, A., & Desideri, U. (2018). Opportunities of power-to-gas technology in different energy systems architectures. Applied Energy, 228, 57–67.

Lohmeier, D., Cronbach, D., Drauz, S. R., Braun, M., & Kneiske, T. M. (2020). Pandapipes: An Open-Source Piping Grid Calculation Package for Multi-Energy Grid Simulations. Sustainability 2020, Vol. 12, Page 9899, 12(23), 9899.

Lu, Y., Pesch, T., & Benigni, A. (2021). Simulation of coupled power and gas systems with hydrogen-enriched natural gas. Energies, 14(22).

Lund, H., Thellufsen, J. Z., Østergaard, P. A., Sorknæs, P., Skov, I. R., & Mathiesen, B. V. (2021). EnergyPLAN – Advanced analysis of smart energy systems. Smart Energy, 1, 100007.

Mazza, A., Bompard, E., & Chicco, G. (2018). Applications of power to gas technologies in emerging electrical systems. Renewable and Sustainable Energy Reviews, 92, 794–806.

Meindl, B., & Templ, M. (2014). Analysis of commercial and free and open source solvers for linear optimization problems. http://www.statistik.tuwien.ac.at

Mesfun, S., Sanchez, D. L., Leduc, S., Wetterlund, E., Lundgren, J., Biberacher, M., & Kraxner, F. (2017). Power-to-gas and power-to-liquid for managing renewable electricity intermittency in the Alpine Region. Renewable Energy, 107, 361–372.

MinIO. (2022). MinIO | High Performance, Kubernetes Native Object Storage. https://min.io/

Mirz, M., Vogel, S., Reinke, G., & Monti, A. (2019). DPsim—A dynamic phasor real-time simulator for power systems. SoftwareX, 10, 100253.

Onile, A. E., Machlev, R., Petlenkov, E., Levron, Y., & Belikov, J. (2021). Uses of the digital twins concept for energy services, intelligent recommendation systems, and demand side management: A review. Energy Reports, 7, 997–1015.

Otto, B., Hompel, M., & Wrobel, S. (2019). International Data Spaces. Digital Transformation, 109–128.

Pau, M., Kapsalis, P., Pan, Z., Korbakis, G., Pellegrino, D., & Monti, A. (2022). MATRYCS—A Big Data Architecture for Advanced Services in the Building Domain. Energies 2022, Vol. 15, Page 2568, 15(7), 2568.

Pelekis, S., Karakolis, E., Silva, F., Schoinas, V., Mouzakitis, S., Kormpakis, G., Amaro, N., & Psarras, J. (2022). In Search of Deep Learning Architectures for Load Forecasting: A Comparative Analysis and the Impact of the Covid-19 Pandemic on Model Performance. 2022 13th International Conference on Information, Intelligence, Systems & Applications (IISA), 1–8.

Pellow, M. A., Emmott, C. J. M., Barnhart, C. J., & Benson, S. M. (2015). Hydrogen or batteries for grid storage? A net energy analysis. Energy & Environmental Science, 8(7), 1938–1952.

PostgreSQL. (2022). PostgreSQL | The world's most advanced open source database. https://www.postgresql.org/

Qadrdan, M. (2012). Modelling of an Integrated Gas and Electricity Network with Significant Wind Capacity.

Qarawlus, H., Hellmeier, M., Pieperbeck, J., Quensel, R., Biehs, S., & Peschke, M. (2021). Sovereign Data Exchange in Cloud-Connected IoT using International Data Spaces. Proceedings - 2021 IEEE Cloud Summit, Cloud Summit 2021, 13–18.

Quarton, C. J., & Samsatli, S. (2018). Power-to-gas for injection into the gas grid: What can we learn from real-life projects, economic assessments and systems modelling? Renewable and Sustainable Energy Reviews, 98, 302–316.

React. (2022). https://reactjs.org/

Robles, J. O., Almaraz, S. D. L., & Azzaro-Pantel, C. (2018). Hydrogen as a pillar of the energy transition. Hydrogen Supply Chain: Design, Deployment and Operation, 3–35.

Sarmas, E., Dimitropoulos, N., Marinakis, V., Mylona, Z., & Doukas, H. (2022). Transfer learning strategies for solar power forecasting under data scarcity. Scientific Reports 2022 12:1, 12(1), 1–13.

Sarmas, E., Spiliotis, E., Marinakis, V., Tzanes, G., Kaldellis, J. K., & Doukas, H. (2022). ML-based energy management of water pumping systems for the application of peak shaving in small-scale islands. Sustainable Cities and Society, 82, 103873.

Sarmas, E., Strompolas, S., Marinakis, V., Santori, F., Bucarelli, M. A., & Doukas, H. (2022). An Incremental Learning Framework for Photovoltaic Production and Load Forecasting in Energy Microgrids. Electronics 2022, Vol. 11, Page 3962, 11(23), 3962.

Schröder, A., Kahlen, C., Martino, M., & Papanikolaou, A. (2018). The EU Research Project PLANET. Smart Microgrids.

SEI. (2020). NEMO: the Next Energy Modeling system for Optimization - SEI. https://www.sei.org/projects-and-tools/tools/nemo-the-next-energy-modeling-system-for-optimization/

Smith, W. (2000). The role of fuel cells in energy storage. Journal of Power Sources, 86(1–2), 74–83.

Sridhar, ©, Suman, A., Adari, K., Alla, S., & Adari, S. K. (2021). What Is MLOps? Beginning MLOps with MLFlow, 79–124.

Streamlit. (2022). https://streamlit.io/

Superset. (2022). https://superset.apache.org/

Tabkhi, F., Azzaro-Pantel, C., Pibouleau, L., & Domenech, S. (2008). A mathematical framework for modelling and evaluating natural gas pipeline networks under hydrogen injection. International Journal of Hydrogen Energy, *33*(21), 6222–6231.

Thurner, L., Scheidler, A., Schafer, F., Menke, J. H., Dollichon, J., Meier, F., Meinecke, S., & Braun, M. (2018). Pandapower - An Open-Source Python Tool for Convenient Modeling, Analysis, and Optimization of Electric Power Systems. IEEE Transactions on Power Systems, 33(6), 6510–6521.

Varone, A., & Ferrari, M. (2015). Power to liquid and power to gas: An option for the German Energiewende. Renewable and Sustainable Energy Reviews, 45, 207–218.

Zhou, L., Zhang, F., Wang, L., & Zhang, Q. (2022). Flexible hydrogen production source for fuel cell vehicle to reduce emission pollution and costs under the multi-objective optimization framework. Journal of Cleaner Production, 337, 130284.

Zimmerman, R. D., Murillo-Sánchez, C. E., & Thomas, R. J. (2011). MATPOWER: Steady-state operations, planning, and analysis tools for power systems research and education. IEEE Transactions on Power Systems, 26(1), 12–19.

TOWARDS INCLUSIVE DIGITAL DEMOCRACY: A CONCEPTUAL FRAMEWORK FOR DIGITAL CITIZEN PARTICIPATION

Jonas Fegert
Karlsruhe Institute of Technology, FZI Research Center for Information Technology, Haid-und-Neu-Street 10-14, 76131 Karlsruhe, Germany

ABSTRACT

E-Participation, a subfield of Digital Government, has fallen short of initial expectations. Despite its potential to enhance democratic processes, it has struggled with inclusivity, particularly with respect to gender, class, and race. This paper proposes the concept of Digital Citizen Participation, which is contrasted with e-Participation research. It is argued that participatory processes can be improved by integrating diverse research disciplines, adopting user-centered design approaches that prioritize the citizen as a user, and incorporating technological innovations such as immersive systems. Thereby, the Digital Citizen Participation framework aims to provide theoretical guidance for public participation in the digital age.

KEYWORDS

Digital Citizen Participation, e-Participation, Digital Democracy, Digital Government, Platform Design

1. INTRODUCTION

In 2021, Meta Platforms presented their vision of the Metaverse, sparking a polarized debate about the future of the digital world. Some see the Metaverse as a promising new environment, while others view it as a potential threat to our already polarized world (Barbaro et al., 2022; Tengtrakool, 2021; Verdi, 2022).[1] However, if the Metaverse becomes the next big thing, who will assure that it is a democratic and deliberative space? Those questions echo the expectations and concerns surrounding the internet at the beginning of the 2000s (Gimmler, 2001), when online social networks (ONS) were seen as promising deliberative spaces that could assist populations in organizing democratic protests and resistance (Wolfsfeld et al., 2013). Unfortunately, these expectations have been diminished in recent years and reached a new low with the acquisition of Twitter through Elon Musk. The transaction highlights the dangers and fragility of allowing private platform operators to control public discourse. Twitter, once seen as a progressive alternative, has experienced a surge in hate speech, disinformation, and misinformation (Frenkel and Conger, 2022; Lavelle, 2022). This underscores the urgent need to continue the search for truly deliberative digital spaces.

E-Participation, as part of e-Government studies, has failed to meet the expectations set for them in their early stages. In 2008 Scholl pointed out how e-Government and its subordinated e-Services were perceived in its initial stages as a novelty in itself. A novelty that was overloaded with expectations that were already back then "seemingly losing its magic" (Scholl, 2008). In the beginning of the 2020s, the relevance of participatory Government services became – due to the pandemic – evident (United Nations, 2020). Nevertheless, the pandemic also showed manifold challenges. Offering digital and independent services for meaningful interactions between citizens and the state seems to be one of the great challenges of this decade. Nevertheless, the e-Participation frameworks does not seem to fit adequately to the challenges of this time: Big Tech has changed the expectations towards platforms and usability dramatically. Through using digital innovations in hard - and software design, including network-effects and gamification, they attract millions of user and

[1] This paper consist on two chapters from a dissertation on the topic of Digital Citizen Participation and how immersive systems might be used for participatory urban planning (Fegert, 2022). Submitting the paper to the e-Society conference 2023 should assist to discuss the concept in a broader setting with the respective scientific community.

successfully keep them on their platform. Their platform mechanism also manage to work across various social groups and milieus. A reality that does not seem to be the same case for e-Participation, where the participants tend to be a rather exclusive group of people. Kim and Lee (2019) found that gender differences exists in the use of e-Participation. Furthermore, motivating factors for public participation through digital means, as identified by Rottinghaus and Escher (2020) and Novo Vázquez and Vincente (2019), include previous political involvement and personal interest or concern of the involved citizens and therefore conclude that the platforms are not being inclusive towards the broader public.

This paper, therefore argues to put the citizen, as the user of digital participation platforms, in the focus of research instead of looking at questions of public engagement from the perspective of governmental units. Thus, it is argued to introduce Digital Citizen Participation (DCP) as a new concept to match the increasingly growing field of Digital Democracy research. This new concept addresses the limitations of e-Participation by incorporating interdisciplinarity, technological innovativeness, interoperability, and an inclusive participatory approach. Furthermore, the DCP framework will prioritize the utilization of cutting-edge technologies, including immersive technologies, public displays, and mobile platform solutions, to enhance public participation in the digital age.

2. THEORETICAL BACKGROUND

E-Participation is defined as the use of information and communication technologies (ICT) to extend and transform participation in democratic and consultative processes. Its goal is to support active citizenship through technology developments that increase access to and availability of participation in order to promote a fair and efficient society and government. E-Participation is a sub-branch of Digital Government research, also known as e-Government. E-Democracy or Digital Democracy, as defined by Van Dijk and Hacker (2000), is a collection of attempts to practice democracy without the limitations of time, space, and other physical conditions, using ICT as an addition to traditional political practices rather than a replacement. The theory of the public sphere by Jürgen Habermas is often used as the theoretical foundation for e-Participation research in Information Systems. Sanford and Rose (2007) argue that e-Participation should improve communication and decision-making between politicians, civil servants, citizens, and other stakeholders. Macintosh (2004) identifies three levels of participation in e-Participation: e-Enabling, e-Engaging, and e-Empowering. E-Enabling is the accessibility and understandability of information, e-Engaging is a top-down approach where citizens are consulted on policy issues, and e-Empowering is a bottom-up approach where citizens can influence policy-making through their contributions and become producers of policy rather than just consumers. Van Dijk (2012) created a classification system for forms of e-Participation that is still relevant for most e-participation platforms available. This classification differentiates between "government-centric" and "citizen-centric approaches" (Van Dijk and Hacker, 2000). In summary, e-Participation research made an important contribution to defining the field of research, to highlighting various online participation modes, and to pointing out both the opportunities and the initial pitfalls and disillusionments.

3. THE DIGITAL CITIZEN PARTICIPATION TRIANGLE

Since the creation of the first online participation platforms, new technological innovations emerged and entered the mass-market. Interconnectivity (often through various devices) became in many societies the status quo. Access to the digital technologies is not anymore the limiting factor when it comes to digital participation. Internet and hardware access became not only mainstream, but in certain societies a necessity for social inclusion. Therefore, today the main limiting factor to make use of state-of-the-art technologies are resources and knowledge. The main initiators (governmental agencies) still seem to lack competences when it comes to designing and developing artifacts. To overcome those limiting factors, the concept of DCP should give guidance on designing public participation for the digital age. Today, there are plenty of technological possibilities – although their applicability still needs to be researched and proven. In the following, three key features of Digital Citizen Participation should be defined. These include interdisciplinarity in research and development, technological innovativeness and interoperability, as well as incorporating, an inclusive democratic approach.

3.1 Interdisciplinarity as a Means to Counter Dominant Platform Mechanisms

The normative ideal of deliberative democracies, as it is presented by Habermas, aims at transforming the needs of citizens from an individual level towards an orientation for the common good (Young, 2004). However, an objective assessment of the common needs can only happen if the inclusion of a diversity of perspectives is ensured since only the different perspectives reflect the pluralistic societies in which we live (Young, 2004). Sanford and Rose (2007) already suggested research disciplines, which should play a role in broadening the perspective on e-Participation. Following the authors, communicational science, computer science, information systems, political philosophy, political science, public administration and sociology are research disciplines, that should be involved in research on political participation using ICT. In contrast to Sanford and Rose, this paper argues, that those disciplines should be involved in the process platform design itself. For non-tokenistic and successful forms of political participation in the digital age, it is necessary to include different disciplines into designing platforms. Thereby a platform logic can be established, that does not purely follow full profit market mechanisms.

Platforms such as Facebook, Uber and Airbnb pursue the goal of winning against the competition in their industry. They strive for dominance, as this increases the attractiveness of their networks. Therefore, they are dependent on reaching a certain dominance if they want to operate their platforms sustainably (Srnicek, 2016) In recent times, calls for regulation of platform providers grew more vocal. For example, Scott Galloway, a professor of business administration, called for large Internet companies to be broken up and suggested that the U.S. Department of Justice should take appropriate measures (Galloway, 2018). But how could this point be reached? In his book "Platform Capitalism" Srnicek (2016) points out that the commercialization tendencies of platform providers would not have been possible without the collapse of the dot-com bubble in the early 2000s. Its collapse forced internet companies to shed their investor earnings. While Google still used user data to improve its search function in its early years, the company began to use the data for targeted advertising after the collapse of the dotcom bubble (Srnicek, 2016).

Therefore, it seems clear that the current factors that measure the success and value of platforms need to be revisited when it comes to designing platforms for societal participation of the public in political affairs. In the following, an exemplary framework for the involvement of different disciplines in platform design for DCP is suggested (Figure 1). Thereby, it is argued, that the mentioned disciplines can become with their methods, in DCP, part of the design process itself. This could help to counter dominant platform mechanisms. If participation processes are to be implemented (more) successfully, then the translation work between disciplines is crucial and should be implemented in platform design for DCP.

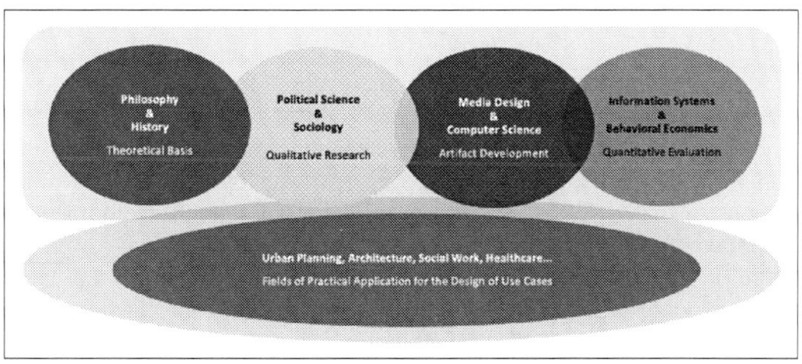

Figure 1. Interdisciplinarity in Digital Citizen Participation

Including the **philosophic and historic** context into platform design does not seem to be an obvious choice. Nevertheless, what is the benefit of including this perspective when starting designing DCP? What is to be considered an ideal form of discourse and public is something suggested and debated in (political) philosophy and history of thought. Habermas theory of the deliberative public still is the theoretical foundation for scientific work on public participation. Every work must either incorporate or differentiate itself from this theoretical basis. Including those core thoughts of how a deliberative form of participation can be reached in a digital setting, is something already acknowledged in early literature on e-Participation (Sanford and Rose, 2007).

Furthermore, it should be argued to put platform design in a historic context to become aware of the origins of some phenomena in the present. A genealogical approach takes a contemporary question as the starting point of analysis and thus makes historical processes and orders of knowledge visible for a critique of the present (Kerchner, 2006). To give an example: Foucault's first volume on "Security, Territory, Population" (Foucault, 2006) deals, in regard to the 18th century, with security mechanisms and the relationship between law and norm, as well as how techniques of empiricism and probability theory took hold. The origins of empiricism are of interest for an examination of current digital platforms, as their algorithms are based on data collection and probability calculations in order to implement, for example, recommender systems. Statistics and empirical data appear as a new instrument of power for the state in the eighteenth-century (Kerchner, 2006). If we want to be aware of the instruments of power of today's economy and the internet corporations as a cornerstone of this economy, we cannot avoid being aware of the origin of these mechanisms. The mechanisms of power can be consciously taken up or intentionally avoided in platform design, but being aware of them, seems necessary.

A core part of DCP is the incorporation of **sociological** methods and methods from **political science**. Especially qualitative methods used and developed in these disciplines can help to develop realistic and true-to-life platform designs. When it comes to designing platforms that should not only be adopted by a specific demographic or sociological milieu, the detection of exclusion mechanisms is key. Therefore, using qualitative methods from those disciplines is especially advantageous. Trust in government and different understandings of the role of government and state have an impact on the willingness to participate (Lee and Schachter, 2019). Evidently, those conditions vary from place to place and are also differential within a state. For this reason, it is important to explore those different starting conditions to design digital participation accordingly. Moreover, for understanding different participation paths and formats, the knowledge of political specifics on a local and federal level is crucial. Understanding political systems and structures on a local and communal level, consequently, appears necessary for the design of DCP. Political science and related disciplines such as public policy and governance have a profound understanding of those political realities and therefore can and should contribute by staking out the framing conditions.

The most obvious disciplines involved with the design of DCP are those who are practically involved with constructing the artifact. The expertise of **media design and informatics** are necessary for the development of advanced and attractive platforms. Structuring the process of artifact design is well researched in information systems. Using methods like Design Science Research based on Peffers (2007) or Kuechler and Vaishnavis framework (2008) which are helpful to structure the design, development and evaluation of a software project. Other methods like participatory software design, a method explored since the 1990s, also puts the user in the center of the development process (Bossen et al., 2016; Mueller et al., 2018; Sanders et al., 2010). Various current system programming approaches seem necessary in informatics for developing DCP projects. A precondition for developing those artifacts is expertise in one or several of the following development fields: backend-, frontend-, full-stack-web and mobile device-development, as well as data science. To conduct and coordinate smooth software engineering processes, today agile forms of software development, which can be found in frameworks like Scrum and Kanban, seem adequate for the development of DCP. Especially the following basics of agile development are fitting to software developments which should cater the needs of a broader population: customer satisfaction, prioritizing software operability and simplicity over complexity (Hazzan and Dubinsky, 2014). When it comes to more complex developments (e.g. adapting voting mechanisms) platforms are built by those who have a clear understanding of roles and access control. This knowledge is crucial for writing fitting code. For this reason, it seems necessary to include information systems and informatics in developing DCP. Design experts, such as graphic and media designers, should assure that the information provided within the DCP platform are presented in a thoughtful and pleasant way. Norman describes in his book "The Design of Every Day Things" (2013) the importance of considerate design choices. Including design experts can help, when it comes for example to forms, typography and color schemes to create user friendly platforms. Therefore, their expertise is crucial for successful platform design.

In their book "The Power of Experiments – Decision Making in Data Driven World" Luca and Bazerman (2020) show how mainstream behavioral economics became as a way for platform providers to test, evaluate and improve their platforms. The authors demonstrate that systemic experimentation is something which e-Commerce businesses can conduct even more easily compared to classical businesses, since their businesses rely on the systemic processing of data. In contrast, however, the authors also provide insights on how traditional institutions, such as government agencies, use experimentation to achieve successful policy making. As an example they present experiments conducted by British government agencies under Tony Blair and David Cameron with the aim of nudging citizens into paying taxes. To name one success: through randomized controlled trials they rewrote and -designed letters asking the citizens to pay their taxes and thereby assured significantly higher tax revenues (Luca and Bazerman, 2020).

Finally, it is necessary to involve those disciplines that have the real-world expertise for use cases. This could be found among others in social work, healthcare, but are in many cases of public participation **urban** or respectively **spatial planning** as well as **architecture**. The latter named disciplines can support designing DCP by adding their knowledge on participatory urban planning as well as construction projects. Including those disciplines means to tackle current questions of urbanism together with the affected citizens. Furthermore, including architecture as a discipline might contribute to design architectural competitions in a way that they are mindful about a possible digital participation process. Thereby, architects can use digital formats that guarantee interoperability between their architectural designs and possible digital participation platforms.

For DCP, it should be argued, that it seems important to engineer platforms that are easy to use and well accepted by the users. Those firms, who design digital participation platforms, tend to not have the resources to research and test the effectiveness of their products. Accordingly, the initiators of digital participation processes might have to become more active in asking for research on the effectiveness of their participatory programs. In experiments it could be researched and established which mechanisms work to keep a broad demographic interested in participating, as e.g. mechanisms of gamification might help to foster interactions on participation platforms. Since governmental agencies are, especially in larger urban contexts, often overwhelmed with the task to create meaningful interactions with their citizens, having perspectives from **psychology, behavioral economics and information systems**, included in the design of DCP seems essential. If communicated properly to the software developers involved, it could enhance the general user experience of the artifact. Nevertheless, experimental methods have to be used carefully and consensual. Therefore, involving an ethics committee can be of assistance to become aware of certain ethical challenges that might arise. Instead of running experiments without knowledge and proper consent of the participants, like some tech companies do, there are other options to test platforms in realistic settings. Besides field experiments, behavioral economic labs pose a valid alternative for conducting ambitious and ethically responsible experiments.

Using data based on experiments can be very powerful for improving platform design. Nevertheless, this power could be – in the hand of state agencies, as shown with the historic example of the eighteenth century – misused by states to control their citizens. Thus, it can be concluded, that using experiments in DCP should be generally about designing software artifacts that empower citizens by making them as useable as possible.

This paragraph can be understood as a plea for the translation work between a number of different disciplines. It is argued that connecting different theories and methods from philosophy, history, sociology, political science, information systems, informatics and behavioral economics and psychology can help to create meaningful DCP artifacts that truly are in the citizens interest. Through this incorporation of a pluralistic perspectives on platform design, the transformation of individual needs and requirements towards the common good could be realized.

3.2 Technological Innovations and Interoperability

In the following, the discrepancy in platform design innovations that exist between current e-Participation and other digital platforms, should be highlighted. The pleasant world of Android and iOS apps, as well as e-Commerce platforms, made customers used to seamless and user-centered platform design. When it comes to games or commerce the adoption of technological innovations, like immersive systems, is in full swing. Already in 2016, a former branch of Google, Ninantic, launched the app Pokémon Go which combined location based GPS technology with AR (Paavilainen et al., 2017). Ikea created with their app Places, for both mobile phone operating systems, a popular app for the visualization of the Ikea furniture catalogue in the homes of their customers using AR. A meta-study on the effectiveness of virtual shopping environments, has already established that the use of the immersive Ikea app increased the customers general interest in products and a purchase (Alves and Luís Reis, 2020). With its rebranding respectively its restructuring from Facebook into Meta, the platform giant also announced to put the company's efforts into immersive systems (Roose, 2021). Apple in contrast broadened the spectrum of its hardware from notebook and desktop computers to portable music players to phones, tablets and watches, which are all connected (Jacobsen, 2017). Google pioneered from early on with collaborative cloud services like Google Docs, Forms etc. and thereby shifted the industry towards comparable cloud solutions.

Compared to this world of technological innovations, what can be found in e-Participation today seems relatively dull. With the new concept of DCP it is reasoned, that the integration of state-of-the-art technologies and hardware needs to become part of designing digital participation platforms. As the results on the acceptance of immersive systems (Fegert, 2022; Fegert et al., 2020) show, there is great interest and curiosity when it comes to using different technologies for public participation.

Another necessity for enabling DCP seems to be system **interoperability**. This wish for high interoperability appears to stand in contrast to the claim for innovative artifacts, but it is the other way around: Interoperability means to be mindful about different access towards technology and to bridge existing gaps between systems and frameworks and thereby making platforms as usable and accessible as possible. Key in including broad parts of the population in participation processes is assuring the ability to use the platform from different operating systems, browsers and hardware. Especially in the search for common standards in e-Government, interoperability has been discussed, mostly for unique states like Brazil (Alves Oliveira and Eler, 2017), South Africa (Manda, 2017) and Uganda (Kanagwa et al., 2018). As a general takeaway of those studies it can be concluded that there is a need for some standardization, which is mindful of different access to soft- and hardware. To guarantee social cohesion, also in DCP the standards need to be as basic as possible to be attentive towards those users who have older soft- and hardware or only use a certain kind of hardware like mobile devices. What should be argued for is a differentiation between classical e-Participation platforms, and something that could be considered to be the next generation of digital participation platforms in DCP. Thiel et al. (2018) already explored some technological innovation and trends such as using smartphones, GPS, wearables, public displays, immersive systems and crowdsourcing. Furthermore, the authors discussed gamification in e-Participation (Thiel, 2016; Thiel et al., 2018) as a promising concept to assure the interest of the population in public participation. That kind of innovative inclusion of up to date technologies is meant, when arguing for more play- and joyful use of technologies and their incorporation into public participation processes.

The German platform "Stimmen auf Knopfdruck" (2021), developed for a participation process in the city of Berlin, made use of an already existing and widely used technology – voice messages. Citizens could leave their comments additionally to classical written content through a recording. Although a study on the effectiveness of this technology is missing, the idea of opening up the dialogue to new forms of interactions seems promising, especially, when it comes to the inclusiveness of participation processes and the question who feels entitled to participate. Another interesting example is the platform Senf.Koeln (2021) developed by UPLab, which placed QR Codes in the city of Cologne and showed an interactive map on a mobile device only webpage to allow the use on the spot of interest. Those specifics alone turned what is shown as a standard upside down: the participation process was accessed through mobile devices, making it more accessible at the site. It can certainly be a barrier to re-envision an urban planning debate at home. Offering opportunities for on-site debates therefore seems overdue. This paragraph argued for more interoperability and including technological innovations into participation processes.

3.3 Incorporating an Inclusivity in the Development Process

According to Habermas, the "political public sphere [...] can fulfill its function of perceiving and addressing problems of society as a whole [...] only to the extent that it is formed from the communication contexts of those potentially affected. It is carried by an audience recruited from the entirety of citizens" (Habermas, 1992, p. 441). The politically relevant challenges are thus based on processes of public negotiation. According to Habermas, they have their origin in the "biographical experiences" (Habermas, 1992, p. 441) the citizens who come together to form such an audience. Therefore, equal access to the public sphere seems to be of central importance for deliberation (Schmidt, 2019). However, studies on e-Participation processes in Germany show that men participate more often than women and that the degree of participation depends, among other things, on the level of education (Rottinghaus and Escher, 2020; Send et al., 2014). This assessment is not at all satisfactory, considering that public participation is supposed to enable an equal discourse between all citizens and decision-making processes for them. As already mentioned and discussed when arguing for using approaches (theories and methods) from sociology and political science, the last pilar of DCP, suggested in this paper, is the inclusion of inclusive democratic approaches.

Online participation undoubtedly created new opportunities to quantitatively involve more citizens, but it seems unclear whether this also leads to more inclusive participation (Schlozman et al., 2018). Qualitative research methods from social science are often used to investigate the inclusivity of deliberative participation platforms (Frisch, 2007; Kies, 2010; Weinhardt et al., 2015). There are obvious mechanisms of exclusion, that come to mind, like the use of language. In German, through the generic masculine version of the third person, the gender neutrality is not given as a default. Weinhardt et al. (2015) therefore rightly pointed out that the use of gender neutral language can promote inclusion. Other language-based aspects need to become center of attention. While, especially in journalism, web accessibility, is already in the focus of research (Giannoumis and Nordli, 2020; Karhunen, 2017), a debate about accessibility of digital participation platforms is urgently needed. How can it be achieved to be mindful about language barriers and how can they be overcome? How can plain language be used to be sensible towards citizens with special needs? Already in 2015, Weinhardt et al. suggested to use translation tools to include parts of the population that do not feel confident about their language skills when it comes to written debate-based e-Participation forums. Also, the platform design itself can be more or less inclusive. Certain color schemes can exclude citizens who are not able to differentiate between certain colors. Here it is reasoned, that the inclusion of a diverse set of citizens into the design of DCP platforms can prevent mechanism of exclusion. A concrete method of inclusion is presented within arguing for qualitative social science methods.

Why does this seem relevant? What is missing when it comes to platform design in Digital Government services is that user-centric design should mean to keep the broader population in mind – in this case all involved stakeholders of the participation processes. There seems to be some kind of misunderstanding, as it appears unclear if the current mostly forum-based e-Participation platforms succeed in catering the needs of the broader population. Some kind of hesitancy in e-Participation concerning technological innovations seems obvious. Although, in 2021 mobile devices are globally clearly the preferred form of internet access and interaction and the one with the higher market share compared to desktops (Enge, 2021; Petrov, 2019), e-Participation platforms continue to be mostly browser based with interfaces that are predominantly made for notebook and desktop computers. Including the realities of general hardware usage into the platform design itself can help to overcome some of those non-inclusive tendencies described by researchers. The fact that the population prefers the casualness of using their mobile devices, should be utilized for public participation. In this case too, research on journalism and technology can help understanding how to create inclusivity (and thereby general relevance) through platform design. Mobile applications showed great potential for local journalism as well as challenges in the example of local news sites in Portugal. Accessibility remains an issue not easily resolved (Santos Gonçalves et al., 2021). Therefore, evaluating platform design and including a pluralistic set of voices into the design process seems highly relevant if digital participation processes claim to be democratic and representative.

Furthermore, new technological possibilities open up new forms of approaching citizens. Advanced data analytics can be used to get in contact with the relevant stakeholder groups in a participation process or can help to target unrepresented or underrepresented groups. Obviously, the practice of advanced data analytics and targeting is debatable. Due to the fact that mostly right-wing extremist took and take advantage of those technological practices (King, 2019; Ramos and Torres, 2020; Wylie, 2019), those who would like to foster democratic practices with their platforms also must become aware of those technics and using data analytics for guaranteeing representativity.

4. CONCLUSION

In this paper’s introduction, the need to explore platform alternatives for the Digital Democracy was highlighted. At such an economically and politically difficult moment, platform operators who do not fulfill their legal duties and obligations (e.g. content moderation regarding hate speech) are a serious threat to democracy. Also due to this vulnerable situation, it appears worthwhile to develop platform alternatives for citizens and their concerns. This paper's contribution lies in the exploration of the conceptual framework of DCP. Thereby, a framework for researching innovative and interdisciplinary forms of Digital Democracy is mapped out and a differentiation between classical e-Participation platforms and DCP platforms created. DCP aims at proving a framework that argues for the necessity of interdisciplinary research approaches, when designing digital public participation formats. It maps out a design framework which includes a variety of academic disciplines and their research methods (philosophy, history, political science, sociology, media design, computer science, information systems and behavioral economics, as well as fields of practical application like urban planning and architecture). Furthermore, the DCP framework pleads for the incorporation of technological innovations (like immersive systems) and guaranteeing interoperability. However, this is only with the aim of reducing access barriers and enabling more inclusive participation. Finally, since e-Participation flourishes even in authoritarian regimes (Åström et al., 2012), DCP makes a strong case for incorporating an inclusive democratic approach in the platform design itself. Thus, with DCP, this paper made the argument to adapt the idea of e-Participation in favor of a modern understanding of digital participation platforms and thereby paving the way for a second wave of digital participation.

As already pointed out by Thiel et al. (2018), there are other promising technological innovations (e.g. smart watches and public displays), which could further be researched and explored for the context of public participation. The latter is currently investigated in a citizen science research project, where researchers also experiment with chatbots for citizen involvement (Greif-Winzrieth and Gau, 2021). The results of this project might be worth considering in future investigations. Especially in the field of human-computer interaction, the attention to inclusivity needs to be a cornerstone of information systems research. Hevner et al. (2004) argued that "[t]he goal of behavioral science research is truth. The goal of design science research is utility" (Hevner et al., 2004, p. 80). If utility is the aspiration of this popular information systems research method, a focus on the inclusiveness of digital participation platforms and processes has to become a major part of further design science research, especially in the field of digital democracy.

REFERENCES

Alves, C., Luís Reis, J., 2020. The Intention to Use E-Commerce Using Augmented Reality - The Case of IKEA Place, in: Rocha, Á., Ferrás, C., Montenegro Marin, C.E., Medina García, V.H. (Eds.), Information Technology and Systems, Advances in Intelligent Systems and Computing. Springer International Publishing, Cham, pp. 114–123. https://doi.org/10.1007/978-3-030-40690-5_12

Alves Oliveira, A.D., Eler, M.M., 2017. Strategies and Challenges on the Accessibility and Interoperability of e-Government Web Portals: A Case Study on Brazilian Federal Universities, in: 2017 IEEE 41st Annual Computer Software and Applications Conference (COMPSAC). pp. 737–742. https://doi.org/10.1109/COMPSAC.2017.222

Åström, J., Karlsson, M., Linde, J., Pirannejad, A., 2012. Understanding the rise of e-participation in non-democracies: Domestic and international factors. Government Information Quarterly 29, 142–150. https://doi.org/10.1016/j.giq.2011.09.008

Barbaro, M., Guillemette, D., Bonja, R., Krupke, E., Ploeg, L.V., Benoist, M., Chow, L., Powell, D., Lozano, M., Ittoop, E., 2022. Microsoft and the Metaverse.

Bossen, C., Dindler, C., Iversen, O.S., 2016. Evaluation in participatory design: a literature survey, in: Proceedings of the 14th Participatory Design Conference: Full Papers - Volume 1, PDC '16. Association for Computing Machinery, New York, NY, USA, pp. 151–160. https://doi.org/10.1145/2940299.2940303

Enge, E., 2021. Mobile vs. Desktop Usage in 2020 [WWW Document]. URL https://www.perficient.com/insights/research-hub/mobile-vs-desktop-usage (accessed 12.29.21).

Fegert, J., 2022. Digital Citizen Participation: Involving Citizens Through Immersive Systems in Urban Planning [WWW Document]. https://doi.org/10.5445/IR/1000147640

Fegert, J., Pfeiffer, J., Peukert, C., Golubyeva, A., Weinhardt, C., 2020. Combining e-Participation with Augmented and Virtual Reality: Insights from a Design Science Research Project, in: ICIS 2020 Proceedings.

Foucault, M., 2006. Die Geburt der Biopolitik. Geschichte der Gouvernementalität II: Geschichte der Gouvernementalität II. Vorlesungen am Collège de France 1978/1979, 5. Auflage [2017]. ed. Suhrkamp Verlag, Frankfurt am Main.

Frenkel, S., Conger, K., 2022. Hate Speech's Rise on Twitter Is Unprecedented, Researchers Find. The New York Times.

Frisch, A., 2007. Das Potenzial deliberativer Demokratietheorie für die Konzeptionalisierung von Demokratie in der Europäischen Union. ZPol 17, 711–733. https://doi.org/10.5771/1430-6387-2007-3-711

Galloway, S., 2018. The four: the hidden DNA of Amazon, Apple, Facebook, and Google. Penguin.

Giannoumis, G.A., Nordli, L.H., 2020. Institutionalizing Universal Design: How Organizational Practices Can Promote Web Accessibility, in: Stephanidis, C., Antona, M., Gao, Q., Zhou, J. (Eds.), HCI International 2020 – Late Breaking Papers: Universal Access and Inclusive Design, Lecture Notes in Computer Science. Springer International Publishing, Cham, pp. 87–102. https://doi.org/10.1007/978-3-030-60149-2_8

Gimmler, A., 2001. Deliberative democracy, the public sphere and the internet. Philosophy & Social Criticism 27, 21–39. https://doi.org/10.1177/019145370102700402

Greif-Winzrieth, A., Gau, M., 2021. MyResearchChallenge.digital - A Participatory Problem Discovery System for Citizen Design Science Research, in: Chandra Kruse, L., Seidel, S., Hausvik, G.I. (Eds.), The Next Wave of Sociotechnical Design, Lecture Notes in Computer Science. Springer International Publishing, Cham, pp. 112–117. https://doi.org/10.1007/978-3-030-82405-1_13

Habermas, J., 1992. Faktizität und Geltung: Beiträge zur Diskurstheorie des Rechts und des demokratischen Rechtsstaats, 7th ed, Suhrkamp Taschenbuch Wissenschaft. Suhrkamp, Frankfurt am Main.

Hazzan, O., Dubinsky, Y., 2014. The Agile Manifesto, in: Hazzan, O., Dubinsky, Y. (Eds.), Agile Anywhere: Essays on Agile Projects and Beyond, SpringerBriefs in Computer Science. Springer International Publishing, Cham, pp. 9–14. https://doi.org/10.1007/978-3-319-10157-6_3

Hevner, A.R., March, S.T., Park, J., Ram, S., 2004. Design Science in Information Systems Research. MIS Quarterly 28, 75–105. https://doi.org/10.2307/25148625

Jacobsen, N., 2017. Die Apple WatchApple Watch: Das erste neue Produkt in fünf Jahren, in: Jacobsen, Nils (Ed.), Das Apple-Imperium 2.0: Die neuen Herausforderungen des wertvollsten Konzerns der Welt. Springer Fachmedien, Wiesbaden, pp. 147–152. https://doi.org/10.1007/978-3-658-09548-2_32

Kanagwa, B., Nakatumba-Nabende, J., Mugwanya, R., Kigozi Kahiigi, E., Ngabirano, S., 2018. Towards an Interoperability e-Government Framework for Uganda, in: Odumuyiwa, V., Adegboyega, O., Uwadia, C. (Eds.), E-Infrastructure and e-Services for Developing Countries, Lecture Notes of the Institute for Computer Sciences, Social Informatics and Telecommunications Engineering. Springer International Publishing, Cham, pp. 16–28. https://doi.org/10.1007/978-3-319-98827-6_2

Karhunen, P., 2017. Closer to the story? Accessibility and mobile journalism. Reuters Institute for the Study of Journalism. University of Oxford.

Kerchner, B., 2006. Wirklich Gegendenken. Politik analysieren mit Michel Foucault, in: Foucault: Diskursanalyse der Politik. VS Verlag für Sozialwissenschaften, pp. 145–164. https://doi.org/10.1007/978-3-531-90475-7_7

Kies, R., 2010. Promises and Limits of Web-Deliberation. Palgrave Macmillan US : Imprint: Palgrave Macmillan, New York.

Kim, S., Lee, J., 2019. Gender and E-Participation in Local Governance: Citizen E-Participation Values and Social Ties. International Journal of Public Administration 42, 1073–1083. https://doi.org/10.1080/01900692.2019.1575669

King, K., 2019. Education, digital literacy and democracy: the case of Britain's proposed 'exit' from the European Union (Brexit). Asia Pacific Educ. Rev. 20, 285–294. https://doi.org/10.1007/s12564-019-09594-0

Kuechler, B., Vaishnavi, V., 2008. On theory development in design science research: anatomy of a research project. European Journal of Information Systems 17, 489–504. https://doi.org/10.1057/ejis.2008.40

Lavelle, T., 2022. The Musk Bump: Quantifying the rise in hate speech under Elon Musk [WWW Document]. Center for Countering Digital Hate | CCDH. URL https://counterhate.com/blog/the-musk-bump-quantifying-the-rise-in-hate-speech-under-elon-musk/ (accessed 1.7.23).

Luca, M., Bazerman, M.H., 2020. The power of experiments: decision making in a data-driven world, First editon. ed. The MIT Press, Cambridge, Massachusetts.

Macintosh, A., 2004. Characterizing E-Participation in Policy-Making, in: Proceedings of the Proceedings of the 37th Annual Hawaii International Conference on System Sciences (HICSS'04) - Track 5 - Volume 5, HICSS '04. IEEE Computer Society, Washington, DC, USA, p. 50117.1-.

Manda, M.I., 2017. Towards "Smart Governance" Through a Multidisciplinary Approach to E-government Integration, Interoperability and Information Sharing: A Case of the LMIP Project in South Africa, in: Janssen, M., Axelsson, K., Glassey, O., Klievink, B., Krimmer, R., Lindgren, I., Parycek, P., Scholl, H.J., Trutnev, D. (Eds.), Electronic Government, Lecture Notes in Computer Science. Springer International Publishing, Cham, pp. 36–44. https://doi.org/10.1007/978-3-319-64677-0_4

Mueller, J., Lu, H., Chirkin, A., Klein, B., Schmitt, G., 2018. Citizen Design Science: A strategy for crowd-creative urban design. Cities 72, 181–188. https://doi.org/10.1016/j.cities.2017.08.018

Norman, D.A., 2013. The design of everyday things, Revised and expanded edition. ed. Basic Books, New York, New York.

Novo Vázquez, A., Vicente, M.R., 2019. Exploring the Determinants of e-Participation in Smart Cities, in: Rodríguez Bolívar, M.P., Alcaide Muñoz, L. (Eds.), E-Participation in Smart Cities: Technologies and Models of Governance for Citizen Engagement. Springer International Publishing, Cham, pp. 157–178. https://doi.org/10.1007/978-3-319-89474-4_8

Paavilainen, J., Korhonen, H., Alha, K., Stenros, J., Koskinen, E., Mayra, F., 2017. The Pokémon GO Experience: A Location-Based Augmented Reality Mobile Game Goes Mainstream, in: Proceedings of the 2017 CHI Conference on Human Factors in Computing Systems, CHI '17. ACM, New York, NY, USA, pp. 2493–2498. https://doi.org/10.1145/3025453.3025871

Peffers, K., Tuunanen, T., Rothenberger, M.A., Chatterjee, S., 2007. A Design Science Research Methodology for Information Systems Research. Journal of Management Information Systems 24, 45–77. https://doi.org/10.2753/MIS0742-1222240302

Petrov, C., 2019. 51 Mobile Vs Desktop Usage Stats You Should Know in 2021 [WWW Document]. TechJury. URL https://techjury.net/blog/mobile-vs-desktop-usage/ (accessed 12.29.21).

Ramos, J.M., Torres, P., 2020. The Right Transmission: Understanding Global Diffusion of the Far-Right. Populism 3, 87–120. https://doi.org/10.1163/25888072-BJA10001

Roose, K., 2021. The Metaverse Is Mark Zuckerberg's Escape Hatch. The New York Times.

Rottinghaus, B., Escher, T., 2020. Mechanisms for inclusion and exclusion through digital political participation: Evidence from a comparative study of online consultations in three German cities. Zeitschrift für Politikwissenschaft 30, 261–298. https://doi.org/10.1007/s41358-020-00222-7

Sanders, E., Brandt, E., Binder, T., 2010. A framework for organizing the tools and techniques of participatory design, in: Proceedings of the 11th Biennial Participatory Design Conference, PDC '10. Association for Computing Machinery, New York, NY, USA, pp. 195–198. https://doi.org/10.1145/1900441.1900476

Sanford, C., Rose, J., 2007. Characterizing eParticipation. International Journal of Information Management 27, 406–421. https://doi.org/10.1016/j.ijinfomgt.2007.08.002

Santos Gonçalves, T., Ivars-Nicolás, B., Martínez-Cano, F.J., 2021. Mobile Applications Accessibility: An Evaluation of the Local Portuguese Press. Informatics 8, 52. https://doi.org/10.3390/informatics8030052

Schmidt, M.G., 2019. Beteiligungsfreundliche Demokratietheorie: Partizipation und Deliberation, in: Schmidt, M.G. (Ed.), Demokratietheorien: Eine Einführung. Springer Fachmedien, Wiesbaden, pp. 227–244. https://doi.org/10.1007/978-3-658-25839-9_15

Scholl, H.J. (Jochen), 2008. Discipline or Interdisciplinary Study Domain? Challenges and Promises in Electronic Government Research, in: Chen, H., Brandt, L., Gregg, V., Traunmüller, R., Dawes, S., Hovy, E., Macintosh, A., Larson, C.A. (Eds.), Digital Government: E-Government Research, Case Studies, and Implementation, Integrated Series In Information Systems. Springer US, Boston, MA, pp. 21–41. https://doi.org/10.1007/978-0-387-71611-4_2

Send, H., Ebert, J., Friesike, S., Gollatz, K., Schildhauer, T., 2014. Online Mitmachen und Entscheiden–Partizipationsstudie 2014. Berlin: Alexander von Humboldt Institut für Internet und Gesellschaft.

Srnicek, N., 2016. Platform Capitalism. Polity, Cambridge, UK ; Malden, MA.

Stimmen Auf Knopfdruck, 2021. Offen für Neues: Das Rathaus der Zukunft [WWW Document].

Tengtrakool, M., 2021. Owning the Metaverse: Blockchain Democracy in a Virtual World [WWW Document]. Harvard Technology Review. URL https://harvardtechnologyreview.com/2021/08/22/owning-the-metaverse-blockchain-democracy-in-a-virtual-world/ (accessed 1.31.22).

Thiel, S., 2016. A Review of Introducing Game Elements to e-Participation, in: 2016 Conference for E-Democracy and Open Government (CeDEM). Presented at the 2016 Conference for E-Democracy and Open Government (CeDEM), pp. 3–9. https://doi.org/10.1109/CeDEM.2016.14

Thiel, S.-K., Fröhlich, P., Sackl, A., 2018. Nutzerorientierte Gestaltung von interaktiver E-Partizipation, in: Leitner, M. (Ed.), Digitale Bürgerbeteiligung: Forschung und Praxis – Chancen und Herausforderungen der elektronischen Partizipation. Springer Fachmedien Wiesbaden, Wiesbaden, pp. 127–161. https://doi.org/10.1007/978-3-658-21621-4_6

United Nations, 2020. Embracing digital government during the pandemic and beyond [WWW Document]. Economic Analysis & Policy Division. URL https://www.un.org/development/desa/dpad/publication/un-desa-policy-brief-61-covid-19-embracing-digital-government-during-the-pandemic-and-beyond/ (accessed 4.22.20).

UPLab, 2021. Senf.Koeln [WWW Document]. URL senf.koeln

Van Dijk, J.A.G.M., 2012. Digital democracy: Vision and reality. Innovation and the Public Sector 19, 49–62. https://doi.org/10.3233/978-1-61499-137-3-49

Van Dijk, J.A.G.M., Hacker, K.L. (Eds.), 2000. Digital democracy: issues of theory and practice. SAGE, London Thousand Oaks, Calif.

Verdi, B., 2022. Welcome to the Metaverse: The Peril and Potential of Governance. Fair Observer.

Weinhardt, C., Lenk, A., Hellmanns, A., Niemeyer, C., Wagenknecht, T., 2015. Gute Beispiele für Online-Bürgerbeteiligung an der Parlamentsarbeit – Gutachten für den Deutschen Bundestag.

Wolfsfeld, G., Segev, E., Sheafer, T., 2013. Social Media and the Arab Spring: Politics Comes First. The International Journal of Press/Politics 18, 115–137. https://doi.org/10.1177/1940161212471716

Wylie, C., 2019. Mindf*ck: Cambridge Analytica and the Plot to Break America. Random House Publishing Group.

Young, I.M., 2004. Situated Knowledge and Democratic Discussions, in: Andersen, J., Siim, B. (Eds.), The Politics of Inclusion and Empowerment: Gender, Class and Citizenship. Palgrave Macmillan UK, London, pp. 19–35. https://doi.org/10.1057/9781403990013_2

DESIGN PRINCIPLES FOR PUBLIC DELIBERATION SYSTEMS

Georgia Rokkou, Vassilios Tsakanikas and Vassilios Triantafyllou
Electrical and Computer Engineering Department, University of Peloponnese Megalou Alexandrou 1, GR26334, Patra, Greece

ABSTRACT

In this report, various categories of e-deliberation systems are researched and the most widely used e-deliberation systems developed worldwide are analyzed. Some types of degree of participation are described as they are supported during the process of a discussion. A questionnaire is presented, from which certain results were extracted in order to design a system based on user preferences.

KEYWORDS

E-Deliberation, E-Democracy, Participation, Transparency, Informed

1. INTRODUCTION

The expectation that information technology will enrich democracy is one that has been on the surface for many years, as discussed in broader terms through the democratizing power of concepts such as the «WorldBrain» (Wells, 1937) or the «MemexMachine» (Bush, 1945), (Barnet, 2013).

In our time this is no longer just theoretical but also empirical and realistic. There is a widespread concern about the removal of citizens from the government. Democratic citizens need reasons for solitary reflection, ways of thinking cut off from political strife (Talisse, 2021). Democracy is a system of government governed by certain constituent conditions and guiding principles, where citizens exercise power through a voting process (Tangian, 2020).

E-democracy is a well-known term that describes a wide range of practices, including the online engagement of the public in political decision-making and opinion-making. (Kneuer, 2016) But as far as the theoretical concepts of democracy are concerned, e-democracy is based primarily on models of participatory and deliberative democracy. (Päivärinta & Sæbø, 2006)

Public deliberation expresses views on any scope, priorities for new initiatives or evaluation of existing policies and legislation. (Solomon & Abelson, 2012)

The introduction of deliberative elements can delay decision making, but it can also create smart solutions and creative moves beyond the impasse. (Dryzek, et al., 2019)

There are many deliberative systems, but most of them do not follow the basic principles of democracy.

In the present work we mapping the area of e-deliberation as well as to export some functional requirements that such systems should have, based on the needs of users.

The research contribution of this work is that, at least from our experience, there is no other corresponding axis comparison of systems as well as there are no recent studies looking at the needs of users for such systems. The aim is to create a system that can combine as many basic principles as possible in order to create a successful e-deliberation.

In section 2 we present and describe the different categories of e-deliberation systems as we analyze the types and degrees of participations of some e-deliberation systems, while in section 3 we present the design of the questionnaire in four pillars. In section 4 we talk about the results and functional specifications that resulted from the processing of the questionnaire. Finally, we see discussion and future work.

2. STATE OF THE ART

There are different categories of e-deliberation systems that can be used, depending on the subject of the discussion, the goals, the profile and the experience of the participants and the coordinators in the relevant processes, but also the general characteristics of the environment in which all these take place.

The main formats of such systems include the following categories.

- **Online forums.** Their main use is for large-scale public discussions and consultations, especially when several people can participate in a discussion at the same time. They can also be used for information, for debate on an issue as well as for decision making by voting. The technology they use includes e-voting, text messaging, e-polls, etc. (Holtz, Kronberger, & Wagner, 2012)
- **Deliberative poll.** The deliberative poll is used specifically to form an opinion. The selection of samples is random but representative of the citizens. There is a discussion, where there is a thorough presentation of views and the community also participates through the transmission of the media. But it does not create the feeling of wide participation but requires a lot of time from those involved.
- **Votes.** E-deliberations voting is usually part of deliberations where the combination of voting and deliberation is achieved. In most deliberations, the impact on public policy is indirect and difficult to exploit. The aim is to influence public opinion and to include them in policy-making beyond those who show interest in such issues and processes.
- **Discussion.** The goal of deliberative discussion is to create a means of attracting people and communities for dialogue with each other. Essentially, a deliberative discussion asks participants to discuss and evaluate the impact of a variety of solution options on a public problem. (Cavalier, Kim, & Sam Zais, 2009)
- **Questionnaires (e-surveys).** By creating structured questionnaires, it is possible for everyone to participate, anonymously or by name. The mass participation is positive of the electronic surveys and the analysis of the results is easy and immediate as it can give long-term results. Questions should be asked with great care and the answers should be relatively simple.

To conduct this structured research review, an analysis of the most widely used e-deliberation systems developed worldwide to find the most relevant and important studies in the field was applied. Based on (Tsakanikas, Rokkou, & Triantafyllou, 2022) the main systems that are involved in deliberative processes are e-dialogos, Mi Senado, Parlement et Citoyens, E-Democracia, Liquid Feedback, DebateHub, Online Consultation Platform (GR0059) and DESIDIM.

Table 1. Types of e-deliberation services. Analyzes what different categories of deliberation systems the systems follow

Systems / Types	e-dialogos	Mi Senac	Parlement et Citoyens	E-Democracia	Liquid Feed back	Debate Hub	Online Consultation Platform (GR0059)	DESIDIM
Questionnaires	✓							
Forum	✓			✓		✓		✓
DeliberativePoll	✓	✓			✓	✓		
Discussion	✓	✓	✓	✓	✓		✓	✓
Vote							✓	✓

E-dialogos and DESIDIM systems seem to be the systems that include most types of e-deliberation services. As it seems to a very large extent most systems follow the service of discussion.

The process of a deliberation is followed by some types of degree of participation in which in each of them the participants and the result between the different systems change.

Some of the types of degree participation of such systems are the following.

- **Issue.** The issue that is open to deliberation can be submitted by different users, depending on the system.
- **Proposal.** The proposals that will be submitted are addressed to open issues, in order to display the views of users.
- **Survey.** The survey of the process in such a system.
- **Output.** The output of each system.
- **Scope.** The way each system will utilize the results of such a deliberation.

Table 2. Degree of participations

System / Types	e-dialogos	Mi Senado	Parlement et Citoyens	E-Democracia	Liquid Feed back	Debate Hub	Online Consultation Platform (GR0059)	DESIDIM
Issue	Authority	Authority	Authority	Coordinator	All	Citizen	Authority	Authority
Proposal	Citizen	Authority	Citizen	Citizen	Citizen	Citizen	Citizen	Citizen
Survey	Citizen	Citizen	Citizen	Citizen	Citizen	Citizen	Citizen	Citizen
Output	Final council decision	Poll of authority proposals	Collection of proposals	Suggested amendments	Opinion formation	Poll of proposals	Collection of proposals	Collection of proposals
Scope	Collect opinions of established proposals	Collect opinions of established proposals	-	Formula teproposals	Decision making	Collective ideation deliberation and democratic decision making.	Collect comments, results and statistics.	Result decision from the proposals

The systems in the process of an e-deliberation follow different degrees of participation in each type. The production of the issue is developed mainly by the authority while in the proposals and surveys the citizens have a greater participation. However, the output and scope are different in each system.

3. MATERIALS AND METHODS

Some results have already been verified by previous research such as LiquidFeedback (https://liquidfeedback.com/en/), which provides users the possibility of either creating or supporting initiatives. The new results after the procedure followed will help to design a system based on user preferences.

A questionnaire with 49 questions was created for the proper operation of the project, with the aim of involving citizens in the design of the system that will allow to include all those features that will ensure the completeness and usefulness of the system.

The questioner was designed in four pillars.

- In the first pillar, we tried to determine the public commitment and the way of the citizens' intervention. The questions that existed had to do with the participation of citizens in an e-deliberation system but also with the means of distribution of power between citizens and the state.
- In the second pillar we tried to identify characteristics of the technical system. These are mainly for the identification of users in an e-deliberation system, for the possible influence of such a system in terms of political principles in the decision-making process, but also for the final results that will result from this system and the way their utilization. Other things also had to do with users' access to the system and how they think it is optimal, given that there are also vulnerable groups (digitally illiterate, technophobic, elderly, etc.). Of course, there are questions about collective entities and how they could participate.
- In the third pillar we tried to determine the quality of deliberation as it is another part that concerns, asking questions about the coordination of public deliberation and how it will be managed as well as the usability of the system and the time of e-deliberation. Questions about the administrative levels and the solutions that such a system could bring could not be omitted. A major issue is also the voting process in an e-deliberation system and the method of gathering citizens' preferences in it.
- In the fourth and last pillar we tried to determine the demographics of the participants in terms of level of education, their status as participants, profession and much more.

The information that was extracted from the above questions will be utilized in such a way that the system manages to approach, as much as possible, the desired characteristics of the citizens regarding an e-deliberation system.

It was passed on to people who play a key role in their involvement with the public and politics, as the authorities can use the proposed technology as a social and political tool to listen to the opinion of the people in a structured way. There were 160 participants who submitted their opinions, of which there were many with a remarkable educational level of 68.4% and quite good familiarity with social media, with the percentage reaching 82.7%.

4. RESULTS

The following elements were obtained from the processing of the questionnaire.

4.1 Types of Participation

There are 3 types of citizen participation that should be included in an e-deliberation system.

- Passive participation through public communication with a preference rate of 2.2%
- Almost active participation in public deliberation with a preference rate of 23.3% and
- Active participation achieved through public participation with a preference rate of 74.5%.

4.2 Process of Identification and Self-Determination

The process of identification and self-determination is in the direct wishes of the citizens for an e-deliberation system.

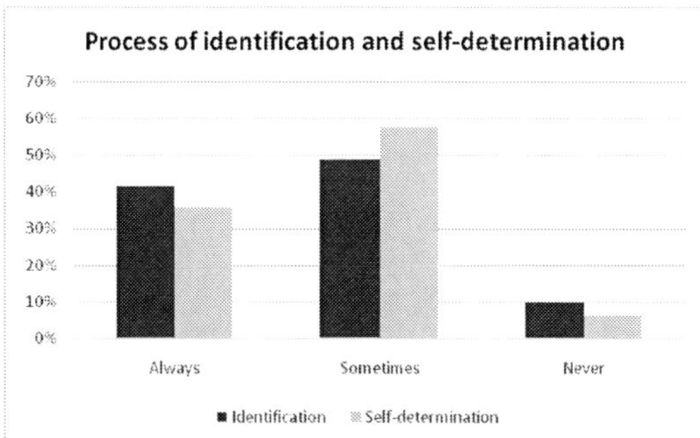

Figure 1. Extent to which citizens must identify and self-identify as users of an e-deliberation system

4.3 Raise the Issues

Citizens believe that it is the right of the public authority to raise the issues, but the majority wants to shape the outcome.

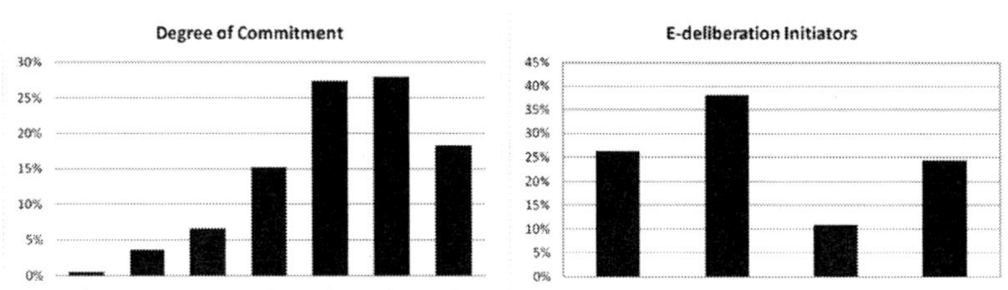

Figure 2. In Graph A is the degree of commitment of public authorities to the results of a public e-deliberation (1. Not at all 2. Very Low 3. Low 4. Neutral 5. Moderate 6. High 7. Extremely High). Graph B is the measures needed so that laws / decisions can be formulated with the result of public e-deliberation. Relevant social issues should: A. To be proposed by the citizens and to be voted by the public authorities B. To be proposed by the public authorities and to be voted by the citizens C. To be proposed and voted by the public authorities D. To be proposed and voted by the citizens

4.4 Cases of Users to Be Informed

It is obvious that the majority of citizens, over 80%, consider their information on matters of public interest as the basis for such a system.

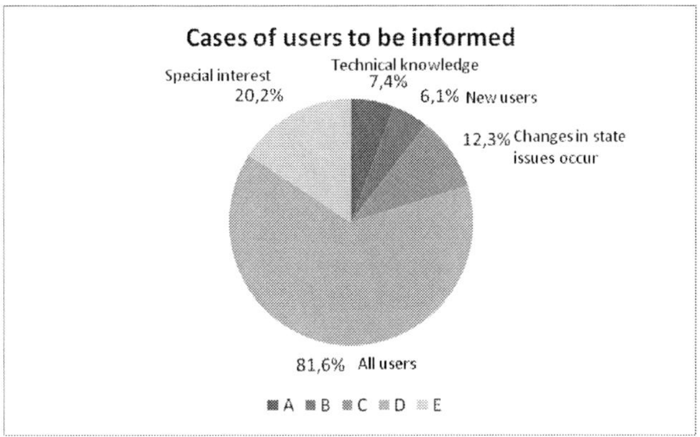

Figure 3. Cases when the system should be available to be used to inform citizens on matters of public interest A. Only for those who have some technical knowledge about a specific topic. B. Only for new users C. Only when changes in state issues occur D. For all users every time they use the system E. For those who have a special interest

4.5 Time for the Deliberation Process

More than 50% of the participants would suggest that the deliberation process continue until at least 2 completed proposals emerge or until the majority decides that the process should be closed.

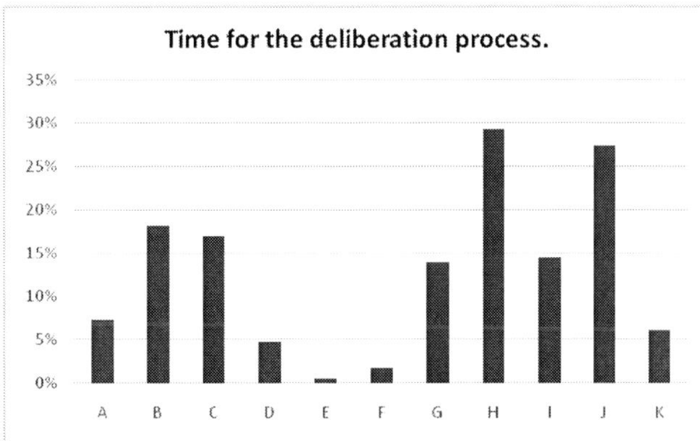

Figure 4. Time that the deliberation process should take A. A week B. A month C. Three months D. Six months E. A year F. More than a year G. Until a consensus is reached between all parties H. Until more than two solutions are created for each problem I. Until the majority of citizens choose to close the discussion J. Until the maximum agreed number of citizens chooses to close the discussion K. Until the citizens choose to close the discussion

4.6 Deliberation Process

One of the things that end users want is for each proposal to be able to be substantiated by relevant supporting material.

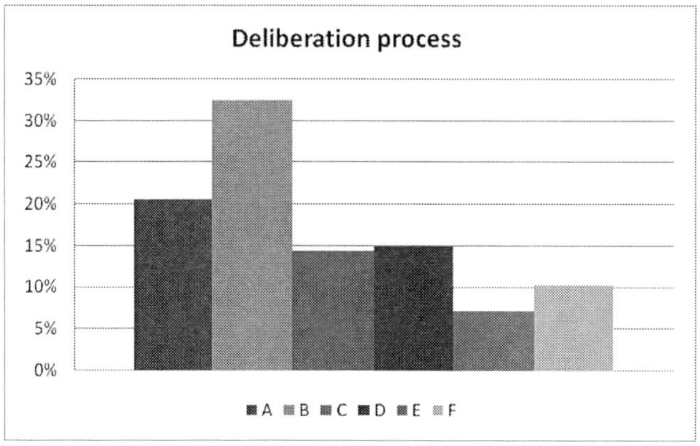

Figure 5. Deliberation process that should be included in a system A. Dialogue for each proposal B. Creating a publicly visible list of pros and cons for each proposal C. Monitoring changes in proposals D. Working in small groups defined by users (family, friends, neighbors, etc.) to create the pros and cons of arguments and solutions, followed by community contributions to proposals E. Submit personalized pros and cons lists for arguments and solutions to a facilitator F. Citizens create solutions and use communication tools to win votes

4.7 Collective Entities

The choice of citizens to be the represented collective entities is evident, with a percentage of 73.5%, nevertheless there is a strong argument in the participation of collective entities in such a system, as while they believe that a large percentage should participate, 43.8 %, believe that it should be done under specific conditions.

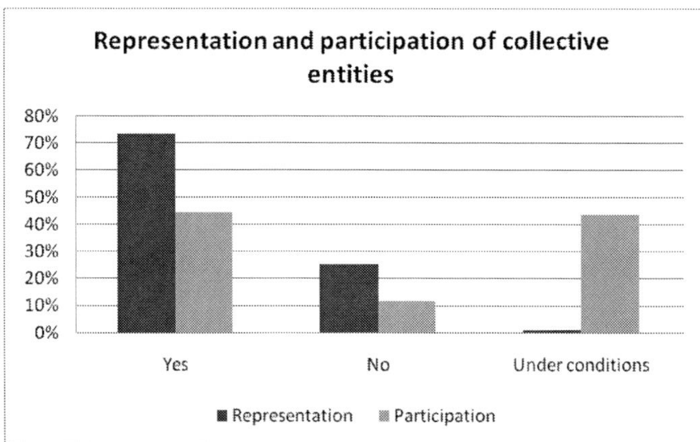

Figure 6. A. Organized collective entities such as organizations, private companies, trade unions and other stakeholders should be represented within this system of public deliberation B. Collective entities must be able to participate

4.8 Design Principles

Bases on the user requirements recording from the analysis of the questionnaire, the function specifications of an e-deliberation system can be written.

4.8.1 Citizen Participation

When configuring the system:

- the issue should be raised by the respective decision-makers, but there should be the possibility for citizens to state their proposals on it.

- it should be possible for users to comment on the proposals submitted in each topic, but also to adapt those comments to the proposals.
- users should be informed about matters of public interest.
- representatives from certain entities should be able to participate, enabling them to contribute to the process in the same way as users.

4.8.2 Authentication

Upon entering the e-deliberation system, should be a service for identification process with the possibility of self-identification.

4.8.3 Integrity

E-deliberation should be ensured, with proper coordination, which is achieved with the participation of an administrator/coordinator.

4.8.4 Electronic Folder

The system should support an electronic folder where the supporting material can be located.

5. DISCUSSION AND FUTURE WORK

A large part of society is made up of digitally literate people, who usually make up the highest participation rates in e-participation initiatives. However, no citizen should put aside of e-deliberation platforms. E-democracy requires smart cities to give all citizens equal and just access to policy and decision-making processes, in such a way that no individual is disadvantaged. A society that is informed and participative becomes stronger and is closer to achieving a true democracy. With the electronic participation and support of citizens, public authorities and governments can perform their tasks in a more efficient way and as a result create a stronger state of which we can encounter smart cities. E-deliberation, especially through a "consensus-driven" platform, is a remarkable mean for enhancing participation of citizens in management and micro-management of a smart-city.

The proposed e-deliberation system has some unique features that make it stand out from other similar solutions. By conducting a questionnaire survey and comparing our system to others, we were able to gather valuable feedback and insights that allowed us to identify areas where our system excels. This is a great way to improve the user experience and ensure that our system is meeting the needs of its users.

According to the analysis we did in the existing systems, we found some blanks concerning specific pillars for an e-deliberation system. These blanks included citizen participation issues, authentication issues and integrity issues.

Based on the results from the questionnaire we developed for 160 participants with 49 questions, we found that citizens are active and want to participate in these deliberation systems if a system contains the following design principles:

- Authentication is important for an e-deliberation system because it helps to ensure the security and integrity of the platform. By requiring users to authenticate their identity, the system can verify that they are who they claim to be and prevent unauthorized access. This can help to prevent malicious actors from infiltrating the platform and disrupting the discussion or manipulating the decision-making process. Additionally, authentication can help to prevent spam and other forms of abuse, such as trolling or harassment, by allowing the system to identify and block suspicious or malicious accounts. Overall, authentication is an important safeguard that helps to ensure the smooth and secure operation of an e-deliberation system.
- Supporting material is important for an e-deliberation system because it provides context and background information that can help participants to better understand the topic or issue being discussed. This can include things like data, statistics, research studies, and other relevant documents that can help to inform the discussion and provide a basis for more informed decision-making. By providing supporting material, an e-deliberation system can help to ensure that participants are able to engage with the topic at hand in a meaningful and productive way, and can ultimately lead to more informed and fair decision-making.

- Having a main authority and allowing for user participation without barriers are both important for an e-deliberation system for several reasons. First, a main authority can help to ensure that the discussions and decision-making processes on the platform are fair and unbiased. This can help to build trust among users and encourage more people to participate in the discussions. Additionally, allowing for user participation without barriers is important because it allows for a more diverse range of perspectives and opinions to be heard. This can help to ensure that the discussions are inclusive and representative of the wider community. It can also help to foster a sense of ownership and involvement among users, which can help to drive engagement and participation on the platform. Overall, having a main authority and allowing for user participation without barriers can help to create a more transparent and inclusive e-deliberation system.

In summary, this paper leads to some basic conclusions. Initially, we suggest that the opinions of experts can be collected to inform the design and development of e-deliberation tools based on the evaluation of some variables such as: i) Democracy Type, ii) Makes a difference, iii) Quality of discussion, iv) Integrity, v) Type of deliberation, vi) Anonymity, vii) Efficacy, viii) Type of deliberative system, ix) Transparency, x) Tailored to circumstances, xi) Is the system part of a larger participatory process?, xii) Scope, xiii) The right number and types of people, xiv) Treats participants with respect, xv) Type of interactions facilitated by the system, xvi) Kept informed, xvii) Access limitations, and xviii) Preference aggregation method (Triantafyllou, Tsakanikas, Asimakopoulos, & Christodoulopoulos, 2019). Then, based on the reviewed literature on the revitalization of public spaces, e-deliberation tools can be envisioned to provide power for change on issues of public interest. And finally we suggest that scaling is facilitated by adding data from multiple small-scale forums, organizing large-scale discussion only on the common links suggested by citizens and citizen groups, and allowing a fine-grained structure for qualitative analysis and database-based abstraction.

To confirm the above these principles should be implemented and a test should be done to have a more thorough opinion on the evaluation of these principles and we should move to the next stage of implementation and creation. In the next phase, this evaluation should be carried out in a large-scale analysis.

REFERENCES

Barnet, B. (2013). *Memory Machines: The Evolution of Hypertext*. Anthem Press.

Bush, V. (1945). As we may think. *The atlantic monthly, 176*(1), 101-108.

Cavalier, R., Kim, M., & Sam Zais, Z. (2009). Deliberative Democracy, Online Discussion, and Project PICOLA (Public Informed Citizen Online Assembly). In T. Davies, & S. Peña Gangadharan, *ONLINE DELIBERATION Design, Research, and Practice* (p. 71).

Dryzek, J. S., Bächtiger, A., Chambers, S., Cohen, J., Druckman, J. N., Felicett, A., et al. (2019). The crisis of democracy and the science of deliberation. *Science, 363*(6432), 1144-1146.

Holtz, P., Kronberger, N., & Wagner, W. (2012). Analyzing Internet Forums: A Practical Guide. *Journal of Media Psychology: Theories, Methods, and Applications, 24(2),* 55.

Kneuer, M. (2016). E-democracy: A new challenge for measuring democracy. *International Political Science Review,* 37(5), 666-678.

Päivärinta, T., & Sæbø, Ø. (2006). Models of e-democracy. *Communications of the Association for Information Systems, 17*(1), 37.

Solomon, S., & Abelson, J. (2012). Why and when should we use public deliberation? *The Hastings Center Report, 42(2)*,17.

Talisse, R. (2021). *Sustaining Democracy: What We Owe to the Other Side*. Oxford University Press.

Tangian, A. (2020). Analytical theory of democracy. *Studies in Choice and Welfare.*

Triantafyllou, V., Tsakanikas, V., Asimakopoulos, G., & Christodoulopoulos, J. (2019, April). Public On-Line Deliberation System (PODS). *17th International Conference on e-Society 2019.*

Tsakanikas, V., Rokkou, G., & Triantafyllou, V. (2022). Towards e-deliberation 2.0. In P. Fitsilis, *Building on Smart Cities Skills and Competences: Human factors affecting smart cities development* (pp. 229–246). Springer International Publishing, Cham.

Wells, H. (1937). The Idea of a Permanent World Encyclopaedia. In *World Brain.*

OVERCOMING CIRCLE OF POVERTY? HUMAN AND SOCIAL CAPITAL-ENHANCING DIGITAL USES AMONG SINGLE MOTHERS – FINDINGS OF REPEATED CROSS-SECTIONAL STUDY 2014-2019

Sabina Lissitsa[1] and Svetlana Chachashvili-Bolotin[2]
[1]Ariel University, Kiryat Hamada, Ariel, Israel
[2] Ruppin Academic Center, Emeq Hefer, Israel

ABSTRACT

Using data from large scale Annual Social Surveys of the CBS in Israel, the current research focused on patterns of digital inequality among Israeli mothers between 2014–2019. The main purpose of the current study was to investigate the differences within a group of single mothers according to their SES as well as differences between single and married mothers and whether these patterns are stable or changeable over time. The highest percentage of digital uses adoption was found among high SES mothers, both single and married. The most disadvantaged group was low SES married mothers. Digital inequality among mothers is best explained by social class, rather than by the difficulties and restrictions of single motherhood. Groups were consistent in their pace of digital uses adoption over time. Policymaker implementation of our specific recommendations may produce beneficial effects for promotion of Internet use among single mothers.

KEYWORDS

Single Mothers, Digital Inequality, Internet Use for Study, Social Media, E-Government

1. INTRODUCTION

Economically and socially disadvantaged groups experience generational suffering due to a range of exclusion types. In Western countries, belonging to a vulnerable group (i.e., lower education, income, disability, or disadvantaged minority status) is a strong predictor of non-online access (Helsper and Reisdorf, 2016, Lissitsa and Madar, 2018). Thus, most socially excluded members of society are also the most likely to be digitally excluded (Witte and Mannon, 2010). There is ample research addressing digital exclusion of various vulnerable groups such as elderly, minorities or people with disabilities (Adkins and Sandy, 2020). However, digital inequality based on single vs. partnered motherhood and its social and economic implications have yet to be explored.

Single-mother households are increasingly common and have become a social concern in global contexts (Li, 2020). Low wages, lack of spousal and social support, limited access to resources and public services, and the burdens of raising children have made single mothers especially vulnerable (Nieuwenhuis and Maldonado, 2018). Compared to coupled-parent families, children from single mother households more often suffer from economic deprivation (Treanor, 2018), lower educational performance (de Lange and Dronkers, 2018), and greater levels of behavioural difficulties. Considering these difficulties, there is a growing interest in whether and how digital technologies, tools, and services can make a difference to single mothers' social inclusion and welfare.

Previous research on single mother families has largely focused on poverty, whereas much less is known about single parent families who are above the poverty threshold. For these mothers, middle and high social class economic resources may afford the services of hired babysitters and high educational level may result in jobs with flexible working hours or from home work opportunities. Thus, life circumstances of single mothers from different socio-economic background may vary. Only a handful of studies have highlighted the relevance of social class in this context, focusing on the heterogeneity of single mothers as a group and suggesting that their economic and social difficulties are class-related. Due to these reasons and the importance of SES status in creating digital inequality (Scheerder et al., 2019, Bach et al., 2013), this research addresses the heterogeneity between single mothers and differentiates between them on the basis of their SES. Accordingly, the main purpose of this paper is to investigate the differences *within* a group of single mothers based on their SES as well as the differences *between* single and married mothers and whether these patterns are stable or changeable over time.

It is fitting for this type of research to be conducted in Israel, given its position as a global leader in the adoption of Internet use and mobile devices (Poushter, 2016). In addition, Israel is characterized by distressed economic conditions for single mothers (Natanzon et al., 2017). In fact, 25 percent of single parent families live below the poverty line compared to 18 percent among Israel's total population (Endeweld et al., 2018).

2. LITERATURE REVIEW

2.1 Internet Use as a Potential Source for Human Capital for Single Mothers

The poverty status of single mothers has been shown to be highly related to their educational level (Härkönen, 2018). Several barriers prevent impoverished single mothers from upgrading their education, among them shortage of financial resources, costs of child care and transportation, lack of access to resources, and limited social support (Bryant-Davis et al., 2010). Therefore, many mothers cannot even consider education as an attainable goal and as a means of escaping the cycle of poverty (Russell, 2019). Some of these barriers, however, can be overcome by using ICTs for study, information seeking and communication. Through the Internet, mothers may gain access to educational resources and broaden their cultural and social perspectives (Abdel-Basset et al., 2019). Research has shown a positive correlation between Internet use for study and for seeking information and growth in earnings, greater extrinsic rewards and job security. This correlation indicates that at least some of the skills and behaviours associated with Internet use reap rewards in the labour market (Lissitsa, 2015, Lissitsa and Chachashvili-Bolotin, 2016, Lissitsa et al., 2017, Czaja and Urbaniec, 2019).

2.2 Social Media as a Potential Source for Social Capital for Single Mothers

Mainstream social relationships are much weaker for single mothers than for their married counterparts. Single mothers often experience less emotional and parental support, less contact with family members and friends, and more unstable social networks than married mothers (Li, 2020). Social judgment may attach "guilty" stigmas to single mothers for not waiting to have children within a heterosexual marriage or for not being able to "hold on" to a partner (Zartler, 2014). They are often stereotyped as unhappy, deviant, troubled, and lacking in child-rearing abilities. Compared with their counterparts in two-parent families, single mothers suffer higher levels of depression and family stress. As the sole parent, they must face in-family and external stressors on their own, often with limited resources. Economic hardship can isolate many single mothers because they do not have discretionary funds to socialize. Their inability to spend time outside the home on their own, going out with friends, or taking children on family outings can result in low self-esteem, helplessness, or a feeling that their world is shrinking.

Social media may help to increase available options. Through the Internet, single mothers can connect with other parents in new ways. They can exchange parenting experiences, tips, details and materials, and respond to comments. Although the social benefits for single mothers of using social media has been generally overlooked, to the best of our knowledge, studies conducted among mothers suggest that social media use contributes to a generally high perception of support and empowerment. It may also be equal in effect to the support traditionally found in neighbour communities (Lin et al., 2019). Facebook group pages for single mothers can help to locate other singles in the area for face-to-face meetings, exchanging advice, relieving feelings of isolation and loneliness, answering questions about child care and helping to fulfil emotional needs (Lupton et al., 2016).

2.3 Internet Use as a Potential Source for Public Services for Single Mothers

The rapid development of e-government service systems objectively improves citizen access to government information and services. E-government promises greater accountability and transparency (Wilson, 2012), enhances direct democratic processes and reduces bureaucracy (Zernik, 2017). Accessing e-government service provision forms via the Internet is an 'anytime, anywhere' resource - as long as access to the Internet is available.

There is ample evidence that e-government services are especially relevant for vulnerable social groups: elderly, people with disabilities, and people from low SES (Lines et al., Mosehlana, 2019, O'Sullivan and Walker, 2018, Lissitsa and Chachashvili-Bolotin, 2021). E-government services use creates the great opportunity to the disadvantaged groups, as those with the greatest need for interpersonal social services are often least likely to have access to adequate human-delivered services. For example, a visit to governmental offices can create unnecessary difficulties for single mothers due to their limited mobility, high number of working hours, and time spent on child care. Filling out and submitting forms and checking account status or eligibility for assistance, discounts and allowances using online services are no longer constrained by physical collection or telephony services that may hinder access to service provision. In contrast to submitting a printed form, submitting an online form may facilitate detecting data omissions and/or inaccuracies and requesting 'corrected' information before submission, in this way preventing service delays. However, e-government usage rates are stagnating on rather low levels and the access of vulnerable groups to e-government services still faces various barriers. For instance, scholars note lack of awareness of e-services, low usability of e-government websites, lack of government support, the existence of digital divide and low trust in government and in Internet technology (Shah and Lim, 2011, Distel, 2018). As a result, those who experience the most problems online also have the most difficulty obtaining high-quality support even when it is available, creating an even larger 'gap' between those who do and do not need support. In the last decade, Israel has emerged as one of the world's leading nations in the field of online government services (Zernik, 2017). However, despite Israeli innovation and advanced technologies, there are significant disparities in Israeli society, and the members of vulnerable groups are also the least likely to be able to effectively engage online, either due to a lack of digital infrastructure or digital literacy.

2.4 Research Questions

RQ1. Is there digital inequality between mothers based on their marital and socio-economic status?

RQ2. What trends, if any, were observed over time in digital uses among the examined groups?

3. METHODOLOGY

3.1 Source of Data

The current research is based on a repeated cross-sectional study. We used data which were collected by means of Annual Social Surveys conducted by Israel's Central Bureau of Statistics (CBS) in the period between 2014 and 2019. CBS interviewers carried out face to face interviews in the field between January and December of each year. The duration of each of the interviews, which were conducted in Hebrew, Russian and Arabic, was about one hour. The surveys provide up-to-date information about living conditions and the welfare of the population in Israel. The formulation of all the questions used in the study was identical throughout this period.

3.2 Population and Sampling Method

The survey pool population comprises the permanent non-institutional population of Israel aged 20 and older, as well as residents of non-custodial institutions (such as student dormitories, immigrant absorption centers and independent living projects for the elderly). New immigrants are included in the survey population if they have been resident in Israel for at least six months. Each year the CBS sample size was about 7,500 persons aged 20 and older, representing about 4.5 million people in that age bracket. The response rate was around

80%. The sample design involved defining groups based on a combination of three demographic variables: population groups (Israeli-born Jews, immigrants and Arabs), age and gender. The expected size of each design group was to be proportional to its size in the population. The social survey samples are based on random selection and the sampling method enables generalization of the results to the entire Israeli population.

We created our database using 6 years of CBS Social Survey data (N=43,485). Our final sample included 7,040 Jewish mothers[1] aged up to 60 years old who have children under age 17, among them 1,046 (15%) are single mothers (see Table 1).

Table 1. Descriptive statistics and t-test results

		Single	Married	Total	t-value	Sig.
	N	827	4110	4937		
	%	16.8	83.2			
Dependent variables: Internet use for						
Study	Mean	0.37	0.38	0.38	-0.791	0.429
	SD	0.48	0.49	0.49		
Seeking information	Mean	0.91	0.95	0.94	-3.721	0.001
	SD	0.29	0.23	0.24		
Social media	Mean	0.89	0.91	0.91	-1.804	0.072
	SD	0.31	0.28	0.29		
E-government services	Mean	0.55	0.62	0.60	-3.384	0.001
	SD	0.50	0.49	0.49		
Independent variables						
Education	Mean	3.02	3.46	3.38	-7.721	0.000
	SD	1.48	1.31	1.35		
Income per person	Mean	2.98	4.08	3.90	-13.669	0.000
	SD	2.06	2.32	2.32		
Control variables						
Age	Mean	43.19	39.85	40.41	11.651	0.000
	SD	7.51	7.61	7.69		
Religiosity level	Secular (%)	56.2%	45.1%	46.9%		
	Traditional (%)	38.1%	37.7%	37.7%		
	Religious (%)	5.7%	17.3%	15.3%		

4. RESULTS

4.1 Segmentation and Descriptive Statistics

Firstly, in order to address the research questions, we ran a cluster analysis that included five socio-economic variables (see Table 2). As a result of the analysis, interviewees were divided into two distinct groups. As Table 2 indicates, the greatest distinction between the groups (according to F values) was found for income per person and education. Those who belong to the first cluster had lower income, education, lower percentage of car use, and ownership of a dwelling (and higher living density), compared to the second cluster. We defined the first cluster as the "Low SES" group and the second one as "High SES".

[1] Among the Israeli Arab female population, the percentage of single mothers is estimated at less than 6% (N=86) during the whole period 2014-2019, therefore we focused only on Jewish single mothers.

Table 2. Cluster analysis findings. Division of the respondents into groups according to the socio-economic variables, Mean and F-values

	Mean		F	df
	Low SES	High SES		
N	5231	1809		
Income per person (NIS)	2,530	6,950	11933.014**	6008
Education	2.88	4.3	1873.305**	6807
Current use of car	0.75	0.98	461.264**	7038
Ownership of a dwelling	0.66	0.81	147.586**	7038
Household density	1.9	1.55	567.096**	7025

** $p<0.01$

Secondly, mothers were divided, by both marital and socio-economic status, into four distinct groups: single mothers from low SES, single mothers from high SES, married mothers from low SES, and married mothers from high SES. As Table 1 shows, among single mothers about 80 % belong to low SES, while among married mothers this rate was 74%. Low SES single mothers had the highest percent of immigrants compared to other groups. Regarding RQ1, the descriptive analysis shows similar patterns of between-group differences for all types of digital uses. The highest percentage of digital uses adoption was found among high SES mothers, both single and married. The percentage of taking advantage of all types of digital uses among low SES mothers was significantly lower. The most disadvantaged group was low SES married mothers. Our important finding is that more similarity was found *between* single vs. married mothers than *within* groups of single or married mothers.

4.2 Multivariate Analyses: Predicting Digital Uses

For a better understanding of the differences between four groups of mothers in digital uses, four logistic regressions (predicting four dependent variables) were applied. The findings show that four examined digital uses increased over time (see Table 3).

Table 3. Predicting digital uses – logistic regressions

	Using for Study Model A		Seeking Information Model B		Social media Model C		E-services Model D	
	B	Exp(B)	B	Exp(B)	B	xp(B)	B	Exp(B)
Years of survey	0.08**	1.08	0.10**	1.11	0.29**	1.34	0.13**	1.14
Group (compared to low SES SM)								
Low SES MM	0.05	1.05	0.38**	1.46	0.18	1.19	0.15	1.16
High SES MM	0.53**	1.69	1.90**	6.69	0.94**	2.57	0.71**	2.04
High SES SM	0.58**	1.79	0.94*	2.57	0.39	1.48	0.71**	2.04
Religiosity	-0.16**	0.85	-1.07**	0.34	-1.33**	0.26	-0.45**	0.64
Age	0.00	1.00	-0.01*	0.99	-0.02**	0.98	-0.02**	0.98
Immigrants	-0.14*	0.87	-0.20*	0.81	0.07	1.07	-0.53**	0.59
Number of children	-0.10**	0.90	-0.19**	0.82	-0.17**	0.84	-0.01	0.99
Child aged 6-17	0.27**	1.31	0.06	1.07	0.02	1.02	-0.12	0.89
Center	-0.21**	0.81	-0.10	0.90	-0.07	0.93	-0.01	0.99
Weekly working hours	0.00*	1.00	0.02**	1.02	0.01**	1.01	0.02**	1.02

Constant	-0.66**	0.52	4.42**	83.04	4.79**	119.73	1.12**	3.06
Nagelkerke R2	0.057		0.406		0.476		0.160	
Cox & Snell R2	0.041		0.230		0.301		0.120	

).05** p<0.01

After controlling for background variables, low SES single mothers had significant disadvantage in all digital uses compared to other groups (except for social media for high SES single mothers). The differences between single mothers and married mothers from the low SES were insignificant (except the low SES married mothers advantage in seeking information). The most advantaged groups in digital uses were high SES mothers both single and married. In most regression models level of religiosity, age, and number of children were negatively associated with digital uses. In general, immigrants were disadvantaged in digital uses compared to Israeli-born citizens. Weekly working hours had a tiny positive significant association with digital uses. Raising young children (aged less 6 years old) and living in a centre decreased the odds of using the Internet for study. It should be noted that model fit indices for seeking information and social media were substantially higher compared to using the Internet for study and e-government.

Addressing RQ2, we found insignificant interactional effects between the wave of data collection and belonging to a group according to family and SES status. Thus, the groups preserve their pace of digital uses adoption. These findings thus translate into the assumption that if effective intervention strategies are not applied, between-groups gaps will continue to exist.

5. CONCLUSION

In the research literature, single mothers are often presented in terms of poverty, disadvantage and exclusion, and treated as one of the most vulnerable groups. However, our study revealed heterogeneity *within* single mothers. In order to extend the literature on digital inequality of vulnerable groups, this finding should be addressed. We found that digital inequality among mothers is more likely to be explained by social and economic inequality (e.g., social class) (Breen and Breen Jr, 2004) than by difficulties and restrictions of single motherhood. One of the most important findings of our study is that we identify the most vulnerable group of mothers in terms of digital inequality – the low SES married mothers. Researchers of digital inequality traditionally address elderly, low educated, immigrants and minorities, and people with disabilities with low SES (Helsper and Reisdorf, 2017, Silver, 2014). However, they overlook the digital exclusion of low SES married mothers. As such, this group should be distinguished within the group of low SES women and treated properly by researchers and policymakers.

The current paper is based on data collected between 2014-2019, before the outbreak of COVID 19, which may lead to significant changes in the labour market such as digitalization, streamlining of work processes, and remote work. Such changes may provide both threats and opportunities for single mothers. Those who have yet to acquire digital skills or adopt digital uses may find themselves unemployed and without means of subsistence. In light of our findings, low SES single mothers are most likely to face such a situation, which may exacerbate their economic and social vulnerability due to their status as the single breadwinner for their family. In contrast, those with digital skills and who know how to use the Internet for study, work, communication and services consumption may enjoy staying home with their children. Simultaneously, they may be able to take advantage of digital uses as a means for empowerment and channel for economic and social mobility.

It is important to mention the limitations of this study, which derive from the CBS social survey database. While this study was unique in its use of data collected over time, the data were still cross-sectional. Only a single questionnaire item examined each Internet use, so we cannot distinguish what kind of information mothers seek online - whether their Internet use for study belongs to formal or informal education as well as what social media and e-government platforms they use. The CBS database does not provide information about respondent digital skills, which may offer deeper understanding of single mother digital inequality. Further research should thus address these issues.

REFERENCES

Abdel-Basset, M., Manogaran, G., Mohamed, M. & Rushdy, E. 2019. Internet of things in smart education environment: Supportive framework in the decision-making process. *Concurrency and Computation: Practice and Experience,* 31, e4515.

Adkins, D. & Sandy, H. M. 2020. Information behavior and ICT use of Latina immigrants to the US Midwest. *Information Processing & Management,* 57, 102072.

Bach, A., Shaffer, G. & Wolfson, T. 2013. Digital human capital: Developing a framework for understanding the economic impact of digital exclusion in low-income communities. *Journal of Information Policy,* 3, 247-266.

Breen, R. & Breen Jr, R. 2004. *Social mobility in Europe*, Oxford University Press on Demand.

Bryant-Davis, T., Ullman, S. E., Tsong, Y., Tillman, S. & Smith, K. 2010. Struggling to survive: Sexual assault, poverty, and mental health outcomes of African American women. *American Journal of Orthopsychiatry,* 80, 61.

Czaja, I. & Urbaniec, M. 2019. Digital Exclusion in the Labour Market in European Countries: Causes and Consequences. *European Journal of Sustainable Development,* 8, 324-324.

De Lange, M. & Dronkers, J. 2018. Single parenthood and children's educational performance: inequality among families and schools. *The triple bind of single-parent families*, 125.

Distel, B. 2018. Bringing Light into the Shadows: A Qualitative Interview Study on Citizens' Non-Adoption of e-Government. *Electronic Journal of e-Government,* 16.

Endeweld, M., Gottlieb, D., Heller, O. & Karady, L. 2018. Poverty and Social Gaps in 2018, annual report. Jerusalem: National Insurance Institute of Israel.

Härkönen, J. 2018. Single-mother poverty: How much do educational differences in single motherhood matter. *The Triple bind of single-parent families*, 31-50.

Helsper, E. J. & Reisdorf, B. C. 2016. The emergence of a "digital underclass" in Great Britain and Sweden: Changing reasons for digital exclusion. *New media & society*, 1461444816634676.

Helsper, E. J. & Reisdorf, B. C. 2017. The emergence of a "digital underclass" in Great Britain and Sweden: Changing reasons for digital exclusion. *New media & society,* 19, 1253-1270.

Li, Q. 2020. Mothers left without a man: Poverty and single parenthood in China. *Social Inclusion,* 8, 114-122.

Lin, J., Vijayalakshmi, A. & Laczniak, R. N. 2019. Toward an Understanding of Parental Views and Actions on Social Media Influencers Targeted at Adolescents: The Roles of Parents' Social Media Use and Empowerment. *Frontiers in psychology,* 10, 2664.

Lines, L., Ikechi, O. & Hone, K. S. Accessing e-government services: design requirements for the older user. 2007. Springer, 932-940.

Lissitsa, S. 2015. Digital use as a mechanism to accrue economic capital: a Bourdieusian perspective. *Innovation: The European Journal of Social Science Research,* 28, 464-482.

Lissitsa, S. & Chachashvili-Bolotin, S. 2016. The less you know, the better you'll sleep–Perceived job insecurity in the Internet age. *Computers in Human Behavior,* 62, 754-761.

Lissitsa, S. & Chachashvili-Bolotin, S. 2021. E-government services use among single Israeli mothers. *Israel Affairs,* 27, 936-949.

Lissitsa, S., Chachashvili-Bolotin, S. & Bokek-Cohen, Y. A. 2017. Digital skills and extrinsic rewards in late career. *Technology in Society,* 51, 46-55.

Lissitsa, S. & Madar, G. 2018. Do disabilities impede the use of information and communication technologies? Findings of a repeated cross-sectional study–2003-2015. *Israel journal of health policy research,* 7, 1-17.

Lupton, D., Pedersen, S. & Thomas, G. M. 2016. Parenting and digital media: from the early web to contemporary digital society. *Sociology Compass,* 10, 730-743.

Mosehlana, M. B. An E-Government Opportunity: Implications for the African Poor and Vulnerable Groups. 2019 2019. International Conference on Public Administration and Development ….

Natanzon, R., Gazela, I. & Porat, M. 2017. Single parent families in Israel. Jerusalem: Macro: The Center for |Political Economies.

Nieuwenhuis, R. & Maldonado, L. C. 2018. The triple bind of single-parent families: Resources, employment and policies. *The triple bind of single-parent families: Resources, employment and policies to improve wellbeing*, 1-30.

O'sullivan, S. & Walker, C. 2018. From the interpersonal to the internet: social service digitisation and the implications for vulnerable individuals and communities. *Australian Journal of Political Science,* 53, 490-507.

Poushter, J. 2016. Smartphone ownership and internet usage continues to climb in emerging economies. *Pew Research Center,* 22.

Russell, P. 2019. Why we gatta be da poorest?: Disrupting the Cycle of Poverty for Single Mothers in the Bahamas by the Assessment of their Needs and the Mapping of Community and Educational Institutions Resources.

Scheerder, A. J., Van Deursen, A. J. & Van Dijk, J. A. G. M. 2019. Internet use in the home: Digital inequality from a domestication perspective. *new media & society,* 21, 2099-2118.

Shah, B. P. & Lim, N. Using social media to increase e-government adoption in developing countries. 2011 2011. 205-213.

Silver, M. P. 2014. Socio-economic status over the lifecourse and internet use in older adulthood. *Ageing and Society,* 34, 1019.

Treanor, M. C. 2018. Income poverty, material deprivation and lone parenthood. *The triple bind of single-parent families: Resurces, employment and policies to improve well-being*, 81-100.

Wilson, S. C. e-government legislation meets the poverty threshold: issues for the economically disadvantaged. 2012 2012. 74-83.

Witte, J. C. & Mannon, S. E. 2010. *The internet and social inequalitites*, Routledge.

Zartler, U. 2014. How to deal with moral tales: Constructions and strategies of single-parent families. *Journal of Marriage and Family,* 76, 604-619.

Zernik, J. E-government in Israel-transformation into the post-truth era. 2017 2017. 270.

CROWDFUNDING SCIENTIFIC RESEARCH: A CASE STUDY BASED ON USER RESEARCH

Chinasa Odo, Stefano De Paoli, Paula Forbes and Andreea Oniga
Abertay University, Bell St, Dundee, United Kingdom

ABSTRACT

Over the years, funding scientific projects have been the responsibility of traditional research funding institutions. Many projects were not getting funded due to the difficulties of accessing government funds. Crowdfunding has provided an alternative means of providing financial solutions to projects which ordinarily are not of interest to government funding agencies and other major funders of research. A crowdfunding platform is an internet-based matchmaker where the citizens (the funders) are matched with the researchers who are seeking funds to finance their projects. This paper investigates the users of a nascent crowdfunding channel for Social Sciences and Humanities. The users are the Social Sciences and Humanities researchers who seek financial support on scientific projects and the funders who are motivated to invest in a project. The goal of this research was to find out about the user needs and preferences to help in the decision-making about this nascent crowdfunding channel. We utilized the mixed method of research design to collect both qualitative and quantitative data about the users and their needs. This included codesigning work and a Europe-wide questionnaire. The outcome of this work was formalized in a set of practical recommendations for the new crowdfunding channel.

KEYWORDS

Crowdfunding, Crowdfunding Platform, Scientific Research, User Experience

1. INTRODUCTION

Crowdfunding is an innovative practice where many people fund projects by giving small sums, using internet-based platforms. Crowdfunding clearly is an increasingly important practice in our digital society. According to Calic (2018), crowdfunding is a process of sourcing small contributions from many individuals to support a proposed idea through an online platform. Crowdfunding can be applied and used in many areas which include supporting product development Belleflamme et al., (2013), the creation of artistic projects Dalla and Dekker, (2021), in taking stakes in a start-up (Belleflamme et al., 2014). Recently, the potential of using crowdfunding for scientific research has been highlighted in the literature, as a novel avenue of funding research (Dahlhausen et al, 2016, Sauermann et al, 2019, Vachelard et al, 2016, Wheat et al 2013). Traditionally, it is the responsibility of government agencies to fund research projects (Deng et al, 2022). However, the difficulties in accessing government-funded projects in many countries made crowdfunding an alternative means of providing funding for research projects (Laurell et al, 2019, Moritz and Block, 2016). According to some authors, crowdfunding of science could bring a more democratic decision process to research by allowing the public to be part of the research they believe in, including curiosity-driven scientific research Perlsterin, (2013), and allowing to fund projects which are not funded by public agencies.

In line with this assumption, the EU TRIPLE project has launched its own crowdfunding initiative, crystallised in the creation of a new crowdfunding channel. The project's aim is to design and develop the (https://www.gotriple.eu/) discovery platform for Social Sciences and Humanities (SSH) publications, data, and projects. In addition to the core discovery services, GoTriple discovery platform has several innovative services including a trust-building system, an annotation tool, a crowdfunding solution, a recommender system, and a visual search interface. Alongside the creation of the main platform, research was conducted for setting up the GoTriple innovative services, which included research for a tailored crowdfunding channel dedicated to SSH projects. It is this work on crowdfunding we are concentrating on in this paper.

One important consideration is that in the crowdfunding landscape, one could identify three main types of actors: the funders (people giving money), the people proposing a project, (researchers in the case of science, inventors, etc.), and the crowdfunding organisations (the intermediary platform). Much focus in the literature has been on the motivations of funders and why they decide to give money to a specific project or endeavours. Similarly, a significant amount of research has been devoted to understanding how to set up a specific campaign, i.e., the point of view of those proposing a project. However, there is comparably less research focused on crowdfunding organisations. Particularly, on the challenges that creating a new intermediary approach may entail and what knowledge is important to acquire to create a new crowdfunding initiative, with a focus on the crowdfunding of science and SSH more specifically.

To address this and answer the main research problem of "what elements should be taken into account when creating a new channel for the crowdfunding of research, with a focus on SSH?", we have designed research encompassing two different studies: 1) a codesign study conducted with both potential funders as well as proposers (i.e. researchers) and 2) a Europe wide questionnaire aimed specifically at funders. With both activities, our goal was to provide knowledge to address the practical problem of setting up a new intermediary for SSH crowdfunding with a major focus on the users.

In this context, the users of the crowdfunding platforms are people who either put money into a project of their choice or researchers who seek funds to carry out a project. These individuals are further explained in this study as the crowdfunding stakeholders. With the codesign, our goal was to gain some qualitative and experiential insights allowing us to discuss directly with participants. The questionnaire instead was designed to have potentially a broader overview. In any case, both activities were functional to the goal of the research. The analysis of the data generated by both studies resulted in a series of recommendations for the project and in influencing the decision-making about the crowdfunding initiative.

2. REVIEW OF RELATED LITERATURE

This literature review will focus on previous findings regarding scientific crowdfunding which are relevant to inform the design of a scientific crowdfunding platform, followed by a review of the limited findings on general crowdfunding from a user perspective.

2.1 Crowdfunding Stakeholders

There are three key players involved in the crowdfunding process according to Tomczak and Brern (2013), the fundraisers, the intermediaries, and the investors. These were also described by Moritz and Block (2016) as capital providers, capital seekers, and intermediaries. Other authors such as Jovanovic (2019) and Petruzzelli et al (2019) identified these key players as the project creator, the campaign to be funded, the supporters (i.e., the crowd), and the crowdfunding platform. In this research, we refer to these key players as the proposers, the intermediary, and the funders.

2.1.1 Proposers

The proposers are individuals or organisations seeking funds to carry out a project. Generally, we can understand that crowdfunding helps to finance new project ideas (Lehner, 2016). The researcher (as the proposers), in the case of the crowdfunding of science, will take the project idea to the crowdfunding intermediary which will review the importance of the project and will coordinate the fundraising through their crowdfunding platform. According to Mollick (2014), the portfolio/track record of the researcher is important as it is a proxy that should signal the quality of the project to be funded. To gain funding, the proposer needs to capture the attention of many people by convincing them that the proposed project is worthy of their investment (Wheat et al, 2013). The proposer needs to clearly state the problem they are trying to solve and how they intend to solve it to enable the funders to understand how their gifts can make a difference (Mollick, 2014). If a proposer can demonstrate beyond reasonable doubt how they will address the problem with a tangible action plan, potential funders will likely invest in it.

2.1.2 Funders

These are the group of individuals (the supposed crowd) who offer their money to a preferred innovation or project. The crowd is the central element of any successful crowdfunding campaign, including for science (Mollick, 2014). The funders not only offer their money but also their opinions (Stonko and Henard, 2017). Some funders can support the creator's ideas and strengthen connections with people in their social networks without any rewards (Bi et al, 2017). Funders often want to be engaged in the project alongside the innovating research, as that experience is typically considered to be a rewarding part of the process (Agrawal et al, 2015). As noted by Bi et al (2017), a funder or investor will consider the information provided about a project before considering whether to invest or not.

2.1.3 Crowdfunding Organisation/Intermediary

The crowdfunding organization, the intermediary, provides the Internet-based platform or the crowdfunding platform, normally a website that enables matchmaking between proposers and funders (Agrawal et al, 2015). Financial pledges can be made and collected through the crowdfunding platform. The project will be published on their website, then the funders can look at the information advertised and decide whether they want to invest in the project or not (Bi et al, 2017). So, in simple terms, the crowdfunding platform is a matchmaker between the fundraiser and the investor (Belleflamme et al, 2013, Calic, 2018). A study by Hemer, (2011) has categorized crowdfunding platforms into four main types: donation-based, reward-based, lending, and equity base platform. Crowdfunding of research is normally donation-based (Allison et al, 2015). Crowdfunding platforms generally provide two keyways to pitch a project: a narrative and a short video (Mollick, 2014).

2.2 Crowdfunding Models

A project or business idea may be appealing to a funder, and they may be interested to invest in such a project. The attraction to fund a project may be self-determined to achieve a desired goal and this could be dependent on the crowdfunding type/model.

2.2.1 Reward-Base Model

In this type of model, funders receive a reward for backing a project (Mollick, 2014). Reward-based crowdfunding allows individuals to donate to a project or business with expectations of receiving in return a non-financial reward, such as goods or services, at a later stage in exchange for their contribution (Calic, 2018, Zhao and Shneor, 2020). The funder may be motivated by the benefit offered.

2.2.2 Equity-Base Model

This is a crowdfunding model that allows the funder to invest in a business idea while they are offered equity in that business. This model is like selling a stake in a business to several investors in return for investment (Moritz and Block, 2016).

2.2.3 P2P Lending Model

This is a type of crowdfunding where funds are offered as a loan, with the expectation of some return. In this model, Mollick (2014) noted that the lender may be more interested in the social good promoted by the venture than any return generated by the loan, thus including patronage model elements as well. According to Allision et al (2015) lenders respond positively to narratives highlighting the venture as an opportunity to help others, and less positively when the narrative is framed as a business opportunity.

2.2.4 Donation-Based Crowdfunding or Patronage Model

This model places the funders in the position of philanthropist and the investor expects no return for their donations. Donation-based crowdfunding according to Hemer (2011) is a form of fundraising where backers provide funding based on motivations without expecting any form of rewards. This type of crowdfunding is different from traditional base fundraising as it provides a way for potential donors to reach people/groups in need of help without the constraints of physical distance (Tanaka and Voida, 2016). This is supported by Agrawal et al (2015) who noted that donation-based crowdfunding allows greater efficiencies in terms of geographical reach.

Scientific research can be considered a type of donation-based crowdfunding, as there is usually no tangible reward for the funders (Schafer et al, 2018, Mollick, 2014). However, some projects also provide non-monetary rewards such as photographs, lab visits, guest lectures, dinners, etc. Sauermann et al, (2019), Mollick, (2014), and in these cases, scientific crowdfunding may overlap with reward-based crowdfunding.

2.3 Crowdfunding from a User Perspective

In scientific research, crowdfunding has broadened access to resources for groups that have been excluded or disadvantaged in traditional funding systems (Sauermann et al, 2019). While there is ample literature on crowdfunding Agrawal et al, (2015,) Belleflamme, (2014), Mollick, (2014), especially on the motivations of funders Gerber, (2012), we want to concentrate on literature that studied users of crowdfunding platforms. A limited number of studies have attempted to explore user needs for the crowdfunding platform and refer to more general crowdfunding, rather than scientific crowdfunding. A study by Prom et al (2016) observed that the content and interface elements on crowdfunding platforms convey necessary information for the users to process. User research on a crowdfunding website in Indonesia identified user needs such as user profile customization, receiving information and news through the platform, a variety of payment methods and funding model types, and user support for creating campaigns and for campaign marketing (Perdana et al, 2017). In the context of equity crowdfunding, user research found that individuals lacked information about financial terminology and pay most attention to the risks presented at the top of a risk warnings page (as opposed to the bottom), suggesting platforms should present major risk warnings first and provide either a list of technical or financial terms to facilitate users' investing (Prom et al, 2016). A study by Lipusch et al (2021) explored the design elements that encourage co-creation (conceptualised as involving feedback and funding) on reward-based crowdfunding platforms. They tested the role of three design principles in influencing co-creation: the provision of multiple sources of information about the project (e.g., external reviews), encouraging funders to express their preferences (e.g., through participatory updates where they can provide feedback), and involving funders in product decisions (e.g., through voting on product features). The purpose of this research is to seek user preference in the codesign process in setting up a new intermediary crowdfunding platform.

3. METHODOLOGY

As stated in the introduction, our goal was to gather knowledge for the set-up of a new "intermediary channel" - i.e., a new crowdfunding initiative for Social Sciences and Humanities (SSH). For this purpose, we utilized both qualitative and quantitative data collection methods as this combination could ensure that the limitations of one type are balanced by the strengths of the other. This mixed method design was assumed to enable us to gain insights into what matters and in which way it matters to the users-funders when it comes to crowdfunding. Moreover, the integration of both methods would help us to gain more insight into answering the research questions. For this purpose, we conducted research articulated around two studies: a qualitative and design-oriented study (study 1) and a quantitative study (study 2) based on a questionnaire.

3.1 Study 1 and 2

In study 1, we collected qualitative data through codesign both one-on-one sessions and workshops. A total of 19 participants were selected using a purposive sampling technique: 9 participants took part in the workshops and 10 participants took part in one-on-one interviews, see Table 1. In study 2, quantitative data was collected through an online questionnaire. A total of 586 respondents took part in study 2, see Table 1. To facilitate an Europe-wide response, the questionnaire was prepared in English and then translated into six other languages. We utilized a snowball sampling method in reaching out to the audience. The questionnaire contained largely Likert scales aimed at measuring the perception of respondents on specific issues, such as the kind of project respondents would be willing to fund or questions about what should happen after the funding. The questionnaire data were analysed with descriptive statistics. Later in the presentation of results of the results, we will assume that the positive response is the sum of the positive items of a Likert scale (e.g., the sum of "strongly agree" and "agree" responses), whilst the negative response is the sum of the negative items of the scale (e.g., the sum of "strongly disagree" and "disagree" response).

Table 1. The number of participants for the workshops, interviews, and surveys

User	Workshop	One-on-One interview	Survey
Funder	4	5	586
Proposer	5	5	–
Total number of participants	9	10	586

4. FINDINGS

4.1 Study 1

4.1.1 Why Do Funders Invest in Crowdfunding Projects?

Participants in the workshops explained that the reasons they had made donations in the past were based on having empathy with the crowdfunding cause, and this made them feel that donating would have a positive effect on the common good. This is in line with Belleflamme (2013) who believe that funders are motivated when they felt that they were contributing because of the project cause.

4.1.2 What Would Guarantee the Quality of a Project?

Participants mentioned that proposing researcher should collaborate with researchers from other institutions and ensure that researchers have sufficient expertise in the chosen topics. Receiving recommendations from other researchers about the quality of the projects was seen as important. Moreover, ensuring high ethical standards and open access were also seen as relevant. The proposal should show the profile of the person responsible for the project with a good description of the proposed methodology and expected outcome. A researcher should show transparency about what the funding will be used for/how exactly the money will be spent using accessible language. Researchers should also show similar projects concluded, disclosing any conflict of interest, and show a calendar for the follow-up (disseminating results). Researchers prefer a platform with a guide on how to put together a good proposal giving a clear description of whom the target audience is going to be.

4.1.3 How Would Funds Be Managed?

The researcher agreed that the researcher's institution should manage the fund or via an associated bank account where movements can be traced by funders. Another suggestion is by using a virtual 'wallet' created via the platform. Researchers should provide a quarterly report on how money was spent. The research should as well be peer-reviewed.

4.2 Study 2

4.2.1 What Type of Research Are Potential Users More Likely to Support?

In the questionnaire, we asked what projects would be of interest to participants. The rationale for this data was to obtain knowledge for prioritizing decisions on the initial projects that could appear on our crowdfunding channel, especially during an initial bootstrapping phase. The proposed statements did not focus on research topics but rather on various aspects that could compose a project proposition, including the nature of the proposers, the impact of the project, and aspects of direct interest for potential funders. The results in Figure 1 show a strong positive response to the statement on willingness to fund projects that have a clear social impact (S1_societal_impact), with 85.8% positive responses. Of relevance are projects that are local to the geographical area of the funders (with a positive response at 60.9%, S1_geographical_area) and projects that see the involvement of civil society partners (at 61.8% of positive response, S1_civil_society). An interesting consideration is in relation to risks, respondents regard slightly more favourably projects which carry low risk (and are less ambitious, S1_low_risk_projects with 41.6% of positive response) than high-risk and more ambitious projects (S1_high_risk_projects with 33.4% of positive response). The question with the lowest positive response (and the highest negative) is the one on whether people would prefer to fund projects proposed by a university in the area where they live (S1_University_my_area with just above 20% positive responses and 43.3% negative). Perlsterin, (2013) mentioned that projects are supported based on their impact.

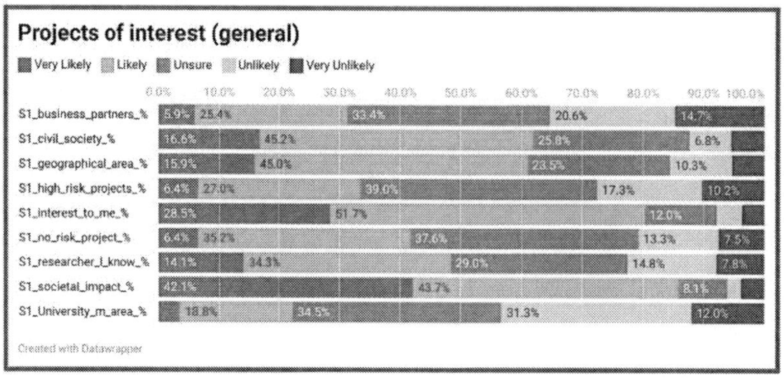

Figure 1. Projects of interest, that participants would be more likely to fund

4.2.2 What Are the Expectations of Users After the Project Conclusion?

In the questionnaire, we also asked respondents to tell us what should happen after the end of funding. This is an important component of success for crowdfunding. Results are presented in Figure 2. Respondents provided a strong positive response to the question about being informed of the project completion (A1_project_completed) with 95.5% of positive responses. Clarity on the ethical implication (A1_ethical_implications) of the project also is significant to note with 93.9% of positive responses. Three other statements received positive responses above 90%, the ones related to the acknowledgment in publications that the project was crowdfunded (A1_acknowledge_crowdfunded); the possibility to receive information about the progress of the project (A1_progress_information); the importance of the data collected by the crowdfunded project to be released as open data, where possible (A1_data_open). Two statements received if compared to the previous ones, relatively low positive responses (nonetheless still above 50%). The first one is the statement asking participants if they would be interested to be involved more in a project (e.g., as citizen scientists) (A1_involved_more) at 62.1%. The other statement was asking whether respondents would be interested to discuss the results of the project with the researchers (A1_discuss_results). This presents 57.3% of positive responses.

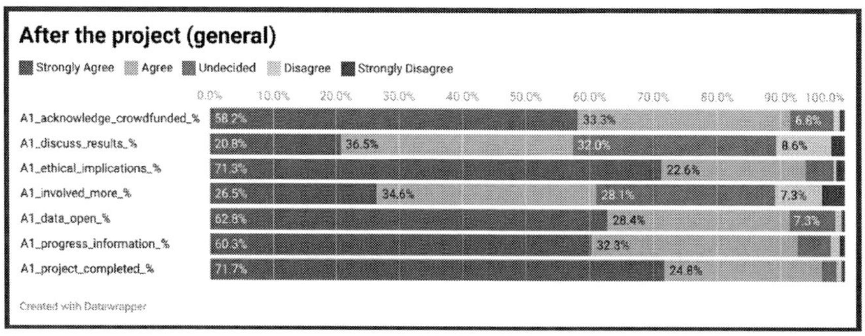

Figure 2. Expectations of users after the project

5. RECOMMENDATIONS/DISCUSSION

The results from studies 1 and 2 were formalised in a set of recommendations for setting up the GoTriple crowdfunding SSH channel. The results revealed that funders believe that projects with societal impact, especially projects that focus on the common good, should be promoted. Therefore, a first recommendation would be for the new channel to prioritize projects with clear societal impact. It was clear from the results they need to prioritize during the bootstrapping phase of the new crowdfunding channel, projects which are team-based rather than individual-based. Moreover, a further recommendation was to prioritize projects which carry low risks but that can reach their objectives, rather than risky projects. This may help build trust toward the platform and its capacity to deliver on the projects promoted in the platform. Whenever possible, it should be a condition of the publication of the project on the crowdfunding platform, that the researchers should make their data open at the end of the project (once the relevant publications have been completed). It was also clear the need to accompany the project proposal with reference letters and to include with the project an ethical statement. These were additional recommendations formulated by this research.

The results of this research have provided the project team with important material for setting up a new crowdfunding channel for SSH. This channel (https://wemakeit.com/channels/operas) is now managed by OPERAS, the Research Infrastructure supporting open scholarly communication in the social science and humanities. GoTriple is one of the OPERAS services. To date, two projects have been successfully funded through the OPERAS crowdfunding channel.

6. LIMITATIONS OF THE STUDY

6.1 Study Focus

This study focused on understanding the needs and preferences of users on a research-based crowdfunding platform with a focus on deriving recommendations for setting up a new crowdfunding channel initiative for SSH. As users of other platforms differ in their aim of investing in a particular project, this study should be repeated on other types of crowdfunding to understand the differences or similarities of users' needs and preferences of those crowdfunding types.

6.2 Sample Size (Qualitative Data)

One of the limitations of this study was the number of participants that took part in the workshops and one-on-one interviews were relatively small and may not necessarily be a good representation of the study population. However, in codesign, it is common to work with a small sample to derive insights.

6.3 Sampling (Quantitative Data)

Another limitation of this study is the distribution of the study sample of the quantitative data. The sample consisted of more researchers although we collected a reasonable quantity of data from the public, we believe that this may likely have an impact on the results. The distribution of the questionnaire was through the project's social media network. This medium may have attracted more researchers to take part in the study as the researchers have more of their colleagues in their contact.

6.4 Implications of the Study/Future Work

The result of this research has revealed that the interface should be able to convey transparency about the potential research project, the funding, and how it will be managed. Additionally, the result of the quantitative survey revealed several important insights from the funder's perspective and preference for low-risk projects and the need to receive regular updates about the research progress and findings. Future work should concentrate on the participants of the projects piloted with the new crowdfunding channel. This will help us understand what works and what could be improved in the new solution.

ACKNOWLEDGEMENT

The project has received funding from the European union's horizon 2020 research and innovation program under grant agreement no 863420. The funders had no role in the study design, data collection, analysis, decision to publish, or preparation of the manuscript.

REFERENCES

Agrawal, A., Catalini, C., and Goldfarb, A. 2015. Crowdfunding: Geography, social networks, and the timing of investment decisions. Journal of Economics & Management Strategy, 24(2):253–274

Allison, T. H., Davis, B. C., Short, J. C., and Webb, J. W. 2015. Crowdfunding in a prosocial microlending environment: Examining the role of intrinsic versus extrinsic cues. Entrepreneurship Theory and Practice, 39(1):53–73

Belleflamme, P., Lambert, T., and Schwienbacher, A. 2013. Individual crowdfunding practices. Venture Capital, 15.

Belleflamme, P., Lambert, T., and Schwienbacher, A. 2014. Crowdfunding: Tapping the right crowd. Journal of business venturing, 29(5):585–609

Bi, S., Liu, Z., and Usman, K. 2017. The influence of online information on investing decisions of reward-based crowdfunding. Journal of Business Research, 71:10–18

Calic, G. 2018. Crowdfunding pages 112–114.

Dahlhausen, K. E., Krebs, B. L., Watters, J., and Ganz, H. H. 2016. Crowdfunding campaigns help researchers launch projects and generate outreach. Journal of Microbiology & Biology Education, 17:32 – 37

Dalla Chiesa, C. and Dekker, E. 2021. Crowdfunding artists: beyond match-making on platforms. Socio-Economic Review, 19(4):1265–1290

Deng, L., Ye, Q., Xu, D., Sun, W., and Jiang, G. 2022. A literature review and integrated framework for the determinants of crowdfunding success. Financial Innovation, 8(1):1–70.

Gerber, E. M., Hui, J. S., and Kuo, P.-Y. (2012). Crowdfunding: Why people are motivated to participate. In ACM Conference on Computer Supported Cooperative Work, Working Paper, Northwestern University

Hemer, J. 2011. A snapshot on crowdfunding. Technical report, Arbeitspapiere Unternehmen und Region.

Jovanović, T. 2019. Crowdfunding: what do we know so far? International Journal of Innovation and Technology Management, 16(01):195-199

Laurell, C., et al 2019. Assessing the interplay between crowdfunding and sustainability in social media. Technological Forecasting and Social Change. 141:117–127.

Lehner, O. M. 2016. Crowdfunding social ventures: a model and research agenda. Routledge Handbook of Social and Sustainable Finance. pages 139–160.

Lipusch, N., Dellermann, D., Bretschneider, U., Ebel, P. A., and Leimeister, J. M. 2021. Designing for crowdfunding co-creation how to leverage the potential of backers for product development

Mollick, E. 2014. The dynamics of crowdfunding: An exploratory study. Journal of Business Venturing. 29:1–16.

Moritz, A., Block, J.H. 2016. Crowdfunding: A Literature Review and Research Directions. In: Brüntje, D., Gajda, O. (eds) Crowdfunding in Europe. FGF Studies in Small Business and Entrepreneurship. Springer, Cham.

Perdana, R., Suzianti, A., and Ardi, R. 2017. Crowdfunding website design with lean product process framework. p369–374

Perlstein, E. O. 2013. Anatomy of the crowd4discovery crowdfunding campaign. SpringerPlus, 2(1):1–3.

Petruzzelli, A. M., Natalicchio, A., Panniello, U., and Roma, P. 2019. Understanding the crowdfunding phenomenon and its implications for sustainability. Technological Forecasting and Social Change, 141:138–148

Prom Tep, S., Senecal, S., Courtemanche, F., and Gohier, V. 2017. Equity Crowdfunding and the Online Investors' Risk Perception: A Co-created List of Web Design Guidelines for Optimizing the User Experience, pages 301–311

Sauermann, H., Franzoni, C., and Shafi, K. (2019). Crowdfunding scientific research: Descriptive insights and correlates of funding success. PLoS ONE, 14

Schäfer, M. S., Metag, J., Feustle, J., and Herzog, L. 2018. Selling science 2.0: What scientific projects receive crowdfunding online? Public Understanding of Science, 27(5):496–514

Tanaka, K. G. and Voida, A. 2016. Legitimacy work: Invisible work in philanthropic crowdfunding. In Proceedings of the 2016 CHI conference on human factors in computing systems, pages 4550–4561

Tomczak, A. and Brem, A. 2013. A conceptualized investment model of crowdfunding. Venture Capital, 15(4):335–359.

Vachelard, J., Gambarra-Soares, T., Augustini, G., Riul, P., and Maracaja-Coutinho, V. (2016). A guide to scientific crowdfunding. PLOS Biology, 14(2).

Wheat, R. E., Wang, Y., Byrnes, J. E., and Ranganathan, J. (2013). Raising money for scientific research through crowdfunding. Trends in Ecology Evolution, 28(2):71–72

Zhao, L. and Shneor, R. (2020). Donation Crowdfunding: Principles and Donor Behaviour,. Springer International Publishing, Cham.

CITIZEN IDENTIFICATION IN CONTEXT OF ELECTRONIC GOVERNANCE – THE CASE OF MOZAMBIQUE

Paulo Maculuve and Luis Amaral
School of Engineering, Centro Algoritmi, University of Minho, Braga, Portugal

ABSTRACT

An efficient citizen identification system is fundamental in the context of the digital economy, both for the citizen and for the state as a public service provider and promoter of social justice, as there will be no justice without a correct identification of the actors, with the risk of penalizing the innocent and glorifying the ceremonious (Hoover, 1972).
The Mozambican Citizen Identification System (CIDS), based on the Information and Communications Technologies (ICTs) potentials, is being improved, therefore, the purpose of this article is to describe the current situation, its problems and forward some ideas to overcome the current problems, based on the Working Systems Theory (WST) (Alter, 2008).
Therefore, at the end of the article, recommendations are presented focused on the rationalization of the identification system, aiming at proposing a Conceptual Model that maximizes the ICT potentials, interoperable and working system.

KEYWORDS

Citizen, Citizen Identification, Interoperability, Electronic Governance, Working Systems

1. INTRODUCTION

Currently, most goods and services are made available using ICTs, through Electronic Governance (e-Gov), so, an indisputable identification of the main actor, the citizen, is essential. The CIDS are crucial tools for achieving Sustainable Development Goal (SDG), as stated in SDG#16.9 - to "provide legal identity for all, including birth registration" by 2030 and is a key enabler or contributor to many other SDG targets, such as financial and economic inclusion, social protection, healthcare and education for all, gender equality, child protection, agriculture, good governance, and safe and orderly migration (Dahan & Gelb, 2015). However, there are still more than one billion of people without proof of identity (Desai et al., 2018), so it is important that government and other players to take actions in CIDS and the appropriate conceptual model suitable for each reality is fundamental.

The Mozambican CIDS is comprised of various sub-systems that work as an "island", that is why it is worth conducting a study to propose a working Citizen Identification Conceptual Model in the context of e-Gov, which will respond to current and future challenges, because a well-structured identification system, conceived in a holistic approach, triggers the reduction of harmful aspects to the Public Administration, as it is the case of corruption and organized crime, which causes a lot of harm in many nations.

The research question is: *What is the appropriate Model of the Citizen Identification System (CIDS) for Mozambique?* This question directs the focus to the research of the conceptual aspects of Management Information Systems (MIS), contemplating the organizational, social and technological aspects, based on the work system Theory (Alter, 2013). To answer the research question, the study could be directed towards one of the following options: (a) developing several alternative models of CIDS, based on the best practices and/or based on principles theorists; (b) guide the study in an incremental development perspective, where the problems of the current Model are described and, based on the techniques of normalization of processes and the specificities of the Mozambican reality (case study), build the solution leading to the Proposed Model. Considering the object of the study and, given an analysis of the strengths and weaknesses of each one, the best option for the nature of the research matter is the second one, incremental development, as it allows a better understanding of the model to be developed, as it results from the cumulative resolution of the problems identified using scientific abstraction according to the selected methodology, visualizing the benefits of the model, thus facilitating the involvement of stakeholders and the ownership of the proposed model. The research methodology adopted to answer the research question is Design Science Research (DSR), as it allows rigor and precision in the description of facts, advocates the design of artifacts, which responds to the need to propose a Conceptual Model of CIDS for Mozambique (Hevner et al., 2004).

The purpose of this article is to describe the current situation of the CIDS, its problems, and propose a working Conceptual Model under the WST perspective. That is why the article structure includes introduction, some concepts, methodological aspects, description of the current system, its problems, proposal of the model, and towards the end, the conclusions and recommendations.

2. FUNDAMENTAL CONCEPTS

After the introductory notes, and for a better framework of the study object of the article, as well as for the reader´s better understanding, this section conveys a concise bibliography review about some concepts addressed in the article.

2.1 Citizen Concept

Among several studies about citizenship concept, there is a common understanding that the concept remotes to classic antiquity and to the French revolution, in 1789, when there was an increase in citizenship awareness, which advocated the effective participation of an individual in a given community, according to the rights and obligations established in that community (Palazzo, 2021).

Since then, nations incorporated in their constitutions and/or ordinary laws, the concept of citizenship. As an example, the Republic of Mozambique Constitution, establishes that man and woman are equal before the law within the political, economic, social and cultural domain("Lei 1/2004," 2004).

Therefore, a citizen can be defined as a set of rights and obligations (or duties), which allows the citizen to engage in political, social, cultural and economic activities (Furtado, 2010). In the context of identification system, the citizen concept is broad-ranging, and defined in two perspectives, namely, (a) citizen as a simple, singular person and, (b) citizen as a singular, complex person(Maculuve & Amaral, 2022).

2.2 Citizen Identification

Identification is the consistent image of the subject about himself, formed by abilities and beliefs, which is built throughout life, being particularly active during adolescence (Santos, 2013).

By definition, identification is the action and effect of identifying and being identified, and it is related identity, which is the set of personal characteristics of a person or community in relation to other (Amicci, 2015). Several identification methods (name, photography, ferrite, tattoo, dental arch, mutilation, anthropometry, papilloscopy, among others) have been developed and adopted over time to ensure undisputed identity and the use of papilloscopy, commonly known as biometry, proved effective, and with the evolution of technology this identification method is being consolidated with usage of smart cards (Maculuve & Amaral, 2022).

2.3 Electronic Governance (e-Gov)

E-Gov is the process of modernizing the governance using virtues of the ICT, allowing: (a) production of better-quality information; (b) improved access to services (public and private); (c) increased opportunities in civic and democratic participation; (d) more effective and efficient and less costly and more accountable of Public Administration. Therefore, e-Gov can be defined as the use of ICTs to promote governmental efficiency in providing public goods and services less bureaucratized and more cantered in the citizen, both within government to government (G2G) and between government the economy (G2B) external relations and from the government to the citizen (G2C) (Gartner, 2000).

2.4 System Interoperability

In the knowledge economy era (where internet is the driving force in institutional business), information from several sources and using different technologies, requires dialogue between different systems in a timely, secure and comprehensive manner, without jeopardizing the desired results (Marques, 2021).

Interoperability can be defined as the information and services exchanged, in a coherent manner, between systems and allows for the replacement of used component or product in the interconnection point without compromising the functionality of the system (UK-Governament, 2000).

Interoperability comprises 3 dimensions, namely, (1) organizational; (2) semantics; and lastly (3) technology (ENAP, 2015). Interoperability require a paradigm shift from isolated to integrated systems based on business rules where several systems obey a set of business rules (procedures and actions) in order to yield harmonized results. Thus, in the case of integrated systems, each system belonging to the architecture must obey the rules on how to produce harmonized results, resulting from normalized processes within organizational environment. Figure 1 illustrates the process of paradigm shift.

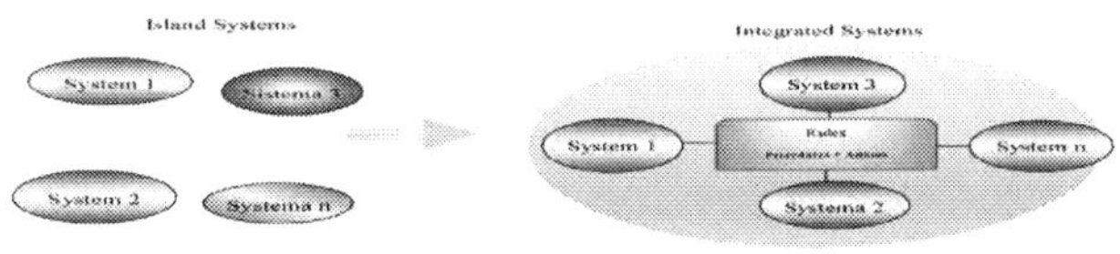

Figure 1. The movement from Island Systems to Integrated Systems

For an effective interoperability, it is important that (Mesquita & BRETAS, 2010). (a) Systems must be based in open standards; (2) services and components of reusable systems must be in the same architecture.

The Service Oriented Architecture interoperability (SOA) define a set of the best practices of the business processes. In figure 2 they are designated Rules Engine, where a set of procedures and actions (which will be common services being shared with different systems and/or with other organizational partners, within the scope of e-Gov) are normalized, aiming at a common understanding. Therefore, the interoperability service oriented architecture emphasizes business processes and the entities being served, and not the specific technology. Figure 2 illustrates the architecture oriented to services, pointing to the interconnection between different systems of a given organization and different networks from partners, who need to share a variety of business processes (services) within the scope of e-Gov.

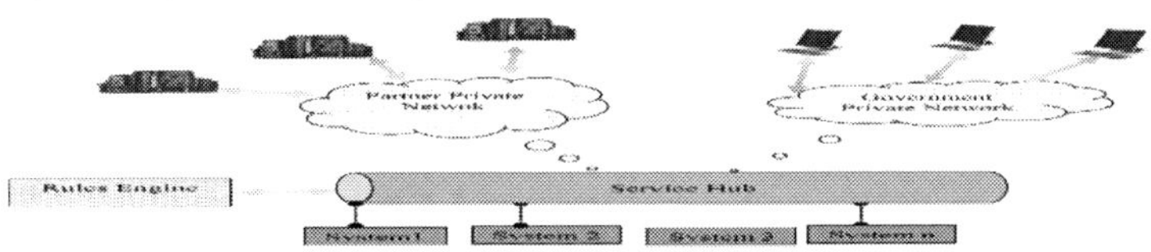

Figure 2. Service oriented architecture in the context of e-Gov

2.5 The Concept of a System

Considering that the article is devoted to the citizen identification system, it is relevant that the concept of systems is correctly understood, because, most of the times the term system is considered a technological solution or a software that operates in a given infrastructure (hardware).

The system can be defined as a group of people, procedures and technology, which, as a whole, can achieve a goal, in a socio-technological context, that is, the organizational, and social issues, as well as the surrounding environment must be considered in the definition of the system concept (Trauth et al., 2006). According to the WST perspective, the system is working if it provides services for which it was conceived for (Alter, 2008).

3. METHODOLOGICAL ASPECTS

The study aims to answer the following research question: *What is the appropriate Model of the Citizen Identification System for Mozambique?* Regarding the nature of the investigation, a combination of exploratory and descriptive was adopted (Diana, 2022), since the object of the study is CIDS for Mozambique, in a perspective of the evolution of the current model, combined with the nature of investigation, the research strategy adopted was a Case Study, because (Yin, 1994): (a) the study in question is knowledge obtained from experience and observation of facts relating to the functioning of the current CIDS model in Mozambique; (b) concerns about CIDS are a contemporary phenomenon for the world in general and for Mozambican society in particular; (c) the functional constraints of the Mozambican CIDS are a phenomenon that happens in real life in Mozambican society; (d) the scope is well delimited and stakeholders are also clearly identified.

Once the nature and research strategy had been defined, the Design Science Research (DSR) methodology was selected as appropriate to answer the research question, on the following grounds (Hevner et al., 2004): (a) it allows for rigor and precision in the description of the facts; (b) advocates the design of artefact's, which responds to the need to propose a Conceptual Model of CIDS for Mozambique; (c) ensures the involvement of people, organizations, processes and procedures. The problem that is intended to be solved with the Conceptual Model of CIDS, requires the creative and cyclical involvement of people, organizations, processes and procedures, within in an organizational environment.

Figure 3. summarize the methodological aspects for the present study, to answer the research question.

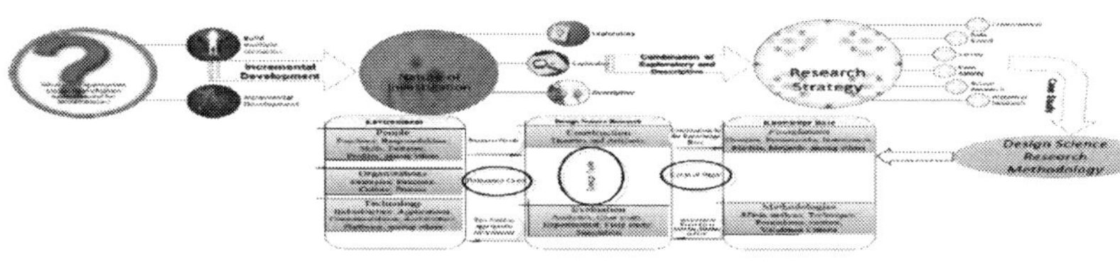

Figure 3. Summary of methodological aspects

Following the DSR methodology the research process carried out as follows: (a) Carry out a bibliographical review on the various concepts related to CIDS, which corresponds, in DSR methodology, the use of the Knowledge Base, for the resolution of the identified problem; (b) Collection of information in the various sources on CIDS both in Mozambique and in some countries, specially selected, this process, in DSR methodology, it fits into the component of studying the environment, where the people, organizations and technologies with the identified problem are. Therefore, the space where the phenomenon under study is observed; (c) In addition to collecting data from various documents that govern the Mozambican CIDS, the data collection strategy included interviews and discussions in focus groups.

The scope of study was limited to the CIDS subsystems that allow citizens to exercise or fulfil their constitutional rights and duties. In this line of action, the following entities were identified as main stakeholders (a) Ministry of Justice, which deals with the Birth Registration subsystem; (b) Ministries of the Interior, which manages the Civil Identification subsystem; (c) Ministry of National Defence, manager of the Military identification subsystem; (d) Technical Secretariat for Electoral Administration (STAE), responsible for managing the electoral identification subsystem; (e) National Institute of Terrestrial Transport (INATRO) manages the Driver identification subsystem, it should be noted that although this identification is not for the fulfilment of constitutional rights and duties, it only enables the citizen to driving motor vehicles, was included in the study due to its relevance in the CIDS, for Mozambican context; (f) Tax Authority of Mozambique, manages the fiscal identification subsystem; (g) Ministry of Health, manager of the Health identification subsystem; and, (h) National Institute of Social Security (INSS), is responsible for the Social Security subsystem.

Discussions in focus groups began, first with main stakeholders and then with other stakeholders. For this propose, a working group was formally created by the Minister of Science and Technologies involving all main stakeholders, with mandate and deadline (MCT, 2006). To support working group as well as to ensure that the assessment process included all those interested in the CIDS, an Advisers Group was created, consisting of high-level personalities who represented different institutions, namely, Judges, Member of parliament, top managers of various institutions, religious leaders, members of political parties, among others.

The outcome of the working group was adopted by Mozambican Government, such as: (a) adoption of Unique Citizen Identification Number (NUIC) ("Lei 12/2018," 2018); (b) new format of ID (BI)based on biometric which allow the citizen to access the BI on birth ("Decreto 11/2008," 2008); (c) new format of Passport based on biometric data ("Decreto 13/2008," 2008); among others.

Phenomenology, or rather, the experience and knowledge of the Mozambican reality was the object of analysis and consideration in the data collection process, which fits perfectly into the investigation strategy, Case Study (Yin, 1994).

4. IDENTIFICATION SYSTEM OF THE MOZAMBICAN CITIZEN, CURRENT SITUATION

This section presents a summary description of the current citizen identification system, aligned with the two perspectives of the citizen concept from the point of view of identification system.

4.1 The Citizen Identification: Singular Simple and Pure Person

The citizen identification in this perspective includes the following subsystems:

(a) Civil Registration, which deals with management of birth registration. From this subsystem, the citizen acquires the following documentation ("Lei 14/2020," 2020): (a) Birth Bulletin, assigned to the citizen at birth by the health authorities, sometimes, even before a name is given (innominate), resorting to the parents identification; (b) Birth Certificate, assigned to the citizen during born registration and it is the basis for acquiring subsequent identification papers, namely, the ID, Passport, among others; (c) Personal Ballot equally assigned during registration, which should have been used to register other events within the citizens' life cycle.

(b) Civil Identification, a subsystem that stores the data base about the national or naturalized (who acquire Mozambican nationality) citizens and the documents resulting from that subsystem are: (a) ID document (BI), assigned at birth, based on the birth registration documents (Bulletin, Certificate or Ballot) ("Decreto 11/2008," 2008); (b) ID for Foreign Residents (DIRE), assigned to foreign citizens with a residence permit ("Decreto 12/2008," 2008); and, (c) Passport (travel document), assigned to a citizen with the need to travel abroad, at any time, upon presentation of the birth registration documents or BI or DIRE ("Decreto 13/2008," 2008).

4.2 Citizen Identification: Singular Complex Person

The citizen identification in this perspective includes various subsystems, namely:

(a) Health, keeps citizens´ database from public hospital units, assigning them a Patient Identification Number (NID), in order to access the clinical process;

(b) Fiscal, keeps citizens´ database to ensure compliance with tax obligations, the essential of this subsystem is the assignment of the Unique Number Tax Identification (NUIT).

(c) Military, keeps database from national citizens above 18 years old, eligible for military service and for those who are already serving the military or are in the military career. The subsystem assigns two documents: (a) Military Ballot; and (b) Militar Identification Card

(d) Electoral, keeps database from citizens with electoral capacity, and the document in this subsystem is the voter card;

(e) Drivers´, keeps database from citizens enabled do drive automobile vehicles, and the document in this subsystem is the Driver's License.

(d) Social Security, keeps database for social security purpose (contributors e beneficiaries), resulting in the creation of two identifiers, namely: (1) Contributor Identification Number (NIC); e (2) Beneficiary Identification Number (NIB). Figure 4, summarize the Mozambican citizen identification system.

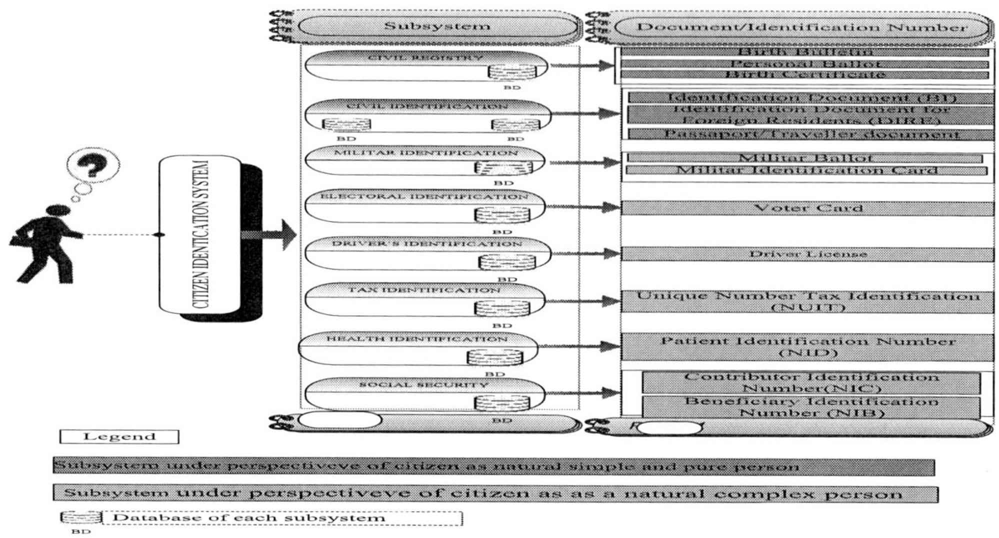

Figure 4. Macro vision of citizen identification system

As illustrated in figure 4, each subsystem maintains its processes and database, producing the respective documents in isolation, in a sort "island" system. There are cases of databases of the same subsystem, for example, Civil Identification subsystem, working in isolation way (one for BI issuance and another one for the issuance of passports (travel documents) and DIRE).

Table 1. Macro Vision of subsystems attributes

N/O	Documents (Subsystems)	Attributes																						
		Name	Father	Mother	Residential Address	Professional Address	Document Number	Birth Day	Marital status	Place of Birth	Tel	Fax	Email	Biometry	Nationality	Sex	Height	Expiry Date	Issuing Entity	Issuing Date	Place of Issue	Profession	Signature	photography
Subsystem under perspective of citizen as natural simple and pure person																								
1.	Birth bulletin	•	•	•	•	•	•	•	X	•	X	X	X	X	•	•	X	X	•	•	•	X	X	X
2.	Personal Ballot	•	•	•	•	•	•	•	X	•	X	X	X	X	•	•	X	X	•	•	•	X	X	X
3.	Birth certificate	•	•	•	•	•	•	•	•	•	•	•	•	X	•	•	X	X	•	•	•	•	X	X
Subsystem under perspective of citizen as natural complex person																								
4.	Identification Document	•	•	•	•	•	•	•	•	•	•	•	•	•	•	•	•	•	•	•	•	•	•	•
5.	Identification Document for Foreign Residents (DIRE)	•	•	•	•	•	•	•	•	•	•	•	•	•	•	•	X	•	•	•	•	•	•	•
6.	Passport/Traveller Document	•	•	•	•	•	•	•	•	•	•	•	•	•	•	•	X	•	•	•	•	•	•	•
7.	Military Identification	•	•	•	•	•	•	•	•	•	•	•	•	X	•	•	•	•	•	•	•	•	•	•
8.	Electoral Identification	•	•	•	•	•	•	•	•	•	•	•	•	•	•	•	X	•	•	•	•	•	•	•
9.	Drivers´ Identification	•	•	•	•	•	•	•	•	•	•	•	•	•	•	•	X	•	•	•	•	•	•	•
10.	Tax Identification	•	•	•	•	•	•	•	•	•	•	•	•	X	•	•	X	•	•	•	•	•	X	X
11.	Health Identification	•	•	•	•	•	•	•	•	•	•	•	•	X	•	•	X	•	•	•	•	•	X	X
12.	Social Security Identification	•	•	•	•	•	•	•	•	•	•	•	•	X	•	•	X	•	•	•	•	•	•	•

Each one of the identification subsystem holds its own set of attributes. In Table 1, we present a macro vision of the different subsystems attributes. As shown in table 1, many attributes are repeated in several subsystems, some of which, in the case of biometric data (which is being collected in the civil identification subsystem, drivers´ identification and electoral subsystem) have high maintenance costs. The subsystem does not have a common identifier (the attribute document number are not uniform).

According to the description of the current system, it is understood that the citizen life cycle in the identification system, as illustrated in figure 5, begins with a new birth registration or a request for nationality or permanent visa residency, going through several stages (qualities) that the citizen acquires throughout its life cycle, specifically, as a health system user, as a tax payer, as a voter, as a potential military, as a driver, as a social security tax payer and/or beneficiary. It also involves change in marital status, and many more, until the end of the citizen´s life cycle, the death, implemented in legal relations through issuance of the Death Certificate or when a foreign resident leaves permanently the country ("Lei 14/2020," 2020).

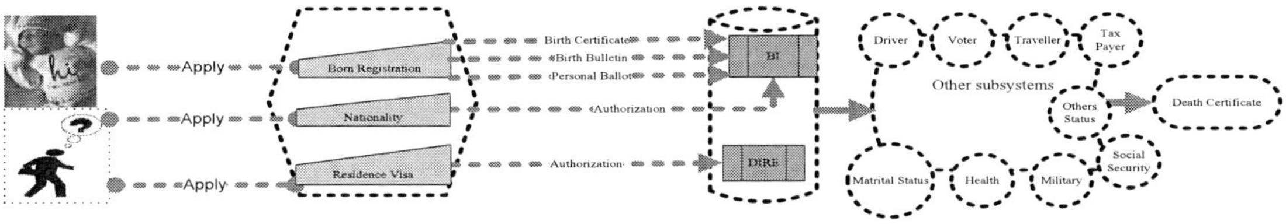

Figure 5. Simplified vision of the citizen life cycle under the identification point of view

A high-level analysis of the life cycle, figure 5, combined with the analysis of table 1, points to the need for simplification and rationalization of the civil registration subsystem, being able, for example, to eliminate some documents currently issued, namely, Birth Bulletin and Personal Ballot, as they have repeated information similar to that contained in the Registration Certificate. Therefore, out of the 3 it would be enough to keep one, the Registration Certificate.

5. CHALLENGES OF THE MOZAMBICAN IDENTIFICATION SYSTEM

After a brief exposure of the current system in the previous section, we bring up a critical analysis of the current system. The strategic use of ICTs is an opportunity for governments to focus their attention on the citizen, with the aim of providing them with goods and services in a responsive manner (available, timely and secure) according to their needs.

In legal terms, in Mozambique, the birth registration is mandatory and free of charge within 180 days after the citizen´s birth ("Lei 14/2020," 2020). However, many children, particularly in rural areas are not registered at birth, due to many reasons, mainly, (1) lack of parents awareness about the importance of the registration (they request it when the child is applying for school for the first time); (2) for some parents the name assignment is anticipated by traditional rites, which delays the registration; (3) The coverage of the infrastructure for providing the birth registration service is limited.

Legally, a Mozambican citizen has access do the BI at birth, upon presentation of birth registration evidence ("Decreto 11/2008," 2008). Nevertheless, this right is affected due to lack of registration at birth, with long lasting impact in their lives, mainly in rural areas, because it prevents them from exercising their rights, such as, access to educational system, among others.

Each institution collects, processes, stores and manages citizen´s data, without observing standardization principles, resulting in duplication of records within several subsystems, consequently, a positive identification of the citizen becomes complex and waste generators.

The exchange of information between different subsystems is manual, and the citizen acts like a facilitator of the process, providing information about changes on its registry along their life cycle, making it difficult and complex the development of new public services.

Lack of interoperability between identification subsystems, forces the citizen to go to numerous government institutions to request for identification documents, prompting high levels of bureaucracy and high cost for the citizen and the state.

Each institution, which manages citizen´s identification system, spends many resources (human, material and financial) to maintain common citizen data, a situation that can be avoided if there was interoperability.

Majority of the documents generates form the identification subsystems lack common and unique identifier of the citizen. In an incipient phase, the BI number is being included in the documents of other subsystems such as Passport, Voter Card and Driver's License, but this practice is still not producing the desired effects because the processes of these subsystems are not standardized and do not use the BI number as a systems common "key" (Information system primary key).

Most of the systems do not include biometric data, putting at stake the principle of undisputable identity.

The registration content and attributes 'structure is variable, because there are no standards to define formats and/or structures of the identification system (example: name format, date of birth format, among others).

The current situation regarding dispersed management of citizen identification highlights the insecurity of the current documentary file about the citizen´s data, placing the country in an inevitable challenge of re-thinking and re-structuring, at all levels, the citizen´s identification system.

In view of this reality, it is essential to carry out a study that culminates in the proposal of a Conceptual Model of the CIDS suited to the Mozambican reality, with a view to enabling the Mozambican citizen for the digital economy.

6. MODEL PROPOSAL

The current trend for the citizen´s identification systems is moving from traditional way to electronic (e-ID) and usage of smart cards, thus, allowing portability of necessary information for the citizen´s undisputable identification, as well as the accessibility to digital services.

According to figure 5, the life cycle of the citizen, evidence the need to rationalize the civil registration subsystem and a correct interconnection with other systems, to ensure citizen´s data integrity throughout its life cycle, in a perspective of a working system(Alter, 2008).

The development of CIDS must be in line with 10 principles, namely (The-World-Bank-Group, 2021): (a) Principle #1- ensure universal access for citizens and free from discrimination; (b) Principle #2-Remove Barrier, direct and indirect costs, information asymmetry, gaps in access to technology and inclusion at birth must never constitute a barrier to citizens accessing, using and obtaining legal identity; (c) Principle #3-Establish a trusted identity (unique, secure and accurate); (d) Principle #4-Create a responsive and interoperable platform; (e) Principle #5-use open standards to avoid dependence on technologies and suppliers; (f) Principle #6-protect privacy and personal autonomy in system design; (g) Principle #7-ensure financial and operational sustainability; (h) Principle #8-protect personal data, maintain cybersecurity and protect citizens' rights through a comprehensive legal and regulatory framework; (i) Principle #9-establish clear institutional mandates and accountability procedures; (j) Principle #10-ensure legality and trust through independent oversight and grievance resolution mechanisms.

Given the current reality and taking into account current and future challenges, as well as trends in identification systems, a Conceptual Model is proposed as systematized in figure 6.

The proposed Model take in consideration the following assumptions: (1) effective adoption of the concept of the Single Citizen Identification Number (NUIC), as a "unique key" for all citizen identification subsystems ("Law 12/2018, of 4 December," 2018); (2) reduce the Mozambican CIDS to 3 subsystems, with harmonized and interoperable processes based on the NUIC, namely: (a) Civil Registry; (b) Civil Identification; and, (c) Driver Identification; (3) the citizen identification system would be limited to issuing 4 types of documents, namely: (a) BI; (b) DIRE; (c) Passport (Travel Document); and, (d) Driver's License; and, (4) the Registry Certificate would be maintained, as an intermediate document for the certification and/or updating of citizen registration events in their life cycle; (5) Adhere to at least 8 out of the 10 principles, specifically principles 1, 2, 3, 4, 6, 7, 8 and 9 (The-World-Bank-Group, 2021).

Accordingly, to the proposed Model, the current identification subsystems of the military, electoral, fiscal, health and social security, that allow the citizen to exercise its constitutional rights and duties, will no longer be identification subsystems and become processes by which the citizen participates, and are interconnected with the CIDS through NUIC, with the BI as a core document and in a consolidated stage, it could be clumped, for example, the driver´s license and the BI.

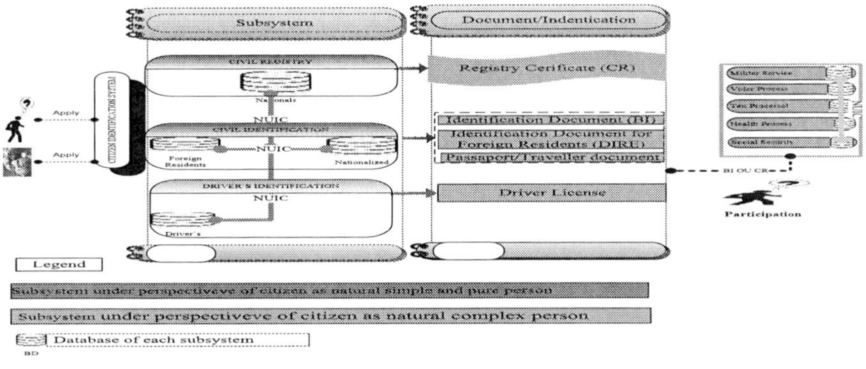

Figure 6. High level proposed conceptual model

7. CONCLUSIONS AND RECOMMENDATIONS

The trend of CIDS is moving to electronic identification system(e-ID), however is crucial to have traditional process well-structured based on appropriate and suitable conceptual model according to the WST(Alter, 2013).

The e-Gov strategy aims to respond to the following challenges: (1) Focus on the citizen; (2) Transparency; (4) Accountability; and, (4) e-participation. However, with an inefficient identification system, as is the case under study, it is difficult to achieve this goal.

There is an effort by the government of Mozambique to implement e-Gov, and since the late 1990s a facilitating legal framework has been developed. However, some challenges still persist, namely: (a) The lack of sustainable ICT infrastructure; (b) higher population concentration in rural areas with limited access to internet and about 39% of the rural population is illiterate, which can compromise the maximization of the virtues of ICT (INE, 2020); (c) the inefficient institutional coordination does not allow synergies in the implementation of e-Gov projects; (d) the inefficient CIDS, among others.

Inefficient CIDS makes public administration complex and it poses problems in two dimensions, namely: (1) to the citizen, it imposes avoidable costs; (2) to the state, it does not allow the existence of responsive information about the citizen identification to assist needs for administrative action.

The current system does not allow interoperability. Therefore, it is not a working system, as it does not produce the results for which it was efficiently designed (Alter, 2008).

The high-level analysis of the current system reveals the need for restructuring and rationalization, which is why the study leading to the implementation of the proposed Conceptual Model is recommended. The proposed model will allow citizens to enjoy the virtues of ICTs and access to digital services and for the state, it will allow the availability of responsive information for the various needs of administrative action.

The article describes the current situation of the Mozambican CIDS, its problems and proposes a working Conceptual Model, with a view to answering the research question, *What is the appropriate Model of the Citizen Identification System for Mozambique?* The Appropriate Conceptual Model for Mozambique or countries with similar socio-economic characteristics is the Model based on the following assumptions: (a) based on the NUIC; (b) that is compliant with at least 8 out of the 10 principles established by the World Bank; (c) that responds to current and future generations' challenges with regard to CIDS; (d) that allows citizens to participate in the digital economy; (e) Interoperable and rationalized as proposed on section 6; among others.

Finally, in addition to the need to detail the proposed Conceptual Model, it seems to us to be justifiable and recommendable a future study on the matter in two lines of action, with a view to: (a) Creating an institutional basis for management, maintenance and technical control-legal of the citizen identification system, in a holistic view, based on a sustainable architecture, which would assume the role of coordinator of the proposed model; (b) assess the need to review some legislation to adapt to the model.

The study becomes relevant because a citizen identification system based on modern architecture that responds to the present and future challenges contributes to the public administration modernization, as well as to the democratization and promotion of social justice(Hoover, 1972).

REFERENCES

Alter, S. (2008). Defining Information Systems as Work Systems: Implications for the IS Field. *Business Analytics and Information Systems*, *2*(1), 44. https://repository.usfca.edu/at/22

Alter, S. (2013). Work System Theory: Overview of Core Concepts, Extensions, and Challenges for the Future. *Business Analytics and Information System*, *14*(2), 72-121, Article 35.

Amicci, P. (2015). IDENTIFICAÇÃO CRIMINAL. In (Vol. 5, pp. 1-22). Brasil: Escola Técnica "Professor Fausto Mazzola" de Avaré.

Aprova Novos Modelos de Visto e de Autorização de Residencia para o Cidadão Estrangeiro, baseado em elementos biometricos e electronicos, 1 Decreto 12/2008, de 29 de Abril § I Serie - Número 17 129 (2008).

Código de Registo Civil, Lei 12/2018, Parlamento da Republica de Moçambique, I Serie - Número 236 Cong. Rec. 48 (2018).

Constituição da Republica de Moçambique, Lei 1/2004, Parlamento da Repaublia de Moçambique, I Serie - Numero 115 Cong. Rec. 40 (2004).

Cria novo Modelo de Passaporte para Cidadãos Nacionais, baseado em elementos biometricos e electrónicos, 1 Decreto 13/2008, de 29 de Abril § I Serie - Número 17 129 (2008).

Dahan, M., & Gelb, A. (2015). The Role of Identification in the Post-2015 Development Agenda [Working Paper]. *Open Knowledge Repository* (The World Bank Working Paper), 12. https://openknowledge.worldbank.org/handle/10986/22513

Desai, V. T., Diofasi, A., & Lu, J. (2018, 25-04-2018). *The global identification challenge: Who are the 1 billion people without proof of identity?* The World Bank Group. Retrieved 27-10-2022 from https://blogs.worldbank.org/voices/global-identification-challenge-who-are-1-billion-people-without-proof-identity

Diana, J. (2022). Qual a diferença entre pesquisa descritiva, exploratória e explicativa? In. www.diferenca.com.

ENAP. (2015). *Introdução à Interoperabilidade* Brasilia.

Estabelece os princípios e normas de organização e funcionamento do Sistema de Administração Financeira do Estado, abreviadamente designado por SISTAFE, Lei 14/2020, Parlamento da Republica de Moçambique, I Serie - Número 246 Cong. Rec. 20 (2020).

Gartner. (2000). What Is E-Government? Gartner's Definitions. 3. http://www.gartner.com/technology/about.jsp.

Hevner, A. R., March, S. T., Park, J., & Ram, S. (2004). Design Science in Information Systems Research. *MIS Quarterly*, *28*(1), 32.

Hoover, J. E. (1972). The Role of Identification in Law Enforcement: An Historical The Role of Identification in Law Enforcement: An Historical Adventure. *46*, 1-20.

INE, I. N. d. E.-. (2020). *Anuário Estratítico*. Maputo: INA Retrieved from http://www.ine.gov.mz/estatisticas/publicacoes/anuario/nacionais/anuario-2020_final-1.pdf/view

Introduz o Bilhete de Identidade (BI) para o Cidadão Nacional Baseado em elementos Biométricos, 2 Decreto 11/2008, de 29 de Abril § I Serie - Número 17 129 (2008).

Maculuve, P., & Amaral, L. (2022, 12-13- 03-2022). Citizen Identification: Concepts, Principles and Opinions – The Case of Mozambique. International Conferences e-Society 2022 and Mobile Learning 2022, Porto, Portugal - Virtual.

Marques, J. R. (2021). Entenda o Conceito de Interoperabilidade entre Sistemas e sua Utilidade para uma Empresa. https://www.ibccoaching.com.br/portal/entenda-o-conceito-de-interoperabilidade-entre-sistemas-e-sua-utilidade-para-uma-empresa/

Mesquita, C. S. F., & BRETAS, N. L. (2010). Panorama da Interoperabilidade no Brasil, .

Palazzo, F. P. (2021). A cidadania e as três leis de Newton.

Santos, C. M. D. (2013). Hermenêutica e o conceito jurídico de cidadão na ação popular no paradigma do Estado Democrático de Direito. In (pp. 1-2).

The-World-Bank-Group. (2021). Princípios de Identificação para o Desenvolvimento Sustentável (Principles on Identification for Sustainable Development : Toward the Digital Age). *I4D*, 24. Retrieved 26-10-2022, from https://documents1.worldbank.org/curated/en/147681573203575593/pdf/Principles-on-Identification-for-Sustainable-Development-Toward-the-Digital-Age.pdf

Trauth, E. M., Howcroft, D., Butler, T., Fitzgerald, B., & Degross, J. I. (2006). *Social Inclusion: Societal and Organizational Implication for Information Systems*. IFIP TC(WG8.2).

UK-Governament. (2000). *UK Government Interoperability Framework* UK: UK Government

Yin, R. K. (1994). *Case Study Research: Design and Methods*. SAGE Publications. https://books.google.co.mz/books?id=8U9qAAAAMAAJ

EDUCATIONAL, SOCIAL AND ETHICAL ASPECTS OF AI IN THE OPINION OF IT AND PEDAGOGY STUDENTS - A CASE STUDY

Eugenia Smyrnova-Trybulska[1], Małgorzata Przybyła-Kasperek[1] and Piet Kommers[2]
[1]*University of Silesia in Katowice, Bankowa 12, 40-007 Katowice, Poland*
[2]*University of Twente, Netherlands*

ABSTRACT

Artificial Intelligence (AI) is currently one of the most important and contemporary scientific developments in an interdisciplinary context. The EU approach to artificial intelligence centres on excellence and trust, aiming to boost research and industrial capacity while ensuring security and fundamental rights (A European approach to artificial intelligence). Strengthening the promotion of excellence in AI will enhance Europe's potential to compete globally. At the same time, many challenges and problems remain to be solved. The *problem* addressed in the article is to explore and analyse IT and pedagogy students' attitudes to educational, social and ethical aspects of AI implementation. The *purpose* is to discover and analyse the attitudes of IT and pedagogy students towards the educational, social and ethical aspects of AI implementation.

KEYWORDS

Artificial Intelligence (AI), Educational, Social and Ethical Aspects, Students, Opinion

1. INTRODUCTION

There are numerous definitions of Artificial Intelligence (AI). Some authors (like LeCun, 2022) consider AI as "[...] a possible path towards autonomous intelligent agents, based on a new modular meta-cognitive architecture and a somewhat new self-supervised training paradigm. The centerpiece of the proposed architecture is a configurable predictive world model that allows the agent to plan." The researcher emphasised that "[t]he world model uses a new type of energy-based model architecture called H-JEPA (Hierarchical Joint Embedding Predictive Architecture). H-JEPA offers hierarchical abstract representations of the world that are simultaneously maximally informative and predictable." (LeCun, 2022).

According to (Rosenzweig, 2021) "[...] [w]hen discussing artificial intelligence, or what many prefer to call autonomous learning machines, an important distinction must be made, which lies in the word 'learning'. There are many autonomous machines in existence already. While these machines can operate independent of human control, they're not, generally, adaptive. They don't learn from experience. They don't adapt to unanticipated situations. They only do what they're programmed to do." (Rosenzweig, 2021)

The authors from different countries analyse the educational, social and ethical aspects of AI implementation in different dimensions.

In the study (by Malyshkin, 2019) the author analyses the ethical and religious problems associated with the creation and dissemination of artificial intelligence systems, and proposes ways of legally regulating social relations related to the use of artificial intelligence (Malyshkin, 2019).

Other researchers emphasize that "despite the human rights harms of hiring algorithms, the AI ethics literature has predominantly focused on abstract ethical principles. This is problematic for two reasons." (Yam & Skorburg, 2021).) In particular, the authors identified: "First, AI principles have been criticized for being vague and not actionable. Second, the use of vague ethical principles to discuss algorithmic risks does not provide any accountability. This lack of accountability creates an algorithmic accountability gap." (Yam & Skorburg, 2021).

"The growth of AI and automated processes often create concerns that the human touch will be removed from the health-care delivery process. What the industry is finding, however, is that the opposite is true: AI can extend the resources and capabilities of overworked health-care professionals and vastly improve processes for medical interventions." (How artificial intelligence is making health care more human, 2021)

The aim of the study (Karnouskos, 2022) was to understand a wide range of potential legal and social issues by exploring the interplay of law, robots and society from different angles, such as legal, social, economic, gender, and ethical perspectives. (Karnouskos, 2022)

The research (Ziosi, Hewitt, Juneja, *et al.* 2022) "considers a host of definitions and labels attached to the concept of smart cities to identify four dimensions that ground a review of ethical concerns emerging from the current debate". The authors identify and describe: "(1) network infrastructure; (2) post-political governance; (3) social inclusion; and (4) sustainability, with a specific focus on the environment as an element to protect but also as a strategic element for the future" (Ziosi, Hewitt, Juneja, *et al.* 2022).

Cox, A. (2022) describes eight ethical scenarios for AI that have been developed specifically for information professionals to understand these issues. The author stressed that "[i]nformation professionals need to navigate these ethical issues effectively because they are likely to use AI in delivering services as well as contributing to the process of adoption of AI more widely in their organisations." Cox, A. (2022).

The ethical risks of employing algorithms using international human rights law as a universal standard for determining algorithmic accountability were emphasized by (Yam & Skorburg, 2021). Four types of algorithmic impact assessments were evaluated in terms of how effectively they address the five human rights of job applicants implied by in hiring algorithms. (Yam & Skorburg, 2021)

Some issues of Artificial Intelligence in the Social Context were analysed in the video: AI and diversity – the cultural and societal context behind artificial intelligence. "... Terah Lyons is the Founding Executive Director of the Partnership on AI, which was established to study and formulate best practices on AI technologies and advance the public's understanding of AI." (Lyons, 2019).

The *problem* of the article is to explore and analyse IT and pedagogy students' attitudes to educational, social and ethical aspects of AI implementation.

The *purpose* of the article is to explore and analyse IT and pedagogy students' attitudes to educational, social and ethical aspects of AI implementation.

The contribution of the paper is to present the result of the research on the analysis of IT and pedagogy students' attitudes towards the educational, social and ethical aspects of AI implementation in one of the Polish universities. The conclusions will highlight interesting reflections on the variation of attitudes of IT and pedagogy students according to their field of study, age, gender, specialisation, to the subject as well as selected aspects of AI implementation and propose some solutions to improve these results.

The two main hypotheses whose validity is tested in the study are:

- Students still have a relatively low level of AI competence and this needs to be developed.
- Students' perceptions of the possibilities offered by AI and areas of its application differ significantly according to their field of study, gender, year of study and previously graduated school.

2. DATA AND ANALYSIS OF THE QUESTIONNAIRE RESULTS

This section presents a preliminary analysis of the questionnaire results obtained. The survey was conducted in December 2022 and January 2023. Students of the University of Silesia in Katowice, Poland of two faculties – Faculty of Science and Technology, Faculty of Arts and Educational Science – were asked to respond. They were mainly students of two specializations – Computer Science and Pedagogy. A total of 103 responses were received. The questionnaire was prepared and completed online. Invitations to complete the questionnaire were sent to students of all years of study. The response rate was about 50%.

2.1 Sociological Metrics

In order to study the relationship between student characteristics and knowledge of AI or attitudes towards AI, the questionnaire included sociological questions. The sociological characteristics questions and possible responses in the questionnaire are presented below:

- age – <15-18>, <19-21>, <22-25>, <26-30>, >30

- name of previous school, university – open question, (optional question)
- name of current school, university – open question
- gender – male, female
- year of study – 1st, 2nd, 3rd, 4th, 5th, secondary school
- study specialization – e.g. pedagogy, social work, IT, humanities, economics, technical but not AI

Descriptive statistics on the responses obtained related to sociological metrics are presented in Table 1.

Table 1. Descriptive statistics on responses to sociological questions

Age	Quantity/ Percentage	Name of previous school, university	Quantity/ Percentage	Name of current school, university	Quantity/ Percentage
<15-18>	0/0	Technical secondary school	31/30.10	University	103/100
<19-21>	33/32.04	General secondary school	33/32.04		
<22-25>	55/53.40				
<26-30>	10/9.71	University	17/16.50		
>30	5/4.85	Polytechnic	12/11.65		
Gender	**Quantity/ Percentage**	**Year of study**	**Quantity/ Percentage**	**Study specialisation**	**Quantity/ Percentage**
Male	54/52.43	1st	18/17.48	Education	42/40.78
Female	49/47.57	2nd	19/18.45	Social	0/0
		3rd	35/33.98	IT	61/59.22
		4th	23/22.33	Humanities	0/0
		5th	8/7.77	Economics	0/0
				Technical but not AI	0/0

Based on the results obtained, it can be concluded that the majority of respondents are between 22 and 25 years old. They are mainly secondary school graduates – the vast majority of them received not technical but general education. All students are currently studying at the University of Silesia in Katowice. In terms of gender, it can be said that the sample is balanced – an almost equal number of men and women were interviewed, with only 5 more men than women. The largest group of respondents is currently in their third year of study. Four-year students are also a numerous group. Together they account for more than half of the sample. First-year and second-year students make up about 36% of the total sample. Fifth-year students are the least represented. Students from two specialisations – pedagogy and computer science were surveyed, with computer science students accounting for 59.22% of the total sample.

2.2 Experience and Self-Assessment of AI Competence

The next part of the survey included questions about experience with AI. The main purpose of this part was to find out whether respondents had encountered AI issues at university or in their personal lives, and at what level they rate their knowledge of specific AI issues. The questions in this part and possible responses to the questions, defined using the Likert scale to the 7-point scale included in the questionnaire, concern their encounter with AI; the definition of AI; identified own level of AI competence (designated as question 1) in seven-point qualitative scale, 1 being the lowest level, 7 being the highest level, as well as competence in the area of AI supporting in programming languages (e.g. Python); Ethical and social aspects of AI? Data Preprocessing Techniques; Knowledge Machine Learning; Deep Learning; Natural Language Processing; Learning Analytics; cyber security; Recommender systems (designated as questions 2-11).

As many as 98 respondents answered that they encountered AI issues, representing 95.15% of the sample. Five respondents answered that they had not encountered AI, which means that they are not aware of using AI issues on a daily basis through their smartphones or search engines. To the question "What do you think Artificial Intelligence is?", the largest number of respondents indicated intelligent machines (31 responses), followed by learning based on experience (23 responses), machine learning (22 responses), robots (12 responses), all other possibilities were indicated by individual respondents.

Table 2 shows the basic statistics of the responses obtained. Bar charts of the responses obtained related to the assessment of AI competences are shown in Figure 1.

Table 2. Basic statistics of the obtained responses

Question	Average	Median	Mode	Minimum	Maximum	Standard deviation
1	3.0	3	3	1	7	1.3
2	2.5	2	1	1	7	1.4
3	2.9	3	multimodal	1	7	1.4
4	2.8	3	2	1	7	1.5
5	3.4	3	3	1	7	1.5
6	2.7	3	3	1	6	1.3
7	2.5	2	2	1	6	1.3
8	2.7	3	3	1	7	1.5
9	2.3	2	1	1	7	1.3
10	2.6	2	multimodal	1	7	1.5
11	2.7	2	2	1	7	1.4

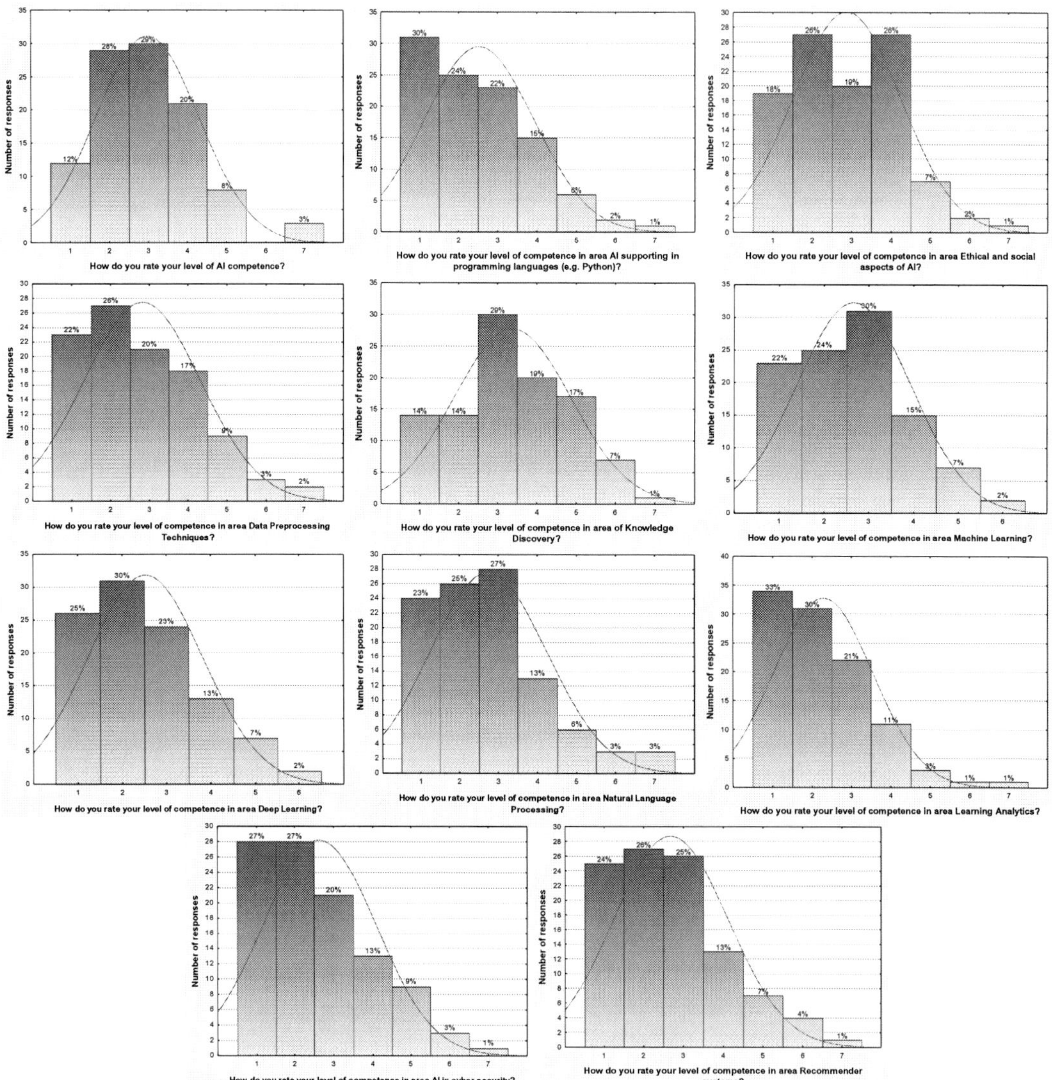

Figure 2. Bar charts of the responses obtained related to the assessment of AI competences

As can be seen from the results, students do not rate their knowledge and competences related to AI highly. For all questions presented in Figure 1, the most frequent answers are 1-3 which means low. It can be concluded that students rated their knowledge and competencies in the following areas: Knowledge discovery and Ethical and social aspects of AI. On the other hand, they rated their competences lowest in the areas of AI supporting programming languages, AI in cyber security and Learning analytics. Thus, the first hypothesis posed is valid.

2.3 AI and Social, Educational and Development Aspects

The next part of the survey is related to the social, educational and development aspects of AI. Also, the questions about the prospects of using AI in education and society were included in this section of the questionnaire. The aim of this study was to analyse the attitudes and concerns about AI among students of different study specialisations, age, gender, year of study and previous schools. The questions in this part and possible responses included in the questionnaire were defined using Likert scales to the 7-point scale listed below e.g.: Can and should AI be used more actively, for example, in education to personalise teaching-learning?; Can social robots be helpful in the development of children including those with special needs? Where could AI be most useful and effective: For people – seven-point qualitative scale, 1 being the lowest level, 7 being the highest level; as well as for education; for medicine; for transport for business, finance and banking; for space and NASA; for economy and management; for IT (Information Technology); for public services; cybersecurity and safety (questions 1, 2, 3a)-3j)). Table 3 shows the basic statistics of the responses. Bar charts of the responses related to the assessment of AI competences are shown in Figure 2.

Table 3. Basic statistics of the responses obtained

Question	Average	Median	Mode	Minimum	Maximum	Standard deviation
1	4.6	5	4	1	7	1.5
2	4.6	5	5	1	7	1.6
3 a)	5.1	5	multimodal.	2	7	1.5
3 b)	4.9	5	5	1	7	1.5
3 c)	5.8	6	7	1	7	1.4
3 d)	5.4	6	7	2	7	1.5
3 e)	5.6	6	7	1	7	1.4
3 f)	5.9	7	7	1	7	1.5
3 g)	5.3	5	7	1	7	1.4
3 h)	6.0	6	7	3	7	1.2
3 i)	5.1	5	6	1	7	1.6
3 j)	5.3	5	7	2	7	1.6

As the figures shows, respondents have no doubt that artificial intelligence can be useful in areas such as: medicine, transport, business, finance and banking, space and NASA, information technology and cybersecurity. In all of these questions, the highest response – rate 7 – was indicated by about 35% to even 50% of respondents. By far the highest responses were given to the use of AI in space and NASA. However, in the case of AI applications for people, education or public services, respondents were not so strongly convinced. In these cases, AI received support, but the results are rather spread around an intermediate intensity: responses of 4, 5, 6 were the most frequent. Respondents also gave moderate support for more active use of AI issues in education to personalise teaching-learning and the use of social robots in the development of children including those with special needs. Negative answers to these two questions were rather rare. But the most frequently indicated answers were average intensities 4, 5, 6.

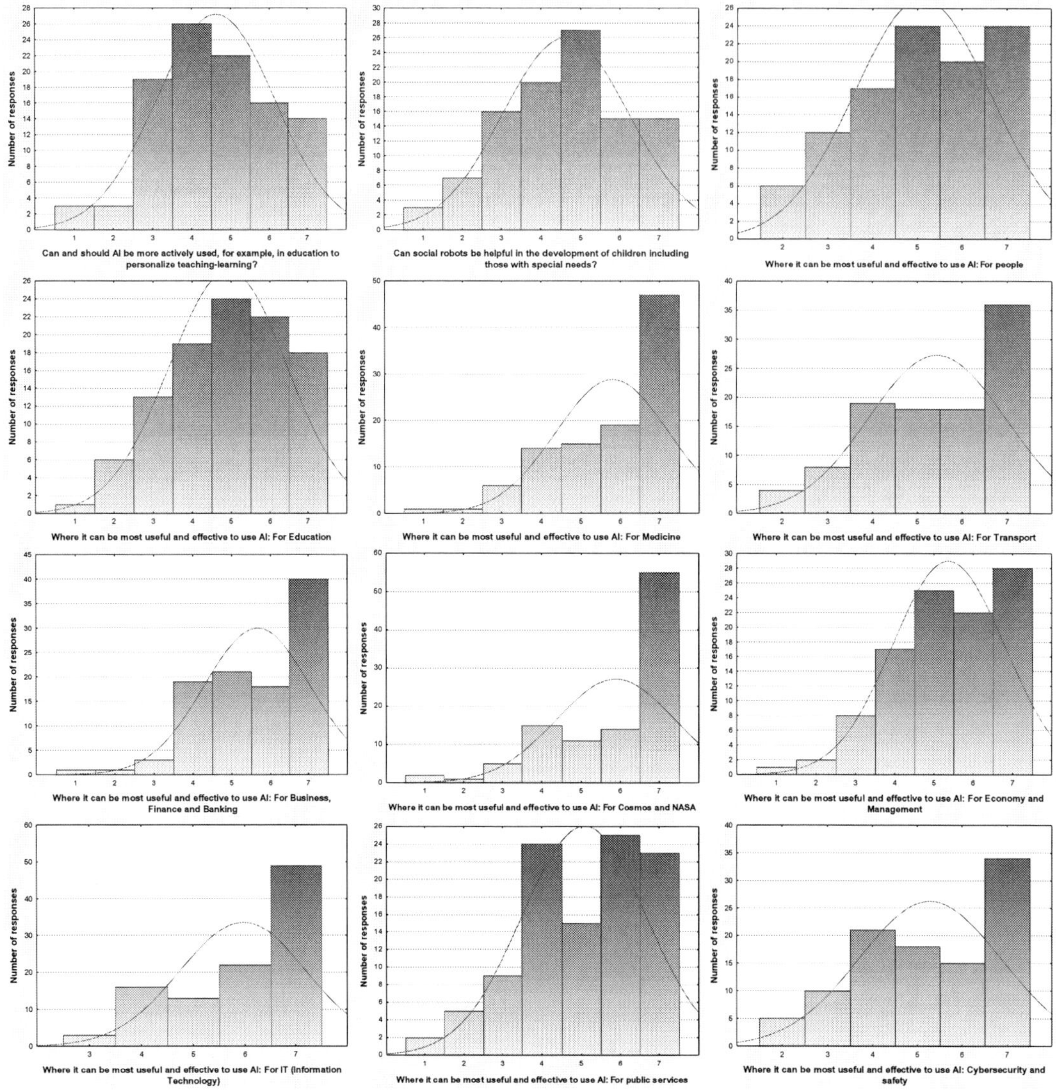

Figure 2. Bar charts of the responses obtained related to social, educational and development aspects of AI

Statistical tests were performed in order to test the significance of differences in the results obtained for groups defined by: study specialization, age, gender, year of study and previous school (each issue was considered separately). All results examined are for the ordinal variable. The Mann-Whitney test was used to detect differences in the two independent samples defined by: field of study and gender. The results obtained are presented in Table 4: sum of ranks across groups and p-value. There are statistically significant differences in the results obtained for all aspects studied – questions 1, 2, 3a)-3j) – in the groups defined by study specialisation. It can be seen that IT students rate the possibility of using AI issues in all aspects studied higher and better than pedagogy students. Perhaps this is due to a greater awareness of the possibilities offered by AI. As far as groups defined by gender are concerned, practically in all questions the differences in ratings are significant – the only exceptions being the questions on: Can and should AI be used more actively in, for example, education to personalise teaching-learning? Where can the application of AI be most useful and effective: cyber security and safety? Analysing the results, it was found that the majority of women study education, and the majority of men study computer science (only 7 women in IT specialisation took part in the questionnaire, the remaining 54 were men). Thus, the results obtained for groups defined by gender are probably also related to the specialisation of students.

Table 4. The Mann-Whitney test results for groups defined by study specialization and gender

Question	Groups defined by the study specialization: education and IT			Groups defined by gender: male and female		
	Sum of the ranks for IT	Sum of the ranks for education	p-value	Sum of the ranks for male	Sum of the ranks for female	p-value
1	3462	1894	**0.048**	3049	2308	0.106
2	3525	1831	**0.016**	3113	2243	**0.041**
3 a)	3661	1695	**0.001**	3254	2103	**0.003**
3 b)	3515	1842	**0.019**	3101	2255	**0.049**
3 c)	3555	1801	**0.007**	3217	2139	**0.004**
3 d)	3692	1665	**0.000**	3333	2024	**0.000**
3 e)	3626	1730	**0.002**	3150	2206	**0.019**
3 f)	3494	1862	**0.019**	3101	2255	**0.035**
3 g)	3531	1825	**0.014**	3110	2246	**0.041**
3 h)	3509	1847	**0.016**	3104	2252	**0.037**
3 i)	3498	1858	**0.026**	3066	2291	0.083
3 j)	3544	1812	**0.010**	3146	2211	**0.026**

In the next stage of the study, the Kruskal-Wallis tests were performed for groups defined by: age, year of study and previous school (in each case the group size was greater than 2). The significance of differences in responses was analysed for all questions from 1 to 3 j), but for readability, only the results obtained (group size, group rank mean, p-value and test statistic value) for questions at which statistical significance of differences was found are presented in Table 5. Significant results are shown in bold. As can be seen, age, type of previous school and year of study have little influence on the evaluation of the applicability of AI issues in different fields. Among the grouping conditions tested, it can be seen that the year of study has the greatest influence. We notice a regularity that students in the first and fifth year of study rate the applicability of AI for people, education, economy and management and computer science higher than students of the second, third or fourth year of study. This may be related to the first fascination with AI issues in the first year of study, and the greatest knowledge about the possibilities of AI in the fifth year of study. In the final conclusion, we can say that the second hypothesis posed is valid.

Table 5. The Kruskal-Wallis test results for groups defined by age, year of study and previous school

	Groups defined by age				
	<15-18>	<19-21>	<22-25>	<26-30>	>30
n	1	32	55	10	5
Question	Rank avg and results				
3 c)	20	43	55	73	41
	H(4,103)=11.227; p-value=0.024				
3 d)	41	46	53	64	55
	H(4,103)=3.117; p-value=0.539				

	Groups defined by previous school			
	Technical secondary school	General secondary school	University	Polytechnic
n	31	33	17	12
Question	Rank avg and results			
3 c)	47	38	56	59
	H(3,93)=8.543; p-value=0.036			
3 d)	42	41	60	58
	H(3,93)=9.013; p-value=0.029			

	Groups defined by year of study				
	1st	2nd	3rd	4th	5th
n	18	19	35	23	8
Question	Rank avg and results				
	H(4,103)=11.871; p-value=0.018				
3 b)	68	40	46	57	54
	H(4,103)=11.085; p-value=0.026				
3 g)	67	45	43	56	63
	H(4,103)=10.952; p-value=0.027				
3 h)	67	40	46	59	55
	H(4,103)=11.957; p-value=0.018				

3. CONCLUSION

In conclusion, it is possible to emphasise some of the findings regarding the attitudes of IT and pedagogy students to the educational, social and ethical aspects of AI implementation, as well as their competence in AI. Their self-assessment has shown an unsatisfactory level in the main areas of AI, while at the same time the students' attitude towards the prospect of using AI in some social areas was positive. Among the grouping conditions examined, it can be seen that the year of study has the greatest influence. We notice a regularity that students in the first and fifth year of studies rate the possibilities of using AI for people, education, economy and management and computer science higher than students in the second, third or fourth year of study. This may be related to an initial fascination with AI issues in the first year of study and the greatest knowledge about the possibilities of AI in the fifth year of study. Their interest in the topic is the motivation for the development of a platform and courses in the research area for students to deepen their knowledge and use it in their education and future professional career, which is what the FITPED-AI project serves (Skalka, & Drlik, 2022; Smyrnova-Trybulska, Drlik, & Skalka, 2023).

ACKNOWLEDGEMENT

The following grant funded this research: European Commission under the ERASMUS+ Programme 2021, KA2, grant number: 2021-1-SK01-KA220-HED-000032095 "Future IT Professionals Education in Artificial Intelligence".

REFERENCES

A European approach to artificial intelligence. European Commission https://digital-strategy.ec.europa.eu/en/policies/european-approach-artificial-intelligence

Cox, A. 2022. The Ethics of AI for Information Professionals: Eight Scenarios, *Journal of the Australian Library and Information Association,* 71(3), 201-214, https://doi.org/10.1080/24750158.2022.2084885

How artificial intelligence is making health care more human 2021. https://www.healthcaredive.com/spons/how-artificial-intelligence-is-making-health-care-more-human/606994/

Karnouskos, S. 2022. Symbiosis with artificial intelligence via the prism of law, robots, and society. *Artif Intell Law* 30, 93–115. https://doi.org/10.1007/s10506-021-09289-1

LeCun, Y. 2022. From Machine Learning to Autonomous Intelligence. https://www.youtube.com/watch?v=YwJwQLktebU

Lyons, T. 2019 AI and diversity – the cultural and societal context behind artificial intelligence https://www.youtube.com/watch?v=qfmwLwtqxOw

Malyshkin, A.V. 2019. Integrating Artificial Intelligence into Public Life: Some Ethical and Legal Issues. Herald St. Petersburg University. *Law 3*: 444–460. https://doi.org/10.21638/spbu14.2019.303

Rosenzweig, P. 2021. The Pros and Cons of Autonomous Learning Machines https://www.wondriumdaily.com/the-pros-and-cons-of-autonomous-learning-machines/

Skalka, J. & Drlik, M. 2022. Proposal of Artificial Intelligence Educational Model Using Active Learning in a Virtual Learning Environment. In E. Smyrnova-Trybulska (ed.) *E-learning in the Transformation of Education in Digital Society. „E-learning" Series.* Vol. 14 Katowice-Cieszyn: STUDIO NOA for University of Silesia. (pp. 15-25) ISSN 2451-3644 (print edition), ISSN 2451-3652 (digital edition), ISBN 978-83-66055-31-5 https://doi.org/10.34916/el.2022.14.02

Smyrnova-Trybulska, E., Drlik, M., & Skalka, J. 2023. Wymiana doświadczeń i najlepsze praktyki w nauczaniu AI. [Exchange of experiences and best practices in teaching AI.] *Gazeta Uniwersytecka, [University Newspaper]* 304, s. 28-29

Yam, J. & Skorburg, J. A. 2021. From human resources to human rights: Impact assessments for hiring algorithms. *Ethics and Information Technology* 23 (4): 611-623. https://doi.org/10.1007/s10676-021-09599-7

Ziosi, M., Hewitt, B., Juneja, P. et al. 2022 Smart cities: reviewing the debate about their ethical implications. *AI & Soc* 2022. https://doi.org/10.1007/s00146-022-01558-0

CONCEPTUALIZING NETWORKED KNOWLEDGE ACTIVITIES: RELATED AND CO-OCCURRING ACTIVITIES IN ONLINE SPACES

Vanessa P. Dennen, Dan He, Hui Shi and Dawn Adolfson
Florida State University, Tallahassee, FL, USA

ABSTRACT

This study examines how college students conceptualize the relationship between different types of networked knowledge activities. The purpose was to determine where there is greater or lessons conceptual consensus among students, which can serve as an indicator of areas where networked knowledge skills may be weak or underused. Using an interview with an embedded card sort activity, 63 college students shared how they would organize different social media actions given larger activity categories (network, collect, curate, share, broker, negotiate, and create). Findings showed greatest consensus under the network and collect categories, especially when familiar actions were represented. Less familiar actions, like different ways of tagging resources and sharing tags, were not highly associated with any particular networked knowledge activity. These findings have implications for teaching digital literacy skills at the college level.

KEYWORDS

College Students, Information Seeking, Knowledge Networks, Networking, Sharing, Social Networking, Social Media

1. INTRODUCTION

In a typical day, most people find themselves in need of information and human interaction. They also might have information of use to others or be able to meet the interaction needs of others. These needs are the driving forces behind networked knowledge activities, and the building blocks of online social networks. Most daily activities, including those supporting work, school, home, and relationships, may be enhanced or enabled by information seeing and interaction in online networks (Rainie & Wellman, 2012). These networks tend to incorporate social media platforms, which offer tools for sharing, searching, and otherwise engaging with both people and information. In a professional context, online networks offer work-related sharing and mentoring opportunities that support informal learning and professional development (Dennen & Wang, 2002). Although the motivation may be different from work contexts, the two dimensions of everyday life information seeking per Savolainen (1995) are orienting information (information about the world and world events) and practical information (information for problem solving), both of which are supported by online networks. Finally, people use social media to maintain personal relationship, including while at work. This latter option offers the ability to connect to their non-work lives in ways that are beneficial to both contexts (Kühnel et al., 2020). In short, online spaces support knowledge networking in its broadest sense for those people who know how and chose to engage in it.

Young adults, a group that includes most traditional-aged college students, occupy an interesting position in the online sphere. They are labeled digital natives because they were born at a time when technology was all around them, although the omnipresence of technology in their lives has not innately made them better than prior generations at online knowledge seeking and network building (Kirschner & De Bruyckere, 2017). They been hailed as active participants in participatory culture (Jenkins et al., 2009) and in transmedia activities (Scolari, 2018; Scolari et al., 2018), although for many their actual online activities may be far more mundane. Still, their regular use of social media is well documented from their teenage years (Anderson & Jiang, 2018; Anderson et al., 2022) and onward into their early adult years (Perrin & Anderson, 2019). Prior research on this population has found that heavy users and non-users experience the greatest satisfaction from their online information-seeking activities (Kim et al., 2014), and that psychological and sociocultural factors may affect information behaviors as well (Kim & Sin, 2015).

This study investigates how college students conceptualize and organize different online and social media activities using the Networked Knowledge Activities (NKA) framework (Dennen, 2019). This framework was original developed to help educators break down online activities into meaningful, related actions when designing lessons, but has also been used to analyze social network activities in naturalistic online settings (Dennen et al., 2020). While the framework provides clarity about activity intent and outcomes and helps structure content analysis for researchers interested in functional activities in online environments, less is known about how individuals conceptualize their online activities and whether they see the relationship between those activities.

2. PURPOSE AND RESEARCH QUESTIONS

This purpose of this exploratory study was to determine how college undergraduates perceive a variety of online activities, and in particular the relationship between different activities. In other words, it explores which activities participants view as being highly related, using the NKA framework as an organizational device.

1. To what extent do college students agree on the social media actions related to each networked knowledge activity category?
2. What social media actions are most associated with each networked knowledge activity?
3. Which social media actions were not closely associated with a specific networked knowledge activity?
4. Which category of social media actions are most and least familiar to college students?

These research questions put an emphasis on practices rather than tools, as recommended by Greenhow et al. (2019). Certain tools may enable specific practices, practices tend to transcend specific tools.

3. METHOD

3.1 Participants

The participants in this study were 63 undergraduate college students at a large research university. Participants were recruited from a research participation pool. All participation was voluntary, and students in the research participation pool could opt to complete an alternate assignment for their classes if they were not comfortable or interested in participating in research. Participants opted into each study they completed, including this one. The study was approved by the researchers' Institutional Review Board and all participants provided consent to participate and to be recorded.

3.2 Data Collection and Analysis

Data collection occurred via one-hour interviews on zoom. During these interviews, participants first completed a brief demographic survey. Then they were asked some general questions about their social media use. Next, they engaged in three rounds of a card sort activity hosted on the ProvenbyUsers platform. Finally, they debriefed the card sort activity with the researcher.

To complete the card sorts, participants followed a URL supplied by the researcher and shared their screen. During the card sort activities, they were asked to use a think-aloud process while sorting cards. All three card sorts used the same 41 cards, but each sort provided participants with different sorting categories. The 41 cards represented different types of social media actions (e.g., use social media to find resources; tag another person to call attention to a resource), The card list was initially developed by the researchers, and then refined with the assistance of a focus group of undergraduate students. The intent was to develop a comprehensive list of activities that might be supported on different online platforms. To maintain cross-platform applicability, general terms like connect, bookmark, and tag were used rather than platform-specific ones like friend, hashtag, and favorite.

The third card sort activity is the focus of this paper. During this card sort, participants were asked to sort their cards into six piles representing the main components of the NKA framework: share, collect, curate, broker, create, and negotiate. Each NKA category was defined for the participants at the start of the card sort and definitions appeared on screen. During the card sort, which typically took 15 minutes or less, participants had to place each card onto a pile. No card could be left out at the end, and cards could only appear in one pile. However, once placed on a pile, cards could later be moved around. At the

Data analysis focused on the calculating overall consensus levels across participants for each NKA category (research question 1) and using frequency counts to determine which actions were most commonly associated with each category (research question 2) or not distinctly associated with any category (research question 3). Qualitative data from the think-aloud portion of the study and the card sort debrief was used to address the fourth research question.

4. FINDINGS

4.1 Overview of Participants

Of the 63 college students who participated in this study, most were under the age of 25 (59; 93.7%). Of the remaining four participants, two were between 25-34, one was 45-54, and one declined to answer. Only 7 (11.1%) considered themselves very savvy social media users, whereas 3 (4.8%) reported being not very savvy. The majority of participants self-reported that they were savvy (31; 49.2%) or somewhat savvy (22; 34.9%). For these participants, the primary purpose for using social media was connecting with close ties (i.e., family and friends) and entertainment, which each were selected by 60 (95.2%) participants. Following this, 42 (66.7%) use it for school/schoolwork, 40 (63.5%) for news consumption, 39 (61.9%) for learning about hobbies, 28 (44.4 %) for meeting new people, and 20 (31.7 %) for work or seeking employment information. In addition, participants were asked about what social media platforms they often use for personal and educational purposes. Most mentioned platforms include Instagram, Snapchat, TikTok, Facebook, YouTube, Pinterest, LinkedIn, Twitter, and blogs.

4.2 Overall NKA Category Sort Consensus

To answer the first research question, participant agreement was calculated at the category level. With a maximum possible value of 1.00, it was unsurprising to see that agreement levels overall were low (see Table 1). The highest agreement was within the network category. All 63 participants sorted cards into this category, and while the participants in aggregate placed greatest number of cards in this category, the number of unique cards in this category was similar to the number of unique cards placed in other categories. The lowest agreement is in the broker category, which received the lowest aggregate number of cards, but the same number of unique cards as the network category. Additionally, 3 participants did not sort any cards into the broker category, making it the only category in the framework not used by all participants during the card sort activity.

Table 1. Students' consensus on the categorical functions of social media actions

NKA	# Participants Used	# Cards[1]	# Unique Cards [2]	Agreement [3]
Network	63	617	27	0.36
Collect	63	358	20	0.28
Curate	63	389	23	0.27
Negotiate	63	350	26	0.21
Create	63	294	26	0.18
Share	63	374	33	0.18
Broker	60	201	27	0.12

Notes: 1. Total number of cards placed into the group across all participants. 2. Number of unique cards placed into the group across all participants. 3. Level of participant consensus about which cards belong in a group. The maximum value of 1.00 would mean that all participants sorted cards into the category identically.

4.3 Within Category Consensus

To identify similarities in thinking about different social media actions, the most commonly sorted cards were noted for each of the NKA categories. The ***network*** category is the overarching category of the NKA framework, and it involves actions that help people build and maintain their connections with others. The social media actions sorted into this category by the greatest number of participants are:

- Send connection requests to people (60; 95.2%)
- Follow people who I know (60; 95.2%)
- Follow people with whom I do not yet have established relationships (60; 95.2%)
- Send a private message to someone with whom I do not have an existing relationship (58; 92.1%)
- Send a private message to someone with whom I have an existing relationship (54; 85.7%)

The 6.4% discrepancy between these last two items is interesting, with four participants differentiating the function of private messages depending on type of relationship.

The ***collect*** category had the second highest agreement score. This category was defined as finding and saving an online item. The actions most frequently sorted into this category are:

- Download interesting resources to my computer (55; 87.3%)
- Email things I find online to myself (55; 87.3%)
- Use search engines to find resources (47; 74.6%)
- Use social media to find resources (45; 71.4%)
- Bookmark resources (42; 66.7%)

In the collect category it is evident that participants most readily identified with downloading and emailing items to store them locally or in personal accounts. However bookmarking, while still firmly in this category, does not reach such high recognition as a collection strategy.

To ***curate*** is to select and organize a group of items, and curation is highly related to collecting. The top cards appearing in this category are:

- Organize online resources by topic (58; 92.1%)
- Apply tags to resources for organizational purposes (51; 81.0%)
- Apply tags to resources to help describe them for myself (44; 69.8%)

Organization as a component of curation clearly resonated with the participants, although some were unable to see that applying tags to organize items is essentially the same as applying tags to describe those items.

The ***negotiate*** category was defined for participants as discussing knowledge with other people. The four cards most sorted into this category are:

- Offer my opinion in response to someone else's post (57; 90.5%)
- Offer my expertise in response to someone else's post (57; 90.5%)
- Correct misconceptions or misinformation that others have posted online (53; 84.1%)
- Ask for advice online (43; 68.3%)

Interestingly, the three of these four items with the highest agreement all focus on giving information to others. The item that involves asking others for assistance had a lower frequency of being sorted into this category, suggesting that participants

The ***create*** category focuses on generating knew knowledge objects or resources. The three most frequently appearing cards are:

- Develop media to share expertise online (55; 87.3%)
- Develop media to share opinions online (48; 76.2%)
- Make a remix or mashup of existing online items (47; 74.6%)

Based on the cards sorted into this category, participants appear to associate creation with expertise more frequently than with opinions, and with unique productions rather than derivative ones.

Share is a simple concept given the prevalence of "share" buttons in most social media tools, although it was one of the categories with lowest consensus. Sharing occurs when one person makes items available to others, The items with greatest agreement were:

- Email things I find online to other people (45; 71.4%)
- Post resources that I have created to an online group or community (35; 55.6%)
- Tag another person to call their attention to a resource (33; 52.4%)

These agreement levels are notably lower than agreement levels in other categories.

Broker was defined for participants as an intermediary behavior, where an individual draws upon knowledge or objects originating with one party or location and purposefully makes it available to another party. With the lowest overall category consensus, the three most frequently appearing cards in this category did not reach sorting frequencies comparable to those of other categories:

- Share or post resources from one social media platform to another (36; 57.1%)
- Share resources from my face-to-face network with my online network (33; 52.4%)

During the think-aloud and debrief, participants expressed that this was a largely unfamiliar concept. Still, a little more than half of the participants recognized brokering as a highly specific form of sharing.

4.4 Actions Lacking a Clear Category

Whereas many cards were sorted into a primary category, as noted above, others were sorted into multiple categories, with less than 50% categorical consensus. Table 2 presents a sample of these items along with the two highest sorting categories. All of these low sorting consensus items were sorted into at least four unique categories and, in most instances, six or seven. The varied sorting patterns indicate the breadth of ways that participants thought about the different activities, and in many cases have a logical connection. For example, Writing a description of an item before saving or sharing is an act of annotation that is associated with curation, but 14 participants felt this was an act of creation, albeit a small act. When following an account that shares interesting things a person is building their network, but the underlying intent may be to collect knowledge objects. The act of evaluating an item before sharing it online resonates with the intentionality behind curation, but 12 participants sorted it into the category related to the next action in the sequence. Finally, applying tags to resources to describe them for others made some participants consider tags as a means of curation, whereas other participants focused on the idea of an audience for those items and sorted the action under share or broker.

Table 2. Sample items with less than 50% category consensus

Action	Highest NKA	Second Highest NKA
Write a description of an item before saving or sharing	Curate (44%)	Create (22%)
Follow an account that shares interesting things	Collect (41%)	Network (37%)
Evaluate an item before sharing it online	Curate (37%)	Share (19%)
Apply tags to resources to help describe them for other people	Curate (35%) and Share (35%)	Broker (14%)

In other instances, actions co-occurred in the same categories with greater frequency than they appeared in any single category. For example, 57 (90.5%) participants placed the cards for unfriending or unfollowing a person and leaving an online group in the same category, although these cards appeared in the networking category with respective frequencies of 79.4% (50 participants) and 76.2% (48 participants).

4.5 Most and Least Familiar Categories and Actions

During the card sort process, participants were free to ask researchers questions about the actions on each card and researchers could provide clarification or examples so long as they did not suggest a specific sorting category. Participants were also asked to use a think-aloud process to indicate their rationale as they sorted cards. Prior to the NKA card sort, the NKA framework was reviewed with each participant. At that time, all participants had already sorted all the cards twice using different frameworks. Based on participant comments during this overall process, brokering was the least familiar category to participants. Curation, while a familiar term, yielded a wide range of participant familiarity; some participants indicated that they regularly curate online resources and talked about making selection and organizational decisions as well as describing or annotating their curated resources. Others appeared to understand the general concept, but struggled to fully differentiate curation from collecting. When discussing the negotiate and create categories, participants commented about their own participation in these activities, generally falling into two user types. The majority indicated discomfort with these activities, wanting to avoid both perceived conflict that might occur through negotiation and vulnerability associated with creation. Participants who engaged in these activities, however, appeared to either hold more nuanced views of the categories (e.g., negotiation as a means of navigating conversation and creation as any act that produces something new, regardless of scope or size) or to be comfortable with public interactions.

In terms of specific actions, tagging was the most confusing to participants. Tagging actions of various types appeared on eight cards, six of which achieved less than 50% frequency in any one category. Comments during the think-aloud confirmed participants' uncertainty about tag use in various contexts. Similar questions arose when piloting the cards. During the first card sort, which focused on frequency of activity, there were four cards focused on resource tagging. For each of these four resource tagging activities, 28-41 of participants indicted it was a practice in which they never or rarely engage.

5. DISCUSSION

Overall, the findings suggest that the were best able to see the functional relationships among familiar networking, negotiation and collection activities that are part of typical information-seeking practices. However, there are many less familiar and practiced networked knowledge activities among this population. Specifically, the findings showed that tagging actions were poorly understood, as were annotation and resource evaluation activities, echoing earlier studies (Cates et al., 2019; Dennen et al., 2018). Although tags can be used in varied ways across social media contexts (La Rocca & Boccia Artieri, 2022), play a critical role in information aggregation, which means that skills related to selecting and applying meaningful tags are important. Tags enable effective information seeking behaviors (Jiang, 2013), and increased tagging literacy can help improve information storage and retrieval activities across various online social platforms and contexts (Keck & Heck, 2019; Shi et al., 2023). For individuals who know tagging primarily as a performative activity, this use of tags may challenge their knowledge and skills, and creates tensions in how people understand tag purpose and use in the broader social media landscape (McCosker, 2017).

Classifying one's everyday online activities using a framework may seem like a largely academic exercise, but it offers participants the opportunity to reflect on their practices. By discussing online practices in terms of isolated actions, it also highlights practices that may be less often invoked or less well understood. It may not be important for individuals to label their networked knowledge activities in order to perform them, but it is nonetheless important for them to understand the range of activities that might be used to support networked knowledge tasks. For example, if individuals are not taught to effectively tag and annotate online resources, or that tags and annotations may be available to help them locate resources, their networked knowledge interactions may be unsatisfactory or at the surface level. Individuals who do not understand curation and its underlying activities, for example, are unlikely to be effective online curators.

Although tagging has been highlighted in this discussion, it is not the only skill area of concern. Curation is an important skill for navigating online information across different life contexts. For example, individuals' curation activities related to online news consumption affect not only the quantity but also the veracity and perspective of the news to which they are exposed (Merten, 2020). Alternately, individuals who cannot differentiate general sharing from targeted brokering may not fully understand the purpose of either. People who engage in knowledge brokering typically exhibit greater depth of knowledge and also are successful at developing and promoting novel ideas (Resch & Kock, 2021). Their knowledge and skills are highly valued in communal knowledge settings. Essentially, all of the skills falling under the umbrella of networked knowledge activities play an important role in being an effective information user.

The findings generated by this study show variability in how people understand networked knowledge activities. Among traditional college-aged people, such as the students in this study, formal education on networked knowledge activities may be lacking. Although demonstrated time and again that the digital natives moniker has little bearing on actual digital skills (Kirschner & De Bruyckere, 2017), this erroneous belief persists. Digital skills vary widely among youth, although they generally increase as education levels increase (Correa, 2016), and meaningful generational differences about social media use may be more about cultural elements than about skill sets (Evans & Robertson, 2020). What his means for educators is that there are latent opportunities for developing these skill sets among their students and smoothing the transition from school settings. Whereas the focus of digital and related information skill development in schools may be limited to certain academic-specific activities (e.g., locating and assessing the quality of scholarly articles), perhaps it should extend to helping students develop broader abilities to navigate the information and sharing landscapes of the Internet in general and social media more specifically. To address this call, educators may need to improve their own skills as well. Regardless, opportunities are plentiful across the academic disciplines to teach students how to effectively engage in activities like information curation and brokering, and these skill sets will serve students well as they enter the workforce.

6. CONCLUSION

The connections made by these participants, individually and in aggregate, demonstrate how they think about their online and social media actions. These findings suggest areas where transfer of skill or knowledge may be weak, specifically in the places where participants did not commonly or consistently see connections between different activities and overall activity categories. In this sense, the study has implications for how social media networking skills and related digital literacy and communication skills are taught to teenagers and young adults. Rather than just assuming frequent use of and familiarity with activities due to time spent on social media platforms, educators might identify and focus on knowledge networking skills that enhance both professional development and everyday life information seeking in their disciplines. Then they can assess the degree to which college students are able to apply skills in these contexts, noting that skill application is not just mechanical (e.g., type a tag), but also conceptual (e.g., identify meaningful tags). They can also use frameworks like NKA to help identify areas where college students may lack confidence in online environments, such as network development, and use their classes to foster skill development.

This study has several limitations as well as implications for future research. Although interviewing 63 participants is a labor-intensive process, it does not yield sufficient insights to support broad generalizability. Data collection relied on self-report and did not extend into measurements of how effectively participants can engage in the different activities. This study represents analysis of a partial dataset. Analysis of the full dataset is ongoing and will include comparison of self-reported activity frequency to effectiveness of activity classification. Additionally, future research could focus on better understanding different naturalistic approaches to engagement in networked knowledge activities as well as the formative experiences that help develop awareness, skills, and use of these activities.

ACKNOWLEDGEMENT

The software used in this research was funded by an Undergraduate Research Opportunity Program Materials grant at Florida State University. We thank the UROP students who assisted with data collection.

REFERENCES

Anderson, M., & Jiang, J. (2018). *Teens, social media & technology 2018*. Pew Research Center.

Anderson, M., Vogels, E. A., Perrin, A., & Rainie, L. (2022). *Connection, creativity and drama: Teen life on social media in 2022*. Pew Research Center.

Cates, M. L., Dennen, V. P., & Bagdy, L. M. (2019). Building pre-service teacher knowledge communities through social bookmarking: A design case. *Technology, Instruction, Cognition & Learning, 11*(2/3), 193-217.

Correa, T. (2016). Digital skills and social media use: How Internet skills are related to different types of Facebook use among 'digital natives'. *Information, Communication & Society, 19*(8), 1095-1107. https://doi.org/10.1080/1369118X.2015.1084023

Dennen, V. P. (2019). Frameworks for designing and analyzing learning: Activity interactions in online courses. In M. G. Moore & W. Diehl (Eds.), *Handbook of Distance Education* (pp. 244-259). Routledge.

Dennen, V. P., Bagdy, L. M., & Cates, M. L. (2018). Effective tagging practices for online learning environments: An exploratory study of approach and accuracy. *Online Learning, 22*(3), 103-120.

Dennen, V. P., & Wang, M. (2002). The keyboard-based job coach: Informal learning via the Internet. *Advances in Developing Human Resources, 4*(4), 440-450. https://doi.org/10.1177/152342202237521

Dennen, V. P., Word, K., Adolfson, D., Arechavaleta, V., He, D., Hsu, C.-W., Hur, J., Jung, D., Kent, H., Russell, A., & Toth, K. (2020). Using the networked knowledge activities framework to examine learning on social networking sites. In P. Kommers & G. C. Peng (Eds.), *Proceedings of the international conference on Web-based Communities and Social Media 2020* (pp. 165-172). IADIS Press.

Evans, C., & Robertson, W. (2020). The four phases of the digital natives debate. *Human Behavior and Emerging Technologies, 2*(3), 269-277. https://doi.org/https://doi.org/10.1002/hbe2.196

Greenhow, C., Cho, V., Dennen, V. P., & Fishman, B. J. (2019). Education and social media: Research directions to guide a growing field. *Teachers College Record, 121*, 14.

Jenkins, H., Purushotma, R., Weigel, M., Clinton, K., & Robison, A. J. (2009). *Confronting the challenges of participatory culture: Media education for the 21st century*. Macarthur Foundation.

Jiang, T. (2013). An exploratory study on social library system users' information seeking modes. *Journal of Documentation, 69*(1), 6-25. https://doi.org/10.1108/00220411311295306

Keck, H., & Heck, T. (2019). *Improving tagging literacy to enhance metadata and retrieval for open educational resources.* DIPF| Leibniz-Institut für Bildungsforschung und Bildungsinformation.

Kim, K.-S., & Sin, S.-C. J. (2015). Use of social media in different contexts of information seeking: Effects of sex and problemsolving style. *Information Research: An International Electronic Journal, 20*(1), n1.

Kim, K.-S., Sin, S.-C. J., & Yoo-Lee, E. Y. (2014). Undergraduates' use of social media as information sources. *College & Research Libraries, 75*(4), 442-457.

Kirschner, P. A., & De Bruyckere, P. (2017). The myths of the digital native and the multitasker. *Teaching and Teacher Education, 67*, 135-142. https://doi.org/https://doi.org/10.1016/j.tate.2017.06.001

Kühnel, J., Vahle-Hinz, T., de Bloom, J., & Syrek, C. J. (2020). Staying in touch while at work: Relationships between personal social media use at work and work-nonwork balance and creativity. *The International Journal of Human Resource Management, 31*(10), 1235-1261. https://doi.org/10.1080/09585192.2017.1396551

La Rocca, G., & Boccia Artieri, G. (2022). Interpreting the changeable meaning of hashtags: Toward the theorization of a model. *Frontiers in Sociology, 7*, 1104686. https://doi.org/10.3389/fsoc.2022.1104686

McCosker, A. (2017). Data literacies for the postdemographic social media self. *First Monday, 22*(10).

Merten, L. (2020). Block, hide or follow—Personal news curation practices on social media. *Digital Journalism, 9*(8), 1018-1039. https://doi.org/10.1080/21670811.2020.1829978

Perrin, A., & Anderson, M. (2019). Share of U.S. adults using social media, including Facebook, is mostly unchanged since 2018. In. Pew Research Center. https://www.pewresearch.org/fact-tank/2019/04/10/share-of-u-s-adults-using-social-media-including-facebook-is-mostly-unchanged-since-2018/

Rainie, L., & Wellman, B. (2012). *Networked: The new social operating system*. The MIT Press.

Resch, C., & Kock, A. (2021). The influence of information depth and information breadth on brokers' idea newness in online maker communities. *Research Policy, 50*(8), 104142. https://doi.org/https://doi.org/10.1016/j.respol.2020.104142

Savolainen, R. (1995). Everyday life information seeking: Approaching information seeking in the context of "way of life". *Library & Information Science Research, 17*(3), 259-294. https://doi.org/https://doi.org/10.1016/0740-8188(95)90048-9

Scolari, C. A. (Ed.). (2018). *Teens, media and collaborative cultures: Exploiting teens' transmedia skills in the classroom.* Transmedia Literacy H2020 Research and Innovation Action/Universitat Pompeu Fabra.

Scolari, C. A., Masanet, M.-J., Guerrero-Pico, M., & Establés, M.-J. (2018). Transmedia literacy in the new media ecology: Teens' transmedia skills and informal learning strategies. *El profesional de la información (EPI), 27*(4), 801-812.

Shi, Y., Cao, H., & Chen, S. (2023). Order and disorder in the evolution of online knowledge community: an investigation of the chaotic behavior in social tagging systems with evidence of stack overflow. *Aslib Journal of Information Management*. https://doi.org/10.1108/ajim-08-2022-0353

FACT CHECKERS IN DEMOCRACY: PERCEPTION OF INDEPENDENT FACT CHECKERS AND NEWS ORGANIZATIONS

Chang Sup Park
Associated Professor, Ph.D., Affiliation: University at Albany, State University of New York, USA

ABSTRACT

This study compares U.S. adults' perception about the performance of news organizations and independent fact checkers. Drawing upon a survey of 1,652 respondents, this study finds that perceptions of objectivity of news organizations is significantly higher than those of fact checkers. Fact checkers, however, are thought to be more objective and give more contextual information about current topics than news organizations. In terms of media trust and transparency of the information collection process, no significant difference is found between news organizations and fact checkers. The analysis also finds that perceptions about objectivity, transparency, contextualization, and trust have a positive association with fact checking use. The results suggest that fact checkers play a substantial role in relation to journalism, possibly showing a new form of journalism.

KEYWORDS

Fact Checkers, News Organizations, Objectivity, Transparency, Media Trust

1. INTRODUCTION

Although the practice of checking facts has long been an essential part of journalism, the establishment of dedicated independent fact-checking organizations is only a recent phenomenon. To some extent, fact checking has been fueled by the abundance of misleading information circulating on social media, and by populist politicians promoting "alternative facts" and denouncing anything they do not like as "fake news." Fact checking's main goal is to provide accurate information by objectively evaluating the veracity of any claim and calling out misinformation, lies, and deception (Graves, 2018). This goal is well reflected in the mission statements of leading fact checkers, which note that their purpose is to "reduce the level of deception and confusion in U.S. politics" (factcheck.org, 2022), and to help citizens "find truth in politics" (politifact.com, 2022).

The increase of independent fact checkers also stems from the disappointment in the inability of conventional journalism to challenge untruthful claims (Graves, 2016), which could account, in part, for the steady decline of public trust in the institution of news (Jones, 2018). As fact checking plays an increasing role in truth in information, it is imperative to evaluate how news consumers perceive and evaluate the roles and performance of independent fact checkers, who strive to set the record straight for as many news consumers, opinion leaders, politicians, and even mainstream news outlets as possible.

This paper examines news consumers' perceptions of the role of independent fact checkers in relation to major news organizations. Specifically, this study compares audience perceptions of news organizations and fact-checking sites on major tenets of solid journalism (objectivity, contextualization, and transparency), as well as trust in fact checkers and news organizations. The results are from a survey of 1,240 U.S. adults conducted in 2020.

2. LITERATURE REVIEW

2.1 Fact Checkers as a New Form of Journalism

The emergence of contemporary fact checkers can be attributed to the perceptions of biased media reports (Graves, 2016). Fact checking may be seen as an outcome of the declining trust in journalism organizations. With diminishing trust, fact-checking organizations are becoming a "new journalistic institution" seeking to "revitalize the 'truth seeking' tradition in journalism" (Graves, 2016, p. 6).

In the last decade, a new class of dedicated fact-checking organizations has emerged using trained staff to objectively assess the truth of controversial, polarizing, and contentious issues and public claims. These fact-checking organizations bridge the media and political spheres. The goal that most fact-checkers share is the promotion of truth in public discourse. Although some fact-checking outlets are subunits of established news organizations, about two-thirds of all fact checkers across the world are independent or run by civil society organizations, such as PolitiFact and MediaWise.

A primary mission of independent fact checkers is to examine and evaluate the accuracy of information and then publicize corrections (Graves, 2016). Fact-checking organizations also take on the role of watchdogs of the government, analyzing and evaluating whether declarations delivered by politicians and reported by journalists are truthful. Fact checking adds context and truth to journalism by fearlessly and objectively setting the record straight.

Fact checkers differ from news media in several ways. Fact checks integrate original sources and, "stand out for the richness and diversity in the use of verification mechanisms" (Vázquez-Herrero et al., 2019, p. 4). Fact checkers aim to provide the most accurate account of an issue by means of thorough verification. Fact checking has developed as a form of accountability journalism. In its current form, fact checkers mainly scrutinize data gathered or produced by others. For instance, they seek credible sources and scrutinize claims, utterances, and data. Fact checkers do not generate data or perform many of the news-gathering activities that are a central part of news journalists' work, such as on-the-spot reporting. Rather than initiating stories, fact checkers react to and focus on verifying reports that have already been published. Fact checkers are experts at uncovering the truth. They know how to break out statistics and explain complex issues, and they know how to use software for geo-location, detecting manipulated videos, and for conducting other types of research.

2.2 Tenets of Journalism and Perceptions about Fact Checkers

The practice of American journalism has been challenged by the fact-checking movement. In 2009, PolitiFact received a Pulitzer Prize, American journalism's highest honor, for its coverage of the 2008 presidential campaign. Within the profession the award was taken as validation of a claim often made by PolitiFact itself: fact checking constitutes "a new form of journalism," reinventing the watchdog tradition for a digital age (Amazeen, 2015). To the degree that fact checking is perceived as an alternative form of journalism, its diffusion can be construed as improving the profession of journalism.

Most communication scholars see ideal journalism in terms of normative democratic viewpoints, and assert argue that news media should contribute to a vibrant and informed democratic society and serve as watchdogs for the public's interests. Investigation and analysis of important public matters are also crucial part of journalists' work. Other principal journalism traits include acting with autonomy, accuracy, and objectivity and providing impartial and reliable facts to the public. These functions are held as universal standards of the journalism profession (Gil de Zúñiga & Hinsley, 2013).

The standards that normatively comprise good journalism may differ among scholars and media practitioners. The three core features of good journalism that are consistent across diverse journalism studies are objectivity, contextualization, and transparency (Iyengar, 1991; Revers, 2014).

Objectivity is a long-standing journalistic principle, as well as a key element in the journalistic code of ethics (Mindich, 1998). The central principle of objectivity in American journalism is the notion that facts can and should be separated from values or opinions, with journalists reporting only the facts. In the 1920s, the objectivity norm was formally articulated as part of a journalistic code of ethics, and it cemented the contemporary notion of the press as a neutral observer of happenings (Schudson, 2001). Professional journalism has continued to embrace objectivity since then.

RQ1: Is there a difference in the way objectivity, transparency, and contextualization of news organizations is perceived compared with independent fact checkers?

2.3 Media Trust

Media trust is "the willingness of the audience to be vulnerable to news content based on the expectation that the media will perform in a satisfactory manner" (Hanitzsch et al., 2018, p. 5). Trust in media organizations plays a role in the way news reports are perceived. Individuals who are skeptical of mainstream media are less likely to regard news stories reported in mainstream media as the most salient problem affecting society, and those with low media trust are less tolerant of factual errors made by the mainstream press. Trustworthiness is key for both journalists and fact checkers to maintain a central role in information dissemination and in American democracy, thus the next research question asks:

RQ4: Are news organizations or fact checkers deemed more trustworthy?

2.4 Reliance on Fact Checkers and Perceptions

In general, people who regularly consume media of any type are more likely to have positive perceptions of particular medium they use most often. News consumers value several features of journalism, including being watchdogs for the public, acting with objectivity, and providing context and explanation of the news. Individual belief that a particular medium or journalist is 'good' depends on whether the audience member's expectations are met.

H1: Positive public perceptions about objectivity, transparency, and contextualization predicts frequent use of fact checking.

H2: A high level of trust in fact checkers is positively associated with frequent fact checker use.

3. METHOD

A survey was conducted in March 2020, using MTurk (www.mturk.com), an online marketplace for work, an Amazon crowdsourcing platform. Each participant was given 50 cents as an incentive. It took about seven minutes to complete the survey. This study allowed only those who indicated that they use the mainstream media outlets, such as *The New York Times*, *The Washington Post*, ABC, NBC or CBS network news, CNN, and Fox News, and independent fact checkers such as PolitiFact and Snopes.com. In total, 1,652 responses were used for the final analysis.

3.1 Measures

Political efficacy is measured with three items on a 5-point agreement scale (1 = strongly disagree, 3 = neither agree nor disagree, 5 = strongly agree): (1) People like me can influence government; (2) I consider myself well-qualified to participate in politics; and (3) I have a pretty good understanding of the important political issues the U.S. is facing (α = .81, M = 3.21, SD = 1.56). Political interest is assessed by the question, "Would you say that you are: (1) not at all interested, (2) barely interested, (3) somewhat interested, (4), interested, and (5) very much interested?" (M = 3.04, SD = 1.75).

Respondents' opinions of the tenets of good journalism, objectivity, transparency, diversity, contextualization, and media trust are assessed using a 5-point Likert scale (1 = strongly disagree, 3 = neither agree nor disagree, 5 = strongly agree). Respondents were asked how much thought news media and fact-checking organizations live up to the three standards of good journalism. Multiple items for each statement were added into a single index.

Objectivity: "clearly distinguish between facts and opinions"; "focus on arguments over emotions"; "report based on evidence." (Objectivity index of news media Cronbach's α = .87, M = 3.66, SD = 1.33; objectivity index of fact checking organizations Spearman Brown coefficient = .68, M = 3.30, SD = 1.67)

Transparency: "present news sources transparently"; "use verified sources"; "give people a chance to express their views." (Transparency index of news media $\alpha = .89$, $M = 3.98$, $SD = 2.64$; transparency index of fact checking sites Spearman Brown coefficient = .62, $M = 4.07$, $SD = 2.55$)

Contextualization: "provides analyses and interpretation of complex problems"; "gives enough background information"; "places occurrences within a wider context"; "presents substantial background information about current topics." (Contextualization index of news media $\alpha = .81$, $M = 3.15$, $SD = 1.48$; contextualization index of fact checking organizations Spearman Brown coefficient = .62, $M = 3.47$, $SD = 1.77$)

Trust was operationalized by the question, "How much do you trust news media (or fact checking organizations)?" (1 = not at all, 5 = very much) (news media $M = 3.19$, $SD = 1.38$; fact checking organizations $M = 3.22$, $SD = 1.40$).

Fact checker use was measured with a question about how often respondents access fact checking sites run by independent non-journalist organizations, such as Snopes.com, Politifact.com (a 7-point scale ranging from "never" to "all the time"). ($M = 3.44$, $SD = 2.06$).

Traditional news media use was obtained by asking respondents how often they use the following news media to get information about current events, public affairs, and politics (a 7-point scale ranging from "never" to "every day"): (1) local television news; (2) national network news such as ABC, NBC; (3) cable news such as CNN, Fox News; (4) national newspapers in print or online; and (5) local newspapers in print or online. An index was constructed by averaging the scores ($\alpha = .83$, $M = 3.08$, $SD = 1.87$).

3.2 Statistical Analysis

To test the gap between news consumers' views of the performance of fact checkers and news organizations, independent sample t-tests were also performed, as well as two sets of ordinary least squares (OLS) hierarchical regressions, one for each dependent variable to test whether public perceptions about the main features of good journalism were associated with media use.

4. RESULTS

Regarding the first research question about objectivity, the t-test is significant, $t(1{,}238) = 2.43$, $p = .02$. Respondents perceive the objectivity of news organizations ($M = 3.30$) significantly lower than that of fact checking organizations ($M = 3.66$). The results of the second research question about transparency, are not significant, $t(1{,}238) = 1.65$, $p = .263$. Respondents do not believe news organizations ($M = 3.98$) are more transparent than fact checking organizations ($M = 4.07$). For the third research question about contextualization, the t-test is significant, $t(1{,}238) = 2.50$, $p < .01$. Respondents think fact-checking organizations provide significantly more context ($M = 3.47$) than mainstream media ($M = 3.15$). The fourth research question pertaining to trust shows there is no statistical difference $t(1{,}238) = .28$, $p = .842$ between the trustworthiness of mainstream media ($M = 3.19$) compared to fact-checking organizations ($M = 3.22$).

Regarding the four hypotheses linking the features of good journalism to use of fact checking, there a positive and statistically significant relationship with respect to perceptions about *objectivity* and fact checker use ($\beta = .106$, $p < .05$), and between perception about *transparency* and fact checker use ($\beta = .173$, $p < .01$), and between perception about *contextualization* and fact checker use ($\beta = .244$, $p < .001$), supporting H1. The analysis also found a significant association between perception about trust and fact checker use ($\beta = .208$, $p < .001$), supporting H2 (Table 1). This finding underscores that trustworthiness is key to the continuation of fact checking. [Table 1 and 2].

Table 1. OLS regression models predicting fact checker use and traditional news use

	Fact Checker Use	Traditional News Use
Block 1: Demographics		
Age	.054	.127*
Gender (male = 0)	–.015	–.009
Education	.113*	.166**
Income	.082	.086
Race (white = 0)	–.064	–.058
Inc. R^2(%)	5.2***	6.9***
Block 2: Political Antecedents		
Political Affiliation (Democrat = 0)	.104*	.067
Political Efficacy	.284***	.351***
Political Trust	.210***	.277***
Inc. R^2(%)	8.8***	9.5***
Block 3: Journalism Traits		
Objectivity	.106*	.149**
Transparency	.173**	.126*
Contextualization	.244***	.081
Trust	.208***	.133*
Inc. R^2(%)	15.8***	13.9***
Total R^2(%)	29.8***	30.3***

Note: N = 1,240. Cell entries are final entry OLS standardized beta (β) coefficients. * $p < .05$, ** $p < .01$, *** $p < .001$.

Table 2. Difference between news consumers' views on fact checkers and news organizations

	Views on Fact Checkers		Views on News Organizations			
	Mean	SD	Mean	SD	Mean Difference	*t*-test *p* values
Objectivity	3.30	1.67	3.56	1.33	–.26	< .001
Transparency	4.07	2.55	3. 98	2.64	.09	.263
Contextualization	3.47	1.77	3.15	1.48	.32	< .001
Trust	3.22	1.40	3.19	1.38	.03	.842

Note: Independent sample t-test with N = 1,240.

5. DISCUSSION

Drawing upon the tenets of good journalism, this study compared U.S. news consumers' perception of independent fact checkers with news organizations on objectivity, transparency, contextualization, and trust. The study found some notable theoretical outcomes. First, the respondents believe that professional news media are more *objective* than independent fact checkers. This result can be explicated by looking into the background in which the fact-checking movement originally began and spread. In their mission statements, fact checkers assert that their goal is to verify facts and determine whether the facts are supported by evidence (Graves, 2018) by sifting facts from opinion and rating pieces of information as fake, misleading, twisted, or recontextualized. Independent fact checkers not only tackle viral rumors, conspiracies, trolls, lies, or hoaxes by counteracting them, but they also balance public narratives with 'empiricism.' Thus, the result about objectivity suggests that fact checkers are not necessarily bound by the long-standing norms of journalistic objectivity, usually considered as balance, but are dedicated to evaluating the accuracy of any claims and determining its truth.

The second notable finding is that respondents believe that fact checkers are doing a better job than news organizations in terms of *contextualization* of information, and they appreciate that fact checkers add context and scrutinize various perspectives. Respondents believe that fact checkers deliver not just a 'fact' but the context and background surrounding the 'fact' as well as evidence that either supports or refutes the 'fact.' The result indicates that respondents might rely on fact checkers to reduce the likelihood that misinformation or disinformation influences civic discourse, and to reduce the likelihood that politicians' inaccurate claims will make the headlines (Nyhan & Reifler, 2015).

The above finding reflects news audiences' expectation about a 'better' form of journalism. News media often fail to contextualize news events, and report on claims of misinformation without explicitly rebutting them or providing a more factual context (Pingree et al., 2014). This practice makes news consumers vulnerable to false claims that are unaccompanied by clear corrective information, and leaving many news readers wishing that journalists would actively clarify factual questions (Stroud et al., 2016). By not providing interpretations and contextualization mainstream media compel news consumers to turn to fact checkers, which increases favorable perceptions and cements fact checkers as reputable entities.

Although respondents deem fact checkers as more objective and as providing more context than journalists, they do not see a significant difference between news organizations and fact checkers regarding *transparency* - both fact checkers and news organizations are rated moderately high in transparency. Respondents thus believe that both traditional journalists and fact checkers satisfy the criterion of letting them decide for themselves what information or who they should trust or distrust (Kovach & Rosenstiel, 2021). Transparency possibly gives respondents a sense of participation in the fact checking and journalism process.

This study's respondents also deem fact-checking entities and news organizations as equally trustworthy. The mean of trust in both organizations is moderate at best (M = 3.19 out of 5 for news organizations, and M = 3.22 for fact checkers). This result may reflect the public's declining trust in journalism in general because journalists are failing to adequately practice core journalism values (Gil de Zúñiga & Hinsley, 2012).

Although fact checkers are perceived as more objective and as providing more contextualization that journalists, positive perceptions of objectivity, contextualization, and trust are associated with frequent use of fact checking (H1 and H2). These findings deserve attention because they expand the understanding about the role of fact checkers in relation to journalism, and show that use of fact checking is influenced by public perceptions of whether fact checkers adhere to the tenets of good journalism.

The public's appreciation of journalistic performance facilitates increased media consumption, which has a host of positive implications for a healthy democracy. As political persuasion and propaganda efforts continue to grow around the world, the increase of fact checkers equipped with journalistic traits will help citizens have a more accurate and educated understanding of important social and political matters and make informed decisions for a healthy democracy. Fact checkers can improve the social power of journalism, by assessing the authenticity of public claims and placing them in the right context particularly during troubled times. Journalists and fact checkers need not be adversaries in competition for followers, but could work together to build audience trust by presenting the news objectively, by explaining the news gathering process, and by providing context to increase news consumers' understanding of the world.

REFERENCES

Amazeen MA (2015) Revisiting the epistemology of fact-checking. *Critical Review* 27(1): 1–22.

Factcheck.org. (2022) Our mission. https://www.factcheck.org/about/our-mission/

Gil de Zúñiga H and Hinsley A (2013) The press versus the public: What is "good journalism?" *Journalism Studies* 14(6): 926–942.

Graves L (2016) *Deciding what's true: The fact-checking movement in American journalism*. New York: Columbia University Press.

Graves L (2018) Boundaries not drawn: Mapping the institutional roots of the global fact-checking movement. *Journalism Studies* 19(5): 613–631.

Hanitzsch T, Van Dalen A and Steindl N (2018) Caught in the nexus: A comparative and longitudinal analysis of public trust in the press. *The International Journal of Press/Politics* 23(1): 3–23.

Iyengar S (1991) *Is anyone responsible? How television frames political issues*. Chicago, IL: University of Chicago Press.

Kovach B and Rosenstiel T (2021) *The elements of journalism: What newspeople should know and the public should expect*. New York: Crown Publishing Group.

Mindich DTZ (1998) Just the facts: How 'objectivity' came to define American journalism. New York, NY: New York University Press.

Nyhan B and Reifler J (2012) *Misinformation and Fact-checking*. New American Foundation. https://www.issuelab.org/resources/15316/15316.pdf

Pingree RJ, Brossard D and McLeod DM (2014) Effects of journalistic adjudication on factual beliefs, news evaluations, information seeking, and epistemic political efficacy. *Mass Communication and Society* 17(5): 615–638.

Politifact.com. (2022) *The principles of the Truth-O-Meter.* https://www.politifact.com/article/2018/feb/12/principles-truth-o-meter-politifacts-methodology-i/

Revers M (2014) The twitterization of news making: Transparency and journalistic professionalism. *Journal of Communication* 64(5): 806–826.

Schudson M (2001) The objectivity norm in American journalism. Journalism 2(2): 149–170.

Stroud NJ, van Duyne E and Peacock C (2016) News commenters and news comment readers." http://engagingnewsproject.org/research/survey-of-commenters-andcomment-readers/

Vázquez-Herrero J, Direito-Rebollal S and López-García X (2019) Ephemeral journalism: News distribution through Instagram Stories. *Social Media + Society* 5(4): 1–13.

AUGMENTED REALITY IN FASHION E-COMMERCE

Lisa Hilpert and Darius Zumstein
Zurich University of Applied Sciences, E-Commerce Lab, Institute of Marketing Management, Theaterstrasse 17, 8400 Winterthur, Switzerland

ABSTRACT

As a result of digitalisation and the Covid-19 pandemic, the demand for online shopping is increasing. In the fashion sector, this implies changes in buying behaviour, especially due to different sizes, size systems and the ability to visualise clothes on one's own body. Customers' incorrect purchases result in a high number of returns, a big challenge for all fashion online retailers. Augmented reality (AR) is to be used to optimise the customer's shopping experience and to counteract the problem of returns. The aim of the research is to determine the drivers and barriers of AR in fashion e-commerce from the consumers' and fashion retailers' perspective. The aim is to analyse the influence of AR on the fashion shopping experience. The strongest drivers of the willingness to use AR from the customer's perspective are the right size selection, the reduction of incorrect purchases and the fit of the garments. The biggest barriers to AR are data security, technical challenges, and a lack of trust in AR. For fashion retailers, the main added value of AR is the reduction of returns. There is a significant, positive correlation between the convenience of customers and the usefulness of AR in fashion online shopping and the intention to use AR. In future, consumers will more likely shop for fashion online via a smartphone and AR glasses.

KEYWORDS

E-Commerce, Fashion, Online Shopping, Augmented Reality, 3D Body Scan, Virtual Try-On

1. INTRODUCTION

In times of digitalisation, the need for and supply of online retailers is constantly increasing. In particular, the ongoing Covid-19 pandemic is causing an *increase in the importance of online shops* for numerous consumers, for example in the fashion industry (Zumstein & Oswald, 2020). The buying behaviour of customers is changing and leading to an increased change in the distribution channels involved in fashion online shopping (Hohmann, 2020). Consumers face major challenges with the **size selection** of garments, different body shapes and inconsistent product specifications by retailers, as well as the resulting incorrect purchases. On the part of fashion online retailers, the problem is particularly reflected in the high number of returns (Henkel, 2020).

With augmented reality (AR), it is possible to counteract these problems and to achieve an optimised online shopping experience for consumers. AR is already being applied in different industries, such as games, cosmetics, medicine and fashion. The fashion online retailer Zalando has bought *Fision*, a software start-up from the ETH Zurich, to implement AR in its platform. With the help of three-dimensional (3D) body scans, customers will be recommended individual sizes and be able to try on clothes using 3D avatars (Henkel, 2020).

This research examines the *factors that influence the willingness to use AR in fashion e-commerce*. Both the drivers and the barriers of AR are examined. This contribution provides new insights into this young field of research regarding the combination of AR and fashion e-commerce to demonstrate the current research relevance (Tißler, 2018; Gilliland, 2019). Based on this work, the research outlook implies further possibilities for a deeper understanding of the drivers and barriers of AR.

2. AUGMENTED REALITY IN FASHION E-COMMERCE

2.1 Theoretical Foundations

The term **augmented reality** (AR) implies an *extension of the real world through additional, virtual elements* (Azuma, 1997). These include graphics, information, animations as well as a linking of these visualisations with acoustic components. AR is characterised by the following three core features: the combination of the real and virtual world, interaction in real time and representation in 3D (Seiler & Klaas, 2016).

Virtual reality (VR) is distinguished from AR by the *creation of an artificial world that is computer-generated.* In contrast to AR, VR completely hides the real world from the consumer (Nikic-Cemas, 2020, p. 72). The basis of this demarcation is the reality–virtuality continuum, which represents a completely real environment on the left and a completely virtual environment on the right (Milgram & Kishino, 1994, p. 3). In between lies mixed reality (MR) through the connection of both worlds by means of AR (Seiler & Klaas, 2016).

E-commerce (electronic commerce) is understood as the digital initiation, negotiation and/or settlement of transactions between economic entities (Clement et al., 2001, p. 56). According to Olbrich et al. (2019, p. 3f.), the focus of e-commerce is on *distribution policy.* All transactions within e-commerce are carried out as a result of an electronic network (Olbrich et al., 2019, p. 6). According to Holland (2014, p. 828), the customer makes contact with the company or product views or clicks of various touchpoints. In the age of digitalisation, customers interact with different digital channels and several touchpoints at the same time (Lemon & Verhoef, 2016, p. 69), making the process increasingly complex from a company''s perspective (von Gizycki & Elias, 2018; Fachinger, 2019).

2.2 Practical Fields of Application in AR

AR offers an attractive global **growth market**, forecast to be worth around $97 billion by 2028 (Deloitte, 2020; Gilliland, 2019). Worldwide sales of over 50 million VR and AR glasses are expected by 2026 (IDC, 2022). As a result of the gaming industry, especially through the apps *Pokémon Go and Snapchat*, AR technology has experienced a significant upswing in recent years and now has great potential in various fields of application. So far, AR has found practical application in the automotive, logistics, interior design, marketing, beauty and fashion sectors (Orsolits & Lackner, 2020).

In **fashion online shopping,** the potential of using AR lies in *individualised product presentations* and informed product decisions for consumers (Tißler, 2018; Gilliland, 2019). The e-commerce company Mister Spex is considered as one of the pioneers, offering a glasses online shop and a virtual fitting in two or three dimensions (2D/3D; Malev, 2020). In the luxury brand sector, the implementation of future-proof technologies, such as AR, is of increasing importance, especially for the pre-purchase phase of the customer. Gucci is the first brand to implement a *virtual sneaker fitting* in its app through an embedded AR technology. A digital overlay shows 19 different sneakers that customers can virtually try on their own foot by swiping (House of Eden, 2020; Gilliland, 2019). Burberry uses AR technology to display products in Google Search. Customers can view the products, for instance the Arthur Check sneaker and bag, in their individual environment instead of on their own body. Thus, they experience a *simulated in-store experience.*

AR technology is used in physical fashion stores with the help of so-called **magic mirrors.** This mirror allows customers to try on different products virtually in the shop. Magic mirrors offer fashion shoppers the advantage of not having to change clothes or find the garments in the fashion store. In addition, products that are not physically available in the shop can be tried on virtually. The magic mirror takes on the function of a personal shopping assistant and recommends products to customers individually.

The following chapter explains how AR is used specifically by the leading fashion online retailer Zalando.

2.3 AR Shopping Service of Zalando

Zalando currently owns the digital shopping service **Zalon**, which is integrated into the online platform and offers customers *personal advice with the help of stylists*. This takes place in the following three steps: (1) customer input on needs, budget and size, (2) stylists put together the outfit and (3) free delivery of the styling box to customers (Zalando, 2020a). In addition, Zalando offers *individualised size recommendations* based on general customer feedback, personal purchase and return history, as well as retailers' information on product dimensions (Henkel, 2020). Currently, this service is available for about half of Zalando's products.

The technology start-up **Fision** was acquired by Zalando in October 2020. Fision acts as a *3D body scan specialist* via the innovative *AR app meepl* (Zalando, 2020b). Using the smartphone, the customer takes two pictures from the front and the side of their body via the meepl app (see Figure 1, picture left and centre). The body shape is analysed and measured to a **3D body scan.** Based on the 3D body scan, a personal **3D avatar** of the customer is created (see Figure 1 on the right) and more than *50 body masses* are derived.

Figure 1. 3D body scan of the author using the meepl app (Source of images: meepl app, own realisation)

3D body scans and 3D avatars enable both *customised garments and a virtual changing room* for the customer. Moreover, the use of meepl offers consumers an *individual size recommendation* for all products, a pictorial representation of the clothes on their own body and an interactive online shopping experience (Fision, 2020).

The individual body scan and avatar can be stored in the user's own profile for size recommendations, independent of size systems and brands. Consequently, the user *saves time when choosing sizes and reduces the number of incorrect purchases*. This goes hand in hand with Zalando's strategic ecological goal of reducing returns (Fision, 2020; Zalando, 2020b).

3. RESEARCH METHOD AND SAMPLE

For this research contribution, a mixed research approach was chosen to guarantee well-founded findings from different perspectives. To gain insights about the potential of AR in fashion e-commerce, in a preliminary study two **qualitative expert interviews** with AR specialists were conducted. Expert 1 is a professor of business administration with a focus on international management and expert 2 is a research assistant and PhD student in digital marketing and consumer behaviour.

Secondly, a **quantitative user survey** was used to analyse the willingness to use, benefits and challenges of AR in fashion e-commerce. Based on these results, a **hypothesis model** on the willingness to use AR in fashion e-commerce was derived. Finally, the hypotheses were tested for statistical significance using a multivariate regression analysis using SPSS.

The quantitative survey was designed for users of AR in fashion e-commerce. This includes those users who have previously shopped online for fashion using AR or can imagine doing so in the future. The survey was conducted online from 22nd of April 2021 to 31st May 2021 and distributed via the snowball principle in the network of the authors. A total of 152 respondents took part in the survey. By the end of the survey in this non-representative study, 79 persons (52%) had participated, resulting in a sample of 76 participants. Due to the snowball principle, the external validity of the results is not given.

The survey comprises 39 questions and is thematically divided into four sections. At the beginning, psychographic characteristics are examined, in the second part, general questions regarding fashion in e-commerce and in connection with AR, followed by specific questions on the use of AR in fashion e-commerce.

The questionnaire concluded with the collection of demographic data. The majority of the questions were measured with a five-point Likert scale. The intention to use AR was measured using individual variables and three constructs whose scales can be rated as sufficient to very good due to the Cronbach's alpha value (Kline, 2011). The following chapter is devoted to the results of this study, including hypothesis tests.

4. RESEARCH RESULTS

4.1 Expert Interviews on AR in Fashion E-Commerce

According to the expert interviews, there is an assumption that, due to the **technological innovations** with *AR Kit and AR Core*, the future trend development of AR apps will go in the direction of app-based applications and, in the long term, towards smartglasses. In contrast, no broad application intention in private use can be predicted for AR glasses. With regard to AR in fashion, the shopping experience and the shopping process can be identified as the two trend directions.

From the customers' perspective, the **benefits and value of AR** technology lie in its fast *availability, independence of location, time savings and product presentation at the point of use*. Furthermore, the virtual fitting of garments and the receipt of individualised size recommendations as a result of a 3D body scan are essential. On the part of the fashion online retailers, the benefit or added value lies in particular in the *reduction of returns* and the technical advantage through AR.

From the fashion retailers' point of view, the **problems and challenges** lie in the creation of awareness of AR among customers, in the use of AR and its integration into the corporate strategy. The limitations lie in the current technology, including movements and moods that cannot yet be implemented. In addition, the technological gap of small and medium-sized enterprises (SME), compared to pioneers such as Zalando, is considered a challenge, too.

With regard to the customer journey and the entire **shopping experience**, an optimisation for the user and a higher conversion rate for the fashion online retailer can be assumed. The customer journey is influenced by the medium used, i.e. AR glasses provide a seamless experience when using AR, whereas *smartphones provide a higher immersion*. The AR application will have an impact on other customer touchpoints, such as social media marketing and branding. Furthermore, an individualisation of advertising can be assumed through user-generated content (UGC) and a user approach with concrete product recommendations.

4.2 User Survey on AR Fashion E-commerce

The user survey revealed that the absolute majority of the sample is made up of women (59%) and the main age category is 25 to 34 year olds (59%). The findings of the **reasons for online fashion purchases** showed that they are primarily *location independence* (57% of the respondents totally agree in Figure 2), *time independence* (54%), a *larger selection of products and brands* (47%) and *time savings* (45%).

The individualisation of articles as well as anonymity were seen by the fewest people as reasons to shop for fashion online (34% and 30% did not agree at all respectively). Figure 2 provides an overview of the general reasons for fashion online purchases.

With regard to the **future use of AR for fashion online shopping using the smartphone**, the majority of respondents (57%) stated that they would probably do so, and 11% would definitely do so. On the other hand, 40% of respondents probably do not intend to use AR glasses. The **online shopping experiences** in the fashion sector led to satisfaction for two thirds (63%) of the respondents, and dissatisfaction for seven precent only. The reasons for their dissatisfaction were mainly incorrect purchases corresponding to item returns due to "*it doesn't fit*" (22%), and the general fit of the garments according to the wrong size or wrong cut (21%).

Regarding **privacy and personal data**, 21% named *trust in the company* as the most important aspect. This was followed by the *credibility of the company* (17%), a *confidentiality agreement* (17%) and *trust in the added value of AR* (nine percent). Regarding automatic measurement via an AR app or video camera, for example 3D body scans, the absolute majority (46%) gave partial consent and 24% gave full consent. Additionally, the majority of respondents (41%) said they had confidence in AR features and results. If an AR app is offered for free, 44% would probably download the AR fashion application, and 44% would download it for sure.

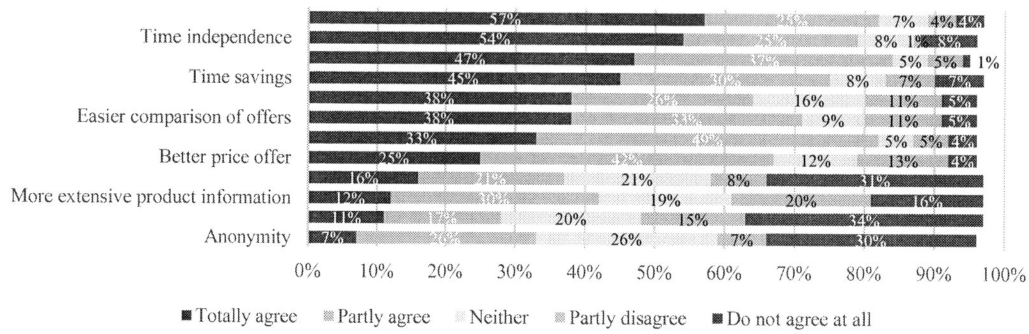

Figure 2. Reasons for fashion online purchases

Figure 3 illustrates the **benefits and added value of AR in fashion online shopping** from the customer's point of view. According to the mean values, the *correct choice of size*, the *reduction of incorrect purchases* due to "doesn't fit", the *fit of the garments* and the *ability to visualise the clothes* on one's own body can be identified as central aspects. 38% would fully agree with a *virtual try-on of glasses* using AR, 32% would agree with a *virtual try-on of clothes*, 16% would agree with a virtual *try-on of sneakers* and 15% would agree with a virtual presentation by models. Overall, 34% of respondents said they find *AR useful* in online shopping.

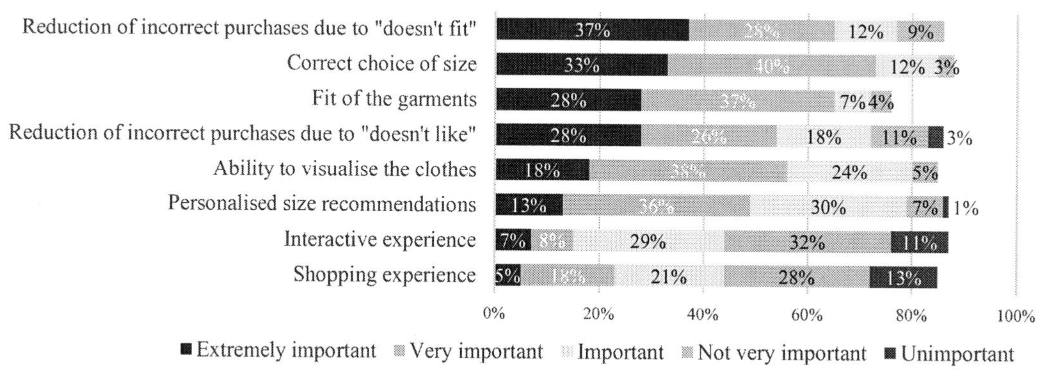

Figure 3. Benefits and added value of AR in online fashion shopping

An expert of the interviews said *"the biggest benefit would be that it reduces the **return rate** and/or if the company naturally does more business or has more conversions and converts more".*

In contrast, 32% said they would *not buy fashion online via a smartphone using AR*, due to **data protection** issues. Other reasons given by customers were a **lack of trust** in AR technology for 26% and a **lack of affinity for technology** for 17% of the respondents. In addition, 42% of respondents shared their satisfaction with fashion online shopping without AR. Therefore, the biggest potential challenges and problems in fashion online shopping are technical issues, data security and a lack of trust in AR technology.

Regardless of this technical **concern,** one expert of the interviews believes in additional five percent of the return quote due to this technical advance, as well as a *stronger customer retention.*

Finally, it should be noted that the absolute majority of consumers (53%) gave their partial consent to a fundamental improvement of the shopping experience by means of AR applications, while 21% gave their full consent. While 43% agreed that they would buy more fashion online thanks to AR applications, 32% would not prefer fashion online purchases via AR to fashion shopping in physical shops.

In the following chapter, the hypothesis model is statistically tested and discussed.

4.3 Hypothesis Model

The hypothesis testing is carried out using a multivariate regression analysis in SPSS. The dependent variable (DV) ***intention to use AR*** represents a construct from the variables *intention to use a smartphone* and *to use AR glasses.* Since the use of AR for fashion online shopping via a smartphone and via AR glasses are independent of each other, the two variables were examined as a construct. The DV implies the customer intention to use or not use AR for fashion online shopping in the future under the drivers and barriers of AR used (in Figure 4). Table 1 shows an overview of the independent variables (IV) and of the ten hypotheses (H).

Table 1. Overview of variables and hypotheses

#	Variable	#	Hypothesis
IV1	Size selection as a challenge	**H1**	The more problems customers have with size selection due to different size systems in fashion online shopping, the more likely they are to use AR.
IV2	Usefulness of AR	**H2**	Overall, the more useful customers find the use of AR in fashion online shopping, the more likely they are to use AR in fashion e-commerce.
IV3	Convenience	**H3**	The more comfortable customers are with online fashion shopping, the more likely they are to use AR in fashion e-commerce.
IV4	Time independence	**H4**	The more important time independence is to customers when shopping online, the more likely they are to use AR in fashion e-commerce.
IV5	Location independence	**H5**	The more important location-independence is to customers when shopping online, the more likely they are to use AR in fashion e-commerce.
IV6	Dissatisfaction due to incorrect purchases	**H6**	The more dissatisfied customers are due to fashion online shopping mistakes, the more likely they are to use AR in fashion e-commerce.
IV7	Frequency of fashion online	**H7**	The less often customers have shopped online for fashion since Covid-19, the less they use AR in fashion e-commerce.
IV8	Technical challenges	**H8**	The more customers agree that there are technical challenges in the use of AR in fashion online shopping, the less they use AR in fashion e-commerce.
IV9	Lack of confidence	**H9**	The greater the lack of trust in AR technology, the less they use AR in fashion e-commerce.
IV10	Gender	**H10**	Women show a higher willingness to use AR in fashion e-commerce than men.

Table 2. Overview of the standardised regression coefficients

Variable	Beta	T	Significance
Size selection *(IV1)*	-0.001	-0.006	0.996
Usefulness *(IV2)*	0.257	2.263	**0.027**
Convenience *(IV3)*	0.517	3.351	**0.001**
Time independence *(IV4)*	-0.309	-1.827	0.072
Location independence *(IV5)*	-0.163	-1.115	0.269
Dissatisfaction due to mispurchases *(IV6)*	0.083	0.699	0.487
Frequency *(IV7)*	0.061	0.535	0.595
Technology *(IV8)*	-0.064	-0.532	0.597
Trust *(IV9)*	0.200	1.693	0.095
Gender *(IV10)*	-0.232	-2.012	**0.048**

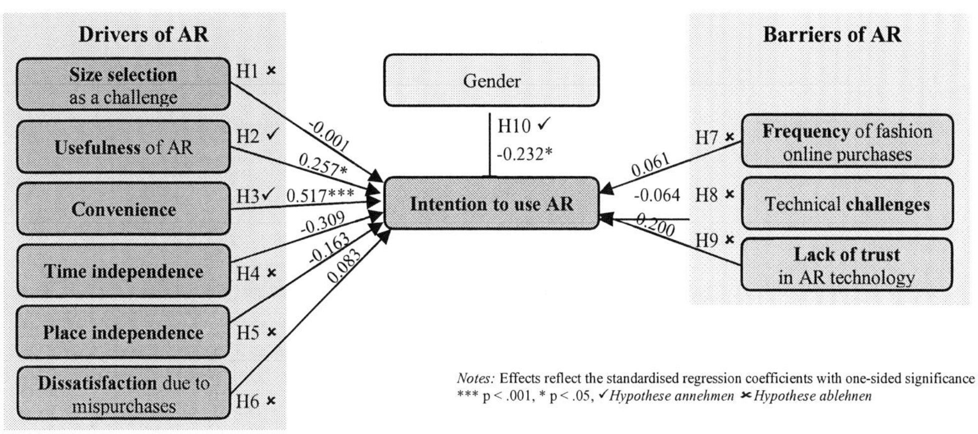

Notes: Effects reflect the standardised regression coefficients with one-sided significance test.
*** p < .001, * p < .05, ✓*Hypothese annehmen* ×*Hypothese ablehnen*

Figure 4. Hypothesis model with effects

According to the **mean values,** the variables IV3 (M = 4.05, SD = 0.985), IV4 (M = 2.21, SD = 1.174) and IV5 (M = 4.32, SD = 1.038) can be identified as the *most important model predictors*.

The statistical testing of the **individual regression coefficients** of the model shows that there are two significant regressions, *usefulness* (IV2) and *gender* (IV10), and one highly significant regression, convenience (*IV3*). The other variables tested have no significant influence on the intention to use AR in fashion e-commerce. Table 2 shows the effect size of all model variables.

5. DISCUSSION

The main objective was to identify the drivers and barriers of AR in relation to the intention (willingness) to use AR in fashion e-commerce. According to the regression analysis, **convenience** (ß = 0.517) has the strongest influence on the intention to use AR. This is followed in descending order by time independence (ß = -0.309), usefulness (ß = 0.257) and gender (ß = -0.232). The lowest influence on the intention to use AR is the frequency of fashion online purchases since Covid-19 (ß = 0.061), dissatisfaction due to incorrect purchases (ß = 0.083) and size selection (ß = -0.001).

Although size selection was identified as the second strongest aspect according to the mean statistics (M = 3.97, SD = 0.984) and as a decisive challenge in fashion e-commerce as a result of the desk research and expert interviews, this effect on the intention to use AR is the smallest and at the same time negative. This means that a higher number of size selection problems in fashion e-commerce correlates with a lower intention to use AR in fashion e-commerce. The contradiction could be attributed to the fact that the hypothesis test only included size selection as a challenge due to different size systems, and excluded other influencing factors, such as missing retailer information regarding size and fit.

Gender has a significant influence on the intention to use AR in fashion shopping (ß = -0.232, t = -2.012, p = 0.048), i.e. *women's willingness* to use AR is higher than men's willingness to use it. This corresponds to the researchers' expectations. Since the proportion of women in the sample is 59%, it is obvious that this is an influence and it is questionable whether the result would be identical with a different gender distribution. There is a negative but non-significant correlation between dissatisfaction through incorrect purchases due to "not fitting" as well as "not liking" and the willingness to use AR. This could be due to the *free shipping and returns policy* of the fashion online retailers. Time independence shows no significant but positive correlation with the willingness to use AR in fashion e-commerce. Consequently, an increasing importance of time independence for customers can be associated with an increasing willingness to use AR in fashion e-commerce. The mean comparisons (M = 4.05, SD = 0.988) and expert interviews support this finding. The effect of the two variables is positive, i.e. a higher frequency of fashion online purchases since Covid-19 correlates with a higher willingness to use AR in fashion e-commerce. It can be assumed that this is due to the convenience for consumers and the change in purchasing behaviour with regard to online shopping.

The analysis of the technical component as a potential challenge in fashion e-commerce using AR leads to discrepancies in the statements of the interviewed experts. On the one hand, the technology is not considered a future barrier, but must function without problems for customer use and to guarantee a satisfactory customer shopping experience. According to the user survey, the **technical challenges** on the part of consumers are to be identified as the strongest challenges.

In addition, the test of the 3D body scan using the meepl app revealed measurement inaccuracies on the part of the researchers, which led to a reduction in satisfaction. Consequently, the technical component is seen as a challenge until new usage studies of AR argue to the contrary.

According to the results of the expert interviews and user survey, the customer journey is positively changed by AR, especially through a *virtual dress fitting, the 3D body scan and personalised size recommendations*. The AR applications increase the time customers spend on the website, which leads to a higher conversion rate for fashion online retailers and a reduction in the number of returns. Contrary to the authors' expectations, customer touchpoints will not be completely digitised, but a combination of physical and digital touchpoints, such as product purchase by advertising posters and AR codes on the street, is a conceivable possibility.

Both the expert interviews and the user survey have shown that AR glasses will not be the common form of AR use for private customers, despite higher immersion. In the future, it is expected that customers will be much more likely to use AR applications in fashion e-commerce *via a smartphone* than AR glasses.

6. CONCLUSION

6.1 Recommendations for Fashion Online Shops

Based on these findings, the following five general implications arise for **fashion online retailers**:

1. **Alternative option for AR applications:** SMEs should offer customers an alternative to AR use for fashion online shopping in order to strengthen their market position against large fashion online retailers, such as Zalando.
2. **User survey:** Before implementing AR technology, SMEs should conduct a user survey on the specific intention to use AR applications. This should provide fashion online retailers with information on whether the absolute majority of their customers would only claim AR applications from the pioneers in the online fashion industry and whether this would consequently be unprofitable for them.
3. **Pilot project:** If the user survey shows a demand for AR applications, a pilot project of six to twelve months would be recommended in order to test fashion online shopping operationally and to optimise it.
4. **Joint venture with software companies:** SMEs should enter into a joint venture with a software company in, for example, the Indian or Chinese market that provide the AR technology, in order to benefit from their industry knowledge and technological edge.
5. **Cooperation with Zalando & Co.:** Instead, a cooperation with a large fashion online retailer, such as Zalando, H&M or Zara, which already has AR technology, would be conceivable. Possible points of negotiation would be a share of the profits when selling garments via AR as well as an image enhancement through the positive sustainability policy of the SME.

6.2 Further Research and Outlook

It is recommended that future research be conducted based on this research. As a priority, the study should be repeated in an international context with a representative sample to generalise the findings and increase external validity. The hypothesis model could be expanded with additional predictors from the user survey regarding the drivers and barriers of AR in order to substantiate the understanding of the willingness to use AR in fashion e-commerce. Furthermore, a mediation analysis would be useful so that in addition to gender, the moderating effect on the willingness to use AR in fashion e-commerce of other demographic variables, such as age or education, could be examined. In addition, based on the survey, hypotheses should be derived in relation to the customer journey and the shopping experience on the part of the customers and then tested for statistical significance.

The following **research questions** serve as suggestions for future studies:

1. Is there a significant positive correlation between the effective use of AR in fashion e-commerce and customer satisfaction with fashion online shopping using AR?
2. What factors influence the use of AR, such as smartphones, in fashion e-commerce?
3. To what extent does a higher intention to use AR in fashion e-commerce increase the conversion rate of fashion online retailers?
4. To what extent does the integration of AR technology influence the strategy of fashion online retailers?
5. How much do AR services like 3D body scans or avatars decrease the return rate of online retailers?
6. What influence does the emerging AR market and thus the intention to use AR have on the e-commerce market in general or on other industries?

REFERENCES

Azuma, R. (1997). A survey of augmented reality. *Presence: Teleoperators and Virtual Environments, 6*(4), 355-385.

Clement, M., Peters, K., Preiß, F. (2001). *Electronic Commerce*, In: Marketing mit interaktiven Medien: Strategien zum Markterfolg. Frankfurt am Main: FAZ-Inst. für Management-, Markt- und Medieninformationen, 2001, pp. 56-70.

Deloitte (2020). *Extended Reality Study 2020: Market Analysis and Forecast. Consumer XR: Future prospects for virtual, augmented and mixed reality.* Retrieved from https://www2.deloitte.com/de/de/pages/technology-media-and-telecommunications/articles/extended-reality-xr-studie-2020.html.

Fachinger, V. (2019). *Customer journey analysis & touchpoint management: What online shops can learn from Amazon!* Retrieved from https://piwikpro.de/blog/customer- journey-analysis-and-touchpoint-management-in-ecommerce/.

Fision (2020). *Creating technology that suits you.* Retrieved from https://www.meepl.com.

Gilliland, N. (2019). *14 examples of augmented reality brand experiences.* Retrieved from https://econsultancy.com/14-examples-augmented-reality-brand-marketing-experiences/.

Hilpert, L. (2021). *Augmented Reality im Fashion E-Commerce am Beispiel von Zalando* (Master thesis). Winterthur: Zurich University of Applied Sciences, School of Management and Law.

House of Eden (2020). *Top 6 brands for augmented reality shopping experiences: We show 6 examples of how brands are embracing the augmented reality trend to set new standards in innovation.* Retrieved from https://www.hausvoneden.de/technology/augmented-reality-shopping/#inline.

Henkel, R. (2020). *Zalando acquires 3D body scan specialist Fision from Switzerland.* Retrieved from https://fashionunited.ch/nachrichten/business/zalando-uebernimmt-3d-body-scan-specialist-fision-from-switzerland/2020101623570.

Hohmann, M. (2020). *Do you want to continue buying fashion and accessories online in the future?* Retrieved from https://de.statista.com/statistik/daten/studie/1178326/umfrage/umfrage- to-buy-fashion-online-after-corona/.

Holland, H. (2014). *Digital Dialogue Marketing: Basics, Strategies, Instruments.* Wiesbaden: Springer Gabler.

IDC (2022). *Forecast for sales of virtual reality and augmented reality glasses worldwide from 2020 to 2026 (in millions of units).* Retrieved from https://de.statista.com/statistik/daten/studie/539653/umfrage/prognose-zum-absatz-von-virtual-reality-hardware.

Kline, R. B. (2011). *Principles and practice of structural equation modelling.* New York: Guilford.

Lemon, K. N., & Verhoef, P. C. (2016). Understanding Customer Experience Throughout the Customer Journey. *Journal of Marketing, 80*(6), 69-96.

Malev, M. (2020). *Technology: added value or gimmick? Augmented reality in e-commerce.* Retrieved from https://dmexco.com/de/stories/mehrwert-oder-spielerei-augmented-reality- in-e-commerce/.

Milgram, P., & Kishino, F. (1994). A Taxonomy of Mixed Reality Visual Displays. *IEICE Transactions on Information and Systems*, *77*(12), 1-15.

Nikic-Cemas, I. (2020). Virtual Reality as a novel communication instrument of internal, identity-based brand communication: A scientific investigation on the case study of the corporate brand Merck. In C. Burmann & M. Kirchgeorg (Eds.): *Innovative brand management.* Wiesbaden: Springer Gabler.

Olbrich, R., Schultz, C. D., & Holsing, C. (2019). *Electronic commerce and online marketing: an introductory textbook and exercise book.* 2nd ed. Berlin: Springer Gabler.

Orsolits, H., & Lackner, M. (2020). *Virtual reality and augmented reality in digital production.* Wiesbaden: Springer Gabler.

Seiler, R., & Klaas, M. (2016). Augmented and Virtual Reality the New Silverbullet of Marketing? An Overview of Applications with the AIDA Model. *Journal of WEI Business and Economics*, *5*(2), 1-10.

Tißler, J. (2018). *Future: Augmented reality in marketing: 8 current examples.* Retrieved from https://dmexco.com/de/stories/augmented-reality-im-marketing-8-aktuelle-beispiele/.

Von Gizycki, V., & Elias, C. A. (2018). *Omnichannel branding: digitalisation as the basis of experience-and relationship-oriented brand management.* Wiesbaden: Springer Gabler.

Zalando SE (2020a). *Group strategy: Our business segments.* Retrieved from https://corporate.zalando.com/en/company/our-business-fields.

Zalando SE (2020b). *Zalando invests further in customer experience with acquisition of Swiss 3D body scan specialist Fision.* Retrieved from https://corporate.zalando.com/de/newsroom/news-storys/zalando-investiert-mit-uebernahme-von-schweizer-3d-body-scan-spezialist-fision.

Zobel, B., Werning, S., Metzger, D., & Thomas, O. (2018). Augmented and virtual reality: state of the art, potential benefits and areas of application. In C. De Witt & C. Gloerfeld (Eds.): *Handbook of Mobile Learning,* pp. 123-140. Wiesbaden: Springer Gabler.

Zumstein, D., & Oswald, C. (2020). *Online Retailer Survey 2020: Sustainable growth of e-commerce and challenges in times of crisis. A study by the Institute of Marketing Management.* Winterthur: Zurich University of Applied Sciences, School of Management and Law.

TECHNOLOGY READINESS OF INSURANCE SERVICES: A CASE STUDY OF NEPAL

Sushant Subedi, Aayush Dip Giri, Saugat Aadhikari and Sushil Shrestha
Kathmandu University, Dhulikhel, Nepal

ABSTRACT

Technology infrastructure plays a crucial role in determining the readiness of E-services in any organization. The rapid evolution of technology and the diversification of customers have made it increasingly important to research the appropriate services and technologies to implement. This research paper examines the technology readiness of insurance companies in Nepal in relation to the growing expectations of customers. Insurance companies are inherently risky businesses for customers to trust. To gain the trust of customers and sustain the insurance business, it is necessary to plan and improve the quality of services. Once customers are willing to accept the services provided by these insurance companies and the right technologies are implemented for different services, it can ensure the technological readiness of insurance companies. The Technology Acceptance Model (TAM) is used to analyze the readiness of customers using current online services provided by insurance companies. A survey-based analysis helped in mapping the technological infrastructure readiness of insurance companies in relation to the services provided to customers. Five different domains of technical infrastructure have been used to analyze the readiness of insurance companies in Nepal, i.e., Infrastructure, DBMS, Applications Assessment Criteria, ICT Management, and Technical Skills. The findings of this research suggest that customers using insurance online services in Nepal trust the technologies and believe that using such services will enhance their daily experiences. However, the technological infrastructure implemented for providing quality service in the future is not sufficient. To be technically ready, it is necessary to constantly access customers' experiences and expectations to increase the capacity and implementation of technological infrastructure. This study can be beneficial to E-Governance practitioners, IT officers of insurance companies, and researchers of E-Governance.

KEYWORDS

E-Governance, E-Readiness, Insurance, Technology Acceptance Model (TAM)

1. INTRODUCTION

E-government (short for electronic government) uses technological communications devices, such as computers and the Internet, to provide public services to citizens and other persons in a country or region. The e-government's ultimate objective is to offer an enhanced portfolio of public services efficiently and cost-effectively to citizens (Ao-Itc, 2019). E-Governance has always been one of the primary focuses of developing countries like the Democratic Republic of Nepal. E-governance's main application is developing all the sectors using (Information and Communication Technology) ICT to enhance better relationships between people, government, and businesses. We can see the emerging growth of ICT applications in health, education, insurance, etc. This paper discusses the readiness of the insurance sector to use ICT technology.

A vital prerequisite for successful economic development is a strong and functional insurance sector (Outreville, 1990). Insurance is a critical component of any economy, providing financial protection against unforeseen events such as accidents, illnesses, and natural disasters. Nepal, a developing country in South Asia, is no exception. However, insurance penetration in Nepal is relatively low compared to other countries in the region, with only 27 percent of the population currently insured (Republic, 2021). The objective of insurance is to provide financial security to individuals, organizations, and businesses. E-insurance, which can be broadly defined as the utilization of the Internet and Information Technologies (IT) for the production and delivery of insurance services, can be further characterized as the provision of insurance coverage through an online mechanism, including the offer, negotiation, and execution of insurance policies. While it is possible for payment, policy issuance, and claim processing to be conducted electronically, certain technical and legislative constraints may impede the full implementation of e-commerce in certain jurisdictions. (Sanayei et al., 2009).

Prior research investigating the e-readiness of the insurance sector in Nepal is non-existent. However, the insurance industry in Nepal is experiencing a significant annual growth rate of 16.48% (Dhungana, 2022), indicating that it is an emerging market. As such, there is a need for research to examine the utilization of Information and Communication Technologies (ICT) within the insurance sector. This research aims to provide an overview of the technological readiness of insurance scenario in Nepal. The study aims to shed light on the potential for growth of technological improvement for facilitating e-Services in Insurance sector for Nepal with two major objective.

RQ1. Are customers ready to accept the services provided by the technologies implemented by Insurance Companies?

RQ2. Are insurance companies fully ready to implement E-Services with the existing technologies?

This paper is divided into two major section for readers to comprehend our work. The first section checks the e-readiness of the insurance and the second section accesses the technological infrastructure.

2. LITERATURE REVIEW

The establishment of e-government readiness is a multifaceted endeavor that cannot be accomplished solely by government organizations. The e-government readiness index is influenced by a variety of dimensions, including user perceptions, institutional frameworks and strategies, human resources, financial resources, interdepartmental cooperation, national infrastructure, economic prosperity, public education, information policies, private sector development, and other factors related to e-government readiness (Omari et al., 2006). While a plethora of readiness assessment tools are readily available to the public, there is a lack of clear guidance on how to utilize these tools as frameworks for conducting assessments in specific contexts, such as the development or implementation of e-government.

2.1 Component Based Framework

Previous research has identified a variety of tools that have been used to evaluate the readiness of countries for e-government services, including the UNDESA e-Government Survey, the Brown University Global e-Government, the Accenture e-Government Leadership, the WU-IEGOV e-Government Ranking, and the UNU e-Readiness Assessment (Shareef et al., 2008). In order for these frameworks to be effective, a well-coordinated set of policies and strategies is crucial for directing the development of regulatory frameworks, organizational and technical infrastructures, and necessary information systems. Despite the availability of these tools, there is a lack of clear guidelines and parameters for utilizing them in the assessment of e-government readiness during implementation (Omari et al., 2006; Shareef et al., 2008). A component-based framework, which involves evaluating eight distinct components to determine readiness, has been implemented in the Maldives and has been found to provide the necessary information for specific planning contexts (Shareef et al., 2008).

2.2 Importance of Technology in Adopting Online Services

E-Governance is defined as the utilization of electronic means to streamline and enhance democratic, governmental, and commercial aspects of governance through interactions between government and citizens, government and businesses, as well as within government processes (Backus, 2001). Every individual in every country expects their government to produce and provide high-quality services; such demands put pressure on the government to deliver quality services. As a result, several initiatives for e-governance implementation are the outcome of citizen pressures and expectations combined with the capabilities attained through the use of Information and Communication Technology (ICT) (Agrawal, 2007). Research has also shown that ICT's e-Readiness increases the level of service and public trust, thus its adoption has become a crucial tool for the government to develop policies and procedures (Gumilang et al., 2019).

2.3 Trust vs. Readiness of Insurance Company

The insurance industry is inherently risky, as the difference between expected and actual losses is a fundamental concept in risk insurance theory (Green et al., 2004; Reigel et al., 2004; Rejda, 2005). Insurance companies base their premium rates on evaluating typical projected losses and damage. An insurer must undertake several fundamental actions in order to ensure a risk against a specific cause of injury, such as determining the premium rate (for instance, when insuring homes or cars against fire or theft) and setting up sufficient reserves to offset variations from typical, anticipated losses. Additionally, the insurer must decide how to adjust the prices it proposes to each client and determine whether any particular clients are likely to have worse claims than usual. The processing of policies, premium notices, market analysis, sales predictions, and bookkeeping are all frequently handled by technological infrastructures. Insurance is an information-intensive industry, making it suitable for e-commerce businesses (Sanayei et al., 2009).

To assess the readiness of E-Services in organizations, several dimensions play an important role. In the current technological era, a crucial factor in the successful implementation of services revolves around implementing technologies to provide quality services to customers by earning their trust in the technologies. Several studies have identified different methods for evaluating E-readiness assessments.

However, only a limited number of studies suggest a theoretical framework for assessing technology readiness. Technical readiness can be evaluated by understanding how well the services align with the technological implementation concerning customers' expectations. A similar gap in the research world allows us to assess the readiness of insurance companies with technological infrastructure concerning customer expectations.

3. METHODOLOGY

3.1 Survey Measures

This study employed a qualitative approach to evaluate the readiness of users to utilize different services within the insurance industry. The Technology Acceptance Model (TAM) served as the theoretical framework for the analysis. A survey questionnaire was developed to assess user readiness and was divided into two sections: one for individuals who had not previously used online insurance services and another for those who had. The survey included eight questions designed to measure three primary factors: perceived ease of use (measured by three questions), perceived usefulness (measured by two questions), and privacy and security concerns (measured by three questions). The survey index ranged from "Extremely Likely" to "Extremely Unlikely".

In addition to the survey, a sample of ten individuals from among the survey respondents who held insurance policies was further interviewed to gain deeper insight into the technological readiness of insurance companies. The interviews explored the respondents' experiences using online services across five dimensions of the ICT framework: Infrastructure, Database Management Systems, Application assessment criteria, ICT management, and Technical skills (as described by Aqeel, 2014). The interviewees were asked open-ended questions about their experiences with online services in relation to various insurance-related tasks.

3.1.1 Survey Methodology

The total sample size for this survey was determined to be n=56. The survey instrument was designed using Google Forms and distributed among the researcher's peers and family through social media platforms.

3.1.2 Data Collection and Analysis

For the initial data collection, a snowball sampling methodology was employed, taking into account the fact that only 25% of the population in Nepal holds insurance (Republica, 2021). The survey respondents were informed that the collected data would be used solely for research purposes, and only those respondents who consented to participate were included in the data analysis. The mean was calculated for each question to determine the most likely response. Additionally, box plots were generated for each question to assess the skewness of the data. Finally, the standard deviation was calculated to provide a measure of the distribution of responses across all questions.

4. RESULT

The survey yielded a total of 56 responses. Of the respondents, 78.6% belonged to the age group of 18-25, 7.1% to the age group of 26-30, and 14.3% belonged to the age group of 35 and above. The survey participants were also asked to identify their gender, 58.9% of the respondents identified as male, and 41.1% identified as female. In terms of insurance coverage, 62.5% (n=35) of the respondents reported having insurance, while 37.5% (n=21) reported not having any insurance policy.

Of those who reported having insurance, 75% (n=27) had life insurance, while 25% (n=9) had non-life insurance. Among those with life insurance, 22.2% had insurance with Rastriya Beema Sansthan, 18.5% had insurance with National Life Insurance, 7.4% had insurance with Union Life Insurance, Reliance Life, Citizen Life Insurance, and Metlife Insurance respectively, 11.1% with Prabhu Life Insurance and Life Insurance Corporation each, and 3.7% with Sun Life Insurance and Jyoti Life Insurance each. Among the respondents who had non-life insurance, 33.3% were affiliated with Ajod Life Insurance, 22.2% with Prabhu Life Insurance, Nepal Health Board Insurance, and Nepal Insurance Company Ltd with 11.1% respectively, and 22.2% were not sure of their insurance policy.

Regarding the use of online services, 72.7% of the respondents reported not having used online services, while 27.3% reported having used such services. The Cronbach Alpha Value which measures the internal consistency of the data was found to be $\alpha = 0.89$ for the eight survey questions that were calculated using the insurer data (n=37). The mean and variance of the results of the questions are displayed in Figure 1.

Technology Acceptance Model Questions	Mean	Variance
Using Insurance online services in my daily life would enable me to accomplish tasks more quickly.	2.54	4.40
Using Insurance online services would enhance my effectiveness while accessing my insurance services.	2.55	2.94
I would find insurance online services useful in my daily life.	2.43	2.93
Learning to operate Insurance online services would be easy for me.	2.33	3.03
I would find it easy to get insurance online services to do what I want it to do.	2.50	2.29
I trust in the technology an online service is using.	2.37	1.78
I trust in the ability of online services to protect my privacy.	2.37	1.63
I find using insurance online services financially secure.	2.53	1.21

Figure 1. Mean and Variance Calculation of TAM questions

Figure 1 suggest us that the data obtained from the last 3 questions are less scattered as compared to first 5 questions. Most the respondents have similar thought process due to which they have similar opinion on survey questions.

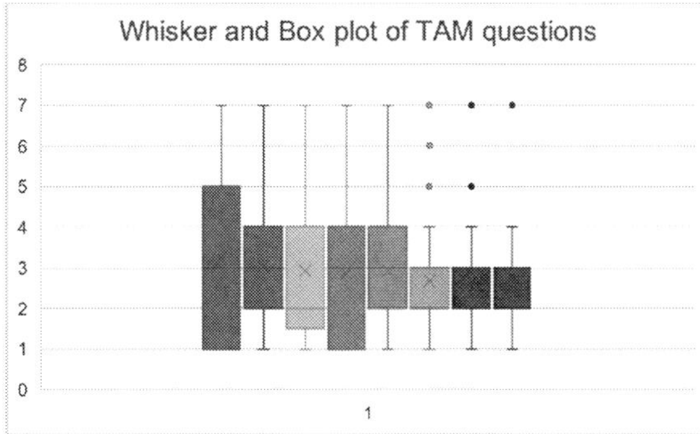

Figure 2. Whisker and Box plot of TAM questions

Based on the responses of 10 participants, the study found that the implementation of various technological dimensions within the context of e-insurance services is illustrated in Figure 3.

Technological Infrastructure	Checklist
Infrasturcture	
Hardware	☑
Communication Network	☐
ICT Facility	☑
DBMS	☑
Applications Assement Criteris	
Application functional maturity	☐
Application integration ability	☐
Application Security	☐
ICT Management	
Effectiveness	☐
Efficiency	☐
Confidentiality	☑
Integrity	☑
Availiability	☐
Reliability	☐
Compliancy	☐
Technical Skills	
Level of Maturity of ICT function	☐
E-Governance Strategic Plan	☑
Approaches to gain new skills and abilities	☐

Figure 3. Technology Infrastructure Checklist

The study employed a technological infrastructure checklist that assesses five different dimensions of technology implementation. These dimensions includes Infrastructure, Database Management Systems, Application Assessment Criteria, ICT Management, and Technical Skills.

5. DISCUSSION AND FINDING

This study aimed to analyze the readiness of E-Insurance services in Nepal through the use of the Technology Acceptance Model (TAM) and Technology Assessment. The results obtained from the TAM questions revealed that the general public is generally ready to accept and trust the ICT infrastructure in the insurance industry, as evidenced by the mean and variance of responses on the security and privacy factors, which were approximately 2.5 and 1.4 respectively. However, the technological infrastructure in Nepal's insurance sector appears to be lacking in certain areas. Specifically, none of the sub-structures in the application assessment criteria checklist were implemented, and only 2 out of 7 sub-structures in the ICT management checklist were implemented and ready for use. This suggests that while users may be ready to accept the technology, the infrastructure itself may not be fully prepared to deliver the necessary services. Additionally, it was found that only 27.9% of respondents had used online services, indicating a significant portion of the population may not be aware of these services or lack the technical skills necessary to utilize them.

Furthermore, the calculated α value of 0.89 suggests that the survey results were consistent with each other and may be generalizable to a larger population. However, future studies could benefit from utilizing the Nepal Stock Exchange (NEPSE) index to investigate investment behavior in the insurance sector, and comparing the results obtained from this survey to investigate the level of trust the public has in the insurance sector in Nepal.

It is important to note that the survey implemented in this study was conducted among individuals in the Kathmandu Valley, and primarily targeted the younger age group (18-25 years) which accounted for 78.6% of the sample. Future research should aim to include a more diverse age group and individuals from different regions of the country.

6. CONCLUSION

In this study, the e-readiness of the insurance industry in Nepal is assessed by utilizing the results from Technology Acceptance Model (TAM) and interview questions. The findings reveal that the insurance sector in Nepal is lacking in the management and integration of Information and Communication Technology (ICT) facilities, despite the availability of infrastructure. Additionally, the survey results indicate that the general public who currently use online services is ready to adapt to digital change, even if the industry is not yet mature in terms of e-readiness. However, a significant gap is observed among individuals who do not currently use the online services of insurance companies. It is important to note that in today's digital age, providing fast and accurate information services to users requires the observation of e-readiness indicators. Therefore, it is the responsibility of the insurance industry in Nepal to access these indicators and take appropriate action. By assessing the readiness of customers who use online services and mapping their focus on technology implementation, insurance companies can increase their own e-readiness. This study may be beneficial for researchers, practitioners of e-governance, and IT officers of insurance companies.

REFERENCES

Ao-Itc. (2019, October 2). *What is e-government and why it is important?* Gräbner Omahna IT Consulitng.

Aqel (2014.). *Toward an organizational e-readiness model.* Share and Discover Knowledge on SlideShare.

Agarwal, A., & Ramana, V. V. (2008). EGOSQ – Users' Assessment of e- Governance Online-Services: A Quality Measurement Instrumentation. In *Foundations of e-government.* Essay, GIFT Publishing, Global Institute of Flexible Systems Management.

Dhungana, R. (2022, September 7). *Current status of insurance business in Nepal.* Instapaper.

Gumilang, S. F. S., Nugroho, H., Lubis, M., & Jacob, D. W. (2019). *E-Government Readiness Model Development for Successful ICT Adoption at Government Institutions in Indonesia.* DlineInfo

Green, M. R., & Treischmann J. S. (2004). Risk & insurance (6th ed.)

Omari, A., & Hussein, H. A. (2006, November). *E-Government Readiness Assessment Model*. Research Gate.

Republica. (2021, September 1). *Nepal's 25 PC population has access to insurance*. My Republica.

Shareef, M., Ojo, A., & Janowski, T. (2008).

A readiness assessment framework for e-government planning: design and application. *ICEGOV '08: Proceedings of the 2nd International Conference on Theory and Practice of Electronic Governance*, 403–410.

Sanayei, A., & Torkestani, M. S. (2009).

Readiness Assessment of Iran's Insurance Industry for E-Commerce and E-Insurance Success. *International Journal of Information Science and Management*, *7*.

TRANSPARENCY IN INFORMATION MARKETS

Daphne Ruth Raban and Efrat Marmur
[1]*School of Business Administration, University of Haifa, Israel*

ABSTRACT

This study focuses on the effects of market transparencies on consumers' perceived value of information. Information goods have two key special characteristics: they are experience goods, and they are often given away for free. The study implements three transparencies related to market goods – cost, operational, and price transparencies - in an experimental information market to examine their effect on the perceived value of information goods. Perceived value is assessed by willingness-to-pay (WTP). The research method is a controlled experiment including preliminary questions, a visual vignette depicting a health app and two value elicitation questions.

Three groups of participants were exposed to each transparency form when price is not known. When cost transparency is applied, participants are more likely to download the app. Operational transparency has no effect on information goods. Price transparency diminishes the perceived value of the information good (WTP changes by -61.8%) and participants are 80% less likely to download the app.

When users received cost information related to a free information good, the perceived value of that good increased by +122.7% compared to the control. Operational transparency did not produce a statistically significant difference in WTP. The combined transparencies produce WTP which is higher than for operational transparency alone, but lower than for cost transparency alone.

Overall, in the case of information goods, cost transparency enhances value perception while price transparency diminishes it. To date, cost transparency is rarely practiced in information markets. The current results suggest that the cost of producing information should be visible to information consumers. The lower combined effect of cost and operational transparencies may be indicative of information overload and the diminishing value of additional information.

KEYWORDS

Information Markets, Transparency, Willingness-to-Pay, Perceived Value

1. INTRODUCTION

Markets rely on varying implementations of excludability, rivalry, and transparency to ensure competition. Information markets are a special type of market where excludability and rivalry are often challenged as evidenced by the vast availability of free information and by easy copying. Furthermore, it seems that transparency in information markets is taken as a given because most markets are digital and inherently offer data and metadata. However, the special nature of information as experience good raises questions regarding the assumption of transparency. This study applies forms of transparency to an information good and examines their effect on people's value perception of the information good.

Experience goods are the case in which consumers are only able to learn about their preferences for a certain product after experiencing it (Villas-Boas, 2006). Before experiencing information products, a consumer knows: (1) the price (zero or else), (2) partial content such as title or description, (3) metadata such as author, publication, date, etc. In addition to the information they know, consumers may have scant indication regarding the quality of content, but they do not know the actual value to them for their needs and expectations. The full evaluation of the information good is revealed after actual use (Rusho & Raban, 2020). Therefore, there is an inherent "gap" of information between experience goods and their ability to present full transparency, an inherent opacity. On one hand, consumers wish to experience the information good prior to the decision to purchase, and on the other hand, if they experience the good, the good may become redundant.

Transparency in markets is generally defined as a key mechanism that reduces the information asymmetry among market participants thereby promoting market efficiency (Bleck & Liu, 2007). What is the role of transparency in the case of experience goods? Can firms that sell experience goods risk full transparency? How can sellers and buyers overcome this "gap" of knowledge? For example, in the consultancy reports market, full transparency can be a double-edged sword. Consumers would like to know exactly what they are paying for or if the specific information they desire is fully researched in the report, while firms can only disclose a high-level abstract.

According to Buell (2019), the consumer-firm relationship is based on three types of transparency: cost, operational and price. Transparency requires clear disclosure of information in each of these areas. Information markets raise new challenges. What happens to transparency when the price is zero, i.e., when products are given for free (at least, without a direct pecuniary charge), as is the case for information? Do the other types of transparency become more salient, or do they also fade? Focusing on the special case of transparency in information markets may offer relief to both challenges raised here: information as experience good and the abundance of free information.

This paper proceeds as follows. First, we describe the special case of information as a market good, followed by an explanation about willingness-to-pay as a form of value perception and defined as the dependent variable in this research. Then, we describe the three types of transparency (cost, operational and price) in consumer goods markets and their expected behavior in the information goods market. Finally, we outline the experiments hypotheses, presented in the research, across a variety of instantiations of the different transparencies.

2. RESEARCH BACKGROUND

Since digital goods are often non-rival, they have some unique characteristics, such as zero cost of duplication and transportation and no geographic boundaries. While the production costs and effort may be considerable, the marginal costs are zero or close to zero (Shapiro & Varian, 1999). This unique cost structure results in a tendency for pricing to often be set at zero, explaining why information is freely available. However, free availability may come at other, social, costs, such as information overload which may bear a negative effect on personal productivity (Sabeeh & Ismail, 2013) or fake news, conspiracy theories, urban legends and the like (European Parliament & Frau-Meigs, 2020). It stands to reason that transparency of and about information may help to reduce these social costs and at the same time, increase the perceived value of information.

The next section describes value perception which is operationalized as willingness-to-pay (WTP), which is the dependent variable in the research.

2.1 Value Perception

Due to the nature of information goods, consumers' perceived value before using the information is related only to the initial description they have about the information. This stands in contrast to physical goods, in which value is mostly known in advance (Rusho & Raban, 2018). From an economic point of view consumers' willingness-to-pay (WTP), reflects their perceived value of information (Lopatovska & Mokros, 2008). Therefore, in the research we use willingness-to-pay (WTP) as the dependent variable to measure individual value perception for each state of transparency.

WTP is the maximum amount an individual is willing to pay for a product or a service (Hanemann, 1991). WTP is a fairly common measure of subjective value which combines the economic and psychological approaches to allocating value to information (Rusho & Raban, 2018). It provides a behavioral assessment of value perception (Horowitz & McConnell, 2003) and as such, it is an indicator of preferences.

In the following, we explain the nature of cost, operational and price transparencies. Each transparency has different effects on consumers perception regarding the value of information.

2.2 Cost, Operational, and Price Transparencies

A firm's disclosure of cost information reveals information about its profit margins, which could make the firm vulnerable to negative consequences, such as consumer ire or supplier price increases (Derlega et al., 1993; Mohan et al., 2020). Although cost transparency is considered sensitive information for a firm, it can engender trust and deepen the relationships among companies and consumers (Aron et al., 1997; Sedikides et al., 1999). Firms typically treat their costs as tightly guarded secrets, however, Mohan et al. (2020) demonstrated that when cost transparency is voluntary rather than forced by regulation, it increases purchase interest by enhancing consumer perceptions of a firm's trustworthiness. In addition, willingness to buy was higher in the presence of cost transparency due to increase in trust even when prices were unexpectedly low.

The challenge in information markets is to set a positive price given the widespread norm of free information. We posit that revealing the cost associated with the production of an information good may provide part of the needed description to enhance its value as perceived by its users. Cost transparency may contribute to reducing the inherent information asymmetry leading to the first hypothesis:

Hypothesis 1 (H1): Cost transparency in information goods markets will increase WTP.

Recent research revealed that operational transparency increases sales and increases people's trust and satisfaction in online services (e.g. digital travel agents), retail (i.e. highlighting the costs and processes involved in manufacturing) and even in settings where trust is otherwise low, such as government services (Ryan W. Buell et al., 2021).

Operational transparency increases perceptions of value because of increased perceptions of effort and resultant feelings of reciprocity between consumer and the firm (Chinander & Schweitzer, 2003; Gershoff et al., 2012). Operational transparency is a driver not only of perceived value but also of satisfaction and repurchase intentions (Ryan W Buell & Norton, 2011).

Following the same logic, we suggest that operational transparency may increase value perception in the information goods market. Free availability of information does not mean free or effortless production process. Consumers do not know the extent of effort put into creating the information good. If consumers become aware of the effort invested in producing the information good, it may increase their perception of value. Therefore, we posit that revealing the process associated with the production of information may have similar effect as in consumer goods markets, leading to the second hypothesis:

Hypothesis 2 (H2): Operational transparency in information goods markets will increase WTP.

Price transparency is defined as the extent to which information available about prices organizes, explains, clarifies, or projects the contextual direction and/or rationale for the seller's pricing (Hanna et al., 2019). An example of price transparency is price partitioning which refers to the common technique of revealing the price of the component parts of a product; for example, by dividing a product's price into its base price and shipping and handling (Bertini & Wathieu, 2008; Morwitz et al., 1998). Price transparency and price partitioning have both been found to increase purchase intentions, and to do so via a cognitive process (Morwitz, 1998).

Price transparency is effective at influencing consumer behaviour, especially when combined with low variability pricing strategies. Consumers are not only willing to pay more when pricing is clear and transparent but also likely to accelerate their purchase (Hanna et al., 2019). In the case of information goods, the lack of pricing (availability at no direct monetary charge) drives consumers towards hoarding behaviour and overconsumption (Edelman, 2009). Free availability may be interpreted as maximum price transparency which supports over-consumption. Imposing a price where the norm is free availability is likely to reduce the rate of transactions, but the implication for WTP is unclear. We posit that the effect of price transparency, when price is not zero, for information goods is similar to the effect of transparency on consumer goods. Therefore,

Hypothesis 3 (H3): Price transparency in information goods markets will increase WTP.

All three types of transparencies have different underlying mechanisms such as enhanced trust for cost transparency, increased effort perception for operational transparency, and increased value perceptions for price transparency (Mohan et al., 2020). Moreover, because consumers do not typically think about firms' costs, when they encounter an unexpectedly high price, they are likely to infer the high price as a reflection of high margins (as opposed to high costs). Since a firm's voluntary revelation of its costs increases trust, it also increases purchase interest both when prices are surprisingly high as well as when prices are surprisingly low (Mohan et al., 2020). But what happens in information markets when price is zero? Increased value perception via price transparency is not a possible underlying mechanism. In that case, trust and effort perception may alone become the underlying mechanism. Therefore, we posit that where price is zero, cost transparency and operational transparency in information goods can increase the rate of transactions. Therefore,

Hypothesis 4a (H4a): Cost transparency will increase WTP for free information goods compared to the control.

Hypothesis 4b (H4b): Operational transparency will increase WTP for free information goods compared to the control.

Hypothesis 4c (H4c): Cost and operational transparencies will increase WTP for free information goods compared to the control.

Hypothesis 5 (H5): transparencies increase the rate of transactions for information goods compared to the control.

3. METHOD

The purpose of the research is to examine the effect of cost, operational, and price transparencies, and interrelations among the three transparencies on the perception of value of information. The research building blocks are expressed in the hypotheses above and are shown in Figure 1.

To investigate the effects of the three types of transparency in a market for information goods, we conducted an experiment eliciting the participants' perceived value as WTP when they were presented with transparency related to an information good. The independent variable was transparency, which had three levels (cost, operational and price). The dependent variables were the consumer's WTP – the private value a consumer was willing to pay for an information good and the willingness to download an app.

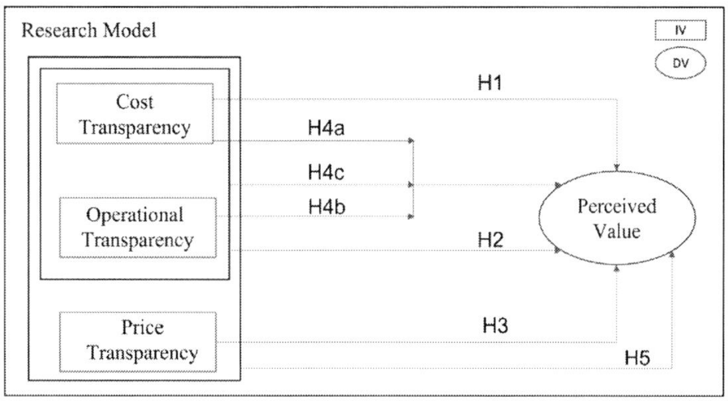

Figure 1. The research model for the study of transparency in information markets

A controlled experiment served to test the causal relations described in the hypotheses. The experiment included preliminary questions, a visual vignette and an elicitation of subjective value (WTP). Forms of transparency were manipulated via the visual vignette. Each manipulation was presented to a new group of participants to avoid dependence. To test the five hypotheses, we needed a control group and six experimental groups. The information good was an app that checks the combination of symptoms and personal information against the aggregated knowledge and experience of thousands of doctors and their clinical insights to provide a possible diagnosis, along with the resources to provide help the ailing the patient.

Research participants were recruited via Midgam Project Web Panel, a company specializing in services for internet research to academic scholars and research companies. Each group included about 35 participants for a total of approximately 245 participants. The sample included Israeli adults who are regular users of mobile phone apps at the ages of 20-75. The independent variable: Types of transparency (cost, operation, and price). The dependent variables: 1. Willingness-to-pay (WTP) – the sum consumers were willing to pay for an information good; 2. The rate of app download transactions (in H5). Participants were randomly assigned to the control and six experiment groups. Each participant opened a link that directed him/her to the experiment comprising the following sequence of web pages: 1. Welcome page and consent form; 2. Background questions (age, gender, education level, apps used); 3. Activity instructions; 4. An infographic with the information good details; 5. Transparency manipulation followed by an input window with a prompt regarding WTP for the presented information good; 6. Closing and thank you. Figure 2 summarizes the screens that comprise the experiment interface.

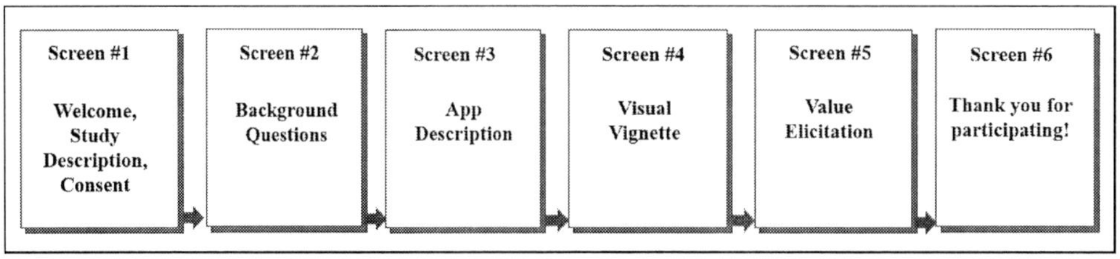

Figure 2. The experiment flow

4. RESULTS

This study set out to discover the influence of market transparencies on the perceived value of an information good. The control group was exposed to the health app without market transparency and the experimental groups saw the same app with the addition of market transparencies. Descriptive data and two-tailed t-test statistics appear in Table 1. The unit of measurement of WTP is virtual money, New Israeli Shekels.

Table 1. Descriptive statistics and two-tailed t-test for the dependent variable, WTP of an information product

Group	Manipulation	Group Size	WTP Range	WTP Mean	Std. Dev.	t-Test*
Control	none	35	0-100	25.06	34.28	
1	Cost transparency	34	0-250	43.68	78.65	1.28
2	Operational Transparency	34	0-100	17.15	30.28	-1.02
3	Price Transparency	34	0-80	9.56	19.28	**-2.31***
4	Cost transparency, free app	36	0-300	55.83	86.24	**1.97***
5	Operational transparency, free app	37	0-150	38.19	49.10	1.31
6	Cost & operational transparency, free app	35	0-300	49.69	66.34	**1.95***

* $p<.05$ in a two-tailed t-test comparing the control group with each of the experiment groups

An important observation (Table 1) is that the introduction of cost transparency is associated with the highest average WTP (M=43.68). The absence of a main effect is likely due to the high standard deviation.

For price transparency in information goods, a statistically significant difference at $p=.024$ in WTP was found. When the users are exposed to price transparency, the perceived value of the app decreases (WTP changes by -61.8%).

A one-way ANOVA (Table 2) compared the means of groups 1-3 where transparency manipulations were applied to the information product while users were not aware whether the product was free or fee-based. A statistically significant difference was found ($F(2,99)=4.379$, $p=.015$). A post-hoc test revealed a statistically significant difference ($p=.016$) between cost transparency (group 1, M=34.68) and price transparency (group 3, M=9.56).

Table 2. ANOVA post hoc Tukey's test for mean WTP in the presence of cost, operational and price transparencies

Group (I)	Group (J)	Mean Difference (I-J)	Std. Error	Sig.	Lower Bound	Upper Bound
1 Cost	2 Operation	26.529	12.106	.078	-2.28	55.33
	3 Price	34.118*	12.106	.016	5.31	62.92
2 Operation	1 Cost	-26.529	12.106	.078	-55.33	2.28
	3 Price	7.588	12.106	.806	-21.22	36.39
3 Price	1 Cost	-34.118*	12.106	.016	-62.92	-5.31
	2 Operation	-7.588	12.106	.806	-36.39	21.22

* The mean difference is significant at the 0.05 level

A t-test comparing group 4 to the control group indicated a statistically significant difference. When users received cost information related to a free information product, the perceived value of the information product increased by +122.7% compared to the control. In the experiment, the zero price of the app was presented as a temporary price. A t-test for independent samples comparing group 5 to the control group was not statistically significant ($p=.195$). To test the effect of combining cost and operational transparency on WTP when the price of the good is zero, a t-test for independent samples compared group 6 to the control group. An effect was found at p =.055. We consider this to be statistically significant. When the users know the app is free and they receive information regarding the costs and operations associated with developing the app, the perceived value of the app increases (WTP changes by +98.3%). This effect is smaller than the effect of cost transparency alone.

H5 results: To test the effect of transparency type on the rate of transaction (willingness to download the app) we conducted a logistic regression. Table 3 displays a statistically significant difference related to cost transparency at p=0.02 with positive Exp(b)=2.4 value. According to these findings, cost transparency increases the likelihood to download the app by +140% (2.4 times) compared to other forms of transparency. A statistically significant difference found for price transparency p=.001 with negative Exp(b)=.214 explains the opposite effect. Price transparency reduces the likelihood of downloading the app by -80%.

In summary, H1, H2, H4b are rejected, H3, H4a, H4c are accepted and H5 is partially accepted.

Table 3. Binary regression results of willingness to download the app per type of transparency

Group	B	S.E.	Wald	df	Sig.	Exp(B)
1 Cost	.875	.376	5.410	1	.020	2.400
2 Operation	.236	.345	.468	1	.494	1.267
3 Price	-1.540	.450	11.725	1	.001	.214
4 zero price cost	-.223	.335	.443	1	.506	.800
5 zero price operation	.054	.329	.027	1	.869	1.056
6 zero price cost and operation	-.651	.356	3.338	1	.068	.522
99 Control		.374	5.997	1	.014	2.500

5. DISCUSSION

This study set out to assess how forms of market transparency affect people's value perceptions of an information product and their willingness to download the product. The main research objective was to establish causality by comparing experimental treatments with a control. Another objective was to evaluate the relative influence of the various transparencies. The study relates to two sub-groups of hypotheses. One sub-group examining a scenario when users are not aware whether the product is free and the other sub-group analyzing similar scenarios with a clear indication that the product is available at no cost for a certain time.

The difference between the group exposed to cost transparency and the control group was not statistically significant. Nevertheless, cost transparency produced the highest average WTP compared to the control group and the other two experimental groups exposed to operational and price transparency, respectively.

Revealing cost information increased the likelihood of downloading the health app by +140% compared to other transparencies. The findings that when cost transparency was observed participants were willing to pay the highest price and were more likely to download the app established that cost transparency increased value perception. This finding was aligned with earlier findings where willingness to buy was higher in the presence of cost transparency (Mohan et al., 2020). The present findings indicate that a similar effect occurs for purely digital goods that carry no particular company or provider information. This attests to the subjective nature of information value perception and to the importance of cost transparency in the market for information products. A future study could establish whether there is an added effect by adding an identity or a brand name to the information provider.

When comparing the operational transparency group to the control group, the difference was not statistically significant. Previous literature indicated that operational transparency increased perceptions of value because customers appreciated the effort involved in the process which led to increased customer satisfaction (Ryan W. Buell et al., 2021). The present results highlight an interesting difference in the effect of operational transparency between market goods and information goods. To better understand the effect of operational transparency on WTP, we suggest conducting the same experiment with a larger sample size to reduce statistical errors. In addition, examining a finer manipulation check of the operational transparency may help to determine whether, indeed, there is no statistically significant difference.

When users are unaware of app pricing, price transparency diminishes the perceived value of the product (WTP changes by -61.8%). Participants are 80% less likely to download the app. When price becomes salient, users are considerably less willing to make a transaction. This finding is noteworthy because the users' natural inclination to pay is higher (control group) when they are not told that payment is required as compared to the case of group 3 in which the users were told that payment is mandatory. Along this line of thinking, a recommendation for companies developing experience goods, would be to allow users to experience the good prior to showing the prices. For example, offering a trial and separately providing the price. The emphasis in a product trial should be on product experience rather than on emphasizing a "free period" which draws attention to pricing. While price transparency is known to support market transactions for regular market goods (Hanna et al., 2019), an opposite effect appears in the case of a digital information product. In the case of information goods, consumers usually expect to find free availability of information and zero pricing. Therefore, price transparency (a non-zero price indication) may contradict with this basic axiom, leading to diminishing market transactions.

The statistically significant difference in WTP between the cost transparency group and the price transparency group is aligned with the theory explaining that cost transparency information is the most sensitive information a company can share, and users value the disclosure of this information (Mohan et al., 2020). Overall, in the case of information products cost transparency enhances value perception while price transparency diminishes it. Cost transparency is rarely practiced in information markets. According to the present results, cost transparency would be a substantial catalyst for transactions in information markets.

Taking an in-depth look at the impact of transparency when price is zero offers some surprising insights. When users know that price is zero and they receive information about cost associated with developing the app, they are willing to pay +123% more for the app as compared to the control group. When they are presented with both cost and operational information, they are willing to pay +98% more as compared to the control group. Interestingly, the combined effect of two transparencies is a WTP value which is higher than for operational transparency alone, but lower than for cost transparency alone. One interpretation could be that since operational transparency does not have a significant positive effect, adding it to cost transparency diminishes the effect of the latter. Another interpretation could be a diminishing value of additional information, an indication of information overload. This should be further explored in a future study presenting additional general information in order to distinguish the general informational effect (i.e. information overload) from the specific operational information effect.

A practical recommendation to companies based on the current findings is to be short and focused on transparency information and not to overload users with information. The results indicate that the combination of free trials of experience goods and cost transparency lead to increased WTP. While many companies implement the logic of offering free goods, the shift to payment is non-trivial. This research offers insight into how to use specific transparencies to elicit and encourage consumers' willingness to pay for an information good.

Next, we offer analyses that were possible using the available data, however, these analyses were not associated with specific hypotheses.

6. FURTHER ANALYSIS

When comparing group 2 (operational information with no price indication) to group 5 (operational information with indication of price zero), a statistically significant difference in WTP was found. When the users know the app is free and they receive information regarding the operations associated with developing the app, the perceived value of the app increases as compared to when users do not know that the app is free or fee-based (WTP changes by +122.7%). This finding provides insight regarding the relation between highlighting that the price is zero, even if temporarily, and operational transparency. Comparing each operational transparency (groups 2 and 5) to the control did not produce a statistically significant difference, however, comparing the groups to each other produced a significant difference. The increased WTP in group 5 is associated with the interplay between operational transparency and zero price information.

Another interesting finding is the statistically significant difference when comparing group 3 in which app pricing was not stated to groups 4-6 where the stated price was zero (group 4 $p=.003$; group 5 $p=.002$; group 6 $p=.001$). In group 3, participants saw price information of similar apps and were asked to submit their willingness to pay for the health app. This resulted in 61.8% decline in WTP of and an 80% decline in the willingness to download the app. In groups 4-6, participants were told that the current price of the app is zero and then they submitted their WTP bids. The results indicate that users value the free trial period and would be willing to pay more afterwards by as much as +484%, +299%, +420% in groups 4, 5, and 6, respectively. These findings indicate that when information products are concerned, the accompanying information should not refer to price alone, but to other elements, which in the current setup are cost and operational transparencies.

7. LIMITATIONS

The different manipulations were descriptive paragraphs of the specific relevant transparency for each group. Although the questionnaires were identical in color scheme and infographic, the length of the transparency paragraphs were not identical. The operational transparency descriptive paragraph was longer than the other paragraphs. Future research may include identical length of descriptive information for each group.

Probably due to small sample sizes and large variances, some differences were not statistically significant. The immediate conclusion is that when eliciting WTP, which is a subjective measure characterized by large variance, larger group sizes are needed. Statistical power will be examined and implemented in selection of the sample size in a future study.

Another angle to consider is related mostly to selecting experiments as the main research tool. It is well-known that the external validity of experiments is limited, however, we rely on the long tradition of behavioral economics while striving to present realistic cases.

8. CONCLUSION

While transparency has been shown to be vital in markets, it has not received sufficient attention in information markets. Beyond the academic interest, transparency has important practical implications because information is critical in affecting people's choices and actions. Transparency in information markets is largely taken as a given because most markets are digital and inherently offer data and metadata. However, the abundance of free information implies that market mechanisms are lacking.

This research focused on three forms of market transparency (cost, operational and price) based on the consumer-firm relationship. Similar to previous studies on transparency in market goods, participants exposed to cost transparency information were willing to pay the most as compared to participants exposed to other forms of transparency. Hence, cost transparency increases value perception also in information goods markets. Interestingly, we found an opposite effect with price transparency in information goods and no effect regarding operational transparency. Further research should assess additional forms of transparency that might be unique for information goods market. By studying how separate and combined forms of transparency affect the perceived value of information, future research will provide theoretical and practical insights relating to people's information consumption.

REFERENCES

Aron, A., Melinat, E., Aron, E. N., Vallone, R. D., & Bator, R. J. (1997). The Experimental Generation of Interpersonal Closeness: A Procedure and Some Preliminary Findings: *Https://Doi.Org/10.1177/0146167297234003*, *23*(4), 363–377. https://doi.org/10.1177/0146167297234003

Bertini, M., & Wathieu, L. (2008). Attention arousal through price partitioning. *Marketing Science*, *27*(2), 236–246. https://doi.org/10.1287/MKSC.1070.0295

Bleck, A., & Liu, X. (2007). Market Transparency and the Accounting Regime. *Journal of Accounting Research*, *45*(2), 229–256. https://doi.org/10.1111/J.1475-679X.2007.00231.X

Buell, R. W. (2019). Operational Transparency: Make Your Processes Visible to Customers and Your Customers Visible to Employees. *Harvard Business Review*, *97*(4), 102–113. https://www.hbs.edu/faculty/Pages/item.aspx?num=55804

Buell, Ryan W. (2019). Operational Transparency: Make Your Processes Visible to Customers and Your Customers Visible to Employees. *Harvard Business Review*, *97*(4), 102–113.

Buell, Ryan W., Porter, E., & Norton, M. I. (2021). Surfacing the Submerged State: Operational Transparency Increases Trust in and Engagement with Government. *Manufacturing & Service Operations Management*, *23*(4), 781–802. https://doi.org/10.1287/msom.2020.0877

Buell, Ryan W, & Norton, M. I. (2011). The Labor Illusion : How Operational Transparency Increases Perceived Value. *Management Science*, *57*(9), 1564–1579.

Chinander, K. R., & Schweitzer, M. E. (2003). The input bias: The misuse of input information in judgements of outcomes. *Organizational Behavior and Human Decision Processes*, *91*(2), 243–253. https://doi.org/10.1016/S0749-5978(03)00025-6

Derlega, V., Sandra, M., Sandra, P., & Margulis, S. T. (1993). *Self-Disclosure*. https://us.sagepub.com/en-us/nam/self-disclosure/book3320

Edelman, B. (2009). Priced and Unpriced Online Markets. *Journal of Economic Perspectives*, *23*(3), 21–36. https://doi.org/10.1257/JEP.23.3.21

European Parliament, D.-G. for I. P. of the U., & Frau-Meigs, D. (2020). *Societal costs of "fake news" in the Digital Single Market - Publications Office of the EU*. https://op.europa.eu/en/publication-detail/-/publication/ac4db4f9-2496-11eb-9d7e-01aa75ed71a1

Gershoff, A. D., Kivetz, R., & Keinan, A. (2012). Consumer response to versioning: How brands' production methods affect perceptions of unfairness. *Journal of Consumer Research*, *39*(2), 382–398. https://doi.org/10.1086/663777/2/M_39-2-382-FG1.JPEG

Hanemann, M. W. (1991). Willingness to pay and willingness to accept: How much can they differ? *American Economic Review*, *81*(3), 635–647.

Hanna, R. C., Lemon, K. N., & Smith, G. E. (2019). Is transparency a good thing? How online price transparency and variability can benefit firms and influence consumer decision making. *Business Horizons*, *62*(2), 227–236. https://doi.org/10.1016/J.BUSHOR.2018.11.006

Horowitz, J. K., & McConnell, K. E. (2003). Willingness to accept, willingness to pay and the income effect. *Journal of Economic Behavior & Organization*, *51*(4), 537–545.

Lopatovska, I., & Mokros, H. B. (2008). Willingness to pay and experienced utility as measures of affective value of information objects: Users' accounts. *Information Processing & Management*, *44*(1), 92–104. https://doi.org/10.1016/J.IPM.2007.01.020

Mohan, B., Buell, R. W., & John, L. K. (2020). Lifting the veil: the benefits of cost transparency. *Marketing Science*, *39*(6), 1105–1121.

Morwitz, V. G., Greenleaf, E. A., & Johnson, E. J. (1998). Divide to and prosper: Consumers' reactions to partitioned. *Journal of Marketing Research*, *4*(35), 453–463. https://doi.org/10.1287/mnsc.16.8.b566

Rusho, Y., & Raban, D. R. (2018). Value Perception of Information Sources in the Context of Learning. *Open Information Science*, *2*(1), 83–101. https://doi.org/10.1515/opis-2018-0007

Rusho, Y., & Raban, D. R. (2020). Hands on: Information Experiences as Sources of Value. *Journal of the Association for Information Science and Technology*, *71*(6), 671–684. https://doi.org/10.1002/asi.24288

Sabeeh, Z. A., & Ismail, Z. (2013). Effects of information overload on productivity in enterprises: A literature review. *International Conference on Research and Innovation in Information Systems, ICRIIS*, 210–214. https://doi.org/10.1109/ICRIIS.2013.6716710

Sedikides, C., Campbell, K. W., Reeder, G. D., & Elliot, A. J. (1999). The relationship closeness induction task. *Representative Research in Social Psychology*, *34*, 1–4. https://psychology.uga.edu/sites/default/files/RCITarticle1999.pdf

Shapiro, C., & Varian, H. R. (1999). *Information Rules: A Strategic Guide to the Network Economy*. Harvard Business School Press.

Villas-Boas, J. M. (2006). Dynamic Competition with Experience Goods. *Journal of Economics & Management Strategy*, *15*(1), 37–66. https://doi.org/10.1111/J.1530-9134.2006.00091.

AN EMPIRICAL STUDY OF CUSTOMER SATISFACTION AND LOYALTY IN B2C E-COMMERCE AMONG INDIAN YOUTHS

Bussu Srikar Reddy, Sumanth Cholleti, Sriram Kalpathy Viswanathan and Asish Oommen Mathew
Manipal Institute of Technology, Manipal Academy of Higher Education, Manipal, India

ABSTRACT

Loyal customers are essential for a business' success in an e-commerce environment. Despite the e-commerce industry's explosive expansion and popularity, businesses continue to have trouble winning over and keeping customers. Therefore, businesses must research the factors influencing customer loyalty in order to ensure their survival in a highly competitive market. This study assesses the influence of variables including online shop image, online shopping expectation, purchasing experience, perceived value, customer satisfaction, and website trust on B2C E-commerce customer loyalty. Indian youths were the study's target group, and a questionnaire survey was used to collect data from them. The main findings of this study show that customer satisfaction and the online shopping image have a substantial impact on customer loyalty. Online shopping image, privacy, and buying experience were proven to have a substantial impact on customer happiness. This study contributes to a deeper knowledge of the variables influencing customer loyalty and happiness in an e-commerce environment, particularly among young people.

KEYWORDS

E-Commerce, Customer Satisfaction, Brand Loyalty, Online Shop Image, Trust, Security, Privacy

1. INTRODUCTION

The internet has become an important medium for business transactions and developing marketing strategies. Online businesses are developing quickly due to their advantages, such as increasing efficiency, reducing rates, saving costs, shifting market size and structure, as well as removing intermediaries and allowing suppliers to meet the right customers (Ebrahimi, 2019; Srivastava, 2020). Previous studies have shown that customer loyalty has a huge effect on company performance, and most companies see it as a major source of competitive advantage. Most companies see consumer loyalty as a major source of competitive advantage. Loyal customers are too important when it comes to sustainability (Kassim N. M., 2009). E-loyalty has become a necessity for businesses to thrive, and it is important to recognize the factors that influence customer loyalty. This includes customer satisfaction, trust, and the effect of the design features of a seller's site. The key to long-term success for e-commerce businesses is developing consumer trust, and consumer satisfaction and customer loyalty to a company's services can both be significantly impacted by consumer trust in online purchasing websites. These ideas have been employed in the context of e-commerce in earlier studies.

Brick-and-mortar businesses have evolved into brick-and-click businesses due to the digital revolution. In December 2014, businesses that completed online sales made up 24.7% of the overall national total. China had 648.75 million internet users in 2014 (CNNIC, 2015) and 55.7% had done at least some online shopping in the year prior (Huang, 2019). According to a Statista report, global retail internet company sales will increase by three times to $4.5 trillion by 2021 from the $1.3 trillion in 2014 (Sharma, 2019).

India's e-commerce market is projected to reach US$ 111 billion and US$ 200 billion by 2024 and 2026, respectively (IBEF, 2022). This increase in sales is due to e-commerce companies providing more services than their offline counterparts, supported by government regulations. Customers have easy access to organizational and product details through e-shopping websites, can access consumer reviews and feedback, compare prices, and much more. This high level of demand for e-commerce websites has created a need for companies to recognize the purchase patterns of people to make sure they survive in the long run.

2. BACKGROUND THEORY

Customer loyalty is a long-term version of customer trust on a website, which gives it an edge over its competitors. It is all about earning the trust of the customer so that they are more likely to recommend the website to others (Gefen, 2002). Multiple definitions of loyalty have been put forward, and they all agree that customer loyalty includes both behavioural and attitudinal components. Loyalty is a valuable asset for companies, as it helps gain new customers and reduce marketing costs (Yang, 2019). It is also seen as a reward for customers, as it encourages them to purchase again and suggest or give favourable remarks to others. Research suggests that satisfaction is also important.

Customer loyalty in an e-commerce setting has been studied deeply, and several interpretations have been given (Abumalloh, 2020). Recent studies have shown that the product's price and promotion are no longer the main factors that drive the customer to make a purchase decision (Azam, 2012). Instead, customers' expectations and demands are the driving forces to create the need for new technology and state-of-the-art features and services (Pereira, 2016). This has enabled businesses to react swiftly to improvements made by rivals, reducing the market impact of product differentiation. Only customer-centric relationships have emerged as a wise way to set businesses apart from their competitors. It is important to examine and comprehend customer online behaviour and buying habits because they are not linear. According to scholars, customer behaviour changes over time because experience shapes perception.

In previous studies, consumer satisfaction has been shown to be the main factor in the formation of loyalty in e-commerce. However, some experts have said that even though customers are satisfied, they tend to go for other alternatives. This ambiguity has led to a need to consider other related factors when assessing customer loyalty (Safa, 2019). Every company in the field of e-commerce is in the red ocean and must find a way to sustain in this high competition with the loyalty factor as the crucial factor contributing to the sustainability of business (Ranggadara, 2019). This study aims to develop and evaluate a model that can be used in corporate management settings and raise scientific awareness in the field of marketing. It aims to establish a deeper understanding of online customer behaviour and the purchase decision process in the e-commerce scenario, as it is essential for companies to evaluate the findings from data analysis and the new insights that are discovered.

3. HYPOTHESIS DEVELOPMENT

3.1 Online Shop Image/Brand Image

The term "online shop image" describes the general perception of e-commerce firms created by a number of signals, including store characteristics, marketing tactics, operational style, etc (Chen, 2010). Consumers develop a mental image and sense of trust for a brand when they associate it with associations they can recall (Hermawan, 2019). A positive brand image will entice buyers to make additional purchases. The brand image is frequently referred to in the psychological elements of the image that are ingrained in the consumer's subconscious through the expectations and experience of adopting the brand through a product or service, creating a positive brand that is increasingly significant to the company. The brand image is also viewed as a description of the business that includes the symbolic meaning connected to the specific characteristics of the goods or services. Providing cost-effective products ensures customer satisfaction and loyalty in addition to enhancing brand image if a website has a positive shop image (Aslam, 2019). Considering this, the following assumptions can be made:

H1a: Online shop image has a significant influence on online shopping expectation.

H1b: Online shop image has a significant influence on the perceived value.

H1c: Online shop image has a significant influence on customer satisfaction.

H1d: Online shop image has a significant influence on customer loyalty.

3.2 Online Shopping Expectation

Before customers utilise an online store to make a purchase, they have certain expectations for the product (Chen, 2010). It is the seller's job to live up to the customer's expectations and to give them confidence that the website can fulfil them (Othman, 2020). It is a crucial psychological test before engaging in online purchasing and has a big impact on how those transactions are regarded and their value. When a person makes a purchase, for instance, their expectations are frequently very high. As a result, even if a tiny issue arises or the person receives a product that falls short of their expectations, the purchasing experience becomes negative and is negatively evaluated as a result. Therefore, the following hypotheses are put forward:

H2a: Online shopping expectation has a significant influence on purchasing experience.

H2b: Online shopping expectation has a significant influence on perceived value.

3.3 Purchasing Experience

The actual psychological reactions to in-store purchases are a focus of the online shopping experience (Chen, 2010). According to its definition, the online customer experience is a psychological condition that shows itself as a user's subjective response to the website. When a client uses an online platform to get information, they participate in the cognitive and emotive processes that produce information that leaves a lasting impression. Numerous studies highlight the crucial part that customer experience plays in online commerce. Numerous publications stress how crucial it is for organisations to provide a positive online consumer experience because it influences client satisfaction. Additionally, the consumer experience is intricate and includes cognitive, social, emotive, and physical components. They are related because perceived value and the buying experience are both cognitive elements. Researchers have concluded that consumers' perceptions and intents are favourably impacted by their online shopping experiences. Individually, more experience increases online buying happiness and the quantity of actual transactions made (Dabrynin, 2019). Based on these reviews, the following hypotheses are proposed:

H3a: Purchasing experience has a significant influence on perceived value.

H3b: Purchasing experience has a significant influence on customer satisfaction.

3.4 Perceived Value

The ability of a product to satisfy the wants and expectations of the consumer is measured by their perception of its perceived value, which is a comparison between the resources they invested and the value they received from the product they purchased (Suhartanto, 2019). In essence, it refers to the cost and resources people are willing to spend on a good or service. Customers may quickly compare product features and costs in the internet business environment, which emphasises the significance of perceived value. Perceived value is high when from the customer's perspective the product or service has a high ability to compensate for the resources spent by the customer in buying that particular product. Hence, the customer deems the product to have a high value or return on investment. Along the same lines, we can talk about why a product has less perceived value. Hence the seller or e-retailer has to make sure that the products have high perceived values in monetary and non-monetary terms, so as to maintain a healthy relationship with the customer.

The perception of the goods and the online store following an online purchase can also be included in the perceived value. The comparison of a product's material and intangible benefits, its added level, and its overall production and use expenses is what is specifically meant by perceived value. The majority of researchers claimed that perceived value was strongly situational and context-dependent (Wang, 2020). The whole of all subjective and objective, qualitative and quantitative, and qualitative aspects that go into the overall shopping experience is what is referred to as value. However, perceived value is not just a comparison of money spent versus the value for money returned in the form of the item purchased, but it is the comparison of effort, time, money spent versus the returns we get in the form of the item. Perceived value just doesn't mean only about pricing, it is also about the product's quality and repurchasing intention. From analyzing many models and literature it is found that perceived value was one of the most important drivers of customer satisfaction (Ali, 2019). Privacy and Security are the components of perceived value and these components indeed affect trust on the website through perceived value.

So, we assume that:
H4a: Perceived value has a significant influence on trust on the website.
H4b: Perceived value has a significant influence on customer satisfaction.

3.5 Customer Satisfaction

Customer satisfaction can be defined as customers' evaluations of a product or service concerning their needs and expectations (Ferreira, 2020). Kotler defines it as a feeling in the form of one's pleasure or disappointment resulting from comparing the perceived product (Widjaja, 2019).

Customer Satisfaction is the result of a good shopping experience. This cognitive state the consumer has is compensated for the price paid. It represents the particular purchasing experience along with the customer's feelings about the experience before the actual buying point. Web design/appearance and privacy/security will also focus on customer satisfaction. After buying online, it's a psychologically pleasant experience. Satisfaction is the satisfaction of a consumer with his or her previous purchase experience with a particular retail website.

Researchers have long been interested in the link between customer satisfaction and loyalty. According to earlier research, the majority of researchers thought that loyalty was significantly influenced by satisfaction. Similar findings were made regarding loyalty in e-commerce, where a review of 45 loyalty articles revealed that more than 30 of them (or more than two-thirds of the literature) analysed and confirmed the link between loyalty and satisfaction, highlighting how improving customer satisfaction could increase customer loyalty. Additionally, there is also significant evidence to suggest that in order to accurately measure loyalty, customer satisfaction must be considered an important indicator of loyalty (Wang, 2020). Thus, we presume:

H5: Customer satisfaction has a significant influence on customer loyalty.

3.6 Trust on the Website

The ability to monitor or control the other party is not a requirement for trust; rather, trust is the desire to be exposed to the acts of the other person (Choi, 2019). Trust is of great importance for long-term success in e-commerce. This trust is transformed into loyalty in the long term through good customer satisfaction. It is important to note that consumers who do not trust a particular website are unlikely to buy back from this website in the future even after a satisfactory shopping experience. In other words, satisfaction doesn't necessarily mean loyalty, but customer loyalty leads to satisfaction. This is because the dissatisfied customer will choose to buy from other websites. Therefore, e-stores have to satisfy customers to make them trust the website. In the process of satisfying the customer, the initial step is to build trust (Mofokeng, 2019). Consequently, as trust increases, the repurchasing intention also increases, affecting customer satisfaction and hence indirectly affecting loyalty (Lin, 2007). So it is assumed that:

H6: Trust on the website has a significant influence on customer satisfaction.

3.7 Information Quality

Website IQ is the customer's assessment of the level of the product or service information offered on the website. Information is an essential part of sites and its quality is viewed as a marketing device to ensure the smooth execution of transactions in web-based shopping (Kim, 2009). The IQ of a website is often defined as the capacity to deliver the knowledge that it needs to offer to its users. When evaluating website usage, website quality is a key success element for e-commerce service providers. The IQ of a website is typically influenced by the products offered there, the provider's service quality, the design of the website or system, its usability, and the product quality (Aslam, 2019). Customer acceptability, for instance, has a favourable link with website IQ. A website's information quality leaves a lasting impact on users, leading them to believe it is the best option for them to proceed with the purchase process. Nonetheless, IQ does not affect the purpose of customers to conduct website transactions. Several researchers suggested a favorable association between website IQ and social image on the website. So, the assumption is that:

H7: Information quality has a significant influence on online shop image.

3.8 User Interface Quality

Previous research indicates that the user interface is directly tied to the website design dimension, which is vital in fostering satisfaction (Kassim, 2008). These aspects of material service quality include visually beautiful, captivating, and eye-pleasing website content, organisation, and structure. In spite of this, developing trust can be significantly influenced by the first impression of a retail website, and maintaining trust can be made simpler by excellent communication. For instance, user-friendliness or content design aesthetic aspects have been purposefully created to express trust in the e-commerce environment.

When customers connect with an e-service provider, the user interface serves as the store's front and ambiance. This element is crucial since it affects a customer's initial perception of the website and how easily they can navigate and grasp its contents. The user interface is referred to as a tangible aspect of e-commerce. More effective and efficient the website is, the more swimmingly the process goes, resulting in higher satisfaction levels (Faraoni, 2019). Hence a well-designed website will create a positive social image among users. So the assumption is that:

H8: User interface quality has a significant influence on online shop image.

3.9 Security Risk

E-transaction protection refers to the customer's perception of online security while dealing with e-commerce service providers when purchasing goods or services. In general, security risk is a major reason why customers are hesitant and doubtful in completing e-transactions through debit or credit cards (Tzavlopoulos, 2019). E-commerce systems should provide protection of customer information and also details about their Internet shopping transactions. Many issues such as stolen information, fraudulent transactions, etc. are consequences of poor protection of customer information which is highly undesirable. Hence security risk is a very important factor in an e-commerce setting (Othman, 2020). If a payment goes wrong or if the site is fraudulent, the perception of the customer towards the site completely changes. So, it is assumed that:

H9: Security Risk has a significant influence on perceived value.

3.10 Privacy

Access to unwanted private information on the website is not entertained by any customer other than the required information. Since a data leak can cause big issues such as identity theft, the privacy of personal information has been a major concern for customers, and any problem in protecting their personal information will deter them from purchasing from the website (Faraoni, 2019). If the website does well in maintaining the privacy of information, it instills confidence in customers which is the genesis of trust. Hence, it is up to the e-service provider to change the customer's perception of the website's competency and policies in protecting private information (Aslam, 2019). If the customer is unhappy or suspicious with the type of information the site is asking, the customer's perception changes and might even lead to damage to the trust the customer had on the website. So it is assumed that:

H10: Privacy has a significant influence on perceived value.

4. METHOD

4.1 Data Collection

This research is a quantitative study for which the tool used is a survey questionnaire to get the responses from the target group. The questionnaire items were adopted form previous literature. Data was collected from 300 participants from the generation Z cohort belonging to different regions of the country using convenience sampling approach. People of this age were considered since they are very active in online shopping.

4.2 Measurement Model Analysis

Measurement model analysis needs to be completed before hypothesis testing to validate the research instrument. All the constructs have Cronbach's Alpha values and Composite Reliability values of more than 0.7 (threshold value) which means that all the items (questions) for all constructs are internally consistent and hence reliable (Hair et al., 2016). Additionally, it was discovered that all constructs have AVE (average variance extracted) values greater than 0.5. This proves the validity of the constructs because more variance is captured by all constructs than there is due to measurement error.

Discriminant validity is a measure of the extent to which a construct is which is supposed to be distinct is actually distinct or different from other constructs in the model. Therefore, we can infer that a construct is distinct and describes phenomena that are not represented by other constructs by demonstrating discriminant validity. The square root of AVE for all constructs exceeds the inter-construct correlation coefficients. Heterotrait-Monotrait correlation ratio (HTMT) values were also found to be less than 0.90 for all constructs thus further establishing the discriminant validity.

4.3 Structural Model Analysis

To test the hypotheses, structural model analysis was performed after measurement model analysis. Table 1 presents a summary of the hypothesis findings.

Table 1. Hypothesis testing results

Hypothesized Relationship		Path Coefficients(β)	T-Statistic	p-value	Hypothesis Result
H1a	OSI ----> OSE	0.818	24.669***	0.000	**Supported**
H1b	OSI ----> PRV	0.334	4.658***	0.000	**Supported**
H1c	OSI ----> CSF	0.277	4.164***	0.000	**Supported**
H1d	OSI ----> CLY	0.185	1.955*	0.051	**Supported**
H2a	OSE ----> PUE	0.811	22.828***	0.000	**Supported**
H2b	OSE ----> PRV	0.057	0.882	0.378	Not Supported
H3a	PUE ----> PRV	0.174	2.414*	0.016	**Supported**
H3b	PUE ----> CSF	0.240	3.843***	0.000	**Supported**
H4a	PRV ----> TRU	0.855	34.629***	0.000	**Supported**
H4b	PRV ----> CSF	0.294	2.891**	0.004	**Supported**
H5	CSF ----> CLY	0.711	6.930***	0.000	**Supported**
H6	TRU ----> CSF	0.158	1.272	0.204	Not Supported
H7	INF ----> OSI	0.541	7.630***	0.000	**Supported**
H8	UIQ ----> OSI	0.357	5.027***	0.000	**Supported**
H9	SER ----> PRV	-0.034	0.353	0.724	Not Supported
H10	PRI ----> PRV	0.493	7.373***	0.000	**Supported**
NOTE :	***$p<0.001$, **$p<0.01$, *$p<0.1$				

5. DISCUSSION & IMPLICATIONS

The key findings of this research indicate that customer satisfaction and online shopping image has a significant influence on Customer Loyalty. Factors significantly influencing customer satisfaction were found to be online shopping image, privacy, and purchase experience. Due to advances in online technology, online retailers are under strong pressure to offer customers a unique, satisfactory, swimmingly, worthy shopping experience compared to the traditional offline shopping experience. Online marketing through different communication channels such as e-mails, websites, direct mails, etc. has also enabled customers to obtain detailed product/service information and quickly compare offers. This emphasises the need to identify the variables influencing consumers' online shopping behaviour. The results show that customer satisfaction has the greatest impact on customer loyalty, leading us to the conclusion that e-commerce businesses must create their marketing plans, pricing structures, and other elements with the customer in mind. According to a number of earlier research, happy customers tend to share favourable reviews and opinions about a business's offerings, and these are crucial in the marketing and referral processes. So, companies should keep in mind that if they want to gain loyal customers they must be satisfied with the purchase on their website. We can also see that security risk has the least effect on customer loyalty which is sensible because it is very rare that an online purchase goes wrong because of a wrong transaction or fraud websites. So, we can also say that according to our responses, customers don't care much about security risk in determining their loyalty towards the website since security issues are very rare nowadays on online shopping websites.

There is evidence to demonstrate the link between customer loyalty and satisfaction. This has several significant ramifications for online retailers. The most important factor is that web users prefer websites that can accomplish the purpose for which they were designed. According to the findings, customer satisfaction has a significant impact on loyalty. As a result, businesses should place a high priority on ensuring that their customers are happy. This can be done by helping them form a positive perception of the company's online store in their minds. This perception is largely influenced by the website's information quality and user interface. So, website designers of the company should take care that the website is designed in such a way that information quality and website interface quality should be of superior quality and should make that first impression on the website and also maintain the brand image among the customers.

The second highest affecting factor of customer satisfaction is purchasing experience, so managers of the company should take care that if a person shops from the website, they should have a good experience, this can be achieved by the quality of goods supplied by the vendor who sells his/her goods through the website. So, the managers of the company should make sure that all these conditions are met by the company to make sure that their customers are left satisfied.

6. LIMITATIONS & FUTURE SCOPE

The research topic should be broadened to include other types of e-commerce since this study only looked at the B2C internet consumption sector. Since data analytics is a fast-growing field, the results we obtain from the customers of today can be used to analyse the buying patterns and behaviours of potential customers of tomorrow. This data can help build product recommendation systems which are a future advancement in the field of analytics and machine learning. Future studies may want to investigate additional potentially relevant factors, such as the ethnicity of the customer, potential income (if the customer is a teenager), parent's income, background, interests, etc. As with many research models, there is a chance that additional significant factors have not been incorporated in the framework. This study has a limitation of being restricted to the youth group and hence cannot be generalised to all customers. Secondly, a big drawback of the survey method is that the respondent's mood, competence, and willingness to candidly fill up the survey form affects the responses to the survey questionnaire which can create in biased responses.

REFERENCES

Abumalloh R., Ibrahim O., and M. Nilashi, (2020) "Loyalty of young female Arabic customers towards recommendation agents: A new model for B2C E-commerce," Technology in Society, p. 101253.

Ali, A. and Bhasin J., , (2019). "Understanding Customer Repurchase Intention in E-commerce: Role of Perceived Price, Delivery Quality, and Perceived Value," Jindal Journal of Business Research, vol. 8, no. 2, pp. 142-157.

Aslam, W. A. Hussain, K. Farhat and I. Arif, , (2019) "Underlying Factors Influencing Consumers' Trust and Loyalty in E-commerce," Business Perspectives and Research, 2278533719887451.

Azam A., Qiang F. and M.I. Abdullah. (2012). "E-satisfaction in business-to-consumer electronic commerce," The Business & Management Review, vol. 3, no. 1, p. 18

Chen J., G. Zhao and Y. Yan, (2010) "Research on customer loyalty of B2C E-commerce based on structural equation modeling," In 2010 International Conference on E-Business and E-Government, IEEE, pp. 2245-2248.

Choi E. and K.C. Lee, (2019) "Effect of Trust in Domain-Specific Information of Safety, Brand Loyalty, and Perceived Value for Cosmetics on Purchase Intentions in Mobile E-Commerce Context," Sustainability, vol. 11, no. 22, p. 6257.

Dabrynin H. and J. Zhang, (2019) "The investigation of the online customer experience and perceived risk on purchase intention in China," Journal of Marketing Development and Competitiveness, vol. 13, no. 2.

Ebrahimi L., V.R. Mirabi, M.H. Ranjbar and E.H. Pour, (2019) "A Customer Loyalty Model for E-Commerce Recommendation Systems," Journal of Information & Knowledge Management, vol. 18, no. 3, p.1950036.

Faraoni M., R. Rialti, L. Zollo and A.C. Pellicelli, (2019) "Exploring e-loyalty Antecedents in B2C e-Commerce," British Food Journal, vol. 121, no. 2, pp. 574-589.

Ferreira V.M.R., J. Parente, M.C. Ponchio and F. Zambaldi, (2020) "Building loyalty in e-commerce: does consumer income matter?," International Journal of Business and Systems Research, vol. 14, no. 1, pp. 74-94.

Gefen D., (2002) "Customer loyalty in e-commerce," Journal of the association for information systems, vol. 3, no. 1.

Hermawan D., (2019) "The Importance of Digital Trust in E-Commerce: Between Brand Image and Customer Loyalty" International Journal of Applied Research in Management and Economics, vol. 2,no. 3, pp. 18-30.

Huang G., (2019) "The relationship between customer satisfaction with logistics service quality and customer loyalty of china e-commerce market: a case of SF express (Group) Co., Ltd.," Journal of Rangsit Graduate Studies in Business and Social Sciences, vol. 5,no. 1, pp.120-137.

IBEF, E-commerce Industry in India, (2022) Retrieved from https://www.ibef.org/industry/ecommerce.

Kassim N.M. and N.A. Abdullah, (2008) "Customer loyalty in e-commerce settings: an empirical study," Electronic Markets, vol. 18, no. 3, pp. 275-290.

Kassim N.M. and S. Ismail, (2009) "Investigating the complex drivers of loyalty in e-commerce settings," Measuring business excellence, vol. 13, no. 1, pp. 56-71.

Kim H. and L.S. Niehm, (2009) "The impact of website quality on information quality, value, and loyalty intentions in apparel retailing," Journal of interactive marketing, vol. 23, no. 3, pp. 221-233.

Lin H.F., (2007) "The impact of website quality dimensions on customer satisfaction in the B2C e-commerce context," Total Quality Management and Business Excellence, vol. 18, no. 4, pp. 363-378.

Mofokeng T., (2019) "Website Information Security and Privacy Concerns in 4IR: The Moderating Role of Trust in B2C e-Commerce," In Proceedings of 4th International Conference on the vol. 12, pp. 180-201.

Othman A.K., L.F.A Hassan, M.A.M. Ibrahim, M.S. Saripin, N.S.A. Sapuan and Z.N.Roslan, (2020) "Factors that influence customer loyalty in using e-commerce," Journal of Islamic Management Studies, vol. 2, no. 2, pp. 43-58.

Pereira H.G., M. de Fátima Salgueiro, and P. Rita, (2016) "Online purchase determinants of loyalty: The mediating effect of satisfaction in tourism," Journal of Retailing and consumer Services, vol. 30, pp.279-291.

Ranggadara I., G. Wang and E.R. Kaburuan, (2019) "Applying Customer Loyalty Classification with RFM and Naïve Bayes for Better Decision Making," In 2019 International Seminar on Application for Technology of Information and Communication (iSemantic), pp. 564-568, IEEE.

Safa N.S. and M.A. Ismail, (2013) "A customer loyalty formation model in electronic commerce," Economic Modelling, vol. 35, pp. 559-564.

Sharma H. and A.G. Aggarwal, (2019) "Finding determinants of e-commerce success: a PLS-SEM approach," Journal of Advances in Management Research, vol. 16, no.4, pp. 453-471.

Srinivasan S.S., R. Anderson and K. Ponnavolu, (2002) "Customer loyalty in e-commerce: an exploration of its antecedents and consequences," Journal of retailing, vol. 78, no. 1, pp.41-50.

Srivastava A., P.K. Bala and B. Kumar, (2020) "New perspectives on gray sheep behavior in E-commerce recommendations," Journal of Retailing and Consumer Services, p.53.

Suhartanto D., M. Helmi Ali, K.H. Tan, F. Sjahroeddin, and L. Kusdibyo, (2019) "Loyalty toward online food delivery service: the role of e-service quality and food quality," Journal of foodservice business research, vol. 22, no. 1, pp. 81-97.

Tzavlopoulos I., K. Gotzamani, A. Andronikidis and C. Vassiliadis, (2019) "Determining the impact of e-commerce quality on customers' perceived risk, satisfaction, value and loyalty," International Journal of Quality and Service Sciences, vol. 11, no. 4, pp. 576-587.

Wang L. and M. Prompanyo, (2020) "Modeling the relationship between perceived values, e-satisfaction, and e-loyalty," Management Science Letters, vol. 10, no. 11, pp. 2609-2616.

Widjaja A., W. Astuti, and A. Manan, (2019) "The relationship between customer satisfaction and loyalty: evidence on online transportation services in Indonesia," International Journal of Advances in Scientific Research and Engineering, vol. 5, no. 4, pp. 214-222.

Yang K.F., H.W. Yang, C.H. Huang, J.Y. Yang and W.Y. Chang, (2019) "Research on the Service Quality, Customer Satisfaction and Customer Loyalty-Taking Corporate Image as a Moderating Variable," In Proceedings of the 2019 5th International Conference on Industrial and Business Engineering, pp. 117-122.

A CONCEPTUAL FRAMEWORK FOR ASSESSMENT OF DIGITAL GOVERNMENT STRATEGY ENVIRONMENT. APPLICATION TO DIGITAL GOVERNMENT DEVELOPMENT IN AFRICA

Sara Halim and Bouchaib Bounabat
ALQUALSADI Team, ENSIAS, Mohammed V University in Rabat, Rabat, Morocco

ABSTRACT

Digital technologies are significantly disrupting the public sector as they offer new opportunities to pursue more innovative goals. The strategic objectives set for a government must result from the assessment of its digital environment in order to meet the needs of its citizens and to target a high-value and in real-time transformation. The contribution of this article consists in describing how governments can assess their digital environment in order to set the right future objectives using the strategic planning method. This article addresses key transformational issues such as evaluation of government readiness level, strategic planning method adoption to set the future objectives, and assessment of these objectives' maturity level. It also presents an application of the proposed model to the digital development in the African context.

KEYWORDS

Digital Government, Strategic Environment, Assessment, Maturity Model

1. INTRODUCTION

The vision targeted by the digital transformation of public services may differ from one government to another as each country provides a different digital ecosystem. This prompts governments to ask the question: How can the assessment of the digital environment help in the strategic planning of the digital government?

This paper presents a conceptual framework for the assessment of digital Government strategy environment, and proposes a model for African countries seeking digital transformation.

This paper is organized as follows. Section 2 describes the Digital Government Strategy, which aims to define a shared vision government's digitalization. This vision is a set of strategic objectives (SOs), composed of Sub-Strategic Objectives (SSOs), and aiming to improve customer (citizen and enterprise) satisfaction and increase government's efficiency. The targeted objectives are identified by analyzing the customers and public administration needs. The Digital Government Strategy Environment embraces legal, financial, technical, human, governance and organizational dimensions, shaping any digital transformation strategy, as they provide the ecosystem for the strategy to evolve. Section 3 describes the Digital Government Strategy Assessment (DGSA), which aims to analyze the digital environment and identify all barriers encountered when developing digital government initiatives. The DGSA framework presents the guidelines to follow to: (i) assess the digital government environment' preparedness to embrace the digital transformation; and (ii) evaluate the achievement level of DGS strategic objectives. In this context, two perspectives are highlighted: (i) the Digital Government Environment perspective describes how the environment dimensions combine to support Foundational Technologies (FTs) implementation, illustrated by the Rwanda use case; and (ii) the Digital Enablers perspective encompasses FTs necessary to an SSO achievement, accordingly to their importance rate or weight. The achievement indicator is calculated based on the maturity model in public agencies (Gonzalo & al., 2011). Section 4 consists in the application of the DGSA framework to the digital-by-design SO by leveraging Data Analytics tool Dedoose to weight each FT necessary to the achievement of each SSO by inspection of international practice and expert opinion present in several World Bank reports.

2. DIGITAL GOVERNMENT STRATEGY

2.1 From e- Government to Digital Government

e-Government systems generally consists in handling the vast majority of administrative transactions through electronic integration. The accessibility and rapidity of such online modes represent a real opportunity to improve hugely the internal administrative performance (Rombach and Steffens, 2009), to enhance coordination between different agencies, and to ensure faster delivered services for citizens. Government 2.0 is a more communicative and interactive version of e-Government, re-shifting the focus to citizens as active contributors to public affairs' management mainly through the use of Web 2.0 social tools (e.g. social web, social media, participative web and user-generated web, etc.) (Meijer, et al., 2012) More recently, the incorporation of new services supported by public sector "open data" (Davies, 2015) and other disruptive technologies, leads to the extension of the e-Government model by the Digital Government concept, and the adoption by several governments of a "digital by default" based strategy (GOV-UK, 2012). Such transition represents an optimal use of electronic communication channels to : (i) improve citizens satisfaction in service delivery, by enabling them to co-design and co-produce public services; (ii) forge new levels of both institutional engagement and trust, based on bidirectional, dynamic and real time communication; and (iii) achieve a better functioning of public agencies with a positive impact on economic competitiveness and prosperity (Accenture, 2014a) (NICTA, 2014) (Accenture, 2014b).

2.2 Digital Government Strategy

Strategic Planning helps organizations set future objectives and sub-objectives to achieve more stable and predictable growth (Hall, 2013), and to identify actions required to reach them. On the other hand, to take advantage of the digital revolution, there is a need for having a digital strategy and evaluation system of the digital transformation (Korachi, 2020). In this vein, Digital Government Strategy (DGS) (OECD, 2019) is developed with the goal to become a real governance tool for the public sector modernization. A DGS has to put forward a shared vision statement for the digitalization of government and the future of public service delivery, in order to improve government services, to increase competitiveness, and to open up more opportunities for citizens. A strategy can be considered as a set of SOs, each one of them composed of SSOs, related respectively to customer's specific requirements through digital Government services, and to the improvement of the operations performance into and between public sectors.

2.3 Technical Foundations

Technical Foundations (FT) consist in technical pillars and tools necessary to achieve DGS strategic objectives. In this vein, new digital trends are key to meeting the growing needs for innovation, and quality of service delivery. FTs that this paper focuses on are:

- Interoperability, ability of government organizations to share information and integrate information and business processes by use of common standards and work practices (State Services Commission, 2007)
- One-Stop-Shop, a centralized platform for delivering e-government services to citizens: "a single point of access to electronic services and information offered by different public authorities" (Wimmer, 2002).
- Multi-Channels Services, extending e-Government to all kinds of wireless and mobile technology, services, applications, and devices to help governments become more efficient (ITU-OECD, 2011).
- Emerging Technologies, already altering traditional business models and pathways to development, yielding significant efficiency and productivity gains, increased convenience, as well as supporting better access to services for consumers (The World Bank, 2020b).
- Data Management, set of data collecting, keeping, and using data practices securely, efficiently, and cost-effectively (Oracle, 2021). This aspect also includes all phases related to Open Government Data life cycle management (Belhiah, 2017).
- Digital Identity, schemes in which the three functions of identification, authentication and authorization are all performed digitally (Nyst et al., 2016).

2.4 Digital Government Strategy Environment

Digital Government Strategy Environment (DGSE) embraces a set of dimensions that can shape any digital transformation strategy:

- Governance dimension, encompassing the readiness of a Government to establish or not a strong governance structure, and reinforce stakeholder predispositions to collaborate with each other to achieve defined SOs.
- Human dimension, related to the capacity to adopt and apply a digitally inclusive approach, targeting two main objectives: (i) to improve the society digital readiness level; and (ii) to enable a digitally-savvy and innovative public sector workforce.
- Legal dimension, considering several principles such as: (i) citizens personal data protection, (ii) consistency between copyright obligations and data transparency; (iii) suppression of legal texts contradictory interpretations; (iv) balance between each governmental sector needs in individual regulations; and (v) celerity to adopt new laws in the digital area (O'Hara, 2011) (Goodspeed, 2011) (Veit and Huntgeburth, 2013) (Debbagh, et al, 2012) (Simes et al., 2015).
- Organizational dimension, indicating the government's aptitude to openness and transparency, and determine whether its internal practices are: (i) collaborative or not to mutualize IT resources; and (ii) participative or not to allowing user participation in the code sign of digital information systems (Jarke, 2021).
- Financial dimension, encompassing the readiness of the department to promote IT investment, to identify expected economic, social and political benefits (OECD, 2014), and to offset savings against ICT investments, and thus encourage long-term digital transformation (Simes et al., 2015).
- Technical dimension, consisting in technical prerequisites related to the IT maturity level of the public entities, in particular their ability to leverage foundational and/or emerging technologies. This dimension also deals with challenges essential to adopt IT Governance practices (Cater-Steel, 2009) in the public context.

3. PROPOSED DGS ASSESSMENT FRAMEWORK (DGSA)

The proposed DGSA framework presents the guidelines to follow in order to: (i) assess the digital government environment preparedness to support any targeted digital transformation; and (ii) evaluate current DGS strategic objectives achievement level.

3.1 Digital Government Environment (DGE) perspective

The proposed framework aims at identifying DGS Strategic Objectives achievement level, by scrutinizing two perspectives: DGS environment enablement degree, and its contribution to each SO achievement.

3.1.1 DGE Assessment Conceptual Model

DGE perspective describes how governance, people, technologies, financial resources, regulatory arsenal and organization, combine to support Foundational Technologies Implementation, and thus a DGS execution. The dimensions (governance, financial, legal, etc.) embraced by DGE, are high-level attributes, each one materialized through specific factors, that are lower levels attributes, measuring the preparedness of a governmental agency to leverage a FT to accelerate the digital transformation process (see Figure1).

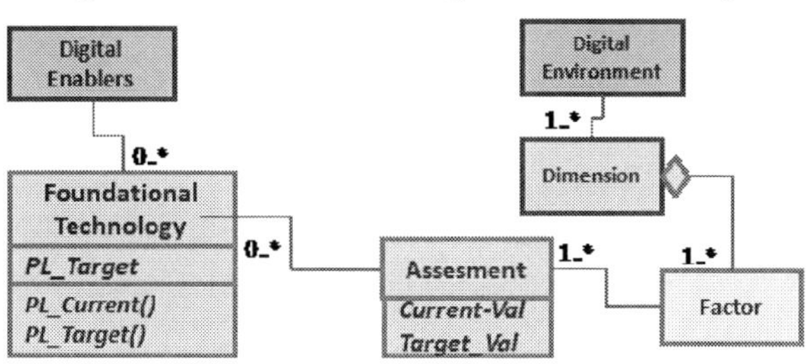

Figure 1. DGE perspective conceptual model

As shown below in Eq. (I) and Eq. (II), the calculation of each FT Preparedness Level (PL) relies on public agencies maturity model described in (Gonzalo & al., 2011).

$$\mathbf{Value(dim_{jk}) = (\sum RL(Factor_{jkp}) / NF_k)} \qquad \text{(I)}$$

NF_k : Number of Factors composing the dimension$_k$, and

$RL(Factor_{jkp})$: Readiness Level of the Factor$_p$, composing the dimension$_k$, to make the FT_j better leveraged. $RL_{jkp} \in \{1,2..5\}$, and it is estimated through specific questionnaire.

$$\mathbf{PL(FT_j) = (\sum Value(dim_{jk})) / ND\_DGE} \qquad \text{(II)}$$

Where ND_DGE: Number of DGE dimensions

The readiness level (RL) of each factor measures the state of readiness that support the implementation of each FT. It is estimated through specific questionnaire and has to be defined between the level 1 and 5 where each level' signification is detailed in Table 1.

Table 1. Readiness Level signification

Readiness Level	Signification
1	Government is aware of the considered factor importance vis-à-vis a specific FT
2	Government starts implementing dedicated actions to reinforce the factor role to set-up the FT
3	Government starts developing dedicated and planned actions to reinforce the factor role to set-up the FT.
4	Dedicated strategic action plans and policies are regularly measured
5	Dedicated strategic plans are regularly updated and continually improved to respond to changes.

3.1.2 Rwanda Use Case

This use case aims to define the maturity of Rwanda's digital environment based on the World Bank report "Rwanda Digital Economy Assessment" (The World Bank, 2019a) which assesses the level of development of digital economy in Rwanda based on the DE4A (Digital Economy for Africa) framework. The first step is to define the readiness level of each factor. Then, using the equations (I) and (II), the value of each dimension composing the digital environment perspective can be calculated (see Table 2).

Table 2. Environment Dimensions' preparedness levels

Environmental Dimensions	Factors	Data Management	Interoperability	Digital Identity	Multi-channels' Digital Services	One-Stop-Shop Portal	Emerging Technologies
Governance	Strong Political leadership	2	2	3	1	1	2
	Governance structure of National D-Gov strategy	2	2	2	1	3	3
	Clear IT Governance in public institutions	1	1	1	1	2	1
	Value (Governance)	1,67	1,67	2,00	1,00	2,00	2,00
Human	Internal human resources IT Skills	2	1	2	3	3	1
	Cultural aspects	1	1	1	1	1	1
	Citizen digital readiness	1	2	1	2	2	2
	Value (Human)	1,33	1,33	1,33	2,00	2,00	1,33
Financial	D-Gov initiatives Funding	1	2	2	2	2	1
	Investment Promotion	2	1	2	1	2	2
	Institution of awards schemes	1	1	1	1	1	1
	Public procurement financial management	1	2	1	1	2	1
	Value (Financial)	1,25	1,50	1,50	1,25	1,75	1,25
Organizational	Simplified and harmonized administrative procedures	1	2	2	1	3	1
	Clear definition of internal roles and responsibilities	1	1	3	1	2	1
	IT acquisition policies autonomy of Public institutions	2	2	1	1	1	1
	Value (Organizational)	1,33	1,67	2,00	1,00	2,00	1,00
Technical	Persistence of a heavy IS legacy	1	1	1	1	1	1
	Infrastructure Access sharing capacities	1	2	1	1	2	1
	Converged networks and services Support	1	1	1	1	1	1
	Disruptive IT adoption (SMAC, IA)	2	2	1	1	1	3
	Value (Technical)	1,25	1,50	1,00	1,00	1,25	1,50
Legal	Citizen protection	1	1	2	1	1	1
	Coverage legal framework	1	3	2	2	1	1
	Quality of IT regulation	1	1	1	1	1	1
	Intellectual Property protection	1	1	1	1	1	1
	Value (Legal)	1,00	1,50	1,50	1,25	1,00	1,00
PL-Value (FT)		**1,31**	**1,53**	**1,56**	**1,25**	**1,67**	**1,35**

Rwanda has rated first in 2016, by the World Economic Forum's Networked Readiness Index (NRI), among East African nations in terms of readiness to exploit the opportunities offered by ICT. To support this evolution, Rwanda adopted the ICT Hub Strategy (2019-2024) with three main objectives: to build skilled workforce, to foster national culture of innovation, and to develop technological capability in selected niche areas. On the organizational level, Rwanda has established a clear list of institutions to implement the government's digital vision such as the Ministry of Information and Communications Technology and Innovation. Over the past decade, Rwanda has digitized many public services using ICTs or more advanced technologies such as cloud infrastructure and identification systems. However, data protection and sharing remains a big challenge that Rwanda lacks in terms of digital transformation. Finally, several regulations have been issued to regulate the use of ICTs in the country but there is a need to continuously update the IT laws according to digital evolution.

3.2 Digital Enablers Perspective

Digital Enablers perspective encompasses Foundational Technologies (FT) necessary to an SSO achievement, accordingly to its importance rate or weight.

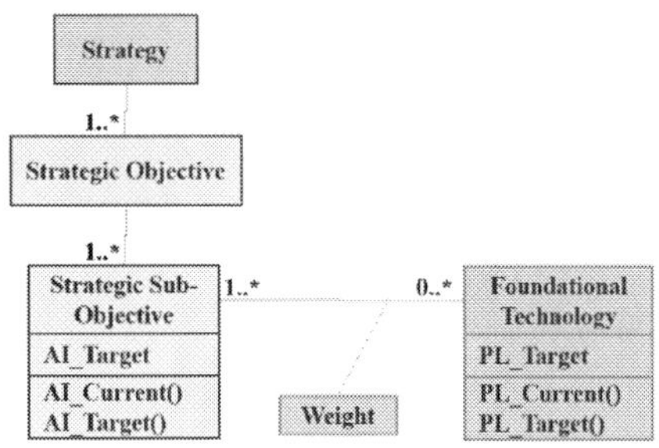

Figure 2. Foundational Technologies perspective conceptual model

The Achievement Indicator (AI) of an SSO indicates the degree of FTs' environment preparedness to contribute to achieve SSO's achievement. Consequently, and according to (Gonzalo & al., 2011), the Achievement Indicator (AI) of an SSO is the weighted average of the weighted Preparedness Level (PL) of its associated FTs, as shown in Eq. (III).

$$\mathbf{AI(SSO_i) = \sum (Weight_{ij} * PL(FT_j)), \text{ where } \Sigma\ Weight_{ij} = 1} \quad \text{(III)}$$

Achievements thus evaluated depicts the maturity degree of each SSO, accordingly to Table 3

Based on Readiness Levels presented in Table 1, the definition of the maturity levels listed in Table 3 are also inspired by (Valdés, et al., 2011) the capability levels defined, and (CMU/SEI, 2010) Capacity Maturity Model.

Table 3. Maturity level of sub-strategic objectives

Maturity level	AI(SSO)	Signifiance : The environment necessary to achieve the SSO is
0 - Initial	[0,1[	limited, and its development process is unpredictable
1 - Developing	[1,2[	being implemented by dedicated projects, and its development process is frequently reactive
2 - Defined	[2,3[	being implemented through dedicated and planned projects, and its development process is more proactive than reactive
3 - Managed	[3,4[	being implemented by dedicated, proactive and regularly measured strategic action plans and policies
4 - Integrated	[4,5[	being implemented by dedicated measured and continually improved strategic plans and policies

4. APPLICATION TO DIGITAL BY DESIGN STRATEGIC OBJECTIVE

A government is Digital by Design (DbyD) when it approaches "digital" with an understanding of the strategic activities involved with successful and long-lasting transformation. Digital technologies are leveraged in order to rethink government to deliver an efficient and sustainable public services, regardless of the channel used by the user.

4.1 Identification of the Digital by Design Strategic Sub-Objectives

DbyD based digital transformation results in the absence of paper procedures requiring significant processing times and the provision of redundant supporting documents. In this study, DbyD is achieved through the 3 SSOs: End-to-End digitalization process, Simplification, and Innovation (See Table 4).

Table 4. Definition of the Digital by Design Strategic sub-objectives

SO	SSO	Signifiance
Digital	End-to-End	Digitize the administrative processes without needing a human intervention
By	Simplification	Rethink business processes and internal operations to simplify procedures
Design	Innovation	Reengineer internal operations using emerging technologies to innovate public services

Indeed, end-to-end digitalization process of public e-services, makes traditional e-government methods seemed to be "so passé" with an increasing need for agencies to turn their focus from automation and cost-cutting to citizens and businesses experience and innovation (Gardiner, 2015). Secondly, the procedures simplification translates into new business processes using emerging technologies and customer data to deliver personalized journeys. For instance, in the context of the digital transformation, emerging technologies, such as artificial intelligence and Blockchain, carry a significant disruptive potential (Ubaldi et al., 2019) as they can help provide more practical and tailor-made delivery. Finally, the scope of the DbyD approach aims to innovate business processes and internal operations by rethinking them and creating new channels of communication between the different stakeholders.

4.2 Definition of FTs Weights

The study of the SSO's achievement level related to the "Digital by design" SO is out based on several reports published by The World Bank group concerning governments digital transformation in Africa (The World Bank, 2022; 2020a; 2020b; 2020c; 2020d; 2020e; 2020f; 2020g; 2020h; 2019b; 2019c; 2019d; 2019e; 2016; 2014). The weights presented below have been generated via data analytics tool Dedoose.

Regarding the analysis of the weight, the first step is to create, the code tree concerning the different FTs and SSOs. Then, excerpts are created by highlighting paragraphs and attaching them to the codes that the snippet refers to. Once all the excerpts created, the Code Co-Occurrence Table was used to present the frequencies for which all code pairings were applied to the same excerpt and, by default, overlapping excerpts.

Table 5. Dedoose Analysis results related to FT weights vis-à-vis SSOs

Digital Enablers Perpsective	Digital by Design		
	Simplification	End-to-End	Innovation
Data Management	0,118	0,098	0,222
Digital Identity	0,098	0,049	0,111
Emerging Technologies	0,059	0,049	0,422
Interoperability	0,412	0,610	0,111
Multi-channels Digital Services	0,059	0,073	0,089
One-Stop-Shop Portal	0,255	0,122	0,044

4.3 SSO's Achievement Indicator for Rwanda

The Achievement Indicator of an SSO is the weighted average of the weighted Preparedness Level (PL) of its associated FTs, as shown in Eq. (III). Based on the PL for each FT calculated in section 3.2 and the weights generated through Dedoose (Table 5), the achievement indicator for each SSO can be deducted (Table 6).

Table 6. The Maturity Level of digital by design SSOs

Strategic Objective	Sub-Strategic Objective	Achievement Indicator	Maturity Level
Digital By Design	Simplification	1,507	1 - Developing
	End-to-End	1,493	1 - Developing
	Innovation	1,381	1 - Developing

The three SSOs areas did not reach the second maturity level (defined), stating SSO's procedures definition, documentation and communication. Indeed, many initiatives to achieve these SOSs are being developed in Rwanda but have not been completed yet. For instance, the emerging Kigali Innovation City, a tech hub that aims to boost Rwanda's economy through digital transformation, has been launched in 2022. The innovation objective is expected to increase in the years to come. On the other hand, end-to-end SSO can be developed using interoperability between public institutions or more specifically between the digital financial services. Finally, the simplification has been noticed in Rwanda with the use of digital services that increase accessibility and efficiency. The simplification maturity level can increase, for example, with the development of multi-channels digital services that offer a choice to the citizen, according to his need, to access services via multiple online and offline channels.

5. DISCUSSION AND CONCLUSION

Governments around the world are targeting new approaches to improve the public services. Each government sets the targeted approach as a strategic objective to achieve its growth and respond to the citizen's needs and administration productivity. These objectives make up the overall vision for digital transformation and can be achieved by the definition of a digital government strategy. The DGSA framework, proposed in this paper, has as objective to help governments to assess the digital environment, and therefore to set government digital strategies targeting relevant and realistic objectives.

This framework presents two perspectives: (i) Digital Government Environment Perspective aiming at assessing the digital government environment in order to define its preparedness level to embrace the digital transformation and; (ii) Digital Enablers perspective evaluating the achievement level of DGS strategic objectives encompassing Foundational Technologies.

This framework is highly recommended for developing countries, especially African countries. It can help them to define the right DGS based on their cultural aspects, financial constraints, technical capabilities, governance structure, legal model and organizational specificities. The application to digital government development in Africa has highlighted the importance of weighting of each FT within a strategic objective. The use of a data analytics tool is highly recommended in order to inspect a large set of international practices and expert opinions. The use case has also revealed the importance of the digital environment perspective as it represents the action plan which makes it possible to achieve defined SOs toward. Finally, this framework is highly adaptable, as it can be adjusted and replicated to any government's vision.

This article can lead us to question: "What are the other strategic objectives that can be analyzed using the DGSA framework?" or "How can governments improve the achievement indicators related to each strategic objective?"

REFERENCES

Accenture, (2014a). *Digital Government Pathways to Delivering Public Services for the Future. A comparative study of digital government performance across 10 countries.*

Accenture, (2014b). *Delivering Public Service for the Future: How Europe can lead Public-Sector Transformation.* The European Centre for Government Transformation. The Lisbon Council asbl, the College of Europe and Accenture

Aileen Cater-Steel, (2009). *Information Technology Governance and Service Management: Frameworks and Adaptations.*Steel University of Southern Queensland, Australia Hershey,New York Information, USA.

Belhiah, M., Bounabat, B. (2017). *A user-centered model for assessing and improving open government data quality.* Proceedings of the 22nd MIT International Conference on Information Quality, ICIQ 2017, 2017

CMU/SEI, (2010). *CMMI for Development, Version 1.3. Improving processes for developing better products and services.* November 2010 TECHNICAL REPORT CMU/SEI-2010-TR-03. ESC-TR-2010-033

Davies, R., (2015). *eGovernment Using technology to improve public services and democratic participation.* European Parliamentary Research Service.

Dedoose. Available at: https://www.dedoose.com

Elpez, I., and Fink, D, (2006). *Information systems success in the public sector: Stakeholders perspectives and emerging alignment model*, Issues in Information Science and Information Technology, V.3. Australia

Feyza Hall, (2013). *The Importance of Strategic Planning.* Strayer University

Gardiner, B. (2015). *Where e-gov looks to improve existing processes, digital gov means service transformation and innovation.* Available at: https://www.cio.com.au/article/590551/e-government-pass-digital-government-future-report/

Gonzalo Valdés ⁎, Mauricio Solar, Hernán Astudillo, Marcelo Iribarren, Gastón Concha, Marcello Visconti, (2011). *Conception, development and implementation of an e-Government maturity model in public agencies.* Government Information Quarterly 28 (2011) 176–187

Goodspeed, Robert, (2011). *From Public Records to Open Government: Access to Massachusetts Municipal Geographic Data.* Journal of the Urban & Regional Information Systems Association 23 (2): 21–32.

GOV-UK, (2012). Government Digital Strategy. Cabinet office. Available at: https://www.gov.uk/government/collections/government-digital-strategy-reports-and-research

International Telecommnications Union, ITU Report. 2011, available at: www.itu.int/ITU-D/cyb/app/

ISACA, (2019). *COBIT 2019 Framework: Introduction and Methodology*

ITU-OECD. (2011). M-Government: Mobile Technologies for Responsive Governments and Connected Societies.

Juliane Jarke, (2021). *Co-creating Digital Public Services for an Ageing Society. Evidence for User-centric Design.* Public Administration and Information Technology Volume 6 Series Editor, Spain.

Korachi, Z., Bounabat, B, (2020) *Towards a Maturity Model for Digital Strategy Assessment,* Advances in Intelligent Systems and Computing, 2020, 1105 AISC, pp. 456–470

Meijer A, Koops B, Pieterson W, Overman S and ten Tije S., (2012). *Government 2.0: Key Challenges to Its Realization. Electronic Journal of e-Government.* Vol. 10, Issue, pp 59-69, available at: www.ejeg.com.m-gov.html.

NICTA, 2014. *New models for Digital Government: The role of service brokers in driving innovation* National Information and Communications Technology Australia.

Nyst, C., Makin, P., Pannifer, S., & Whitley, E. (2016). *Digital identity: Issue analysis: executive summary.*

OECD, (2014). *Recommendation of the Council on Digital Government Strategies.* Public Governance Committee.

OECD, (2019). *The governance of digital government strategies.*

O'Hara, Kieron, (2011). *Transparent government, not transparent citizens: a report on privacy and transparency for the Cabinet Office.* London: Cabinet Office: 84pp

Oracle, (2021). *What is Data Management?* https://www.oracle.com

Rombach, D., Steffens, P. , (2009). *e-Government. Springer Handbook of Automation*, Nof(Ed.), West Lafayette, USA.

State Services Commission, (2007). New Zealand E-government Interoperability Framework, www.e.govt.nz

Taeib Debbagh, Amr Hashem, Bouchaib Bounabat, (2012). *Telecom/ICT Regulatory reform evolution: achievements and way forward*. Arab-Book 2012. International Union of Telecommunications– BDT/ITU.

The World Bank Group, (2020b). *Togo Digital Economy Diagnostic Report.*

The World Bank, (2014). *ICTs for modernizing government in Africa.*

The World Bank, (2016). *Bringing Government into the 21st Century: The Korean Digital Governance Experience.*

The World Bank, (2019a). *Rwanda Digital Economy Assessment*

The World Bank, (2019b). *Nigeria Digital Economy Diagnostic Report.*

The World Bank, (2019c). *Mozambique Digital Economy Diagnostic.*

The World Bank, (2019d). *Digital Economy for Africa: Country Diagnostic of Senegal.*

The World Bank, (2019e). *Ghana Digital Economy Diagnostic.*

The World Bank, (2020a). *Digital Economy for Africa Country Diagnostic Tool and Guidelines for Task Teams.*

The World Bank, (2020c). *Kenya Digital Economy Assessment: Summary report.*

The World Bank, (2020d). *Burundi Digital Economy Assessment.*

The World Bank, (2020e). *The digital transformation strategy for Africa (2020-2030).*

The World Bank, (2020f). *Cameroon Digital Economy Assessment: Country Diagnostic.*

The World Bank, (2020g). *Sierra Leone Digital Economy Diagnostic.*

The World Bank, (2020h). *The Future of Work in Africa: Harnessing the Potential of Digital Technologies for All.*

The World Bank, (2022). *Future of Government: Reimagining Government for Good.*

Ubaldi, B. et al., 2019. *State of the art in the use of emerging technologies in the public sector.* OECD Working Papers on Public Governance, No. 31, OECD, Paris.

Veit Daniel; Huntgeburth Jan, (2013). Foundations of Digital Government Leading and Managing in the Digital Era

Wimmer, M. A., (2002). *A European perspective towards online one-stop government: The eGOV project.* Electronic Commerce Research and Applications, 1(1), 92–103.

EXAMINING CUSTOMER SATISFACTION AND BRAND LOYALTY OF GENERATION Z CUSTOMERS IN OTT MEDIA SERVICES

Pratik Kumar and Asish Oommen Mathew
Manipal Institute of Technology, Manipal Academy of Higher Education,Karnataka, India

ABSTRACT

In today's digital age, there has been an exponential growth in the popularity and demand of over-the-top (OTT) media services. This research aims to identify the antecedents of customer satisfaction leading to brand loyalty in young OTT media consumers. This research's target group is the Indian Generation Z cohort, the most extensive customer base of OTT platforms globally. This research employs a quantitative approach, using a questionnaire survey method. Data is collected from OTT subscribers belonging to the Generation Z cohort from the country's various regions. The antecedents of customer satisfaction analyzed through this research are perceived quality, the perceived value of cost, usefulness, usability, lifestyle congruence, brand identification, and equity. The most significant influence on customer satisfaction factors were perceived usability, overall brand equity, and perceived cost value. Customer satisfaction was also found to have a strong impact on brand loyalty. Primary data was collected from the generation Z cohort in India to test the theoretical model developed through literature review. The study is first of its kind in an emerging economy setup and gives practical insights into the youth population's consumer behavior and preferences. The outcome of this research provides Generation Z's perspective of OTT media consumption behavior. The study also highlights the importance of developing OTT platforms' brand equity, usefulness, and competitive pricing to drive customer satisfaction and brand loyalty.

KEYWORDS

Structural Equation Modelling, Customer Satisfaction, Brand Loyalty, Over-The-Top Media Services, Online Video Services, Brand Identification

1. INTRODUCTION

OTT platforms are becoming exceedingly customer-oriented and are constantly innovating to hold the user's attention. By combining this with analytics, platforms can now suggest certain movies and series based on prior content consumption. These platforms are also helping bridge a language barrier by having a wide range of content from all over the world and providing options for audio and subtitles in desired languages. Users can pause and view content whenever they want and return and start at the same point where they left it last. Also, unlike traditional media, the content on streaming services is not restricted by censor boards, demographics, or box office businesses (Gupta and Singharia, 2021). Thanks to improved network coverage across the country and an increase in the number of smartphones available at a reasonable price, the number of Indian customers to the Over-The-Top (OTT) platform is increasing. In response to the increased demand, several media and entertainment companies have either developed their platform or partnered with other OTT platforms to stream their content (Indian Brand Equity Foundation, 2020).

The COVID-19 pandemic, which resulted in a lockdown and compelled people to stay inside their homes, is one of the main reasons for the OTT platform experiencing an increase in the number of subscribers in recent times. As a result, many filmmakers release their new films through OTT platforms. According to IBEF (Indian Brand Equity Foundation, 2020), the Indian OTT market grew 30% from 22.2 million to 29 million paying customers between March and July 2020. The top five metro cities account for 46% of total viewers in July 2020, with tier I cities accounting for another 35%. Over the next decade, India's over-the-top (OTT) video streaming market might develop at a compound annual growth rate (CAGR) of more than 20%, reaching $13 billion–$15 billion, thanks to original content and pricing improvements. According to All

About Screens, a report by international professional services network Deloitte, paid subscribers are expected to grow at a 17% CAGR from 102 million in 2016 to 224 million in 2026. The demand for geo-demographic-based OTT streaming content is increasing, both within India and worldwide, thanks to the large Indian diaspora. In 2021, OTT platforms spent an estimated $665 million on content, with Netflix, Amazon Prime Video, and Hotstar Disney+ expenditure $380 million combined (Jha, 2022).

Customers are willing to pay more for OTT platforms due to convenience and ease of use, and brand loyalty is seen as a need for a company's long-term success and viability (Chaudhuri and Holbrook, 2001). Marketers are working to sustain and build brand loyalty when product differentiation decreases, resulting in a shorter maturity period and increased unpredictability in the product's market. Previous researches have been inconclusive regarding the relationship between brand loyalty and customer-based brand equity, with Aaker (1991) and Keller (1993) suggesting that loyalty is an outcome of brand equity, not a determinant of it.

Previous research has found that product participation and robust product involvement are significant predictors of brand loyalty (Iwasaki and Havitz, 1998). The primary target for this research is Generation Z (GenZ), the newest cohort encompassing 1.8 billion people born between 1995 and 2015. India has the largest GenZ population of 472 million, and Hameed and Mathur (2020) opined that GenZ in India exhibit behaviors and preferences similar to those of their global counterparts. OTT is a new platform in India, and research of its impact on perceived usefulness and ease of use should be done among those who have accepted it. GenZ, having grown up during the technological revolution, relies on technology in every area of their existence, and their digital information practices are significantly high (Davis et al., 2020, Budiman and Dananjoyo, 202; Subramaniam, et al. 2020). Furthermore, when it comes to using information technologies, the Generation Z cohort has extremely distinct behaviors, priorities, and preferences (Dospinescu et al., 2021; Kamble et al., 2021; Podara et al., 2021; Kymäläinen, 2021; Sadana and Sharma, 2021). Therefore, this research aims to identify the important antecedents of customer satisfaction of OTT media services and examine the extent to which the identified antecedents influence customer satisfaction and brand loyalty in the context of GenZ customers.

2.1 Customer Satisfaction

Customer satisfaction is defined as the difference between expected and experienced performance (McQuitty, 2000, Oliver, 1999). It can impact business property, conflict, and profit in both direct and indirect ways (Gomez et al., 2004). There is a distinction between customer happiness and customer satisfaction regarding service experiences due to services' intangibility and perishability (Veloutsou et al., 2015). Hoest and Andersen (2004) opines that customer satisfaction can be transactional (encounter satisfaction) or cumulative (satisfaction over time). This research considers customer satisfaction as a client's overall opinion of a service provider (Levesque and McDougall, 1996).

2.2 Perceived Quality

Perceived quality (Netemeyer et al., 2004) is an individual's appraisal of a particular brand's predominance compared to other brands. It is different from quality, which is the tangible superiority of a product or service over competitors. Consumer satisfaction has been found to be affected by perceived quality, and a high-quality brand perception leads to a high level of satisfaction. Therefore, we propose:

H1: Perceived quality has a significant influence on customer satisfaction.

2.3 Perceived Value of Cost

Perceived value is the link between the worth of benefits obtained and the amount sacrificed to acquire the same use. Netemeyer et al. (2004) defined it as an individual's estimation of the return based on the perceived benefits gained and sacrifices made to obtain the product or service. Research suggests that satisfaction is associated with perceived value, meaning perceived value has a significant impact on satisfaction (Anderson and Mittal, 2000; Theodorakis et al., 2014). McDougall and Levesque (2000) opine that perceived value directly influences customer satisfaction and loyalty. Based on these reviews, we propose the following hypothesis:

H2: Perceived value of cost has a significant influence on customer satisfaction

2.4 Perceived Usefulness

The Technology Acceptance Model (Davis et al., 1989) revealed that perceived usefulness influenced a person's behavioral intentions and attitude through indirect and direct influence. This observation is based on the motivation theory, which argues that if people recognize the importance of activity in helping them achieve their goals, they are more inclined to accept a new product or service. Perceived usefulness is positively related to customer usage and adoption, and online purchases are perceived to be more profitable if customers believe they will improve transaction performance. Alreck et al. (2009) found that online sellers who emphasize time-saving, completing tasks faster, or focusing on just one of these benefits are more likely to attract customers. Additionally, self-efficacy and usefulness are essential perspectives to explain consumer satisfaction. Therefore, we propose:

H3: Perceived usefulness has a significant influence on customer satisfaction.

2.5 Perceived Usability

The presentation of a product on a website is an important aspect of increasing customer satisfaction (Bhat et al., 2021). Researchers have discovered that the usability of a website plays a big role in an online application's success, and that customers form effective links due to web usability (Casalo et al., 2010). OTT platforms should continue to improve the user interface, including the design, impression, and performance. Usability is an important factor that customers perceive as a fundamental characteristic of a good website. Venkatesh and Agarwal (2006) developed a usability model that examines the interaction between content, usability, and marketing. Based on these reviews, we propose the following hypothesis:

H4: Perceived usability has a significant influence on customer satisfaction.

2.6 Lifestyle Congruence

Lifestyle (Solomon, 2010) is the extent to which brand consumption supports an individual's distinctive way of life, as affected by their subjective preferences. Companies should offer products that appeal to the customer's specific tastes, as lifestyle congruence is an important factor determining customer satisfaction. According to Nam et al. (2011), lifestyle congruence is an important factor determining customer satisfaction. Therefore, the following hypothesis is proposed:

H5: Lifestyle congruence has a significant influence on customer satisfaction.

2.7 Brand Identification

Consumer-brand identification is the degree to which the brand represents and enhances the customer's identity, while personal identification occurs when an individual's self-schema overlaps with the schema for a brand (Long and Schiffman, 2000). Brand identity influences consumer loyalty and happiness, and Shirazi et al. (2013) concluded that brand identification affects consumer satisfaction. The emotional attachment, symbolic consumption, and brand loyalty developed by brand recognition can be attributed to a brand when the consumers' expectations are met. Brand identity influences consumer loyalty and happiness (Kim et al., 2001; Gimpel, 2015). Hence, the following hypothesis is proposed:

H6: Brand identification has a significant influence on customer satisfaction.

2.8 Brand Equity

Brand equity is the value addition through customers' association and perception towards a selected product. Brady et al. (2008) opine that brand equity is a broader concept than brand loyalty since it encompasses general familiarity and brand image. Lehmann and Srinivasan (2014) defines brand equity from the customers' perspective as how they perceive, react, and associate with brands and nonbranded products. Brand equity can also be defined as the financial present value of future purchases of a brand. Brands inspire confidence, loyalty, and trust through establishing identities and relationships. Aaker (1992) recognized happiness as a possible outcome of brand equity.

H7: Overall brand equity has a significant influence on customer satisfaction.

2.9 Brand Loyalty

Brand loyalty is a measure of consumer interest in continuing to consume products or services from a brand, and is used to measure brand resonance among customers. Attitudinal loyalty, which captures commitment, trust, and other similar aspects toward a brand, is operationalized as brand loyalty and is more likely to express good feelings about a company and pay higher costs. Research has shown that increased customer satisfaction has a considerable impact on attitudinal and behavioral loyalty, and that good customer satisfaction increases market share and premium pricing (Bowen and Shoemaker, 2003; Back and Parks, 2003). However, few researchers estimate that customer satisfaction does not always imply brand loyalty (Hosseini and Ahmadi Nejad, 2009). As a result, more research into the relationship between consumer satisfaction and brand loyalty is required. Based on these reviews we postulate that:

H8: Customer satisfaction has a significant influence on brand loyalty.

3. METHODOLOGY

3.1 Research Instrument

This research uses a quantitative approach and data is analysed using Partial Least Squares-structural equation modelling (PLS-SEM) method to test the hypotheses. This study's questionnaire included validated items from previous investigations, such as Kataria (2019), Tandon (2015), and Rambocas (2017). Further, the questionnaire was subjected to content validity by experts in consumer behavior and marketing. The questionnaire consists of 35 items measured on a 5-point Likert Scale. Care was taken to include GenZ respondents from various regions across the country to get a comprehensive national representation.

3.2 Sampling

Data was gathered from the GenZ population in various parts of the country who had subscribed for at least one OTT media provider and have been using it for at least a year. If the respondents had multiple OTT subscriptions, they were asked to take the survey based on the most frequently used OTT platform. Over four months, 236 responses were obtained, out of which eight responses had to be omitted from the analysis due to straight-lining and inconsistent responses. Finally, 228 replies met all the criteria and were incorporated in the final analysis. There were 134 male responders (58.8%) and 94 female respondents (41.2%) in total from different regions of India.

3.3 Statistical Analysis

The partial least square structural equation modelling (PLS-SEM) approach was utilised to examine the hypothetical research model using Smart PLS V3.0 (Hair et al., 2016). The PLS method makes no assumptions regarding the data's normality and can be applied to data sets with smaller sample sizes (Aguirre-Urreta and Marakas, 2010). As a result, the PLS method was used for this investigation. The measurement and structural models are the two layers of analysis in the PLS-SEM analysis. The purpose of measurement model analysis is to determine the instrument's validity and reliability. After completing these tests, the structural model is examined to determine the links between the constructs.

3.3.1 Measurement Model Analysis

In measurement model analysis, the survey instrument's validity and reliability are evaluated. Convergent and discriminant validity analyses are used to assess the validity (Chan et al., 2010). The degree to which two or more items measuring the same variable agree is known as convergent validity (Thong, 2001). The average variance extracted (AVE) and outer loading values are used to determine convergent validity. The AVE values of each dimension should be larger than 0.50 (Fornell and Larcker, 1981), and the outer loadings of each construct item should be greater than 0.60 (Lee at al., 2015) to prove convergent validity (Lee at al., 2015). According to the measurement model analysis, all of the constructs' AVE values were in the range of 0.509 to 0.832. All of the constructs' items had outer loading values ranging from 0.689 to 0.933. Both criteria for assessing the constructs' convergent validity were met, and the model's convergent validity was established. Cronbach's alpha and Composite Reliability were used to evaluate item reliability (CR). Reliability levels greater than 0.60 are considered acceptable. All of the constructs were judged to be sufficiently reliable.

3.3.2 Structural Model Analysis

After the measurement model was validated, the structural model evaluation was carried out to evaluate hypotheses. To determine the adequacy of the suggested model, the R-square value of the structural model was assessed. The PLS-SEM result revealed that 49.1% variance in BLY was explained by the construct SAT, and the constructs OBE, BRI, LSC, PRQ, USB, USF, and PVC explained 62.7% variation in SAT. The hypothesis results are presented in table 1.

Table 1. Hypothesis testing results

Hypothesised Relationship		Path coefficients (β)	T Statistics	Hypothesis Result
H_1	PRQ -> SAT	0.164	2.781**	Supported
H_2	PVC -> SAT	0.202	3.331**	Supported
H_3	USF -> SAT	0.300	5.797***	Supported
H_4	USB -> SAT	-0.027	0.479	*Not Supported*
H_5	LSC -> SAT	0.130	2.218*	Supported
H_6	BRI -> SAT	0.010	0.186	*Not Supported*
H_7	OBE -> SAT	0.272	3.972***	Supported
H_8	SAT -> BLY	0.688	18.418***	Supported

***p<0.001, **p<0.01, *p<0.05

Note: OBE = overall brand equity, BRI = brand identification, BLY = brand loyalty, SAT = customer satisfaction, LSC = lifestyle congruence, PRQ = perceived quality, USB = perceived usability, USF = perceived usefulness, PVC = perceived value of cost

4. DISCUSSION

The relationship between OBE and SAT has been studied and found statistically significant (Rambocas et al., 2017), thus supporting our research findings. Similarly, as advocated in our study, the influence of PRQ and PVC on SAT has also been reported as significant by earlier researchers (Kataria and Saini, 2019; Hallencreutz and Parmler et al., 2019). A previous study conducted in the Indian context found that young consumers consider OTT content quality an essential factor (Sadana and Sharma, 2021). This observation is in concurrence with our results. The influence of LSC on SAT has been well researched, and the relationship was found to be significant in different contexts (Nam et al., 2011; Kataria and Saini, 2019). Our research findings also supported the association of lifestyle congruence on customer satisfaction. The influence of USF on satisfaction, supported by this research, was also in line with past studies that have examined this relationship (Ha and Stoel, 2009; Alreck et al., 2009). Convenience, a factor closely related to USF, was found to significantly influence young consumers' OTT adoption (Sadana and Sharma, 2021); this result is also in line with the results of this research. Another factor, PVC, was also a significant factor influencing the OTT consumption behavior of youths in earlier studies (Sadana and Sharma, 2021). Previous studies revealed that ease of use, convenience, and monetary value have less influence among millennial consumers of OTT (Walsh & Singh, 2021). But, our research proves that all these factors are significant factors that influence customer satisfaction among Gen Z consumers.

The relationships, BRI → SAT and USB → SAT was not statistically supported in this research. Past researchers who have studied the influence of BRI on SAT have found this relationship to be significant (Kim et al., 2001; Casalo et al., 2010; Pérez and Rodriguez del Bosque, 2015); but there have also been studies that found this relationship to be insignificant (Kataria and Saini, 2019). Brand identification with customers is expected to grow with time. Therefore, the GenZ population, who are most likely to have lesser involvement with any single OTT platform, could be why this relationship was insignificant. Also, procuring OTT services is a low involvement purchase due to the affordability and lower cost involved in the subscriptions. Therefore, the customers' focus here would be more on the functional benefits rather than having an affection towards the brand. While usefulness to customer satisfaction was statistically significant, usability was not. This finding was not in line with past studies which proposed that USB and SAT are related (Nielsen, 2012; Ha and Janda. 2014; Tandon et al., 2015). This result may be because GenZ cohorts are naturally tech-savvy, and they find it easy to use online platforms with much ease compared to other generations.

5. CONCLUSION AND IMPLICATIONS

5.1 Theoretical Implications

This study empirically validates a model for OTT media service brand loyalty based on the predictor variables such as perceived quality, brand identification, perceived cost, perceived usefulness, perceived usability, lifestyle congruence, and overall brand equity. The most important factor determining consumer satisfaction is overall brand equity, followed by perceived usefulness. Perceived quality also has a moderate but significant effect on customer satisfaction, while the perceived value of cost is critical to customer retention and satisfaction. Customer satisfaction was unaffected by brand identification, and customers purchase OTT media services not just out of habit but also because of the brand's practical benefits. This study stands out as a first of its kind in an emerging economy setup that evaluates the OTT media consumption behavior of the GenZ cohort.

5.2 Practical Implications

The OTT business has become highly competitive due to international competitors and the creation of new product categories. To sustain a loyal consumer base, marketers must take the efforts necessary to differentiate the brand from competitors and increase functional utility. Overall brand equity and perceived usefulness have a more significant impact on customer satisfaction than other constructs. Major players are also focusing on releasing new films on their platforms, and the perceived value of cost is a crucial variable in determining brand loyalty. Marketing strategies should be devised based on the utility of the platform to the client and the value for money it provides.

This research highlights the importance of customer satisfaction for developing brand loyalty for OTT media services. Perceived usefulness of product had the most significant effect on consumer satisfaction in the case of GenZ consumers, while brand equity had the second most significant effect. OTT companies must focus on improving the usability quotient of their platform to enhance customer satisfaction. The perceived value of cost is a significant factor influencing satisfaction, but it ranks below OBE and USF in its effect on SAT. OTT platforms should evaluate the quality of content being delivered through their platform and provide competitive pricing. It is suggested that the OTT companies conduct thorough market research to identify the changing preferences of the target consumers to deliver the content that the customers want.

6. LIMITATIONS AND FUTURE SCOPE

The sample pool is restricted to India, but more data from countries with a significant GenZ cohort population could lead to a more detailed analysis of this generation and their OTT preferences. There is a chance of reverse causality, as different constructs with customer satisfaction were shown to mediate brand loyalty in the study. A more extensive study with a wider range of product categories and qualitative research through interviews and focus group discussions among OTT consumers can provide more insights into customer satisfaction and loyalty behavior of GenZ customers in comparison with other cohorts.

REFERENCES

Aaker, D. (1991), Managing Brand Equity: Capitalizing on the Value of a Brand Name, The Free Press, New York, NY.

Aaker, D.A. (1992), "The value of brand equity", Journal of Business Strategy, Vol. 13 No. 4, pp. 27-32.

Aaker, D.A. (1996), "Measuring brand equity across products and markets", California Management Review, Vol. 38 No. 3, pp. 102-120.

Aguirre-Urreta and Marakas, G. M. (2010). "Is it really gender? An empirical investigation into gender effects in technology adoption through the examination of individual differences", An Interdisciplinary Journal of Humans in ICT Environments, Vol.6 No. 2, pp. 155–190.

Alreck P. L., DiBartolo G.R., Diriker M., Dover H.F., Passyn K.A. and Settle R.B. (2009), "Time pressure, time saving and online shopping: Exploring a contradiction", Journal of Applied Business Research, Vol. 25 No. 5, pp. 85–92.

Anderson, E.W. and Mittal, V. (2000), "Strengthening the satisfaction-profit chain", Journal of Service Research, Vol. 3, No. 2, pp. 107-120.

Back, K. J., and Parks, S. C. (2003), "A brand loyalty model involving cognitive, affective, and conative brand loyalty and customer satisfaction", Journal of hospitality & tourism research, Vol.27 No. 4, pp. 419-435.

Bhat, S., Islam, S. B., and Lone, U. M. (2021), "Antecedents and consequences of online buying behavior: a mediation study", South Asian Journal of Business Studies., Vol. ahead-of-print No. ahead-of-print. https://doi.org/10.1108/SAJBS-07-2020-0223

Bowen, J. T., & Shoemaker, S. (2003), "Loyalty: A strategic commitment", The Cornell Hotel and Restaurant Administration Quarterly, Vol. 44 No.5-6, pp. 31-46.

Brady, M.K., Cronin, J.J. Jr, Fox, G.L. and Roehm, M.L. (2008), "Strategies to offset performance failures: the role of brand equity", Journal of Retailing, Vol. 84 No. 2, pp. 151-164.

Budiman, S., and Dananjoyo, R. (2021), "The Effect of Cafe Atmosphere on Purchase Decision: Empirical Evidence from Generation Z in Indonesia", The Journal of Asian Finance, Economics and Business, Vol. 8 No. 4, pp. 483-490.

Casalo, L.V., Flavian, C. and Guinalıu, M. (2010), "Generating trust and satisfaction in e-services: the impact of usability on consumer behavior", Journal of Relationship Marketing, Vol. 9 No. 4, pp. 247-263.

Chan, F. K. Y., Thong, J. Y. L., Venkatesh, V., Brown, S. A., Hu, P. J. W., andTam, K. Y. (2010)., "Modeling citizen satisfaction with mandatory adoption of an e-government technology", Journal of the Association for Information Systems, Vol. 11 No. 10, pp. 519–549.

Chaudhuri, A., and Holbrook, M. B. (2001), "The Chain of Effects from Brand Trust and Brand Affect to Brand Performance: The Role of Brand Loyalty", Journal of Marketing, Vol.65 No.2, pp. 81–93.

Davis FD (1989), " Perceived usefulness, perceived ease of use and user acceptance of information technology" , MIS Quarterly, Vol 13 No. 3, pp. 319–340.

Davis, K., Charmaraman, L., and Weinstein, E. (2020), "Introduction to special issue: Adolescent and emerging adult development in an age of social media", Journal of Adolescent Research, Vol.35 No.1, pp.3-15.

Dospinescu, O., Dospinescu, N., & Agheorghiesei, D. T. (2021), "Fintech services and factors determining the expected benefits of users: evidence in Romania for millennials and generation Z", E+M Ekonomie a Management, Vol. 24, No. 2, pp. 101-117

Fornell, C., and Larcker, D. F. (1981), "Structural Equation Models with Unobservable Variables and Measurement Error: Algebra and Statistics" , Journal of Marketing Research, Vol. 18 No. 3, pp. 382–388.

Gimpel, G. (2015), "The future of video platforms: Key questions shaping the TV and video industry", International Journal on Media Management, Vol .17 No. 1, pp. 25–46.

Gomez, M.I., McLaughlin, E.W. and Wittink, D.R. (2004), "Customer satisfaction and retail sales performance: an empirical investigation", Journal of Retailing, Vol. 80 No. 4, pp. 265-278.

Gupta and Singharia(2021), "Consumption of OTT media streaming in COVID-19 lockdown: Insights from PLS analysis 2021", Vision: The Journal of Business Perspective, Vol. 25 No.1, pp. 36–46

Ha HY and Janda S (2014), "The effect of customized information on online purchase intentions" , Internet Research, Vol.24 No.4, pp. 496–519.

Ha S and Stoel L (2009), "Consumer e-shopping acceptance: Antecedents in a technology acceptance model" , Journal of Business Research, Vol. 62 No. 5, pp. 565–571.

Hair Jr, J. F., Hult, G. T. M., Ringle, C., and Sarstedt, M. (2016), "A primer on partial least squares structural equation modelling (PLS-SEM)." Sage Publications, California.

Hameed, S. and Mathur, M. (2020), "Generation Z in India: Digital Natives and Makers of Change", Gentina, E. and Parry, E. (Ed.) The New Generation Z in Asia: Dynamics, Differences, Digitalisation (The Changing Context of Managing People), Emerald Publishing Limited, Bingley, pp. 89-104. https://doi.org/10.1108/978-1-80043-220-820201010

Hosseini, M.H. and Ahmadi Nejad, M. (2009), "Examining the effects of customer satisfaction and trust and specific trademark value in customer loyalty and attitudinal behavior: a case study of Refah Bank", Commerce Review, Vol. 33, pp. 42-51.

IBEF Knowledge Center (2020), "India'S OTT Markey: Witnessing a rise in number of paid subscribers", available at : https://www.ibef.org/blogs/india-s-ott-market-witnessing-a-rise-in-number-of-paid-subscribers, (Accessed on 22 July 2021).

Iwasaki, Y. and Havitz, M.E. (1998), "A path analytic model of the relationships between involvement, psychological commitment, and loyalty", Journal of Leisure Research, Vol. 30 No. 2, pp. 256-280.

Kamble, A., Desai, S., and Abhang, N. (2021), "Wearable Activity Trackers: A Structural Investigation into Acceptance and Goal Achievements of Generation Z", American Journal of Health Education, Vol. 52 No.5, pp. 307-320.

Kataria, S., & Saini, V. (2019). "The mediating impact of customer satisfaction in relation of brand equity and brand loyalty", South Asian Journal of Business Studies, Vol. 9 No.1 , pp. 62–87.

Keller, K.L. (1993), "Conceptualizing, measuring, and managing customer-based brand equity", Journal of Marketing, Vol. 57 No. 1, pp. 1-22.

Kim, C.K., Han, D. and Park, S.B. (2001), "The effect of brand personality and brand identification on brand loyalty: applying the theory of social identification", Japanese Psychological Research, Vol. 43 No. 4, pp. 195-206.

Kymäläinen, T., Seisto, A., and Malila, R. (2021) , "Generation Z Food Waste, Diet and Consumption Habits: A Finnish Social Design Study with Future Consumers", Sustainability, Vol. 1 No. 4, pp. 2124.

Lee, V. H., Ooi, K. B., Chong, A. Y. L., and Lin, B. (2015), "A structural analysis of greening the supplier, environmental performance and competitive advantage", Production Planning & Control, Vol. 26 No. 2, pp. 116-130.

Lehmann, D.R. and Srinivasan, S. (2014), "Assessing brand equity through add-on sales", Customer Needs and Solutions, Vol. 1 No. 1, pp. 68-76.

Levesque, T., & McDougall, G. H. (1996), "Determinants of customer satisfaction in retail banking" International Journal of Bank Marketing, Vol. 14 No. 7, pp.12–20.

McDougall, G.H. and Levesque, T. (2000), "Customer satisfaction with services: putting perceived value into the equation", Journal of Services Marketing, Vol. 14 No. 5, pp. 392-410.

McQuitty, S., Finn, A. and Wiley, J.B. (2000), "Systematically varying consumer satisfaction and its implications for product choice", Academy of Marketing Science Review, Vol. 10 No. 1, pp. 231-254.

Nam, J., Ekinci, Y. and Whyatt, G. (2011), "Brand equity, brand loyalty and consumer satisfaction", Annals of Tourism Research, Vol. 38 No. 3, pp. 1009-1030.

Netemeyer, R.G., Krishnan, B., Pullig, C., Wang, G., Yagci, M., Dean, D., Ricks, J. and Wirth, F. (2004), "Developing and validating measures of facets of customer-based brand equity", Journal of Business Research, Vol. 57 No. 2, pp. 209-224.

Nielsen J (2012), "Usability 101: Introduction to usability", available at : https://www.nngroup.com/articles/usability-101-introduction-to-usability/ (accessed on August 2021).

Oliver, R.L. (1999), "Whence customer loyalty?", Journal of Marketing, Vol. 63 No. 4, pp. 33-44

Pérez, A. and Rodriguez del Bosque, I. (2015), "Corporate social responsibility and customer loyalty: exploring the role of identification, satisfaction and type of company", Journal of Services Marketing, Vol. 29 No. 1, pp. 15-25.

Podara, A., Matsiola, M., Nicolaou, C., Maniou, T. A., and Kalliris, G. (2021), "Transformation of television viewing practices in Greece: Generation Z and audio-visual content", Journal of Digital Media & Policy, Vol. 00 No. 00, pp. 1–23.

Rambocas, M., Kirpalani, V. M., & Simms, E. (2018), "Brand equity and customer behavioral intentions: a mediated moderated model", International Journal of Bank Marketing, Vol. 36 No. 1,pp. 19–40.

Sadana, M. and Sharma, D. (2021), "How over-the-top (OTT) platforms engage young consumers over traditional pay television service? An analysis of changing consumer preferences and gamification", Young Consumers, Vol. 22, No. 3, pp. 348-367. https://doi.org/10.1108/YC-10-2020-1231

Shirazi, A., Zeynvand Lorestani, H. and Karimi Mazidi, A. (2013), "Investigating the effects of brand identity on customer loyalty from social identity perspective", Iranian Journal of Management Studies, Vol. 6 No. 2, pp. 153-178.

Subramaniam, M., Pang, N., Morehouse, S., and Asgarali-Hoffman, S. N. (2020), "Examining vulnerability in youth digital information practices scholarship: What are we missing or exhausting?", Children and Youth Services Review, Vol 116 No.105241, pp.1-12.

Tandon, U., Kiran, R., and Sah, A. N. (2015), "Customer satisfaction using website functionality, perceived usability and perceived usefulness towards online shopping in India. Information Development", Vol. 32 No. 5 , pp. 1657–1673.

Theodorakis, N.D., Howat, G., Ko, Y.J. and Avourdiadou, S. (2014), "A comparison of service evaluation models in the context of sport and fitness centres in Greece", Managing Leisure, Vol. 19 No. 1, pp. 18-35.

Thong, J. Y. L. (2001), "Resource constraints and information systems implementation in Singaporean small businesses" , Omega, Vol. 29, pp .143–156.

Veloutsou, C. (2015), "Brand evaluation, satisfaction and trust as predictors of brand loyalty: the mediator-moderator effect of brand relationships", Journal of Consumer Marketing, Vol. 32 No. 6, pp. 405-421.

Venkatesh V and Agarwal R (2006), "Turning visitors into customers: A usability-centric perspective on purchase behavior in electronic channels" Management Science, Vol. 52 No. 3, pp. 367–382.

Walsh, P. and Singh, R. (2021), "Determinants of Millennial behaviour towards current and future use of video streaming services", Young Consumers, Vol. ahead-of-print No. ahead-of-print. https://doi.org/10.1108/YC-08-2021-1374

USING A MOBILE APP TO CREATE RELEVANT AND PARTICIPATORY MUSIC LEARNING SPACES

Heather J. S. Birch
Tyndale University
Toronto, Ontario, Canada

ABSTRACT

This case study features pedagogical strategies that were used in the context of a mobile app for learning to encourage relevant engagement and participation. For 20 weeks, a group of 18 piano students, ages 10 through 15, used a mobile app known as PracticeCactus. This self-contained social media platform allowed young participants to create and post audio recordings of their piano practice to share with their peers, which could then be 'liked' and commented on. Giving the mobile app to music learners without any direction at first, to provide them with freedom to engage with the app as they chose, resulted in limited engagement, due to individualism and a performance-based mindset. To encourage participatory engagement with the app, four pedagogical strategies were enacted, including: a) inviting students to take on the identity of 'content creator;' b) celebrating process over product; c) initiating goal-setting projects; and d) scaffolded instruction. These strategies resulted in the students using the app more frequently, but more importantly, fostered a different type of engagement, i.e., new opportunities for musical thinking and learning. Teachers who want to foster participatory engagement in music learning may benefit from this discussion of pedagogical strategies in the context of a mobile app.

KEYWORDS

Music Education, Participatory Culture, Students as Content Creators, Affordances of Mobile Tech, Pedagogical Strategies

1. INTRODUCTION

Mobile apps designed to facilitate learning are often insufficient, in themselves, to guarantee that relevant and participatory learning takes place. The pedagogical strategies a teacher uses to guide and direct students' use of a mobile app can have a crucial impact. This paper articulates the value of using a mobile app as a learning tool in the context of formal music learning to foster a sense relevance and participatory practice among learners, where each person feels they can be fully engaged, and has a voice as a content creator. In this case study, a mobile app was used as the learning context and over time, there were changes in how the students engaged with the app for learning. The students were a group of piano students, (n=18), ranging in age from 10 to 15. For 20 weeks, they used a mobile app called PracticeCactus—a self-contained social media platform accessible by the students and their music teacher. The mobile app allowed the students to share musical creations and musical thinking with their peers. Over time, the students began to use the app in ways that were more frequent, more creative, and more deeply engaged with the learning content. The mobile app itself was not solely responsible for these positive trends. Rather, the affordances of the app, in combination with the pedagogical strategies that were employed, resulted in increased opportunities for learning. The research question in this qualitative study was: 'What social and cultural practices do piano students enact when invited to use a mobile app designed to facilitate music learning'? The findings and discussion are meant to support teachers as they consider ways to use a mobile app as a learning context, keeping in mind some limiting factors that could hinder meaningful engagement, and suggesting pedagogical strategies that may be effective for fostering participation and socially engaged music learning.

2. LITERATURE REVIEW

Educational technology is not neutral, and the choice to integrate a digital tool into an educational space has impacts on what can and what will take place in that space (Scardamalia & Bereiter, 2008). Many mobile apps designed to facilitate music learning are focused on tracking errors such as wrong notes and rhythms, and testing to see if users, once their errors are identified, can correct them. These mobile apps convey a specific message about what music learning is. The mobile app used in this study was intended to go beyond the conceptualization of music learning as building skill to play the right notes at the right time, and to encourage meaningful music making in ways that are relevant to students' social and cultural contexts.

2.1 Theoretical Foundation

This study assumes the epistemological stance that meaning is constructed (Confrey, 1990; Dart et al., 2000), and that meaning-making happens when learners actively explore, in relation to others (Nurrenbern, 2001). Constructivist theory, as applied to music learning, expands the possibilities for learning beyond building technical skill, and envisions music learning as musical inquiry, musical connections, and musical discoveries (Garnett, 2013; Shively, 2015). Sociocultural learning, as a lens in this study, understands learning to be embedded within interactions themselves, in that space which is between the self and others (Glăveanu, 2010). Knowledge, then, does not simply exist within the mind of an individual, but also exists between people and in cultural contexts; it exists within social practices themselves (Gee & Green, 1998; Lave & Wenger, 1991). As described by Gaztambide-Fernández (2013), the production of culture, or cultural production, is the way that humans represent themselves, the way they perceive others, and the way they think about and experience the world through symbolic means.

In the world of music, distinct cultural and social practices take place in different musical genres (e.g., jazz and rock), and within different musical contexts (e.g., school music classes, Indigenous pow wows, or hip-hop concerts). Music learning, then, consists of making use of a rich set of tools to understand and create music (Wallerstedt, 2013) within various social contexts. Over the course of this study, participants were encouraged to engage in music learning in social and culturally situated ways, to foster this type of meaningful, situated learning.

2.2 Relevant and Participatory Learning

Students live in a world of user-generated content, i.e., content created and shared on social media by any individual who is part of the general public (Daugherty et al., 2008) for the purposes of self-expression and actualization (Buf & Ştefănită, 2020; Stoeckl et al., 2007). Empowering students toward production and interaction is possible because of accessible, affordable, and user-friendly digital tools (Gee, 2010; O'Hear & Sefton-Green, 2004). Therefore, creating a learning environment where students are invited into the world of user-generated content is a way of providing relevant, culturally situated experiences for students. Music students, as they engage in authentic creation and sharing, are empowered to be part of participatory culture.

The significant role of music in the life of young people today is heightened by unprecedented access to all music, any time, thus increasing opportunities and urges to 'participate' with music (Allsup et al., 2012; Tobias, 2014). Participating with music includes spending time practicing to develop technical skill, but also includes improvising, composing, listening, and dancing (Folkestad, 2006; Green, 2005; Tobias, 2014). Small (1998) describes the act of engagement with music as participating in relationships that bring meaning to the act of music-making. Relationships are embedded between musical notes, between musical ideas, and between people who enact and facilitate a musical performance. Music educators, then, have an opportunity to create opportunities for learners to experience these relationships. Mobile technology is ideally suited to fostering such relationships, in partnership with supportive pedagogical practices. Within the mobile app used in this study, students took on various musical roles and engaged in various ways, through relationships with music and with one another.

3. METHODS

3.1 Research Design Overview

The research design is an instrumental, qualitative case study, as described by Stake (1995). The case is bounded by a particular mobile app for learning which was used by a group of 18 music students over a period of 20 weeks. The goal of examining this case was to investigate the musical artifacts that students created, shared, and interacted with, as well as the students' reflections on what they created and shared, and then to use rich description to illustrate the case. The researcher, a music teacher who also took on the role of app designer, wanted to explore how piano students would choose to use a mobile app when it was provided to them as a context for their learning. Halfway through the study, it became apparent that the students had not used the app very often, and only in limited ways. Therefore, some specific pedagogical strategies were enacted to encourage further and more meaningful involvement.

3.2 Participants

The researcher, along with all the participants in the study, reside in a medium-sized town in Ontario, Canada. Before proceeding with this study, ethical clearance from the researcher's University was obtained, and then a colleague of the researcher, (another music teacher), along with 18 of her students, 9 females and 9 males ages 10 through 15, were recruited to participate. The students agreed to use a mobile app as part of their musical instrument practice sessions which they routinely engaged in at home between weekly, in-person lessons with their teacher. The researcher and the music teacher worked together to communicate with the student participants to ensure that ethical protocols were faithfully enacted, and that the students knew they could opt out of participation at any time, as well as to monitor and guide the students' musical participation within the app.

3.3 Data Collection

The primary data collection source was the set of audio recordings, 'likes,' and comments that students contributed to the mobile app. The students used the mobile app, (which was a self-contained social media platform), while they were practicing at home as a way of sharing some of the things that were happening as they practiced, with their peers. As they posted audio recordings of their practice sessions for others to hear, these posts appeared in the app's news feed, and others responded with 'likes' and comments. The other data source consisted of four, in-person music-sharing sessions where all the participants met at their music teacher's house for one hour. These were modified focus group sessions, which included opportunities for musical games and snacks, as well as group discussions about the students' experiences of using the app. Some activities and discussions at the music-sharing sessions were planned in advance, while others evolved according to the students' queries and emerging needs. These sessions were audio-recorded and transcribed.

3.4 Data Analysis

The semiotic signs created and enacted by the participants were observed, collected, and analyzed for patterns and themes. These signs included posts, comments, and 'likes' that the participants added within the mobile app, and these were examined holistically (Baxter & Jack, 2008). In addition, transcripts of the music-sharing sessions were analyzed to determine common themes that were part of the students' experiences. Each piece of data, taken together, was a source that led toward understanding the behaviour of the community, and to a nuanced understanding of the case. Patterns that emerged regarding when students posted, and what they posted, were noticed and described. While this single case is not meant to be definitive, knowledge of a certain case does provide a tangible, real-life example of general principals of human behaviour which can prompt reflection and imagination—of what was and what might be (Flyvbjerg, 2018). The phenomenon presented by the analysis of the case may be useful to teachers who are seeking information about ways to foster relevant and participatory learning environments in the context of music education, or other content areas where sociocultural production is part of the learning process.

4. RESULTS

There were three main findings, in answer to the question, 'What social and cultural practices do piano students enact when invited to use a mobile app designed to facilitate music learning'? First, it became evident that when left to decide how they would engage with the app, participants contributed rarely, and in specific limited ways. Second, it was discovered that there were two specific reasons that seemed to be the cause of this limited participation. Third, it was found that, with the enactment of four pedagogical strategies, the participants experienced some freedom the limiting beliefs that had hindered meaningful participation with the app, and as a result, engaged more frequently and meaningfully in music learning.

4.1 Participation Patterns

Throughout the study, a total of 74 audio recordings were shared within the mobile app. Over the first 10 weeks of the study, 12 recordings were posted by participants, most of which were full musical pieces, i.e., an entire song played from beginning to end without stopping. After week 10, the participants posted 62 audio recordings, and these posts included partial pieces, technical exercises, tutorials, and invitations to respond. Partial pieces were excerpts of songs that students recorded and shared, either because they wanted to highlight a particular section they were doing well, or that they needed more work on. Technical exercises are often assigned by music teachers as required practice items for warming up and developing facility on a musical instrument in specific skill areas. Participants shared audio recordings of these exercises, including scales and chords in various keys. Invitations to respond were those audio recordings posted by students where they invited a response from their listeners. For example, they asked their audience to listen to their playing and to try to identify the tune or attempt to find a mistake.

By Week 10 of the study, two factors that were limiting the students' participation were identified, including their mentality of individualism, and their focus on performance. To address these limiting mindsets, four pedagogical strategies were initiated during music-sharing sessions, including: a) inviting students to take on the identity of 'content creator;' b) celebrating process over product; c) initiating goal-setting projects; and d) scaffolded instruction. These strategies will be described more fully in the Discussion section. When these strategies were put in place by the researcher and the music teacher, the students' use of the mobile app increased, as previously illustrated, in both number and creativity. Students began to post more, and they also began to post a variety of different types of recordings, according to their emerging needs and interests.

4.2 Limiting Mindsets

Through conversations with the participants during focus group sessions, it was revealed that these students came to the research study with two limiting mindsets, including individualism and an emphasis on performance. It is not surprising that the students in the study had an individualistic view of piano practice. They had been practicing for years, mostly at home, alone, likely without many experiences that allowed them to view their piano practice as a community activity. When these young participants were asked why they had not posted in the app, they did not give excuses such as running out of time or forgetting. Rather, it seemed that they did not know why they were not posting, since they could not articulate a reason. But neither could they articulate a reason why they would choose to record something from their piano practice and post it for the community to see and hear. They did not have, as part of their understanding of music learning, that practice, before a piece is ready to be performed, could be understood as a socially engaged act that is situated within a community experience.

Students also came to the study with a performance mindset, which limited their participation with the app. They began the research study by only posting full pieces that they deemed ready to perform for their peers, or in other words, pieces they could play from beginning to end without stopping. When students came to the mobile app with this narrow perspective on what kinds of audio recordings could be shared, they were limited to only performance-ready pieces. Just as the individualistic mindset was not surprising to encounter, this focus on performance was not surprising either. Some music teachers might only invite certain students to perform in public, because they want these performances to reflect well on them and their teaching skill, and those who are invited may only be asked to share their very 'best' performances publicly (Webster,

1993). Even though the mobile app used in this study was a self-contained learning environment where only the students of one music teacher could hear the audio recordings posted, the idea that only those who had something worthy of public performance pervaded.

4.3 Pedagogical Strategies

Four pedagogical strategies were introduced to help students overcome these limiting mindsets – two in relation to individualism, and two in relation to valuing performance-based participation.

To empower learners to engage more deeply with using the app, and to interact with one another in ways that resulted in musical listening and thinking, it was first decided that the mindset of individualism would be addressed, using two pedagogical strategies. First, to prompt students to participate in the learning community, they were invited to take on the identity of 'content creator.' This pedagogical strategy may resonate with young learners who are immersed in the world of rich media-sharing, whereby one's social and cultural capital can be defined by the content that one creates and shares. At first, the students had difficulty conceiving of how their independent musical practice sessions at home might be thought of as part of a community experience, and so a new identity was offered for them to take on, which could make content creation and sharing a part of their lived experience. At a focus group session, the researcher led a discussion with the young learners about the difference between content consumers and content creators. As a group, they brainstormed a list of some typical habits and identifiers that would be part of each of these roles. The intent of the discussion was to help students explicitly realize and acknowledge that nothing is going to happen in a learning community if there aren't any content creators. This discussion, then, was meant to empower each participant to, going forward, take on the task of creating content, not just for what benefit they might have perceived for themselves, but also because of the benefit that others in the community might experience through hearing their posts and seeing their comments.

Second, the individualistic mindset was addressed through introducing small group goal setting. At the next focus group session, the students divided themselves into five small groups, and each group decided how often, how many, and what types of posts they would like to share with one another within the mobile app. They wrote down their group goals on paper, signed their names, and handed these plans to the researcher. This second pedagogical strategy, then, was meant to address the individualistic mindset by encouraging the participants to work together, and to creatively imagine how they might use an app for music learning. This empowered the students to create recordings and post them in the app, as part of a group, and as a team effort, instead of having to come up with their own ideas about what to record and post, and then posting on their own.

To overcome the performance mindset that was limiting students' participation with the app, two pedagogical strategies were invoked. First, the celebration of process over product was introduced. At one of the focus group sessions, the researcher facilitated a discussion of how the process of musical learning is just as valuable as the final product of musical instrument practice. Examples of audio recordings that contained excerpts of piano pieces and imperfect recordings were shared, and the students were asked what would happen if they heard something like this posted within the mobile app. The students listened to one another share how they would add a comment to encourage the person, cheer them on to keep practicing, or suggest a helpful practice technique. Because the sharing in the group was positive, it built a feeling of trust whereby each participant realized that they had the freedom to post musical progress, and they were not required to have a perfect offering to share. After this discussion, they were ready to share parts of pieces (e.g., only the left hand of a piece or only one section of a piece), and they shared pieces where they were clearly having difficulty with one or more aspects of the piece.

Second, to address the performance mindset, (because the students did not have much practice hearing others' in-progress music), time at a focus group session was devoted to scaffolded instruction about what to do when you encounter a post that someone else has shared, which clearly has mistakes, an uneven tempo, or some other musical challenge. We wanted to prompt the students to use their musical listening skills as they heard a recording, and to use their musical thinking skills to construct a comment that would be valuable to the person who had posted that recording. The music students, ages 10 through 15, did not necessarily already have this skill. To scaffold the instruction, as a group, we brainstormed ideas for different types of comments that could be posted, which might prove helpful. Then we crafted a list of sample comments that they could use, as is, if they found an audio recording where they wanted to express one of those sentiments. We also encouraged the participants to create their own comments based on this learning.

5. DISCUSSION

When the study began, the students were intentionally given a minimal amount of instruction with regard to how often and in what ways they should use the app. This was part of the study design, in that naturally emerging choices, interactions, and patterns were anticipated and hoped for. When it became clear that students were posting in a singular, traditional manner (full, performance-ready pieces), and many were not posting at all, mainly due to two limiting mindsets, four pedagogical strategies were introduced to increase student involvement and interaction. This highlights the fact that the affordances of a mobile app do not always reside within the app itself, but rather, come forth as various activities enabled by the app are enacted (Beach, 2017). Simply introducing a mobile app and hoping that learners will use it in rich and meaningful ways puts too much onus on the learners who, while they may be digitally proficient, need guidance to know how to use mobile apps for learning. This study demonstrates that even in a content area such as music, where performance is an integrated social practice in many genres and contexts, a mobile app, paired with pedagogical strategies, has the potential to change the mindset of the learners to adopt new, participatory social practices.

5.1 Relevant Mobile Learning

This study uses the term 'content creator,' which may evoke ideas of vloggers and famous Instagram influencers, and this is intentional. A survey of 3000 children in the US, UK, and China revealed that 30% indicated 'YouTuber' as their career aspiration (The Harris Poll, 2019). The career of a content creator is not without challenges. Some of these challenges include being subject to manipulation by brands (Harms et al., 2022) and by social media companies (Arriagada & Ibáñez, 2020), and feeling pressure to relentlessly post content and cater to viewers' desires (Törhönen et al., 2018). But content creators want to communicate something valuable to an audience in creative and productive ways (Buf & Ştefănită, 2020), to build self-confidence (Snelson, 2015), and to imagine new identities and statuses (Berryman & Kavka, 2017; Choi & Behm-Morawitz, 2017), and this is something that teachers can play a role in supporting among their students. Learning to be a content creator usually happens through social interactions in distributed, online communities (Harlan et al., 2012). Educators who take on some responsibility for teaching learners about the role of content creators can potentially help their students toward critical reflection and wise decisions regarding content creation, perhaps as a career for some, but also, as a regular part of life for anyone who is active on social media and creates and shares content. Ultimately, encouraging music students to create and learn about music within a social community, as part of cultural expression, can happen within the context of a mobile app with affordances that reflect the values of socially engaged music learning.

5.2 Participatory Mobile Learning

The mobile app in this study became a useful tool, not only for engaging students, but for shifting students' conceptualization of musical identity and musical participation. The app was a social media platform that facilitated creation and sharing of content. That alone may not be powerful for learning. But students in this study realized that sharing in the mobile app could be a different kind of sharing than they were used to, i.e., mostly in performance contexts. This shift from purely performance-oriented sharing to the progress-focused sharing is significant because it allowed students to enact music making in a participatory fashion such that they were sharing their 'doing' of music on a regular basis. More opportunities to represent the self throughout the stages of learning rather than waiting until some final product is reached provides more practice of authentic, consistent cultural expressions. Being freed from sharing only final products provides more access for students to participate with music and does not restrict the amount of sharing and expressing someone can do based on their ability to reach certain skill or technical levels. Understanding how to support one another's music learning, through the messy parts of progress, before performance-level is reached, can empower learners to recognize the value of the process of learning, and engage in meaningful musical thinking as they reflect on their own in-progress learning, as well as others.'

6. CONCLUSION

At the outset, participants were given a mobile app to use for learning, but without any details or direct guidance. This was intentional, to determine if the students had ideas about the social and cultural practices they would like to enact together as a group. When little to no engagement happened, and some limiting mindsets were discovered, instruction and strategies were implemented to support the learners. Therefore, this study may provide ideas to instructors who want to conduct learning within mobile spaces, and who want to positively influence social engagement.

This study discusses pedagogical strategies that can be used in the context of a mobile app for learning that empowers students to engage deeply with learning, and to participate meaningfully with the learning content. One typical way to increase engagement in a learning environment is to link participation to assessment. For example, to earn 10% of their grade in a course, a student may be required to post a certain number of times. What is assessed is what students do. But this study suggests a different approach, including offering a new identity for learners, and scaffolded instruction to empower students to participate as a socially and culturally connected experience.

A study about content creators has shown that they tend to represent a singular, privileged socioeconomic group (Brake, 2014). Therefore, empowering all students with the critical thinking skills and practical skills necessary to engage in content creation and sharing has the potential to disrupt this imbalance, and provide more equitable access to the career of content creator for all learners. Admittedly, this study was limited in that it made use of a self-contained social media platform that only facilitated the sharing of audio content and text, and not video, which is currently the most popular mode for content creation sharing. Future studies could investigate the impact of a mobile app for music learning, in tandem with pedagogical strategies that facilitate a shift from performance-oriented to participatory-oriented engagement, on the mental health of music learners.

REFERENCES

Allsup, R. E., Westerlund, H., & Shieh, E. (2012). Youth culture and secondary education. In G. E. McPherson & G. F. Welch (Eds.), *The Oxford Handbook of Music Education* (Vol. 1, pp. 460–475). Oxford University Press.

Arriagada, A., & Ibáñez, F. (2020). "You need at least one picture daily, if not, you're dead": Content creators and platform evolution in the social media ecology. *Social Media and Society*, *6*(3), 1–12. https://doi.org/10.1177/2056305120944624

Baxter, P., & Jack, S. (2008). Qualitative case study methodology: Study design and implementation for novice researchers. *The Qualitative Report*, *13*(4), 544–559.

Berryman, R., & Kavka, M. (2017). 'I guess a lot of people see me as a big sister or a friend'': The role of intimacy in the celebrification of beauty vloggers.' *Journal of Gender Studies*, *26*(3), 307–320. https://doi.org/10.1080/09589236.2017.1288611

Brake, D. R. (2014). Are we all online content creators now? Web 2.0 and digital divides. *Journal of Computer-Mediated Communication*, *19*(3), 591–609. https://doi.org/10.1111/jcc4.12042

Buf, D. M., & Ştefănită, O. (2020). Uses and gratifications of youtube: A comparative analysis of users and content creators. *Romanian Journal of Communication and Public Relations*, *22*(2), 75–89. https://doi.org/10.21018/rjcpr.2020.2.301

Choi, G. Y., & Behm-Morawitz, E. (2017). Giving a new makeover to STEAM: Establishing YouTube beauty gurus as digital literacy educators through messages and effects on viewers. *Computers in Human Behavior*, *73*, 80–91. https://doi.org/10.1016/j.chb.2017.03.034

Confrey, J. (1990). What constructivism implies for teaching. In *Journal for Research in Mathematics Education* (pp. 107–210). National Council of Teachers of Mathematics.

Dart, B. C., Burnett, P. C., Purdie, N., Boulton-Lewis, G., Campbell, J., & Smith, D. (2000). Students' conceptions of learning, the classroom environment, and approaches to learning. *Educational Research*, *93*(4), 262–270.

Daugherty, T., Eastin, M. S., & Bright, L. (2008). Exploring consumer motivations for creating user-generated content. *Journal of Interactive Advertising*, *8*(2), 16–25. https://doi.org/10.1080/15252019.2008.10722139

Flyvbjerg, B. (2018). Case Study. In N. K. Denzin & Y. S. Lincoln (Eds.), *The Sage Handbook of Qualitative Research* (pp. 301–316). Sage Publications Inc.

Folkestad, G. (2006). Formal and informal learning situations or practices vs formal and informal ways of learning. *British Journal of Music Education*, *23*(2), 135–145.

Garnett, J. (2013). Beyond a constructivist curriculum: A critique of competing paradigms in music education. *British Journal of Music Education*, *30*(2), 161–175.

Gee, J. P. (2010). *New digital media and learning as an emerging area and "worked examples" as one way forward.* MIT Press.

Gee, J. P., & Green, J. (1998). Discourse analysis, learning, and social practice: A methodological study. *Review of Research in Education*, *23*(1), 119–169.

Glăveanu, V. P. (2010). Paradigms in the study of creativity: Introducing the perspective of cultural psychology. *New Ideas in Psychology*, *28*(1), 79–93. https://doi.org/10.1016/j.newideapsych.2009.07.007

Green, L. (2005). *How popular musicians learn: A way ahead for music education.* Ashgate Publishing Limited.

Harlan, M. A., Bruce, C., & Lupton, M. (2012). Teen content creators: Experiences of using information to learn. *Library Trends*, *60*(3), 569–587. https://doi.org/10.1353/lib.2012.0001

Harms, B., Hoekstra, J. C., & Bijmolt, T. H. A. (2022). Sponsored influencer vlogs and young viewers: When sponsorship disclosure does not enhance advertising literacy, and parental mediation backfires. *Journal of Interactive Marketing*, *57*(1), 35–53. https://doi.org/10.1177/10949968221075834

Lave, J., & Wenger, E. (1991). *Situated learning: Legitimate peripheral participation.* Cambridge University Press.

Nurrenbern, S. C. (2001). Piaget's theory of intellectual development revisited. *Journal of Chemical Education*, *78*(8), 1107–1110.

O'Hear, S., & Sefton-Green, J. (2004). Style, genre and technology: The strange case of youth culture online. In I. Snyder & C. Beavis (Eds.), *Doing literacy online: Teaching, learning and playing in an electronic world* (pp. 121–144). Hampton Press.

Scardamalia, M., & Bereiter, C. (2008). Pedagogical biases in educational technologies. *Educational Technology*, *48*(3), 3–10.

Shively, J. (2015). Constructivism in music education. *Arts Education Policy Review*, *116*(3), 128–136.

Small, C. (1998). *Musicking: The meanings of performing and listening.* University Press of New England.

Snelson, C. (2015). Vlogging about school on YouTube: An exploratory study. *New Media and Society*, *17*(3), 321–339. https://doi.org/10.1177/1461444813504271

Stake, R. (1995). *The art of case study research.* Sage.

Stoeckl, R., Rohrmeier, P., & Hess, T. (2007). Motivations to produce user generated content: Differences between webloggers and videobloggers. *Proceedings of BLED Conference*, 398–413.

The Harris Poll. (n.d.). *LEGO Group kicks off global program to inspire the next generation of space explorers as NASA celebrates 50 years of moon landing.* 2019. https://theharrispoll.com/briefs/lego-group-kicks-off-global-program-to-inspire-the-next-generation-of-space-explorers-as-nasa-celebrates-50-years-of-moon-landing/

Tobias, E. S. (2014). 21st century musicianship through digital media and participatory culture. In M. Kaschub & J. Smith (Eds.), *Promising Practices in 21st Century Music Teacher Education* (pp. 1–23). Oxford University Press.

Törhönen, M., Sjöblom, M., & Hamari, J. (2018). Likes and views: Investigating internet video content creators perceptions of popularity. *GamiFIN Conference Proceedings*, *2186*, 108–114.

Wallerstedt, C. (2013). Here comes the sausage: An empirical study of children's verbal communication during a collaborative music-making activity. *Music Education Research*, *15*(4), 421–434. https://doi.org/10.1080/14613808.2013.812626

Webster, P. (1993). Where are we and where should we be going? *Proceedings of the National Conference on Piano Pedagogy.*

REMOTE TEACHING DURING THE COVID-19 PANDEMIC: CHALLENGES AND POTENTIALITIES OF USING M-LEARNING IN LITERACY CLASSES IN BRAZIL

Emely Crystina da Silva Viana, Hélio José Santos Maia, Danielle Alves de Oliveira Tabosa, Daniel Alves da Silva, Fábio Lúcio Lopes de Mendonça and Rafael Timóteo de Sousa Júnior
Universidade de Brasília, Brazil

ABSTRACT

The research presents the objective of analyzing the challenges and potentialities of teaching with the use of m-learning, in literacy classes during remote teaching caused by the COVID-19 pandemic, based on learning results regarding the appropriation of the writing system alphabetical. In view of the constant social and educational changes caused by the COVID-19 pandemic, in which social isolation became a security measure imposed to reduce the circulation of the virus, they led to the reconfiguration of educational spaces and the adoption of strategies for the continuation of formal education, as an alternative, emergency remote teaching was adopted. Remote teaching has driven changes in education, such as the use of mobile and wireless technologies, cell phones, tablets and notebooks, m-learning, to facilitate the teaching-learning process. A bibliometric review was carried out in order to study and explore the phenomenon with the identification of relevant scientific publications, which were obtained by applying quality and approach evaluation criteria, which showed scientific interest in m-learning and remote teaching. This is a qualitative research on the challenges and potential of using mobile learning with Brazilian children in literacy classes and is configured as an ethnographic case study. The locus of the research were two classes of the 1st year of Elementary School in a public school of the State Department of Education of the Federal District - SEEDF, Brazil, Brasília, Federal District, with a temporal cut of the 1st semester of 2021, having as research subjects 26 children of approximately 6 and 7 years old. The results indicate that despite the challenges faced, the data presented reveal that activities mediated by educational tools such as Google Classroom, Google Meet and the use of student interaction platforms such as the use of digital games and presentation of videos, music and stories interactive activities, among many other factors, demonstrates the potential of m-learning, with the appropriate interventions and pedagogical mediations, however, it is worth noting that access to the online teaching-learning process is still worrying, due to the difficulty of students accessing the internet and the lack of technological devices to monitor the educational proposals, such as computers or smartphones, and the formative weaknesses in relation to the use of TDIC's, therefore, teaching mediated by m-learning, can be considered as a modality of high potential, among other factors, if it is accessible to all.

KEYWORDS

COVID-19 Pandemic, Remote Teaching, M-learning, Literacy

1. INTRODUCTION

The emergence of new technologies redefines communication and interaction environments and, consequently, learning spaces, enabling the (re)creation and development of other teaching and learning modalities and methodologies supported by new technologies in the educational field, such as m-learning or mobile learning, spread worldwide. According to Saikat, et al. (2021), m-learning presents itself as a subdivision of online learning, a type of remote education that takes place in different environments, through the exchange of content mediated by mobile devices, such as cell phones, tablets and notebooks.

Over decades, the discussion about the use of technologies for pedagogical mediation, as well as its limits and potential, has been presented and questioned. With the need for social distancing as a measure to combat the new Corona virus, in a short period of time, the educational field had to be reinvented, institutions interrupted face-to-face teaching and the use of technologies was quickly incorporated as an alternative for the continuation of activities education.

The pandemic caused by COVID-19, socially, provoked the global challenge of saving lives, human losses are irreparable, educationally, it challenged the (re)invention and (re)signification of educational spaces and teaching approaches used so far. There were countless challenges and limitations emerging from remote teaching, mainly in relation to internet access and the acquisition of mobile technological equipment for the class camp. In Brazil, data from the Internet Management Committee in Brazil (2020), revealed that in 2020, 47 million people did not have access to the internet and according to the UNICEF report on the scenario of school exclusion in Brazil, 3.7 million students enrolled did not have access to school activities and were unable to keep studying and learning at home during remote teaching, this situation of exclusion mainly affected those who already lived in a situation of greater vulnerability, which makes the data even more worrying (UNICEF, 2021).

Silva (2022, p.8) points out that remote teaching was a provisional and emergency alternative for maintaining the teaching-learning process in which classes took place synchronously and asynchronously. Still in this regard, the author points out that "we need to rethink, already in the 'hybrid' form of teaching, [...] alternative ways to realign our organization of pedagogical work", in addition to the duty to inform the extent to which there was a diversity of scenarios experienced during remote classes in view of the Brazilian regional diversity and the multiple difficulties encountered in monitoring classes.

Amid the educational challenges caused by the COVID-19 pandemic, teachers needed to reinvent their practices. In literacy classes, advancing students in learning the Alphabetic Writing System became even more challenging.

In view of this, the central objective of this research is to analyze the challenges and potentialities of teaching with the use of m-learning, in literacy classes during remote teaching caused by the COVID-19 pandemic.

With this research, it is expected to answer the following question: what were the challenges and potentialities of teaching with the use of m-learning regarding the teaching and learning process of the Alphabetic Writing System?

Therefore, this research is configured as a contribution to the educational field, especially to the area of literacy, as it presents challenges and learning potential with the use of m-learning in literacy classes in Brazil, as an alternative found for the continuity education during the COVID-19 pandemic.

2. RELATED STUDIES

In the last five years, there has been a significant amount of academic work and articles published on the subject of m-learning and remote teaching, in view of the global pandemic scenario.

M-learning refers to a learning style, based on the mobility of contexts, individual, cultural or learning content interactions, mediated by mobile electronic devices such as smartphones, laptops and tablets (Zhonggen & Xiaozhi, 2019.)

Teaching mediated by technologies, resulting from one of the biggest health emergencies, the COVID-19 pandemic, forced teachers to think differently about methodologies and technologies for training and supporting education, these new educational guidelines form a set of of radical innovations in terms of form, organization and efficiency (Barletta et al., 2022).

Due to the worldwide closure of schools at all levels of education, the educational system has experienced a shift from face-to-face education to the paradigm of online education, however, the online support offered in response to the global education crisis does not have the characteristics of education online, which is why it was called Emergency Online Education (EOE) in India (Mahanta & Sharma, 2022). In Brazil, in the same sense that it should not be confused with Distance Education (EaD), teaching, due to its emergency nature, was called Emergency Remote Teaching (ERE).

Technologies have changed the way information is accessed and the current educational model. Mobile devices, compatible with the constant and rapid changes in our communication situations, offer quick and easy access to knowledge available online, which encourages reflection on teaching and learning models and the roles played by educators and students, who present an increasingly active profile regarding the educational process. (Criollo et al., 2021). The mobile application facilitates the learning process, but the problems and difficulties faced by students regarding the lack of access to the internet and mobile devices, challenges and limitations of the modality should be considered (Lima & Isotani, 2021). The low internet connection was a challenge and limitation mainly in emerging countries, where economic conditions for students and teachers may not be favorable (Lima & Isotani, 2021).

The pandemic caused many changes in people's lives, including education, and although these tools were a viable option for continuing classes, a major difficulty encountered by students was access to the internet linked to the quota for accessing materials on the internet. and internet instability to watch videos, participate in games (Lima & Isotani, 2021). There are still several obstacles emerging from the implementation of m-learning, as it is mediated by the use of mobile devices and internet use. Many communities, particularly in rural areas, lack electricity, lack an internet connection, or lack mobile devices capable of supporting mobile learning. Despite the numerous challenges, schools have used mobile learning as an alternative for continuing education during the academic process. (Chibisa & Mutambara, 2022).

In addition to these difficulties, for teachers, another gap found was about the lack of adequate training in the use of technologies and the need to change methodologies that this teaching requires. On the part of educational institutions, there was difficulty in providing adequate technological infrastructure and effective training support for teachers (Barletta et al., 2022).

Access to the online teaching-learning process is still worrying, m-learning can be considered a powerful tool with high potential as a learning modality, if it is accessible to all (Mahanta & Sharma, 2022).

The intensive use of m-learning during this period revealed many enlightening experiences, adding a new perspective for the use of this modality of education, aiming at the present and projecting the future (Saiakat et al., 2021), despite the need to consider the challenges regarding students' lack of access to the internet and mobile devices.

Throughout remote teaching, tools such as Whatsapp, Google Classroom, Zoom, Google Meet were the most common learning strategies during the class period. As online support and instruction tools for students adopted by educational institutions, the most used were videos, audios, Power-Point presentations, text messages, and YouTube video links (Shrutidhara & Chander, 2022). In addition, the combination of more than one of these tools was an alternative found for the widest possible range of students.

The use of these tools was essential to enable communication between teachers and students, so governments and ministries of education need to consider investing in these tools as essential for school success. Google Classroom has good usability and accessibility in addition to the good performance of the tool, it is easy to learn to use.

The correlation between these studies and the present research is identified, since they highlight the challenges and potential of using m-learning in teaching during the COVID-19 pandemic.

3. RESEARCH METHODOLOGY

The objective of this work is to analyze the challenges and potentialities of teaching with the use of m-learning, in literacy classes during remote teaching caused by the COVID-19 pandemic. To achieve this objective, learning outcomes will be observed regarding the appropriation of the alphabetic writing system in literacy classes.

This is a qualitative research on the challenges and potentialities of using mobile learning with Brazilian children in literacy classes, configured as an ethnographic case study.

The ethnographic type case study allows an in-depth study of a given reality, makes it possible to know in depth a particular instance taking into account its context, complexity and own dynamism. It is especially indicated when the focus of the research is a phenomenon that is happening in a real situation and that is contemporary (André, 2005).

For the collection of empirical information, the ethnographic techniques of participant observation were associated, which consists of verifying the largest possible number of situations during the course of the research, to apprehend actions; and document analysis, to contextualize the phenomenon, collecting information from different types of documents (André, 2005). Participant observation of synchronous classes and documental analysis of activities carried out in asynchronous classes were chosen.

The locus of the research was a public school of the State Department of Education of the Federal District - SEEDF, Brazil, Brasília, Federal District. Having as part of the study, the result of learning regarding the appropriation of the alphabetic writing system in literacy classes. The research was carried out in two classes of the 1st year of Elementary School, with a time frame of the 1st semester of 2021, with 26 children aged approximately 6 and 7 years old as research subjects.

The methodology used to carry out a bibliometric review on the subject was the Theory of the Consolidated Meta Analytical Approach - TEMAC, which allows the integration between the current demands of the literature about scientific works with a view to precision, validity, functionality (Mariano & Rocha, 2017).

As for research preparation, the construction of the research string was carried out, based on words that reflected the theme, involving expressions related to remote teaching during the COVID-19 pandemic, the use of m-learning and the time frame of 5 years, as shown in table 1.

Table 1. Search string

Base de dados	String
SCOPUS	*TITLE-ABS-KEY(("m-learning" OR "m learning" OR "mlearning" OR "mobile learning") AND ("covid" OR "covid-19" OR "pandemic")) AND (LIMIT-TO (PUBYEAR,2023) OR LIMIT-TO (PUBYEAR,2022) OR LIMIT-TO (PUBYEAR,2021) OR LIMIT-TO (PUBYEAR,2020) OR LIMIT-TO (PUBYEAR,2019))*

Source: authors (2023)

To gather research carried out and related to the topics under discussion in this study, the Scopus database was used, as it is a consolidated and robust base, based on the keywords highlighted in the table above, with the time frame of the last 5 years, from 2019 to 2023. From this query, 314 publications associated with the theme were found, based on a careful analysis considering: number of citations, relevance of the publication to the chosen theme and more recent publications. From the quantitative found, 9 publications were chosen that provide a wide spectrum of information on the subject, including the challenges and potentialities of teaching with the use of m-learning, during remote teaching caused by the COVID-19 pandemic.

The results of this selection, presented in the previous section, allowed the identification of studies that addressed topics similar to the present research, providing scientific evidence and an updated panorama on the application of mobile learning in the teaching-learning process during remote teaching, in addition to providing subsidies for understanding and analyzing the theme in greater depth.

4. REMOTE TEACHING

Despite the challenges and significant educational impacts caused by the COVID-19 pandemic, the biggest pandemic of the 21st century, educational institutions needed to continue to develop ways to (re)invent pedagogical practices to ensure that teaching and learning activities continued despite of the numerous obstacles encountered.

Considering the need for social isolation as a measure to face the global health crisis, the COVID-19 pandemic and the consequent closure of schools, on July 13, 2020, the public education network of the Federal District adopted non-face-to-face teaching alternatives. A little over a year later, on August 5, 2021, based on an escalation scheme, students began to return face-to-face, however, still maintaining hybrid teaching, with face-to-face activities and activities mediated by digital technologies .

For the purpose of checking attendance and learning assessment, the SEEDF adopted as a strategy, for students with internet access, asynchronous activities made available by teachers on the Google Classroom platform and synchronous activities carried out via Google Meet. For students without access to the internet or mobile devices, such as smartphones, tablets and notebooks, printed material was delivered in line with the content available on the platform (DISTRITO FEDERAL, 2020).

According to a UNICEF report (2021) on how municipal education networks in Brazil promoted non-attendance teaching during the year 2020, the most used strategy was the use of printed material (95.3%), followed by by Whatsapp (92.9%), recorded video classes (61.3%), online guidelines by apps (54.0%), educational platforms (22.5%), TV classes (4.1%), radio classes (2.6%) and no remote activities were offered (2.4%).

In the classes in which the study was carried out, 77% of the students used the educational platforms provided by SEEDF, Google Classrrom and Google Meet or carried out activities through Whatsapp and 23% followed the activities proposed by the printed material strategy.

Teaching mediated by digital technologies, as a result of the COVID-19 pandemic, has highlighted and expanded the inequalities of access to formal education, especially for public school students, exposing the difficulty of accessing the internet and the lack of technological devices for monitoring educational proposals and training weaknesses in relation to the use of TDIC's.

However, this reality also provoked a reflection and redefinition about teaching, providing in the educational field, the appearance of educational tools and methodological innovations, which modified and will modify forever the relationship of the school with the use of mobile electronic learning devices, the m-learning.

4.1 Pedagogical Practices for Carrying out Remote Teaching Using M-learning

The pedagogical activities presented concern, in general, the practice of the two teachers in which the research was carried out, considering that they carried out the planning and execution of activities together, due to the proximity of the students regarding the needs regarding understanding about alphabetic writing. The variations were punctual, however the proposals presented here contemplate the practice of the two teachers.

The alphabetic writing system is a system that represents the sound chains of speech by graphic signs, that is, the representation of speech sounds with the letters of the alphabet. The appropriation of the alphabetic writing system requires the internalization of the rules and conventions of the alphabet, it is necessary to understand the properties of the alphabet as a notational system (Morais, 2012; Soares, 2021).

As highlighted by Soares (2021), the appropriation of this system is a complex process, which requires interaction between cognitive and linguistic processes, in addition to learning carried out systematically and explicitly in the school environment. From the dialogue between development and learning, mediated by someone more experienced, whether a teacher or peers in the social, cultural and school context in which the child's development takes place (Vigotsky, 2007).

Based on strategies that could be attractive, effective and based on digital technologies for students to interact with, such as the use of digital games, YouTube videos and interactive story channels, with a view to advancing students in terms of the alphabetic writing system, practices Pedagogical practices developed with the use of m-learning demanded that the teachers, from the classes in which the research was developed, reinvent their practices from spaces and resources of multimodal communication. Multimodal communication is defined by the different modes that allow for interaction based on semiotic resources in the design of a product (Ribeiro, 2021).

In view of this, the challenge posed to teachers of literacy classes was regarding the realization and effectiveness of this complex process without face-to-face interaction, based on teaching with the use of m-learning.

The specificities experienced by these teachers during remote teaching were complex and challenging, considering that they had to manage multifaceted learning environments with the use of m-learning, with their own technological infrastructure and without having had support regarding training for the use of strategies and methodologies for this teaching.

The use of screens and information and communication technologies influence reading and writing practices and social and communication behaviors (Ribeiro, 2021), mainly due to the COVID-19 pandemic, however, it is worth highlighting, regarding the locus of this research in literacy classes, that the situation of literacy teachers was perhaps one of the most challenging, due to the age of the students (approximately 6 and 7 years old.), which required constant assistance from those responsible for the participation and execution of the proposals and the the fact that the students are not literate, which also reduces their autonomy when using commands that require reading and writing.

In addition, the planning of activities should be satisfactory for students who did not have the opportunity to participate in these proposals, but who should also have their rights to the same learning guaranteed.

Bearing in mind that this change in the educational environment requires a change in teaching methodologies, based on learning supported by new technologies, the teachers carried out different educational proposals during classes, which took place synchronously through Google Meet (three times a week). And asynchronously through the Google Classroom platform or via Whastapp with the posting of a file, in PDF format, which began with a page organizing the students' weekly routine (with the themes that would be addressed in that period), followed by the weekly activities (organized by day and theme).

Lima and Isotani (2021), regarding the use of Google Classroom, point out that this platform is more effective if combined with other learning platforms such as Google Meet or Whatsapp and that the emerging obstacles of Google Classroom indicate emphasis on teaching methods, which must be adapted to this teaching environment.

The authors' statement reinforces the work that was already being developed by these teachers, who adapted the teaching methodologies to the context of remote teaching, and even combined with the use of Google Classroom, used other learning tools such as Google Meet and Whatsapp as a possibility to increase students' access to education.

About the activities aimed at learning alphabetic writing, in Google Meet, classes were carried out from some supports such as youtube (with the presentation of videos, stories and songs), canva (with the presentation of stories and contents using characteristics of communication digital technology such as the use of interactive images and emojis), Google Jamboard (which the teachers used to make specific explanations about a certain subject, such as getting children to reflect on the graphic similarities of words that share the same sound). In addition, at times the teachers used strategies in which Meet was the means of interaction and communication, for example with the performance of games and virtual dynamics involving, in an interdisciplinary way, the study of alphabetic writing with object hunting at home (from of the initial sounds of the words or some other similarity), presentation of objects that started with the studied letter, production of collective text.

The teachers made use of the available resources and at times tried to adapt practices used in face-to-face teaching, without measuring efforts towards the desired, that the children reached the end of the 1st year, despite the remote teaching, having understood the alphabetic writing system and have arrived at the alphabetical hypothesis of writing (Morais, 2012).

The weekly activities file was sent via Google Classroom, posted on the platform on Mondays and should be returned, with the proposed activities carried out on Fridays. This was a material planned and constructed by the teachers on a weekly basis. Based on the students' advances and difficulties, the teachers planned the proposals for the following week. Furthermore, bearing in mind the specificities of the use of m-learning in literacy classes, the material was proposed considering the digital medium, consisting of hyperlinks that directed the student to videos, stories, educational games, music and pages of curiosities. These weekly activities dialogued with the classes developed on Google Meet.

Students without access to the internet and mobile devices to follow the synchronous and asynchronous proposals, received the material with the same proposals and contents contemplated in the realization in digital media, but with the restructuring of the material contemplating the methodological change that the realization in the paper support requires. The activities were carried out without the help of the teacher, considering that the only form of communication was the digital medium and these students did not have access.

5. DISCUSSIONS

In order to analyze the students' learning results regarding the learning process of the Alphabetic Writing System towards the appropriation of alphabetic writing, we focused our attention on the considerations made about the diagnoses regarding the students' level regarding the comprehension of writing carried out in two moments of the learning path.

The pedagogical practices developed by the teachers with a view to the students' advancement in relation to learning alphabetic writing were based on carrying out an initial diagnostic assessment of the students' level regarding writing comprehension, carried out at the beginning of the semester, based on the psychogenesis of the language writing proposed by Emília Ferreiro and Ana Teberosky (1985).

To carry out the evaluation, the teachers used their own means to contact students and families, via Whatsapp or via Google Meet. Whatsapp presented the feature of being an application already installed on most smartphones and, according to reports from family members, being more practical for users. This strategy was used with students who had mobile devices and internet access, with those who did not have the resources to carry it out, given the need for social distancing, the diagnosis was not carried out in the 1st semester.

Starting from the initial diagnostic evaluation of the students' writing, carried out at the beginning of the 1st semester, the teachers planned their classes and guided their practices. At the end of the semester, after carrying out the educational proposals and with a view to planning the 2nd semester, the teachers carried out a final diagnostic evaluation, through which it was possible to analyze the students' advances in relation to alphabetic writing.

Graph 1 presents data about the progress of students in relation to the writing hypothesis of those who had access to mobile technologies, such as cell phones, tablets and notebooks to enable the teaching-learning process mediated by technology. In the graph, the students' writing hypothesis levels are presented in an increasing way towards alphabetical writing.

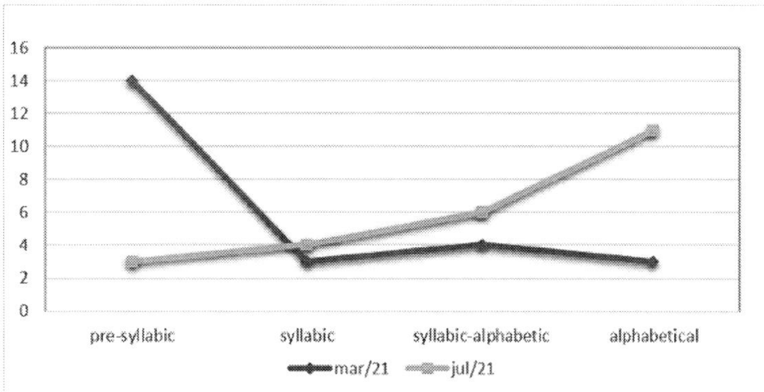

Source: authors (2023)

Graph 1. Evolution of writing levels

Students who used printed material did not have access to the internet, so it was impossible to carry out the diagnostic test, but with the hybrid return, in the second half of 2021, it was observed that these students were in a pre-syllabic hypothesis in relation to to writing, demonstrating the importance of equal access and permanence in school and the fragility of any educational proposal without proper teacher intervention.

6. CONCLUSION

Remote teaching and the educational conditions imposed by the COVID-19 pandemic, in the reality of public schools in Brazil, highlighted and widened the inequalities of conditions of access and permanence in formal education, especially for those in situations of greater social vulnerability.

As for the results of learning with the use of m-learning in literacy classes, the data presented reveal that students who were able to access and remain in remote teaching, showed significant advances in terms of learning towards alphabetic writing. In this way, activities mediated by educational tools such as Google Classroom, Google Meet and the use of student interaction platforms such as the use of digital games and presentation of videos, music and interactive stories, among many other factors, demonstrate the potential of m-learning, with the necessary interventions and pedagogical mediations.

The students who did not have the opportunity to participate in the remote proposals and had their teaching mediated by printed material, without pedagogical assistance, presented the level of comprehension of writing in the first hypothesis, pre-syllabic, at the end of the semester, making it even more The inequalities caused by the pandemic scenario are evident, especially regarding access to education. Thus, it is worth noting that access to the online teaching-learning process is still a matter of concern, due to the difficulty for students to access the internet and the lack of technological devices to monitor educational proposals, such as computers or smartphones, and the weaknesses training in relation to the use of TDIC's.

Regarding the role of teachers during remote teaching, it is worth highlighting the results achieved regarding the appropriation of the alphabetic writing system, which were only possible due to the interventions and planning of educational proposals carried out by literacy teachers with the use of m-learning, ratifying the essential and irreplaceable character of the work of these professionals, who reinvented their practices and methodologies based on the demands imposed on them by remote teaching, even without the training, technical and financial apparatus of educational institutions.

The data presented reflect a specific reality of the locus of this research, therefore, they cannot be generalized, however, as highlighted in this study and based on the studies related to it, teaching mediated by m-learning can be considered as a modality of high potential, among other factors, if it is accessible to all. In addition, it is necessary for teachers to receive adequate training in the use of educational technologies, which did not happen during remote teaching.

ACKNOWLEDGEMENT

The authors are grateful for the support of the University of Brasília, Faculty of Education, in particular the support of the Graduate Program in Professional Master's Education, as well as the Faculty of Technology, Laboratory of Decision-Making Technologies.

REFERENCES

Andre, M. E. D. A. (2012). *Etnografia da prática escolar*. Papirus.

Barletta, V. S., Cassano, F., Marengo, A., Pagano, A., Pange, J., & Piccinno, A. (2022). *Switching learning methods during the pandemic:* A quasi-experimental study on a master course. Applied Sciences (Basel, Switzerland), 12(17), 8438. https://doi.org/10.3390/app12178438

Chibisa, A., & Mutambara, D. (2022). *Determinants of high school learners' continuous use of mobile learning during the Covid-19 pandemic.* International Journal of Learning Teaching and Educational Research, 21(3), 1–21. https://doi.org/10.26803/ijlter.21.3.1

Criollo-C, S., Guerrero-Arias, A., Jaramillo-Alcázar, Á., & Luján-Mora, S. (2021). *Mobile learning technologies for education: Benefits and pending issues.* Applied Sciences (Basel, Switzerland), 11(9), 4111. https://doi.org/10.3390/app11094111

Ferreiro, E., & Teberosky, A. (1985). *Psicogênese da língua escrita.* Porto Alegre: Artes Médicas.

Governo do Distrito Federal Secretaria de Estado de Educação. (2020). *Gestão Estratégica para a Realização das Atividades Pedagógicas Não Presenciais no Distrito Federal.* Agência Brasília. https://agenciabrasilia.df.gov.br/2020/05/20/educacao-promove-debate-sobre-plano-de-volta-as-aulas/

Lima, D. A., & Isotani, S. (2021). *Constraints, effectiveness and solutions in using Google Classroom as a Learning Management System during Covid-19 pandemic: a systematic literature review.* 2021 XVI Latin American Conference on Learning Technologies (LACLO).

Morais, A. G. (2012). *Sistema de Escrita Alfabética: como eu ensino*. Melhoramentos.

Saikat, S., Dhillon, J. S., Wan Ahmad, W. F., & Jamaluddin, R. A. (2021). *A systematic review of the benefits and challenges of mobile learning during the COVID-19 pandemic.* Education Sciences, 11(9), 459. https://doi.org/10.3390/educsci11090459

Soares, M. (2021). *Alfaletrar: toda criança pode aprender a ler e a escrever*. Contexto.

Undime. (2021). *Undime apresenta "Pesquisa Volta às Aulas 2021" em coletiva de imprensa*. Undime. https://undime.org.br/noticia/12-03-2021-20-36-undime-apresenta-pesquisa-volta-as-aulas-2021-em-coletiva-de-imprensa

UNICEF. (2021). *Cenário da Exclusão Escolar no Brasil: Um alerta sobre os impactos da pandemia da COVID-19 na Educação.*

Mahanta, S., & Sharma, R. C. (2022). *Challenges, prospects, and strategies of emergency online education at secondary level in the Assam state of India during COVID-19 pandemic.* Education & Self Development, 17(4), 34–51. https://doi.org/10.26907/esd.17.4.04

Mariano, A. M., & Rocha, M. S. (2017). *Revisão da Literatura: Apresentação de uma Abordagem Integradora.* XXVI Congreso Internacional de la Academia Europea de Dirección y Economía de la Empresa (AEDEM), v. 26, n. 427–443.

Ribeiro, A.E. (2021). *Multimodalidade, textos e tecnologias: provocações para a sala de aula.* Parábola.

Silva, F. T. (2022). *Gestão, política curricular e algumas lições de um Brasil pandêmico: Reflexões a partir da pedagogia histórico-crítica.* Revista on Line de Política e Gestão Educacional, e022105. https://doi.org/10.22633/rpge.v26iesp.4.17119

Vigotsky, L.S. (2007). *A formação social da mente: o desenvolvimento dos processos psicológicos superiores*. Martins Fontes.

Zhonggen, Y., & Xiaozhi, Y. (2019). A*n extended technology acceptance model of a mobile learning technology.* Computer Applications in Engineering Education, 27(3), 721–732. https://doi.org/10.1002/cae.22111

CONSTRUCTING A STUDENT ENGAGEMENT AND LEARNING DEVELOPMENT MODEL IN MOBILE LEARNING BY SEM

Shu-Jing Wu[1], Feng-Lan Liu[2], Yan-Yu Xu[2], Tin-Chang Chang[3] and Zeng-Han Lee[4]
[1]*Guangzhou Institute of Science and Technology, China*
No.638, Xingtai 3rd Road, Taihe, Baiyun District, Guangzhou, Guangdong, P.R. China
[2]*School of Education Science, Nanning Normal University, China*
No. 175, East Mingxiu Road, Nanning, Guangxi, P.R. China
[3]*Department of Business Administration, Asia University, Taiwan*
Department of Business Administration, Asia University, 41 354 Taichung, Taiwan
[4]*Minnan Normal University, China*
No. 36, Qianzhi Street, Xiangcheng District, Zhangzhou City, Fujian, P.R. China

ABSTRACT

This study aimed to build a model to detect the factors to enhance student engagement and learning development in mobile learning during the COVID-19 Pandemic. Data from a total of 400 junior-high-school students were collected in China in the fall semester of 2020, and a large proportion of students preferred accessing their study with cellphones (67.0%) than with computers (11.8%), laptops (11.3%) or pads (10.0%). Exploratory factor analysis and structural equation modeling (SEM) were used for data analysis. The fitness of the items for each scale of the student engagement and learning development indicated a sufficient fit ($\chi^2_{(19)} = 41.252$, GIF = 0.974, AGFI = 0.951, CFI = 0.986, RMSEA = 0.054, NNFI = 0.979, IFI = 0.986). The results of SEM analysis show that emotional engagement is the most important factor ($r^2 = 0.859$) in the model, and student engagement has a significant positive impact on learning development in mobile learning. The findings of this study provide a good reference for enhancing student engagement or fostering students' learning development in mobile learning.

KEYWORDS

Mobile Learning, Student Engagement, Learning Development, Junior High School, COVID-19 Pandemic, Structural Equation Modeling (SEM)

1. INTRODUCTION

COVID-19 has resulted in schools being shut all across the world since 2020. While countries are at different points in their COVID-19 infection rates, worldwide there are currently more than 1.2 billion children in 186 countries affected by school closures due to the pandemic (UNESCO, 2021). Due to school closures and learning loss across the world, the use of technology in online education has exploded all over the world. In response to significant demand during the COVID-19 pandemic, many mobile learning platforms are offering free access to their services, including platforms such as Alibaba's distance learning solution, DingTalk, Cloud Class, etc. With this sudden shift away from the classroom in many parts of the globe, whether the adoption of mobile learning will continue to persist post-pandemic, and how such a shift would impact worldwide education will be an imperative issue in education research.

[4]Corresponding author: Zenghan88@gmail.com

2. LITERATURE REVIEW

2.1 Student Engagement in Mobile Learning

For most students, engagement can positively predict students' academic achievement and provide an excellent theoretical framework for predicting learning performance. Previous studies defined student engagement as a relevant and multidimensional conception with good construction that reflects the level of academic motivation (Skinner & Belmont, 1993), a concept that requires psychological connections within the academic environment (Chapman, 2003; Furlong et al., 2003; Kuh, 2001), or the concept classified into behavioral, emotional, and cognitive dimensions (Fredericks, Blumenfeld, & Paris, 2004; Jimerson, Campos, & Greif, 2003).

Behavioral engagement indicates to what extent learners engage in learning based on their behavior in learning activities which show positive associations with course achievement and completion (Kahan et al., 2017). Emotional engagement refers to learners' perceptions of their learning in mobile learning, such as their course satisfaction, perceptions of learning experiences, and benefits (Post et al., 2019). Cognitive engagement refers to a knowledge test, of which quizzes, assignments, tests, examinations, surveys, self-assessments, discussion forums, exercises, essays, labs, and writing projects were employed to assess the intellectual skills that learners acquired in mobile learning (Chiu & Hew, 2018; Krasny et al., 2018).

2.2 Learning Development

It is encouraged to cultivate students' core competences (2009) and to promote the high-level competences in educational settings. The high-level competences are classified into five dimensions as collaboration (Chuang et al., 2012; Huang et al., 2012), communication (Lan et al., 2012), complex problem solving (Hung et al., 2012a; Hwang et al., 2014), critical thinking (Hung et al., 2012b; Kuo et al., 2012), and creativity (Wu et al., 2013). Several studies have further signified the positive impacts of incorporating mobile technologies into school curriculums on students' higher-order thinking performances, such as their problem-solving, critical thinking and creativity (Kim et al. 2015; Kong and Song 2014). According to Hwang's study, students' engagement in communication and collaboration are important mediators between their technology preferences and higher-order thinking tendency (e.g., problem-solving, critical thinking, and creativity)(Hwang, et al., 2018). The performance of these competences could be regarded as a reference for measuring high-level learning development.

2.3 Mobile Learning

Mobile learning refers to a learning context in which learners utilize their individual portable devices to access a mobile network to conduct their learning, whether in or out of the classroom (Song, 2014).With the rapid advancement and popularity of mobile technology, researchers have further indicated using mobile technology to support learning could be an effective learning mode for facilitating student-centered learning (Chang, et al., 2011). This study addresses students studying remotely, specifically handheld devices. The connection between engagement and mobile devices is confirmed by 88.2% of the sample in this study.

3. METHODOLOGY

A students' self-reporting opinion survey collected in the fall semester of 2020 regarding student engagement and high-level competences development in mobile learning was developed as a quantitative measure. The data analysis in this study has been shown to be a flexible and powerful means of examining the relationships among constructs. This study developed nine hypotheses regarding junior-high-school students' engagement and learning development in mobile learning. The Theoretical framework is as shown in Figure 1.

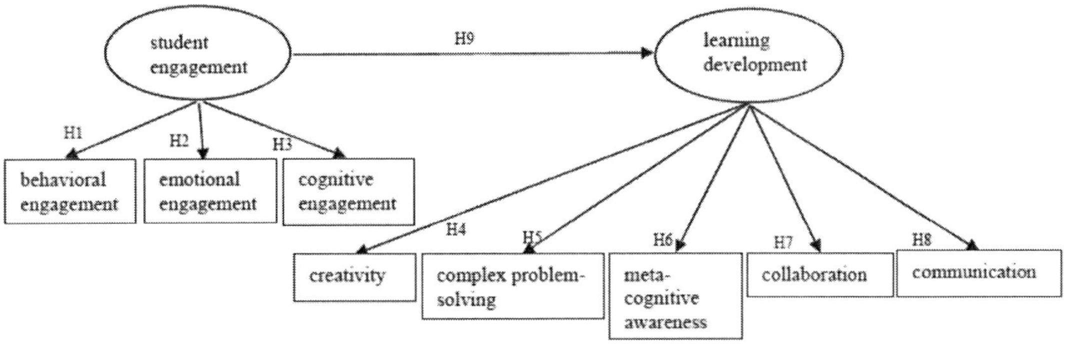

Figure 1. Theoretical framework of student engagement and learning development

3.1 Participants

The survey sample was a non-probability sample of convenience, consisting of eight junior high schools in Nanning City, Guangxi, China. The ranking of the schools was around the average. A total of 400 junior high school students (14.0 years old on average), including 193 males (48.3%) and 207 females (51.8%), 142 (35.5%) 1st grade, 131 (32.8%) 2nd grade, and 127 (31.8%) 3rd grade, were surveyed. The responses of the learning equipment used in mobile learning indicated that a large proportion of students preferred accessing with cellphones (67.0%) than with computers (11.8%), laptops (11.3%) or pads (10.0%). The return rate was approximately 83%. Ethical approval clearance and informed consent clearance were granted due to the use of anonymous questionnaires.

3.2 Instruments

To achieve the research objectives, a survey consisting of two dimensions, learning engagement and high-level competences, was adopted to measure the students' perceptions. All of the items in the questionnaire were presented using a 5-point Likert scale, ranging from 1 - *strongly disagree* to 5 - *strongly agree*.

The aspect of student engagement consisted of three scales: behavioral engagement (BE), emotional engagement (EE), and cognitive engagement (CE), with seven, seven, and six items, respectively. Behavioral engagement included basic behaviors such as participation, motivation, and support from teachers. Emotional engagement refers to the students' attitudes towards mobile learning. Cognitive engagement values the learning outcomes that assess multidimensional students' perceptions of mobile learning.

In addition, the learning development measure was developed by Lai and Hwang (2014), which was modified from the surveys cited as follows: (1) Creativity represents the creative tendencies of the students; creativity (CRE) was modified from the Creativity Assessment Packet (Lin & Wang, 1994). (2) Complex problem solving represents the students' ability when they are solving problems; complex problem solving (CPS) was modified from the problem-solving questionnaire by Pan (2001). (3) Meta-cognitive awareness is for assessing the students' metacognition when they are learning; meta-cognitive awareness (MCA) was developed based on metacognitive awareness (Schraw & Dennison, 1994). (4) Collaboration represents the students' experience of collaborating with others; collaboration (COL) was modified from the knowledge integration capability survey developed by Jeng and Tang (2004). (5) Communication represents the interactions when students communicate with others. Communication (COM) was revised from the Communicative Adaptability Scale (Duran, 1992).

3.3 Data Analysis

With the statistical software of SPSS and AMOS, the exploratory factor analysis and confirmative factor analysis were utilized to identify the structure of each survey. Variable difference was examined by exploratory factor analysis and SEM. The Structural Equation Modeling (SEM) was implemented to determine the relationship of each source of student engagement on learning development. The results determined the magnitude and consistency of any relations.

4. RESULTS

4.1 Exploratory Factor Analysis of Student Engagement and Learning Development

To validate the questionnaire of student engagement and learning development, exploratory factor analysis (EFA) with varimax rotation was performed to clarify the structure. According to the results of EFA of student engagement, the participants' responses were grouped into three factors: behavioral engagement (BE), emotional engagement (EE), and cognitive engagement (CE). Hair et al. (2006) noted that an item is remarkable if its factor loading is greater than 0.50. The factor loadings of all the items in the measure range from 0.654 to 0.836, thus meeting the threshold (0.50), and demonstrating convergent validity at the item level. The Cronbach's alpha coefficients for the factors were .87, .89 and .87, with 56.09%, 61.27%, 60.31% of variance explained, respectively, the overall alpha was .94, and the total variance explained was 60.46%. The KMO value was 0.939, and the Bartlett χ^2-value was 4474.127 (p<0.000), as shown in Table 1, suggesting that these factors have highly acceptable reliability for assessing student engagement.

Table 1. Rotated factor loadings, Cronbach's alpha values, item means, and standard deviations for the three factors of student engagement

Items	Factor 1	Factor 2	Factor 3
Factor 1: behavioral engagement (BE), α = .87, mean = 3.47, *SD* = 0.72			
BE_1	0.755		
BE_2	0.777		
BE_3	0.749		
BE_4	0.654		
BE_5	0.762		
BE_6	0.799		
BE_7	0.737		
Factor 2: emotional engagement (EE), α = .89, mean = 4.37, *SD* = 0.71			
EE_1		0.815	
EE_2		0.836	
EE_3		0.806	
EE_4		0.818	
EE_5		0.740	
EE_6		0.736	
EE_7		0.720	
Factor 3: cognitive engagement (CE), α = .87, mean = 3.69, *SD* = 0.71			
CE_1			0.826
CE_2			0.805
CE_3			0.785
CE_4			0.743
CE_5			0.734
CE_6			0.762
% of variance	56.09%	61.27%	60.31%

Note. loading less than 0.50 omitted, N = 400, overall α = .94, total variance explained is 60.46%.

According to the results of EFA of learning development, the participants' responses were grouped into five factors: creativity (CRE), complex problem-solving (CPS), meta-cognitive awareness (MCA), collaboration (COL), and communication (COM). The factor loadings of all the items in the measure range from 0.665 to 0.854, thus meeting the threshold (0.50), and demonstrating convergent validity at the item level. The Cronbach's alpha coefficients for the factors were .86, .85, .86, .82 and .85, with 64.42%, 63.19%, 64.60%, 58.86%, 62.63% of variance explained, respectively, the overall alpha was .92, and the total variance explained was 64.35%. The KMO value was 0.919, and the Bartlett χ^2-value was 5266.870 (p<0.000), suggesting that these factors have highly acceptable reliability for assessing the learning development.

Table 2. Rotated factor loadings, Cronbach's alpha values, item means, and standard deviations for the five factors of learning development

Items	Factor 1	Factor 2	Factor 3	Factor 4	Factor 5
Factor 1: creativity (CRE), α = .86, mean = 3.69, *SD* = 0.82					
CRE_1	0.693				
CRE_2	0.820				
CRE_3	0.841				
CRE_4	0.828				
CRE_5	0.822				
Factor 2: complex problem-solving (CPS), α = .85, mean = 3.79, *SD* = 0.70					
CPS_1		0.751			
CPS_2		0.797			
CPS_3		0.819			
CPS_4		0.813			
CPS_5		0.791			
Factor 3: meta-cognitive awareness (MCA), α = .86, mean = 3.64, *SD* = 0.73					
MCA_1			0.775		
MCA_2			0.803		
MCA_3			0.817		
MCA_4			0.852		
MCA_5			0.768		
Factor 4: collaboration (COL), α = .82, mean = 3.58, *SD* = 0.71					
COL_1				0.794	
COL_2				0.810	
COL_3				0.668	
COL_4				0.756	
COL_5				0.798	
Factor 5: communication (COM), α = .85, mean = 3.89, *SD* = 0.72					
COM_1					0.768
COM_2					0.665
COM_3					0.854
COM_4					0.846
COM_5					0.809
% of variance	64.42%	63.19%	64.60%	58.86%	62.63%

Note. loading less than 0.50 omitted, $N = 400$, overall α = .92, total variance explained is 64.35%.

4.2 Results of SEM

The results of SEM, along with the recommended values for the common model fit, and the suggested saturated and independence models, are shown in Table 3. Most of the model-fit indices exceed their respective common acceptance levels suggested by previous research, thus demonstrating that the default measurement model exhibits a good fit with the data collected ($\chi^2_{(19)} = 41.252$, GIF = 0.974, AGFI = 0.951, CFI = 0.986, RMSEA = 0.054, NNFI = 0.979, IFI = 0.986), as shown in Table 8. This implies that the suggested model is a good fit.

The paths from the behavioral engagement, emotional engagement, and cognitive engagement factors to student engagement showed significant difference. As expected, the results support H1, H2, and H3. The result reveals that emotional engagement is the most important factor ($r^2 = 0.859$), with 85.9% variance explained, then behavioral engagement ($r^2 = 0.811$), with 81.1% variance explained, and cognitive engagement ($r^2 = 0.807$), with 80.7% variance explained in the model. In the meantime, as expected, the results support H4, H5, H6, H7 and H8. The result reveals that communication is the most important factor ($r^2 = 0.827$), with 82.7% variance explained, then meta-cognitive awareness ($r^2 = 0.741$), with 74.1% variance explained, complex problem-solving ($r^2 = 0.735$), with 73.5% variance explained, collaboration ($r^2 = 0.730$), with 73.0% variance explained, and creativity ($r^2 = 0.415$), with 41.5% variance explained in the model.

There is also a significant path from student engagement to learning development. According to the standardized regression coefficient ($r^2 = 0.830$), and the Criteria Ratio (C.R.) = 7.648 > 3.29, $p < 0.01$, 83.0% of variance explained, it means that the correlation between student engagement and learning development is fairly high. As expected, the results support H9. It is confirmed that the standardized coefficients show high validity and reliability by SEM. Student engagement has a direct effect on learning development in the model, as shown in Figure 2.

Table 3. Fit indices for structural and independence models

Fit indices	Recommended	Default_m	Saturated_m	Independence_m
		Model fit summary		
χ^2/df	$\leq$ 3.00	2.171	-	56.954
GIF	$\geq$ 0.80	0.974	1.0	0.354
AGFI	$\geq$ 0.80	0.951	-	0.169
CFI	$\geq$ 0.90	0.986	1.0	0.000
RMSEA	$\leq$ 0.1	0.054	-	0.374
NNFI	$\geq$ 0.90	0.979	-	-
IFI	$\geq$ 0.90	0.986	1.0	0.000
AIC (relative)	smaller	75.252	72.000	1610.712

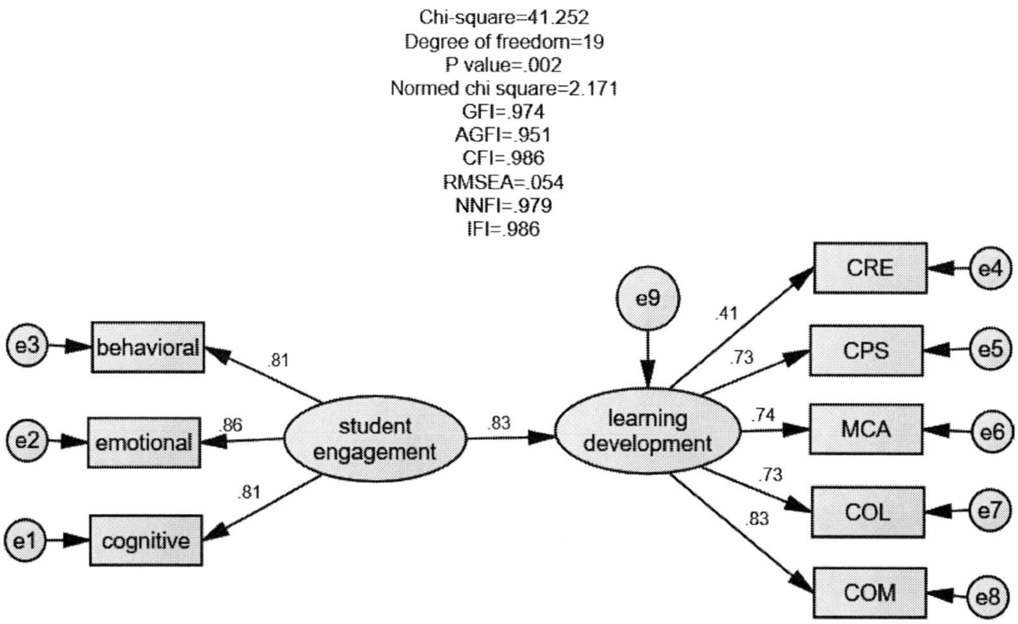

Note. The figure shows standardized path coefficients; $p < 0.05$.

Figure 2. Paths of student engagement to high-level competences development in mobile learning

5. CONCLUSION

5.1 Educational Implications

The pandemic has brought about a paradigm shift in education which has resulted in new modes of educational delivery and new learning processes. While the pandemic and the extended school closures in 2020 have changed students' learning methods and habits, a comprehensive measure is required for monitoring and support to ensure students' learning outcomes.

According to the exploratory factor analysis in this study, the questionnaire showed good reliability for assessing student engagement and learning development. The item means and standard deviations for student engagement showed that the degree of students engaged in mobile learning was quite high, which implied that they commonly recognized the value of mobile learning during the COVID-19 pandemic. However, behavioral engagement had a lower mean than the other factors, which implied that some students had poor self-regulation and had trouble concentrating on lectures in mobile learning. As Barnard et al. (2009) advocated that the mobile learning environment is characterized by autonomy, self-regulation becomes a critical factor for success in mobile learning.

It was confirmed that the standardized coefficients show high validity and reliability by SEM in this study. The fitness of the items for each scale of the student engagement survey and learning development survey indicated a sufficient fit and also confirmed the questionnaire's structure. The SEM analysis shows that student engagement has a significant positive impact on learning development in mobile learning. The SEM results provided a valuable reference that student engagement is critical to determining how students perceive mobile learning and their learning development.

5.2 Implications for Research and Practice

This study contributes to our understanding of the effect of student engagement in mobile learning on learning development in junior high schools. Bozkurt et al. (2015) addressed that mobile learning is no longer peripheral or supplementary, but rather has become an integral part of mainstream society. An understanding of junior high school students' engagement in this study can provide references for improving the efficiency of students' learning development and adjusting teachers' teaching approaches. As engagement is an important factor affecting students' efficient learning and academic achievement, it directly affects the learners' learning results and learning effectiveness (Authors, 2021). An essential conclusion of this study is that teachers or developers must design mobile learning environments to match not only the expectations of the students but their engagement and competences development as well.

5.3 Limitations and Suggestions for Future Research

First, this study focused only on a special population of junior-high-school students in China. Discretion must be exercised in extending the results to other disciplines. Second, this study was an exploratory study of how student engagement affects learning development in mobile learning, but it provides little discussion on the arrangement of mobile learning platforms or system management. Third, whereas measuring methods of engagement by questionnaires have several strengths, they also have limitations, including the difficulty of interpretation without additional contextual information. In addition, the resulting model has not been compared with any other similar model, which makes it difficult to use the results in practice to improve learning and teaching processes. It is suggested that more models be constructed in mobile learning settings to improve learning and teaching designs for future research. The findings of this study could be a good reference for those who intend to develop a specific topic of learning on technology for enhancing student engagement or fostering students' learning development.

REFERENCES

Bozkurt, A., et al., 2015. Trends in Distance Education Research: A Content Analysis of Journals 2009-2013. *International Review of Research in Open and Distributed Learning*, Vol. *16*, No. 1, pp. 330–363.

Chang, C. S., et al., 2011. The Study on Integrating WebQuest with Mobile Learning for Environmental Education. *Computers & Education*, Vol. 57, No. 1, pp. 1228–1239.

Chapman, E., 2003. Alternative Approaches to Assessing Student Engagement Rates. *Practical Assessment, Research and Evaluation*, Vol. 13, No. 8, pp. 1-7.

Chiu, T. K. F., and Hew, T. K. F., 2018. Factors Influencing Peer Learning and Performance in MOOC Asynchronous Online Discussion Forum. *Australasian Journal of Educational Technology*, Vol. 34, No. 4, p. 16.

Chuang, P. J., et al., 2012. Social Networks-based Adaptive Pairing Strategy for Cooperative Learning. *Educational Technology & Society*, Vol. 15, No. 3, pp. 226–239.

Fredericks, J. A., et al., 2004. School Engagement: Potential of the Concept, State of the Evidence. *Review of Educational Research*, Vol. 74, pp. 59-109.

Furlong, M. J., et al., 2003. Multiple Contexts of School Engagement: Moving toward a Unifying Framework for Educational Research and Practice. *California School Psychologist*, Vol. 8, pp. 99-114.

Hair, J. F., et al., 2006. *Multivariate Data Analysis* (6th ed.). New Jersey, NJ: Prentice-Hall International.

Huang, H. W., et al., 2012. The Effectiveness of Using Procedural Scaffoldings in a Paper-plus-smartphone Collaborative Learning Context. *Computers & Education*, Vol. 59, No. 2, pp. 250–259.

Hung, C. M., et al., 2012a. A Project-based Digital Storytelling Approach for Improving Students' Learning Motivation, Problem-solving Competence and Learning Achievement. *Educational Technology & Society*, Vol. 15, No. 4, pp. 368–379.

Hung, P. H., et al., 2012b. A Concept-map Integrated Dynamic Assessment System for Improving Ecology Observation Competences in Mobile Learning Activities. *Turkish Online Journal of Educational Technology*, Vol. 11, No. 1, pp. 10–19.

Hwang, G. J., et al., 2014. Improving Learning Achievements, Motivations and Problem-solving Skills Through a Peer Assessment-based Game Development Approach. *Educational Technology Research and Development*, Vol. 62, No. 2, pp. 129–145.

Hwang, G. J., et al., 2018. A long-term experiment to investigate the relationships between high school students' perceptions of mobile learning and peer interaction and higher-order thinking tendencies. *Education Tech Research Dev*, Vol. 66, pp. 75-93.

Jimerson, S. R., et al., 2003. Toward an understanding of definitions and measures of school engagement and related terms. *California School Psychologist*, Vol. 8, pp. 7-27.

Kahan, T., et al., 2017. Types of Participant Behavior in a Massive Open Online Course. *International Review of Research in Open and Distance Learning*, Vol. 18, No. 6, pp. 1–18.

Kuh, G. D. (2001). Assessing What Really Matters to Student Learning: Inside the National Survey of Student Engagement. *Change*, Vol. 33, No. 3, pp. 10-17, 66.

Kuo, F. R., et al., 2012. A Hybrid Approach to Promoting Students' Web-based Problem-solving Competence and Learning Attitude. *Computers & Education*, Vol. 58, No. 1, pp. 351–364.

Lai, C. L. and Hwang, G. J., 2014. Effects of Mobile Learning Time on Students' Conception of Collaboration, Communication, Complex Problem-solving, Meta-cognitive Awareness and Creativity. *Int. J. Mobile Learning and Organisation*, Vol. 8, No. 3/4, pp. 276–291.

Lan, Y. F., et al., 2012. Comparing the Social Knowledge Construction Behavioral Patterns of Problem-based Online Asynchronous Discussion in E/m-learning Environments. *Computers & Education*, Vol. 59, No. 4, pp. 1122–1135.

Partnership for 21st century skills. (2009). *Museums, libraries, and 21st century skills*. Washington, DC: Institute of Museum and Library Services.

Post, L. S., et al., 2019. Effects of Remote Labs on Cognitive, Behavioral, and Affective Learning Outcomes in Higher Education. *Computers & Education*, Vol. 140. https://doi.org/10.1016/j.compedu.2019.103596

Song, Y. J., 2014. "Bring Your Own Device (BYOD)" for Seamless Science Inquiry in a Primary School. *Computers & Education*, Vol. 74, pp. 50–60.

Tsai, C. C., 2005. Preferences toward Internet-based Learning Environments: High School Students' Perspectives for Science Learning. *Educational Technology & Society*, Vol. 8, No. 2, pp. 203–213.

UNESCO., 2021. *UNESCO's education response to COVID-19*. Paris, France: UNESCO Publishing.

Wu, C. H., et al., 2013. A Mindtool-based Collaborative Learning Approach to Enhancing Students' Innovative Performance in Management Courses. *Australasian Journal of Educational Technology*, Vol. 29, No. 1, pp. 128–142.

Wu, S. J., et al., 2021. An Integrated Model for Exploring College Students' Engagement and Competences Development in Flipped Learning Using Partial Least Squares Path Modeling, *Interactive Learning Environments*, DOI: 10.1080/10494820.2021.1881799

TECHNOLOGY IN THE PERCEPTION OF ENGLISH TEACHERS IN SOUTHERN BRAZIL SCHOOLS

Paula Behenck Machado[1], Patricia Jantsch Fiuza[1] and Graziela Fátima Giacomazzo[2]
[1]Universidade Federal de Santa Catarina - UFSC
Rodovia Governador Jorge Lacerda, 3201 - Urussanguinha, Araranguá/SC – Brazil
[2]Universidade do Extremo Sul Catarinense - UNESC
Avenida Universitária, 1105 - Universitário, Criciúma/SC - Brazil

ABSTRACT

Due to the advance of technologies and the increase of their use around the world, it shows a need to include them in education, as tools that could help the current teaching methods. Taking into account that most English classes in Brazilian public schools have been happening in the same way for many years, and considering the importance of learning a foreign language in this new technological world scenario, the objective of this study, that is part of a Master Degree dissertation, is to understand the perception of Brazilian English teachers in relation to the use of games and digital technologies, in the practice of face to face and remote language teaching classes, in different educational environments. Based on the participation of English teachers in the research stages, it is possible to explore their experiences and points of view, directly related to the English teaching and the use of technologies and digital games. This research collected information through a focus group research method. In this way, it was possible to verify that teachers, together with technologies and digital games, are very important in the classroom and those are extremely important tools to be used in teaching, including English. It was also noticed that keeping learning and qualifications are very important for the updating and practice of teaching. In addition, it was possible to conclude that, through the planning of activities, visualizing the right moment to insert digital games and technologies in their classes, teachers have support tools in these, which will help to engage and motivate students in learning a new language.

KEYWORDS

English Language, English Education, Teaching-Learning, Digital Technology, Digital Games

1. INTRODUCTION

Languages are an integral part of the universal exchange of knowledge. The English language is one of the most needed languages across the world. It is considered the language of international communication and business because it is the official language of many countries, and it is being taught as a foreign/second language all over the world (Menni, 2020).

The English language has always had its importance throughout history, but it was globalization and technology that expanded horizons and brought new opportunities and also urgent needs. The more economies, technologies and societies are intertwined, the more a way to communicate externally is needed. Therefore, the use of English has spread around the world in recent decades, unevenly but incessantly (First, 2021). Today, English is probably the main example of a global language. It is used to communicate in areas such as workplaces, science and technology, arts and business world (Holden; Nobre, 2021). From the 2.5 billion English speakers in the world, only about 400 million have this language as their mother tongue. People are learning English because they realize its importance in different situations. English increases inclusion as it enables professional development and puts people from different backgrounds on the same level (First, 2021).

Much has changed and evolved over time, and the area of education has not been left behind. Approximately a decade ago, Prensky already stated that today's students are no longer the same people our educational system was developed for (PRENSKY, 2010). Then, it is necessary to realize the importance of using new tools to mediate knowledge for these new people. The digital natives, people who were born in the age of knowledge, in order to have meaningful learning, aspirate for a teaching that includes a little of their life realities. Learning a foreign language has become more accessible with the help of technology, which brings to hands several online resources, such as videos, audios and materials to learn wherever you are. With so many enabling devices, the ideal would be to connect what is taught in the classroom with what the world offers digitally.

Given the above and focusing on the importance of learning a second language, it is noticed the necessity to use auxiliary tools capable of encouraging students learning. Therefore, this study proposes a reflection on the current way of teaching English in schools, analyzing the perception of Brazilian English teachers in relation to the use of games and digital technologies, in the practice of language teaching using the focal group method, taking into account the reality of each teacher and technologies available.

Learning a language has become more accessible with the help of technology and, according to Anjos-Santos et al. (2014), the English language and digital technologies have assumed an increasingly important role in the contemporary world. Learning English today has become a fundamental requirement for citizenship. In the same way that the English language has become increasingly present, the use of different digital technologies has been incorporated into the most diverse contemporary social practices (Anjos-Santos; Gamero; Gimenez, 2014).

From this point, considering the English language learning and Technologies, as well as the use of digital games, the focus group method will be explained and how it was done with the participants' teachers.

2. FOCUS GROUP

The focus group is a technique that stimulates and favors the interaction between its participants. This interactivity facilitates the development of studies that seek to understand attitudes, preferences, needs and feelings (ROLOFF, 2021). It is the data collection mechanism based on group discussions focused on a specific topic. The direction, guaranteed by a moderator, must occur in a non-structured and natural way (Duarte, 2007). Another relevant point of this methodological approach is to enrich quantitative research, due to its power to scan issues that, not always, can be measurable numerically (Abreu; Baldanza; Gondim, 2009).

Focus group is defined, therefore, as a joint discussion, between six to twelve participants (maximum number of participants), guided by a moderator/facilitator. The moderator (which in the case of academic research should be the researcher himself) must be able to guide the progress of the discussion in order to respect opinions, avoiding introducing any preconceived ideas (Duarte, 2007).

The social distance resulting from the COVID-19 pandemic has strengthened the already emerging process of virtual connections between people, also bringing implications for conducting research. With the introduction of New Communication and Information Technologies, focal groups began to use virtual rooms. The online focus group is an information gathering method similar to the face-to-face focus group. Its main characteristic is that it is performed in a virtual environment, dispensing with the physical presence of the participants so that there is interaction and consequently communication between them. This differentiation is pointed out as one of the main advantages of online focus groups (Abreu; Baldanza; Gondim, 2009).

The main purpose of this research modality is to extract from the attitudes and responses of the group participants, feelings, opinions and reactions that would result in new knowledge. Through the observation of everyday things, it is possible to see what is hidden, hear what was not said and read what is not written (Gomes, 2005). From this knowledge about focus groups, it is important to explain about the online focus group conducted with the Brazilian teachers.

2.1 Brazilian Teachers Focus Group

When it comes to data collection, the focus group was used as a research resource. This was done through data and information from discussions in the online focus group, carried out with Brazilian English teachers from public and private schools, language schools, university and remote teaching.

In the second semester of 2021, English teachers from Torres, state of Rio Grande do Sul, Brazil, and the region, were contacted to be invited to participate in the online focus group. From all these contacts, a positive response was obtained from ten teachers, who agreed to participate in the focus group. Of these ten respondents, seven of them participated in the focus group: two teachers from a language school, two teachers from public schools - two private online teachers, who have already taught in private and public schools - and one university teacher, who works at the university of a native English speaking country, with experience in national and international language schools and private online classes.

Next is shown the analysis of the focus group results, performed with the teachers, a mediator and the author, responsible for the study. These are organized into three categories: Teaching practices and challenges, use of digital resources in the classroom and teachers' shared experiences, and each category is reasoned with some author's ideas.

2.1.1 Teaching Practices and Challenges

This category addressed how teachers see teaching English in their classes and what their biggest challenges are.

Teacher 1: *teaching, like, it has a lot of positive parts, because I'm not teaching them to speak English, you know, I'm teaching them to write an introduction in English, I'm teaching them to do research and use bibliographic references, etc. So, the difficulty is the issue of the students' English level when they arrive, and another difficulty too, with the pandemic and such, and even before the pandemic as well, it was even a bit of the students' interest. Their motivation is also a difficulty for me here.*

Teacher 2: *A student doesn't want to spare even a little extra time to learn the language, so he/she hopes that magic will happen in the classroom. They need to expose themselves to the language in other environments, at other times, formally and informally, but they don't want that exposure, they say they don't have time, that they can't, that it's a lot, but they want to learn, they want to see the end result, but they don't want to work towards the learning outcome.*

According to Holden and Nobre (2021), what students may not fully realize is that learning a foreign language requires a lot of work and requires practical and memorizing activities, as well as communicative and creative ones. Likewise, learning to play a musical instrument, or to drive a car, also requires extensive student practice.

Teacher 3: *The most nerve-racking point of all, getting the students involved and getting them to understand that it's not magic, there's no miracle, if there's no effort. Learning a language, we know very well that it's not like that, right, it requires time, dedication, so for me, this was and will continue to be the teacher's great challenge, how to involve your students, how to bring all of them, you know, to accomplishing what needs to be done, it's a process, you know, it has stages, everything.*

Widodo (2006, p. 122-141 apud Kurlishchuk, 2016, p. 88-89) reports numerous benefits of using games, such as increasing motivation among shy students who cannot express their feelings or talk in front of other people. By using games, students can be more active, autonomous and energetic, learn about the environment, the world they live in and get involved in the teaching-learning process (Kurlishchuk, 2016).

Teacher 4: *Our methodologies are still very expositive due to the fact that our schools are not equipped, so we don't have an English-only room, we don't have the electrical equipment. These difficulties are crossed by the teaching of the English language, mainly in state schools. There are also several students who arrive throughout the year and as our city is a touristic city, them you are with that group that is already on the way, which has such a level, then a student arrives who don't know anything, you know, several students actually, or who don't like English because of a series of things that happened along their path, you know, at school.*

Granito and Chernobilsky (2012 apud Rad, 2017, p. 9) suggests that inserting different forms of technology can help teachers create enjoyable and motivational classes for students of all levels (Rad, 2017).

Teacher 6: *When we talk about a private course, right, that is extracurricular, we have a slightly higher level of interest, but still with this feeling that it is magical. In the classroom, what I noticed in addition to this issue, you know, wanting everything to happen, the student's lack of interest, there is also the issue of unevenness, so you work with a student who does not know what the verb to be is, and you already have that student who is already doing 5 years of language school and who is super advanced, and you have to make an interesting class for all these levels, right? So I see this as the greatest difficulty in the classroom, this issue of the student's unevenness.*

“In the current educational context, being a teacher has become a challenging issue, since the classes are diverse, each with its own particular characteristics, which requires a more elaborate pedagogical work on the part of the educator. perfection of their practice."(Gomes et al., 2016, p. 90).

Teacher 7: *Despite the dream, if you don't have the motivation, the dream is not enough, you have to have a motivation to learn and this issue of unevenness and we are always afraid of exposing ourselves, of talking about silly things. I think more than the use of technology, that it facilitates some things, you create new*

activities, give this engagement, technology brings these opportunities, but it is not enough, because there is also a factor that I usually say in relation to my students, the experience of their lives.
The use of collaborative technologies is advised to help English learners to participate more actively in their own learning. English students not only learn English, but also acquire more information and knowledge, improve their communication skills, make friends and expand their social contacts using English (Franco-Madrigal, 2016).

Teacher 8: *I deal a lot with the difficulty of working in a school which is considered a school in a neighborhood on the outskirts here in the city, you know, there is a lot of prejudice in the issue of English, of teaching English, they don't think it is important because their reality is very different and I realize that there are few who are really interested in the language, you know. So I realize that we have to create a lot of that affectivity and playing things, if we don't have that, we lose the student, you know.*

Socioeconomic inequality is still an important factor for the lack of meaning of discipline in classrooms. (Trevisan, 2018).

There are still some specific difficulties in relation to the work of English teachers that can be attributed to the use of a traditional methodology, as well as the lack of student awareness regarding the importance of learning a foreign language (Gomes et al., 2016).

It is understood, therefore, that teachers and students face many challenges in terms of teaching and learning English. There is resistance on the part of students to dedicate themselves and practice, as well as a lack of motivation and a sense of learning. To the teachers, the scarcity of materials and resources to try to innovate and involve all students.

2.1.2 Use of Digital Resources in the Classroom

In this category, the use of games and digital technologies in the practice of English language teaching, the importance of these digital tools for teachers, and whether there have been changes, comparing before and during the pandemic, with the use of technology and games.

Teacher 1: *I always liked using games, when I taught English as a second language, but it's something that we have to take care of, too, not to get that pressure of always having to bring a game to the classroom, sometimes you can adapt that goal with a little game. But it is something that is important for us to think that the games are important, they are part of learning, the students end up getting more involved, but it can generate pressure for the teacher. So I think there has to be a little bit of balance, but I agree that games are very important and technology is there to help, right?*

Teacher 2: *One point that I think is that we always need to have a goal, which has also been mentioned, so playing Kahoot just for the sake of playing will not lead anywhere, it will make the student a little more coquettish, but what was the pedagogical objective of that activity? It's valid, but there has to be a dose, so I think we also have to know how to measure each thing, each activity that we do in the classroom, always with a purpose, to feel to know the class, to feel/know the student, then to know the class, there is a class that will do very well with more technological activities and games, another not so much, so I think you also have to know the reality of each student and each class, to know what to offer is very important too.*

Teacher 3: *I work 80% of the time with online, individual classes, so it's a very different thing, the technology I use are video conference platforms. I don't use games much, I use more interaction with students. But from the experience I had while I was a teacher, I remember well that I took the whole transition, I took the issue of technology being introduced, the need, the demands of the students, so I participated a lot in all the stages, the discussions, reality was changing. So if we are in a class with 30 children, 30 teenagers, the challenge is immense and these resources come to help us.*

It is salutary to understand that digital technologies will not replace or diminish the importance of the role and function of the teacher, but rather that they serve as important tools to bring formal education closer to the new generations and expand and intensify the learning process (Cruz, 2021).

Teacher 4: *So, we still use little digital technology in the classroom, we use a lot of technology, in the game that a colleague showed you, you also use the technology to print, to choose images. I have students who are very uneven, just like I have students who know a lot of English, I have students there who know almost nothing, so we have to make the necessary adaptations, I also do a lot of them creating their own games with other groups, organize themselves, learn, you know, so more in that sense that I use technology there.*

According to a study by the British Council, English teachers say that didactic resources are more relevant in teaching their subject than in other subjects. They also state that English is a discipline that requires more playful, collective and interactive activities to generate student engagement and practical involvement with the language. Therefore, teaching resources, especially technological ones, are the main demand of teachers (Council, 2015).

Teacher 5: *As soon as we jumped in there for these online classes, and from day to night we had to find a way, first we had to get on digital platforms, which was not our reality, you had to adapt everything, right, for that environment without ever having studied, thought or imagined that we were going to have to teach classes that way, right, so it was like that, it turns you around, so I wanted to show you something that is zero technological, but it was a crazy success with my students, here I hid the flashcards and the children had to find out what I was showing, so it's really needed.*

Buckingham (2006 apud Cruz, 2021) warns that we need to have the courage to deal with and prepare students (and here we include teachers) for this new world, in which they can be active and critical. The focus on the use of games in learning situations is justified by allowing the development of different skills, such as autonomy, systemic and strategic thinking and problem solving (Cruz, 2021, p.151).

Teacher 6: *When I was a student, technology was that movie on a TV tube they brought and dragged around the whole school until I got to the classroom to watch a movie, in terms of technology, that was it. So, I see it like this, really as a resource, an option that you can use, but it is very dangerous when used without purpose. Because I know that games facilitate the teaching-learning process. Another thing that worries me about the game is the competition. When you are going to make the students compete, I start to think about the anxiety, the frustration, of dealing with losing or winning. So I'm already starting to take this idea away from the competition and go more to the collaborative, to the cooperative.*

The pedagogical use of digital games can go beyond the construction of knowledge in specific areas, treating them not as mere teaching machines, but rather as cultural artifacts, which exist within a context (social, cultural, economic, historical). This implies that, when digital games are used in a pedagogical initiative, the cultural character of these productions should not be ignored (Cruz, 2021, p.151).

Teacher 7: *Before the pandemic I thought I mastered things on the internet, but with the pandemic I realized that there were many resources that I didn't know about. We had the opportunity to take a postgraduate course in education technology and we did it, and then I learned quite a lot. Because in classes when it was online, I analyzed myself a lot. I left a lot to be desired because of many things I didn't know. Now I realize that it's different, we also received computers for the municipal students, so they play online games and I see that they like it a lot, so I think it contributes to our reality in the classroom. I really like games. And I see that a lot of people are still stuck in that traditional education, even with the whole issue of technology.*

With the decreed pandemic and the release of non-face-to-face activities, institutions or teaching networks, in order to carry out remote activities, needed changes in pedagogical practices, that is, the teacher needed pedagogical support that would provide conditions to act in this context. differentiated moment. Unfortunately, many were not able to include non-face-to-face activities and the use of methodologies for this teaching process, due to their initial professional training, which did not provide them with such skills (Cruz, 2021). Considering that the new scenario of technological innovation in education calls for a renewed posture of the teacher, with the role of guiding and mediating the students' learning, above all a guide, who explores the critical sense in everything that the student learns (Carvalho et al., 2020).

It is observed that, with the pandemic, technology entered the lives of students and teachers, breaking barriers and coming to stay. The educator's role goes far beyond teaching, and this was noted in the teachers' speeches. Technology needs to be seen as an ally for teaching, and teachers have to gather with it.

2.1.3 Teachers Shared Experiences

In this last category, the subject was developed regarding possible changes in teaching practices during the COVID-19 pandemic, and perceptions of what can be improved in English language teaching, by teachers. "Analyzing challenges based on evidence is always a good starting point" (Council, 2019, p.6).

Teacher 1: *We are continuously, constantly adapting and changing, you know, now I think it won't just be going back to what it was, there will be a lot of things that we will still miss, even the online part there that was easy, right, but in relation to one thing that could improve, especially in Brazil with this financially, the needy to have good access to the internet, because that's what made this inequality so wide open. So, thinking about a governmental issue, I think that an initiative to subsidize resources for needy students, so that they can have access to the internet. I think it is an ideal world, right, but if I were to choose any thing, maybe that would be an interesting thing.*

Teacher 2: *I think that before the pandemic, in a way, some professionals managed to escape the use of technology a little bit and it worked and they made it happen, and after the pandemic this was no longer an option. I think that has changed, we learned a lot from it and I think what is left of teaching is that there is a lot of room for learning and training. So what remains is, we cannot escape the use of technology in the classroom, regardless of how this use will be, because it's already part of what our students are today and just as technology was very present in the pandemic and fundamental, I think affectivity is too.*

It will be necessary to invest in teacher training as a language user and in more integrated teaching methodologies for the use of English. (Council, 2019, p.34).

Teacher 3: *I think it changed everything, right, the teachers come out much better. So my admiration for everything you've done and are still doing in this period of pandemic, and overnight they had to learn and manage, and make things happen, you know, because the families were waiting, the students too, we know that a lot was lost in this period, especially those who are in the state school, many students were also lost. Last week, the result of a survey in Brazil regarding internet access was published and one third of the Brazilian population does not have any access. What we come out of this pandemic is that our country needs more equality. We have to always be looking, keep studying, searching.*

Teachers struggle to deal with social issues and more the pedagogical one. This is in addition to the problems of infrastructure and access to inputs at school. That very traditional class, sometimes, is what is possible to do within a very complex context (Council, 2019, p.42).

Teacher 4: *We are having the reality of high school, I'm with them, you know, and they are coming back in this post-pandemic, I don't know if it's a post-pandemic, right, but not all of them are coming back, so that makes it a lot difficult. What I'm trying to do is try to give a projection of the pedagogical for that cell phone, because they know how to use the cell phone, they use it all the time, but then doing things that will collaborate with their lives, they don't know. For example, producing a curriculum, which is there in high school, right, making a Powerpoint, a slide, a presentation on a topic, they don't know that, I think we have now to teach them to use their cell phones as a pedagogical resource.*

Teacher 5: *I think it was a moment to shake things up, you know, so there were a lot of people who were really accommodated there, I'm not going to say that they didn't, because they were really scared and didn't want to go through this evolution, but I think it was really very positive in the sense of it, that we were actually forced to enter the digital world, right, that was really cool and I think it was the opportunity for us to learn a lot. I think we are slowly coming back and I think we are, as professionals, even more strengthened. One thing that I found very interesting was the moment we started the online classes, we exposed our class, our day, our moment to the whole family, everyone started to participate in our classes, right, it was also a huge challenge for us to expose ourselves.*

Teacher 6: *I think that some initiatives are already being taken, I see from the micro to the macro, I saw some city halls, for example, they bought a lot of tablets but they don't know what to do with them because they think it's just changing the book for the tablet, it's not, because then you have to train the teacher, you have to think about how you can use that, so I see the biggest total disorganization like that. One thing that I noticed was that we couldn't teach the same online class time as the classroom time, so there's something wrong there. It seems that the face-to-face class has more contact there, the class is more productive, I felt that online people were very lost.*

Teacher 7: *On the issue of the pandemic, I think the municipality woke up a little, a lot of resources are coming, many students don't have this contact at home, so that's one more reason for them to go to school, because for many it is demotivating. Of course, many teachers are still thinking that the technology is difficult, and with the issue of age, they don't want to update themselves. It happened at my school, with teachers resigning because they didn't want to deal with technology, they got desperate because they didn't know when we would return face-to-face. I think that a teacher is an eternal construction. As I say to them, it's not just us who teach, they teach us a lot, right, and it's a nice exchange.*

Based on the reports, an important movement can be noticed with regard to leaving the comfort zone and going in search of new knowledge. Teachers did everything possible and impossible to reach their students during the COVID 19 pandemic. Many went further and strengthened ties with their students through affection. There is still a lack of greater perception from government officials, to look at the urgent needs of public education classrooms, as well as the neediest students.

3. CONCLUSION

Based on the results obtained through the focus group, raising the practices of English language teaching and the experience lived by the teachers, as well as the use of digital resources in the classroom in formal schools of regular education and language schools, present that teachers have some knowledge about the use of technologies and digital games, and it was possible to see how much the pandemic accelerated, even forced, many times, the attempts and learning of new technologies by teachers. It was also noticed how essential the teacher's role is in the classroom, as mentioned by the participants' teachers.

In addition, it was found that the teacher, through the planning of classes and activities, visualizing exactly where to insert digital games and technologies, has support tools in them, which will help to facilitate, engage and motivate students. in learning a new language. York, Poole and DeHaan (2021) state that if the vision of games transforming education is to be realized, and if the use of games in the classroom is to be normalized, this will be done by teachers. Thus, research must turn its focus to the language classroom and how educators can teach with games. Opportunely mentioned, studies and qualifications are of paramount importance for updating and practicing teaching. Holden and Nobre (2021) state that, as teachers, it is necessary to continuously develop, and it is the teacher's responsibility to keep up to date and learn more about the language and different teaching methods. According to the reports of the focus group, in addition to technology, teachers opened their horizons for qualifications, in search of new learning related to their teaching, as well as for technologies to help them with remote classes.

After this study, it is concluded that technology and digital games are extremely important tools to be used in teaching, including the English language. There are several impasses that hinder this progress in the classroom, such as schools without inputs and teachers without the necessary qualifications. However, there was a strong desire for change on the part of the teachers, for themselves and for education and teaching in Brazil. This will be a daily work to change this scenario.

In the event that students do not have access to the internet at school, it is possible to survey who has the internet and cell phone and/or computer at home, and make games available as homework. The teacher can monitor the student's performance in the activity, as well as review the points in which he/she had greater difficulty. In case the student does not have internet and/or cell phone, the school does not have internet and computer, it is still possible to play some games on the teacher's computer (with its shared internet), games that are for the whole group, that do not need cell phones. There are many possibilities, even with few resources. May the teacher continue to plant seeds in the lives of his students. If he can get one to flourish, he has accomplished a great achievement.

For future studies, it is possible to think about training through an English cultural immersion for English teachers, which addresses different types of digital games and technologies. In this opportunity, teachers practice the target language and learn new game platforms to apply in their classes. Studies and meetings with other teachers also help in sharing experiences and ideas. As well, new research about offline games, that could include all students, in classes or at home. Technology sometimes distances people, but if used in the right way and at the right time, it brings them closer, helps to relax, motivate and make things more interesting.

REFERENCES

Abreu, N. R. de; Baldanza, R. F.; & Gondim, S. M G.., (2009). *Os grupos focais on-line: das reflexões conceituais à aplicação em ambiente virtual. pp.* 5–24.

Anjos-Santos, L. Mo. dos; Gamero, R.; & Gimenez, T. N.., (2014). *Letramentos digitais, interdisciplinaridade e aprendizagem de língua inglesa por alunos do Ensino Médio.* Campinas, SP, Brazil. pp. 79–102.

British Council (2015). *O ensino de inglês na educação pública brasileira.* São Paulo, Brazil.

British Council (2019). *Políticas Públicas para o Ensino De Inglês. Um Panorama das Experiências na Rede Pública Brasileira.* São Paulo, Brazil.

British Council (2021). *Observatório para o Ensino da Língua Inglesa. Professoras e Professores de Inglês no Brasil: Retratos de uma Profissão a partir do Censo Escolar e do Censo da Educação Superior.* São Paulo, Brazil.

Carvalho, A. A., et al., (2020). *Atas do 5 Encontro sobre Jogos e Mobile Learning.* Coimbra, Portugal.

Cruz, S. (2020). *Atas do 5 Encontro sobre Jogos e Mobile Learning.* Coimbra, Portugal.

Cruz, D. M. (2021). *Professor Midiático em Tempos de Pandemia: Novos Conteúdos e Habilidades, Desafios e Possibilidades Criativas*. pp. 48.

Duarte, A. B. S. (2007). *Grupo focal online e offline como técnica de coleta de dados*. Minas Gerais, Brazil.

First, Education., 2022. *Índice de proficiência em Inglês da EF*. São Paulo, Brazil.

Franco-Madrigal, M. C. (2016). *Teacher Perspectives in Using Technology To Support English Learners*. Pomona, California, USA.

Gomes, A. A. (2005). *Apontamentos sobre a pesquisa em educação: usos e possibilidades do grupo focal*. EccoS – Revista Científica, São Paulo, v. 7, n. 2, pp. 275-290.

Gomes, J. de F. P. et al. (2016). *O Uso de Recursos Tecnológicos como Ferramentas Motivacionais no Ensino de Língua Inglesa para Estudantes Jovens e Adultos da Escola Pública*. Revista Científica Interdisciplinar, nº 2, v. 3. pp. 8411.

Holden, S.; & Nobre, V. (2021). *Teaching English Today*. The Editorial HUB, Buckingham, UK.

Kurlishchuk, I. (2016). *The impact of educational game use on young children's foreign language communication*. Ukraine. pp. 85–92.

Menni, S. (2020). *Board Race Game as a Strategy to Boost EFL Learners Engagement to Learn Grammar. The case of first year EFL LMD Students at Mohamed Kheider University of Biskra*. Biskra, Algeria, pp. 17.

Prensky, M. (2010). *Não me atrapalhe, mãe–Eu estou aprendendo*. Phorte, São Paulo, Brazil.

Rad, P. N. (2017). *Investigating Motivation and Language Performance in Esl Classrooms Through the Use of Tablet Applications*. Kuala Lumpur, Malaysia.

Roloff, L. M. (2021). *Perspectiva metodológica formativa: um estudo no curso de Engenharia Civil*. Criciúma, Brazil.

York, J.; Poole, F. J.; Dehaan, J. W. (2021). *Playing a new game: An argument for a teacher-focused field around games and play in language education*. ACTFL, v. 54, Issue 4.

DEVELOPMENT OF DIGITAL COMPETENCES IN TEACHING GEOGRAPHY THROUGH THE CREATION OF MULTIMEDIA EDUCATIONAL MATERIAL IN THE H5P APPLICATION

Magdaléna Závodná and Kateřina Kostolányová
University of Ostrava, Czech Republic

ABSTRACT

In today's modern age, digital technologies are an essential part of everyone's life, so students must learn to use them in primary school. The specific competences defined in the European Digital Competence Framework DigComp 2.1 (2017) are divided into six areas. The Ministry of Education of the Czech Republic has subsequently drawn on this document to add digital competences to its Framework Education Programme (FEP). For this reason, a research experiment was conducted in the context of primary school teaching, which included the design of several specific lessons. The aim of this experiment was to test the research question of whether online collaboration between students using the BYOD model would lead to the acquisition of the subject curriculum, as well as the acquisition of selected digital competences. Therefore, the aim of this paper is to present a design of a Geography teaching method in which students develop not only their subject knowledge but also selected digital competences, using the H5P application and the creation of a multimedia learning object, and to present the results of the research carried out. The paper includes a description of the individual lessons, the tasks set for the pupils and the methodology for the teachers.

KEYWORDS

Digital Competence, H5P Application, Multimedia Learning Object, Primary School

1. INTRODUCTION

Every school should prepare students for life in society. It doesn't matter what the individual is good at or what field he or she will pursue. Every person, without distinction, must be able to integrate into society. These skills, which are supposed to prepare a student for life in society, are called competences. In each culture, country or society, these skills may vary slightly, but the principle remains the same. Each individual must be able to communicate, for example, or to learn new things. Nowadays, these basic skills are being supplemented by a new competence, namely the mastery of digital technologies.

In 2017, the European Digital Competence Framework DigComp 2.1 was published, summarising all the areas of digital competences that primary school pupils should learn. However, these competences should not be acquired by pupils primarily in Computer Science classes, but should occur across all subjects from Geography, to Humanities, to Mathematics or Physics. Many teachers, however, had and still have some problems with this area, not only because of their lack of experience with the use and integration of digital technologies into teaching or the actual manipulation of them, but also because some lack inspiration, an example of what digital technologies offer and what they can be used for in the classroom actively, but above all effectively.

For this reason, we decided to create a lesson plan and test our research question, i.e. whether online collaboration between students using the BYOD model will lead to the acquisition of the subject matter, and at the same time to the acquisition of selected digital competences. For the purpose of the experiment, we also created a multimedia object that contains not only the assignment tasks for the pupils, but also short educational videos, sample solutions, but most importantly a detailed description of the teaching, which is divided into five lessons of 45 minutes each. This proposed lesson is intended for Geography lessons, but every teacher can be inspired by this proposal and create a similar form of teaching for their own subject, e.g. History, Mathematics, Physics, or Natural History.

The original intention was only to test the possibilities of engaging students in online learning and activating them during group work, which was a very topical issue in the time of covid. However, in the end, a comprehensive proposal for project-based learning was created, which can be easily used not only in online learning, but also in the traditional face-to-face form of teaching using the BYOD model. Thus, in this paper, we present the instructional design and the created multimedia object, which contains all the assignments for students as well as educational materials and develops selected digital competencies and subject matter knowledge of students. The proposed teaching meets the requirements set by the Ministry of Education of the Czech Republic and is based on the theoretical foundations of general didactics. The proposed teaching has also been practically tested at the second level of primary school in the Czech Republic.

2. DIGITAL COMPETENCE

As already mentioned, according to the *DigComp Digital Competence Framework 2.1* (2017), digital competences can be divided into six different areas. Each area then contains several points that fall here. These areas are information and data literacy, communication and collaboration, digital content creation, security, problem solving and technological competences. As well as other competences such as learning, communicative or work competences, pupils need to acquire digital competences in all subjects in primary school.

The proposed project-based learning is primarily designed to develop the areas of communication and collaboration, digital content creation, but it also develops information and data literacy and, of course, technological competences. As the titles suggest, pupils are to learn how to use digital devices to create files of various types, from simple text, to graphics and sound files, to videos or directly multimedia objects. They should also learn how to interact with each other and share different types of files using technology, as well as how to use digital technologies effectively to obtain different types of information, which they must be able to access critically, while respecting copyright when sharing this information. To acquire these skills, students must, of course, learn to operate the digital devices themselves and other necessary hardware and software, and be able to deal with a variety of technical problems. And, as with most activities in human life, there is a need for safety when working with digital technologies, both in terms of physical health (associated with, for example, excessive use of digital technologies) and mental health (which can be compromised by, for example, cyberbullying), and avoiding data loss and other attacks or computer viruses.

3. METHODS

In order to implement our intended research experiment, it was necessary to create a lesson plan, which we had to base not only on the RVP of Czech education, but also on many professional didactics, for example, Modern Teaching G. Petty (2013) and R. Čapek's Modern Didactics (2015), from which we had to draw information for the choice of appropriate methods and forms of teaching, the formation of groups, the motivational and final part, the evaluation of group work and the overall organization of the teaching. It was necessary to set a goal for the students to reach during the teaching, set a timetable and create a detailed methodology describing the individual tasks, group formation and the whole project-based learning. Most importantly, however, was to create a multimedia object that is the centre of all this project-based learning, see below.

3.1 Application

In the creation of the multimedia object, not only the text editor Microsoft Word was used, in which all the information had to be written, i.e. the assignments of the tasks and some teaching materials, but above all the methodology itself for the teachers. In the editing of the photographs, several graphic editors or applications used to work with photographs and other graphic objects were used. These were PhotoFiltre and the online tools Photopea and Polarr. The DaVinciResolve application, which is freely available for download but still offers professional video work at the level of applications such as Premiere Pro from the well-known Adobe company, was used to create individual video tutorials. The main part of the creation of the multimedia object took place in the H5P application.

3.1.1 H5P

This is a web-based application that can be accessed from anywhere, but only with internet access. This application is used to create interactive materials that have great potential in teaching. Registration and use of the basic features of this application is available for free, but the full version, which contains a wide variety of different types of interactive content, is chargeable. New users can at least try the full version for free for 30 days. Some of the files that can be created in this app include interactive images, videos, quizzes, books and much more.

The advantage of this app is not only that it is very easy to use and learn for both teachers and students, but also that the resulting interactive files used in lessons motivate and awaken students' interest in the subject matter and contribute to greater understanding and retention of the material.

For the purpose of the proposed project-based learning, a multimedia object (see below) containing text as well as images and videos was created in this application. The Image hotspots file type was used for this multimedia object. This file type works by placing a cover image, which can be anything from a photograph to an infographic. Subsequently, individual hotspots are inserted on top of this cover image, which then contain other files. This can be classic text (Figure 2), other images, or even a video (Figure 1), which can be uploaded directly from a computer, or by using a link from an existing video on the internet, e.g. from youtube.com. The user can then modify the appearance of these points, both in terms of colours and the symbol displayed on the points themselves.

Figure 1. Clicked point with video tutorial

Figure 2. Clicked point with text

3.1.2 Graphic Editor

The graphic editor was the most frequently used tool in the creation of the documents for the proposed project-based learning, for this reason not only one program was used. Three photo editing applications were used in turn, but each offered different functions that were needed for the final form of the photographs used. All the image material, especially the photographs used, was sourced in-house, so there can be no problem of copyright infringement. The resulting files are then licensed under CC BY-SA 4.0.

In the first stage of the work it was necessary to use the online application Polarr, which is used to work with filters. This allows you to adjust the brightness, contrast, light, shadows, colour tone and so on in a given photo. In the second phase, the work was done with the PhotoFiltre application, which is available for free and works on a similar principle to other graphic editors, but the main difference is that this application does not allow working with layers and mask, which can have its advantages and disadvantages. If it was necessary to work with layers, another online application Photopea was used, which offers many interesting features, and its environment is similar to working in the well-known Photoshop from Adobe. The advantage of all these applications is their availability for free, their ease of use and the abundance of necessary features.

3.1.3 Video Creation

For better clarity and clarity, it was also necessary to create short video tutorials used to introduce the different applications that the students had to work with. Thus, three videos were created. One video introduces the pupils working with the H5P application itself, in which the pupils had to create their own multimedia object of the Image hotspots type. Another video focuses on working with a graphical editor, specifically working with the PhotoFiltre application. This video explains the complete basics, which are the same for all graphic editors, so it would not be a problem if the students chose a different graphic editor for their work. The last video then introduces working in Windows' MovieMaker. This introduces the basic features that can be used to create a video. This program is used by most primary schools in the Czech Republic, but even here it would not be a problem if the pupils chose another program to create their own videos, as these programs are based on a similar principle.

3.1.4 File Sharing

The most challenging aspect in terms of preparation was to figure out how to communicate the created multimedia file to the pupils and to choose a file sharing platform for the pupils to work in during the project-based learning. The first method that was tried was to create a custom website using Google Sites, where all the necessary materials, the multimedia object and the final quizzes were placed. Unfortunately, a month before the practical verification of the teaching, technical problems occurred in this application and the multimedia object created there stopped working. The replacement solution was the Moodle application, which is widely used especially in Czech universities. In this application, a special course was created (Figure 3), which again contained all the necessary materials created for this project-based learning. Another great advantage is that students can access this course using the "guest login" function and do not need to create accounts. This course can be found at https://amos.pdf.osu.cz/moodle/course/view.php?id=424.

Within the framework of the implemented teaching, the school itself was left free to choose the appropriate application for online collaboration between students, but it was assumed that the school would choose one of the two most widely used platforms for online learning in the Czech Republic, which are Microsoft Teams and Google Classroom. This school eventually chose Google Classroom, which the pupils were already used to working with and where all pupils had already created their accounts.

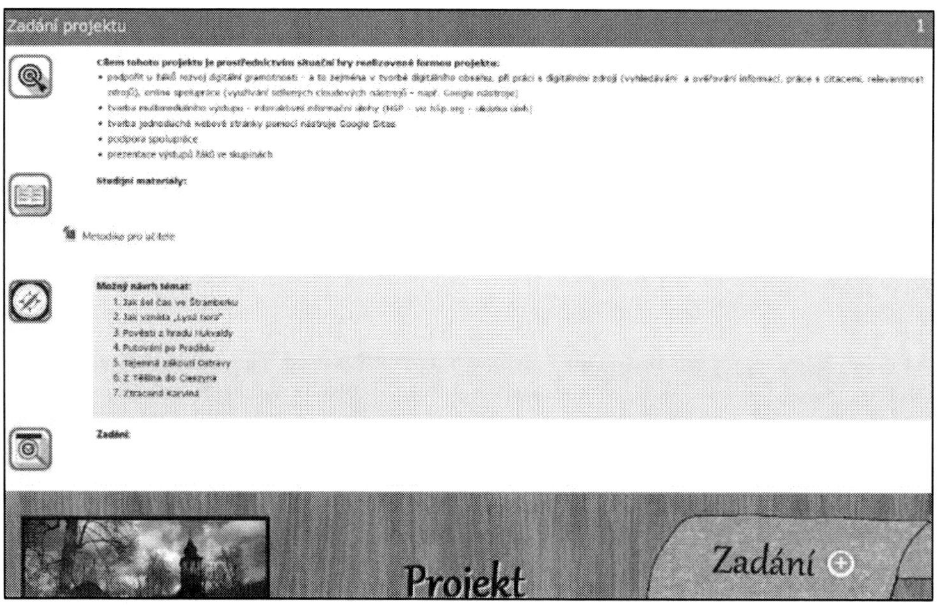

Figure 3. Project entry in Moodle

3.2 Multimedia Object

The multimedia object created is the core of the whole project-based learning. This multimedia object (Figure 4) is divided into three parts. On the top right there are the assignments for all the tasks, the evaluation criteria for the whole project-based learning, tips that students can use to create their own materials, a final quiz and a questionnaire used to evaluate the designed project-based learning. At the bottom there are teaching materials. Some of the learning materials are text-only, some are in the form of video tutorials. On the top left there is a sample solution that students can use for inspiration when creating their own multimedia object.

The main task of the students is to create the same type of multimedia object. Each group has to choose a suitable title image and creatively edit it. Each group must then place a text describing the location, several other images from around the location and a short video to serve as an advertisement for the location.

Figure 4. Multimedia object

3.3 Lesson Plan

The entire project-based learning is designed to take five lessons. In each lesson, the students complete different tasks, which are interconnected, and finally combine everything into one coherent set using the H5P application. Throughout the project-based learning, working with shared storage and shared documents is important, with pupils working in groups all at the same time on a given task and saving the files they have created on the shared storage. Pupils are also able to choose which digital devices they use for their work, so that they can all use their own mobile devices, following the BYOD model. Our original lesson plan also included the inclusion of a field trip where students could use their mobile phones to take their own photos needed to create a multimedia object. Unfortunately, this plan had to be cancelled for organizational reasons.

In the first lesson, the pupils are introduced to the whole project through appropriate motivation, which is an essential part of project-based learning. In this case, it was a situation where the pupils became employees of a travel agency for which they had to create advertising files for a selected location in the Czech Republic. The pupils were divided into groups by the teacher based on his experience with the class. In these groups, they then chose their own tourist area, about which they collected the necessary data using the Internet and wrote it down in a coherent form. This lesson was thus designed to acquire and deepen knowledge of the Czech language, Geography, but especially digital competences in the field of information and data literacy, digital content creation and technological competence.

The second lesson focuses on working with a graphic editor. Also in this lesson, the students had to find the necessary photographs and other visual material they wanted to work with, taking into account the respect of copyright. From the photographs obtained, the pupils had to create an introductory image, which had to be representative, and three other photographs to be used at different points in the multimedia file. In this lesson, the pupils again deepened their knowledge of Geography and skills in the digital competences of digital content creation, information and data literacy and technological competences and now also their knowledge of Computer Science.

In the next lesson, pupils followed the same process. This time, however, they created their own promotional video, for which they could use both photographs and other short videos.

The following lesson is dedicated to map work. Now the pupils were asked to explore the area around the monument using online maps and to create their own map with important places such as a bus stop, a parking lot, a restaurant or important landmarks of the area. In this lesson, in addition to specific knowledge about the area, pupils were also acquiring general knowledge of Geography, specifically cartography. Again, they were deepening their digital competences.

In the last lesson, the pupils were given the space to complete the whole project, inserting the individual files into the H5P application and creating the final Image hotspots file. The main part of this lesson, however, is the presentation of each pupil's work, which each group has to present to the other pupils and introduce them to the site. In the last part of the lesson there is a space reserved for discussion of the results of the group work, feelings, impressions, knowledge gained, etc. After this discussion, the pupils then fill in the quizzes that they could have prepared for the others during the project-based learning, but if they did not manage to create these quizzes, they can use the already prepared quizzes (Figure 5), which focus on the general knowledge that the pupils should have acquired during the project-based learning.

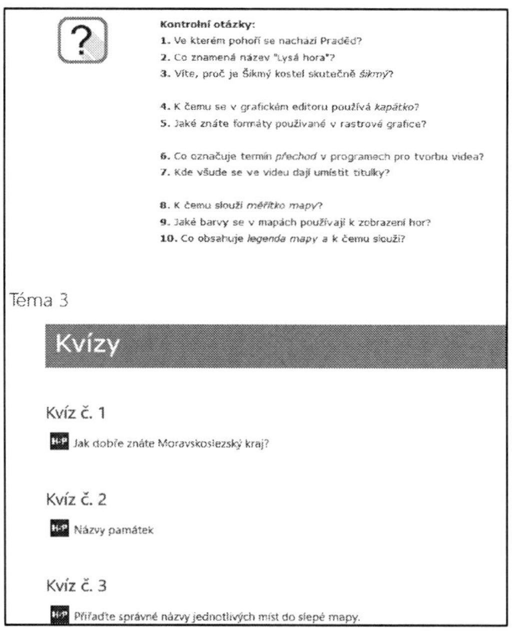

Figure 5. Review questions and quizzes in Moodle

Figure 6. Sample solution in Moodle

Thanks to the Moodle course, the pupils had at their disposal at all times a multimedia object which, as already mentioned, contains detailed assignments for all the tasks, a proposal of possible topics, sample solutions (Figure 6), criteria for evaluating group work, quizzes and detailed instructions, hints and tips.

4. RESULTS

After the practical verification of the proposed project-based learning, the students were asked to fill in a questionnaire to determine the effectiveness of the proposed learning. In addition to this questionnaire, the teacher who had implemented this teaching was asked to evaluate the proposed teaching and his/her professional opinion on the course and results of the teaching.

The questionnaire contained thirty-two questions, which were divided into four thematic headings on questions related to group work and the chosen topic, acquired knowledge in the field of Geography, Czech language and digital competences.

The results of the questionnaire show that 66.7% of the pupils perceived the atmosphere in the groups as rather pleasant, which is always important for the pupils to acquire the necessary knowledge and skills. The involvement of all group members was perceived differently by pupils. 83.4% of pupils were satisfied with the involvement of other group members, but less than 20% were not satisfied with the involvement of other members. Overall, the results of the survey show that pupils enjoyed working in groups, but at the same time had some problems with it, which may be due to the fact that pupils do not work in groups very often in this class. In terms of the topic, 80% of the pupils liked the topic, 15% of the pupils would have preferred a topic focused on zoology and 5% of the pupils were not interested in the topic. The chosen topic thus contributed again to a higher motivation of the pupils due to this high popularity.

On average, 75% of the pupils found the materials comprehensible, but the majority of pupils (83.3%) turned to their teachers or found the information they needed on the Internet. The overall success rate for group work and final quizzes was greater than 70%. For the quizzes, pupils were on average 75% successful and for the individual assignments, pupils were on average 79% successful. The success rate of the designed instruction was on average 6% higher than the learning outcomes of the class in the regular instruction.

All pupils (100%) agreed that they had gained new knowledge in Geography, both in cartography and within individual geographical locations. Half of the pupils (50%) also reported that information relating to copyright was new to them. Pupil responses varied in the area of Computing and Digital Competence, with each pupil learning something different. Some pupils learnt how to share files, others learnt how to search the internet, some pupils improved their skills in using a graphic editor, and other pupils improved their skills in video production.

The teacher who participated in the implementation of the proposed project-based learning evaluated the proposed learning rather positively. From his point of view, the pupils were most interested in the creation of the video, although this activity was the one that caused the pupils the most problems. He was very positive about the H5P application, which he found simple and intuitive. In his opinion, working in this application motivated the pupils. The teacher evaluated the created multimedia object as understandable and the project-based learning as suitable for the chosen age category of pupils. Compared to the usual way of teaching (in the case of this teacher, without the use of digital technologies, mobile devices and online collaboration between pupils), the proposed way of teaching was more motivating and the pupils were more actively involved in the lesson, which generally contributes to a deeper understanding of the curriculum. In his view, the proposed teaching fulfilled its purpose, as the pupils acquired the necessary knowledge in Geography, Czech language and Computer Science, but especially in the area of digital competences.

5. CONCLUSION

The aim of our research was to find out whether online collaboration between students using the BYOD model would lead to the acquisition of the subject matter, as well as the acquisition of selected digital competences. To this end, we created a learning design together with a multimedia object that was intended to develop selected digital competences of the students together with the specific subject material. Thus, based on the results of our scientific experiment, it can be said that the designed teaching met the set objectives and online collaboration between students is possible and leads to the development of selected digital competences together with the subject knowledge, while offering effective cross-curricular relationships. Thanks to data sharing, pupils could work from their own mobile devices, not only at school but also at home, but especially all members of one group at the same time, which made this group work more effective.

In this paper, a lesson plan designed for teaching Geography at the second level of primary schools was presented, but it can also be used as a general model for teaching any subject, whether it is Physics or Civics. And if the possibilities of the school or the organisation of the lessons allow it, the pupils can go on a trip and, thanks to the work with their own mobile device, take their own photographs as a basis for their work.

REFERENCES

Belz, H. & Siegrist, M. (2011). *Key competences and their development*. Portál, Prague, Czech Republic.

Carretero, S., Vuorikari, R. & Punie, Y. (2017). *DigComp 2.1: The Digital Competence Framework for Citizens with eight proficiency levels and examples of use*. Publications Office of the European Union, Luxembourg.

Čapek, R. (2015). *Modern didactics: a lexicon of teaching and assessment methods.* Grada, Prague, Czech Republic.

Collective of authors (2021). *Framework curriculum for primary education*. MŠMT, Prague, Czech Republic.

Petty, G. (2013). *Modern teaching*. Portál, Prague, Czech Republic.

PANDEMIC-DRIVEN MOBILITY IN HIGHER EDUCATION: THE GOOD, THE BAD AND THE USEFUL

Orly Calderon[1], Susan Penque[2], David Luhr[1], Caryn Nahum[1] and Lauren Scardigno[1]
[1]*Long Island University, 720 Northern Blvd, Brookville NY 11548, USA*
[2]*Sacred Heart University, 5151 Park Avenue, Fairfield, CT 06825, USA*

ABSTRACT

The purpose of this mixed method research study is to describe the experiences of faculty and students in post-secondary education institutions as they shifted to remote education at the start of the COVID-19 pandemic, and to understand these experiences in the context of previous research about pre-pandemic remote or mobile education. One hundred and two participants in the study include full-time and adjunct faculty, undergraduate and graduate students. A convergent mixed method survey queried about participants' demographics, mobility experiences in terms of frequency of access to technology and a suitable learning/teaching environment and usefulness of various web and video conferencing and Learning Management Systems (LMS) tools to support education in this format. The findings indicate that on average, faculty and students report positive experiences, especially for participants who had prior involvement with online education. Qualitative data highlight challenges associated with access to technology, managing the out-of-classroom physical environment and balancing personal and education responsibilities at the time of the pandemic outbreak. These results have implications that may be relevant as the world of education evolves, applying lessons learned during the pandemic. Resource allocation, training faculty in remote education pedagogy and providing infrastructure support for students to improve mobile education experiences are crucial for success in the new normal world of higher education.

KEYWORDS

Emergency Remote Education, Mobility in Higher Education, Faculty and Students Experiences

1. INTRODUCTION

The COVID-19 pandemic is entering its third year, and its impact on higher education has been significant (Robinson-Neal, 2021). The sweeping mandatory shift to emergency remote education in March of 2020, forcing the world of education to quickly adapt to a mobile learning mode, has presented multiple challenges for students and faculty. Research emerging about the experiences of faculty and students during the pandemic reveals obstacles ranging from varying computer literacy levels, limited accessibility to mobile learning technology (Onyema et al., 2020), and adjustments in pedagogy and learning styles (Berger, Mallow & Tabag, 2022). While some studies found no significant differences in students' academic performance after the emergency shift to an online learning environment (Barletta et al., 2022), others noted that students required additional support in order to successfully navigate this change, such as more frequent communication with professors, extension on due dates and encouraging dialogue among students (Basford, 2021). Likewise, instructors have reported challenges in adapting to online teaching and emphasized the importance of adjusting expectations and reexamining goals (Ross & Disalvo, 2020). Yet remote education has existed long before the pandemic. During the half decade preceding the pandemic, nearly three quarters of all public, private, and for - profit institutions of higher education have been offering online courses and full online programs (Calderon & Sood, 2018). There is a wide body of research about remote learning experiences that highlights the following challenges, to name but a few: students' acculturation to remote learning especially in regards to technology-related interruptions and distractions (Cilezis, 2015), institutional infrastructure needed to support successful remote learning (Snow et al., 2018), preferred modes of communication (Snow et al., 2018) and students' reduced sense of social connectedness in remote education (Irani et al., 2014; Stewart et al., 2011). At the same time, the literature offers evidence of positive outcomes of remote learning including higher student satisfaction, and grades (Ling, 2017; Simon, et al., 2014), decrease in teaching costs, and the role of mobility in enhancing integration of social, family, and personal life with education, along with an increase in students' active participation and empowerment (Gonzalex-Yebra, 2019). However, these findings may or may not apply to an emergency shift to remote education during tumultuous times such as the pandemic. Therefore, the purpose of this article is to describe the experiences of faculty and students in post-secondary education institutes during the emergency shift to remote education, thus adding the body of knowledge on what is becoming an increasingly wide, and possibly a permanent format, of higher education (Yeigh & Lynch, 2020). We hope that results of this study will contribute to a better understanding of the challenges and advantages of remote education during an emergency state and how pre-pandemic knowledge about remote learning may have been useful when adjusting to the increased mobility in higher education.

2. METHODS

2.1 Sampling and Participants

The target population for this study is comprised of faculty and students in post-secondary education, who, due to COVID-19, experienced an abrupt shift to emergency remote education during the spring semester of 2020. A random sample was obtained through recruitment via the first two authors' professional organizations in the United States. One hundred two participants include full-time and adjunct faculty, undergrad and graduate students. Table 1 illustrates the sample characteristics.

Table 1. Participants' characteristics

Gender Distribution Among All Participants			
Female		*Male*	
91%		9%	
Ethnicity Distribution Among All Participants			
White	*Hispanic*	*Asian*	*Black*
60%	14%	10%	6.5%
Average Household Income Range			
Undergraduates Students		$70,000-79,000	
Graduate Students		$90,000-99,000	
Faculty		$100,000 – 149,000	

2.2 Instrument

This study utilized two mixed-method surveys, designed by the first two authors for the purpose of this research project. The two surveys were geared towards investigating the respective experiences of students and faculty after the shift to remote learning in March 2020. Although the language of some items differed between the students and faculty surveys, to reflect learning vs. teching experiences, the two surveys covered the same content areas. The parallel in the surveys' content allowed for evaluating teaching and learning experiences in relationship to similar aspects of the emergency shift to a remote education environment. The surveys consist of 5 content areas, each: Section A asked a few demographics questions to gain a better understanding of who our participants are. The rationale for the items in this section was to provide context within which we could interpret data about students and faculty experiences in relationship to Socio-Economic-Status (SES), ethnic diversity, and previous experience with the online educational environment. Section B asked students and faculty to rate the frequency with which they were able access technology learning and teaching tools (e.g., desktop computers, laptops, Ipads) during the spring or summer 2020 semesters. Items in this section utilized a 3-point ordinal sale response option, ranging from daily access to no access. The purpose of this section was to investigate the respective variability in students' and faculty's access to technology when they were not able to rely on school-based devices.

Section C asks students and faculty to rate the frequency with which they were able to access a suitable learning and teaching environment, respectively, during the spring or summer 2020 semesters. Items in this section addressed access to suitable place to join or teach online class as all as access to a suitable place to study or do homework (student survey), or prep classes and grade papers (teachers survey). The rationale for this section was to investigate students' and faculty's access to a physical environment from which to engage in remote education during campus closure.

Section D asked students and faculty to rate the helpfulness of web conferencing tools, including Learning Management System (LMS) features, in learning and teaching, respectively. Items included web conferencing tools such as webcam, break out rooms, as well as other online pedagogical tools such as online exams and assignments, and course digital communication applications such as emails and announcements. Items in this section utilized a 4-point ordinal scale response option, ranging from not at all helpful to very helpful. The purpose of this section was to gain an understanding of the degree to which various online tools contribute to learning and teaching.

Open ended questions followed each set of the quantitative questions in sections B ,C, and D, inviting participants to add comments on their accessibility to technology, suitable environment and helpfulness of online teaching and learning tools.

Finally, section E comprised of open-ended questions about motivation for learning/teaching during the COVID 19 pandemic, and general life experiences during the pandemic. The purpose of this section was to allow participants to share general reflections on the pandemic in order to gain a wider context for a deeper understanding of participants' experiences during the shift to emergency remote learning and teaching. However, data from section E are not included in the current analysis and will be reported in future papers.

2.3 Procedure

This study was approved by the first author's University's Institutional Review Board, under an exempt category. A link to the survey utilizing the Anthology platform was included in a recruitment email distributed via the respective professional national listserv the first two authors are members of. The survey was available for a period of 4 weeks in the summer of 2020, during which two reminders were posted on the respective listservs.

2.4 Data Analysis

Quantitative data about faculty and students' access to technology and a suitable environment and their respective rating of web-based learning and teaching tools helpfulness were analyzed using descriptive statistics. T tests and two-by two factorial analysis was used to compare faculty and students' responses to items within these dimensions. Pearson correlation was used to examine the relationship between faculty and students' rating of their experiences along the various dimensions, and the rating of participants' overall teaching and learning experience during the emergency shift to remote education.

The constant comparison method (Grinnell, Williams, & Unrau, 2019) was used to analyze participants' comments on their experiences within each dimension of the survey.

3. RESULTS

3.1 Access to Technology Tools and a Suitable Learning and Teaching Environment

On average, faculty reported regular access to computer technology for teaching (M = 1.03, SD = .17). On the other hand, students had more difficulties accessing technology for learning. On average, students reported that they had only a somewhat regular access to technology tools (M = 1.63, SD = .56). Access to a laptop was most frequent (M = 1.04; SD = .28), whereas access to a desktop computer was least frequent (M = 2.03, SD = .96). On average, faculty and students reported they had regular daily access to a suitable environment from which to prep classes, teach, do homework and join classes. Analysis of Variance revealed that level of household income did not differentiate among levels of students' and faculty's frequency accessing technology and a suitable environment for earning and teaching.

3.2 Helpfulness of Video or Web Conferencing Tools

On average, students reported that web conferencing tools were moderately helpful to learning (M= 1.55, SD = .50). Virtual white board, audio, chats, and share screen were the most helpful tools for learning. Interestingly, while faculty reported regular use of video or web conferencing technology in teaching, (M = 1.03, SD = .17), faculty's use of the type of tools varied. In fact, some faculty did not use the very tools that students found to be most helpful in learning. Students reported that nearly 19% of their professors did not use the virtual white board and nearly 7% of the professors did not use the chat tool. On the other hand, students reported that all their professors used the share screen tool. Faculty members reported that, on average, web conferencing tools were moderately helpful in teaching (M= 1.53; SD = .53). Faculty reported that screen share was the most helpful in teaching (M= 1.09, SD = .40), while breakout rooms were least helpful in teaching (M= 2.6; SD = 1.15).

3.3 Helpfulness of LMS Tools

On average, students reported that Learning Management System (LMS) tools were moderately helpful in their online courses (M = 1.54; SD = .49). Students reported that use of emails, course content posted online and online exams were very helpful in the online courses. On the other hand, blogs, journals and announcement were rated as only moderately helpful in the online courses. It is interesting to note that while announcements were considered only moderately helpful in the online course, 99% of the students reported their professors used this tool. On the other hand, all, or most of the students, reported their professors communicated with them by email (100%), posted course content online (99%), and used online exams (96%), all of which students found to be very helpful in their online course. Ninety seven percent of faculty reported using LMS tools in their remote classes. Posting course content on the LMS was rated as most helpful in teaching (M = 1.06, SD = .24), while blogs were rated as least helpful (M = 2.56, SD = .88).

3.4 Overall Teaching and Learning Experiences During the Shift to Emergency Remote Education

On average, both students and faculty reported their respective learning and teaching online experience was good (M_{students} = 1.87, SD = .87; M_{faculty} =- 1.82, SD = .63).

A two-tail independent T test revealed significant differences in overall rating of online teaching and learning experience between faculty and students who did and did not have previous experience with online or blended courses ($t_{faculty}$ = -3.3 (32), p = .002; $t_{students}$ = -.2.06 (52), p = .045). For both faculty and students, those with previous online involvement reported a better experience during the emergency shift to remote education environment. A two-tail Pearson correlation revealed that students' overall rating of their online learning experience is positively correlated with their frequency of accessing a suitable environment, (r = .362 , p = .007) but not with their frequency of access to technology (r = .142 , p = .315). Even so, only 13% of students' overall online learning experience was explained by their access to technology. On the other hand, students' overall rating of their online learning experience is positively correlated with their rating of web conferencing tools and LMS tools helpfulness to learning. Students' rating of web conferencing tools to learning explains 19% of the variability in their overall online learning experience (r = .44, p = .002). Students' rating of LMS tools helpfulness to learning explains 28% students' overall rating of their online learning experience is positively correlated with their (r = .530, p = .000). A two-tail Pearson correlation revealed that faculty's rating of the overall online teaching experience was not associated with either frequency of access to technology (r = -.232, p = .186) or with access to a suitable place to teach (r = .252, p = .150). similarly, no correlation was found between faculty's rating of the overall online teaching experience and faculty's rating web conferencing tools helpfulness to teaching (r = -.283, p = .111) , or faculty's rating of LMS tools helpfulness to teaching (r = .025, p = .890).

3.5 Comments on Emergency Shift to Remote Learning

Students and faculty were invited to comment on their respective experiences accessing technology, a suitable environment, helpfulness of web conferencing and LMS tools. A constant comparison content analysis yielded 348 units of meaning, which have been coded and grouped into 17 categories. These yielded five themes that reflected both negative and positive experiences. Table 2 illustrates the results of this analysis.

Table 2. Content analysis of students' comments

Themes	Categories	Select Units of Meaning
The basic components of remote learning	Place	"studied from Home"
	Web conferencing tools or features	"zoom"; " recorded lectures"
	Device type Mentioned	"personal laptop"; "my phone"
	Financial considerations	"needed a new laptop but could not afford it";
Challenges in remote learning	Interruptions in the learning environment	"hectic"; "less noise"
	Input/say over the environment	"I enjoy…that I can control my environment's noise"
	Personal circumstances interference with the learning environment	"it can be hard with my family and dog around"
	Web conferencing tools interference with learning experience	"We had some ghosts appear in our classes through zoom"; "We could not access some of the video materials"
	Device-related experiences	"mine did not have the right camera"; [computer] very slow"
	Connection issues	"Internet was sometimes a problem"
Positive experiences in remote learning	Positive experiences in the environment	"without the interruptions encountered in the classroom"
	Web conferencing tools contributing to learning experience	"Zoom was very helpful during lectures"; "Classes were clear using web conferencing"
	Positive experience	"had no issues";" The technology was easy to access"
User's input/contribution to remote education	Input/say over the environment	"once I developed a routine of classes…I found a good balance"
	Faculty/administration management of web conferencing tools	"Professor had class room noise under control"; "The breakout rooms need to be led by an instructor"
General reflections on remote learning	Perspectives on others' experiences	"I have talked with others about their online sessions, and …they have a harder time focusing on their classes"
	General reflections on web conferencing tools	"the experience felt similar to attending class in-person"; " I think it was an adjustment for everyone"
	Reflections on technology and learning	"different type of learning"; "prerecorded lecture were helpful"; zoom classes should be an option in future; regardless of covid 19"

3.5.1 Challenges Associated with the Emergency Shift to Remote Education

Students discussed challenges such as managing out-of-classroom learning environment, financial hardship due to cost of devices or software needed for their remote classes, and balancing personal and educational responsibilities while accessing classes from home. Students described how positive or negative management of web conferencing tools by faculty and administration has contributed to, or detracted from, their remote education experience. For example, students commented that the quality of the remote classes depended on the professors' grasp on the use of the technology and on the tools provided to the faculty by the university.

3.5.2 Positive Experiences Associated with the Emergency Shift to Remote Education

Students commented on the enjoyable aspects of remote learning (e.g., preferred way of learning, peaceful without the interruptions typical to the in-person class environment). Students explained how web conferencing tools helped their learning (e.g., tools gave students the information they needed, prerecorded lectures were helpful because students were able to review them as their convenience). Finally, students noted how important it was for them to have a say in regards to their learning environment, such as controlling their space and preferring to study from home.

4. CONCLUSION

The purpose of this study was to describe the experiences of faculty and students during the COVID-19 emergency shift to remote learning. Unlike some of the previous research on adjusting to the emergency remote education, the current results suggest faculty and students had positive experiences, with no significant difficulties in adjusting to the use of LMS and web or video conferencing tools. However, while faculty reported no difficulties accessing the technology needed for remote teaching, students had some challenges accessing technology needed for remote learning.

Neither faculty nor students reported difficulties accessing a suitable environment for teaching and learning. However, environment, not technology access, has emerged as a correlate of students' experience in the remote education, highlighting a challenge of mobile learning that is relevant for students, but not for faculty. Interestingly, SES did not differentiate in frequency of access to either technology or environment, suggesting this may not be a factor of finances but rather of lifestyle. Possibly students' living arrangements (dorm rooms, shared apartments etc.) are less conducive to learning outside of the traditional classroom. Indeed, qualitative data revealed more nuanced students' experiences, highlighting challenges managing the learning environment and the cost of devices needed for remote learning.

Interestingly, positive experiences were associated with previous involvement with remote education, suggesting that the prevalence of pre-pandemic remote education helped faculty and students to adjust during the COVID-19 emergency shift. Consistent with Gonzalex-Yebra, 2019, the current findings indicate that students appreciate having greater say in their educational environment. Similar to findings by Snow et al. (2018) There were some differences between faculty and students in terms of preferred features of LMS and web conferencing tools, but in general faculty and students found these tools to be helpful. Consistent with Snow et al., (2018), institutional support has emerged as an important factor impacting the quality of faculty and students' experiences during the shift. Thus, unique mobile learning advantages and challenges that are evident in the pre-pandemic world, have also emerged during the emergency shift to this modality, suggesting that such advantages and challenges are typical in the mobile learning environment regardless of the circumstances that prompt choosing this education model. On the hand, the current findings did highlight pandemic-unique challenges for students, such as having to balance educational with personal responsibilities during a health emergency situation.

The current findings have important implications that may be relevant as the world of education evolves to reflect greater mobility in higher education. Faculty should consider attaining certification in online education and attending regular classes to enhance their online teaching skills. Universities may want to consider requiring this as a professional development opportunity for faculty. Pedagogy must take into consideration students' preferred modes of communication to enhance effective connectedness in the mobile education environment. When students begin their orientation at a university, more education on the learning management system should be given so students are prepared, especially in unforeseen circumstances such as a pandemic or another emergency. Resource reallocation may be needed to support successful mobile education and meet emerging needs of faculty and especially of students, such as providing students with appropriate devices and access to technology. Special attention should be paid to pedagogy and resources that support students learning in the mobile environment, taking into consideration students' appreciation for more control of their learning environment on the one hand, and the challenges students face in accessing a suitable learning environment outside of the traditional classroom. Experts in remote education design should be added to a university Information Technology team to facilitate effective use of technology in teaching and learning.

The mixed method design used in this study was a strength in that it allowed for richer data, expanding on both students and faculty perspectives. However, the study is limited in that the sample is small and insufficient in scope since recruitment has taken place mostly in the northeast region of the United States. Many of the faculty and students were from two disciplines only (nursing and social work). Therefore, it is difficult to generalize the results of this study. Future studies should include faculty and students from across the country, and possibly internationally, and from varied disciplines to deepen the understanding of faculty and students experiences in remote education and its implications in the increasingly mobile world of academia.

REFERENCES

Barletta, V.S., Cassano, F., Marengo, A., Pagano, A., Pange, J., & Piccinno, A. (2022). Switching learning methods during the pandemic: A Quasi-experimental study on a master course. *Applied Science 12*, 8438. https://doi.org/10.3390/

Basford, L. (2021). "COVID keepers": The teaching strategies we should hold onto after the pandemic ends. *Academia Letters*, Article 2332. https://doi.org/10.20935/AL2332

Berger, R., Mallow, A., Tabag, K., et al (2021). Teaching and learning in a time of CORONA: A Social Work experience. *Clinical Social Work Journal*. doi.org/10.1007/s10615-021-00804-0.

Calderon, O., & Sood, C. (2018). Evaluating learning outcomes of an asynchronous online discussion assignment: A post-priori content analysis. *Interactive Learning Environment*. https://www.tandfonline.com/eprint/CSuZmcHIfMGYRwvYnZUI/full

Cilesiz, S. (2015). Undergraduate students' experiences with recorded lectures: towards a theory of acculturation. *Higher Education*, *69*(3), 471–493. https://doi.org/10.1007/s10734-014-9786-1

González-Yebra, Ó., Aguilar, M., Aguilar, F., & Lucas, M. (2019). Co-Design of a 3D virtual campus for synchronous distance teaching based on student satisfaction: experience at the University of Almería (Spain). *Education Sciences*, *9*(1), Article 21. doi.org/10.3390/educsci9010021

Grinnell, R.M., Williams, M., & Unrau, Y.A. (2019) *Research methods for social workers: An introduction* (12th ed). Pair Bond Publications.

Irani, T., Wilson, S., Barbour, S., Lynn, D., Rieger, M. et al. (2014). Graduate Student Experiences on and Off campus:Social Connectiveness and Perceived Isolation. *Journal of Distance Education*, 28,1, 1-16.

Ling, W., Lee, T., & Tho, S. (2017). A technological acceptance of remote laboratory in chemistry education. *Asia-Pacific Forum on Science Learning and Teaching*, *18*(2), 1-20.

Onyema, E. M., Nwafor, C. E., Obafemi, F. A., Sen, S., Antonye, F. G., & Sharma, A. (2020). Impact of Coronavirus Pandemic on Education. *Journal of Education and Practice. 11*(13), 108-121.

Robinson-Neal, A. (2021). Reflections on educational practice: COVID-19 influences. Academia letters, 176, 1-6.

Ross, A. F., & DiSalvo, M. L. (2020). Negotiating displacement, regaining community: The Harvard Language Center's response to the COVID-19 crisis. Foreign Language Annals, 53(2), 371-379. https://doi.org/10.1111/flan.12463

Simon, J., Burton, K., Lockhart, E., O'Donnell, S. (2014). Post-secondary distance education in a contemporary colonial context. *International Review of Research in Open and Distance Learning*, Athabasca, 15,1. doi.org/10.19173/irrodl.v15i1.1357.

Snow, W., Lamar, M., Hinkle, S., & Speciale, M. (2018). Current Practices in Online Counselor Education. *The Professional Counselor*, 8, 2, 131-145. doi:10.15241/whs.8.2.131.

Yeigh, T., & Lynch, D. (2020). Is online teaching and learning here to stay? *Academia Letters, Article 24*, 1-4. https://doi.org/10.20935/AL24

EDU-SOCIAL ALGORITHM: A METHODOLOGICAL MODEL FOR USING SMARTPHONES AND INSTAGRAM IN GENERATION ALPHA'S EDUCATION THROUGH A COMMUNITY OF VIRTUAL PRACTICES

Alessio Castiglione
Department of Psychology, Educational Sciences and Human Movement, University of Palermo, Viale delle Scienze, Ed.15, 90128, Palermo, Italy

ABSTRACT

The Edu-social Algorithm research project aims to construct a micro-pedagogical, experimental, digital research action to create a methodological model using the functions and algorithms found in social media used by Generation Alpha (specifically Instagram). The project is the manifestation of an explorative research path seeking to alter the algorithms that form the basis of all the major platforms in current cyberspace, and in "Big Tech". This alteration is possible through the development of a community of virtual practice, consisting of students and faculty working within Instagram through an interactive approach, to take pedagogical advantage of their mobile phones and apps. The qualitative results show a series of media-educational content evidencing the pedagogical potential of the social media platform Instagram, and the possibility of reproducing the developed methodological model. The relationships between digital education, social media, and active learning are the prevalent components of this work. Along with these main aspects, this research will also treat the relationship between educational reciprocity and the ownership of knowledge, though the goal of the research action is not only to create a digital methodological model, but a community of virtual practices founded on the approach derived by the didactic strategies intrinsic to the Edu-social Algorithm. The practical aspect of this research involves a target group of classes in the final year of middle schools, reaching a total of 98 students and 57 teaching faculty, participating in the Edu-social Algorithm across seven classrooms in three different schools in Palermo (Italy). The students in the experimental classrooms showed, compared with the control classrooms which followed a traditional model, the possibility of learning through social media and improving one's own scholastic performance, intentionally leaving smartphones on in the classroom, when used in conjunction with educational strategies designed for healthy smartphone use in teaching and learning.

KEYWORDS

Mobile Learning, Community of Virtual Practices, Media Education, Information and Communication Technologies, Generation Alpha

1. INTRODUCTION

Automated thinking was made possible by procedures known as *algorithms*. In information technology, the algorithm is a basic concept. Unlike equations, which have one result, algorithms limit themselves to recording the process for solving a problem (Foer, 2018). They are made up of a series of instructions that regulate and facilitate the at-times chaotic digital activity of human life. Over the years, the term has extended beyond the confines of information technology, accumulating new meanings for understanding and expressing simple and complex actions. Inspired by mathematics, today algorithmic thought is easily converted into a useful practice of organizing actions and ideas in order to behave according to certain determined standards. Education might be treated as a problem needing translation from the conceptual to the practical. Algorithms can allow, through a series of automatically ordered options, a person's process of discovering ideas aiding their own growth. Exploring the vocabulary of information technology inspired and became the foundation of, the general hypothesis guiding the reflections in this pedagogical research. This project looks to the future, but the results are largely grounded in the daily post-modern reality of constant technological inter- and hyper-connections. For a list of instructions to be considered an algorithm, only the following requisites must be satisfied:

completeness: every algorithm must be complete, meaning that each instruction must be able to be executed in a finite time and number of times; generality: every algorithm must provide the solution for a category of problems: at the same time, it must be applicable to any group of data and must produce results; non-ambiguity: each step to be followed must be defined distinctly, without paradoxes, contradictions, and ambiguities. Furthermore, these steps must be elementary, that is, unable to be broken down further; able to be understood in a direct and unambiguous by the executor, whether human or artificial; and completed in a defined time with an unambiguous result (Palladino, 2020). The algorithm tool which follows (figure 1), named *Edu-social Algorithm,* was built following these criteria. The end goal is to accompany students in forming a community of virtual practice called *Edu-social Algorithm.*

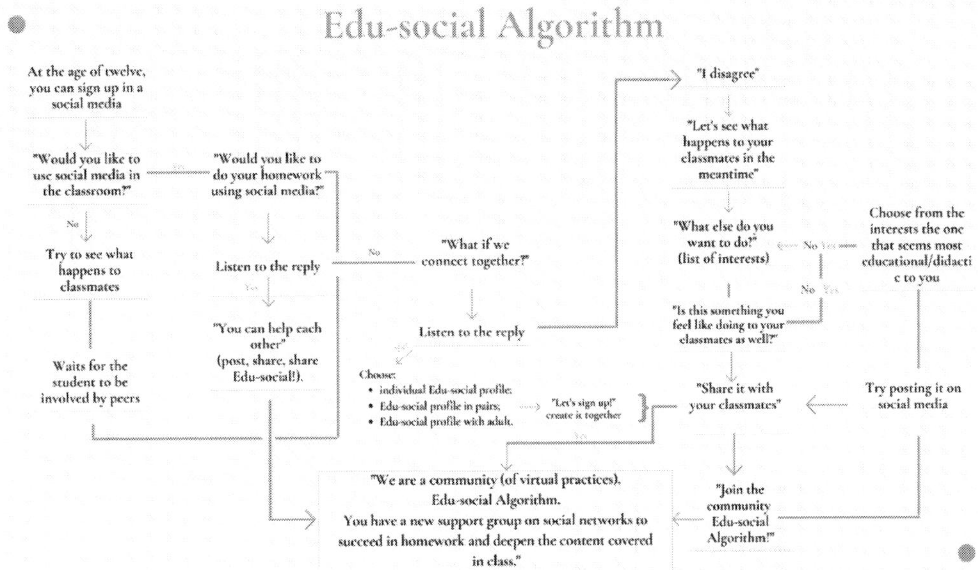

Figure 1. Algorithmic tool for the application of Edu-social Algorithm

There were two fundamental components of this research-action. On the one hand, pedagogy, to try and understand how the methodologies in education studies are responding to the new complexities of cyberspace. For this research, we adopted a heuristic-experimental research perspective of content and action, taking into account the significant pedagogical factors in Generation Alpha's educational experience thus far, and going beyond traditional, ready-made models of in-person and virtual education. The main objectives of the research-action were:

- to verify the pedagogical validity of social networks as media-educational tools;
- ideate, plan, and develop a community of virtual practice called the *Edu-social Algorithm;*
- to educate on a healthy use of social networks, when seen as tools functioning for students' scholastic performance and teachers' sense of self-efficacy.

2. CHOOSING A TARGET: GENERATION ALPHA AND DIGITAL LAUNCH

We can already see glimpses of education's future in how and where Generation Z spends its free, social, and alone time. Today, no adolescent does not have at least one tech device in front of their eyes, on their wrist, in their ears, or in their pockets (Gheno & Mastroianni, 2018). The next generation, Generation Alpha, affirms this picture even further. The psychologist Lancini in an interview with ANSA (2020) defines it as "the first generation that perceives technology not only as a means but as an integral aspect of existence. Raised with a tablet and a cell phone always right there, they are the children of parents who invest a lot of time, resources, and care in their education."(https://www.adviseonly.com/economia-e-mercati/economia-politice-esocieta/largo-alla-gen-alpha-veri-nativi-digitali-e-con-unanima-green/). The kids of this generation are digital native speakers, with digital-speaking parents who understand the potentials and risks of the Internet and its ways. The digital world has influenced the last thirty years of human life. Since the 2000s, the Internet has connected a large portion of the global population, with a computer or smartphone, creating the feeling that the risk of potentially unbearable individual isolation has been eliminated. According to the report *Digital 2018: global digital overview* from Global Annual Digital Growth, "Big Tech" has five billion registered users around the world, of which more than three billion are exclusively *social mobile*.

The landscape in Italy is no different, and follows the international trend of an exponential growth in the use of the Internet and various social media. Surveys from We Are Social and Hootsuite show that 57% of the Italian population is active on social networks. L'Atlante annuale dell'infanzia a rischio (Annual Atlas of Childhood at Risk), edited by Treccani in 2016 and born from the work of Save the Children Italy, analyzed the social fabric of youth and reported on numbers regarding minors in Italy: in 2015, more than one out of three minors surfs the internet every day (38.6%). In a sample of one thousand minors between the ages of twelve and seventeen, almost everyone (95%) has a profile on at least one social network. The average age for owning a first smartphone has lowered every year since 2001, reaching age eleven in 2017. A pre-teen owns at least one device that connects to the internet. These digital natives seem to use the internet mainly to stay in contact with their peers, through instant messaging platforms like Whatsapp, Messenger, or Telegram. Many of them know how to independently update their own Facebook and TikTok profiles, add stories and photos on Instagram or Whatsapp, and look for new friends in the hopes of feeling understood, appreciated, seen, desired, validated with an extra like or message (Castiglione et al., 2018). The psychologist Lavanco (2021) observes how children today are born in the world of the possible. With the excess of choice comes the risk of dependence. But what determines that behavior? Narcissism and the importance of being aesthetically affirmed. The need to think of oneself as the strongest, or best, representation of a particular quality, reinforcing natural pre-teen inclinations: to be totally perceived or to disappear completely. Pre-teens and adolescents live in a social media world of appearance and perception, based on images, and it allows for the capacity to seduce, to show one self, expose onself, or behave in extreme ways to attract others: for followers. Another collateral effect, notes Lavanco, is anxiety combined with a widespread lack of language for emotional expression, confusing emotions and roles in the adolescent mind. It is a time when the adolescent cannot distinguish between love and friendship, parents and friends, teachers and parents. On social media, this confusion manifests as a collective incapacity for understanding emotions. This is also the result of lacking and inadequate digital education, which should be guided by adults, working alongside young people, to develop the way together. The pedagogical experience should be seen as a collaborative one, a way to recognize one's own limits and potential.

Today, the algorithm holds a central place in our lives, involving our emotional plane and changing our decision-making processes (Nowotny, 2022). In the last few years, new and ever-more sophisticated systems of artificial intelligence have been developed, and not just for social media. As already discussed, the algorithm has become one of the basic tenets of information technology and artificial intelligence, but originally it was not a purely scientific concept. An algorithm is first and foremost a system, and skills, calculation, and creativity are needed for that system work correctly. Algorithms have always been considered precious, but technological progress has rendered them even more efficient and, at times, risky. Machine-learning has made these systems even more powerful, overthrowing the scientific method, as the designs emerge from data and correlations, rather than being guided by hypotheses (Foer, 2018). Depending on how they are used, algorithms can present amazing feats of logical reasoning, make life on the internet easier, allow old friends to reconnect, locate the book you were desperately trying to cite, find a way for enriching learning, or introduce a work opportunity that could set the digital user on the path to their future.

Recent research commissioned by BNP Paribas Cardif and conducted by Friendz, Technological, Inclusive and Green: Welcome Generation Alpha! (2020) helped show certain significant aspects of the generation of children born after 2010. Some of the most representative data in this research on technology shows a deep relationship to social media. "According to reports from parents, 62% of children begin using technology before age 5; a percentage which is trending upward each year, showing that the age of initial exposure to technology is consistently lowering. As expected, children mainly use smartphones (62%) and tablets (55%). Further, 53% can claim exclusive ownership of at least one device, even if only 9% has complete autonomy in using it, while 45% are always under parental control and 46% sometimes under parental control when using devices. What do they use them for? To play (50%), to watch videos or cartoons (21%), but some also use it for school (10%)" (BNP Paribas Cardif, 2020).

This research gives a first look at understanding the undeniable value and impact of technology in the lives of pre-adolescents of this generation. Knowing what the world was like before the technological revolution allows for a critical view of the present. But there is a risk of a "nostalgic pedagogy" that could condition our response to the new demands that education is being called on to confront. (Lavanco, I social e le dipendenze, from the cycle's online seminar "In trappola nella rete", 2021). We must adapt to the speed and rhythm of this technological evolution, and its many changes. With this perspective, the algorithm can be seen as a useful tool for working in educational contexts, in-person and virtual. The meaning of algorithm has grown far from the definition given to it by the Persian intellectual Muhammad Ibn Musa al-Khwarizmi. Over the course of the last few years, the term "algorithm", thanks to social media, has become part of colloquial language. App developers and tech engineers consider an algorithm a tool that is able to select, from among thousands of possible combinations, a "ranking" of the content that the user sees as soon as they login to their account. This model is created based on data freely offered by users whenever they search, comment, share, like, or even talk about something near a device connected to the internet. It is a sophisticated facilitator of content, able to sift and sort notifications that might be interesting to millions of users with social media accounts. It is a filter of knowledge that adapts itself to the user's interests, and at the same time triggers new interests based on its programmers' intentions (Cappello, edited by, 2020).

These considerations brought forth the Edu-social Algorithm project's general research question: is it possible to use smartphones, and to adapt social media algorithms for media-educational purposes?

In this first experiment 7 classes, 98 students, and 57 teachers were reached, through carefully created social media accounts with the usernames Edu + first name + last name, used by all involved participants (students and faculty) across three different middle schools in Palermo, located in neighborhoods deemed at risk for poor education and high dropout rates. The collective creation of new accounts by the project participants was the launch of this experiment for a community of virtual practices. This community uses algorithms and has a pedagogical focus. It is activated by educational and didactic content uploaded and shared by connected users in a virtual space within Instagram, and aims to promote a positive change in the teaching and learning of students in Generation Alpha. In the four months of executing this project, the smartphone became more than a purely technological object. It began to be considered as, and converted into, a tool for learning, in line with the theories and practices derived from Mobile Learning for the educational future of Generation Alpha and the generations to follow.

In Italy, a law went into action on September 20, 2018, following European regulations (Gdpr, May 25, 2018) that decreed fourteen as the minimum age required for accessing a social network or instant messaging service. Currently, in Italy, no thirteen-year-old minor can sign up for any social media platform, despite the American and Chinese laws that govern the companies that run these platforms. Corroborating these norms is the warning issued by the Italian Data Protection Authority (Garante della privacy nazionale), after a criminal case in Palermo involving an alleged challenge killer and a ten-year-old girl. Parents who want to sign their children up on social media networks between age thirteen and fourteen are liable for the consequences; this rule abides by culpa-in-vigilande (vicarious culpability), a practice at the basis of Italian parental civil responsibility. Despite the fact that by law minors between eight and thirteen are not permitted to sign up for social media or instant messaging platforms, the sale and ownership of sim cards for minors that have turned eight years old, with permission from a parent or guardian, is permitted. This sale often includes offers from phone providers for installing apps with parental controls.

At the international level, today, the main social networks and messaging channels follow these age restrictions:

- Facebook and Instagram: the minimum age requirement is thirteen years old, minors between thirteen and fifteen years need parental consent to use social media;
- WhatsApp, Messenger: if the user resides in a country within the European Economic Area (includes the EU), the user must be at least sixteen years old (or the oldest age required by Country). If the user resides in another country, outside of the European Area, the user must be at least thirteen years old.
- TikTok: since February 9, 2021, the platform blocks users under thirteen through an age verification system;

In Italy, the minimum age requirement has been set at fourteen years old. However, the threshold is thirteen for the main platforms listed above, who have not changed their policies to adapt to Italian law, making it easy for thirteen-year-olds to access social network platforms. Thirteen to fourteen is exactly the range of ages that currently marks the first members of Generation Alpha. With this in mind, this research design has resolved to transform the educational methodological model, based on the tool of the Edu-social Algorithm, in order to create a community of virtual practices within Instagram, the app most used by Generation Alpha along with TikTok. The end goals are to find new educational ways to adopt in scholastic settings (and outside these settings), for the defused use of a new digital methodological model to introduce at the exact moment at which a pre-adolescent can legally become a part of social media cyberspace.

3. METHODOLOGICAL PROCEDURES

In a first investigation, we considered sources and data from a variety of national and international scientific studies, including those on: online teaching contexts (Marcus-Quinn & Hourigan, 2021), learning to cope with complexity and adolescents online (Amendola et al., 2018); digital education and digital teachers (Volpi, 2021); the theory and implementation of Mobile Learning (Kearney et al., 2020); participatory culture and digital competence (Jenkins, 2009); social media education (Kai Wha Chu, 2020); algorithm as educational instrument; education among peers with supervision by educational personnel. A comparison to these educational models will follow, taking into account the evolution of individual generational facts (McCrindle & Fell, 2021), and connecting them to the general progression of the education system. This comparative perspective developed a micro-pedagogy thanks to this previous research, and drawing on reflections of experienced educational personnel in the project as a research resource: e-tutor faculty, researcher-instructors. The faculty was also involved in a training centered around the Edu-social Algorithm methodological model for creating the approach to be used within classrooms. A useful point of reference for the research was the study relating to Dig Comp 2.1: A Framework for Developing and Understanding Digital Competence in Europe (following link: publications.jrc.ec.europa.eu/repository/handle/JRC128415) a tool for improving digital competency in citizens, applicable to educational contexts. DigComp provided a dynamic definition for digital competence, not defined by the use of specific tools, but to the needs that each citizen holds (Cartesio M.L., 2020).

Along with pedagogy, the main focus point was the digital world and its algorithms. This research focus deepened the theme of digital education through social media. The chosen methodology was research-action (RA). The main purpose of this style of research consists in actively involving all subjects included in the study. An informal involvement, aimed at promoting change (Benvenuto, 2015). To answer these questions, the research-action Edu-social Algorithm was developed in three phases:

I. Phase I (plan): identification of subject definition of project and collective problems with the involvement of target teachers.
   a. Intervention description: Along with source and data collection from pedagogical research on digital education, in this first phase of research partner schools were chosen. Project was shared with the schools, and the involved school education staff was chosen. From subject, project definition, and research-action questions, a methodological format was created from the theme, definition, and research-actions questions, focused on using smartphones during class as educational resources, in order to collect significant positive and/or negative experiences useful for the development of an educational model that has a phenomenological approach to social networks. On this occasion, a handbook will be created using DigComp sizes, Netiquette concepts, and a relevant glossary on digital education for the diffusion of a common digital pedagogical culture. Focus points: problem identification; analytically examine and explore possibilities and understand limits; conceive a methodological format known as Edu-social Algorithm; plan phase II. Assessment tools: focus group and training (teachers); participatory observation (researcher); focus group's reflective report (researcher).

II. Phase II (act): Application of methodological template related to Edu-social Algorithm + creation of the empirical basis.
   a. Intervention description: This second phase of research is entirely characterized by the launch of the practical experiment. The experimental group and control groups in classes were chosen by the researchers, after completing training, learning the tool Edu-social Algorithm and choosing the teachers to work in Generation Alpha's classes. The implementation phase included the creation of a methodological model with the teachers and the experimental group students in order to create a time and space for digital education. This step involved paying

attention to all the components and activating the students through the Edu-social Algorithm, with the purpose of developing a community of virtual practice on social networks. In addition, this step provided the empirical base with the first collected data.

   b. Focus points: launching and promotion of experiment; data collection; creation of a community of virtual practices.
   c. Assessment tools: research diary (researcher); journal on insights and observations (teachers); digital storytelling on Instagram (teachers and students).

III. Phase III (observe & reflect): final theorization and elaboration of collective processes.

   a. Intervention description: after the practical experimentation in Generation Alpha's educational contexts with the methodological template produced by the research-project Edu-social Algorithm; the last phase was dedicated to the collection of qualitative and quantitative data produced in the first two phases, for the drafting of an article for academic publication. This phase referred back to the use of assessment techniques and methods with the tools used in previous actions.
   b. Focus points: critically assess the process; discuss, deepen, analyse (comparison forum).
   c. Assessment tools: Narrative inquiry (Clandinin & Connelly, 2004) on the collected data (researcher); report (researcher).

Methods: complicating factors and variables were considered valuable in this experiment, following the explorative-interpretive method regarding the observation of faculty and student behaviors within the designated social networks. An experimental method was used for the application of the Edu-social Algorithm in training contexts for teachers who took part in the experiment. Evaluation tools were developed in order to track students' progress, and for understanding the positive and/or negative effects of the research.

Research Queries:

- Can education go viral thanks to smartphones and social media?
- Can you create social media teachers, or media-educational students—*nano influencers* (F. Pira, 2020)?
- Can we configure social networks to create a new methodological model as a response to the new educational challenges facing Generation Alpha's teachers?

4. RESULTS AND MATERIALS

The overall results (figure 1 and figure 2) demonstrate the reactions of the participants using the Edu-social Algorithm methodological model. They used media as an education tool for the planning, theoretical development, and practical execution of a methodological model aimed towards the creation of a community of virtual practices, to be used in the teaching and learning of Generation Alpha, who uploaded, shared, and commented on media-educational content. In the pilot class, after faculty training and focus groups with students, we developed additional materials for evaluating learning with the Edu-social Algorithm. Throughout this project, we also grappled with the means and function of smartphones used in the classroom within a delineated time and space. A community of practices, in line with this research project's aims, grew within Instagram. This community was made up of teachers and students who continue to use these educational accounts to upload core lesson materials. An activity sheet (figure 3) and evaluation (figure 4) aided faculty and students as they integrated material from the Edu-social Algorithm model into their classroom.

Measuring Progress and Early Results

The key indicators of progress for the Edu-social Algorithm model are the student posts on the community feed. Here are a few examples of the educational content students have shared on Instagram*

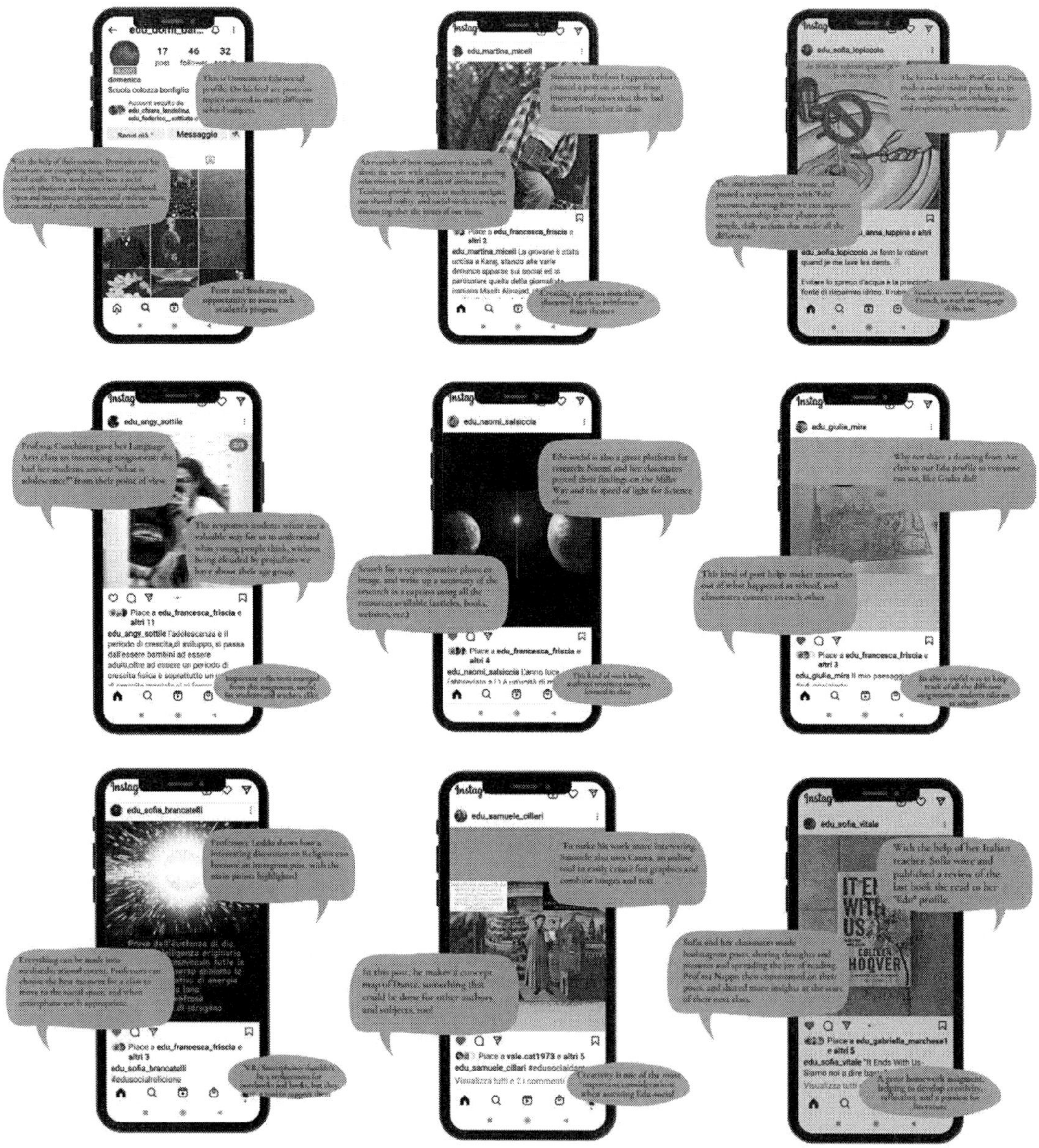

*FURTHER INFORMORMATION ON THE PROJECT CAN BE FOUND ON THE INSTAGRAM PROFILE "EDU_SOCIAL_ALGORITHM"

Figure 1. Posts published by Edu-social students

Figure 2. Posts published by Edu-social teachers

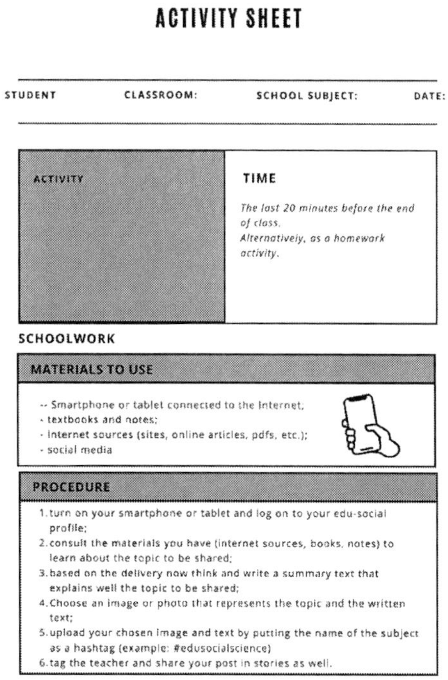

ACTIVITY SHEET

STUDENT CLASSROOM: SCHOOL SUBJECT: DATE:

ACTIVITY

TIME

The last 20 minutes before the end of class.
Alternatively, as a homework activity.

SCHOOLWORK

MATERIALS TO USE

-- Smartphone or tablet connected to the Internet;
- textbooks and notes;
- Internet sources (sites, online articles, pdfs, etc.);
- social media

PROCEDURE

1. turn on your smartphone or tablet and log on to your edu-social profile;
2. consult the materials you have (internet sources, books, notes) to learn about the topic to be shared;
3. based on the delivery now think and write a summary text that explains well the topic to be shared;
4. Choose an image or photo that represents the topic and the written text;
5. upload your chosen image and text by putting the name of the subject as a hashtag (example: #edusocialscience)
6. tag the teacher and share your post in stories as well.

Figure 3. Activity Edu-social Sheet

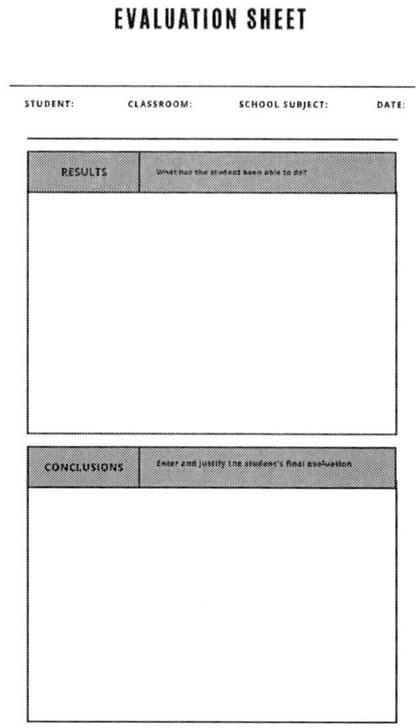

EVALUATION SHEET

STUDENT: CLASSROOM: SCHOOL SUBJECT: DATE:

RESULTS	What has the student been able to do?

CONCLUSIONS	Enter and justify the student's final evaluation

Figure 4. Evaluation Edu-social Sheet

The e-tutor faculty showed, through the training, a model of how to exist online in a human and authentic way, learning how to created meaningful relationships online, overcoming instinctive or primitive attitudes. This study provided an occasion for true intergenerational exchange, and educational reciprocity in the enormous and experiential territory that makes up most of every day in the lives of Generation Alpha students and their adult reference points. With this educational framework, we also kept in mind the potential risks to the lives of youth online, regarding: identity theft; security failures; phishing; hate-speech and incitement; online child grooming; conditions and behaviors of extreme risk (challenge killer); cyberbullying, etc. At the same time, given the widespread attention to the prevention of these increasing phenomena, we tried to understand with the teachers how and how much the approaches and policies of social networks, within Europe and outside of Europe, affect the regulation of online behaviors. This action aimed for horizontal work online, involving everyone: students, social media teachers, and research teams, collaborating to find ways to make education viral, and to create a cultural pedagogy of social media, with educational clicks powerful enough to change the algorithm.

5. CONCLUSION AND DISCUSSIONS

"Edu-social Algorithm: a Methodological Model for Evaluating the Impact of Social Media Network Algorithms on Generation Alpha's Education Through a Community of Virtual Practice" is the complete title of this research design, presented for the doctorate in the Department of Psychology, Educational Sciences and Human Movement at the University of Palermo. The project involved three middle schools in Palermo for the implementation of a methodological model that has followed the increased classroom use of smartphones connected to Instagram with specific "Edu" accounts. In these last few months, 7 classrooms, 98 students, and 57 faculty across three different schools in Palermo ("I.C.T. Principessa Elena di Napoli", "I.C.T Colozza-Bonfiglio", "I.C.T Lombardo Radice"), participated in beginning to create a new kind of school, within social networks. Thanks to the participants, the virtual space has become a learning space, a space for sharing pedagogical content, working on assignments, doing homework, giving information, and uploading classroom work. The project, with school cooperation, will continue, with possible developments and the hope of bringing other schools into this experiment of transforming social media into a tool for education. The initial student response has been positive, and teachers have also started to notice improvements in participation and scholastic performance. While it is too early to understand its long-term value, the general attitude and the first media-educational content that has emerged from the methodological model in action are hopeful indicators for the pedagogical potential of social media. With teachers, we addressed the time and space given to this new model, specifying that the intention is not to substitute learning with notebooks, books, and computers, but to use the smartphone as another resource for Generation Alpha's education. This Generation, after Generation Z, sees technology as an integral part of their lives. For that reason, it is fundamental to help them develop, in a protected context like school, a healthy relationship with social networks and smartphones, as suggested by Mobile Learning, the pedagogical style integrating mobile technology in scholastics settings as useful instruments for learning, inside and outside of school. This experiment has tried to build a bridge between different generations, to create a new pedagogical path, full of surprises and new ideas for rethinking school, smartphones, and social media.

REFERENCES

Ansa. (2020). *Inclusivi e ambientalisti, così i bambini della Generazione Alpha guidano il cambiamento.* https://www.ansa.it/canale_lifestyle/notizie/teen/2020/10/14/inclusivi-e-ambientalisti-cosi-i-bambini-della-generazione-alpha-guidano-il-cambiamento_8900c192-38ca-49e0-b5e4-1ffa0aa8ca66.html.

Amendola, A., Beniamino, G., Monti, A., M. (2018). *Adolescenti nella rete. Quando il web diventa una trappola* (Tr. IT.). Rome: L'Asino d'oro edizioni.

Benvenuto, G. (2015). *Stili e metodi della ricerca educativa* (Tr. IT.) Rome: Carocci editore.

BNP Paribas Cardif. (2020). *Tecnologica, inclusiva e green: benvenuta Generazione Alpha!,* https://ifmagazine.bnpparibascardif.it/2020/11/02/benvenuta-generazione-alpha.

Buckingham, D.. (2020) *La media education a scuola. Un approccio olistico per la costruzione della cittadinanza digitale* (Tr. IT.), Gianna Cappello (edited by), in *Un manifesto per la media education.* Florence: Mondadori Università.

Cartesio, M. L., *La competenza digitale nel DigComp e nel DigCompEdu* (Tr. IT.), in "Educazione, didattica e comunità", 1 (2020), pp. 317-323.

Castiglione A., Coppola G., Alessi Batù G., Palma S., *Affrontare il cyberbullismo in classe. Comprendere e riconoscere gli effetti collaterali dei social network* (Tr. IT.), in Psicologia di comunità, 2 (2018), pp. 112-119.

Clandinin D., J., Connelly, F., M. (2004). *Narrative inquiry. Experience and Story in qualitative Research.* New York: Jossey-Bass.

Demetrio, D. (2020). *Micropedagogia. La ricerca qualitativa in educazione* (Tr. IT.). Milan: Raffaello Cortina Editore.

Digital 2020 Italia. (2018). *We Are Social Italia*, www.wearesocial.com.

EU Science Hub. (2017). *DigComp 2.1: The Digital Competence Framework for Citizens with eight proficiency levels and examples of use.* publications.jrc.ec.europa.eu/repository/handle/JRC128415)

Foer, F. (2018). *I nuovi poteri forti, come Google, Apple, Facebook e Amazon pensano per noi* (Tr. IT). Milan: Longanesi.

Global Annual Digital Growht. (2018). *Digital 2018: global digital overwiev*, https://datareportal.com/reports/digital-2018-global-digital-overview, www.datareportal.com.

Gheno, V., Mastroianni, B. (2018). *Tienilo acceso. Posta, commenta, condividi senza spegnere il cervello* (Tr. IT*).* Milan: Longanesi.

Jenkin, H. (2009) *Confronting the Challenges of Participatory Culture: Media Education for the 21st Century.* Cambridge: The MIT Press.

Kearney, M., Burden, K., Schuck, S. (2020). *Theorising and implementing Mobile Learning. Using the iPAC Framework to Inform Research and Teaching Practice.* Singapore: Springer Nature Singapore.

Kai Wah Chu, S. (2020*). Social Media Tools in Experiential Internship Learning.* Singapore: Springer Nature Singapore.

Lavanco, G. «I social e le dipendenze», presentato per il ciclo di incontri In trappola nella rete. Palerm, 23/02/2021.

Marcus-Quinn, A., Hourigan, T. (2021). *Handbook for Online Learning Contexts: Digital, Mobile and Open. Policy and practice.* Cham: Springer Nature Switzerland.

McCrindle, M., Fell, A. (2021). *Generation Alpha.* Sydney: Hachete Australia.

Nowotny, H. (2022). *Le macchine di Dio. Gli algoritmi predittivi e l'illusione del controllo* (tr. ITA). Rome: Luiss University Press.

Palladino, M. (2020) *Gli algoritmi nella vita di tutti i giorni*. https://www.marcopalladino.it/it/algoritmi-nella-vita-di-tutti-i-giorni/#:~:text=L'algoritmo%20%C3%A8%20presente%20un,motore%20di%20ricerca%20sul%20Web.

Pira, F. (2020) *Figli delle app. Le nuove generazioni digital-popolari e social-dipendenti*. (Tr. IT.), Milan: FrancoAngeli.

Save The Children Italia. (2016) *Atlante annuale dell'infanzia a rischio*, Treccani, Rome: Treccani Libri.

Volpi, B. (2021) *Docenti digitali. Insegnare a sviluppare nuove competenze nell'era di Internet* (Tr. IT). Bologna: Società editrice il Mulino.

Fundaro, A. (2021). *Social media per bambini e adolescenti: cosa devono sapere docenti e genitori*, https://www.orizzontescuola.it/social-media-per-bambini-e-adolescenti-cosa-devono-sapere-docenti-e-genitori-scarica-elenco-app-piu-usate/, www.orizzontescuola.it.

GENERATION OF PRODUCTIVE EXPERIENCES IN THE DIGITAL ERA 4.0

Sonia Armas-Arias[1,]*, María Esther Alcántara Gutiérrez** and Mireya Ramírez Martínez**
*Universidad Técnica de Ambato, Equador
**Universidad Popular Autónoma del Estado de Puebla, Mexico

ABSTRACT

The digital age 4.0 governs the progress of society and individuals require the acquisition of skills to face this reality. Education is the only way that will allow human beings to adapt to the new global challenges. Therefore, the achievement of productive experiences must be the priority of the current educational system to train competent professionals. This research aimed to diagnose the elements involved in the generation of productive experiences in the digital age 4.0. The methodology worked through a quantitative approach, of a descriptive nature, supported by a non-experimental and field design. The research sample was made up of 25 teachers from the "Nueva Era" Educational Institution, who participated in a survey consisting of a questionnaire of questions related to learning experiences and the digital age. The results of the study showed that an average of 3.82 interviewers, at a high level, pay special attention to the causal processes in the approach to such learning. Therefore, it was concluded that the main elements that intervene in the generation of productive experiences in the digital age 4.0, are the technical, contextual, and pedagogical processes, as well as the intervention of teaching strategies and technological tools, directly influencing in the development of digital skills for life.

KEYWORDS

Productive Experiences, Digital Age 4.0, Digital Skills, 21st Century Society

1. INTRODUCTION

As technological advances increase, the requirements of society become more demanding. The digital age no longer depends on mechanical individuals, but on subjects prepared to face current problems. For this reason, the training of professionals should be directed to the development of abilities and skills applicable to life, where they become executors of innovative processes. Consequently, the educational field plays a fundamental role in creating the exit profile of students, providing a wide range of theoretical, practical, and evaluative knowledge, focused on the use of TIC and globalization.

The generation of productive experiences is the possible response to the change that the world demands because it allows acquiring significant learning that facilitates the resolution of conflicts of daily life. However, the biggest obstacle is found in the so-called digital age 4.0, since the gaps between one context and another have made innovation almost impossible for certain sectors of society. Therefore, the insertion of technological tools in education is a complex task and requires proper resource management. In other words, not only is it enough to acquire virtual equipment and platforms, but also to plan their effective use.

The use of TICs in educational units has not shown major change when compared with the results obtained by the same institutions in previous years. The high school exit profile, despite having the management of technology and innovation as a strength, has not been sufficiently reflected in the labor field. So, it is not possible to speak of productive experiences, since there are individuals who have only acquired theoretical knowledge, but do not know how to use it properly for their personal and collective benefit.

In this way, the main objective of the research was to diagnose the elements that intervene in the generation of productive experiences in the digital age 4.0, applied by the teachers of the "New Era Educational Institution". In this way, the study emphasized the interrelation between technical, contextual, and pedagogical processes, which directly affect the achievement of learning for life supported using technological tools.

[1] Corresponding Author: sp.armas@uta.edu.ec

Students, through the development of digital skills, can actively participate in solving current problems under a well-prepared professional profile.

The aspects that intervene in the generation of productive experiences in the context of the digital age 4.0 must consider the needs of the 21st century society. The technical, contextual, and pedagogical processes involved in the generation of learning experiences must be fully understood to improve current education. However, we must not forget the role that the educator plays in teaching and the development of skills that allow the learner to form a comprehensive profile. Based on these approaches, it is essential to analyze the global panorama of the study phenomenon and determine the influence of the elements that intervene in the educational and professional training field.

2. STATE OF THE ART

According to Casillas and Ramírez, 2019, The digital culture has modified the population, causing social interactions to change in all sectors. Technological transformation forces human beings to redesign their way of communicating and acting, however, adequate preparation is necessary to face the panorama of the 4.0 age. Therefore, educational institutions must be ready to train versatile students, capable of easily adapting to the new way of life, through processes that identify strengths and weaknesses that directly affect the achievement of learning, especially in the technological context.

Mogollón (2020) mentioned that educational innovation faces various obstacles such as the use of technological tools, the design of learning experiences in digital contexts and the formation of a culture of digital literacy, however, he considers that they do not represent a challenge. The correct planning of the use of ICT can provide fruitful results, however, if they are not used, unfortunately there will never be a significant change. Thus, the resources that schools have, regardless of their quantity, must be used to the maximum to achieve the desired skills.

Mobile devices and some technological devices such as computers and tablets have become essential tools for society. The increase in technologies that include the internet and mobile connection forms an imminent possibility to establish a wide set of processes that facilitate feedback and learning (Gelb, Mital and Mukjerjee, 2020). In other words, people who have digital resource should make the most of its benefits and use its full potential for the benefit of knowledge and its applicability to everyday life.

According to Mercado, L., Mercado, T., Ziritt, G., and Consuegra, S. (2018), they argue that the vertiginous technological advance and the social transformations of the 21st century society have caused the response capacity of the school sector is not up to the level and requires urgent innovation alternatives. So, even though students have various electronic devices, education has not shown any progress by not properly taking advantage of the resources available to them. Therefore, it is necessary to plan activities that use the available tools to achieve the rhythm of the digital age 4.0.

The achievement of productive experiences must go hand in hand with the use of all available physical and human resources to ensure educational progress. In this sense, to generate true learning experiences in the digital age, school actors must seek the integration of capacities, both technological and academic, to consolidate interdisciplinary knowledge (Ureta and Rossetti, 2020). To do this, it is necessary to identify the goals to be achieved and design plans based on objectives, strategies, methods, activities, and evaluations that allow checking theoretical and practical learning.

In addition to proper planning, educational agents must consider the dizzying progress of TICs and how they affect the development of education for the 21st century. Apolo (2019) mentioned the importance of identifying trends in the field of technology for formal education and highlights the need to be applied in a study context, to distinguish weaknesses and strengths of use in school establishments. Various platforms and free digital resources are created every day and go unnoticed by society. Therefore, education must be attentive to changes and be ready to transform its traditional method of work.

Hernández R., 2017 mentioned that technology, therefore, has become the generator of opportunities for change and transformation of education, where the results cause a great impact that provides timely solutions to educational and social problems useful for the social progress. However, it should be noted that to achieve these results it is essential that there is a correct use of digital and technological resources, without ignoring the part that falls on the development of life skills. Therefore, prioritizing students to achieve productive experiences in the digital age 4.0 must become the global mission of education.

It is not enough to know the concept of technological devices or how to handle the main text editors, because digital competence encompasses more than that. Under this scheme, Álava, Illescas and Loor (2017), emphasize that students demand improvements in the exit profile, where the achievement of job skills aimed at the effective management of virtual platforms and the use of TIC is ensured. Therefore, education must analyze, from the social reality, the requirements of the new generations in terms of their training and professional development as functional subjects.

An alternative is to opt for the design of educational programs based on active methodologies that insert technology as an applicable means for academic training. Learning based on virtual platforms should be considered as an opportunity for educational actors to create their own digital resources, use e-learning strategies and apply interactive evaluations that work as support for current teaching (Clavijo, Loiza, Ramirez, and Pacheco, 2021). In other words, taking advantage of all the available tools will make it possible to meet the expectations of students in acquiring skills for the 21st century society.

Under this scheme, Garzón (2021) maintains that educational competencies are not static, much less unmodifiable, or rigid, since they must be adapted to the context and its particularities, considering the key factors that surround it. Therefore, education can no longer aspire to the formation of mechanical people, experts in replicating actions and following orders, since that is no longer required by society. Currently, the needs are focused on the search for solutions to the great problems of society, so the ability to solve and manage technologies are the most desired skills.

There are countless skills that have caught the attention of young people today, such as adaptability, capacity for interrelation and teamwork, as well as creativity, innovation and leadership, which will ensure the creation of a profile based on competencies (Tamayo, Tinitana, Apolo, Martínez, and Zambrano, 2021). The inclusion of such skills will allow the development of productive experiences in children and adolescents, who will be able to apply their knowledge in activities that stand out for innovation and the use of technological tools. Therefore, the use of digital resources is a key factor in the design of these study plans.

The main actor in educational change is the teacher, becoming the protagonist of the TIC inclusion process. The achievement of applicable skills for the digital age 4.0 continues to be perceived as a challenge, however, it should not be considered as an impossible challenge to meet. Hernández, Orrego and Quiñones (2018), assure that the teaching role is cataloged as a mediator of learning, which values the recent challenges of education in the so-called era of knowledge and innovation. So, although the educator is aware of the challenge of inserting technology in the school, he looks for ways to take advantage of it to improve the teaching and learning process.

According to Melo, 2018, the insertion of ICT in education leads to the development of sequential programs with all the stages of planning, application, and evaluation by the teacher. In addition, the teacher requires preparation and training processes that allow him to monitor compliance with educational plans and teaching strategies that include the use of technological tools. Consequently, the educator becomes an active subject, interested in learning new forms of teaching and the use of virtual resources that prepare students for life.

Therefore, active methodologies have gained strength in those interested in educational innovation by ensuring significant learning in students. The construction of knowledge from experiences supported by theoretical, practical, and technological knowledge will always be classified as a great educational success. In this sense, educational institutions must make the most of the benefits of such strategies.

The teacher oversees designing didactic activities, based on the use of technologies, where the search for adaptable teaching strategies and collective individual work, form in the student a profile attentive to the contents and practice (Rodríguez, R., Orozco, Rocha and Rodríguez, O., 2017). Therefore, the work of the innovative teacher will bear fruit if he develops an active plan that develops skills for daily living. Through human, digital, and physical resources, students will be able to acquire skills focused on the significant contribution they can make to society.

Internal factors such as motivation and aptitude, inherent to the teacher, need to be strengthened through strategies such as training in TIC skills, the use of digital tools and their incorporation into educational processes (Sosa, 2018). In this sense, the teaching profile, as well as the student profile, must be redesigned to meet the requirements of today's society. Teachers, being the subjects that directly influence student learning, need to innovate their methodology and expand the range of resources used during class hours.

According to Ramírez, Monroy and Vargas (2017), they assure that teachers must be constantly updated, causing them to appropriate the use of TIC and apply it in the classroom, achieving a drastic improvement in pedagogical performance. The benefits of inserting digital tools in the classroom continue to stand out by developing transversal skills that lead to critical thinking and the motivation to transform traditional education. Innovation in the educational field derives in the success of the subjects that are trained in the different educational establishments. However, it depends on the efforts that all the actors involved in such a process are willing to make.

However, there are sectors that do not have basic resources such as devices or Internet access and, therefore, it is imperative that the authorities rethink government and institutional policies in order to keep pace with technological advances, making possible their insertion in education (Melo, 2018). Although there are establishments that have a wide range of digital resources, there is still a shortage of them in socially disadvantaged sectors. Therefore, state actions must be directed to the benefit of education, since it will mean, in the future, the development of the country.

The changes that 21st century society reflects day by day create new challenges in all sectors (Ramírez, et al., 2017). Education does not face its economic problems, but also of ideology and innovation. Not having sufficient technological resources for the development of a significant educational process is a serious obstacle, but there are institutions that have the necessary tools and do not know how to use them. Therefore, the preparation of future professionals should not remain stagnant and requires the search for alternatives that allow the formation of great skills in the future.

According to Callis and Basto 2020, technological culture is classified as a concrete process, in which thoughts and actions are combined for social benefit. An outdated education, focused on creating docile professionals who do not think and do, is no longer essential for global advancement. Therefore, the interest of creating true productive experiences in the digital age 4.0 must be perceived as the ideal objective for the society of the 21st century, since it is the salvation letter for the great problems of today.

3. METHODOLOGY

The study worked under a quantitative, descriptive approach, supported by a non-experimental and field design. Taking into consideration the theoretical construction and the obtaining of data on the fundamental circumstances that allow the generation of productive experiences in the digital age, the chosen methodology starts. A rational method of deductive hypothetical analysis was selected in relation to the type of knowledge generated by teachers in a technological context in favor of the education of the students of the "Nueva Era" Educational Institutional.

To approach this method, it was necessary to achieve the following order of steps: define the problem, formulate the hypothesis, contrast the empirical information with the scientific one, and deduce the results obtained.

The teachers of the educational institution were the protagonists of the study, who provided the field information required to comply with the methodological design of the research. The events raised are currently found for what is considered a contemporary temporality at work, emphasizing the pandemic caused by Covid-19, since the use of the necessary technological means in a virtual modality education was highlighted.

The events raised are currently found for what is considered a contemporary temporality at work, emphasizing the pandemic caused by Covid-19, since the use of the necessary technological means in a virtual modality education was highlighted. In the same way, the data collection approach was quantitative for its subsequent treatment and generation of statistical graphs that support the investigative work, the following scales being the ones selected to fulfill this task.

Table 1. Scale for the Interpretation of the average or arithmetic mean

Range	Interval	Category
5	4,21 – 5	Higher Level
4	3,41 – 4,20	High level
3	2,61 – 3,40	Moderate Level
2	1,81 – 2,60	Low level
1	1 – 1,80	Lower Level

Source: Armas, S (2022).

The scale that has been designed represents the levels that the results can reach taking into account the scores obtained on a measurement scale from zero to four represented in intervals and categories. Regarding the arithmetic mean and standard deviation, the tables indicate the degree of dispersion between the findings obtained, as well as their level of reliability.

Table 2. Scale for the Interpretation of the standard deviation

Range	Interval	Category
5	3.21 – 4	Higher Level
4	2.41- 3.20	High level
3	1.61 – 2.40	Moderate Level
2	0.81 – 1.60	Low level
1	0 – 0.80	Lower Level

Source: Armas, S (2022).

4. RESULTS

As a result of the work carried out, with the help of the data collection instruments and the purpose of achieving the objectives determined in the investigation, the most relevant results for this document were taken. The following results were obtained:

Table 3. Causal processes in 21st century education

Dimension	Subdimensions	Average	Category	Standard deviation	Category
Causal Processes	Technical	4.08	High level	0.43	Lower dispersion
	Contextual	3.48	High level	0.19	Lower dispersion
	Pedagogical	3.89	High level	0.62	Lower dispersion
General average of the dimension		3.82	High level	0.42	Lower dispersion

Source: Armas, S (2022).

Taking into account the data obtained from the teacher survey applied in the “New Era Educational Institution”, there is an average of 4.08 respondents who reflected a high level in the technical subdimension, with a 0.43 standard deviation, resulting in a very low dispersion between the answers. Regarding the contextual subdimension, it was found that an average of 3.48 teachers have a high knowledge of their environment with a very low dispersion according to the interpretation scale of the resulting 0.19 standard deviation. Likewise, in the pedagogical subdimension, an average of 3.82 teachers was obtained, who show that they have a high recognition in pedagogy, reflecting in a very low dispersion between the results with a standard deviation of 0.62.

Table 4. Learning experiences in virtual environments

Variable	Dimensions	Average	Category	Standard deviation	Category
Learning experience	Teaching Strategies	4.24	Very High Level	0.16	Very low dispersion
	Types of technological tools	3.57	High level	0.33	Muy baja dispersión
	Causal Processes	3.82	High level	0.42	Muy baja dispersión
General average of the dimension		3.88	High level	0.30	Muy baja dispersión

Source: Armas, S (2022).

Regarding the findings collected from the teacher survey, it is reflected that there is an average of 4.24 respondents who claim to apply teaching strategies at a high level, showing a 0.16 standard deviation, demonstrating low dispersion. On the other hand, the participants have a high level of knowledge in relation to the types of technological tools with an average of 3.57 and a 0.33 standard deviation, revealing a very low dispersion between the data. Finally, in the causal processes sub-dimension, the teachers ratified having a very high level of comprehension with an average of 3.82, confirming a very low dispersion according to the answers obtained with a standard deviation of 0.42.

5. DISCUSSION

The data reflected in table 3 show that, although the teacher is the owner of the subject and the concepts that he teaches within it, the must be aware that not only the theoretical part intervenes at the time of teaching, since the techniques that he uses, the environment in which it works and who are the beneficiaries of their work are fundamental elements. As Ramírez, Monroy and Vargas (2017) mentioned, who argue that a teacher must be constantly updated to strengthen their performance in the pedagogical field with the help of TIC tools in the classroom. Being corroborated by Sosa in 2018, who asserts that teaching skills are strengthened through self-training and training primarily when they focus on the use of TICs in educational processes.

Due to the fact that people are currently immersed in the digital age 4.0, it is necessary to recognize that the whole world is in constant change and that it is imperative to stay immersed in that change. In order to know how to accompany students in their learning process and the generation of productive experiences, the teacher is the key actor in the educational process. In this situation, it is necessary to take the words of Hernández R. (2017) and Mogollón (2020), who agreed that using technological tools conjectures a solution to the problems and challenges around the development of innovative learning and the generation of experiences, within a virtual educational modality. On the other hand, Hernández, Orrego and Quiñones (2018), supported that the teacher is the protagonist in the mediation of learning, if he knows how to respect and value the challenges that may arise in the new digital and knowledge era.

In addition, it is argued that to achieve a comprehensive education and form productive experiences in the student body, it is a requirement to combine the technical, contextual, and pedagogical field added to the technological advances that exist in contemporary times. According to Callis and Basto (2020), who considered that thought and action were favored within a technological culture that focuses on the social selection of individuals. Given the above, Gelb, Mital and Mukjerjee (2020), ratified that by using digital and mobile technologies added to the Internet, great opportunities can be created for the creation of a vast set of mechanisms and resources for the academic field.

Therefore, the generation of productive learning experiences, useful for everyday life, can only be carried out if there is a conjugation between technical, contextual, and pedagogical processes. Educational actors must focus their efforts on designing recreational activities that allow students to develop digital skills that allow them to form a transversal and innovative profile. The TICS and the changes of the digital age are not an impediment and need to be involved in such a process, so that the skills achieved by students are used to provide solutions and create new opportunities.

Indeed, the main elements that intervene in the generation of productive experiences in the digital age 4.0 are the technical, contextual, and pedagogical processes. These phenomena directly influence the achievement of significant learning, which allows individuals to contribute greatly with innovative solutions that include the use of technological tools. The students, in other case, will achieve through the acquisition of digital skills, the ability to solve problems, innovation and leadership, which will allow them to actively participate in their environment, both individually and collectively. However, changes cannot be evidenced if education is not transformed.

In addition, there is a great variety of technical, contextual, and pedagogical processes that must be applied to develop productive experiences. Technological devices such as cell phones, computers and tablets are the main tools to acquire skills, however, there are other elements that are also essential. The context directly influences, social factors can benefit or affect the insertion of TICs, therefore, educational actors must make the most of all the resources available to them. Pedagogy is a discipline that could not be missing, since, without a good teaching method, unfortunately the educational process cannot be carried out.

On the other hand, the data showed in table 4, showed that there is a much higher level of response when talking about didactic strategies compared to the levels obtained in the types of technological tools and the existing causal processes within the classroom. For this reason, it is worth highlighting the words of Garzón (2021) who maintains that teaching competencies should never remain rigid, static, or immutable, on the contrary, they must be variables that can understand the situations and the context in which the class develops today in day. According to Apolo (2019), he suggested that the most current trends in technology and virtual media intended for formal education should be identified, knowing how to combine them with the context in which students find themselves and differentiate the strengths and needs of the application of these tools in the educational system.

According to Ureta and Rossetti (2020), the learning experiences immersed in digital environments must show the integration between the academic and technological capacities of the students in favor of the construction of knowledge with the use of different strategies, methods, objectives, and activities. On the other hand, Tamayo (2021) and Melo (2018) agreed that educational agents must know how to adapt to the current era, focusing on the design and planning of sequential and continuous programs, taking into account the development, control and evaluation of strategies that include technological tools. Despite this, the reality is so different, since not all students and teachers can use technological means for education properly or conscientiously.

According to Loiza, Ramirez, and Pacheco (2021), maintained that learning can be supported on countless virtual platforms, this symbolizes a great opportunity for educational centers and teachers in order to generate digital materials, information bases, interactive assessments and thereby achieve encourage student learning. But for the before mentioned happen, it is necessary to include different didactic strategies in every academic process through the support of the technological tools within our reach and the recognition of the causal processes that encourage the student to generate productive experiences in a digital age.

In other words, to achieve a generation of productive experiences in the digital age 4.0, educational actors must direct their efforts to redesign the methodologies and resources used until now and transform them from an innovative perspective. Strategies, digital tools, and causal processes are, to a large extent, the main elements involved in achieving learning for life. Therefore, teachers must transform their role as an educator and become a leader, who motivates students to strengthen their skills and together they can achieve the skills that 21st century society so desperately needs.

Although all educational actors play an important role in generating productive experiences in the digital age, the teacher is primarily responsible for the teaching and learning process. Therefore, it is imperative that teachers design new ways of teaching, where the need for practice, criticism and assessment of what has been learned is taken into account, and not just the repetition of content. The insertion of technology can be seen as a great challenge, but after the analysis carried out, the educational rethinking is simpler than what is created thanks to the management of TICs and electronic devices.

REFERENCES

Álava, I., Illescas, M., & Loor, E. (2017). *La plataforma virtual como fortalecimiento al proceso enseñanza-aprendizaje en las aulas de la educación ecuatoriana.* Revista científica Ciencia y Tecnología. https://doi.org/10.47189/rcct.v17i16.135

Apolo, D. (2019). *Tecnología y educación: un largo camino por recorrer. Puntos de acuerdo, tensiones y disputas entre estudiantes, docentes y autoridades para los usos juveniles de internet con fines educativos. Caso: Colegio Nacional Eloy Alfaro, Quito-Ecuador.* Presentada en Universidad Nacional de La Plata. Facultad de Humanidades y Ciencias de la Educación para optar al grado de Doctor en Ciencias de la Educación. https://www.memoria.fahce.unlp.edu.ar/tesis/te.1697/te.1697.pdf

Buzón De La Hoz, Y. (2021). *¿Cómo integrar el modelo pedagógico Constructivista y con las competencias educativas para despertar en los estudiantes un rol más activo dentro del aula de clase?*. Barranquilla: Corporación Universidad de la Costa. https://hdl.handle.net/11323/8353

Callis, Y., & Basto, M. (2020). *La cultura tecnológica una alternativa en la formación protagónica del estudiante en la enseñanza universitaria.* Maestro y Sociedad, 189-203. https://maestroysociedad.uo.edu.cu/index.php/MyS/article/view/5157

Casillas, M., & Ramírez, A. (2019). *Cultura digital y cambio institucional de las universidades*. RESU, 97-111.

Clavijo, L., Loiza, C., Ramirez, S., & Pacheco, E. (2021). *Desarrollo de manual para el manejo de la plataforma lost (Goal Project) para docentes y estudiantes.* EIEI ACOFI, 1-13. https://doi.org/10.26507/ponencia.1868

Garzón, C. (2021). *Las competencias docentes en el siglo XXI. De cara a la virtualidad de la educación con ocasión del COVID-19.* Boletín REDIPE, 10(5), 177-188. https://dialnet.unirioja.es/servlet/articulo?codigo=8116437

Gelb, A., Mital, N., & Mukjerjee, A. (2020). *Hacia la gobernanza en tiempo real: el uso de la retroalimentación digital para mejorar servicios, voz y rendición de cuentas. Estado Abierto.* Revista Sobre el Estado, la administración y las políticas públicas, 165-179. https://publicaciones.inap.gob.ar/index.php/EA/article/view/136

Hernández, R. (2017). *Impacto de las TIC en la educación: Retos y Perspectivas.* Propósitos y Representaciones, 5(1), 325-347. https://dialnet.unirioja.es/servlet/articulo?codigo=5904762

Hernández, R., Orrego, R., & Quiñones, S. (2018). *Nuevas formas de aprender: La formación docente frente al uso de las TIC.* Propósitos y Representaciones, 671-701.

Melo, M. E. (2018). *La integración de las TIC como vía para optimizar el proceso de enseñanza-aprendizaje en la educación superior en Colombia.* Alicante, España. http://hdl.handle.net/10045/80508

Mercado, L. M., Mercado, T. M., Ziritt, G., & Consuegra, S. D. (2018). *Determinantes discursivos del uso de las Tics en el sector educativo oficial del departamento del Atlántico, Colombia.* Revista Espacios, 1 - 7. http://hdl.handle.net/10584/9976

Mogollón, I. (2020). *Tendencias, desafíos y desarrollos de la educación a distancia y virtual en la universidad venezolana.* Universidades, 17-30. https://doi.org/10.36888/udual.universidades.2020.83.73

Ramírez, E., Monroy, S., & Vargas, J. (2017). *Uso de la Tecnologías TIC por los Docentes de las Instituciones Educativas Públicas de la Ciudad de Riohacha.* (R. I. REDIPE, Ed.) Boletín Redipe, 6(6), 113-118. https://revista.redipe.org/index.php/1/article/view/248

Rodríguez, R., Orozco, E., Rocha, C., & Rodríguez, O. (2017). *Transformación de la estructura cognitiva con el uso de herramientas tecnológicas en matemáticas. 37.* Universidad Sergio Arboleda: Colombia. http://hdl.handle.net/11232/1040

Sosa, E. (2018). *Diseño de un modelo de incorporación de tecnologías emergentes en el aula (MITEA) para la generación de estrategias didácticas por parte de los docentes.* España: Universitat de les Illes Balears. http://hdl.handle.net/11201/149058

Tamayo, L., Tinitana, A., Apolo, J., Martínez, E., & Zambrano, V. (2021). *Implicaciones del modelo constructivista en la visión educativa del siglo XXI.* Revista Sociedad & Tecnología, 4(S2), 364-376. https://doi.org/10.51247/st.v4iS2.157

Ureta, L., & Rossetti, G. (2020). *Las TAC en la construcción de conocimiento disciplinar: una experiencia de aprendizaje con estudiantes universitarios.* Revista Iberoamericana de Tecnología en Educación y Educación en Tecnología, (26), e11. https://doi.org/10.24215/18509959.26.e11

GES APP – SUPPORTING GLOBAL EMPLOYABILITY SKILLS FROM THE PERSPECTIVES OF STUDENTS, STAFF AND EMPLOYERS

Sobah Abbas Petersen[1], Maria Iqbal[1], Alan Williams[2] and Gavin Baxter[2]
[1]Dept. of Computer Science, Norwegian University of Science and Technology, Norway
[2]School of Computing, Engineering and Physical Sciences, University of the West of Scotland, UK

ABSTRACT

Global Employability Skills are skills that students acquire during their study period, that are in addition to their academic knowledge and skills, and that would help in their careers. As students continue their university journeys, they often overlook or underestimate the importance of developing Global Employability Skills that employers may consider important for their jobs. In this paper, we present a mobile application, the GES App, designed to help students recognize, document, and articulate their skills to their prospective employees. The GES App is designed to stimulate university students to reflect upon their experiences and assess the skills they may develop outside of their formal university studies. This paper presents how such an app could support students plan their careers and develop their Global Employability Skills that would make them more attractive to their future employers. A use case scenario is described to illustrate the role the GES App could play, from the perspectives of students, staff, and employers.

KEYWORDS

Global Employability Skills, Self-Assessment, Career Planning

1. INTRODUCTION

Global Employability skills (GESs) are defined in the literature as skills that are graduate level abilities that are beyond the content of specific disciplines and also practical and transferrable (Maciejewski et al., 2020), which are needed by an individual to perform a task and would make them employable. The significance of global employability skills for employment is inevitable. The focus of students' attention seems to be discipline specific knowledge and academic performance and they usually fail to anticipate the importance of GES in addition to their discipline specific skills during their academic journey. Literature highlights student's proactive behavior towards career planning and preparing for their futures, e.g. (Clements & C., 2018). However, the challenge for making a connection between the GES acquired by students and what they learn at university and elsewhere during their university journeys still remain. Furthermore, finding the right candidates for fulfilling a company's requirements is not an easy task for employers and they find it hard to spot the right candidate at job fairs or through job applications.

This paper describes the work conducted as a part of the European ERASMUS+ project on GES, with four European universities from Greece, Norway, Poland and the United Kingdom (UK). The main aim of the project is to develop a mobile application to allow students to plan, record and evidence the acquisition and development of GES throughout their university journey. The project started in 2019 and lasted 3 years. The GES mobile app, hereafter referred to as the GES App or the app, aims to support the GES from the perspective of students, academic staff and employers. The perspectives of the three types of users and/or stakeholders have been obtained during the requirement analysis phase of the project where interviews were conducted to investigate their interests and needs for supporting the enhancement and documentation of GES among university students. The requirement analysis highlighted the need for a mobile application by users as the efficacy and ability to provide timely access to learning in authentic working contexts (Herrington et al., 2014). The activities supported by the GES App are designed in the light of requirements defined by the three user groups, supported by the Self-Determined Learning Model of Instructions (SDLMI) (Shogren et al., 2019). This model is student or learner-centered and focuses on the learner's competencies and their capabilities and the capacity to learn and enhance their skills.

The aim of this paper is to show the effectiveness of supporting the enhancement and documentation of GES for students, from the three different perspectives that play significant roles for employability of students in the industry. The main research question we wish to answer is: how can we design a mobile application to support students enhance their understanding of employability skills? To answer this research question, we developed a prototype mobile application and conducted evaluations. In this paper we describe the main functionalities of the GES App and how students may use it in career planning and enhancing their employability skills.

The rest of the paper is structured as follows: Section 2 provides the theoretical foundations for the design of the app's concepts; Section 3 describes the methodology for obtaining requirements and the development of the GES App; Section 4 provides an overview of the requirements from different perspectives; Section 5 provides an overview of the GES App; Section 6 describes a use case scenario and the main functionalities of the GES App, and Section 7 concludes the paper.

2. THEORETICAL FOUNDATIONS

Studies have shown that employment requirements from the perspective of employers vary from that of employees, especially when the employees are students or fresh graduates. It can often result in complaints from employers with regards to workplace skills, work readiness and application of skills in non-academic environments (Jackling & De Lange, 2009). Therefore, to seek employment, students not only need to acquire a wide range of skills but also need to evidence the acquired skills as the significance of generic skills surpasses the need of discipline specific skills (Tomlinson, 2008).

A detail literature review conducted in the ERASMUS+ GES project revealed two important aspects that form the basis of the GES App design. First, employability cannot be guaranteed by skills, attitude, or knowledge individually and it is required to be a combination of the three to achieve the goal. Secondly, application of these skills in a workplace and practical life is more important than only possessing the skills that exhibits the competency required. Thus, the GES App is designed around the skills and knowledge of the user, but also provides resources to evidence and evaluate skills giving a way for users to show their competency.

The Self Determined Learning Model of Instructions (SDLMI) is a learner-centered learning approach, which focuses on the development of competency and the capability of a learner while building the capacity of learning (Shogren et al., 2019). The SDLMI approach has founded the basis of identifying activities of the GES App that allows a user to identify skills with self-determination while enabling them to explore the prospects to learn and practice those skills. The activity to add a skill enables a user to know what they have learned, while the activity of a Dream job enables a user to determine what is needed to be learned, giving the user an opportunity to learn and practice through the activity of practicing skills (Abbas et al., 2022).

Awareness can have a stimulating effect on the self-determined behavior of the student for which the process of reflection has been integrated. The model proposed by Rolfe et al. has been used as the foundation of the reflection process (Rolfe et al., 2001). Rolfe's model of reflection is also known as a reflective cycle and based on simple key questions of What? Now What? And So, What? These guidance questions are tailored as per the objectives of reflection and goal. The self-assessment of skills through a process of reflection is based on these guiding questions, which leads to the awareness and encourages learning.

3. METHODOLOGY

For the development of the GES App, the Design Thinking methodology was used, which not only offers benefits of a user-centered methodology, but is also recursive in nature (Plattner et al., 2015). The five phases of the Design Thinking methodology are empathize, define, ideate, prototype and test and the output of one phase is input to the subsequent phase. An interactive Figma prototype was developed to support the ideation process, which is described in (Iqbal, Fredheim, et al., 2022). The work presented in this paper is focused on the empathize phase where requirements from the users and the stakeholders of the app were gathered, which contributed to the resulting prototype of the GES App.

Requirements were gathered from the four European partners from Greece, Norway, Poland, and UK. Requirements gathering was conducted in two stages; the first was a qualitative study and focus group and semi-structure interviews with the different stakeholder groups: students, employers and academic staff. The second stage was a quantitative study using questionnaires, which was based on the results from the qualitative study. A total of 75 participated in the first stage: 43 students and 19 staff participated in the focus group interviews, and 13 individual employers were interviewed. In the second stage, 153 students responded to a questionnaire. The same questionnaires and interview guides were used for the participants from all the countries and the requirements gathering activities were conducted in the same time period. The results were then analysed for the different countries and user groups to identify the functionalities for the GES App. The focus group discussions and interviews were conducted online due to the COVID-19 related restrictions and the questionnaires were administered using an online survey tool. Greek and Polish translations were used for the respective participants. Based on the requirements, a conceptual framework for the functionalities of the GES App and the activities it should support were defined (Iqbal, Fredheim, et al., 2022).

During the define and ideation phases, user scenarios were described, one of which is used in this paper to describe the functionalities of the GES App prototype, developed using the Unity platform.

4. REQUIREMENTS FROM DIFFERENT STAKEHOLDERS

The relevance of career aspirations and its psychological impacts have been discussed in the literature (Hoff et al., 2021). Studies have also shown that students have proactive career behaviors, such as career planning, skills development, career consultation, network building and show stronger commitment to their career goals, which have a statistically significant relationship with career success (Clements & C., 2018; Moeller et al., 2012). The qualitative analysis of the requirements gathered through interviews and focus group interviews in the EU ERASMUS+ project GES App identified three main groups of stakeholders and their different perspectives. Hence, the mobile application for GES App incorporates three types of users' perspectives through various functionalities, as shown in Figure 1.

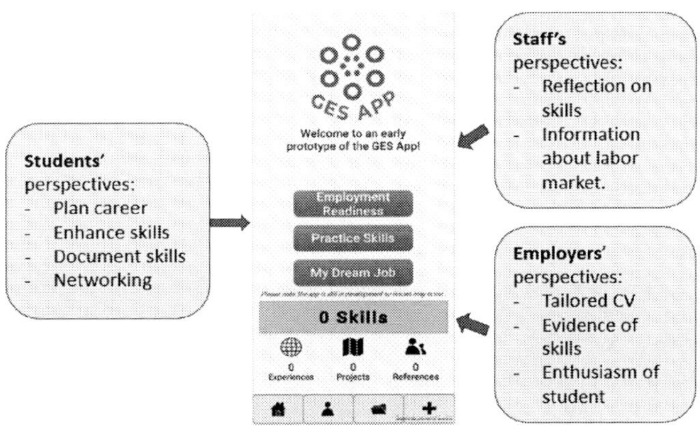

Figure 1. Different perspectives of Global Employability Skills

From the interviews with focus groups of students, it was established that students usually have a specific professional plan, although, they may also consider a plan-B as an alternative career path. Responses from students offer insights regarding their perspective of employability skills and the lack of specific skill-oriented training. It was also observed during the interviews that students acknowledge the fact that mere discipline specific knowledge does not suffice the requirement of employability in the industry and most employers seek extensive skill sets along with the need of experience. Students also identified the need for a mobile application, which could serve as an effective resource and indicate the need of tracking skills development, skill documentation in an authorized way, the need for networking, advice on how to acquire more skills, training for interviews, industry specific skill phrase bank, the possibility to set goals and to track what they know.

The interviews with employers identified some of the important qualities they look in a potential employee which are, apart from the industry specific skills, the ability to learn new things, bring value to the company, a tailored CV and if they are able to keep their enthusiasm of working. The analysis of requirements enabled to envision some important functionalities of the mobile app that could enhance the prospects of employment for students, such as enabling them to present their skills with evidence of the skills, e.g., through experiences.

The perspectives of the academic staff, such as teachers and careers advisers, highlighted the need to support students to prepare for their employment and careers. This group of interviewees mentioned the use of a mobile app for enhancing the learning effects through reflections, modification of curriculum in the light of results acquired, and as an information channel for labor market skills.

5. OVERVIEW OF THE GES APP

The different perspectives highlighted through the requirement analysis identified the major activities that should be supported by the GES App. Thus, the functionalities in the GES App are based on five main activities, that support the development of students' GES. These activities are based on the literature and the key concepts, and the requirements that are summarised in Section 4. The main activities that have been identified to support the different perspectives, mainly the students, are summarised below:

1. Self-reporting, documenting and self-assessing GES: users are able to add one or more Skills to their skill profile, assess their Skills level, set a Goal and relate the Skills to their Goal, reflect upon how and what experiences have helped them acquire the Skills and document the evidence of the Skills by adding Experiences, Artifacts and References (Iqbal, Fredheim, et al., 2022).
2. Dream job: users are able to define a Dream Job and relate to the desired list and level of Skills for the Dream Job (Iqbal, Abbas, et al., 2022).
3. Practice selected skills: users are able to access learning resources that can help them to enhance their Skill set by learning a new Skill(s) or by enhancing the level of an existing Skill, e.g., by playing a game.
4. Networking and Ethics: users are able to connect to other users and share their experiences and communicate through the GES App.
5. Employment readiness: users are able to generate content for their CVs through the GES App, by accessing the Skills, Experiences, Artifacts and References from the GES App, practice for employment related activities such as learn about creating a CV and prepare for an interview.

6. USING THE GES APP

This section illustrates how the GES App supports a use case scenario, which includes three different stakeholders: student, employer and careers advisor. Using ideas from user-centered design, we have created a persona for a student. Sarah is a student, who is focused on getting an interesting job after completing her university studies and she is actively looking for job opportunities and preparing her CV and job applications. She is concerned about creating a good CV that will make her attractive to her potential employers and she is keen to find good ways to present her skills and experiences to potential employers. Thus, Sarah decides to get an appointment with the university's careers adviser, Joe. She was told by the Careers Adviser that she should carefully consider the skills and experiences she lists in her CV, and they should be tailored to the job position, to have maximum effect.

Sarah uses the GES App regularly and records all her skills in the app. She sets a goal using the Dream Job functionality and explores the diverse career paths that are possible with her set of skills. She discovers a selection of learning resources in the GES App, in the form of games, videos, YouTube and other online sources. Sarah browses through her skills stored in the GES App and wonders if she could use some of that information as a part of her CV. Sarah explores the GES App to see if this is possible and she finds the functionality to create a CV. She selects the relevant Skills and the related Experiences, References and Artifacts that she would like to include in her CV and exports them as an editable file. She receives the exported list of Skills as an email message. She copies the contents into her CV template, edits the format and adapts her CV to the needs of the job. Sarah found this to be an effective means of tailoring her CV.

Sarah attends a jobs fair at the university and comes across a company that she would like to apply for a job and meets Helen, the head of Human Resources (HR). Sarah accesses her skills profile overview in the GES App and asks Helen about the possibilities of getting a job in her company. Sarah happily explains her experiences, the skills that she has acquired and how those skills could be relevant for a job in the company. Sarah feels that she has a better idea of the skills that she needs to focus on. Sarah leaves the stand very motivated and excited, and very glad that she had been using the GES App.

The following sub-sections describe how the GES App functionalities support the main activities identified through this user scenario.

6.1 Documenting Skills and Evidence of Skill

To document the skills, the student selects the option of "Add Skill", which provides the possibility to select a skill from a skills repository in the app, as shown in Figure **2** (a), or add a new skill, as shown in Figure **2** (b). The student is asked if she wants to share the added skill as shown in Figure **2** (c) and if option of sharing is selected by the student, the skill is added to crowdsourced skills repository in the GES App. Once the skill is added to the student's profile, the app enables the student to assess the skill through reflecting upon her level of the skill and she can define her level as novice, advanced beginner, competent, proficient, and expert, as shown in Figure **2** (d). A summary of the skill can be viewed in the profile as shown in Figure **2** (e), where the skill is listed with skill level.

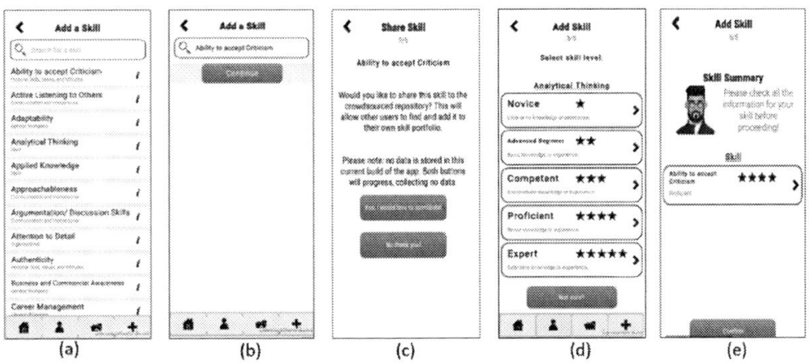

Figure 2. Documentation and self-assessment of Skills in the GES App

Students also need a convincing way to show that they actually have the skill that they have included in the GES App. The evidence for a skill can be recorded in the app in the form of Experiences, Artifacts and References. Recording the evidence to support the reported skill allows student to showcase the practical expertise that can be acquired during a project, a job or an internship as an experience, and an output from the experience in terms of videos, reports, paper, online links, etc. Furthermore, it can also be a human reference that could validate the skills of a student, such as a referee from academia or industry.

After adding a skill in the GES App, as shown in Figure **2**, students can also add the evidence of a skill and can record experiences through the "Add Experience" functionality, as shown in Figure **3** (a). The GES App asks the student to add dates during which the experience was acquired, as shown in Figure **3** (b). Then, the student needs to identify the skills from the list of saved skills that are practiced or acquired through the recorded experience as shown in Figure **3** (c). The GES App also enables students to assess the experience through a series of questions in terms of very good, good, moderate, little, and not at all, as shown in Figure **3** (d). Once all the information is recorded, the student can view the summary of the added experience, which is shown in Figure **3** (e).

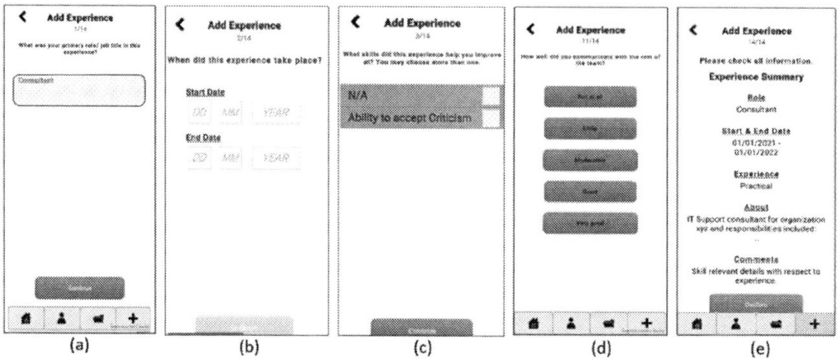

Figure 3. Documentation of evidence of a Skill as Experience in the GES App

Similarly, students can also record and upload artifacts through "Add Artifacts" option of the GES App, and add the relevant details for the added artifact, such as which skills were enhanced during the development of the artifact. The "Add Reference" option allows the student to add referees, similar to those that would be included in a CV, where the student can also add the contact details of a referee, if consent has been sought.

6.2 Creating a CV

Exploring further, students can also extract all the saved information regarding the skills in the form of an editable file. This is a functionality to support "Employment Readiness" as shown in Figure 4 (a), and the "Create CV" functionality, Figure 4 (b), which facilitates students to create tailored CVs for job applications. Students can select the relevant skills from the list of skills in their profile and the experiences, artifacts and references associated with the skills, as shown in Figure 4 (c). The app then displays a summary of skills and other information that have been selected, which could be exported as a text file. This provides an effective way of identifying the relevant skills and starting to create a CV. The contents from GES App could be imported/copied into the desired template for a CV.

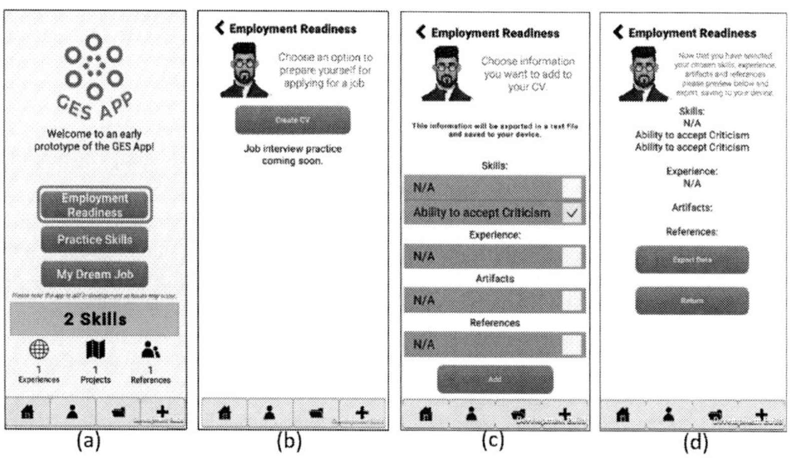

Figure 4. Creating a CV

6.3 Reviewing and Presenting an Overview of Skills

When a student meets the careers adviser or a potential employer, it is helpful to be able to present an overview of their skills. The GES App functionalities support the perspectives of staff and employers. Staff such as career advisers have a need to consider the skills and experiences of a student before giving advice regarding their future possibilities and to encourage students to use tailored CVs for the specific job opportunities. Similarly, an overview of a potential employee's (e.g. a student's) skills and experiences would enable them to obtain an impression of the student. More importantly, how a student assesses her level of skills will, no doubt, help career advisers as well as employers to obtain a sense of the student's enthusiasm and advise them on how to further enhance their relevant skills. The overview of skills that is available in the GES App facilitates all three perspectives.

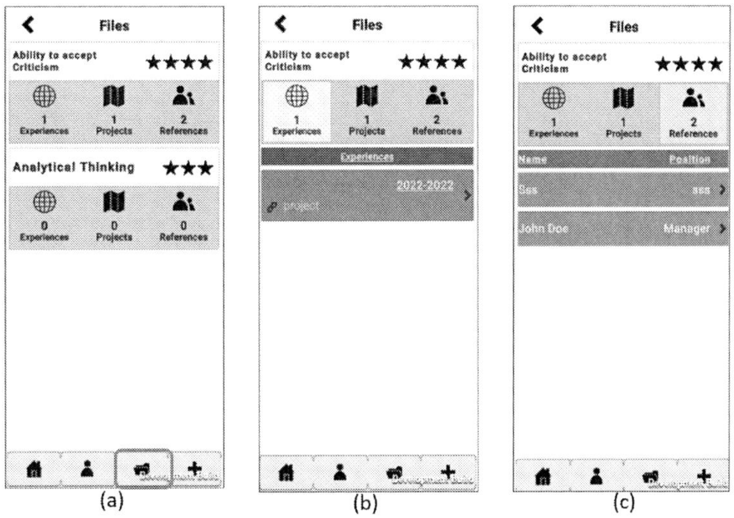

Figure 5. Overview of skills (skills profile of a user) in the GES App

An overview of a student's skills is summarized in the GES App as shown in Figure 5 (a). They are presented as a set of skill cards, where each card displays the details in terms of skill level, number of experiences during which a specific skill has been practiced, number of artifacts for which the skill has been applied and the number of references that validate the acquisition of the skill. Such details could support academic staff to provide personalized counselling services to students and can also guide them for improvement with respect to the student's career goals.

When a skill card is selected from the list, the GES App displays the detailed overview of that skill as shown in Figure 5 (b). The skill recorded by the student can be explored further for details of the evidence recorded, such as the details of experiences recorded, or details of references recorded to support the skill, as shown in Figure 5 (c).

7. CONCLUSION

In this paper, we have presented a mobile application, the GES App, designed to help students recognize, document, and articulate their skills to their prospective employees. The GES App was designed to stimulate university students to reflect upon their experiences and assess the skills they may develop outside of their formal university studies. The main research question for this study has been how we could design a mobile application to support students enhance their understanding of employability skills. To address this, a prototype of the GES App has been developed and some of the main activities supported by the app have been described in this paper. The GES App has been evaluated by students from Greece, Norway, Poland and the UK, where pre- and post-intervention questionnaires were used. The results are currently being analyzed. Preliminary results of the analysis show that the participants had positive comments about the idea of the app, the organization of contents in the app and the functionalities. They found the app meaningful, important, original and motivating towards exploring many aspects of their employability skills and attitudes. They felt that the app has a good level of game flow, usability and learnability and that the expected outcomes are important since the app could support students toward exploring and reflecting on their employability skills.

Furthermore, the results also showed that the participants showed an increase in their understanding of the labour market and how to prepare for employment.

The current version of GES App is available in Google Play for Android devices. In the future, we aim to enhance the functionalities in the app to support students based on the feedback from the evaluations. One of the main limitations of this study is that the evaluations have so far been limited to students and the lack of feedback from the other stakeholders. Furthermore, an evaluation of the GES App from the perspective of the learning and enhancing skills need further investigations.

Our future work will focus on conducting further user evaluations with the different stakeholder groups such as academic staff and employers, in the different countries. In addition, we continue to analyze the results from the studies reported in this paper and the feedback from them will be used to improve the GES App capabilities and improve our evaluation methods.

ACKNOWLEDGEMENT

This work has been conducted as a part of the EU Global Employability skills App (GES-App) project, by a KA203 - ERASMUS + Strategic Partnerships for higher education, grant; KA2, Cooperation for Innovation and the Exchange of Good Practices; Grant Agreement no: 2019-1-UK01-KA203-062146. The authors would like to thank the participants of the interviews and surveys and all the GES App project participants for their contributions.

REFERENCES

Abbas, A., Iqbal, M., Boyle, L., Baxter, G., Williams, A., Petersen, S. A., Topolewska-Siedzik, E., Jimoyiannis, A., Tsiotakis, P., & Scott, G. (2022). Graduate Employability Learning through Self-Determined Learning Model of Instruction (SDLMI) Driven Digital App INTED2022 Proceedings, https://library.iated.org/view/ABBAS2022GRA

Clements, A. J., & C., K. (2018). Understanding students' motivation towards proactive career behaviours through goal-setting theory and the job demands–resources model. Studies in Higher Education, 43(12), 2279–2293.

Herrington, J., Ostashewski, N., Reid, D., & Flintoff, K. (2014). Mobile technologies in teacher education: Preparing pre-service teachers and teacher educators for mobile learning. In J. Ryan et al. (Ed.), Successful Teacher Education (pp. 137-151). https://www.academia.edu/33938952/Mobile_Technologies_in_Teacher_Education

Hoff, K., Van Egdom, D., Napolitano, C., Hanna, A., & Rounds, J. (2021). Dream Jobs and Employment Realities: How Adolescents' Career Aspirations Compare to Labor Demands and Automation Risks. Journal of Career Assessment, 30(1), 134-156. https://doi.org/10.1177/10690727211026183

Iqbal, M., Abbas, A., & Peteren, S. A. (2022). Development of Graduate Employability Skills with Regards to Dream Job Using Mobile App International Conference on Education and New Learning Technologies-EDULEARN 22, https://ges-app.com/index.php/publications/

Iqbal, M., Fredheim, L. J., Olstad, H. A., & Peteren, S. A. (2022). Graduate Employability Skills Development through Reflection and Self-assessment using a Mobile App, International Conference on Mobile Learning

Jackling, B., & De Lange, P. (2009). Do accounting graduates' skills meet the expectations of employers? a matter of convergence or divergence. Account. Educ,, 18(4-5), 369–385.

Maciejewski, G., Simpson, A., Boyle, L., Jimoyiannis, A., McCrory, M., Olstad, H. A., & Scott, G. (2020). A Literature Review Looking at Graduate Employability Skills (GESs): GES App Report 1: Review of the GES literature.

Moeller, A. J., Theiler, J. M., & C., W. (2012). Goal Setting and Student Achievement: A Longitudinal Study. Modern Language Journal, 96(2), 153–169.

Plattner, H., Meinel, C., & Leifer, L. (Eds.). (2015). Design thinking research: Making design thinking foundational. Springer.

Rolfe, G., Freshwater, D., & Jasper, M. (2001). Critical reflection for nursing and the helping professions: A user's guide. Palgrave Macmillan.

Shogren, K. A., Raley, S. K., & Burke, K. (2019). The Self-Determined Learning Model of Instruction Teacher's Guide. https://selfdetermination.ku.edu/wp-content/uploads/2019/05/Teachers-Guide-2019-Updated-Logos.pdf

Tomlinson, M. (2008). The degree is not enough': students' perceptions of the role of higher education credentials for graduate work and employability. British Journal of Sociology of Education, 29(1), 49–61.

RESEARCH ON THE ATTITUDES OF HIGH SCHOOL STUDENTS FOR THE APPLICATION OF ARTIFICIAL INTELLIGENCE IN EDUCATION

Vladislav Slavov[1], Kamelia Yotovska[2] and Asya Asenova[2]
[1]*Technical University of Sofia, Faculty of Automatics, 8 Kliment Ohridski blvd., Sofia, Bulgaria*
[2]*Sofia University "St. Kliment Ohridski", Faculty of Biology, 1164 Sofia, 8 Dragan Tsankov Blvd, Bulgaria*

ABSTRACT

Artificial intelligence (AI) technology is already challenging a variety of societal areas, including education. It is transforming education to data driven. AI-enhanced technologies in education (abbreviated AIinED) will have a significant role in changing the teaching and learning methods, as well as impacting the behavior and organization of the educational system. It is considered that the AIinED will change the paradigm of education in the future. And yet, AIinED is still more in the lab than being practically implemented in education and training. We consider three major players in the implementation of AIinED – students, teachers, and society. All three can benefit from AIinED and at the same time be a potential target of the risks that AIinED brings along with its promises – may be one of the reasons why main stakeholders (UNESCO, EC etc.) have been developing guidelines and recommendations for ethical use of AIinED. The literature shows that the center of AIinED system will be the student, but we consider the student not only as a target but also as a source of ideas for AIinED development with the potential to accelerate the process of adoption of AIinED. Hence, one of the big questions should be how the students foresee the role of artificial intelligence in education. To initiate such a question, though, it is important to know the level of understanding among the students about what and where artificial intelligence is. There are three major aspects that AIinED must be considered accordingly – technological, lawful, and ethical.

This paper presents the results of a study on high school students' understanding of AI technologies and their attitudes to their application in education. A survey was used as a tool to elaborate. The conceptual model of the research was developed on the basis of established theories linking attitudes to behavior and the acceptance of artificial intelligence technologies in education. Each element of this concept is explored with a different part of the questionnaire, which contains a total of 12 questions (some of which with sub-questions). The survey was elaborated online within October-November 2021. A link to the questionnaire in Bulgarian was provided to 178 high and vocational high schools educating students aged 14-19 (grades 8-12) across the country (Bulgaria). 766 students submitted their replies through the online survey form.

Descriptive statistics and analysis of the frequencies of the respondents' opinions were made based on the data. The results show that the students participating in the survey:(a) understand the essence of AI technologies; (b) they are convinced of the usefulness of the application of artificial intelligence technologies in their daily activities and strongly believe that it improves it; (c) are not entirely clear about the benefits of artificial intelligence enhanced technologies in learning and teaching; (d) do not demonstrate sufficient knowledge and understanding of the necessity of ethical use of AI technologies in education;

The latter reduces the positive influence of the perceived usefulness of artificial intelligence technologies in the learning process on students' attitudes.

KEYWORDS

Artificial Intelligence Technologies, Artificial Intelligence in Education, Online Survey, Ethics in AIinED

1. INTRODUCTION

The implementation and later adoption of new technologies has always been a key to the future progress in all areas of our lives. The questions about the risks related to that have always gone along with the opportunities. Even when in the early 80s of the last century, computers called by Steven Jobs "the bicycle of the 20th century" (Jobs, July-August 1981) became part of many people's lives, the questions on the fears and threats were raised (Burnham, 1983). And if the computer was the bicycle of the 20th century, artificial intelligence turns to become its engine (Stephen Lucci, 2016). The risks of using AI raised awareness in 2014 after the release of Nick Bostrom's Superintelligence (Bostrom, 2014). Nowadays, managing the risks of implementation of AI and ethical use of AI are important steps towards the integration of AI in different areas (Benjamin Cheatham, Kia Javanmardian, and Hamid Samandari, 2019), (Galaz *et al.*, 2021).

1.1 Artificial Intelligence

In psychology, intelligence is a generalized concept of a person's thinking abilities, i.e. his ability to understand, to be able to abstract, to solve problems applying his knowledge, and to use language (Gardner, 2010), (Gardner, 2012).

Artificial intelligence (AI) is any result of the work of a computer, which, if it was the product of human activity, would be considered reasonable (Legg and Hutter, 2007). This is enhanced by (Chen, Chen and Lin, 2020) saying that AI is a field of study and the resulting innovations and developments that have culminated in computers, machines, and other artifacts having human-like intelligence characterized by cognitive abilities, learning, adaptability, and decision-making capabilities, adding that AI is the culmination of computers, computer-related technologies, machines, and information communication technology innovations and developments, giving computers the ability to perform near or human-like functions.

Artificial intelligence is a wide-ranging tool that enables people to rethink how we integrate information, analyze data, and use the resulting insights to improve decision-making – and already it is transforming every walk of life (West, 2018; Ross *et al.*, 2022).

1.2 Artificial Intelligence Technologies in Education

There is no doubt that AI is the inevitable future of a lot of industrial sectors but also the future of schools, universities, training centers (Dai and Ke, 2022) bringing them to the fourth education revolution (Seldon and Abidoye, 2018). If we can compare the implementation of AI in education with the human life cycle, the AIinED is still an embryo. AIinED will reshape not only the way of teaching and learning but will significantly impact the organization of educational institutions and systems.

There is a slow adoption rate of technologies in education (Chen X., Xie H., Zou D., Hwang G.-J., 2020), because of mismatch between real needs and supply. The lack of use of technologies is affecting every level of education - from primary schools to universities. There is a need for building the evidence base for more effective learning with technology. This will go hand in hand with tools and processes for collecting, storing, exploring, and reasoning on large-scale educational data. That "big data" will be from students' technology supported learning activities, transforming the data into information, and producing, recommending actions aimed at improving learning outcomes.

Most of the strategic documents and regarding AIinED issued by EU and UNESCO by October 2021, (Duggan, 2020; EUROPEAN COMMISSION, 2021) are focused on the benefits that artificial intelligence will bring to the students. They put the student as the center of the AIinED system, which is inevitable. AIinED though will influence not only the students but also the teachers and should contribute to the wellbeing of the society. The development of successful policies for AIinED the learners, educators and society should be considered as a whole, and the point of view and the benefits for each of these groups should be accounted for.

AIinED will enhance the learning for not only the students who are part of the formal education, but also students from all ages through vocational education and life-long learning programs (van der Vlies R, 2010; Roll and Wylie, 2016). Students' performance is the most significant source of data for AIinED but it will not be correct that data such as grade scores, results from school and state exams, attendance and punctuality records, school reports, comparative scores with regard to peers or classmates is enough as quality, quantity and type.

Although governments will be responsible for the implementation of AIinED, there are three major role players and users in that process: students, teachers, society (not only parents). All their opinions must matter, but also it can be a valuable source of ideas and can reveal the actual expectations to AIinED.

1.3 Schooling and Artificial Intelligence Technologies

According to B. Marr, AI will contribute to the acquisition of better school and university education (Marr, 2018). The effect of so-called smart classrooms and academic learning labs where AI is applied is already being seen. It supports teaching, enhances the individual approach by responding to the needs of learners.

These new methods help teachers and university professors to concentrate on understanding and adapting new knowledge and skills.

The ability for a machine to perform intelligent tasks that are generally assigned to the human mind, and override the problem-solving of information processing, prediction, and choosing the best and most effective action to achieve a certain goal is something that is already a reality.

More and more innovations and best practices are being applied in the direction of how artificial intelligence can change education such as systems, chatbots, semantic analysis, natural language processing, automatic scoring and feedback, audio games and vision-based robotics, problem-solving (Kahn and Winters, 2017).

Platforms have been created that, based on feedback questionnaires, can accurately specify the educational levels, and needs of those using them (Content Science, 2017; Century, 2019).

Such type of platforms can become universal classrooms or learning subjects to be used by everyone, but at a low cost or for free. This will contribute to equality of access (even children who do not know languages can use the functions of an instant translator) and will strengthen the role of Internet technologies in the learning process (Todorova, 2019).

Implementation of AI-based applications can help solve the problems of low quality of education and its inaccessibility in remote areas, and also improve the existing education systems (Ivanova et al., 2020).

According to the EC Communication "Artificial Intelligence for Europe" there are three main challenges facing the EU which underline the fundamental role of education and training, the responsibility of which lies with the Member States. The first challenge is to prepare society as a whole. It means helping all Europeans to develop basic digital skills, as well as skills that are complementary in nature and cannot be replaced by any machine - such as critical thinking, creativity, management ability. Second, efforts should focus on helping people in those jobs that are likely to undergo the greatest transformation or disappear as a result of automation, robotics and AI. Third, more AI specialists should be trained based on long-standing academic traditions, to create a suitable environment for them to work in the EU and, if possible, to attract talents from abroad. Hence, the modernization of education at all levels should become a major national priority (for Bulgaria), and in the field of scientific research, artificial intelligence should become one of the priority areas in information and communication technologies.

In order for the education system in Bulgaria to respond to the challenge of developing knowledge and skills necessary for work in the field and AI, as well as for work in an environment with AI, these priority directions for development in the education system of Bulgaria are enshrined in the Law on Preschool and school education (2016), the Law on Higher Education and other normative acts of the Ministry of Education and Science, the proposals of the Ministry of Education, Culture and Science contained in the document "Artificial Intelligence in Education and Science" (Ministry of Education and Science of Bulgaria, 2020).

The article presents the results of a study on Bulgarian students' understanding of artificial intelligence and their attitudes towards its application in the learning process.

2. METHODOLOGY

The research questions are focused on the attitudes of the relevant age students towards AI. The research was conducted through a survey. The questionnaire was self-constructed for the purposes of the study. The literature lacks a similar off-the-shelf instrument whose reliability and validity have been established. The conceptual model of the study was developed based on established theories relating attitudes to behavior and the adoption of artificial intelligence in education. Each element of this concept is explored with a different part of the questionnaire, which contains a total of 12 questions (some with sub-questions). The survey was conducted online in the period October-November 2021. A link to the questionnaire in Bulgarian was provided to 178 high and vocational high schools educating students aged 14-19 (grades 8-12) across the country (Bulgaria). 766 students submitted their replies through the online survey form. The total number of students enrolled in high schools and vocational high schools in Bulgaria in the 2021/2022 academic year was 255 342. Such, the results confidence level is 95 % results with error margins within 3.5 % (Whitley and Ball, 2002).

The main part of the sample consists of students aged 15-18 years (Table 1). The largest relative share is respondents aged 16 (25.5%), followed by almost the same share of 15-year-olds (24.8%). The surveyed students aged 17 have a relative share of 20.1% (154 students), and 18-year-olds – 16.1% (124 students).

The share of students who completed the survey studying in vocational high schools is significant - 75.2%, and 21.9% are high school students.

It is noticeable that the sex of the students is 62 % to 38 % for the male students. This result is not surprising considering the relative number of male and female students in the vocational schools in Bulgaria, according to statistics. The National Statistical Institute of Bulgaria gives 60 % of male students towards 40% of females in Bulgarian vocational schools in 2021/2022 (Information system "Infostat" of the National Statistics Institute of Bulgaria).

Table 1. Sociodemographic characteristics in the sample (N= 766, ε = 3.5 %, CL= 95 %)

Variables	n	% of the sample
Age		
14 years	74	9,7
15 years	190	24,8
16 years	195	25,5
17 years	154	20,1
18 years	124	16,2
19 years	15	2
Other	14	1,7
Type of school		
High School	168	21,9
Vocational high school	576	75,2
Other	22	2,9
Sex		
Male	475	62
Female	281	38
Total	**56**	**100**

Descriptive statistics and frequency analysis of respondents' opinions were made on the data. Some questions were open to more than one answer.

3. RESULTS AND DISCUSSIONS

3.1 Understanding AI Technologies

The center of the survey is the students' understanding of the nature of artificial intelligence as the students were asked "What is AI?" (Figure 1). The relative share of respondents who associate artificial intelligence with the ability of a machine/device to demonstrate human-like abilities is the largest (74.41%). Students understand that artificial intelligence occurs when a machine thinks, plans, creates, chooses, learns. The relative share of those who answered that artificial intelligence is receiving data from technical systems that register changes in parameters in their environment, process them and perform actions related to achieving a specific goal can be accepted as relatively high - 62.27%. There are fewer students (28.08%) who are recognized as artificial intelligence machines or software capable of adapting their behavior (to some extent) by analyzing the results of previous actions.

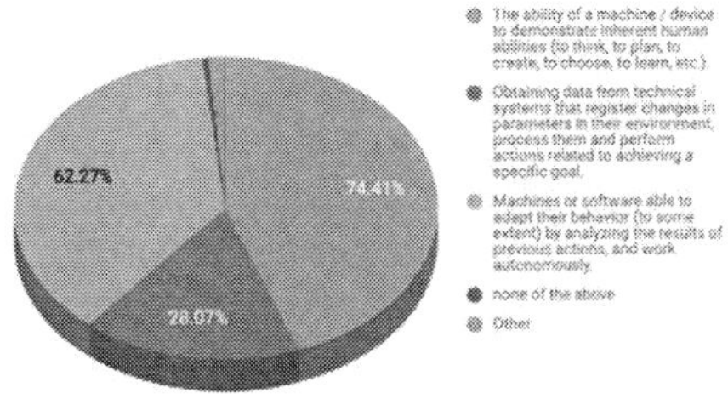

Figure 1. What is artificial intelligence?

From a research point of view, interesting are the answers to the question about examples of artificial intelligence enhanced technologies (Figure 2). Virtual assistants are the most recognizable example of artificial intelligence - 551 of the respondents with a relative share of 71.93%, followed by autonomous cars (cars without a driver) - selected by 547 students with a relative share of 71.41% and almost the same result for robots (selected by 543 the student with a relative share of 70.89%). Speech and face recognition systems are also a recognizable example (chosen by 418 students, with a relative share of 54.57%). The relative share of telephone assistant respondents is smaller (291 students with a relative share 37.99%) and online search engines (235 students with a relative share of 30.68%).

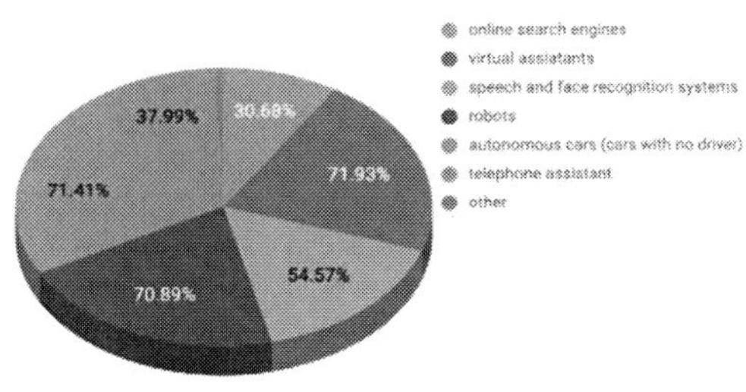

Figure 2. Examples of artificial intelligence

For the students, the most recognizable field in which artificial intelligence is used is digital personal assistants (74.93%). Smartphones offer virtual assistants that answer questions, make recommendations, and organize daily routines (eg Siri, Alexa, etc.). This result is most likely related to the fact that in Bulgaria, 71.8% of individuals aged between 16 and 74 (according to National Statistical Institute data) use mobile phones or smartphones to access the Internet. These devices are affordable and widely used.

In second place in terms of recognition are smart homes (67.62%). Respondents know this application of artificial intelligence from the curriculum content of biology and health education and geography and economics. In this age group, part of the training is related to working on "smart house" projects, with the aim of saving energy. A smart house is also recognized as a dwelling in which devices are installed that are connected to each other and this enables remote monitoring and control of appliances and systems such as locks, video surveillance, heating, etc. – a reality in many homes (Figure 3).

As applications of artificial intelligence, students also recognize smart cities and infrastructure (respondents with a relative share of 54.70%), automatic sensor systems that identify potentially dangerous situations (respondents with a relative share of 53.00%), as well as "automatic" translations (respondents with a relative share of 52.61%). The recognition of these fields of application of AI is largely associated with projects implemented in large cities to improve mobility and reduce congestion through traffic regulation. Popular among students are the use of automatic sensors such as thermal cameras (which recognize people with an elevated temperature), sensors in cars when the distance is reduced, for warnings in case of flood, tsunami, etc.

Less than half of respondents (40.99%) recognize the application of AI when using online search. This result is interesting given the fact that students use search engines on a daily basis. Consequently, most students do not appreciate the role of AI in search engines' processing of large volumes of data to provide increasingly precise and personalized search results. The situation is similar with the application of AI in combating disinformation (40.60%) and online shopping and advertising (40.34%). Among the likely reasons for these results is students' lack of awareness of how to identify "fake" news. It shows the need for app promotion campaigns that analyze social media data and assess the authority of online sources. The surveyed students are aged 14-18 years, which explains the lower results regarding the application of AI in providing personalized purchase suggestions based on products that have been searched for or purchased in the past. Students in this age group in Bulgaria rarely shop online (due to limited access to eligible payment methods), and the lack of this experience is largely associated with the results obtained.

The application of AI in healthcare is relatively recognizable - 298 respondents with a relative share of 38.90% are informed about the possibilities of analyzing large volumes of data and discovering patterns in order to improve the diagnosis of diseases. It is likely that the students' awareness of the pandemic crisis related to the spread of COVID-19 and the mathematical models used in relation to situation analysis and future forecasts have influenced this result in a positive direction.

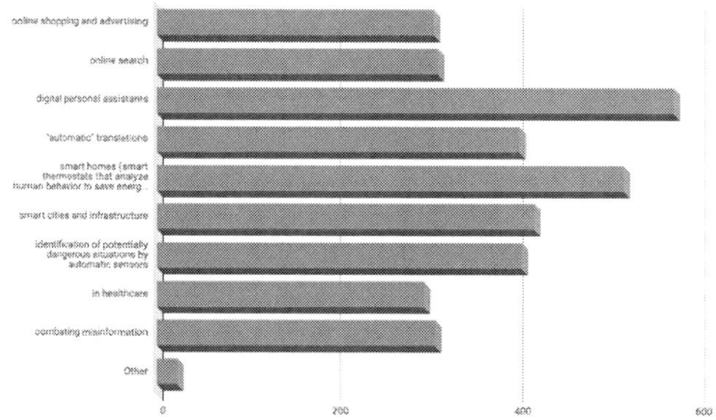

Figure 3. In which areas is artificial intelligence technologies is being used?

3.2 AI Technologies in Teaching and Learning

The research seeks to explore students' views on how artificial intelligence can change education. In this regard, two open questions were formulated in the survey - the place of AIinED n the teaching process and in relation to learning.

The question of how AI technologies could be used in teaching is considered in the following directions - how it could support it and what functions robots/machines could perform in class to support the work of the teacher.

The trends in students' responses are in several aspects (directions). The first of these is artificial intelligence as a teaching assistant. In this aspect, the vision is to offer individual training programs developed with the help of artificial intelligence. Thus, to prepare the student to follow an algorithm instead of a teacher.

Teachers make a lot of effort to help each student, taking into account his individual characteristics. This is especially difficult in classes of thirty or more students. Students perform the same tasks, use the same textbooks, regardless of the success rate of each student in each subject. One part of the class fails to learn the material, while the other learns it quicker and loses interest. Respondents see an opportunity for AI to tackle this problem. What's more, it now helps teachers personalize the learning process. Students are given the opportunity to familiarize themselves with the new material at a pace convenient for them, using special applications. Thus, these applications become assistant teachers and help them realize their maximum potential.

The second general aspect in the opinion of the respondents, regarding the place of artificial intelligence in teaching, is related to the capabilities of AI to analyze the behavior of students. According to some respondents, AI-connected cameras can not only conduct automatic attendance monitoring, but also analyze student behavior. These systems are able to recognize and evaluate how students react to different topics and tasks, how well they cooperate, whether they work alone, or whether they get bored. This would give the teacher information to help him adapt his teaching, depending on the particular situation.

Some typical answers from the students surveyed:

"AI can find easier to understand and curated information, built incrementally by AI throughout the learning process, to be delivered to students in a fast and convenient way."

"They can be used to conduct virtual experiments..."

"AI can make it easier to create and review tests, saving teacher time and fatigue."

"... to increase children's interest and motivation. Of course, artificial intelligence cannot replace the teacher, but it can help him."

AI is unlikely to ever fully replace teacher assessment, but it is increasingly entering the process. In the future, AI-enhanced technologies will fully verify written papers and exam tasks with the help of establishing metrics and benchmarks, excluding bias and favoring certain students.

A significant part of those who answered the question about the place of artificial intelligence in teaching (with a relative share of 54.70%) are not convinced of the usefulness of artificial intelligence in teaching. They prefer the traditional way of teaching, contact with the teacher "face to face" and do not approve of the use of AI in the teaching process. The likely reasons for this result are due to the extended periods of distance learning in an electronic environment during the last two academic years due to the pandemic caused by COVID-19.

The second open-ended question from the survey regarding students' opinion on the connection between artificial intelligence and education is centered on learning (How could artificial intelligence be used in the learning process?). The trends in the students' answers are in the following aspects: through the application of AI, everyone can progress according to their abilities by personalizing the learning content according to the individual achievements of the students; artificial intelligence can be used to self-check homework; to be able to automate and personalize the assessment of knowledge (it is a common practice in schools to assess all students with same standardized tests); detect gaps in knowledge and inform the individual student which part of the learning content to pay attention to again.

Among the students' answers, the following are of interest:

"Voice assistants can tailor what material to keyword search based on a given issue or topic. Now, when doing projects through search engines, a lot of information comes out that we don't need."

"...tests tailored to the individual capabilities and level of each student can easily be created. It's not good to give struggling students and excellent students the same tests."

"...finding out what I haven't learned well and helping me to learn and understand it well."

Students with a relative share of 37.99% are not convinced of the usefulness of artificial intelligence in the learning process.

The respondents gave interesting answers to the question of how they imagine a "smart" classroom. Most of the answers are in the direction of equipment, thanks to which the educational process becomes completely digital, and notebooks and textbooks are replaced by laptops, smartphones, and tablets.

Almost half of the answers are related to energy-saving solutions. Among them are: adjustable light - "controlling the brightness of the lamps in the classrooms so that the light is always suitable for learning for those who study at later hours"; "heat control of radiators and air conditioners in the classroom to save energy" so that "the temperature is constant and does not affect the learning process"; "smart windows that open automatically when it gets too hot or during breaks", a "smart" voice assistant to help with the learning process, etc.

3.3 Attitude to the Risks and Ethical use of AI Technologies

Respondents formulate risks of using artificial intelligence in education (open question from the survey). The answers formulated by the students are related to the experience of emotions in the learning process and "real student-teacher communication with corresponding shared feelings" ("modern robots can simulate some feelings of people, but not feel them"). Other potential risks are related to the danger of the "gradual disappearance of the teaching profession", the sudden interruption of the learning process ("any machine/robot can break down at any moment", "most students will not understand the opportunity they are given, and they will try to trick. In general, the surveyed students realize that as a result of improper use of artificial intelligence technologies, people can lose important skills and knowledge, and professions can disappear. There is a prevailing view that despite the possibility that technology can demonstrate human-like capabilities, it does not mean that it can completely replace humans.

To an open question from the survey why it is necessary to regulate the use of artificial intelligence technologies by law, respondents with a relative share of 52.61% did not give a specific answer (they did not answer anything, or they answered with "I don't know", "I have no idea"). This can be considered as a red flag, alarming responsible policymakers and authorities for the lack of understanding among the young people regarding the ethical use of AI.

The fact that AI-based applications can collect and analyze information about academic performance, reasons for leaving school, teachers' professional habits and other indicators. In this way, the probability of students dropping out of school can be predicted, and appropriate measures can be taken to prevent it.

Of course, disputes about the improper use of these data and technical means are inevitable here (Legg and Hutter, 2007), (van der Vlies R, 2010). The absence of a corresponding legal framework also heightens public anxiety about such systems. It is assumed that the relevant legal regulation will be prepared in a timely manner. For example, it is expected in September 2022 the European Commission to publish "Ethical guidelines on artificial intelligence and data in education and training based on the Ethics Guidelines for Trustworthy Artificial Intelligence" (Commission expert group on artificial intelligence (ai) and data in education and training (E03774), 2021).

Figure 4 represents the results of the question of how important the ethical use of artificial intelligence technologies in education is. It is noteworthy that students find it difficult to assess the importance of this problem - 294 of the respondents (with a relative share of 39 %) do not have an opinion on the issue, and 128 (with a relative share of 16.1 %) think that it is not important. These results incline to more uncertainty and can be interpreted as insufficient knowledge and understanding among the students on application of ethical principle when using AI. This is another signal to how important the awareness raising is in ethical use of AI in education among all the involved parties - teachers, students, and society.

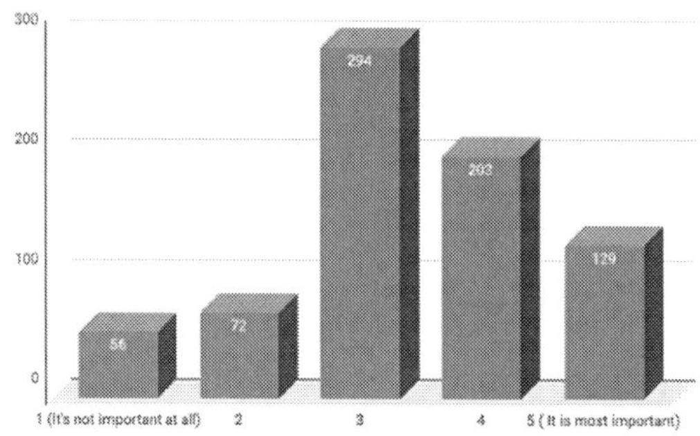

Figure 4. Importance of ethics in using AI technologies in education

The approach to the use of artificial intelligence technologies in education must be based on protecting fundamental European principles and values, to be controlled by the person - human on the loop but not necessarily in, to respect the principles of transparency and responsibility. Practical guidelines are needed for the use of artificial intelligence technologies in education. Because new technologies and artificial intelligence cannot and should not replace the teacher, but AI can allow the educational process to be more individualized, it can also allow education to be very interactive.

4. CONCLUSIONS

The results of the survey show that the students who participate in the survey: (a) correctly understand the essence of artificial intelligence; (b) they are convinced of the usefulness of the application of artificial intelligence technologies in their daily activities and strongly believe that it improves them; (c) are not entirely clear about the utility of artificial intelligence in learning and teaching; (d) do not show understanding of the ethical use of AI in education. The latter reduces the positive influence of the perceived usefulness of artificial intelligence in the learning process on student attitudes.

The results can contribute to the research trends in AI technologies in and for education. They raise the issue on whether the students are ready to be part of education enhanced by AI referring to how important ethics will be in the process. The results can be used as a reference point for future research in other countries, but one thing must be admitted: raising awareness on ethical use of AI technologies among students must begin.

Artificial intelligence has great potential to transform education and training for students, teachers and school staff. It could help reduce early school-leaving, compensate for learning difficulties and support teachers with differentiated or individualized learning through language learning apps, text-to-speech generators, learner mentors and more.

Different applications and software solutions will help, on the one hand, to adapt the learning process to the needs of the individual student, on the other hand, to help those children who have special needs or to reduce dropping out of school.

This is a long process that has begun. With each successive step, finding the balance between artificial intelligence learning and preserving natural social relationships is closer.

What is needed are not ready-made solutions, but a comprehensive vision for the development of education supported by AI technologies and a personal approach to each institution. It is in this way that AI can make education better, cheaper and more accessible.

It is necessary for policymakers to work in the direction of popularizing the benefits of the application of AI in the learning process among learners and teachers. A legislative framework for legally regulating the use of artificial intelligence technologies, including the ethical use of artificial intelligence in education, would be an appropriate act.

ACKNOWLEDGEMENTS

We are expressing our gratitude to all Bulgarian students who participated in that survey and gave their honest opinions. We highly appreciate the support of all Bulgarian teachers and school principals.

The authors would like to thank the Research and Development Sector at the Technical University of Sofia for the financial support.

REFERENCES

Artificial Intelligence for Europe (2018). Available at: https://ec.europa.eu/transparency/documents-register/detail?ref=COM(2018)237&lang=en (Accessed: October 3, 2022).

Benjamin Cheatham, Kia Javanmardian, and Hamid Samandari (2019) *Confronting the risks of artificial intelligence*, *McKinsey Quarterly*. Available at: https://www.mckinsey.com/capabilities/quantumblack/how-we-help-clients (Accessed: February 10, 2022).

Bostrom, N. (2014) *Superintelligence: Paths, Dangers, Strategies*. London, England: Oxford University Press.

Burnham, D. (1983) *The rise of the computer state*

Cannarsa, M. (2021) "Ethics guidelines for trustworthy AI," in *The Cambridge Handbook of Lawyering in the Digital Age*. Cambridge University Press, pp. 283–297.

Century (2019) *Century* Available at: https://www.century.tech/ (Accessed: October 3, 2022).

Chen X., Xie H., Zou D., Hwang G.-J. (2020) "Application and theory gaps during the rise of Artificial Intelligence in Education," *Computers and Education: Artificial Intelligence*, 1. doi: j.caeai.2020.100002.

Chen, L., Chen, P. and Lin, Z. (2020) "Artificial intelligence in education: A review," *IEEE access: practical innovations, open solutions*, 8, pp. 75264–75278. doi: 10.1109/access.2020.2988510

Commission expert group on artificial intelligence (ai) and data in education and training (E03774) (2021) *Europa.eu*. Available at: https://ec.europa.eu/transparency/expert-groups-register/screen/expert-groups/consult?do=groupDetail.groupDetail&groupID=3774 (Accessed: October 3, 2022).

Content Science (2017) *Content technology fact sheet*, *Content Science Review*. Available at: https://review.content-science.com/content-technology-fact-sheet/ (Accessed: October 3, 2022).

Dai, C.-P. and Ke, F. (2022) "Educational applications of artificial intelligence in simulation-based learning: A systematic mapping review," *Computers and Education: Artificial Intelligence*, 3(100087), p. 100087. doi: 10.1016/j.caeai.2022.100087.

Duggan, S. (2020) *AI in Education: Change at the Speed of Learning –, UNESCO IITE*. Available at: https://iite.unesco.org/publications/ai-in-education-change-at-the-speed-of-learning/ (Accessed: October 3, 2022).

European commission (2021) *regulation of the european parliament and of the council laying down harmonised rules on artificial intelligence (artificial intelligence act) and amending certain union legislative acts*. Available at: https://eur-lex.europa.eu/resource.html?uri=cellar:e0649735-a372-11eb-9585-01aa75ed71a1.0001.02/DOC_1&format=PDF.

Galaz, V. *et al.* (2021) "Artificial intelligence, systemic risks, and sustainability," *Technology in society*, 67(101741), p. 101741. doi: 10.1016/j.techsoc.2021.101741

Gardner, H., (2010) Multiple intelligences. *New York.-1993*.

Gardner, H., (2012) The theory of multiple intelligences. *Early professional development for teachers, 133.*, ISBN 1-8536-792-8

Information system "Infostat" of the National Statistics Institute of Bulgaria Nsi.bg. Available at: https://infostat.nsi.bg/infostat/pages/module.jsf?x_2=140 (Accessed: October 3, 2022).

Ivanova, K. *et al.* (2020) *Artificial Intelligence in and for Education in Bulgaria-Measures for Achievement Reliable Intelligent Growth*.

Jobs, S. (July-August 1981) "When We Invented the Personal Computer…," *Computers and People*.

Kahn, K. and Winters, N. (2017) "Child-friendly programming interfaces to AI cloud services," in *Data Driven Approaches in Digital Education*. Cham: Springer International Publishing, pp. 566–570.

Legg, S. and Hutter, M. (2007) "A collection of definitions of intelligence," *Frontiers in Artificial Intelligence and applications*. doi: 10.48550/ARXIV.0706.3639

Marr, B. (2018) *How is AI used in education--Real world examples of today and a peek into the future*. Forbes Magazine.

Ministry of Education and Science of Bulgaria (2020) *Artificial intelligence in education and science (Ideas for the development and use of AI in education and science in the Republic of Bulgaria)*. Available at: https://www.mon.bg/upload/23352/MON+AI+Doc .pdf.

Roll, I. and Wylie, R. (2016) "Evolution and revolution in artificial intelligence in education," *International journal of artificial intelligence in education*, 26(2), pp. 582–599. doi: 10.1007/s40593-016-0110-3.

Ross, J. N. *et al.* (2022) "The power behind the screen: Educating competent technology users in the age of digitized inequality," *International journal of educational research*, 115(102014), p. 102014. doi: 10.1016/j.ijer.2022.102014.

Seldon, A. and Abidoye, O. (2018) *The Fourth Education Revolution: Will Artificial Intelligence liberate or infantilise humanity?* Buckingham, England: University of Buckingham Press.

Stephen Lucci, D. K. (2016) *Artificial Intelligence in the 21st Century*. Dulles Town Center, VA: Mercury Learning & Information.

Todorova, M. (2019) *Artificial Intelligence. A brief history of development and ethical aspects of the subject*. Sofia: East-West.

Vincent-Lancrin, S. and R. van der Vlies (2020), "Trustworthy artificial intelligence (AI) in education: Promises and challenges", *OECD Education Working Papers*, No. 218, OECD Publishing, Paris, https://doi.org/10.1787/a6c90fa9-en.

West, D. M. (2018) *How artificial intelligence is transforming the world*

Whitley, E. and Ball, J. (2002) "Statistics review 4: Sample size calculations," *Critical care (London, England)*, 6(4), p. 335. doi: 10.1186/cc1521.

FRAMEWORK OF BEST PRACTICES FOR UNIVERSITY STUDENTS' MOBILE LEARNING IN STEM SUBJECTS

Shamsul Arrieya Ariffin
Konsortium Kecemerlangan Penyelidikan (KKP)
Research Consortium of Excellence (CoE), Creative Industry and Culture (CICC)
Satellite Special Interest Group (SIG) for Educational Usability Testing
Universiti Pendidikan Sultan Idris, Tanjong Malim, Perak, Malaysia

ABSTRACT

This study investigated the students' experience and impact of using Science, Technology, Engineering, and Mathematics (STEM) related subjects for mobile learning or mLearning. In this study, mobile learning student-generated activities (SGA) focused on Malaysian universities as a developing country. The study approach was a qualitative case study based on mobile technology usage through 18 focus group discussions amongst students in Malaysia from 10 universities. The students participated voluntarily, and a purposive sampling approach was used. This study examined the students' perspectives using STEM mobile learning through activities created by students in Malaysian universities. The data were analysed using thematic analysis approach. The findings established factors or themes derived from data on the impact of mobile learning for STEM activities created by students in mobile learning from 10 Malaysian universities. The mobile learning framework of best practices emerged from understanding the impact of the research themes from students' experiences.

KEYWORDS

Mobile Learning, Universities, Malaysia, Developing Country, Activities, STEM, Students' Experience, Perspectives, Themes, Factors

1. INTRODUCTION

The application of mobile learning is becoming increasingly widespread across many industries, including those in the Science, Technology, Engineering, and Mathematics (STEM) sector (Crompton & Traxler, 2016). Similarly, mobile learning strategy can benefit students majoring in STEM fields because it encourages students to interact with technology using contemporary teaching methods (Alrahmi et al., 2021). This study focused on STEM-related subject areas in developing countries (Tang et al., 2021). Meanwhile, mobile learning could facilitate learning in a contextualised environment (Mohammadi et al., 2020) amongst university students in Malaysia (Ariffin, 2018). Furthermore, this strategy incorporated the study of STEM disciplines in educational institutions from developing countries, such as those found in Malaysia. However, very little has been done in previous studies on developing Asian nations, particularly in understanding mobile learning activities performed by students in STEM fields (Ariffin, 2018). Therefore, this study aimed to get insights into the STEM domains of mobile learning (Adov et al., 2020) from students, mainly to understand students' experiences in a developing country like Malaysia to contribute from developing perspectives. Previously, a limited studies were done to collect local students' voices, particularly on STEM mobile learning for developing nations.

1.1 Limitations

Additionally, not all subjects of STEM were covered, as the nature of this study was to garner in-depth perspectives from selective universities and classes that voluntarily participated. There were some limitations, whereby the study did not cover all the universities in Malaysia due to its in-depth nature. This study focused on public universities, whereby most students were from rural areas, middle-class and low-income family.

1.2 Definition

STEM education is defined as studying and teaching in the domains of science, technology, engineering, and mathematics. On the other hand, this research looked at topics associated with STEM (Mutambara & Bayaga, 2021) in Malaysian universities, such as health promotion, e-commerce, multimedia, artificial intelligence, information technology and society, and three-dimensional animation. Student-generated activities (SGA) involve activities of users in mobile learning (Pachler et al., 2010) that create digital content using mobile devices (Mutambara & Bayaga, 2021; Dyson, 2016), which originated from learning from experience (Kolb, 1984). Moreover, in this study, SGA promoted a digital learning environment, whereby students were digital content producers and consumers, co-creating, collaborating, and sharing their work with other students. Additionally, using their own mobile devices in doing their assignments that related to STEM subjects.

1.3 Study Purpose

The study is aimed at investigating the students' perspectives in Malaysian universities about SGA in the fields of STEM. The main research questions is: What are the students' perspectives using mobile devices in SGA for their STEM subjects? Likewise, SGA has the potential to produce more digital material and engage students in mobile learning. As a result, this study is aimed at analysing and categorising students' opinions towards mobile learning SGA. In addition, this research classified the aspects for students in conjunction with SGA (Ariffin, 2016) in STEM disciplines.

1.4 Value of Digital Content Produced Locally for STEM Fields

In Asia, mobile learning is frequently considered a relatively recent approach to accessing education in this new millennium. For example, mobile learning makes education more accessible for students, allowing them to follow their learning needs according to their schedule and access it whenever convenient (Mutambara & Bayaga, 2021). Similarly, mobile learning has a promising future in enhancing education in Asian countries. However, limited studies for STEM can be applied to mobile learning within the framework of Malaysia's educational system as a developing country. Ariffin (2018) highlighted a limited study conducted in this field of STEM in Malaysia for mobile learning, and the findings indicated that no one cares about it. Consequently, there is a stigma about learning STEM subjects, as it is more difficult to understand and learn. In the context of Malaysia, there is greater availability of western digital content than local digital content, notably for subjects related to STEM. Therefore, this study compared the contents from foreign countries with contents produced locally in Malaysia, which made learning STEM subjects difficult for students in Malaysia (Ariffin, 2018).

1.5 Efforts by the Local Government of a Developing Country

The enrolment of students in Malaysia, who are pursuing degrees in STEM fields is not encouraging for several years. Compared to the government's target of having 60% of students primarily in STEM subjects, a scientific survey conducted in Malaysia in 2015 found that only 21% of students were enrolled in STEM courses. However, Terkowsky et al. (2016) stated that using mobile technology devices in STEM education enabled students to learn actively and creatively, while enhancing their grasp of various topics. The Malaysian education system supports STEM education. According to the Malaysia Education Blueprint 2013–2015 (2015), the low awareness about learning STEM subjects was to be blamed for the falling enrolment numbers and quality of outputs achieved by students in the fields of STEM.

1.6 Theoretical Pedagogy

In mobile learning, one of the strategies is the constructivism theory, which emphasises learning from experience. According to Kolb (1984), the pedagogical approach comprised four different teaching and learning strategies and established the experimental learning theory (Kolb,1984; Ariffin, 2018). During this time, Yin (2018) concentrated his efforts on conducting research based on phenomena associated with mobile technology in an education case study. Moreover, the study of experiential learning through mobile learning was relatively new to Malaysian students. Consequently, the teaching and learning process was more inventive and engaging with mobile learning than the traditional face-to-face approach, which was more acceptable. Meanwhile, the current emergence of learning in advanced countries adapts and adopts new technology (Parsons & MacCallum, 2021). Students develop their activities using mobile devices rather than sitting passively during experiential learning. This learning approach also applies to SGA, emphasising student-centred learning through mobile devices in the students' respective courses (Dyson, 2016). In a similar context, despite the difficulties inherent to the Malaysian context, there are chances for student-led activities to develop digital content for learning purposes (Ariffin, 2016). On the other hand, students can easily access and develop their digital multimedia content using multimedia functionalities built into their mobile devices. The students produced assignments using mobile devices as part of mobile learning. The active learning method in student activities was successful (Ariffin, 2016; Dyson, 2016). It exhibited a strong comprehension and enthusiasm for university learning linked with mobile learning, and was extensively employed worldwide. The overwhelming majority of evidence indicated that mobile devices provided teachers with support for instruction, given that all pupils have smartphones (Tang et al., 2021). Additionally, these mobile learning strategies encouraged learning activities outside or beyond school hours by utilising the students' mobile devices (Ariffin, 2018).

1.7 STEM Learning in Student-Generated Activities

In developed countries, STEM for mobile learning (Traxler & Crompton, 2016) has the potential to be expanded to SGA for STEM topics, in the Malaysian context. Students in Malaysia are demonstrating an increased level of expertise in the utilisation of mobile devices for educational pursuits. However, students tend to avoid STEM courses and are unmotivated to learn about them. Students entrance to universities for STEM courses has yet to accomplish a satisfactory level of enrolment, particularly in Malaysia. In Malaysia, STEM subjects are gaining more attention using mobile learning. For example, a few types of research were conducted in Malaysia on STEM topics related to mobile learning. Consequently, Nithia et al. (2015) stated their evidence of research, even though it was not considered in Malaysia to STEM and mobile learning. Therefore, there are opportunities to investigate STEM-related courses in Malaysia by implementing mobile learning to facilitate the creation of digital material by students. As a result, mobile learning that incorporated mobile SGA (Ariffin, 2018) might be one solution to the problem of getting students interested in STEM education.

2. METHODOLOGY

This is primarily a qualitative study, using case study approaches adapted from Ariffin (2018), that aims to gather in-depth information to find participants' perceptions of mobile learning related to STEM disciplines. The occurrences seen in the case study served as an impetus for the research, and brought perspectives (Yin, 2018). This research utilised a method of data collection, known as focus group discussion (Mertens, 2010) to acquire students' opinions regarding mobile learning application in STEM fields.

No	Grp	Uni	Subject	Pre	Post
1	FG1	A	Health Promotion	10	9
2	FG2	B	E-Commerce	13	11
3	FG3	C	Multimedia	4	3
4	FG4	D	Artificial Intelligence	6	6
5	FG5	A	IT & Society	6	6
6	FG6	E	3D Animation	6	6
7	FG7	F	Computer Science	6	6
8	FG8	C	Weight Lifting	9	7
9	FG9	G	Bio Chemistry	6	6
10	FG10	H	Game Design	7	7
11	FG11	I	Robotic	6	7
12	FG12	J	Educational Tech	6	6
13	FG13	I	Discreet Math	7	6
14	FG14	A	Health Promotion	10	5
15	FG15	A	Health Promotion	3	7
16	FG16	C	Rehabilitation	6	6
17	FG17	K	Cosmetic Eng.	6	6
18	FG18	H	Structure Program	6	6
Total Number of Students				123	116

Note: FG = Focus Group,

Figure 1. Participants

Figure 1 provides the participants' details for this study. The students were recruited voluntarily and involved with subjects associated with STEM. Most of them were tertiary-level students in Malaysian public universities.

2.1 Procedures

There were two stages in this study, which included the stages before and after SGA. In the first stage, 18 focus group discussions were held at 10 universities. The purpose of these focus group discussions was to get in-depth insights into the effects, which previously gained mobile learning experience had on the study of STEM subjects. For instance, the participants communicated using mobile devices, and only a tiny percentage participated in activities that used SGA to learn about STEM-associated subjects. As shown in Figure 1, the study incorporated 18 unique focus groups held across 10 distinct educational institutions or universities in Malaysia. The researcher suggested that the academics included student-created multimedia activities in their teaching to enhance the student's learning experiences. Furthermore, the students were instructed to use their mobile phones to complete their homework for disciplines related to STEM. After the brief introduction of mobile learning activities for STEM, the typical length of time for each interview ranged between 30 minutes and an hour. The semi-structured questions were adapted from the mobile learning literature by Ariffin (2016). These questions were inspired by student-generated experiential learning activities based on research by Dyson et al. (2008) that used experiential learning (Kolb, 1984). On the other hand, data from the interviews were analysed by utilising the thematic analysis method (Braun and Clarke, 2006), and organised by NVivo software. Some examples of semi-structured questions that were used for this study were as follows:

- How did the students utilise mobile devices for activities related to STEM mobile learning student-generated content?
- Which benefits of mobile learning the STEM student-generated activities are in the process of learning STEM subjects?
- What difficulties did students face when carrying out these student-generated mobile learning activities for STEM subjects?

Participants in this study should have a subject associated with one of the STEM fields (science, technology, engineering, or mathematics). Consequently, all participants from 18 different focus groups and 10 universities located in Malaysia contributed to the study voluntarily. In a nutshell, 123 students participated in phase one, whereas 116 students participated during the stage before SGA. Figure 2 shows the research process. In this study, the fields of study associated with STEM included Health Promotion, E-Commerce, Multimedia, Artificial Intelligence, IT & Society, 3D Animation, Computer Science, and Weight Lifting. Likewise, subjects such as Bio-Chemistry, Game Design, Robotics, Multimedia, Education Technology, Discreet Math, Health Promotion Rehabilitation, Cosmetic Engineering, and Structured Programming, were also included.

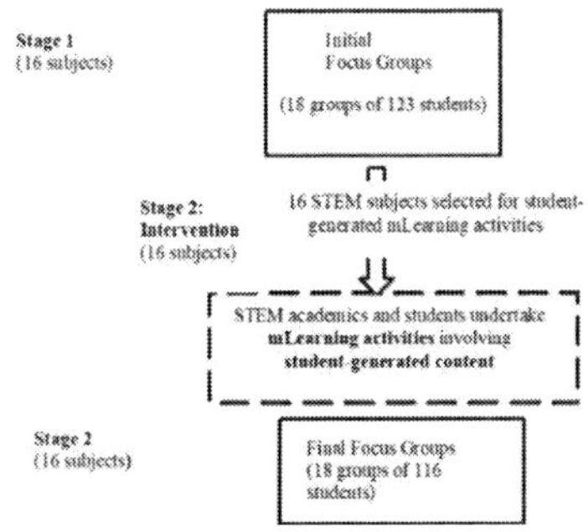

Figure 2. Various Stages of Research in STEM Fields

This article elucidated the findings of a study that focused on the perspectives of students, who participated in mobile learning for STEM courses at universities in Malaysia. These phases included Phase 1, which took place before the students participated in content activities. Furthermore, Phase 2 took place after the students participated in multimedia activities. During this round of activities, the students created STEM-related multimedia content.

2.2 Thematic Analysis Process

A series of repetitive steps, whereby the meaning of data was analysed and interpreted in developing the theme analysis (Myers & Avison, 2002). The factors were extracted from the data through a method, known as theme analysis. Braun and Clarke (2006) emphasised that to conduct thematic analysis, one should be familiar with the transcripts, initialised the code, and grasp the topics. Additionally, the participants' responses were collected by an audio recorder. The researcher provided a Malay language transcription of the audio (Bahasa Melayu or Bahasa Malaysia). To produce an accurate transcription, the researcher needs to listen to the audio recorder more than once. The original recording was in Bahasa Malaysia and translated into English language. Furthermore, the codes were identified from the interview statements. Consequently, if required, the combination of codes was categorised and reorganised in developing the themes (Saldaña 2009). Likewise, Auerbach and Silverstein (2003) came to a similar conclusion, stating that the coding phases were nonlinear processes that might reverse, bringing about changes in coding, and theme processes as topic generation moves forward. Modifying the topics aligns with how the data may be interpreted, and the study corresponds with the thematic background (Braun & Clarke 2006). Finally, the mobile learning findings were organised into a few broad categories, and topics from which the factors or themes were derived.

3. FINDINGS

Table 1. Framework of Emerging Factors from the Best Practises

	Emerging Factors from the Research
1	Affordances of mobile devices for individual use and consumption
2	Affordances for educational usage
3	Challenges of mobile phones for education
4	Affordances of mobile learning, particularly for SGA
5	Mobile learning achievement
6	Opportunities and requirements for overcoming challenges associated with mobile learning
7	Usability of mobile devices

3.1 Affordances of Mobile Devices for Individual Use and Consumption

The first aspect that was discovered was referred to as 'affordability for personal usage of mobile devices'. This element showed that mobile devices could be utilised for daily activities and according to participants' lifestyles, notably in the multimedia function of mobile devices, and utilisation of social media for communication purposes. Some examples were:

> "Because I enjoyed making video calls, WhatsApp programme was one of my favourites to use." (Pre, FG13, S3)

3.2 Affordances for Educational Usage

This topic focused on the significance of mobile devices in education, highlighting their wide range of applications, in particular blended digital online learning, and application of social media platforms for educational reasons. An example:

> "YouTube, Google Chrome, and Google Translate are the three Google products I used constantly." (Pre, FG2, S13)

3.3 Challenges of Mobile Phones for Education

This topic focused on the challenges that arise while attempting to use mobile phones for educational purposes, and access digital content while participating in educational activities. An example:

> "The price is high, but with the quota and internet speed that does not make it worth it." (Pre, FG9, S6)

3.4 Affordances of Mobile Learning, Particularly for SGA

The fourth consideration was 'affordability of mobile devices for mobile learning', particularly concerning SGA. Within this topic, participants reaped the benefits of the influence and results that mobile learning content created for student-driven activities. After participating in SGA, the participants showed vital awareness of using mobile learning in STEM than their understanding before participating in SGA. An example:

> "Makes it easier for the learner to gain knowledge through the process of revising or completing assignment." (Post, FG9, S3)

3.5 Mobile Learning Achievement

Additionally, 'mobile learning achievement' emerged as the fifth criterion. This topic presented the results of mobile learning digital content generation based on SGA that used the multimedia capabilities of mobile devices. An example:

> "The video was such a pleasant and enjoyable experience." (Post, FG4, S3)

3.6 Opportunities and Requirements for Overcoming Challenges

The phrase 'opportunities and requirements for solving mobile learning challenges' is the sixth factor. This issue focused on the prospects and opportunities that mobile learning presents for lowering the barriers to mobile learning. This was by giving students more agency in creating digital material by utilising mobile devices multimedia capabilities. An example:

> "… I can do it." (Post, FG7, S4)

3.7 Usability of Mobile Devices

The capacity to use mobile devices is the seventh criterion to consider. Users discussed their difficulties and worries regarding usability issues while using mobile devices to participate in SGA. This topic emphasised the significance of mobile devices practical use for educational purposes. Some examples were:

> "Doable for anybody and everyone." (Post, FG4, S6)

"It is a form of independent study that may be done at any time and in any location. Mobile learning allows us to obtain information even if we stay in an unfamiliar location without the need to locate the information in a book." (Pre, FG7, S6)

> "...via mobile learning, everyone has the same rights to get this mobile learning since it is accessible, and that there are no restrictions to the boundaries for you to gain the education and access information." (Post, FG5, S1)

4. DISCUSSION

This section discusses the contribution of mobile learning best practices for STEM in a developing country, such as Malaysia (Yin, 2018). Furthermore, this study shed light on the fact that mobile learning encompasses a broader range of topics, including those in the STEM domain when applied in a local, regional setting. On the other hand, this study utilised the experiential learning approach (Kolb, 1984) for the development of a sustainable mobile learning environment in the production of multimedia digital content that embeds to improve the learning of STEM subjects within the context of case studies in Malaysian universities.

4.1 Students Empowerment Implementation

According to the study findings, the students felt more equipped to work on their projects amongst other students when they utilised mobile devices for SGA learning from experience (Crompton & Traxler, 2016). The students were more engaged rather than sitting passively, and produced projects of high levels for subjects related to STEM. As a result of developing the digital content for their group assignments, they improved their knowledge in the respective subjects, and acquired skills in creating digital multimedia (Dyson, 2016; Tang et al., 2021). Additionally, as part of their work assignments, the students should create STEM-related digital multimedia content for the projects. Consequently, they had a more profound comprehension of complex topics, such as STEM as a result of working on the projects using SGA approach for local universities in the Malaysian context.

4.2 Bring Your Own Device (BYOD) for Student-generated STEM Activities

The students acquired the role of digital content creators for the entire SGA when 'bring your own device' (BYOD) strategies were implemented. This study enlightened them that they might become digital content creators with relatively little guidance from their instructors (Ariffin, 2016). Nevertheless, they produced high-quality STEM digital content using BYOD by working collaboratively with their group. This study also found that the students had a greater awareness of using their own mobile devices, such as smartphones, for access to educational purposes (Mutambara & Bayaga, 2021). In particular, the students were more aware of using their mobile devices for SGA in STEM subjects.

5. CONCLUSION

In this research, mobile learning elements garnered from students' perspectives in Malaysia gave new insights. Specifically, this research focused on mobile learning SGA for STEM in developing countries within Malaysian universities. The students benefited from the BYOD policy, as it made the subject matter of STEM more meaningful and easier to comprehend. Future research could investigate other fields, such as creative industries for SGA. Likewise, SGA involves creativity, and therefore, phenomena in STEM topics related to IR 4.0 and creative industries may be further researched.

ACKNOWLEDGEMENT

This study acknowledged the grant contribution to the Consortium of Excellent for Creative Industry & Culture: JPT(BKPI)1000/016/018/25(63), Special Interest Group (SIG) for Educational Usability Testing UPSI: 2021-0042-106-10. Likewise, the author would like to extend her gratitude to the Ministry of Higher Education Malaysia via Universiti Pendidikan Sultan Idris (UPSI), which provided the FRGS grant code: 2017-0074-107-02.

REFERENCES

Ariffin, S. A. (2018). Towards a smart educational environment frame-work for mlearning in a Malaysian context. In Proceedings of the 4th International Conference on Human-Computer Interaction and User Experience in Indonesia, CHIuXiD'18 (pp. 74-81).

Ariffin, S. A. (2016). Academics' Perspectives on the Challenges and Opportunities for Student-Generated Mobile Content in Malaysia. International Journal of Mobile and Blended Learning (IJMBL), 8(3), 49-64.

Barbour, R. (2007). Doing focus group. London: SAGE Publications.

Braun, V. & Clarke, V. 2006, Using thematic analysis in psychology, Qualitative Research in Psychology, 3(2), 77101

Crompton, H., & Traxler, J. (Eds.). (2016). Mobile Learning and STEM: Case Studies in Practice. Routledge.

Dyson, L. E. (2016). Achieving sustainable mobile learning through student owned devices and student-generated multimedia content. In W. Ng & T. M. Cumming (2016), Sustaining mobile learning: Theory, research and practice (212226). New York, NY: Routledge.

Dyson, L. E., Lawrence, E., Litchfield, A., & Zmijewska, A. (2008). Mfieldwork for information systems students. In Proceedings of the 41st Annual Hawaii International Conference on System Sciences (HICSS 2008) (pp. 46-46). IEEE.

Kolb, D. A. (1984), Experiential learning: Experience as the source of learning and development, 1 edn, Prentice Hall, New Jersey USA, 1256.

Mertens, D. M. (2010). Research and evaluation in education and psychology, 3 Ed.,Sage Publications Inc., Oaks California, USA, 1527.

Mohammadi, A., Grosskopf, K., & Killingsworth, J. (2020). Workforce development through online experiential learning for STEM education. Adult Learning, 31(1), 27-35.

Mutambara, D., & Bayaga, A. (2021). Determinants of mobile learning acceptance for STEM education in rural areas. Computers & Education, 160, 1-16.

Myers, M.D. & Avison, D. (2002). An introduction to qualitative research in information systems. London: SAGE Publications Ltd.

Parsons, D., & MacCallum, K. (2021). Current perspectives on augmented reality in medical education: applications, affordances and limitations. Advances in Medical Education and Practice, 12,77-91.

Tang, K. Y., Hsiao, C. H., Tu, Y. F., Hwang, G. J., & Wang, Y. (2021). Factors influencing university teachers' use of a mobile technology-enhanced teaching (MTT) platform. Educational Technology Research and Development, 69(5), 2705-2728.

Yin, R. K. (2018). Case study research and applications. Sage.

STUDY OF THE CORRECTIVE GRAMMATICAL TREATMENT OF ENGLISH SUPPORTED BY MOBILE APPLICATIONS

Adriana Guanuche[1], Osana Eiriz[2] and Roberto Espi[2]
[1]*Universidad Politécnica Salesiana, Ecuador*
[2]*Universidad de la Habana, Cuba*

ABSTRACT

The increasing technological development of computers, tablets and smartphones has enabled a rapid increase in the adoption of mobile technology for language teaching and learning, and numerous applications that provide easy access for any learner without limitations of place and time have been developed. This paper shows the study of grammatical treatment using corrective feedback supported by mobile applications. The study subjects were first-level students of the language institute, where a control and experimental study was carried out. The experimental group was evaluated with paper-based assessments and the control group with the Canvas mobile application. Subsequently, a statistical analysis was performed for data analysis. The results show that there was a 4.9% improvement in the grades of students who used the application and received corrective feedback.

KEYWORDS

Corrective Feedback, English Learning, Mobile Applications

1. INTRODUCTION

During the last decades, technological development has grown at an impressive pace, and this has led to portable devices being increasingly equipped with a variety of applications and WIFI access. Therefore, the use of smart mobile devices is becoming more and more widespread in the population, as the mobile Internet develops (Zou & Li, 2015). Nowadays, students have easy access to more advanced functions in the use of mobile technologies and can use applications for education, including language learning. They are experienced in using online tools and learn by interacting, creating, editing, commenting and sharing documents and ideas, which is highly beneficial due to the unique characteristics of mobile applications: interactivity, ubiquity and portability(Abdel-Reheem Amin, 2020)(Kacetl & Klímová, 2019). Mobile technology has been found to play an important role in learning English, and many countries are investing in ICT-enhanced educational projects, mainly due to the current English language scenario (Irudayasamy et al., 2021).

In addition, there has been a rapid increase in the implementation of mobile technology for mobile-assisted language teaching and learning, which is why numerous applications have been developed to provide easy access for any student, without limitations of place and time (Zhang & Yu, 2022)(Gangaiamaran, 2017). Several Google applications have been developed for the learning and teaching of foreign languages, and it has been proven through various researches that the appropriate use of these applications improves the English level of students (Abdel-Reheem Amin, 2020)(Chen, 2016). It should be considered that most students use mobile devices mainly for entertainment and communication. To teach the new generation called digital natives, teachers must know how to motivate and adapt these digital resources for language learning, instead of prohibiting the use of tablets or smartphones (B.-T. Wang, 2017).

The use of this technology and online resources contribute to the teaching and learning of foreign languages. However, there are still many challenges to be faced regarding the use of these tools in the classroom (Guaqueta & Castro-Garces, 2018)(Zou & Li, 2015). One of the reasons is that most existing applications have not been developed from a pedagogical point of view, due to the gap between application developers and language teachers. It has been found that there are still limitations in several applications for grammar treatment in error recognition, and also that feedback in grammar processing is not fully efficient (Ferreira & Kotz, 2010). In the writing process, it is quite common for students to make mistakes because writing is not a skill that is naturally acquired; it is usually learned or culturally transmitted as a set of practices in instructional settings (Marzban & Arabahmadi, 2013). On the other hand, the process requires the management of grammatical competence that involves the correct use of verb tenses, connectors, prepositions, among others, and many times these parameters have not been fully assimilated by students before undertaking academic writing processes (Ortiz et al., 2019). Feedback is one of the most important tasks of teachers. However, it is time-consuming because of the need to respond to the different expressions of learners who make an error and to provide correct metalinguistic information about the nature of the error (Septiana et al., 2016)(Ellis et al., 2009). Corrective feedback is used to provide information about the correctness of the students' expressions and provide them with the correct answer (Hashemifardnia et al., 2019).

There are some applications for learning English supported by using mobile applications, but most of them have not been validated or tested. Several studies have shown a positive relationship between perceived usefulness and the intention to continue using language learning applications (X. Wang et al., 2022), allowing a new pedagogical approach with the use of applications, so that teachers play the role of facilitators and thus increase the level of participation of students and teachers.

This paper shows the study of the corrective grammatical treatment of English, with corrective feedback supported by mobile applications, for which an evaluation was developed using the Canvas mobile application. The study subjects were first-level students of the language institute, most of them have an elementary knowledge of the English language that was learnt in school and high school. where a control and experimental study was carried out. The experimental group was evaluated with paper-based assessments and the control group with the Canvas mobile application. Subsequently, a statistical analysis was performed to obtain the percentages of improvement with the use of mobile applications.

2. PREVIOUS CONCEPTS

2.1 Corrective Feedback

Corrective feedback is defined as the set of comments provided to students on their production or comprehension of the second language. Its effectiveness and influence on learning has been investigated in recent years in relation to the impact of corrective feedback on students' responses (Li & Vuono, 2019). There are studies that show great acceptance of corrective feedback in learning English grammar due to its contribution to error correction. Providing corrective feedback comments improves grammar learning more than vocabulary learning. The success of the influence of corrective feedback on learning lies in the flexibility and adaptability of the feedback and, above all, its alignment with the linguistic objectives of academic progress(Van, 2022). In addition, different types of corrective feedback are verified, but in this paper, corrective feedback will be considered: positive, self-corrective and metalinguistic feedback.

2.1.1 Corrective Feedback

This type of corrective feedback aims to highlight the error made by the learner immediately through written comments that are received visually, and it focuses on improving the written language skills of the second language (Li & Vuono, 2019). Written corrective feedback is aligned with writing improvement, as it focuses on particular errors that students make the most, as well as giving attention to individual needs (Lee et al., 2021). Previous studies show that teachers should pay close attention to the feedback they provide to their students, as this can have a great emotional and motivational impact on them (Liu et al., 2022). Corrective feedback can also be positive, through comments that praise correct responses (Bagheri & Rassaei, 2021).

2.1.2 Metalinguistic Corrective Feedback

This type of corrective feedback is provided after the student has made the error, and it consists of providing key words that guide the learner to identify the location of the error, motivating self-correction (Li & Vuono, 2019). There are two types of metalinguistic feedback. The first one uses error codes consisting of abbreviated phrases or words representing the different types of errors, which can be located next to the error or at the end of the line. The second one is based on explaining the error to the learner. These types of metalinguistic feedback allow students to diagnose their grammatical inaccuracies and indirectly induce explicit learning of the second language. In both types of feedback, it is important that students first identify the error and then correct it.

2.1.3 Self-Corrective Feedback

The teacher motivates students to pay attention to the answers provided and gives them enough information to correct their mistakes, so that they have the opportunity to actively participate in self-correction (Bagheri & Rassaei, 2021). Self-corrective feedback allows students to benefit from correcting their own errors, and it can be done orally or in written form. The fact that students benefit from feedback allows them to become self- regulators and monitors of their own learning progress (Kingston Pal Thamburaj et al., 2020).

2.2 Mobile Learning

The term "mobile" comes from the word mobility, which in learning refers to the ease of access a student has to learn anywhere using a mobile device. Currently, the positive attitude, the predisposition, and the intention of the students to continue using the applications on cell phones in the learning process is evident. Mobile learning has become an indispensable tool for students and teachers, boosting their level of self-confidence and the ability to stay motivated to meet their academic goals (Huang & Chueh, 2022)(Sanda & Klimova, 2021).

2.3 Canvas

Canvas is an LMS Online platform or learning management system (LMS), which has been adopted lately by several universities in the USA and Canada that are interested in the teaching and learning process, incorporating pedagogical principles and development-based active learning. Its functionality is based on the cloud and the support it provides to initiate new models of learning and personalized education, allowing teachers and students to have access to all the notes. The teacher is allowed to invite students to join the activities in Canvas, manage their content, review the summary notes individually and in general, and thereby identify students with learning needs(Duin & Tham, 2020). The Canvas LMS mobile application is flexible, reliable, adaptive, and intuitive. It also provides accessibility from any iOS or Android device, without the need for a desktop or laptop. All you need is a smart device and an Internet connection via Wi-Fi or a data plan, and it is available in both free and paid versions.

2.4 Applications for Grammar Learning

Current technology offers multiple applications to support English language learning. One source for downloading is Google Play Store, but before using an application, it is important to analyze its effectiveness by analyzing the following aspects: connection to the curriculum, feedback, performance, authenticity, friendliness, and dynamism (Kingston Pal Thamburaj et al., 2020). The use of mobile applications for learning does not replace the grammar learning process, on the contrary, they become a complement that seeks to prolong the efficient knowledge of students. According to previous studies, it is important to use authentic applications for grammatical learning with exercises and corrective feedback, which allow students to be actively involved in their academic process by correcting their mistakes(Guanuche et al., 2021).

2.5 ICT in Education

Technology has been present in English language learning since the 1940s, even though the current availability of openness in place and space did not exist. The advancement of technology in smartphones allows them to be increasingly closer to people in different areas, such as social, learning, entertainment, among others. Thus, English language learning has also been influenced by the use of ICTs, encouraging teachers to examine their methodologies and adapt them to the needs of students in an effective way (Kingston Pal Thamburaj et al., 2020). The use of ICTs in education seeks personalized learning, with constructivist approaches that provide resources available to teachers and students at any time or place, and above all, that motivate academic progress through the use of technologies connected to reality and the needs of students (Putri et al., 2021).

3. STUDY CASE

For the design of the application, it was considered that: it should be user friendly and have an intuitive interface. Four types of questions were selected according to a previous study: (Fill in the blanks, Simple multiple choice, Sentence structuring and Complex multiple choice). For the development of the application, the following actions were carried out. "Figure. 1" shows the scheme that was used

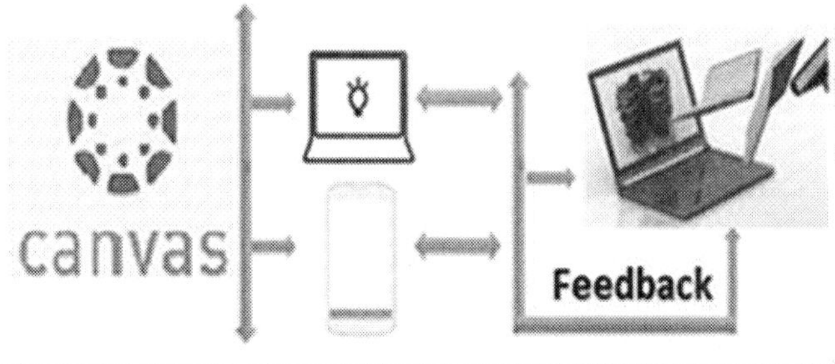

Figure 1. Design application

3.1 Study of the use of Mobile Applications for Learning

Figure 2 shows the survey answered by teachers to find out if they use mobile applications for the English language learning process, or if they would like to use them in different activities of the learning process. This was done to obtain real data and to plan training if necessary. It is important to mention that the data about preferences for ICT tools for grammar learning was taken from the experimental and control group.

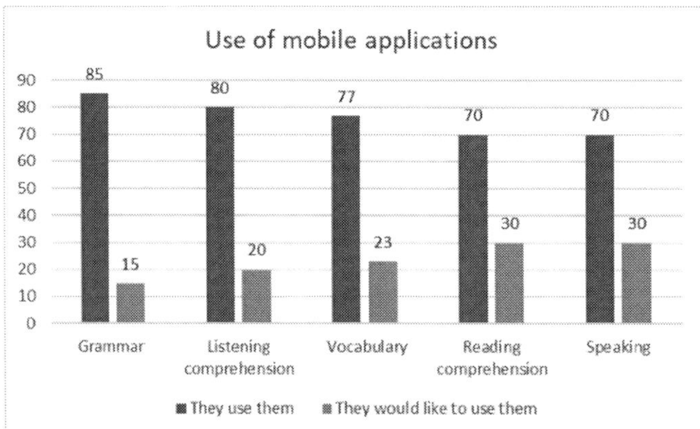

Figure 2. Survey on the use of applications answered by teachers.

The results show that 76.4 % of teachers use mobile applications for English language learning, while 23.6 % want to use such tools. Subsequently, the same survey was applied to UPS students to find out in which skills the applications are being used. The results are shown in Figure 3.

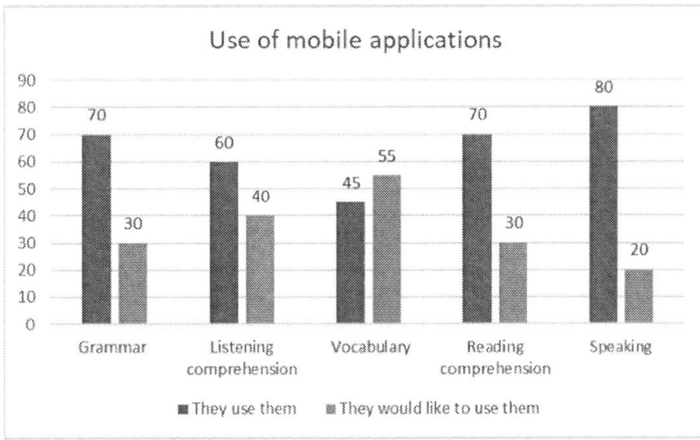

Figure 3. Survey on the use of applications answered by students

The results show that students use mobile devices to complement their studies, thanks to the easy access and availability of applications on the web. An average of 35% of students want to use this technology

3.2 Selection of Topics and Grammar Exercises

The grammatical topics selected correspond to the twelve units of the Cambridge textbook that are studied in the first level. Each unit reviews two grammar contents, so in the Canvas application four types of exercises were created for each grammar topic, with five items for each exercise. The exercises used were: Fill in the blanks, Simple multiple choice, Sentence structuring and Complex multiple choice. The selection was based on the review of exercises used in international examinations, and on the evaluations taken at the institution where the study was conducted. The classroom visits revealed that each course is large, with approximately 40 students in each, which makes it almost impossible for the teacher to provide effective feedback to all students. It was observed that most teachers use explicit collective feedback. The teachers who participated in the study have knowledge in mobile learning.

The study was conducted with 34 students and the questions with corrective feedback were automatically evaluated in CANVAS, as shown in Figure 4, where a simple multiple-choice question that was answered correctly can be seen. To analyze the characteristics and the grammatical contents for the corrective treatment, the questions were asked according to the analytical plans used in English classes.

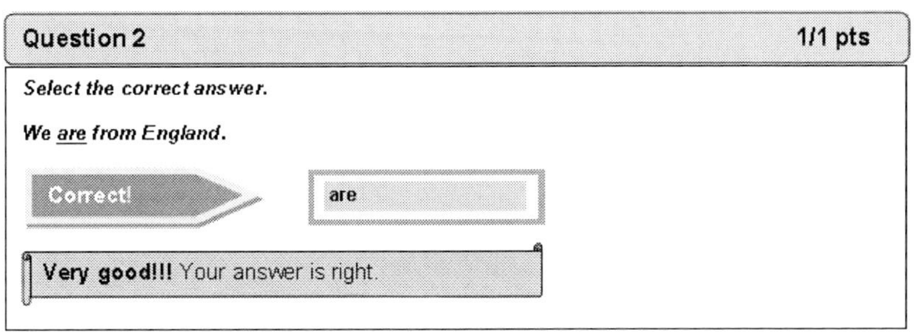

Figure 4. Positive Feedback Model: Correct answer.

Figure 5 shows that the student's answer was incorrect, and CANVAS automatically performed the self- corrective feedback. Thus, the student was able to know that his answer was incorrect and received an explanation about the error made.

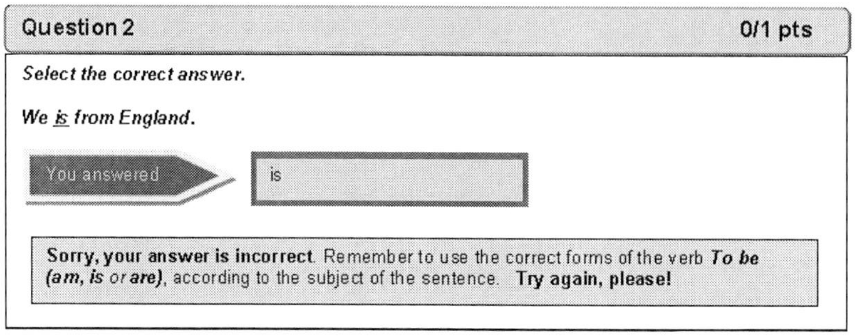

Figure 5. Self-corrective Feedback Model: Incorrect answer

3.3 Evaluation of the Methodology

Results of the proposed evaluation through the use of applications to the students of the first level of English, subsequent evaluation, and analysis of the results. The learning progress was evaluated by the obtained results of the grammar contents learnt in the different units of the study.

Table 1. Percentages according to each type of exercise

	Control	Experimental
Fill in the blanks	74.6%	78.8%
Simple multiple choice	82.7%	90.1%
Sentence structuring	69.7%	73,1%
Complex multiple choice	79%	83.9%
Improvement between contr and experimental	**76.5%**	**81.4%**

Table 1 shows the results control vs. experiment, and it can be seen that the experimental group had a significantaverage improvement of 4.9% with respect to the control groups, analyzing six units with different topics, according to the university's own analytical plans. These results validate the use of the application and the benefits of using applications for learning English grammar. It should be emphasized that the results were obtained from the evaluations made to several groups with different topics and were analyzed considering the type of question, since students have a certain preference, and they are also more didactic when using the application.

After using the application and evaluating it, a survey was conducted with the students of the regular course and those of the intensive course to find out their preference for doing the exercises, as shown in Figure 6.

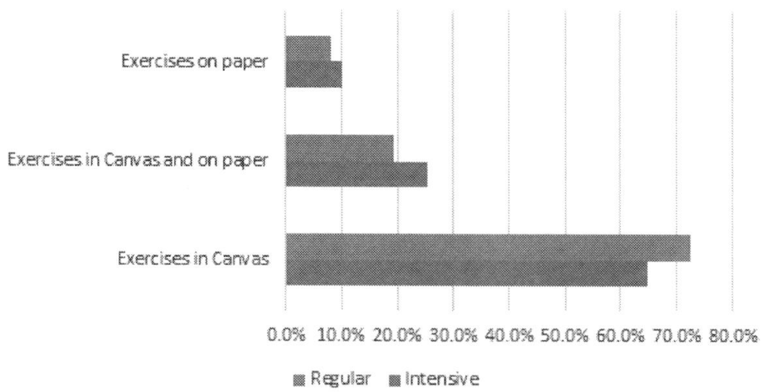

Figure 6. Preference for doing exercises

The results show an average preference of 68.6% for teaching methods using apps. Some 22.4% prefer to use applications in combination with paper and only 9% want to continue using traditional teaching methods.

The results show that the use of the Canvas application and corrective feedback contributed to grammatical learning during the six units studied. In addition, a greater tendency to make grammatical errors in question formulation and less in sentence structuring was identified. At the linguistic level, better learning results were reflected in the morphological area and less impact in the syntactic area. This differentiation of results is attributed to the fact that students show more difficulty in correctly structuring the components of sentences and questions in the foreign language, which for this study was English.

4. CONCLUSION

The use of applications as online learning tools, together with good teacher guidance, can significantly improve language learning, as well as improve student motivation thanks to the advantages of using mobile applications (adaptability, ease, mobility, interactivity, accessibility, interactivity, and cost).

The research results show that mobile technologies for language teaching are increasing significantly. In addition, teachers and students use different technologies to complement the process of teaching and learning English inside and outside the classroom.

The control vs experiment results show that the experimental group obtained an average significant improvement of 4.9% compared to the control groups. This is because, thanks to the use of mobile applications, the strategies used for learning English have been transformed, and now students can determine when and where to learn using online resources.

REFERENCES

Abdel-Reheem Amin, E. (2020). A Review of Research into Google Apps in the Process of English Language Learning and Teaching. *Arab World English Journal*, *11*(1), 399–418. https://doi.org/10.24093/awej/vol11no1.27

Bagheri, M., & Rassaei, E. (2021). The Effects of Two Forms of Written Corrective Feedback and Ambiguity Tolerance on EFL Learners ' Writing Accuracy. *English Teaching & Learning*, 20. https://doi.org/https://doi.org/10.1007/s42321-021-00082-6

Chen, X. (2016). Evaluating Language-learning Mobile Apps for Second-language Learners. *Journal of Educational Technology Development and Exchange*, *9*(2). https://doi.org/10.18785/jetde.0902.03

Duin, A. H., & Tham, J. (2020). The Current State of Analytics: Implications for Learning Management System (LMS) Use in Writing Pedagogy. *Computers and Composition*, *55*. https://doi.org/10.1016/j.compcom.2020.102544

Ellis, R., Loewen, S., & Erlam, R. (2009). Implicit and explicit corrective feedback and the acquisition of L2 grammar.

Implicit and Explicit Knowledge in Second Language Learning, Testing and Teaching, 303–332. https://doi.org/10.21832/9781847691767-015

Ferreira, A., & Kotz, G. (2010). ELE-Tutor Inteligente: Un analizador computacional para el tratamiento de errores gramaticales en Español como Lengua Extranjera. *Revista Signos*, *43*(73), 211–236. https://doi.org/10.4067/S0718-09342010000200002

Gangaiamaran, R. (2017). *Review on Use of Mobile Apps for Language Learning*. *12*(21), 11242–11251. Guanuche, A., Caiza, G., Eiriz, O., & Espí, R. (2021). Development of a Mobile Application for English Language

Learning Through Corrective Feedback. In *Smart Innovation, Systems and Technologies* (Vol. 202). Springer

International Publishing. https://doi.org/10.1007/978-3-030-57566-3_42

Guaqueta, C. A., & Castro-Garces, A. Y. (2018). The Use of Language Learning Apps as a Didactic Tool for EFL Vocabulary Building. *English Language Teaching*, *11*(2), 61. https://doi.org/10.5539/elt.v11n2p61

Hashemifardnia, A., Namaziandost, E., & Sepehri, M. (2019). The effectiveness of giving grade, corrective feedback, and corrective feedback-plus-giving grade on grammatical accuracy. *International Journal of Research Studies in Language Learning*, *8*(1), 15–27. https://doi.org/10.5861/ijrsll.2019.3012

Huang, D. H., & Chueh, H. E. (2022). Behavioral intention to continuously use learning apps: A comparative study from Taiwan universities. *Technological Forecasting and Social Change*, *177*(November 2021). https://doi.org/10.1016/j.techfore.2022.121531

Irudayasamy, J., Uba, S. Y., & Hankins, C. A. (2021). Exploration and Exploitation of Mobile Apps for EnglishLanguage Teaching: A Critical Review. *English Language Teaching*, *14*(4), 43. https://doi.org/10.5539/elt.v14n4p43

Kacetl, J., & Klímová, B. (2019). Use of smartphone applications in english language learning—A challenge for foreign language education. *Education Sciences*, *9*(3), 1–9. https://doi.org/10.3390/educsci9030179

Kingston Pal Thamburaj, Kartheges Ponniah, & Muniiswaran. (2020). the Use of Mobile – Assisted Language Learning in Teaching and Learning Tamil Grammar. *PalArch's Journal of Archaeology of Egypt / Egyptology*, *17*(10), 843-849. https://www.archives.palarch.nl/index.php/jae/article/view/4700

Lee, I., Luo, N., & Mak, P. (2021). Teachers' attempts at focused written corrective feedback in situ. *Journal of Second Language Writing*, *54*(March), 100809. https://doi.org/10.1016/j.jslw.2021.100809

Li, S., & Vuono, A. (2019). Twenty-five years of research on oral and written corrective feedback in System. *System*, *84*, 93–109. https://doi.org/10.1016/j.system.2019.05.006

Liu, Y., Storch, N., & Morton, J. (2022). It takes two to tango: Investigating teacher-student interactions related to written corrective feedback with Activity Theory. *Assessing Writing*, *53*(May). https://doi.org/10.1016/j.asw.2022.100647

Marzban, A., & Arabahmadi, S. (2013). The Effect of Written Corrective Feedback on Iranian EFL Students' Writing.

Procedia - Social and Behavioral Sciences, *83*(3), 1000–1005. https://doi.org/10.1016/j.sbspro.2013.06.186 Ortiz, M. A., Fuica, M. A., & Saez, L. A. (2019). Uso del feedback correctivo indirecto y su efecto en la adquisición de

aspectos gramaticales en estudiantes de Pedagogía en inglés de una universidad chilena. *Revista Educación*, *43*(2),

26. https://doi.org/10.15517/revedu.v43i2.31933

Putri, N. V. W., Munir, A., & Anam, S. (2021). Students' perceptions of teacher feedback in EFL English class and their self-regulated learning after receiving feedback. *Journal on English as a Foreign Language*, *11*(1), 42–60. https://doi.org/10.23971/jefl.v11i1.2237

Sanda, L., & Klimova, B. (2021). Educational mobile applications for learning English as a second language by Czech seniors. *Procedia Computer Science*, *192*, 1848–1855. https://doi.org/10.1016/j.procs.2021.08.190

Septiana, A. R., Sulistyo, G. H., & Effendi Kadarisman, A. (2016). Corrective feedback and writing accuracy of students across different levels of grammatical sensitivity. *Indonesian Journal of Applied Linguistics*, *6*(1), 1–11. https://doi.org/10.17509/ijal.v6i1.2642

Van, X. (2022). Effects of a professional development program on teachers' practices regarding oral corrective feedback.

Elsevier, *110*, 131932.

Wang, B.-T. (2017). Designing Mobile Apps for English Vocabulary Learning. *International Journal of Information and Education Technology*, *7*(4), 279–283. https://doi.org/10.18178/ijiet.2017.7.4.881

Wang, X., Lu, A., Lin, T., Liu, S., Song, T., Huang, X., & Jiang, L. (2022). Perceived usefulness predicts second

language learners' continuance intention toward language learning applications: a serial multiple mediation model of integrative motivation and flow. *Education and Information Technologies*, *27*(4), 5033–5049. https://doi.org/10.1007/s10639-021-10822-7

Zhang, K., & Yu, Z. (2022). Extending the UTAUT Model of Gamified English Vocabulary Applications by Adding New Personality Constructs. *Sustainability (Switzerland)*, *14*(10). https://doi.org/10.3390/su14106259

Zou, B., & Li, J. (2015). *Exploring mobile apps for English language teaching and learning*. *2015*, 564–568. https://doi.org/10.14705/rpnet.2015.000394

MATHEMATICAL MOBILE APPS VIA RURAL CASTING

Ma. Louise Antonette N. De Las Peñas[1], John Chris T. Kwong[1,2], Peter Antonio B. Banzon[2], Philip A. Martinez[1,2], Wilbur Isaac G. Lapada[2], Julian N. Eballa III[2], John Emil C. Sebastian[2], Miguel D. Asido[2], Jan Daryl M. San Juan[2], Debbie Marie B. Verzosa[3], Jumela F. Sarmiento[1], Agnes D. Garciano[1], Mark Anthony C. Tolentino[1], Maria Alva Q. Aberin[1] and Juan Carlo F. Mallari[1]
[1]*Department of Mathematics, Ateneo De Manila University, Philippines*
[2]*Department of Science and Technology - Advanced Science and Technology Institute, Philippines*
[3]*Department of Mathematics and Statistics, University of Southern Mindanao, Philippines*

ABSTRACT

This paper discusses the distribution, through a digital datacasting framework, of mathematical resources for Grades 1 to 7 to two schools in a community in the Philippines. Among the mathematical resources made available, are mathematical applications (apps), which run on mobile technologies, that have been created to help in the mathematical learning of students in a remote setting. The distribution is facilitated by the RuralCasting set-top box, a developed custom set-top box capable of receiving digital TV broadcasts and providing local content access through its Wi-Fi network. This paper presents the performance of the set-top box in distributing the mobile mathematical apps, and a short discussion on the mathematical applications deployed.

KEYWORDS

Mobile Technology in Teaching Mathematics, Datacasting, Mathematical Apps

1. INTRODUCTION

In the Philippines, based on the National ICT Household Survey (Department of Information and Communications Technology, 2019) only about 17.7% of households have access to the internet. As such, the Philippine Department of Education's, blended learning approach during the time of the Covid-19 pandemic, focused largely on non-internet sources such as printed modules, radio and television. There was a need to explore alternative avenues for the delivery of information and resources for teaching and learning. The Department of Science and Technology- Philippine Council for Industry, Energy and Emerging Technology Research and Development (DOST-PCIEERD) and the Department of Science and Technology - Advanced Science Technology Institute (DOST-ASTI) led an initiative aiming to develop technologies that maximize the use of the UHF spectrum (e.g., the use of TV whitespaces for LTE mobile broadband services, use of digital TV datacasting framework) for the deployment of information.

This paper discusses the results of a project under this government initiative, where the datacasting capabilities of the ISDB-T Digital TV standard adopted by the Philippines has been maximized by sending different file formats furthering the cause of distance learning and contributing to the availability of educational resources in areas and communities where internet infrastructure is unreliable or non-existent. In particular, a custom *set-top box* was developed that was able to receive the usual TV programming, along with the attached data content, providing multiple users access to the content thru Wi-Fi, and return information back using alternative transmission methodologies.

One of the resources that were distributed through the set top box were mathematical applications (apps) that run on mobile technologies. Even before the Covid-19 pandemic, there has always been the need to provide support for the mathematics education of Filipino learners. The challenges of achieving the twin goals of mathematics education, as explicated by the Department of Education (2016) are well-documented (Bernardo & Limjap, 2012; Verzosa & Vistro-Yu, 2019). Although the twin goals of mathematics education are critical thinking and problem solving, mathematical learning in the Philippines is still characterized by rule-based methods and rote memorization (Verzosa, 2020). Further, a large number of Filipino students perform poorly in mathematics assessments that demand higher levels of cognitive thinking (Schleicher, 2019). The problem was exacerbated by the Covid-19 pandemic where students were not with their teachers, and remote learning was mostly done through modules, especially in the areas without internet. In this connection, mathematical applications were developed by the math group of the project team. These were interactive, engaging, easy to use with limited supervision, and were designed to address learning competencies prescribed by the Department of Education. One venue of distribution for these mathematical apps is through the set-top box and can be easily downloaded by the parents and students.

The use of datacasting technology for educational delivery to under-resourced communities has already been trialed elsewhere. Recently, in the United States, due in part to the disruption of onsite classes brought about by the COVID-19 pandemic, SCETV, South Carolina state's public educational broadcasting network (South Carolina ETV, 2020), and Pennsylvania PBS, a public television organization (Pennsylvania PBS, 2020), have pioneered a pilot project to explore how the datacasting technology can address the digital divide by providing learning content to students without home internet access. Although datacasting is not meant to take the place of broadband internet, its potential to provide an equitable solution using a well-established technological infrastructure to access online educational materials without home internet connection is boundless.

2. CONCEPTUAL FRAMEWORK

2.1 RuralCasting

The RuralCasting system mainly utilizes Wi-Fi technology to distribute the educational resources that are normally unavailable to users without the internet. As shown in Figure 1, the set-top box can be accessed using any Wi-Fi device or using the set-top box itself as a stand-alone unit. When accessed through the Wi-Fi network, multiple users will be able to download, view, and stream the content made available offline. The content can also be updated periodically using the datacasting transmission.

The contents, namely, the applications, videos, text files, images will be locally stored in the set-top box. A lightweight learning management system like Moodle and Canvas but specifically for the RuralCasting set-top box, named *Edukastv* was created. In *Edukastv*, the content creators or teachers can upload their subject outline, reading modules, quizzes, etc. for the students to access.

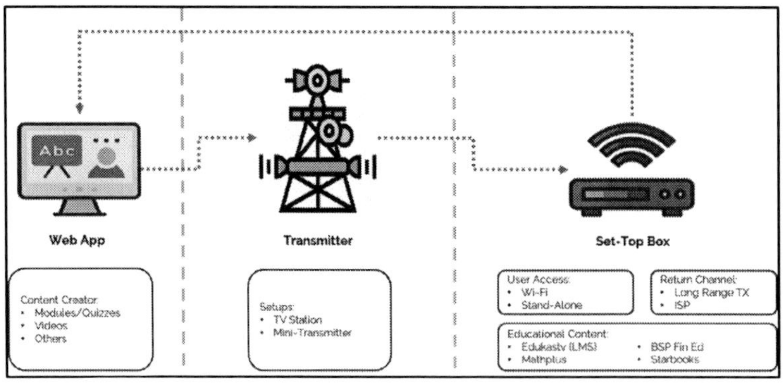

Figure 1. RuralCasting system overview

Users connect to the RuralCasting's Set-Top Box Wi-Fi network and will be able to access the RuralCasting Portal (Figure 2a). Once connected, the user can then navigate through the services hosted by the Set-Top Box, such as Edukastv, Math Applications, and videos on Financial Education produced by the Bangko Sentral ng Pilipinas (BSP). The Set-Top box also hosts an instance of DOST's Science and Technology Academic and Research-Based Openly Operated Kiosk (STARBOOKS) (Figure 2b).

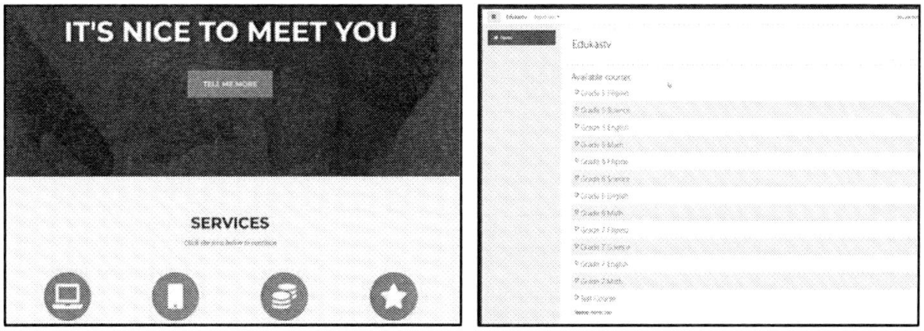

Figure 2. (a) RuralCasting Portal; (b) Edukastv page

For the users to access the mathematical mobile applications, they will need to be connected to the set-top box's Wi-Fi, go to the rcast.local page, and navigate the portal to the Math Applications page. The page will display all the available mathematical mobile apps available for download. An instructional page is also available for the users shown in Figure 3.

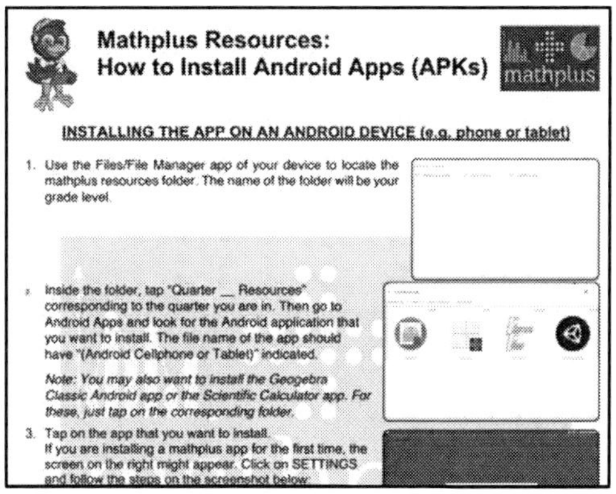

Figure 3. Instructional guide in installing the mobile app

The teachers can incorporate the apps into their learning modules in Edukastv as shown in Figure 4(a). Since the mobile apps have been curated for the learners' grade level, the teachers will have an easier time in assigning the appropriate mathematical concept for their learners. Accompanying the mobile apps are other related resources such as teaching guides, student worksheets, or instructional videos that have been developed through the project. Examples or models for different grade levels on how the apps and these resources can be integrated and organized in Edukastv are also provided to the teachers as shown in Figure 4(b-c).

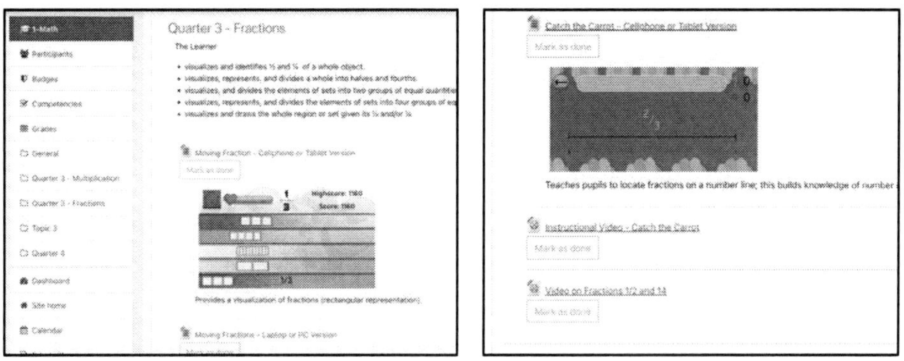

(a) (b)

(c)

Figure 4. (a) Incorporating the mobile app in Edukastv; (b-c) Organizing mobile apps and other educational resources (e.g., videos, teacher's guide, student worksheet) in Edukastv

2.2 Mathematical Applications

The mobile mathematical applications have been designed and developed for Grades 1-6 but can also be used for Grade 7. The applications focus on place value, fraction number sense, and number sense strategies. All these concepts are tied to the understanding of number magnitude, which provides a unifying framework for mathematical understanding (Siegler et al., 2011). Examples of apps that have been developed by the project are *Catch the Carrot* (Verzosa et al., 2021a) and *Grid Game* (Verzosa et al., 2021b).

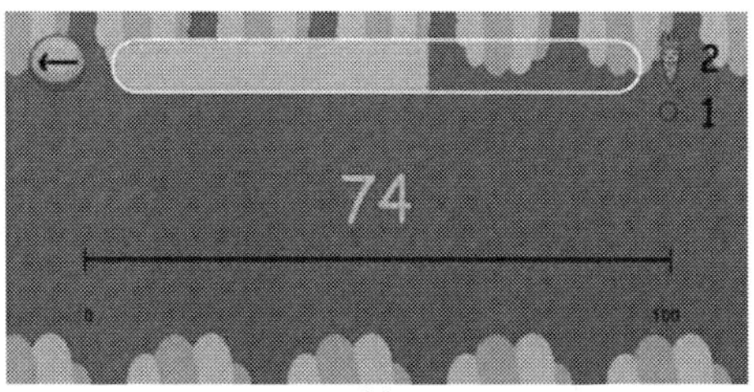

(a)

(b)

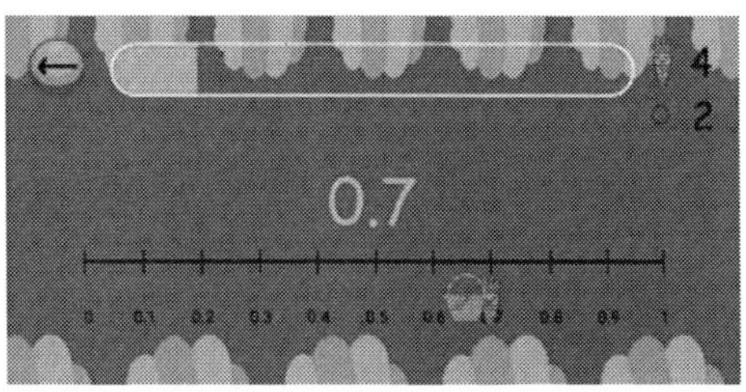

(c)

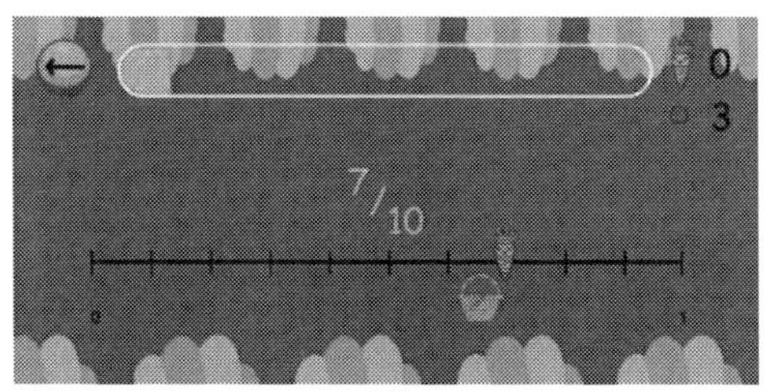

(d)

Figure 5. Screenshots of *Catch the Carrot* consisting of different levels such as (a) whole numbers, (b) integers, (c) decimals, and (d) fractions

Catch the Carrot is a number line mobile app designed to develop students' knowledge of whole number and fraction magnitude, which are important predictors of later mathematical achievement (Siegler, 2016). In the app, a segment of a number line is shown, and students need to estimate the location of a given number on the segment. For example, in Figure 5(a), the segment is from 0 to 100, and the given number is 74. The student then needs to indicate the location of 74 on the number line. After the student enters a response, by tapping or clicking on the number line, a carrot appears and falls into a basket if the student's estimate is close enough. Different levels and challenges are present in the app. Students may choose to play with integers (Figure 5(b)), decimals (Figure 5(c)) or fractions (Figure 5(d)).

On the other hand, *Grid Game* is an app aimed to develop conceptual place value (Ellemor-Collins & Wright, 2011). The app shows a starting number and a target number (Figure 6(a)). The student needs to click on the buttons so that the starting number reaches the target number. In higher levels, the student must perform the task in the minimum number of moves. There is also an option to work with higher levels of abstraction through a blank grid (i.e., a grid with no numbers) as in Figure 6(c) or through no grid at all (i.e., only the starting and target numbers are shown) as in Figure 6(d).

As further detailed by Verzosa et al. (2021a, 2021b), both *Catch the Carrot* and *Grid Game* are based on research in mathematical learning and are aimed to promote mathematical reasoning and visual thinking so that children can learn to think independently. Both apps also contain various levels to address official learning competencies across the elementary mathematics curriculum. Further, both apps have been designed with careful integration of educational game design principles. This has been intentionally done to maximize the apps' potential not only in the classroom or in online synchronous classes but also for students' independent and regular use. Specifically, *Catch the Carrot* has been designed following the Game-based Learning Design Model (Shi & Shih, 2015) where 11 interrelated game-design factors are considered. Meanwhile, the game design of *Grid Game* conforms to the Educational Games Design Model (Ibrahim & Jaafar, 2009), which focuses on game design, pedagogy, and learning content modeling.

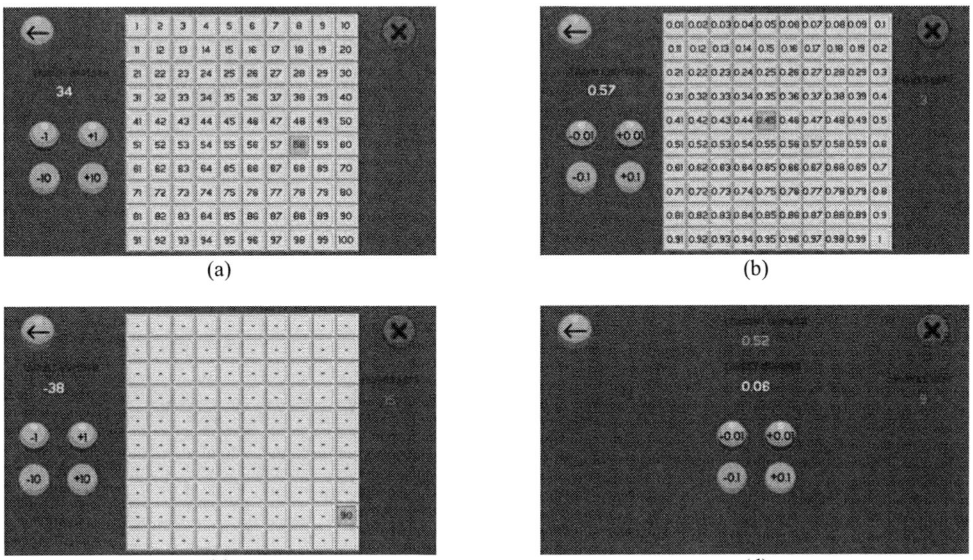

(a) (b)

(c) (d)

Figure 6. Screenshots of the *Grid Game* consisting of different levels such as (a) whole numbers, (b) decimals, (c) integers with a blank grid, and (d) decimals with no grid (for increased abstraction)

The full set of mathematical apps developed by the project can be found on the website https://mathplusresources.wordpress.com/. As is the case with *Catch the Carrot* and *Grid Game*, all the mathematical apps found therein have been developed based on research in mathematics education and with due consideration to their alignment to the official curricula of the Philippines' Department of Education (DepEd, 2020). The design and development of apps that are game-based or gamified also follow educational gaming principles that have been corroborated in literature on technology in mathematics education. All the grade school level apps found in the aforementioned website are included in deployments via the RuralCasting system.

3. METHODOLOGIES

The mathematical applications were deployed by the team to two elementary schools: San Andres Elementary School and Madilaydilay Elementary School in the province of Rizal, Philippines. Location was a crucial component in choosing the schools; the team had to identify schools with low interference in television frequencies for RuralCasting. The deployment had the full support of the Department of Education School Division Office of Rizal, which facilitated the cooperation of school administrators and teachers. Community officials also provided assistance. Meetings were held between the project team and the officials of the school division office, and the school administrators and teachers for the onboarding process. The math project team met with mathematics teachers of both schools and gave them webinars on the use of the mathematical applications.

During deployment, the team devised instructions and scenarios where the participants will be able to access the services, and simultaneously browse and download the applications. The team then tested the maximum number of participants able to smoothly access, stream, and download the content from the RuralCasting set-top box. Also, after downloading the mathematical applications, feedback on the applications (Figures 5 and 6) were gathered. Improvements were done on the mathematical applications based on the feedback. For example, an opportunity for improvement shown in Figure 7 is the integration of audio feedback, which was later on incorporated into the app. Further, the lack of instructions was identified as a weakness. Thus, some video demonstrations of the application were made to accompany the application.

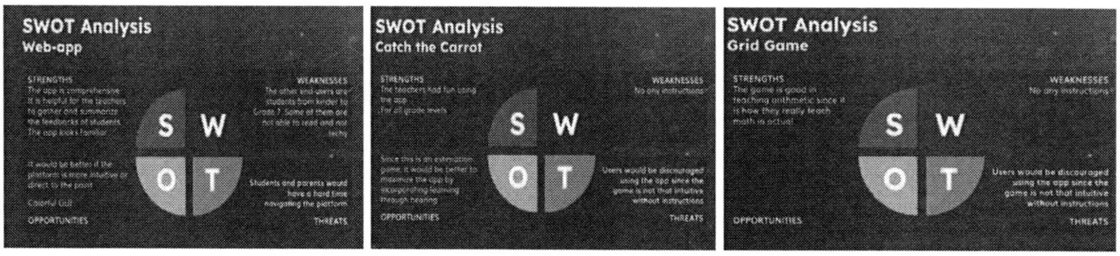

Figure 7. Sample SWOT analyses

4. RESULTS AND DISCUSSIONS

In Table 1, it is shown that issues arose when there were more than 15 devices connected and utilizing the Wi-Fi network simultaneously. The mathematical applications that were given for transmission testing in RuralCasting worked perfectly and were compatible with the set-top boxes (Table 2).

In Table 2, it is shown how the set-top box performs in terms of distributing the mobile mathematical applications with respect to the increase in participants. As shown, it is observed that the participants have no problems in downloading, installing, and using the application. But issues such as delays in downloading and awaiting the pop-up for the device were observed once more than 15 participants simultaneously accessed the custom set-top box. Fortunately, once fully downloaded, the application was successfully installed and was fully utilized.

Table 1. Maximum users, activities, and remarks per set-top box

No. of Participants	Wi-Fi Connected	Browsing	Streaming	Downloading	Remarks
5	5	5	5	5	all were able to connect, browse, stream, and download the available content
10	10	10	10	10	all were able to connect, browse, stream, and download the available content
15	15	10	10	10	all were able to connect, browse, stream, and download the available content
18	16	14	13	15	some were not able to connect, some had issues loading the webpage, some had difficulty in downloading the app

Table 2. Example of app performance with respect to participants and experience

MathPlus App	No. of Participants	Remarks
Catch the Carrot	10	app successfully downloaded from the set-top box, installed in an Android device, and used the app
	15	app successfully downloaded from the set-top box, installed in an Android device, and used the app
	18	not everyone successfully downloaded the app from the set-top box, others had a delay in the download, but once successfully downloaded the app was successfully installed and utilized
Grid Game	10	app successfully downloaded from the set-top box, installed in an Android device, and used the app
	15	app successfully downloaded from the set-top box, installed in an Android device, and used the app
	18	not everyone successfully downloaded the app from the set-top box, others had a delay in the download, but once successfully downloaded the app was successfully installed and utilized

5. CONCLUSION AND OUTLOOK

This paper discusses the deployment of a customized set-top box capable of distributing offline content thru Wi-Fi. The resources offered from the set-top box range from images and texts to videos and Android applications. The users have been able to connect their personal Wi-Fi devices successfully and to navigate through the RuralCasting Portal. The contents have been successfully downloaded, installed, and utilized simultaneously by up to 15 participants during the technical demonstrations in the targeted sites in Rizal, Philippines.

The deployment continues in the current school year, where more schools in remote areas in the Philippines are identified to have access to set-top boxes with more educational content. A point of consideration and improvement in the set-top box is the testing with the participants of the return channel feature that allows information to be returned to the teachers (e.g., grades, scores, feedback from explorations with apps). This will provide valuable information to the teachers, and thus offer a mechanism for an alternative communication system to these areas without internet access.

This school year as well, the Philippines' Department of Education is implementing a "back-to-basics" program in reading and mathematics as part of a learning recovery endeavor to address the serious learning gaps among school children who have been locked down and only learned remotely during the two years of the pandemic. The mathematical apps that have been developed in this project are envisioned to contribute towards this purpose. Part of the outlook for the school year is to conduct studies in the areas of deployment with respect to the effectiveness of the apps in addressing the learning of the students.

ACKNOWLEDGEMENT

The authors would like to acknowledge the support of the Department of Science and Technology- Philippine Council for Industry, Energy and Emerging Technology Research and Development (DOST-PCIEERD) and the Department of Science and Technology - Advanced Science Technology Institute (DOST-ASTI). They are also grateful to the Ateneo de Manila University University Research Council, the School of Science and

Engineering, the Department of Education - Rizal, and all the participants during the initial testing of the set-top box and the deployment/distribution of the mobile mathematical applications. Thanks are also extended to the app developers: Victor Ortega, Nigel Cargo, and Theo Lacson; and to the project managers and deployment team, Pinky Manio, Maria Aya Lei Banzuela, Julius Urbina, and Grace Datiles.

REFERENCES

Bernardo A.B.I. and Limjap A., (2012). Investigating the Influence of Teachers' Pedagogical Beliefs and Reported Practices on Student Achievement in Basic Mathematics. 12th International Congress on Mathematical Education. Seoul, Korea.

Department of Education (DepEd), (2016). K to 12 Curriculum Guide: Mathematics. https://www.deped.gov.ph/wp-content/uploads/2019/01/Math-CG_with-tagged-math-equipment.pdf

Department of Education (DepEd), (2020). K to 12 Most Essential Learning Competencies with Corresponding CG Codes. https://commons.deped.gov.ph/K-to-12-MELCS-with-CG-Codes.pdf

Department of Information and Communications Technology (National ICT Household Survey 2019). https://dict.gov.ph/ictstatistics/nicths2019/

Eballa J. N. et al., (2022). RuralSync: Providing Digital Content to Remote Communities in the Philippines through Opportunistic Spectrum Access. 2022 IEEE Global Humanitarian Technology Conference (GHTC). California, USA, pp. 125-128.

Ellemor-Collins D. and Wright R., (2011). Developing Conceptual Place Value: Instructional Design for Intensive Intervention. Australian Journal of Learning Difficulties, Vol. 16, No. 1, pp. 41-63.

Ibrahim R. and Jaafar A., (2009). Educational Games (EG) Design Framework: Combination of Game Design, Pedagogy and Content Modeling. Proceedings of the 2009 International Conference on Electrical Engineering and Informatics (ICEEI 2009), Bangi, Malaysia, pp. 293-298.

National Telecommunications Commission (NTC), (2016). Memorandum Circular No. 02-03-206, ISDB-T Standards. https://ntc.gov.ph/wp-content/uploads/2016/MC/MC-No-02-03-2016-Attachment.pdf

Pennsylvania PBS, (2020). Datacasting. Retrieved 10/30/2020 from https://pennsylvaniapbs.org/datacasting/

Rusciano A., 2021. ATSC Datacasting Paves Way for Flexibility of ATSC 3.0 in Distance Education - ATSC: Nextgen TV. https://www.atsc.org/news/atsc-datacasting-paves-way-for-flexibility-of-atsc-3-0-in-distance-education/

Schleicher A., (2019). PISA 2018: Insights and Interpretations. OECD, Paris, France. https://www.oecd.org/pisa/PISA%202018%20Insights%20and%20Interpretations%20FINAL%20PDF.pdf

Shi Y.-R. and Shih J.-L., (2015). Game Factors and Game-based Learning Design Model. International Journal of Computer Games Technology, Vol. 2015, pp. 1-11.

Siegler R.S., (2016). Magnitude Knowledge: The Common Core of Numerical Development. Developmental Science, Vol. 19, No. 3, pp. 341-361.

Siegler R.S. et al., (2011). An Integrated Theory of Whole Number and Fractions Development. Cognitive Psychology, Vol. 62, No. 4, pp. 273-96.

South Carolina ETV, (2020). Datacasting. Retrieved 10/30/2020 from https://www.scetv.org/datacasting

Verzosa D.M.B., (2020). Pre-service Elementary Teachers' Reasoning in Introducing Multidigit Subtraction. International Journal of Mathematical Education in Science and Technology, Vol. 51, pp. 876-892.

Verzosa D.M.B. et al., (2021a). Development of a Gamified Number Line App for Teaching Estimation and Number Sense in Grades 1 to 7. Proceedings of the 29th International Conference on Computers in Education. Taoyuan, Taiwan, pp. 648-656.

Verzosa D.M.B. et al., (2021b). Using Mobile Technology to Promote Higher-Order Thinking Skills in Elementary Mathematics. Proceedings of the International Conferences Mobile Learning and Educational Technologies. Lisbon, Portugal, pp. 19-26.

Verzosa D.M.B. and Vistro-Yu C.P., (2019). Prospects and Challenges in Implementing a New Mathematics Curriculum in the Philippines. School Mathematics Curricula, pp. 207-226.

PRACTICE THROUGH PLAY USING MOBILE TECHNOLOGY

Agnes D. Garciano[1], Debbie Marie B. Verzosa[2], Ma. Louise Antonette N. De Las Peñas[1], Maria Alva Q. Aberin[1], Juan Carlo F. Mallari[1], Jumela F. Sarmiento[1] and Mark Anthony C. Tolentino[1]
[1]*Department of Mathematics, Ateneo De Manila University, Philippines*
[2]*Department of Mathematics and Statistics, University of Southern Mindanao, Philippines*

ABSTRACT

This paper discusses the *Just Keep Solving* apps that are designed based on deliberate practice model for developing mathematical skills. Features of deliberate practice include well-defined goals involving areas of weakness as determined by a knowledgeable other such as a teacher. The integration of game design features provides a positive environment wherein the learning goals critical in a deliberate practice model are emphasized. Possible strategies for integrating the apps in a classroom are also discussed using Hughes, Thomas and Scharber's RAT (Replacement, Amplification, Transformation) framework. The games can replace traditional pen-and-paper classroom activities, amplify learning by personalizing a student's experience and providing opportunities for deliberate practice, and transform instruction from being teacher-centered to student-centered.

KEYWORDS

Mobile Technology in Teaching Mathematics, Mathematical Apps, Drill-and-Practice

1. INTRODUCTION

In school year 2022-2023, the Department of Education (DepEd) in the Philippines implemented the gradual transition to the in-person learning modality after purely distance learning due to the Covid 19 pandemic. The DepEd developed the *Basic Education Learning Recovery Plan* to guide schools in addressing learning gaps brought about by the pandemic (DepEd Memo 664, 2022). Under a government-funded project *Mathematical Resources for Distance Learning Utilizing Community LTE Networks and Television Frequencies*, the authors collaborated with local DepEd school divisions to deliver mathematical content that included mathematical applications (apps), teaching guides/instructional videos, and performance tasks or activity sheets that are distributed not just through the internet but also through community LTE networks (De Las Peñas et al., 2022) and local networks powered by datacasting technology (De Las Peñas et al., 2023). The mathematical apps were designed to address the Most Essential Learning Competencies (MELCs) prescribed by DepEd (DepEd, 2020) as well as to help narrow the existing learning gaps on particular competencies determined by the school administrators and teachers.

The apps have also been developed to be compatible with the use of mobile technology, which offer additional advantages. First, given the growing popularity and access to mobile technology (e.g., smartphones, tablets) in the Philippines, majority of the project's apps are compatible with a large range of Android devices and have relatively small storage requirements. Secondly, the use of mobile technology can potentially improve the learning opportunities and experiences of students. The portability and convenience of mobile devices mean that students use them more often (Norris et al., 2011). Consequently, students become capable of personalizing their learning experiences (Shuler, 2009) because their mobile devices are available for use even outside the classroom and/or without the supervision of their teachers.

This paper discusses two particular mathematical apps, namely *Just Keep Solving* and *Just Keep Solving 2,* that focus on linear equations and inequalities, and statistics and probability, respectively. These apps are based on a strategic application of the deliberate practice model for developing mathematical skills, particularly those that have not yet been learned (Lehtinen et al., 2017). The interested reader can access *Just Keep Solving* and *Just Keep Solving 2* as well as all the mathematical apps of the project from the website https://mathplusresources.wordpress.com/.

2. DRILL-AND-PRACTICE AND DELIBERATE PRACTICE IN MATHEMATICS EDUCATION

The approach of using game-based drill-and-practice activities has been previously used and studied in different fields and has been associated with some positive outcomes. For instance, Foss et al. (2014) assessed the use of an online game that provides medical calculation drills intended for student nurses. For learning vocabulary, Yip & Kwan (2006, p.246) report that their research results indicate, "both quantitatively and qualitatively, that learners playing online vocabulary games tend to learn better and could retain the learnt vocabulary for a longer period and retrieve more words than those who simply attended face-to-face lessons without accessing the vocabulary games." It is important to note that the vocabulary games in Yip and Kwan's study are all drill-and-practice games. As a last example, in mathematics education, Ke (2008) has reported that computer math drill games (particularly ASTRA EAGLE, a series of web-based games consisting of drill-and-practice math activities) have a positive effect on students' attitudes towards learning mathematics.

While drill-and-practice is often associated with low-level or procedural skills, deliberate practice involves the learning of higher-order skills (Lehtinen et al., 2017). Deliberate practice is typically associated with music or sport (Ericsson et al., 2006). Applying this concept to mathematics education, Lehtinen summarized features of deliberate practice based on Ericsson's (2016) work. These include developing skills that have not yet been learned but are known by a knowledgeable other (such as a teacher) who can provide support, and the provision for feedback. Further, the emphasis on well-defined goals involving areas of weakness suggests that the process is not necessarily enjoyable (Lehtinen et al., 2017).

Fuchs et al. (2010) investigated whether deliberate practice can improve low-performing mathematics students' skills in strategic counting, which is a skill that typically developing children usually learn on their own. They found that low-performing students who received deliberate practice performed significantly better on strategic counting tasks than the control group who did not receive any form or instruction, and another group who received instruction but no opportunity to practice. By isolating the effect of deliberate practice on learning, they argued that practice is indeed valuable for students with mathematical difficulties.

In another study, Pachman et al. (2013) investigated the effect of deliberate practice on the learning of geometry. Similar to Ericsson (2016), they considered an emphasis on weakness as a critical feature of deliberate practice. They found that more knowledgeable students derived the most benefits from deliberate practice. For these students, the teacher can impose that they focus solely on their weak areas. By contrast, less knowledgeable students improved more if they practiced in both their weak and strong areas. These results suggest that some level of competence must first be attained before students are compelled to focus solely on their weak areas.

3. THE *JUST KEEP SOLVING* APPS

The *Just Keep Solving* apps are designed in a game-like environment to address particular learning competencies in mathematics, based on a deliberate practice model. Both apps are compatible with and run efficiently in a wide range of Android devices (e.g., smartphones, tablets). Versions for use in Windows computers (laptops or desktops) are also available. Each app focuses on topics, and a topic has several levels. The apps show an underwater environment with bombs that threaten to destroy the ocean corrals. The questions are written on the bombs, and to prevent a bomb from reaching the ocean floor, the student must answer the question corresponding to the bomb correctly. A wrong answer results in some destruction to the corals. After a certain number of wrong answers, the game is terminated.

3.1 *Just Keep Solving*

One of the five content areas in the mathematics curriculum given in the K to 12 Curriculum Guide in Mathematics in the Philippines is that of Patterns and Algebra (DepEd, 2016). In particular, one of the Most Essential Learning Competencies (MELCs) in Grade 7 mathematics under this content area is: solve linear equations and inequalities (DepEd, 2020). The achievement of this competency is a prerequisite to solving quadratic and higher order equations.

The *Just Keep Solving (JKS)* app (Figure 1(a)) offers students opportunities to practice solving linear equations and inequalities. It is meant to provide repetitive exercises necessary for students to master algebraic skills.

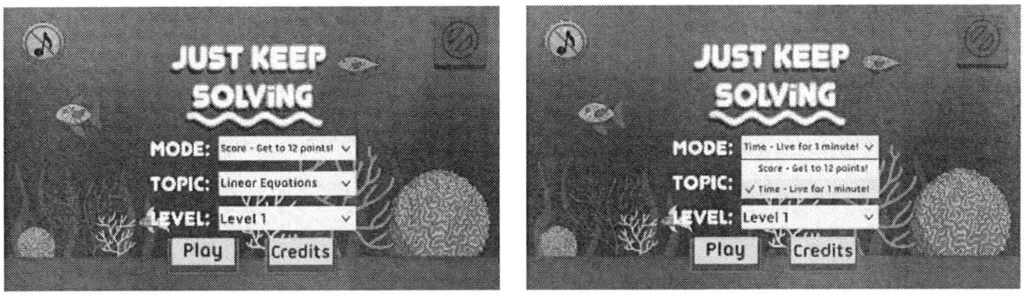

(a) (b)

Figure 1. (a) Home screen of *JKS*; (b) Two modes to play *JKS*

The *JKS* app is divided into two topics: *Linear Equations* and *Linear Inequalities*. Each topic can be played in two modes: one where the student can score up to 12 points before the game ends, and the other, where the student is given one minute to answer as many questions correctly as he can (Figure 1(b)). There are two levels under the topic *Linear Equations*. The first level deals with one-step linear equations (Figure 2(a)) and the second level deals with one and two-step linear equations (Figure 2(b)). When a bomb is selected, a screen containing only the question appears and allows students to focus on solving the question (Figure 2(c)). At this point, the falling of the bombs is paused. The equations are basic and are meant to invite students to play while providing practice needed for procedural fluency in algebra.

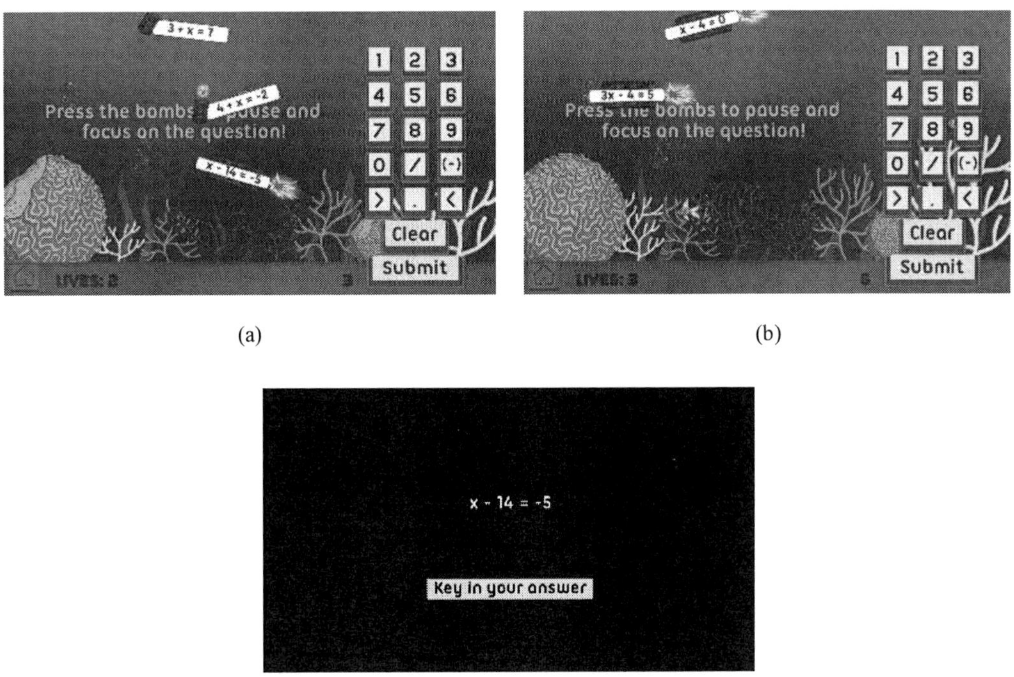

(a) (b)

(c)

Figure 2. *JKS* topic *Linear Equations*: (a) Level 1; (b) Level 2; (c) screen displaying a question

Likewise, there are two levels under the topic *Linear Inequalities*. The first level displays linear inequalities which are solvable using addition or subtraction of positive or negative numbers (Figure 3(a)), while the second level deals with linear inequalities which are solvable using multiplication or division of positive or negative numbers (Figure 3(b)). Under this topic, the correct answer requires the student to provide the appropriate inequality symbol (< or >) as well as the correct number. For example, in answering the question $x - 1 > 0$, the inequality ">" and the number "1" is provided.

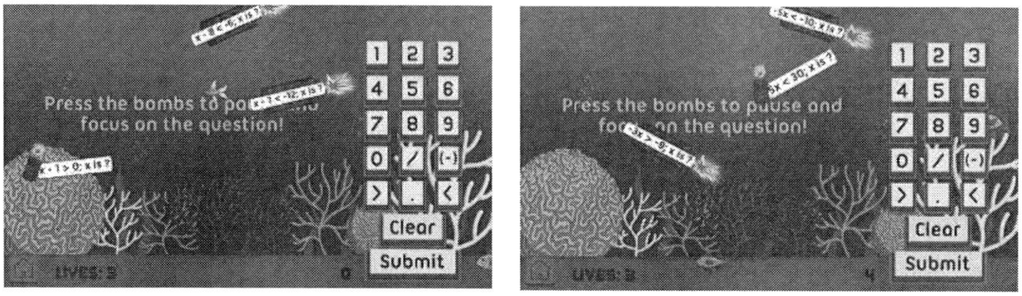

(a) (b)

Figure 3. *JKS* topic *Linear Inequalities*: (a) Level 1 and (b) Level 2

3.2 *Just Keep Solving 2*

Given the potential of *JKS* in developing students' skills on implementing simple computations and applying mathematical formulas, *Just Keep Solving 2* (*JKS* 2) (Figure 4) has been conceptualized as an expansion of *JKS* with topics *Statistics* and *Probability.* The topic *Statistics* has three levels that are intended for Grade 7 students and are focused on the following Most Essential Learning Competencies (MELCs) under Statistics: i) calculates the measures of central tendency of ungrouped data; ii) uses appropriate statistical measures in analyzing and interpreting statistical data; and iii) calculates the measures of variability for ungrouped data (DepEd p.307, 2020). Moreover, there are also two levels on the topic *Probability*. The first level is intended for the following Grade 8 MELCs under Probability: i) finds the probability of a simple event; and ii) solves problems involving probabilities of simple events. (DepEd p.312, 2020) On the other hand, the second level involves MELCs under the Grade 11 content area Random Variables and Probability Distributions. These MELCs are: i) illustrates a probability distribution for a discrete random variable and its properties; ii) computes probabilities corresponding to a given random variable; and iii) solves problems involving mean and variance of probability distributions. (DepEd, 2013; DepEd, 2020).

Figure 4. Home screen of *Just Keep Solving 2*

While *JKS 2* retains most of the features of the first *JKS,* certain changes had to be applied to adapt to the relatively lengthier questions and computations involved in the aforementioned statistics and probability MELCs. The most significant of these changes is that only the first part of each question, or a key phrase to represent the question, is displayed on a falling bomb (Figure 5(a)). The complete question can only be shown by tapping on the bomb itself. The students get access to a full-screen view where the question is displayed (Figure 5(b)). Another change, as shown in Figure 5(a), is that some questions use different icons (e.g., a card or a die) instead of the bomb icon. This is to give a visual cue about the corresponding question's context, when applicable.

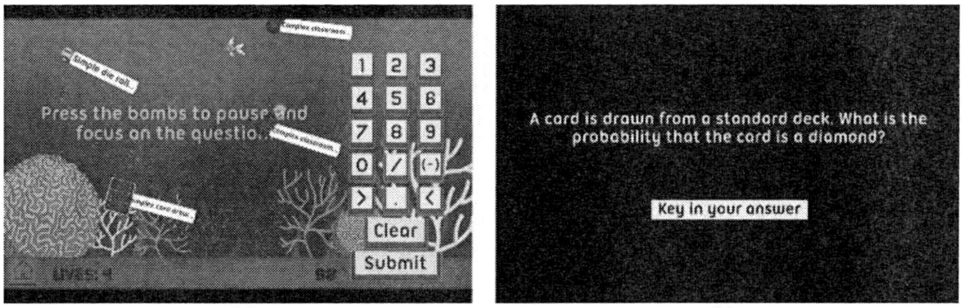

(a) (b)

Figure 5. (a) In *Just Keep Solving 2*, only the first parts of the questions are shown beside the falling bombs. (b) Tapping a falling bomb gives access to the full-screen view of the corresponding question.

Each level of *JKS 2* features six to eight types of questions. Specific questions are generated randomly within prescribed parameters. Due to this variety, some game aspects in *JKS 2* have been adjusted to allow for longer game play. Specifically, the modes are now "Score – Get to 20 points!" (previously 12 points) and "Time – Live for 2 minutes!" (previously 1 minute) while the number of game lives has been increased from three lives in *JKS* to five. At the end of each game, regardless of the player succeeding or failing to complete the mode's goal, relevant game records are displayed (Figure 6) for easy recording (e.g., via a screenshot).

(a) (b)

Figure 6. (a) Game screen after a successful completion of a level of the "Time – Live for 2 minutes!" mode; (b) Game screen after failing to complete a level "Score – Get to 20 points!" mode.

4. GAME DESIGN FACTORS

The *Just Keep Solving* apps have been designed to enhance the potential benefits of traditionally pen-and-paper or flash-card-based activities by transforming them into digital game applications. As many students are fascinated with playing games in smartphones, tablets, and/or computers (Castellar et al., 2014), it is envisioned that the *Just Keep Solving* apps can increase the interest and attention of the students. The gamelike environment can positively transform their experience in doing deliberate practice activities which, due to its demands and emphasis on weak areas, can tend to be unenjoyable (Lehtinen et al. 2017).

While some have expressed that drill-and-practice games may lead to some players developing the undesirable behavior of "try[ing] actions with no reflection on outcomes" (Kiili, 2005 p.14), previous studies (Foss et al., 2014; Ke, 2008 Yip & Kwan, 2006) exemplify that well-designed drill-and-practice games may lead to positive outcomes on learning. Thus, the Just Keep Solving apps were designed to promote features of the deliberate practice model through the integration of game-design factors. For this purpose, we employed Shi and Shih's (2015) Game-based Learning (GBL) Design Model, which has been developed as a result of an extensive review of research on game design factors. The GBL Design model identifies 11 game-design factors (game goals, game mechanism, game fantasy, game value, interaction, freedom, narrative, sensation, challenges, sociality, and mystery) which form the environment wherein learning goals, a critical feature of deliberate practice, can be emphasized.

For both *Just Keep Solving* apps, the *game goal* can be identified by a knowledgeable other, such as a teacher, to enable students to work on weak areas in Algebra, Statistics, or Probability. Since it had been shown that purely focusing on weak areas may not be optimal for the weaker students (Pachman et al., 2013), other game-like features were necessary to make the experience more enjoyable and effective. The *game fantasy* is established by using clear and aesthetically appropriate graphics in the background (i.e., ocean floor with fishes and corals) and other game elements (i.e., falling bombs, damaged corals). These graphics assets, together with the playful background music and sound effects (e.g., for correct or wrong answers), form the multimedia presentation of the game's setting and contribute to players' *sensation*. The game's *narrative* is implied both by the multimedia presentation and the game *mechanism*, which as previously described, requires the players to answer questions that are attached to falling bombs so that they do not fall and explode on the ocean floor.

Players *interact* with the game by tapping the bombs to access a full-screen view of the questions and by using a digital number keypad for inputting answers. While the bombs' falling pauses on the full-screen view of questions, the game's *challenge* is that there is only a limited time for each bomb to reach the ocean floor and explode and that bombs continue to appear as the game progresses. This means that players can only afford a limited number of incorrect answer inputs and, thus, must perform their computations carefully and precisely.

In the *Just Keep Solving* apps, each player has the *freedom* to choose between two game modes and from a variety of levels that are dependent on the topic covered and its difficulty. This freedom also provides less knowledgeable learners the opportunity to achieve a certain level of competence before they are subjected to deliberate practice that focuses primarily on their weak areas (Pachman et al., 2013). Further, the availability of these modes and levels contributes to the game's *mystery* and might lead students to spending more time with the game. Since both apps have been designed to be single-player games, they have limited *sociability*. It is worth mentioning, however, that when used in the classroom setting and with teacher supervision, the *Just Keep Solving* apps may allow for friendly competitions and/or cooperative playing experiences.

The implementation into the *Just Keep Solving* apps of all the game-design factors mentioned above contributes to the game's value. In addition, students might find it more engaging or preferable to conduct their drills and practices, or assessments, using the games instead of pen-and-paper or flash-card modalities. Lastly, as previously mentioned, both *Just Keep Solving* apps are compatible with mobile technologies that can allow students to use the apps even outside the classroom. This enables them to have opportunities for independent or asynchronous learning.

5. INTEGRATION AND USE OF JUST KEEP SOLVING APPS

This section describes how the *Just Keep Solving* apps can be utilized as a pedagogical tool based on the RAT (Replacement, Amplification, Transformation) framework (Hughes, Thomas, & Scharber, 2006).

Using this framework, the *Just Keep Solving* apps can *replace* the traditional method of providing examples and exercises for students to solve without changing the learning goals of a lesson. The printed worksheets or exercises from the textbook are now replaced by the questions which appear in the more inviting game-like setting of the app.

Playing the apps can enrich or *amplify* a student's experience in solving problems. The design of the app enables students to choose to work at just the right level of difficulty and provides elements in which students can be excited and challenged to work on advanced levels. Furthermore, the teacher as a knowledgeable other (Lehtinen et al., 2017) may identify students' areas of strength and weaknesses in order to design appropriate deliberate practice activities for more knowledgeable students, or a combination of deliberate practice and drill-and-practice activities for less knowledgeable students (Pachman et al., 2013).

Finally, the *Just Keep Solving* apps may give impetus to *transform* instruction from being teacher-centered to student-centered. This is possible because the apps have been designed so that students can easily understand and play them with little to no guidance from a teacher or a guardian. Hence, the apps are suited for use by students who are learning asynchronously or remotely. Transformation can also happen when tasks are redefined. For instance, individual tasks can be changed to collaborative activities using the apps. This gives students an opportunity to discuss and teach each other the problem-solving techniques required to answer the questions.

The apps, particularly *JKS* can be used for remediation. As mentioned in the introduction, a *Basic Education Learning Recovery Plan* was set in place in the Philippines to address learning gaps brought about by the pandemic. The repeated solving of similar problems provided by the apps aims to have a transformative effect to help reduce the gaps in specific MELCs. Moreover, a gradual improvement in skills can provide encouragement to weak students and increase their confidence.

6. CONCLUSION AND OUTLOOK

The *JKS* was developed to provide a tool in which students can repeatedly solve certain mathematical problems on linear equations and inequalities while playing a game. Expanding on *JKS*, a second mobile game *JKS 2* was designed using similar mechanics but applied to topics on statistics and probability. The competencies covered by both apps are aligned to the Philippines' Department of Education Most Essential Learning Competencies. Both apps are based on the strategic application of deliberate practice through the incorporation of game design principles with the aim of maximizing the games' value and their potential to enrich students' learning experiences and help students develop the intended learning competencies.

The apps can be used as a pedagogical tool to provide opportunities for deliberate practice in a classroom setting and in an asynchronous or remote learning set-up. The app can also be further extended to include additional mathematical competencies that are identified to be areas of weakness among students. The next step is to study the effectiveness of the apps in addressing the MELCS and/or increasing students' engagement and interest towards learning.

ACKNOWLEDGEMENT

This paper is one of the outputs of the Ateneo Mathplus Resources Laboratory housed at the Department of Mathematics, School of Science and Engineering, Ateneo de Manila University. The authors thank the Department of Science and Technology-Philippine Council for Industry, Energy, and Emerging Technology Research and Development (DOST-PCIEERD) and the University Research Council (URC), Ateneo de Manila University for the support of the development of the mathematical resources for Grades 1 to 11 Mathematics. We thank our app developers Victor Antonio M. Ortega, Mr. Nigel Benedict Cargo, Mr. Jose Teodoro Lacson, and Mr. Amiel Damian F. Justiniani for the apps' assets. Much appreciation is extended to our partners the Department of Science and Technology - Advanced Science Technology Institute (DOST-ASTI), the Ateneo Innovation Center, our partner DepEd School Division Offices Rizal and Quezon City and the teachers and administrators of our partner schools.

REFERENCES

Castellar, E.N. et al., 2014. Improving Arithmetic Skills through Gameplay: Assessment of the Effectiveness of an Educational Game in Terms of Cognitive and Affective Learning Outcomes. *Information Sciences*, Vol. 264, pp. 19-31.

De Las Peñas, M. et al., 2022. Deployment of Mathematical Resources to a Philippine High School through a Community LTE Network. *Electronic Proceedings of the 27th Asian Technology Conference in Mathematics*. Mathematics and Technology LLC, Prague, Czech Republic.

De Las Peñas, M. et al., 2023. Mathematical Mobile Apps Via Rural Casting. To appear: *Proceedings of the Mobile Learning 2023 International Conference*. Lisbon, Portugal.

Department of Education (DepEd), 2016. *K to 12 Curriculum Guide: Mathematics*. https://www.deped.gov.ph/wp-content/uploads/2019/01/Math-CG_with-tagged-math-equipment.pdf

Department of Education (DepEd), 2020. *K to 12 Most Essential Learning Competencies with Corresponding CG Codes*. https://commons.deped.gov.ph/K-to-12-MELCS-with-CG-Codes.pdf

Department of Education (DepEd), 2013. *Senior High School Core Subject (Statistics and Probability)*. https://www.deped.gov.ph/wp-content/uploads/2022/02/SHS-Core_Statistics-and-Probability-CG.pdf

Department of Education (DepEd) Region I, 2022. *Regional Memorandum No. 664, s. 2022: Basic Education Learning Recovery Plan in light of the COVID 19 Pandemic.* https://depedro1.com/wp-content/uploads/2022/06/rm0664s2022.pdf

Ericsson, K.A., 2016. Summing up Hours of Any Type of Practice Versus Identifying Optimal Practice Activities: Commentary on Macnamara, Moreau, & Hambric. *Perspectives on Psychological Science*, Vol. 11, No. 3, pp. 351-354.

Ericsson, K.A., Charness, N., Feltovich, P.J., and Hoffman, R.R. (Eds.), 2006. *The Cambridge Handbook of Expertise and Expert Performance*. Cambridge University Press, Cambridge, England.

Foss, B. et al., 2014. Digital Game-Based Learning: A Supplement for Medication Calculation Drills in Nurse Education. *E-Learning and Digital Media*, Vol. 11, No. 4, pp. 342-349.

Fuchs, L.S. et al., 2010. The Effects of Strategic Counting Instruction, with and without Deliberate Practice, on Number Combination Skill among Students with Mathematics Difficulties. *Learning and Individual Differences*, Vol. 20, No. 2, pp. 89-100.

Hughes, J., Thomas, R., and Scharber, C., 2006. Assessing Technology Integration: The RAT – Replacement, Amplification, and Transformation - Framework. *Proceedings of Society for Information Technology & Teacher Education International Conference 2006.* Association for the Advancement of Computing in Education (AACE), Waynesville, NC USA, pp. 1616-1620.

Ke, F., 2008. A Case Study of Computer Gaming for Math: Engaged Learning from Gameplay? *Computers & Education*, Vol. 51, No. 4, pp. 1609-1620.

Kiili, K., 2005. Digital Game-based Learning: Towards an Experiential Gaming Model. *The Internet and Higher Education*, Vol. 8, No. 1, pp.13-24.

Lehtinen, E. et al., 2017. Cultivating Mathematical Skills: from Drill-and-practice to Deliberate Practice. *ZDM Mathematics Education*, Vol. 49, pp. 625-636.

Norris, C., Hossain, A., and Soloway, E., 2011. Using Smartphones as Essential Tools for Learning. *Education Technology*, Vol. 51, No. 3, pp.18-25.

Pachman, M. Sweller, J., and Kalyuga, S., 2013. Levels of Knowledge and Deliberate Practice. *Journal of Experimental Psychology: Applied*, Vol. 19, No. 2, pp. 108-119.

Shi, Y.-R. and Shih, J.-L., 2015. Game Factors and Game-based Learning Design Model. *International Journal of Computer Games Technology,* Vol. 2015, pp. 1-11.

Shuler, C., 2009. *Pockets of Potential: Using Mobile Technologies to Promote Children's Learning*. The Joan Ganz Cooney Center, New York, USA.

Yip, F.W.M., and Kwan, A.C.M., 2006. Online Vocabulary Games as a Tool for Teaching and Learning English Vocabulary. *Educational Media International*, Vol. 43, No. 3, pp. 233–249.

WEB VIEWERS FOR EDUCATIONAL VR CONTENTS

Yoshihiro Okada[1] and Kanami Oki[2]
[1]Innovation Center for Educational Resources (ICER), Kyushu University Library, Kyushu University
[2]Department of Physics, Faculty of Science, Kyushu University
Motooka 744, Nishi-ku, Fukuoka, 819-0395, Japan

ABSTRACT

This paper introduces web viewers for educational VR contents. Recently, many types of VR goggles have been released as commercial products and many entertainment applications for them have been created. However, educational VR contents have been created so far are not so many because the creation of VR contents is time consuming task. We need to create many educational VR contents to enhance educational efficiency using VR technology. On the other hand, many types of scanning devices have been researched and developed, e.g., Lidar cameras, 360VR cameras and so on. Using these scanning devices, we can obtain 3D data like Point Cloud Data (PCD), 3D model data, 360VR images/videos. To use these 3D data as educational VR contents, we need viewer applications for them. In this paper, the authors propose such viewer applications as web services. The proposed web viewers also have functionality to upload 3D data from users' web-browser to the web-server on that the web viewers are stored. Therefore, it becomes possible for users like teachers to provide other users like students with educational VR contents as web contents. In addition, as the proposed web viewers support VR goggles, they provide students with immersive environments.

KEYWORDS

Web Viewers, 3D Models, 360VR, Point Cloud Data, VR, Educational Materials

1. INTRODUCTION

This paper treats activities of ICER (Innovation Center for Educational Resources), Kyushu University, Japan. The missions of ICER are to provide educational materials using the latest ICT and to support teachers for creating such educational materials. In this paper, we introduce web viewers for educational VR contents that were developed as the activities of ICER. Recently, many types of VR goggles have been released as commercial products and many entertainment applications for them have been created. However, there have been few educational VR contents so far because the creation of VR contents needs much time and human resources. In the near future, our center ICER has to create many educational VR contents to enhance educational efficiency using VR technology. On the other hand, many types of scanning devices have been researched and developed so far, e.g., Lidar cameras, 360VR cameras and so on. ICER has these scanning devices. Using these scanning devices, we can obtain 3D data like Point Cloud Data (PCD), 3D model data, 360VR images/videos. To use such 3D data as educational VR contents, we need viewer applications for them. Then, we propose such viewer applications as web services in this paper. The proposed web viewers also have functionality to upload 3D data from users' browser to the web servers that the web viewers are stored. By this functionality, it becomes possible for users like teachers to provide users like students with educational VR contents as web contents. As the proposed web viewers support VR goggles, they can provide students with immersive environments.

The remainder of this paper is organized as follows: In next section 2, we describe related work. Section 3 introduces scanning devices that ICER possesses, and Section 4 introduces web viewers for each 3D model data, Point Cloud Data (PCD) and 360VR images/videos, respectively and explains how users like teachers prepare educational VR contents of these data. Finally, we conclude the paper in Section 5.

2. RELATED WORK

Usually, we need to use any toolkit systems for creating interactive 3D applications like educational materials. As a research system of our laboratory, there is IntelligentBox (Okada and Tanaka, 1995) that is a development system for interactive 3D graphics desktop applications. There have been many applications including educational materials (Okada and Ogata, 2017, Kosuki et al, 2012, Nomi et al, 2021, 2022) practically developed using IntelligentBox so far. Although there are web-based 3D graphics applications developed using the web-version of IntelligentBox (Okada, 2013), those cannot support VR goggles such as Meta Quest 2. We need to use other toolkit systems for educational VR contents. Unity is one of the most popular game engines in the world (https://unity.com/). We have developed a couple of serious games for educations using Unity (Sugimura, et al, 2014). Although Unity is very powerful, it requires programming knowledge and skills of its operations. So, Unity is not easy for common end-users like teachers to use it. Our proposed web viewers of PCD, 3D model data and 360VR images/videos are developed using Three.js, one of the popular WebGL-based 3D graphics JavaScript library systems (https://threejs.org/). We have developed several web-based 3D educational materials using our development frameworks (Okada. et al, 2016, 2016, 2017, Ma. et al, 2018, Hirayama. et al, 2019, Yamamura. et al, 2020) based on Three.js.

There are many commercial services for creating interactive web contents using 360VR camera images. The service of RICOH (https://www.theta360.biz/) does support 360VR images but not 360VR videos nor PCD. The service of Matterport (https://matterport.com/) does support 360VR images and PCD but not 360VR videos. Our proposed web viewers are supposed to be released as open web services. Then, it is thought that the number of educational VR contents will grow quickly, and as a result, the education using VR technology will be promoted.

3. SCANNING DEVICES AND THEIR SOFTWARE

In this section, we introduce three types of scanning devices, i.e., Artec Leo for 3D model data, Leica BLK 360 for Point Cloud Data (PCD) and Insta360 for 360VR images/videos as shown in Figure 1.

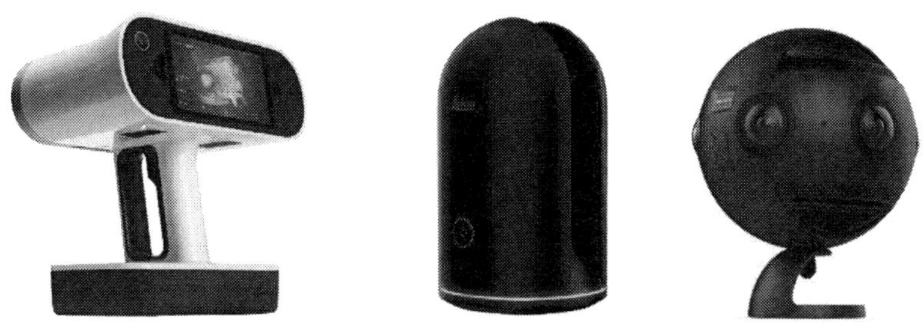

Figure 1. Image of sensing devices of Artec Leo(left), Leica BLK360(middle) and Insta360 Pro(right)

Figure 2. Screen image of Artec Studio

3.1 Scanning Device for 3D Model Data and its Software

As a scanning device for 3D model data, we use Artec Leo as shown in the left part of Figure 1. Artec Leo makes 3D scanning easy because it is the wireless and fully standalone professional 3D scanner consisting of the new NVIDIA Jetson TX2 processor onboard, 5" HD built-in display and battery. It has the ultimate all-in-one 3D scanning function of fast, accurate, and high-quality data capture. You can find the full specifications from https://www.artec3d.com/portable-3d-scanners/artec-leo. Once we obtain 3D points data by scanning any real-world objects, we use Artec Studio that is a dedicated software handling scanned 3D points data to generate 3D model data (https://www.artec3d.com/3d-software/artec-studio) shown in Figure 2.

3.2 Scanning Device for Point Cloud Data (PCD) and its Software

As a scanning device for Point Cloud Data(PCD), we use Leica BLK 360 shown in the middle part of Figure 1. The BLK360 captures the world with full-color panoramic images overlaid on a high accuracy point cloud easily by the single button. Also, it is easy to handle the BLK360 because of its light weight and compact size. By using an iPad and the cyclone field, a dedicated software installed in the iPad, anyone can capture the world around him/her with high resolution 3D panoramic images. Using the software, the BLK360 streams image and point cloud data to the iPad in real time. You can find the more details of the BLK360 from https://leica-geosystems.com/en-in/products/laser-scanners/scanners/blk360. Once we obtain PCD by scanning any real-world rooms or buildings, we use Cyclone REGISTER 360 (BLK Edition), a dedicated software that processes scanned PCD to generate merged PCD (https://leica-geosystems.com/en-gb/products/laser-scanners/software/leica-cyclone/leica-cyclone-register-360) shown in Figure 3.

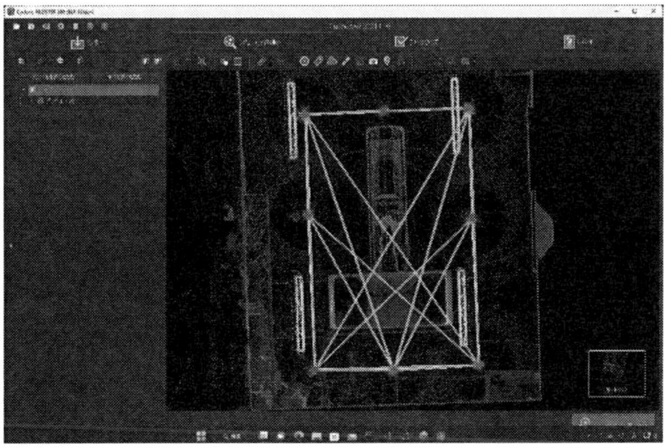

Figure 3. Screen image of Cyclone REGISTER 360

3.3 Sensing Device for 360VR Images/Videos and its Software

As a sensing device for 360VR images/videos, we use Insta360 Pro as shown in the right part of Figure 1. It was created by designing from the ground up with creators in mind. Its compact, spherical frame is custom-milled from aluminum alloy and surrounded with six 200° lenses. A detachable base and easy-to-grip contours make it a versatile on-set companion. You can find more detail specification of Insta360 Pro from https://www.insta360.com/product/insta360-pro/#pro_specs. Once we obtain fish-eye images/videos by scanning any real-world rooms or buildings, we can use Insta360 STITCHER, a dedicated software to generate 360VR images/videos by stitching the scanned fish-eye images/videos (https://leica-geosystems.com/en-gb/products/laser-scanners/software/leica-cyclone/leica-cyclone-register-360) shown in Figure 4.

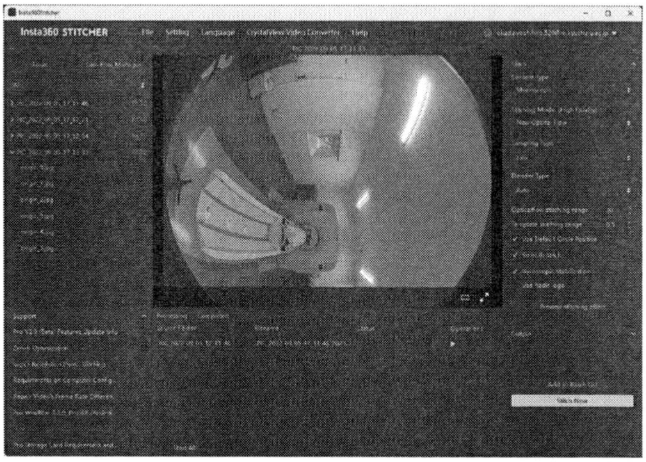

Figure 4. Screen image of Insta360 STITCHER

4. WEB VIEWERS

In this section, we introduce three web viewers for 3D model data, PCD, and 360VR images/videos and explain their functional details to show how users can use them.

4.1 Web Viewer for 3D Model Data

After generating 3D model data, users can upload using a data upload web service for them onto a target web server. Figure 5 shows the screen images of the data upload web service for 3D model data. The texts are Japanese and English. In the left part of Figure 5, there are three file selection inputs, the upper box is for a 3D model file of .obj format, the middle is for a material file and the lower is for a parts names file of the 3D model. Once you choose 3D model file and two subsidiary files in the three boxes and push the send button, the files will be uploaded onto the web server. If the file upload is completed successfully, the message including two URLs (WebGL Ver. and WebXR Ver.) will appear in the browser as shown in the right part of Figure 5. This case, a brain model was uploaded on the server. Furthermore, if you click on the upper URL(WebGL Ver.), the uploaded brain model will appear in the browser as shown in the left part of Figure 6. In the middle part of the browser, there is the menu to specify a manipulation type such as rotate, translate and zoom. You can rotate, translate and zoom the brain model by the mouse drag operation. If you move the mouse cursor on any part of the brain, its corresponding name appears those names are defined in the parts names file. Then, students can learn the details of a brain interactively. If you click on the lower URL (WebXR Ver.), the uploaded brain model will appear in the browse as shown in the right part of Figure 6. You can see 'ENTER VR' button in the right lower part of the browser. By clicking on the button, the web viewer will become VR mode as shown in Figure 7. This means that the user can look the brain model using a VR goggle like Meta Quest 2.

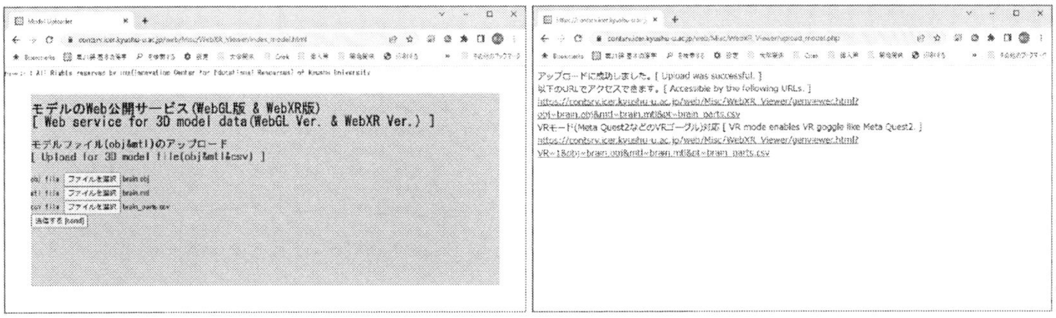

Figure 5. Screen images of the 3D model data uploader before and after uploading the data files (left and right)

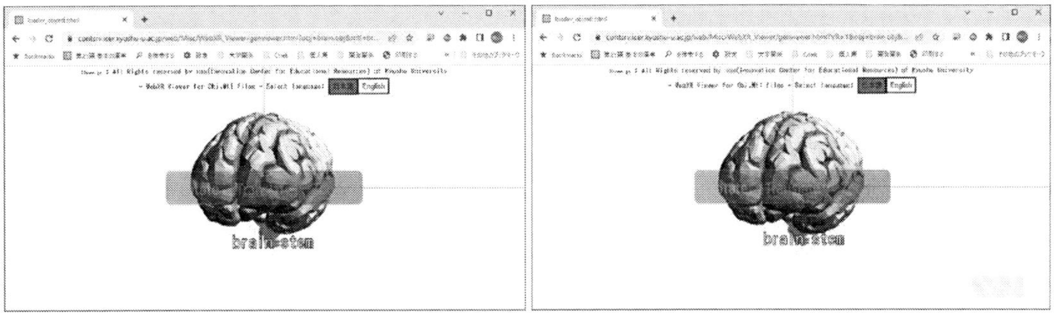

Figure 6. Screen images of web viewer for 3D model data of WebGL mode (left) and WebXR mode (right)

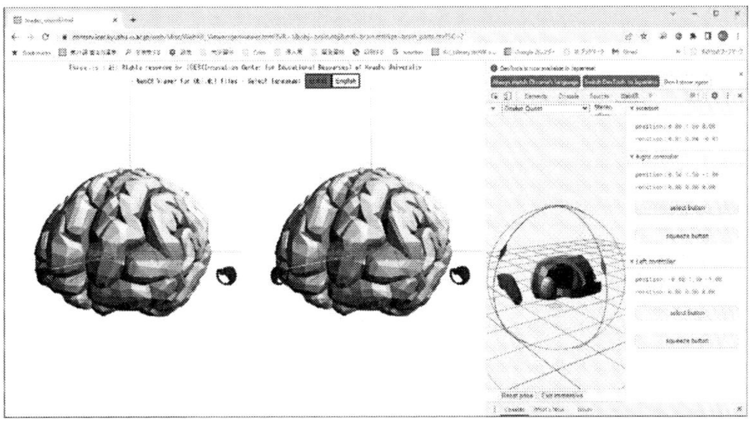

Figure 7. Screen image of web viewer for 3D model data of WebXR mode (stereo view)

4.2 Web Viewer for Point Cloud Data(PCD)

After generating merged PCD, users can upload using a data upload web service for them onto a target web server. Figure 8 shows the screen images of the data upload web service for PCD. The texts are Japanese and English. There is one file selection input box in the left part of Figure 8. Once you choose PCD file in the input box and push the send button, the PCD file will be uploaded onto the web server. If the file upload is completed successfully, the message including two URLs (WebGL Ver. and WebXR Ver.) will appear in the browser as shown in the right part of Figure 8. In this case, PCD of the CT training room was uploaded. Furthermore, if you click on the upper URL(WebGL Ver.), the uploaded PCD will appear in the browser as shown in the left part of Figure 9. You can change your eye position and direction in the room by the mouse drag operation.

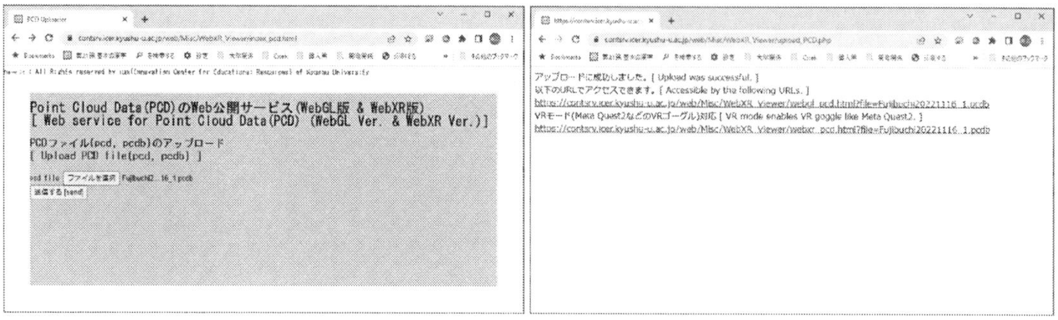

Figure 8. Screen images of PCD uploader before and after uploading the data file (left and right)

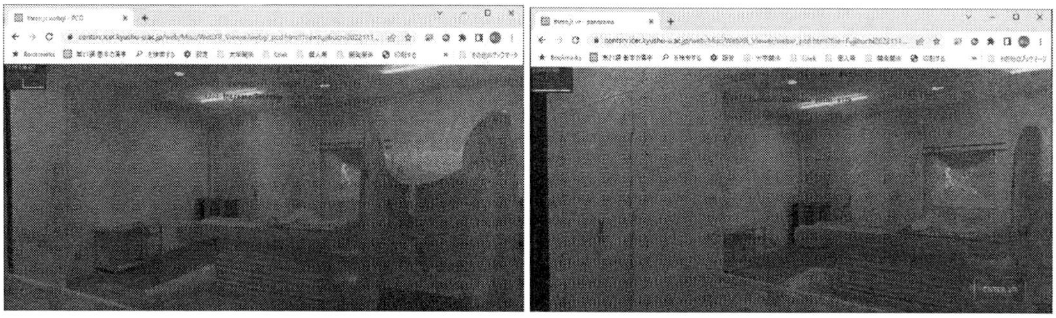

Figure 9. Screen images of web viewer for PCD of WebGL mode (left) and WebXR mode (right)

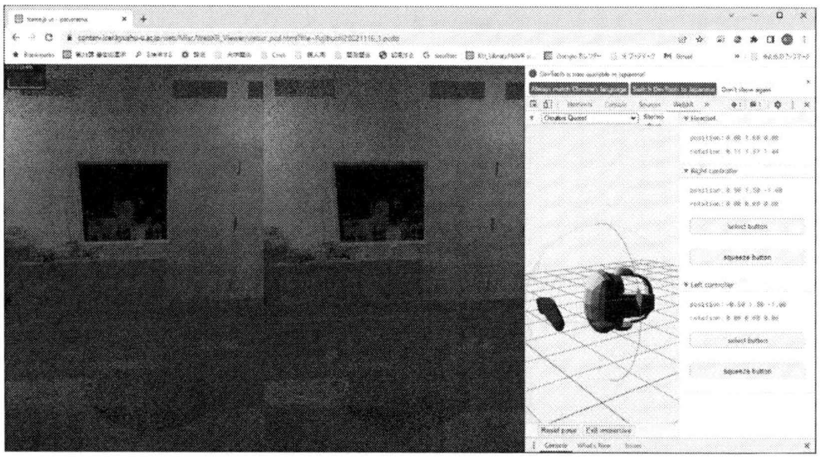

Figure 10. Screen image of web viewer for PCD of WebXR mode (stereo view)

If you click on the lower URL (WebXR Ver.) of the browser of the right part of Figure 8., the uploaded PCD will appear in the browse as shown in the right part of Figure 9. You can see 'ENTER VR' button in the right bottom of the browser. By clicking on the button, the web viewer will become VR mode as shown in Figure 10. This means that the user can see the CT training room using a VR goggle.

4.3 Web Viewer for 360VR Images/Videos

After generating 360VR images/videos, users can upload using a file upload web service for them onto a target web server. Figure 11 shows the screen images of the file upload web service for 360VR image/videos. The texts are Japanese and English. There are two file selection input boxes, the upper box is for 360VR images and the lower is for 360VR videos as shown in the left part of Figure 11. Once you choose 360VR image file in the upper box and push the send button, the file will be uploaded onto the web server. If the file upload is completed successfully, the message including two URLs (WebGL Ver. and WebXR Ver.) will appear in the browser as shown in the right part of Figure 11.

In this case, 360VR image of the CT training room was uploaded onto the server. Furthermore, if you click on the upper URL (WebGL Ver.), the uploaded 360VR image will appear in the browser as shown in the left part of Figure 12. You can change your eye position and direction in the room by the mouse drag operation. If you click on the lower URL (WebXR Ver.) of the browser of the right part of Figure 11, the uploaded 360VR image will appear in the browse as shown in the right part of Figure 12. You can see 'ENTER VR' button in the right bottom of the browser. By clicking on the button, the web viewer will become VR mode as shown in Figure 13. This means that the user can see the CT training room using a VR goggle. Furthermore, once you choose 360VR video file in the lower box in the browser of the left part of Figure 11 and push the send button, the file will be uploaded onto the web server. If the file upload is completed successfully, the message including two URLs (WebGL Ver. and WebXR Ver.) will appear in the browser similarly to the right part of Figure 11. Then, you can watch 360VR video of the CT training room in both WebGL mode and WebXR mode similarly to Figure 12 and Figure 13. Medical students learn how the CT therapy device works.

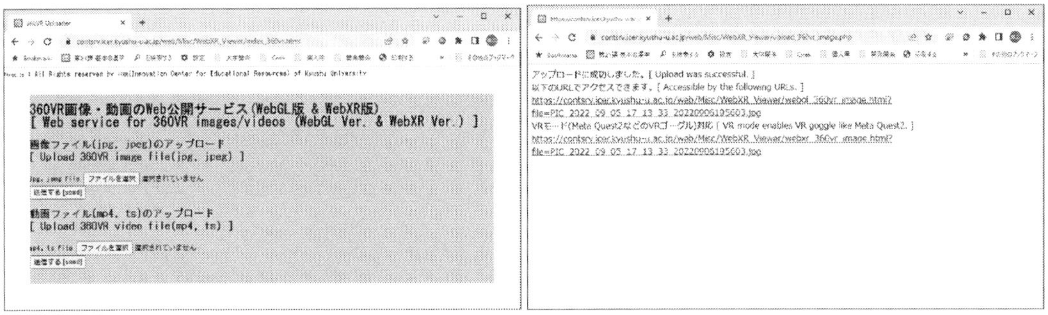

Figure 11. Screen images of the 360VR image/video uploader before and after uploading the files (left and right)

Figure 12. Screen images of web viewer for 360VR images of WebGL mode(left) and WebXR mode (right)

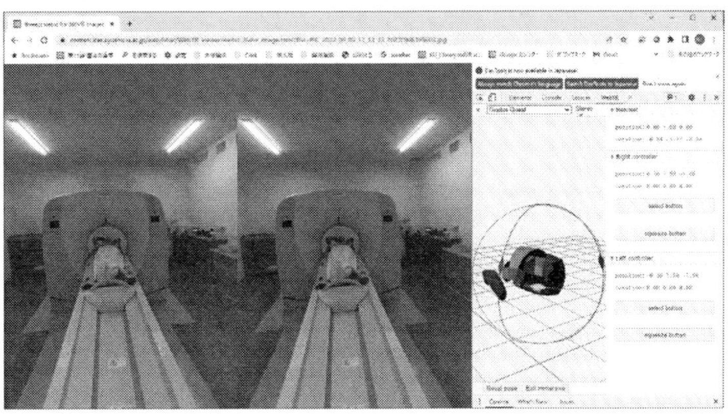

Figure 13. Screen image of web viewer for 360VR images of WebXR mode (stereo view)

5. CONCLUSIONS

Recently, many types of scanning devices have been researched and developed, e.g., Lidar cameras, 360VR cameras and so on. Using these scanning devices, we can obtain 3D data like Point Cloud Data (PCD), 3D model data, 360VR images/videos more easily rather than ever. To use these 3D data as educational VR contents, we need viewer applications for them. In this paper, we proposed such viewer applications as web services. The proposed web viewers also have functionality to upload 3D data from users' web-browser to the web-server on that the web viewers are stored. Therefore, it becomes possible for users like teachers to provide other users like students with educational VR contents as web contents easily. In addition, as the proposed web viewers support VR goggles, teachers can provide students with immersive environments that are regarded to have higher educational efficiency.

ACKNOWLEDGEMENT

This research was partially supported by JSPS KAKENHI Grant Number JP22H03705.

Also, we appreciate Prof. Toshioh Fujibuchi, Graduate School of Medicine of Kyushu University, for his help to obtain 360VR images/videos and PCD of the CT training room.

REFERENCES

Hirayama, D. et al, 2019. Web-Based Interactive 3D Educational Material Development Framework and Its Authoring Functionalities, Proc. of the 22nd International Conference on Network-Based Information Systems (NBiS-2019), ISBN 978-3-030-29028-3, pp. 258-269.

Kosuki, Y. and Okada, Y. 2012. 3D visual component based development system for medical training systems supporting haptic devices and their collaborative environments. Proc. of 6th International Conference on Complex, Intelligent, and Software Intensive Systems, CISIS 2012, pp. 687-692, https://doi.org/10.1109/CISIS.2012.131

Ma, C. et al, 2018. E-Learning Material Development Framework Supporting VR/AR Based on Linked Data for IoT Security Education, Proc. of 6th International Conference on Emerging Internet, Data & Web Technologies (EIDWT 2018), ISBN: 978-3-319-75928-9, pp. 479-491.

Nomi, M. and Okada, Y. 2021. Improvement of Dental Treatment Training System Using a Haptic Device. Proc. of the 15th International Conference on Broad-Band and Wireless Computing, Communication and Applications, BWCCA 2020, pp. 143-153, Lecture Notes in Networks and Systems; Vol. 159 LNNS.

Nomi, M. and Okada, Y. 2022. Dental Treatment Training System Using Haptic Device and Its User Evaluations. Proc. of the 16th International Conference on Complex, Intelligent and Software Intensive Systems CISIS-2022, pp. 569-580, Lecture Notes in Networks and Systems; Vol. 497 LNNS.

Okada, Y. 2013. Web Version of IntelligentBox (WebIB) and Its Integration with Webble World, Vol. 372 of the series, Communications in Computer and Information Science, Springer, pp. 11-20.

Okada, Y. and Tanaka, Y, 1995. IntelligentBox: a constructive visual software development system for interactive 3D graphic applications, Proc. of Computer Animation '95, IEEE CS Press, pp. 114-125.

Okada, Y. el al, 2016. Interactive Educational Contents Development Framework Based on Linked Open Data Technology, 9th annual International Conference of Education, Research and Innovation, pp. 5066-5075.

Okada, Y. et al, 2016. Framework for Development of Web-based Interactive 3D Educational Contents, 10th International Technology, Education and Development Conference, pp. 2656-2663.

Okada, Y. et al, 2017. Interactive Educational Contents Development Framework and Its Extension for Web-based VR/AR Applications, Proc. of the GameOn 2017, Eurosis, ISBN: 978-90-77381-99-1, pp. 75-79.

Okada, Y., Ogata, T. el al, 2017, Component-based approach for prototyping of Tai Chi-based physical therapy game and its performance evaluations. Computers in Entertainment, 14(1), https://doi.org/10.1145/2735383

Sugimura, R., et al, 2014. Mobile Game for Learning Bacteriology, Proc. of IADIS 10th Int. Conf. on Mobile Learning 2014, pp.285-289.

Yamamura, H. et al, 2020. A Development Framework for RP-type Serious Games in a 3D Virtual Environment, VENOA 2020 in Proc. of the 14th International Conference on Complex, Intelligent, and Software Intensive Systems (CISIS-2020), pp. 166-176.

PROMOTING STUDENTS' CRITICAL THINKING & PROBLEM SOLVING SKILLS VIA MOBILE-SUPPORTED LABS

Manolis Kousloglou, Eleni Petridou, Anastasios Molohidis and Euripides Hatzikraniotis
Faculty of Physics, Aristotle University of Thessaloniki, 54124 Thessaloniki, Greece

ABSTRACT

Critical Thinking & Problem Solving belong to 21st century skills that enhance ways of thinking, learning, working and living in the world. When combined with well-designed educational activities, mobile technology has the capacity to foster these abilities. This study evaluates the Critical Thinking & Problem Solving skills of ninth-grade students who participated in mobile-supported labs. According to the findings of a questionnaire provided to students, their skills have improved. Students' written responses to open-ended questions before and after the mobile-supported Labs revealed interesting data about their improvement. Also, records of students' written discussions on the Viber-platform, throughout the process, revealed aspects of critical thinking & Problem Solving development.

KEYWORDS

Mobile Technology, Critical Thinking, Problem-Solving, Greece, Secondary Education

1. INTRODUCTION

Critical thinking is a reasonable, reflective, responsible, and skilled thinking process that focuses on what to believe and do (Cavus & Uzunboylu, 2009). As a result of metacognition, students who can monitor and evaluate their own cognitive processes are more likely to exhibit high-quality thought. When students think critically, they assess the outcomes of their thought processes, such as the quality of a decision or the effectiveness of a Problem-Solving strategy (Halpern, 1998). Problem Solving in the context of education refers to the capacity of students to detect problems, obtain and evaluate pertinent information, develop solution strategies, propose alternative and viable solutions, solve problems and communicate the solutions (Hwang et al., 2018; OECD, 2005). Critical Thinking and Problem Solving skills, along with other skills belong to the 21st century skills that students must master to compete in the workforce of the future.

Mobile learning can engage students in experiential and situated learning without location or time constraints and can enable them to continue learning activities begun inside or outside the classroom through contextual engagement and communication with them and/or teachers. In addition to supporting on-demand access to educational resources independent of students' commitments, mobile technology can facilitate the acquisition of new skills or knowledge (Sharples et al., 2009). Technology can improve students' higher-order cognitive skills, such as Critical Thinking. As critical thinking is a crucial ability for modern students, teaching and learning tools must be able to promote its growth. Mobile technology may help to address this challenge. The virtual engagement of pupils in information retrieval alters both their cognitive processes and mental states. The ability of mobile technology to improve students' Critical Thinking motivates them to become more developed and contemporary individuals (Ismail et al., 2016). By communicating at their own convenience via mobile technology, passive students may become more engaged in class. Mobile devices can enhance their experiences by promoting the reflection required for effective communication and critical thought. Through texting, phone, video, social networking, and other internet technologies, mobile learning may help promote students' critical reflection with others. Students are able to record their thoughts, observations, and activities on mobile devices for instant or later analysis and evaluation. This skill provides a routine and time for reflection, which may lead to a shift in viewpoint and the development of creative and critical thought (McCann & Camp, 2015). Interventions in education that utilise these mobile capabilities go beyond information delivery to develop a platform that decreases the negative effects of time lag and promotes critical thought. Mobile technology permits the creation of new educational models (Fisher & Baird, 2006). In addition, students can utilise mobile devices to improve their graphic representation and critical thinking skills (Saputra & Kuswanto, 2019). Mobile technology is an effective learning medium that helps students to study anywhere and at any time, improves the learning process, and facilitates the mobility of equipment. It has been demonstrated that mobile technology facilitates student engagement in creative, collaborative, critical, and communicative learning activities in science education (Cavus & Uzunboylu, 2009; Saputra & Kuswanto, 2019).

However, mobile technology alone cannot guarantee the efficacy of learning; rather, the success of learning is partly decided by a mobile-based learning process. If mobile technology is used simply to memorize information searches and teachers fail to establish an appropriate teaching method to be used in conjunction with the technology to enhance students' critical thinking, the potential of the technology is lost. Teachers must thus create a class that incorporates mobile technology in a way that not only attracts and motivates students, but also leads to a more meaningful learning experience that improves students' higher-order thinking, particularly their critical thinking (Ismail et al., 2016). In addition, the integration of technology and well-designed educational activities makes the transfer of knowledge and skills across settings and life transitions feasible (McCann & Camp, 2015).

This study claims that well-designed, technology-enabled learning environments provide valuable chances for reflection and critical thinking. The chosen instructional strategy is an inquiry-based approach, which shifts the emphasis of science education from traditional memorization of facts and concepts in separate specific disciplines to inquiry-based learning in which students are actively engaged in using both science processes and critical thinking skills as they seek answers (Zacharia, 2003). Not only does requiring students to undertake original research strengthen their critical thinking in respect to their own work, but it also increases research outputs generally. Research experience boosts students' awareness of how evidence may be used to demonstrate a certain opinion and improves their comprehension of newspaper and website material. Instead of accepting results at face value, they submit questions for data analysis, which significantly increases their engagement in the learning process (Wyatt, 2005).

The importance of investigating the development of Critical Thinking and Problem Solving skills through mobile-supported Labs stems from the correlation between the findings and classroom practices. Critical thinking and Problem Solving skills are usually assessed by using a pretest/post-test quasi-experimental design (Zheng et al., 2016), by using the independent–sample t–test in a large sample (Lai & Hwang, 2014), by administering semi-structured interviews, by doing class observation or a combination of these methods (Agustina et al., 2022). Surveys address either the dispositional dimension of critical thinking (ex. the California Critical Thinking Disposition Inventory – CCTDI, e.g. Unlu & Dokme, 2017), or the actual skills dimension (ex. the California Critical Thinking Skills Test – CCTST, e.g. Stephenson et al., 2019). Although worldwide research has been undertaken on the relationship between mobile technology and critical thinking, the cultural background of each country may impact the findings. In addition, in Greece mobile learning is an underexplored topic and the development of higher-order thinking skills is weak. Consequently, the present research, which was done in Greece, adds to worldwide research, and the findings are anticipated to have significance for researchers and school policymakers.

In this work, students' Critical Thinking and Problem-Solving skills development via mobile-supported labs is investigated. The research question was: *How Critical Thinking & Problem-Solving Skills are evaluated in a mobile-supported Lab sequence and to what extent the Post-Lab Viber communication contributes?*

2. METHOD

2.1 The Sample

This study was conducted in a Junior high school in Kavala, Greece, during the second semester of the academic year 2021-22. The sample consisted of 10 ninth graders (15 years old) who willingly participated in the school's science club. The science club members met once a week after school hours. One of the authors of this study, who also taught science to the pupils, formed this group. Four females and six males with high Physics grades participated in a mobile-supported Lab sequence. The students were skilled with their smart phones but had never been engaged before in mobile learning activities.

2.2 Design of the Lab Sequence

The Lab sequence consists of 4 topics, namely Hooke's Law, Linear Oscillator, Pendulum and Friction. Each topic has 4 experimental (Lab) sessions: familiarize, explore, extend and reflect. Each Lab session lasts one week. Thus, the whole Lab sequence lasted 16 weeks. Each Lab has three phases (pre-Lab, in-Lab, post-Lab). The unfolded structure of the Lab sequence is depicted in Figure 1.

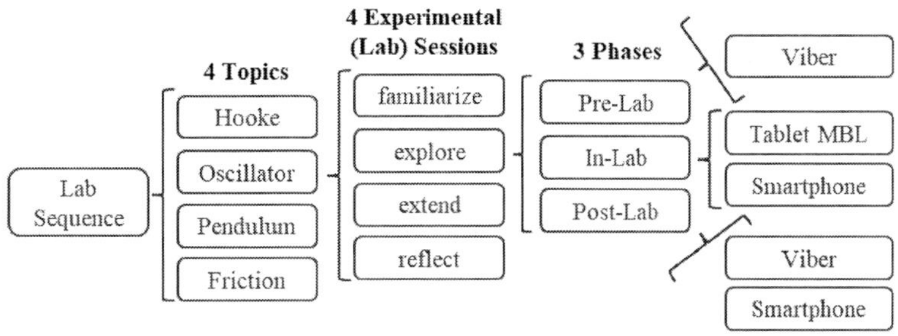

Figure 1. The unfolded structure of the Lab sequence

A short description of the 4 Lab sessions of each topic is as below:

- *familiarize*: Basic theoretical notions are discussed. The students become familiarised with the measurement setup (ex. first glance of elongation - weight)
- *explore*: The basic parameters that affect the experimental result are investigated (ex. spring stiffness, hanging weight)
- *extend*: An exploration of extended features takes place (ex. 2 springs in series/parallel)
- *reflect*: The students reflect on the concepts, the experimental procedures, the way that evidence can be drawn from graphs, the reliability of the measurements, the communication of the findings etc.

A short description of each phase in each Lab session is as below:

- *pre-Lab*: A captivating scenario is provided to spark conversation regarding the inquiry procedure. The students fill an Experiment Design Plan sheet. Questions are asked to promote critical thinking, such as "What are we investigating?", "What is our hypothesis?", "How will we construct an experiment?", and "How will we test our hypothesis?".
- *in-Lab*: The experiment is carried out using wireless sensors and tablets as Microcomputer-based Laboratories (MBL). The students monitor the evolution of relative dynamic diagram representations in their smartphones/tablets via shared session affordance of SPARKvue software. The monitoring takes place in-class or from home for the students who are unable to physically attend the lab owing to an unusual circumstance, such as illness.
- *post-Lab*: Analysis of the results takes place and a reflective procedure about the whole Lab sequence is applied. The students complete a Reflective Experiment Design Sheet. Indicative questions for promoting critical thinking are "What did we investigate?", "What was our hypothesis?", "How was our hypothesis verified?". Students also reflect on the data provided from graphs.

2.3 Implementation of the Lab Sequence Utilizing Mobile Devices

Nowadays, the extensive use of mobile devices has replaced the typical Laboratory equipment in a modern classroom. Actions that in the past years were typically carried out by a computer, are now being performed by a tablet. The use of wireless sensors has eliminated the need for the interface through which older days wired sensors were connected to the computer.

In our Lab sequence, we used both conventional laboratory equipment (springs, weights, bases, clamps, etc.) and mobile technologies (PASCO Force Acceleration Sensors and SPARKvue software on school tablets). Wireless Force Acceleration Sensors monitor force, acceleration, and rotational velocity. These devices link with PASCO SPARKvue suite software through bluetooth for data logging on tablets/smartphones

(SPARKvue, 2014) and visualize data in many ways (graphs, tables, numeric indicators, etc). Students can monitor the evolution of the experiment on their smartphone screen through the *Shared Session* affordance, which also saves the experiment individually so that the data be analyzed afterward. Figure 2 illustrates a smartphone display during the oscillation experiment. Three student groups are connected to a shared session to obtain real-time data and its accompanying graph. One student, who is not physically present in the school laboratory and is connected from home, has the opportunity to observe the experiment, the data-logging diagram and to acquire the experimental data.

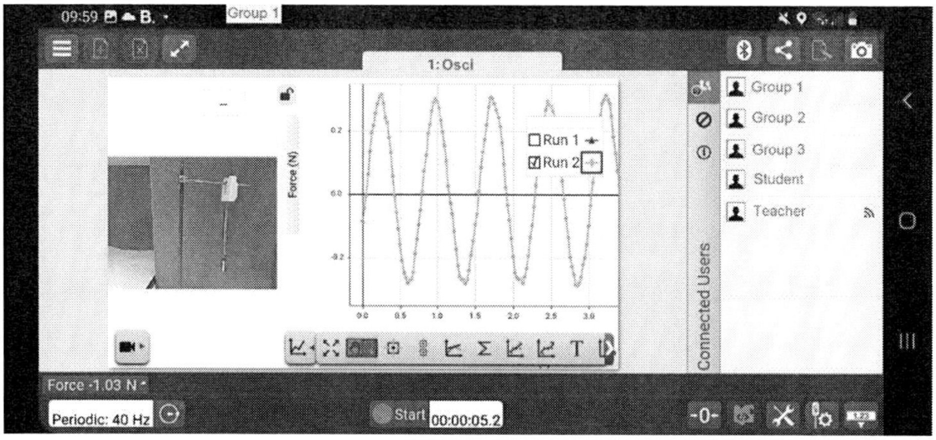

Figure 2. PASCO SparkVue datalogging software shared session

Students also used their smartphones for both student-to-student and student-to-teacher communication and reflection on the experimental procedure. This was accomplished by forming a Viber group, which provided students with an extra channel for information, communication, and cooperation via their smartphones, also outside the classroom environment. A brief description of the utilization of the mobile devices in each phase of the Lab sessions, as depicted in Figure 1, is as below:

- *pre-Lab phases:* The Viber group was employed for discussions on the science club's procedures and the planning and resolution of relevant questions. Thus, during the Labs the participants had more time to focus on issues related to the experimental process. In several circumstances of student absence, links to distance learning platforms (Zoom/Webex) and reports to be completed were distributed through the group to facilitate the active participation of absent students.
- *in-Lab phases:* The tablets were utilised as MBLs for diagram generation and study. Concerning the diagrams resulting from the experimental data, contentious debates between the students were held. In addition, share session affordance and/or a tablet camera were utilised for students' active involvement in distant experiments using their mobile phones.
- *post-Lab phases*: The Viber group was used to settle questions regarding student assignments or charts to be processed, to transmit diagnostics to be filled as reflective, and to resolve questions. In addition, methods of disseminating the findings to the larger scientific school community were discussed. In addition, the students' mobile phones served as MBLs, as the data and diagrams from the experiments were recorded on them for additional examination at home. Lastly, cell phones were utilised to capture the procedure for use in presentations and conferences.

Students worked in groups of three or four and were supported by worksheets. The four topics of the Lab sequence were structured using the same inquiry-based learning framework according to Pedaste et al. (2015). In each Lab, the students were oriented through a story based on everyday life, developed testable questions, formulated hypotheses about the probable answers, designed and conducted experiments to test their hypotheses, analyzed and evaluated the data, drew conclusions, and communicated their findings to the class, receiving feedback and review from their classmates. Although reflection occurred throughout the whole procedure, students reflected on the entire Lab during the final reflect session. They also completed a Reflection Report at home during the entirety of the Lab session using their smartphones.

2.4 The Measuring Instruments

To address the research question, two methods have been employed, namely, the evaluation of the students' Critical Thinking & Problem Solving skills, and the analysis of the messages exchanged in the Viber group, during post-Lab sessions. For the evaluation method, both the students' Critical Thinking & Problem Solving skills have been assessed, as well as the students' perceptions as a self-evaluation process on these skills have been examined.

The instrument for the self-evaluation is based on a questionnaire devised by Hwang et al. (2018). The original questionnaire consists of 23 questions-items that are organized into 4 skill areas (4Cs), namely, collaboration, communication, creativity, and critical thinking & problem-Solving. In our study, only items about Critical Thinking & Problem-Solving skills are analyzed (Appendix A).

Two experienced secondary school teachers, a physics teacher and an English teacher, acted as translators for the translation and adaption of the questionnaire into the Greek language. The translators were native English and Greek speakers who collaborated by discussing the precise phrasing of each question until consensus was reached. The translated questionnaire was reviewed by a small group of five ninth-grade students for semantic accuracy. Each question was read aloud, and the students were then instructed to explain in their own words what they had understood from each question. This approach resulted in some question rephrasing. An experienced Greek language instructor examined the final version of the questionnaire for syntax and spelling. Prior to and following the entire Lab sequence, the final form of the questionnaire was distributed to the science club students.

Before and after completing the Lab Sequence, students were required to answer a set of open-ended questions forming the assessment tool. Appendix B's open-ended questions were based on the topics addressed in the questionnaire in an effort to undertake a more in-depth analysis. The content of the students' free-form written responses was analysed by two authors of this research. Inter-rater reliability of 0.90 was achieved when two researchers separately categorised pre- and post-test student responses and then engaged in a lengthy discussion to resolve any inconsistencies.

Moreover, recordings of students' written dialogues on the Viber platform were evaluated to detect critical thinking and problem solving characteristics. Ethical issues were taken into account according to the new General Data Protection Regulation. The questionnaires were anonymous. Both the school board and the students were notified that all data gathered from the surveys and the Viber group will be utilised only for research purposes.

3. RESULTS AND DISCUSSION

3.1 Analysis of the Post-Lab Viber Communication

Apart from the messages of social type ("hello", "how are you", etc.) a total of 1046 messages referring directly to the Lab activities were exchanged in the Viber group, during the four-month operation of the science club. Viber messages were classified into four categories depending on the content of their discussions: (a) procedural issues, (b) Lab homework, (c) Connectivity issues and (d) Discussion for motivation purposes. 48% of the total 1046 messages refer to Procedural issues, 36% to Lab homework, 3% to connectivity issues and 13% is devoted to motivation purposes. *Procedural issues* concern in discussions of a procedural nature pertaining to the running of the science club, including changes to the meeting schedule, absences, student assignments etc. *Connectivity issues*, such us sending links of distance learning platforms for students that could not participate face to face in the Labs. *Discussion for motivation purposes*, refers to messages between the teacher and the students to cultivate a pleasant context, enhance active participation, engagement and encouragement. Finally, *Lab homework messages* concern on reflective debate between students for the completion of the assignments in the post-lab phase of each Lab. Students in their messages look for evidence in the graphs, consider other interpretations in data analysis, participate in reflective discussions about the experiments and come up with solutions in challenging situations in the experimental setups. Analysis of the Viber-message threads have shown that students seem to examine the "big-picture", avoid emotional reasoning or oversimplifications, question the conclusions and understand the problem they are dealing with. Such items are indicative of the evolution of students' critical thinking & problem-solving skills.

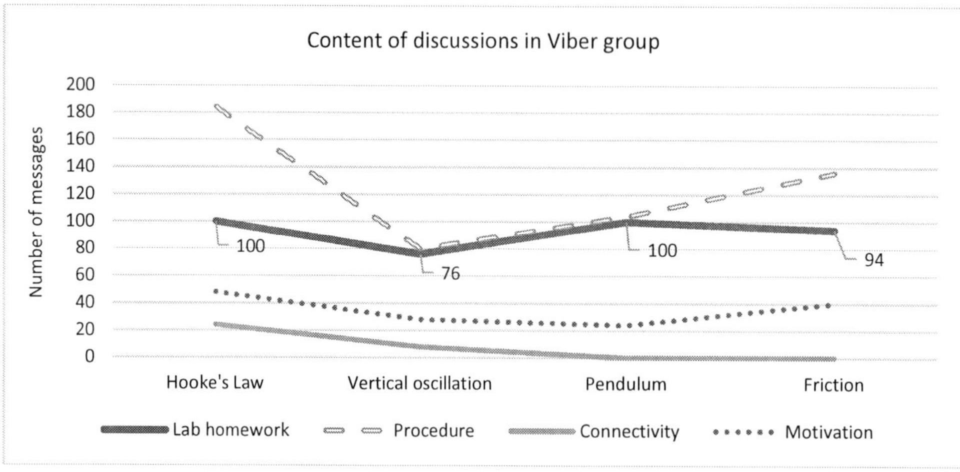

Figure 3. Classification of messages in Viber group

Figure 3 depicts the number of messages per topic for each of the four categories: (a) Procedural issues (b) Lab homework, (c) Connectivity issues, and (d) Discussion for motivation purposes. As can be observed, during the four topics of the Lab sequence, a significant number of messages dealt with issues pertaining to Critical Thinking and Problem-Solving skills. By establishing a Viber group, digital mobile devices were used by students to communicate/argue about methods and scientific practices without regard to space or time limitations. The reflective processes through the possibility of further study of dialogues, but also of the distributed material at any time via their mobile devices, and the students' continuous collaboration in the Viber group may have aided in the development of their Critical Thinking and Problem-Solving skills.

The deep thinking through the study/explanation of the diagrams that MBL created in real time, as well as their storage in the mobile devices of the students for further study and analysis at home, in combination with the reflective processes that inquiry-based learning strategy required (Experiment and Reflective Design Plan sheets) may have contributed to the promotion of students' Critical Thinking & Problem-Solving skills. In addition, the shared session affordance of SPARKvue enabled the involvement of students who were unable to attend some group sessions in person, keeping them involved throughout the whole Lab sequence.

3.2 Students' Perspectives and Assessment of Critical Thinking & Problem-Solving Skills

Six out of ten students agreed with the eight items of the questionnaire regarding Critical Thinking and Problem-Solving before their participation in the mobile-supported Labs, whereas eight of them agreed thereafter. Students' agreement with the items of the questionnaire means their own acknowledgment of the enhancement of Critical Thinking & Problem-Solving skills.

In order to explore in depth the development of Critical Thinking and Problem-Solving skills, students (S1 to S10) were asked open-ended questions before and after the Lab sequence (Appendix B). As shown in Table 1, the responses of the students were categorised and arranged according to four characteristics.

Table 1. Categorizing students' written answers about Critical Thinking & Problem-Solving

	Critical Thinking and Problem-Solving	**PRE**	**POST**
1	Reflecting/monitoring, evaluating processes of thought	**3**	**9**
2	Proposing alternative and viable solutions	**5**	**8**
3	Analysing, synthesizing, and evaluating	**0**	**4**
4	Detecting the Problem	**1**	**2**

As demonstrated in Table 1, three out of ten students reported pausing to reflect during the experiment, suggesting to the critical thinking ability of "reflection and analysis of mental processes." Following the Lab sequence, nine out of ten students reported pausing to analyse and reflect on the process. S1 said, "*Occasionally, I pause to decide if what I'm doing is correct or incorrect*". Additionally, students were asked to define what "alternative options" meant to them. Prior to the Lab sequence, only five out of ten students mentioned alternative viable answers to a Problem. However, following the Lab sequence, eight out of ten students identified alternative viable solutions as a characteristic of Critical Thinking and Problem-Solving skills. Exemplary student responses include: S5 "*For me, alternative solutions involve exploring all potential answers to a Problem while concurrently confirming my results*". Prior to the Lab sequence, no student said that appraisal of a claim or piece of information, analysis of a difficult circumstance, and synthesis are essential factors for finding answers, however, four students did so thereafter. Indicatively, S4 stated, "*I always attempt to consider a suggestion or piece of information that a groupmate provides*", and S8 mentioned that "*each time I attempt to assemble the data I acquire, it is like putting together a puzzle*". One student before the Lab sequence and two students after it acknowledged identifying a Problem as a precondition for proceeding. After the Lab sequence, S8's response to the question "What makes you a competent issue solver?" is "*My ability to utilise past knowledge helps me to tackle the issues I encounter. However, the prerequisite to deal with a Problem, is to identify it*".

4. CONCLUSIONS

The aim of this study was to investigate how Critical Thinking & Problem-Solving Skills are evaluated in a mobile-supported Lab sequence and to what extent the Post-Lab Viber communication contributes. The students' participation in discussions through their smartphones, before and after the Lab experimentation in the class, gave them the opportunity to develop their Critical Thinking & Problem-Solving skills. Specifically, the student's participation in the Viber group, during the pre-phase of the Lab sessions, allowed for reflection on the scenario and the possible ways of controlling their hypotheses. The captured graphs of the experimental data, saved on students' smartphones, were the starting point for each of them to discuss and reflect on the results through the Viber group even outside the Lab class in the school. This fact also ensured the continuous involvement of the students in the reflection both before and after the execution of the experiments.

This study's findings represent a micro-level scenario and can contribute to the expansion of the literature on the subject of mobile learning, which has not been systematically incorporated into the Greece education system's curriculum. This is an ongoing project. Future goals include the investigation of what extent mobile-supported Labs promote other 21st century skills, such as creativity, collaboration, and communication.

REFERENCES

Agustina, N., Mayuni, I., Iskandar, I., & Ratminingsih, N. M. (2022). Mobile learning application: Infusing critical thinking in the EFL classroom. *Studies in English Language and Education*, *9*(2), 16. https://doi.org/10.24815/siele.v9i2.23476

Cavus, N., & Uzunboylu, H. (2009). Improving critical thinking skills in mobile learning. *Procedia-Social and Behavioral Sciences*, *1*(1), 434-438. https://doi.org/10.1016/j.sbspro.2009.01.078

Fisher, M., & Baird, D. E. (2006). Making mLearning work: utilizing mobile technology for active exploration, collaboration, assessment, and reflection in higher education. *Journal of Educational Technology Systems*, *35*(1), 3-30. https://doi.org/10.2190/4T10-RX04-113N-8858

Halpern, D. F. (1998). *Teaching critical thinking for transfer across domains: Disposition, skills, structure training, and metacognitive monitoring. American Psychologist, 53(4), 449–455.* https://doi.org/10.1037/0003-066x.53.4.449

Hwang, G. J., Lai, C. L., Liang, J. C., Chu, H. C., & Tsai, C. C. (2018). A long-term experiment to investigate the relationships between high school students' perceptions of mobile learning and peer interaction and higher-order thinking tendencies. *Educational Technology Research and Development*, *66*(1), 75-93. https://doi.org/10.1007/s11423-017-9540-3

Ismail, N. S., Harun, J., Salleh, S., & Zakaria, M. A. Z. M. (2016). Supporting students' critical thinking with a mobile learning environment: a meta-analysis. In *10th International Technology, Education and Development Conference. Valence, Spain: INTED2016 Proceedings* (pp. 3746-55). https://doi.org/10.21125/inted.2016.1899

Lai, C. L., & Hwang, G. J. (2014). Effects of mobile learning time on students' conception of collaboration, communication, complex problem–solving, meta–cognitive awareness and creativity. *International Journal of Mobile Learning and Organisation, 8*(3-4), 276-291. https://doi.org/10.1504/IJMLO.2014.067029

McCann, S., & Camp Pendleton, C. A. (2015). Higher order mLearning: Critical thinking in mobile learning. *MODSIM World, 208*, 1-11.

OECD. (2005). *PISA 2003 Technical Report*. Paris: OECD

Pedaste, M., Mäeots, M., Siiman, L.A., de Jong, T., van Riesen, S.A.N., Kamp, E.T., Manoli, C.C., Zacharia, Z.C., Tsourlidaki, E. (2015). Phases of Inquiry-Based Learning: Definitions and the Inquiry Cycle. *Educational Research Review, 14*, 47–61. https://doi.org/10.1016/j.edurev.2015.02.003

Saputra, M., & Kuswanto, H. (2019). The Effectiveness of Physics Mobile Learning (PML) with HomboBatu Theme to Improve the Ability of Diagram Representation and Critical Thinking of Senior High School Students. *International Journal of Instruction, 12*(2), 471-490. https://doi.org/10.29333/iji.2019.12230a

Sharples, M., Arnedillo-Sánchez, I., Milrad, M., & Vavoula, G. (2009). Mobile learning. In: Balacheff, N., Ludvigsen, S., de Jong, T., Lazonder, A., Barnes, S. (eds). *Technology-enhanced learning* (pp. 233-249). Springer, Dordrecht. https://doi.org/10.1007/978-1-4020-9827-7_14

SPARKvue (4.7.1.8). (2014). [Mobile app]. PASCO.

Stephenson, N. S., Miller, I. R., & Sadler-Mcknight, N. P. (2019). Impact of peer-led team learning and the science writing and workshop template on the critical thinking skills of first-year chemistry students. Journal of Chemical Education, 96(5), 841–849. https://doi.org/10.1021/acs.jchemed.8b00836

Unlu, Z. K., & Dokme, I. (2017). Science teacher candidates' epistemological beliefs and critical thinking disposition. *Eurasian Journal of Educational Research, 72,* 203-220. https://dergipark.org.tr/en/pub/ejer/issue/42492/511913

Wyatt, S. (2005). Extending inquiry-based learning to include original experimentation. *The Journal of General Education, 54*(2), 83-89. https://www.jstor.org/stable/27798010

Zacharia, Z. (2003). Beliefs, attitudes, and intentions of science teachers regarding the educational use of computer simulations and inquiry-based experiments in physics. *Journal of Research in Science Teaching: The Official Journal of the National Association for Research in Science Teaching, 40*(8), 792-823. https://doi.org/10.1002/tea.10112

Zheng, L., Chen, N. S., Li, X., & Huang, R. (2016). The impact of a two-round, mobile peer assessment on learning achievements, critical thinking skills, and meta-cognitive awareness. *International Journal of Mobile Learning and Organisation,* 10(4), 292-306. https://doi.org/10.1504/IJMLO.2016.079503

APPENDIX A: QUESTIONNAIRE

Critical Thinking & Problem-Solving

- I ask myself periodically if I am meeting my goals.
- I consider several alternatives to a Problem before I answer.
- I find myself pausing regularly to check my comprehension.
- I ask myself questions about how well I am doing once I finish a task.
- When facing Problems, I believe I have the ability to solve them.
- I believe I can put effort into Solving Problems.
- I can solve Problems that I have met before.
- I am willing to face Problems and make an effort to solve them.

APPENDIX B: OPEN-ENDED QUESTIONS

- Do you consider it essential to make pauses and think-over, when you work in Lab or for homework? Please explain.
- What is the meaning of “alternative solutions” to you?
- What makes you a “strong Problem solver”?

VALUE OF A MOBILE GAME-BASED APP TOWARDS EDUCATION FOR SUSTAINABILITY

Rita Rodrigues[1,2], Lúcia Pombo[1,2], Margarida M. Marques[1,2], Sofia Ribeiro[3], João Ferreira-Santos[2] and Julia Draghi[4]
[1]*Research Center on Didactics and Technology in the Education of Trainers (CIDTFF), Portugal*
[2]*Department of Education and Psychology (DEP), University of Aveiro, Portugal*
[3]*Digital Media and Interaction (DigiMedia), University of Aveiro, Portugal*
[4]*Department of Social, Political and Territory Sciences (DCSPT), University of Aveiro, Portugal*

ABSTRACT

The local environment can be explored to sustain effective sustainability learning. With this aim, new learning methodologies can be fostered, namely mobile and game-based learning, as is the case of the EduPARK app. This app supports innovative learning strategies through treasure hunt games, integrating multimedia and augmented reality resources, in natural spaces. This paper presents a pilot case study of a pedagogical approach based on the exploration of a game in the EduPARK app, in the outdoors. The game was developed to be explored in the largest annual event of the University of Aveiro (UA) – XPERiMENTA 2022 – where students of several ages and the wider community are invited to participate in diverse activities on the campuses. The main goal of the activity "XPERiMENTA with EduPARK in the UA Campus" was to raise basic education students' awareness towards nature conservation. Eighteen students (14 and 15 years-old) explored an interdisciplinary educational game that encouraged them to follow a path through the UA Campuses to promote learning related to recycling, renewable energies, food waste, and ocean plastic pollution. Simultaneously, curricular contents of Science, Mathematics, Education for Citizenship, and cultural aspects of the city of Aveiro were articulated. At the end of the activity, an individual and anonymous questionnaire to evaluate the activity was applied. Students revealed a positive attitude towards the EduPARK app, as their answers revealed they felt motivated to learn during the game. Additionally, students reached a good performance in the game, although difficulties in one specific question were identified. This paper presents preliminary results that will inform the development of a new related project, the EduCITY, that aims to promote education for sustainability through a smart learning city environment.

KEYWORDS

Mobile Learning, Outdoor Learning, Game-based Learning, Augmented Reality, Education for Sustainability, EduPARK App

1. INTRODUCTION

We are witnessing a vast set of global challenges, which demonstrate the fragility of the planet and the effective need for human development to be sustainable. To mitigate the decades of exhaustive use of natural resources and the consequences of climate change, the adoption of a set of global, and integrative actions needs to be reinforced, to reduce the effects of human development on the natural and social environments. Actions to address this problem must involve the community and need to be structured and developed both at global and local levels (United Nations, 2015). They should also take place in outdoor environments, in direct contact with the local reality, anticipating benefits in terms of learning and well-being (UNESCO, 2020).

From the above, sustainable development must become an integral part of our daily lives. Education for Sustainable Development is a lifelong learning process and a fundamental part of quality education. It improves the cognitive, social, emotional, and behavioral dimensions of learning, as predicted by the United Nations (UNESCO, 2020). Moreover, the 2030 Agenda for Sustainable Development is a plan of action for people, the planet, and prosperity, so Education for Sustainable Development should consider and contribute to these goals.

Mobile Augmented Reality (AR) technologies can be suitable and engaging pedagogical tools for Education for Sustainable Development, as they enable students to learn and reflect on their behaviors. Altinpulluk (2019) mentions that tablets and smartphones are the most used devices that support AR in

Education, and that its most positive effect is on academic success and learning motivation. In the last decade, the evolution of mobile technology provided the emergence of mobile learning as a natural consequence of the development of new ways of digital communication in society.

Mobile learning is the use of mobile technology to facilitate learning anytime and anywhere. According to Su and Cheng (2015) "mobile devices can create more active learning experiences, which improve student engagement, learning and course retention, and the use of new technologies can amplify motivation, which is a vital aspect of learning, deliver information when needed, and encourage students to solve problems and satisfy their curiosity" (p. 269).

Thus, it is imperative to use mobile technology in order to provide better access to the learning process (Almaiah, Al-Khasawneh & Althunibat, 2020). The proliferation of mobile technology offers possibilities to revolutionize education, combining mobile learning and game-based learning approaches (Li & Tsai, 2013). Game-based learning provides an environment where students can learn using gaming through mobile devices. Students are engaged in it, not only for leisure pursuits but also for educational purposes, consequently, their motivation is improved when they play games while learning (Prensky, 2001). Also, mobile devices can support game-based learning approaches in the outdoors (Özdener & Demirci, 2019). With these devices, the learning environment accompanies the student everywhere.

An example of the promotion of such innovative approaches is the EduPARK project (Pombo, Marques, & Oliveira, 2019). The EduPARK is a research and development project, funded from 2016 to 2019, that developed innovative, attractive, and interdisciplinary teaching strategies. The project created an interactive app for authentic interdisciplinary learning, supported by mobile and AR technologies, in a game-based learning approach, to be explored by educational stakeholders from all school levels and the wider community. One of its innovative aspects is the displacement of the learning experience from the classroom to the outdoors, moving learning to the green park Infante D. Pedro, in Aveiro (Portugal) (Pombo & Marques, 2019). The app was developed to be explored specifically in this park in order to support authentic and contextualized learning, as it prompts users to observe this outdoor environment and to access AR content through image-based markers. This option allows students to physically explore natural spaces, while making connections with curricular content (Paixão, Jorge & Martins, 2013).

The EduPARK project developed a set of interdisciplinary educational games aimed at different publics; however, only one educational game was focused on sustainability topics (Rodrigues, 2021). In order to identify the potential of the EduPARK app to promote Education for Sustainable Development in basic education students, through mobile and game-based learning strategies in the outdoors, a pilot study was conducted. Its preliminary results are presented in this paper and support a set of lessons learned that contributes to the area of mobile AR games for learning. These will also inform the development of a new related funded project, the EduCITY, which aims to promote quality education for sustainability through a smart learning city environment.

The next topic in this work describes the study's methodological options, which include the description of the pedagogical approach, materialized through the "XPERiMENTA with EduPARK in the UA Campus" activity. Data collection and analysis procedures and tools are also presented in this section. Follows the results presentation and discussion section, based on the results obtained through a student questionnaire. Finally, some conclusions are put forward.

2. MATERIALS AND METHODS

This paper reports a pilot study that fits a case study research approach (Amado & Freire, 2017). It aims to answer the research question "What is the potential of a mobile game-based learning strategy, based on the EduPARK game explored in the «XPERiMENTA with EduPARK in the UA Campus» activity, to promote Education for Sustainable Development in basic education students?". The game was designed in alignment with a previous game developed under the Ph.D. work of this paper's first author (Rodrigues, Pombo & Neto, 2020).

This section comprises two subsections: i) a description of the "XPERiMENTA with EduPARK in the UA Campus" activity for context; and ii) data collection and analysis approaches and tools.

2.1 The "XPERiMENTA with EduPARK in the UA Campus" Activity

The developed pedagogical approach comprises an activity framed in the **XPERiMENTA** 2022 event. This is one of the biggest events of the University of Aveiro (UA), directed at basic and secondary school students, as well as at the wider community. This event invites participants to explore hands-on activities, interactive projects, scientific experiments, and guided tours through the UA Campuses. The context of this big annual university event facilitated the recruitment of volunteers to participate in this study.

The main goal of the activity "XPERiMENTA with EduPARK in the UA Campus" was to raise awareness towards nature conservation in basic education students and to promote their learning related to the topics: recycling, renewable energies, food waste, and ocean plastic pollution, articulating curricular contents of Science, Mathematics, Education for Citizenship, and cultural aspects of Aveiro city.

The activity required playing a specific game with the EduPARK app. It was an interdisciplinary educational outdoor quiz, in a treasure hunt approach, that challenges users to find specific locations with AR markers in the UA Santiago Campus and to observe their surroundings to answer the questions.

The game integrates ten multiple-choice questions with images, audios, videos and AR contents. These are virtual information that complements the observable reality in each location. In this game, AR was integrated into the questions with two main aims: i) to promote historic patrimony preservation, which is the case of AR markers that are art tiles of the city (questions 1, 2, 4, and 6); and ii) to promote natural patrimony preservation, where AR markers are identification plaques of trees in the Campus, in this case, the Canary Island palm plaque.

Additionally, multimedia resources, such as animations and images about sustainability issues, help to correctly answer some questions and make the game more appealing (Pombo & Marques, 2019). The players always get feedback to the selected answers, whether right or wrong, explaining the right answer or giving further information on the topic associated to each question, there were AR and multimedia resources. According to Chen (2020) immediate feedback, design principles, student involvement and motivation to learn are considered the greatest advantages of using these resources in learning.

After answering all the questions, the users are challenged to find a virtual treasure on the UA Campuses. Hence, geocaching principles are explored to enhance the gameplay experience for the app EduPARK users, by finding hidden virtual treasures to promote curiosity, a powerful intrinsic motivator (Pombo & Marques, 2019).

Eighteen students of the 9th school year (14/15 years-old, both female and male) participated in this activity, which occurred in the Santiago university campus, on the 29th of April of 2022. Students were organized in seven groups of three elements. Each group played the game for an average of one hour (Figure 1), using a smartphone of the project, to reduce technological issues and concerns. The quiz game was previously downloaded to the mobile devices and no internet connection was required to play.

At the end, symbolic EduPARK prizes were given to teams with the best performance.

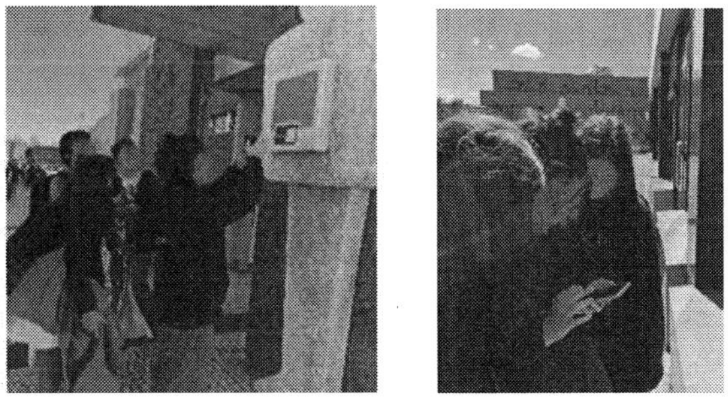

Figure 1. Students at the University of Aveiro during the "XPERiMENTA with EduPARK in the UA Campus" activity

2.2 Data Collection and Analysis

Data collection included anonymous and automatic logs of game performance, and a questionnaire applied right after the game activity. The logs of game performance included scores, the number of correct and incorrect answers, and the time of gameplay. This data was collected directly by the app in an anonymous way and allows to analyze the game's ability to support learning.

After the game, students were asked to fill in an individual and anonymous questionnaire. It comprised three questions with different objectives: i) understanding what students liked the most about the EduPARK app; ii) identifying students' opinions on the value of the game to learn about nature conservation; and iii) knowing which environmental issue from the game most concerned them. This tool included two multiple-choice closed questions (first and second questions) and a challenge with one open-ended question (third question). In this challenge, qualitative data analysis was completed, in the logic of content analysis and resorted to the categorization of responses based on the environmental issue that they choose (Amado & Vieira, 2017). The quantitative data were analyzed through descriptive statistics and the results were triangulated to analyze the value of this game for the promotion of nature conservation attitudes (Coutinho, 2019).

3. RESULTS AND DISCUSSION

Through the analysis of game logs, it is found that out of the ten questions of the game, seven questions were correctly answered by all groups (Graph 1). These questions explored curricular content or cultural aspects of Aveiro city, including the topics: recycling, renewable energy, and plastic pollution.

Regarding the remaining questions, one related to fossilization processes stands out, because only one team selected the correct option. The questions six and seven, about "salineiras" (women who work in salt pans) and food waste, only one team selected an incorrect option in each one. These three questions included image resources that could be analyzed by the students to support the answer. The results suggest that most groups of students achieved a good game performance although the question about fossilization may need improvement.

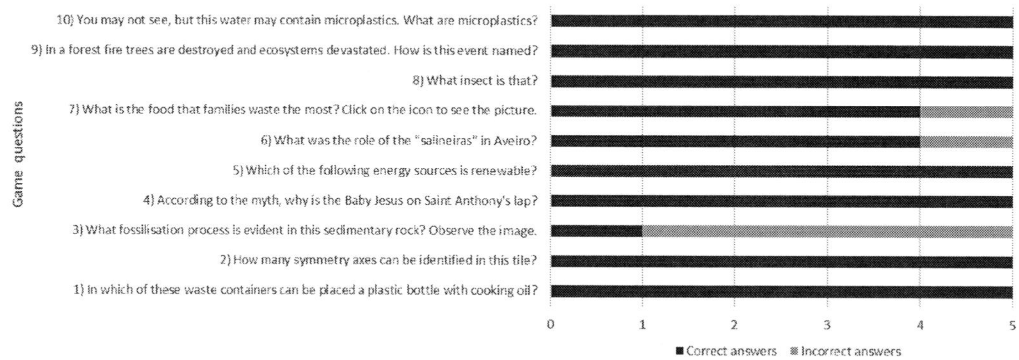

Graph 1. Number of correct and incorrect answers in the game

As referred, after the quiz game, students filled in a questionnaire. Students revealed that the three features they liked the most about the app were being at the UA (16 students), playing an educational game (12), and exploring AR (11). Graph 2 shows this data. Results show that the most valued features are related with new experiences of students revealing that campus visits exploring games and AR are activities valued by the target public.

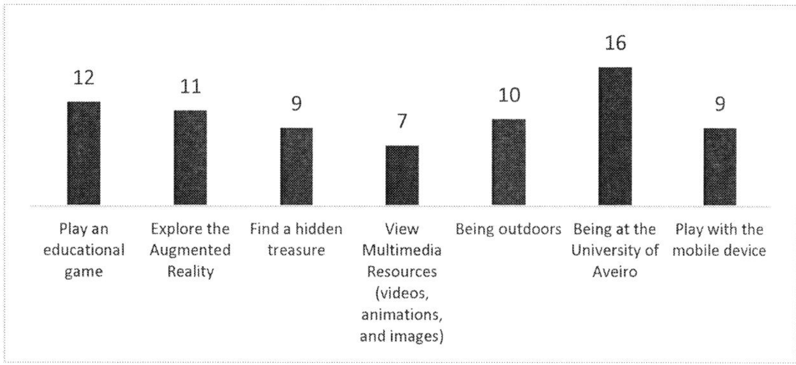

Graph 2. Students' preferences regarding the EduPARK app

The second question on the questionnaire, "What did you think about the value of the EduPARK app for learning about nature conservation?" was divided into eight topics. To answer it, students filled in a table with a Likert scale numbered from 1 to 5 with a degree of agreement (strongly disagree, disagree, neutral, agree, strongly agree). Results are presented in graph 3.

The majority of students felt motivated to learn during the game (11 students "strongly agree" and 6 "agree") and indicated that they had fun while learning with the app (8 students "strongly agree" and 9 "agree"). The majority also indicated that they enjoyed learning curiosities about the city of Aveiro (12 students "strongly agree" and 5 "agree") and felt more capable of conserving nature (9 students "strongly agree" and 7 "agree"). Most students indicated that learning outdoor helped them to better understand the school contents (6 students "strongly agree" and 9 "agree"). Regarding the topic "I will quickly forget what I learned from this app", the majority of students "strongly disagree" (8 students) or "disagree" (8 students) about it. Concerning the topic "Sometimes I answered randomly", most students "strongly disagree" (9 students) or "disagree" (7 students) about it.

The majority of the students indicated that they "strongly disagreed" (9 students) and "disagreed" (7 students) with the item that the app presented confused and difficult to understand information.

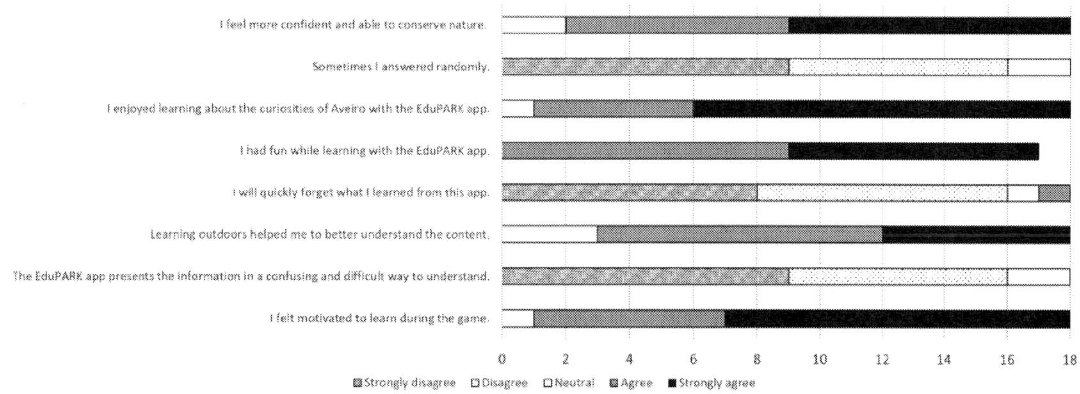

Graph 3. Students' opinion about "What did you think about the value of the EduPARK app for learning about nature conservation?"

An overall view about the answers to those topics indicates that students considered the EduPARK app has a positive potential on learning about nature conservation. Students also pointed out that the outdoor context promoted a better understanding of the school's contents. They also indicated that using the app, promoted enjoyment and motivation during the learning activities in the UA Campuses.

Students in the third, and last question of the questionnaire had to choose which environmental issue most concerned them (Table 1). Among the options "recycling", "renewable energies", "food waste", and "ocean plastic pollution", "ocean plastic pollution" was the one that most concerned them (13 students). Ten students justified their choice with two main reasons: a) Relevance of the topic because it is one of the biggest environmental problems, mentioned by 10 students; and b) Integration in schools' curriculum, as this is a topic rarely discussed in schools, mentioned by 3 students.

About the first sub-category, students said that their generation will have to deal with the consequences of these environmental problems in the future. In the second sub-category, students demonstrated concern about marine ecosystem pollution and the issues about microplastic and its consequences to humans.

The option "renewable energies" was selected by 5 students. They justified their choice with two main reasons: a) Environmental awareness, as "renewable energies" are a less pollutant option (3 students); and b) Interest of the topic, because they are concerned about having a better world, and mention that the resources are limited (2 students).

Table 1. The environmental issue most concerned participating students

Category	Sub-category	Citations Examples	Frequency	
Ocean plastic pollution	Relevance of the topic	"Our generation will deal with the consequences of this problem in the future"; "in addition to killing the fish, people's food is at risk"; "it's more and more common to see plastic in the sea"	10	13
	Integration in schools' curriculum	"Destroys the habitat of many marine animals, some species are endangered"; we must show the consequences of microplastics to the population".	3	
Renewable energies	Environmental awareness	"Non-renewable resources are polluting and finite"; "we can ride more bikes".	3	5
	The interest in the topic	"To have a better world"; "because resources are limited";	2	

No student mentioned recycling and food waste, as probably these are contents they are most familiar with, when compared to the other two topics (Ocean plastic pollution and Renewable energies), which are more comprehensive and difficult to fully understand. Moreover, pollution issues may be a hot topic and a frequent issue explored by students, not only within the school content but also in their everyday life.

4. CONCLUSION

The EduPARK project developed an innovative interactive mobile AR game to promote authentic interdisciplinary learning in a specific urban park (Pombo & Marques, 2019). This paper summarizes the results of an activity of playing a game of the EduPARK app about Sustainable Development.

This game was implemented during the XPERiMENTA event. Regarding the perception of the EduPARK app the aspects that students valued the most were visiting a University through active methodologies, such as games, and exploring innovative educational technologies, namely AR.

The results of the game showed a good game performance for all groups, as most questions were correctly answered. The game question that induced more difficulties among the students was the one regarding fossilization processes, in which two hypotheses can be raised: 1) the used image requires improvements, to become clearer, and 2) this topic has been studied in previous school years, without further mobilization, so it may be difficult to remember these contents and how to apply them. Students considered the game fun to play, appreciated its features, contents, and curiosities about the city of Aveiro. Students also considered that the EduPARK app promotes motivation for learning because they learn in a fun way while walking outside the classroom.

Students also acknowledged the EduPARK app's potential in the promotion of nature conservation learning. After this activity, they revealed feeling more aware of nature conservation problems, in particular in what concerns ocean plastic pollution.

These arguments are similar to the ones described by Chen (2020), in particular the importance of using AR as a learning tool in context, accompanied by the exploration of multimedia resources, promoting mixed realities as an effective learning environment.

By using the EduPARK app, it's possible to explore Sustainable Development theme from different school subjects, but as a common goal, promoting a global understanding of the topic as advocated by international agencies as UNESCO.

These results are in line with other studies that indicate that mobile apps promote student motivation and the construction of learning (Crompton et al., 2017). Therefore, to answer the research question, evidences were collected pointing that the EduPARK app is an educational app with great potential to promote Education for Sustainable Development in basic education students. Innovative interdisciplinary practices, combined with outdoor activities curricularly integrated and supported by mobile technologies, provided the consolidation of knowledge from different curricular areas in students, and the construction of new learning about Education for Sustainable Development.

As a final note, the EduPARK app is an example of a successful mobile AR game for nature conservation learning (Rodrigues, 2021). The great relevance and innovation of EduPARK are related to cross-subject outdoor learning in formal, informal, and non-formal contexts, supported by mobile technology, in an integrated perspective of Science, Technology, Society, and Innovation. In terms of future work, within the EduCITY project, it is proposed to carry out activities related to education for sustainability, with a greater number of students and teachers, from different school contexts, and the general public, replicating the study and enabling the identification of patterns. Furthermore, it is predicted to conceive several teacher training sessions to collect systematic data about the benefits of using this mobile learning strategy in outdoor settings. It is also intended to complement this study with further research allowing a better understanding about the potentialities of mobile AR games in outdoor environments for learning.

ACKNOWLEDGEMENT

This work is funded by Portuguese Funds through FCT – Fundação para a Ciência e a Tecnologia, I.P., under the project UIDB/00194/2020.

The first author's work is funded by Portuguese Funds through FCT with a research grant (SFRH/BD/139048/2018) within the Doctoral Program in Multimedia in Education.

The third author's work is funded by Portuguese funds (state budget), through University of Aveiro, in the scope of the framework contract foreseen in the numbers 4, 5 and 6 of the article 23, of the Decree-Law 57/2016, of August 29, changed by Law 57/2017, of July 19.

The EduPARK project is funded by FEDER – Fundo Europeu de Desenvolvimento Regional funds through the COMPETE 2020 – Operational Programme for Competitiveness and Internationalisation (POCI), and by Portuguese funds through FCT within the framework of the project POCI-01-0145-FEDER-016542.

REFERENCES

Almaiah, MA., Al-Khasawneh, A. & Althunibat, A. (2020), 'Exploring the critical challenges and factors influencing the E-learning system usage during COVID-19 pandemic', *Education and Information Technologies*, vol. 25, no. 6, pp. 5261–5280.

Altinpulluk, H. (2019), 'Determining the trends of using augmented reality in education between 2006-2016', *Education and Information Technologies*, vol. 24, no. 2, pp. 1089–1114.

Amado, J. & Freire, I. (2017), 'Estudo de caso na investigação em educação', in João Amado (ed), *Manual de investigação qualitativa em educação* , Imprensa da Universidade de Coimbra, Coimbra, pp. 123–145.

Amado, J. & Vieira, C. (2017), 'A validação da investigação qualitativa', in João Amado (ed), *Manual de investigação qualitativa em Educação* , Imprensa da Universidade de Coimbra, Coimbra, pp. 359–378.

Chen, CH. (2020), 'Impacts of augmented reality and a digital game on students' science learning with reflection prompts in multimedia learning', *Educational Technology Research and Development*, vol. 68, no. 6, pp. 3057–3076, retrieved from <https://doi.org/10.1007/s11423-020-09834-w>.

Coutinho, C. (2019), *Metodologia de Investigação em Ciências Sociais e Humanas: Teoria e Prática* 2nd edn, Edições Almedina, Coimbra.

Crompton, H., Burke, D. & Gregory, KH. (2017), 'The use of mobile learning in PK-12 education: A systematic review', *Computers and Education*, vol. 110, pp. 51–63.

Li, M.-C. & Tsai, C.-C. (2013), 'Game-Based Learning in Science Education: A Review of Relevant Research', *Journal of Science Education and Technology*, vol. 22, pp. 877–898.

Özdener, N. & Demirci, F. (2019), 'Determining Students' Views about an Educational Game-Based Mobile Application Supported with Sensors', *Technology, Knowledge and Learning*, vol. 24, no. 1, pp. 143–159.

Paixão, F., Jorge, FR. & Martins, H. (2013), 'Aprender no jardim: matemática criativa com a sombra', in *Encontro ensinar e aprender matemática com criatividade dos 3 aos 12 anos*, Associação de Professores de Matemática, Viana do Castelo, pp. 17–29, retrieved from <http://hdl.handle.net/10400.11/2146>.

Pombo, L. & Marques, MM. (2019), 'An app that changes mentalities about mobile learning—the eduPARK augmented reality activity', *Computers*, vol. 8, no. 2, pp. 1–33, retrieved October 18, 2022, from <https://doi.org/10.3390/computers8020037>.

Pombo, L., Marques, MM. & Oliveira, S. (2019), *Lessons Learned EduPARK*, UA Editora, Aveiro, retrieved December 18, 2022, from <https://ria.ua.pt/handle/10773/26979>.

Prensky, M. (2001), 'Fun, Play and Games: What Makes Games Engaging', *Digital Game-Based Learning*, pp. 1–31, retrieved from <http://www.marcprensky.com/writing/Prensky - Digital Game-Based Learning-Ch5.pdf>.

Rodrigues, R. (2021), 'Taking it to the next level: the potential of the EduPARK app to promote nature's conservation in an urban park', in M Menéndez-Blanco, S Yavuz, J Schubert, D Fogli, & F Paternò (eds), *Interactive Experiences and Doctoral Consortium*, CEUR Workshop Proceedings, Bozen-Bolzano, pp. 56–60, retrieved October 20, 2022, from <http://ceur-ws.org/Vol-2892/paper-10.pdf>.

Rodrigues, R., Pombo, L. & Neto, T. (2020), 'Aprender a conservar a Natureza: construção do guião educativo integrado na aplicação móvel EduPARK', in A Carvalho, F Revuelta, D Guimarães, A Moura, C Marques, I Santos, & S Cruz (eds), *Atas do V Encontro sobre Jogos e Mobile Learning.*, Centro de Estudos Interdisciplinares do Século 20 (CEIS20); Universidade de Coimbra -Coimbra, Coimbra, pp. 502–510, retrieved November 30, 2022, from <http://hdl.handle.net/10316/89364>.

Su, CH. & Cheng, CH. (2015), 'A mobile gamification learning system for improving the learning motivation and achievements', *Journal of Computer Assisted Learning*, vol. 31, no. 3, pp. 268–286.

United Nations (2015), *Transforming our world: the 2030 Agenda for Sustainable Development*, retrieved October 18, 2022, from <https://www.refworld.org/docid/57b6e3e44.html>

A STUDY ON THE PATHWAY OF IMPROVING THE SUBJECT CORE LITERACY OF CHINESE RURAL SECONDARY SCHOOL TEACHERS BASED ON MOBILE LEARNING

Jiachao Wei, Chenfei Xiang, Lu Li, Mengmeng Zou and Weiwei Yu
School of Educational Sciences, Nanning Normal University, Guangxi, China

ABSTRACT

In this era of globalization, mobile learning is increasingly becoming a new paradigm to promote teachers' core literacy. In this study, teachers in rural secondary schools in South China were selected as respondents, and the correlation between mobile learning and teachers' subject core literacy was proved by using SPSS22.0 software. The study concluded that mobile learning for Chinese rural secondary school teachers is deficient at the level of social interactivity, the learners (teachers) themselves and mobile learning devices. Therefore, enhancing the social interaction level of mobile learning, stimulating the demand for m-learning among rural secondary school teachers and Increasing Equipment Support are crucial to improving teachers' subject core literacy in rural secondary schools.

KEYWORDS

Mobile Learning, Teachers' Subject Core Literacy, Chinese Rural Secondary Schools

1. INTRODUCTION

Since the 21st century, information and communication technologies have developed rapidly and the Internet is widely used in various fields. Mobile technology has become a new tool for professional development of teachers, and mobile learning is gradually entering the field of teacher development. Mobile learning is a way of learning that transcends geographical limitations and makes full use of portable technology. This learning approach is expected to contribute to the improvement of teachers' subject core literacy through teacher professional development and changes in the form of teacher education. Teachers' subject core literacy refers to the necessary competencies (language skills, learning skills) and required qualities (cultural awareness, thinking skills) of the subjects teachers acquire. As a huge part of Chinese teachers, it is urgent to improve the subject core literacy of rural secondary school teachers. In the context of global informatization and the COVID-19, mobile learning is particularly important for the enhancement of subject core literacy of rural secondary school teachers.

2. LITERATURE REVIEW

In this study, we used 10 November, 2022 as the time point,and "mobile learning" as the keyword, then we searched in the China Knowledge Network (CNKI: www.cnki.net) .. We got a total of 8521 academic papers. and 1253 of the papers were from the CSSCI（Chinese Social Sciences Citation Index） When we entered "teachers' core literacy", 1924 academic papers were shown on, including 507 papers selected by the CSSCI. The third keyword is "rural secondary school teachers", and 105 academic papers were shown, 24 of them were published in core journals selected by the CSSCI. This study composed the above papers and summarizes the main following parts.

2.1 Studies on M-Learning for Teachers' Subject Core Literacy Enhancement

Scholars have focused on the positive impact of mobile learning on teachers' subject core literacy enhancement. Mobile learning has become an important way for teachers to enhance their subject core literacy. For example, American scholars Micah Shippee and Jared Keengwe (2014) pointed out that Internet technology continues to emerge to break geographical barriers in education and teaching on a global scale, build information platforms, narrow opportunity gaps, promote educational equity, and build bridges of communication. Chinese scholar Xiao-yu, Hua (2017) pointed out that with the increasing development of mobile Internet technology, it is proven to explore the path of teachers' subject core literacy development, and the mobile learning model helps teachers understand the frontier knowledge of education, accumulate relevant knowledge and skills, and achieve subject core literacy improvement.

2.2 Challenges of Mobile Learning for Chinese Rural Secondary School Teachers

Scholars have focused on the negative impact of mobile learning on teachers in rural areas where online technologies are not well developed. For example, Chinese scholars Jian-jun, Ma et al. (2017) pointed out that teachers in rural area were not sufficiently prepared to use mobile learning, and they were unfamiliar with the operation of mobile devices. Meanwhile, some of them were less motivated to accept new things on the whole and had a narrower and lower level of cognitive scope, and the conditions and environment of mobile facilities in rural areas were not perfect, so the overall effect was poor. Chinese scholars Shao-rong,Guo and Zhi-ping,Zhou (2021) talked about the serious loss of good students in rural schools, the loss of good students can be traced to the loss of good teachers. Teachers are the first resource for education, so retaining good teachers is fundamental. The workload of teachers in rural schools is heavy, and their welfare and benefits are low. Long-term overload makes teachers physically and mentally exhausted. All of which affects the enthusiasm of the majority of teachers' work.Teachers' low sense of professional achievement and gradual loss of enthusiasm for education will lead to burnout. There are serious challenges to enhance their own subject core literacy.

2.3 Improving the Subject Core Literacy of Rural Secondary School Teachers Based on Mobile Learning

Scholars have focused on the possible paths of mobile learning to enhance teachers' core literacy in the subject, and three different arguments have been formed in the academic community. First, the subject theory, which was pointed out by Chinese scholars such as Qi-guang,Yang(2021)..In order to enhance the awareness of mobile learning among rural secondary school teachers, we must start with rural secondary school teachers themselves. By Changing their cognitive concepts, stimulating their intrinsic motivation to engage in mobile learning, and enhancing their mobile learning. The teachers' confidence in mobile learning should also be enhanced. Second, the institutional theory. Chinese scholars such as Wei-rong, Huang (2017) proposed that to enhance the information technology of Chinese rural secondary school teachers requires the collaboration of government departments, mobile learning researchers, universities, and international organizations. Chinese scholars such as Yan-hong,Cao (2017) agree with this point. Third, the methodological theory. Teachers' subject core literacy enhancement should be carried out in the context of Chinese basic national conditions and local educational realities, and the professional literacy practices of teachers should be tailored to local conditions.

As we can see above, the existing studies on the enhancement of subject core literacy of rural teachers have made a lot of attempts in many aspects and have come up with many useful conclusions, providing many references for the enhancement of subject core literacy of rural teachers. However, the research on mobile learning for teachers is not only few but also unsystematic, most of the studies are based on macroscopic assumptions. And the research on mobile learning and teachers is from a microscopic perspective, research which from the perspective of rural secondary schools is still rare. Therefore, the importance of this study has been highlighted.

3. RESEARCH DESIGN

3.1 Theoretical Foundation

The Framework for the Rational Analysis of Mobile Education (FRAME) is a model for mobile learning analysis that describes the intersection of mobile learning as a process involving mobile technology, human learning capabilities, and social interaction (Ally, 2009). The model was proposed by Marguerite Koole of Athabasca University in Canada in 2006 and has been widely adopted by mobile learning researchers and practitioners in China and abroad in recent years.

In the FRAME model, Koole (2006) primarily views mobile learning as a learning experience in which learners are placed in a specific information environment. Learners individually and collectively use and create information, and this information interaction takes place through technology. It is through this complex interaction that information becomes meaningful and contributes to learning. In this information environment, the FRAME model presents the intersection of three different dimensions through the Venn Diagram, as illustrated in figure 1. The framework shows that in the information context and theory logic, device, learner and society constitute the three core circles of mobile learning, which overlap to form the intersection of Interaction Learning, Social Technology and Device Usability. This study uses the model as an analytical framework to explore the path of enhancing teachers' subject core literacy in the context of mobile learning in practice.

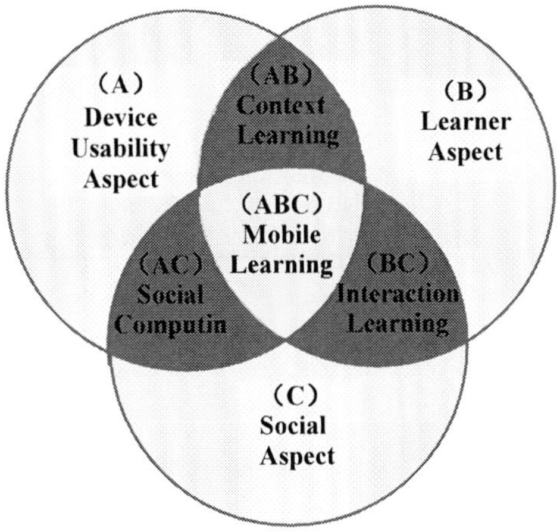

Figure 1. The FRAME modal

3.2 Research Hypothesis

Based on the literature review and the analysis of the questions, this study attempts to investigate the current situation of mobile learning among Chinese rural secondary school teachers and the impact of mobile learning on the development of subject core literacy among rural secondary school teachers. The research hypothesis was also proposed: the subject core literacy development of Chinese rural secondary school teachers is positively related to mobile learning ability.

3.3 Research Objects and Research Tools

3.3.1 Research Objects

The subjects of this study covered rural middle school teachers in South China.1260 questionnaires were distributed and 1245 were collected, excluding invalid questionnaires, 1225 valid questionnaires were obtained, with a recovery rate of 98.80%. The respondents were all rural middle school teachers, including 660 males and 565 females, other basic information of teachers is shown in Table 1.

Table 1. Basic information about the research subjects

Classification	Length of teaching experience 1-3years	4-9years	10-15years	15+ years	Academic Specialized and below	Bachelor's Degree	Postgraduate
Number of people	155	435	405	230	146	380	135
Ratio (%)	12.7	35.5	33.0	18.8	59.0	31.0	7.3

Classification	Qualifications Title Not rated	Secondary Level 2 Teacher	Secondary Level 1 Teacher	Senior Secondary Teacher
Number of people	90	380	730	25
Ratio (%)	7.3	31.0	59.6	2.0

3.3.2 Research Tools

The research instrument for this study was a self-designed questionnaire. The main sources for the question design are form China's Professional Standards for Secondary School Teachers (for Trial Implementation) (2012), Research on the Construction of Professional Core Literacy Models for Primary and Secondary School Teachers (He Zhongqi,2021), and the FRAME Model. The questionnaire consists of four main parts: basic information, society, learner,and device, as shown in Table 2. The second and third parts of the questionnaire are based on the five-point scale of Likert,The Cronbach's alpha coefficient of this questionnaire was 0.921, which was greater than 0.85, and the KMO value was 0.763, which was between 0.7 and 0.8, indicating that the reliability of the questionnaire was good.

Table 2. Questionnaire dimensions

Level 1 Indicators	Level 2 Indicators
1 Basic information	Gender, teaching experience, title, education, IT level
2 Society	2.1 Mobile Learning Community 2.2 Mobile learning sharing platform
3 Learner (Teacher)	3.1 Consciousness of Mobile Learning 3.2 Effectiveness of Mobile Learning
4 Device	4.1 Personal mobile learning device usage 4.2 Mobile Learning Resources Sharing

4. RESEARCH RESULTS

4.1 The General Situation of Mobile Learning for Rural Secondary School Teachers in China

Firstly, the overall situation of mobile learning among Chinese rural secondary school teachers is not bad. The average score of this indicator for the participating teachers was 3.758, and the average scores of the dimensions within mobile learning ranged from 3.63 to 3.90, rated them in descending order.

Secondly, there was no significant gender difference in Chinese rural secondary school teachers' engagement in mobile learning ($t=-0.409$, $p=0.683$). However, it appeared that the overall level of mobile learning was slightly higher among females ($m=4.03$) than males ($m=3.97$) in terms of average scores.

Thirdly, there were significant differences in mobile learning among Chinese rural teachers with different teaching ages and job titles ($F=18.037$, $p<0.001$; $F=21.234$, $p<0.001$). Chinese rural teachers with 1-3 years of teaching experience had the highest average score ($m=4.174$), followed by teachers with 10-15 years of teaching experience ($m=4.052$), 4-9 years of teaching experience ($m=3.758$) and those with more than 15 years of teaching experience ($m=3.589$). In terms of job title, secondary level 2 teachers had the best performance in mobile learning ($m=4.300$), followed by senior secondary teachers ($m=4.176$), unrated teachers ($m=3.917$), and secondary level 1 teachers ($m=3.501$) in descending order.

Fourthly, teachers with different levels of IT skills showed significant differences in mobile learning ($F=10.934$, $p<0.001$). Teachers with appropriate IT training experience or IT certification had an overall higher level of mobile learning than those teachers who did not have IT training before.

4.2 The Correlation Between M-learning Ability and Teachers' Subject Core Literacy Enhancement in Rural Secondary Schools

4.2.1 Calculation of Model Validity

The Pearson correlation coefficient is applicable to the study of continuous linear data, therefore, before analyzing the correlation empirically, the scientific validity of the Pearson correlation coefficient should be verified. The linear correlation between the two variables of "mobile learning" and "subject core literacy" was verified by using SPSS22.0 scatter plots, as shown in Figure 2.

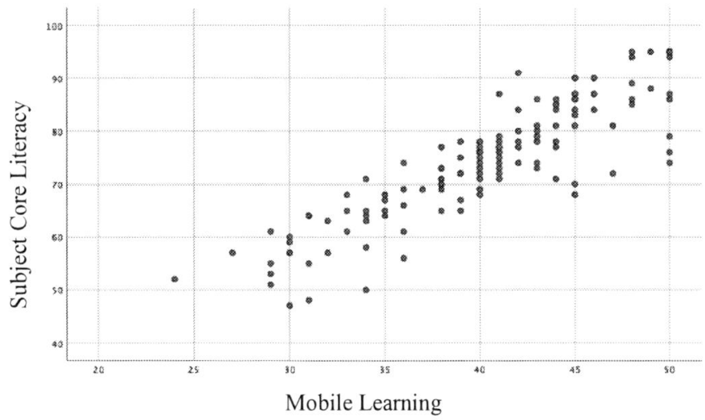

Figure 2. Scatter plot

In this study, the linear correlation between the mobile learning score as the independent variable and the disciplinary core literacy score as the dependent variable was verified. The R^2 equals to0.752 and was obtained. The fitted equation:y =11.944+1.606* x, presenting a linear relationship between the two variables. Regression analysis was performed by using SPSS 22.0. It shows that the model is validity.

4.2.2 The Correlation Between Social Interactions of Mobile Learning and Teachers' Disciplinary Core Literacy

The social interaction of mobile learning in this study is mainly concerned with the interaction between teachers and mobile learning content, but also includes the interactive communication between teachers using mobile platforms. For example, teachers' communication in online forums. The survey showed that most of the schools were slightly inadequate in providing mobile learning social interactions for teachers (M=3.61). In the correlation analysis, it was also revealed that teachers' social interactions using mobile learning were highly correlated with teachers' subject core literacy (r=0.730, p=0.000).

4.2.3 The Correlation Between Learner and Teachers' Subject Core Literacy

Overall, the subject core literacy status of Chinese rural secondary school teachers was average (M=3.89). The score of subject knowledge was 3.77, the score of professional competence was 3.59, and the score of professional affect was 3.85. Based on the validity verification of the previous computational model, this study used SPSS22.0 with Pearson correlation coefficients and conducted a correlation analysis study of the data using a two-sided test (two-tailed). It was found that teachers' mobile learning cognition, knowledge, and competence in mobile learning in general showed a high correlation with teachers' subject core literacy. Where correlation coefficient equals to 0.867 and p = 0.000.

4.2.4 The Correlation Between M-learning Devices and Teachers' Subject Core Literacy

From the data findings, schools are still inadequate in terms of devices support to teachers for mobile learning, the data showed that the average level of input equals to 3.80. The results showed that there is a positive correlation between the equipment situation of schools on mobile learning and subject core literacy of teachers in rural areas (r=0.861, p<0.001).

5. CONCLUSION

In summary, the research hypothesis was verified that teachers' mobile learning competency has a positive relationship with their subject core literacy development. The overall mobile learning competencies of Chinese rural secondary school teachers were average, with teachers' mobile learning competencies showing significant differences in terms of teachers' teaching experience, job title, and information technology level. At the same time, Chinese rural secondary school teachers' m-learning condition was deficient in social interactivity, learners' (teachers themself) performance and mobile learning device.

5.1 Weak Social Interaction of M-learning among Chinese Rural Secondary School Teachers

From the results of the study, there is a deficiency in social interaction in mobile learning for teachers in Chinese rural secondary schools. The average score of social interaction is 3.61 and the standard deviation is 0.896. Teachers were independent of each other and had less interaction when learning online. In the survey of Chinese rural secondary schools, the question "What do you think are the main difficulties of mobile learning for teachers' subject core literacy development?" was asked. 78.05% of teachers believe that schools currently lack effective interactive communication. This is mainly because most teachers only focus on their knowledge during mobile learning, and teachers lack communication and interaction with each other. For example, some online training in the China Teacher Development Network is mainly based on listening to lectures, and learning is evaluated mainly by the total minutes teachers spend when watching online courses (40% of the total) and independently complete assignments. The communication part such as forum and salon occupies only 5% of the score.

5.2 Low M-learning Conscience among Chinese Rural Secondary Schools Teachers

According to the results of the study, mobile learning showed a high positive correlation with teachers' subject core literacy development ($r=0.911$), and the current subject core literacy status of Chinese rural secondary school teachers is average ($M=3.89$), which shows that rural secondary school teachers have more room to improve their subject core literacy and can use mobile learning to promote their own subject core literacy development. However, the overall situation of mobile learning among rural secondary school teachers in China is average ($M=3.758$). Among them, teachers' awareness of mobile learning is at a low level ($M=3.63$), which shows that the internal motivation for mobile learning among rural secondary school teachers is not strong. The study also showed that there were significant differences in mobile learning among Chinese rural teachers with different teaching ages and job titles ($F=18.037$, $p<0.001$; $F=21.234$, $p<0.001$), and rural secondary school teachers' motivation to engage in mobile learning decreases as they grow older and develop professionally, relative to younger teachers. In addition, the situation of rural secondary school teachers conducting mobile learning was closely related to their information technology level, and teachers with different information technology levels showed significant differences in conducting mobile learning ($F=10.934$, $p<0.001$). Some rural secondary school teachers had low awareness of information technology and low initiative in using mobile learning devices.

5.3 Insufficient Device Support Among Chinese Rural Secondary Schools Teachers

According to the survey data, there is a positive correlation between schools' material support on mobile learning and rural secondary school teachers' subject core literacy development ($r=0.861$, $p<0.001$), and according to the questionnaire results, rural secondary school teachers are very concerned about the support of classroom network condition, mobile device performance, learning resources quality and other factors on their mobile learning. But at present, the investment in these resources in rural secondary schools is at an average level($M=3.80$). In addition, funding is also a factor of particular concern to teachers. Because local economic development in rural middle schools is slower than that in cities, educational resources and funds are often limited, and there are still some differences in the use of mobile platforms from urban areas, so teachers' needs in terms of financial investment and information technology in teaching cannot be fully met, and the construction of advanced mobile learning platforms has not been built in rural middle schools. In the open-ended questionnaire, 74.7% of teachers said that the singularity of training content and form is also one of the biggest obstacles to their mobile learning. In terms of training methods, teachers in rural middle schools often participate in group training, online training, and lack of expert guidance and systematic learning.

6. SUGGESTIONS

The level of teachers' subject core literacy will eventually affect the level of students' literacy. According to Koole's framework, improving teachers' mobile learning ability is an inevitable development of the times, and also an important way for rural middle school teachers to improve their professional quality in the context of information society.

6.1 Enhancing the Social Interaction Level of M-learning among Rural Secondary School Teachers

Social interactivity is an essential element of mobile learning. Focusing on the social interactivity of mobile learning is an important way to enhance the effectiveness of mobile learning for teachers. The social interactivity of mobile learning is mainly reflected in online interaction and communication. Therefore, this study proposes the following recommendations.

Firstly, building an interdisciplinary learning community for teachers' mobile learning. The construction of interdisciplinary learning communities can establish close ties among teachers, break the barrier of "non-interaction" among teachers in mobile learning, enhancing emotional communication among different disciplines teachers， and provide emotional and social support for the sustainability of mobile learning. Secondly, building a sharing mechanism for teachers' mobile learning. On the one hand, theme-based social groups can be constructed. This could start with key skills that teachers urgently need for professional development, for example by designing different subject teaching skills exchange themes. Teachers can design mini-lessons through online education platforms such as Tencent Classroom, which is popular in China, in order to share their experiences with each other and thus promote self-reflection and subject skills development. On the other hand, problem-based social groups can be constructed. Design a mobile learning exchange mechanism based on subject teaching problems. For example, with the theme of thorny problems encountered in subject education and teaching practice, teachers in rural secondary schools can use social tools such as QQ and WeChat, to share their confusion and insights in classroom teaching, showcase teaching problems they have encountered, share their problem-solving strategies, etc.

6.2 Stimulating the Demand for M-learning among Rural Secondary School Teachers

While mobile learning as a new learning model has made great strides in some developed countries or regions, there are still many teachers in rural areas of some developing countries who do not have a good understanding of mobile learning models. Targeted training is needed for the teachers concerned.

First, teachers in rural secondary schools should be made more aware of the mobile learning model. Make teachers aware that mobile learning is based on modern multimedia mobile terminals such as mobile phones, laptops and IPDADs, which allow for personalised learning that is not restricted by time and space. This mode of learning, due to its convenience, affordability and speed, can help teachers in rural areas to make up for such shortcomings as limited resources and time and space constraints. This can have a unique and important impact in promoting the development of their subject core literacy. In addition, incentives such as rewards and credit systems can also be set up to enhance the internal motivation of teachers in rural secondary schools to participate in mobile learning. Second, the effectiveness of mobile learning in developing the subject core literacy of rural middle teachers should be improved. To help teachers in rural middle schools master mobile learning skills, regularly conduct centralized training, and invite teachers who are good at mobile learning mode to conduct one-on-one tutoring. On the one hand, we should help teachers in rural middle schools establish the teaching concept of "learning for teaching and teaching for learning" and change the concept of separating learning from teaching. On the other hand, we should improve the application effect of mobile learning tools for teachers in rural middle schools, so that they can personally feel that they will achieve greater and better development in subject core literacy with the help of mobile learning.

6.3 Increasing M-learning Equipment Support For Rural Secondary School Teachers

It should increase investment in mobile learning equipment construction and resources, optimise mobile learning equipment and innovate public mobile learning content, so as to provide the most advanced support for mobile learning for teachers in rural secondary schools.

First, optimise personal mobile learning equipment. On the one hand, the government should increase funding for township secondary schools, enrich the quantity of mobile learning tools and improve the quality of mobile learning devices. On the other hand, it should also accelerate the construction of mobile high-speed Internet networks to ensure smooth, high-speed and efficient network signals, so as to ensure that teachers in township secondary schools can carry out mobile learning effectively. Second, innovate the content of public mobile learning. Large social platforms such as Qzone and WeChat space should be fully utilised to enrich the content of mobile learning resources for teachers in rural secondary schools. For example, teachers should be encouraged to upload their mobile learning materials to their personal social networking platform spaces for sharing and learning. In addition, a school mobile learning database could be established. This means that a school-level teacher subject core literacy learning database can be established based on different subjects and teachers' personal teaching literacy characteristics, and AI technology can be used to select different mobile learning content and learning resources for teachers of different subjects, thus forming a unique and systematic subject core literacy development programme for each teacher. This will enable the mobile learning model to better promote the development of subject core literacy among teachers in rural secondary schools.

REFERENCES

H. X. Wang, and M. Li. (2020). The connotation, components and development path of core qualities of excellent teachers[J]. Education Science,36(06):40-46

J. J. Ma, L. Y. Zhou, and Y. W. Liu. (2017). A survey on the use of modern education technology by teachers in rural middle schools in central China--a case study of four counties in province H[J]. Journal of Educational Science, Hunan Normal University,16(03):89-94.DOI:10.19503/j.cnki.1671-6124.2017.03.014.

Q. G. Yang, and T. T. Xu. (2021). Mobile learning for teachers' professional development:practices, challenges and responses[J]. Journal of Capital Normal University (Social Science Edition),(03):171-180.

S. R. Guo, and Z. P. Zhou. (2021). Self-perceived equity impact and reconstruction of rural junior high school teachers--a perspective based on recognition justice theory[J]. Educational Development Research, 41(02):72-80.DOI:10.14121/j.cnki.1008-3855.2021.02.013.

Shippee , M. and Keengwe,J. (2014). mLearning: Anytime, anywhere learning transcending the boundaries of the educational box[J]. Education and Information Technologies,19(1)

W. R. Huang, and J. Yang. (2017). A study on the hybrid training of information technology application ability of rural secondary school teachers[J]. Teaching and Management,(12):61-64.

X. Y. Hua. (2017). Exploration of teachers' mobile learning model based on new media applications[J]. Primary and secondary school teacher training,(09):27-31.

Y. H. Cao, and Q. G. Yang. (2017). Quality and equity of education supported by mobile learning:new developments in international research and practice[J]. Comparative Education Research,39(03):60-66+88

TRANSFORMER LANGUAGE MODEL-BASED MOBILE LEARNING SOLUTION FOR HIGHER EDUCATION

Silvia García-Méndez, Francisco de Arriba-Pérez and Francisco J. González-Castaño
Information Technologies Group, atlanTTic, University of Vigo,
School of Telecommunications Engineering, Maxwell street, 36310 Vigo, Spain

ABSTRACT

Mobile learning or mLearning has become an essential tool in many fields in this digital era, among the ones educational training deserves special attention, that is, applied to both basic and higher education towards active, flexible, effective high-quality and continuous learning. However, despite the advances in Natural Language Processing techniques, mLearning still does not take full advantage of the great potential of the latter techniques. It is the case of the transformer language models distributed in chatbot form. Accordingly, this work presents a mLearning application based on OpenAI GPT-3 model, which enables user-friendly interactions. The proposed system was tested in two evaluation scenarios, and the experimental results endorse its appropriateness toward learning experience enhancement.

KEYWORDS

Higher Education, Intelligent Virtual Assistant, Mobile Learning, Natural Language Processing, User-Generated Content, Transformer Language Models

1. INTRODUCTION

Mobile learning or mLearning allows to gather knowledge and develop skills by exploiting mobile technologies. mLearning exploits all media types (audio, text, visual data, *etc.*) at any place and time (Crompton & Burke, 2018). Consequently, it has become an essential tool in this digital era, driven by the recent advances in communication networks, information technologies, and learning applications (Bai, 2019). All levels of education have been affected by digitalization which promotes practice-based learning instead of just offering theoretical knowledge. Particularly, mLearning has been extensively used in both basic and higher educational levels, being a critical component in the latter towards high-quality, active, and continuous education (Crompton & Burke, 2018). As a result, mLearning is established as a strategic tool to enhance university student capacities (Pinto et al., 2020). There exist several mobile technologies used in mLearning, such as eBooks, smartphones, tablets, etc. Among them, mobile phones are the most common devices due to their multi-task nature (audio, image, and video recording capabilities, and all kinds of educational software available) (Crompton & Burke, 2018; Hartley & Bendixen, 2019).

Its flexible and convenient nature (Pedro et al., 2018) is highly attractive to digital natives who seek a fully immersive learning experience. However, learning experience enhancement can only be achieved through well-designed learning solutions (Parsazadeh et al., 2018). Accordingly, consideration should be given to advanced mLearning approaches to ensure learning effectiveness. In this line, transformer language models are relevant to this work. They are intended to solve sequence-to-sequence tasks and handle long-term dependencies by relying on the self-attention mechanism based on the encoder-decoder architecture. More in detail, the input word embeddings enter the first encoder, and then they are transformed and propagated to the next encoder. The output is obtained after decoding. These models are the most advanced for Natural Language Generation and are distributed in a chatbot form (Brown et al. 2020). A chatbot is a conversational agent able to interact with users in a natural way using textual or voice-based interfaces in order to answer questions, establish a conversion on any topic or even perform a certain task. This technology has been applied in multiple domains, such as customer service and, especially to education and training (Tallyn et al., 2018). Users can benefit from the instant availability of mLearning applications and the ability to respond naturally using chatbots. Accordingly, this work contributes with a transformer language model-based mobile application which exploits Natural Language Processing (NLP) to enable user-friendly interactions to enhance mLearning acceptance of both educators and learners, inside and outside of the classroom.

The rest of the paper is organized as follows. Section 2 reviews relevant literature on mLearning to support the motivation of the present work. Section 3 presents the proposed solution, while Section 4 details the implementation decisions and displays the experimental results obtained. Finally, Section 5 concludes the article.

2. RELATED WORK

mLearning solutions are nowadays official tools in both classrooms and workplaces, but they are also relevant systems outside these environments, at homes for teleworking and remote education, respectively (Kumar Basak, 2018). They seek to provide new efficient ways of learning and also remove the existing limitations in the process with the ultimate objective of meeting the learner's needs. As previously mentioned, mLearning was originally developed as a way to save resources (money and time) while at the same time enabling high-quality, easier and faster learning. Learning processes involve challenging tasks such as comprehension, design, problem-solving, debugging, etc. (Malik et al., 2020). Thus, Technology Enhanced Learning (TEL) and Learning Analytics (LA) constitute relevant approaches for enhancing users' learning satisfaction in multimodal learning environments compared or combined with traditional methodologies (Mota et al., 2018).

The European Digital Agenda 2020[1] seeks to perform strategic ICT (Information and Communications Technology) research and innovation actions like promoting digital skills and inclusion. Among Good Practice Teaching (GPT) (Romero-Rodríguez et al., 2020), which involves cooperative work, knowledge, and self-regulation training along with the development of digital competence, educational chatbot solutions are appropriate. The latter solutions promote human-machine interaction and engagement (Smutny & Schreiberova, 2020). This is the case with the Ethnobot chatbot (Tallyn et al., 2018), which asks users ethnographic-related questions. However, the most advanced technology for chatbot design is the aforementioned language transformer models. Particularly, OpenAI, an Artificial Intelligence research and deployment company, provides three different models depending on the use case: GPT-3, oriented to NLP, Codex for programming users, and Content filter to detect whether a text may be confidential or insecure (Brown et al. 2020). However, none of them focus on the educational field.

In the particular case of Spain, mLearning has started to be applied to preschool and primary levels (Romero-Rodríguez, 2020). The results obtained show a positive increase in motivating the learners and improving their learning outcomes (Bai, 2019). However, there is still work to be done in digital competence development in Spain (Fuentes et al., 2019), even though it is the fifth country in the world regarding the number of smartphone and Internet users2. Therefore, the Instituto Nacional de Tecnologías Educativas y Formación del Profesorado (INTEF) indicated the necessity to promote the latter digital competence among students (Romero-Rodríguez, 2020) beyond Learning Management System (LMS) software (Antonova & Bontchev, 2020). LMS is very popular at higher levels (Abazi-Bexheti et al., 2018). Examples of LMS include Blackboard, Edmodo, Google Classroom, Moodle, Sakai, and Schoology. In this line, Andrei et al. (2019) presented the Open Virtual Mobility Learning Hub which combines different interactive learning methodologies in open-source frameworks like MOODLE. Learning apps are also very common, the second most popular category on Google Play (Singh & Suri, 2022). Take Duolingo, Quizlet, SoloLearn as representative examples.

Regarding prior research on mLearning, Mota et al. (2018) presented a framework to create applications with augmented reality, while Oyelere et al. (2018) developed MobileEdu focusing on computing education for university students following a blended learning approach, that is, combining mlearning and traditional face-to-face teaching (Nogueira & Paniago, 2022). Furthermore, Parsazadeh et al. (2018) presented a Jigsaw-based mLearning application that combines interactive and cooperative learning to promote peer and group interaction. More recently, Nazar et al. (2022) created an Android app to comprehend the concept of redox in Chemistry for university students. Other popular use cases include language (Brata et al., 2019) and

[1] Available at https://library.educause.edu/resources/2019/4/2019-horizon-report, January 2023.
[2] Available at https://compromiso.atresmedia.com/levanta-la-cabeza/quienes-somos/movimiento-uso-responsable-tecnologia_201901245c49b0f20cf238d4657881bc.html, January 2023.

code (Troussas et al., 2020; App Inventor and Scratch) learning. Accordingly, Liu (2022) developed an mLearning application to improve the English language among college students, which combines gamification and collaborative/competitive learning. More closely related to our work is the WeChat application developed by Ng et al. (2020), the most popular collaborative learning application used among Chinese students.

This work contributes to all the fundamental perspectives of mLearning: (contribution-i) cognitive (how the brain operates during learning), (c-ii) emotional (engagement, motivation, etc.), (c-iii) behavioral (outcomes of the learning process), and (c-iv) contextual (interaction and collaboration). Consequently, the proposed intelligent mobile application seeks learning optimization in a virtual and adaptive environment by exploiting NLP techniques over the content (c-i and c-iii). It also adapts the utterances to the emotional state of the users thanks to its sentiment analysis (SA) and empathetic module to prevent frustration and promote confidence (c-ii). Note that the latter feature is especially relevant since the emotional state of the learner is strongly related to the outcome of the learning process (Singh & Suri, 2022). Finally, the system uses an innovative communication approach with a transformer language model (c-iv).

3. PROPOSED METHOD

The proposed virtual learning assistant is depicted in Figure 1. In this figure, the conversational server and client application are illustrated. The solution is intended for both professors and students and was especially designed for the Spanish language, even though its adaptation to other languages may be considered straightforward. Thanks to the pre-trained model available, this solution will be able to accommodate any educational issue without prior training or additional information. The assistant provides automatic question generation and free dialogue functionalities. In the particular case of students, the virtual assistant enables doubts resolution.

3.1 Conversational Server

The conversational server is the core of the system and allows to automatically generate interactions with the users in the form of questions or free dialogue. The system utterances are enriched following a template-based approach to ensure that the human-machine interaction is satisfactory.

3.1.1 ML Model Selection Module

Once the request is received from the client, it is necessary to select the Machine Learning (ML) model to generate the system output. Accordingly, the model with a higher computational cost is selected. If the latter model is not available, that is, request errors are being produced, or there is a response time greater than 30 seconds, the next model based on higher computational cost is selected.

3.1.2 Playground Manager Module

The playgrounds in OpenAI are composed of templates that contextualize the dialogue in a specific area or topic and ensure that the system response is appropriate. Thus, this module allows to management of the available playgrounds and includes relevant features like personalization, empathy, and feedback.

Personalization stage. It detects the profile of the user (teacher or student), the conversation type (automatic question generation or free dialogue), and the area and topic of the conversation. The history of the interactions is also managed in this stage (maximum history of six utterances). Firstly, the users indicate their role, and since the words teacher or student (or synonyms of these words) may be absent, the system identifies the role with the following template in the playground, "*Si te dijese* [USER ROLE DEFINITION IN NATURAL LANGUAGE], *¿qué dirías que soy un profesor o un alumno? Contesta con una sola palabra*" (If I told you [USER ROLE DEFINITION IN NATURAL LANGUAGE], what would you say I am, a teacher or a student? Answer with one word). The system returns the role of the user, and only when "teacher" or "student" is identified the conversation continues. Otherwise, the system keeps asking the users about their roles. Then, the operation mode is detected using the following templates, "*Soy un/una docente. Si te dijese* [USER OPERATION MODE DEFINITION IN NATURAL LANGUAGE], *¿qué dirías que he elegido de las opciones disponibles: generar preguntas de examen, chat abierto? Contesta con una sola de las opciones de* *la lista*" (I am a teacher. If I told you [USER OPERATION MODE DEFINITION IN NATURAL LANGUAGE], what would you say I have chosen from the available options: exam question generation, free dialogue? Answer with only one of the options from the list) and "*Soy un/a estudiante, si te dijese* [USER OPERATION MODE DEFINITION IN NATURAL LANGUAGE], *¿qué dirías que he elegido de las opciones disponibles: generar preguntas de auto-evaluación, resolver dudas, chat abierto? Contesta con una sola de las opciones de la lista*" (I am a student, if I told you [USER OPERATION MODE DEFINITION IN NATURAL LANGUAGE], what would you say that I have chosen from the available options: generate self-assessment questions, resolve doubts, free dialogue? Answer with only one of the options from the list), for the teacher and student roles, respectively. Finally, if the question generation functionality was previously detected for the teacher or student role, it is time to infer the area and topic of the conversation. Accordingly, a similar template is used, "*Si te dijese* [USER AREA AND TOPIC DEFINITION IN NATURAL LANGUAGE], *¿a qué área y temática me refiero? Contesta siguiendo el siguiente formato, materia: A, tema: B*" (If I told you [USER AREA AND TOPIC DEFINITION IN NATURAL LANGUAGE], what area and topic am I referring to? Answer using the following format, area: A, topic: B).

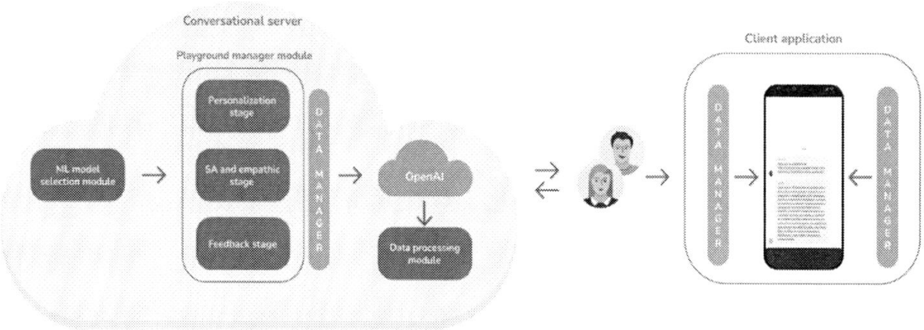

Figure 1. System scheme

SA and empathetic stage. The system generates sentences adapted to the state of mind of the users since it has been trained to follow this template "*El asistente es dinámico, nunca repite dos veces lo mismo, es creativo, es inteligente y muy amable*" (The assistant is dynamic, it never repeats the same thing twice, it is creative, intelligent and very kind). During the quiz with the students (system automatic question generation and user response), if three consecutive mistakes are made by the student, the assistant asks how the student feels. The latter response is analyzed using the template "*Si te digo* [USER STATE OF MIND DEFINITION IN NATURAL LANGUAGE] *dirías que estoy ¿triste o feliz?*" (If I told you [USER STATE OF MIND DEFINITION IN NATURAL LANGUAGE] would you say I am happy or sad?). If the emotion "tristeza" (sad) is detected, questions from a lower difficulty level will be presented to the student.

Feedback stage. The empathetic nature of the assistant defined in the previous stage is combined with the feedback provided to the users. The latter is possible thanks to the template "*Soy un/a estudiante y a la pregunta* [ASSISTANT QUESTION] *he contestado* [USER ANSWER]. *Dime si mi respuesta es 100% correcta, parcialmente correcta o no es correcta. Y explícame el porqué*" (I am a student and to the question [ASSISTANT QUESTION] I have answered [USER ANSWER]. Please tell me if my answer is 100% correct, partially correct or incorrect. And explain to me why).

Finally, for the utterances generation of the virtual assistant, there exist several additional playgrounds depending on the role and action previously chosen.

- **Exam question generation for the teacher role**. The template used is "*Soy un/a docente con conocimientos avanzados, necesitaría generar una pregunta para un examen de* [ASSISTANT AREA AND TOPIC DETECTED]" (I am a teacher with advanced knowledge, I would need to generate a question for an exam [ASSISTANT AREA AND TOPIC DETECTED]).
- **Self-assessment for the student role**. The template used is "*Soy un/a estudiante, necesitaría practicar para un examen de* [ASSISTANT AREA AND TOPIC DETECTED]. *Genérame una pregunta al respecto*" (I am a student, I would need to practice for a [ASSISTANT AREA AND TOPIC DETECTED] exam. Give me a question about it).

- **Doubts resolution for the student role**. The template used is "*Soy un/a estudiante. Necesitaría que me resolvieras esta pregunta* [USER QUESTION IN NATURAL LANGUAGE]" (I am a student. I need you to solve this question [USER QUESTION IN NATURAL LANGUAGE]).

3.1.3 Data Processing Module

Text processing is essential for personalization, SA, and empathetic stages. Thus, this module deletes symbols, URLs, and other non-alphanumeric content.

3.2 Data Manager

The main functionality of this module is to serve as an abstraction layer between the conversational server, the ML model selector, and the client application. Server-client data are sent and received in JSON format. In addition, JSON allows the status of the conversion to be established by identifying the type of interlocutor and the number of interactions, as well as the immediately preceding questions and conversations, thus, acting as an intermediate lazy cache.

3.3 Client Application

It serves as the system access interface for the end users. This module identifies the number of interactions that have been carried out in the free chat functionality. In addition, the cleaning of the user cache is performed when the user ends the conversation with the "terminate" command.

4. EXPERIMENTAL RESULTS

This section presents the implementation decisions. In the end, the evaluation results are discussed.

4.1 Conversational Server

This module was deployed as a Flask server (version 2.2.2) with a Gunicorn traffic balancer (version 20.1.0) using Python programming language (version 3.8).

4.1.1 ML Model Selection Module

For the generation of sentences, the system uses the GPT-3 transformer language model (version 3.5) provided by OpenAI.

4.1.2 Playground Manager Module

In order to either reduce the randomness of the response or guarantee the maximum dynamism of the dialogues, the *temperature* parameter was set as follows (0 and 1, respectively).

- **Personalization stage**. *Temperature* = 0.
- **SA and empathetic stage**. *Temperature* = 0 when using the templates to train the assistant and *Temperature* = 1 when generating empathetic interactions.
- **Feedback stage**. *Temperature* = 1.

4.1.3 Data Processing Module

Regular expressions are exploited to detect both symbols ("#", "´", ";", "`", "~", "&", ".", "?", "¿", "!", "¡") and URLs (starting with http, https, pic, and www).

4.2 Data Manager

The Python http module is used for request management on the client side while, on the server, the Flask library. In addition, for the generation of requests against the transformer language model, the OpenAI Python library is used.

4.3 Client Application

The client has been designed using the cross-platform Flutter language; hence the proposed system is accessible from Windows, macOS, iOS, and Android as a native application or from a browser. For the design of the chat, the Flyer Chat library was used. A model-view-controller paradigm was followed.

4.4 Case Study

In our study, a total of 100 interactions have been manually annotated by two NLP experts. Particularly, two evaluation scenarios have been set.

Scenario 1. Five thematic areas with a single topic (history – World War II, biology – cellular and biochemistry, mathematics – differential equations, medicine – human anatomy, engineering – Python programming) and ten questions each have been generated using the assistant. The following evaluation questions were used, EQ1: Is the question generated by the assistant related to the area requested?, EQ2: Is the question useful for an exam?, EQ3: Are there any grammatical errors, or its construction is inconsistent?

Scenario 2. The answers to the questions generated for the previous scenarios are evaluated using, EQ4: Is the answer related to the question?, EQ5: Is the concept clearly explained to a student?, EQ6: Are there any grammatical errors, or its construction is inconsistent?

4.5 Annotation Results

Tables 1 and 2 show the results obtained for the first and second evaluation scenarios, respectively. Results are provided in terms of the percentage of affirmative answers to the evaluation questions. The values of the first evaluation scenario range from 92% to 100% for EQ1 and EQ2. Thus, the questions generated by the assistant are both within the area and topic of the dialogue and appropriate to be included in the exam. The number of grammatical and coherent errors is minimal (up to 6%). In the second evaluation scenario (see Table 2), the results obtained for EQ4 and EQ5 are even higher, between 94% and 100%. However, grammatical and coherence errors are more frequent (up to 14%). The latter fact is due to the greater difficulty in generating complete answers to the questions generated to be used in an exam (second scenario) compared to creating the questions themselves (first scenario).

Table 1. Percentage of affirmative answers of the two annotators for the first evaluation scenario

	EQ1	EQ2	EQ3
Annotator 1	98%	92%	4%
Annotator 2	96%	100%	6%

Table 2. Percentage of affirmative answers of the two annotators for the second evaluation scenario

	EQ4	EQ5	EQ6
Annotator 1	100%	94%	12%
Annotator 2	100%	98%	14%

5. CONCLUSION

There exist a variety of mLearning solutions that are being exploited in classrooms and workplaces as new efficient tools to meet the learner's needs while removing the existing limitations in the process, such as time and location constraints. The latter proliferation of mLeaning systems has been driven not only by private parties as the end users themselves but also by the European Digital Agenda 2020, and the Spanish INTEF to promote digital skills.

In this line, this work seeks to fully exploit the latest advances in NLP techniques in an intelligent virtual assistant based on the transformer language model GPT-3 by OpenAI. Our solution is composed of a conversational server and a client application. Among its most relevant features are the personalized and emphatic utterances along with the feedback provided during the dialogues with the users. Experimental results show that the questions generated by the assistant are both within the area and topic of the dialogue (up to 98 %), appropriate to be included in the exam (up to 100 %), and fully explanatory (100 %) to a student (98 %). The number of grammatical and coherent errors is minimal (up to 14 %). A real example of a conversation with the virtual assistant is shown in Figure 2. The user, in this case, is a student that wants to practice for a chemistry exam about redox reactions.

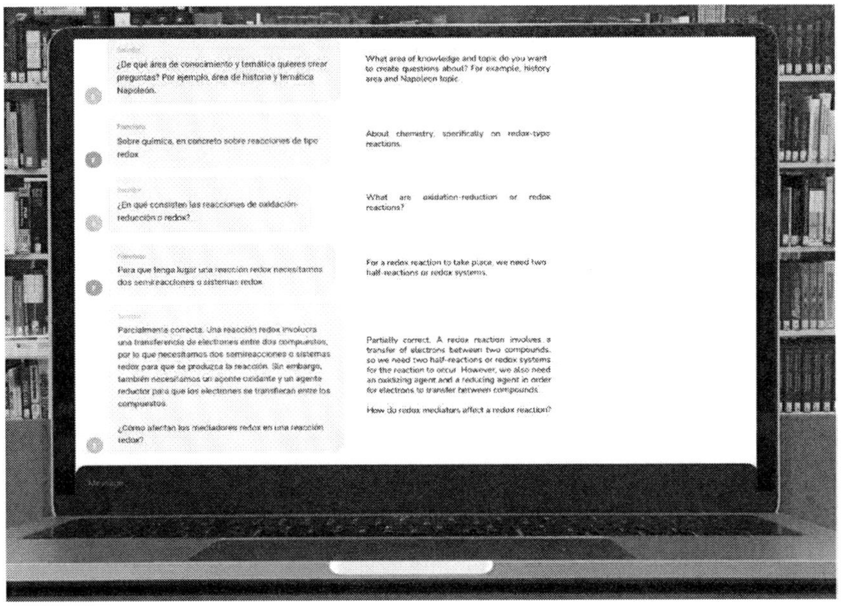

Figure 2. Integration of the system in a multiplatform application

In future work, the dialogues generated in the mobile application can be mined to recommend adjustments in learning methods. Other languages will be considered in the next versions of the assistant.

ACKNOWLEDGEMENT

This work was partially supported by Xunta de Galicia grants ED481B-2021-118, ED481B-2022-093, and ED431C 2022/04, Spain; and Ministerio de Ciencia e Innovación grant TED2021-130824B-C21, Spain.

REFERENCES

Abazi-Bexheti, L., Kadriu, A., Apostolova-Trpkovska, M., Jajaga, E., & Abazi-Alili, H. (2018). LMS Solution: Evidence of Google Classroom Usage in Higher Education. Business Systems Research Journal, 9(1), 31–43. 10.2478/bsrj-2018-0003

Andrei, T., Vasiu, R., Mihaescu, V., & Andone, D. (2019). Integrating Open Technologies in the Virtual Mobility Learning Hub. Proceedings of the International Conference on Advanced Learning Technologies, 24–28. 10.1109/ICALT.2019.00016

Antonova, A., & Bontchev, B. (2020). Investigating mooc platforms as a prospective tool for mobile learning. Proceedings of the International Conference on Mobile Learning, 31–38. 10.33965/ml2020_202004L004

Bai, H. (2019). Pedagogical Practices of Mobile Learning in K-12 and Higher Education Settings. TechTrends, 63(5), 611–620. 10.1007/s11528-019-00419-w

Brata, K. C., Brata, A. H., & Lukman, E. P. (2019). Hanasu: Interactive Japanese Language M-Learning Application to Support Listening and Speaking Exercise. Proceedings of the International Conference on Education and Multimedia Technology, 311–315. 10.1145/3345120.3345155

Brown, T. B., Mann, B., Ryder, N., Subbiah, M., Kaplan, J., Dhariwal, P., Neelakantan, A., Shyam, P., Sastry, G., Askell, A., Agarwal, S., Herbert-Voss, A., Krueger, G., Henighan, T., Child, R., Ramesh, A., Ziegler, D. M., Wu, J., Winter, C., Amodei, D. (2020). Language models are few-shot learners. Advances in Neural Information Processing Systems, 1–25.

Crompton, H., & Burke, D. (2018). The use of mobile learning in higher education: A systematic review. Computers & Education, 123, 53–64. 10.1016/j.compedu.2018.04.007

Fuentes, J. L., Albertos, J., & Torrano, F. (2019). Hacia el Mobile-Learning en la escuela: análisis de factores críticos en el uso de las tablets en centros educativos españoles. Education in the Knowledge Society, 20, 17. 10.14201/eks2019_20_a3

Hamidi, H., & Chavoshi, A. (2018). Analysis of the essential factors for the adoption of mobile learning in higher education: A case study of students of the University of Technology. Telematics and Informatics, 35(4), 1053–1070. 10.1016/j.tele.2017.09.016

Hartley, K., & Bendixen, L. D. (2019). Smartphones and self-regulated learning: opportunities and challenges. Proceedings of the International Conference on Mobile Learning, 149–152. 10.33965/ml2019_201903R001

Kumar Basak, S., Wotto, M., & Bélanger, P. (2018). E-learning, M-learning and D-learning: Conceptual definition and comparative analysis. E-Learning and Digital Media, 15(4), 191–216. 10.1177/2042753018785180

Liu, I.-F. (2022). Gamified mobile learning: effects on English learning in technical college students. Computer Assisted Language Learning, 1–24. 10.1080/09588221.2022.2080717

Malik, S. I., Al-Emran, M., Mathew, R., Tawafak, R. M., & Alfarsi, G. (2020). Comparison of E-Learning, M-Learning and Game-based Learning in Programming Education – A Gendered Analysis. International Journal of Emerging Technologies in Learning, 15(15), 133. 10.3991/ijet.v15i15.14503

Mota, J. M., Ruiz-Rube, I., Dodero, J. M., & Arnedillo-Sánchez, I. (2018). Augmented reality mobile app development for all. Computers & Electrical Engineering, 65, 250–260. 10.1016/j.compeleceng.2017.08.025

Nazar, M., Rusman, Puspita, K., & Yaqin, H. (2022). Android-Based Mobile Learning Resource for Chemistry Students in Comprehending the Concept of Redox Reactions. International Journal of Interactive Mobile Technologies, 16(03), 123–135. 10.3991/ijim.v16i03.24133

Ng, S. F., Azlan, M. A. K., Kamal, A. N. A., & Manion, A. (2020). A quasi-experiment on using guided mobile learning interventions in ESL classrooms: Time use and academic performance. Education and Information Technologies, 25(6), 4699–4719. 10.1007/s10639-020-10191-7

Nogueira, K. A. N., & Paniago, M. C. L. (2022). Understandings and perspectives on blended learning in a brazilian private university in the context of transformations. Proceedings of the International Conference on e-Society and the International Conference on Mobile Learning, 139–146.

Oyelere, S. S., Suhonen, J., Wajiga, G. M., & Sutinen, E. (2018). Design, development, and evaluation of a mobile learning application for computing education. Education and Information Technologies, 23(1), 467–495. 10.1007/s10639-017-9613-2

Parsazadeh, N., Ali, R., & Rezaei, M. (2018). A framework for cooperative and interactive mobile learning to improve online information evaluation skills. Computers & Education, 120, 75–89. 10.1016/j.compedu.2018.01.010

Pedro, L. F. M. G., Barbosa, C. M. M. de O., & Santos, C. M. das N. (2018). A critical review of mobile learning integration in formal educational contexts. International Journal of Educational Technology in Higher Education, 15(1), 10. 10.1186/s41239-018-0091-4

Pinto, M., Sales, D., Fernández-Pascual, R., & Caballero-Mariscal, D. (2020). Attitudes, perceptions and prospectings on mobile information literacy training: Design and validation of the MOBILE-APP questionnaire. Journal of Librarianship and Information Science, 52(1), 208–223. 10.1177/0961000618788726

Romero-Rodríguez, J.-M., Aznar-Díaz, I., Hinojo-Lucena, F.-J., & Cáceres-Reche, M.-P. (2020). Models of good teaching practices for mobile learning in higher education. Palgrave Communications, 6(1), 80. 10.1057/s41599-020-0468-6

Singh, Y., & Suri, P. K. (2022). An empirical analysis of mobile learning app usage experience. Technology in Society, 68, 101929. 10.1016/j.techsoc.2022.101929

Smutny, P., & Schreiberova, P. (2020). Chatbots for learning: A review of educational chatbots for the Facebook Messenger. Computers & Education, 151, 103862. 10.1016/j.compedu.2020.103862

Tallyn, E., Fried, H., Gianni, R., Isard, A., & Speed, C. (2018). The Ethnobot: Gathering ethnographies in the age of IoT. Proceedings of the Conference on Human Factors in Computing Systems, 1–13. 10.1145/3173574.3174178

Troussas, C., Krouska, A., & Sgouropoulou, C. (2020). Collaboration and fuzzy-modeled personalization for mobile game-based learning in higher education. Computers & Education, 144, 103698. 10.1016/j.compedu.2019.103698

RAISING STUDENTS' AWARENESS ABOUT NATURE CONSERVATION: FROM THE PARK TO THE CITY

Rita Rodrigues, Lúcia Pombo and Margarida M. Marques
Research Center on Didactics and Technology in the Education of Trainers (CIDTFF),
Department of Education and Psychology (DEP), University of Aveiro, Portugal

ABSTRACT

Mobile devices, augmented reality (AR), and outdoor games can be mobilized to promote Education for Sustainable Development and, thus, to sensitize to nature conservation. The EduCITY project combines mobile learning, AR, and environmental sensors towards sustainability education and creates opportunities for citizens to contribute to their city's sustainability. This paper presents a study that articulates the previous project, the EduPARK, with the current one, the EduCITY. While EduPARK was developed within an urban park, EduCITY expanded its geographical area to the entire city. This study aims to analyze students' perceptions regarding changes in their nature conservation attitudes after exploring an urban green park in a mobile AR game-based learning activity. For this purpose, 233 basic education students (from school-year 5 to 9) played a game for environmental education, available in the EduPARK app, at the Infante D. Pedro Park (Aveiro, Portugal). Through a mixed method approach, data collection was focused on students and included two questionnaires, applied before and after the game activity; a focus group guide; and an observation grid. Results show a strengthening of positive attitudes towards nature conservation. Moreover, students mentioned that their nature conservation future intentions are focused on preserving natural resources, combating resources' waste, recycling waste, reducing pollution, and protecting fauna and flora. Students also revealed willingness and concern to teach friends and family about what they have learned with the EduPARK game. The EduCITY intends to give continuity to these practices throughout Aveiro city. This is anchored on a community-based participatory project integrating AR location games based on challenges, to be explored in the city, in formal, non-formal, and informal educational contexts, in a socio constructivism approach. This study adds to the literature on education for Sustainable Development, by revealing that it is possible to sensitize school students to nature conservation through mobile AR game-based approaches in the outdoors, which can be a first step to promote positive nature attitudes.

KEYWORDS

Outdoor Learning, Mobile Learning, Game-based Learning, Augmented Reality, Education for Sustainability, Nature Conservation Education

1. INTRODUCTION

In our modern society, the protection of nature and environment is becoming increasingly important. An essential approach to address these issues and change people's behavior is Education for Sustainable Development (ESD). Faced with the challenge of promoting the sustainable development of the planet and humanity over generations, UNESCO decided to invest in education, and its recommendations will guide international and national educational policies to educate citizens to make more informed and responsible decisions (United Nations 2015)

This study adds to research in ESD and intends to contribute to the 2030 Agenda for Sustainable Development goals (UNESCO, 2015). With that aim, an educational quiz game entitled "O Verdinho [The green game]" was developed and integrated into the EduPARK app. Among all the Sustainable Development Goals, the following were selected to be addressed by this educational guide: i) goal 3: good health and well-being; ii) goal 4: quality education; iii) goal 12: responsible consumption and production; iv) goal 13: climate action; v) goal 14: life below water and vi) goal 15: life on land (United Nations Educational Scientific and Cultural Organization, 2017).

Mobile devices, augmented reality (AR) and outdoor games can be mobilized to promote ESD and, thus, to sensitize to nature conservation. Mobile devices can create more active learning experiences, which improve student engagement and learning. Moreover, can amplify motivation, which is a vital aspect of learning, deliver information when needed, and encourage students to solve problems and satisfy their curiosity (Su & Cheng, 2015).

In addition, engagement and motivation are some of the main factors that impact student performance during a learning process (Fatih, Kumalija & Sun, 2018). Mobile AR technologies offer a suitable pedagogical tool for ESD, as they enable students to learn and reflect on their behaviors by exploring the game. Furthermore, AR technology has opened new opportunities for building more attractive and pedagogical learning settings and is regarded as a type of "next-generation" pedagogical media for promoting learning quality, especially for outdoor exploration activities (Huang, 2019).

Teaching and learning that takes place outside the classroom, especially outside the school building, has other values and qualities, such as supporting contextualized and authentic learning by the direct contact with the phenomena to teach and learn, when compared with the more traditional form of education, taking place inside the classroom (Pombo & Marques, 2019). As a pedagogical approach, outdoor learning approaches may have something to offer since they support holistic and experiential learning and enable the integration of knowledge and skills from a range of discipline areas. Outdoor and environmental education research suggests that educational experiences in outdoor settings can be significant in developing environmental sensitivity and knowledge (Paixão, Jorge & Martins 2013).

This paper presents a study that articulates the previous project, the EduPARK, with the current one, the EduCITY. The initial project, EduPARK, developed an app that promotes an interdisciplinary, active, and contextualized learning experience through innovative teaching strategies that combine mobile learning, game-based learning, and AR, and integrates geocaching principles in an outdoor environment. Its educational laboratory was an urban green park, the Infante D. Pedro Park, in Aveiro (Portugal), where students and teachers from nearly all educational levels, and the broad public as well, could play educational treasure hunt games that prompted them to follow a path through several points of interest. The EduCITY project emerged from the need to expand the EduPARK to the city, so EduCITY combines mobile learning, AR, and environmental sensors towards sustainability education and creates opportunities for citizens to contribute to their city sustainability.

The next topic in this work describes the study's methodological options, which include the description of the EduPARK activity. Data collection, analysis procedures, and tools are also presented in this section. Follows the results presentation and discussion section, based on the results obtained through a student questionnaire (before and after the activity), a focus group, and an observation grid. Finally, some conclusions are put forward.

2. MATERIALS AND METHODS

This paper reports a mixed methods study that aims to analyze students' perceptions regarding changes in their nature conservation attitudes after exploring an urban green park in a mobile AR game-based learning activity. To answer the research question "How do the strategies used by EduPARK, with the exploration of "O Verdinho [The green game]", promote students' awareness about nature conservation?", the research team organized 13 activities for students to play the game. These activities involved 233 students (from school-year 5 to 9), from formal (involving schools) or non-formal (involving study and leisure centers) educational contexts. In each activity, students were organized in groups of 2-5 elements, according to the availability of adults to accompany the students in the park. Each group played the game for an average of one hour using a smartphone of the project, to reduce technological problems and concerns. The quiz game was previously downloaded to the mobile devices and no internet connection was required to play *in situ*. The game was developed under the first author's Ph.D. work (Rodrigues, Pombo & Neto, 2020).

This section comprises two subsections: i) a description of the EduPARK activity with "O Verdinho [The green game]"; and ii) data collection and analysis approaches and tools.

2.1 The Activity with "O Verdinho [The Green Game]"

The EduPARK activity was organized in various steps. At the beginning of the activity, all students were briefly informed about the research project and asked to fill in a pre-game questionnaire. All students who participated in the game were authorized by their parents. The game was developed for students of the 2nd and 3rd Cycle of Basic Education in formal and non-formal educational contexts.

In the activity, students played the quiz game "O Verdinho [The green game]" integrated into the EduPARK app (Figure 1) to be played at the Infante D. Pedro Park. The game includes 30 multiple choice questions about Science, Maths, Physical Education, and Citizenship Education. This quiz game was enriched with AR and other multimedia resources, such as videos and images, to promote student learning. Considering the influence that multimedia resources have on student learning, it was considered pertinent to include these resources in the game to assess the impact of their use in outdoor teaching and learning environments.

Figure 1. Students at the Infante D. Pedro Park playing "O Verdinho [The green game]" integrated into the EduPARK app

With this game we intend to influence positively the behavior of students towards nature conservation, focusing on the following topics: a) Waste (reduce, reuse, and recycle), b) Lake and biodiversity, c) Water and Energy, and d) Pollution. All these topics are related to an area of the park.

Students follows a path in the park through fifteen points of interest. In each one, students are prompt to answer one or several questions that require analyzing multimedia resources or their surroundings. For each question it was necessary to develop: i) question introduction and audio narration; ii) image, video, or audio (multimedia resources); iii) the question formulation; iv) four answer options (1 correct option and 3 incorrect options); v) feedback for correct and incorrect answers with audio narration; vi) multimedia resources for the feedback; vii) accumulated points (in correct answers) or points removed (in incorrect answers); viii) associate AR marker; and ix) instructions to find the AR marker (Figure 2).

After answering all the questions about the four topics, the users are challenged to find a virtual treasure in the park. Hence, geocaching principles are explored to enhance the gameplay experience for the users of the EduPARK app, by finding hidden virtual treasures to promote curiosity, a powerful intrinsic motivator (Pombo & Marques 2019).

Figure 2. Game illustrative screens

After the game, the students filled in a post-game questionnaire and participated in a focus group. The activity ended with a small prizes attribution to the teams with the best performance. However, all students received a participation award.

2.2 Data Collection and Analysis

Data collection included two questionnaires, applied before and after the game activity, one focus group interview guide, and an observation grid. Data was collected anonymously and did not include any personal information or set of information allowing the identification of specific participants.

The questionnaires were similar and complement each other. The aim is to: i) Analyze students' knowledge about nature conservation and what changed at this level through the educational game, and ii) Assess the impact of the game-based activity on changing students' attitude concerning of nature conservation, as perceived by the students. For this work, only the second aim was considered. Hence, the students' answers that were analyzed were: a) the open question asking to mention three "environmentally friendly attitudes"; and b) the question with seven sentences in a Likert scale.

The purpose of the focus group was to gather students' opinions regarding the evaluation of the EduPARK game, by collecting data on different kinds of evidence, such as the game's interest, willingness to change attitudes towards nature's conservation, knowledge, and insights. The students involved were randomly chosen by the adult who accompanied each group, and it was clarified that their collaboration was voluntary. Parents authorized their participation through an informed consent statement handed before the game.

Regarding the observation grid, a checklist was created with several inferences, divided into three well-defined categories, to facilitate completion by each observer. For this article, only the category of nature conservation is considered. The grid was given to each observer before the activity, and was filled in during the game, whenever they observed a certain inference, or at the end of the activity. The observers were teachers and monitors who accompanied the groups and members of the EduPARK project.

Regarding the results of the EduPARK game app, descriptive statistics (a quantitative analysis) of the responses to the game "O Verdinho [The green game]" was carried out. Regarding the two questionnaires, all multiple-choice questions were analyzed quantitatively, except an open-ended question that was analyzed qualitatively using the WebQDA software, as well as responses to the focus group, through content analysis. The observation grid was filled in by 46 observers, particularly the researcher, the teachers/monitors who accompanied the students, and some EduPARK researchers, and it was analyzed quantitatively.

In this research, the quantitative data were analyzed through descriptive statistics and presented in the form of tables. The qualitative data were analyzed in the logic of content analysis and resorted to the categorization based on students' responses (Amado & Vieira, 2017). The questionnaire results were triangulated with the student's responses to the focus group to analyze the value of this game for the promotion of nature conservation attitudes (Coutinho, 2019).

3. RESULTS AND DISCUSSION

This section starts with the analysis of students' responses to the open questions of the questionnaires (before and after the activity). Before the activity, the nature conservation measures most mentioned by students were recycling, reducing water consumption, and preserving the atmosphere. After the activity, students mentioned again these nature conservation measures. However, they mentioned as well new measures related to the game topics, namely: recycling cooking oil, reducing microplastics, reducing food and textile waste, and preserving lichens bees, and turtles.

Through the analysis of the questionnaire responses, before the activity, a high percentage of students considered important to preserve nature (Table 1). Regarding the sentence 1 "My actions contribute to the increase of the greenhouse effect", the results do not allow taking conclusions since students' opinion are divided similarly, about 30% of answers are *neutral*, 36.5 % are *disagree* and *strongly disagree*, and 26.2% are *agree* and *strongly agree*.

The same happens in the sentence 5 "I'm not used to check the composition of my hygiene products, to see if they have microplastics in their composition", where 26.2% of students answer neutrally, 34.8% answer *agree* and *strongly agree*, and 30.9% *disagree* and *strongly disagree* with the statement.

On the other hand, students answered with more certainty, answering *agree* and *strongly agree*, to the sentence 2 "At home, I separate the waste for recycling" (71.2%), sentence 6 "I feel good when I have environmentally friendly behaviors" (83.2%), and sentence 7 "I feel capable of encouraging friends/family to conserve nature" (71.1%).

Moreover, 67% of students revealed consciousness regarding one of the biggest environmental problems today, the pollution of beaches and oceans, through their answer to the sentence 4 "When I go to the beach, I don't care about the waste I produce". In addition, 54.1% of students expressed regret when they use more energy, water, or fossil fuels than they need, while 29.2% of students responded neutrally to sentence 3.

Table 1. Students' perceptions before the activity regarding their attitudes toward nature conservation

Sentences	***Likert scale***				
	Strongly disagree	***Disagree***	***Neutral***	***Agree***	***Strongly agree***
1. My actions contribute to the increase of the greenhouse effect.	17,2%	19,3%	29,2%	15,9%	10,3%
2. At home, I separate the waste for recycling.	3,9%	5,2%	11,6%	30,9%	40,3%
3. I feel guilty when I use more resources (energy, water, fossil fuels…) than I need.	4,7%	3,9%	29,2%	28,8%	25,3%
4. When I go to the beach, I don't care about the waste I produce.	42,5%	24,5%	11,2%	9,0%	5,6%
5. I'm not used to check the composition of my hygiene products, to see if they have microplastics in their composition.	13,3%	17,6%	26,2%	24,5%	10,3%
6. I feel good when I have environmentally friendly behaviors.	0,9%	1,3%	6,0%	24,0%	59,2%
7. I feel capable of encouraging friends/family to conserve nature.	2,1%	1,3%	16,7%	36,5%	35,2%

Voided answers: 7,7%

An overall view about the answers to the questionnaire applied after the game indicates that students felt more capable and confident in answering the questions, since the percentage of neutral responses decreased when compared to the questionnaire applied before the game. This may demonstrate that students respond with more certainty after playing the game (Table 2). On the other hand, these data revealed that, after the activity, most students became more aware of the change in their attitude towards nature conservation.

Table 2. Students' perceptions after the activity regarding their attitudes toward nature conservation

Sentences	*Likert scale*				
After this activity...	*Strongly disagree*	*Disagree*	*Neutral*	*Agree*	*Strongly agree*
1....I will contribute to the increase of the greenhouse effect.	56,2%	18,0%	7,3%	5,6%	4,7%
2....I will separate the waste for recycling.	0,9%	1,7%	6,9%	24,9%	57,9%
3....I will do my best not to use more resources (energy, water, fossil fuels, etc.) than I need.	3,4%	3,0%	18,9%	30,0%	36,9%
4....I won't worry about the waste I produce on the beach.	60,5%	16,7%	4,3%	7,3%	3,0%
5.... I will start checking the composition of my hygiene products, to see if they have microplastics, which are harmful to the environment.	4,7%	3,4%	30,0%	30,9%	23,2%
6....I feel that I should always behave in an environmentally friendly way.	0%	0%	2,6%	23,6%	66,1%
7....I feel more able to encourage friends/family to conserve nature.	1,3%	2,1%	11,2%	33,0%	44,6%

Voided answers:7,7%

As mentioned earlier, in the pre-game questionnaire it was not possible draw conclusions regarding the students' opinions about their attitudes towards the greenhouse effect. However, in the post-game questionnaire, the students felt more able to state their opinion in sentence 1 "I will contribute to the increase of the greenhouse effect", as the answers in the *neutral* option dropped expressively (-21.9%) and there was a small number of students (10.3%) who answered *agree* or *strongly agree*. On this matter, during the focus group, only one student reflected on the increase in the greenhouse effect, saying: "*If we continue to pollute as we are now, the animals will be homeless".*

Regarding sentence 2 "I will separate the waste for recycling", the percentage of students stating they will recycle after the activity increased from 71.2% to 82.9%. This indicates that more students were acknowledging the importance of separating waste for recycling. This sentence generated a lot of discussion in the focus group, where the students mobilized topics addressed in the game, particularly the separation of used cooking oil for recycling: *"I intend to separate waste, such as cooking oil."; "I'm going to talk to my parents about using the oil collection tank"* and *"I'm going to talk to my mother about the cooking oil, we usually pour the used oil at home."*

Part of the students (67%) *agree* or *strongly agree* whit the sentence 3 "I will do my best not to use more resources (energy, water, fossil fuels, etc.) than I need". In the focus group, the two ideas most discussed by the students were food waste and water-saving measures. Regarding food waste, the students mentioned game content: *"Buy less bread! I will never go to the bakery again to buy too much bread, just one for each person."* In addition, students valued water and expressed their willingness to save this resource: *"When I'm brushing my teeth, I used to leave the faucet running and now I'm going to start turning it off."*

The sentence 4 "I won't worry about the waste I produce on the beach", purposely written in the negative to assess students' attention when filling in the questionnaires, demonstrates that students are concerned with the waste in the beach. After the activity, more students (+ 10.2%) marked *strongly disagree* or *disagree*. In the focus group, the students demonstrated that they were concerned about the pollution of beaches and oceans and were aware of the need to adopt actions in the future to reduce it, particularly plastic pollution, as shown by the statement: *"The most worrisome thing for me is air pollution and plastic on the ground and in the sea. Poor turtles!".*

The sentence 5 "I will start checking the composition of my hygiene products, to see if they have microplastics, which are harmful to the environment" was the one that obtained the highest percentage of students selecting the *neutral* option (30%), which is most likely associated with the student's lack of knowledge about the topic. After the activity, more students *agree* (+ 6.4%) and *strongly agree* (+ 12.9%) with the statement. In the focus group, the students highlighted this aspect: *"with the videos and images we learned about microplastics"*.

Moreover, students' answers reflect a degree of enthusiasm for the change in nature conservation attitudes, as they revealed feeling more capable of having "environmentally friendly" behaviors. In addition, students felt more confident and able to encourage friends and family to conserve nature, as a minority marked the options *disagree* and *strongly disagree*. It should be noted that more than 9.4% of the students marked the option *strongly agree* in the post-game questionnaire. This is also evident in the responses to the focus group: *"It is important to have knowledge about everything that is going on and apply it and this activity was important for that, for us to learn and change"*.

In short, the data collected through the answers to both questionnaires (before and after the activity) showed that the students were more aware of the relevance of conserving nature and that they intend to change some of their attitudes towards the planet.

Finally, the observation grid emphasized these results. From the perspective of the observers that accompanied the students throughout the game, during this activity, students referred to nature conservation attitudes that they take daily, whilst making associations with the game contents. Moreover, students created expectations about nature conservation attitudes that they would pass on to family and friends. Observers also mentioned that AR and multimedia resources, integrated into the app, promoted motivation and nature conservation learning.

4. CONCLUSION

According to UNESCO (2015), it is essential to raise awareness and sensitize students to environmental problems, intending to raise their awareness to nature conservation. This paper summarizes the results of several activities of playing the "O Verdinho [The green game]" integrated into the EduPARK app, developed with the aim of raising awareness concerning attitudes towards nature conservation.

Firstly, this study results reveal the participant students were already well informed about some of the topics explored through the game. Nevertheless, it was also evident that, after the activity, they became more confident, aware, and sensitized to other environmental problems.

Regarding nature conservation attitudes presented by students, recycling and reducing water consumption were the two most mentioned. However, results indicate that students were more sensitized, after the activity, because they mentioned new attitudes related to the game topics, namely: recycling cooking oil, reducing microplastics, reducing food and textile waste, and preserving lichens, bees, and turtles.

After the activity, students mentioned being concerned about reducing resources waste, recycling waste and used cooking oil, reducing pollution caused by microplastics, and protecting fauna and flora, more specifically protecting bees, as they are endangered species. Moreover, students showed that they felt more capable of conserving nature, as they revealed willingness to sensitize friends and family about what they have learned with the EduPARK game.

The EduPARK app proved to be an educational tool with great potential for Education for Sustainable Development (ESD). Innovative interdisciplinary practices, combined with curricular integrated outdoor activities supported by mobile technologies, allowed to sensitize students for nature conservation. The EduCITY intends to continue these practices throughout Aveiro city. Hence, EduCITY opens the park boundaries to the city, and to other cities, seeking to strengthen the university network with community partners, such as schools, municipalities, and enterprises. This network fosters knowledge further and creates opportunities for everyone to contribute to the cities' sustainability, meaning that other cities can be inspired by it, and replicate the ideas and solutions emerging from this project.

This project is anchored on a community-based participatory approach integrating AR location games based on challenges, to be explored in the city, in formal, non-formal, and informal educational contexts, in a socio constructivism approach. In terms of future work, within the EduCITY project, it is proposed to carry out activities related to ESD with a higher number of students and teachers from different school contexts, and the general public.

This study adds to the literature on ESD, by revealing that it is possible to sensitize school students to nature conservation through mobile AR game-based approaches in the outdoors, which can be a first step to promote positive nature attitudes.

ACKNOWLEDGEMENT

This work is funded by Portuguese funds through FCT – Foundation for Science and Technology within the framework of the EduCITY project "PTDC/CED-EDG/0197/2021". The EduPARK project is funded by FEDER – Fundo Europeu de Desenvolvimento Regional funds through the COMPETE 2020 – Operational Programme for Competitiveness and Internationalisation (POCI), and by Portuguese funds through FCT within the framework of the project POCI-01-0145-FEDER-016542.

The first author's work is funded by Portuguese Funds through FCT with a research grant (SFRH/BD/139048/2018) within the Doctoral Program in Multimedia in Education.

The third author's work is funded by Portuguese funds (state budget), through University of Aveiro, in the scope of the framework contract foreseen in the numbers 4, 5 and 6 of the article 23, of the Decree-Law 57/2016, of August 29, changed by Law 57/2017, of July 19.

REFERENCES

Amado, J. & Vieira, C 2017, 'A validação da investigação qualitativa', in João Amado (ed), Manual de investigação qualitativa em Educação , Imprensa da Universidade de Coimbra, Coimbra, pp. 359–378.

Coutinho, C 2019, Metodologia de Investigação em Ciências Sociais e Humanas: Teoria e Prática 2nd edn, Edições Almedina, Coimbra.

Fatih, Y, Kumalija, J & Sun, Y 2018, 'Mobile learning-based gamification in a history learning context', in 14h International Conference Mobile Learning 2018, Lisboa, pp. 143–147.

Huang, TC 2019, 'Seeing creativity in an augmented experiential learning environment', Universal Access in the Information Society, vol. 18, no. 2, pp. 301–313.

Paixão, F, Jorge, FR & Martins, H 2013, 'Aprender no jardim: matemática criativa com a sombra', in Encontro ensinar e aprender matemática com criatividade dos 3 aos 12 anos, Associação de Professores de Matemática, Viana do Castelo, pp. 17–29, retrieved from <http://hdl.handle.net/10400.11/2146>.

Pombo, L & Marques, M 2019, 'Educational Mobile Augmented Reality EduPARK game: Does it improve students learning?', in I Sánches, P Isaías, P Ravesteijn, & G Ongena (eds), 15th International Conference Mobile Learning 2019, Utreque, pp. 19–26.

Rodrigues, R, Pombo, L & Neto, T 2020, 'Aprender a conservar a Natureza: construção do guião educativo integrado na aplicação móvel EduPARK', in A Carvalho, F Revuelta, D Guimarães, A Moura, C Marques, I Santos, & S Cruz (eds), Atas do V Encontro sobre Jogos e Mobile Learning., Centro de Estudos Interdisciplinares do Século 20 (CEIS20); Universidade de Coimbra -Coimbra, Coimbra, pp. 502–510, retrieved November 30, 2022, from <http://hdl.handle.net/10316/89364>.

Su, CH & Cheng, CH 2015, 'A mobile gamification learning system for improving the learning motivation and achievements', Journal of Computer Assisted Learning, vol. 31, no. 3, pp. 268–286.

United Nations 2015, Transforming our world: the 2030 Agenda for Sustainable Development, retrieved October 18, 2022, from <https://www.refworld.org/docid/57b6e3e44.html>.

United Nations Educational Scientific and Cultural Organization 2017, Educação para os Objetivos de Desenvolvimento Sustentável Objetivos de aprendizagem, retrieved from <http://unesco.org/>

SHORT

PAPERS

CROSS-CULTURAL EDUCATION IN ASIA USING ONLINE COMMUNICATION TOOLS AND THE DIALOGBOOK

Jun Iio[1], Shigenori Wakabayashi[2], Junji Sakurai[3] and Yuya Nakagawa[4]
[1]*Faculty of Global-Informatics, Chuo University,1-18 Ichigaya-tamachi, Shinjuku-ku, Tokyo, 162-8478, Japan*
[2]*Faculty of Letters, Chuo University,742-1 Higashi-nakano, Hachioji-shi, Tokyo, 192-0393, Japan*
[3]*Sekisaibo, LLC.3-7-1 Akebono, Kashiwa-shi, Chiba, 277-0841, Japan*
[4] *Faculty of Education, Mie University 1577 Kurimamachiya-cho, Tsu-shi, Mie, 514-8507, Japan*

ABSTRACT

The significance of intercultural communication has steadily increased in today's global era. However, partly due to Japan's remote geographic location, it is difficult for Japanese people to travel abroad; this is especially true for the younger generations. Since 2020, we have been conducting the Students Meet Internationally through Learning English (SMILE) project to offer opportunities for Japanese students to communicate with other students living in foreign countries. In the SMILE project, students use the online meeting tools to communicate with each other and the Dialogbook, which was developed as a learning portfolio system, to record and support their learning activities. This paper provides an overview of the project and explains the current situation.

KEYWORDS

Cross-Cultural Education, Online Communication Tools, Learning Portfolio System, Dialogbook

1. INTRODUCTION

With the vast and pervasive spread of internet technologies, global communication infrastructure has become a commodity; global communication is now a necessity for businesspeople who work internationally. In addition, since the coronavirus disease 2019 pandemic prevented physical overseas travel, we have become accustomed to using online communication tools, such as Zoom, Webex, Skype, Google Meet, and Microsoft Teams.

Under these circumstances, the significance of cross-cultural education, which enables students to engage in intercultural communication, has steadily increased. To provide such an education, several pedagogical methods have been proposed. One such method is Content and Language Integrated Learning (CLIL), which is expected to foster intercultural understanding. For example, Yang (2021) showed that content-driven CLIL learners obtained slightly higher cultural quotient scores than their language-driven CLIL English-major peers.

The Collaborative Online International Language (COIL; Appiah-Kubi, 2020) is also a typical method of learning international communication in English. However, COIL programs are led mainly by western communities; since many western languages are similar to English, learning English communication is relatively easy for them. However, eastern languages, including Japanese, are very different from western languages. Therefore, learning English could be more difficult for eastern students than for those from the west.

For eastern people like the authors of this paper, it is essential to learn English as the lingua franca. Considering this, the Students Meet Internationally through Learning English (SMILE) project was established to offer Japanese students the opportunity to communicate with other students living in foreign countries (Wakabayashi et al., 2021). The SMILE project started in the academic year (AY) 2020 and is currently in its third year. In this project, students communicate with each other using online meeting tools. Additionally, to record and support students' learning activities, we developed the Dialogbook (Iio and Wakabayashi, 2020).

This paper provides an overview of the SMILE project, the current situation, and the future vision of the project.

2. THE SMILE PROJECT

This section provides a brief introduction to the project.

2.1 An Overview of the Project

As described previously, the SMILE project was created to provide opportunities for students from Japan and its neighboring countries to communicate with each other using online meeting tools. The distinctive features of the project are as follows:

1. Cross-cultural education is conducted between Japanese and foreign schools; the counterpart schools are mainly chosen from Japan's neighboring countries.
2. International communication is conducted using online meeting tools, where two or three students participate from both sides.
3. The project offers specific programs, starting with the preparation and ending with the reflection; it includes at least three online communication lessons and employs coordinators who support the classes.
4. The aim of the project is not only to provide opportunities for learning cross-cultural communication for students but also to allow teachers the experience of facilitating such lessons.

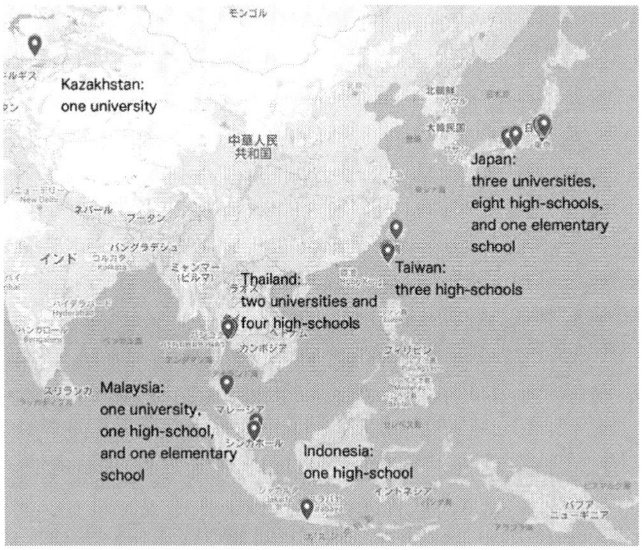

Universities	Faculty of Letters, Chuo University	Japan
	ITL, Chuo University	Japan
	Soka University	Japan
	King Mongkut's Institute of Technology Ladkrabang	Thailand
	King Mongkut's University of Technology Thonburi	Thailand
	Universiti Teknologi Malaysia	Malaysia
	Suleyman Demirel University (SDU)	Kazakhstan
High schools	Dokkyo Senior High School	Japan
	Toshimagaoka-joshigakuen Senior High School	Japan
	Seishin Gakuen Senior High School	Japan
	Tsukuihama Senior High School	Japan
	Ichihara Chuo Seninor High School	Japan
	Chuo University Senior High School	Japan
	Sakainishi Senior High School	Japan
	Taweethapisek school in Bangkok	Thailand
	Rattaphumwittaya School, Songkhla	Thailand
	Rajprachasamasai Phaimathayom Rachadabhisek	Thailand
	Watsuthiwararam School	Thailand
	Fu Cheng Senior High School	Taiwan
	Taipei Municipal Yong Chun Senior High School	Taiwan
	SMK Sri Mersing	Malaysia
	SMA Negeri 1 Yogyakarta (SMAN1)	Indonesia
ES	Kurima Elementary School	Japan
	SJK(T) Taman Tun Aminah	Malaysia

Figure 1. The map (left) and the list (right) of the schools participating in the SMILE project in AY 2022

2.1.1 Participating Schools

Figure 1 is a map containing the locations of the schools participating in the SMILE project. In AY 2022, approximately 500 students from six universities, seventeen high schools, and two elementary schools from Japan, Taiwan, Thailand, Malaysia, Kazakhstan, and Indonesia, will participate in the project. The fundamental criteria for choosing the counterpart countries are: 1. the time difference with Japan should be two or three hours at most, and 2. they should be non-English native countries.

It is relatively difficult to make the schedule for the communication classes because of the differences in education systems; daily timetables and school year calendars between the participating countries deviate. Therefore, choosing counterpart schools from countries with minor time differences is preferable. In addition, countries with minor time differences easily accommodate real-time online communication.

It is also significant that the counterpart countries should be non-English native countries. We choose the counterpart schools from the east-Asian and south-east Asian countries, excluding Singapore, Hongkong, and the Philippines. The project considers English to be a lingua-franca and global communication tool. Hence, both parties should not be native English speakers or use English as a daily conversation tool. Several third parties in Japan provide English conversation training programs outside of schools. Nevertheless, most students lack the chance to meet other students of their generation who are not native English speakers. In that sense, our project can provide students with better opportunities than others.

2.1.2 Online Group Meetings

When international communication classes are conducted, most students enjoy conversing in English, even though they may speak English incorrectly. Since the students are unfamiliar with using English, conducting one-by-one English communication sessions could be challenging. To solve this problem, the project divides the classes into small plural groups and arranges communication groups with two or three members on either side (see Figure 2).

Figure 2. Group members, students from a Taiwanese school (left) and a Japanese school (right), participated in the SMILE project

Students nowadays are familiar with using IT devices such as smartphones and personal computers. Therefore, if they feel uncomfortable with the conversation, they can employ various other communication methods, such as drawing figures on paper, showing pictures on smartphones, writing text messages, and chatting. The project allows them to use all these forms of interaction because the aim is not to learn English conversation but to get accustomed to cross-cultural communication.

2.1.3 Typical Curriculum and Coordinators

The project offers a typical program template, starting with preparation and ending with a reflection session, and includes at least three international communication classes. From our experience in the three years of operation, we have accumulated some valuable materials, such as students' worksheets, presentation materials, and informed consent forms for collecting data from the participants. Those resources can also be used as educational materials.

The project also provides session coordinators. They help the teachers conduct the lessons thoroughly by facilitating previous and subsequent meetings for the international communication classes, setting proper information on the Dialogbook, and preparing informed consent forms.

2.1.4 Learning Opportunities for Both Students and Teachers

Finally, the essential point of the project is to provide opportunities for students and teachers alike. The project offers practical lessons on how to foster teachers' skills.

2.2 Tools Used in the Project

The online meeting tools and the Dialogbook are critical for conducting cross-cultural education.

2.2.1 Online Meeting Tools

Students should converse using online meeting tools. The project does not specify which online meeting tool should be used because of many conditions and problems in choosing such tools on educational sites. For example, Taiwan's educational board prohibits using Zoom for security reasons, so the schools interacting with Taiwanese schools should use other software, such as Webex and Google Meet.

Configurations must be considered in addition to tool choice. Japanese public schools tend to restrict the functions of the software they use. Therefore, checking availability is critical before conducting practical classes.

2.2.2 Dialogbook

Contemporary schools use learning management systems (LMS). However, normal LMSs are only available within one school range, meaning that only students, teachers, and staff in the school can access the system. This restriction in using LMSs is an obstacle to the interaction between schools. It is the main reason for developing the Dialogbook for the project.

The Dialogbook has several functions; meeting management is the primary one. Managing connecting information is essential, as is providing accurate information to the students to get into their assigned meeting rooms. This information can be shared between the participants from the Japanese and counterpart schools. Additionally, functions for rubrics management and simple chatting between students and teachers are provided by the Dialogbook.

3. CONCLUSION

This paper presented an overview of the SMILE project and its IT tools. The project aims to provide low-cost intercultural education by connecting schools in Japan and neighboring countries via online conference systems. The information system called Dialogbook was developed to conduct the project efficiently.

In AY 2022, approximately 500 students from 25 institutes participate in the project. We are planning to expand the size of the project larger. If the readers of this paper are interested in it, please feel free to contact us.

ACKNOWLEDGMENT

This project is supported by "Grant for Establishing Interdisciplinary Research Cluster, Chuo University," and JSPS KAKENHI Grant Number 22K00689. We thank all the students and teachers for participating in the project and providing valuable data for research on their learning activities.

REFERENCES

Appiah-Kubi, P. and Annan, E., (2020). A review of a collaborative online international learning. *International Journal of Engineering Pedagogy*, 10(1), 109-124.

Iio, J. and Wakabayashi, S., (2020). Dialogbook: A Proposal for Simple e-Portfolio System for International Communication Learning, *International Journal of Web Information Systems,* 16(5), 611-622.

Yang, W., (2021). Developing intercultural competence: A comparison of CLIL and language majors before and after industrial placements. In *International Perspectives on CLIL,* pp. 129-148. Palgrave Macmillan, Cham.

Wakabayshi, S., Iio, J., Ramayah, K., Komoto, R., and Sakurai, J., (2022). How ICT Tools Support a Course Centered on International Collaboration Classes, *IFIP WCCE 2022: World Conference on Computers in Education,* 2C-3, Hiroshima, Japan.

A DATA ACQUISITION FRAMEWORK FOR BUILDING ENERGY MANAGEMENT

Konstantinos Touloumis, Panagiotis Kapsalis, Elissaios Sarmas, Stathis Stamatopoulos, Vangelis Marinakis and Haris Doukas
Decision Support Systems Laboratory, School of Electrical and Computer Engineering, National Technical University of Athens, 9 Iroon Polytechniou Str., 15773 Athens, Greece

ABSTRACT

Collecting data for providing energy analytics services has closely been dependent on Building Management Systems (BMSs). A BMS connected to a set of sensors and other electronic devices aims at observing a collection of rooms in terms of temperature, humidity, and other energy related metrics with the goal of maximining user comfort while preserving energy consumption. The tasks of collecting, preprocessing, storing and querying data on a BMS faces the same challenges with those of querying big data in terms of scalability, data heterogeneity, and integration. This paper presents a framework that addresses the problem of collecting sensor data in one enriched data warehouse which follows a common ontology model. Data from various data sources is homogenized by appropriate data preprocessing and feature extraction techniques. The framework allows timeseries-oriented querying with the target outcome of providing stakeholders high detailed analytics services for decision making on energy consumption optimization, building renovation and financing.

KEYWORDS

Building Energy, Analytics, Big Data Pipeline, Energy Data Modelling, Building Data Processing

1. INTRODUCTION

Managing data on the energy sector is of significant importance since the building sector accounts for almost one fourth of the energy consumed worldwide (International Energy Outlook 2016), for electric lighting (Yun et al., 2012) and appliances (Ridi et al., 2014). The problem becomes even greater when it comes down to CO_2 emissions as the building sector is responsible for almost 40% of the global CO_2 emissions (Hu, 2022). The rapid rise in the energy demand of the building sector comes along with the exponential growth of networking capabilities including the Internet of Things (IoT) (Marinakis & Doukas, 2018), which has led to an outburst of data collected by sensors in large scale networks. Thus, efficient management on the building sector is of crucial importance for preserving energy consumption and further reducing environmental harm. Big data querying frameworks try to leverage the problem of collecting, processing, and providing data analytics services. Many approaches have integrated big data analytics methods for efficient data management on the building sector and will be analyzed thoroughly in the next sections.

The problem of handling data from buildings addresses a number of challenges as mentioned in (Pau et al., 2022). Firstly, the problem of automated data integration, as data is collected from various data sources and includes both real time and historical data. Secondly, the problem of data scaling, as sensors produce densely populated data on a high rate leading to large quantity of data within a small-time frame. The data heterogeneity is another major concern, as data is stored in different formats between sensors which makes data preprocessing a complex task, so a common ontology model is needed to project data from various data sources onto a common dataspace. Finally advanced monitoring and querying both real time and historical data along with aggregations is a complex but essential task for supporting high level user driven services (Marinakis et al., 2020).

The purpose of this paper is to present a framework for managing big data from the building sector. The proposed framework manages to efficiently deal with the aforementioned challenges. The steps of the framework are the following: Collecting data, to support efficient big data management and scalability the solution is built upon a data warehouse which receives real time streams of data from various sensors.

Preprocessing data, with appropriate feature extraction, normalization, data harmonization techniques and ontology modelling. A common ontology model will be used to address the problem of data heterogeneity which not only reuses existing ontologies models like BRICK (Balaji et al., 2016) and SAREF (Daniele et al., 2015) but is also FIWARE compliant (Rodriguez et al., 2018) to ensure data sovereignty and protection. Storing the processed data in a timeseries database that will allow high level time series querying thus allowing users to have a deeper understanding on how the energy consumption varies on different indoor and outdoor parameters.

2. BACKGROUND

As mentioned in (Minoli et al., 2017) a traditional BMS comprises of the following layers: The field layer, which consists of all the sensors installed on the building premises. The automation layer, which applies strategies derived from a set of rules. The management layer, that manages the functionality of a BMS. BMSs are often limited in storage capacity and act isolated from the entire network. In the same research a system for collecting building data is structured that uses the notion of virtual objects that can be mapped to a real sensor through an ID created by a specialized collector. Tokens are used to protect the data flow and a MySQL database is used to augment metadata with a virtual object and transmit it through Kafka messaging. However, the research later mentions that at the storage level the NoSQL databases are compromising between consistency, availability and partition tolerance known as the CAP theorem (Davoudian et al., 2019). Also, Kafka messaging is not suitable for computing time-based aggregations on streams (le Noac'h et al., 2017).

Similarly, another big data system for analytics on the building sector is analyzed in (Pau et al., 2022) that firstly preprocesses data to remove incomplete or inaccurate data, and then uses Kafka for transmitting data because of its high throughput and latency but ignores its inefficiency for time-based aggregation on time-series streams. Data is then harmonized and projected onto a common data model. The enriched data is stored in a Mongo DB that acts as the enriched data warehouse. On top of the warehouse the Presto (Sethi et al., 2019) technology is used, a distributed query engine that provides high level of abstraction for querying different data sources. However, it should be mentioned that Presto is not tailor made for querying time series data in contrast to other databases like InfluxDB (Nasar & Kausar, 2019) which can query large scale time series data without extract, transform, load (ETL).

Efficient management and monitoring of energy consumption data can benefit stakeholders in many ways. Analytics services can be built upon the upper layer of the proposed framework that will assist decision making for the following purposes: Monitoring the energy consumption, aimed at improving the building energy performance. Predicting, by using appropriate models, the energy demand towards minimizing energy consumption across different weather conditions (Karakolis et al., 2022). Designing and enhancing building infrastructure, aimed at assisting the design and development of building infrastructure, retrofitting and refurbishment actions. Designing climate resilient buildings that will ensure people comfort and well-being while preserving energy consumption (Yang et al., 2022). Creating green policies towards building sustainability, aimed at assisting policy making towards sustainable action plans, energy performance certificates, and assessing the impact of EU policies for buildings (El-Diraby et al., 2017). Decision making for energy efficient buildings, aimed at assisting in making accurate predictions on energy consumption, towards contributing to Energy performance contract conditions, EU financing institutions, and centralizing building stock data (Marinakis, 2020).

3. ARCHITECTURE

The proposed framework collects both building sensor and electricity consumption data and is depicted in Figure 1. The framework follows a modular architecture with every layer strongly interoperating with its previous and next one.

BMS: The Building Management System is an embedded system that includes sensors, meters and actuators for measuring energy related data in the building rooms. Such data includes the humidity and the temperature of the monitored building, as well as electricity consumption data from lighting, A/C meters and ventilation. All the collected information is reported in CSV files every 5 minutes. The CSV files are transformed to ZIP files and are sent to the FTP Staging Area.

Staging Area: The Staging Area uses the FTP (File Transfer Protocol) to send the collected data to the central data warehouse. The staging area authentication information and credentials should be declared in the BMS to transfer the measured data. The Staging Area is used as the intermediate layer of the framework where raw data is persisted and can further be analyzed by the next modules.

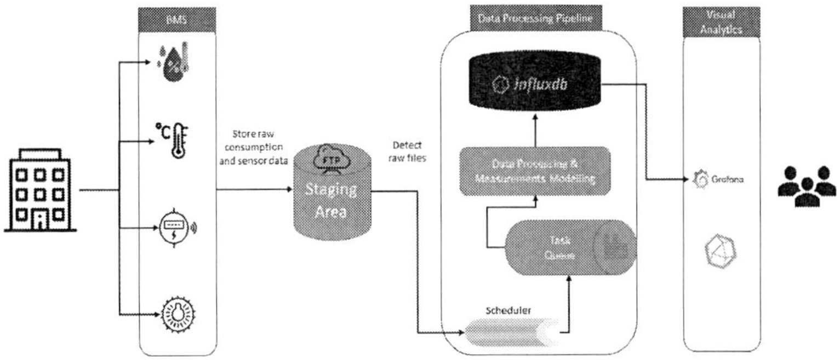

Figure 1. Building data processing pipeline

Data Processing Pipeline: The Data Processor is the module responsible for detecting the incoming raw information from the FTP Staging Area, scheduling and prioritizing data pipeline workers, pre-processing and cleaning raw data, modelling the processed information and finally storing it to an InfluxDB instance. More specifically each sub-module functionality is described below:

- **Data Processing Pipeline Scheduler**: It is a software component implemented with Python 3.7. It uses the Celery Task Scheduling Framework that is triggered periodically every 1 hour and collects all new raw information from the Staging Area. By leveraging the functionalities of the Celery framework, the tasks and the computational load are distributed to machine threads. The information is then sent to the Task Queue to be processed from the Data Processing and Measurements Modelling sub-modules.
- **Task Queue**: It is a RabbitMQ instance, connected to the Framework Scheduler that manages the collected data for processing and modelling.
- **Data Processing & Measurements Modelling**: This module receives events to be processed and modelled from the Task Queue. It is implemented with Pandas DataFrame and InfluxDB Python drivers. It conducts the pre-processing steps (removing duplicates, handling null values, detecting outliers, transforming dates) to improve the data quality. The collected data is divided in smaller data collections according to the measured information.
- **InfluxDB Storage**: It is the timeseries database that structures the stored information in measurements and tags. In the current design the metrics measured are the humidity, temperature and electricity consumption from lighting, ventilation, and air-conditioning. The tags are the device names that the measured information originates from.

Visual Analytics: The Grafana visualization engine will be used for visualizing analytics. Grafana is a well-known opensource interactive visualization web platform that allows users to create customized dashboards, charts and graphs. Grafana is connected to the InfluxDB storage and will allow users to visualize analytics that will let them further explore and infer logical relations between data coming from various data sources.

In order to define a data model to project various data sources onto a common dataspace, the ontology development 101 (Pullmann et al., 2017) is being followed which defines the steps needed for that purpose. The FIWARE smart data model offers data models for modeling many domains including the building and energy domains, since it defines the properties and the facets of the slots, but it lacks hierarchy between smart cities domain (Kapsalis et al., 2022). The BRICK ontology can be used for representing relationships between buildings and sensors, but it lacks properties and facets. SAREF defines many recurring objects from different ontologies in the building domain which can provide features and assist less experienced modelers.

However, control strategies over spaces are not included in all SAREF extensions. The EPC4EU models the energy performance certificate datasets in different geographical scales, however, the EPC4CEU doesn't store information about sensors. Finally, the created ontology is translated to a data model by following the ontology development 101 method. The model is depicted in Figure 2.

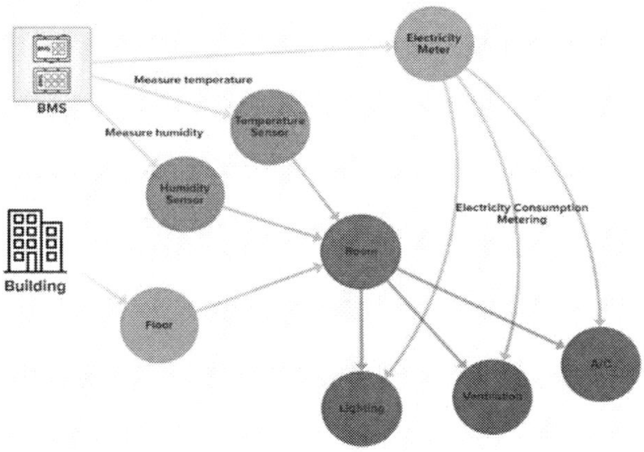

Figure 2. Constructed data model

The constructed data model is aligned with the information stored in the Influx timeseries database. More specifically, the timeseries information includes the measured values of electricity consumption from lighting, ventilation, and air-conditioning functionalities of the room. A logical entity of the constructed ontology model is the "Building", that has floors and rooms. The main entity of the conceptual Building data model is the "Room", facilitating lighting, air conditioning and ventilation. The logical model "BMS" represents the temperature, the humidity of the room and its electricity consumption from lighting, ventilation, and air-conditioning. In our experiment we have established a first level of tags, the room IDs, and a second level of tags, the source types that produce the recorded information (lights, ventilation system, air-conditioning).

4. CONCLUSION & FUTURE OUTLOOK

The framework presented in this research collects, analyzes, and homogenizes data coming from various energy sources to monitor the energy consumption of buildings. The power market to stay competitive needs to predict the electrical power consumption in both short and long term. Load forecasting aims at predicting the demand of energy consumption towards efficient power distribution construction and planning (Fekri et al., 2021). The proposed framework can be used in forecasting the energy consumption of buildings. By adding weather data such as the wind speed, solar radiation and by applying Deep Learning (DL) techniques, models can be trained to predict the energy consumption on different weather conditions and further assist building administrators in efficient energy planning. Deep learning techniques can handle big data by capturing the inherent non-linear features through automatic feature extraction methods. This work will be expanded by adding an offline training stage where data captured by the framework will be used to train robust predictive models, such as RNNs, LSTMs, for both short- and long-term energy consumption.

ACKNOWLEDGEMENT

This work has been co-funded by the European Union's Horizon Europe research and innovation programme under the DigiBUILD project, Grant Agreement No 101069658.

REFERENCES

Balaji, B., Bhattacharya, A., Fierro, G., Gao, J., Gluck, J., Hong, D., Johansen, A., Koh, J., Ploennigs, J., Agarwal, Y., Berges, M., Culler, D., Gupta, R., Kjærgaard, M. B., Srivastava, M., & Whitehouse, K. (2016). Brick. *Proceedings of the 3rd ACM International Conference on Systems for Energy-Efficient Built Environments*, 41–50. https://doi.org/10.1145/2993422.2993577

Daniele, L., den Hartog, F., & Roes, J. (2015). *Created in Close Interaction with the Industry: The Smart Appliances Reference (SAREF) Ontology* (pp. 100–112). https://doi.org/10.1007/978-3-319-21545-7_9

Davoudian, A., Chen, L., & Liu, M. (2019). A Survey on NoSQL Stores. *ACM Computing Surveys*, *51*(2), 1–43. https://doi.org/10.1145/3158661

El-Diraby, T., Krijnen, T., & Papagelis, M. (2017). BIM-based collaborative design and socio-technical analytics of green buildings. *Automation in Construction*, *82*, 59–74. https://doi.org/10.1016/j.autcon.2017.06.004

Karakolis E., Pelekis S., Mouzakitis S., Markaki O., Papapostolou K., Korbakis G., & Psarras J., (2022). Artificial Intelligence for Next Generation Energy Services across Europe–The I-NERGY Project. *IADIS International Conference E-Society 2022 (e-Society 2022)*, 61–68.

Fekri, M. N., Patel, H., Grolinger, K., & Sharma, V. (2021). Deep learning for load forecasting with smart meter data: Online Adaptive Recurrent Neural Network. *Applied Energy*, *282*, 116177. https://doi.org/10.1016/j.apenergy.2020.116177

Hu, M. (2022). Embodied Carbon Emissions of the Residential Building Stock in the United States and the Effectiveness of Mitigation Strategies. *Climate*, *10*(10), 135. https://doi.org/10.3390/cli10100135 International *Energy Outlook 2016*. (n.d.).

Kapsalis, P., Kormpakis, G., Alexakis, K., Karakolis, E., Mouzakitis, S., & Askounis, D. (2022). A Reasoning Engine Architecture for Building Energy Metadata Management. *2022 13th International Conference on Information, Intelligence, Systems & Applications (IISA)*, 1–7. https://doi.org/10.1109/IISA56318.2022.9904419

le Noac'h, P., Costan, A., & Bouge, L. (2017). A performance evaluation of Apache Kafka in support of big data streaming applications. *2017 IEEE International Conference on Big Data (Big Data)*, 4803–4806. https://doi.org/10.1109/BigData.2017.8258548

Marinakis, V. (2020). Big Data for Energy Management and Energy-Efficient Buildings. *Energies*, *13*(7), 1555. https://doi.org/10.3390/en13071555

Marinakis, V., & Doukas, H. (2018). An Advanced IoT-based System for Intelligent Energy Management in Buildings. *Sensors*, *18*(2), 610. https://doi.org/10.3390/s18020610

Minoli, D., Sohraby, K., & Occhiogrosso, B. (2017). IoT Considerations, Requirements, and Architectures for Smart Buildings—Energy Optimization and Next-Generation Building Management Systems. *IEEE Internet of Things Journal*, *4*(1), 269–283. https://doi.org/10.1109/JIOT.2017.2647881

Nasar, M., & Kausar, M. A. (2019). Suitability Of Influxdb Database For Iot Applications. *International Journal of Innovative Technology and Exploring Engineering*, *8*(10), 1850–1857. https://doi.org/10.35940/ijitee.J9225.0881019

Pau, M., Kapsalis, P., Pan, Z., Korbakis, G., Pellegrino, D., & Monti, A. (2022). MATRYCS—A Big Data Architecture for Advanced Services in the Building Domain. *Energies*, *15*(7), 2568. https://doi.org/10.3390/en15072568

Pullmann, J., Petersen, N., Mader, C., Lohmann, S., & Kemeny, Z. (2017). Ontology-based information modelling in the industrial data space. *2017 22nd IEEE International Conference on Emerging Technologies and Factory Automation (ETFA)*, 1–8. https://doi.org/10.1109/ETFA.2017.8247688

Ridi, A., Gisler, C., & Hennebert, J. (2014). A Survey on Intrusive Load Monitoring for Appliance Recognition. *2014 22nd International Conference on Pattern Recognition*, 3702–3707. https://doi.org/10.1109/ICPR.2014.636

Rodriguez, M. A., Cuenca, L., & Ortiz, A. (2018). FIWARE open source standard platform in smart farming-a review. *Working Conference on Virtual Enterprises*, 581–589.

Sethi, R., Traverso, M., Sundstrom, D., Phillips, D., Xie, W., Sun, Y., Yegitbasi, N., Jin, H., Hwang, E., Shingte, N., & Berner, C. (2019). Presto: SQL on Everything. *2019 IEEE 35th International Conference on Data Engineering (ICDE)*, 1802–1813. https://doi.org/10.1109/ICDE.2019.00196

Yang, B., Lv, Z., & Wang, F. (2022). Digital Twins for Intelligent Green Buildings. *Buildings*, *12*(6), 856. https://doi.org/10.3390/buildings12060856

Yun, G. Y., Kim, H., & Kim, J. T. (2012). Effects of occupancy and lighting use patterns on lighting energy consumption. *Energy and Buildings*, *46*, 152–158. https://doi.org/10.1016/j.enbuild.2011.10.034

DAO IMPLEMENTATION CHALLENGES MODEL IN IRANIAN COMPANIES

Masoumeh Afsharinezhad [1] and Mohammad Ali Sarlak[2]
[1]Ph.D Candidate, Department of Public Management, Payame Noor University, Tehran, Iran
[2] Professor, Department of Public Management, Payame Noor University, Tehran, Iran

ABSTRACT

Decentralized autonomous organizations (DAOs) are blockchain-based organizations fed by a peer-to-peer (P2P) network of contributors. Their management is decentralized without top executive teams and built on automated rules encoded in smart contracts, and their governance works autonomously based on a combination of on-chain and off-chain mechanisms that support community decision-making. There is no comprehensive study to classify the obstacles and challenges of DAO implementation in recent researches. So, in this research we propose an integrative model that reveals five main pillars of every organization (goals, individuals, structure, technology, and environment) and explain how to classify them.

KEYWORDS

Blockchain, Challenges, Decentralized Autonomous Organization (DAO), The Five Organizational Pillars

1. INTRODUCTION

What is Decentralization? Decentralization is one of the words most frequently used in the field of blockchain, and even it is often viewed as a kind of blockchain itself. However, it is also the word most difficult to define. The decentralized system can be said to be the system that has no point to decide the system's status at one's own will, which means that peer-to-peer consensus is required. For the decentralization system, users do not need to trust anyone but trust the system. In addition, it means that the measurement of decentralization is related to the measurement of how reliable the system itself is (Lee et al., 2021).

The first references to actual Decentralized Autonomous Organization (DAO) only emerged in the 1990s to describe multi-agent systems in an internet-of-things (IoT) environment (Dilger, 1997).While the academic literature on DAOs is still fairly limited, there is a significant number of papers from the field of computer sciences focusing on blockchain technology as a technical platform for building new blockchain-based business models, such as decentralized exchanges (Lin et al., 2019) or market-based platforms such as prediction markets (Clark et al., 2014) that operate as decentralized organizations with automated governance (Singh & Kim, 2019). For the purposes of definition, a DAO, is a virtual entity managed by a set of interconnected smart contracts-operate as computer programs which are deployed on a blockchain (Takagi, 2017), where various actors maintain the organization state by a consensus system and are able to implement transactions, currency flows, rules and rights within the organization. Members of a DAO are able to propose options for decisions in the organization and to discuss about and vote on those through transparent mechanisms (Zichichi, 2019). By their decentralized nature, indeed, these technologies have the potential to make processes more democratic, transparent and efficient.

Due to its origins linked to cryptocurrencies, blockchain has been mostly applied to financial and insurance applications and also in exchange markets. However, in recent years it is increasingly applied to other fields (Hassan et al., 2020). In this paper, the challenges of decentralized autonomous organization should be classified so that it can be managed accordingly. In other words, managers should discover the challenges and impediments of implementing a DAO structure in companies, then manage them according to the level and degree of the priorities based on the five organizational pillars. So, the researchers seek to answer the following questions:

- What is the comprehensive model of decentralized autonomous organization to the five pillars of the organization?
- What are the priorities of each challenge based on the proposed model?

2. RELATED WORK AND STATED CHALLENGES

A decentralized organization is not a new concept but has existed in organization theory since the 1960s (Freeland and Baker, 1975). However, technology-led decentralized organization implementation literature dates back to the 1990's leveraging internet and connecting physical devices (things) (Dilger, 1997). Proponents and enthusiasts, these days say that DAOs will eventually replace many of the world's corporations. Although this may seem farfetched for most traditionalists, DAOs continue to expand their potential capabilities in conjunction with technological advancements (Tse, 2019).

There is also an emerging body of literature from the field of economic and legal theory concerning DAOs. While most of these works focus on the new opportunities of decentralized blockchain-based organizations in the realm of economics and governance (Kaal, 2020), others focus on the legal issues of DAOs from either a theoretical (De Filippi & Wright, 2018) or practical perspective (Werbach, 2018). On the other hand, the political discourse around DAOs is more pronounced, at least in the context of many existing blockchain communities (Scott, 2015; DuPont, 2019). This survey is done to provide proper classification for all the challenges faced in the existing systems to facilitate effective use of blockchain technology in future, other than in the field of cryptocurrency.

A decentralized organization is also linked to corporate governance and audit. So, in terms of governance, diverse scholars recently started investigating the opportunities of blockchain technology and smart contracts to experiment with open and distributed governance structures (Rozas et al., 2018; Jones, 2019), along with the challenges and limitations of doing so (Hutten, 2019).

3. PROPOSED MODEL

Leavitt (1965) defines the four internal elements of organization (technology, structure, goals and individuals) as organizational pillars, however does not consider the environment as a separate independent element. The environment is a constitutive and inevitable component of the organizational model and every organization is also located in the specific physical, technical, cultural and social environment that it must adapt to (Scott, 1995). Therefore, culture is embedded in the infrastructure section as one of the basic components in the model. Sarlak and Koulivand (2016) define the conception of the organization as a human based organization, structured, equipped with technology, purposeful and enclosed in the environment. According to this definition which is consistent with Leavitt's diamond model (Scott, 1995), all organizations have at least five important pillars. In this research we have classified the critical challenges of implementing a DAO based on the proposed model elements as presented in figure 1.

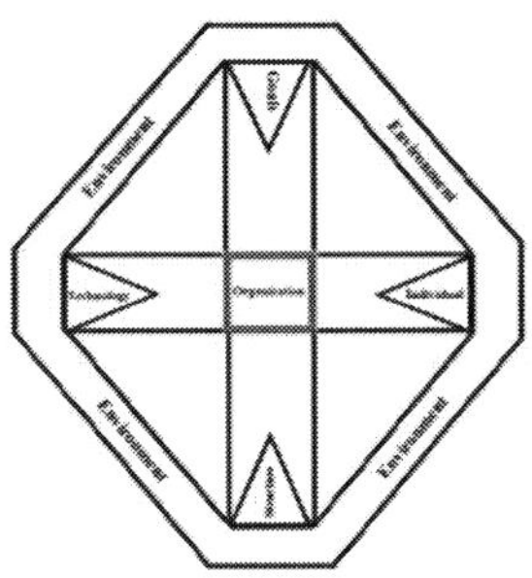

Figure 1. Organizational pillars model (Sarlak and Koulivand, 2016)

By considering this classification taking cyber cover, a Cyber Insurance Company (available at www.cyber-cover.tech), as an example which is pioneered in the implementing blockchain technology in its organization in Iran. At the beginning of the establishing, it encountered some challenges such as determining the decision-making procedure, rebuilding the existing structure in a new way, availability of experts for designing and managing the new system and so on. Based on the proposed model, these problems can be classified in two main categories: structural and individual domains.

4. RESEARCH METHODS

The purpose of this research is to identify the challenges of implementing a DAO in Iranian companies. For this purpose, the effective indicators in the implementation of a DAO have been identified through a systematic review and asking experts' opinions in the form of the organizational pillars model and the Delphi method. Kendall test has been used to analyze the experts' findings and determine the harmony of their views. Since it is impossible to coordinate the opinions of experts in one stage, in the current research, experts were asked for their opinions in three different time periods using the Delphi method, and finally, in the third round, the coordination of experts' opinions was at a high level. If the Kendall coefficient is more than 0.7, it can be concluded that the coordination of the experts' point of view is at a high level (Schmidt, 1997).

5. RESEARCH FINDINGS

In this research, the Delphi method and the model of the organizational pillars were used to identify the indicators of the implementation of a DAO in Iranian companies. In order to reach a common point of view regarding the challenges of implementing the decentralized autonomous organization, the Delphi method and the Kendall test have been used in three stages.

Table 1 presents the results of Kendall test stages of the Delphi method. In the first stage, 35 sub-indicators were introduced by experts. It can be seen that in the first stage, the Kendall coefficients for the main indicators do not differ much from each other, but the coordination between the opinions of the experts in relation to the extracted sub-indicators is not very high. At this stage, there have been two overlapping semantic indicators for the dimensions of technology, structure, goals and individuals, and three overlapping indicators for the environment dimension, and these indicators have become a sub-index. In the second stage 24 sub-indicators have been identified. It can be seen that in this stage, the Kendall coefficient for the five dimensions has increased significantly compared to the first stage, which indicates the existence of a greater coordination in the experts' point of view. However, the coordination of experts' views is at a low level, and a third step is needed to improve the experts' views.

In the third step, 15 sub-indicators have been extracted for the five dimensions. It can be seen that the values obtained for the Kendall coefficients are more than 0.7, in other words, there is a high coordination in the third stage of the Delphi method regarding the sub-indicators (Table 2). Based on the Kendall coefficient and the coordination of views, goals are ranked first, structure is ranked second, technology is ranked third, individuals are ranked fourth, and environment is ranked fifth.

Table 1. Findings of the Kendall coefficient for the results of the Delphi method

Indicators	Kendall test- 1st stage			Kendall test- 2nd stage			Kendall test- 3rd stage		
	Significance level	Chi-square	Kendall coefficient	Significance level	Chi-square	Kendall coefficient	Significance level	Chi-square	Kendall coefficient
Technology	0.040	13.217	0.088	0.001	39.214	0.318	0.001	39.214	0.784
Structure	0.032	12.197	0.098	0.001	40.519	0.240	0.001	40.519	0.810
Goals	0.023	14.679	0.098	0.001	41.551	0.323	0.001	41.551	0.831
Individuals	0.030	13.934	0.093	0.001	37.881	0.302	0.001	37.881	0.758
Environment	0.040	13.217	0.088	0.001	36.171	0.242	0.001	36.171	0.723

Table 2. Findings of effective indicators in the implementation of a DAO based on the organizational pillars model

Indicators	Sub-indicators
Technology	The affordability of smart software
	Appropriate use of information
	Information storage and documentation
Structure	Organizational hierarchy
	Exchange of information
	Coordination of tasks
Goals	Managers' awareness of the quality of activities
	Sufficient budget and credit to do things
	Dependence of activities on decentralized management
Individuals	Suitability of jobs and people's expertise
	Software and hardware knowledge
	Creativity and innovation of people
Environment	Technical infrastructure
	District rules and regulations
	Beneficiaries and users

6. CONCLUSION

DAOs are becoming more common, and now is an exciting time for industrial and organizational experts to address this new phenomenon with new theory and empirical study. Also, brands must keep up with current developments that may impact how they interact with customers or vice-versa. The growing of DAOs has driven new research on this new organizational form that integrates the entanglement between blockchain-enabled technology and decentralized, automated, and autonomous governance in organizations. This new research has also prompted the analysis of DAOs main environmental, technological, individual, structural challenges and also organizational goals concerns.

Some studies supported the technological aspects of the proposed model and revealed the challenges of information security, limitations of smart contracts and code-is-law in the decentralized organization based on the blockchain technology (Wang et al., 2019, Zainal, et al., 2022). From the structural aspects some studies have the same survey. For example, zhou et al. (2019) proposed the decision-making model to overcome the possible challenges in this type of organizations. Moreover, some researches revealed governance challenges and its limitations (Hutten, 2019). Relevant studies to the environmental issues can be referred to DAOs' reputation system research (DuPont, 2019), political concerns (Scott, 2015) and legal issues of DAOs (De Filippi & Wright, 2018, Werbach, 2018).

Two other challenges, goals and individual, were identified in this research by the proposed model. However, there are some theoretical studies in these fields, there are no similar practical research. As mentioned in the literature of the research, Cyber cover company as an example facing individual concerns at the beginning of its activity. On the other hand, goal dimension is ranked first based on the Kendall coefficient and the coordination of views in this research. Therefore, it is recommended to other researches to identify and determine the priorities of DAO implementation challenges based on their proposed model to enlighten the path for managers for controlling and overcoming the obstacles.

DECLARATION OF COMPETING INTEREST

The authors declare that there are no conflicts of interest.

REFERENCES

Clark, J., Bonneau, J., Felten, E. W., Kroll, J. A., Miller, A., & Narayanan, A., (2014). On decentralizing prediction markets and order books. *13th Annual Workshop on the Economics of Information Security, Pennsylvania State University.*

De Filippi, P., Wright, A., (2018). Blockchain and the law. The rule of code. *Harvard University Press*, Cambridge, MA.

Dilger, W., (1997). Decentralized autonomous organization of the intelligent home according to the principle of the immune system'. *IEEE International Conference on Systems, Man, and Cybernetics. Computational Cybernetics and Simulation*, 351–356.

DuPont, Q., (2019). Cryptocurrencies and blockchains. *John Wiley & Sons.*

Freeland, J.R. and Baker, N.R., (1975). Goal partitioning in a hierarchical organization. *Omega*, Vol. 3, No. 6, pp. 673-688.

Hassan, S, Brekke, J, Atzori, M, Bodó, B, Meiklejohn, S, De Filippi, P, Beecroft K, et al., (2020). In: Pólvora A, Hakami A, BolE, editors. Scanning the European Ecosystem of Distributed Ledger Technologies for Social and Public Good: What, Why, Where, How, and Ways to Move Forward. *Luxembourg: Publications Office of the European Union.*

Hütten, M., (2019). The soft spot of hard code: Blockchain technology, network governance and pitfalls of technological utopianism. *Global Networks*, 19(3), 329–348.

Jones, K., (2019). Blockchain in or as governance? Evolutions in experimentation, social impacts, and prefigurative practice in the blockchain and DAO space. *Information Polity*, 24(4), 469–486.

Kaal, W. A., (2020). Decentralized Corporate Governance via Blockchain Technology. Annals of Corporate Governance, 5(2), 101–147.

Lee, Jaeseung, Lee, Byungheon, Jung, Jaeyoung, Shim, Hojun, Kim, Hwangnam, (2021). DQ: Two approaches to measure the degree of decentralization of blockchain, *The Korean Institute of Communications and Information Sciences, ICT Express* 7 (2021) 278–282.

Lin, L. X., Budish, E., Cong, L. W., He, Z., Bergquist, J. H., Panesir, M. S., & Wu, H., (2019). Deconstructing Decentralized Exchanges. *Stanford Journal of Blockchain Law & Policy,2019.*

Rozas, D., Tenorio-Fornés, A., Díaz-Molina, S., & Hassan, S., (2018). When Ostrom Meets Blockchain: Exploring the Potentials of Blockchain for Commons Governance. https://eprints.ucm.es/id/eprint/59643/1/SSRN-id3272329.

Sarlak, M.A., Koulivand, P.S., (2016). Factors causing organizational trauma in private hospitals and solutions to reduce it, *Governmental organizations management Journal*, 3(9), Tehran, Iran.

Schmidt, RC., (1997). Managing Delphi surveys using nonparametric statistical techniques, *decision Sciences*, - Wiley Online Library.

Singh, M. and Kim, S., (2019). Blockchain technology for decentralized autonomous organizations, *in Advances in Computers, Elsevier*, Vol. 115, pp. 115-140.

Scott, B., (2015). Visions of a techno-leviathan: The politics of the bitcoin blockchain,2015.

Takagi, Soichiro, (2017). Organizational Impact of Blockchain through Decentralized Autonomous Organizations, (2017) 12 *IJEPS* 22.p25.

Tse, Nathan, (2019). Decentralized Autonomous Organization and the corporate form, Law Clerk, Russell McVeagh. *Submitted for the LLB (Honours) Degree, Faculty of Law, Victoria University of Wellington*, 2019.

Wang, S., Ding, W., Li, J., Yuan, Y., Ouyang, L. and Wang, F.Y., (2019). Decentralized autonomous organizations: concept, model, and application, *IEEE Transactions on Computational Social Systems,* Vol. 6 No. 5, pp. 870-878.

Werbach, K., (2018). Trust, but verify: Why the blockchain needs the law. Berkeley Tech. LJ, 33, 487.

Zhou, Z., Xu, G., Wang, C., & Wu, J., (2019). Modeling undesirable output with a DEA approach based on an exponential transformation: An application to measure the energy efficiency of Chinese industry. *Journal of Cleaner Production,* 236, Article 117717. https://doi.org/10.1016/j.jclepro.2019.117717

Zainal, M. Anna and et al., (2022). A decentralized autonomous personal data management system in banking sector. *Computers and Electrical Engineering* 100 (2022) 108027.

Zichichi, M., Contu, M., Ferretti, S., D'Angelo, G. (2019). Like Starter: A Smart-contract based Social DAO for Crowdfunding. *Inn Proceedings of the INFOCOM 2019—IEEE Conference on Computer Communications Workshops (INFOCOM WKSHPS), Paris, France*, 29 April–2 May 2019.

DISRUPTIVE CHALLENGES OF REMOTE WORK IN THE CONTEXT OF E-SOCIETY

Katarina Šiber Makar[1], Ivana Ogrizek Biškupić[2] and Mihaela Banek Zorica[3]
[1]in2 & ALGEBRA University College, Zagreb, Croatia
[2]ALGEBRA University College, Zagreb, Croatia
[3]Faculty of Humanities and Social Sciences University of Zagreb, Zagreb, Croatia

ABSTRACT

The aim of this paper is to analyse the workplace disruption caused by the paradigm shift due to the digital transformation process and the context of hybrid/remote work. The authors analyse benefits, challenges and approaches companies are facing within the segment of workplace regulation as well as e-leaders' tactics for remote work performance, result-based metrics, and performance indicators. The authors have noticed huge discrepancy between research on remote work subjects in business and teaching and learning industry sector (in business there's a lot of pros, and in the education especially during the pandemic, cons). Remote work represents one of the most important segments, especially in the segment of teaching, that also affects the satisfaction level in the process, which is often neglected by setting out the focus on the technologies or/and teaching methods in the e-learning environments and performance, and at the same time dropping out from the focus working conditions, policies, and institutional support for workers/teachers. In this paper authors analyse challenges and benefits of hybrid/remote work in general by observing possible applicability to various sectors of e-Society.

KEYWORDS

Remote Work, Disruptive Models, Digital Transformation, E-Society

1. INTRODUCTION

The digital transformation has influenced workplace disruption by digitizing processes and enabling communication and cooperation between employees and managers in a remote or hybrid work model. Hybrid/remote work model has become so relevant for employees that majority is ready to change an employer if current does not offer an option to work in hybrid/remote model. On the other hand, the lockdown generated by the COVID 19 pandemic has forced European universities to move their teaching activities to the online environment. This ad hoc shift to digital environment resulted in emergency remote teaching which is a different concept than the e-learning. Unfortunately, by the majority of the teachers and management there is not a clear understanding of the difference between these two concepts creating difficulties in moving towards a proper digital transformation. It is evident that questions about the preparedness, designing and effectiveness of e-learning is still not clearly understood (Muthuprasad, 2021). From the body of the research, we can see that teachers as employees working inside disruptive models in higher education industry need a clear definition and guidance. Only this way can we have a truly modernized education. But how do we reach this, where do we learn from? Could flexibility that other industries have achieved become something that could open different approach to teaching and learning thus enabling full digital transformation of educational environment. Could we learn from the business environment regarding the remote work and what are obstacles and advantages.

2. DIGITAL TRANSFORMATION INFLUENCE ON WORKPLACE DISRUPTION

The digital transformation has been mainly driven by global trends, such as changes in customers' expectations that demand 24x7 availability from product and service providers, higher speed of execution, close to real time, and clear preference for digital channels for many of the customers. The superb digital experience some of the industries are providing has created demand from other industries to do the same, although that might be a much higher challenge, hard to realize. Globalization and digitalization have made products and services easily available anywhere in the world, creating additional competitive pressure even for those companies that do not operate globally. Not only that products and services became globally available, the workers too. More and more companies have people employed across the globe and operate as one team regardless of their geographical dispersion. These companies have started applying remote work model as pioneers, but many more joined the same path because of Covid-19 pandemic that significantly speeded up both digitalization and adoption of remote and hybrid work models. Technology pace is increasing and is fundamentally changing the nature of job tasks, resulting in many new job roles that were created in the last decade, while others have become obsolete and fully automatized by robots, artificial intelligence, machine learning, chat bots and other digital technologies and solutions. By 2025 machines and humans will be equal in terms of how tasks will be divided (Zahidi, 2020).

2.1 Hybrid/Remote Work History Context

Some form of remote work model was here for more than 50 years, slowly developing as new technology were entering the workplace. In 1973, Nilles working on decreasing pollution and improving air quality questioned the necessity of daily travel to office without the real need (Nilles, 1998). First adopter of remote work were technology companies. Cisco, launched in Silicon Valley in 1993, had one of the first systematic remote work programs where employees could work either fully remotely or were offered flexible working hours and communicating via broadband technology. 10 years later, after a decade of working under remote and hybrid model, Cisco reported an increase in employee productivity and savings in 2003 of 195 mill $ (Neeley, 2021). Back in 1991, Drucker declared that in the future "office work, rather than office workers, will do the traveling" (Drucker 2020). Many international companies started to introduce telework as possible working conditions, like American Express, IBM, AT&T. The European Union realized in the year 2002 how the increase of information technology is changing working habits and requirements. In July 2002 a European Framework Agreement on Telework was concluded, the act that regulates employment and working conditions, health and safety, training, and collective rights of teleworkers (Eurofound, 2005). The USA Government in 2010 issued Telework Enhancement Act by which telecommuting officially was more secure and effective for Federal employees (Allied Telecom, 2022). From 2015 many fully remote companies were born, like GitLab, Toptal, DuckDuck Go, WeWorkRemotely, etc. In 2015 19% of EU employees worked from home remotely or in a hybrid model using collaboration technologies, where Scandinavian countries were leading with 30%-38% working in remote or hybrid model (Samek Ladovici, 2021). According to a study by the International Labor Office from Geneva from 2019, 40% of US workers work remotely occasionally (Lister & Harnish, 2019). Since 2017 remote working started to be a common working option possibility, required by employees. Since the Covid-19 pandemic outbreak, telework (fully remote or hybrid) became the new normal, where almost 50% of all the employees all over the globe during some point worked remotely and continues to do so. "Flexible work is here to stay" according to findings done by Microsoft in 2021 (Microsoft, 2021).

2.2 Challenges and Benefits of Hybrid/Remote Working

Hybrid and remote work do not come without challenges. Management typically questions if employees will be fully engaged without continuous monitoring, while there is a challenge of work-life balance, sense of loneliness and isolation on employees' side, as well as lack of socialization with their colleagues. According to 2020. BCG research, success of hybrid/remote work depends on several factors like transparent remote-work vision, selecting right operating model, enhancing trust-based management, establishing the technological foundation and solutions (BCG, KRC; José Ferreira, Pablo Claver, Pedro Pereira, and Sebastião Thomaz, 2020). Leadership proved to have a key role in motivation and communication among employees. Additionally, without a company culture built on trust and clear goal settings, it is hardly possible to successfully introduce hybrid and remote working models. According to BCG survey from 2020, 24% of managers believe that it's harder to control and drive productivity while working remotely vs in-office work, 39% of managers believe it is harder to ensure team engagement and connection, and 30% of managers believe in less innovation while working remotely. Global Workplace Analytics survey (Lister, Kate; Kamouri, Dr.Anita, 2020) points out that 35% of managers believe that main struggle of remote work is employee engagement, 34% believes that the main struggle is a lower performance of teamwork and cohesion among team members, followed by lower creativity and innovation and lower availability of manager's control over employees work performance. 2021 research from

Gartner shows that employees were very engaged in remote/hybrid model even when their work had not been under constant company control and monitoring. According to research data of 2.865 participants, 70% of leaders confirmed that remote work performance was the same or better as on-site (in office) work (Kamouri, Anita, PhD; Lister, Kate, 2020). BCG study from 2020 shows that two major employees benefit in hybrid/remote work are work-life balance (mainly related to less commute time which allows extra time to be spent for their personal needs and family) and cost reduction of living costs (mainly due to lower cost of commute, cost of meals, etc.). OWL Labs study from 2021. shows that more than 80% of respondents considers that main benefits of remote working are more time with their family 86%, that they are happier 84%, better able to handle work-life balance 83% and that hybrid work is better for their mental health 82% (OWL, 2021). Main **benefits for employers/companies** are (Florentine, Sharon, 2020): employee engagement and productivity increase, retention, morale, expanding talent pool, cost reduction. BCG survey from 2020 shows that companies have the following benefits from hybrid/remote work model: cost saving, talent attractiveness, productive workforce. Applying hybrid/remote working model allows companies to employ experts from any geography, allowing them to choose the best talents, but also surveys as a way to expand their business in new geographies. What comes across all research and surveys investigated as common **benefits of hybrid/remote working for employees and employers** are following: work/life balance for employees; more personal and family time for employees; cost reduction for both employees and employers; increased flexibility and autonomy for employees; development of digital competences for employees; higher performance in well managed hybrid/remote work for both employees and employers; improved work satisfaction and expanding talent pool for employers. On the other hand, research has shown many **challenges** of this type of work, such as: sense of loneliness and isolation on employees' side, as well as lack of socialization with their colleagues and losing team spirit; no clear boundaries between work and home time; too much of virtual communication; difficulty focusing on fully remote work model; staying motivated especially in fully remote work model; new colleagues onboarding; and appropriate communication with managers and team members.

McKinsey Global Survey on digital transformation from 2018 lays down five characteristics of successful digital transformation as prerequisite for successful remote / hybrid work: leadership by having the right, digital-savvy leader in place, capability building for the workforce of the future (engaging integrator and technology-innovation manager who would support employees to bridge the gap between traditional and digital parts of business - they will translate and integrate new digital methods and processes into the existing way of working), empowering employees to work in new ways, continuous upgrading of tools used for collaboration and process digitalization, frequent communication via traditional and digital ways (McKinsey & Company, 2018). In a new remote and hybrid work model, relationships between manager and employees have become more important than ever, while through manager employee validate employer as well (Kropp & McRae, 2022). Important criteria for successful remote work and productive teams are (Neeley, Tsedal, 2021): delivering results, individual growth facilitation, building team cohesion. For productive remote and hybrid team, there are tactics for successful leading remote workers (Neeley, Tsedal, 2021): a) minimize location differences - leaders should not make differences in leading people who are working on a different location, no matter if locations are geographically different, or on site or off site working; b) strengths, not status emphasize - leaders should emphasize individual strengths, not working status for remote workers, common purpose promotion vs faultiness – key for leaders is to promote group-level identity and stress out that each individual represents one part of a team (chain link); c) create structure – predictability is important for remote workers, leaders should give clear direction to each team member with direct communication and clear job description and responsibilities; d)give feedback – in order to motivate team members, leaders must give appropriate and constructive feedback as an individual support for career development no matter if working in office or remotely; e) promote engagement, but not avoid conflicts – bonding of remote and hybrid workers through informal parts of the meetings in order to encourage engagement and fruitful discussion.

Taking all of the challenges employers and employees are facing in full remote work, hybrid work model seems to be more widely adopted by majority of employers, where applicable. It is considered that the optimum balance could be around two to three days of remote work a week (Samek Ladovici et.al., 2021) giving possibility to the worker to organize work to maximize benefits of both options (in office and home office).

2.3 Measuring Work Performance

Hybrid/remote work model requires defining of measurable targets (Key Performance Indicators - KPIs) for achieving its purpose which will provide clarity about the goals and boost engagement of employees to achieve targets. The Performance Management must be adapted to a new way of working through (BCG, 2020): 1) Trust-based management – as a first enabler for successful hybrid/remote work, means shifting towards measuring workers' output (e.g., achievement of settled KPIs and quality and timeliness of the work); 2) KPIs and OKRs (Objectives and Key Results) – use measurable targets, which should be equally accessible and fair for both remote and onsite employees, by providing tools and information that enable reaching targets, and provide reporting for regular tracking of performance; 3) Coaching and feedback – important in driving employee's individual development and managing employee expectation, which could be very challenging in remote work model. New flexible working models require new practices and routines which could improve efficiency in daily tasks.

3. DIGITAL TRANSFORMATION IN EDUCATION

Starting from the context of the pandemic and the reflection it had on the education system, the short-term transition to a completely online/remote way of working, according to the many research papers, often has negative context or repercussions. This negativity is also influenced by the fact that some segments of the process and human resources were not ready for a complete transition to the online/remote way of working. However, e-learning and digital tools were already in use, planned and integrated 20 years ago and as such quite successful, which indicates that only certain segments could be the one giving the online learning/working a negative context, and they, on the other hand, can be easily detected by conducting quality performance measurement metrics. Digital transformation of educational institutions should therefore be viewed in a comprehensive context as companies tend to do by analysing all the segments, which is much broader than just delivery of teaching and learning with the use of technologies but integrating all its processes with all stakeholders (and also using the capabilities of AI bots to help personalize communication, especially in communication with external stakeholders (including the wider social community). Digital skills are becoming indispensable competencies that the labour market requires today. Education that prepares employees for this digital market is also changing attitudes towards 21st century skills development. The University, as the umbrella institution of higher education, is also expected to act proactively. Digital transformation in higher education was one of the key strategic priorities of the International Association of Universities (IAU, 2020) and their policy wish sets out key principles and values that are key to shaping the digital transformation of higher education and human-centered, ethical, inclusive and holistic transformation for the common good. If we are to develop future workers that are employable the disruption emerging in the educational environment needs to be recognized and solved.

The project DIGITOOLS - Innovative Tools for Enhancing E-Learning Solutions in Universities (the Erasmus+ KA 226 Partnerships for Digital Education Readiness Project. Project Number: 2020-1-IE02-KA226-HE-000781) is aimed at introducing enhanced digital tools and methods to help university staff deliver quality education through online means. It supports and cultivates innovative pedagogies and methods for teaching, learning and assessment, encouraging educators and learners to use digital technologies in creative, collaborative and efficient ways to help them to quickly adapt to this fast evolving and complex situation caused by this global pandemic. In particular, the project promotes effective digital-age learning and digitally competent educational organisations actively building on the European Framework for Digitally Competent Educational Organisations. Digital technologies are enablers of a step change in learning and teaching practices. The project is effectively tackling skills gaps and mismatches particularly with regard to preparedness to remote work, learning and teaching in the digital environment promoting more flexible and innovative learning. (DIGITOOLS, 2022).

4. CONCLUSION

Digital transformation with many disruptive models has been successfully applied in many industries in the last decade (e.g. media and entertainment, retail, financial services, telecommunications, hospitality and travel, transportation, insurance, manufacturing, healthcare, utilities, wholesale, etc.). Research shows that most employers and organizations still feel more in control of the work process when it takes place on-site than when it's been organized hybrid/remotely despite the fact that by implementing certain performance measurement methods and techniques the same effect can be achieved. Flexibility is a positive thing that both sides, employers and employees emphasize, which then consequently has an impact on all other processes of the system as a whole (for example, education, library's, healthcare etc.). Digital transformation experienced in the labour market definitely have influence on the education institutions that represent central place in preparing students for their future jobs and their flexibility to work in the context of different working models and simultaneously remotely connected to wide segment of e-Society.

REFERENCES

Allied Telecom. (2022). https://www.alliedtelecom.net/the-history-of-telecommuting/

BCG, KRC; Ferreira, J., Claver, P., Pereira, P. and Thomaz, S. (2020). Remote working and the platform of the future. The path to remote-working maturity: https://www.bcg.com/publications/2020/the-path-to-remote-working-maturity

BCG. (2020). Remote working and the platform of the future. https://web-assets.bcg.com/80/e1/8db524dc4b80abf09f0575cd0eea/bcg-remote-working-and-the-platform-of-the-future-oct-2020.pdf

DIGITOOLS project. (2022). Retrieved from https://www.digi-tools.eu/

Drucker, P. (2020). Peter F. Drucker on practical leadership (ISBN: 978-1-63369-931-1 ed.). (e. 978-1-63369-932-8, Ed.) Boston, Massachusetts: Harvard Business Review Press. Eurofound. (2005).

Eurofound. (2005). https://www.eurofound.europa.eu/sites/default/files/ef_files/docs/eiro/tn0910050s/tn0 910050s.pdf. Retrieved from https://www.eurofound.europa.eu/sites/: https://www.eurofound.europa.eu

Florentine, S. (2020). The keys to succesful remote work strategy. Retrieved from https://www.cio.com/article/230829/the-keys-to-a-successful-remote-work-strategy.html: https://www.cio.com/article/230829/the-keys-to-a-successful-remote-work-strategy.html

IAU. EAG Draft IAU Policy statement for Membership consultation. September 2020. Access date 11.08.2020. Available at: https://www.iau-aiu.net/IMG/pdf/draft_iau_policy_statement_september_2020_-_final.pdf

Kamouri, A., PhD; Lister, K. (2020). Global Work-From-Home Experience Survey. Retrieved from globalworkplaceanalytics.com:https://globalworkplaceanalytics.com/global-work-from-home-experience-survey#:~:text=About%20the%20Global%20Work-from-Home%20Experience%20Survey%20Nearly%203%2C000,the%20largest%20global%20post-COVID%20employee%20survey%20to%20date .

Kropp, B., & McRae, E. R. (2022). 11 Trends that will shape work in 2022 and beyond. Retrieved from Harvard Business Review: https://hbr.org/2022/01/11-trendsthat-will-shape-work-in-2022-and-beyond

Lister, K., & Harnish, T. (2019). Telework and its effects in the United States. In J. C. Messenger, Telework in the 21st Century (p. 128). Northampton, Massachusetts; Geneva: Edward Elgar Publishing, Inc.; International Labor Office. doi:10.4337/9781789903751

Lister, K.; Kamouri, A. (2020). Global work-from-home Experience Survey. Retrieved from Global Workplace Analytics: https://globalworkplaceanalytics.com/global-work-from-home-experience-survey

McKinsey&Company. (2018). Unlocking success in digital transformation. McKinsey&Company. Retrieved from https://www.mckinsey.com/business-functions/people-and-organizational-performance/our-insights/unlocking-success-in-digital-transformation

Microsoft. (2021). The next great disruption is hybrid work - are we ready? Microsoft. The Next Great Disruption Is Hybrid Work—Are We Ready? (microsoft.com)

Muthuprasad, T. A. (2021). Students' perception and preference for online education in India during COVID -19 pandemic. Social Sciences & Humanities Open, 3(1).

Nilles, J. M. (1998). Strategies for Managing the Virtual Workforce 1st Edition (ISBN-13 : 978-0471293163 ed.). Wiley.

Neeley, T. (2021). Remote work revolution: Succeeding from Anywhere (ISBN:978-0-06- 306832-2 ed.). New York: HarperCollins Publishers Inc.

OWL Labs. (2021). Retrieved from OWL Labs:State of remote work: https://owllabs.com/state-of-remote-work/2021/

Samek Ladovici, M. (2021). The impact of teleworking and digital work on workers and society / Special focus on surveillance and monitoring, as well as on mental health of workers. European Parliament. Policy Department for Economic, Scientific and Quality of Life Policies https://www.europarl.europa.eu/RegData/etudes/STUD/2021/662904/IPOL_STU(2021)662904_EN.pdf

Samek Ladovici et.al., M. (2021). The impact of teleworking and digital work on workers and society. doi:10.2861/691994

Zahidi, S. (2020). How COVID-19 can change work for the better. World Economic Forum. - the World Economic Forum's Saadia Zahidi on the Jobs Reset Summit: https://www.weforum.org/agenda/2020/10/jobs-reset-saadia-zahidi/

EMOTIONAL EVALUATION OF MOVIE POSTERS

Takashi Hanagaki and Jun Iio
Faculty of Global-Informatics, Chuo University, 1-18 Ichigaya-Tamachi, Shinjuku-ku, Tokyo, 162-8478, Japan

ABSTRACT

This study examines the impressions that movie posters give people and analyzes movie poster trends. The primary objective was to determine whether movie posters have any characteristics, which was done through clustering using arousal–valence maps. Thereafter, we tried to determine whether these characteristics are related to other indicators, such as box office revenue and audience satisfaction. A prototype of the proposed emotion evaluation system to conduct the survey was implemented, and an its overview and functions were elucidated. The system randomly displayed 6 movie posters from a list of 100 poster images prepared in advance. A small case study was conducted wherein participants were asked to rate each poster, and their ratings were saved. The evaluation values were analyzed, and several findings were obtained.

KEYWORDS

Arousal, Valence, Movies Posters, Emotion Analyses

1. INTRODUCTION

Advertising is widely used by companies to promote their products and work. There are several types of advertising, such as TV commercials, internet advertisements, and movie posters. Posters are known to influence and increase the interest of moviegoers. Recently, with the advent of over-the-top media services such as Amazon Prime Video and Netflix, people are offered more opportunities to decide whether to watch a movie based on its poster, which suggests that the impressions they acquire through movie posters can influence their viewing.

This study focused on movie posters and analyzed their impressions on people. Participants' impressions of each poster were collected using a questionnaire and quantitatively evaluated. This study introduces an emotion evaluation system that was developed to conduct the questionnaire, and reports the results of the data analysis performed using the data generated through this system.

The system adopted the arousal–valence (AV) index proposed by the psychologist James A. Russell (1980). Arousal involves evaluating the activation performance of an object; for example, whether it imparts a calm feeling or makes an individual nervous when they see it. In contrast, valance involves evaluating positivity/negativity, that is, whether the impression obtained when looking at the object is anxious, sad, confident, or happy. The primary objective of this study was to determine some characteristics of movie posters and to achieve this goal, clustering was performed using the aforementioned (AV) map. Subsequently, we expected to gain insight into whether these features are related to other indicators, such as box office revenue and audience satisfaction.

The following are some previous studies related to this research:

Kutsuzawa et al. (2022) analyzed the relationship between emojis, which are frequently used worldwide to express feelings and emotional states. Using the emotional value-arousal scale, they determined that emojis comprehensively express human emotions.

Kato (2022) evaluated the arousal and emotional valence for images selected from the International affective picture system dataset. The measured arousal and emotional valence differed among the cases wherein participants were instructed to rate the emotion aroused by the stimulus and those wherein they were instructed to identify the sentiment contained in the stimulus.

Kimura et al. (2020) aimed to create a list of stimulus words suitable for emotional arousal. They presented university students with two-character phrases and asked them to rate the emotional valence and arousal level imparted by each phrase. Consequently, they created a list of emotional words that minimized the interdependent effects of emotional valence and arousal levels.

Goto (2019) investigated the emotional valence and arousal levels of single-kanji characters to create an emotion word list. The 7-point Likert scale survey included 45 students and a list of 95 words selected from Kanji in contemporary magazines. Consequently, 29, 33, and 30 words were assigned negative, positive, and neutral values, respectively.

Sasaki et al. (2013) recommended songs that matched the impression of a scene by mapping the input image to the song impression. In this method, the image and music features were transformed into AV value, which is a psychological index of liveliness, to map them in the AV space.

Although most of these studies have evaluated emotional valence and arousal of words, this study attempted to do this for images.

2. EXPERIMENT AND RESULTS

This section provides an overview of the experiment and inferences of the results obtained.

2.1 Experiment Overview

An experiment was conducted to determine the impressions movie posters make on people. The experimental system was designed to randomly display 6 movie posters from a list of 100 different movie posters prepared in advance, and participants were asked to rate the impression they obtained from each image. The poster images were obtained from an online database called the Movie Database (TMDB). By using the application programming interface of this website, various information about any movie can be collected, such as the country of production, year of production, names of actors, and satisfaction level. Moreover, it is possible to collect information and posters of all movies around the world. The 100 poster images prepared in advance were those of the top 100 movie titles according to their world box office revenue rankings. The terms and conditions of use of TMDB allow free use of movie poster images. It was confirmed that no intellectual property rights were infringed.

The AV index was used to evaluate the posters. Because Russell's model plots various emotions on two axes, each AV value could be represented as a 2D representation of the corresponding emotion. The average AV values for the posters were calculated from the accumulated results, which were analyzed by applying them to the corresponding emotions.

2.2 Emotion Evaluation System

The emotion evaluation system randomly displayed 6 movie posters out of the selected 100 movie posters, and stored the arousal and emotional values entered by the users.

After a participant completed the evaluation, the system showed them other participants' scores, which was expected to impart gamification. Thus, users could intuitively identify the differences between their and others' scores, which was intended to encourage them to assess other posters.

The jQuery-UI and Bootstrap 5 CSS libraries were used at the front end, and the back end (server side) was built using the Rails 7.0.2.3 framework. Figure 1 shows a screenshot of the evaluation system, which shows six posters randomly selected from TMDB.

Figure 1. Evaluation system called "Emotion Analysis for Movie Posters"

2.3 Experiment and Result Analyses

The experiment was conducted using a previous system on May 16, 2022. Twenty members of our laboratory participated in this study, and their multiple responses resulted in 372 evaluation results. The results were displayed in the format of Russell's model, with the vertical axis representing arousal level and the horizontal axis representing the emotional valence (Figure 2).

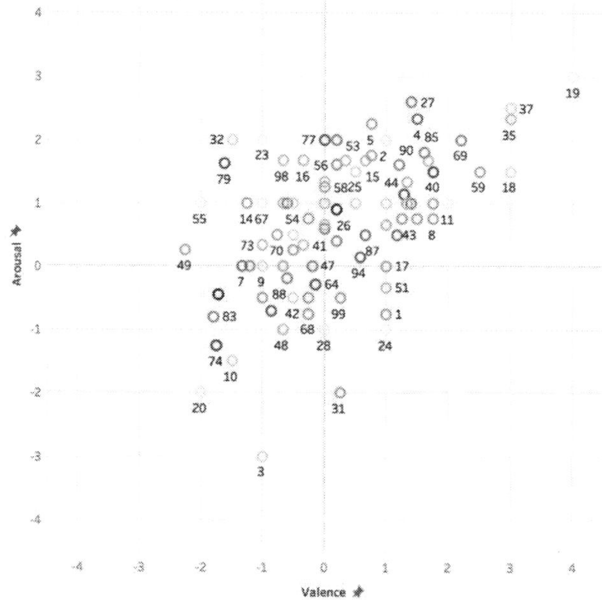

Figure 2. Scatter plot of emotion evaluation

The colored circles indicate the number of evaluations; the darker the color, the more times the assessment was made, and the higher the evaluation validity. The numbers displayed near the circles indicate box office rankings. For example, item 1 indicates the movie with the highest box office revenue, whereas item 100 indicates the one with the lowest.

Three findings were obtained through this experiment. First, there is a positive correlation between arousal and valence; the correlation coefficient was 0.513, indicating that there was indeed a correlation. Second, currently there is no direct correlation between the evaluation value of posters and box office revenue. The numbers in the graph indicate the box office revenue rankings; however, large and small numbers are scattered. Third, very few posters were rated as having low arousal and positive valence. The following figure shows the number of poster images in each quadrant. The number of posters evaluated as having low arousal and positive valence, that is, in the fourth quadrant, was only five, which was lower than in the other quadrants. The following hypothesis is proposed based on these results: there is a lower number of posters in the fourth quadrant for some reason (e.g., they do not lead to sales) and participants rarely evaluated the posters in this quadrant. Because the evaluation hurdle was high in this quadrant, posters were rarely classified in this area.

3. CONCLUSIONS AND FUTURE WORK

This study attempted to examine the impressions that movie posters impart to people. The characteristics and trends of movie posters were analyzed by clustering them using AV maps and examining whether these characteristics were related to other indicators, such as box office revenue and audience satisfaction. The evaluation system was constructed based on Russell's AV model, and an experiment was conducted using the proposed system. The data obtained were mapped and analyzed using the AV model. The results did not show a correlation between the evaluation value and box office revenue, and posters rated as having low arousal and positive valence tended to be less favored than others.

Although this study was conducted using movie posters, the vital outcome is the evaluation system that was created. In other words, this system does not have to be limited to movie posters, and could be used to evaluate paintings, brand advertisements, etc. Because this study evaluated the impression people acquire when they see an object, we believe it can be used to anticipate user experience. We hope that this study will aid future research in this field.

However, more experiments are required to ensure the validity of the evaluation values. Therefore, it is expected that the number of evaluations can be increased in the future by recruiting students from the same faculty as participants (our faculty has approximately 600 students). Additionally, a similar experiment should be conducted using posters of movies that did not have high box office collections and its results should be compared with those obtained in this study. We will continue to examine the relationships between the evaluation results. Because this study did not find a direct relationship with box office ranking, we plan to investigate the correlation between the number of PV views and the level of audience satisfaction in future work.

REFERENCES

Gotoh, F., 2019, Affective Valence and Arousal from Single-character Kanji Words. *Bulletin of DEN-EM-CHOFU UNIVERSITY* 14, 35–49.

Kato, M., 2022, Comparison of different ratings of arousal and emotional valence for emotional stimuli. *Tama University journal of management and information science* 26, pp. 69–79.

Kimura, T. and Suzuki, N., 2020, Development of a list of emotional words comprising two-character idioms. *Japanese Journal of Research on Emotions*.27(2), pp. 43–50.

Kutsuzawa, G., et al, 2022, Classification of 74 facial emoji's emotional states on the valence-arousal axes. *Sci Rep* 12, 398.

Russell J. A, 1980, A Circumplex Model of Affect; *J. of Person. and Soc. Psychol*. 39(6), pp. 1161–1178.

Sasaki, S., et al, 2013, Affective Music Recommendation System based on Input Image. *Information Processing Society of Japan*. 75(1), 45–46.

CONCEPTUAL MODEL FOR EXAMINING THE CONTINUANCE USAGE INTENTION OF SMART GOVERNMENT SERVICES

Omar Hujran[1] and Mutaz M. Al-Debei[2]
[1]*College of Business and Economics, United Arab Emirates University, Al Ain, United Arab Emirates*
[2]*Business School, Al-Ahliyya Amman University, Amman, Jordan*

ABSTRACT

Until recently, little attention has been paid to citizens' continuance usage (i.e. post-adoption) of emerging technologies. Recognizing this gap in the literature, this research aims at developing an integrative research model by extending the Unified Theory of Acceptance and Use of Technology (UTAUT) framework with public satisfaction and trust constructs which are considered as imperative factors in continuance usage of e-government services. As part of a larger research project, this model will be then applied to examine citizens' continuance usage intention of smart government services in the United Arab Emirates (UAE).

KEYWORDS

Smart Government, E-government, Continuance Usage, UTAUT, Trust, Satisfaction

1. INTRODUCTION

Smart government, the next-generation e-government, refers to the use of breakthrough technologies such as Artificial Intelligence (AI), Machine Learning (ML), Internet of Things (IoT), Mobile Computing, Open Government Data, Cloud Computing, Social Media, Blockchain and Big Data Analytics by the public sector (Hujran et al., 2021). Smart government has the potential to modernize the public sector by enabling governments to provide intelligent, integrated, personalized, and interactive public services to their stakeholders (Althunibat et al., 2021). Despite its numerous benefits, however, the literature on smart government is still in its infancy. In contrast to e-government and m-government, little consideration has been paid to exploring issues related to smart government (Al-Hujran et al., 2022). Hence, the first contribution of this research is to address this gap in the literature.

As smart government initiatives are increasingly being implemented by some countries around the globe including the UAE, certain technical and non-technical challenges need to be considered including citizen adoption and continuance use (Althunibat et al., 2021). Recent studies frequently reported that electronic public services and associated innovative technologies have been often underutilized (Xiong et al., 2021; Alruwaie et al., 2020) with a discontinuance rate being high (Islam et al., 2021; Xiong et al., 2021; Alruwaie et al., 2020; Li and Shang, 2020). Hitherto, prior information systems (IS) literature showed that the success of any IS and the feasibility of its long-term strategies is highly dependent on its continued use (i.e. post-adoption) rather than on initial acceptance (Alruwaie et al., 2020; Li and Shang, 2020; Bhattacherjee, 2001). Several researchers argued that the problem of underutilization of Information and Communications Technologies (ICT) applications is because organizations tend to overlook the post-adoption period (Islam et al., 2021; Alruwaie et al., 2020). After a comprehensive review of the e-government literature, the current research found only a few studies explored the continuance use of e-government services (e.g. Alruwaie et al., 2020; Li and Shang, 2020; Naranjo-Zolotov et al., 2019), m-government services (e.g. Xiong et al., 2021) and open government data (e.g. Islam et al., 2021). Therefore, studies related to the post-adoption of smart government services are still needed to make this innovation successful. Filling this gap in the literature represents the second contribution for the current study. Accordingly, this study aims at developing an integrated model of smart government continuance usage by extending the UTAUT model.

2. LITERATURE REVIEW

The e-government literature has witnessed an increasing number of studies that have been devoted to understanding citizens' perspectives toward the acceptance and adoption of e-government services (e.g. Mustaf et al., 2020; Al-Hujran et al., 2015; Al-Hujran et al., 2014; Al-Hujran and Al-dalahmeh, 2011). As a result, numerous e-government adoption models have been developed, and a wide range of factors affecting adoption have been pinpointed. For example, Mustaf et al. (2020) identified around 50 different influencing factors from 41 e-government adoption studies that have been published during the years 2007-2018. However, neither the acceptance nor the adoption is enough to ensure the success of e-government services, but the continuance use or the post-adoption does (Li and Shang, 2020). While acceptance and adoption might represent the initial stage of use of an information system, post-adoption represents the repeated or continuance use, and the latter deserves more specific attention (Yan et al., 2021).

The lack of citizens' continuance use of e-government services has been frequently recognized and highlighted in the recent literature (Gupta, 2021; Li and Shang, 2020), which also have called for further attention to be placed on understanding citizens' continuous use of e-government services. Accordingly, more recent studies started to focus on determining the underlying factors that influence citizens' continuance use of e-government services (e.g. Gupta and Maurya, 2020; Li and Shang, 2020), mobile government services (Xiong et al., 2021) and open government (Islam et al., 2021). Nevertheless, the post-adoption or continuance use of smart government services has been rarely been investigated, especially in developing nations such as the UAE. The continuance usage of technology, as a wider domain, has received little attention compared with technology acceptance and/or adoption (Yan et al., 2021). A recent examination of the use of UTAUT2 theory (from 2012 -2017) has found that, among 650 studies cities UTAUT2, only three studies focused on user post-adoption of ICT applications (Tamilmani et al., 2021). Another recent study but a broader systematic review of 147 papers in the context of continuous use of technologies at the time period from 2001 to 2019, found only 10 studies addressed continuance use of ICTs (Yan et al., 2021). Apparently, this knowledge gap also exists in the smart government literature.

3. HYPOTHESES DEVELOPMENT

This research proposes an integrative model by extending the UTAUT (Venkatesh et al., 2003) through the integration of two significant predictors of e-government continuance usage identified in the relevant literature: public satisfaction and public trust constructs (See Figure 1). The UTAUT theory is one the most broadly employed theoretical models that have effectively replicated numerous occasions and used to investigate the adoption of a wide range of technologies (Venkatesh, 2021; Hujran et al., 2020). In the UTAUT model, behavioral intention and use behavior are influenced directly by four independent constructs. These constructs are performance expectancy (PE), effort expectancy (EE), facilitating conditions (FC), and social influence (SI).

3.1 Impact of Performance Expectancy on Public Satisfaction

Performance expectancy refers to the degree to which a user believes that the usage of a particular system would lead to enhancing his/her job performance (Venkatesh et al., 2003). Smart government has the potential to enhance citizens' performance and create greater values for them such as offering greater convenience, transforming government-citizen relationships, improving citizens' experiences, and transforming public decision making (Hujran et al., 2021). Thus, it could be argued that citizens are more likely to be satisfied with their experience of utilizing smart government services when they realize a higher level of utilitarian value in using such innovative services. The significant relationship between PE and satisfaction has been validated in similar contexts (e.g. Alalwan, 2020; Singh, 2020). Hence, the following hypothesis is proposed:

H1. *Performance expectancy positively influences public satisfaction.*

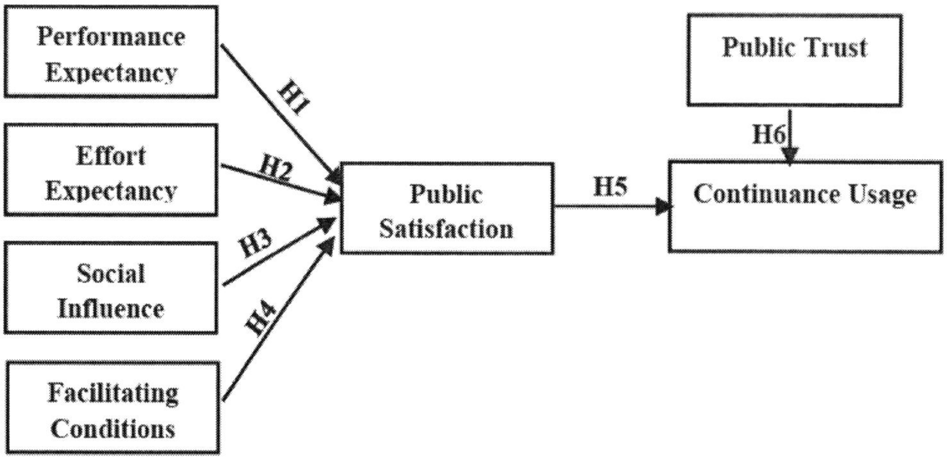

Figure 1. Research model

3.2 Impact of Effort Expectancy on Public Satisfaction

Effort expectancy is deified as the degree to which the user believes the use of a new technology to be free of effort and easy to use (Venkatesh et al., 2003). The use of various novel technologies such as Chatbots, IoT-related services, Virtual reality, and Smartphones would enable the public to complete their transactions with minimal effort and without needing help from government staff. Accordingly, it could be proposed that whereas citizens perceive that using smart government services is effortless, they will be satisfied with their experience in utilizing such services. Previous studies confirmed the significant impact of EE on end-user's satisfaction across similar contexts (e.g. Hope and Zhang, 2015). Thus, we posit:

H2. *Effort expectancy positively influences public satisfaction.*

3.3 Impact of Social Influence on Public Satisfaction

Social influence denotes the degree to which a user believes that other important individuals to him/her (i.e. family, peers, friends) think that he/she should use a technology or system (Venkatesh et al., 2003; Khasawneh et al., 2018). The current study argues that citizens are more likely to be influenced by the opinions and word-of-worth of those around them when judging their experience (satisfied or dissatisfied) with smart government services. The positive link between SI and user's satisfaction was empirically proved by prior ICT adoption literature (e.g. Chen et al., 2020). Therefore, this study suggests the following hypothesis:

H3. *Social influence positively influences public satisfaction.*

3.4 Impact of Facilitating Conditions on Public Satisfaction

Facilitating conditions are defined as users' perceptions of the availability of proper organizational resources and infrastructure that support the use of a specific system or technology (Venkatesh et al., 2003). It is anticipated that when citizens perceive that the government provides them with enough resources and support when using smart services, they are more likely to have conformable experiences and, hence, would be more satisfied. Earlier research reported that FC is a strong predictor of user satisfaction (e.g. Alalwan, 2020; Chan et al., 2010). Thus, we hypothesize:

H4. *Facilitating conditions positively influence public satisfaction.*

3.5 Impact of Public Satisfaction on Continuance Usage

The satisfaction concept has been extensively studied in different domains including marketing, management, commerce, and information systems. According to Bhattacherjee (2001), satisfaction is regarded as "experience-specific affect" and it represents a psychological state connected to and generated from a comparison between expectations and experience (i.e., confirmation). Previous research showed that satisfaction is a strong determinant of the continuance intention to use a product, service, or technology (Alalwan, 2020; Singh, 2020). Accordingly, we posit:

H5. *Public satisfaction positively influences the continuance usage of smart government services.*

3.6 Impact of Public Trust on Continuance Usage

According to Williamson (1993), trust is viewed as a calculative process and a particular level of subjective probability with which an individual weighs available evidence associated with possible benefits and risks to decide whether to rely on another agent to perform a particular activity. Thus, if a user does not trust particular smart government services, he or she may stop using them. Past studies indicated the important role of trust in predicting a user's intention to continually use a product, service, or technology (e.g. Benlian et al., 2012). Therefore, the following hypothesis is proposed:

H6. *Public trust positively influences the continuance usage of smart government services.*

4. CONCLUSION

While most studies on smart government have focused on Western countries, just a handful have looked at how it has been used in Arab countries like the United Arab Emirates. In addition, there is a scarce of studies that examine the continuance usage intention of smart government services. This study, therefore, proposed a conceptual model to examine the continuance intention to use smart government services. As a future work, an extensive empirical survey research will be carried out in the UAE to empirically validate the proposed research model.

ACKNOWLEDGEMENT

This study is supported by the CBE Annual Research Program (CARP) from the United Arab Emirates University.

REFERENCES

Alalwan, A. A. (2020). Mobile food ordering apps: An empirical study of the factors affecting customer e-satisfaction and continued intention to reuse. *International Journal of Information Management*, 50, 28-44.

Al-Hujran, O., & Al-dalahmeh, M. (2011). The role of national culture on citizen adoption of eGovernment web sites. In *Proceedings of the 11th European Conference on e-Government, ECEG 2011* (pp. 17-26).

Hujran, O., Al-Debei, M. M., Al-Adwan, A. S., Alarabiat, A., & Altarawneh, N. (2022). Examining the antecedents and outcomes of smart government usage: An integrated model. *Government Information Quarterly*, 101783. In Press.

Hujran, O., Abu-Shanab, E., & Aljaafreh, A. (2020). Predictors for the adoption of e-democracy: an empirical evaluation based on a citizen-centric approach. *Transforming Government: People, Process and Policy*, *14*(3), 523-544.

Al-Hujran, O., Al-Debei, M. M., Chatfield, A., & Migdadi, M. (2015). The imperative of influencing citizen attitude toward e-government adoption and use. *Computers in human Behavior*, 53, 189-203.

Al-Hujran, O., Al-Debei, M. M., & Al-Lozi, E. (2014). Examining eDemocracy adoption intention for digital society: An integrative model. In *The eighth international conference on digital society* (pp. 39-47).

Alruwaie, M., El-Haddadeh, R., and Weerakkody, V. (2020). Citizens' continuous use of eGovernment services: The role of self-efficacy, outcome expectations and satisfaction. *Government Information Quarterly*, 37, 101485.

Althunibat, A., Binsawad, M., Almaiah, M.A., Almomani, O., Alsaaidah, A., Al-Rahmi, W., and Seliaman, M.E. (2021). Sustainable Applications of Smart-Government Services: A Model to Understand Smart-Government Adoption. *Sustainability*, 13, 3028.

Benlian, A., Titah, R., & Hess, T. (2012). Differential effects of provider recommendations and consumer reviews in e-commerce transactions: An experimental study. *Journal of Management Information Systems*, 29(1), 237-272.

Bhattacherjee, A. (2001). Understanding information systems continuance: An expectation-confirmation model. *MIS quarterly*, 25 (3), 351-370.

Chan, F. K., Thong, J. Y., Venkatesh, V., Brown, S. A., Hu, P. J., & Tam, K. Y. (2010). Modeling citizen satisfaction with mandatory adoption of an e-government technology. *Journal of the association for information systems*, 11(10), 519-549.

Chen, C. C., Hsiao, K. L., & Li, W. C. (2020). Exploring the determinants of usage continuance willingness for location-based apps: A case study of bicycle-based exercise apps. *Journal of Retailing and Consumer Services*, 55, 102097.

Gupta, K.P. (2021). Impact of e-government benefits on continuous use intention of e-government services: the moderating role of citizen trust in common service centres (CSCs). *International Journal of Electronic Governance*, 13, 176–191.

Gupta, K. P., & Maurya, H. (2020). The role of access convenience of common service centres (CSCs) in the continued use of e-government. *Digital Policy, Regulation and Governance*, 22 (5/6), 437-453.

Hope, P., & Zhang, X. (2015). Examining user satisfaction with single sign-on and computer application roaming within emergency departments. *Health informatics journal*, 21(2), 107-119.

Hujran, O., Alarabiat, A., Al-Adwan, A. S., & Al-Debei, M. (2021). Digitally Transforming Electronic Governments into Smart Governments: SMARTGOV, an Extended Maturity Model. *Information Development*, 02666669211054188.

Islam, M.T., Talukder, Md.S., Khayer, A., and Islam, A.K.M.N. (2021). Exploring continuance usage intention toward open government data technologies: an integrated approach. *VINE Journal of Information and Knowledge Management Systems*, ahead-of-print.

Khasawneh, M. H. A., Hujran, O., & Abdrabbo, T. (2018). A quantitative examination of the factors that influence users' perceptions of trust towards using mobile banking services. *International Journal of Internet Marketing and Advertising*, *12*(2), 181-207.

Li, Y., and Shang, H. (2020). Service quality, perceived value, and citizens' continuous-use intention regarding e-government: Empirical evidence from China. *Information & Management*, 57, 103197.

Mustaf, A., Ibrahim, O., and Mohammed, F. (2020). E-government adoption: A systematic review in the context of developing nations. *International Journal of Innovation: IJI Journal*, 8, 59–76.

Naranjo-Zolotov, M., Oliveira, T., Casteleyn, S., & Irani, Z. (2019). Continuous usage of e-participation: The role of the sense of virtual community. *Government information quarterly*, 36(3), 536-545.

Singh, S. (2020). An integrated model combining ECM and UTAUT to explain users' post-adoption behaviour towards mobile payment systems. *Australasian Journal of Information Systems*, 24.

Tamilmani, K., Rana, N. P., Wamba, S. F., & Dwivedi, R. (2021). The extended Unified Theory of Acceptance and Use of Technology (UTAUT2): A systematic literature review and theory evaluation. *International Journal of Information Management*, 57, 102269.

Venkatesh, V. (2021). Adoption and use of AI tools: a research agenda grounded in UTAUT. *Annals of Operations Research*, 308, 641–652.

Venkatesh, V., Morris, M. G., Davis, G. B., & Davis, F. D. (2003). User acceptance of information technology: Toward a unified view. *MIS quarterly*, 27(3), 425-478.

Williamson, O. E. (1993). Calculativeness, trust, and economic organization. *The journal of law and economics*, 36(1, Part 2), 453-486.

Xiong, L., Wang, H., and Wang, C. (2021). Predicting mobile government service continuance: A two-stage structural equation modeling-artificial neural network approach. *Government Information Quarterly* 101654.

Yan, M., Filieri, R., and Gorton, M. (2021). Continuance intention of online technologies: A systematic literature review. *International Journal of Information Management*, 58, 102315.

ROLE OF NAMED ENTITIES IN UNDERSTANDING SEMANTIC SIMILARITY OF ENGLISH TEXT

Sumit Kumar and Shubhamoy Dey
Indian Institute of Management Indore, Rau-Pithampur Road, Indore – 453556, India

ABSTRACT

Understanding semantic similarities between documents is challenging but have enormous benefits, like plagiarism detection and information retrieval. Various techniques are available in Natural language processing, which help in understanding similarities between text documents. Every approach aims to find a unique set of features that help differentiate between two or more documents.

Names of persons, organizations, locations, medical codes, acronyms, technical terms, date & time expressions, quantities, monetary values, and percentages (collectively known as Named Entities) and the order in which they appear in a document contribute a great deal to the uniqueness of the document (Li et al., 2020). If two documents share them, they must present the same information or discuss the same concept. Another advantage of Named Entities (NE) in the context of plagiarism detection is that they do not have synonyms – replacing words with their synonyms to avoid detection is, therefore, not an option. Thus, NEs have a high potential for detecting similarities between documents. Yet, going by the availability of literature, it is an under-researched concept.

In this article, we discuss and explore the concept of NEs and their meta characteristics, and propose a way of using that information to find similarities between documents.

Our initial experimental results, discussed in this article, demonstrate the efficacy of the approach intuitively argued above. This article is unique in its methodology, thus comparing the results with other available methods on textual similarity is inappropriate. We have compared the results of the proposed NE based approach with existing approaches based on Term Frequency and TF-IDF.

The future goal of the ongoing research work is to combine NEs and their meta characteristics with other characteristics to develop a robust and comprehensive framework for finding semantic similarities between documents.

KEYWORDS

Text Similarity, Semantic Similarity, Named Entity

1. INTRODUCTION

We use the concept of semantic text similarities in day-to-day life without being aware of their existence. Human civilization will progress further if machines can understand human language. Finding similarity is one step in the direction where machines can understand human language. For example, applications like human-machine interfaces (such as Seri, Alexa or Cortana) can become more flexible and useful. They depend on how machines find similarities between human language and their trained modules. Finding semantic similarities has various other applications in information retrieval, automatic question answering, machine translation, dialogue systems, and document matching (Pradhan et al.,2015).

The general approach is to extract features unique to each document and convert these features into numerical representations that can be easily converted into machine language. Named Entities are among the unique features of documents. Named Entity Recognition (NER) are a set of techniques that help in finding these unique words present in documents. Grishman and Sundheim (1996) discussed named entities in the 6th Message Understanding Conference. They have used NER to identify persons, places, or organization names, dates, currency, and numerical values. After many advancements in the NE proposed subsequently, researchers have segregated NEs into two broad categories: Generic NEs and domain-specific NEs. NER uses one of these four methods: Rule-based method (on hand-crafted rules), unsupervised (based on unlabelled data), feature-based supervised learning (feature engineering later followed with supervised learning approach), and deep learning based approach (detect similar patterns of words on which a model trained) (Li et al.,2020).

2. NAMED ENTITY RECOGNITION

"a named entity is a word or a phrase that identifies one item from a set of other items with similar attributes." (Sharnagat, 2014, pp.1-27). Examples of named entities are organizations, persons, location names, gene, protein, drug and disease names in the biomedical domain—the fundamental of NER is to find the location of such words and tag the words in the document.

Formally defining NER: consider a document with a unique set of words S = { W1, W2, W3, ..., WN}, where a subset of those words are a list of NEs, i.e. { I1, I2,... IM}.

At the time of MUC-6 (Grishman, & Sundheim, 1996), each NE was assigned a single tag. This was popularly known as coarse-grained NER. Another kind of NER developed recently is known as fined-grained NER, which can allocate more than one tag to some of the NEs where required.

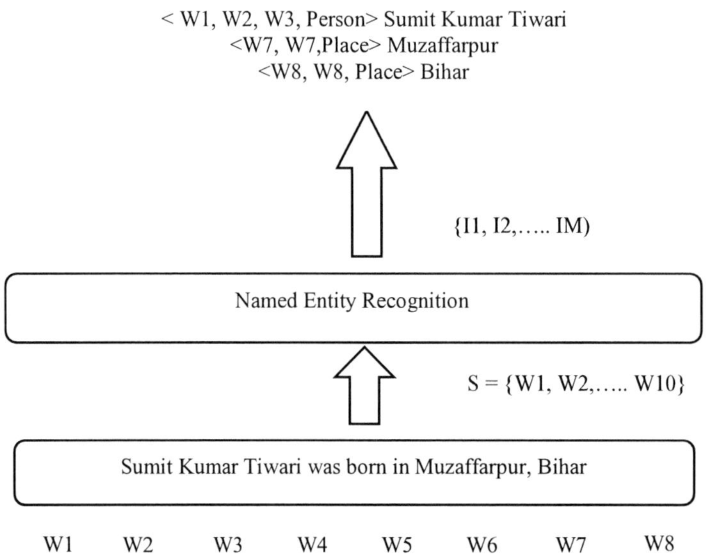

Figure 1. Illustration of named entity recognition

3. PROPOSED METHODOLOGY

3.1 Pre-Processing Prior to NER

Generally, while writing any document, if any proper noun or common noun repeats itself, the document's writer replaces it with a pronoun. The pronouns hide some important named entities and their location within the documents. It therefore, makes the task of NER more challenging. Fortunately, there are many tools and techniques available in Natural Language Processing (NLP) to resolve pronouns. Coreference resolution is a technique for finding all the expressions referring to the same entity in a document (Mitkov, 2001). Researchers have been working on the Co-reference resolution problem since the late 1970s when Hobb's naïve algorithm was proposed. It is a rule-based algorithm that focuses on syntactical characteristics of language to capture the NEs present in the form of pronouns. Advancement of statistical and machine learning techniques in the early 1990s led to the development of several new methods for coreference resolution. Probabilistic techniques such as the Bayesian rule, decision tree and genetic algorithm were some of the early approaches used for pronoun resolution (Aone & William, 1995; McCarthy & Lehnert, 1995). The next stage of development was the neural network and deep learning based approaches – eliminating the dependency on handcrafted rules. These models were able to understand the semantic structure. Clark and

Manning (2016) and Lee et al. (2017) have done some significant work in the area. Notably, Lee et al. (2017) have modelled end-to-end coreference resolution systems using character-level convolutional neural networks.

Our work uses a state-of-the-art method to resolve the coreferences. It is the spanBERT method based on the concept of span, where each span is numerically embedded. These spans are useful in reducing the size of the coreference cluster, and the leftover span uses the transitivity principle to find out the co-referent (Lee et al., 2018). The SpanBERT Model is available in allenNLP pre-trained package.

3.2 Finding Named Entities

Coreference resolution ensures that each coreference (i.e. pronoun) of an NE in a document is replaced by the actual NE. Various methods are available for tagging each document word with its proper named entities tag. In recent years, deep learning-based methods gained quite a lot of popularity due to their high accuracy over various document contexts. The strength of deep learning algorithms is that they are pre-trained and use transfer learning methodologies to achieve higher accuracy and low biasedness (Kitaev & Klein, 2018).

This current work uses the AllenNLP coreference resolution package for tagging NEs present in the documents. Internally AllenNLP uses ElMo, a sequence-to-sequence neural language model. Peters et al. (2018) have proposed ELMO representation with two layers of bi-directional language model.

The forward language model predicts the future token based on past available tokens. The backward language model runs over the sequence in reverse order, predicting the previous token given its future context. Given the token sequence $t_1, t_2, \dots. t_N$ the forward and backward model compute the sequence of probability of token t_k.

This, somewhat complex representation of the document has capability to capture both syntactical and semantic characteristics. Also, ELMo is a pre-trained deep bidirectional Transformer that works by jointly conditioning on both left and right context in all layers. It provides a lot of strength to the model for finding NEs accurately.

3.3 Named Entities and Similarity

It is therefore clear from the foregoing discussion that NEs contribute to the determination of a document's uniqueness. While there has been substantial research on finding textual similarity (Friburger et al., 2002), the specific role played by NEs has received only scant attention of researchers.

3.3.1 NE Frequency Similarity

Basic Concept: The existence of unique NEs and their frequency is a characteristic contributing to the uniqueness of a document. If two documents share a list of named entities it increases the similarity of the documents. Adding frequency to the context means that the documents not only share the same NEs but the NEs also occur in each of them in the same proportion. This increases the possibility of the documents being similar to a great extent. It will be clear with the help of a small example:

Text 1: Mahatma Gandhi is the father of our nation. Gurudev Rabindranath Tagore had given him the title of Mahatama.

Text 2: At one point in time, Gurudev Rabindranath Tagore gave the Mahatma title to Mohandas Karamchand Gandhi, who came to be popularly known as Mahatma Gandhi after that.

It is clear from the above two pieces of text that they are very similar and carry almost the same information. In this example, Mahatma Gandhi, Gurudev Rabindranath Tagore, and Mohandas Karamchand Gandhi, that is two out of three NEs are common between the two pieces of text, with the exact frequency count.

This example shows that documents sharing the same NEs with equal frequency counts must be similar or would at least be discussing the same topic.

Table 1. NE Frequency

NE words	Text-1 Frequencies	Text-2 Frequencies
Mahatama	1	1
Mahatma Gandhi	1	1
Gurudev Rabindranath Tagore	1	1
Mohanddas Karamchand Gandhi	0	1
Gurudev	1	1

Euclidean distance suffers from high sensitivity to magnitudes (Xia et al., 2015). Due to this, information retrieval and related studies widely use cosine similarity (Rahutomo et al., 2015) to compare similarity of document vectors. Cosine similarity is the angle between two document vectors. It does not depend on magnitude.

The cosine similarity between the abovementioned texts is 0.895, which is understandable because they share many NEs with compare frequencies. This illustrative example clearly shows that above mentioned concept will play a significant role in understanding the similarity between documents.

3.3.2 NE Order Similarity

Basic Concept: the last subsection shows the importance of NE frequencies in the determining similarity. Wang et al. (2016) discussed ranking the NEs in the document based on their importance. However, that previous work is only confined to web documents and uses a tripartite graph for understanding the NE rank based on "importance". Want et al. (2016) did not leverage the order of occurrence of the NEs in the document.

This work focuses on the Concept of the order of occurrence of the NEs within the documents. It will capture the order information of each NEs in a document and compare it with their order of occurrence in another document. The argument being that if two documents share the same NEs in the same order of occurrence, the possibility of them being similar is very high. It signifies both documents present context and concepts in the same order, and even the unique building blocks of the documents (i.e. NEs) are similar. It will be clear with the help of a small example:

Text 1: Mahatma Gandhi is the father of our nation; Gurudev Rabindranath Tagore had given him the title of Mahatama.

Text 2: At one point in time, Gurudev Rabindranath Tagore gave the Mahatma title to Mohandas Karamchand Gandhi, who came to be popularly known as Mahatma Gandhi after that.

Table 2. NEs and their location in the documents

NE words	Location in Text-1	Location in Text-2
Mahatama	15	11
Mahatma Gandhi	1	24
Gurudev Rabindranath Tagore	8	6
Mohanddas Karamchand Gandhi	0	14
Gurudev	8	6

Table 3. NEs and their consecutive order in the documents

NE words	Order in Text-1	Order in Text-2
Mahatama	4	3
Mahatma Gandhi	1	5
Gurudev Rabindranath Tagore	3	2
Mohanddas Karamchand Gandhi	0	4
Gurudev	2	1

Once again, for calculation of NE order similarity between two documents, cosine similarity is useful. The cosine similarity between the abovementioned examples is 0.714, which is understandable because they share most of the NEs in nearly the same order. This illustrative example clearly shows that the above mentioned concept will play a significant role in understanding the similarity between the two documents.

4. EXPERIMENTS & RESULTS

Dataset: For experimentation purposes, this work uses a set of four documents. Two are on Mother Teresa (Mohita, 2014; Panda, 2022), and the other two are news reports on the Djokovic vaccine controversy (Kershaw, 2022; Rajan, 2022). In order to avoid bias, all four document sizes are in the range of 1000-1200 words.

Experimentation: In this work we have compared NEs between similar documents, i.e. between the two Djokovic news reports and between the two Mother Teresa documents, and dissimilar documents: one of the Djokovic reports with one of the Mother Teresa documents.

Obtained Results: The results obtained on both similar and dissimilar sets reflect the cosine similarity of NE frequencies and NE order. The results shown in the tables below justify our hypothesis. The assumption was that similar documents would have a high value of NE frequency and order similarity, and dissimilar documents would have a low value of NE frequency and order similarity, which is what is observed from the entries in Table 4. Table 5 shows the corresponding cosine similarity between the same pairs of documents when the conventional measures Term Frequency (TF) and Term Frequency – Inverse Document Frequency (TF-IDF) are used. While, the cosine similarity values between the "similar" pairs are higher than those between dissimilar pairs, the differences between the similar and dissimilar pairs are significantly lower. Also, notably TF-IDF performs worse than even TF based similarity values. This is because TF-IDF, having been developed to discriminate between documents, loses all the common words, including the common NEs between them, (the IDF part evaluates to zero) which makes TF-IDF weak in measuring similarity.

Table 4. NE Frequency and Order Cosine Similarity

	Similar Documents		**Dissimilar Documents**	
	Mother Teresa 1 Vs Mother Teresa 2	**Djokovic (BBC) Vs Djokovic (iNEWS)**	**Mother Teresa 1 Vs Djokovic (BBC)**	**Mother Teresa 2 Vs Djokovic (iNEWS)**
Frequency Similarity	0.964	0.675	0	0.0003
Order Similarity	0.445	0.255	0	0.004

Table 5. TF and TF-IDR similarity

	Similar Documents		**Dissimilar Documents**	
	Mother Teresa 1 Vs Mother Teresa 2	**Djokovic (BBC) Vs Djokovic (iNEWS)**	**Mother Teresa 1 Vs Djokovic (BBC)**	**Mother Teresa 2 Vs Djokovic (iNEWS)**
TF Similarity	0.413023	0.382043	0	0.005
TF-IDF Similarity	0.27693711	0.26206084	0.03841347	0.08569649

5. DISCUSSION

NEs have the potential to uncover latent semantic characteristics present in the documents. The frequency and order meta characteristics of NEs can enormously impact information retrieval, textual similarity, text summarization, voice command identification, and many other application areas. Semantic similarity of texts using named entities is an under-explored area; NE frequency and order information help in the semantic understanding of the text. Available plagiarism detection software is based only on syntactical or lexical comparisons. A proper understanding of NEs and their meta-characteristics would help improve the effectiveness of plagiarism detection software.

This current work demonstrates the advantages of NEs over conventional TF or TF-IDF based similarity measures in understanding text. In this research experiments were conducted with the help of a limited set of experiments. A more extensive analysis is required over a large set of documents to analyze the proposed method's full potential and limitations. Natural language processing is an evolving area with interesting developments due to the advancement of deep learning techniques among others. Some recently proposed techniques for co-reference resolution and extraction of NEs have the potential to produce more accurate results.

6. CONCLUSION

The work presented in this article has demonstrated the potential of meta characteristics of NEs in understanding semantic similarity between documents. The work in its current form is restricted by the effort required due to manual calculations. The entire algorithm will be automated in the near future to run more comprehensive tests over a large set of documents of various sizes and types to establish the strength and robustness of our proposed method.

REFERENCES

Aone, C., and William, S., (1995). Evaluating automated and manual acquisition of anaphora resolution strategies. In 33rd Annual Meeting of the Association for Computational Linguistics, pp. 122-129.

Clark, K., and Manning, C. D., (2016). Improving coreference resolution by learning entity-level distributed representations. arXiv preprint arXiv:1606.01323.

Friburger, N. et al, (2002). Textual similarity based on proper names. In Proc. of the workshop Mathematical/Formal Methods in Information Retrieval, pp. 155-167.

Grishman, R., and Sundheim, B. M., (1996). Message understanding conference-6: A brief history. In COLING 1996 Volume 1: The 16th International Conference on Computational Linguistics.

Kershaw, T., (2022), January 20. Novak Djokovic's controversial beliefs and why he is opposed to the vaccine. The Independent. https://www.independent.co.uk/sport/tennis/novak-djokovic-vaccine-australian-open-2022-b1995236.html

Lee, K. et al, (2017). End-to-end neural coreference resolution. arXiv preprint arXiv:1707.07045.

Lee, K. et al, (2018). Higher-order coreference resolution with coarse-to-fine inference. arXiv preprint arXiv:1804.05392.

Li, J. et al, (2020). A survey on deep learning for named entity recognition. IEEE Transactions on Knowledge and Data Engineering, Vol. 34, No. 1, pp 50-70.

McCarthy, J. F., and Lehnert, W. G., (1995). Using decision trees for coreference resolution. arXiv preprint cmp-lg/9505043.

Mitkov, R., (2001). Outstanding issues in anaphora resolution. In International Conference on Intelligent Text Processing and Computational Linguistics Springer, Berlin, Heidelberg, pp. 110–125.

Mohita, N., (2014), February 27. Mother Teresa: Essay on Mother Teresa. Your Article Library. https://www.yourarticlelibrary.com/essay/mother-teresa-essay-on-mother-teresa/28438

Panda, I., (2022), June 2. The Life and Work of Mother Teresa - 1163 Words | Essay Example. Free Essays. https://ivypanda.com/essays/the-life-and-work-of-mother-teresa/

Pradhan, N. et al, (2015). A Review on Text Similarity Technique used in IR and its Application. International Journal of Computer Applications, Vol. 120, No. 9, pp. 29-34.

Rahutomo, F. et al, (2012). Semantic cosine similarity. In The 7th international student conference on advanced science and technology ICAST, Vol. 4, No. 1, p. 1.

Rajan, B.A., (2022), February 15. Novak Djokovic willing to miss tournaments over vaccine. BBC News. https://www.bbc.com/news/world-60354068

Wang, C. et al, (2016). Nerank: Bringing order to named entities from texts. In Asia-Pacific Web Conference, Springer, Cham, pp. 15-27.

Xia, P. et al, (2015). Learning similarity with cosine similarity ensemble. Information Sciences, Vol. 307, pp. 39-52.

ANALYSIS OF CLAIM EXPRESSIONS IN JAPANESE ASSEMBLY MINUTES USING SENTENCE EMBEDDINGS

Ryo Kato and Minoru Sasaki
Ibaraki University, Japan

ABSTRACT

There are many expressions in bills included in the minutes of local assembly meetings that represent not only stances but also suggestions. These expressions are different for each party and member of the assembly to express their opinions. In this paper, we analyse the statements made by each party in the minutes of several local assemblies such as Tokyo, Osaka, and Ibaraki. Moreover, we analyse whether differences in the expression of opinion exist across areas using word frequency and sentence embeddings from BERT model on the minutes of several assemblies. The results of the experiments indicate that some specific opinion expressions tend to represent similar content. Moreover, we show that there are differences in the use of wording to express opposite stances between urban and local assemblies.

KEYWORDS

Stance Analysis, Claim Expressions, BERT, Claim Embeddings, Clustering

1. INTRODUCTION

In Japan, there are many assemblies, including the Diet, prefectural assemblies, and the assemblies of the various local governments. In these assemblies, a wide range of social issues are actively discussed by their members. The assembly minutes record discussions on these issues. However, reading the assembly minutes is time-consuming and it is difficult to understand these social issues being discussed. Therefore, we consider that it is important to effectively understand which stance each assembly member takes (e.g., agree or disagree) by extracting the statements made by all assembly members in the assembly.

In this paper, we analyse the statements made by each party in the minutes of several local assemblies such as Tokyo, Osaka, and Ibaraki. In the Japanese assemblies, delegates from each party provide their opinions on the bills. When analysing opinions across these local assemblies, expressions of opinion in the statements tend to differ across different areas. However, it is difficult for existing methods using word frequencies to distinguish differences in the stances taken in the expressions of the opinions. Therefore, we analyse whether differences in the expression of opinion exist across areas using word frequency and sentence embeddings from BERT model on the minutes of several assemblies.

2. ANALYSIS OF TOKYO METROPOLITAN ASSEMBLY MEETING PROCEEDINGS

We conduct an analysis using feature expressions in the Tokyo Metropolitan Assembly. The analysis will deal with the statements of the Japanese Communist Party (JCP). The Communist Party has been consistently positioned as an opposition party for the past decades. Therefore, we consider that we can extract features of opinion more stably by targeting the negative stance of the statements of JCP members.

2.1 Tagging of Content

A topic label is assigned to a statement to identify which topic the statement belongs to. Even within a single response, many areas are discussed for or against. We divide the text into sections that address each of these areas, and manually tag each section. Tags are roughly categorized by field, such as "medical," "education," and so on. For example, the following statement is tagged as the 'Olympic Games' label.

次に、二〇二〇年東京オリンピック・パラリンピックについてです。五輪費用の削減の…

(Next, I would like to discuss the Tokyo Olympics and Paralympics in 2020. The reduction of the cost of the Olympics...)

2.2 Extraction of Characteristic Expressions

We extract "characteristic expressions" from the statements. We manually extract the parts of the sentences tagged with "～することを求める。(～seek to ~ be)"、"～に反対する。(I am opposed to ~)", etc., that are arguments or requests for each proposal as follows:

東京五輪の選手村用地は、…直ちに全面公開するよう、改めて(厳しく求めるものです)。

The same nouns and verbs are often used in these extracted feature expressions. In some cases, they are used in exactly the same way, while in others, there are differences in the words before and after. We investigate whether there are differences or characteristics in this usage.

2.3 Sentence Embeddings of Statements and Clustering

For each statement sentence extracted in the previous section, we use a pre-trained BERT model to derive a sentence embedding from the input sequence. We make use of the "反対(opposite)" word token's output vector as a sentence embedding. For the obtained embeddings, we use the k-means clustering to obtain clusters. From the results, we also classify the tags that were added in advance and investigate whether the content of the utterance has any characteristics.

2.4 Comparison of Clusters between Different Assemblies

The characteristics of each word obtained using the minutes of the Tokyo Metropolitan Assembly proceedings will be compared with those of statements made in the assemblies of other prefectures. For comparison, we will focus on the assemblies of Osaka Prefecture, Japan's second largest city, and Ibaraki Prefecture, a regional city. In Ibaraki, the Communist Party is the largest opposition party, as is the case in Tokyo, so we focus on the Communist Party's statements. In the Osaka assembly, the Liberal Democratic Party (LDP) is the largest opposition party, so we will focus on this statement and make a comparison. For each assembly, tagging and feature expression extraction are performed as in 2.1.1 and 2.1.2, and as in 2.1.3, the words used in the feature expressions and the vectors of whole sentences are obtained. This will be used to make comparisons with the Tokyo Metropolitan Assembly.

3. EXPERIMENTAL RESULTS USING THE MINUTES OF THE TOKYO METROPOLITAN ASSEMBLY

In this section, we use the method described in the previous section to analyse the statements of the JCP. As experimental data we use the statements of the JCP in the plenary proceedings of the Tokyo Metropolitan Assembly from 2000 to 2020. For the set of input sentences, we obtain the clustering results of the word vector of the word '反対(opposite)' in the input sentences and the clustering results of the embeddings in the sentences containing the characteristic expressions using BERT, and analyse whether the words and expressions used in the sentences in each cluster have features.

Table 1. The labels of the sentences belonging to each cluster and its frequency

1	('事業', 2), ('都政', 1), ('築地・豊洲', 1), ('オスプレイ', 1), ('コロナ', 1)
2	('都政', 1), ('教育', 1), ('事業', 1), ('議員', 1), ('条例', 1)
3	('事業', 2), ('福祉', 2), ('築地・豊洲', 2), ('教育', 1), ('安部', 1), ('議員', 1), ('議会', 1), ('消費税', 1), ('オリ ンピック', 1)
4	('福祉', 2), ('予算', 2), ('事業', 1), ('議員', 1), ('議会', 1), ('消費税', 1)
5	('事業', 4), ('教育', 2), ('都政', 1), ('築地・豊洲', 1), ('議案', 1), ('福祉', 1)

Table 2. Characteristic Expressions Included in each Cluster and Their Frequency

①	('反対です', 5), ('反対であります', 1)
②	('反対するものです', 3), ('反対します', 1), ('反対をするものです', 1)
③	('反対するものです', 5), ('反対します', 2), ('反対するに至りました', 1), ('反対するものであります', 1), ('断固反対する ものです', 1), ('反対いたします', 1), ('厳しく反対するものです', 1)
④	('反対です', 5), ('本条例案には反対です', 1), ('反対であることを申し述べておきます', 1), ('反対であります', 1)
⑤	('反対するものです', 7), ('反対します', 3)

Table 3. Characteristic words in the "opposite" word vector

Cluster 1	Cluster 2	Cluster 3	Cluster 4	Cluster 5
地域:0.325418	立場:1.000000	立場:0.239666	開発:0.237000	教育:0.259043
整備:0.325418	うたい文句:0.000000	予算:0.198944	今回:0.235922	管理:0.259043
開発:0.290582	すべて:0.000000	中央:0.198039	地下:0.235922	後退:0.194282
再生:0.216945	まち:0.000000	卸売:0.198039	投資:0.235922	知事:0.194282
可能:0.216945	やり方:0.000000	大学:0.198039	重要:0.235922	行政:0.194282

Table 1 shows the labels of the sentences belonging to each cluster obtained from the word vector of the word "反対(opposite)". Comparing the word and sentence vectors, the representation of "するものです" was similarly distributed in both the word and sentence vectors. Table 1 shows that the same labels can be found in the multiple clusters. Therefore, there are no features representing content in the clusters. Table 2 shows the characteristic expressions included in each cluster and their frequency. From Table 2, characteristic expressions "反対するものです", "反対です" and "反対します" are frequently used in the Tokyo Metropolitan Assembly. This result indicates that "反対です" and "反対であります", which express opinions more directly, tend to belong to the same cluster. Table 3 shows the top five words with the highest TFIDF in the sentences included in each cluster. Table 3 indicates that the NCP expresses a direct opposition stance on topics such as local redevelopment and renewable energy.

4. COMPARISON OF CLAIM REPRESENTATION BETWEEN LOCAL ASSEMBLIES

In analysing the characteristics of the Tokyo Metropolitan Assembly, a comparison will be made with the Osaka Prefectural Assembly and the Ibaraki Prefectural Assembly. Comparisons will be made for Tokyo and Ibaraki, and for Tokyo and Osaka, respectively, with respect to "反対(opposite)" using cosine similarity. The word vectors are also calculated for Osaka and Ibaraki as in Section 2.

4.1 Data Set

In the experiment, we use the minutes of the Tokyo Metropolitan Assembly (2000-2020) (Kimura et al. 2020), the Ibaraki Prefectural Assembly (2011-2020) and the Osaka Prefectural Assembly (2012-2020).

4.2 Experimental Results

In the experiment, Tables 4, 5 and 6 show the similarity of claim expressions between Tokyo and Osaka, Tokyo and Ibaraki, Osaka and Ibaraki respectively. Table 4 shows that the similarity between Tokyo and Osaka exceeded 0.8 for about 84% of the claimed expressions. Therefore, the result shows that Tokyo and Osaka use similar expressions to express opposite stance. Tables 5 and 6 show that about 42% of the claim expressions in Tokyo and Ibaraki, and about 44% in Osaka and Ibaraki, had a similarity exceeding 0.8. Therefore, the results show that in Ibaraki, the opposite stance is expressed in somewhat different expressions compared to Tokyo and Osaka. These results suggest that there are differences in the use of wording to express opposite stances between urban and local assemblies. Therefore, we consider that we can analyse opinions from the minutes more effectively by using this analysis method to capture these differences.

Table 4. The similarity of claim expressions between Tokyo and Osaka

	1~	0.9~0.8	0.8~0.7	0.7~
number	31	336	68	2
ratio	7.09%	76.89%	15.56%	0.046%

Table 5. The similarity of claim expressions between Tokyo and Ibaraki

	1~0.9	0.9~	0.8~0.7	0.7~
number	10	454	525	115
ratio	1.01%	41.46%	45.90%	11.63%

Table 6. The similarity of claim expressions between Osaka and Ibaraki

	1~	0.9~0.8	0.8~0.7	0.7~
number	12	351	363	91
ratio	1.47%	42.96%	44.43%	11.14%

5. CONCLUSION

In this paper we analyse the statements made by each party in the minutes of several local assemblies such as Tokyo, Osaka, and Ibaraki. Moreover, we analyse whether differences in the expression of opinion exist across areas using word frequency and sentence embeddings from BERT model on the minutes of several assemblies. The results of the experiments indicate that some specific opinion expressions tend to represent similar content. Moreover, from the results of analysis of the statements made by each party in the minutes of several local assemblies such as Tokyo, Osaka, and Ibaraki, there are differences in the use of wording to express opposite stances between urban and local assemblies. Therefore, we consider that we can analyse opinions from the minutes more effectively by using this analysis method to capture these differences.

REFERENCES

Ryo Kato, Minoru Sasaki, 2021, Predicting the Approval or Disapproval of each Faction in a Local Assembly Using a Rule-based Approach, *Proceedings of the Thirteenth International Conference on Information, Process, and Knowledge Management* (eKnow2021), pp.42-46.

Yasutomo Kimura, Hideyuki Shibuki, Hokuto Ototake, Yuzu Uchida, Keiichi Takamaru, Madoka Ishioroshi, Teruko Mitamura, Masaharu Yoshioka, Tomoyosi Akiba, Yasuhiro Ogawa, Minoru Sasaki, Kenichi Yokote, Tatsunori Mori, Kenji Araki, Satoshi Sekine and Noriko Kando, 2020, Overview of the NTCIR-15 QA Lab-PoliInfo-2 Task, *Proceedings of the 15th NTCIR Conference*, pp.101-112.

FACT-CHECKING IN 2022: MISINFORMATION THEMES AND FACEBOOK USERS' REACTIONS

Tereza Zichová[1] and Shudipta Sharma[2]
[1]*Faculty of Informatics and Statistics, Prague University of Economics and Business, Churchill Square 4, 130 67 Prague 3, Czech Republic*
[2]*Bowling Green State University, Bowling Green, OH 43403, USA*

ABSTRACT

The daily life of most of today's society is intertwined with misinformation and social media. Fake news can pose a significant threat. Social media offer space for spreading misinformation, so it is important to continuously monitor and analyse them. The purpose of this article is to identify the presence of the most common themes of misinformation in 2022 listed on the Facebook page of fact-checking website FactCheck.org. The paper reveals the character of the news by analysing 322 Facebook page posts and their reactions, comments, and shares. This makes it possible to better understand which topics resonate most with the tens of thousands of followers of this page. The results summarise the thematic areas and people's reactions to one year of fake news and show which topics can have the greatest social impact and are therefore important to monitor in the future. The findings can be useful for targeting the activities of fact-checking sites, for journalists, media, and government representatives to base their statements and speeches more often on evidence-based information.

KEYWORDS

Misinformation, Fake News, Social Media, Content Analysis, Facebook, Users' Reactions

1. INTRODUCTION

Information technologies help people all over the world every day. However, they also have their dark sides. One of them represents the simplicity of the creation of misinformation and its ultra-fast online dissemination. Their controlled dissemination can have disastrous consequences for society and the government (Muhammed & Mathew, 2022; Rapp & Salovich, 2018). Therefore, any initiatives and projects supporting the verification of information and coming to people with facts are essential. Fact-checking teams attached to media companies can assemble audiences vastly exceeding most independent fact-checkers reach (Graves & Cherubini, 2016). Many researchers are into the topic of fake news in the context of fact-checking websites (Al-Zaman, 2021; Brennen et al., 2020). Misinformation is characterized as inaccurate or false information that is spread intentionally or unintentionally. Misinformation can be represented by rumours, conspiracy theories, hoaxes, propaganda, misleading or edited content, social media bots or false news stories. It can be disseminated through various channels, such as social media, word of mouth, traditional media, or other communication channels.

One of the channels where fake news can spread quickly is social media (Luo et al., 2021). Social media has evolved too quickly to have sufficiently effective control mechanisms to prevent dangerous information. Fortunately, the situation has been improving in recent years, and artificial intelligence is also helping control fake news (Landon-Murray et al., 2019). The study aims to answer the following research questions (all of them regarding the year 2022).

RQ1: What were the dominant themes of misinformation on the FactCheck.org Facebook page?
RQ2: Which reactions were used by Facebook users regarding misinformation news?
RQ3: Which posts were the most commented and the most shared?

The paper is divided into five sections. The introduction gives a broader overview of the types of misinformation and the importance of analysing them on social networks. The next two sections describe the used methods and the emerging results of the study. These are subsequently put into the literature context in the discussion section. Finally, the paper addresses the results regarding the research objectives and suggests possible next steps.

2. RESEARCH METHODS

The data for this study was collected from the Facebook page of fact-checking website FactCheck.org. There are different reasons why the Facebook page of this website was chosen. It has around 836.000 followers and it is considered unbiased in the United States. FactCheck.org became the inspiration for other European projects dedicated to fact-checking statements by politicians (Graves & Cherubini, 2016). The goal of FactCheck.org is to monitor the factual accuracy of what is said by major United States political players in the form of TV ads, debates, speeches, interviews and news releases. From 2014-2019, FactCheck.org won the Webby Awards (the "Oscars of the Internet") from the International Academy of Digital Arts and Sciences for being the best Politics site. In recent years, the organisation's work has been recognized with other prizes, among others: Sigma Delta Chi fact-checking awards (in 2019 and 2020) for their in-depth stories about claims made by former President Donald Trump and the Media Consumer Excellence Award (in 2022) for their commitment to monitoring and reporting on the factual accuracy of what political figures say or espouse (FactCheck.org, 2023).

Facebook posts containing overshared articles from websites from 1st January to 31st December 2022 were analysed. The data set was composed of 412 posts of which 90 did not refer literally to fake news or were irrelevant. It was either a summary report, general information or discussion (SciCheck Talks). FactCheck.org sometimes publishes the same posts bilingually in English and Spanish, only those published in English are included in the analysis. On the other hand, posts with updated news published the second time remain in the data set because the article has been modified. However, there are not too many such cases. The final sample contains 321 posts mentioning the title, and a short description of the fake news with a page link to the original article. Excel was chosen as a sufficiently satisfactory analytical tool, which provides all the necessary functions for the chosen research method.

The authors coded misinformation articles using the qualitative content analysis method to build meaningful theme categories and map Facebook users' reactions. The analysis consists of familiarising with data, generating initial codes, searching for themes and reactions, reviewing, defining and naming, and producing the report (Braun & Clarke, 2006; Zhou et al., 2022). Articles are coded separately and they are assigned one theme according to dominant expressions of the fake news and coders' intuition. Different types of reactions and forms of engagement reflect the total numbers of A. Likes, B. Shares, and C. Comments. Posts' likes are additionally divided into seven possible reactions according to the meaning of the emoticons: A.I Like, A.II Love, A.III Haha, A.IV Wow, A.V Care, A.VI Sad, A.VII Angry.

3. RESULTS

FactCheck.org published 1.13 posts per day in 2022. Following an iterative coding technique, the authors found four main thematic areas of misinformation news: politics, COVID-19, the war in Ukraine, and miscellaneous. The ratio of individual areas is: 36.4% politics (117 posts), 25.9% COVID-19 (83 posts), 7.2% war in Ukraine (23 posts), and 30.5% miscellaneous (98 posts). Miscellaneous could be divided into smaller thematic areas like election 2022, immigration, economy (taxes, budget), abortion, climate change/global warming, guns/gun violence, and Medicare/social security, about which fake news was dealt with most often. Each article on the website also contains tags, according to which topics can be sorted based on other areas (month, people, issue, location). Graph 1 shows the distribution of posts themes by month with the evenest presence of COVID-19 articles.

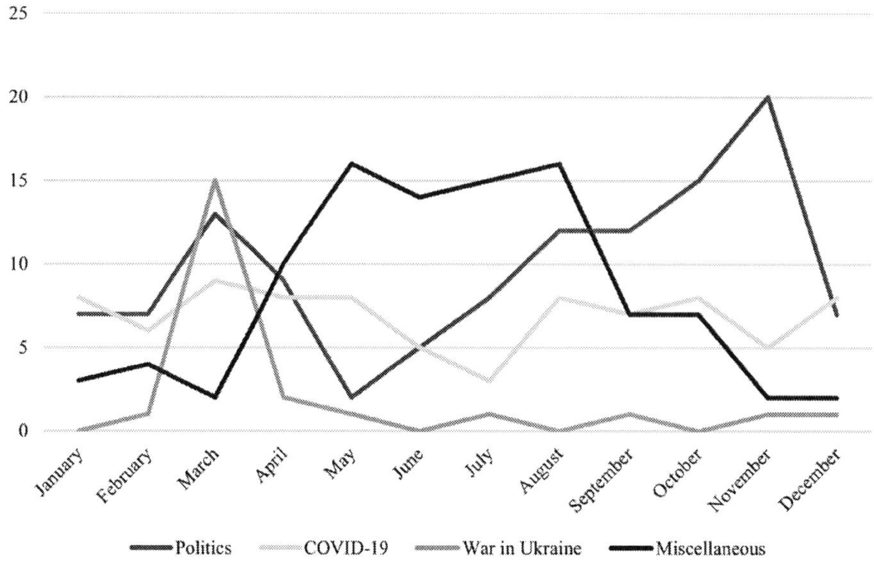

Graph 1. Fact-checking in 2022: FactCheck.org posts themes by month

Overall, the posts got 63,595 likes (198 on avg. per post), and 67,058 comments (209 on avg. per post) and they were shared 21,032 times (66 on avg. per post). As expected, A.I Like was the most common interaction displayed in the analysis of our sample. It was given 39,854 times in 2022. Likes are followed by the reaction A.III Haha with occurrences of 10,377 and A.VII Angry with occurrences of 9,186. Almost the same frequency values are reached by reactions A.IV Wow (1,758 times) and A.VI Sad (1,320 times). Facebook users use the least frequent reactions A.II Love (706 times) and A.V Care (394 times) in case of misinformation posts on the FactCheck.org Facebook page.

The majority of posts are dominated by reaction A.I Like, but in some cases reactions A.III Haha and A.VII Angry are used more. The greatest preponderance of A.III Haha reactions were caused by the news: 1. Crude Oil Prices Down Due to Recession Fears, Contributing to Lower Gasoline Prices; 2. Viral Video Spouts Baseless Claim About Early Voting in Arizona and 3. Trump Rally Photo Is From 2020, Not Recent Wisconsin Rally, as Social Media Posts Claim. On the contrary, Facebook users were mostly angered by fake news: 1. Ted Nugent Posts Fake Headline, Claim About Sotomayor's Health; 2. GOP Ads Use Outdated Federal Report to Attack Democrats on 'Higher Taxes' and 3. What Happens if Roe v. Wade Is Overturned? With an absolute preponderance of 20,529 comments, the most commented and most shared post was 1. Democrats Misleadingly Claim 'Republicans' Plan' Would 'End' Social Security, Medicare (highest number of reactions - 5,700). Other important topics for the long discussion and sharing were: 2. Social Media Claims Misrepresent Election Software CEO's Arrest and 3. Sorting Out the Partisan Tax Spin on Inflation Reduction Act.

4. DISCUSSION

Different studies divide fake news into several different categories. Common categories of misinformation are: Health Misinformation (health and medical topics), Political Misinformation (politics and government), Financial Misinformation (finance, investing, or economics), Scientific Misinformation (climate change or evolution), Social Misinformation (racism, gender identity, or social justice), Historical Misinformation (historical events or figures). The study findings show that most of the misinformation on the FactCheck.org Facebook page was connected to politics and COVID-19 in 2022. Many researchers deal with the connection between fake news and COVID-19 (Al-Zaman, 2021; Caceres et al., 2022; Kim & Tandoc, 2022). Caceres et al., 2022 want to increase awareness of the negative impact of misinformation on the pandemic and highlight the need to prevent the dissemination of misinformation. Interactions with false content on Facebook have dropped dramatically. Have also risen on Twitter. Still, lots of people continue to click on, comment on, like and share misinformation (Allcott et al., 2019). In 2022 fake news spread widely on social media. Evon (2022) mentions as frequent areas of misinformation topics like Russia's invasion of Ukraine, Anti-vaccination falsehoods, Election fraud allegations, Economic conspiracies, Faked multimedia, Fake litter boxes and anti-transgender claims and Flat Earth and climate-change lies.

The study brings with it some assumptions and limitations. The thematic analysis divided the articles into four general categories. News often contained a combination of different themes. In these cases, the authors selected the prevalent one or assigned a category miscellaneous. The most difficult process was to differentiate between the categories of politics and miscellaneous which could be widely discussed. However, the topic of COVID-19 and the war in Ukraine was mostly unambiguous. By definition, a certain political aspect could be observed in the majority of posts. Categorization is influenced by the researchers' experience and judgement. The results of the study provide basic insights for the future development of the topic by segmenting the main categories into subcategories. The information overview could be used as a basis for the application of specific methods and the incorporation of theoretical approaches. The issue of summing different types of A. Like reactions (A.I-A.VII) occurs for posts where there are more than 1,000 reactions. While the exact number of B. Shares, and C. Comments can be displayed on Facebook from the user's account, reactions A.I-A.VII above 1000 is displayed in a rounded form. Therefore, the data consists of raw numbers (e.g. 1.2K is counted as 1,200). The number of reactions and their combination can be influenced by several factors. In terms of the type of reaction when you click on A. Like, A.I Like is automatically given, therefore this reaction usually prevails. The number of reactions is then affected by different factors such as the date and time of post-publication, its description, used photo/graphics/video, events in the world etc. The psychology of Facebook reactions is very complex, as they are influenced by a range of factors, including personal emotions, cognitive biases, and social norms. Results are based on reactions by the followers and fans of the FactCheck.org Facebook page. Although they do not apply to the entire company, they are related to a significant group of individuals representing fact-checkers.

5. CONCLUSION

The paper provides findings regarding misinformation on the FactCheck.org Facebook page in 2022. It shows the development of four thematic areas over time: politics, COVID-19, the war in Ukraine, and miscellaneous. The number of mapped reactions draws attention to the reach and importance of fact-checking websites and to the fake news that is perceived as the most fundamental. Sharing is of great importance in this case as well as commenting options offer sometimes good space for an open discussion. People mostly reacted to the news regarding politics. The post that was most commented on and most used by users was related to the 2022 election, Medicare, and social security.

Studies of misinformation are important for several reasons. They can help protect the public, preserve democracy, improve communication, and advance science like psychology, sociology, and communication studies. Fake news and social media are closely intertwined, as social media platforms have become key drivers of the spread of misleading information. They can become a great tool to mitigate the negative effects of misinformation and promote truthful and reliable information.

The contribution of this study lies primarily in the fact that it is one of the first evaluations analysing the fake news of fact-checking social media page in the whole year 2022. Secondly, users' reactions can point to interesting connections with users' perceptions of the news. The general findings provide many possibilities for future research. The field of fact-checking and misinformation research is very broad, which makes it possible to follow up on it in several ways. Research on different types of comments and their meaning could be incorporated into the analysis of posts. A follow-up paper could provide extensions to other fact-checking websites, e.g. PolitiFact which focuses on investigating specific statements made by politicians and rating them for accuracy (PolitiFact, 2023). An interesting finding would be a geographical comparison with other countries' websites on different continents. Last but not least, the area of research could be extended to other social networks like Twitter and Instagram which are used by different social and age groups.

REFERENCES

Allcott, H., Gentzkow, M., & Yu, C. (2019). Trends in the Diffusion of Misinformation on Social Media. *National Bureau of Economic Research*. https://doi.org/10.3386/w25500

Al-Zaman, M. S. (2021). A Thematic Analysis of Misinformation in India during the COVID-19 Pandemic. *International Information & Library Review*, 1–11. https://doi.org/10.1080/10572317.2021.1908063

Braun, V., & Clarke, V. (2006). Using thematic analysis in psychology. *Qualitative Research in Psychology*, 3(2), 77–101. https://doi.org/10.1191/1478088706qp063oa

Brennen, J. S., Simon, F. M., Howard, P. N., & Nielsen, R. K. (2020). *Types, sources, and claims of COVID-19 misinformation*. UK: University of Oxford.

Caceres, M. M. F., Sosa, J., P., A Lawrence, J., Sestacovschi, C., Tidd-Johnson, A., UI Rasool, M., H., Gadamidi, V., K., Ozair, S., Pandav, K., Cuevas-Lou, C., Parrish, M., Rodriguez, I., & Fernandez, J., P. (2022). The impact of misinformation on the COVID-19 pandemic. *AIMS Public Health*, 9(2), 262–277. https://doi.org/10.3934/publichealth.2022018

Evon, D. (2022). *2022, the year in misinformation: News literacy takeaways*. The News Literacy Project. https://newslit.org/updates/2022-in-misinfo-news-literacy/

FactCheck.org (2023). *Our Mission*. The Annenberg Public Policy Center of the University of Pennsylvania. https://www.factcheck.org/about/our-mission/

Graves, L., & Cherubini, F. (2016). *The Rise of Fact-Checking Sites in Europe. In Digital News Project Report*. Reuters Institute Digital News Report. Reuters Institute for the Study of Journalism.

Kim, H. K., & Tandoc E. C. Jr. (2022). Consequences of Online Misinformation on COVID-19: Two Potential Pathways and Disparity by eHealth Literacy. *Front. Psychol*, 13. https://doi.org/10.3389/fpsyg.2022.783909

Landon-Murray, M., Mujkic E., & Nussbaum, B. (2019). Disinformation in Contemporary U.S. Foreign Policy: Impacts and Ethics in an Era of Fake News, Social Media, and Artificial Intelligence. *Public Integrity*, 21(5), 512–522. https://doi.org/10.1080/10999922.2019.1613832

Luo, H., Cai, M., & Cui, Y. (2021). Spread of Misinformation in Social Networks: Analysis Based on Weibo Tweets. *Security and Communication Networks 2021*, 1–23. https://doi.org/10.1155/2021/7999760

Muhammed T, S., & Mathew, S. K. (2022). The disaster of misinformation: a review of research in social media. *International Journal of Data Science and Analytics*, 13, 271–285. https://doi.org/10.1007/s41060-022-00311-6

PolitiFact (2023). *The Principles of the Truth-O-Meter: PolitiFact's methodology for independent fact-checking*. Poynter Institute. https://www.politifact.com/article/2018/feb/12/principles-truth-o-meter-politifacts-methodology-i/#How%20PolitiFact%20Started

Rapp, D. N., & Salovich, N. A. (2018). Can't We Just Disregard Fake News? The Consequences of Exposure to Inaccurate Information. *Policy Insights from the Behavioral and Brain Sciences*, 5(2), 232–239. https://doi.org/10.1177/2372732218785193

Zhou, L., Tao, J., & Zhang, D. (2022). Does Fake News in Different Languages Tell the Same Story? An Analysis of Multi-level Thematic and Emotional Characteristics of News about COVID-19. *Inf Syst Front*. https://doi.org/10.1007/s10796-022-10329-7

CYBERPHARMACY: A FUTURE PLATFORM OF SERIOUS GAMES FOR HEALTHCARE

Yong-Young Kim
Department of Business Administration, Konkuk University,
268 Chungwon-daero Chungju-si Chungcheongbuk-do 27478, Republic of Korea

ABSTRACT

Digital technologies have had an innovative impact on healthcare and medicine. In order to grow the serious games for healthcare (SGHs) market, it is necessary to identify issues related to the establishment and operation of a distribution platform. In particular, a platform strategy needs to distribute efficiently and effectively SGHs by participating various stakeholders such as game developers, consumers (patients), medical experts, and government officials. Therefore, this study presents a distribution platform called *CyberPharmacy* as a strategy necessary to establish and operate a SGHs distribution platform.

KEYWORDS

CyberPharmacy, Serious Games for Healthcare, Digital Therapeutics (DTx), Distribution Platform, Hyper-Personalization

1. INTRODUCTION

The term serious game began in 1970 with the book "Serious Games" by sociologist Clark C. Abt (Abt, 1970), who defined serious games as 'games whose main purpose is education, not play and pleasure for users'. Since then, the applied area of serious games has expanded not only to the field of education but also to military, healthcare, and business. Serious games for health (SGHs) are categorized by a set of users such as personal, professional, research/academic and public health cross related with a set of serious games objectives including preventive, therapeutic, assessment, education, and informatics. (Wattanasoontorn et al., 2013).

Recently, digital therapeutics (DTx) is emerged as a new therapeutic approach for the prevention management, or treatment of chronic, behaviour-changeable diseases (Kim & Choi, 2021). DTx is "an evidence-based therapeutic intervention using high-quality software programs to prevent, manage, or treat a medical disorder or disease" (DTA, 2020). DTx is implemented in various forms, such as applications, virtual reality, and chatbots, as well as (serious) games. The medical paradigm shift triggered by the FDA's DTx approval and rapid development of digital technologies such as extended reality (XR), artificial intelligence (AI), big data, machine learning (ML) and 5G networks are leading digital healthcare innovation.

In order to grow the SGHs market, it is necessary to identify issues related to the establishment and operation of a distribution platform. In particular, a platform strategy needs to distribute efficiently and effectively SGHs by participating various stakeholders such as game developers, consumers (patients), medical experts, and government officials. Therefore, this study presents a distribution platform called *CyberPharmacy* as a strategy necessary to establish and operate a SGHs distribution platform.

2. RELATED WORK

2.1 Comparison between Serious Games for Health and DTx

Based on the primary commercialization approach (Gautam *et al.*, 2020), SGHs can be divided into three types: DTC, OTC, and Rx. First, there are direct-to-consumer (DTC) SGHs. The DTC type refers to serious games for health that consumers can choose and use without going through the hands of doctors or pharmacists. The

DTC type covers a wide range of general health and wellness concepts as opposed to specific indications. The second type is the over-the-counter (OTC) SGHs. The OTC type means serious games for healthcare that are not prescribed by a doctor, but can be handed over to a patient at the judgment of a pharmacist. In other words, although approval from the Ministry of Food and Drug Safety in Korea is not required, SGHs belonging to the OCT type can be used to retain clinical data, help manage diseases, or optimize medication. Finally, it is a medical prescription (Rx) type of SGHs. The Rx type is a cure for disease, which should be used according to the degree of disease and may have serious side effects, so it is illegal to medicate, prescribe, use these SGHs without a doctor's prescription.

In general, SGHs are distributed through games developers, publishers, and distributors and delivered to consumers. Given the aforementioned commercialization approach of SGHs, it can be classified in the type of DTC. However, after *EndeavorRx*® was first approved by the FDA, a lot of SGHs have been developed in the form of Rx. In the future, Rx-type SGHs are expected to increase through government approval. In addition, SGHs in the type of DTC and OTC and SGHs in the type of variants are expected to increase rapidly, and the market size of SGSs is expected to be growing sharply.

2.2 Healthcare Paradigm Shift

Tarakji *et al.* (2020) suggested that digital technologies have had an innovative impact on healthcare and medicine. Traditional models required collaboration between doctors, scientists, and industries to create drug therapy or device therapy, and to undergo comprehensive testing and clinical trials before physicians could apply it directly to patients. Recent emerging models follow the process of innovative companies developing products, presenting them directly to consumers, and introducing some FDA-approved products to the medical community. With the new model, doctors and healthcare providers often find themselves on the receiving end and realize that they cannot keep up with technological advances. In the case of the DTC-type SGHs, its effectiveness has been verified based on data obtained while using the SGHs and has emerged as a new way to enter the medical community.

According to Goldsmith *et al.* (2022), the paradigm shift in healthcare can be summarized as follows. First of all, AI and ML will lead the current human-driven drug screening and development in the future, and human capabilities will be dramatically expanded by utilizing these technologies. Second, medication is now often prescribed to everyone in a one-size-fits-all manner, and patients are left to mass market therapeutics. However, in the future, personalized treatment optimized by developing genome sequencing, precision dosing, and data analytics will be possible. In addition, advances in these technologies will help patients save money and optimize their healthcare systems. Finally, prevention, detection, and treatment of diseases are currently managed preferentially through episodic in-person consultations for patients. In the future, however, healthcare will take advantage of the accessibility provided by technology. Health risks can be proactively analysed using DTx, genomics, ML, and telehealth. Keywords for future healthcare can be summarized as (1) technology (ML and AI), (2) personalization and optimization, and (3) accessibility.

3. CYBERPHARMACY MODEL

CyberPharmacy is a distribution platform for SGHs. The participants of the SGHs may vary for each distribution stage according to the type of DTC, OTC, and Rx. For example, Rx-type SGHs are diagnosed by a physician, but in the case of a DTC, the consumers (patients) are diagnosed by themselves. SGHs are more likely to be selected through recommendations by AI as well as medical experts such as doctors and pharmacists based on the actual effects and data experienced by consumers (patients) after SGHs use rather than being verified for safety and effectiveness by the government such as FDA. Therefore, beyond the stages of research/development, approval, manufacturing, distribution, and consumption of traditional medicines, the development of SGHs and the use of consumers (patients) will evolve into a method of applying them to the pharmaceutical community.

CyberPharmacy is a multi-sided distribution platform involving various stakeholders such as medical experts, game developers, consumers (patients), and pharmaceutical companies. As shown in Figure 1, the distribution process goes through diagnosis, prescription, design, computing, personalized SGHs, and remote monitoring. It is noteworthy here that SGHs allow consumers (patients) to have an optimal medical experience through remote monitoring. In addition, intelligent recommendation systems and diagnostic systems using AI and ML may be applied to lead to full cusomizaiotn and optimal health coutcomes. The data collected through these monitoring can be used to optimize the current state of the consumers (patients) as well as to provide SGHs that are highly effective to other consumers (patients).

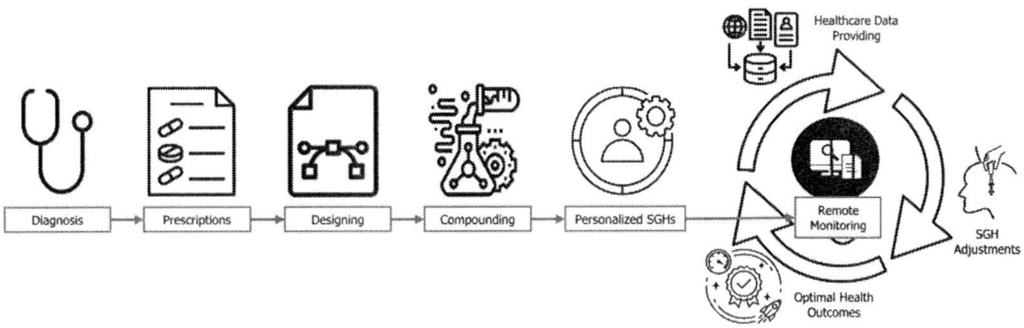

Figure 1. Cyberpharmacy process model

4. CONCLUSIONS

CyberPharmacy plays the following role as a distribution platform. First, *CyberPharmacy* integrates the knowledge of various stakeholders such as medical experts, game developers, consumers (patients), and pharmaceutical companies to provide services ranging from the development of SGHs components and modules for diagnosis, prescription, designing, compounding, and remote monitoring. Second, *CyberPharmacy* can provide full customization through hyper-personalization, which is an advanced and real-time customization of offering, content and customer experience at an individual level. Third, experiential knowledge can complement mechanisms that can provide various services in real time and streamline governance. As customized services are developed, diagnosed, prescribed, designed, and used through *CyberPharmacy*, learning occurs, and data related to *CyberPharmacy* operation are accumulated through this experience. By analysing and utilizing the data, it is possible to supplement the current maintenance mechanism and streamline governance.

ACKNOWLEDGEMENT

This research was supported by "Regional Innovation Strategy (RIS)" through the National Research Foundation of Korea (NRF) funded by the Ministry of Education (MOE) (2021RIS-001).

REFERENCES

Abt, C. C., 1970, *Serious Games*, The Viking Press, New York.

Digital Therapeutics Alliance (DTA), 2020. *A New Category of Medicine*. Available from: https://dtxalliance.org.

Gautam, L., Opler, T., & Xu, V. *Digital Therapeutics and the Future of Pharma*, Torreya (2020).

Goldsmith, P. et al., 2022. *One Size Doesn't Fit All, Closed Loop Medicine : A New Age in Healthcare*. Availablefrom: https://www.closedloopmedicine.com/white-paper/

Kim, M. and Choi, H. J., 2021. Digital Therapeutics for Obesity and Eating-Related Problems, *Endocronololgy and Metabolism*, Vol. 36, No. 2, pp. 220-228.

Tarakji. K. G. et al., 2020. Digital Health and the Care of the Patient with Arrhythmia, *Circulation: Arrhythmia and Electrophysiology*, Vol. 13, No. 11, pp.1397-1408.

Wattanasoontorn, V. et al., 2013. Serious Games for Health Care. *Entertainment Computing*, Vol. 4, No.4, pp. 231-247.

DICOM METADATA - A USEFUL RESOURCE FOR BIG DATA ANALYTICS

Francisco Maestre[1], Ana Paula Sorrell[2], Christian Mata[2,3] and Miguel Cabrer[1]
[1] *Idonia Medical Exchange, Palma de Mallorca, Spain*
[2] *Universitat Politèctica de Catalunya, Barcelona, Spain*
[3] *Fundació de Recerca Sant Joan de Déu, Barcelona, Spain*

ABSTRACT

This project provides an overview of new ways to represent data combining patient access and Medical Images (DICOM) information, advanced use of medical imaging metadata and the process to anonymize the personal health information contained to facilitate medical research.

KEYWORDS

DICOM Metadata, Big Data, Personal Health Information, Anonymization

1. INTRODUCTION AND OBJECTIVES

Data is the world's most valuable resource and it is possible to find data everywhere. In medical images, data covers not only gigapixel images, but also metadata and quantitative measurements (Aiello et al. 2021). DICOM (Digital Imaging and Communications in Medicine) is a clear source of medical data, since it is the current standard for storing and transmitting medical images (Aiello et al. 2021) and related information (Savaris et al. 2014); this means it contains raw data imaging and all metadata related to the procedures of image acquisition and curation (Aiello et al. 2021).

Idonia is a medical imaging exchange platform that facilitates the collection, storage, delivery and visualization of medical images for medical centers, professionals and patients. Over 200 million medical images (DICOM) have been processed and delivered up to today; with them, a necessity arose: this was studying the medical data contained in them in order to see if any conclusions could be drawn from such examination. This was possible thanks to a service called Magic Link, a tool to deliver medical images to patients that replaces the use of CD/USB, which simplified the process of accessing the data.

So the purpose and objectives of the internal research project were basically two:

- Analyze that the metadata contained into the DICOM images is valuable data with concreate patient related information.
- Demonstrate that DICOM metadata and medical reports can be processed and anonymized to facilitate clinical research and collaboration between organizations.

2. DATA LAKE FOR MEDICAL IMAGING ACTIVITY

DICOM is the current standard for storing and transmitting medical images (Aiello 2021) and it is defined as the international standard for medical images and related information. It was originally developed by the American College of Radiology (ACR) and the National Electrical Manufacturers Association (NEMA) (Savaris et al. 2014). Its first publication, in 1993, revolutionized the practice of radiology, allowing the replacement of x-ray film with a fully digital workflow (Aiello et al. 2021).

The DICOM standard comprises a set of specifications regarding structure, format, and exchange protocols for digital-based medical images. In other words, it defines the formats for medical images that can be exchanged with the data and quality necessary for clinical use (Aiello et al. 2021). This means it contains raw data imaging and all metadata related to the procedures of image acquisition and curation (AAPM 2008).

DICOM images consist of textual metadata (Kathiravelu et al. 2021); in fact, a DICOM file contains both the image and a large variety of data in the header (Aiello et al. 2021). Physically, the content of a DICOM file can be seen as structured at the data element level (Savaris et al. 2021), which means that the information recorded on the file are the attributes; these shall be ordered by increasing data element tag number and shall occur at most once in a data set (Aiello et al. 2021).

After two years of research, we created the Data Lake under an R&D project supported by the CDTI (*Centro para el Desarrollo Tecnológico Industrial*) from the Ministry of Science and Innovation of Spain. The purpose of this tool was to analyze all the information provided by the clients –hospitals at most– to provide them with relevant and new information about their own data and also to facilitate a way to analyze, process, anonymize, extract and exchange data in a legal way to facilitate clinical research and collaboration.

So, the data lake metadata information was created with standard data warehouse techniques based on cloud computing (ETLs, Bigquery and Google Cloud). The datalake was containing the metadata information combined with the accessibility information, who has accessed the images obtained from Idonia Magic Link functionality.

The Data Lake obtains and analyses some relevant information from DICOM metadata:

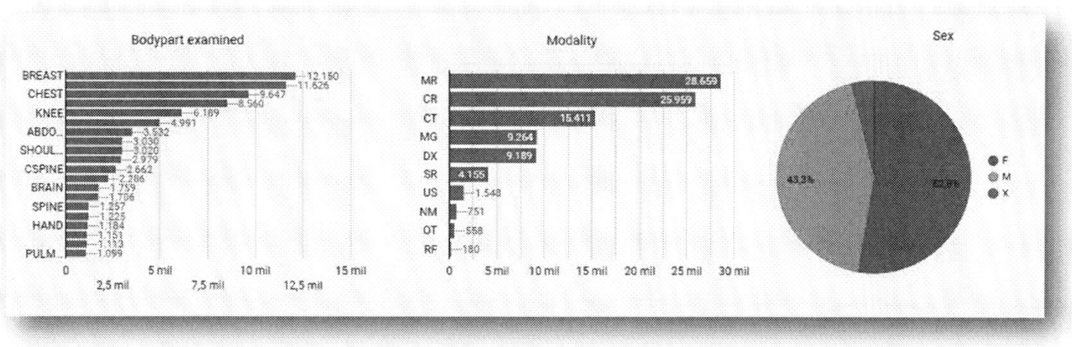

Figure 1. DICOM Metadata analyzed by Data Lake

The first analysis was done around medical imaging activity combined with some information stored in DICOM images, such as the imaging technique, manufacturer of the medical device, the patient's body part examined and modality of study, etc. This information was shared with clients via the development of a command center functionality that went beyond traditional dashboards: it also contained access information from both professionals and patients.

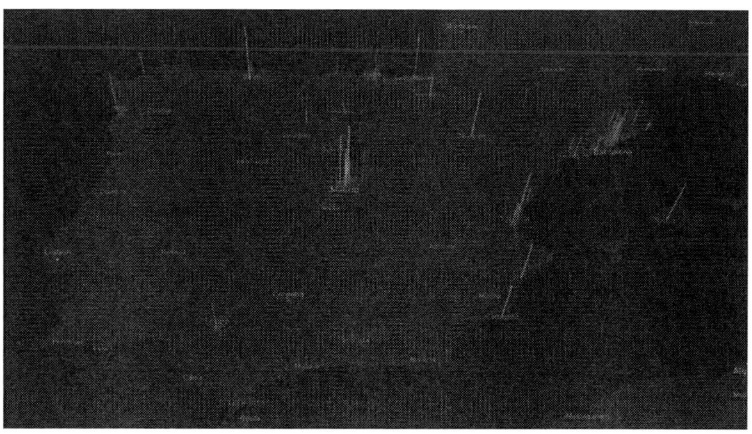

Figure 2. Example of information from patients accessing their medical studies

It was also possible to generate a *medical device activity map*, that provided some useful information about medical devices, generated information, their activity and remote access to their generated content.

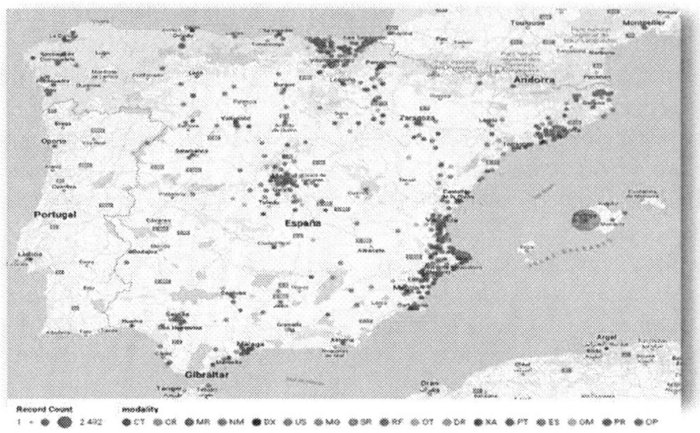

Figure 3. Example of information from medical devices

2.1 Data Analytics Around Radiation

In the first objective of the research, we analyzed several DICOM Metadata Tags willing to encounter valuable concrete medical information that is relevant and is normally out of the scope of a traditional Electronic Medical Record. The radiation information contained in the DICOM Images was capturing our attention.

After years of studying medical related information, it was found that the most relevant data relied on radiation dose parameters, and from this, the idea of developing a digital tool to analyze radiation-related data originated.

In the current defined Directives and Regulations, no limits on the radiation dose are stipulated for patients undergoing diagnostic nor treatment procedures. There is proof that ionising radiation has direct implications in human health (ICRP 1990), which is why measures need to be taken as soon as possible.

These actions start with being able to quantify the radiation received by a patient in studies over time, which can be done by means of a DICOM dataset of metadata. With the available DICOM data, it is possible to quantify radiation with the effective dose, a parameter that serves as a dose descriptor (AAPM Report 2008).

The purpose of this research part of the project (Sorrell et al. 2022) was to extract and analyze the data and compare it with the SEPR (*Sociedad Española de Protección Radiológica*) and the ICRP (*International Commission on Radiological Protection*) recommendations. The result of this is differently structured/organized data sets, which makes data analysis a complex challenge. Since the information is valuable, different techniques can be applied in order to collect that information.

The imparted ionising radiation to a patient has always been the main concern in radiology, since there is substantial evidence of adverse effects due to radiation exposure. The process of ionization that occurs when imparting radiation to a patient changes atoms and molecules and may sometimes damage cells (ICRP 1990).

The European Council Directive 2013/59/EURATOM, of 5 December 2013, establishes uniform basic safety standards for the protection of the health of individuals subject to occupational, medical and public exposures against the dangers arising from ionizing radiation. It defines medical exposure as the exposure incurred by patients in order to be diagnosed or treated of any disease. In disparity with the dose limits for professional workers and the public in both occupational and public exposures, neither the Directive nor any of the Spanish Regulations establishes any limits on patient dose. In fact, in Article 6.1, it says that the radiological protection of the exposed patient will be optimized in order to keep the individual doses *as low as reasonably possible* (ALARP). Article 6.2 follows up with this and establishes that, in medical exposures, dose restrictions will only apply with respect to the protection of caregivers and volunteers involved in medical or biomedical research.

Let's take Computed Tomography (CT) as an example. CT scans consist of a computerized x-ray imaging procedure in which a narrow beam of x-rays is aimed at a patient and quickly rotates around the body.

CT images are based on the different x-ray absorption rates of the various organs of the human body, which is why it provides both good soft tissue resolution (contrast) as well as high spatial resolution

(Zhanli et al. 2009). To ensure the best resolution, the dose imparted must be considerably high; in fact, the dose levels imparted in CT exceed those from conventional radiography and fluoroscopy and the use of CT continues to grow, often by 10% to 15% per year, which leads to a discussion of radiation risk versus medical benefit (AAPM Reports 2008). At the end of the day, what matters are the long-term repercussions of radiation exposure, which is why the American Association of Physicists in Medicine (AAPM) has defined several dose parameters to provide guidance on reasonable CT dose levels on routine examinations (AAPM 2008).

3. PROCESSING DICOM METADATA AND MEDICAL REPORTS FOR RESEARCH PURPOSES

The research organizations need real medical content in order to analyze the information and be able to cross data, build AI models or medical research. Idonia has been creating a relevant database of medical images (200 millions) combined with access information from patients and doctors. This allows to profile patients and medical devices and brings interesting information that can be analyze or combined with a medical data warehouse to complement and cross more information.

The Medical information is a high-level protected information by all country regulations (GDPR in Europe, HIPAA in the United States). So, in order to be able to facilitate a data lake that can be used for researchers or collaboration purposes between organizations, it has to be properly anonymized / de-identified.

Once the Data lake was created, the second step was to create a tool to search and navigate on the data lake and build the processes to anonymize data and process.

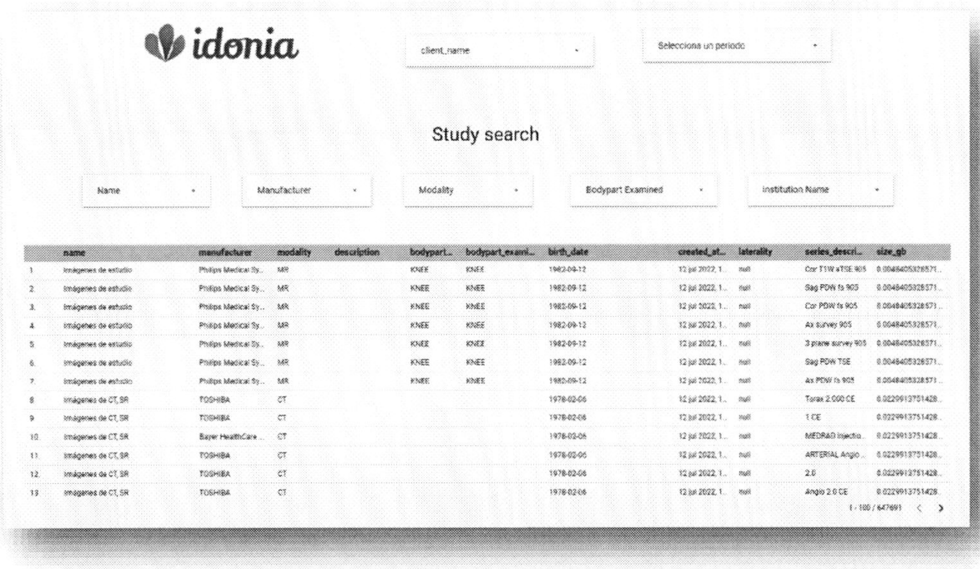

Figure 4. Tool to search for medical images on the DICOM Metadata Data Lake

The information associated to medical images is normally containing a DICOM structure (metadata and images) and medical reports (normally PDFs). The process of data manipulation the data was divided in two:

- DICOM Anonymization: through tag morphing techniques and ID Hash (tag removal, tag redaction, tag shifting) combined with PixelData De-identification in case image has printed data on it.
- Reports in SR, PDF, TXT format conversion, identification and removal of sensitive data, translation in multiple languages (to facilitate international research initiatives) exporting a de-identify and translated report.

The process took around 8 months to be implemented with double processed in some cases to ensure personal data is not involved. Techniques used for all the processes were OCR, Reports Translation, Tag removal, Hashing, data loss prevention, pixel data analysis.

4. CONCLUSION

The delivery of medical images in a secure and efficient way is a necessary functionality up to date, and specially patients are taking benefit from it. Accumulating those delivered images in a cloud infrastructure, analyze the data generated around them may bring great benefits for the medical centers to better understand their patient profiling and medical activity and promote research. An infinite loop of value is created.

DICOM files contain both the image and a large variety of metadata. This metadata provides valuable information for many different applications, including a radiation-related study. At the presented project, a Metadata Data Lake was created with deep analysis of valuable DICOM Tags (like radiation dose).

The data exploration executed was remarkable throughout and allowed a deep understanding on how DICOM files are constructed. The value of aggregating all the information from different sources in one common dataset (Data lake) opens new possibilities to analyze or enrich the data that can benefit all data providers.

Then the objective of demonstrating that that can be prepared, manipulated, combined and extracted without patient information and in a way that researchers can reuse it for their R&D projects was also achieved. It took time and the need of combining different techniques but finally a successful test was performer and validated by some institutions involved.

DICOM has some very interesting medical metadata available, thus can complement a Big Data and Analytics project in the medicine scope. The medical imaging delivery service based on cloud technology allows to combine disparate information like the remote accessibility from patients and professionals with the DICOM metadata. A proper data warehousing and personal data removal techniques offer the possibility to reuse the content for medical research purpose. This unique way to analyze the information is just a first step but the potential is huge. The aggregate information obtained from different sources through cloud infrastructure not only enriches the data source but provides more potential capabilities for deep learning data analytics.

REFERENCES

Aiello M, Esposito G, Pagliari G et al. (2021) *How does DICOM support big data management? Investigating its use in medical imaging community*. Insights into Imaging. 12(1):1-21.

Savaris A, Härder T, von Wangenheim A (2014) Evaluating a row-store data model for full-content DICOM management. Proceedings - IEEE Symposium on Computer- Based Medical Systems. 193–198.

Zhanli H, Hairong Z, Jianbao G, Ying Z (2009) *Real-time gray and coordinate statistics methods of medical CT image*. 3rd International Conference on Bioinformatics and Biomedical Engineering. 1-4.

Juszczyk J et al. (2021) *Automated size-specific dose estimates using deep learning image processing*. Medical Image Analysis. 68:101898.

Kathiravelu P, Sharma A, Sharma P (2021) *Understanding Scanner Utilization with Real-Time DICOM Metadata Extraction*. IEEE Access. 9:10621–10633.

ICRP (1990) ICRP Publication 60: 1990 *Recommendations of the International Commission on Radiological Protection*. Available at https://journals.sagepub.com/doi/pdf/10.1177/ANIB_21_1-3

American Association of Physicists in Medicine (2008). *The Measurement, Reporting, and Management of Radiation Dose in CT*. Available at https://www.aapm.org/pubs/reports/rpt_96.pdf

SEPR, "*SEPR - Requisitos básicos para los sistemas de registro y gestión de dosis en pacientes sometidos a exploraciones de diagnóstico por imagen*," 2020. Accessed: Jun. 14, 2022. [Online]. Available: https://revistadefisicamedica.es/index.php/rfm/article/view/328

"*Computed Tomography (CT)*." https://www.nibib.nih.gov/science-education/science-topics/computed-tomography-ct (accessed Jun. 14, 2022).

Ana Paula Sorrell Meriño, Christian Mata. *Analysis of Radiation Dose Using DICOM Metadata*. EEBE, Universitat Politècnica de Catalunya (UPC), Bachelor's Degree in Biomedical Engineering, defended 28/06/2022, Barcelona, Spain

TOWARDS THE E-SOCIETY: SOCIAL MEDIA AS A TOOL TO SUPPORT E-PARTICIPATION

Tereza Zichová
Faculty of Informatics and Statistics, Prague University of Economics and Business, Czech Republic

ABSTRACT

E-governance consists in the application of information and communication technologies to government functions and processes to increase efficiency, transparency, and e-participation. The level of society's participation in electronic government services is an important element in assessing the success of the entire system. However, e-participation values in the context of negotiations with public administration remain low in the European Union. State institutions are trying to encourage citizen participation in various ways, one of which is the use of social networks. The purpose of the paper is to analyse the use of a wide range of social media by European financial e-administrations and tax e-offices in order to highlight the differences and discuss their potential benefits. The data comes from an online research analyses of 31 European financial authorities' portals. The findings show significant variation in the strategies for setting up systems of online communication for national financial institutions, and there is considerable potential for mutual inspiration on how to achieve effective public e-government. The results of the paper reveal new findings and insights for inspiration and development across disciplines (strategic, content, and social media management), for discussion among politicians and decision-makers, and for application by public authorities. The findings may also stimulate and inspire various possibilities of future research.

KEYWORDS

E-Society, E-Participation, E-Administration, E-Government, Tax Portal, Social Media

1. INTRODUCTION

Society faces many challenges and opportunities brought about by the fourth industrial revolution (Chen et al., 2018). Citizens around the world are increasingly using technology to simplify everyday activities – a challenge for governments and public institutions, which are not as exposed to the competitive environment as companies that seek to retain their customers. The latest available data from a joint analysis by Hootsuite and We Are Social shows that the number of internet users has more than doubled in the last decade, from 2.18 billion to 4.95 billion. The compound annual growth rate for the period of 2012–2022 is 8.6% (Kemp, 2022a). As of July 2022, of the world's total population of 7.98 billion, 63% use the internet, 59% actively use social networking sites and 67% have some form of mobile phone. The information society saw an especially high growth during the peak of the COVID-19 pandemic. The main reason people are using the internet most is to find information (61% respondents aged 16–64 have stated this motivation). A vast majority of the respondents (95.2%) have used or visited social networks. Around 4.7 billion people (59% of the total population, 93.6% of total internet users) are social media users, with the average number of social platforms used each month equal to 7.4. The proportion of social media users in the total population is highest in Northern and Western Europe (Kemp, 2022b). Members of Generation Z and Generation Alpha in particular have grown up in the era of technology and the internet. The birth years of each generation are not officially anchored and vary in scientific studies. For Generation Z, the range of birth years is usually 1997–2012 (Pew Research Center, 2019) or 1995–2010 (Jha, 2020). Jha (2020) identifies the birth years of Generation Alpha as 2011–2025. These are highly technologically literate generations that have high expectations for simplicity and interactive design and communicate primarily through social media. These facts indirectly influence their thinking and decision-making process (Hariadi et al., 2016). The user-friendliness of communication with the financial administration represents an important factor influencing citizens' perception when paying taxes and insurance premiums (Zichová, 2022). This concerns both offline and online channels.

The e-society is multi-dimensional phenomenon where information technologies are integrated into the society's mindsets and lifestyles. Jayashree & Marthandan (2010) define e-society as the society that uses digital media in most relationships. E-Participation is based on public participation in governance through information and communication technologies. Electronic participation as a socioeconomic movement propagates the increased level of cooperation between public and civic institutions through various digital platforms (Macintosh, 2004). The interorganizational relations theory, especially in relationship to the investigation of participatory trends, could be traced in various digital collaborative projects and related social media platforms (Kassen, 2020). The number and character of social media offered by e-government can increase level of e-participation. The average e-participation rate in the context of dealing with public administrations in the 25 evaluated European countries is 58%. The data comes from the Czech Statistical Office (CSO) and Eurostat, with the CSO reporting data for people aged 16 and over, whereas Eurostat publishes data for people aged 16–74. The highest activity is observed among citizens in the Nordic countries of Sweden and Finland, closely followed by the Netherlands, Estonia, and France. The lowest proportion is in Romania, where only 15% of citizens used the internet to communicate with public administrations in 2021. A similar ranking of countries can logically be observed when comparing the number of people aged 16–74 in EU countries who have completed and submitted an online form to public administrations, but the overall EU average is lower (ČSÚ, 2022; Eurostat, 2021).

The popularity and importance of social media use is constantly growing, especially among the younger generations. Therefore, it is worthwhile to address their coverage by the public e-administration. Social networks are changing the purpose of the internet as a tool to propagate products and promote sales. They offer less expensive and more effective means of online marketing and new approaches to communication, helping companies develop their business and communication strategy (Drahošová & Balco, 2017). Raising awareness through effective public communication campaigns is becoming a prerequisite both for informing people about the benefits of digital services and for ensuring wider use of online platforms. If people do not realize the value of e-government online services, they will not be willing to use them. Governments have countless tools through which to inform – from banners, materials for public campaigns, videos for television and materials for personal face-to-face sessions with people to a wide range of social networks (with Twitter and LinkedIn more on the formal side, and less formal options including Facebook, Instagram, YouTube, TikTok, Pinterest, Snapchat, Tumblr) (United Nations, 2020).

2. RESEARCH METHODS

The research method consists of online research analyses of 31 European public financial institutions – ministries of finance and tax portals. States use different terminology, which is based on the legislative setting of responsibility for the given area (Tax portal – summarizing all taxes or specifically income tax, Financial Administration / Ministry of Finance / Tax Administration and similar institutions). Content analysis refers to finding the occurrence of their associated social media. The information is translated from foreign languages using Google Translator, an automatic translator, supplemented where necessary by DeepL Translator. The types of social platforms used by ministries and tax portals are inductively developed and documented manually in Microsoft Excel, which was chosen as it provides a sufficient overview tool for the intended analysis. Data is obtained from the websites of European Union member states plus the four countries of the Schengen area or the countries of the European Free Trade Association, searched on the European Union website (Iceland, Liechtenstein, Norway and Switzerland). Their relevance is verified by the presence of a link on government portals. Social network page links are searched for on the websites of state financial institutions; the information is usually contained on the website of the tax administration (Tax Administration, Tax Agency, Federal Public Service, Ministry of Taxes, etc.) and the website of the tax portal. Their existence is also directly verified on the relevant social networks: Facebook, Instagram, YouTube, LinkedIn, TikTok, Twitter, SoundCloud, Flickr, Dailymotion and WhatsApp. Non-functional links (e.g., the Scribd profile of the Croatian Ministry of Finance) are omitted from the analysis. The analysis includes all the social networks mentioned by both portals. The main subject of the analysis is Financial e-Government, in some cases countries provide tax information directly from the Ministry of Finance instead of the online tax administration. Secondarily, the author tracks the content of the tax portals to the extent accessible to her as a resident of the Czech Republic, as well as content on the associated social networks. Links to social networks most often appear in the footer of the website as symbols, in some cases as text or even as a written link (e.g., the Lithuanian Ministry of Finance website https://finmin.lrv.lt/). In rare cases, social networking links are not a standardised part of the footer of the website but are found in the site header, in the body of the page as a banner (the Malta Ministry of Finance website http://www.mfin.gov.mt/), as icons or in the contacts.

3. RESULTS

The analysis produced results summarising the use of social networks by financial e-administrations and tax portals across European countries (see Table 1). All the ministries and tax portals of e-governments use at least one social media. Public financial institutions of European countries most often use Facebook, followed closely by Twitter. The third most common social media used is YouTube, which serves primarily for instructions on how to use tax forms and fulfil the obligations of citizens. Some social networks were only used in 1–3 cases (TikTok, Flickr, Dailymotion – a French social platform, SoundCloud, WhatsApp). No data could be traced for the Republic of Liechtenstein. Finland is the most active on social media, dominating with 7 actively used platforms. On average, 3.5 social networks are used per country.

Table 1. Use of social networks by European financial e-administrations and tax portals

Country	Facebook	Instagram	YouTube	LinkedIn	TikTok	Twitter	Flickr	Dailymotion	SoundCloud	WhatsApp	Total
BE	X		X	X		X					4
BG	X		X	X							3
CZ	X	X	X			X					4
DK	X		X	X		X					4
EE	X		X			X					3
FI	X	X	X	X	X	X			X		7
FR	X	X	X			X		X			5
HR	X	X	X	X		X					5
IE				X		X					2
IT	X	X	X			X					4
CY			X			X					2
LT	X										1
LV	X	X	X			X	X				5
LU	X			X		X					3
HU	X	X	X			X					4
MT	X										1
DE						X					1
NL	X	X				X				X	4
PL	X	X	X			X					4
PT	X	X	X			X					4
AT	X		X				X				3
RO	X	X	X			X				X	5
GR	X		X			X					3
SK	X	X	X	X							4
SI	X		X			X					3
ES	X	X	X	X	X	X					6
SE	X		X	X		X					4
NO	X	X		X		X	X				5
IS	X					X					2
LI											-
CH				X		X					2
Total	26	14	21	12	2	25	3	1	1	2	

4. DISCUSSION

The governments of European countries use different types of social networks. An interesting perspective is provided by their comparison with the world's most frequently used and most popular social media platforms, based on Kemp's (Kemp, 2022b) global report. The world's most-used social platform in July 2022 (per global active users) was Facebook with 2,936 million users followed by YouTube and WhatsApp. The fourth position with the highest number of users was Instagram. The remaining top ten social networks per active user count, from 5th to 10th place, are the following: WeChat, TikTok, Facebook Messenger, Telegram, Snapchat and Douyin. In Europe, Twitter is a more relevant social media for the tenth position. However, from the point of view of popularity the most favorite platforms are (in order from the most popular): WhatsApp, Instagram,

Facebook, WeChat, TikTok, Douyin, Twitter, Facebook Messenger, Telegram and Line (Kemp, 2022b). The research brings some limitations. Social media is not homogeneous. Therefore, their comparison within a single table could be arguable. Due to the simplistic type of research method, the paper mainly provides thematic areas and a basis for follow-up in-depth studies. The research could be supplemented with details regarding the level of cooperation/usage, goals, scope (public/private, citizen/clerk), percentage of cases compared to traditional data exchange and social cooperation.

Several factors may account for the low e-participation rate. The United Nations survey (United Nations, 2020) recommends that governments should: 1. Clarify the objectives of e-participation activities and understand the needs, interests, motives and incentives of stakeholders in relation to e-participation. 2. Facilitate the institutionalization of e-participation processes within government departments. 3. Pay attention to the legal, regulatory and administrative environment in which e-participation takes place. 4. Establish clear linkages between e-participation activities and formal decision-making processes. 5. Promote the acquisition of e-participation skills in the population. 6. Understand how e-participation is affected by people's trust in public institutions, the internet and social media. 7. Strengthen the evaluation of e-participation initiatives.

5. CONCLUSION

The study provides an overview of the different social networks used by the financial administrations of the European Union. The problem of the use of social networks in e-government offers a wide range of possibilities for further research. Through interviews and questionnaires, it would be possible to penetrate deeper into the perception of e-government social networks by citizens. This could also reveal interesting opinions on how to improve their content and bring it closer to users to increase e-practice. Another useful focus for research would be a comparison of mutual dependencies based on statistical methods. A comparison not only at the level of Europe, but also of other continents, including developing countries, taking into account cultural, historical and socio-economic differences, would also bring stimulating results. The challenges and opportunities of the use of social media by e-government and the tax portal also bring a wide range of possibilities for meta-analysis and thematic or cross-sectoral comparisons with regard to geographical differences. Last but not least, the content analysis of the social platforms of tax portals and relevant social networks can also be followed up in many directions, either by extending it to other e-government websites, to the image presented in the media or by focusing on different elements of the content analysis (e.g., the position and content of the headlines, information in the first paragraph, formatting of the text, informational value, choice of words and phrases, context, meaningfulness of the text and other linguistic elements). A more in-depth analysis of the amount and types of multimedia tools used (use of photos, videos, infographics, podcasts, etc.) would also be offered as part of the content analysis. Possible suggestions for future research activities are summarised in Table 2, framing the main methods embedded in the related disciplines and extending them with possible research questions and areas.

Table 2. Overview of future research opportunities

Method	Relevant disciplines	Research questions/areas
Interview	public financial institutions, social media, citizens' perception	*How do citizens perceive social media websites and e-government applications?* *What value do citizens attach to the social platforms of public institutions?*
Questionnaire survey	e-participation, social media, citizens' perception	*Are there statistically significant differences in the perception of the use of social networks by e-government between individual age groups, between genders, on the basis of residence or educational attainment?* *If people perceived the use of social networks more positively, would they use e-government social platforms more often?*
Systematic mapping	e-government, strategy, social media	*What are the latest insights into the challenges and opportunities of government use of social media from studies over the past decade?* *Which areas of the given field are attracting the most attention from researchers?* *On which continents/in which countries/universities/research centres?*

Content analysis	tax portal, e-government websites and applications, e-participation, media, social media, multimedia	*What future challenges in the context of the use of social media by digital government can be expected given the transformational tendency towards Society 5.0 and Industry 5.0?* *Does the information content of different e-government applications and sites differ?* *What percentage of the population of each country follows the local social media of public financial institutions?* *How often and how do they react to different types of social network posts?* *Can differences also be seen internationally/intercontinentally?* *Which multimedia tools are used most frequently on e-government websites and applications?*

REFERENCES

Chen, B., Wan, J., Shu, L., Li, P., Mukherjee, M. & Yin, B. (2018). Smart Factory of Industry 4.0: Key Technologies, Application Case, and Challenges. *IEEE Access*, vol. 6, pp. 6505–6519.

ČSÚ (2022). *Informační společnost v číslech* [Information society in numbers], Czech Republic and European Union. https://www.czso.cz/documents/10180/164503431/06100422.pdf/69ccf5e2-92e8-4dcd-b22a-cb3df3e8119a?version=1.3

Drahošová, M., & Balco, P. (2017). The analysis of advantages and disadvantages of use of social media in European Union. *ANT/SEIT*.

Eurostat (2021). *Comprehensive Database*. Eurostat. https://ec.europa.eu/eurostat/web/digital-economy-and-society/data/comprehensive-database

Hariadi, B., Sunarto, M. J. D. & Sudarmaningtyas, P. (2016) Development of Web-Based Learning Application for Generation Z, *International Journal of Evaluation and Research in Education (IJERE)*, vol. 5, no. 1, pp. 60–68. https://doi.org/10.11591/ijere.v5i1.4523

Jayashree, S. & Marthandan, G. (2010). Government to E-government to E-society. *Journal of Applied Sciences*, vol. 10, pp. 2205–2210. https://doi.org/10.3923/jas.2010.2205.2210

Jha, A. (2020). *Understanding Generation Alpha*. https://doi.org/10.31219/osf.io/d2e8g

Kemp, S. (2022a). *Digital 2022: Digital Adoption Doubled Over the Past Decade. DataReportal – Global Digital Insights*. https://datareportal.com/reports/digital-2022-digital-adoption-doubled-over-the-past-decade

Kemp, S. (2022b). *Digital 2022: July Global Statshot Report*. We Are Social a Hootsuite. https://wearesocial.com/uk/blog/2022/07/the-global-state-of-digital-in-july-2022/

Macintosh, A. (2004). Characterizing e-participation in policy-making. In: System Sciences, Proceedings of the 37th Annual Hawaii International Conference on System Sciences, pp. 10–pp. Big Island, Hawaii: IEEE.

Maxat Kassen (2020) E-participation actors: understanding roles, connections, partnerships, *Knowledge Management Research & Practice*, vol. 18, no. 1, pp. 16–37, https://doi.org/10.1080/14778238.2018.1547252

Pew Research Center (2019). *Defining Generations: Where Millennials End and Generation Z Begins*. Pew Research Center. https://www.pewresearch.org/fact-tank/2019/01/17/where-millennials-end-and-generation-z-begins/ft_19-01-17_generations_2019/

United Nations (2020). *E-Government Survey 2020*. ISBN 978-92-1-123210-3. https://publicadministration.un.org/egovkb/Portals/egovkb/Documents/un/2020-Survey/2020%20UN%20E-Government%20Survey%20(Full%20Report).pdf

Zichová, T. (2022). Public e-administration: Understanding the perception of taxes by Generation Y and Generation Z. In: *Proceedings of the international conferences on e-society 2022 and mobile learning 2022*. online, 12.03.2022 – 14.03.2022. Portugal: IADIS Press, 2022, pp. 248–252. eISBN 978-989-8704-38-2.

ZOOM APPLICATION FOR ONLINE LANGUAGE LEARNING

Charito Ong and Grace Pimentel
Professors, University of Science and Technology of Southern Philippines, Cagayan De Oro City, Philippines

ABSTRACT

Flexible learning in this pandemic combines a specific percentage of synchronous and asynchronous sessions. In this research, the adoption of Zoom as a discussion platform tool in teaching communicative English skills to tertiary education students in a public HEI is discussed; based on the Leapfrog Principle. The study investigated the effectiveness of Zoom as a language teaching tool in Language courses. It also examined the platform's role in new learning spaces with today's learners. Data for the study was collected via online class observation, followed by a recorded interview conducted among fifty-five students. The analysis of the data was done qualitatively. The findings of the study indicated that Zoom is perceived as an effective teaching tool; in terms of both delivery and pedagogy in Intensive English programs. It was also believed to cater to a flexible and motivating language learning environment for the current flexible learning academic scenarios. The integration of zoom application into the intensive Language courses for tertiary level learners, enriched the teaching-learning experiences.

KEYWORDS

Flexible Learning, Zoom Application, Effectiveness

1. INTRODUCTION

Su (2022) posits that success rate in language learning in these difficult and trying times is highly dependent on the kind of application that teachers utilize. This was found specifically true among Higher Education research studies conducted by Twainy (2021) and Zurik (2022). As the essential pillar in the educational system in this pandemic, zoom application assured learning gains. Hence, educational organizations are now motivated to accomplish language competence, efficacy and proficiency by remote means. This indicates the necessity of utilizing break out rooms, aside from the virtual teaching preparation teachers do for daily academic engagement.

However, engaging students in a variety of remote activities is not sufficient. To measure if they successfully enhanced their language competencies, the priority to conduct engaging remote communicative sessions are necessary. In their paper, Strei (2022) and Buor (2021) conclude that when zoom break out session rooms are activated, more students are able to freely share their ideas. Hence, this vital information to design the research plan was deemed necessary. The study therefore investigated the effectiveness of Zoom as a language teaching tool in Language courses. It also examined the platform's role in new learning spaces with today's learners.

2. METHODOLOGY

Discussed as follows are the methods and procedures of this study.

This research employed the descriptive and investigative research designs. The researchers gathered data from the research respondents through online class observation, Focus Group Discussion sessions and recorded interviews among the student-respondents. The need to develop communication skills through online discussion utilizing break out session rooms were identified; focusing on teaching strategies and communicative activities.

The paper utilized focus group discussion prompts modified from Zurong (2018). The same set of transcripts were employed during the individual interviews. The online class observation scrutinized the communicative measures used by the Language teachers. Nunan's (2015) communicative teaching observation tool was used. These validated instruments formed the descriptive and investigative research processes.

The respondents of this research were the fifty-five Higher Education students who were enrolled in English subjects for the second semester of school year 2021-2022. They were purposively chosen based on their teachers' recommendation to participate in the research plan, being the less participative. The researchers kept in touch with them through their language teachers. Group chats and zoom conferences were also conducted.

3. DATA GATHERING PROCEDURE

In this study, the researchers facilitated five focus group discussion sessions among the student-respondents. The modified FGD prompts were utilized for this purpose. The same group of respondents participated in the individual interview via zoom. This highlighted on their perception about the impact of zoom usage to their language competencies; the types of teaching strategies employed with their motivation to use the application, how the zoom sessions enhance their communicative abilities and critical thinking skills.

4. RESULTS AND DISCUSSION

The results of the study are discussed subsequently.

Table 1. The benefits of Zoom application as a learning tool

Zoom Application advantage	Number of Respondents
Increased motivation	16
Self-directed learning	10
Active interaction	35
Enhance communicative ability	33
Avenue to develop critical thinking skills	19

Table 1 shows that among the identified zoom application advantage, active interaction ranks first. The data is similarly situated with the study conducted by Levin (2022) which revealed that more students perceive zoom to be an enabler for discussion. This implies that the break out rooms helped the respondents to freely express their ideas, without fear of being corrected. Similarly, more students responded that zoom sessions are avenues to develop their critical thinking skills. This accordingly happened during break put sessions.

Table 2. Satisfaction levels with Zoom video conferencing

Satisfaction level	Number of Respondents
Very satisfied	40
satisfied	10
normal	3
dissatisfied	2
Very dissatisfied	0

Table 2 presents the satisfaction level of the respondents in zoom video conferences. Majority of the respondents were very satisfied of the application. Only ten ticked satisfied while three opted for normal satisfaction and two very dissatisfied. Consequently, the respondents found zoom nice even in listening to lectures. They were able to look at the professor's face which gave them the feeling similar with that of face-to-face lectures. More respondents shared that it was good to communicate with the professor, and it was also good that the professor listened to their opinion. With the screen sharing function, they found it easy to understand the subject by taking classes while watching PPT and class materials together. Some respondents also commented that zoom is a good application because it was like a customized class for them. The annotation button likewise made them share ideas in writing.

The study of Roiersy (2022) revealed similar findings. The paper discussed that the respondents of the study likened zoom to an actual physical class session. The only difference was that they were online. Moreover, Zerty (2021) in his study on zoom application implied that break out rooms provide comfort for the learners to express their interest in sharing ideas to topics that were assigned to them. They had interactive sessions as they were not governed by anxiety.

5. CONCLUSIONS & RECOMMENDATIONS

In conclusion, zoom application was found to gain popularity in the academe which was perceived by the respondents to enhance their communicative competence. Most universities converted their classes from face-to-face to online lectures in the duration of the COVID-19 pandemic. Within this context, the existing study attempted to examine the effect of real-time remote video lessons using Zoom on learners' English communication skills. The study also investigated learners' opinions on and satisfaction with real-time zoom video lectures. The study's purpose is to provide a better direction for instructors who wish to use zoom video lectures for real-time lessons in the future by more clearly understanding the efficiency of zoom video lectures and considering important points that must be supplemented. The results of this study showed that real-time zoom video lectures have a positive effect on learners' English reading achievement.

From the perspective of both learners and instructors, zoom is recommended to be supplemented with automatic attendance processing, convenient data uploading and downloading, and more efficient video screen management functions. Language instructors, must become further aware of the efficiency of Zoom technology in the EFL classroom. If remote classes must be prolonged due to the spread of COVID-19, instructors must learn how to implement technological tools including Zoom and develop class activities and teaching strategies suitable for video lectures that can encourage learners' active participation.

REFERENCES

Buor (2021). The challenges confronting the remote learning in higher education. International Journal of Language Management, 14, 18479790211049706.

Levin, M. (2022). Aligning the Needs of Students. European Journal of Education and Pedagogy, 3(1), 7-15.

Nunan, D. (2015). Views of Pre-service Teachers in Different Disciplines about Zoom Application. Malaysian Online Journal of Educational Technology, 9(2), 1-14.

Roierty, P. (2021). Communication games: Their contribution to developing speaking skills. International Journal of Instruction, 14(4), 643-658.

Strei, G. M. (2022). The effectiveness of alternative training activities in changing teaching practices. American educational research journal, 23(2), 217-225.

Su, G. (2022). College Communicative Teaching. International Association for Development of the Information Society.

Twainy, M. E. (2021). Teaching during a pandemic: do university teachers prefer online teaching?. Heliyon, 8(1), e08663.

Zerty, J. M. (2021). Student attitudes toward communicative and non-communicative activities: Do enjoyment and effectiveness go together?. The Modern Language Journal, 77(1), 1-10.

Zurik, R. (2022).Basic Training For Zoom Application. The Spirit of Society Journal, 1(1).

Zurong, C. (2018). Using collaboration to enhance communication skills in language classroom. In Proceedings of EDUTEACH conference (pp. 8-12). Thailand.

REFLECTION

ITERATIVE DEVELOPMENT OF AN INCLUSIVE LEARNING ENVIRONMENT FOR HUMAN ANATOMY STUDIES: FROM ONLINE ENGAGEMENT WITH 3D MODELS TO VIRTUAL REALITY

Martine Pellerin and David Vergote
University of Alberta, Canada

ABSTRACT

In the fields of medicine and health, there is a growing interest in resorting to the affordances offered by game-based learning and 3D interactive platforms. In human anatomy education, interactive learning environments can indeed foster higher levels of learner engagement and more effective learning of abstract and complex anatomy concepts. Though evolving quickly in the last decade, the design of learning environments has been accelerated by the pandemic and the associated need for online and hybrid learning. This paper presents the process of designing and developing a prototype for an interactive learning environment for human anatomy education anchored in educational theories of learning, especially the Universal Design for Learning framework. In this context and with the purpose of helping students understand the content of human anatomy courses in a more intuitive and interactive manner, we developed a multimedia teaching tool called Anatomy 3D. Our learning environment leads students through anatomical topics using an interactive scenario-based quiz with a 3D model. Our quizzes follow "pathways" throughout the body, where each question builds on the previous one. After each question, the student gets feedback tailored to their response. Anatomy 3D is unique among the wide range of tools already existing, as it highlights the functional relationships between anatomical elements, the understanding of which is important to building an accurate mental representation of human body systems. Anatomy 3D is also bilingual, with all content available in both French and English. The development of our learning environment involved an iterative process with regular inputs from students and designers. Our more recent development has been to adapt Anatomy 3D to a virtual reality system, allowing an even more immersive experience for learners.

KEYWORDS

3D, Bilingual, Human Anatomy, Interactive, Learning Environment, Virtual Reality

1. INTRODUCTION

Immersive learning environments foster learner engagement and facilitate learning abstract and complex concepts [Kuhail et al., 2022; Lui et al., 2020; Alharbi et al., 2020]. The affordances offered by game-based learning and 3D interactive platforms are of particular interest in the fields of medicine and health education [Ali et al., 2015; Singh et al., 2019; Estai & Bunt, 2016].

The paper presents the process we used to design and develop a prototype for an interactive learning environment dedicated to human anatomy education anchored in educational theories of learning, especially the Universal Design for Learning framework [CAST, 2018]. With the purpose of helping learners understand the content of human anatomy courses in a more intuitive and interactive manner, we used an iterative process involving input from students and designers at each step to develop a multimedia teaching tool called Anatomy 3D.

2. ANATOMY 3D PLATFORM

2.1 Description of Anatomy 3D

Anatomy 3D is an interactive, multimedia teaching tool. Its purpose is to help students understand the content of anatomy classes in a more intuitive and interactive manner. It leads students through anatomical topics using an interactive quiz with a 3D model (Figure 1).

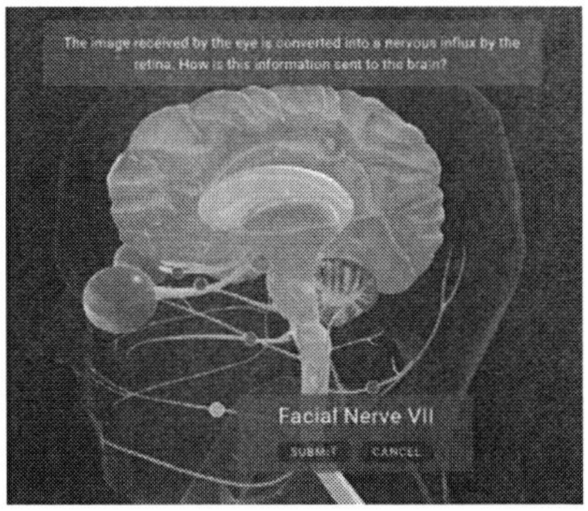

Figure 1. 3D image and question illustrating the visual appearance of Anatomy 3D

The quizzes follow "pathways" throughout the body, meaning each question builds on the previous one. After each question, students are provided with context-aware feedback based on their answers (Figure 2).

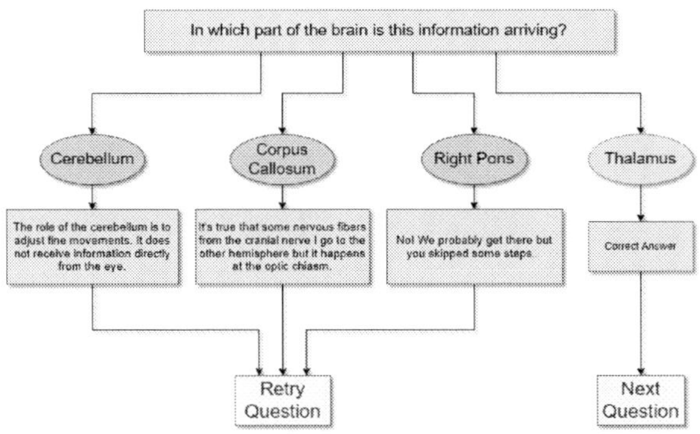

Figure 2. Typical structure of a question associated with response-tailored feedback

2.2 Scenarios

We currently have developed four scenarios using models of the brain, skin, and ear (Figure 3). Each module is five to ten questions and is designed to be completed in one sitting.

Scenario development is supported by a domain-specific language and a corresponding editing tool to enable instructors to efficiently develop multiple high-quality modules using the same 3D anatomical model, if desired. Anatomy 3D is bilingual, with all content available in both French and English.

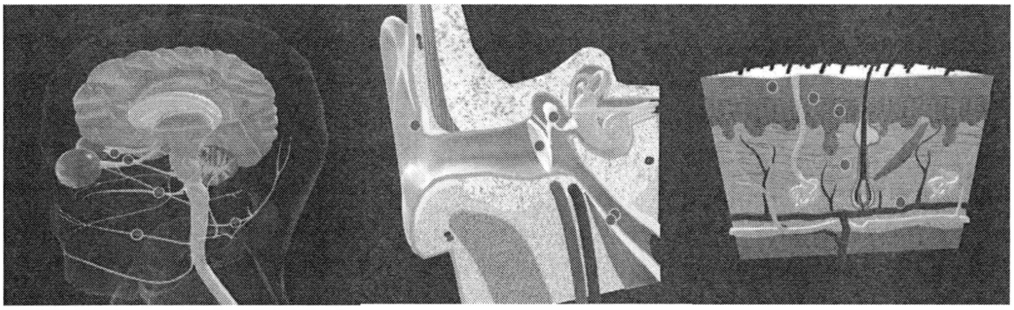

Brain And Vision **Hearing** **Vaccination**

Figure 3. Three scenarios using models of the brain, the ear and the skin

2.3 Iterative Improvement of Anatomy 3D

Iterative design is a process of continuous step-by-step refinement, alternating the testing and updating of a product [Enginess, 2021]. Our initial prototype was presented to students taking a first/second-year human anatomy course in the Fall 2019 semester. This course is typically offered annually in both the Fall and the Spring terms. Using the iterative process illustrated by Figure 4, three additional improved versions of Anatomy 3D were prepared and shared with students over three years until the Fall 2022 semester.

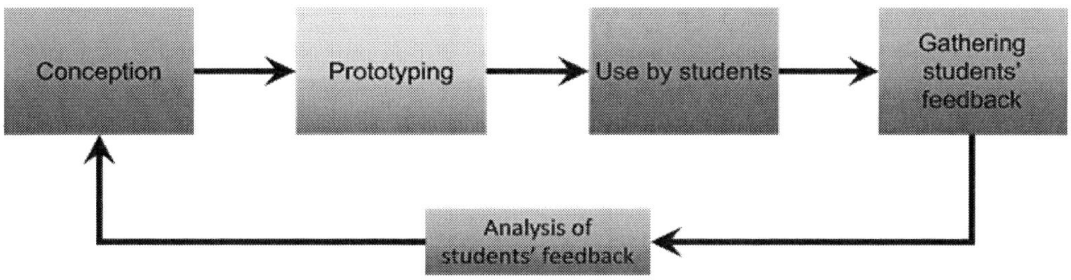

Figure 4. Process used for the iterative improvement of Anatomy 3D

3. METHODOLOGY

3.1 Participants

The prototype was tested by first- and second-year undergraduate students enrolled in the introductory Anatomy course taught by one of the authors, Dr. David Vergote. We used an online questionnaire to gather students' perceptions of and feedback on the prototype. This research was approved by the University of Alberta ethics approval committee.

3.2 Data Collection

The students' perceptions and feedback regarding the prototype, such as its usefulness, design, and usability, were gathered through the use of an online questionnaire involving students enrolled in an anatomy course. Students were encouraged to fill up the survey by rewarding them with bonus points on their final exam. Although every student who filled up the survey received bonus points, only the answers of those who agreed to be part of this study are considered here.

The platform also collects data (average time to answer, difficulty, common wrong answers) from the system-learner interaction for further learning analytics (Figure 5). To date, we have used this data to evaluate the usability of the platform.

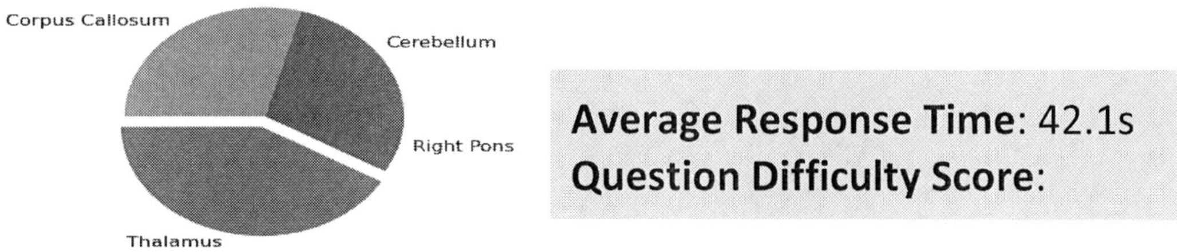

Figure 5. Example of the analysis of answers to a question

3.3 Recent Development

A more recent development has been to adapt Anatomy 3D to a virtual reality system, allowing for an even more immersive experience for learners. However, we have not shared this latest improvement with students yet.

4. CONCLUSION

The novelty of Anatomy 3D among the wide range of tools already existing lies in the fact that it highlights the functional relationships between anatomical elements, the understanding of which is important to build an accurate mental representation of human body systems as complex as the brain, for example. The content or teaching methods can be adjusted to improve student success using the collected data. In the future, there is potential to personalize question content based on users' past performance to optimize the difficulty and topic of the next question displayed.

ACKNOWLEDGEMENT

This project is funded by the University of Alberta through a Teaching and Learning Enhancement Fund (TLEF) Grant with Dr. Martine Pellerin as Principal Investigator, and Drs. David Vergote and Eleni Stroulia (Department of Computing Science, University of Alberta) as Co-Principal Investigators. The contributions from Dr. Victor Fernandez Cervantes (Department of Computing Science, University of Alberta), and Patrick von Hauff and Sheldon Roberts (Faculty of Medicine and Dentistry, University of Alberta) were paramount to the completion of this work.

REFERENCES

Alharbi, Y., Al-Mansour, M., Al-Saffar, R., Garman, A., & Alraddadi, A. (2020). Three-dimensional Virtual Reality as an Innovative Teaching and Learning Tool for Human Anatomy Courses in Medical Education: A Mixed Methods Study. *Cureus*, 12(2):e7085.

Ali, A., Khan, Z. N., Konczalik, C. P., & El Sayed, S. (2015). The perception of anatomy teaching among UK medical students. *The Bulletin of the Royal College of Surgeons of England*, 97(9):397–400.

CAST. (2018). Universal design for learning guidelines version 2.2. http://udlguidelines.cast.org

Enginess. (2021). What is Iterative Design? (and Why You Should Use It). https://www.enginess.io/insights/what-is-iterative-design.

Estai, M., & Bunt, S. (2016). Best teaching practices in anatomy education: A critical review. *Annals of Anatomy*, 208:151-157.

Kuhail, M. A., ElSayary, A., Farroq, S., & Alghambi, A. (2022). Exploring immersive learning experiences: A survey. *Informatics*, 99(4):75.

Lui, M., McEwen, R., & Mullally, M. (2020). Immersive virtual reality for supporting complex scientific knowledge: Augmenting our understanding with physiological monitoring. *British Journal of Educational Technology*, 51(6):2181-2199.

Singh, K., Bharatha, A., Sa, B., Adams, O. P., & Majumder, M. A. A. (2019). Teaching anatomy using an active and engaging learning strategy. *BMC Medical Education*, 19:249.

REIMAGINING TEACHING AND LEARNING FOR A NEW ERA: HYBRIDIZATION OF THE TEACHING AND LEARNING MODALITIES IN THE K-12 EDUCATIONAL CONTEXT

Martine Pellerin
University of Alberta, Edmonton, Alberta, Canada

ABSTRACT

The paper aims to explore the concept of hybridization as a digital transformation process of teaching and learning in the K-12 educational context. The discussion is informed by the results of a research project involving elementary and secondary school teachers and their students and how they have experimented with the concept of hybridization of their teaching modalities and learning environment. The paper examines various examples of hybridization of teaching modalities that have emerged from the project. In particular, it examines the use of 360-degree digital cameras and video conferencing to promote the hybridization of teaching modalities in in-person classrooms. It also examines the use of interactive and digital tools and online platforms to contribute to the hybridization of the learning environment in in-person classrooms. Finally, the paper demonstrates how the hybridization of teaching modalities and learning environments contributes to promoting students' engagement, collaboration, and creativity as well as the emergence of learning communities beyond the classroom walls.

KEYWORDS

Hybridization, Digital Transformation, Teaching Modalities, Digital Learning Environment, K-12educational Context, Pandemic

1. INTRODUCTION

The COVID-19 pandemic contributed to accelerating digital transformation across educational systems. New teaching modalities and digital learning environments have emerged as a result of the transfer to online learning during the pandemic and contribute to the renewal of educational practices in the K-12 educational context. One of the lessons learned from the online shift during the pandemic (Bates, 2021) is that the educational approaches and digital tools used in an online teaching context can be used for in-person teaching. Specifically, we have a growing understanding that the hybridization of both online and in-person teaching methods and learning environments can potentially create new teaching and learning modalities. We are now in a new educational era where digital and online technologies contribute to reimagining teaching and learning through the hybridization of teaching modalities and learning environments (Laker,2021).

Hybridization is a move away from traditional teaching modalities (Garrison and Kanuka, 2004; Graham,2006) and learning environments that were limited by in-person interaction within the boundaries of a classroom. It is also the reconceptualization of blended and hybrid learning that dominated the field of education (Hrastinski, 2019), prior to the pandemic. The conceptualization of the integration of online and digital technologies in the in-person classroom needs to evolve beyond the guidelines offered by traditional blended and hybrid approaches that were popularized before the pandemic. The integration of online technologies into the K-12 classrooms requires a new conceptualization aligned with the digital transformative phenomenon accelerated by the pandemic and that allows the emergence of the natural phenomenon of hybridization. The adoption of new teaching modalities supported by new emergent technologies (e.g., 360-degree digital camera and video conferencing) and digital and online interactive learning environments that emerged during the pandemic is now contributing to reimagining teaching and learning beyond traditional approaches. The hybridization of the teaching modalities and learning environments corresponds to our adaptation to a changing world where digital technologies and their affordances (Pellerin, 2018) allow the emergence of new and innovative ways to interact, communicate, collaborate, solve problems and be creative like never before.

2. METHODOLOGY

The research methodology for the project presented in this article is anchored in a qualitative and participative approach (Denzin & Lincoln, 2008). The project took place during the 2021-2022 school year. It involved 12 school teachers (elementary and middle school) in their respective classrooms in Canadian context. Data collection included digital documentation as artifacts gathered by teachers including audio and video recordings as well as screen shots of the activities completed on digital and interactive platforms (e.g., Flipgrid; Jamboard, etc.). Qualitative research approaches are used for the data analysis and aligned with the grounded theory method of qualitative data analysis. Through a coding process of the various digital sources of data gathered, initial key themes as well as emerging themes were identified in accordance with the qualitative methodology.

3. RESULTS AND DISCUSSION

Although the transfer to online teaching during the pandemic created many pedagogical challenges and forced teachers to adapt new pedagogical practices with new teaching modalities, new modes of teaching delivery have emerged such as co-modality, which refers to teaching that combines in-person and online modes simultaneously by using 360-degree cameras and videoconferencing tools like ZOOM. These teaching modalities were first adopted in the context of the pandemic to support emergency remote learning for the K-12 educational context as well as in higher education. The hybridization of online modality with face-to-face teaching gave rise to innovative pedagogical practices. New videoconferencing tools like ZOOM also grew in popularity during the pandemic, allowing synchronous learning to take place in order to provide social interaction and a sense of connectivity between the teachers and their students and between students, especially during the confinement period. Teachers are now experimenting with the combination of both online teaching modalities and in-person teaching. The hybridization of in-person and online teaching and learning modalities leverages the affordance offered by the new online and digital tools, thus contributing to the creation of new pedagogical practices and new learning environments.

3.1 Using The 'Owl' 360-Degree Camera: Fostering Greater Learner Engagement and Building Communities of Learning That Extend Beyond the Traditional Classroom Walls

In this first example, two secondary school teachers used the 360-degree 'Owl' camera to connect their students. Their classrooms were located on opposite sides of the same school and the pandemic did not allow for the mixing of student cohorts. The teachers used an interactive online platform (Kahoot) to review the content of a learning module that they had completed. They engaged their students in a friendly competitive game. The 360-degree 'Owl' camera's visual sensor allowed the students from each class to see and interact with the teacher as well as their classmates and access the online board game presented on the whiteboard. The students' engagement was enhanced by the connection of the two classrooms, as it increased student motivation, facilitated interactions with other learners, and supported the creation of a learning community.

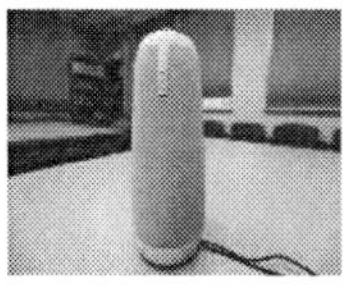

Figure 1. The use 360-degree 'Owl' camera to fostering learner engagement and building communities of learning that extend beyond the traditional classroom walls

Another example of the hybridization of the teaching modalities using the 360-degree 'Owl' camera involved two secondary French teachers in two schools located in two different rural towns within a 45-minute driving distance. The students were first engaged in a guessing game to find out where the other group was located. Afterward, the students spent time chatting with each other in the target language. The teachers shared the students' enjoyment in meeting other students who were also learning French and going through similar learning experiences, in turn creating a real sense of learning community. Students asked their respective teachers to repeat the experience several times with their new friends from the other school.

The following example demonstrates how a videoconferencing tool like ZOOM was utilized in the in-person classroom resulting in the hybridization of the teaching modalities. Elementary teachers from the same school and later from different schools outside of the urban center teamed up to experiment with using ZOOM to provide early literacy activities with the young second language learners. Even though schools reopened during the pandemic in 2021 and 2022, the sanitary measures implemented to avoid the spread of the COVID-19 virus did not allow teachers to create literacy learning cohorts and reading 'buddies' as they used to prior to the pandemic. Having experienced the ZOOM tool during the confinement period and for emergency remote learning to provide synchronous education, these elementary teachers felt compelled to combine the online teaching modalities in the in-person classroom. Therefore, they first teamed up with classrooms in the same school reading aloud activities. Then, the teachers extended the hybridization of their reading aloud activities by teaming up with other teachers from the same grades but in different schools in different towns in the same school districts. The young learners (grades 1 and 2) were engaged in a synchronous way through the videoconference with others students. Neither the physical restrictions imposed by the pandemic in the schools or the physical distance from other schools inhibited the possibility to connect with other students, engage in collaborative learning, and create literacy communities of learning. The hybridization of teaching modalities in these examples demonstrate that it can contribute to further develop a sense of connectivity and community between the teachers and their students and between students, especially beyond the walls of the traditional classrooms.

3.2 Hybridization of the Learning Environments: Promoting Student Engagement, Collaboration, and Creativity

Although many digital tools and platforms were used in the classroom prior to the pandemic, they were mainly adopted as a complement or replacement (Hrastinski,2019) to in-person learning. The hybridization of the learning environment goes beyond this conceptualization of traditional blended and hybrid learning. The affordances offered by the new digital tools and online platforms such as Flipgrid, Book Creator, Jamboard, to name of few, allow learners to engage actively in their learning by collaborating, problem-solving, and sharing, all in ways that were not possible before. The hybridization of the learning environments also gives learners multi-sensory access (Pellerin, 2018) as well as multiple means of representation, interaction, and engagement. Therefore, by reimagining learning through the hybridization of the learning environment, greater inclusive pedagogical approaches emerged following the guidelines of the Universal Design for Learning (UDL) framework (2018).

In the following example, elementary school teachers from two different grades teamed up to engage their language learners in collaborating in the creation of an online story. They used the Book Creator online application to create multimodal and digital books for their story. The project contributed to fostering a sense of learning community between young learners and older learners and through the affordance of the application, the digital book could be downloaded to share with the school community and beyond the classroom.

The next example demonstrates how the hybridization of the teaching modalities and digital learning environments was experimented with by elementary teachers to promote social interaction and collaboration among students. After participating in reading aloud through ZOOM with other classrooms, teachers invited their students in reading comprehension and writing activities using the Flipgrid digital tool and shared their multimodal products and artifacts including video of the learning on the online platform.

Interactive and digital whiteboards like Jamboard were integrated into synchronous online learning during the pandemic. This type of platform allows students to interact and collaborate on a digital whiteboard. Through the hybridization of the learning environment, teachers are now integrating interactive online platforms in in-person approach to allow learners to benefit from greater engagement, and interaction, while also gaining access to multiple ways of representing and expressing their understanding and knowledge. As an example, as an early literacy activity, the teacher used a picture of a snowman as a backdrop on the Jamboard platform. Images of different clothing and objects were displayed on the digital board by the teacher. Students were able to interact with the online platform to demonstrate to their learning by manipulating the different objects they wanted to use to represent their snowmen. The multimodal affordances of the application allow learning and thinking to become visible and increase student interaction, which in turn contributes to better engagement. The hybridization of the learning environment in the in-person classroom contributes to enhancing student engagement through active learning, social interaction, collaboration, and creativity.

4. CONCLUSION

The acceleration of the digital transformation in K-12 education following the COVID-19 pandemic contributes to the emergence of new possibilities to reimagining teaching and learning for a new digital era. We can no longer afford to teach the way we used to teach. The traditional in-person teaching modalities and learning environments are no longer adequate to prepare our students for a digital world in constant evolution. The affordances of the new online and digital technologies allow us to learn, interact, communicate, collaborate, engage and be creative in ways that were not possible before. Therefore, the hybridization of the teaching modalities and learning environments needs to go beyond the traditional blended and hybrid teaching and learning approaches. Like in nature, the phenomenon of hybridization corresponds to the combination of two species that goes on to create a whole new one. The hybridization of the teaching modalities and learning environment contribute to reimagine teaching and learning for a new era.

ACKNOWLEDGEMENT

The research project received financial support from the government of Canada through the national organization (ACUFC) and the support of the Rocky View Schools district in Alberta, Canada by allowing 12 French Immersion teachers and school leaders to participate in the project. We thank them and their students for their participation even during the challenging time brought about by the pandemic.

REFERENCES

Bates, T. (2021), "A Review of Online Learning in 2021." *Online Learning and Distance Education Resources*. Available online: https://www.tonybates.ca/2021/12/10/a-review-of-online-learning-in-2021/

CAST. (2011), Universal Design for Learning Guidelines version 2.0. Wakefield, MA: Author.

Denzin, N. K. & Lincoln, Y. S. (2008), *Collecting and interpreting qualitative materials* (3rd ed.). London, England: Sage.

Garrison, D. R. & Kanuka, H. (2004), "Blended learning: Uncovering its transformative potential in higher education." Internet and Higher Education, 7, 95–105. https://doi.org/10.1016/j.iheduc.2004.02.001.

Graham, C. R. (2006), "Blended learning systems: Definition, current trends, and future directions." In C. J. Bonk & C. R. Graham (Eds.), The handbook of blended learning: Global perspectives, local designs (3–21). San Francisco: Pfeiffer.

Hrastinski, S. (2019), "What Do We Mean by Blended Learning?" TechTrends, 63, 564–569. https://doi.org/10.1007/s11528-019-00375-5

Laker, B. (2021), Why 2021 Will Be the Year of Hybridization. Available online: https://www.forbes.com/sites/benjaminlaker/2021/01/08/why-2021-will-be-the-year-of-hybridization/?sh=a48564279da7

Pellerin, M. (2018), "Affordances of New Mobile Technologies: Promoting Learner Agency, Autonomy, and Self-Regulated Learning." *Journal of Interactive Learning Research*, 29(3): 335-350.

USABILITY EVALUATION OF MOBILE INTERFACES FOR MATH FORMULA ENTRY

Yasuyuki Nakamura
Graduate School of Informatics, Nagoya University
Nagoya, 464-8601, Japan

ABSTRACT

STACK is an online testing system that can automatically assess mathematical formulae. When working with STACK on a smartphone, inputting mathematical formulae is time-consuming; therefore, to solve this problem a mathematical formula input interface for smartphones has been developed based on the flick operation. However, since the time of development, an increasing number of smartphone types have been developed, making the verification of such interfaces important. We organised the problems of each device and verified the effectiveness of the flick operation for formula input compared with conventional text input.

KEYWORDS

Mathematics E-learning, Mobile Interface for Math Input

1. INTRODUCTION

Due to the Covid-19 pandemic, online education has attracted attention in recent years, and the introduction of e-learning using LMS is rapidly accelerating. One of the important functions of an LMS is online testing, and the conventional formats of online tests that can be automatically graded include correct/incorrect, multiple-choice, numerical input, and short-answer input. However, when trying to measure students' understanding of science and mathematics subjects through online tests, it is important, for example, for students to input answers to calculation questions using mathematical formulae rather than selecting the correct answer from a list of options. In view of this need, the use of systems that can automatically grade answers entered in mathematical formulae, that is, mathematics e-learning systems, is becoming increasingly widespread. Representative mathematics e-learning systems include STACK (Sangwin, 2013), Numbas[1], WeBWorK,[2] and Möbius[3]. A barrier to the use of these systems is the effort required to input mathematical formulae, and it is usually difficult to input complex mathematical formulae in the systems. This is especially true when using a mathematics e-learning system on a mobile device, such as a smartphone.

To solve this problem, Nakamura et al. developed FlickMath, a mathematical formula-input interface for STACK that can be used on mobile devices (Nakamura, 2017). This dramatically reduces the number of taps on the smartphone when entering mathematical expressions. Shirai et al. also developed an interface that, like kana-kanji conversion in Japanese input, presents candidates with mathematical formulae using a machine-learning algorithm and allows the user to input mathematical formulae by selecting them (Shirai, 2014).

However, since the development of such formula input interfaces, various smartphones have been launched, and screen sizes have become more diverse. Even though they are developed in JavaScript and have fewer hardware and software dependencies, they still need to be validated on a larger number of devices. It is also important to investigate the types of interfaces that are effective for students these days. Therefore, we conducted a survey with 65 students on the use of the FlickMath formula input interface.

[1] https://www.numbas.org.uk/
[2] https://webwork.maa.org/
[3] https://www.digitaled.com/mobius/

2. USAGE SURVEY

In the usage survey, 65 students were asked to input three mathematical expressions, $(a+b)^2, \frac{y}{2x+1}, \frac{1}{\sqrt{x^2+y^2}}$ from a smartphone using both the conventional text and flick input methods. The input time and input error rate were obtained as objective data, and choice of preferred input method between text and flick input and their impressions were obtained as subjective data.

First, the smartphone types used by the 65 respondents were iPhone 8, iPhone XR, iPhone SE, iPhone SE3, iPhone 11, iPhone 11 Pro, iPhone 12, iPhone 12 mini, iPhone 12 Pro, iPhone 13, iPhone 13, iPhone mini, iPhone 13 Pro, iPhone 14, iPhone 14 Pro, Galaxy, Pixel 6, OPPO Reno3 A, and Xperia 1 II. Most of the respondents were iPhone users (89.2 %) which is more than the 67% share of smartphones in Japan[4]. Of the 65 respondents, 38 found it easy to input text, and 27 found it easy to input flicks. Eight of the 38 participants who answered that text input was easier to use said that flick input might be easier once they got used to it, thus indicating the potential for flick input.

The data of 39 of the 65 respondents who answered both text and flick input, excluding those who took more than 30 minutes to input both, were then included in the analysis and are summarised in Table 1. It can be observed that the input time is shorter for flick input than for text input. Histograms of the input times for text and flick inputs are shown in Figure 1. Text input has a relatively large amount of data with long input times and a wide distribution, whereas flick input shows, on average short input times, except for exceptionally long-time data. Paired two-sample t-tests showed no significant differences in the input time. A scatterplot of the input times for the text and flick inputs is shown in Figure 2. There was a weak positive correlation, except for the data of the maximum text and maximum flick input. It can be assumed that the students in the data with the maximum value of flick input were those with fast text input times and were relatively familiar with the operation of the device. Therefore, it is expected that once students become accustomed to flick input, the input time will be much shorter. Table 1 shows that the error rate of the flick input is higher. As mentioned earlier, flick input is easier to use once the user is used to it, and it was assumed that the error rate was high because the user was not used to it.

Table 1. Comparison of the average time taken to enter the three formulae for text and flick input, respectively, and the percentage of incorrect entries

Input method	Average input time [s]	Incorrect entries [%]
Text	525.9	12.0
Flick	516.5	16.2

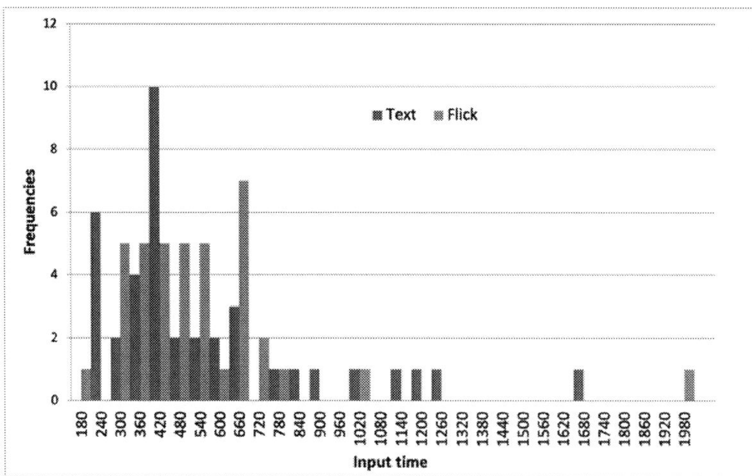

Figure 1. Histogram of input time for text and flick input

[4] https://gs.statcounter.com/vendor-market-share/mobile/japan

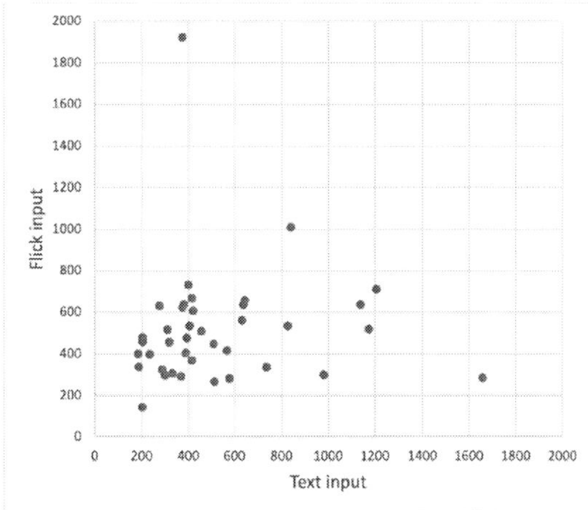

Figure 2. Scatterplot of input times for text and flick input

As for operation problems, it was reported that the flick input interface did not appear and flick input operations were not reflected, but same problem did not occur on the same device repeatedly, therefore, the problem is not reproducible and needs to be investigated in more detail.

3. CONCLUSION

We conducted a usage survey to determine whether flick input, which was developed for inputting mathematical formulae on smartphones, could be used without problems on a range of new devices. Although the reduction in input time of flick input was not superior to that of conventional text input, we were able to identify a potential situation in which flick input would be preferred, as it would increase efficiency once the user becomes familiar with it.

Our conclusion that once people are familiar with flick input, it is more effective for inputting mathematical formulae may be optimistic. However, given that flick input reduces key taps for input dramatically (Nakamura, 2017), it is a reliable prediction that flick input is more effective once users are familiar with it. Free-text student comments have been included. “I found the flick operation difficult as I am not used to it, but once I learnt the operation, I thought I could answer faster than with text”. “I found it difficult because it was not the keyboard I normally use. However, I thought that once I got used to it, flicking might be easier”. “Flick input was confusing at first, but once I got used to it, I thought it would be very easy”. “I did not understand it at first, but once I got used to it, I thought I could use it quickly”.

In addition a student noted, “I found it difficult at first to input formulas by flick because I was not used to the input method, but once I understood it, I could easily input formulas with a single click, and it was easy to use because there was no need to input extra formulas. I also felt that the input system was highly effective as it utilised the characteristics of computers, and education is also progressing on tablets”. As mobile devices are increasingly used in the field of education in the future, it will be important to improve the input method. For this reason, it is expected that flick input will improve formula input and, in turn, expand the possibilities for learning with mobile devices.

ACKNOWLEDGEMENT

This work was supported by JSPS KAKENHI Grant Number 21H04412.

REFERENCES

Nakamura Y. and Nakahara T., 2017. A New Mathematics Input Interface with Flick Operation for Mobile Devices. *MSOR Connections*, Vol. 15, No. 2, pp. 76082.

Sangwin, C., 2013. *Computer Aided Assessment of Mathematics*, Oxford University Press.

Shirai, S. and Fukui, T., 2014. Development and Evaluation of a Web-Based Drill System to Master Basic Math Formulae Using a New Interactive Math Input Method, *Proceedings of the 4th International Congress on Mathematical Software*, Seoul, Korea, Lecture Notes in Computer Science 8592, Springer, pp.621-628.

POSTERS

ONLINE APP FOR THE EVALUATION OF CLIMATE CHANGE IMPACT IN URBAN GREEN AREAS

Zacharoula Andreopoulou, Dimitra Papagiannopoulou and Thekla Tsitsoni
School of Forestry & Natural Environment, Laboratory of Silviculture, P.O. Box 262, 54124, Aristotle University of Thessaloniki, Thessaloniki, Greece

ABSTRACT

Information and Communication Technologies (ICTs) play an important role in addressing the major challenges related with climate change and sustainable development. ICTs are tools for the monitoring of climate change, the mitigating and adapting to its effects contributing at the same time to the development of the green economy. Green development is a proposal for a new kind of pioneering development, where the environment and quality is not a parameter or another industry policy, but the main axis and basis of an innovative and alternative development plan of a country in the global socioeconomics. According to researches, the air temperature shows an increasing trend in recent years. Urban trees have an important value in urban ecosystems because they are carbon sinks and they help urban areas to mitigate the impacts of climate change. Nowadays, the new information technologies (ICTs) and their services are modern tools via them a big amount of knowledge and data can be transferred. These tools promote new improved relationships between people and environment that is necessary for a sustainable natural environment. They also provide benefits for both recipients. Aim of this paper is to describe the online app which was constructed within the framework of the project LIFE CliVut (Climate Value of Urban Trees) LIFE18 GIC/IT/001217 and the process by which the phenological data is entered into the app. Online app (lifeclivut.treedb.eu) is a modern tool, an online database that provides data on the behavior of urban trees in climatic conditions via the science of phenology to both experts and citizens. Experts can monitor the behavior of the trees and shrubs over the years and they also will detect changes that happens in the urban species immediately. Online database app was created to be used as a user-friendly tool for environmentalists, biologists, foresters, urban planners, landscape architects, local authorities, aiming to support urban green. This app will help experts to compare data that entered in years and derive results that shows the impact of climate change in phenological stages of urban trees.

KEYWORDS

Climate Change, Urban Areas, Urban Trees, Online App, Phenology, ICTs

1. INTRODUCTION

Green Informatics is a new term in the science of information that describes the utilization of informatics in the frame of the natural environment and the natural resources taking into consideration sustainability and sustainable development (Andreopoulou, 2012). New technologies have significantly entered our lives and online services offer the opportunity for sustainable regional development. Electronic services offered by the new Information and Communication Technologies (ICT's), have proved an important decision making tool (Kirkenidis and Andreopoulou, 2015). Literature suggests that introducing IT tools into urban design provokes a new paradigm that involves new modes of thinking that would increase the quality of the design and decision-making process (Al Douri, 2022). The rapid development and global spread of modern information and communication technology (ICT) led to the implementation of its applications to agroforestry. One of the most important benefits of using ICT is the dissemination of knowledge to extension agencies via appropriate information models can be fed back to the international agroforestry community on research or policy making level (Andreopoulou et. al., 2011). The benefits of Green Informatics are the reduction of energy consumption, the rise of environmental awareness, the effective communication for environmental issues and the environmental monitoring and surveillance systems, as a means to protect and restore natural ecosystems potential (Andreopoulou, 2012). Plant Phenology is the scientific study of biological stages, such as flowering, leaf unfolding, seed set, and senescence in relation to climatic conditions (Davi et. all, 2011). Environmental factors such as temperature and humidity can affect phenological stages (Rousi et. all, 2011). Climate change affects bioclimatic conditions during the growing period of trees (Meier et. all. 2011; Farooq and Meraj, 2016). Global warming is disrupting the phenological phases (Paltineanu and Chitu, 2020) The time of leaf development, the time of the beginning of flowering, the time of development of fruit, the time of leaf fall are the main phenological stages (Davi et. all, 2011). The recording of the start date of phenological stages and relating them to temperature has an important role in plant phenology study (Tiwari et. all 2021). The sensitivity of phenology to temperature changes makes it an indicator of vegetation response to environmental changes and can be used to monitor the effects of climate change globally (Garcia and Townsend, 2016). As phenology is an indicator to detect climate variability and climate change the monitoring of phenophases of species is important to extract results for climate change. So, the online app in which the data is entered is an important tool that contributes to the processing and extraction of the results. The LIFE CliVUT (LIFE18 GIC/IT/001217) project is coordinated for Greece by the Forestry Laboratory of the Department of Forestry and Natural Environment of the Aristotle University of Thessaloniki. A key objective of the project is to leverage academic expertise to better assess the importance of urban green in climate change mitigation and CO_2 sequestration dynamics. The project partners are the University of Perugia, the Municipalities of Bologna and Perugia, the Italian Institute CESAR and the Portuguese Institute ISG. The main aim of LIFE CLIVUT project is to develop and implement a Strategic Management of Urban Green Spaces, with focusing on the mitigation of Climate Change, adapted to medium-sized Mediterranean cities. Aim of this paper is to enter the phenological data into a database so that it is easier to process them and correlate them over the years as the project provides for observation and data entry for at least 10 years.

2. CLIVUT APP DESCRIPTION

Online app, a tree database, was constructed via the project LIFE CliVut LIFE18 GIC/IT/001217 and contains the data of the monitoring of the phenological stages of the urban trees in the three Phenological Monitoring Areas that also was created within the framework of the same project. Each PMAs contains 100 individuals (5 per species), 10 species of trees and 10 species of shrubs. The forest species are presented in Table 1. The tree database includes: Plant census database which contains the specific dendrometric data for each tree as a botanical species, tree height etc. The phenological data carried out by the trees present in the phenological monitoring areas (PMA), always identical by a genetic point of view, introduced in the public parks. Environmental behaviors of each individual tree species in terms of GHG absorption, particulate matter absorption, shadow effect, biodiversity increase. Georeferenced data of the urban green asset available on the web by a specific GIS server, based on open source software.

Table 1. Species in Phenological Monitoring Areas

Trees		Shrubs	
Acer campestre	*Carpinus betulus*	*Spartium junceum*	*Phillyrea latifolia*
Tilia cordata	*Sorbus domestica*	*Euonymus europaeus*	*Salix caprea*
Quercus pubescnens	*Alnus glutinosa*	*Berberis vulgaris*	*Cornus sanguinea*
Quercus ilex	*Fraxinus angustifolia*	*Corylus avellana*	*Ligustrum vulgare*
Prunus avium	*Populus canescens*	*Sambucus nigra*	*Punica granatum*

Trees were planted at a distance of 5m from each other and shrubs were planted at a distance of 4m. The phenological stages of the plants were studied from March to December 2021 and throughout 2022 till now. For each individual, leaf development, flower development, development of fruit and leaf fall were recorded on a weekly basis taking into consideration BBCH scale. BBCH scale as a standard system for describing the phenological stages of plant development has been introduced by The Global Phenological Monitoring Network (Meier et. all 2009). Zadoks et al. (1974) developed the decimal code, which is divided into principal and secondary growth stages.

LIFE CLIVUT project has developed an online app which is available in lifeclivut.treedb.eu to increase knowledge about the trees in the cities and the awareness of their contribution to the environment and climate change mitigation. It is an innovative tool that allows to visualize the trees and their ecosystem contribution. The user can map the trees in an area, and with georeferenced information via GPS, including photos, the data can be acquired for the plant census. This app allows also to identify the best management techniques to maximize the tree climate functions. It reports the climatic and biodiversity value of the trees, for example the $C0_2$ storage per tree, or the PM10 captured. This reliable operative tool enables: Urban planner to design and implement effective Urban Climate Green Assets Strategy valuing all the factors related to environmental benefit, climatic effect, and socio-economic impact. Citizens to monitor and manage the private urban green area adopting climate-oriented and ecosystem-based approach. This app is available for computers, smartphones and tablets and it can be used by experts and citizens. Available application language is English and it is operating independent. There are specific instructions for using the application in the official site of LIFE CLIVUT project (www.lifeclivut.eu). To insert a tree with the necessary information it takes a little time at about 5 minutes. Till now 10 census areas of Thessaloniki exist in the database (Figure 1). There is information for the trees in the parks such as dendrometric characteristics, CO_2 absorption. The user can use other applications in order to recognize the species. Also, is easy to delete the tree in case wrong information was entered. The phenological data of the monitoring in the three PMAs can only be entered by experts. To insert phenological data of trees that exist in other areas, citizens must be trained. The time required for a complete training is about 3 hours. Till now about 200 citizens attended educational seminar about the application. It is expected that more than 10.000 citizens will participate to the plant census. Application related to the planting and management of trees in urban areas in the three countries. In this paper the input of phenological data is described. The home page of the online app is shown in Figure 2.

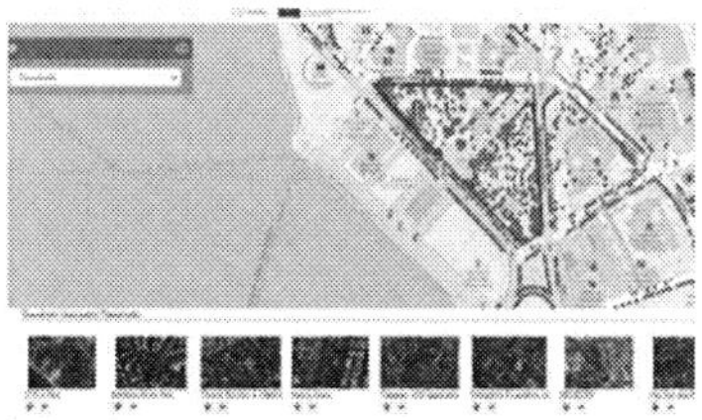

Figure 1. Census areas in Thessalonik

Figure 2. Home page of the online app

Then, we choose the PMA that we want to insert the data. There are two options: PMA and PMA list (Figure 3). The species appears in the left side. We choose the date and the species that we want to insert the data of the monitoring and then, we insert the data in the right stage (Figure 4 and 5). After, after entering the data of the monitoring of the species the information of the phenological montitoring is shown in aggregate for each species (Figure 6).

Figure 3. Options PMA and PMA list

Figure 4. Trees and shrubs list

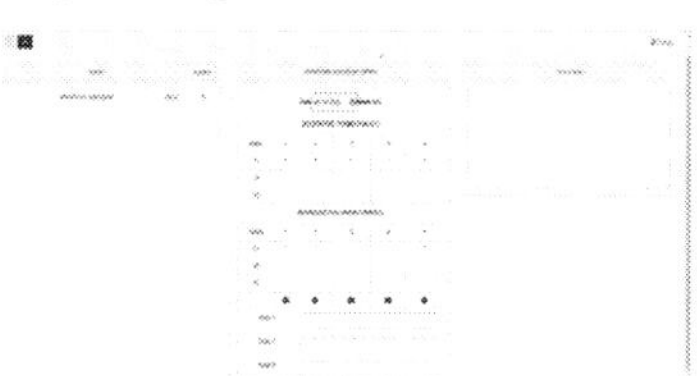

Figure 5. Stages of species on specific dates

Figure 6. The data of the monitoring of trees and shrubs aggregated

3. CONCLUSION

In the LIFE Clivut web app the data from the phenological monitoring in the three PMAs are entered. The growth of trees and shrubs is clearly visible via the online app. This app shows the phenological stages of each species and provides the possibility for correlations and processing of the data depending on the climatic conditions. Decision making process is an important activity especially in designing of urban green spaces. So, a special attention has to be paid when making decisions in designing open green spaces in urban areas. Once the app is installed in a portable device, it is easy to be used. Therefore, end users of the app are not IT specialists, they do not need to have advanced computer literacy, as the app is especially designed to serve their needs and data registration is facilitated with pre-designed input boxes, with drop down menus of options. Thus, ICT could improve the decision-making in this sector.

REFERENCES

Andreopoulou, Z. Manos, B. Polman, N. and Viaggi D. (Eds.) (2011). *Agricultural and Environmental Informatics, Governance and Management: Emerging Research Applications*. IGIGLOBAL.

Andreopoulou, Z. (2012). Green Informatics: ICT for green and Sustainability, *Journal of Agricultural Informatics*, 3(2), 1-8.

Al-Douri, F.A. (2022). How information and communication tools (ICT) affect the processes and decision-making in professional urban design practice?, *URBAN DESIGN International* [Preprint]. Available at: https://doi.org/10.1057/s41289-022-00196-8.

Davi, H., Gillmann, T., Cailleret, M., Bontemps, A., Fady, B., Lefevre, F. (2011). Diversity of leaf unfolding dynamics among tree species: new insights from a study along an altitudinal gradient, *Agric For Meteorol*, 151(12):1504-1513.

Farooq, M. and Meraj, G. (2016). *Tree Phenology and Climate Change* DOI: 10.13140/RG.2.2.24621.08166.

Garcia, M., and Townsend, P. A. (2016). Recent climatological trends and potential influences on forest phenology around western Lake Superior, USA, *Journal of Geophysical Research: Atmospheres*, 121(22), 13,364-13,391.

Kirkenidis, Y. and Andreopoulou, Z. (2015). E-learning and the aspect of students in Forestry and Environmental Studies, *Journal of Agricultural Informatics*, 6(1). Available at: https://doi.org/10.17700/jai.2015.6.1.158.

Liang, L. (2019). A spatially explicit modeling analysis of adaptive variation in temperate tree phenology, *Agricultural and Forest Meteorology*, 266-267, pp. 73–86. Available at: https://doi.org/10.1016/j.agrformet.2018.12.004.

Meier, U. et. all. (2009). Phenological Growth Stages of Roses (rosasp.): Codification and description according to the BBCH scale, *Annals of Applied Biology*, 154(2), pp. 231–238.

Meier, M., Vitasse, Y., Bugmann, H. and Bigler, C. (2021). Phenological shifts induced by climate change amplify drought for broad-leaved trees at low elevations in Switzerland, *Agricultural and Forest Meteorology*, 307, p. 108485. Available at: https://doi.org/10.1016/j.agrformet.2021.108485.

Paltineanu, C. and Chitu, E. (2020). Climate change impact on phenological stages of sweet and sour cherry trees in a continental climate environment, *Scientia Horticulturae*, 261, p. 109011. Available at: https://doi.org/10.1016/j.scienta.2019.109011.

Rousi, M., Heinonen, J. and Neuvonen, S. (2011). Intrapopulation variation in flowering phenology and fecundity of silver birch, implications for adaptability to changing climate, *Forest Ecology and Management,* 262(12), pp. 2378–2385. Available at: https://doi.org/10.1016/j.foreco.2011.08.038.

Tiwari, P., Verma, P. and Raghubanshi, A.S. (2021). Forest phenology as an indicator of climate change: Impact and mitigation strategies in India, *Springer Climate*, pp. 185–205.

.Zadoks, J.C., Chang, T.T., Konzak, C.F. (1974). A decimal code for the growth stages of cereals, *Weed Research*. 14 (6), 415–421.

E-LEARNING ACTIVITIES DURING PANDEMIC: PROJECT LIFE CLIVUT

Thekla Tsitsoni, Dimitra Papagiannopoulou and Zacaharoula Andreopoulou
School of Forestry & Natural Environment, Laboratory of Silviculture, P.O. Box 262, 54124, Aristotle University of Thessaloniki, Thessaloniki, Greece

ABSTRACT

New technologies have significantly entered our lives and online services offer the opportunity for sustainable regional development. Electronic services offered by the new Information and Communication Technologies (ICT's), have proved an important tool in efforts to disseminate e-learning in modern education during the pandemic especially in confinement. E-Learning is the delivery of learning and training via digital resources. E-Learning is based on formalized learning and it is provided through electronic devices such as computers, tablets and even smartphones that are connected to the internet. The global pandemic has drastically changed the way that people learn worldwide. Citizens, experts, students from all around the world have suddenly shifted from classroom learning to online learning. This type of learning that is independent of place and time, extends learning to people around the world. This paper describes seminars that took place online in the framework of LIFE CLIVUT project (Climate value of urban trees-LIFE18 GIC/IT/001217).

KEYWORDS

E-Learning, Green Development, Tele-Education, Social, ICTS

1. INTRODUCTION

According to the rapid change in technological progress and the globalization trend in education, new methods and perspectives such as E-learning have opened to educational practice (Hassan Ja'ashan, 2020). E-learning refers to the learning that utilizes electronic technologies to access educational curriculum outside of a traditional classroom (Al-Atabi and Al-Noori, 2020).

The electronic services provided by the new Information and Communication Technologies (ICT's). They are an important tool in efforts to disseminate the electronic learning (e-learning) in modern education. The new technologies have entered our lives dynamically and online services are the lever for sustainable regional development (Andreopoulou, 2008; Kirkenidis and Andreopoulou, 2011). The extreme development of technology and the trend of continuing education in all fields make the tele-Education one of the highest form of modern education (Kirkenidis and Andreopoulou, 2011). Distance learning is a modern field of education that focuses on teaching methods and technology with the aim of delivering teaching, to students, citizens, experts who are not physically present in a traditional educational setting. It has been described as "a process to create and provide access to learning when the source of information and the learners are separated by time and distance, or both" (Bušelić, 2017). The pandemic created new challenges and caused disruption in the Education sector. The face-to-face teaching replaced by E-learning (Bashir et. all., 2021). As a result, the higher education market has become increasingly competitive with the addition of distance and open education models (Cunha et al., 2020).

E-learning is a tool via it the direct transmission of knowledge is provided, without spatial limitations (Kirkenidis and Andreopoulou, 2011). In recent years, the countries need to adopt a new development model for them· a development model that serves people and their real needs. E-learning is a promising educational medium and a new teaching methodology that contributes to effective student learning (Encarnacion et. all., 2021).

Green development is a proposal for a new kind of pioneering development, where the environment and quality is not a parameter or another industry policy, but the main axis and basis of an innovative and alternative development plan of a country in the global socioeconomics (Andreopoulou et. al., 2006). One of the main advantages of using ICT is the dissemination of knowledge to extension agencies through appropriate information models can be fed back to the international agroforestry community on research or policy making level (Andreopoulou et. al., 2011). Also, electronic services offered by the new Information and Communication Technologies (ICT's), is important decision making tool (Black, 2002; Koutroumanidis and Andreopoulou, 2009; Kirkenidis and Andreopoulou, 2015). Expect for e-learning, during the pandemic the use of social networks increased. Social media are interactive Internet applications that facilitate creation, curation, and sharing of user-generated content (Davis, 2016). Social media during the pandemic played an important role in dissemination of information across the world (Demuyakor, 2020).

The LIFE CliVUT - Climate value of urban trees (LIFE18 GIC/IT/001217) project is coordinated for Greece by the Forestry Laboratory of the Department of Forestry and Natural Environment of the Aristotle University of Thessaloniki. A key objective of the project is to leverage academic expertise to better assess the importance of urban green in climate change mitigation and CO_2 sequestration dynamics. The project partners are the University of Perugia (Università degli Studi di Perugia - Dipartimento di Ingegneria Civile ed Ambientale), the Municipalities of Bologna and Perugia, the Italian Institute CESAR (Centro per lo Sviluppo Agricolo e Rurale) and the Portuguese Institute ISG (Instituto Superior de Gestão, ENSINUS-Estudos Superiores SA). The main aim of LIFE CLIVUT project is to develop and implement a Strategic Management of Urban Green Spaces, with focusing on the mitigation of Climate Change, adapted to medium-sized Mediterranean cities. Both its planning and its implementation will be based on participatory processes, between the local government, scientists, professionals and citizens. During, the pandemic seminars took place online that many experts, students, citizens and stakeholders attended them. Also, the LIFE CliVUT project has a website (www.lifeclivut.eu) and pages in social media to inform citizens, students and stakeholders on issues related to climate change, urban greening as one of the main purposes is to increase awareness.

2. E-LEARNING COURSES

In the framework of the action C.1.1 'Urban planners capacity building' of the European LIFE program LIFE_CLIVUT_LIFE18 GIC/IT/001217 the laboratory of Silviculture, Department of Forestry and Natural Environment, Faculty of Agriculture, Forestry and Natural Environment, of the Aristotle University of Thessaloniki, have organized four 4-day online courses via platform ZOOM. These educational seminars addressed both at experts and at students were foreseen by the project by physical presence. Due to confinement the educational seminars carried out online. The positive point of this process was that that experts and students from all over Greece attended the training seminars who otherwise would not have been able to attend.

The first step of the planning process is the construction of a deep Knowledge of the existing situation (structure, performance, location, ownership and accessibility of green spaces) and the awareness in these actors of the existing and potential contribution of green spaces to the mitigation of Climate Changes in Cities and to citizen well –being. The capacity building will be based on: short basic courses (8 session of 4 hours each. Each session had a different topic) managed by professors and researchers of the university and with the engagement of international lecturers: urban tree dendrometric and phenological characteristics and function in urban environment the ecosystem approach in urban planning, management technics and planning rules improving the environmental and climate performance of urban trees, How to plan and manage urban green asset through Urban Green Asset Management System. Experts, students and citizens attended the courses.

The 2-day online courses 'Urban Planners capacity building for designing and implementation of Urban Climate Green Asset Strategy' addressed to experts and the other 2-day online courses 'Climate Value of Urban Trees' to citizens and students. In total 150 people attended the online courses (Figure 1). The lectures presented their subject in Greek language.

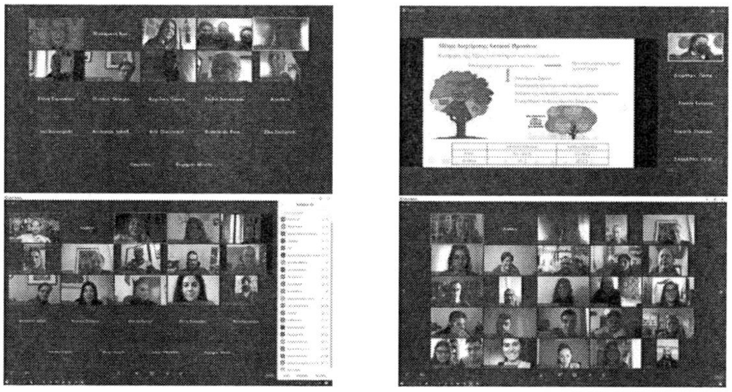

Figure 1. Online courses in the framework of Action C.1.1

In the context of the action C4.1 "Business awareness'' of the European LIFE program LIFE_CLIVUT_LIFE18 GIC/IT/001217, the laboratory of Silviculture, Department of Forestry and Natural Environment, Faculty of Agriculture, Forestry and Natural Environment, of the Aristotle University of Thessaloniki, have organized four 4-day online courses through ZOOM platform. The aim was to increase the awareness of the different business sectors that present in the urban areas regarding the benefit for their business and for the Urban Community to actively participate in the Urban Climate Green Asset Strategy planting and maintaining trees in private places also for public use. According to action C4.1 "Business awareness'' For business, sustainability and in particular Zero Emissions strategy can mean greater competitiveness and represents a continuation of its inevitable drive towards efficiency. The importance of this Strategy increases where there is local shared strategy promoted by local authorities and by citizens. This sub-activity is finalized to increase the awareness of entrepreneurs on the benefit of a more sustainable behavior and in participating in the Urban Climate Green Asset Strategy as a mean to exchanges their mission with the sequestration capability of new planted trees.

The courses were divided into four groups according to the four sectors (retail, industry, transport, tourism). The courses took place on November 30th & December 1-3th 2021. All groups carried the title: ''The Role of Corporate Social Responsibility in Climate Change and Urban Green Management'', mainly for the businesses of Greece. 90 people attended the seminars (Figure 2). The seminars were uploaded in Greek language to the YouTube where everyone can watch them.

Figure 2. Online courses in the framework of C.4.1

3. CONCLUSION

The extreme development of technology and the trend of continuing education in all fields make the e-learning (tele-Education) the highest form of education. The services and goods was available through the Internet and other forms of data transmission, especially during the pandemic. The perfect organization, design, development and completion by a full team of associates present the needs and the professionalism needed for running online courses. This professionalism is linked inextricably with the evolution of technology and the offered solutions. The online courses that took place in the framework of LIFE CliVut project promoted the environmental awareness during the pandemic as many people had the opportunity to attend them. The new web technologies and their applications in e-learning are the tools for broad dissemination of knowledge without spatial and temporal constraints. The participants liked the educational seminars as evidenced by their participation in subsequent activities.

REFERENCES

Al-Atabi, A. J. and Al-Noori, B. S. (2020). E-Learning In: Teaching. *E-learning.* https://www.researchgate.net/publication/341684491_E-Learning_In_Teaching/citations#fullTextFileContent

Andreopoulou Z. S., Arabatzis G, Koutroumanidis T., Manos B. 2006. "E-learning Model for the Afforestation of Agricultural Land", Proc. of the 18th Conference of the Hellenic Society for Operational Research –HELORS 06, with title '*Planning, Information Retrieval and Knowledge Management'*, 15–17 June 2006, Kozani, Vol. II, 661 670.

Andreopoulou, Z. (2008). ''*New technologies, environmental sustainability and sustainable development.*'' Chapter 15 in the book "Natural Resources, Environment and Development 'ed. G. Arampatzis. Tziola publication, Thessaloniki. pp. 385-404 ISBN 978-960-418-153-7.

Bashir, A., Bashir, S., Rana, K., Lambert, P., & Vernallis, A. (2021). Post-COVID-19 adaptations; the shifts towards online learning, hybrid course delivery and the implications for biosciences courses in the Higher Education Setting. *Frontiers in Education*, 6. doi:10.3389/feduc.2021.711619.

Black, G. (2002). 'A Comparison of Traditional, Online and Hybrid Methods of Course Delivery', *Journal of Business Administration Online, Spring*, 1 (1). Retrieved from http://jbao.atu.edu/old/Journals/black.html.

Bušelić, M. (2017). "Distance learning – concepts and contributions," *Oeconomica Jadertina*, 2(1), pp. 23–34. Available at: https://doi.org/10.15291/oec.209.

Cunha, M. N., Chuchu, T., and Maziriri, E. 2020. Threats, Challenges, and Opportunities for Open Universities and Massive Online Open Courses in the Digital Revolution. *Int. J. Emerging Tech. Learn.* (Ijet) 15 (12), 191–204.

Davis, J. (2016). 'Social Media', *The International Encyclopedia of Political Communication.* DOI: 10.1002/9781118541555.wbiepc004.

Demuyakor, J. (2020). "Social Media and COVID-19 pandemic: Enhancing panic or preventing it?," *International Journal of Humanities, Arts and Social Sciences*, 6(5), pp. 211–222. Available at: https://doi.org/10.20469/ijhss.6.20005-5.

Encarnacion, R. E., Galang, A. D., & Hallar, B. A. (2021). The impact and effectiveness of e-learning on teaching and learning. *International Journal of Computing Sciences Research*, 5(1), 383-397. doi: 10.25147/ijcsr.2017.001.1.47

Kirkenidis, Y. and Andreopoulou, Z. (2011). "The use of internet new technologies on e-learning model for green development in Greece," *Agricultural Informatics Conference, Innovative Information Tecnologies in Agriculture*, 1, pp. 40-45.

Kirkenidis, Y. and Andreopoulou, Z. (2015). "E-learning and the aspect of students in Forestry and Environmental Studies," *Journal of Agricultural Informatics*, 6(1). Available at: https://doi.org/10.17700/jai.2015.6.1.158.

Koutroumanidis, T., & Andreopoulou, Z. S. (2009). E-learning in the internet supporting quality of life and Environment within sustainability in the EU, *Journal of Environmental Protection and Ecology*, 10 (4), 1227–1242.

Mohammed Nasser Hassan Ja'ashan, M. (2020). The challenges and prospects of using e-learning among EFL students in Bisha University. *Arab World English Journal*, 11(1), 124-137. doi:10.24093/awej/vol11no1.11.

COLLABORATIVE LEARNING IN STEAM TEACHING FOR STUDENTS IN THE CENTRAL AMAZON

Juliana Gisele Corrêa Rodrigues[1], Adan Sady de Medeiros Silva[2]
and Jucimar Maia da Silva Junior[3]
[1]Post-graduation program in Biodiversity and Biotechnology from BIONORTE, Amazonas State University, Brazil
[2]Dept. of Meteorology, Amazonas State University, Brazil
[3]Dept. of Computer Engineering, Amazonas State University, Brazil

ABSTRACT

The State of Amazonas has one of the most modern industrial and technological centers in Latin America. As a result, the search for skilled professionals for this job market is constantly growing. It is believed that STEAM teaching is an important tool to improve engagement, creativity, innovation, problem-solving skills, and other cognitive benefits generating more skilled professionals in the technology market. One approach that can be applied to STEAM teaching in schools is collaborative learning through maker culture. From mobile labs the STEM Academy Project takes STEAM teaching to high school students in public schools in the state of Amazonas. In the courses taught, collaborative learning is also applied in order for students to understand topics such as basic electronics, robotics, and programming, thus stimulating students' social skills and shared mutual learning, and attracting them to degree courses in STEAM fields.

KEYWORDS

Maker Culture, Social Skills, Cognitive Benefits, Mobile Labs

1. INTRODUCTION

The State of Amazonas is a Brazilian state located in central Amazonia. It is home to one of the most modern industrial and technological centers in Latin America, the Industrial Park of Manaus. As a result, the demand for qualified professionals to work in this market is constantly growing. It is believed that a tool that can train skilled professionals to work in this job market is STEAM education.

STEAM (Science, Technology, Engineering, Arts, and Mathematics) education has emerged as a new pedagogy in response to the need to increase student interest and skills in Science, Technology, Engineering, and Mathematics (STEM) (Quigley, Herro, & Jamil, 2017). STEAM education merges the arts with STEM subjects with the goal of improving engagement, creativity, innovation, problem-solving skills, and other cognitive benefits and to enhance employability skills (e.g., teamwork, communication, adaptability) needed for career and economic advancement (Root-Bernstein, 2015; Perignat & Katz-Buonicontro, 2018). As STEAM grows in popularity in schools, pedagogical models and approaches are proposed to employ this teaching methodology in these settings.

One approach that can be applied to STEAM education in schools is the maker culture. The maker culture has the potential to promote collaborative learning in education in formal and non-formal spaces, providing practical situations in which students are the protagonists in the construction of their own knowledge and the teacher is the mediator of this process, whether technological or manual. These spaces, whether in a school environment or not, awaken skills such as creativity, proactivity, teamwork, and manual skills in students and/or users, which are fundamental for the formation of citizens with a holistic and complete view of the universe around them (Medeiros et al, 2022). Therefore, this work aimed to employ collaborative learning in STEAM teaching for public high school students.

2. METHODOLOGY

With the search for more qualified professionals for the technological market, the STEM Academy project, developed by the Amazonas State University (UEA), has as one of its goals to take STEAM education to high school students from low-income schools in order to awaken their interest in science, technology, engineering, arts, and mathematics.

Courses are offered in mobile laboratories based on the maker culture. The Project's Mobile Laboratories are trailer-like structures transformed into Maker spaces and equipped with smart TVs, laptops, smartphones, 3D printers, laser cutters, among other electronic components and tools, and have a maximum capacity of 40 students simultaneously. The laboratory structure has 8 tables so that group activities can be developed (Figure 1a).

During the courses, which last one week, the participants learn concepts of microelectronics, robotics, programming, and Industry 4.0, when they build, along with the monitors, prototypes that simulate a semi-autonomous assembly line. First, classes are given on basic concepts about microelectronics, robotics, programming, and Industry 4.0. After that, collaborative learning is employed. Groups are formed where students are encouraged, through group activities, to solve challenges such as assembling a traffic light using Tinkercad software, printing parts in 3D printers for use in later projects (semi-autonomous assembly) and encouraging teamwork.

3. RESULTS

During group activities it is possible to verify the mutual shared responsibility, where everyone is responsible for the success or failure of the group. The engagement of students in solving the proposed challenges demonstrates teamwork and the sharing of knowledge. In these activities, they learn to relate to their peers, understand the opinions of others, and make decisions together. The proposed challenges make the students seek knowledge outside the maker environment, bringing solutions and ideas for the development of the activities. In this way students end up promoting collaborative learning because they are encouraged to develop the activities and challenges proposed during the course and characteristics such as autonomy, initiative, and leadership skills are observed.

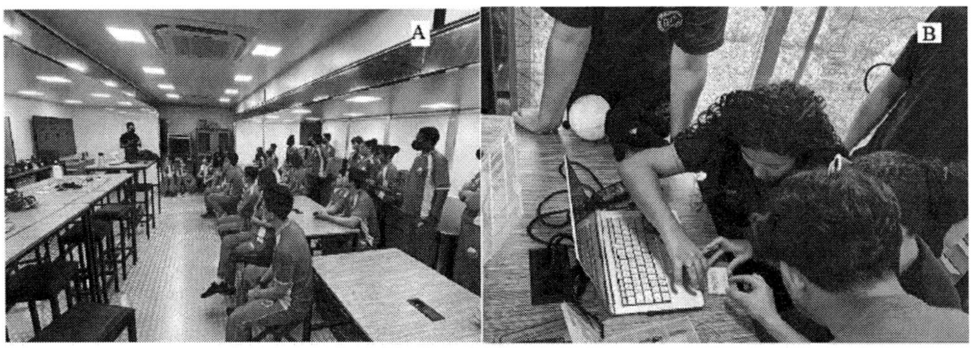

Figure 1. A: Internal structure of the mobile laboratory; B: Group activity stimulating collaborative learning

In the last 8 months, the project has already assisted and certified approximately 1000 high school students, who, through their activities after the course, such as school activities in makers rooms and participation in events that involve the STEAM themes, it is possible to identify the interest these students have in the areas of science, technology, engineering, arts and math, developing indispensable skills for the job market, such as leadership, proactivity, and technical conditions to deal with technology. Another result we obtained with the course was the approval of students who took the course through the STEM Academy Project in undergraduate courses in the STEAM area at the Amazonas State University (Figure 2). Of the courses taken in December, 106 students were certified. Of these 106 students, 32 were approved at the University of the State of Amazonas, 15 of them in STEAM area courses, this shows a 47% conversion of the students who were approved heading towards the STEAM area.

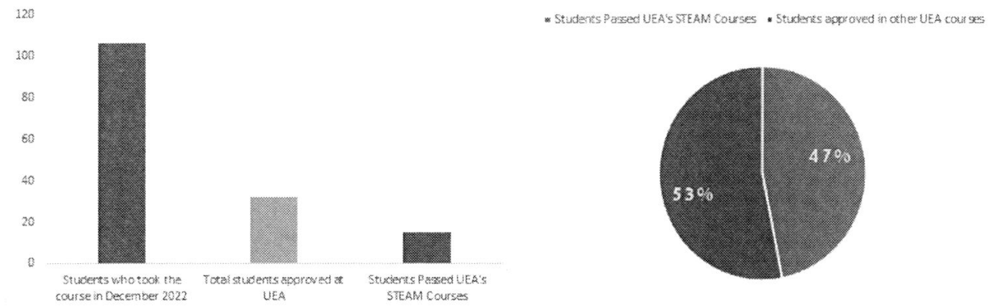

Figure 2. Students who entered the Amazonas State University and took the STEM Academy Project course

4. CONCLUSION

Thus, collaborative learning employed in maker culture through collaborative methodology in STEAM education becomes an important tool to improve engagement, creativity, innovation, problem-solving skills, and other cognitive benefits that will help students in the state of Amazonas to develop and be prepared for the complexities of today's world and to assume a leading role in the technological landscape, as well as direct them to graduate courses in STEAM areas.

ACKNOWLEDGEMENT

This article is the result of the project "Academia STEM", carried out by the University of the State of Amazonas (UEA), in partnership with Samsung Eletronica da Amazônia Ltda, using resources from Samsung, resulting of the IT Law for The Western Amazon (Federal Law Nº 8,387/1991), and its publicity is in accordance with the provisions of article 39 of Decree Nº 10,521/2020.

REFERENCES

Medeiros, A.S.; Almeida, W. A.; Rodrigues, J. G. C. (2022). *6th International Symposium on Academic Makerspaces.* Itinerant MakerSpaces in Central Amazon. Atlanta, United States of America.

Perignat, E., & Katz-Buonincontro, J. (2018). *STEAM in Practice and Research: An Integrative Literature Review.* Thinking Skills and Creativ, Vol. 18, pp. 1-42.

Quigley, C. F., Herro, D., & Jamil, F. M. (2017*). Developing a conceptual model of STEAM teaching practices. School Science & Mathematics*, Vol. 117, No 1, pp. 1-12.

Root-Bernstein, R. (2015). Arts and crafts as adjuncts to STEM education to foster creativity in gifted and talented students. *Asia Pacific Education Review*, Vol. 16, No. 2, pp. 203-212.

ONLINE COURSE ON BASIC CONCEPTS OF ROBOTICS AND INDUSTRY 4.0 FOR STUDENTS FROM PUBLIC SCHOOLS IN MANAUS - AMAZONAS

João Victor Pessoa da Silva and Jucimar Maia da Silva Junior
Department of Production Engineering, Amazonas State University, Brazil

ABSTRACT

The present work aims to address the impact of STEAM teaching in public school students through an online course of basic robotics. Considering the increasing use of automation in Industry 4.0 in the city of Manaus, it is of utmost importance the process of training students who enter the academic context through a free and online course, which merges concepts of everyday life with topics from the universe of robotics, in order to bring students closer to this reality, as well as serve as a facilitating tool in the learning process.

KEYWORDS

Robotics Course, STEAM Education, Video Lessons

1. INTRODUCTION

In view of the advances in technology and their consequences on society, robotics has a great impact on sociocultural aspects. According to Schiavicco and Siciliano (1995), robotics is designated as the scientific mechanism in which the study of robots and the dynamics of the human relationship with robotic apparatuses is allocated. Robotics, in turn, elucidates its innovations in several fields, either by adapting certain employment modes or by creating new ones; in medicine, where doctors perform delicate surgeries at a distance; in war conflicts, and even in domestic use, as well as in social relations, besides the extensive use of robots on the factory floor, which, in turn, perform repetitive and precise tasks.

Continuing the exposed principles and entering the facilitating factors linked to the use of robotics in the teaching and learning process, Zilli (2004) says about the educational character of robotics, which is aligned in the extension and elaboration of valences estimated within the learning scenario, such as: The manual and aesthetic skills, the nuances of logical reasoning, the intrapersonal and interpersonal connections, the integrative elements of elaborative concepts acquired in the most diverse areas of knowledge for the constructive development of projects, as well as the investigation and understanding of representative nuances of communication.

In allusion to the structures arranged by the use of technological tools, it is worth mentioning to elucidate in a practical way, according to Brazil (2017), the Industrial Pole of Manaus (PIM), located in the city of Manaus, situated in a strategic area region, in the central axis of the Amazon, configuring itself as one of the most modern industrial and technological poles of all Latin America, currently bringing together more than 500 cutting-edge industries, concentrating on the margin of the optics of the growth of technological practices, with a view to greater market complacency in the production orders and maintenance of existing structural processes. Thus, establishing a dynamic demand for skilled professionals, with tendencies to increase this dynamic in relation to the demands presented by the market.

With this, the course 'Basic Robotics and Industry 4.0 Concepts' makes use of the precepts of everyday life, together with the topics of robotics, in order to facilitate learning and bring students into this reality, through classes and real-life situations associated with the course content.

2. METHODOLOGY

Within a modern context, it can be evidenced that the demand for qualified labor is becoming increasingly assiduous, thus, this course aims to provide high school students through free online classes available on YouTube, in order to make accessible the convergence of socially esteemed knowledge.

Based on these elements, the course has as content subjects related to programming and basic robotics using programming tools in blocks by the Blockly platform, as well as expanding the conceptual notions involving Industry 4.0. The learning capital generated through the expository lectures ranges from the fundamental understanding of introductory concepts of the elaboration and systematic operation of everyday robotic functions to the explanation about the programmatic structuring in blocks. The didactics employed is configured as a great differential of the course, in which, in all classes, associations of the contents presented are made with situations analogous to the real ones of everyday life, with the insertion of examples inherent to the contexts currently experienced, with a basic principle of facilitating the students' understanding, allowing a more qualitative and assertive learning dynamic.

Following the above guidelines, the course was taught by students from the Amazonas State University (Figure 1), with a workload of 10 hours, with a certificate available after the conclusion of the course. To obtain the certificate it is necessary that the students attend and assimilate all the classes and subjects taught, performing at the end a questionnaire through the Google Forms platform, which provides an evaluation with multiple choice questions with a maximum score of 130 points, being necessary to reach 70 points to receive the certification.

Figure 1. Recordings from the online course

3. RESULTS

The results related to the number of students enrolled and certified in this course are available in table 1.

Table 1. Status and number of students participating in the course

Status	Quantity
Enrolled students	**310**
Certified students (approved)	**158**
Failed (dropouts)	**152**

Upon completion of the course, it was possible to observe that 310 students attended all classes, while 158 students were certified. As this is an online course, the numbers found were classified as satisfactory, with respect to possible difficulties encountered during the course.

According to Santos & Silva (2017) the evasion of students in online technical courses can reach up to 75%. The course presented here showed an evasion rate of less than 50%.

4. CONCLUSION

In this way, it is evident the great value of the contents addressed throughout the methodological process of the course, which addresses various areas of technology, through the introduction to the constructs of robotics and its inferences within the educational parameters, as well as the social results. It is possible to notice that the inherent course seeks to establish a certain academic bond with the high school students, configuring proximity bonds with the theoretical and practical processes of topics related to technology, which are not very frequent in the conventional high school contexts.

ACKNOWLEDGEMENT

This article is the result of the "STEM Academy" project, carried out by the Amazonas State University (UEA), in partnership with Samsung Eletronica da Amazônia Ltda, using Samsung resources, resulting from the Informatics Law for Western Amazonia (Federal Law No. 8.387/1991), and its publicity is in accordance with the provisions of Article 39 of Decree No. 10.521/2020.

REFERENCES

Brasil, Ministry of Economy. Industrial Pole of Manaus. Brasília, 2017. available at: https://www.gov.br/suframa/ptbr/assuntos/polo-industrial-de-manaus

Costa, R.L.D. The evasion in distance learning Technical courses, Brasil, dez./2005. Available at: https://doi.org/10.1590/0104-4060.50700

Schiavicco, L., Siciliano, B., Robotica Industriale - Modellistica e Controllo di Manipolatori, 1 ed., McGraw-Hill Inc., Milano, 1995.

Zilli, S. do R. A Robótica Educacional No Ensino Fundamental: Pespectivas E Práticas. Santa Catarina, 2004. Dissertação (mestrado) – Programa de Pós-Graduação em Engenharia de Produção, Universidade Federal de Santa Catarina.

THE CREATION OF VIDEO CONTENT FOR TEACHING AND LEARNING ABOUT STEAM

Vinicius Schramm Caldas[1] and Adan Sady de Medeiros Silva[2]
[1]*Dept. of Computation, Amazonas State University, Brazil*
[2]*Dept. of Meteorology, Amazonas State University, Brazil*

ABSTRACT

The work brings as a discussion the viability of technological advancement in the spheres of educational applications, validating the practices of using the creation of content in video format for teaching and learning the STEAM theme. Thus, the STEM academy, a project run by the Amazonas State University, aims to reach high school students using social networks as a teaching tool for this theme through videos that pique the interest of these young people. According to the restructuring moment experienced in the spheres of education not only in Brazil, but throughout the world, there is a need to search for a way to disseminate the m STEAM approach, such as creating videos for social networks, a communication tool widely used by young people. The results of this way of disseminating the STEAM theme have allowed for a better way of valuing the teacher as a whole, besides enabling the improvement of working conditions, along with teaching, and also the application of new teaching methods to teachers. In conclusion, it is understood that the insertion of new technologies enables the full development of the teaching-learning process, thus bringing possible improvements in education excellence and better working conditions.

KEYWORDS

Social Media, Videos, Learning, STEAM

1. INTRODUCTION

Education has changed over time, and so have some teaching models. Thus, there was a need for new configurations in the ways technologies were applied so that there would be less distance between the teacher and the student. The sudden change from face-to-face teaching to remote teaching can prove to be one of the most complex tasks for teachers and students. However, digital technologies can be used in educational activities as long as teachers are also open to new teaching models; and aware of the numerous possibilities offered by technological resources (MELO and MAIA, 2019). Thus, it is necessary that the applicability of digital technologies in the development of this learning process be increasingly interconnected with the teaching mode. This becomes challenging because most Brazilian schools and colleges face such a dilemma.

Nowadays, most people own cell phones, which enable them to access social media and become an allied tool for teaching. Such a tool can be applied in different approaches, including the STEAM (Science, Technology, Engineering, Arts and Math) approach.

So, in order to arouse the will of young people to know more about this approach, one has as a strategy the creation of content in video format for social networks, as a way to attract the viewer (high school students). Thinking about this approach, the STEM Academy (project developed by the Amazonas State University), through the Attraction Pillar (one of the pillars of the project that aims to reach high school students), uses the creation of video content to introduce these young people to the STEAM world, bringing content that is interactive, intriguing and fun, showing that the areas of technology and engineering are more accessible and interesting than one might imagine.

2. METHODOLOGY

The STEM Academy project has as one of its objectives to attract new students to courses involving the STEAM area (Science, Technology, Engineering, Arts and Mathematics). In this aspect, one of the strategies employed is the dissemination of the STEAM approach through social networks. As a mechanism to attract these young people is the creation of content in video format, being these, videos of curiosities, videos of reactions, and educational videos, mixing with everyday things, making fun the knowledge about the STEAM theme, showing more about the experiences of how the university life is, so that high school students feel lighter when they eventually enter this world.

To create these videos, first we search for content that involves the STEAM theme. After this search, the process of script assembly begins. This process is important because in it we can evaluate the best way to deliver the content with quality to the viewers. After the creation of the script, we move on to the video production and recording process. For the recording we use equipment such as: camera, microphone, lighting, software that helps capture the audio and create the scenery. After recording the video, the post-production process begins, which is the audiovisual editing. The last step is to post the video on the social network. All these steps can be observed in a flowchart shown in Figure 1.

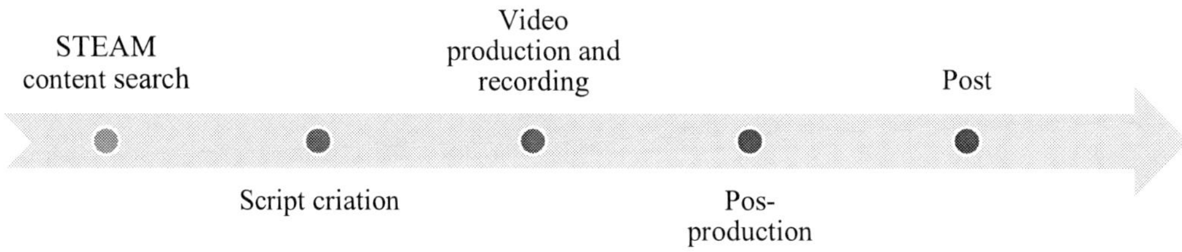

Figure 1. Flowchart of steps for video creation

3. RESULTS

Analyzing the last 6 months of video posts in one of the social networks of the STEM Academy Project (August/2022 to January/2023) 66 videos involving the STEAM theme were created (Figure 2a). From these posts it was possible to observe that the involvement of students with access to these themes has been extremely important for the continuity of the contents created in video, the feedbacks are always positive to those who didn't even have the basic knowledge of this area, thus encouraging them to experience this universe that is little talked about in the classroom. As an example, we can cite a post about a curiosity about the world's first train, reaching 15100 views (Figure 2b).

With the results obtained, it was possible to observe how this tool can help the dissemination of the STEAM theme reaching young audiences. It can also be observed how the technological tools for creating the videos helped to achieve the proposed goal.

Figure 2A. Social Network feed with the produced videos
2B. Comments on the videos indicating the identification of the content with young people

4. CONCLUSION

From this study it was possible to verify that the technological tools associated with the STEAM approach provide better knowledge retention and stimulus to individual learning, providing collective and teacher support in the preparation of classes, making them more attractive. Therefore, the STEM Academy Project included this tool as a teaching disclosure, thus reaching the target audience, the youth and teenagers. The videos meet this demand, helping in the implementation of STEAM in schools by providing students access to sources of information and promoting questions about the world we live in. At the same time, STEAM aims to promote a sense of curiosity. Videos also help in this aspect, as they are tools capable of turbocharging the methodology because, using engaging narratives, they help students identify new interests and become critical thinkers. and, in this way, all that is needed is access, understanding, and the proper application of the subject to which it needs to be addressed.

ACKNOWLEDGEMENT

This article is the result of the project "Academia STEM", carried out by the University of the State of Amazonas (UEA), in partnership with Samsung Eletronica da Amazônia Ltda, using resources from Samsung, resulting of the IT Law for The Western Amazon (Federal Law Nº 8,387/1991), and its publicity is in accordance with the provisions of article 39 of Decree Nº 10,521/2020.

REFERENCES

Marques, A. Dos S. Veloso. Collaborative Learning: A Methodological Proposal for Knowledge Construction in Organic Chemistry. Manaus, AM: PPGECEM/UFMT/Polo Manaus. (Thesis).197p.

Martins, Lilian C. Bacich - Bacich, Lilian; Holanda, L. STEAM in the Classroom Project-Based Learning Integrating Knowledge in Basic Education - Series: Education Challenges. 1. ed. Porto Alegre: Penso, 2020. v. 1.244p.

Meira, S. R. de L. Profession that does not require creativity will undergo dramatic changes. 2016. São Paulo newspaper. Interview with D. Ferrasolli. Acess at: 13 fevereiro. 2019.

THE PROCESS OF CONTENT PROSPECTION IN STEAM AREAS AIMED AT HIGH SCHOOL STUDENTS

Beatriz Freitas de Souza[1] and Jucimar Maia da Silva Junior[2]
[1]*Department of Production Engineering, Amazonas State University, Brazil*
[2]*Department of Computer Engineering, Amazonas State University, Brazil*

ABSTRACT

The present work seeks to find a suitable process for the prospection of content intended for STEAM areas, which have simple and efficient steps to be used in a development project located in the Amazon. Taking advantage of social media as a means of propagation of this educational content, one tends to carefully and cautiously choose topics that are attractive and that convey veracity in their posts. Therefore, the care that must be taken in the process of searching for this content and in its stages is of paramount importance and becomes decisive to achieve your goal.

KEYWORDS

Social Media, Content, Teaching, STEAM

1. INTRODUCTION

The STEAM methodology is a movement that proposes an education based on five specific disciplines (science, technology, engineering, arts, and mathematics), integrated in an innovative interdisciplinary approach. In this sense, D'Ambrosio (2020, p. 155) states that the STEAM approach favors broad appropriation of the subjects about the concepts of the components that compose it and, therefore, "(...) it is a transdisciplinary and transcultural proposal for Education". The search for an efficient and dynamic tool to disseminate STEAM content to young people and teenagers becomes indispensable. One of these tools that can be used are social networks.

Social networks are one of the most effective and widely used means of communication in the 21st century. For Torres (2009, p.44) "the internet is a network of millions of people, from all social classes, who search for information (...), interact and interfere in any and all activities related to society and business" and with this immense variety of applications, it has become over the years an ally of student education. The process of inserting virtual learning through digital channels is growing on a large scale. For Leopoldo (2015, p.13) "Online learning opportunities and the use of open educational resources and other technologies can increase educational productivity by accelerating the rate of learning."

Taking advantage of social media as a means of propagating this educational content, one tends to carefully and cautiously choose topics that are attractive to this audience. Thus, prospecting, which originates from the Latin "prospectione" and means the action of prospecting and researching something, is a means of selecting the content that is posted on social networks, that is, seeking differentiated subjects and ideas in articles, websites, and network pages to achieve a set goal regarding the creation of content.

The way in which subjects are researched and their transformation into a post for the internet is given in a systemic way and divided into steps for the proper functioning, validation, and verification of these contents. So, this work aimed to find a more appropriate process for the prospection of content that will be used in the social networks of the project is a case to be studied exclusively.

2. METHODOLOGY

The content prospection process was developed and discovered through field research with people from the STEM Academy project's social media team. The STEM Academy is a project of the Amazonas State University (UEA) and has as one of its goals to increase the interest of high school students in STEAM (Science, Technology, Engineering, Arts and Mathematics) degree courses. One of the project's social networks is called ManoSTEM, in which all the content aimed at teenagers is posted.

For the development of the prospecting process, a mapping of opinions, suggestions and ideas for the creation of each stage was done through a brainstorm with all team members. From the ideas a flowchart of the stages of this process was developed (Figure 1). Finally, the collected data were equated and consolidated, thus determining the effectiveness of the process through the results of the conversion of content into posts from the prospection carried out.

Figure 1. The ideal process found for content prospecting

Having ideas for content is the first step of the process, thinking of interesting subjects or that are on the rise at the moment and that involve STEAM is the first step, with this we begin the bibliographic research on websites and articles, to prove the scientific nature of this idea. The validation of the information is given in a referential way based on what was found in the previous step, always checking two or more sources to ensure the veracity of the information is fundamental. The phase of presenting the content to the team is crucial for the good progress of the posts, to check if everyone thought this idea was cool, if it is feasible to use it, and if everyone agrees with the content presented. After the team's approval, a script is created for a possible educational video or digital art about the subject, where the format of the post is designed.

3. RESULTS

The predetermined process was used for 2 months. It was possible to observe the change that happened in content prospecting when compared to the previous scenario. During this period about 95 types of STEAM-themed content were prospected, and of this number about 57 were used as posts on the project's social networks, distributed between videos and digital arts. In relation to the previous scenario of this methodology, with the same number of 95 prospected contents only 32 were used for posts (Figure 2).

Therefore, from these results one can observe an increase of approximately 30% in the use of the content found through the proposed process, with this process being more assertive in terms of relevance and transformation of the researched subjects into posts for the social networks, thus showing its effectiveness for use in the studied social network.

With a high rate of utilization of the researched content, the rework time decreased and consequently its frequency. The number of assertive subjects that fit into the editorial line of the ManoSTEM social networks increased, consequently the engagement in the posts was proportional to what was expected. The contents presented a high rate of acceptance by the followers, reflecting directly in the number of likes and comments that were made.

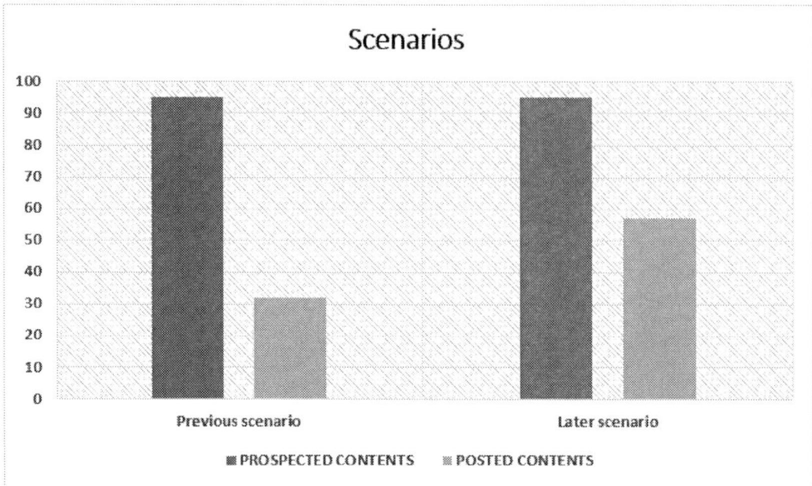

Figure 2. Presentation of the scenarios before and after the use of the process found

4. CONCLUSION

Therefore, it is noted that the process of content prospection found for use in one of the STEM Academy project's social networks proved to be effective and efficient to the proposed objectives. With this process it was possible to obtain an increase of posts up to 30% in the prospected content, thus reducing the time of rework, increasing the rate of acceptance of the content, and generating greater engagement in the project's social network.

ACKNOWLEDGEMENT

This article is the result of the "STEM Academy" project, carried out by the Amazonas State University (UEA), in partnership with Samsung Eletronica da Amazônia Ltda, using Samsung resources, resulting from the Informatics Law for Western Amazonia (Federal Law No. 8.387/1991), and its publicity is in accordance with the provisions of Article 39 of Decree No. 10.521/2020.

REFERENCES

D'Ambrósio, U. (2020) On STEM and STEAM curricular proposals and the Ethnomathematics Program. *Revista Paradigma (Fortieth Anniversary Edition: 1980-2020)*, vol. XLI, p.151-157.

Leopoldo, L. P. (2015) New Technologies in Education: Reflections on the practice Teacher training and new technologies. 2nd ed. Maceió: Editora Ufal

Torres, R. C. (2009) The digital marketing bible. 1st edition. São Paulo: Novatec.

APPLYING STEAM EDUCATION FOR HIGH SCHOOL STUDENTS ON SOCIAL MEDIA THROUGH GEEK CONTENT

Andreison Santos da Silva[1] and Adan Sady de Medeiros Silva[2]
[1]*Dept. of Production Engineering, Amazonas State University, Brazil*
[2]*Dept. of Meteorology, Amazonas State University, Brazil*

ABSTRACT

The work in question aims to apply STEAM education in social networks through geek content, aiming to improve the acceptance and learning of physics, mathematics and science among high school students. Short videos and posts to social networks using geek-themed movies and series, mixing science fiction with real concepts, will be applied and evaluated in order to verify the degree of acceptance and learning of high school students about the topics addressed, through associations and allusions to geek content and the real world.

KEYWORDS

Social Media, STEAM, GEEK, Physics, Mathematics, Science

1. INTRODUCTION

STEAM (Science, Technology, Engineering, Arts, and Mathematics) education emerged in response to the need to increase students' interest and skills in Science, Technology, Engineering, and Mathematics (STEM) fields (Quigley, Herro, & Jamil, 2017). Learning basic concepts of physics, math, and science through theoretical textbooks with fancy language is not appealing to young people in today's. Given the world they are immersed in, with the amount of technology available, it is increasingly difficult to continue with somewhat archaic and monotonous teaching methods. The STEM Academy project, a partnership between Samsung and the Amazonas State University, has as one of its goals STEAM education for high school students in Amazonas and uses social media as a tool for outreach.

Social networks are groups of Internet applications built on the ideological and technological foundations of Web 2.0, and that enable the creation and exchange of User Generated Content (UGC) (Kaplan Andreas M., Haenlein Michael, 2010). Social networks have assumed gigantic proportions in the last decades in modern society due to their high capacity to propagate a large amount of information enabling communication and bringing science closer to society. Targeting young people, who end up spending many hours on social networks (Instagram, TikTok, etc.), and with this consume a lot of content, among which can be mentioned the geek content, which focuses on science fiction movies (Star Wars, Star Trek, Marvel Cinematic Universe, DC). Therefore, this study aimed to insert Geek content to promote STEAM teaching in social networks.

2. METHODOLOGY

The social network @manostem is one of the STEM Academy Project's social networks dedicated to promoting STEAM education to young people and teenagers. This social network is used to post information about the project, online and on-site courses, content about university entrance exams and STEAM education. For STEAM education, strategies are devised to attract these young people. One of these strategies is the use of geek contents.

The use of geek contents that are part of this world in which they are immersed, through series and movies, is used, trying to make an association to teach theoretical concepts of science, physics, and mathematics in a didactic way and with a language they are already used to. Thus, the short videos (reels) in which the themes will be merged, explaining how physics applies or not, in these science fiction scenarios.

The contents covered in the videos, are prospected through websites, science magazines, science channels, among others. These contents go through a selection process in which the most appropriate ones are chosen. Then, the scripts are developed with the objective of retaining the maximum attention of the followers. As a tool, the mental triggers are added, which are tools of persuasion used to keep the interlocutors in the first 3 seconds of the video, then the scenario is set up for the recording that is thought to refer to the subject matter, using panels and led lights to create the best environment and increase quality, and then the recording is made. After going through all the previous process, the video goes to editing, in which changes will be made to make it even more attractive, which is done with the use of images, sound effects, visual effects and various other graphics resources. The video when completed goes to the post on social network entitled as @manostem on Instagram and thus delivered to the public of these contents.

3. RESULTS

The possible contents that went through the funnel phase (selection) were prospected, where we obtained those that would be used to make short videos or posts that went to the social network page on Instagram (@manostem), so that we could get the results, if it was accepted or not by the public.

An example of content created would be to associate the high speed of flash, a DC Comics character who has super speed, and physics in the real world, explaining how kinetic energy works and what are the consequences of a human being reaching 98% of the speed of light. The video got a total of 1564 views and 84 likes, a satisfactory amount considering the amount of followers of the page, which is 3000 thousand followers.

Another example was that of Spiderman, a character from the MCU (Marvel Cinematic Universe), which aimed to demonstrate if Spiderman's spear could stop a train, using physical concepts and comparing the materials of the spear with steel. The video got 8942 views and 261 likes, more than satisfactory numbers.

Figure 1. A: Flash Video B: Spiderman Video

The results were quite significant taking into account the number of views and likes that the videos obtained. Proving that this approach to content has an adhesion and much greater among young people and teenagers, and also that association can be very significant to better introduce STEAM teaching to these students. We can evaluate this performance, through the views of 8 contents that were posted in the month of

December 2022, 4 of them being geeks and the other 4 non-geeks, which were arranged in a table, and then a comparison was made between the contents as shown in the graph below:

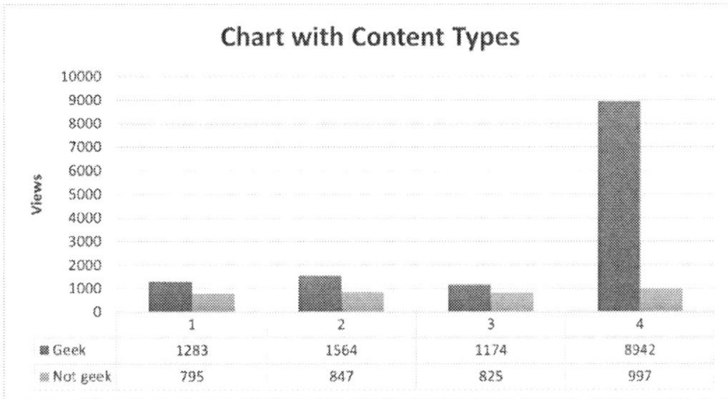

Figure 2. Geek and non-geek content comparison chart

The graph shows the progression of each content that was posted. Videos 1, 2, and 3 had a similar progression when compared to non-geek content, they had a growth of approximately 62%. Content 4 had a much higher performance, when compared to non-geek content it had an 897% growth. This result of the last video is due to Instagram, which, realizing that the video got more views than usual, delivered it much more on the platform, raising this significant number.

4. CONCLUSION

Therefore, its use in the geek content application method can be very useful, because it allows a much greater absorption and in a more effective way, due to the high habituation to the subject by young people who are in high school and who consume a large amount of information through the media, learning concepts of physics, mathematics or science in a faster, more didactic and fun way, and with the passage of time, it can become as habitual as watching a simple video or seeing a simple post.

ACKNOWLEDGEMENT

This article is the result of the "STEM Academy" project, carried out by the Amazonas State University (UEA), in partnership with Samsung Eletronica da Amazônia Ltda, using Samsung resources, resulting from the Informatics Law for Western Amazonia (Federal Law No. 8.387/1991), and its publicity is in accordance with the provisions of Article 39 of Decree No. 10.521/2020.

REFERENCES

Kaplan A. M., & Haenlein M., (2010), Users of the world, unite! The challenges and opportunities of social media, *Business Horizons*, *53*(1).

Quigley, C. F., Herro, D., & Jamil, F. M. (2017). Developing a conceptual model of STEAM teaching practices. *School Science & Mathematics*, 117(1), 1-12.

AUTHOR INDEX